CONCEPTS OF
TAXATION

1993 Edition

The Dryden Press Series in Accounting

INTRODUCTORY

Bischoff
Introduction to College Accounting
Second Edition

PRINCIPLES

Hanson, Hamre, and Walgenbach
Principles of Accounting
Sixth Edition

Hillman, Kochanek, and Norgaard
Principles of Accounting
Sixth Edition

COMPUTERIZED

Bischoff and Wanlass
The Computer Connection
Second Edition

Brigham and Knechel
Financial Accounting Using Lotus 1-2-3

Wanlass
Computer Resource Guide: Principles of Accounting
Third Edition

Yasuda and Wanlass
The Real Time Advantage

FINANCIAL

Backer, Elgers, and Asebrook
Financial Accounting: Concepts and Practices

Beirne and Dauderis
Financial Accounting: An Introduction to Decision Making

Hanson, Hamre, and Walgenbach
Financial Accounting
Seventh Edition

Hoskin and Hughes
Financial Accounting Cases

Kochanek, Hillman, and Norgaard
Financial Accounting
Second Edition

Stickney, Weil, and Davidson
Financial Accounting: An Introduction to Concepts, Methods, and Uses
Sixth Edition

MANAGERIAL

Ketz, Campbell, and Baxendale
Management Accounting

Maher, Stickney, Weil, and Davidson
Managerial Accounting: An Introduction to Concepts, Methods, and Uses
Fourth Edition

INTERMEDIATE

Williams, Stanga, and Holder
Intermediate Accounting
Fourth Edition

ADVANCED

Huefner and Largay
Advanced Financial Accounting
Third Edition

Pahler and Mori
Advanced Accounting
Fourth Edition

FINANCIAL STATEMENT ANALYSIS

Stickney
Financial Statement Analysis: A Strategic Perspective
Second Edition

AUDITING

Guy, Alderman, and Winters
Auditing
Third Edition

THEORY

Belkaoui
Accounting Theory
Third Edition

TAXATION

Everett, Raabe, and Fortin
Fundamentals of Taxation

Sommerfeld, Madeo, Anderson, and Jackson
Concepts of Taxation

REFERENCE

Miller
HBJ Miller GAAP Guide
College Edition

Miller and Bailey
HBJ Miller GAAS Guide
College Edition

The HBJ College Outline Series includes these fine study aids:

Campbell, Grierson, and Taylor
Principles of Accounting I
Revised Edition

Emery
Principles of Accounting II

Emery
Intermediate Accounting I

Emery
Intermediate Accounting II

Frigo
Cost Accounting

CONCEPTS OF
TAXATION

1993 Edition

RAY M. SOMMERFELD
UNIVERSITY OF TEXAS

SILVIA A. MADEO
UNIVERSITY OF MISSOURI–ST. LOUIS

KENNETH E. ANDERSON
UNIVERSITY OF TENNESSEE

BETTY R. JACKSON
UNIVERSITY OF COLORADO AT BOULDER

THE DRYDEN PRESS

Harcourt Brace Jovanovich College Publishers

Fort Worth   Philadelphia   San Diego   New York   Orlando   Austin   San Antonio
Toronto   Montreal   London   Sydney   Tokyo

Editor in Chief	Robert A. Pawlik
Acquisitions Editor	Tim Vertovec
Developmental Editor	Bill Teague
Project Editor	Cheryl Hauser
Assistant Project Editor	Jill Prince-Klancnik
Production Manager	Alison Howell, Eddie Dawson
Book Designer	Diana Jean Parks
Electronic Composition	Julie Warren

Cover Photo: © 1992 Elle Schuster.

Address for Editorial Correspondence
Harcourt Brace Jovanovich College Publishers, 301 Commerce Street, Suite 3700, Fort Worth, TX 76102

Address for Orders
Harcourt Brace Jovanovich College Publishers, 6277 Sea Harbor Drive, Orlando, FL 32887
1-800-782-4479, or 1-800-433-0001 (in Florida)

ISBN: 0-03-096384-2

Library of Congress Catalog Number: 92-70389

2 3 4 5 6 7 8 9 0 1   0 6 9   9 8 7 6 5 4 3 2 1

Printed in the United States of America

The Dryden Press
Harcourt Brace Jovanovich

CONCEPTS OF
TAXATION

1993 Edition

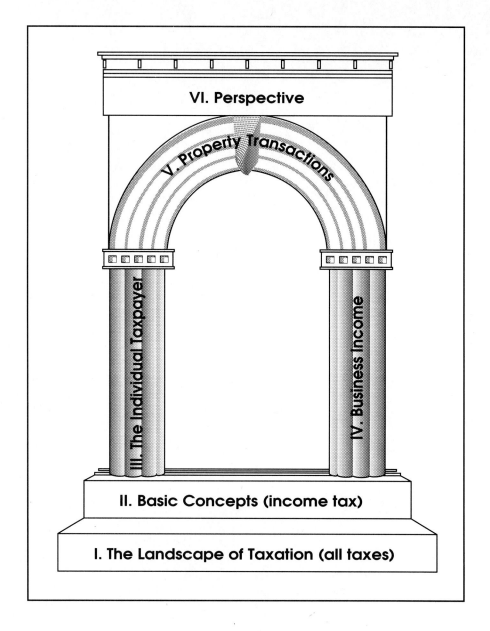

Preface

Concepts of Taxation, 1993 Edition, is a completely redesigned introductory tax course emphasizing the U.S. income tax and its broad implications. The entire textbook can be covered in one semester, although some instructors will choose to skip selected chapters. As described later in the preface, this new textbook provides ample material in the form of thought problems, group projects, and research assignments to maximize the kind of real learning experience that will last for a lifetime rather than for just one term. The textbook stresses the important fact that only *one* U.S. income tax is imposed on *three* different taxpayers (individuals, corporations, and fiduciaries). The textbook further explains the taxation of income earned both inside the United States and abroad by individuals, partnerships, S corporations, estates, and trusts.

THE GOAL OF THIS TEXT

Concepts of Taxation was created in direct response to the challenge for new and more conceptual educational material, as articulated by the Accounting Education Change Commission, the Bedford Committee Report, the Big Eight White Paper, and other leading business education authorities. As implied by the title, this textbook places primary emphasis on concepts, yet it draws liberally on specific details of the U.S. income tax law to illustrate how concepts are routinely applied in actual situations. The overriding objective of this textbook is to instill in each reader a clear appreciation for the important impact that taxes have on individual behavior, business activity, and civilized society in general. See Figure A for an overview of

• • • •
The overriding objective of this text is to instill in each reader a clear appreciation for the important impact that taxes have on individual behavior, business activity, and civilized society in general.
• • • •

the organization of the textbook into six parts. A separate mission statement is provided for each part so that students can clearly understand the intended interrelationship between the the six parts and 19 chapters of the textbook. In addition, learning goals are articulated at the beginning of each chapter so that every student can determine continuously and independently whether or not he or she is comprehending the most important information contained in that chapter. Thereafter each learning goal is clearly identified in the margin to help students associate textual material with the chapter goals. The margins also contain a running glossary to define technical words and phrases used in both the textbook and in real-world tax discussions.

The same educational authorities identified earlier further call for a reduced emphasis on memorization and a corresponding increase in learning to learn. To facilitate the achievement of this recommendation, all problem materials are subdivided into two clearly identified categories, namely (1) recall and (2) thought questions. All recall questions can be answered directly from the material presented in the chapter. Thought questions, on the other hand, require a higher level of comprehension. By using either inductive or deductive logic, or through the synthesis of multiple notions introduced earlier as separate topics, students are encouraged to think beyond the words of the textbook and to apply a conceptual understanding to similar but different circumstances, not specifically addressed in any chapter. Every question, in both the recall and thought categories, is specifically identified with one or more of the learning goals identified for that chapter. By the careful selection of advanced problem assignments, instructors can thus emphasize memorization of detail, learning to learn, or a balance between both objectives, on a chapter-by-chapter basis.

Finally, the same education authorities call for an increased use of group projects to facilitate greater teamwork and improved communication skills. Our response to these recommendations is a series of group assignments located at the very end of every chapter. By making frequent assignments from the group projects, tax instructors can better respond to this final challenge for new and improved methods of teaching the traditional introductory tax course in the business curriculum.

In summary, our goal in writing this textbook was to give the student a foundation for a lifetime of learning rather than a litany of detailed rules that have value only in the short term. As faculties struggle to respond to the growing demand for change, we encourage them to investigate the breadth of educational experience available through our conceptual approach to the tax component of the accounting curriculum.

• • • •

Concepts of Taxation was created in direct response to the challenge for new and more conceptual material, as articulated by the Accounting Education Change Commission, the Bedford Committee Report, the Big Eight White Paper, and other leading business education authorities.

• • • •

nontaxable entities to taxable entities. Chapter 7 introduces the important accounting-period and -method rules. And finally, Chapter 8 synthesizes several concepts introduced in the four preceding chapters to illustrate how tax information is captured in the basis concept.

Part Three introduces many of the details of income taxation unique to individual taxpayers. Although these four chapters (9–12) contain more detail than most others, they continue to stress underlying concepts as much as possible. The goal is to give students an understanding of current rules while providing a conceptual framework for understanding future changes in the law.

Part Four consists of three chapters. Chapter 13 details with special problems in the measurement of business income. Chapter 14 is devoted to cost recovery (or depreciation) rules applicable to business properties. Chapter 15 introduces the special tax rules that may be applicable to certain related-party transactions encountered in everyday business.

Part Five has two chapters that concentrate on the income derived from property transactions. Chapter 16 covers the capital gain and loss provisions. Chapter 17 contains the general rules for certain tax-deferred transactions, commonly known as the "nontaxable exchange" provisions.

Part Six also contains two chapters. Chapter 18 gives students a perspective of what tax accountants do and how individuals become tax specialists. Chapter 19 illustrates what can happen when tax planning is too successful! It illustrates the typical congressional reaction to widespread tax avoidance schemes through a discussion of (1) the passive activity loss rules and (2) the alternative minimum tax rules.

_____ TOPICAL ORGANIZATION

Part One offers an overview of the U.S. tax system. Chapter 1 is a general introduction to all forms of taxation. Chapter 2 contains a brief history of the income tax and a discussion of possible near-term changes in the U.S. tax structure. Chapter 3 reviews the process that produces and interprets our tax laws and thereby lays the groundwork for independent research assignments.

Part Two introduces the basic concepts of income taxation. Chapter 4 explains the concept of *gross income*, the starting point in the tax determination process. Chapter 5 explains the general notion of *deductions*, including the deduction for certain losses. Chapter 6 explains the various tax rates that are applicable to income earned by the three taxable entities, as well as the method used to allocate the income earned by

INSTRUCTOR'S _____ ANCILLARIES

To support the efforts of the instructor, the authors and publisher have created a number of teaching tools. Most of these are gathered in the Instructor's Manual. For each chapter, the Instructor's Manual includes

✓ a chapter outline for the use of the instructor in developing class lectures.

✓ author comments and suggestions.

✓ expanded solutions with comments for all recall problems, thought problems, and class projects.

✓ miscellaneous teaching transparencies.

All of these materials are provided by the authors of the textbook themselves. The final section of the Instructor's Manual consists of a Test Bank, by Marci A. Flanery (University of Kansas), of more than 570 test items in all. For each chapter, the test bank includes the following items:

> 10 purely conceptual multiple-choice items.

> 10 multiple-choice items that involve both conceptual understanding and an understanding of procedures or computation.

> 5 problems requiring moderate computations.

> 3 challenging objective questions.

> 2 essay questions.

This test bank is also available in the form of the Exa-Master™ computerized test bank software for both the IBM PC and the Macintosh microcomputers.

• • • •

Our goal in writing this text was to give the student a foundation for a lifetime of learning rather than a litany of detailed rules that have value only in the short term.

• • • •

AUTHORS

Many of the ideas utilized in this textbook build on *An Introduction to Taxation,* previously published by Harcourt Brace Jovanovich, Inc. Professors Ray Sommerfeld (The University of Texas at Austin) and Silvia Madeo (University of Missouri—St. Louis) contributed to both volumes. Joining them as co-authors of our new textbook are Professors Ken Anderson (University of Tennessee at Knoxville) and Betty Jackson (University of Colorado at Boulder). All co-authors are actively involved in both accounting education and research and all are highly respected by the professional accounting community.

ACKNOWLEDGMENTS

Thanks are due a number of colleagues who reviewed various stages of this textbook. Among them we especially want to thank Caroline K. Craig, Illinois State University; Douglas A. Shackelford, The University of North Carolina at Chapel Hill; James P. Trebby, Marquette University; and George E. Volkmann, Walsh College. We would also like to thank our students who previewed some of the material.

SUGGESTIONS FOR CHANGE

The textbook will be revised during the fall of 1992 and spring of 1993. We urge all adopters to communicate their suggestions for improvements and their identification of errors to any one or all of the authors—or to the publisher, in care of Bill Teague, Managing Developmental Editor, The Dryden Press/HBJ College, City Centre Tower II, 301 Commerce Street, Suite 3700, Fort Worth, TX 76102.

Ray M. Sommerfeld

Silvia A. Madeo

Ken E. Anderson

Betty R. Jackson

Brief Contents

PREFACE   vi

PART ONE   THE LANDSCAPE OF TAXATION   1

   1   THE TAX TOPOGRAPHY   3

   2   EVOLUTION OF THE U.S. TAX SYSTEM   41

   3   LEGAL PROCESSES AND RESPONSIBILITIES   71

PART TWO   BASIC CONCEPTS   **113**

   4   INCOME: GENERAL CONCEPTS   115

   5   DEDUCTIONS: GENERAL CONCEPTS   137

   6   TAXABLE ENTITIES, RATES, AND TAX CREDITS   165

   7   TAX ACCOUNTING   225

   8   TAX BASIS   271

PART THREE   THE INDIVIDUAL TAXPAYER   **299**

   9   INDIVIDUAL EXCLUSIONS AND ADJUSTED GROSS INCOME   301

   10   DEDUCTIONS FROM AGI   325

   11   CALCULATING THE INDIVIDUAL TAX LIABILITY   371

   12   INCENTIVES FOR SAVING: RETIREMENT PLANS AND DEFERRED COMPENSATION ARRANGEMENTS   397

PART FOUR   THE TAXATION OF BUSINESS INCOME   **423**

   13   CHALLENGING TAX ISSUES IN BUSINESS   425

   14   DEPRECIATION AND COST RECOVERY   455

   15   RELATED-PARTY TRANSACTIONS   515

PART FIVE   PROPERTY TRANSACTIONS   **547**

   16   CAPITAL GAINS AND LOSSES   549

   17   NONTAXABLE EXCHANGES   599

PART SIX   PERSPECTIVE   **645**

   18   TAX PRACTICE, PLANNING, AND EDUCATION   647

   19   LEGISLATIVE BACKSTOPS   665

APPENDIXES   A1

INDEX   I1

Contents

PREFACE   *vi*

Part One   **THE LANDSCAPE OF TAXATION**   **1**

1 *THE TAX TOPOGRAPHY*   **3**

CHAPTER OBJECTIVES   3
LEARNING GOALS   3
"READ MY LIPS"   4
THE WORD *TAX* DEFINED   4
    Nonpenal   4
    Compulsory Transfer of Resources, from the Private to the Public Sector 5
    Levied without Receipt of Specific Benefit of Equal Value   6
    On the Basis of Predetermined Criteria   7
    Enforced to Accomplish Economic and Social Objectives   8
CRITERIA USED IN THE SELECTION OF A TAX   10
    Equity   10
    Convenience   11
    Certainty   11
    Economy   12
    Productivity   12
    Visibility   13
    Political Considerations   14
KEY CONCEPTS   14
    Tax Bases   15
    Tax Rates   16
    Average versus Marginal Tax Rates   17
    Nominal versus Effective Tax Rates   18
    Tax Incidence   19
    Implicit Taxes   19
    Tax Burdens in General   20
COMMON TAX BASES   21
    Income Taxes in General   22
    Income Taxes Paid by Individuals   23

Social Security Taxes   25
Income Taxes Paid by Corporations   27
Transactions Taxes   29
Excise Taxes   29
Consumption Taxes   30
Wealth (or Ownership) Taxes   31
Wealth-Transfer Taxes   32
CONCLUSION   33
KEY POINTS TO REMEMBER   33
RECALL PROBLEMS   34
THOUGHT PROBLEMS   35
CLASS PROJECTS   39

2 *EVOLUTION OF THE U.S. TAX SYSTEM*   41

CHAPTER OBJECTIVES   41
LEARNING GOALS   41
EVOLUTION OF THE PRESENT SYSTEM   42
Tax Bases by Levels of Government   42
INCOME TAXATION PRIOR TO 1913   45
The Colonial Faculties Taxes   46
The Civil War Income Tax   46
The Constitutional Question   47
The 1909 Corporate Income Tax   50
THE U.S. INCOME TAX SINCE 1913   51
The Period 1913–1939   51
The Period 1939–1954   52
The Period 1954–1969   52
The Period 1969–1978   53
The Period 1978–1986   54
The 1986 Tax Reform Act   55
The Period 1987–1991   57
Assessing the Effects of the 1986 Act and Successor Acts   58
Unaddressed Problems   59
SIGNIFICANT FACTORS FOR THE FUTURE OF OUR TAX SYSTEM   62
CONCLUSION   66
KEY POINTS TO REMEMBER   67
RECALL PROBLEMS   67
THOUGHT PROBLEMS   68
CLASS PROJECTS   69

3 *LEGAL PROCESSES AND RESPONSIBILITIES*   71

CHAPTER OBJECTIVES   71
LEARNING GOALS   71

THE SOURCE OF TAX LAW 72
THE STRUCTURE OF TAX LAW 74
ADMINISTRATIVE INTERPRETATION 75
    Treasury Regulations 75
    Revenue Rulings 76
    Revenue Procedures 76
JUDICIAL INTERPRETATION 77
TAXPAYER COMPLIANCE 77
    Responsibilities of Taxpayers 77
    The Role of the Practitioner 82
    The Role of the IRS 85
    Judicial Review 90
TAX RESEARCH 93
    The Importance of Facts 93
    Identifying the Issues 93
    Searching for Authoritative Solutions 94
    Evaluating Potential Authority 94
    Reaching a Defensible Conclusion 95
CONCLUSION 95
APPENDIX 3A: SEARCHING FOR AUTHORITATIVE SOLUTIONS ... 96
    Organization of Primary Tax Law 96
    Tax Services 102
    Editorial Sources 103
    Computer-Assisted Research 103
    Expert Systems 104
KEY POINTS TO REMEMBER 105
RECALL PROBLEMS 105
THOUGHT PROBLEMS 108
CLASS PROJECTS (APPENDIX 3A) 109

Part Two   **BASIC CONCEPTS**   **113**

4 *INCOME: GENERAL CONCEPTS*   **115**

CHAPTER OBJECTIVES 115
LEARNING GOALS 115
INCOME CONCEPTS 117
    The Income of Economics 117
    The Income of Accounting 119
    The Income of Taxation 120
GROSS INCOME FOR TAX PURPOSES—INCLUSIONS AND EXCLUSIONS ... 125
    Inclusions 125
    Exclusions That Apply to all Taxpayers 127

KEY POINTS TO REMEMBER 132
RECALL PROBLEMS 133
THOUGHT PROBLEMS 134
CLASS PROJECTS 135

5 *DEDUCTIONS: GENERAL CONCEPTS* 137

CHAPTER OBJECTIVES 137
LEARNING OBJECTIVES 137
DEDUCTIONS 138
    The Basic Authorization: The Revenue Code 139
    Limits on Deductions 147
LOSSES 148
    Net Operating Losses 149
    Passive Activities and the Passive Loss Limits 150
    Capital Losses 152
    Casualty and Theft Losses 153
    Other Considerations 156
CONCLUSION 157
KEY POINTS TO REMEMBER 159
RECALL PROBLEMS 159
THOUGHT PROBLEMS 162
CLASS PROJECTS 163

6 *TAXABLE ENTITIES, RATES, AND TAX CREDITS* 165

CHAPTER OBJECTIVES 165
LEARNING GOALS 165
WHO ARE THE TAXPAYERS 166
    The Statutory Foundation 166
    Statutory Exceptions to the General Rule 172
    Summary 182
    The Taxation of Income Earned by Other Entities 182
    Critical Definitions 185
AT WHAT TAX RATE ARE TAXPAYERS TAXED? 187
    Tax Rates for Individual Taxpayers 187
    Tax Rates for Corporate Taxpayers 192
WHAT ARE TAX CREDITS AND PREPAYMENTS? 202
    Tax Credits 202
    Tax Prepayments 204
USE OF ENTITIES IN TAX PLANNING 205
    Comprehensive Illustration 205
    Matching Entity Attributes with Objectives 208
    Multiple Corporations 210
    Other Entities 211

KEY POINTS TO REMEMBER   212
RECALL PROBLEMS   213
THOUGHT PROBLEMS   218
CLASS PROJECTS   221

7 *TAX ACCOUNTING*   225

CHAPTER OBJECTIVES   225
LEARNING GOALS   225
TAX ACCOUNTING VERSUS FINANCIAL ACCOUNTING   226
    Reasons for Differences   226
    Categories of Differences   227
THE IMPORTANCE OF TIMING   228
THE ACCOUNTING PERIOD   229
    The Annual Accounting Concept   229
    The Tax Year   230
    Special Rules for Certain Entities   230
    Adopting a Tax Year   233
    Changing the Tax Year   234
THE CLAIM OF RIGHT DOCTRINE AND THE TAX BENEFIT RULE   235
    The Claim of Right Doctrine   235
    The Tax Benefit Rule   237
METHODS OF ACCOUNTING—GENERAL REQUIREMENTS   238
    The Book Conformity Requirement   239
    The Clear Reflection of Income Requirement   241
METHODS OF ACCOUNTING—SPECIFIC METHODS   242
    The Cash Method   242
    Restrictions on the Use of the Cash Method   245
    The Accrual Method   246
    Hybrid Methods   252
    Special Methods   252
ADOPTING AND CHANGING ACCOUNTING METHODS   257
INVENTORY METHODS   258
    Inventory Valuation   259
    Uniform Capitalization   260
    Inventory Flow   261
KEY POINTS TO REMEMBER   262
RECALL PROBLEMS   264
THOUGHT PROBLEMS   268
CLASS PROJECTS   270

8 *TAX BASIS*   271

CHAPTER OBJECTIVES   271
LEARNING GOALS   271

INCOME FROM PROPERTY DISPOSITIONS   272
    Amount Realized   272
    Adjusted Basis   273
COST BASIS IN GENERAL   274
    Original Basis   275
    Allocations   275
    Subsequent Adjustments   277
INVESTMENTS IN TAX CONDUIT ENTITIES   279
    Original Investment   279
    Subsequent Increases in Basis   280
    Subsequent Decreases in Basis   281
    Effect of Debt on Investor's Basis   282
    Determining Gain or Loss on Sales during the Year 282
LOSS LIMITATION   284
PROPERTY ACQUIRED BY INHERITANCE   286
PROPERTY ACQUIRED BY GIFT   287
CONCLUSION   290
KEY POINTS TO REMEMBER   290
RECALL PROBLEMS   291
THOUGHT PROBLEMS   294
CLASS PROJECTS   296

Part Three THE INDIVIDUAL TAXPAYER   299

9 INDIVIDUAL EXCLUSIONS AND ADJUSTED GROSS INCOME   301

CHAPTER OBJECTIVES   301
LEARNING GOALS   301
AN OVERVIEW   302
    Statistical Profile of the Individual Taxpayer   302
    The Tax Formula Revised   303
EXCLUSIONS FOR INDIVIDUAL TAXPAYERS   304
    Exclusions Related to Illness and Personal Injury 304
    Exclusions Related to Death   307
    Exclusions Related to Age—Social Security Benefits 308
    Exclusions Related to Double Taxation   309
    Exclusions Related to Education   309
    Exclusions Related to Employment   310
ADJUSTED GROSS INCOME DEFINED   312
    Deductions Related to the Conduct of a Trade or Business 314
    Trade or Business Expenses of Employees   314
    Losses from Sale or Exchange of Property   315
    Deductions Related to Transactions Entered into for Profit 315
    Alimony Payments   315
    Contributions to Retirement Plans   316

KEY POINTS TO REMEMBER   316
RECALL PROBLEMS   317
THOUGHT PROBLEMS   321
CLASS PROJECTS   323

10 *DEDUCTIONS FROM AGI*   **325**

CHAPTER OBJECTIVES   325
LEARNING GOALS   325
DEDUCTION FOR PERSONAL AND DEPENDENT EXEMPTIONS   326
    Exemptions for Taxpayers   326
    Exemptions for Dependents   327
THE STANDARD DEDUCTION   329
ITEMIZED DEDUCTIONS   331
    Interest   332
    Taxes   336
    Charitable Contributions   339
    Medical Expenses   345
    Casualty and Theft Losses   348
    Miscellaneous Itemized Deductions   350
KEY POINTS TO REMEMBER   357
RECALL PROBLEMS   357
THOUGHT PROBLEMS   368
CLASS PROJECTS   369

11 *CALCULATING THE INDIVIDUAL TAX LIABILITY*   **371**

CHAPTER OBJECTIVES   371
LEARNING GOALS   371
NOMINAL RATE SCHEDULES FOR INDIVIDUAL TAXPAYERS   372
    Filing Status   372
    Unearned Income of Minor Children   375
MARGINAL TAX RATES FOR INDIVIDUAL TAXPAYERS   376
    The Limitation on Itemized Deductions   376
    The Phaseout of Personal and Dependent Exemptions   377
    Other Factors That Change Effective and Marginal Tax Rates   378
TAX CREDITS FOR INDIVIDUALS   379
    Earned Income Credit   379
    Credit for Child-Care Expense   380
    Credit for Elderly and Disabled   382
    Foreign Tax Credit   383
    The Order for Subtracting Credits   384
SOME MISCELLANEOUS PROCEDURES   385
    Use of Tax Tables   385

KEY POINTS TO REMEMBER   387
RECALL PROBLEMS   388
THOUGHT PROBLEMS   394
CLASS PROJECT   394

12 *INCENTIVES FOR SAVING: RETIREMENT PLANS AND DEFERRED COMPENSATION ARRANGEMENTS* — 397

CHAPTER OBJECTIVES   397
LEARNING GOALS   397
LIFE INSURANCE AND ANNUITY CONTRACTS   399
    Life Insurance Contracts   399
    Annuity Contracts   400
PUBLIC RETIREMENT PROGRAMS   403
PRIVATE RETIREMENT   404
    Qualified Plans—General Rules   405
    Corporate Qualified Plans   407
    Self-Employment Retirement Plans (Keough Plans)   411
    Individual Retirement Accounts (IRAs)   412
    Simplified Employee Pensions (SEPs)   414
    401(k) Plans   414
    Nonqualified Corporate Plans   415
    Controversies over Treatment of Qualified Plans   415
OTHER SAVINGS INCENTIVES   417
    Deferred Compensation   417
    Incentive Stock Options (ISOs)   417
KEY POINTS TO REMEMBER   418
RECALL PROBLEMS   419
THOUGHT PROBLEMS   421
CLASS PROJECTS   422

Part Four   **THE TAXATION OF BUSINESS INCOME** — 423

13 *CHALLENGING TAX ISSUES IN BUSINESS* — 425

CHAPTER OBJECTIVES   425
LEARNING GOALS   425
DEFINITIONAL CHALLENGES   426
    Repairs   427
    Professional Fees   427
    Rental Payments   428
    Interest Expense   429
    Feasibility Studies   429

Valuation Studies   430
Start-Up Costs   430
Organization Costs   431
Environmental Cleanup Costs   432
Package Design Costs   433
STATUTORY CHALLENGES   433
Capital Expenditures Revisited   434
RECORD-KEEPING CHALLENGES   435
Travel and Transportation Expenses   436
Meal Expenses   439
Entertainment Expenses   440
Reporting and Accounting Requirements   443
TAX CREDITS RELATED TO BUSINESS   445
The Investment Tax Credit   446
Credit for Rehabilitation of Older Structures   446
The Targeted Jobs Credit   447
The Alcohol Fuels Credit   447
The Research Credit   447
The Low-Income Housing Credit   448
The Enhanced Oil Recovery Credit   448
The Disabled Access Credit   448
KEY POINTS TO REMEMBER   448
RECALL PROBLEMS   449
THOUGHT PROBLEMS   452
CLASS PROJECTS   453

14 *DEPRECIATION AND COST RECOVERY* 455

CHAPTER OBJECTIVES   455
LEARNING GOALS   455
THE ECONOMICS OF DEPRECIATION   456
How Depreciation Affects Returns on Capital Investments   456
Immediate Expensing versus Economic Depreciation   459
Depreciation and Implicit Taxes   462
Depreciation and Inflation   466
EVOLUTION OF DEPRECIATION REQUIREMENTS   467
Early History: Development of the Straight-Line Concept, 1913–1932   467
The Era of Bulletin F, 1933–1953   469
The Emergence of Accelerated Depreciation, 1954–1980   469
The Era of Accelerated Cost Recovery, 1981–Present   470
DEPRECIATION OF PROPERTY PLACED IN SERVICE BEFORE 1981   471
Depreciation Methods   472
Changes in Depreciation Method and Useful Lives   475
ACCELERATED COST RECOVERY SYSTEM FOR PROPERTY PLACED
IN SERVICE IN YEARS 1981 THROUGH 1986   475
Recovery Property   475
Unadjusted Basis   476

     Applicable Percentage under ACRs   477
     Section 179 Expense Election   480

MODIFIED ACCELERATED COST RECOVERY SYSTEM FOR
PROPERTY PLACED IN SERVICE AFTER 1986   480
     Property Subject to MACRS   481
     Classes of MACRS Property   481
     Applicable Methods, Recovery Periods, and Conventions   482
     Straight-Line Election   487
     Alternative Depreciation System   488
     Other Depreciation Methods after 1986   489
     Section 179 Expense Election   489
     Special Limitations on Listed Property and Luxury Automobiles   490

AMORTIZATION OF INTANGIBLE ASSETS   492

DEPLETION IN THE EXTRACTIVE INDUSTRIES   493
     Depletion for the Producer   494
     Depletion for the Royalty Owner   498

KEY POINTS TO REMEMBER   498

RECALL PROBLEMS   500

THOUGHT PROBLEMS   504

CLASS PROJECTS   506

APPENDIX 14A: SELECTED ACRS TABLES (1981–1986)   507

APPENDIX 14B: SELECTED MACRS TABLES (1987 AND AFTER)   510

15 *RELATED-PARTY TRANSACTIONS*   515

CHAPTER OBJECTIVES   515

LEARNING GOALS   515

WHO IS RELATED TO WHOM?   516

LEGAL AUTHORITIES   517
     Statutory Authorities   517
     Judicial Authorities   521

OWNER-ENTITY TRANSACTIONS   524
     Symbols   524
     Sale Transactions   525
     Compensation Transactions   528
     Dividend Transactions   529
     Stock-Redemption Transactions   531
     Family Partnerships   534

OTHER RELATED-PARTY TRANSACTIONS   535
     Multiple Corporations   535

KEY POINTS TO REMEMBER   539

RECALL PROBLEMS   540

THOUGHT PROBLEMS   543

CLASS PROJECTS   545

Part Five PROPERTY TRANSACTIONS   547

16 *CAPITAL GAINS AND LOSSES*   549

CHAPTER OBJECTIVES   549
LEARNING GOALS   549
THE CAPITAL GAIN CONCEPT   550
   Judicial Concept of a Capital Gain   551
   Economic Concept of a Capital Gain   552
   Accounting Concept of a Capital Gain   552
   Tax Concept of Capital Gain   552
ARGUMENTS FOR PREFERENTIAL TREATMENT OF CAPITAL GAINS
WITH COUNTERARGUMENTS   553
   The Lock-In Effect   553
   Incentives   554
   Competitiveness   554
   Bunching   555
   Inflation   555
   Revenue   556
ARGUMENTS AGAINST PREFERENTIAL TREATMENT OF CAPITAL GAINS
WITH COUNTERARGUMENTS   556
   Deferral of Gain   556
   Simplicity   557
   Equity   557
CURRENT PROVISIONS: THE PURE CASE   557
   Capital Gain and Loss Defied   558
   Tax Treatment of Capital Gains and Losses   560
   Planning Implications   568
CURRENT PROVISIONS: MODIFICATIONS TO THE PURE CASE   569
   A Historical and Conceptual Overview of Section 1231 and
     the Depreciation Recapture Provisions   569
   Section 1231: Some Additional Details in Current Law   574
   Depreciation Recapture: Some Additional Details in Current Law 578
   Section 165(h): Personal Casualty (and Theft) Gains and Losses 581
   Section 1272: Original Issue Discount   582
   Section 165(g): Worthless Securities   583
   Section 1244: Losses on Small Business Stock   583
KEY POINTS TO REMEMBER   585
RECALL PROBLEMS   586
THOUGHT PROBLEMS   592
CLASS PROJECTS   594

17 *NONTAXABLE EXCHANGES*   599

CHAPTER OBJECTIVES   599
LEARNING GOALS   599
SECTION 1031: LIKE-KIND EXCHANGES   600
  Requirements for Like-Kind Exchanges   603
  The Role of Boot in Like-Kind Exchanges   605
  Exchanges of Property Subject to Liabilities   607
  Basis and Holding Period of Property Received in Like-Kind Exchanges   608
  Exchanges of Multiple Properties   611
  Three-Party Exchanges and Deferred Exchanges   612
SECTION 1033: INVOLUNTARY CONVERSIONS   613
  Nonrecognition Requirements and Basis of Replacement Property   613
  Eligible Replacement Property   615
  Time Requirements   616
SECTION 1034: ROLLOVER OF GAIN ON THE SALE
OF A PRINCIPAL RESIDENCE   617
  Statutory Requirements   617
  Special Exclusion for Taxpayers Age 55 or Older   619
  Comparison of Sections 1031, 1033, and 1034   621
FORMATION OF A CORPORATION   622
  Statutory Requirements   623
  Transfers of Property Subject to Liabilities   624
  Basis of Stock and Property   625
CORPORATE REORGANIZATIONS   626
KEY POINTS TO REMEMBER   630
APPENDIX 17A: MULTIPLE PROPERTY EXCHANGES   631
RECALL PROBLEMS   632
THOUGHT PROBLEMS   637
CLASS PROJECTS   642

Part Six   PERSPECTIVE   645

18 *TAX PRACTICE, PLANNING, AND EDUCATION*   647

CHAPTER OBJECTIVES   647
LEARNING GOALS   647
TAX PRACTICE   648
  Public Practice   648
  Private Industry   649
  The Government   649
TAX PLANNING   650
  Avoidance versus Evasion   651
  The Critical Variables   651
  The Timing of Income and Deductions   656

TAX EDUCATION   657
KEY POINTS TO REMEMBER   660
RECALL PROBLEMS   660
THOUGHT PROBLEMS   662
CLASS PROJECTS   664

19 *LEGISLATIVE BACKSTOPS*   **665**

CHAPTER OBJECTIVES   665
LEARNING GOALS   665
THE NECESSITY FOR BACKSTOP PROVISIONS   666
THE ALTERNATIVE MINIMUM TAX   667
   Overview of the AMT   669
   Basic Computation   669
   Adjustments and Preferences   671
   The AMT Exemption   675
   AMT Credits   676
   The AMT and Tax Planning   677
PASSIVE ACTIVITIES AND THE PASSIVE ACTIVITY LOSS LIMITS   677
   What Is a Tax Shelter?   678
   Congressional Response—The PAL Sledgehammer 682
   Taxpayers Subject to the Limits   682
   Passive Activities Defined   683
   Applying the Limits on Passive Losses   686
   Recoupment of Losses at Disposition   688
   Is the Tax Shelter Extinct?   689
   PIGs and PTPs   689
CONCLUSION   690
KEY POINTS TO REMEMBER   690
RECALL PROBLEMS   691
THOUGHT PROBLEMS   694
CLASS PROJECTS   695

APPENDIXES   **A1**

APPENDIX A: 1992 TAX RATE SCHEDULES   A2
APPENDIX B: 1991 TAX TABLES   A4
APPENDIX C: 1991 EARNED INCOME CREDIT   A10
APPENDIX D: GIFT AND ESTATE TAX RATES   A14

INDEX   **I1**

Part One

THE LANDSCAPE OF TAXATION

Part One provides an overview of taxation in general. Before we study the details of any specific tax provision, it seems appropriate to provide the introductory student with a bird's-eye view of the entire tax landscape. The overview is intended to provide the intellectual coordinates necessary to place taxes into the larger economic and political realm in which they are conceived, grow to maturity, and pass into history. This overview will eventually help students distinguish between the tax equivalents of Mount Everest and haystacks.

> *"Something is wrong when—in the country born of a tax revolt—the most important document regulating individual social behavior, after the Bible, and the most important document affecting the relationship of the individual to the state, after the Constitution, is that uninspiring mass of convoluted prose called the Internal Revenue Code."*
>
> *MORTIMER ZUCKERMAN, EDITOR-IN-CHIEF, U.S. NEWS AND WORLD REPORT (1988)*

note and emphasize this fundamental distinction between this textbook and others because instructors, who are more accustomed to the traditional approach, may be tempted to skip Part One as unnecessary. We could not disagree more. If a conceptual orientation is ever to become a reality in accounting and business courses, it must begin with a reorientation of the introductory courses, including the introductory tax course.

Part One also provides historical perspective. This feature permits you to distinguish between tax equivalents of an ancient Smokey Mountain and the top of a Mount St. Helens. We concentrate our historical perspective on the U.S. federal income tax because it dominated our domain for at least the last half century. We also note and explain why there is reason to believe that a major shift in our tax landscape could occur within the near future.

Our approach can be analogized to the study of physical geography. In that discipline students ordinarily begin with a look at the globe, if not the galaxy. Before physical geography students examine any local phenomena, they typically become acquainted with continents and oceans, major mountain ranges, rivers, forests, and other macro landmarks of the earth's surface. As obvious as this approach might seem, it is not the approach followed in most introductory tax courses. Tax courses traditionally focus, from the very first meeting, on the study of one or another detail found only in the U.S. federal income tax law. We

In summary, just as anyone has a better sense of comprehension when he or she begins an unfamiliar journey with the study of a map of the ground to be covered, we believe that your comprehension of the material encountered later in this text will be significantly improved if you begin with the overview provided in Part One. An appreciation of both forests and trees is important; neither is sufficient alone.

To accomplish our mission, we provide three chapters with these overriding objectives:

CHAPTER 1:
THE TAX TOPOGRAPHY—to define taxes and to distinguish them from other sources of government revenue, to identify criteria for judging a tax system, to introduce key concepts, and to describe the most common types of taxes.

> *"Taxes are what we pay for civilized society. . . ."*
>
> *JUSTICE OLIVER WENDELL HOLMES, JR., COMPANIA DE TABACOS V. COLLECTOR (1927)*

CHAPTER 2:
EVOLUTION OF THE U.S. TAX SYSTEM—to review the history of taxation in the United States, to emphasize recent developments, and to consider what these developments suggest about the future.

CHAPTER 3:
LEGAL PROCESSES AND RESPONSIBILITIES—to describe the federal income tax process from inception of new law to compliance with specific provisions, and to introduce the tools tax professionals use to solve complex problems.

If you know the position a person takes on taxes, you can tell their whole philosophy. The tax code, once you get to know it, embodies all the essence of life: greed, politics, power, goodness, charity. Everything's in there. That's why it's so hard to get a simplified tax code. Life just isn't simple.

FORMER IRS COMMISSION, SHELDON COHEN[1]

THE TAX TOPOGRAPHY

CHAPTER OBJECTIVES

In Chapter 1 the student will encounter the difficulty of defining words for tax purposes; be exposed to the criteria most commonly used to judge both specific taxes and tax systems in general; become familiar with seven key concepts of taxation; and explore the tax bases used in the United States and other tax systems.

LEARNING GOALS

After studying this chapter, students should be able to

1 Define the word tax and explain the major components of the authors' definition of it;

2 Explain the objectives of taxation, including: raising revenues, achieving economic objectives, attaining social objectives, and maintaining economic neutrality;

3 Discuss and evaluate the criteria that are commonly used in the selection of a tax base, including: equity, convenience, certainty, economy, productivity, visibility, and political factors;

4 Understand seven key concepts of taxation, including: tax bases, tax rates, average versus marginal tax rates, nominal versus effective tax rates, tax incidence, implicit versus explicit taxes, and tax burdens in general; and

5 Describe the most common tax bases used in the U.S. tax system.

---

1 As quoted by Jeffery Birnbaum and Alan Murray in *Showdown at Gucci Gulch* (New York: Random House, 1987).

In the first part of this chapter we define that simple but elusive three-letter word, *tax*. It would be much easier, and certainly much more comforting, to simply get on with it. That is, it would be much easier for both you and your instructor if we would start with some nitty-gritty detail of the unbelievably complex law governing our federal **income tax**. Once on such a path we could simply continue to focus on procedural details until time ran out at the end of the term.

To do so, however, would be grossly misleading. For those of you who pursue a career in taxation, much of your professional challenge will derive from the constant need to define and redefine words. Specifically, you will need to define and redefine, in an operational way, both everyday or common words and new technical terms and phrases as used in federal income tax parlance. For all of you, regardless of profession, much of your challenge as a taxpayer will derive from the need to deal with taxes as one of the annually recurring hard facts of life. That is why we will spend much of this first chapter defining the word *tax* operationally.

The apparent security of definition-by-example, a frequent definitional technique, is wholly illusory. We believe that it is much better to learn at the outset just how difficult and frustrating the tax of definition can be. This more vexing path will better prepare you for the truly interesting challenges that can be found in the landscape of taxation.

> The **income tax** can be neatly defined as a tax on the income of individuals and businesses. This definition tells us nothing if we fail to understand what *tax* and *income* really mean: In simple terms, **income** is the monetary gain that derives from capital or labor; the concept of income as something *taxable* includes many other factors. Tax is defined later in this chapter.

> **Goal #1**
> Define the word *tax* and explain the components of the authors' definition.

> A **tax** is any nonpenal yet compulsory transfer of resources, from the private to the public sector, levied without receipt of a specific benefit of equal value and on the basis of predetermined criteria, enforced to accomplish some of a nation's economic and social objectives.
>
> **Topology** is the study of the configuration of a surface and its features.
>
> **Penal** means that a monetary charge (fine) is being levied to dissuade certain behavior.

"READ MY LIPS"

The significance of terminology in taxation is graphically demonstrated by recent debates over what constitutes a tax. During the 1988 presidential campaign, candidate George Bush made his now famous pledge, "Read my lips: No new taxes." With that pledge, Bush set the stage for what has become an intense political battle over the definition of the word *tax*. The battle derives from the need for additional sources of government revenues that can be defined as something other than a tax. President Bush's appointee, Office of Management and Budget (OMB) Director Richard G. Darman, attempted to punch holes in the political rhetoric, and entered the definitional fray with his equally famous response: "If it looks like a duck, walks like a duck, and quacks like a duck, then it *is* a duck."

Although Darman's definition is both clever and intuitively correct, it helps very little when one is faced with the real problem of defining the word. Darman's definition is not *operational*; it offers little help when we try to decide exactly what is and what is not a tax.

THE WORD *TAX* DEFINED

We define the word **tax** as *any nonpenal yet compulsory transfer of resources, from the private to the public sector, levied without receipt of a specific benefit of equal value and on the basis of predetermined criteria, enforced to accomplish some of a nation's economic and social objectives*. To help you fully understand this definition, we will flesh out the meanings of each phrase. After you have considered each of its parts, you will have a direct appreciation for the contours and **topology** of taxation.

NONPENAL

We can distinguish a tax from a **penal** transfer (a criminal or civil penalty, usually a fine), at least crudely. Usually authorities devise a penalty solely to dissuade a person from engaging in an act deemed detrimental to society. For example, a government may impose a $10,000 fine for possession or sale of a specified drug or for striking a police officer. In these instances, the government demands a relatively large exaction for a single act. The government intends to discourage the specific act because it runs counter to a broad objective (such as maintaining a healthy populace or maintaining general order).

Taxes, on the other hand, generally do not have such a specific objective, even though the government often intends to influence general behavior. Taxes typically provide for lesser exactions, often for more general categories of behavior. For example, a relatively small tax increase may be devised to discourage spending (or more accurately, to decrease aggregate demand). Or a small tax may be imposed to discourage the consumption of products that place extra costs on the individual and society.

But the line is not clear-cut. Taxes on alcohol and tobacco have often been called *sin taxes,* connoting a penalty for undesirable behavior. (Historically, these two taxes have been popular because alcohol and tobacco are characterized by a relatively inelastic demand curve.) Other penalty taxes have been enacted and imposed in the United States. A good example is the tax on personal holding companies. In those cases the tax rate is set so that the undesirable action (using corporate entities to reduce tax liabilities on certain kinds of investment income) is more expensive than the desirable action (paying fairer taxes on said income).

Traditionally the United States has preferred to influence behavior through granting tax privileges rather than imposing tax penalties. For example, for years the federal government has granted businesses an income-tax credit for the purchase and installation of certified pollution control devices, even though some critics believe that government could better limit pollution by imposing taxes on those who pollute the air and water.[2]

In summary, the two major differences between a tax and a penalty are (1) the relative size of exaction demanded and (2) the specific objective behind the exaction. The larger the exaction and the more restrictive the objective, the more likely that the exaction should be classified as a penalty rather than a tax.

COMPULSORY TRANSFER OF RESOURCES, FROM THE PRIVATE TO THE PUBLIC SECTOR

The U.S. income tax system is sometimes described as a voluntary self-assessment system. Individuals and entities are responsible for calculating their income tax liabilities and reporting these amounts to the government. However, this system is *voluntary* and *self-assessed* in only a very narrow sense. A *compulsory transfer of resources* more aptly characterizes this system, since substantial penalties—including jail sentences in extreme cases—may be imposed on those who do not self-assess and pay the amount of tax the IRS deems proper.

As we will discuss in Chapter 3, the IRS attempts diligently to monitor compliance. The two broad approaches used are auditing tax returns and matching information documents (provided by third-party payors) to individual tax returns. The last decade saw a major shift in emphasis from auditing returns to information reporting and

---

2 See Wallace Oates, "A Pollution Tax Makes Economic and Social Sense," *Tax Policy in the Twenty-First Century* (New York: John Wiley & Sons, 1988).

matching. These changes have sparked a significant amount of debate culminating in congressional hearings regarding the effectiveness and fairness of current tax administration policies.[3] In the face of the enforcement mechanisms used to administer our tax system, it appears accurate to characterize income taxes as a compulsory, rather than voluntary, transfer of resources *from the private to the public sector.*

In the private sector, you must pay a price before you can receive a specific private good. Suppose that you desired to purchase both a refrigerator and a microwave oven. Unfortunately, you cannot afford both items. If you decide to buy the refrigerator and to forgo buying the microwave oven, you automatically receive the full benefit of the one but get no benefit whatsoever from the other. You may be disappointed by not having the microwave, but you would likely recognize the conditions of the marketplace that led to your decision.

Private goods and services are defined as those items and services that can be satisfactorily rationed or allocated among all would-be benefactors solely by the means of a price mechanism, that is, by operation of the laws of supply and demand. In a purely competitive economy, the consumer decides how to allocate resources in response to individual needs and individual price tags.

On the other hand, we may enjoy the benefit of another category of goods, even if we do not pay for them. **Public goods and services** are those items for which a reasonable price and an optimum output level cannot be determined or maintained by the market forces of supply and demand. The national defense force, the legal system, and food safety inspection are three services that U.S. voters have determined cannot be parceled out to a nation's populace in any *acceptable* manner by a free-market mechanism. This distinction allows us to proceed to the next part of our definition.

> **Private goods and services** are those items that can be satisfactorily rationed or allocated among all would-be benefactors solely by means of a price mechanism.
>
> **Public goods and services** are those items that a nation decides should not, or cannot, be allocated by means of a price mechanism. Everyone benefits from the mere existence of the good, whether or not he or she directly consumes it.

LEVIED WITHOUT RECEIPT OF A SPECIFIC BENEFIT OF EQUAL VALUE

Our society has deemed it imperative that public goods and services be equally available to everyone, whether or not they are used directly and without regard for the degree of use. Therefore taxes should not be confused with a payment for specific personal goods. By definition, the benefits of public goods are independent of payment.

A government, like a private business, can produce and sell private goods. When it does, the government charges a price for the good or service produced, just like any other provider. For example, the charge imposed on the user of the postal services and the price paid for TVA-produced electrical energy cannot be accurately described as taxes because (1) the purchaser receives a good or service equal in value to the charge imposed; (2) the decision to use the service or receive the good is an elective rather than a coerced decision; (3) persons not paying the charge are unable to receive the good or service; and (4) the price paid is not significantly different from what it would have been had the same good or service been provided by private enterprise. Such goods and services are not public goods even though they are publicly provided goods.

To gain acceptance for revenue increases (and thus to free general revenues for other purposes), politicians are increasingly likely to argue that a tax is really a reasonable price for a benefit received. Thus, federal and state **excise taxes** on gasolines, lubricants, and tires are frequently rationalized as a reasonable charge for the use of public highways. OMB Director Darman, for instance, suggested that a

> An **excise tax** is levied on a specified good only and may be imposed at the manufacturing or retail-sales level.

---

3 See J. Dubin, M. Graetz and L. Wilde, "The Changing Face of Tax Enforcement, 1978–1988," *Tax Lawyer* (Summer 1990), 43: 894.

gasoline tax can be justified by the negative effects that gasoline has on the environment, the nation's infrastructure, public health, and national security. According to Darman, if a tax's *primary* purpose is not to raise revenue (even though it would), it might not be a tax but rather a way of balancing **negative externalities**.[4] These arguments supported large rate hikes in excise taxes in the 1990 Act. Revenue projections for 1991, based on these rate hikes, show increases of $9.9 billion in excise tax collections.[5]

> **Negative externalities** are detrimental consequences created by a given activity, such as the pollution effects of gasoline use.

The notion of benefit received is further reinforced by the practice of earmarking taxes for specified government funds or accounts. For example, gasoline tax receipts are often channeled into a Road-Use Tax Fund that can be used only for building or improving public highways.[6] This tactic frees general funds that would otherwise be used for public highways and may facilitate raising more revenue than the public would otherwise tolerate.

State and local users fees imposed for benefits received (for example, garbage disposal or water) are not deductible *as a tax* for federal income tax purposes. On the other hand, state and local income and property taxes are deductible. Thus both the courts and the IRS have been called on to decide whether a service fee is really a tax. The Supreme Court has held that "only those costs attributable to the provision of a particular service to a particular individual properly can be called fees."[7] Consistent with the Court's position, the IRS holds that a general charge imposed on the *value* of tangible personal property owned within a city, to support the police and fire departments, is a tax and not a user fee or a price (Revenue Ruling 61–152). On the other hand, a trash collection fee charged with additional levies depending on the service provided was held to be a user's fee rather than a tax (Revenue Ruling 77–29), even if based on the value of real property.

To summarize, a primary criterion for any tax is that it involves a compulsory transfer of resources without the receipt of a private good or service of equal value. Prices are voluntary transfers made in free markets, involving exchanges of equal value. This basic distinction between prices and taxes is important in evaluating all proposals that divert resources from the private to the public sector.

ON THE BASIS OF PREDETERMINED CRITERIA

Taxes, unlike an outright confiscation of resources, are levied on the basis of predetermined criteria and on a recurring basis. Hence, occasional national expropriations—whether they involve copper mines, railroads, or other property—cannot be correctly classified as a form of taxation. The fact that taxes are based on predetermined criteria is important for at least two reasons. First, predetermination gives every taxpayer a chance to modify his or her business or personal behavior in a way that will minimize taxes, if the taxpayer deems it desirable. Second, taxpayers who vote have the opportunity to assess the criteria used in raising taxes and thus have the opportunity to remove from political office those individuals who select or modify a **tax base** unwisely.

> A **tax base** is an item or event made subject to taxation, usually measured by value.

---

4 J. Andrew Horner, "What's a Tax, Anyway?" *Tax Notes*, April, 24, 1989, p. 381.

5 BNA Special Supplement, House Ways and Means Committee Report, "Overview of the Federal Tax System," 1991 Ed. (WMCP:102–7), Part IV, Table 1, "Receipts by Source, 1981–1991," p. S–68. *Source:* OMB, Budget of the United States Government, Fiscal Year 1992.

6 In 1991, the search for new revenues led to a great deal of support for an additional 5¢ earmarked gasoline tax.

7 See discussion by J. Andrew Horner, *op. cit.,* p. 381.

Historically the predetermined criteria for selection of new tax bases, and for the extension of old taxes, have been as confused with political rhetoric as is the definition of the word tax. Because these issues are important and complex, we will discuss them separately later in this chapter.

ENFORCED TO ACCOMPLISH ECONOMIC AND SOCIAL OBJECTIVES

> **Goal #2**
> Explain the objectives of taxation.

The most obvious reason for imposing taxes—that is, taxing to raise government revenues—is often of much greater significance to lower levels of government than to national (or federal) governments. Many national governments are at least as interested in achieving various economic and social objectives via taxation as they are in raising government revenues. To complicate matters more, the achievement of various economic and social objectives sometimes can be accomplished only at the price of conflicting criteria. For example, greater simplicity is often cited as a criterion that conflicts with improved equity.

Raising Revenues

In one sense, taxes are to governments what incomes are to businesses and individuals. For all nonfederal levels of government, this characterization is essentially accurate: most taxes at the state and local levels are imposed solely for the purpose of raising revenues—that is, to provide the governmental unit with an income. The federal government, however, is wholly unlike state and local governments, private businesses, and individuals. Theoretically, the federal government can expend any amount of money it wishes without ever collecting taxes, because the federal government alone controls the power to create money. Lest anyone doubt this conclusion, note that the U.S. federal government currently has a debt of approximately $4 trillion.

Economic Objectives

Perhaps the federal government's two most fundamental reasons for taxing citizens are to provide a reasonable degree of price stability and to foster economic growth within the nation. Whether the government does this for the benefit of its citizens or for its own self-preservation is a moot question. If a government purchases any substantial amount of goods and services without taxing, and if few underemployed resources exists, spending by the public and private sectors can generate a strong excess demand and create an inflationary bias in the economy. The closer the nation is to a full-employment equilibrium without government spending, the greater the inflationary dangers of government spending without taxation. During periods of underemployment, Congress often reduces taxes (and increases deficits) to try to jump-start the economy and generate economic growth.

The subtle difference between taxing to raise revenues and taxing to achieve economic goals is an important difference that explains many changes in the U.S. tax law. Certainly our federal government relates aggregate revenues to aggregate expenditures when it considers a budget proposal each year. At the all-important margin—at least prior to the **Gramm-Rudman Act of 1985**—the federal government did *not* accept or reject any single expenditure proposal on the grounds that it did or did not have the wherewithal to pay for the project. Rather the U.S. government traditionally committed the nation to selected projects with only limited or secondary concern for the source of payment; then it *separately* set the tax policy for the next year, duly

> The **Gramm-Rudman Act of 1985** set deficit reduction targets that must be met by Congress.

considering both the expenditures budget it had approved and the economic milieu in which it had to operate.

Although Gramm-Rudman has not really changed the basic strategy—witness the massive deficits accumulated in the past five years—it has forced politicians to spend more time and effort explaining how each new program is supposed to be financed. Politicians and citizens alike harbor honest differences of opinion over what part of federal spending can and should be decreased. Ultimately any decision concerning the amount of federal spending must be made in the political arena; lawmakers are therefore quite aware of various sensitivities as they develop and defend their plans.

Once spending decisions are formulated, the government should be ready to set tax policy. In this way, taxation can be made the residual buffer that keeps demand more or less in line with supply. Taxation can therefore be a primary method of achieving various economic goals of a nation. It should be remembered that tax policy is not the only weapon available to a government; monetary policy can also promote or hinder the achievement of economic objectives.

Social Objectives

Some tax policy objectives are purely social. For example, U.S. income tax law has historically provided financial assistance through tax breaks to homeowners because many lawmakers believe home ownership helps preserve family values. Recent proposals to provide a credit for first-time homebuyers reinforce this notion. More recently legislators cited the increased employment of the hard-core unemployed as the primary objective of yet another socially motivated tax provision.

The motivation for a single tax can be either social or economic. Consider the case of wealth redistribution. Legislators may propose a redistribution of wealth because of an economic judgment that redistribution is required for a desired level of economic health. This economic argument is based on the premise that high-income earners spend a smaller proportion of their incomes than persons with smaller incomes and the large concentration of wealth and income tends to reduce aggregate demand. However, wealth redistribution may as easily be supported by the social value judgment that excesses in the distribution of private wealth are undesirable.

Neutrality as an Objective

The use of tax law to achieve specific economic and social objectives inherently conflicts with the concept of **tax neutrality**. Tax neutrality means that the tax law does not favor one economic decision or activity over another. United States history provides many examples of our tax law favoring certain groups or individuals in the name of economic and social goals, such as the preferential treatment given the oil and gas industry in 1918. A more current example is the child-care credit.

Over 100 adjustments to the income-tax base have been identified as tax preference items, sometimes called **tax expenditures** to draw public attention to the fact that they have the same effect as direct government subsidies. Each preferential provision violates the objective of economic neutrality. The 1986 Tax Act reflected a growing sentiment for economic neutrality; recent proposals for restimulating the economy are anything but neutral.

In trying to meet the overall goals of the tax system, a number of commonly accepted criteria for evaluating a tax have emerged.

Tax neutrality is the concept that tax law should not favor one economic decision or activity over another.

Tax expenditures are an estimate of the tax revenues forgone because of provisions in the tax law that favor certain types of economic activities or choices.

CRITERIA USED IN THE SELECTION OF A TAX

Goal #3
Discuss and evaluate criteria used in the selection of a tax.

One of the earliest attempts to identify the criteria for designing a tax system is credited to Adam Smith who, in 1776, suggested that a good tax ought to be equitable, convenient, certain, and economical. He called these criteria the "canons of taxation."[8] A review of the current literature shows that Smith's criteria are still considered useful today. As you may by now suspect, however, the terminology used is less than clear, and additional criteria have emerged over time.

EQUITY

The phrase **tax equity** is commonly used to mean the equal treatment of similarly situated taxpayers. But little agreement exists as to the specifics of how to measure that equality.

Taxable income is a technical term for the amount equal to the statutorily defined tax base for the federal income tax.

Horizontal equity means equal tax treatment for similarly situated taxpayers.

A valid measure of the **ability to pay** a tax would include such factors as income, accumulated wealth, and prospects of future income—but in practice, there is no accepted formula to measure it.

Vertical equity means that those who have a greater ability to pay should bear a larger portion of total taxes.

Both the tax literature and political discussions commonly define **tax equity** as the equal treatment of similarly situated taxpayers. One obvious problem with this criterion is that the definition fails to provide a method or basis for measurement to determine under what conditions two or more taxpayers are similarly situated. The term *tax equity* seems to suggest that the appropriate measure is implicit in the tax base. In other words, a tax imposed on the purchase of a given commodity is assumed to be equitable as long as all purchasers of that commodity (with possible modifications for such things as quantity, quality, or price) pay an equivalent tax. By this same standard, a tax imposed on **taxable income** is deemed equitable as long as two persons earning the same *taxable income* during a given time period pay the same amount of income tax.

The larger problem is that this standard (equal treatment for similarly situated taxpayers), known as **horizontal equity**, considers only one dimension of the total taxpayer. In many cases this dimension is not the most significant for purposes of taxation. Example 1-1 easily demonstrates the problem.

EXAMPLE 1-1

Suppose that each of two taxpayers purchase a loaf of bread with a sales tax or an excise tax of 8¢. The bread is for personal consumption. Since each taxpayer pays an identical tax on an identical purchase, the tax may be said to be equitable. If we expand the number of variables to include incomes, wealth, marital status, physical condition, or any of hundreds of other possible factors common to these two taxpayers, then we may decide that the tax is not truly equitable in any meaningful sense because the taxpayers are not equally situated. The 8¢ tax on the loaf of bread may be grossly inequitable in a social sense if one purchaser is married, has 10 dependent children, and spends his or her last dollar to purchase this loaf of bread to feed the children, whereas the other purchaser is single, independently wealthy, and buys the bread to feed a swan.

The shortcomings of horizontal equity lead us to a related but somewhat different notion of equity—that of **ability to pay** or **vertical equity**. This criterion suggests that those who have a greater taxpaying ability should pay a larger part of total taxes. This Robin Hood notion, of taking relatively more from the rich to give to the poor, is considered equitable by some because it results in a more nearly equal distribution of after-tax incomes. The U.S. income tax system reflects vertical equity in two principal

8 *The Wealth of Nations*, Book V, Chapter II, Part II (New York: Dutton, 1910).

ways. First, our rate structure taxes people with higher incomes at higher tax rates. Second, the amount of income subject to taxation is reduced by the approximate costs of meeting a minimum standard of living for different family sizes.

Even if one could measure each person's ability to pay, there is still the problem of determining how much more the most able should pay than the least able. This problem has led to frequent changes in the tax-rate structure and adjustments to the tax base—almost always in the name of equity—with little consensus on the correctness of the result. Fortunately, the three other tax criteria proposed by Adam Smith are somewhat easier to explain and therefore less subject to the wide differences of opinion that exist on the subject of tax equity.

CONVENIENCE

Taxpayers and tax administrators alike place great stock in administrative simplicity, and in practice the criterion of **convenience** plays the predominant role. Any tax that can be easily assessed, collected, and administered seems to encounter the least opposition. Thus, for example, the **retail sales tax** is popular in many jurisdictions at least in part because most taxpayers find it relatively convenient to pay 6¢, 7¢, or 8¢ per dollar of purchase. Individually, these small sums seem immaterial; no formal tax return must be completed by the purchaser, and few additional records must be maintained by the vendor. Even the income tax, which is generally conceded to be a most inconvenient tax, has been made more tolerable by the creation of the standard deduction, withholding, and tax tables.

> **Convenience** means that a tax can be easily assessed, collected, and administered.
>
> A **retail sales tax** applies to the sales price of every item sold in a retail sale.

CERTAINTY

Certainty, like convenience, is high on most taxpayers' lists of criteria for a good tax. Most citizens like to know with a reasonable degree of certainty what their tax bill will be, given any set of circumstances. Obviously, the existence of certainty also permits a maximum of advance planning. The major problem with using certainty as a criterion for the selection of tax policy is the fact that different economic and social conditions may demand different tax provisions. Therefore, to the extent that taxation is used to achieve nonrevenue objectives, this criterion is de-emphasized—at least from the government viewpoint.

> **Certainty** means that taxpayers can predict with relative accuracy their tax liabilities.

Tax administrators have attempted to increase the certainty of some aspects of income taxation by providing detailed instructions, advance rulings, regulations, and other interpretations of the law. Property taxation often is made more palatable by widespread publication of annual tax rates, infrequent property reappraisals, and provisions for review boards. These and other efforts to increase the certainty of many taxes have added to their general acceptance in the United States.

Historically, the term *certainty* has also meant consistency in the amount of revenue collected in aggregate. For many years, taxes that produced widely fluctuating amounts of revenue were considered undesirable, while those providing stable amounts were favored. Government administrators solely dependent on revenue collections to conduct their operations were particularly concerned about this aspect of tax certainty. Since the 1950s, however, the notion that tax collections should vary with the economic cycle has been increasingly accepted as the desirable alternative to certainty of collections. This change, obviously, necessitated nontax sources of revenue (including debt financing).

ECONOMY

> An **economical tax** involves a minimum cost of compliance by taxpayers and administration by the government.

A good tax should involve a minimum cost for compliance by taxpayers and administration by the government. That is, it should be an **economical tax**. The income tax's historic position as a cheap tax to collect has come into serious question in recent years. In fiscal year 1987, the IRS collected over $450 billion in individual income tax revenue with an agency budget of about $4.4 billion. For 1990, individual income tax collections were $465 billion, but the agency budget had increased by 25% to $5.5 billion (for a workforce of 115,000 employees).[9] These costs represent only the administrative costs. Estimates of taxpayer compliance costs, comparing 1982 to 1989, show increases in time from 22 to 27.5 hours per person, and increases in money from $44 to $79 on average for assistance.[10]

When taken together, the costs of compliance (taxpayers' costs plus administrative costs) are estimated to equal 5% to 10% of all tax revenues.[11] The compliance and administrative burden of the income tax on taxpayers and on the government is substantially greater than that of other major revenue sources, such as Social Security and sales taxes.

PRODUCTIVITY

> A **productive tax** produces relatively large amounts of revenue.

Although Adam Smith did not include the ability to produce large amounts of revenue as one of the canons of taxation, this factor is given much consideration by politicians today. Obviously a **productive tax** holds much appeal as a source of tax revenues. Since a major objective of any tax system is to raise revenue, taxes that do not produce a significant amount of revenue are not viewed favorably even if they are equitable, convenient, certain, and economical. Pollution taxes appear to be held in disfavor for this reason. As a practical matter, most taxes could not have limited productivity and still be economical. A relatively unproductive tax is typically as expensive to enforce as a productive one.

> A **luxury tax** is an excise tax on certain luxury goods; it may be more important for its symbolic value than for its productivity.

Sometimes taxes are enacted because of their symbolic value. The 1990 Tax Act added a **luxury tax** on cars, boats, aircraft, jewelry, and furs that sell for more than specified thresholds. This new tax is expected to cost more than it will yield. It was enacted despite these projections because the increases in excise taxes on alcohol, tobacco, and gasoline impose a disproportionate burden on lower income taxpayers. Therefore, the symbolic value of imposing luxury taxes on the rich was believed to justify them, despite their low or even negative productivity.

Many state and local governments are currently searching out and deleting the less productive taxes while increasing already productive ones. A typical casualty of this process has been the tangible personal property tax on such items as household furniture and art work, which has often been deleted in favor of increased real property taxes. The only taxes on the horizon that are not already used but that could be highly

---

9 BNA Special Supplement, Part III, Section 9, Compliance Issues, Table 5, p. S-67, and Part IV, Historical Tables, Table I, p. S-68.

10 Joel Slemrod and Nikki Sorum, "The Compliance Cost of the U.S. Individual Income Tax System," *National Tax Journal*, December 1984, pp. 461–74; and Marsha Blumenthal and Joel Slemrod, "The Compliance Costs of the U.S. Individual Income Tax System: A Second Look After Tax Reform," manuscript in process, Office of Tax Policy Research, The University of Michigan, 1991.

11 Blumenthal and Slemrod, *op. cit.*

productive are a national sales tax and a value-added tax. These two taxes have essentially the same potential revenue yield and equity implications. However, a value-added tax involves taxing each transfer in the production process and thus would be less economical, since an entirely new administrative system would be needed to collect the tax.[12] Furthermore, a value-added tax ranks low in terms of the next criterion, visibility.

VISIBILITY

For taxpayers in a democracy to evaluate costs and benefits properly, they need to understand how much they are paying in taxes and the public benefits their tax dollars are buying. Political theory suggests, however, that politicians will tend to highlight benefits while obscuring taxes.[13] The **visibility** of taxes helps educate the public to the price they are paying for government. But politicians may resort to various **fiscal illusions** to disguise the true size or incidence of the tax burden.[14] These illusions can take various forms, such as excise taxes that are buried in the cost of a good; corporate taxes shifted to consumers; and deficit spending.

> The **visibility** of a tax is measured in terms of taxpayers' ability to understand the amount of taxes they pay and the benefits obtained for their tax dollars.

Deficit spending results when government spending exceeds the amount raised in tax revenues in the current year. To make up the difference between revenues and expenditures, the government issues interest-bearing debt. Thus, even though deficit spending is not an explicit tax, it can be viewed as a low-visibility form of taxation on future generations. This characterization of debt as a tax is consistent with our definition of tax except that the levy is not made on the basis of predetermined criteria.

> **Fiscal illusions** disguise the true size or incidence of the tax burden.

The federal government operated with a deficit in 53 of the years from 1926 through 1991 and with a surplus in the other 13 years. The *annual* target deficits currently exceed $300 billion, and the accumulated gross federal debt is projected to be $4.4 trillion at the end of fiscal year 1993. At the end of the Carter administration in 1981, total public debt was less than $1 trillion. Therefore, if the 1993 projections are correct, the public debt will have more than quadrupled in the most recent 12-year period. The tax current and future generations increasingly must bear is the *interest* on the dramatically increasing debt. Interest on federal debt in fiscal 1994 is projected to be $1,278 for each person in the United States.[15]

> **Deficit spending** occurs when the government spends more money than it raises in tax revenues in the current year.

More troubling to some are the less visible deficits that are not reflected in the dollar deficits. These are **infrastructure deficits** resulting from patterns of underfunding. Two important examples are in education and in transportation (including roads, bridges, and so on). Over the period from 1980 to 1988, education spending as a percentage of GNP has declined by 44%; transportation has declined by 29%. The burden of these undenominated costs on future generations is not even being estimated.[16]

> **Infrastructure deficits** result from underfunding of public goods and are like an undenominated tax on future generations.

---

12 See J. Due and A. Friedlaender, *Government Finance: Economics of the Public Sector* (Homewood, IL: Irwin, 1977), for a discussion of the relative merits of a national sales tax versus a value-added tax.

13 See Benjamin Page, *Choices and Echoes in Presidential Elections* (Chicago: University of Chicago Press, 1978); see also Albert Hirschman, *Exit, Voice, and Loyalty* (Cambridge, MA: Harvard University Press, 1970).

14 Susan Hansen, *The Politics of Taxation: Revenue without Representation* (New York: Praeger, 1983), p. 39.

15 See Allen D. Manvel, "Marking an (Unhappy) Anniversary," *Tax Notes*, April 8, 1991, pp. 119–21.

16 Allen D. Manvel, "Federal Spending Shifts: 1988 versus 1980," *Tax Notes*, April 3, 1989, pp. 101–103.

POLITICAL CONSIDERATIONS

Tax law is not made in a vacuum. It is important to recognize that members of Congress are influenced by **political action committees (PACs)**, large corporations and lobbyists promoting particular interests. From 1974 to 1988, PAC spending on congressional campaigns increased almost 900% (from $12.5 million to $120 million). During the same period, the number of PACs grew from 400 to more than 4,500. On average, payments by PACs and lobbyists to members of Congress far exceeded the amount paid in congressional salaries. Furthermore, in 1988 PACs gave incumbents $17 for every $1 they donated to challengers. This money facilitated the reelection of 99.2% of the House of Representatives' incumbents in 1988.[17] PAC money has also been an issue in the Senate. Senate Finance Committee chair Lloyd Bentsen disbanded his $10,000-per-seat breakfast club for lobbyists because of negative publicity.[18]

Assuming that PAC expenditures are made because they pay off, it can be concluded that many of the provisions in the following chapters are not pure reflections of the predetermined criteria discussed in this chapter. Special interest lobbying is usually packaged with rhetoric asserting that it fits under the general rubric of at least one of the criteria discussed. You must learn to evaluate the rhetoric critically.

In the following section, we review terms that are essential to sorting out whether a tax is structured according to the predetermined criteria associated with a good tax or according to political considerations.

_____ KEY CONCEPTS

In mechanical or arithmetic terms, a **tax** can also be defined as the product of a tax base times the tax rate. In equation form, this alternative definition is

$$T = B \times R$$

where T stands for tax, B stands for the tax base, and R stands for the tax rate. This quantitative definition will be the focal point for our discussion of seven key concepts in taxation: (1) tax bases, (2) tax rates, (3) average versus marginal rates, (4) nominal versus effective rates, (5) incidence of taxes, (6) implicit taxes, and (7) tax burdens in general.

In the equation of $T = B \times R$, the two critical variables in any tax are (1) the measure of the item or event that is made subject to tax (called the tax base), and (2) the portion or percentage of the tax base that must be paid to the government (called the tax rate). The product of the multiplication is the tax that the taxpayer must pay to the government. Example 1-2 illustrates this alternative definition.

EXAMPLE 1-2

Imagine that a strange government imposed a 10% tax on the value of any ring(s) individuals wore on their left hand. The value of any ring worn on anyone's left hand would be the tax base for this tax. The tax rate, which must be clearly stated in any law that imposes a tax, is 10% in this example. The tax is simply the product

Continued

---

17 Brooks Jackson, "Michel Joins Swelling Chorus of Republican Voices Calling for PAC Funding to Be Curbed or Ended," *The Wall Street Journal*, December 5, 1988, p. A12.

18 Mary Gael Timberlake, "Revelation of Member's Breakfast Clubs Renews Controversy over PACs' Influence," *Tax Notes*, February 9, 1987, pp. 541–43.

EXAMPLE 1-2 (Con't.)

of a multiplication. Thus if an individual in this imaginary country were to wear a ring, valued at $5,000, on the left hand, that individual would owe the government a $500 tax.

Collecting this silly tax would be another matter! Problems of discovery, enforcement, valuation, and definition would be so great that no tax revenues would ever be forthcoming. The example, however unrealistic, emphasizes the more important considerations that must be thoroughly investigated before any government attempts to impose and collect any tax. Thinking about the many creative ways in which individuals could adapt their behavior to escape this tax is particularly instructive. Definitional problems are equally fascinating. For example, how long must a ring remain on a finger before it is deemed to have been worn? If a band encompasses two fingers, rather than the traditional one finger, is it still a ring? Might one escape the tax by wearing the ring on some mechanical device attached to one's hand not directly connected to a finger? The possibilities are endless. Similar problems are encountered with every tax base known to humankind.

TAX BASES

As the prior example demonstrates, the wise selection of a tax base presents a very difficult task. Administrative considerations, social consequences, and yield (or, the amount of tax revenue derived) are paramount. In countries that are less economically developed, administrative considerations are typically more important than social consequences. As countries develop and populations become more educated, social consequences assume greater importance. As social issues gain prominence, entirely new problems in measurement and definition arise.

To illustrate this point, we will focus on a tax base that has withstood the test of time. If one ignores social consequences, the retail sales tax presents relatively few administrative problems. Even in its most rudimentary form, however, this tax demands that retail sales be distinguished from all other sales. Valuation is not a big problem. The amount subject to the retail sales tax is simply the sales price of any item sold in a retail sale. Collection of the tax is difficult but not impossible because the government can readily identify and coerce compliance from the vast majority of all vendors engaged in the retail sales business. Although the tax may be imposed on the ultimate consumer, the vendor making the sale typically becomes responsible for maintaining the records and remitting the tax to the government.

Now note how social considerations can quickly complicate an otherwise simple tax. In an attempt to make the retail sales tax less regressive (a term that will be defined momentarily), many governments have elected to exempt from it such things as retail sales of food for off-premises consumption; housing; medicine and medical services; and other goods and services that must be consumed by even the poorest taxpayer in daily living.

Such exceptions introduce many new definitional questions. What for example, is food? Does it include soft drinks? Beer? Candy? Cookies? If food is purchased in a delicatessen and taken to one's workplace for consumption, should it be taxed like food bought in a restaurant or exempted like food bought in a grocery store? The list of exemptions from the retail sales tax varies from one state to another, as do definitions. These differences radically vary the social consequences of the retail sales tax from state to state.

Different but equally pesky issues dog the heels of other tax bases (to be covered later in this chapter), such as income or ownership of real property. You may now begin to appreciate the human complexities that lurk behind the abstract values in our mathematical formula of $T = B \times R$. We turn next to the multiplier in that formula.

TAX RATES

Tax rates are commonly described by one of three adjectives, namely (1) proportional, (2) progressive, or (3) regressive. *In a purely technical sense* these three adjectives can be easily explained in terms of the formula ($T = B \times R$). Through elementary algebraic manipulation this formula can be rearranged to read as follows:

$$R = \frac{T}{B}$$

This rearranged equation puts greater emphasis on tax rates and is useful in explaining one of two concepts implicit in the words proportional, progressive, and regressive.

> A **proportional tax rate** structure applies a constant tax rate to every level of the tax base.

A **proportional tax rate** is one that applies a constant tax rate to every possible level of any tax base. Or, in other words, if the ratio T/B is constant for all levels of the tax base, the tax rate is a proportional tax in a purely technical sense.

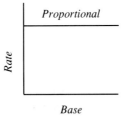

> A **progressive tax rate** structure takes an increasing proportion of the tax base as it rises.

A **progressive tax rate** is one that takes an increasing proportion of the tax base as the tax base increases. Or, in arithmetic terms, if the ratio T/B increases as the tax base increases, the tax rate is progressive in a technical sense. Progressive tax rates are commonly used in a technical sense for income, estate, inheritance, and gift taxes.

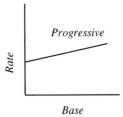

A **regressive tax rate** is one that takes a decreasing proportion of the tax base as the base increases. Or, in terms of our revised formula, if the ratio T/B decreases as the tax base increases, the tax rate is technically described as a regressive rate. Social Security taxes have a regressive tax rate structure, using this definition.

> A **regressive tax rate** structure takes a decreasing proportion of the tax base as it rises.

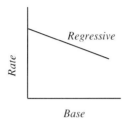

Politicians, newspaper editors, television commentators, and other interested parties often use these same three words—proportional, progressive, and regressive—to describe both specific tax bases and overall tax systems. This shift from a technical description of tax *rates* to a description of tax *bases* or overall tax *systems* is a subtle but extremely important one for students of taxation to understand clearly. To grasp the many important definitional distinctions in these two uses of the same three words, let us repeat that the pertinent ratio in a technical description of tax *rates* is the ratio of *tax payable/tax base*. As the words are used to describe tax bases and tax systems in the popular media, the ratio that is pertinent is the ratio of *actual tax burden/ability to pay*. Unfortunately, there are serious (possibly insurmountable) problems in the measurement of both the numerator and the denominator used in the more popular definition. Before we begin to examine those measurement problems in greater detail, let us note in passing two other key concepts.

AVERAGE VERSUS MARGINAL TAX RATES

The ratio of *tax payable/tax base* is also used to determine a taxpayer's **average tax rate**. The average tax rate will not equal the marginal tax rate for any tax imposed using either a progressive or a regressive tax rate structure. The **marginal tax rate** is the rate which applies to any *incremental* change in the tax base. To demonstrate the difference between marginal and average tax rates, consider the 1992 U.S. income tax rates for single individuals. This rate structure involves three different tax brackets: a 15% bracket applicable to taxable incomes of less than $21,450; a 28% bracket applicable to taxable income in excess of $21,450 but less than $51,900; and a 31% bracket for taxable income in excess of $51,900. (See Appendix A.) Thus a single individual who reports a $25,000 taxable income in 1992 would owe an income tax of $4,211.50 (15% x $21,450 plus 28% x $3,550). This person's average tax rate is 16.846% or $4,211.50/$25,000; that is, the ratio of *tax payable/tax base* or $4,211.50/taxable income$.

> The **average tax rate** is derived by dividing the tax by the tax base.
>
> The **marginal tax rate** is the rate applied to any *incremental* change in the tax base.

If this individual were to receive a raise which increased his or her taxable income by $1,000, the extra tax would amount to $280 ($1,000 x 28%). The marginal tax rate is 28% because it is the rate, stipulated in our federal income tax law, for any amount of taxable income of more than $21,450, but less than $51,900, for single (unmarried) taxpayers. Observe that the marginal tax rate will always exceed the average tax rate if (1) the tax involves a progressive tax rate schedule and (2) the taxpayer's tax base exceeds the maximum amount subject to the lowest tax rate. For unmarried persons subject to the U.S. income tax in 1992, this means that their marginal tax rate will always exceed their average tax rate if their taxable income is in excess of $21,450 (the maximum amount subject to the 15% rate).

It is important to grasp the significance of the marginal tax rate early in the study of taxation because the marginal rate determines how knowledgeable taxpayers will act in many circumstances. As a practical matter, the marginal tax rate is to business what the law of gravity is to physics; tax bases tend to seek their lowest level just as water does. In other words, taxpayers tend to arrange their financial affairs so that any tax base is subject to tax at the lowest possible marginal tax rate.

NOMINAL VERSUS EFFECTIVE TAX RATES

The average tax rate determined by dividing a taxpayer's tax liability by his or her tax base minimizes the significance of exemptions or deductions that are allowed in the calculation of the tax base. Many commentators have carefully pointed out that the allowance of any exemption or any deduction automatically turns a proportional tax into a progressive tax.[19] The arithmetic of their conclusion is simple. Suppose, for example, that a (flat) 15% tax on all income in excess of a $2,000 per year exemption is imposed. The progressive nature of this otherwise proportional tax is shown in Table 1-1. In other words, the tax rate is a proportional (constant) 15% tax on the tax base (defined as all income over $2,000) but it results in a progressive (increasing percentage) tax base on total income.

The assumptions used in the creation of Table 1-1 clearly involve the application of a proportional (15%) tax rate. Nevertheless, the mere existence of a single $2,000 exemption available to every taxpayer converts an otherwise proportional income tax into a progressive income tax. This subtle shift in focus from tax rates to the tax base is easily overlooked and even more easily misunderstood.

Whether a tax is judged to be proportional, progressive, or regressive depends in part on the measure used in the denominator of the equation $R = T/B$. If taxable income—defined previously as the statutorily defined tax base for the federal income tax—is the denominator, the resulting rate may best be described as the **average nominal tax rate**. If we adjust the denominator to do a less technical but more realistic

> The **average nominal tax rate** is the percentage applied to the tax base to determine the tax liabillity.

TABLE 1-1

The Progressive Effect of the Personal Exemption

	Taxpayer 1	Taxpayer 2	Taxpayer 3
Income earned	$5,000	$10,000	$15,000
Less exemption	2,000	2,000	2,000
Taxable income (tax base)	$3,000	$ 8,000	$13,000
Times tax rate	0.15	0.15	0.15
Equals tax liability	$ 450	$ 1,200	$ 1,950
Average effective tax rate	$450/$5,000	$1,200/$10,000	$1,950/$15,000
	=9%	=12%	=13%

---

19 For example, see Walter J. Blum and Harry Kalven, Jr., *The Uneasy Case for Progressive Taxation* (Chicago: University of Chicago Press, 1953), p. 4.

job of measuring the intended tax base—for example, if we adjust taxable income to reflect real or economic income—the resulting percentage may best be described as the **average effective tax rate.** Although individuals might not agree on a hard and fast definition of economic income, almost everyone would agree that it is a broader concept than taxable income. In very general terms, economic income would include adjustments for a number of income items that are exempted from the U.S. income tax law by statute; it would also include both positive and negative adjustments for various deductions authorized in the calculation of taxable income. The precise inclusions and exclusions in this set of adjustments might vary from one commentator to another and from one purpose to another.

> The **average effective tax rate** is derived by dividing the tax by an amount representing economic income.

TAX INCIDENCE

A second problem in measurement arises when determining the distribution of a tax burden. This is the problem of economic **incidence**, which concerns the correct identification of the person who ultimately bears any tax. You might initially assume that a tax is borne by the person who pays it. That assumption, however, need not be correct, especially when many taxpayers are artificial legal entities (corporations) rather than living individuals. It is far easier to determine who writes the tax check than who ultimately bears a tax burden for many different taxes.

> The **incidence** of a tax involves a determination of who actually bears the economic burden of any tax.

Recall our earlier discussion of the retail sales tax. We noted that the sales tax is typically paid by the consumer but that the record-keeping and tax-collection-remission functions ordinarily are made the responsibility of the retailer. That is, the retailer first collects the retail sales tax from the buyer when the retail sale is made. Sometime later the retailer will remit the sales tax to the government. Although the retailers may ultimately write the check to the government, in most cases the actual burden of the retail sales tax is clearly borne by the initial purchaser, not the vendor.

The burden of many other taxes is far more difficult to determine. Who, for example, bears the burden of the real property tax? The corporate income tax? Payroll taxes? In each of these cases it is easy to identify the apparent taxpayer; that is, the landowner pays the real property tax, the corporation (a legal entity) pays the corporate income tax, and the employer pays the payroll taxes. Those observations do not, however, justify the conclusion that landowners, corporations, or employers ultimately bear the burden of these three taxes. Depending on market conditions, these taxes may be passed on to others in ways that are difficult, if not impossible, to determine with precision. If the landowner, the corporation, or the employer function as either a monopoly or oligopoly, they may be able to shift part or all of the real economic burden from themselves to purchasers (in the form of higher prices); to suppliers of labor (in the form of reduced wages); or to others (in yet other ways). Although economists can model the problem and estimate the ultimate distribution of taxes under varying conditions, their conclusions are often suspect because the information required in the modeling process is often incomplete.

IMPLICIT TAXES

So far we have been talking only about *explicit* taxes. Attention has recently focused on **implicit taxes** because of their significance in tax policy and investment decisions.[20] To understand the concept of implicit taxes, it is necessary to refer to a

> **Implicit taxes** are measured by the reduction in the before-tax return an investor accepts to invest in a tax-favored investment.

---

20 For a thorough discussion of implicit taxes, see Myron S. Scholes and Mark A. Wolfson, *Taxes and Business Strategy: A Planning Approach,* (Englewood Cliffs, NJ: Prentice-Hall, 1992), Ch. 5. Much of the discussion of implicit taxes in this text is derived from that source.

basic economic principle: The value of an asset is determined by the present value of the after-tax income stream that the asset will produce. This principle leads to the conclusion that investors will bid up the price of tax-favored investments until the after-tax rates of return on tax-favored and benchmark investments are equal, after adjustments for differences in risk. Implicit taxes occur when before-tax rates of return on tax-favored investments decrease as a result of this bidding process.

Consider the comparison of returns on municipal bonds (which generate tax-exempt interest) to returns on fully taxable bonds. Investors accept a lower rate of return on municipals when their after-tax rate of return equals or exceeds that on taxable bonds. These investors clearly pay lower explicit taxes. The question is do they also pay implicit taxes in an amount equal to the lower before-tax return that they will accept?

An implicit tax can be calculated as the difference between the before-tax return on a taxable bond and the before-tax return on a municipal bond of equal risk. For example, if benchmark taxable bonds are earning 10% and the return on tax-exempt bonds (risk-adjusted) is 7%, the 3% difference is an implicit tax. The total tax is the sum of the implicit and explicit taxes. As you can see in this example, the *total* tax on either investment is the same. In the taxable bond case, the tax is an explicit tax; in the tax-exempt bond case, the tax is an implicit tax. The implicit taxes in this example accrue to the municipal governments who are able to pay a lower rate of interest to borrow money.[21]

In the past, most calculations of the distribution of tax burdens have not taken implicit taxes into account. The result is that most of these calculations systematically underestimate the relative progressivity of our tax system because implicit taxes are borne largely by higher income taxpayers.

In this introduction, we do not examine the actual calculations for implicit taxes. Rather, our intent is to expose you to the concept and to make it clear that the calculation of tax burdens involves much more than initially meets the eye.

TAX BURDENS IN GENERAL

As already noted, a completely accurate measure of the proportionality, progressivity, or regressivity of any tax rate or structure (or of any tax system overall) requires a valid measure of both (1) a taxpayer's actual tax burden and (2) that taxpayer's ability to pay taxes. Valid measures of the former would include adjustments for both tax incidence and implicit taxes. Valid measures of the latter would include more factors than the taxpayer's income for a single year.

Because most people who make statements about distributions or tax burdens fail to explain exactly what they measured, or how they measured it, you can often dismiss their conclusions as little more than political rhetoric. Even tax scholars who make a serious effort to measure all of the critical factors correctly must be viewed as less than accurate because there is no accepted measure of anyone's ability to pay taxes. Lacking a more formal measurement, tax scholars may accept taxable income as a reasonable proxy for one's ability to pay in a tax sense. What is problematic in this approach? While our tax system incorporates many factors in defining taxable

---

21 Sometimes implicit taxes can accrue to parties other than a government. Under certain conditions, the new buyer of an asset pays an implicit tax which benefits the seller. For a whimsical description of this situation, see Boris I. Bittker, "Tax Shelters and Tax Capitalization, or Does the Early Bird Get a Free Lunch?" *National Tax Journal*, Volume 28, No. 4, 1987, pp. 416–19.

income—factors including age, marital status, health expenditures, and number of dependents—it fails to include such indicators as accumulated wealth and future earning prospects.

Table 1-2 illustrates the fact that a proportional income tax can become regressive if deductions are distributed unevenly. As you will learn later in this text, our income-tax law permits individual taxpayers to claim a personal exemption and the larger of either (1) a standard deduction or (2) their "itemized" deductions. IRS records show that about 75% of all itemized deductions are actually claimed by taxpayers reporting the highest 40% of all family incomes. Further, 50% of those deductions are claimed by taxpayers reporting the highest 20% of all family incomes.[22]

Although the data used in the construction of Table 1-2 are somewhat contrived, they illustrate a potentially important distributional feature of our federal income tax. It would be incorrect to conclude from this limited data that the U.S. income tax is, in fact, a regressive tax. Many other factors would have to be investigated and quantified before one could justify that conclusion. Mathematical precision often masks major difficulties in both definition and measurement. Because you have studied these key concepts of taxation, however, you should be better prepared than most others to challenge doubtful conclusions based on incomplete and inaccurate information.

_____ COMMON TAX BASES

For all levels of government in the aggregate, more revenues are generated from income taxation than from any other tax. Figure 1-1 illustrates the heavy federal reliance on income taxation in the United States. This predominance of income taxation is perhaps a major distinguishing characteristic of U.S. taxation; many other countries rely more heavily on other tax bases. It is therefore appropriate that we start our discussion of common tax bases with income. The discussion will continue with social security taxes, transactions taxes, excise taxes, consumption taxes, wealth (or ownership) taxes, and wealth-transfer taxes.

> **Goal #5**
> Describe the common tax bases used in the United States and their relative importance.

TABLE 1-2

The Potentially Regressive Effect of Itemized Deductions

	Taxpayer 1	Taxpayer 2	Taxpayer 3
Income earned	$5,000	$10,000	$15,000
Less exemption	2,000	2,000	2,000
Adjusted earnings	$3,000	$ 8,000	$13,000
Less itemized deductions	500	3,200	6,000
Taxable income (tax base)	$2,500	$ 4,800	$ 7,000
Times tax rate	0.15	0.15	0.15
Equals tax liability	$ 375	$ 720	$ 1,050
Average effective tax rate	$375/$5,000	$720/$10,000	$1,050/$15,000
	=7.5%	=7.2%	=7.0%

22 Daniel H. Weinberg, "The Distributional Implications of Tax Expenditures and Comprehensive Income Taxation," *National Tax Journal*, June 1987, pp. 237–54.

FIGURE 1-1

**Federal Revenues
by Source as
Shares of GNP**

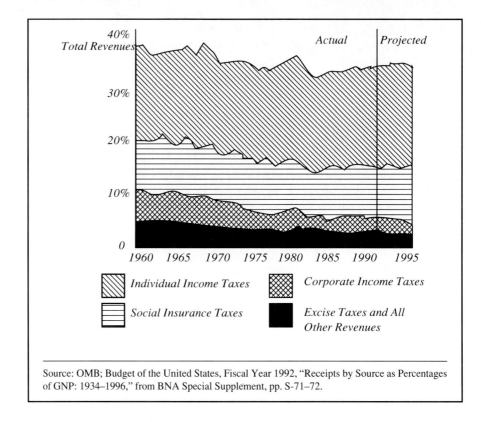

Source: OMB; Budget of the United States, Fiscal Year 1992, "Receipts by Source as Percentages of GNP: 1934–1996," from BNA Special Supplement, pp. S-71–72.

INCOME TAXES IN GENERAL

An income tax can be imposed in various forms. The most common form is, of course, a tax on ordinary taxable income. A decision to tax income also necessitates an identification of the basic entities subject to this tax. In the United States, the three taxable entities are individuals, corporations, and fiduciaries (estates and trusts). Ignoring for the moment important details, we may generalize that the ordinary incomes earned each year by individuals, corporations, and fiduciaries have been a common tax base since 1913.

Refer again to Figure 1-1. For 1991–1996, 45% to 47% of total federal revenues are projected to be derived from the individual income tax and slightly less than 9% from the corporate income tax. Note that tax from fiduciaries is not a significant revenue source and is lumped into the "other" category. As will be discussed shortly, if social insurance (FICA) taxes are considered taxes on income, then income taxes on individuals constitute about 85% of federal taxes in the United States today.

Striking trends emerge from a review of Figure 1-1. Social insurance payroll taxes have been growing slightly as a percent of total revenues. And, despite a recent emphasis on users fees and excise taxes, the "other" category in total is projected to stay flat. Notice also that the share of revenues provided by the corporate sector was decreasing until 1987. The 1986 Tax Reform Act shifted some of the burden from individuals to the corporate sector, but the corporate tax burden is still much lower now than it was in the 1960s.

To some of you it may be a surprise that in the United States we do not have a single tax base for our income tax. Instead we have two income taxes: the regular income tax and the **alternative minimum tax (AMT)**. Taxpayers must pay the larger of these two income-based taxes. Lawmakers enacted the AMT in recognition of the fact that

The **alternative minimum tax (AMT)** is a tax on a variation of the regular income tax base as adjusted for certain exclusions and deductions; taxpayers must pay the larger of the regular income tax and the AMT.

the regular tax system failed miserably to measure ability to pay in some relatively unusual situations. The tax base for the AMT starts with the tax base for the regular income tax and adjusts for certain exclusions and deductions that were motivated by reasons other than measuring ability to pay. Thus, one can think of the AMT tax base as being the regular income tax base after a purge of many (but not all) items subject to special tax treatment.

INCOME TAXES PAID BY INDIVIDUALS

Although the tax base for the income tax paid by individuals begins with income broadly conceived, practical matters constrain the tax definition of gross income. For example, if asset values appreciate, the resulting increase in an individual's net worth is income in an economic sense. However, our tax system omits such an increase from gross income because of the administrative difficulty of capturing subjectively determined values in the tax base on an annual basis.

The tax formula in Figure 1-2 gives an overview of the tax base for individuals. The formula begins with personal income. Like income broadly conceived, personal income is difficult to quantify with accuracy because it is not captured on tax returns.

FIGURE 1-2

Tax Formula for Individuals

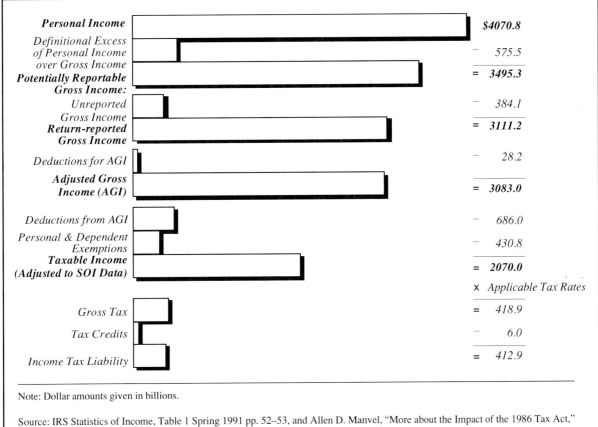

Personal Income	$4070.8
Definitional Excess of Personal Income over Gross Income	− 575.5
Potentially Reportable Gross Income:	= 3495.3
Unreported Gross Income	− 384.1
Return-reported Gross Income	= 3111.2
Deductions for AGI	− 28.2
Adjusted Gross Income (AGI)	= 3083.0
Deductions from AGI	− 686.0
Personal & Dependent Exemptions	− 430.8
Taxable Income (Adjusted to SOI Data)	= 2070.0
	x *Applicable Tax Rates*
Gross Tax	= 418.9
Tax Credits	− 6.0
Income Tax Liability	= 412.9

Note: Dollar amounts given in billions.

Source: IRS Statistics of Income, Table 1 Spring 1991 pp. 52–53, and Allen D. Manvel, "More about the Impact of the 1986 Tax Act," *Tax Notes,* December 10, 1990, pp. 1259–61.

As we will discuss later in the text, items such as gifts, inheritances, life insurance proceeds, and nontaxable fringe benefits are exempt from gross income for tax purposes even though they constitute personal income in an economic sense and are conducive to measurement. For political and social considerations, Congress has decided to exempt these amounts from taxation.

> **Adjusted gross income (AGI)** is a statutory subtotal in the calculation of taxable income. It includes all income but only certain deductions.

The tax base is further narrowed by deductions *for* and deductions *from* **adjusted gross income (AGI),** including exemption deductions. Deductions for AGI tend to be more of a business or investment nature, whereas deductions from AGI tend to be more of a personal nature, although a clear conceptual distinction is not always evident. Thus, partnership losses, deductions attributable to a business carried on by the taxpayer, reimbursed expenses of employees, and contributions to IRAs and Self-Employed Retirement Plans (SERPs) are all deductible *for* AGI. Table 1-3 estimates the composition of AGI for 1989. Note that deductions *for* AGI will already have been deducted in determining net income from the sources listed in the figure. Individuals can deduct a stipulated amount from AGI, or they can choose to itemize deductions if the latter total is higher. The major itemized deductions *from* AGI include home mortgage interest, state and local income and property taxes, charitable contributions, and medical expenses. Table 1-4 details the amounts taxpayers deducted for these amounts in 1989. Like the standard deduction used by nonitemizers, exemptions are rather straightforward. An exemption of $2,300 in (1992) is generally permitted for each taxpayer and each dependent.

In contrast to how our tax system treats income earned by an individual, business are taxed on net profits, not gross revenues. That is, a business has no taxable income if gross income does not exceed deductions. Individual taxpayers generally may not deduct such personal expenses as food, shelter, clothing, and transportation. Thus an employee typically has taxable income even if his or her gross income fails to exceed expenditures. Ask policymakers why they deny employees so many deductions, and they might respond that most employees' expenses are personal in nature and would have to be incurred even if they earned no income. The policymakers might also note that individuals make purely personal choices about the amount to expend on such

TABLE 1-3

Composition of Adjusted Gross Income—1989

	In Billions
Salaries and wages	$2,467.5
Interest and dividends	298.0
Net business income*	204.0
Net capital gains	144.1
Pensions and annuities	149.4
Unemployed compensation and taxable Social Security benefits	29.7
Rents, royalties, estate and trust income	.4
Statutory adjustments for IRAs and SERPs	(17.3)
Other statutory adjustments and adjustments to total AGI	15.6
Total AGI	$3,291.4

*Includes sole proprietorships, partnerships, S corporations, and farming operations

Source: Statistics of Income, Spring 1991, Table 1, page 52.

	In Billions
Itemized deductions	
Interest	$188
Taxes	131
Charitable contributions	55
Other	31
Medical expenses	20
Total	$425
Standard Deduction	$311

Source: Statistics of Income, Spring 1991, Table 1, page 53.

TABLE 1-4

1989 Deductions from Adjusted Gross Income

items. For a majority of all individuals, this inconsistency is resolved by allowing a flat standard deduction for each tax return (the amount varies by filing status) and an additional deduction for each personal and dependent exemption claimed on the tax return. Congress generally tries to keep the amount of the standard deduction and the exemption deduction in a range that will exempt a poverty level of personal income from taxation.

The data graphed in Figure 1-3 demonstrate that the distribution of the tax burden has flattened (become less progressive) over time. One point is important to remember. Although high income taxpayers pay a larger percentage of their income in taxes, they make up a relatively small portion of the population. Most taxpayers are in the middle. Thus, in the remainder of the text, as we discuss provisions that involve high income taxpayers, remember that the percentage of taxpayers affected is small. Consequently, the tax dollars gained or lost from changing provisions that affect only the top payers are sometimes small in terms of total revenue raised. Any big surge in tax dollars generally comes from changing provisions that affect the middle class—the bulk of the taxpayers.

SOCIAL SECURITY TAXES

If you are encountering the contribution formula for **Social Security,** or **Federal Insurance Contributions Act (FICA)** for the first time, you may have to accept our word that at one time it was actually simple. The 1990 Tax Law continued a long history of tampering with this formula. Currently two different bases are used for funding three different trusts. (These trusts are for *OASI* or *Old Age and Survivors Insurance, DI* or *Disability Insurance,* and *MI* or *Medicare Hospital Insurance.*) Each trust has a separate tax rate.

In brief the formula works like this. At least for 1992, OASI and DI share a base of $55,500, and MI derives from a base of $130,200. Rates are 11.2% for OASI, 1.2% for DI, and 2.9% for MI. Thus, for 1992, the total Social Security tax paid is 15.3% on incomes up to $55,500 ($8,492) and 2.9% on incomes from $55,500 to $130,200 ($2,166) for a maximum of $10,658.

As an employee, you pay half of the tax and your employer pays half. If self-employed, you pay the full amount of the tax. (Despite this surface difference between

The **Social Security,** or **Federal Insurance Contributions Act (FICA)** allows for benefits to be paid to retired or disabled workers, and (under certain conditions) their spouses and children. To qualify, workers must meet age and contribution requirements.

FIGURE 1-3

Federal Individual Income Tax as a Percent of Taxable Income (for a Married Couple with Two Dependents)

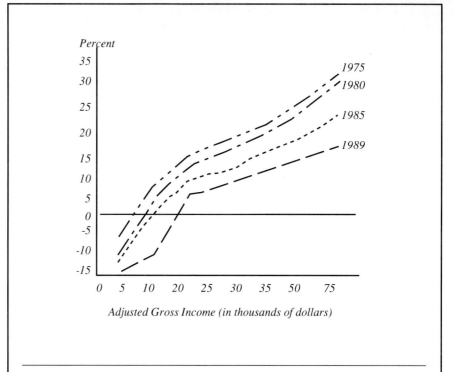

Note: Negative percentages and percentages less than 2% reflect refundable earned income credit.
Source: Tax Foundation, Inc., *Facts and Figures on Government Finance,* (Baltimore: Johns Hopkins University Press, 1991), Table C38, pp. 127.

the burdens of the employed and the self-employed, most economists believe that the incidence of all payroll taxes falls on the employee.) Because of steady increases in the contribution rate and tax base (see Table 1-5), two out of three taxpayers now pay more in self-employment or combined employee/employer Social Security taxes than they do in federal income tax.[23] Of low-income families paying any federal taxes, at least 97% pay larger Social Security than income taxes.[24]

Social Security taxes and individual incomes taxes tap essentially the same tax base. Table 1-3 showed that about 75% of all AGI is derived from employment income (*Salaries and Wages ÷ Total AGI* = $2,467.5 billion ÷ $3,291.4 billion = .7497). And most business income included in AGI is also subject to self-employment taxes. Therefore, upwards of 85% of the tax base is subject to both income and Social Security tax. Further, most of individuals' employment income is fully subject to Social Security taxes because it falls below the exempt levels. This has critical implications for the relative marginal tax rates of low-income versus high-income workers. A typical low-income worker faces a combined Social Security rate of 15.3% plus a 15% federal income tax rate, or a marginal rate of 30.3%. The high-income worker faces a marginal rate of 33.9% on income over $53,400 and 31% on income over $130,200 (ignoring some modifications that we will encounter later).

---

23 Gene Steuerle, "Economic Perspective," *Tax Notes*, Dec. 11, 1989, pp. 1371–72.

24 "Tax Progressivity and Income Distribution," House Ways and Means Committee Report, 101st Congress, 2d Sess. (Committee Print 1990); 33.

Year	Contribution Rate for Employer and Employee (Each) (in percent)	Annual Maximum Taxable Earnings (in nominal dollars)
1975	5.85	14,100
1976	5.85	15,300
1977	5.85	16,500
1978	6.05	17,700
1979	6.13	22,900
1980	6.13	25,900
1981	6.65	29,700
1982	6.70	32,400
1983	6.70	35,700
1984	7.00	37,800
1985	7.05	39,600
1986	7.15	42,000
1987	7.15	43,800
1988	7.51	45,000
1989	7.51	48,000
1990	7.65	51,300
1991	7.65	53,400*
1992	7.65	55,500+

TABLE 1-5

Social Security Contribution Rates and Maximum Taxable Earnings, 1975–1992 (by calendar year)

*In 1991, the 2.9% MI tax was payable on income of up to $125,000.
+In 1992, the 2.9% MI tax is payable on income of up to $130,200.

Source: *Social Security Bulletin, Annual Statistical Supplement*, 1990.

The Social Security contribution is more aptly characterized as a tax than as an insurance premium or retirement saving because, after certain minimums are met, the amounts eventually received are determined by Congress rather than by an individual's lifetime payments into the system. This point is well illustrated by one Congressional Research Service estimate that a 65-year-old retiree in 1980 will have received all contributions plus interest back by his or her 70th birthday, whereas the same retiree in the year 2040 will not break even until the age of 97. Notice that social insurance payments would still fit our definition of a tax even if earmarking were abandoned and the program were financed out of general revenues.

INCOME TAXES PAID BY CORPORATIONS

The income tax paid by corporations is a very controversial tax. Conceptually, it is a bad tax because it is unclear which individuals (shareholders, employees, or consumers) ultimately bear or share the burden of the tax. Politically it has been a source of contention because some (like former President Reagan) have advocated repeal while others (like Citizens for Tax Justice) have agitated for increases. Whatever the merits, it is clear that the public supports corporate income taxation. Stories of rich corporations not paying any taxes fueled the 1986 tax reform movement (projected to shift $120 billion in taxes from individuals to corporations) just as stories of rich individuals not paying any taxes had fueled the 1969 tax reform legislation 17 years earlier.

Although examples of specific corporations paying no taxes generated adverse publicity, the aggregate statistics are also quite dramatic. Figure 1-1 shows the significant reduction in corporate tax revenues as a share of the Gross National Product (GNP). The Tax Reform Act of 1986 essentially reversed this trend by broadening the tax base. Even though corporate rates were lowered, the net effect of the 1986 Act was to increase corporate taxes to 2% of GNP. Although this percentage was higher than that in any of the preceding seven years, the taxes collected from corporation income taxes have fallen short of the Treasury Department's estimates. Government officials apparently underestimated the extent of corporate America's desire and ability to adapt and adjust to avoid taxes.[25]

As the formula in Figure 1-4 suggests, the corporate income tax is conceptually similar to the individual tax since it is predicated on a tax base determined by subtracting allowable deductions from gross income. Certain differences are obvious, however. Because corporations aren't people, incurring basic living expenses, they are not entitled to personal and dependency exemptions or a standard deduction. But corporations do receive some considerations not afforded individuals, as noted earlier. Generally, all losses are deductible because all activities of a corporation are considered business activities, whereas individuals are severely restricted in their ability to deduct personal losses. Also a corporation that is a shareholder of another corporation is allowed a *dividend received deduction*. Such a corporation may generally deduct either 70% or 80% of any dividend received to mitigate double taxation on the allowed income. Double taxation of dividend payments would otherwise occur, because they are not deductible in the calculation of the payor corporation's taxable income.

FIGURE 1-4

Formula for Corporations

Gross Income =	*$9,581 billion*
– Deductions and Adjustments:	*$9,269 billion*
= Taxable Income:	*$312 billion*
x *Applicable Tax Rate*	
= Gross Tax Liability:	*$118 billion*
--Tax Credits:	*$31 billion*
= Net Tax Liability:	*$87 billion*

Source: *IRS Statistics of Income,* Spring 1991, Table 13, pp.117–18.

---

25 For further details, see Lee Burton, "Business as Usual: Under New Tax Law, Corporations Still Find Ways to Reduce Rates," *The Wall Street Journal*, June 2, 1988, p. 1.

TRANSACTIONS TAXES

Transactions taxes are levied on transactions or events such as stock transfers, severance of natural resources from the earth, and official registration of selected legal and business papers. In certain jurisdictions the transfer of stock ownership from one party to another, whether or not by sale, has been a taxable occasion. In other jurisdictions the separation of a natural resource from the earth (for example, natural gas, petroleum, and iron ore) is a taxable event. In yet other jurisdictions a stamp tax is imposed on the registration of a deed, the notarization of a document, or the filing of a business paper.

> **Transactions taxes** are taxes levied on certain transactions or events.

EXCISE TAXES

The manufacture, sale, or consumption of various commodities has been singled out as a base for taxation. Taxes imposed on only *selected* commodities are widely referred to as excise taxes. The 1990 Tax Act increased excises tax on many items, most notably tobacco and alcohol products, motor fuels, and airplane tickets. Since 1970 Congress has imposed an excise tax on airplane tickets. That tax was increased from 8% to 10% in 1990. Other common federal excise taxes cover distilled spirits (increased from $12.50 to $13.50 per gallon), cigarettes (increased from 16¢ to 20¢ per pack through 1992 and increased to 24¢ per pack thereafter), and gasoline (increased from 9¢ per gallon to 14¢ per gallon). The newly enacted luxury tax is a 10% tax on autos, boats, aircraft, jewelry, and furs that cost an amount in excess of varying threshold values.

You may be surprised to learn that among the bases for U.S. excise taxes are such items as fishing equipment; pistols and revolvers, shells and cartridges; tires; truck parts; teletypewriter service; wagers and the occupation of accepting wagers; sugar; narcotic drugs; white phosphorous matches; adulterated butter; filled cheese; cotton futures; and machine-gun transfers. Because lower-income taxpayers must generally consume all of their income, excise taxes (like other consumption taxes) are typically assumed to be regressive.

Some years back a Congressional Budget Office study found that a family with an income of $15,000 spends 14% of its income on items that are subject to excise taxes, whereas a family with income of more than $50,000 spends only 6% of its income on such items.[26] However, due to spending variations among income classes, not all excise taxes are regressive. Increasing the airline ticket excise would have a slightly progressive effect, whereas increasing the excise tax on cigarettes would be extremely regressive. Raising the gasoline excise would have a relatively even, though somewhat regressive, effect across all income classes, if not geographical areas. (Residents of the western states drive more than residents of the eastern states.)

Opponents of higher excise taxes condemn them as regressive. In rebuttal, proponents argue that tax law should discourage behavior that imposes negative externalities (extra costs) on society. These proponents note that in real terms, our taxes on tobacco products are lower than they were at the time the Surgeon General of the United States issued his report concerning the hazards of tobacco smoke. Taxes on alcohol products are likewise lower than they were before there was an organization known as MADD (Mothers Against Drunk Driving).[27] The implication is that higher

---

26 Lee Sheppard, "CBO Finds Excise Taxes Largely Regressive," *Tax Notes*, February 23, 1987, pp. 750–51.

27 Remarks of Lawrence Summers, Professor of Economics at Harvard University and currently Chief Economist at the World Bank, at the conference "U.S. Tax Policy for the 1990s: Staying Competitive in a Global Economy," sponsored by Coopers & Lybrand and New York University, November 1990.

excise taxes would reduce the ill effects of known social hazards. Despite these graphic examples, considerable question remains as to precisely how the taxation of alcoholic beverages, cigarettes, or machine-gun transfers helps reduce consumption to non-abusive levels or compensates for negative externalities.

These arguments are consistent with the notion that the (immediate) highway user ought to pay for the cost of highways through taxes on gasoline, tires, lubricants, and so on. The same basic idea can as easily apply to the excise taxes on airfares, alcoholic beverages, and wagers. Obviously, this justification presumes that the incidence of these taxes rests with the person who makes the expenditure necessary in the first instance.

A more plausible rationalization for the existence of many excise taxes is that they are good revenue producers. This attribute of most excise taxes has been particularly important in the current environment of seemingly intractable budget deficits, with particular attention given to the gasoline tax.[28]

Politicians have found it relatively easy to sell the public on excise taxes because revenues from most of them have decreased as a percentage of GNP since 1975—in large part because many major ones are levied on a per-unit basis. In 1992 approximately $5 billion is expected to be raised by the excises tax on tobacco, $8 billion by the tax on alcoholic beverages, and $15 billion by the tax on gasoline. The most highly visible new excise tax, the luxury tax, is not even expected to raise half a billion dollars.[29] It is clear that President Bush's pledge of "no new taxes" did not preclude revenue enhancement through higher excise taxes.

CONSUMPTION TAXES

> **Consumption taxes** are taxes on expenditures for goods or services.
>
> A **value-added tax (VAT)** is a tax imposed on the incremental value added to a product at various stages of production.

Consumption taxes include a host of taxes on goods and services, including the excise taxes just discussed. Other common consumption taxes are sales taxes and **value-added taxes (VAT)**. A VAT extending through the retail level is basically identical to a retail sales tax, except that the tax is collected in increments throughout the production and distribution channels, instead of entirely from the retailers.[30] Still other consumption taxes are imposed on an entire class of transactions, with limited exceptions, and are always applied to value.

Consumption taxes in the form of sales taxes are currently applied only at the state and local levels (see Chapter 2). Five states (Alaska, Delaware, Montana, New Hampshire, and Oregon) have no sales taxes, but other states and many local governments rely heavily on these taxes. The only consumption taxes collected at the federal level in the United States are excise taxes. The United states has never had a federal VAT but the current deficit problems are drawing substantially more attention and more vocal proponents of the tax despite historical opposition. Liberals oppose such taxes because of their regressivity and conservatives oppose them because they believe such taxes would cause the size of government to balloon by providing a cash cow that could be used to finance new spending. (This political alignment has prompted pundits to declare that consumption taxes will be adopted when liberals figure out that

---

28 For example, see David Wessel, "Volcker Urges Cut of Up to $40 Billion a Year in Deficit, Asks Gasoline Tax Rate Rise," *The Wall Street Journal,* December 1, 1988, p. A16; Andrew Tobias, "A Modest Proposal," *Time,* November 21, 1988, p. 46; and "How to Cut the Deficit by $50 Billion," *Business Week*, November 28, 1988, p. 190.

29 BNA Special Supplement, House Ways and Means Committee Report, "Overview of the Federal Tax System" 1991 Edition (WMCP: 102–107), Part III, Section 5, pp. S-36–S-37.

30 J. Due and A. Friedlaender, *Government Finance: Economics of the Public Sector* (Homewood, IL: Irwin, 1977), p. 392.

such taxes are a cash cow and conservatives figure out that they are regressive.) Since Japan has adopted a modest 3% VAT, the United States and Australia are now the only major industrialized countries that do not have either a national sales tax or a VAT.

Consumption taxes are generally deemed to be inferior to income-based taxes in terms of equity because they permit few adjustments for the personal circumstances of individuals. Regressiveness can be reduced by exemptions and credits, but only at the expense of adding complexity to the system and by creating economic distortions.[31]

Is the VAT a good tax? In terms of the criteria discussed earlier both a national sales tax and a VAT would be relatively convenient and certain, and very productive (estimates are that each one percent of tax rate would yield approximately $20 billion of revenue). A national sales tax could be more economical than a VAT (45 of the 50 states have a retail sales tax).[32] A national sales tax would also satisfy the criterion of visibility; a VAT would not. Everywhere a VAT is imposed, except in Denmark, it is hidden from the final consumer.[33] However, this invisibility may be the essential ingredient for political palatability.

WEALTH (OR OWNERSHIP) TAXES

Wealth taxation, like income taxation, has various forms. Selective forms of wealth taxation—such as taxes on the ownership of real property or certain personal properties, such as autos—are far more common than a comprehensive net-wealth tax. A tax on wealth technically does not duplicate an income tax. A **wealth tax** is a levy on aggregate accumulation of net wealth at one moment in time (hence a *stock concept*) whereas an income tax is a levy on the net increase in wealth during a given period of time (hence, a *flow concept*). You should immediately recognize the parallel between these two tax bases and the two basic financial statements—the balance sheet (or statement of financial position at one moment in time) and the income statement (or statement of profit and loss for a given period of time).

A tax based on aggregate net wealth would be far more equitable than the typical selective wealth taxes, because the former tax would apply equally to all forms of wealth and only to the net excess of the fair market value of property owned over debt owned. Under a wealth tax, individuals would not always be taxed on the full value of their home or car, but only on the portion that represents their equity in the asset. Nevertheless, net wealth has never been popular as a tax base. Its unpopularity may be attributed to the administrative difficulties of valuing a multiplicity of assets at frequent time intervals, as well as to the ease of concealing ownership of many assets. Another likely problem is that the government would have to amass a considerable amount of information on individuals to administer a comprehensive wealth tax. Collection of such information would clash with the traditional American values of privacy.

> A **wealth tax** is a levy on aggregate accumulation of net wealth at one moment in time.

---

31 Due and Friedlaender, *op cit.*, p. 392.

32 George Carlson and Charles McLure, "Pros and Cons of Alternative Approaches to the Taxation of Consumption," *1984 National Tax Association Annual Conference Proceedings,* p. 148.

33 Sijbren Cnossen and Richard Bird, "Foreign Experience with National Sales Taxes," *1986 National Tax Association Annual Conference Proceedings,* p. 146. Also, for a further discussion of VAT, see *Tax Notes,* "Consumption Tax Symposium" beginning in the March 7, 1988, issue, p. 1110; *The Value-Added Tax: Lessons from Europe,* Henry J. Aaron, ed. (Washington, DC: The Brookings Institute, 1981); and Charles E. McLure, *The Value-Added Tax: Key to Deficit Reduction?* (Washington, DC: American Enterprise Institute, 1987).

Wealth taxes are not a significant source of federal revenue. (As Figure 1-1 suggests, the "other" category is small, and it consists mainly of excise taxes). However, there is one area of wealth taxation in which the federal government does get involved: *wealth-transfer* taxes.

WEALTH-TRANSFER TAXES

> A **wealth-transfer** tax is a tax imposed on the transfer of an individual's ownership interest to anyone other than a bona fide purchaser.
>
> A **donative transfers tax** is a tax imposed on the transfer of wealth by lifetime gifts or at death.

In addition to the various taxes on selected forms of ownership per se, governments frequently impose a **wealth-transfer tax** on the *transfer* of an individual's ownership interest to anyone other than a bona fide purchaser. For example, the federal **donative transfers tax** and the state inheritance taxes are based on the gratuitous transfer of an ownership interest.

The Tax Reform Act of 1976 combined what previously had been two separate wealth-transfer taxes—the federal gift tax and the federal estate tax—into a single donative transfer tax. Conceptually, this tax is relatively simple. If in any year during a donor's life he or she makes a *taxable* gift, then that donor must pay a tax determined by applying the tax rates to the aggregate value of all taxable gifts made since birth, less a tax credit (similarly determined) for all taxable gifts made in prior years. In this manner, current gifts are taxed at progressively higher marginal tax rates. At the donor's death, a similar tax calculation is made, as follows:

Compute the value of the *taxable* estate	$XXX
Add the aggregate value of *taxable* gifts made during life	$XXX
The sum equals the base of the donative transfers tax	$XXX
Compute the gross tax on the above value (this tax rate schedule is printed in Appendix B)	$XXX
Subtract the aggregate gift tax paid on all gifts made during life (also using the tax rate schedule in Appendix B)	$XXX
The remainder is the federal estate tax payable at death	$XXX

> The **decedent** is the person who has died and left behind an estate of assets and debts.

The federal estate tax is payable by the executor from the assets left by the **decedent**. This estate tax is equivalent to a true net-wealth tax because it is based on the excess of the fair market value of the decedent's assets over the debts owed (plus certain other special exemptions written into the law) at one moment in time. Technically, however, it is considered a wealth-transfer tax. As noted, the law contains a long list of special provisions (or exceptions), most of which were enacted either to allow smaller estates to escape taxation or to make the law's administration feasible.

Most estates wholly escape the federal estate tax by applying the $192,800 unified credit.

EXAMPLE 1-3

A person dying with an estate of less than $600,000 will pay no estate tax because the $192,800 credit will negate the tax otherwise payable on an estate of exactly $600,000. In addition, a decedent may leave any amount of property to his or her spouse free of the estate tax.

Because of these generous exemptions, it is estimated that only 0.5% of the estates of all persons dying in 1986 was subject to the federal donative transfers tax.[34]

---

34 This is due to the concentration of wealth. For instance, the Joint Economic Committee estimated that in 1983 the top 0.5% of the population owned 25% of the wealth.

The federal gift tax is made administratively feasible by allowing every individual to make gifts of $10,000 per year to as many donees as he or she wishes without incurring a gift tax. In other words, the law provides that no *taxable* gift occurs until one person gives more than $10,000 to another person in any year. In addition, gifts to charity are excluded from the gift tax base. Without these exemptions and deductions, the IRS would face the truly Herculean task of discovering small gifts among family members and exacting a tax from the donor for each gift made.

On the other hand, because of the generous deductions, exemptions, and credits, less than 1% of federal tax revenue is obtained from the donative transfers tax. Does this suggest that the expenditure of time, effort, and money required to enforce the law is greater than the benefit received? That conclusion is doubtful for two reasons. First, the donative transfers tax has the primary objective of reducing the concentration of great amounts of wealth. Second, because of the combined effects of our realization criterion and certain basis rules (explained later in this book), the appreciation in value that occurs between the time a taxpayer acquires a property and the time he or she dies is never subject to an *income* tax as long as the property is not sold or exchanged in a taxable transaction. Thus a significant amount of income—at least as that word is defined by economists—wholly escapes income taxation. Gift and estate taxes may be viewed as an attempt to impose an income tax on unrealized appreciations in value.

_____ CONCLUSION

The purpose of this chapter has been to give you a broad overview of some of the important structural components of tax systems, particularly that of the Untied States. We continue this overview in the next chapter, focusing more narrowly on income taxes. First, we consider the development of our present income tax law. Then we consider the future of our tax system and the international evolutionary forces that are altering our perspectives on how our tax system should be structured.

_____ KEY POINTS TO REMEMBER

✓ We define the word *tax* as any nonpenal yet compulsory transfer of resources, from the private to the public sector, levied without receipt of a specific benefit of equal value and on the basis of predetermined criteria, enforced to accomplish some of a nation's economic and social objectives.

✓ Taxation has objectives other than raising revenue. Federal governments also use the tax system to redistribute wealth and to accomplish various other social and economic objectives.

✓ Multiple criteria should be considered in designing any tax system. The primary criteria are

    equity

    convenience

    certainty

    economy

    productivity

    visibility

The relative importance of these criteria varies depending on many factors. Political considerations often influence the emphasis placed on other criteria.

✓ You must understand several key concepts in taxation before you have a firm grasp on the economics of taxation. These concepts include

1. tax bases,

2. tax rates,

3. average versus marginal tax rates,

4. nominal versus effective tax rates,

5. tax incidence,

6. implicit taxes, and

7. tax burdens in general

✓ Although we are primarily concerned with income taxes, there are other common tax bases that are important in both our tax system and those of other countries. It is likely that the other tax bases may become more important in our tax system over the next decade.

———— RECALL PROBLEMS

#1
1. Citizens frequently make payments other than taxes to governmental units. Write a short essay distinguishing taxes from penalties (or fines), from charges for goods or services (or beneficiary's charges), and from confiscation.

#1
2. FICA (Social Security) has often been described and justified as old-age insurance. Are payments made to the government under this act beneficiary's charges or taxes? Why?

#1
3. Which of the following payments would you classify as a tax? How would you classify the other payments?

   a. Payment for automobile registration (that is, license plates)

   b. Payment for a hunting or fishing license

   c. Payment for a safety sticker on an automobile

   d. Payment for parking on a metered street

   e. Payment for federal stamps required on transfer of a real estate deed

   f. Payment for riding a city-owned and -operated bus

   g. Payment for a bottle of liquor purchased in a state-owned store

#1
4. Is the price paid for postage more accurately classified as a price (beneficiary's charge) or a tax? Explain your answer.

#1
5. Assume that a city requires that every dog be licensed and that the fee for this annual license is $5. Assume further that the money collected in this way is put into a special fund used to pay the cost of the city dog patrol operation. Is this $5 fee better labeled a price or a tax? Explain your answer.

6. Consider the taxes normally paid by consumers in the United States. Make a list of the ones that have some characteristics of a penalty; make a separate list of those that have some characteristics of a beneficiary's charge.

`#1`

7. Explain why the federal government collects taxes rather than just printing the money it needs.

`#2`

8. Define both horizontal and vertical equity.

`#3`

9. If taxpayer X has a taxable income of $10,000 and pays an income tax of $2,000 and taxpayer Y has a taxable income of $50,000 and pays an income tax of $8,000, what statement can you make concerning horizontal equity in that taxing jurisdiction? concerning vertical equity?

`#3`

10. Governmental units in the United States depend primarily on property, income, and sales taxes to raise revenue. Rate each of these tax bases in terms of Adam Smith's canons of taxation.

`#3`

11. a. Taxpayer Kane earned a total income of $10,000 in 1991. Only $6,000 of his income, however, was included in the tax base for the income tax. Kane paid a tax of $1,200 during 1991. What average nominal tax rate does Kane pay? What average effective rate does Kane pay?

`#4`

  b. In 1992, Kane had taxable income (tax base) of $8,000. That year he paid a tax of $1,700. Assuming that the tax-rate structure was not changed by the government unit imposing the tax, what marginal tax rate did Kane pay on the additional income of $2,000 in 1992? What average nominal rate did Kane pay in 1992?

12. Taxpayer A, a single individual, has a total income of $50,000. Taxable income for the current year, however, is only $40,000. Using the 1992 tax rates

`#4`

  a. Determine A's marginal tax rate.

  b. Determine A's average nominal tax rate.

  c. Determine A's average effective tax rate.

13. What are implicit taxes? Explain the implicit tax that is borne on municipal bonds.

`#4`

14. List the principal tax bases and describe significant characteristics of each.

`#5`

15. Excise taxes are a special form of consumption tax. Describe arguments for and against these taxes.

`#5`

—— THOUGHT PROBLEMS

1. Must taxes involve the transfer of money? Under what circumstances might you expect a government to impose a nonpecuniary tax?

`#1`

2. Politicians seldom increase their popularity by advocating a tax increase. Nevertheless, in spite of the fact that the U.S. federal government does not need to collect taxes before it can spend, no federal politician has ever advocated the end of all tax collections at the federal level of government. Explain the apparent contradiction.

`#1`

#1

3. Section 164(a) of the Internal Revenue Code (the basic statutory authority for the U.S. federal income tax) authorizes a taxpayer to deduct certain taxes in the determination of taxable income. That subsection reads, in part, as follows:

> Except as otherwise provided in this section, the following taxes shall be allowed as a deduction for the taxable year within which paid or accrued:
>
> (1) State and local, and foreign, real property taxes.
>
> (2) State and local personal property taxes.

Based on the authority of Sec. 164(a)(2), taxpayers in some states can deduct the cost of their automobile license plates, whereas taxpayers in other states cannot claim that same deduction. How might you explain the apparent conundrum?

#2

4. An increase in any federal tax is often justified as necessary to pay for a war. How adequate is this explanation? Why? If Congress refused to enact a requested tax, how would the United States pay for various government programs, including a war?

#2

5. In what significant way are the fiscal resources of the federal government significantly different from those of state and local governments?

#2

6. "The primary purpose of federal taxes may be significantly different from the primary purpose of state or local taxes." Discuss.

#2

7. Imagine that you are the minister of finance in a small third-world nation. What features might you incorporate in your tax program to encourage economic development?

#3

8. Early in the 1960s, a new national party, the Constitutional Party, was formed. Its principal platform was elimination of the federal income tax and substitution of a general sales tax and beneficiary's charges. On what grounds could such a movement be criticized?

#3

9. Some tax scholars have noted that as the economy moves from the very primitive to the highly industrialized state, tax systems typically evolve from poll taxes (a flat tax on each human or head tax), to property taxes, to flat-rate income taxes, to graduated income taxes. Furthermore, these scholars suggest, at the various stages of economic progress each of these taxes can be said to approximate some social measure of ability to pay.

   a. Explain how a poll tax or a property tax might reflect an ability to pay.

   b. What sociological factors augur well for this sequence in tax systems?

#4

10. Write a short essay supporting the idea that mandatory military service is a form of progressive taxation.

#4

11. Two objectives of the United Nations are peaceful settlement of international disputes and encouragement of cultural and economic intercourse between nations and peoples. Under its present charter, the U.N. has no taxing power. Assume that everyone agreed that the U.N. should have the power to tax the citizens of member nations. What problems would arise in selecting a tax base?

#4

12. Prepare three graphs representing tax *rates* and another set representing tax *burden* under proportional, progressive, and regressive tax systems. Record the amount of taxes paid on the vertical scale and the tax base on the horizontal scale.

13. Is the tax *rate* for FICA progressive, proportional, or regressive? In a technical sense, is the present FICA (Social Security) tax progressive, proportional, or regressive in relation to income? Explain with a simple diagram.

14. What do salt, white phosphorous matches, motor fuels, tobacco, and alcoholic beverages have in common as far as a tax base is concerned? If the retail sale of marijuana is legalized in the United States, what good reason(s) do you have for predicting that it will become a common tax base?

15. Consider the effect of Congress's passing laws that reduced depreciable lives of assets. Now consider the effect of doubling depreciable lives. What are the economic effects of such action by Congress? What are the implications for the implicit tax analysis?

16. Assume that your state legislature enacted, and your governor signed, a new law that imposed a tax on the sale of all new and used gasoline engines at the following rates:

0 to 50 horsepower	—		$5 per horsepower
50 to 100 horsepower	$250	plus	$4 per horsepower over 50
100 to 150 horsepower	$450	plus	$3 per horsepower over 100
150 to 200 horsepower	$600	plus	$2 per horsepower over 150
over 200 horsepower	$700	plus	$1 per horsepower over 200

a. If A purchased a Buick with a 175-horsepower engine and B purchased a Ford with a 90-horsepower engine, who would pay the greater tax, A or B?

b. Who would be in the higher marginal tax bracket, A or B?

c. What would A's average nominal tax rate per horsepower be?

d. In a technical sense, would this new tax be progressive, proportional, or regressive?

e. If the new tax applied only to gasoline engines, what should happen to the price of diesel-powered automobiles? Explain briefly.

17. The government of Neverneverland, a small, strange, island republic in the middle of the Ancient Ocean, imposes two taxes on its citizens and resident aliens. One monthly tax is based on the size (measured in cubic feet) of the taxpayer's residence, an igloo, according to the following rates:

First 3,000 cubic feet	¢10 per cu. ft.
Next 3,000 cubic feet	¢18 per cu. ft.
Next 6,000 cubic feet	¢34 per cu. ft.
Next 12,000 cubic feet	¢62 per cu. ft.
Remainder	¢100 per cu. ft.

(Note: The basic monetary unit in this imaginary country is the cube, or ¢)

The second tax is the tax of ¢5 per ounce of wonderdrug, which is made and distributed by a secret agency of the government. Neverneverland, you see, is a very strange country indeed: humans can live there only if they take exactly one ounce of wonderdrug on the first day of each full moon. If they fail to take this drug at the prescribed time or in the prescribed amount, they will die within 20 hours.

a. In a technical sense, is the tax imposed on igloos progressive, proportional, or regressive?

b. In a technical sense, is the tax imposed on wonderdrug progressive, proportional, or regressive?

c. In a popular sense, is the tax imposed on wonderdrug progressive, proportional, or regressive?

d. Fred Jidair's home in Neverneverland contains 9,000 cubic feet of space. Is the average nominal tax paid by Fred on his home less than, equal to, or more than ¢34 per cubic foot?

e. If Fred decides, after the birth of his seventh child, to expand the size of his igloo from 9,000 to 12,000 cubic feet, would his marginal tax rate be less than, equal to, or more than ¢34 per cubic foot?

18. Sam Sharp lives in the Empire of Konform, which is ruled by King Kon. Sam, an employee of King Kon, earns a annual salary of $20,000 (his only source of income). The income tax in Konform is determined according to the following rate schedule:

$0—$1,000	—		5% of income
$1,001—$5,000	$ 50	plus	7% of income in excess of $1,000
$5,001—$100,000	$330	plus	10% of income in excess of $5,000

In addition, any relative of King Kon may deduct 50% of his or her salary in the calculation of income tax base; any employee of King Kon may deduct 10%.

a. Technically, should the income tax in Konform be classified as proportional, progressive, or regressive?

b. Determine Sam's average nominal tax rate.

c. Determine Sam's average effective tax rate.

d. Determine Sam's marginal tax rate.

#4

19. What can be done to make a sales tax (relatively) more progressive in relation to income? Explain.

#4

20. If a government desired to decrease consumption spending and increase investment, other things being equal, you would expect it to advocate regressive rather than progressive taxes. True or false? Explain briefly.

#5

21. Large cities often impose a heavy tax (for example, 10%) on the cost of hotel and motel rooms. What good reasons can be given in support of such a tax?

#5

22. Proposals to eliminate the federal income tax have been made. For each of the alternative bases listed below, indicate briefly the major political and economic problems that would arise in shifting to such a base at the federal level.

a. Wealth tax

b. Employment taxes

c. Excise taxes

23. What good reasons might a free-world government have for imposing a fee of, say, $20 on a pack of cigarettes? If that were done, would it be correct to refer to the $20 charge to the consumer as a tax? Explain briefly.

24. In the recent past, personal property taxes—that is, taxes on the value of bank accounts, stocks, bonds, furniture, television sets, refrigerators, and similar personal assets—have been disappearing from the list of tax bases used by state and local governments. Why are these particular taxes disappearing despite the fact that almost every state and local government is currently looking for new sources of revenue?

25. Forty-six states now impose an income tax. What practical problem does this present for businesses engaged in interstate commerce? What comparable problem exists with the federal government?

26. The maximum wage or salary subject to Social Security taxes, as well as the maximum Social Security tax payable by an employee and his or her employer, has increased dramatically over the past 50 years, as demonstrated in the following table:

Year	Maximum Base	Maximum Tax
1937	$ 3,000	$ 60
1959	4,800	240
1972	9,000	936
1979	22,900	2,808
1984	37,800	5,066
1987	43,800	6,264
1990	51,300	7,849
1991	53,400 + 2.9% up to 125,000	10,246
1992	55,000 + 2.9% up to 130,000	10,658

What political response to do you predict for further changes?

——— CLASS PROJECTS

1. Some states have recently tried lotteries to raise revenues. Find information in state legislative documents, the popular press, or academic journals discussing the use of lotteries as an alternative to raising taxes. Write a brief essay evaluating lotteries in the context of the criteria used to evaluate taxes. Compare the arguments made in the information you found to your analysis.

2. Consumption taxes have recently drawn attention as a potential source of new revenue for the federal government. Divide into groups to develop arguments supporting (opposing) increased use of consumption taxes. Do whatever research you feel is necessary to understand more fully the issues and to gather relevant data. Debate the issue in four-person groups with two supporters and two opposers. Following the debate, write a two-page essay supporting your assigned position on the issue. On the day the essays are due, be prepared to be selected as part of a three-person debate team to argue your side of the issue.

3. How much federal income tax do you believe each of the following four persons *should* pay on the income they earn? (Note: this question is asking for your personal opinion, not what the current law demands.)

Person	Income	Occupation
Andrew	$ 25,000	Factory worker
Beverly	150,000	Medical doctor
Calvin	300,000	Football player
Diane	600,000	Actress

4. Compare your answer to question 3, above, with that of all your classmates and determine how the majority would define vertical equity.

Taxation involves the power of one person to take property from another. Not surprisingly, it has from the earliest times inspired a wide range of human emotions—from anger to fear to jealousy.

JAMES A. BAKER III, U.S. SECRETARY OF THE TREASURY (1987)

EVOLUTION OF THE U.S. TAX SYSTEM

CHAPTER OBJECTIVES

In Chapter 2, you will review the history of taxation in the United States, focusing on recent developments and considering what these developments suggest about the future of our tax system.

LEARNING GOALS

After studying this chapter, you should be able to

1 Explain trends in tax revenue collections by level of government, with special emphasis on understanding the role of income taxes in the overall scheme of taxation in the United States;

2 Describe the evolution of income taxation in the United States that culminated in the Sixteenth Amendment to the Constitution;

3 Describe the distinctive features of each of six periods of income taxation, including the current period which began with the Tax Reform Act of 1986;

4 Discuss the principal motivations for, and significance of, the 1986 Tax Reform Act;

5 Describe the important trends and developments in tax law in the period following the 1986 Tax Reform Act;

6 Describe the major problems that persist with the U.S. tax system; and

7 Identify the forces that are likely to have a significant impact on future changes in the U.S. tax system and explain their importance.

The tax system of every country is in a constant state of flux and the United States of America is no exception to this somewhat obvious observation. In this chapter we review the major ways in which the overall U.S. tax system has changed over the twentieth century before we examine the most important recent changes in our federal income tax in somewhat greater detail. At the end of this chapter, we attempt to assess the recent changes and speculate on the tax future of this country.

Among the more interesting issues is that of intergovernmental fiscal relations. Because relatively few taxes produce the vast bulk of all tax revenues collected, two or more levels of government increasingly impose and collect taxes on essentially the same tax base. For example, our federal government, most state governments, and a growing list of municipal governments all utilize an income tax. Most states and more and more city governments impose a retail sales tax, while at least some government officials consider the possibility of a federal value-added tax. This tendency to rely on overlapping tax bases raises numerous important questions at every level of government. For example: Should two or more governments consolidate their separate taxes if they are imposed on essentially a single tax base? If so, which level of government should have the responsibility of collecting that tax? How can the proceeds of a consolidated tax best be redistributed without the recipient becoming unduly beholden to the distributor? In the face of such complex future issues, the nostalgia associated with somewhat simpler times is inviting.

——— EVOLUTION OF THE PRESENT SYSTEM

<table>
<tr><td>

Goal #1
Explain trends in tax revenue collections by level of government.

</td></tr>
</table>

Less than 70 years ago, the U.S. tax structure was dominated by locally collected taxes, and total tax collections were relatively small, both absolutely and as a percentage of national income. After the Great Depression of the 1930s, and especially during World War II, this picture changed drastically. By 1945, our tax structure was dominated by a rather sizable federal tax. Table 2-1 clearly demonstrates these changes in our tax structure.

In reviewing these data, note that even though state and local taxes decreased as a percentage of total tax collections between 1934 and 1960, they continued to increase significantly in absolute amounts. State tax receipts have increased so rapidly that they now approximate their depression position relative to total tax receipts. The increasing claims on tax funds at all levels make intergovernmental fiscal relations an important issue today.

TAX BASES BY LEVELS OF GOVERNMENT

The various levels of government tend to rely on different tax bases as their primary sources of revenue. Local governments in the United States have traditionally depended heavily on property taxation; state governments have historically relied on sales and excise taxes but have placed growing emphasis on income taxes; while the federal government has relied on personal and corporate income taxes. Table 2-2 reveals the distribution of tax collections among the various tax bases, by level of government, in a recent year.

This table demonstrates clearly that the income tax is by far the most productive tax utilized today. Of total tax collections, *excluding* social insurance taxes, about 60% came from income taxes alone. At the federal level, about 88% came from the income tax. At the state level, nearly 50% came from sales and excise taxes; another 40% came from income taxes. At the local level, almost 75% came from property taxes. Of total tax collections, 30% is from social insurance taxes, or taxes on labor income, primarily collected at the federal level.

Year	Receipt (in millions) Total	Federal	State	Local	Percentage Distribution Total	Federal	State	Local
1902	$ 1,373	$ 513	$ 156	$ 704	100.0	37.4	11.4	51.3
1913	2,271	662	301	1,308	100.0	29.2	13.3	57.6
1934	8,854	2,942	1,979	3,933	100.0	33.2	22.4	44.4
1942	22,962	13,351	4,979	4,633	100.0	58.1	21.7	20.2
1950	54,799	37,853	8,958	7,988	100.0	69.1	16.3	14.6
1960	126,678	88,419	20,172	18,088	100.0	69.8	15.9	14.3
1970	274,996	185,670	50,486	38,840	100.0	67.5	18.4	14.1
1980	727,984	492,846	148,691	86,447	100.0	67.7	20.4	11.9
1988	1,504,057	877,241	355,467	271,349	100.0	58.3	23.6	18.0

Note: Because of rounding, detail may not add to total.

Source: Tax Foundation, Inc., *Facts and Figures on Government Finances,* (Baltimore: Johns Hopkins University Press, 1991), Tables A14 and A15, pp. 16 and 17.

* Includes social insurance taxes.

TABLE 2-1

Federal, State, and Local Tax Receipts* for Selected Fiscal Years, 1902–1988

Tax Base	Total	Federal	State	Local
Individual income	$ 489	$401	$ 80	$ 8
Corporate income	118	94	22	2
General sales	105	—	87	18
Excise	104	53	43	8
Property	132	—	5	127
Motor vehicle and operator licenses	10	—	9	1
Death and gift	11	8	3	—
All other	28	7	14	7
Total taxes, before social insurance taxes	$ 997	$563	$263	$171
Social Insurance Taxes*	425	320	91	14
Total taxes	$1,422	$883	$354	$185

Note: Because of rounding, detail may not add to totals.

Source: Adapted from Tax Foundation, Inc., *Facts and Figures on Government Finance,* (Baltimore: Johns Hopkins University Press, 1991), Table A11, p. 13.

*Social Security, Unemployment, etc.

TABLE 2-2

Tax Revenues by Tax Base and Level of Government, Fiscal Year 1988 (in billions)

The reliance on different tax bases by the various levels of U.S. government are summarized as follows:

Tax Base	Level of Government		
	Federal	State	Local
Income	Primary	Secondary	
Property			Primary
Sales and excise		Primary	Secondary
Social Security	Secondary		

Before proceeding, take a moment to comprehend the sheer magnitude of the numbers involved in Table 2-2. The statement that our federal, state, and local governments collect more than $1,422 billion in taxes each year does not really mean much to most of us. We can comprehend the number $1,422, but we really cannot sense the meaning of one billion, let alone $1,422 billion. To put these magnitudes in perspective, consider the fact that roughly one billion *seconds* ago the Vietnam War was escalating. Christ died slightly more than one billion *minutes* ago. And a billion *hours* ago, man lived in caves! Then recall that our governments collect about two billion dollars in tax revenues every single day of the year! And taxes are only a part of government revenues. Each level of government also receives funds from nontax sources. For example, all state and local governments receive funds from the federal government and many operate utility companies, manage airports and recreation facilities, and dispense liquor. Therefore, total government revenues are always greater than tax receipts.

The tax bases traditionally relied on by the various levels of government are often jealously guarded. Congressional discussions and actions involving more excise taxes and possible value added tax (VAT) are of more than passing interest to state and local governments. These governments, facing increasing budget difficulties, are understandably concerned about overburdening tax bases they see as theirs.[1] Table 2-3

TABLE 2-3

Total Government Revenues by Major Source, Various Years (percentage distribution)

Major Source	Fiscal Year			
	1960	1970	1980	1988
Individual income taxes	28.2	30.3	30.7	27.6
Corporation income taxes	14.8	11.0	8.4	6.6
Social insurance taxes	8.9	12.6	16.6	18.7
Property taxes	10.7	10.2	7.3	7.4
Sales and gross receipts	16.0	14.6	12.0	11.8
Death and gift	1.3	1.4	0.9	.6
All other	2.9	2.4	2.3	2.1
Total taxes	82.7	82.4	78.2	74.8
Nontax revenues	17.3	17.6	21.8	25.2
Total revenues	100.0	100.0	100.0	100.0

Source: Adapted from Tax Foundation, Inc., *Facts and Figures on Government Finance*, (Baltimore: Johns Hopkins University Press, 1991), Table 13, p. 15.

---

1 For a discussion of recession effects on state revenues, see Steven D. Gold, "No Sign of Recovery Yet in State Tax Revenue," *State Tax Notes*, Sept. 16, 1991, pp. 90–92.

shows the percentage of total revenues contributed by each tax base for all levels of government from 1960 through 1988. This table reveals major trends in different tax bases. Noteworthy trends since 1970 include a reduction in corporate income taxes (to less than 50% of their 1960 levels); a doubling of the relative contribution from social insurance taxes; and a large increase in nontax revenues.

Table 2-3 also makes clear how heavily the United States depends on the income tax. There can be no doubt that the income tax dominates the U.S. federal tax structure. The largest single source of federal tax revenues is the income tax paid by individuals; the second largest, the Social Security tax; and the third largest, the income tax paid by corporations. Because of this dominance, and because this tax is so amenable to modification, we will restrict our attention in most of this text to the federal income tax.

Before we examine the details of our present income tax, however, let us consider the general development of those provisions in broad historical context. Although income taxation has conceptual roots that are over 2,000 years old, most of the current rules have evolved in the past 75 years. In the next part of this chapter, we will divide our discussion into two major periods—that prior to the Sixteenth Amendment (1913) and the years after that constitutional change. The later period is further divided into six periods that can be distinguished from each other by the kind of legislation that dominated those years.

—— INCOME TAXATION PRIOR TO 1913

Income taxation is nothing new. Historians suggest that elementary forms of income taxation were imposed by the Roman Empire even before the birth of Christ. Indeed, the fact that Christ was born in the city of Bethlehem could be attributable to some form of income taxation. Saint Luke relates the events in this manner: "There went out a decree from Caesar Augustus, that all the world should be taxed . . . . And all went to be taxed, everyone into his own city. And Joseph also went up from Galilee, out of the city of Nazareth, into Judea, unto the city of David, which is called Bethlehem; (because he was of the house and lineage of David) to be taxed with Mary his espoused wife . . . ."[2] Although no details concerning this tax are available, the fact that the taxpayer was required to respond to the tax personally and with his family suggests that it may have been some form of the poll or head tax as well as a census mechanism. A poll tax with graduated tax rates—often called a *faculties tax*—constitutes the most elementary form of the income tax. Essentially, a faculties tax is a tax on *estimated* income. This form of income taxation is not uncommon today in preindustrial societies.[3]

Other early traces of income taxation are seen in the Florentine Republic in Italy in the fourteenth and fifteenth centuries.[4] What began as a tax on property evolved into a tax on income. By 1451, much income and wealth could be attributed to established industry and commerce rather than to the more traditional forms of property. Consequently, the value base for taxation became a capitalization of the earnings stream. Because of administrative complications and political favoritism in

> **Goal #2**
> Describe the evolution of income taxation in the United States.

---

2 Luke 2:1–5 (King James Version).

3 The progressive poll tax is still used today in some African countries. See John F. Due, "The African Personal Tax," *National Tax Journal*, XV (December 1962), pp. 385–98.

4 The authors owe a considerable debt to Professor Edwin R. A. Seligman for much of the early history of income taxation. Persons interested in additional details should see his book, *The Income Tax*, published by Macmillan in 1911 and again in 1914 in an enlarged and revised edition.

the earnings calculations, this early income-based tax fell into disrepute and was largely replaced by indirect taxation on consumption.

THE COLONIAL FACULTIES TAXES

The **faculties tax** was a tax on personal faculties and abilities.

The earliest variant of the income tax in the Untied States appeared in 1643 in the colony of New Plymouth as a tax based on a a person's faculties, or **faculties tax**. Although no measurement techniques were provided in this law, the appointed assessors were supposed to base the tax on "personal faculties and abilities."[5] Three years later (1646), the Massachusetts Bay Company enacted a similar tax based on the returns and gains of artists and tradesmen. Early in the eighteenth century, faculties taxes based on estimated incomes were commonplace among the New England colonies, and the definitions of the tax base slowly became increasingly comprehensive definitions of income. This gradual expansion is attributed to recognition that taxation based only on selective forms of property does not adequately recognize every citizen's tax capacity or ability to pay. Thus, income taxation began in this part of the world as a supplement to more traditional forms of property taxation.

The colonial faculties taxes had largely disappeared by the middle of the nineteenth century, to be replaced by partial income taxes in a few of the new Southern states, including Virginia, North Carolina, and Alabama. These newer forms of income taxation can be traced to England, where, under the leadership of William Pitt, the first modern income tax was adopted in 1799. Generally, the Northern and Middle states avoided income taxation before the twentieth century, although during the Civil War the federal (Union) government did utilize such a tax.

THE CIVIL WAR INCOME TAXES

The first U.S. federal income tax was enacted into law on August 5, 1861, to raise revenue in support of the Civil War. Although this law was never enforced, the 1861 tax was extended by a law adopted on July 1, 1862, and limited collections were made under the latter act. The law imposed a 3% tax on most incomes between $600 and $10,000 and a 5% tax on all income in excess of $10,000. Enforcement of the law was greatly confused, and evasion was widespread.[6] The 1863 tax return form is of historic interest, and a copy appears in Figure 2-1.

The 1864 Revenue Act revised the earlier income tax rates and provided a maximum tax rate of 10%, applicable to incomes in excess of $10,000. The rate structure was again revised in 1865 and in 1867. The latter change instituted a flat (proportional) tax of 5% on most incomes in excess of $1,000. All Civil War income taxes lapsed in 1872, when the need for war financing was eliminated.

Although the Civil War income taxes were not an overwhelming success, they did illuminate some important aspects of income taxation. First, although the income tax never challenged the dominance of the tariff duties during this period, it was a major revenue producer. During the 10-year period that they were enforced, the Civil War income taxes provided the federal government with $376 million. The largest single year was 1866, when approximately $73 million (of a total of $490 million of federal revenue) was collected in income taxes.

5 *Ibid.* (1911 edition), p. 368.

6 The first Commissioner of Internal Revenue, George S. Boutwell, was appointed by President Lincoln in 1862.

FIGURE 2-1

Pages 2 and 3 of the Income Tax Form Used in the 1860s

DETAILED STATEMENT OF SOURCES OF INCOME AND THE AMOUNT DERIVED FROM EACH, DURING THE YEAR 1863.

☞ *Gross Amounts must be stated.* ☜

	AMOUNTS
1. Income of a resident in the United States from profits on any trade, business, or vocation, or any interest therein, wherever carried on	
2. From rents, or the use of real estate	
3. From interest on notes, bonds, mortgages, or other personal securities, not those of the United States	
4. From interest on notes, bonds, or other securities of the United States	
5. From interest or dividends on any bonds or other evidences of indebtedness of any railroad company or corporation	
6. From interest or dividends on stock, capital, or deposits in any bank, trust company, or savings institution, insurance or railroad company, or corporation	
7. From interest on bonds or dividends on stock, shares or property in gas, bridge, canal, turnpike, express, telegraph, steamboat, ferry-boat, or manufacturing company or corporation, or from the business usually done thereby	
8. From property, securities, or stocks owned in the United States by a citizen thereof residing abroad, not in the employment of the Government of the United States	
9. From salary other than as an officer or employee of the United States	
10. From salary as an officer or employee of the United States	
11. From farms or plantations, including all products and profits	
12. From advertisements	
13. From all sources not herein enumerated	
TOTAL	

DETAILED STATEMENT OF DEDUCTIONS AUTHORIZED TO BE MADE

	AMOUNTS
1. Expenses necessarily incurred and paid in carrying on any trade, business or vocation, such as rent of store, clerk hire, insurance, fuel, freight, &c	
2. Amount actually paid by a property owner for necessary repairs, insurance, and interest on incumbrances upon his property	
3. Amount paid by a farmer or planter for—	
(*a*) Hired labor, including the subsistence of the laborers	
(*b*) Necessary repairs upon his farm or plantation	
(*c*) Insurance, and interest on incumbrances upon his farm or plantation	
4. Other national, state, and local taxes assessed and paid for the year 1863, and not elsewhere included	
5. Amount actually paid for rent of the dwelling-house or estate occupied as a residence	
6. Exempted by law (except in the case of a citizen of the United States residing abroad.) $600	
7. Income from interest or dividends on stock, capital, or deposits in any bank, trust company, or savings institution, insurance, or railroad company, from which 3 per cent. thereon was withheld by the officers thereof	
8. Income from interest on bonds, or other evidences of indebtedness of any railroad company or corporation, from which 3 per cent. thereon was withheld by the officers thereof	
9. Salaries of officers, or payments to persons in the civil, military, naval, or other service of the United States, in excess of $600	600 00
10. Income from advertisements, on which 3 per cent. was paid	
TOTAL	

Source: Income Taxes 1862–1962. A History of the Internal Revenue Service, *IRS Publication No. 447* (U.S. Government Printing Office), p. 9.

A second important lesson learned during that decade was that a detailed taxpayer guidance system is essential to successful income taxation. Major administration problems were encountered. Surprisingly, perhaps, these early laws did provide for withholding at the source on wages and salaries, interest, and dividends. But other aspects of the administrative machinery were not so advanced. For example, it remained for the state of Wisconsin to demonstrate (in 1911) the importance of a central tax commission, autonomous from local officials.

Perhaps the most surprising fact of that decade of income taxation is that the tax functioned as well as it did. Richard Goode, an economist with special competence in tax matters, once suggested that there are six prerequisites to a successful income tax: (1) a money economy, (2) general literacy, (3) minimum accounting records, (4) acceptance of the idea of voluntary compliance with tax laws, (5) political acceptance of an income tax, and (6) an efficient administrative machine.[7] Considering the situation in the United States in 1872 with regard to each of these six criteria, it is not surprising that the income tax was permitted to lapse once the pressure for war financing ended.

THE CONSTITUTIONAL QUESTION

Even many educated persons are surprised to learn that the U.S. government imposed and collected an income tax prior to 1913, for the common belief is that this form of taxation was unconstitutional prior to the ratification of the Sixteenth Amendment. This belief, however, is only partially accurate.

Article I, Section 9, Clause 4 of the Constitution reads as follows: "No Capitation, or other direct, Tax shall be laid, unless in Proportion to the Census or Enumeration herein before directed to be taken." Since incomes are not equally distributed between people or states, an income tax cannot be divided among states in proportion to population. When the Civil War income tax was tested in the Supreme Court, the question the Court decided was, therefore, a straightforward one: Is an income tax a "direct tax" as that term was understood by those who drafted the Constitution?[8]

The most important early decision of the Supreme Court on this question was in the 1880 case of *Springer v. United States*, and the decision was unanimous and negative—that is, the income tax was deemed to be an indirect tax. The Court said, "Our conclusions are, that *direct taxes*, within the meaning of the Constitution, are only capitation taxes, as expressed in that instrument, and taxes on real estate; and that the tax of which the plaintiff in error complains is within the category of an excise or duty."[9] Fourteen years later, the Court changed its mind.

Between the *Springer* decision in 1880 and the Revenue Act of 1894, income taxation was a political football. Generally, the states of the West and the South favored the income tax, whereas the Eastern states opposed it. The income tax was part of the Populist program, along with railroad regulation, expanded currency, and the direct election of senators. This was the program of an "oppressed" agrarian midland, revolting against the Eastern bankers and industrialists—in short, a program for the

---

7 Richard Gode, "Reconstruction of Foreign Tax Systems," *Proceedings of the Forty-Fourth Annual Conference of the National Tax Association* (1951), pp. 212–22.

8 Here we are discussing only the legal (or constitutional) meaning of the phrase "direct tax." Actually, the phrase is originally one adopted from the economics literature. For a discussion of that matter see C. J. Bullock, "Direct and Indirect Taxes in Economic Literature," *Political Science Quarterly*, XIII (1898), pp. 442–86.

9 *Springer v. United States*, 102 US 602 (1880).

poor against the rich.[10] No less than 124 income tax bills were introduced into Congress between 1873 and 1879, but none of them gained the majority necessary to become law. Finally, on August 28, 1894, such an act was made law, without the signature of President Cleveland. By this date, the lines were well drawn and a final political showdown was inevitable.

Once the income tax had found its way through the halls of Congress, the battle was transferred from the legislative arena to the judicial, with the executive standing by. *Pollock v. Farmers' Loan and Trust Co.*[11] was instituted by a stockholder (Pollock) to restrain the corporate officers from paying a tax the stockholders deemed unconstitutional. The issue in the case was almost identical to that raised in the earlier *Springer* case. However, slight factual differences existed. In *Springer*, the income in question involved income from personal property and from professional earnings; in *Pollock*, the income was derived from land. The plaintiff argued that if a tax on real estate is a direct tax, then a tax on the income from real estate must also be a direct tax. The first *Pollock* decision was a 6-2 decision, holding that the 1894 Act was unconstitutional to the extent that it taxed income from real estate (as well as income from municipal bonds).[12] Because so many other aspects of income taxation were unanswered by this decision, the counsel for the appellants requested a rehearing, which was granted.

On the rehearing, the nine justices on the bench reaffirmed the earlier decision in a second opinion by a scant 5–4 vote. Interestingly, the reports do not reveal the name(s) of the vacillating judge(s). This second opinion extended the earlier decision to income derived from personal property and, for all practical purposes, to all income.

Today, most historians would concede that the decision was heavily influenced by the political and social tenor of the times. Although Chief Justice Fuller's words were clear, they had a hollow ring. He noted that "the distinction between direct and indirect taxation was well understood by the framers of the Constitution and those who adopted it."[13] Justice Field, in a long concurring opinion, concluded his statement with more telling words:

> Here I close my opinion, I could not say less in view of questions of such gravity
> that go down to the very foundation of the government . . . . The present assault
> upon capital is but the beginning. It will be but the stepping-stone to others, larger
> and more sweeping, till our political contests will become a war of the poor against
> the rich; a war constantly growing in intensity and bitterness.[14]

It is hard for us today, when the income tax is an accepted part of economic and political life, to comprehend the political heat generated by the issue in 1895. The following quotes from editorials in the popular press at the time of the *Pollock* decision seem to come from a different world:

---

10 See Richard Hofstadter, *The Age of Reform* (New York: Vintage Books, 1955), for a most informative history of this politically tumultuous period. The Populists were never successful as a party, but their program was certainly successful after it was adopted by other reform groups.

11 157 US 429 (1895); 158 US 601 (1895).

12 The latter portion of the decision is not particularly germane to the immediate discussion and is, therefore, dismissed. Later statutes have carefully exempted this income from tax, although many persons are now prepared to argue again the constitutionality question.

13 *Pollock v. Farmers' Loan and Trust Co.*, 157 US 429 (1895), p. 573.

14 *Ibid.*, p. 607.

The St. Louis Post Dispatch: Today's decision shows that the corporations and plutocrats are as securely entrenched in the Supreme Court as in the lower courts which they take such pains to control.

The New York Tribune: The great compromises which made the Union possible still stand unshaken to prevent its overthrow by communist revolution. The fury of ignorant class hatred, which has sufficed to overthrow absolute power in many lands . . . has dashed itself in vain against the Constitution of the United States, fortified by the institutions which a free people have established for the defence of their rights.

In short, the issue of income taxation at the turn of the twentieth century was as controversial as, say, abortion is today.

Edwin Seligman's analysis of the constitutional issue is both more thorough and more convincing than the analysis offered by the bench. After a lengthy study, Seligman concludes:

With this general uncertainty as to the use of the older terms, it need not surprise us to find that there was no agreement at all as to the use or meaning of the newer term, "direct tax." As a matter of fact, the term was scarcely employed at all before 1787. We have found only one instance of its use in the United States before that date, namely, in a Massachusetts act of 1786.

From the above review of the origin of the direct-tax clause it is clear that it was due simply and solely to the attempt to solve the difficulty connected with the maintenance of slavery. But for that struggle Gouverneur Morris would never have introduced the term "direct tax," and there would have been no reason to introduce it anywhere else.[15]

The battle for the income tax did not end with the Supreme Court. The proponents of the tax decided that a constitutional amendment would provide a surer route to acceptance than would a new statute and another judicial review. Thus, in 1909 the Congress was persuaded to pass a joint resolution that on February 25, 1913, was ratified as the Sixteenth Amendment to the U.S. Constitution. It states that "[T]he Congress shall have power to lay and collect taxes on incomes, from whatever source derived, without apportionment among the several States, and without regard to any census or enumeration."

THE 1909 CORPORATE INCOME TAX

Even before ratification of the Sixteenth Amendment, the income tax had reappeared in a limited form. In 1909 Congress enacted, and President Taft signed, a bill that imposed a 1% tax on all corporate incomes in excess of $5,000. In 1911, this tax was tried again on constitutional grounds, in *Flint v. Stone Tracy Co.*[16] This time the Supreme Court found that the tax on corporate incomes was not a direct tax but rather a special form of excise tax on the privilege of doing business.

This special corporate tax was short-lived, for the 1913 revenue measure included provisions for both personal and corporate income taxes. During the next half-century,

---

15 Seligman, *op. cit.*, pp. 555, 561.

16 *Flint v. Stone Tracy Co.*, 220 US 107 (1911).

the income tax was transformed from a levy of minor importance to the position of preeminence it holds today.

THE U.S. INCOME TAX SINCE 1913

The history of the federal income tax from 1913 to the present is a mirror reflecting the economic and social environment of the times. Like the Civil War, World War I necessitated vast changes in federal fiscal operations. Income tax collections rose more than a hundredfold from some $35 *million* in 1913 to nearly $4 *billion* in 1920. With the end of the war, tax collections decreased, but they never returned to prewar levels. In 1930, the combined individual and corporate income tax collections totaled approximately $2.5 billion, slightly more than half of total federal receipts. This pace of taxation was roughly maintained until World War II. During the years 1941–1945, income tax collections averaged nearly $20 billion annually, representing approximately two-thirds of total federal receipts. The Cold War, the Korean conflict, and the Vietnam involvement have all contributed significantly to the maintenance of record-level tax collections since 1945. Income tax collections today exceed $600 billion annually, which is approximately 60% of total government tax-revenues excluding social insurance taxes. The sheer magnitude of these numbers makes any meaningful comprehension difficult. In 1913, however, the income tax was not so difficult to comprehend.

<table>
<tr><td>

Goal #3
Describe distinctive features of periods of income taxation.

</td></tr>
</table>

THE PERIOD 1913–1939

The 1913 income tax was a modest affair. The tax applicable to individual incomes began at 1% on taxable incomes in excess of $3,000 and increased to a maximum of 7% on taxable incomes in excess of $500,000. The $3,000 exemption was increased to $4,000 for a married taxpayer who lived with a spouse. The tax imposed on corporate incomes was a flat 1%, with no exemption provisions. Withholding was provided at the source for interest, rents, salaries, and wages but not for domestic dividends.

The 1913 law, and particularly the progressive nature of the tax, was subject to judicial review in the case of *Brushaber v. Union Pacific Railroad Co.*[17] Counsel for the plaintiff argued that the progressive rate structure was tantamount to an arbitrary abuse of power and therefore violated the due process clause of the Fifth Amendment. The Supreme Court, however, disagreed, and since 1916, progressive income taxation has never really been threatened, either by the legislative or judicial branch of the government.

The legislative branch has, of course, frequently modified earlier statutes. In 1916, for example, the tax rates were increased to range from 2 to 12% (on incomes in excess of $2 million). That year also ushered in the first U.S. war-profits tax on munitions manufacturers, which was broadened into an excess-profits tax in 1917. The withholding provisions were eliminated in 1916.

A limited dependent's deduction ($200 for one child) was introduced in 1917 and was extended (to $200 for each dependent) in 1918. The Revenue Act of 1918 also introduced discovery-value depletion, the predecessor of percentage depletion. Special provisions for capital gains were introduced in 1921—a modification that has provided more complexity than any other single provision ever enacted—and

---

17 240 US 1 (1916).

provisions for loss deductions were frequently modified during the period 1918–1934. A graduated corporate income tax was introduced in 1936.

Between 1913 and 1939, some 17 income-tax-related laws were enacted by Congress. Although the language of each act tended to reflect closely the earlier provisions, a single codification, to unify these many laws, was deemed desirable. By the joint efforts of the Justice Department and the Bureau of Internal Revenue, this desire was realized with the enactment of the Internal Revenue Code of 1939. All revenue acts passed between 1939 and 1954 were integrated into the 1939 Code, whose framework was thus used until 1954.

THE PERIOD 1939–1954

In 1939, less than 6% of the U.S. population was required to pay a federal income tax. Just six years later (1945), more than 74% of an enlarged population had to pay that same tax.[18] As a mass tax, the income tax is a relative newcomer to our country. Its drastically increased coverage is attributable largely to a major reduction in exemptions during a period of rapidly rising personal income and inflation. Wide coverage was facilitated by the reintroduction of withholding provisions in the Current Tax Payment Act of 1943. To avoid the doubling up of two years' tax liabilities in a single year, the federal government in 1943 forgave 75% of the lower of the 1942 or 1943 tax liabilities.

During the period 1940–1954, several changes were enacted to simplify the administration of the income tax laws. For example, the optional tax table, now familiar to every taxpayer, was introduced in 1941 and extended to larger incomes in 1944, when the exemption and dependent rules also were simplified. The administration of the law was further improved by the reorganization of the Bureau of Internal Revenue in 1952. The old Bureau operated through 64 collectors, who were political appointees. The new Internal Revenue Service operated through 9 regional commissioners and 64 district directors selected on a merit system.

Social and economic equity considerations also weighed heavily in the income tax modifications enacted between 1939 and 1954. For example, a deduction for personal medical expenses was first introduced in 1942. A special exemption for the blind was granted in 1942; another for old age was permitted in 1948. Income splitting, to equalize the federal tax treatment of incomes earned in community and noncommunity-property states, was also enacted in 1948. A head-of-household provision was adopted in 1951 to give single persons with family responsibilities some of the tax advantages that previously existed only for married couples. By 1954, Congress decided to organize and rewrite the 1939 Code.

THE PERIOD 1954–1969

The Internal Revenue Code of 1954 constituted a comprehensive revision of the 1939 Code. It rearranged many of the old provisions in a more logical sequence; deleted much obsolete material; sought to make the language of the Code more understandable; and instituted numerous substantive changes.[19] All revenue measures

18 For more details of this growth see Richard Goode, *The Individual Income Tax* (Washington, D.C.: The Brookings Institution, 1964), pp. 2–4.

19 The objectives of the 1954 revision are stated clearly in both the House Ways and Means Committee Report [H.R. Rept. No. 1337, 83d Congress, 2d Session 1 (1954)] and the Senate Finance Committee Report [S. Rept. No. 1622, 83d Congress, 2d Session 1 (1954)].

modifying the income tax between 1954 and 1986 were incorporated into that codification.

The dominant objectives of the revisions between 1954 and 1969 were economic, although matters of equity and administration received considerable attention. In the former category, two innovations deserve special comment. The investment credit provisions—introduced in 1962, liberalized in 1964, suspended in 1966, reinstated in 1967, deleted in 1969, reintroduced in 1971, further liberalized in 1975 and 1978, and repealed in 1986—had as their primary purpose the stimulation of *investment* spending. The second major innovation of economic significance enacted between 1954 and 1969 was the general tax reductions of 1964 and 1965, which were granted to stimulate *consumption* spending. The proponents of the tax reductions argued that the cut in taxes would even reduce the budget deficit by stimulating the economy to the point that more income taxes would actually be collected at the lower rates than would have been collected at the old, higher rates. This experiment is now generally conceded to have been successful.

Experiments intended to improve tax administration took various forms. Perhaps the greatest advance was the computerization of much tax information by the Internal Revenue Service in Regional Service Centers. In addition, a Small Claims Division of the Tax Court was introduced to handle informally the adjudication of many small tax disputes without much cost to the taxpayer. Finally, a revised tax form was devised to help simplify the reporting process.

THE PERIOD 1969–1978

Historical periods are, of course, arbitrary classifications. Additionally, the closer in time an observer is to the events, the more difficult it is to determine whether a change of such magnitude has occurred that it is meaningful to speak in terms of a new period. We believe, however, that the Tax Reform Act of 1969 marked the beginning of a distinctive period in U.S. tax history, which ended with the Revenue Act of 1978. That period was characterized by periodic and systematic attacks, supported by well-documented studies, on the tax provisions that had permitted large-scale tax avoidance in prior years. The same theme seemed to reoccur in 1986, thereby leaving the years 1978–1986 as either an aberration to a longer period (1969 to present) or a separate and brief period of its own.

Clearly, the effectiveness of many notorious tax avoidance schemes was seriously curtailed between 1969 and 1978. The relative advantage of capital gains was substantially reduced; major avoidance opportunities in charitable contributions and private charitable foundations were eliminated; the ability to claim a deduction for losses from oil and gas properties, motion pictures and video tapes, vacation properties and certain farm-and-ranch operations, citrus groves, and livestock operations was sharply limited; percentage depletion allowances were drastically cut; the early deduction of prepaid interest was eliminated; the deduction of investment interest was limited; and the minimum tax on tax preferences was significantly increased.

The Tax Reform Act of 1976 also made major changes in the federal gift and estate taxes. Major revisions to those two taxes had been promised for many years, but not until 1976 was something finally done to correct many well-known shortcomings of the prior law. President Jimmy Carter campaigned strongly for still greater tax reforms including the well-publicized elimination of deductions for the three-martini lunch. Shortly after taking office, Treasury Secretary Blumenthal announced the new administration's support of a drastic simplification proposal.

The Carter administration's support for additional reforms and drastic simplification in income taxation was short-lived. By midsummer 1977, the president had given up on the more dramatic tax changes initially considered. Even with a large Democratic majority, there was little chance of getting Congress to approve further tax reform measures. Furthermore, public opinion surveys revealed that the general public would neither understand nor fully appreciate many of the recommended tax law changes that had great theoretical merit. In summary, President Carter quickly accepted the political realities that had constrained many prior administrations in making tax reform proposals.

THE PERIOD 1978–1986

Instead of continuing the trend of tax reform started in 1969, the Revenue Act of 1978 was, in many ways, a direct reversal of the recent past. Most important, it made major cuts in the taxation of capital gains (effectively returning them to their pre-1969 preferred position), deferred the effective date on the carryover basis rules for inherited property (which had represented a hard-fought victory for reform proponents in the 1976 Act), and effectively reduced the minimum tax on tax preference items. Although the 1978 Act included a few reform-type provisions, those provisions were clearly of minor significance. The reason for this dramatic turn of events appears to be the stagnating and inflationary state of the economy. By 1978, **stagflation** was a national concern, and the tax code was viewed as part of the problem. As Joseph Minarik relates

> **Stagflation** exists when the economy is stagnant and inflationary at the same time.

> inflation was distorting the measurement of income in the tax base—overstating the income of lenders and understating the income of borrowers (because inflation allowed borrowers to pay their debts with cheaper dollars); eroding the depreciation deductions of investors in business equipment and structures; and creating and inflating phantom capital gains. These effects created all the wrong incentives. . . .[20]

In view of the prevailing conditions, Congress reversed its field and once again gave economic considerations top billing.

A provision of the 1979 Windfall Profits Tax Bill made permanent the originally temporary deferral of the 1976 carryover basis rules for inherited property. President Carter had previously threatened to veto *any* bill that included a provision to modify carryover basis. However, the proponents of repeal knew that Carter wanted the Windfall Profits Tax too badly to veto that bill to achieve a lesser objective. Thus, the opponents of carryover basis adroitly achieved a major reversal of one tax reform that had looked certain just four years earlier.

The shift away from the concerns of tax reform and the reemphasis on economic impact was accelerated with the election of President Ronald Reagan in 1980. Reagan campaigned hard on promises to make major reductions in both personal and business income taxation. To the surprise of many, he quickly made good on both promises with the passage of the Economic Recovery Tax Act of 1981. It appears that the tax revenue increases that followed the 1964–1965 tax reductions noted earlier had made a lasting impression on those who recommended tax policy to Reagan, including economist Arthur Laffer. Laffer, a former chief economist in the OMB, observed that a reduction in the effective income tax rates does not necessarily reduce government

---

20 Joseph Minarik, "How Tax Reform Came About," *Tax Notes* (December 28, 1987), pp. 1361–62.

revenues. He noted that both at a zero tax rate and at a 100% rate, income tax revenues should be nonexistent.[21] The shape of the rest of the curve representing tax revenues, however, is unknown.[22]

One problem with tax policy is that no one knows either (1) the general shape of the real Laffer curve or (2) exactly where we are on that curve at any time. The widely divergent opinions on these two unknowns were implicit in some of the early estimates of the federal budget deficits that would attend the passage of the 1981 Act. The following three comparisons are illustrative:

Early Estimates of 1981 Act-induced Budget Deficits by

Year	Reagan Administration	House Budget Committee	Chase Econometrics
1982	$43 billion	$ 85 billion	$118 billion
1983	35 billion	110 billion	144 billion
1984	23 billion	120 billion	162 billion

The Reagan administration alleged that the 1981 Act would so stimulate saving and investment that, via a multiplier effect, the productive capacity and gross national product of the country would increase. Subsequent economic events, however, have shown that even Chase Econometric's effect projections were too optimistic.

THE 1986 TAX REFORM ACT

> **Goal #4**
> Discuss the principal motivations for, and significance of, the 1986 Tax Reform Act.

The 1986 Tax Reform Act, passed during President Reagan's second term, was a momentous event in U.S. tax history. We will frequently reference the 1986 Act because it turned existing tax law upside down in many important respects. The 1986 Act is viewed as revolutionary because it created fundamental changes of broad scope in the basic structure of our tax law: making drastic rate cuts, eliminating long-standing exclusions and deductions from the tax base, and inverting the relative rate structures of corporations versus individuals.

The process of passing this Act presents a classic study in political compromise. Eventual enactment required the active support of such amazingly diverse political bedfellows as President Ronald Reagan, a champion of conservative causes, and Congressman Dan Rostenkowski, a leader of liberal Democrats and chair of the powerful House Ways and Means Committee. The Act succeeded because it proposed an irresistible blend of old-fashioned tax reform (in the form of a dramatically broadened tax base) and new-style economics (in the form of a drastically flattened rate structure, with top rates slashed). Another important ingredient was the principle of **revenue neutrality**. That is, the entire package was designed to neither increase nor decrease overall federal tax revenues. The political goal of significantly lower top

> **Revenue neutrality** means that a bill must neither increase nor decrease *overall* federal revenues.

---

21 The justification for the assertion that a tax rate of 100% produces no tax revenues is that people would find no reason to engage in productive efforts if the government took all the income generated. For a critical review of these ideas see Walter Heller, "The Kemp-Roth-Laffer Free Lunch," in *The Economics of the Tax Revolt: A Reader*, Arthur B. Laffer and Jan P. Seymour, eds. (New York: Harcourt Brace Jovanovich, 1979), pp. 46–49.

22 For an interesting and scholarly discussion of the Laffer curve, see Charles E. Stuart, "Swedish Tax Rates, Labor Supply and Tax Revenues," *Journal of Political Economy* 89(5), October 1981, pp. 1020–38; see also Don Fullerton, "On the Possibility of an Inverse Relationship between Tax Rates and Government Revenues," *Journal of Public Economics* 19 (1), 1982, pp. 3–22.

marginal tax rates had to be paid for by expanding the definition of taxable income. Conventional wisdom held that such fundamental changes would never happen. The fact that the Act was passed caused many of the tax wizards to put away their crystal balls, at least for a short while.

Tax reform was achieved through the base broadening technique introduced earlier in the 1969 Act: the systematic elimination of many Code provisions that allowed some taxpayers to reduce their federal income tax liabilities to little or nothing, even though they earned substantial amounts of income in both economic and financial accounting terms. Using this approach, the 1986 Act became the most radical base broadening bill in our history. The 1969 Act reduced 20 tax expenditure provisions and expanded 8; the 1986 Act eliminated 14, reduced another 72, and expanded 12. Only 5 years earlier, under the same president, the 1981 Act enacted 7 new tax expenditures, expanded 30, and narrowed 2. One commentator describes these two tax bills as the "historic extremes of tax reform and anti-reform legislation."[23] The 1981 Act's overriding purpose was to stimulate the economy through tax provisions. The 1986 Act's overriding purpose was a complete reversal: to create a more **level playing field** that would minimize tax factors in economic decisions.

> A **level playing field** is an environment in which tax factors do not have a significant impact on economic decisions.

The list of provisions targeted for extinction in the 1986 Act included, among others, capital gains incentives, investment credits, deduction of sales taxes, ultrarapid depreciation, income averaging, and loss deductions generated by tax-sheltered investments. To keep tax revenues neutral—that is, to raise enough revenue to pay for the significant rate cuts—many other deduction provisions had to be severely curtailed. That hapless list included deductions for interest, individual retirement accounts (IRAs), medical expenses, miscellaneous itemized deductions, and other items too numerous to mention here.

Economic stimulus was to be generated by significantly lower marginal tax rates. The rate cuts were dramatic: the top marginal rate for individuals dropped from 50% to 28%; for corporations, from 46% to 34%. The paramount importance of delivering on the promise of lower and flatter rates focused much of the debate on the tax base issues discussed above.

An important structural component of the 1986 Act was a projected shift over five years of approximately $120 billion in income taxes from individual to corporate taxpayers. Despite the obvious significance of tax incidence questions, that issue was never seriously debated.[24] Congress avoided debate of this issue because of the political sensitivity caused by periodic news releases noting that some of the largest corporations in America paid less in federal income tax than did the proverbial widow in Dubuque. Nevertheless, data for 1987–1989 show that corporate tax payments were $76 billion lower than the initial projections, but that individual payments were higher by about the same amount. Reasons for the shortfall were lower corporate profits than projected (in part because taxpayers shifted to S corporations and partnerships), less revenue generated than projected by certain base broadeners, and an unexpectedly high use of ESOPs (which reduce corporate taxable income).[25]

---

23 John F. Witte, "Congress and Tax Policy: Problems and Reforms in a Historical Context," presented at the American Law Institute and American Bar Association conference "Improving the Tax Legislative Process: A Critical Need," April 26–27, 1991.

24 Gregory Ballentine discusses this further in "Three Failures in Economic Analysis of Tax Reform," *National Tax Journal, 1986 Annual Conference Proceedings*, pp. 3–6. (Indicative of accounting firm involvement in tax policy matters, Ballentine is with KPMG Peat Marwick.)

25 Emil M. Sunley and Randall D. Weiss, "The Revenue Estimating Process," presented at the American Law Institute and American Bar Association conference "Improving the Tax Legislative Process: A Critical Need," April 26–27, 1991, pp. 53–54.

THE PERIOD 1987–1991

The massive tax law changes of 1986 were followed by relatively minor tax laws in each year, until 1991. The single most distinctive feature of this period is a focus on the deficit. Most of the annual changes were driven either by the need to make technical corrections to prior changes, or to raise additional revenues needed to meet deficit targets. The budget process itself was changed for 1991 and subsequent years in an attempt to forestall further changes of major significance to both tax laws and government expenditure programs, at least in the near term.

A substantial portion of the alleged tax revenue increases or **revenue raisers** involve changes in accounting provisions. These changes modify tax accounting for long-term contracts, installment sales, and other specific items of income and deduction. Although the accounting changes serve only to accelerate tax collections, they receive a lot of press coverage because they count as revenue increases in the deficit projection. In other words, even though none of these changes will increase overall tax revenues in the long run, they will increase tax revenues in the short run, and only the short run is of significance in deficit projections. The extra and permanent costs imposed on businesses in complying with the revised accounting rules do not get counted in government deficit projections. The problem is that there are no more easy targets for raising large amounts of additional tax revenue. Hence business taxpayers are increasingly required to contribute more through (1) accelerated tax payments and (2) increased compliance costs.

Two other general trends during the period from 1987 to 1991 are noteworthy. First, emphasis increased on excise taxes as a source of additional federal revenues (see Chapter 1). Second, the deductions that can be claimed by individual taxpayers with high incomes have slowly but steadily eroded. Both of these trends may accelerate in the future for reasons explained later in this chapter.

Although many other tax policy issues—including capital gains and the need for simplification—were the subject of recurring and vigorous debate, no action was taken on those issues. Two bills of general interest to taxpayers, however, were enacted. In 1988 Congress passed a "Taxpayer Bill of Rights" largely in response to public outcries concerning the imbalance of power between taxpayers and the IRS. Early evidence suggests this bill was a step in the right direction, but more legislation may be required to resolve the problem. And, in 1990, Congress passed the **Omnibus Budget Reconciliation Act** (or **OBRA**).

OBRA followed quickly on the heels of the shutdown of many highly visible government services. These shutdowns were mandated by the budget sequester requirements of the Gramm-Rudman Act. The fact that Boy Scouts and other visitors to our nation's capital could not ascend the Washington Monument, because it was closed by the **sequester** provisions, created enormous pressure for Congress to find a new way to deal with budget matters. OBRA does not directly affect tax revenues, but it does dramatically affect the tax-writing process. Before OBRA, Congress would annually direct the House Ways and Means and the Senate Finance Committees to produce revenues sufficient in amount to meet deficit reduction targets. As a result, every year, tax legislation centered on finding new sources of revenue or cutting expenditures. OBRA changed this process by replacing *deficit* targets with *spending* targets. The new system establishes categories or **baskets** for different programs. For each basket, spending changes can be enacted only on a pay-as-you-go basis. The major categories are revenues, tax expenditures, **nondiscretionary spending** programs (such as Social Security) and discretionary spending. The first three

---

Goal #5
Describe the important trends and developments in tax law in the period following the 1986 Tax Reform Act.

Revenue raisers are tax provisions that are projected to increase net revenues over the five-year projection period.

OBRA is the **Omnibus Budget Reconciliation Act** of 1990 that significantly changed the budget procedures.

A **sequester** is a freeze of funds, terminating government activities. The Gramm-Rudman Act set deficit reduction targets that must be met annually by Congress. Failure to meet these targets triggers sequestration.

Baskets are categories used to group government expenditures.

Nondiscretionary spending refers to categories where the amounts to be spent are controlled by legal requirements.

categories are placed within one basket. Various trade-offs within this one large basket are possible as long as they are revenue neutral.

Discretionary spending
refers to categories over which Congress can exert some control.

Discretionary spending now operates under different rules than the other categories. It is made up of three baskets: defense, international, and domestic, each subject to its own spending cap. A spending cap means that any increase in expenditures in one of the discretionary baskets must be offset by a decrease in another expenditure within that same basket. For example, increases in defense spending cannot be offset by decreases in domestic or international programs. Exceeding an expenditure cap results in a sequester of all programs within that same basket.

In summary, talk of budget deficits and revenue increases dominated the period from 1987 to 1991. The tax acts passed each year had their primary goal of raising revenue. Tax reform and tax equity issues were only incidental.

ASSESSING THE EFFECTS OF THE 1986 ACT AND SUCCESSOR ACTS

The equity effects of the 1986 tax law were rather immediate and apparent for both low and high income taxpayers but were generally a wash for those in the middle. Most significantly, the 1986 legislation removed 6 million poor families from the tax rolls. As shown in Figure 2-2, in 1979 a family of four began to owe an income tax only after it earned about 18% *over* the poverty line. By 1985, the same household was required to pay an income tax after earning only $9,500, 14% *below* the $11,000

FIGURE 2-2

Ratio of Income Tax Threshold to Poverty Level, 1975–1990

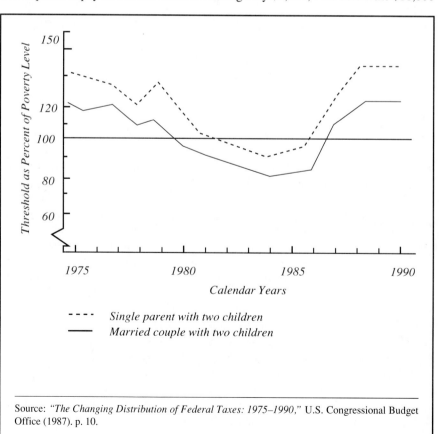

Source: *"The Changing Distribution of Federal Taxes: 1975–1990,"* U.S. Congressional Budget Office (1987). p. 10.

estimated poverty level. Indexation for inflation and increases in the earned income credit, the standard deduction, and the personal exemption allowed the working poor to retain over $4 billion a year more of their earnings. Figure 2-2 shows that these changes in the law raised the tax-exempt level of income to at least 120% of the poverty threshold for a married couple with two children in 1988 and are expected to keep them in the same position relative to the poverty line thereafter.[26]

Just as the new law treated lower income taxpayers more equitably, it also improved the *horizontal* equity of people in the upper income classes. Prior to the 1986 Act, individuals who earned a real economic income of between $100,000 and $500,000 per year often paid very different tax rates. The amount of tax paid ranged from nearly 50% of income (for about 5% of the group) to little or nothing (for 2–3% of the same group). Although some high income taxpayers continue to pay little in taxes due to substantial sums of nontaxable interest and fringe benefits, the vast majority of all affluent taxpayers are now expected to pay at least 15–20% of their real income in federal income taxes.[27] This result is due to the base broadening aspects of the 1986 Act geared toward obtaining a relatively accurate measure of economic income. A measure of the effectiveness of the 1986 changes in accomplishing this goal is the comparison of salary and wage income to nonwage income as a percentage of gross reported income. Nonwage income steadily increased from 19.7% in 1985 to 24.9% in 1988.[28]

While the 1986 Tax Act was generally expected to improve both horizontal and vertical equity, critics of the law initially predicted dire economic consequences.[29] But today the general consensus is that tax reform helped remove economic distortion and did not depress overall investment.[30] Real estate values probably were more affected than anything else. Indirectly this effect also had an impact on the construction, savings and loans, banks, and insurance industries.

Although the tax changes appear to be neutral or positive overall, significant reshuffling has taken place. Tax shelters are dying.[31] Shareholders are increasingly electing Subchapter S rather than C corporation form. And an estimated three-fourths of the decline in consumer credit (nondeductible interest expense) has been replaced with added home mortgage borrowing (deductible interest expense).[32]

UNADDRESSED PROBLEMS

> **Goal #6**
> Describe problems that persist with our tax system.

At least four major underlying issues have not been addressed by the recent tax legislation. First, the 1986 Act was designed to shift a substantial portion of the overall tax burden to corporations. As we noted in the first part of this chapter, corporate tax

26 This discussion is based on the 1987 U.S. Congressional Budget Office Report "The Changing Distribution of Federal Taxes: 1975–1990"; David Wessel's "U.S. Rich and Poor Increase in Numbers; Middle Loses Ground," *The Wall Street Journal* (September 22, 1986), pp. 1 and 16; and Kenneth Bacon's "The Rich Get Richer, but Congress Avoids Changing Inheritance Taxes," *The Wall Street Journal* (August 5, 1986), p. 13.

27 Hilary Stout, "Tax Act of 1986 Proves a Winner: It Spawns a Lot of Rich Losers," *The Wall Street Journal,* April 17, 1989, p. 1.

28 Allen D. Manvel, "Measuring the Income Tax Base," *Tax Notes*, July 22, 1991, pp. 485–488.

29 Gerald Brannon, "An Early Review of Tax Reform," *Tax Notes*, November 20, 1989, pp. 943–48.

30 J. Andrew Hoerner, "Tax Reform Improved the Economy, Michigan Tax Conference Concludes," *Tax Notes*, November 20, 1989, pp. 942–43.

31 William Power, "Shearson Cuts Back on Partnerships: Some Fear Pullout," *The Wall Street Journal,* December 18, 1989, p. C1.

32 Jonathan Skinner and Daniel Feenburg, "The Impact of the 1986 Tax Reform on Personal Saving," University of Virginia working paper (1989).

collections have dwindled substantially over the past three decades. Congress's response to the perception that corporations have not been paying their "fair share" was to tighten up the regular tax system and substantially broaden the base for the corporate alternative minimum tax. This action begs the critical question of the incidence of the corporate tax burden, an issue introduced earlier. In drawing conclusions about the relative progressivity and equity of our tax system as a whole, it would be highly desirable to resolve the question: Who bears the corporate tax burden?

The second issue is related to the first but involves a fundamentally more critical issue. Until 15–20 years ago, the post–World War II era had been marked by a trend in the United States toward income becoming divided a bit more evenly in the population each year. The rich got richer, but the middle class got richer, too; and it grew. Poverty didn't disappear, but it dwindled. This trend has reversed in the past 15 years. David Bloom, a Harvard University economist, states that "the country has moved in the direction of becoming a nation of haves and have-nots, with less in between."[33] Census bureau data for 1990 show that 13.5% of the population lived below the poverty line ($13,359 for a family of four). This was an increase of 2.1 million individuals, the first increase since 1983. Further detail shows that 20% of all children, 28% of all Hispanic-Americans, and 32% of all African-Americans fall into this group.[34] Only 15% of children were below the poverty line in 1970. It is projected that by the year 2000 about half of all American children will have lived at least some part of their lives in poverty.[35] Figure 2-3 reflects the growing inequality in the distribution of income over the past 15 years. When incomes stated in 1992 dollars are compared from the lowest to the highest income taxpayers, we see that the lowest 20% of taxpayers will earn 10% less in 1992 than they did in 1977. Meanwhile, the top 1% of all taxpayers have experienced a real increase in income of 113%. Nominal tax rates for both groups have decreased: for the lowest 20%, by about 8%; for the upper 1%, by 19%. Effective income tax rates for all groups are lower but the income tax rates of taxpayers in the upper half, and especially in the top 10%, have decreased relatively more than the lower half. When the income tax burden is combined with the Social Security tax burden, the overall burden falls much more heavily on the lower 80% of the population. Only the lowest 20% and the upper 5% have seen a decrease in their effective tax rates during this period.[36]

Taxes are obviously not the only factor affecting the income distribution; several other important factors are at work. The economy continues a trend toward more service-oriented jobs and it is not producing as many middle-wage jobs as union-shop manufacturing once did. The average hourly wage (stated in 1982 dollars) was $7.78 in 1980 and $7.54 in 1990. Compared with earlier postwar years, the unemployment rate in the past two decades has been relatively high. Furthermore, a growing number of households are headed by poor, single mothers rather than by two parents and there have been cutbacks in welfare programs. The tax system alone cannot cure the problems of poverty and the distribution of wealth in the United States. However, its design and relative progressivity are intended to smooth out the distribution of income to some degree, a goal that does not appear to have been achieved. For whatever

33 Wessel, *op. cit.,* "U.S. Rich and Poor Increase in Numbers: Middle Loses Ground."

34 Pat Carr and Trevor Johnston, "One of Seven Americans Below Poverty Level in 1990," *Knight-Ridder Tribune News,* Sept. 27, 1991.

35 Wessel, *op. cit.,* "U.S. Rich and Poor Increase in Numbers: Middle Loses Ground."

36 "The Changing Distribution of Federal Taxes: 1975–1990," U.S. Congressional Budget Office (1987), pp. 42, 44.

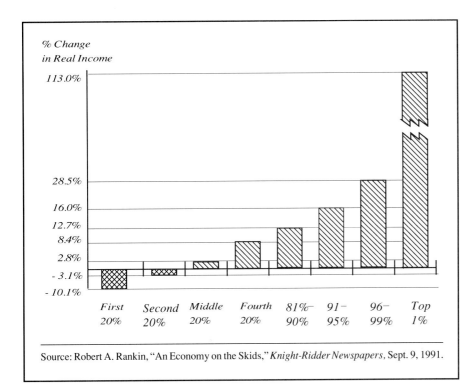

FIGURE 2-3

Percentage Change in Incomes from 1977–1992 by Percentiles

Source: Robert A. Rankin, "An Economy on the Skids," *Knight-Ridder Newspapers,* Sept. 9, 1991.

reason, we apparently are living in an era in which the rich are getting richer and the poor are getting poorer.

A third problem is that, for those fortunate taxpayers with higher incomes, the new laws add an almost draconian degree of complexity. This added complexity is a major problem for about 30% of all individual taxpayers and nearly all corporate taxpayers. One commentator notes that "compromise is the root of complexity."[37] As you will see in later chapters, the current tax law is a parade of seemingly unending compromises buttressed by a shadowy system of minimum taxes. Not only have new distinctions emerged regarding types of income and deductions, but the changing law has necessitated thousands of transition rules. Since 1976, more than 8,500 subsections of the Internal Revenue Code have been changed—including more than 2,700 subsections that were changed by the 1986 Tax Act.[38] In 1988, Dow Chemical Company filed a tax return nearly 7,000 pages long, up from 5,500 pages in 1987 and 4,800 pages in 1986.[39] This state of affairs is thought by many to be seriously impairing the U.S. tax system because compliance becomes such a daunting task and predicting tax outcomes of prospective transactions becomes virtually impossible.

An important tax simplification movement is being led by practitioners working through national organizations of accountants and attorneys. One speaker at a simplification conference for tax accountants and tax attorneys lent a cynical note to this movement by saying, "It's like going to a Hell's Angels conference on the decline of social graces in America. . . . We are the problem."[40] Regardless of the causes of

---

37 Michael Graetz, "The Truth about Tax Reform," *University of Florida Law Review, 1988.*

38 *BNA Daily Report for Executives*, "Moratorium on Change," October 11, 1988, p. H-1.

39 Robert Norton, "The Corporate Tax Mess," *U.S. News and World Report*, October 11, 1988, p. H-1.

40 Former Joint Committee on Taxation Chief of Staff David H. Brockway, at the AICPA/ABA Joint Conference on Reduction of Complexity, January, 1990.

complexity in the tax system, sufficient outcry by taxpayers, practitioners, and administration officials has lead to the recent introduction of several bills devoted solely to simplifying the Internal Revenue Code. Practitioner groups are also developing suggestions and procedures to ensure that the legislative and administrative processes elevate simplification to a higher level of priority.

The final issue not adequately addressed by tax legislation in the 1980s is that of budget deficits. As indicated in Chapter 1, the United States has generated unprecedented budget deficits during this decade. Although federal receipts have remained close to their norm of 19–20% of GNP (individual income tax cuts have offset increases in Social Security and other taxes), spending has risen.[41] Oliver Blanchard of the Massachusetts Institute of Technology suggested that former President Reagan's budget policy would create, via deficits, sufficient political pressure to reduce government spending.[42] OBRA is the result of that pressure. Time will tell if it will be effective.

The main evil of a federal budget deficit (estimated at $338 billion in 1991) is that it represents public dissaving. Charles Schultze, a senior fellow at the Brookings Institution and former chairman of the President's Council of Economic Advisers, expressed the problem this way: "At Christmas, kids get what they want, and adults pay for it. With federal deficits, grownups get what they want, leaving the kids to pay for it."[43] As a result, net national savings—the sum of personal and corporate savings, plus government surpluses or deficits—fell to 3.7% of net national product in the 1980s. This is less than half the 8.0% average experienced from 1952 through 1979.[44]

Savings are essential to investment and economic growth. Furthermore, U.S. international competitiveness is threatened because the current rate is one-fifth the national savings rate of major industrialized nations and only one-eighth the savings rate of Japan.[45] Because of the impact of savings on future productivity, we can expect numerous tax law proposals designed to address this issue in the next few years.

SIGNIFICANT FACTORS FOR THE FUTURE OF OUR TAX SYSTEM

Goal #7

List forces that will have a significant impact on future directions of change in our tax system. Explain their importance.

We believe that three factors will have a significant impact on the direction of changes in the tax system in the future. The overriding concern will be the deficit because of its unprecedented growth.[46] OBRA was spawned by congressional realization that spending cuts are no longer optional: The only issue is where cuts will be made. OMB Director Richard G. Darman's introduction in the 1992 budget proclaimed a "new emphasis for reform: increasing fairness in the distribution of benefits [and] reducing subsidies for those who do not need them." The growth of spending on all people, compared to spending on the poor, has grown dramatically over the past 30 years. (See Figure 2-4.)

41 The editorial, "Tax and Pretend," *The Wall Street Journal,* November 4, 1987, p. 30.

42 As quoted in the editorial, "The Struggle for Economic Equilibrium," *The Wall Street Journal,* December 2, 1987, p. 1.

43 As reported in *Tax Notes,* December 31, 1990, p. 1502.

44 U.S. Congressional Budget Office, *The Economic and Budget Outlook: Fiscal Years 1990–1994,* January 1989, p. 84.

45 Kenneth Bacon, "The Savings Slump: No Easy Solution," *The Wall Street Journal,* December 19, 1988, p. 1.

46 Our discussion on the budget incorporates data from Coopers & Lybrand "Current Legislative Report," March 1991, p. 1.

FIGURE 2-4

**Mandatory
Spending by
Income (Outlays)**

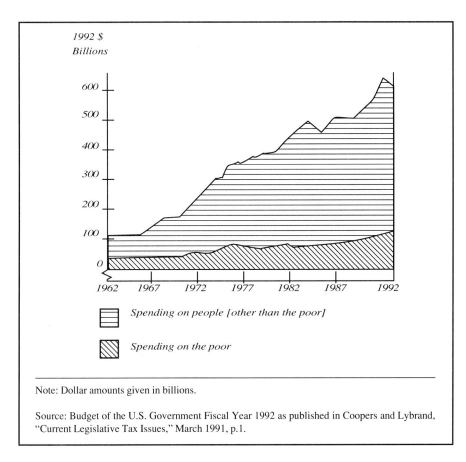

1992 $
Billions

Spending on people [other than the poor]

Spending on the poor

Note: Dollar amounts given in billions.

Source: Budget of the U.S. Government Fiscal Year 1992 as published in Coopers and Lybrand, "Current Legislative Tax Issues," March 1991, p.1.

The federal debt is conservatively projected to be $4.4 trillion by the end of fiscal year 1993. This estimate may be understated because it is based on economic assumptions that appear to be unrealistic in this recessionary period. The good news is that interest rates are lower than the 7.4% used in the projections.

The annual interest on that debt is estimated to be $1278 per person. Consequently, the portion of federal spending that is clearly nondiscretionary continues to grow rapidly. Another aspect of spending that is virtually uncontrollable relates to entitlement programs such as Medicare and Social Security. These two elements make up 62% of the 1992 budget, but only 37% of the budget in 1970 and 53% in 1980. Faced with these projections, the attention of Congress must be drawn to the next significant factor: spending through tax expenditures.

Tax expenditures are a measure of governmental decisions to achieve economic and social goals through the tax system. Examples are accelerated depreciation, home mortgage interest, pension provisions, and deductions for charitable contributions. The cost to the government is calculated in terms of the tax revenues forgone. The forgone revenues, labeled *tax expenditures*, are tallied in the annual budget in the same way direct expenses are reflected. Table 2-4 shows the projected cost of the 12 largest tax expenditures for both 1992 ($276.6 billion) and for the five year period of 1992–1996 ($1,615.8 trillion). Of these 12 expenditures, 11 primarily benefit individuals and are skewed toward middle- to high-income individuals. The only major expenditure targeted toward businesses is accelerated depreciation of machinery and equipment. That expenditure is now the seventh largest; it was fourth largest in the fiscal 1989 budget.

TABLE 2-4

**The Twelve
Largest Tax
Expenditures
Fiscal 1992 and
Fiscal 1992–1996
(in billions)**

	Fiscal 1992	Fiscal 1992–96
1. Net exclusion of pension contributions and earnings	$54.0	$295.0
2. Deductibility of mortgage interest on owner-occupied homes	38.8	231.2
3. Exclusion of employer contributions for medical insurance premiums and medical care	37.7	226.4
4. Exclusion of OASI benefits of retired workers	25.6	142.3
5. Deductibility of nonbusiness state and local taxes other than on owner-occupied homes	23.8	137.9
6. Exclusion of interest on state and local debt	22.1	123.9
7. Accelerated depreciation of machinery and equipment	18.1	97.0
8. Deductibility of charitable contributions	12.5	96.3
9. Deductibility of property taxes on owner-occupied homes	11.0	69.0
10. Exclusion of untaxed medicare benefits	11.1	67.3
11. Deferral of capital gains on sales of principal residences	11.5	65.3
12. Carryover basis of capital gains at death	10.5	64.2

Source: BNA Special Supplement, House Ways and Means Committee Report, "Overview of the Federal Tax System," 1991 ed. (WMCP: 102–107), Part V, Table 1, pp. S-76–S-79, "Tax Expenditure Estimates by Budget Function, Fiscal Years 1992–1996," April 19, 1991.

Untaxed employee pension contributions, medical insurance, and other fringe benefits now represent about one-third of all personnel expense. They will cost the federal government approximately $100 billion in lost revenue in 1992. Recent tax legislation has left this area virtually untouched despite the inequity that arises between individuals when one person receives one-third of his or her total income in tax-free benefits while another, generally the low-income worker, has to pay for health insurance, life insurance, and other benefits with after-tax dollars.

Three items in the top 12 measure the large cost to the government of subsidizing home ownership: (1) deductibility of mortgage interest, (2) property taxes, and (3) deferral of capital gains on sales of principal residences, are expected to cost $61.3 billion in lost tax revenues in 1992. Inequity among taxpayers is also a problem with the home ownership tax benefits. Because the home-ownership-related deductions reduce the after-tax cost of home ownership, the prices of homes rise, increasing the barrier to those who do not already own homes. Furthermore, for reasons described more fully in later chapters, many deductions are of little or no value to lower income taxpayers. As Emil Sunley, Director of Tax Analysis for Deloitte & Touche, notes:

> There are no easy pickings for base broadening on the individual side. A strategy to raise additional individual income tax revenues through base broadening is a strategy to go after the major itemized deductions (state and local taxes, mortgage interest, and charitable contributions), the major employee benefits (pensions and group medical), or unrealized capital gains at death or to tax Social Security retirement benefits and interest on state and local debt.[47]

---

47 Emil Sunley, "The Tax Challenge for the 1990s," *Tax Notes*, August 8, 1988, pp. 621–26.

Despite the nearly sacred status that these expenditures have attained, Darman's statement that increasing fairness will entail "reducing subsidies for those who do not need them" signals the prospect of a frontal attack on these particular expenditures. At the very least, his statement suggests more aggressive use of phaseouts of these deductions as income increases, a technique initiated in the Revenue Reconciliation Act of 1990.

Finally, we can expect Congress to keep an eye on the position of the United States relative to other countries with regard to three important measures of the tax burden: taxes as a percentage of gross domestic product, individual income taxes as a percentage of all federal taxes, and taxes on goods and services (consumption taxes) as a percentage of total tax revenues (see Table 2-5). The United States is tied with Japan for the lowest total tax burden as measured in terms of gross domestic product. The middle column in the table reveals the United States's relatively high reliance on the individual income tax (fifth out of the fourteen countries listed). The last column clearly indicates our relatively low reliance on taxes on goods and services as a percentage of total tax revenues. Japan ranks lower on consumption taxes, but these figures do not reflect the 3% value-added tax (VAT) that Japan legislated in 1989. In addition, although Canada's consumption taxes were already substantially higher than those of the United States, Canada also legislated a national goods and services tax of over 6% effective for 1991. That change is not reflected in Table 2-5.

Another comparative measure significant to taxation is the level of debt as a percentage of Gross Domestic Product (GDP). When comparing Germany, Japan, the United States and the United Kingdom, Japan has debt of about 270% of GDP while

TABLE 2-5

International Comparisons— 1987

Country	Taxes as Percent Gross Domestic Product	Percent Income Taxes to All Taxes	Percent Consumption Taxes to All Taxes
Sweden	57	41	24
Denmark	52	55	34
Norway	48	33	40
Netherlands	48	27	26
Belgium	46	39	25
France	45	18	29
Austria	42	26	32
United Kingdom	38	37	31
Germany	38	34	25
Italy	36	37	26
Finland	36	50	38
Canada	35	47	29
United States	30	44	17
Japan	30	47	13

Source: Adapted from Revenue Statistics of OECD Member Countries, 1965–1985, Table 1. Adapted from Tax Foundation, Inc. *Facts and Figures on Government Finance*, (Baltimore: Johns Hopkins University Press, 1991), Tables A33 and A34, pp. 36–37.

the other three countries have debt of between 150% and 200% of GDP. Only the United Kingdom has seen a decrease in this debt ratio over the past 20 years. Japan's debt as a percentage of GDP has nearly doubled, while Germany's is up 44% and the United States is up 34.5%[48]

These comparisons are especially important in an era of growing concern over international competitiveness. The House Ways and Means Committee held a series of hearings in 1991 on long-term international competitiveness issues. On May 30, the Joint Committee on Taxation published an extensive analysis of the effect of the tax system on international competitiveness. Michael J. Graetz, Deputy Assistant Secretary of the Treasury for Tax Policy, views these developments as "the opening shots in what will be the next long-term examination of the U.S. tax system [and] the focus over the next decade or so is going to be far more international than it has been in the past." In Graetz's opinion, the U.S. system must converge with those of other industrialized nations, especially with respect to consumption taxes. He expects these issues to be a subject of continuing and growing debate.[49]

——— CONCLUSION

Taking all of these factors into account, what changes in our tax system will take place in the future? The pressure of the deficit has grown to the point that major players in the administration (Darman and Graetz) are signalling two important areas for change. With no easy targets for significant spending cuts, the benefits of some of the larger tax expenditure categories appear to be vulnerable, at least for high income taxpayers. Two recurring suggestions for enlarging the tax base involve further limiting the home mortgage interest deduction and making Social Security benefits fully taxable for higher income taxpayers. These two measures would probably raise less than $10 billion initially, but they would enhance income tax progressivity and help staunch the flow of even more red ink in the future.

Consumption taxes are almost certain to get more attention. It is easy to justify such consideration because the United States has tapped that tax base relatively lightly compared to its trading partners. The 1990 Act made modest moves in tapping this base through excise taxes, but a much larger source of new revenues could be found through a national sales tax or a value added tax. The lure of big money may prove irresistible as Congress once again goes on a frustrating hunt for places to cut spending. Given the hard, cold facts on the intractability of the budget, the hunt is doomed to turn up only Easter eggs and no large treasure.

Capital gains and IRAs are also likely to get continuing attention, but given the budget problems and new budget procedures, they are weak candidates for action in the near term, unless they can be tied in to a reduction in some other tax expenditure.

In these first two chapters, we have touched only the surface of some complex subjects. Some of you may be sufficiently stimulated by this brief introduction to make a more exhaustive examination at another time. The remainder of this textbook is concerned exclusively with income taxation because that is the dominant form of taxation in today's economy. Bear in mind throughout, however, that the income tax is but one part of a complex tax structure. As taxpayers and tax practitioners, we must be concerned with how much tax must be paid in a given situation. As citizens and

---

48 "News Report: Is the United States Hooked on Debt?" *Journal of Accountancy*, September 1991, p. 17.

49 As reported in *Tax Notes*, June 17, 1991, pp. 1363–64.

students of taxation, we must also strive to gain an appreciation of the place of the tax laws in the social, economic, and political fabric of our time.[50]

_____ KEY POINTS TO REMEMBER

✓ Each level of government relies primarily on different tax bases. The income tax is the most productive tax in the United States and federal tax collections make up over 60% of total tax collections.

✓ Various income taxes were used in the United States before the Sixteenth Amendment to the Constitution laid the foundation for our current income tax system.

✓ There are several distinct periods in the evolution of the income tax from 1913 to the present. One can relate economic circumstances, as well as changing views on equity and incentive considerations, to the thrust and ultimate shape of legislation during each of these periods.

✓ The 1986 Act is the starting point of the current period in tax history. The view of the legislators responsible for this period was that the role of tax law in economic decisions should be minimized. That view was reflected in a broader tax base, flatter rate structure, lower overall marginal tax rates, and an inversion of the historical position of the highest marginal corporate rate relative to the highest marginal individual rate.

✓ A distinctive feature of the post-1986 Act period is an almost singular focus on the deficit. Recent changes in tax law have been primarily revenue raisers, many of which have affected businesses through changes in accounting rules. Efforts to find new revenue sources have led to increased excise taxes.

✓ The major problems that face tax legislators today include the difficulty of determining the incidence of the corporate income tax, growing gaps in the well-being of the rich and the poor, escalating complexity in the tax law, and persistent deficits.

✓ The continuing problems noted above and the issue of international competitiveness will have a dominant influence on the shape of tax legislation in the near-term future.

_____ RECALL PROBLEMS

1. To which level of government (federal, state, or local) does the largest portion of all taxes go? What is the relative share each level collects? How stable are those shares? What is the principal tax base for each level of government?

2. Approximately what percentage of total tax collections do income taxes produce? What is the relative amount collected for income taxes versus social insurance taxes for individuals?

---

50 The following intermediate-level public finance texts can provide additional insight into the economics of taxation: Harvey S. Rosen, _Public Finance,_ 3rd ed. (Homewood, IL: Irwin, 1992); Edgar K. Browning and Jacqueline M. Browning, _Public Finance and the Price System,_ 3rd ed. (New York: Macmillan, 1987); Richard A. Musgrave and Peggy B. Musgrave, _Public Finance in Theory and Practice_, 5th ed. (New York: McGraw-Hill, 1989); and David N. Hyman, _Public Finance: A Contemporary Application of Theory to Policy,_ 3rd ed. (Chicago: Dryden, 1990).

#2

3. If the income tax was truly unconstitutional prior to the ratification of the Sixteenth Amendment in 1913, how could the United States actually impose and collect an income tax for approximately 10 years in the 1870s and 1880s?

#2

4. What is a direct tax? What is an indirect tax?

#2

5. Between 1861 and 1872, several revenue acts passed by Congress included an income tax.

   a. Was the constitutionality of these acts ever tested before the U.S. Supreme Court? If so, what did the Court find?

   b. List four reasons why these early experiments in income taxation may be considered significant for subsequent income tax laws.

#3

6. How would you characterize the major changes in the federal income tax between 1913 and 1939? between 1939 and 1954? between 1954 and 1969? between 1969 and 1977? between 1978 and 1986?

#3

7. The federal income tax on individuals did not become a *mass tax* until about 1942. Explain what this means and what was necessitated by the transition from a select tax to a mass tax.

#4

8. How did Congress and the administration achieve the dramatic reduction in the marginal income tax rates of individual taxpayers in the Tax Reform Act of 1986 without, supposedly, precipitating a major decline in the overall federal tax revenues?

#4

9. List distinctive characteristics of the 1986 Act.

#5

10. What tax law changes have occurred since the 1986 Act?

#6

11. What are the principal problems that have not been resolved by recent tax legislation?

#6

12. What is the size of the budget deficit predicted to be? List some of the major components of the deficit.

#7

13. What are tax expenditures? What are the five largest tax expenditures in the budget? Who benefits most from tax expenditures?

#7

14. How does the U.S. compare to other major nations in terms of significant economic indicators?

———— THOUGHT PROBLEMS

#1

1. Is it likely that either the corporate or personal income taxes will be repealed in the near future? Explain briefly.

#1

2. A majority of individual taxpayers pay more in Social Security or self-employment taxes than they do in income taxes. These taxes are imposed only on labor income. Is taxing labor income at a higher rate than capital income a good idea for the economy? How do you think this feature of our tax system is justified?

#3 #4 #5

3. As this book is being written, the economic indicators are very weak. This status has prompted President Bush to call for tax breaks to stimulate the economy. If you were a member of Congress, would you argue for or against using the tax

system to influence economic activity under such conditions? Explain why you would take that position. Explain the weaknesses you see in your position.

4. Review Table 2-4 to recall the tax expenditure budget for items related to home ownership. What is your opinion about the merits of directing resources to support home ownership? What are the direct and indirect economic effects of allowing tax deductions for these home ownership–related deductions?

#6 #7

5. Write a brief essay developing the issues surrounding the question of who bears the corporate tax burden.

#6

6. To what extent should the tax system be used to attempt to redress problems of the rich getting richer and the poor getting poorer? Prepare an outline of the advantages and disadvantages of relying on the tax system to cure this problem.

#6

7. If the United States adopts an approach of placing increasing reliance on consumption taxes, what problems are presented for the tax system?

#7

8. Critique the policy our tax system has adopted of allowing significant amounts of benefits such as pensions, health and life insurance, and other fringe benefits to be provided tax-free to employees.

#6 #7

CLASS PROJECTS

1. Using the daily newspapers or weekly newsmagazines available in your library, determine what changes in tax laws have been proposed or enacted within the past six months. Evaluate the arguments given in support of these provisions in light of the things you have learned about our tax system and the canons of taxation.

2. Using the daily newspapers, weekly newsmagazines, or other sources available in your library, find information about current projections on the budget deficit. In particular, determine what factors are being blamed (or credited) for revisions from earlier estimates. Write a brief essay explicating your opinion about the seriousness of the budget deficits.

Most people simply can't understand our tax laws. The basic tax law is more than 2,000 pages long—and tax regulations are almost 10,000 pages more, plus thousands of pages of interpretations and judicial opinions . . . . It has been said, accurately I might add, that "Laws, like sausages, cease to inspire respect in proportion as we know how they are made."

SENATOR BILL BRADLEY, THE FAIR TAX (1984)

LEGAL PROCESSES AND RESPONSIBILITIES

CHAPTER OBJECTIVES

In Chapter 3, you will learn about the federal income tax process from the creation of new tax law to compliance with specific provisions. IRS administration of the laws, taxpayer and practitioner responsibilities, and dispute resolution procedures are also discussed. Finally, you will gain an introduction to the tools tax professionals use to solve complex tax problems.

LEARNING GOALS

After studying this chapter, you should be able to

1 Describe the process by which tax laws are made;

2 Describe the sources available to determine both the current tax law applicable to any situation and the legislative history of that law;

3 Identify sources of administrative interpretation of the statutory tax law and describe their relative weight of authority;

4 Explain the role of the judiciary in the interpretation of tax law;

5 Describe a taxpayer's responsibilities and broad indicators of taxpayers' general compliance with those obligations;

6 Identify the more significant penalties that may be imposed on taxpayers who do not satisfy their legal responsibilities;

7 Explain the significance of tax practitioners in the U.S. tax system and describe their responsibilities to the system;

8 Identify the most significant penalties that may apply to those individuals who advise taxpayers inappropriately;

9 Explain the function of IRS in the administration of tax law;

10 Describe taxpayer options to resolve tax disputes; and

11 Define tax research and explain the sources used by tax professionals in doing tax research.

The body of tax law is ever changing. In recent years, this dynamic nature has been evidenced by the fact that each year Congress has passed a new tax law. In most years, the new tax law made only slight amendments to previous provisions. In other years, as in 1986, the new tax law introduced vast changes from past provisions. Whether the changes are minor or extensive, new tax law tends to generate considerable debate in Congress.

While the interaction of the social, political, and economic factors influencing tax legislation seemingly results in endless complexity, an understanding of the process by which this law is created, and the structure for its administration, is an invaluable tool in demystifying the complexity that is innate in tax laws. Because most tax practitioners not only prepare tax returns but also help clients with tax planning, an understanding of tax law creation and administration enhances a practitioner's ability to anticipate changes and effectively plan for clients. Although this chapter is not a complete and definitive review of either the political process related to tax legislation or the legal research tools that practitioners need, it does provide a general overview of the components of the process and the information relevant to planning.[1]

In this chapter, we will discuss the various sources of legal pronouncements collectively known as the tax law. At this point, our concern will not be with what the tax law is but rather with how the various legal pronouncements come into existence. In addition, we will discuss the taxpayer's responsibility for compliance with the existing law and the role tax practitioners and the IRS play in the functioning of the system. Finally, we will illustrate how tax practitioners, with their knowledge of the system and research skills, can help clients solve their tax problems.

—— THE SOURCE OF TAX LAW

Goal #1
Describe the process by which tax laws are made.

Hundreds of bills, dozens of them focusing on the tax law, are introduced in Congress each year. For instance, the Bradley–Gephardt tax bill (the forerunner of the 1986 Tax Reform Act) was first introduced in the House of Representatives in August 1982. This bill was one of 2,151 introduced in the House of Representatives and one of 1,119 introduced in the Senate that year.[2] Since only several hundred bills, and generally only one tax bill, ever become law, it is instructive to review sources of influence in the legislative process.

Although most major proposals for changes in tax laws are presented to Congress by the Secretary of the Treasury, all tax bills, like other revenue measures, must originate in the House of Representatives and be introduced by one of its members. Once introduced into the House, tax bills are referred to the Committee on Ways and Means. Because no action by the House is possible until the bill is reported to the floor of the House by the committee, the chairperson of the Committee on Ways and Means is given considerable power through the control of the committee's agenda. Using this power and various other strategies, the chairperson can block all action on a tax bill. Therefore, it is the chairperson who often effectively initiates successful tax legislation. In general, tax legislation reported from the committee to the floor of the House is *not* subject to amendment from the floor.

On passage by the House, a tax bill goes to the Senate. Here the bill is referred to the Committee on Finance, where it is refashioned to suit the persuasions of the

---

1 For a detailed guide to research materials and techniques, see Sommerfeld, Streuling, Gardner, and Stewart, *Tax Research Techniques,* 3rd ed. (AICPA, New York), 1989.

2 Jeffrey H. Birnbaum and Alan S. Murray, *Showdown at Gucci Gulch* (New York: Random House, 1986), p. 31.

committee members. If and when the bill is reported by the committee to the Senate floor, amendments may be generally offered freely from the Senate floor. Thus, the bill passed by the Senate is inevitably different, often considerably different, from the one passed by the House. The bills are then referred to a Conference Committee for compromise. Birnbaum and Murray describe the crucial nature of this process as follows:

> Now, virtually everything that had been done would be put on the conference table for a small group of senators and representatives to dispose of as they pleased. The two tax bills were in many ways mirror images: The House bill closed many corporate loopholes, but left the tax preferences used by individuals largely untouched, while the Senate bill made sweeping reforms on the individual side of the code, but left many of the biggest corporate tax breaks unchanged. That meant the twenty-two conferees had wide leeway to determine the final shape of the most comprehensive tax overhaul bill in the nation's history.[3]

Once members of the Conference Committee reach a compromise, the rest of the process is typically anticlimactic. In 1986, the revised bill was reported back to both bodies for final ratification in August, affirmed by the House on September 25, passed by the Senate on September 27, and signed by President Reagan in October, 1986.

Many scholars blamed legislative reforms instituted in the early 1970s for both the current state of the budget and tax problems in general.[4] Those legislative reforms decentralized power and increased visibility of the law-making process in an attempt to overcome the damage perceived to be done by allowing a few powerful Congressmen to create tax law largely behind closed doors. However, these reforms had serious side effects. More widely spread power and visibility led to increased pressure by constituents and special-interest groups for tax breaks and more pressure from congressional colleagues to trade support for various provisions.

The 1986 Act was a return to pre-reform days in three significant ways. Committee chairs regained some of their earlier power in (1) setting agendas, (2) establishing working rules, and (3) deciding compromises. Important markups of a bill were made in executive or closed sessions. Amendments to a bill on the floor were severely restrained. Although a **closed rule** (no amendments to the Committee bill allowed from the floor) in the House was traditional, a closed rule was imposed for the first time ever in the Senate. These recent changes are not engraved in stone. Rather, they are dependent on the power of the committee chairs, who imposed them by fiat in 1986. In the current environment, the leaders of both the House Ways and Means and Senate Finance Committees wield a great deal of power. If these leaders are replaced by weaker individuals or with smaller party majorities (particularly in the House), the tax legislative process might well return to open forums and amendments from the Senate floor.

Two less obvious influences in the present process are also noteworthy. One is the influence of staffers (staff aides). With the increasing complexity of the tax law, a great deal of influence has shifted to key members of Congress and to the staff aides of key committee members. Personal congressional aides number around 1,200, the House Ways and Means Committee has almost 100 staffers; the Senate Finance

A **closed rule** means that no amendments to a bill can be made from the floor.

---

3 *Op. cit.*, p. 254.

4 The following discussion is based on remarks by John Witte, Professor of Political Science, University of Wisconsin, Madison, at the American Law Institute–American Bar Foundation Invitational Conference, "Improving the Tax Legislative Process: A Critical Need," April 26–27, 1991.

Committee, 50. Although most of these staffers lack practical tax experience, many have the technical tax expertise essential to understanding the proposed legislation that elected officials do not have. Birnbaum and Murray report that with the 1986 tax legislation, as with other technical matters, "aggressive staffers dominated much of the legislative process. They controlled the information, and that was what drove events."[5]

The second somewhat hidden influence involves the role of **transition rules.** Transition rules are supposed to help phase in new tax legislation, but they are most generally used to grease the wheels of the legislative process by doling out favors to members of Congress in order to win votes. Literally billions of dollars of tax revenue are lost due to hundreds of transition rules. Birnbaum and Murray note that the 1986 Senate Finance Committee bill alone granted generous transition rules to 174 beneficiaries, including General Motors, the New Orleans Superdome, the University of Delaware, and the estate of James Thompson (a wealthy silk merchant who disappeared mysteriously). Usually these beneficiaries are disguised in the legislation. For instance, General Motors was not named directly but was described as an automobile manufacturer that was incorporated on October 13, 1916.[6]

Transition rules are provisions applicable during a phase-in period following law changes to smooth the transition to a new regime.

THE STRUCTURE OF TAX LAW

Goal #2
Describe the sources available for determining the current tax law and its legislative history.

A tax bill passed by Congress is usually enacted as a revenue act that amends the existing Internal Revenue Code. The most recent exception to this practice occurred in 1986, when the Tax Reform Act of 1986 also created the Internal Revenue Code of 1986. From 1954 to 1986, tax legislation simply amended the Internal Revenue Code of 1954. Before 1954, revenue acts amended the tax laws first codified in the 1939 Revenue Code. Prior to the 1939 Code, the tax provisions consisted of an accumulation of separate revenue acts, passed on irregular intervals. A public outcry for a more systematic organization of the numerous tax laws passed between 1913 and 1938 convinced Congress to authorize the creation of the first Revenue Code in 1939.

Even though tax laws typically amend an existing Internal Revenue Code, laws passed in any given year also have their own formal and informal names. Some revenue acts are named to reflect a specific objective of Congress, such as the Tax Reform Act of 1986, the Economic Recovery Act of 1981, and the Tax Reduction and Simplification Act of 1977. Officially, however, a revenue bill is signed into law as a public law. For example, the Tax Reduction and Simplification Act of 1977 is officially known as Public Law 95-30; the Tax Reform Act of 1986, as Public Law 99-514. But it should be remembered that each year's tax laws become part of an accumulating and revised Code.

Once Congress passes a new provision, the revised Internal Revenue Code becomes the *primary* authority for all research and planning in taxation. Other sources must be consistent with the Code. They derive importance from their ability to clarify the interpretation of the Code. The legislative process itself creates the original documents that are used to indicate congressional intent.

- *Committee reports.* Each revenue bill from the Committee on Ways and Means is accompanied by a House Report that explains the problem as well as the changes in the law proposed in response to the problem. Reports also accompany the bills

5 *Op cit.,* p. 217.

6 *Op. cit.,* pp. 240–41. See also Donald L. Barlett and James B. Steele, "The Great Tax Giveaway," *The Philadelphia Inquirer* (April 10–16, 1988).

reported by the Senate Finance Committee and the Joint Conference Committee. The **committee reports** are the most important sources for interpretation.

- *Hearings.* **Hearings** before the Committee on Ways and Means and the Committee on Finance are often published. These hearings provide insight into the political, economic, and social problems the legislators are attempting to address. However, the published hearings are of no significance in the determination of Congressional intent. They represent the views of taxpayers and lobby groups and not the intent of Congress.

- *Text of floor debates.* The ***Congressional Record*** contains the floor debates in the House and Senate on revenue bills. Often the responses to questions shed some light on congressional intent. Hence the *Congressional Record* can also be a source for determining congressional intent.

These sources often relate in plain language what Congress hopes to accomplish with any amendment to the extant Code. Because the Code's language rarely achieves the same clarity, an understanding of Congressional intent is important: deviations from this intent (which may occur with the implementation of the law) are potential targets for future legislation.

> **Committee reports** are documents supporting a bill that describes problems motivating the new provision and the purpose of the new provision.
>
> **Hearings** are testimony provided to Congress on the expected impact on proposed law changes.
>
> The ***Congressional Record*** documents floor debates on revenue bills.

———— ADMINISTRATIVE INTERPRETATION

TREASURY REGULATIONS

Once a revenue bill has been passed through the legislative process, its evolution is far from complete. A provision of the Internal Revenue Code requires that the Treasury Department issue regulations interpreting the law. To accomplish this task, new **Treasury regulations** are usually issued first as proposed regulations, inviting the comments and criticisms of interested parties, either in writing or at hearings. Proposed regulations provide taxpayers with an advance indication of the likely IRS position and signal areas of potential disagreement.

> **Treasury regulations** are the Treasury Department's interpretation of the Internal Revenue Code.

Because proposed regulations are still merely proposals, however, they have no value as precedents. Consequently, when a major tax law is enacted, the Treasury Department may skip the proposed regulation step and issue temporary regulations instead. When, and if, final regulations are issued, they generally apply retroactively to the time when the Code section first went into effect.

As a practical matter, the regulation process often bogs down. There are currently 500 regulations projects under way. At times, regulations exist for years in proposed or temporary form without being finalized. At other times, there is no timely guidance from the Treasury Department in critical areas long after the enactment of new law. Although there is an initial presumption that final regulations have the same authoritative weight as the Code, they may be challenged by taxpayers in court. A taxpayer will not prevail against the government, however, unless it can be shown that the regulations are inconsistent with the Code, represent an unreasonable interpretation of the Code, or are beyond the scope of power delegated to the Treasury Department. In assessing an argument that the Treasury has exceeded the scope of its power, a judge will consider whether the regulation is interpretative or legislative. Legislative regulations are also called *statutory regulations* because Congress specifically states in the Code section that the Treasury shall prescribe such regulations as deemed necessary. Thus, legislative regulations are even more difficult to challenge success-

> **Goal #3**
> Identify sources of administrative interpretation and describe their relative weight of authority.

fully than are the more routine interpretative regulations because, in the former, Congress has explicitly delegated its rule-making authority to the Treasury.

In addition to assessing whether a regulation is proposed, temporary, or final, and whether it is interpretative or legislative, there are three other factors to consider in evaluating the weight of authority given to a regulation. First, *has the regulation been tested in court?* Through court decisions, definitive interpretations of the tax law are made; a court finding that a regulation is consistent with congressional intent usually settles the issue. Second, *how long has the regulation been in existence?* Age lends respectability to a regulation, presumably because Congress itself would have changed the regulation if it violated congressional intent. Third, was the regulation issued soon after the passage of the law? Contemporaneous issuance of the law and Treasury interpretation enhances the likelihood that the regulation's draftsman has followed the measure through Congress and understands its purpose. Judges are less likely to upset regulations promulgated on a timely basis.

REVENUE RULINGS

A **private letter ruling** is an interpretation of specific provisions in response to a taxpayer's request for a ruling.

Taxpayers who are uncertain about the correct tax treatment of a prospective transaction can ask the IRS for a **private letter ruling** on how the transaction will be taxed. While the IRS has no legal obligation to make advanced rulings on prospective transactions, their general policy is to offer guidance when requested. In many cases, taxpayers use private letter rulings to reduce the uncertainty of the tax law on prospective transactions. In other cases, taxpayers and tax advisors ask for rulings not because application of the law is particularly doubtful, but because the transaction involves large amounts of money and affects large numbers of taxpayers. Corporate reorganizations and changes in employee pension plans are two common examples that make use of this alternative. However, the issuance of an unfavorable ruling does not preclude the taxpayer from subsequently challenging the IRS's position. It must be remembered that the IRS is a strategic actor in the process and may provide an overly conservative interpretation.

Revenue Rulings are interpretations of specific provisions of tax law published by the IRS.

From the thousands of private letter rulings issued each year, the IRS selects the ones that it feels offer guidance to the public and, after deleting facts that might identify the taxpayer, publishes them as Revenue Rulings. The facts ruled upon in published **Revenue Rulings** are highly individualized, but these rulings *may be* used as precedent by other taxpayers with similar tax situations. Although a ruling generally is binding on the government with respect to the facts on which the ruling was requested, the Commissioner is not required by law to follow the interpretation in other cases. Private letter rulings issued after 1984 may also be relied on by other taxpayers as authoritative after they have been released to the public.

REVENUE PROCEDURES

Revenue Procedures explain procedures and other duties of the taxpayer.

Tax information releases deal with timely topics of general interest and are released to the popular press. The most important of these information releases are **Revenue Procedures**, which explain procedures and other duties of the taxpayer. Historically, Revenue Procedures have included such items as the original depreciation guidelines.

Of the various sources of administrative interpretation, the Treasury Regulations are a higher source of authority than Revenue Rulings and other releases issued by the IRS.

JUDICIAL INTERPRETATION

As suggested in the preceding discussion, the Treasury Department and the Internal Revenue Service both publish administrative interpretations of the Code in such pronouncements as Treasury Regulations and Revenue Rulings. However, not everyone agrees with the government's interpretations of the Code. Disputes frequently develop between IRS agents and taxpayers. As we will discuss later in the chapter, the IRS provides a review and appeals process. If the parties cannot reach an agreement through this process, the only way to resolve a disputed interpretation of the Code is through a court decision. This judicial interpretation applies the constitutional concept of separation of powers to tax law, and helps prevent abuse by the IRS.

Arguments decided in the courts can be used as precedents by other taxpayers in similar situations. However, taxpayers must be aware of the possibility that the IRS may still fight for its interpretation. Decisions of any court can be appealed until they ultimately reach the Supreme Court. But because it is rare for the Supreme Court to agree to hear a tax case,[7] appeals rarely go higher than the Circuit Court of Appeal or the Circuit Court for the Federal Circuit. The higher the court in which the case is decided, the greater the authority of the decision. The taxpayer must be aware that decisions in a given circuit may not necessarily be followed in other circuits; hence the taxpayer's place of residence may affect his or her chances of winning. The strategy of choosing a court to which to appeal is discussed further in a later section.

> **Goal #4**
> Explain the role of the judiciary in interpretation of tax law.

TAXPAYER COMPLIANCE

The forgoing discussion explained the process by which the tax law comes into existence and the interpretation to which the law is subject. As the law evolves, every taxpayer has the responsibility of complying with it. Because the federal income tax is a self-assessed tax, this compliance includes the accurate calculation of the tax, proper completion and submission of a return form, and payment of the tax.

> **Goal #5**
> Describe taxpayer responsibilites and broad indicators of taxpayers' compliance with those obligations.

RESPONSIBILITIES OF TAXPAYERS

Tax Returns

The compliance process requires each taxable entity (individual, corporation, fiduciary) that is subject to federal income tax to file a return form. Individuals may file Form 1040EZ, Form 1040A, or Form 1040 depending on the sources of the taxpayer's income and the nature of deductions (see Figure 3-1).

In addition to determining the tax due and filing a return, the taxpayer is also required to pay the tax. Individual taxpayers are on a pay-as-you-go system that is accomplished in one of two ways. The most common form of payment is through **withholding** from wages. However, for those individuals not subject to withholding or whose withholding is not sufficient, **estimated tax payments** may be required to be paid in four installments. Given these prepayments, a final payment or refund is then made when the annual return is filed.

Two other entities besides individual taxpayers are required to file tax returns. Fiduciaries (for example, executors of estates or trustees of trusts) file their returns on

> **Withholding** is any amount withheld from a payment to another individual, most commonly on wages, to meet the taxpayer's tax obligation.
>
> **Estimated tax payments** are quarterly payments made to the IRS in prepayment of the amount taxpayer estimates will be due for taxes.

---

7 The Supreme Court usually hears only six to eight tax cases a year. The cases selected generally involve important tax policy issues where there are conflicting opinions among two or more of the Circuit Courts of Appeal or where the issue is of such broad applicability that it is deemed critical to resolve promptly.

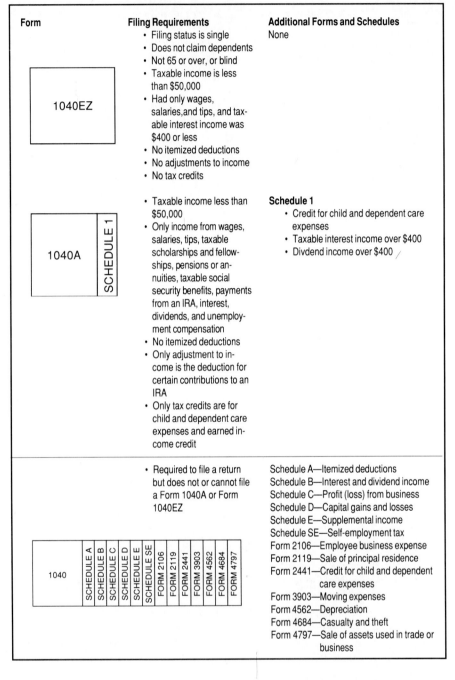

FIGURE 3-1

Report Forms for Individuals

Form	Filing Requirements	Additional Forms and Schedules
1040EZ	• Filing status is single • Does not claim dependents • Not 65 or over, or blind • Taxable income is less than $50,000 • Had only wages, salaries,and tips, and tax-able interest income was $400 or less • No itemized deductions • No adjustments to income • No tax credits	None
1040A SCHEDULE 1	• Taxable income less than $50,000 • Only income from wages, salaries, tips, taxable scholarships and fellow-ships, pensions or an-nuities, taxable social security benefits, payments from an IRA, interest, dividends, and unemploy-ment compensation • No itemized deductions • Only adjustment to in-come is the deduction for certain contributions to an IRA • Only tax credits are for child and dependent care expenses and earned in-come credit	**Schedule 1** • Credit for child and dependent care expenses • Taxable interest income over $400 • Divdend income over $400
1040 SCHEDULE A SCHEDULE B SCHEDULE C SCHEDULE D SCHEDULE E SCHEDULE SE FORM 2106 FORM 2119 FORM 2441 FORM 3903 FORM 4562 FORM 4684 FORM 4797	• Required to file a return but does not or cannot file a Form 1040A or Form 1040EZ	Schedule A—Itemized deductions Schedule B—Interest and dividend income Schedule C—Profit (loss) from business Schedule D—Capital gains and losses Schedule E—Supplemental income Schedule SE—Self-employment tax Form 2106—Employee business expense Form 2119—Sale of principal residence Form 2441—Credit for child and dependent care expenses Form 3903—Moving expenses Form 4562—Depreciation Form 4684—Casualty and theft Form 4797—Sale of assets used in trade or business

> **Self-assessment** means that each entity subject to tax must file a tax return accurately reporting all income and deduction items.
>
> The **tax gap** is the measure of revenue losses due to noncompliance.

Form 1041, and because they are not required to pay the tax in advance, the entire amount is generally due with the return. Corporations report their incomes on Form 1120. They are on a pay-as-you-go basis and must declare their estimated tax and pay the tax on a quarterly basis during the taxable year just like individual taxpayers.

While the **self-assessment** process requires all entities subject to tax to file a tax return and accurately report their income and deduction items, not all taxpayers comply. Tax revenue losses due to noncompliance (called the **tax gap**) are estimated to be $114 billion for 1992 alone. This estimate is based on the underpayments of taxes by only legitimate or legal business ventures and money-making activities. No estimates of the illegal sector tax gap (from illegal drug sales, prostitution, and so on) are considered reliable. The estimated tax gap includes both underreported income and overstated deductions. The IRS estimates that about 75% of this $114 billion is from under reported income.

The ratio of taxes actually reported to taxes that *should* be reported is called the **voluntary compliance level (VCL).** As shown in Figure 3-2, there was a VCL of 99% on wages, dividends and interest for 1987 versus a 41.4% VCL on income of informal suppliers and sole proprietors. In 1981, the VCL for dividends was estimated at 84%; for interest, at 86%; and for wages and salaries, at 94%. The improvement in these three VCLs is attributable to the level of **third-party reporting** that accompanies these income sources. Virtually all wages, dividends and interest are now subject to reporting by third-party payors. The reporting rules and enforcement were tightened significantly between 1981 and 1987. Much of the income received by self-employed persons is still not subject to third-party reporting; hence underreporting is difficult for the IRS to discover.

In recent years, the focus on VCL's has shifted somewhat from the individual to the business sector. Recent data show that smaller corporations are less compliant than larger ones. For small corporations (those with assets under $10 million), the estimated

> The **voluntary compliance level (VCL)** is the ratio of taxes actually reported to taxes that should be reported.
>
> **Third-party reporting** refers to the process of payors reporting transactions involving a taxpayer. Examples are reports of wages and interest submitted by employers, banks, S&Ls, and so on.

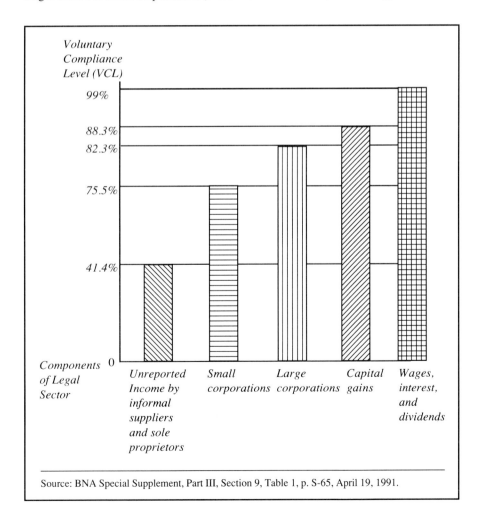

FIGURE 3-2

Compliance Rates in Components of the Legal Sector—1987

Source: BNA Special Supplement, Part III, Section 9, Table 1, p. S-65, April 19, 1991.

VCL is 75%, compared to 82% for large corporations. The General Accounting Office (GAO) studied reasons for noncompliance among those in the business sector and found very different profiles for different categories of taxpayers. Sole proprietors both understated income and overstated deductions. Those in fixed-location sales and transportation businesses had the largest percentages of underreported income. Informal suppliers (home repairs supplies and child care providers, for example) underreported income by $7.7 billion. Their income, often received in cash, is not subject to third-party reporting.

Small corporations' noncompliance is about evenly divided between underreported income and overstated deductions. The smaller the corporation, the larger its level of estimated noncompliance. This trend shows up most in services and retail sales. For large corporations, the problem is of a different nature. Unlike other segments, large corporations tend to report all of their gross income and take only those deductions for which they have adequate documentation. The adjustments to large corporations' returns on audit tend not to be for blatantly hiding income or overstating various deductions, but for what the IRS considers to be "misreporting" of income and deductions. These differences are due to the taxpayers either interpreting the law or applying the law in a way that is inconsistent with the IRS's interpretation or application. Examples are "misallocation" of income and deductions between foreign and domestic subsidiaries or "misstatement" of the periods over which an asset's cost must be allocated. Based on IRS examination results, the highest noncompliance for large corporations occurs in the banking and petroleum industries.[8]

Noncompliance presents a serious problem for tax administration because it can undermine the social and economic objectives built into the law and thus distort fair competition and redistribute resources from honest to dishonest taxpayers. Noncompliance also increases the economic resources that must be expended by the IRS to enforce compliance. In addition, noncompliance can erode the sense of moral commitment citizens feel toward the federal government.

Documentation

A primary responsibility of the taxpayer is to document transactions that affect the tax computation. In any dispute with the IRS, the taxpayer has the burden of proof. If the IRS questions the amount of a deduction, the taxpayer must provide documentation in some form (a receipt, bill, cancelled check, estimate, and so on) in order to substantiate the allowance of the deduction. Without the proof, the IRS may disallow part or all of the deduction, even if there is strong circumstantial evidence.

Goal #6
Identify significant taxpayer penalties.

Playing the audit lottery means gambling that one's tax return will not be selected for audit.

Penalties and Interest

Taxpayers who fail to meet their self-assessment obligations are subject to a myriad of penalties and interest assessments. This area of the law has been modified frequently in the last 15 years. Numerous new penalties have been imposed in response to taxpayer's **playing the audit lottery**. This term refers to taxpayers taking aggressive tax return positions and gambling that their returns will not be selected for audit. Even when their returns were selected for audit, the possible penalties imposed a few years ago were minor enough to be worth the risk for many taxpayers. The proliferation of penalties enacted to address this problem resulted in more than 150 penalties, many of which were overlapping. Although Leona Helmsley, the self-proclaimed hotel

8 BNA Special Supplement, House Ways and Means Committee Report, "Overview of the Federal Tax System," 1991 ed. (WMCP: 102–107), Part III, Section 9, *Compliance Issues*, pp. S-65–S-67.

queen, generated little sympathy when convicted of tax evasion, the fines levied against her are a good example of the potential effect of overlapping penalties. Her $1.2 million of alleged tax cheating turned into a total assessment of $7 million due to penalties and interest.[9]

While there was no public reaction to Helmsley's personal situation, there was a storm of protest from taxpayers and practitioners over the severity of the general penalty regime. This public protest led to a series of congressional hearings and to significant penalty reform in 1989. The more important taxpayer penalties today relate to the failure to file a return, the failure to pay tax when due, and inaccurate returns.

If a taxpayer fails to file a return, a penalty of 5% of the "amount required to be shown as tax on such return" is added *for each month* or part of the month the return is delayed, to a maximum of 25%. Note that this penalty is assessed on the tax *liability*, not on the *tax due.*

EXAMPLE 3-1

Taxpayer X fails to file her return when required. Her total tax liability is $2,000. Even though her employer withheld $2,500, and she will have a refund of $500 when she files her return, the failure to file penalty will be calculated as 5% of $2,000 ($100) per month, up to the maximum of 25% ($500).

If the taxpayer files a return, but fails to pay the tax due, an additional 0.5% per month penalty is assessable. This penalty is in addition to interest due. Interest is calculated at the federal short-term rate plus 3 percentage points. (It is interesting to note that the interest rate the government must pay taxpayers on overpayments is only the federal short-term rate plus 2 percentage points.) The penalties, but not the interest, are subject to abatement if it can be shown that the error is due to reasonable cause rather than willful neglect.

The taxpayer also faces "accuracy related penalties" equal to 20% of the portion of an underpayment attributable to either negligence or disregard of rules and regulations. A 20% penalty may also be levied for "substantial understatement" of an income tax liability or any "substantial valuation overstatement." Valuation overstatements typically involve the estimation of fair market values of items that can be deducted in the determination of taxable income. An understatement of a tax liability is regarded as substantial if it exceeds the larger of (a) 10% of the correct tax or (b) $5,000 ($10,000 for a corporation). The amount of understatement is reduced by the portion of any understatement for which the taxpayer's position is supported by **substantial authority.** It is also reduced by amounts for which the taxpayer does not have substantial authority, but which are disclosed on the return as required by statute. Substantial authority is difficult to define precisely. In general it means that significant administrative or judicial authority lends support to the taxpayer's interpretation of the law. Finally, if any portion of a taxpayer's underpayment is found to be attributable to fraud, a penalty of 75% of that portion of the underpayment applies.

> **Substantial authority** generally means that either administrative or judicial authority lends support to the taxpayer's interpretation of the law.

Criminal penalties, involving substantial fines and imprisonment, can be invoked for the willful failure to pay the tax, to file a return, or to keep adequate records; for attempting to evade or defeat the tax; or for willfully making and subscribing to a false return. Out of over 10 million taxpayers a year, only about 1,600 a year are sentenced

---

9 Wade Lambert, "Leona Helmsley Is Found Guilty of Evading Taxes," *The Wall Street Journal,* August 31, 1989, p. A3.

to jail for tax offenses.[10] To be imprisoned, the fraud must generally be blatant. Leona Helmsley was convicted of billing personal items—such as a swimming pool and a dance floor at her Connecticut estate—as business expenses. Stockjobber Patrick Rooney was convicted of filing a false tax return after deducting a $50,000 contribution to the American Cancer Society and getting $45,000 kicked back to him. Fraud charges usually are pressed only if the investigating agent uncovers willful evidence such as back-dated documents, falsified names on invoices, or double sets of books.[11]

Criminal penalties can only be imposed by a court after the taxpayer has been found guilty in criminal proceedings. The other penalties, however, are administratively imposed by the IRS. The assessment of penalties by the IRS is subject to administrative and judicial review. These processes will be explained later in this chapter.

Statute of Limitations

A **statute of limitations** is a period of time beyond which legal action cannot be taken against a party.

Both taxpayers and the government generally have a **statute of limitations** of three years, from the date a return is filed, to correct errors. If a return is actually filed *before* the due date, the period runs from the due date, not from the filing date.

EXAMPLE 3-2

T, a calendar year taxpayer, files his income tax return for 1991 on April 1, 1992. The return is treated as filed on April 15, 1992, its due date. The statute of limitations expires on April 16, 1995. Both T and the IRS have until April 15, 1995, to correct the 1991 return.

There are many exceptions to the three-year statute of limitations just explained. The most important exceptions are

1. Refund claims—Refund claims can be initiated by taxpayers within three years from the filing date of the return, or two years from the date when the tax is paid, whichever is later. To illustrate, assume that T (in our example above) does not pay his 1991 tax until June 1, 1993. T has until June 1, 1995, to file a refund claim against his 1991 tax. (Note that T will be subject to interest and penalties for failure to pay his tax on a timely basis.)

2. Statutory fraud—The statute of limitations runs for six years, rather than three years, if a taxpayer omits gross income in excess of 25% of the gross income reported. Such an omission also subjects the taxpayer to the special penalties for statutory fraud.

3. Criminal fraud—The government can bring charges of criminal fraud against a taxpayer at any time. Neither the three-year nor the six-year limitation period affords protection to the taxpayer who willfully defrauds the government.

Goal #7
Explain the significance of tax practitioners in our system and describe their responsibilities to the system.

THE ROLE OF THE PRACTITIONER

Given the complexity of the Code and the potential consequences of noncompliance, many taxpayers hire a professional to help them comply with the law. About 44% of the 114 million individual federal income tax returns for 1990 were signed by a paid

---

10 William Baldwin, "How to Stay Out of Trouble," *Forbes*, October 2, 1989, pp. 218–22.

11 *Ibid.*

preparer. Of the returns filed by preparers, about 10% were filed under a new electronic filing system in which no *paper* return is submitted. Instead the return information is transmitted and stored electronically. The use of tax practitioners roughly reflects the complexity of the tax law. Immediately following the 1986 Act, approximately 50% of taxpayers used paid preparers. The decline from 50% in 1987 to 44% in 1990 indicates that many taxpayers have gained enough familiarity with the 1986 changes to file their own returns. Only 3% of all Form 1040EZ filers pay a preparer, whereas 53% of those filing Form 1040 used a preparer.

Except for relatively simple tax situations, it appears that paying a preparer is cost effective. A recent study analyzing actual return data found average cost savings ranging from $300 to $3,000 for middle- and higher-income taxpayers who use a tax preparer.[12] Because of tax preparers' widespread exposure to compliance issues and their expertise in identifying potential tax savings, practitioners play a prominent role in the present system.

In an effort to better understand this role, the IRS analyzed characteristics of tax returns signed by paid preparers and preparer attitudes.[13] CPAs for instance, prepare less than 20% (and lawyers less than 2%) of all paid preparer returns, but they are associated with the most complex returns and charge the highest fees. At the time of the study, fees for CPAs and lawyers generally ranged from $75 to $275 an hour; the fee for a return of modest complexity averaged about $400. In contrast, H&R Block did relatively straightforward returns and charged about $50 for an average return.[14] In terms of attitude, CPAs and lawyers stand apart from other preparers in expressing strong pro-taxpayer attitudes and showing less of an inclination to review client documentation when they prepare a return.

Aggregate audit statistics show that although less than one-half of the returns are professionally prepared, such returns are associated with about 75% of the audit adjustments. Independent analysis of this statistic indicates that differences in the complexity and income level of the professionally prepared returns explain the higher rate and amount of audit adjustments.[15] Detailed examination of tax return data on this issue suggests that tax preparers are linked to higher-than-average compliance when the legal issues are clear but to lower-than-average compliance when the items involve some ambiguity.[16] Consistent with their expressed attitudes, accountants and lawyers resolve doubtful items in their clients' favor.

Although a number of bills were introduced into Congress in the mid-1970s to require licensing of tax preparers, the government has opted instead to regulate preparers through penalty provisions. Preparer responsibilities include signing a return and providing identifying information, maintaining either copies of all returns prepared or a list of clients, and not understating a client's tax liability. Preparer penalties are targeted toward motives of preparers rather than on their competence. Higher penalties apply as the taxpayer's responsibility for the understatement decreases (see Table 3-1). In contrast to taxpayer penalties, preparer penalties are imposed as flat dollar amounts rather than as a percentage of the tax understatement.

Goal #8
Identify significant preparer penalties.

---

12 James E. Long and Steven B. Caudill, "The Usage and Benefits of Paid Tax Return Preparation," *National Tax Journal*, March 1987, pp. 35–46.

13 U.S. Internal Revenue Service, *Survey of Tax Practitioners and Advisors: Summary of Results by Occupation*, June 1987.

14 *U.S.A. Today*, "Taxes '87: Cutting Your Tax Bill," December 7, 1987, p. 3B.

15 Kent Smith and Karyl Kinsey, "Showdown at the 1040 Corral: Confrontations Between the IRS and Tax Practitioners,"American Bar Foundation, August 1987.

16 Steven Klepper and Daniel Nagin, "The Role of Tax Practitioners in Tax Compliance," Carnegie Mellon University, July 1987.

TABLE 3-1

Preparer Penalties

Violation	Date of Inception	Penalty
Administrative Penalties Sec. 6695		
Failure to furnish copy of return to taxpayer	1/1/77*	$50 per return
Failure of preparer to sign return	1/1/77*	$50 per failure
Failure to furnish identifying numbers	1/1/77*	$50 per failure
Failure to maintain copies of returns prepared or maintain a listing of all clients	1/1/77*	$50 per failure
Failure to file correct information on return regarding preparers employed	1/1/77*	$50 per failure
Negotiation of taxpayer's refund check	1/1/77*	$500 per incident
Penalties Related to Understatement		
Understatement due to unrealistic positions	1/1/77+	$100
Willful or reckless conduct in understatement of taxpayer liability	1/1/77+	$1,000
Aiding and abetting understatement of tax liability	9/4/84	$1,000 ($10,000 for corporation) per return
Fraudulent understatement		$100,000 fine and/or 5 years imprisonment

*Fines increased in 1989.
+Revisions in 1989.

Negligence penalties were replaced in 1989 by penalties based on a tax advisor's taking a position "for which there was not a realistic possibility of being sustained on its merits." This change was made in an attempt to increase the objectivity of the old negligence standard. Preparers are now responsible not only if they actually knew, but also if they "should have known" that the position they were taking was unrealistic. The penalty for each such offense is $250. This penalty will not be imposed on the preparer if either (1) there is "substantial authority" for the position taken or (2) the position is adequately disclosed on the tax return. If a preparer takes an unrealistic position in a "willful attempt" to understate the taxpayer's liability or if the preparer is guilty of "reckless or intentional disregard of rules or regulations," the penalty increases to $1000. A $1000 penalty also attaches to a finding that the preparer aided and abetted a taxpayer's understatement. That penalty increases to $10,000 if the taxpayer is a corporation, presumably because the stakes with corporate returns are higher than those with individuals' returns. The aiding-and-abetting penalty was enacted to enable the government to prosecute fraud cases that could not meet the more rigorous evidence requirements associated with criminal fraud.[17] Finally, a finding of criminal fraud carries a $100,000 penalty for individuals, $500,000 for a corporation.

17 For a discussion of civil tax penalties, see Denzil Causey and Frances M. McNair, "The New Civil Penalty Structure," *Journal of Accountancy* (August 1990), pp. 43–48.

The large number of possible penalties may convey the impression that tax preparer penalties are very common. In fact, they are rather infrequent. As you can see from Table 3-1, most of the penalties went into effect in 1977. During the next three years, fewer than 15,000 tax preparer penalties involving tax liability understatement were proposed on the approximately 270 million tax returns filed. Over 80% of the penalties proposed were for mere negligence. Even in cases in which the preparer ignored information provided by the taxpayer, the government was unwilling or unable to bear the burden of proof necessary to assess the willful understatement penalty.[18] After the penalties had been in effect for 10 years, a national survey of tax practitioners indicated that 14% of all tax-return preparers had had some type of preparer penalty asserted against them by the IRS at some time, but that only 8% had actually been assessed a penalty.[19] Of those penalized, only a few egregious offenders were subject to criminal prosecution.

During the 1980s, the role of tax practitioners underwent a serious re-evaluation. The IRS increasingly wants tax practitioners to take a more active role in policing taxpayers such as checking client documentation and probing in depth for other sources of income. Tax practitioners, especially CPAs and lawyers, see themselves as client advocates; hence they generally resent pressure to police their clients. The professional conduct guidelines of both the American Bar Association (ABA) and the American Institute of Certified Public Accountants (AICPA) were revised to reflect a compromise with the revised penalty provisions of the Code. In July 1985, the ABA issued a "Formal Opinion" that replaced its prior "reasonable-basis" standard with a new "good-faith-argument" standard. This new standard, applicable to tax attorneys, requires "some realistic possibility of success if the matter is litigated." The AICPA, in a revised "Statement of Responsibilities in Tax Practice," currently suggests that a CPA not recommend a tax-return position unless he or she has a good-faith belief that if the position is challenged, it has a "realistic possibility of being upheld . . . on its merits." The AICPA rule is similar to Code Section 6694 that requires that a position must have a "realistic possibility of being sustained on its merits." So, for now, it appears that a meeting of the minds has been achieved with respect to reporting and advising responsibilities of tax practitioners.

THE ROLE OF THE IRS

Goal #9
Explain the function of the IRS.

Once a return is filed, the IRS has the responsibility of reviewing and auditing returns. The purpose of this administrative review is to ensure that the tax is computed properly and that the correct tax is paid.

Return Examination

All returns received by the IRS undergo a check for mechanical accuracy, which includes the following:

1. Arithmetic, including the application of the appropriate tax rate to taxable income.

2. Verification of the existence of all appropriate supporting schedules for the return and transfer of the correct amount from these schedules to the return.

18 Edward J. Schnee, Kathleen J. Bindon, and Craig A. Ellis, "The Policy Implications of and Experience with Preparer Penalties," *Nevada Review of Business and Economics*, Spring 1987, pp. 21–30.

19 U.S. Internal Revenue Service, *op. cit.*

3. Matching information returns, filed by other taxpayers, with the income reported on the return. For example, the employer submits a copy of each employee's Form W-2 (withholding) to the IRS. The IRS also receives Form 1099 showing the amounts of interest, dividends, and other payments paid to taxpayers by financial institutions, corporations, and certain other entities. Over the past several years, the IRS has increased the matching of these informational reports with tax returns to the point that nearly 100% of the Forms W-2 and 1099 are presently matched. There has also been a dramatic increase in the number of information returns to be matched: from about 600 million in 1980 to about 1 billion in 1988. The number of items of income reported has also increased from 16 in 1980 to 29 in 1988. Items that are commonly deducted by individual taxpayers have historically not been subject to third-party reporting. But, because of perceived abuses in reporting home mortgage interest and child-care expenses, an information report is now required to support those deductions. Discrepancies between the amounts reported on an individual's return and the information reports trigger automatic notices called **CP 2000s**. These notices ask taxpayers to reconcile discrepancies or pay the amount the IRS calculates is due. This system has been quite effective from a cost/benefit analysis, but has been burdened with a high error rate because of the difficulty of accurately cross-checking reported amounts.

> **CP 2000s** are computer-generated notices of discrepancies between what the taxpayer has reported and what third parties have reported.

The IRS computers are also programmed to select high-potential returns for audit. Returns receive a computer-generated score, called a DIF score, based on their revenue generation and error potential. Consequently, tax returns with either (1) high income amounts not subject to information reporting or (2) unusually large or disproportionate deductions are more likely to be selected for audit than are returns filed on a Form 1040A or Form 1040EZ. The IRS uses a priority system, linked to particular line items or issues, to choose returns most likely to provide the government with favorable results. For example, before the large-scale elimination of many tax shelters by the Tax Reform Act of 1986, some districts (for instance, California, Colorado, and Texas) were unable to audit many returns beyond the large number that contained tax-shelter issues because of the priority given these issues.

Over one million individual returns are audited annually. Although that sounds like a large number, when compared to the approximately 110 million individual returns filed annually, the rate of audit is now less than 1%. Audits sometimes produce good news for taxpayers. An IRS report for 1990 shows that audits of 47,269 individual returns led to refunds of almost $190 million. The probability of being audited varies dramatically by income level for individuals, and by asset level for corporations. Data for 1965, 1978, and 1988 audit rates by various income and asset categories are reflected in Figure 3-3. This figure also demonstrates that the percentage of returns audited each year continues to decline. This decline is due in part to the diversion of audit resources from routine DIF audits to audits focused on particular issues such as tax shelters; in part to the shift toward more computer-matching techniques; and in part to lower budget allocations to the IRS by Congress (at least in current dollars). As illustrated in Figure 3-3, the audit rate for both individual and corporate taxpayers has dropped significantly in the last 10 years. Large corporations still face a 50% chance of being audited; high-volume individuals, only a 2% chance.

> The **Taxpayer Compliance Measurement Program (TCMP)** is a random sample of about 50,000 tax returns, selected for detailed audit. Results are used to establish taxpayer profiles and error rates.

In addition to the annual strategic audits, the IRS conducts a special, in-depth audit program once every three years. About 50,000 tax returns are selected from a stratified random sample of all returns for this special program, called the **Taxpayer Compliance Measurement Program (TCMP).** These results are used to statistically infer

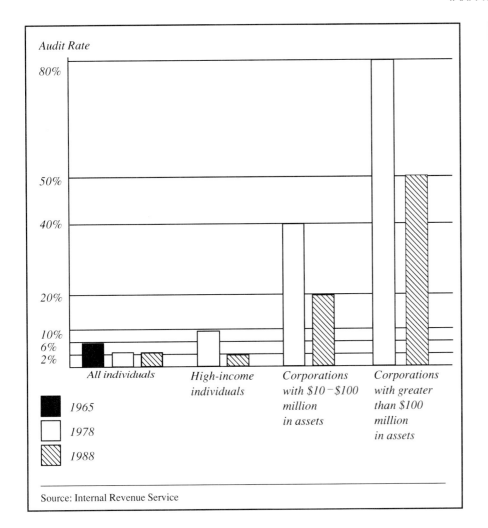

FIGURE 3-3

**Audit Rate
Comparisons
by Type**

Source: Internal Revenue Service

the error rate on all returns and to adjust the computer program for selecting tax returns for future audits. Data from these audits are also used to estimate the VCLs discussed earlier. In contrast to the strategic audits which target specific items on a return for examination every amount on the tax return is subject to verification in a TCMP audit.

Audit Process

Returns selected for audit are assigned to revenue agents who meet with the taxpayers to examine appropriate records and supporting documents. When the examination is complete, any one of three outcomes is possible. First, the agent may find that the return is correct as filed. Second, the agent may propose adjustments, which normally increase the tax, and the taxpayer may agree. Third, the agent may propose adjustments resulting in a deficiency, and the taxpayer may disagree. In this final case, when no agreement is reached between the agent and the taxpayer, the taxpayer may either request a conference in the Appeals Office or proceed directly to judicial review. The IRS auditing process is depicted in Figure 3-4.

If the taxpayer refuses to agree with the agent's proposed adjustments, the agent prepares a complete report of the findings, which is submitted to the review staff. After review (and changes, if required), the **revenue agent's report (RAR)** is mailed to the

A **revenue agent's report (RAR)** is the IRS agent's summary of points of disagreement in the audit.

FIGURE 3-4

**Income Tax Audit
Procedure of the
Internal Revenue
Service**

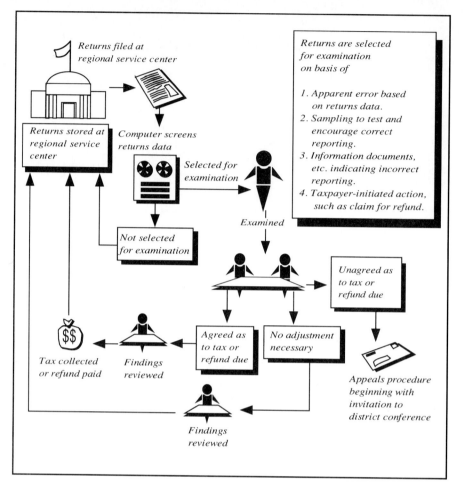

FIGURE 3-4

Income Tax Audit Procedure of the Internal Revenue Service

A **30-day letter** is a notification to the taxpayer by the IRS of a tax deficiency that gives the taxpayer 30 days to reply.

A **90-day letter** is the formal deficiency letter issued by the IRS.

Goal #10
Describe taxpayer options to resolve tax disputes.

taxpayer. The cover letter, called the **30-day letter**, notifies the taxpayer of the proposed deficiency and normally gives the taxpayer a 30-day period in which to decide on a course of action. The taxpayer may take any one of three different courses of action. First, he or she may accept the examiner's findings and thereby close the case. Second, he or she may request a conference with the Appeals Office of the IRS. Third, he or she may ignore the 30-day letter and wait for the formal deficiency notice, called the **90-day letter**. In deciding on a course of action, the taxpayer must consider both the monetary costs and the time demands involved with each option.

The Appeals Process

On receipt of the 30-day letter, the taxpayer has the right of appeal to the Appeals Office. If the amount of the taxpayer's deficiency is more than $2,500, the taxpayer is required to file a written protest before the conference. The protest generally includes all the issues that the taxpayer intends to raise during the conference. Although no rule prohibits the taxpayer from raising new issues, surprise moves during the conference are rarely effective.

In the conference, there are no formal rules of procedure. If the taxpayer is represented by an accountant or lawyer, which is common practice, the taxpayer's representative must present a power of attorney that evidences the right of the representative to act for the taxpayer. The points of disagreement are typically enumerated in the RAR and the **taxpayer's protest**, if one is filed. The factual or legal points at issue are then discussed to determine if the parties can reach some sort of agreement.

During this conference process, the Appeals Office has exclusive jurisdiction over the dispute, and the conferees are required to consider the hazards of litigation without regard to the amount involved. The purpose of the Appeals Office is to keep disputes out of the courts. If the law is uncertain, the appellate conferees welcome offers to compromise the issues. Conferees may also make such offers. Agreements reached, if any, are reviewed by the head of the Appeals Office. If on review the settlement is not acceptable, the taxpayer is generally given an opportunity to hold a final conference with the reviewer.

> A **taxpayer protest** is the taxpayer's summary of points of disagreement in the audit.

The 90-Day Letter

If either no agreement is reached in the Appeals conference or the taxpayer ignores the 30-day letter, a statutory deficiency notice, or 90-day letter, is issued. Upon issuance of this notice, if the taxpayer elects not to pay the tax, the taxpayer may file a petition to have his or her case heard in the Tax Court. Once this petition is filed, the Appeals Office no longer has exclusive authority to compromise, and the case is assigned to an attorney who represents the Justice Department and works on behalf of the IRS. After the case has been assigned, but before a date for a trial is set, an effort may still be made to reach a settlement. For the IRS, during this period authority to settle is shared between the Appeals Office and the office of the District Counsel of the IRS, although the latter has formal power. After the case is set for trial, settlement authority rests solely with the government counsel. Figure 3-5 summarizes the steps of this process.

JUDICIAL REVIEW

The Tax Court

Filing a petition for a hearing in the **Tax Court** is the most common course of judicial action for taxpayers. While this court is completely independent of the IRS, it is specially organized to hear tax cases. The Tax Court is a trial court at which taxpayers may either represent themselves or be represented by counsel. The IRS is represented by their own attorneys. At the hearing, both oral and documentary evidence may be presented. Formal rules of evidence apply and written briefs are submitted. It is generally important that the taxpayer be represented by an attorney (or someone authorized to practice before the Tax Court) because the taxpayer has the burden of proving the IRS acted improperly. In the Tax Court, there is no jury: the judge makes all decisions. When the court arrives at its decision, its findings are presented to the parties in an opinion.

> The **Tax Court** is a trial court which only hears tax cases.

Concern about the expense of litigation for issues involving relatively small tax deficiencies prompted Congress to establish a small claims division of the Tax Court. In the small claims division, a taxpayer has less need for an attorney. This division has jurisdiction to handle disputes when the amount contested does not exceed $10,000 plus any amount conceded by the parties. In assessing this option, the taxpayer should weigh the value of simplified proceedings against the loss of any right to appeal. Hearings in the small claims division are not before judges but before commissioners appointed by the Chief Judge of the Tax Court; formal rules of evidence need not be followed. The findings of the commissioner of the small claims division are not

FIGURE 3-5

**The Taxpayer's
Three Courses of
Action in
Response to an
Audit**

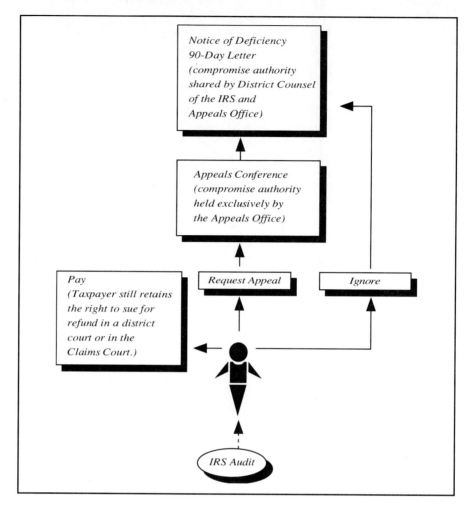

reported in formal written opinions, and these opinions cannot be used as precedent in other cases.

Other Judicial Routes

The taxpayer has two other options for judicial review. To gain access to other courts, the taxpayer must pay the deficiency proposed by the IRS. Upon payment of the deficiency, the taxpayer may then file with the IRS a claim for a refund of the deficiency paid. This filing once again sets the IRS review and appeals process in motion. If the refund claim is denied or if six months lapse without any IRS action, the taxpayer has a statutory right to sue the government on the grounds that in the opinion of the taxpayer, the tax was illegally assessed and collected. These suits may be brought against the IRS in either a U.S. district court or the Claims Court.

In a **U.S. district court**, the taxpayer must be represented by an attorney. On the other side, the government is represented by an attorney from the Tax Division of the Department of Justice. A jury may be used to determine any question of fact, but the district court judge decides any questions of law. As an alternative to the district court, the taxpayer can file suit before the **Claims Court.** Here, as in the Tax Court, a judge sits without a jury to hear and decide all of the issues in cases involving claims against the U.S. government.

A **U.S. district court** is a court which hears all types of cases and may have a jury to determine factual issues.

The **Claims Court** is a court which only hears those cases involving claims against the U.S. government.

Regardless of the judicial route chosen—Tax Court, district court, or Claims Court—the unsuccessful party has the right to **appeal** the decision. Cases decided in both the Tax Court and district courts can be appealed to the appropriate circuit court of appeals (see Table 3-2). Appeals from the Claims Court are decided by the Court of Appeals for the Federal Circuit. Decisions from either appeals courts can in turn be appealed to the Supreme Court, but the Supreme Court is under no obligation to grant its review of any lower court decision. Figure 3-6 summarizes the court routes available to the taxpayer.

> An **appeal** of a court decision means that the case is presented to a higher court. On appeal, issues of law are routinely reviewed, but issues of fact generally are not.

Strategy in Court Choice

The taxpayer has three different options for judicial review, and the choice may have a critical influence on the outcome. In making this decision, the taxpayer should weigh the following factors:

1. Payment of tax. Can the taxpayer afford to pay the tax deficiency at the time it is issued? Large amounts can impose substantial hardship and opportunity cost.

2. Jury versus judge. Does the taxpayer believe he or she may benefit by having a jury determine the facts of the case? A jury may be more sympathetic to nontechnical issues involved in a tax case.

3. Formality of the court. Is it possible that the taxpayer may be able to effectively represent himself or herself (as in the small claims division of the Tax Court) and thereby avoid the costs of representation? The potential benefits of a favorable judgment must be weighed against the costs of hiring counsel.

TABLE 3-2

United States Courts of Appeals

Federal Circuit	Geographical Areas Served
First (CA-1)	Maine, New Hampshire, Massachusetts, Rhode Island, Connecticut, Puerto Rico
Second (CA-2)	New York, Vermont
Third (CA-3)	Pennsylvania, New Jersey, U.S. Virgin Islands
Fourth (CA-4)	West Virginia, Maryland, Delaware, Virginia, North Carolina, South Carolina
Fifth (CA-5)	Texas, Louisiana, Mississippi
Sixth (CA-6)	Michigan, Ohio, Kentucky, Tennessee
Seventh (CA-7)	Wisconsin, Illinois, Indiana
Eighth (CA-8)	North Dakota, South Dakota, Nebraska, Minnesota, Iowa, Missouri, Arkansas
Ninth (CA-9)	Washington, Montana, Oregon, Idaho, California, Nevada, Arizona, Alaska, Guam, Hawaii
Tenth (CA-10)	Wyoming, Utah, Colorado, Kansas, Oklahoma, New Mexico
Eleventh (CA-11)	Alabama, Georgia, Florida, Canal Zone
District of Columbia (CA-DC)	Washington, D.C.

FIGURE 3-6

Judicial Routes
Available to the
Taxpayer

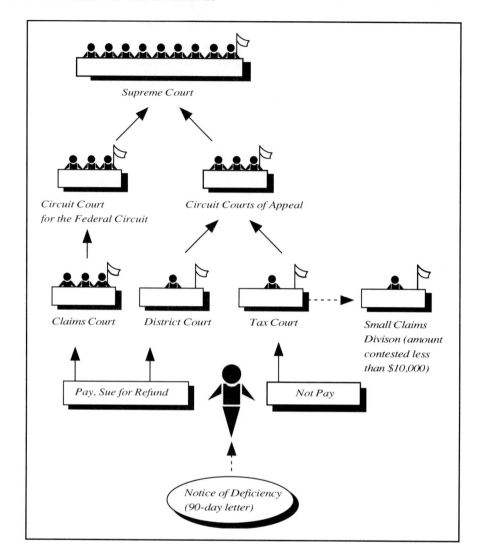

4. Jurisdictional precedents. Are there different precedents for the three courts in cases similar to that of the taxpayer? Has one jurisdiction consistently ruled in favor of individuals in the taxpayer's position, or at least not ruled consistently against them? Precedents can vary for long periods of time without higher court resolution, causing differences in interpretation among jurisdictions.

By weighing the various costs and benefits associated with each attribute, the taxpayer may be able to increase the odds of winning the case.

Only a small percentage of all tax disputes reach the judicial process. Nevertheless, the total number of dollars in dispute before the Tax Court has increased from $3 billion in 1978 to $31 billion in 1991, including one single case for $6.5 billion.[20]

In 1990,[21] less than 9% (or, more precisely, 99,407 of the 1,139,247 audited taxpayers) appealed the IRS's findings. Most disputes are either settled by the Appeals Office or compromised before the case goes to trial. The government fares better in

---

20 Internal Revenue Service data reported in *Journal of Accountancy*, September 1991, p. 18.

21 The following discussion is based on the *Wall Street Journal*, Tax Report, August 14, 1991.

court than taxpayers do. In one recent year, the Tax Court heard 1270 cases and decided 37% in favor of the IRS, 4% in favor of the taxpayer, with the remainder split. In that same year, 359 cases were taken to the Claims and District Courts. Of these cases, the IRS won 66%. The appeals courts, which heard 253 cases, decided 75% of those cases in the government's favor. The Supreme Court heard only 4 tax cases, deciding 3 for the government.

Criminal cases are an area of special concern. Out of the 5243 criminal inquiries the IRS completed, it proposed 3228 prosecutions. This process yielded 2472 convictions and 1609 prison sentences. Criminal cases are often characterized by links to drugs or organized crime; relatively little activity occurs with respect to tax crimes on legal sources of income. The criminal tax statutes are often used by the IRS Criminal Investigation Division in cooperation with other law-enforcement agencies to prosecute criminals for tax evasion in tandem with prosecution on other grounds or when they cannot perfect a case for other criminal activities.

This overview of the IRS/taxpayer conflict-resolution procedure has not adequately captured the importance of tax research to the income-tax process in general. Taxpayers, tax advisors, and IRS personnel are equally dependent on a common tax research process to locate, interpret, and apply our tax laws.

────── TAX RESEARCH

Each taxpayer who consults a tax practitioner presents the practitioner with a new problem. While some basic questions may be nearly the same as in other cases, each case will involve a slightly different set of facts. To determine how to comply properly with the Tax Code, the practitioner must recognize the unique nature of each case. Despite the uniqueness of every case, the tax research that the practitioner performs always involves five key steps: (1) determining the facts, (2) identifying the issues, (3) searching for authoritative solutions, (4) evaluating that authority, and (5) reaching a defensible conclusion.

> **Goal #11**
> Explain the process of tax research and the sources used by tax professionals in giving tax advice.

THE IMPORTANCE OF FACTS

The first task the tax adviser must master is properly gathering the facts. While some facts may initially seem unimportant to the taxpayer, the seasoned tax practitioner will ensure that all relevant facts have been determined. Because of the often complex and intricate nature of the tax law, small differences in facts can sometimes result in totally different tax outcomes. In addition to ascertaining the facts, the practitioner should advise the taxpayer of his or her responsibility to provide necessary documentation.

IDENTIFYING THE ISSUES

Once the tax adviser has determined all pertinent facts, he or she must identify the issues so that the necessary authority can be located. Asking the right questions (to identify the issues) is a critical tax skill that can best be developed through practice. The form in which the issues are stated typically varies with experience. A tax adviser with limited experience, and only a passing knowledge of the Internal Revenue Code, will usually phrase issues in a very general way. The initial search for satisfactory conclusions to broadly worded tax questions ordinarily raises additional questions (issues) in the mind of the tax adviser. Sometimes more appropriate, detailed questions completely escape the attention of an inexperienced researcher until he or she has studied the tax law relative to the more general issues.

An experienced tax adviser might phrase the original questions differently. With a greater knowledge of the Code, the adviser's question will likely refer directly to a specific Code section, focusing the research effort on the relevant law. In some instances, a particular court decision, or a line of decisions, can be the focus of the issue raised. In these cases the beginning point is even more precise.

Experience cannot be overrated. The most seasoned tax researcher realizes that lengthy periods of contemplative thought may be necessary before a complex tax issue becomes obvious. In addition, a good imagination and considerable creativity are important traits of every successful tax adviser.

SEARCHING FOR AUTHORITATIVE SOLUTIONS

Before resolving tax issues, a researcher must first locate, interpret, and evaluate all of the authorities relevant to a particular situation. Pertinent authorities include both the statute and interpretations issued by the IRS and the courts. Ordinarily, the search should begin with statutory authority—the Internal Revenue Code. From that point, some researches go next to administrative authority, then to judicial authority, and finally to secondary references. Other researchers contend that one should avoid reading administrative authority as long as possible because it represents the IRS point of view. Regardless of which order the researcher follows, he or she must assess and interpret all pertinent authority to reach a defensible conclusion and to advise a client.

Appendix 3A following this chapter identifies in more detail authoritative sources and research tools: primary tax law, tax services, other editorial law sources, computer-assisted search programs, and expert systems.

EVALUATING POTENTIAL AUTHORITY

In searching for a defensible solution to a tax problem, a person must keep in mind that the primary authority ordinarily involves some statute—in other words, some part of the Internal Revenue Code of 1986 as amended. Frequently, however, the specific problem the researcher is facing is not explicitly addressed in the Code. The second line of authority to be considered is often such primary authority as administrative interpretations (Treasury Regulations, Revenue Rulings, Revenue Procedures, and so on) or judicial interpretations. Secondary authority may be consulted either to aid in making a more intelligent search or to fill in the gaps found in primary authorities.

Consideration of judicial authority should include a review of the court that rendered the decision; the year in which the decision was rendered; and subsequent cases addressing similar facts. Tax Court decisions have general application throughout the United States. However, Tax Court decisions that are unfavorable to the IRS may be subject to an IRS nonacquiescence, a clear signal that it will *not* follow the decision, even though it may choose not to appeal it. Alternatively, the IRS may announce an acquiescence, which lets taxpayers know that it *will* follow the decision in similar situations. The commissioner, through this acquiescence policy, has taken the liberty of putting taxpayers on notice that the IRS will either follow a decision or take a hard-line position opposing a Tax Court decision. A Tax Court decision to which the commissioner has not publicly announced acquiescence or nonacquiescence is nevertheless an important precedent.

The Tax Court is not required to follow universally a circuit court decision that overturned an earlier Tax Court decision. The Tax Court has held in *Jack E. Golson,* 54 TC 742 (1970), however, that it will consider itself bound by a circuit court decision, but only for other cases litigated in that particular circuit. Hence the taxpayer's place of residence will sometimes be an important factor in determining how the Tax Court will decide a particular issue. Any taxpayer may attempt to take a position contrary to that rendered by a circuit court in a circuit in which he or she does not reside. Obviously, however, the risks are high that, in the event of litigation, the local circuit will follow the decisions of other circuit courts if the precedent appears logical and there seems to be no more definitive recourse.

When a researcher finds conflicting authority due to disagreement between courts or between administrative and judicial authorities, such disagreements are usually resolved in favor of the conclusion rendered by the court of highest authority. Conflicting decisions between the Tax Court and a district court, between two district courts, or between the Tax Court and a circuit court of appeals must be considered temporary authority. In those instances, there is a high probability that further litigation on similar facts will be appealed for clarification. The risk of receiving an adverse decision in these cases, therefore, is higher than normal.

REACHING A DEFENSIBLE CONCLUSION

After researching the authoritative sources, the tax researcher often will be able to reach a defensible conclusion. However, a tax researcher may encounter a situation for which he or she is unable to locate applicable authority. In such cases, authority from a set of related facts may be used. For example, a Tax Court decision or revenue ruling dealing with the valuation process of stock in a closely held corporation may help to determine the value of a partnership interest. Without any authority, a researcher may need to apply analogous reasoning to deduce a solution. In this way, new authority may be created.

In conclusion, tax research involves a continuing challenge as new fact situations are encountered, as Congress alters the laws, and as administrative and judicial interpretations evolve. A manual research process utilizing one or more of the popular tax services—and involving the Internal Revenue Code, Treasury Regulations, IRS Rulings, and court cases—is still most common. However, the new computer databases offer the exciting prospect of eliminating much of the drudgery of tax research in the future and are more widely used each year.

_____ CONCLUSION

The legal processes and responsibilities involved in creating, complying with, and administering the tax law are considerable. Members of Congress attempt to fashion a tax law that is responsive to the social and economic needs of their constituencies. These same constituents seek to minimize their tax liabilities and avoid unpleasant encounters with the IRS. Because of the complexity of the tax system, taxpayers often seek professional assistance in tax planning and compliance matters. Thus, tax practitioners play an important role in the process and they, in turn, have certain responsibilities. Within this framework, the IRS tries to protect tax revenues in order to facilitate smooth functioning of the government. Finally, the judiciary acts to help ensure the integrity of the entire system by adjudicating disputes.

It is obvious that ample opportunities arise for the taxpayer and the IRS to disagree vigorously. It is also obvious that through its system of penalties and powers granted by Congress, the IRS has the upper hand in many disputes. Relatively few cases have been publicized in which the IRS has allegedly treated taxpayers in an unfair and heavy-handed manner. Frequently taxpayers have been punished for omissions or commissions alleged to have resulted from mistakes by the IRS itself. As a result, there has been a growing demand for Congress to protect taxpayers from unfair treatment. As part of the Technical and Miscellaneous Revenue Act of 1988, Congress passed a Taxpayer Bill of Rights. The new law is designed to improve relations between the IRS and taxpayers and to provide assistance to taxpayers who believe they have been mistreated because of IRS blunders. Some of the provisions merely codify existing procedures and practices, but additional protection is given to taxpayers involved in administrative and judicial proceedings.

For example, the IRS is required to provide taxpayers with a written statement of taxpayer rights and the obligations of the IRS during audit, appeal, and refund and collection processes. Another new provision that is likely to be popular with taxpayers requires the IRS to abate any portion of penalties or tax attributable to erroneous written advice provided by the IRS. The public should also be happy to learn that the Act prohibits the IRS from using tax-enforcement results as a basis for evaluating its employees or for imposing or suggesting production goals or quotas for its employees. Another provision, of great interest to preparers, and one that will create a hardship for the IRS, prevents temporary regulations from remaining in effect for longer than three years.

APPENDIX 3A: SEARCHING FOR AUTHORITATIVE SOLUTIONS

In searching for authoritative solutions to tax questions, tax professionals turn to such authoritative sources and research tools as primary tax law, tax services, other editorial law sources, computer-assisted search programs, and expert systems.

ORGANIZATION OF PRIMARY TAX LAW

Internal Revenue Code

The organizational scheme of the Internal Revenue Code of 1986 is depicted in Table 3-3. Chapter 1, titled "Normal Taxes and Surtaxes," contains Subchapters A through V. Because Subchapters R and U were repealed in 1969 and 1986, respectively, only 20 subchapters are currently operative. Table 3-4 lists some of the more commonly referenced subchapters and parts of Chapter 1 of the Internal Revenue Code.

Nearly all of the popular income tax literature refers only to the section or some lower subdivision of the Code. Thus, for example, Sec. 301 refers (without specific mention) to the 1986 Code, Subtitle A, Chapter 1, Subchapter C, Part I. The abbreviated reference is definitive because the sections are numbered progressively beginning with Subtitle A, Chapter 1. There is only one Sec. 301. Also, not all numbers were used originally, enabling Congress to add sections at the end of any subchapter or part. In a sense, the Code is like a constantly evolving chart of accounts in an accounting system. To illustrate, Subchapter A, Part I, uses section numbers 1 through 5—currently, no sections numbered 6 through 10 exist; Part II uses section numbers 11 and 12; Part III uses number 15 only; Part IV uses a further organizational division, namely, subparts. Subpart A of Part IV uses section numbers 21 through 26; Subpart B, section numbers 27 through 29; Subpart C, section numbers 32 through 35; and so on.

Division	Designation
(9) Subtitles	Designated by uppercase English letters A–G; Subtitle A is titled "Income Taxes."
(60) Chapters	Designated by Arabic numerals 1–98 (some numbers unused); Chapter 1 is titled "Normal Taxes and Surtaxes."
Subchapters	Designated by uppercase English letters, as required; Chapter 1 has 20 Subchapters (Subchapters R and U repealed), A–V.
Parts	Designated by Roman numerals, as required; Chapter 1, Subchapter A, has 6 Parts, I–VII (Part V repealed).
Subparts	Designated by uppercase English letters, as required.
Sections	Designated by Arabic numerals, as required. See text for important details of this subdivision of the Code.
Subsections	Designated by lowercase English letters in parentheses, as required.
Paragraphs	Designated by Arabic numerals in parentheses, as required.
Subparagraphs	Designated by uppercase English letters in parentheses, as required.
Sub-subparagraphs	Designated by lowercase Roman numerals in parentheses, as required.

TABLE 3-3
Internal Revenue Code Organizational Scheme

Location in Code*	Description
Subchapter A	Determination of tax liability
Part I	Tax on individuals
Part II	Tax on corporations
Part III	Changes in rates during a taxable year
Part IV	Credits against tax
*	
Part VI	Alternative Minimum Tax
*	
Subchapter B	Computation of taxable income
Part I	Definition of gross income, adjusted gross income, taxable income, etc.
Part II	Items specifically included in gross income
Part III	Items specifically excluded from gross income
Part IV	Tax exemption requirements for state and local bonds
Part V	Deductions for personal exemptions
Part VI	Itemized deductions for individuals and corporations
*	
Part VIII	Special deductions for corporations
Part IX	Items not deductible
*	
Subchapter C	Corporate distributions and adjustments
Part I	Distributions by corporations
Part II	Corporate liquidations

Continued on page 98

TABLE 3-4
Subtitle A— Income Taxes Chapter 1 Normal Taxes and Surtaxes

TABLE 3-4 (Con't.)

Subtitle A—
Income Taxes
Chapter 1
Normal Taxes
and Surtaxes

Location in Code*	Description
Part III *	Corporate organizations and reorganizations
Subchapter D *	Deferred compensation, etc.
Subchapter E	Accounting periods and methods of accounting
Part I	Accounting periods
Part II	Methods of accounting
Part III	Adjustments
Subchapter F *	Exempt organizations
Subchapter G *	Corporations used to avoid income tax on shareholders
Subchapter H *	Banking institutions
Subchapter I *	Natural resources
Subchapter J	Estates, trusts, beneficiaries, and decedents
Part I	Estates, trusts, and beneficiaries
Part II	Income in respect of decedents
Subchapter K	Partners and partnerships
Part I	Determination of tax liability
Part II	Contributions, distributions, and transfers
Part III	Definitions
Subchapter L	Insurance companies
Subchapter M *	Regulated investment companies and real estate investment trusts
Subchapter N *	Tax based on income from sources within or without the United States
Subchapter O	Gain or loss on disposition of property
Part I	Determination of amount of and recognition of gain or loss
Part II	Basis rules of general application
Part III *	Common nontaxable exchanges
Subchapter P	Capital gains and losses
Part I	Treatment of capital gains
Part II	Treatment of capital losses
Part III *	General rules for determining capital gains and losses
Subchapter Q *	Readjustment of tax between years and special limitations
Subchapter R	Repealed
Subchapter S	Tax treatment of S corporations and their shareholders
Subchapter T *	Cooperatives and their patrons
Subchapter U	Repealed
Subchapter V	Title 11 cases

* Indicates an omission of parts.

Regulations

Upon adoption, regulations for all federal taxes are printed in Title 26 of the Code of Federal Regulations. Title 26 is divided into parts that correspond with the subtitles in the Internal Revenue Code. Thus, Part 1 of the Regulations deals with Subtitle A of the Code, the income tax. In addition, the parts are subdivided into sections that correspond with the second numbers of the Code. Thus, Part 1, Section 162 of the Regulations deals with the ordinary and necessary expenses of carrying on a trade or business. The complete citation for that section of the Regulations is 26 CFR 1.162, which can be interpreted as Title 26, Code of Federal Regulations, Part 1, Section 162. For brevity, the citation is usually reduced to Treas. Reg. Sec. 1.162-x or even Reg. 1.162-x. A complete citation to any treasury regulation has four distinct parts:

1. The number to the left of the decimal point indicates that the regulation deals either with a specific tax or with a procedural rule, as follows:

1.	Income tax
20.	Estate tax
25.	Gift tax
31.	Employment tax
48 or 49.	Excise tax
301.	Administrative and procedural rule
601.	Statement and procedural rules

2. The number between the decimal point and the hyphen (-) indicates the Code section which the regulation is interpreting.

3. The first number to the right of the hyphen indicates the sequential number of the regulation interpreting the Code section already identified.

4. The letters and/or numbers following the first number to the right of the hyphen indicate subreferences within a regulation to help the reader find a particular point of interpretation.

Revenue Rulings and Other Releases

Revenue Rulings are consecutively numbered each calendar year and are cited as Rev. Rul. 1992-1, Rev. Rul. 1992-2, and so on. Revenue Procedures are cited in a similar manner. The *Internal Revenue Bulletin*, which is published weekly by the Internal Revenue Service, contains much of the information referred to in the preceding paragraphs. For example, the *Bulletin* includes copies of any newly enacted Internal Revenue Acts, committee reports on these acts, and all Treasury Decisions, as well as all Revenue Rulings. The material in the *Bulletin* is reorganized and printed in a bound volume on a semiannual basis. The bound volumes are called *Cumulative Bulletins* and are cited C.B. Thus, 1992-1 C.B. would contain Rev. Rul. 1992-1, as well as other information.

Tax Court

The Chief Judge of the Tax Court classifies each of the court's decisions (other than those rendered in the Small Claims Division) as either regular or memorandum decisions. Technically, only regular decisions have precedential value. Regular decisions are reported by the U.S. Government Printing Office in *Tax Court Reports*. Memorandum decisions are decisions that, in the Chief Judge's opinion, add little or nothing to the tax law. Consequently, Tax Court Memorandum Decisions are published by the government only in mimeograph form. Because these decisions may be informative to taxpayers and their advisers, both Commerce Clearing House (CCH) and Prentice-Hall (P-H) publish all memorandum decisions, first in loose-leaf advance sheets and later (at the end of each year) in hard-bound copy. The CCH publication is titled *Tax Court Memorandum Decisions* (cited TCM); the P-H edition is titled *Prentice-Hall Memorandum Decisions* (cited PH Memo TC).

District Court

At the judges' discretion, district court decisions may be released and reported in the *Federal Supplement*, commonly cited F. Supp. Appeals from the district courts as well as from the Tax Court to the U.S. Circuit Courts of Appeals are reported in the *Federal Reporter*, Second Series, commonly cited F.2d.

Claims Court

Decisions of the Claims Court are published in the *U.S. Claims Court Reports,* typically cited *Cl. Ct.* Cases heard by the Court of Appeals for the Federal District appear with the cases of the U.S. Circuit Courts of Appeals in the *Federal Reporter*, Second Series, cited F.2d.

Other Court Reporters

In addition to these common citations, court decisions are often published in a number of other commercial reporters. All of these citations follow the same general format shown in Figure 3-7. The first set of numbers refers to the volume number of a particular reporter series. The letters refer to the reporter series. The last set of numbers usually refers to the page number on which that particular judicial interpretation begins. For example, "54 AFTR 2d 310" refers to volume 54 of the American Federal Tax Reporter, second series, beginning at page 310. Ordinarily, the name of the case immediately precedes such a citation. Additional information—such as the court and, possibly, the year in which the decision was rendered—follows the citation. See Table 3-5 for a list of the more commonly encountered reporter series.

FIGURE 3-7

Citation Format

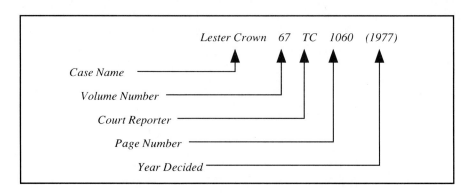

TABLE 3-5

Publication Summary of Court Decisions

Courts		Publisher	Title	Citations
Tax Court				
Regular Decisions:				
1924–1942	P*	GPO	U.S. Board of Tax Appeals Reports	*Nellie G. Dodge,* 40 BTA 209 (1939)
1943–present	P	GPO	Tax Court of U.S Reports[+.]	*Lester Crown*, 67 TC 1060 (1977)
Memorandum Decisions:				
1924–1942	P	P-H	P-H BTA Memorandum Decisions	*R. Olsen*, 38 BTA 1531, Dock 86970 (Memo) Aug. 16, 1938 P-H ¶ 6.413
1943–present	P	P-H	P-H TC Memorandum Decisions	*John C. Kenny*, 1966, P-H TC Memo 66-1027
1942–present	P	CCH	Tax Court Memorandum Decisions	*John C. Kenny*, 25 TCM 913 (1966)
District Court				
1924–1932	P	West	Federal Reporter 2nd	*Obispo Oil Co. v. Welch*, 48 F.2d 872 (DC Cal., 1931)
1932–present	P	West	Federal Supplement	*Armstrong v. O'Connell*, 451 F.Supp 817 (DC Wisc., 1978)
1900–present	S	P-H	American Federal Tax Reports	*Nickerson v. Gilbert*, 42 AFTR2d 78-5886 (DC RI, 1978)
1913–present	S	CCH	United States Tax Cases	*Nick v. Dunlap*, 50-2 USTC ¶ 9436 (DC Tex., 1950)
Claims Court[‡]				
1982–present	P	West	U.S. Claims Court Reports	*Raphan v. US.*, 3 Cl.Ct. 457 (1983)
1982–present	S	P-H	American Federal Tax Reports 2nd	*Raphan v. US.*, 52 AFTR2d 83-5984 (Cl.Ct., 1983)
1982–present	S	CCH	United States Tax Cases	*Raphan v. US.*, 83-2 USTC ¶ 9613 (Cl.Ct., 1983)
Circuit Court of Appeals[¥]				
1900–present	P	West	Federal Reporters 2nd	*Vishnevsky v. US*, 581 F.2d 1249 (CA-7, 1978)
1900–present	S	P-H	American Federal Tax Reports 2nd	*Vishnevski v. US.*, 42 AFTR2d 78-5681 (CA-7, 1978)
1913–present	S	CCH	United States Tax Cases	*Vishnevsky v. US.*, 78-2 USTC ¶ 9640 (CA-7, 1978)
Supreme Court				
1900–present	P	West	Supreme Court Reporter	*Commr. v. Kowalski*, 984 S.Ct. 315 (1977)
1900–present	P	GPO	United States Reports	*Commr. v. Kowalski*, 434 US 77 (1977)
1900–present	S	P-H	American Federal Tax Reports 2nd	*Commr. v. Kowalski*, 40 AFTR2d 78-5681 (S.Ct., 1977)
1913–present	S	CCH	United States Tax Cases	*Commr. v. Kowalski*, 77-2 USTC ¶ 9748 (S.Ct., 1977)

* "P" = Primary Citation; "S" = Secondary Citation.
[+] After 1969, "Tax Court of the U.S. Reports" is referred to as "United States Tax Court Reports."
[‡] In 1982, the predecessor Court of Claims was merged into the new U.S. Court of Appeals for the Federal District. In its place the Claims Court was created. Cases of the old Court of Claims can be found in the following services:

F. Supp (West) 1932–60	AFTR2d (P-H) 1900–82
F.2d (West)1929–32; 1960–82	USTC (CCH) 1913–82

[¥] Includes since 1982 the new U.S. Court of Appeals for the Federal District.

TAX SERVICES

To facilitate the tax research process, publishing companies sell tax services that conveniently assemble, in one set of reference works, the basic research materials relating to a specific tax topic. (See Table 3-6 for a list of major service publications.) Two popular tax services are the Standard Federal Tax Reporter, published by Commerce Clearing House, Inc. (CCH), and Federal Taxes, published by Prentice-Hall (P-H). These two services (as well as several others) provide the researcher with background information on tax issues as well as citations that are helpful for finding further authority.

The Standard Federal Tax Reporter is composed of five major parts. The first component is the set of Code Volumes. These two volumes contain the complete Internal Revenue Code arranged sequentially by Code section. The second component of the service is the Index Volume, which allows the researcher to look up key words to pinpoint the location of applicable materials. All references in the index are to *paragraph* numbers, not *page* numbers. These paragraph numbers generally lead the researcher to the third component—the 11 income tax Compilation Volumes. The Compilation Volumes are organized by Code section. Each portion of each compilation volume begins with the specific portion of the Code and Regulations, complete with all amendments to date. Following the Code and Regulations, each volume contains digests of and citations to revenue rulings and court decisions relating to that topic. The fourth component consists of new matters contained in Volume 10. By using this current cumulative index, the researcher can determine if any new ruling was published after the compilations volume was printed. Finally, the fifth component is the Citator Volumes. These volumes allow the researcher to search for additional authority by case name. The CCH citator provides the judicial history of each case, the court of original jurisdiction, subsequent appeals, and subsequent cases in which the original case was cited.

	Title of Service	Publisher	Organization According to	Arrangement of Content
TABLE 3-6 **List of Major Tax Service Publications**	Federal Taxes	Prentice-Hall	Code Section	Code Section, Regs., Editorials, Synopsis of Cases & Rev. Rul.
	Mertens Law of Federal Income Taxation	Callaghan & Co.	Topic	Editorial treatise with footnotes
	Rabkin & Johnson, Federal Income, Gift & Estate Taxation	Matthew Bender & Co.	Code Section	Editorial discussion with references in body of text
	Standard Federal Tax Reporter	Commerce Clearing House, Inc.	Code Section	Code Section, Regs., Editorials, Synopsis of Cases & Ref. Rul.
	Tax Coordinator 2d	Research Institute of America	Topic	Editorial discussion with footnotes
	Tax Management Portfolios	Bureau of National Affairs	Topic	Editorial discussion with footnotes

Federal Taxes by P-H is organized by Code section in much the same way as the CCH service. It also has five components, with the first being a two-volume set of the Internal Revenue Code. The second component, Volume 1, contains not only the topical index but also the main table to cases, the main table of rulings, and the index to tax articles. The index is referenced by paragraph number found in the compilations Volumes 2 through 10. As with CCH, these volumes contain segments with the Code, followed by the Regulations, and finally the digests and citations to revenue rulings and court cases that pertain to the topic. Volume 11 of the P-H service contains the current matter. Finally, the citator volumes disclose case citations in the same manner as CCH, with two exceptions. Case citations of subsequent cases in the P-H citator disclose whether earlier decisions were followed, overruled, or modified. In addition, subsequent cases in which the original case is cited are listed in order of the specific issues enumerated in the original case.

While both of these tax services are similarly arranged, each may emphasize a different facet of a particular law, and each service has a unique indexing system. A researcher should check a tax problem through more than one service to ensure that he or she has located and defined all aspects of a defensible position.

EDITORIAL SOURCES

In addition to the various tax services, other potential editorial sources for locating answers to tax research problems include books, magazines, and newsletters. One widely respected treatise is Bittker and Eustice's *Federal Income Taxation of Corporations and Shareholders*, published by Warren, Gorham & Lamont. Numerous other reference works can be found in any tax library.

Tax magazines (for example, *The Journal of Taxation, The Tax Adviser, TAXES—The Tax Magazine*, and *Taxation for Accountants*), as well as various law journals, are an excellent source of discussion on current tax topics and can assist a researcher in finding a solution to a difficult tax issue. Most tax professionals personally subscribe to one or more of these journals. All are standard items in a good tax library.

A number of tax newsletters are also published on a monthly, biweekly, weekly, and even daily basis. For instance, CCH and P-H provide weekly updates titled *Taxes on Parade* and *Accountant's Weekly Report*, respectively. Because tax advisers work in a dynamic field, newsletters are an important means of keeping informed of recent developments at the congressional, administrative, and judicial levels.

COMPUTER-ASSISTED RESEARCH

Since computers have the ability to store large quantities of information and to retrieve information quickly, it is not surprising that their capability has been utilized to assist tax advisers with their research. Two companies, Mead Data Central, Inc., and West Publishing Company, market their computer libraries under the brand names LEXIS and WESTLAW, respectively. Both libraries contain all types of statutory, administrative, judicial, and editorial source documents. Since these computerized libraries are not limited to tax-related materials, they are especially popular with attorneys. Large CPA firms also subscribe to LEXIS, primarily for the tax materials. However, since computer libraries are still relatively expensive, individual practitioners and small firms often cannot justify their cost. Some CPA firms that subscribe to computerized tax services reduce operating costs by limiting access to LEXIS to a few designated experts in each office.

CCH and P-H also market their respective tax services as a computer library. CCH uses the title CCH ACCESS, while P-H markets its product under the name PHINET. To utilize any computer in tax research efficiently, one must first become a proficient manual researcher. Because the computer search is organized under a key word system, the researcher needs to have sufficient technical tax knowledge to identify key words. Only then will using the computer become cost efficient.

EXPERT SYSTEMS

Expert systems are computer programs that help to solve problems or answer difficult questions about a specific domain (area). They are called expert because they solve problems at a level comparable to that of a human expert in the same domain.

Tax applications lend themselves to expert systems for several reasons. First, many expert systems use rules to reason through problems. Since tax laws are essentially rules, they lend themselves to this methodology. Second, to develop an expert computer system, human experts must exist to develop the expert system and human tax experts exist.

Several expert systems have already been developed in the tax area.[22] TAXMAN I analyzes the tax consequences of various corporate reorganization transactions. TAXMAN II extends TAXMAN I with an advanced representation of legal arguments. TAXADVISOR makes recommendations about income, estate, and gift tax planning for individuals. INVESTOR advises users in the selection of tax shelters tailored to suit particular needs. ExperTAX assists users in the corporate tax accrual and planning process. FINANCIAL ADVISOR advises users on projects, mergers, products, and acquisitions. FINANCIAL ADVISOR's advice is based on the general financial consequences of an alternative, not just taxation issues. It is a more generalized application than the other expert systems mentioned. FINANCIAL ADVISOR was the first commercially available system.

The exert systems just mentioned assist a taxpayer or tax preparer. The IRS also uses expert systems. It has established an AI lab and trains employees in artificial intelligence (AI). Although expert systems are just one part of AI, they are often considered the most successful part. Therefore, it is reasonable that the IRS AI lab emphasizes the development of expert systems. At least 13 systems are in varying stages of development in different areas. These areas include identification of major audit potential from forms 1040, 1040A, and 1040EZ; assisting IRS employees with taxpayer correspondence; and managing the computer and printing systems at IRS service centers.

Because it takes so long to develop expert systems, it may be some time before they are in general use. Furthermore, each system is expert in a very limited area of taxation. This limitation is a general characteristic of expert systems. Even a relatively narrow specialty can require years of development and experimentation before it is made available for general use.

Annual changes to the tax code plus the lengthy development time for expert systems make it unlikely that expert taxation systems will ever encompass large portions of the taxation problem. However, expert system technologies are continually improving, and taxation has proven to be a suitable subject for expert system solutions. Consequently, the continued application of expert systems to specialized taxation problems seems likely.

22 For an excellent review of these programs, see R. Michaelsen and W. Messier's article, "Expert Systems in Taxation," *Journal of the American Taxation Association*, Spring 1987, pp. 7–21.

KEY POINTS TO REMEMBER

✓ Tax bills are initiated in the House of Representatives. After passage by the House, they go to the Senate. Since the Senate inevitably passes a bill that is different from the one passed by the House, the bills are referred to a Conference Committee for compromise.

✓ The tax statutes were last codified in the Internal Revenue Code of 1986. Congressional intent implicit in the 1986 Act and other acts can be found in Committee Reports and the *Congressional Record.*

✓ Tax law is interpreted by the administration through Treasury Regulations, Revenue Rulings and Revenue Procedures. It is further interpreted by the judiciary through Tax Court, district courts, Courts of Claims, appellate courts and the Supreme Court.

✓ Taxpayers are responsible for assessing their own tax liabilities. Several different IRS forms are available to help taxpayers fulfill this obligation.

✓ Noncompliance is a problem of serious magnitude in the United States. The rates and types of noncompliance vary widely by category of taxpayer and source of income.

✓ Taxpayers who do not fully comply with the tax law are subject to various penalties and interest. There have been many changes in the penalty structure in recent years.

✓ Practitioners play an extremely important role in the tax system. The balancing of their responsibilities to the tax system and to the interests of their clients is sometimes difficult. This inherent conflict has been a source of contention between the IRS and tax advisers over the past decade.

✓ Practitioners who do not fulfill their responsibilities to the tax system are subject to various penalties. These penalties have been changing in recent years as greater responsibilities to the tax system have been formalized.

✓ The IRS uses various procedures in its attempt to ensure a high level of compliance by taxpayers. The audit rate has been steadily decreasing, but the computer-matching capability of third-party reports has dramatically improved both in terms of quantity of items matched and accuracy of matching.

✓ The taxpayer has several avenues of recourse when there is an unsettled dispute from an audit. There are appeals procedures within the IRS. Failing resolution there, the taxpayer may present the issue to a court of his or her choice.

✓ (Appendix 3A) Researching complex tax issues involves five key steps: (1) determining the facts, (2) identifying the issues, (3) searching for authoritative solutions, (4) evaluating that authority, and (5) reaching a defensible conclusion.

RECALL PROBLEMS

1. Indicate whether each of the following statements is true (T) or false (F). If you feel the statement is false, explain why it is false.

    a. Tax proposals for consideration by Congress may be introduced in either the House or the Senate.

b. The House Ways and Means Committee and the Senate Finance Committee hold separate hearings on the same proposed tax bill.

c. Committee Reports are the only general source from which interested parties can obtain an understanding of the underlying reasons for passage of a particular tax provision.

d. Amendments to a tax bill, made during the bill's debate on the floor of either the House or Senate, are reported in the Congressional Committee Reports.

e. Treasury Regulations are published by the Treasury Department to assist taxpayers with a general interpretation of the Internal Revenue Code.

f. Since passage of the Sixteenth Amendment, Congress has passed only two Internal Revenue Codes. The most recent Code is known as the Internal Revenue Code of 1954.

g. Revenue Rulings are issued regularly by the IRS. Taxpayers may rely on rulings when their fact situations are identical with those mentioned in the published rulings.

h. Revenue Rulings are similar to Revenue Procedures except that rulings apply to income tax issues while procedures apply to gift and estate tax issues.

i. Private letter rulings issued to taxpayers by the IRS are published by commercial publishers like CCH and P-H. They have no precendential value, however, other than for the taxpayer by whom the ruling was requested and then only for the identical fact situation mentioned in the ruling request.

j. If a taxpayer cannot reach an agreement through the normal appeals process with the IRS over a tax issue, he or she must pay the contested tax liability. The taxpayer may then file suit in the United States Tax Court and request a refund.

k. Decisions by the Tax Court can be appealed by either the taxpayer or the IRS to a Circuit Court of Appeals.

2. a. What are the three courts in which legal action may be initiated in income tax matters?

b. Which of these courts may include a trial jury?

c. To which court are the majority of tax disputes taken?

d. What is the appeal route from each court?

3. What types of tax forms are used by individual taxpayers? What are the differences between these forms?

4. What is meant by the term self-assessment? Describe the factors affecting the level of voluntary compliance in the United States.

5. On May 1, Arlo tells you that he did not file his return on April 15 because he had been told by a friend that penalties were only assessed on net tax due with the return. He thought that since his total tax bill was $10,000 and his withholdings were $11,000, he could file the return anytime. Do you agree? Will there be any penalties due with his return if he files it immediately? If he files it in December?

6. Angela received $50,000 in a legal settlement. The tax treatment of the item is not certain. Angela did some research that led her to believe the income was probably taxable. However, because there was some doubt and she did not think

she would be audited, she decided to take the position that the income was not taxable. Therefore, she did not include the income in her tax return. Her taxable income excluding the $50,000 in question is $60,000.

    a. Describe any penalties she might be liable for.

    b. Would your answer be any different if she was certain the amount was taxable but decided to exclude it from her return anyway?

7. What is a statute of limitations? What is the significance of the statute of limitations to taxpayers?

8. a. In the previous year, the taxpayer reported gross income of $6,000, on which he paid a tax of $150. In reviewing his records during the current year, he discovered a remittance advice for $120 that he had received in the previous tax year and that he had failed to report on his tax return for that year. What is your advice to him? What types of liabilities will he have if he follows your advice?

    b. A friend of the taxpayer in part a, above, suggests to the taxpayer that he should "just forget that $120. They [the IRS] never audit returns with income as low as yours." Reply to this, including in your answer a review of the procedures by which returns are selected for audit.

9. Does a practitioner have any responsibility for ensuring that positions on a return he or she has prepared are supported by substantial authority?

10. What is a CPA's responsibility with respect to preparing a return or recommending a position when there is some ambiguity as to the correct tax treatment?

11. John Price recently received a letter from the IRS stating that John's return for a recent year is being examined. John, an engineer, prepared the return himself. The letter asks John to bring his records for the year under examination when he appears for the office audit. John is convinced that he has made some terrible mistake in the computation of his tax and is worried. What can you tell him that will ease his mind?

12. On his return for 19X1, Omar claimed a dependency exemption for his mother. His return was audited, and an agent disallowed the dependency exemption. Omar received a 30-day letter notifying him of a proposed additional tax liability of $182. Omar is very perturbed over this assessment and says to you, a tax expert, "I'll take it to court. I'm just not going to pay this $182."

    a. What procedure do you suggest that Omar follow?

    b. What procedure would be necessary to literally take it to court?

13. What alternatives are available to a taxpayer on receipt of the 30-day letter? the 90-day letter?

14. Below are statements about the tax process. State whether each is true or false. If false, explain why.

    a. The statutory notice of a tax deficiency is issued following the completion of the audit process.

    b. A taxpayer cannot obtain court action on a tax case until he or she has exhausted all procedures for relief within the IRS.

c. Most disputes between the IRS and taxpayers are settled at the appeals conference.

d. Taxpayers must have a formal protest prepared before they are entitled to a hearing at the appeals conference.

e. Most taxpayers elect to carry their disputes to the federal district courts, if they decide to go to court.

#11 15. In researching a tax case, you find a decision of the Fifth Circuit Court of Appeals that supports a favorable outcome of your situation. Is it certain that the IRS will follow this decision? What if you reside in California (Ninth Circuit)?

#11 16. When can a taxpayer unquestionably rely on a Tax Court decision, given the same facts?

#11 17. What signal or signals does the IRS give taxpayers to indicate that a Tax Court decision will not be followed?

#11 18. Indicate whether each of the following statements is true (T) or false (F). If you feel the statement is false, explain why it is false.

a. Decisions rendered by the United States Tax Court are published by CCH in a publication titled *U.S. Tax Cases.*

b. The IRS publishes Revenue Rulings and Revenue Procedures in a weekly publication titled *Internal Revenue Bulletin.* The weekly bulletins are then compiled in an annual publication of two or three volumes under the title *Cumulative Bulletin.*

c. The Tax Court issues both regular and memorandum decisions. Only the regular decisions are published, however, while memorandum decisions are only informally announced to interested parties. Memorandum decisions therefore have no precedential value.

d. A number of commercial publishers produce tax services that are a helpful tool to tax professionals.

e. Each publisher uses a unique system organizing the various tax resource materials. Consequently, most tax professionals subscribe to that one tax service with which they can most readily identify. Subscription to more than one tax service is an unnecessary expense that most tax professionals can ill afford.

f. The IRS is required by law to comply with decisions handed down by the Tax Court and to dispose of subsequent fact situations by other taxpayers in the same manner.

g. Most tax services are updated weekly. It is therefore a waste of money to subscribe to any of the many tax newsletters available on a weekly, biweekly, or monthly basis.

——— THOUGHT PROBLEMS

 1. Discuss the advantages and disadvantages of having relatively closed or open proceedings in the legislative process.

 2. Explain how the U.S. system of checks and balances is reflected in the tax system.

3. Present the arguments that might support having tax cases heard only by a court with expertise in tax issues. Present the arguments for having a variety of judicial forums to hear tax cases.

4. Write an essay that develops your views on the reasons for noncompliance in the United States. To the extent that you think a penalty system is an important component of an enforcement system, address the quality of our current system for dealing with noncompliance.

5. Until very recently, lawyers and CPAs took the view that they could ethically take a position on a tax return as long as the position had a reasonable basis. That standard was judged to be so weak that one student interpreted it to mean a practitioner could take any position as long as it didn't cause him to laugh aloud. That standard has been modified by both the ABA and the AICPA. Describe the current ethical standard for lawyers and CPAs. Explain your opinion on the appropriateness of that standard.

6. Evaluate the strength of the penalty structure on tax return preparers in terms of modifying behavior.

7. Assume that you are the Commissioner of the IRS. Write a several paragraph paper outlining the views you think you would have in that position on the most important changes needed in the tax system for improving taxpayer compliance.

8. Are taxpayers provided adequate recourse for settling tax disputes? Why or why not?

9. Explain why the initial steps of determining all relevant facts and identifying all relevant tax issues are so important in tax research.

_____ CLASS PROJECTS (APPENDIX 3A)

1. Visit your campus library and determine which of the following publications it has available:

   a. Standard Federal Tax Reporters (CCH)

   b. Federal Taxes (P-H)

   c. Law of Federal Income Taxation (Mertens)

   d. Tax Management Portfolios (BNA)

   e. United States Tax Court Reports (GPO)

   f. United States Tax Cases (CCH)

   g. The American Federal Tax Reports (P-H)

   h. Prentice-Hall T.C. Memorandum Decisions (P-H)

   i. Tax Court Memorandum Decisions (CCH)

   j. Cumulative Bulletin (GPO)

2. Locate the case cited at 77-2 USTC Par. 9536.

   a. What court heard the case?

   b. Name the judge who issued the opinion.

    c. How many issues were enumerated in this case?

    d. Can you give a primary citation for the case?

3. Locate Volume 67 of the *Tax Court of the United States Reports (TC)*.

    a. What is the time period covered by this volume?

    b. How many regular judges served on the Tax Court for the period covered by Volume 67?

    c. List the various indexes found in Volume 67.

    d. Locate the case cited at 67 TC 352 and indicate how many issues were presented in the case.

4. Locate *1976-1 Internal Revenue Cumulative Bulletin (CB)*.

    a. What time period is covered by Volume 1?

    b. What do you find on page 1?

    c. What items are printed in Part I of the bulletin?

    d. In what order are the items presented in Part I?

    e. What items are printed in Part II?

    f. What items are printed in Part III?

5. Locate the case cited at 28 AFTR2d 71-5676.

    a. What court heard the case?

    b. List the judge(s) who heard the case.

    c. Who wrote the opinion?

    d. Name the court of original jurisdiction.

    e. What is the primary citation for this case?

    f. Where did you find the primary citation?

    g. Write the complete citation to a CCH publication in which the same case is located.

6. a. Locate and read the two cases cited below:
      Robert N. Hewitt, 16 TCM 468, TC Memo 1957-112.
      John Thomas Blake, 29 TCM 513, TC Memo 1970-117.

    b. Enumerate, in outline form, the important facts of each case.

    c. Suggest, in outline form, the facts that you feel most influenced the judges to reach opposite conclusions in the two cases.

7. a. Locate and read the two cases cited below:
      FS Services, Inc., 413 F.2d 548, 69-2 USTC Par. 9539 (Ct. Cls., 1969).
      Dearborn Company, 444 F.2d 1145, 71-1 USTC Par. 9478 (Ct. Cls., 1971).

    b. Enumerate, in outline form, the important facts of each case.

    c. Suggest, in outline form, those facts that you feel most influenced the judges to reach opposite conclusions in the two cases.

8. a. Locate and read the two cases cited below:
      Martha S. Cowarde, 35 TCM 1066, TC Memo 1976-246.
      C.E.R. Howard, 28 TCM 1435, TC Memo 1969-277.

b. Enumerate, in outline form, the important facts related to casualty losses in each case.

c. Suggest, in outline form, those facts that you feel most influenced the judges to reach opposite conclusions in the two cases.

Part Two

BASIC CONCEPTS

T he mission of Part Two is to explain the general income tax formula in broad terms. To accomplish this mission we provide five chapters with the following objectives:

CHAPTER 4:
INCOME: GENERAL CONCEPTS—to introduce the income concept as found in economics, financial accounting, and taxation.

CHAPTER 5:
DEDUCTIONS: GENERAL CONCEPTS—to present an overview of the items that can be subtracted from gross income in the calculation of taxable income.

CHAPTER 6:
TAXABLE ENTITIES, TAX RATES, AND TAX CREDITS—to introduce the provisions that establish the

> *"I guess you will have to go jail. If that is the result of not understanding the Income Tax law I shall meet you there. We will have a merry, merry time, for all of our friends will be there. It will be an intellectual center, for no one understands the Income Tax law except persons who have not sufficient intelligence to understand the questions that arise under it."*
>
> *ELLHU ROOT, QUOTED IN RANDOLPH E. PAUL, TAXATION IN THE UNITED STATES*

basic taxable entities for federal income tax purposes, to explain how these entities are taxed, and to explain how the gross tax liability of any entity may be reduced by tax credits and prepayments.

CHAPTER 7:
TAX ACCOUNTING—to provide insight into various aspects of tax accounting with emphasis on differences between financial and tax accounting.

CHAPTER 8:
TAX BASIS—to introduce the concept of tax basis and explain some critical relationships that exist between income measurement and the notion of taxable and nontaxable entities.

113

The first nine pages of the Internal Revenue Code define income; the remaining 1,100 pages spin the web of exceptions and preferences. The average taxpayer rarely gets beyond the nine pages.

SENATOR WARREN MAGNUSON, CONGRESSIONAL RECORD (1966)

INCOME:
GENERAL CONCEPTS

CHAPTER OBJECTIVES

In Chapter 4 you will be introduced to the concept of income from the perspectives of economics, accounting, and income taxation.

LEARNING GOALS

After studying this chapter, you should be able to

1 Understand why and how accounting and income tax concepts of income differ from the concept used in economics;

2 Explain how the realization criterion of income taxation differs from the realization criterion of accounting;

3 Explain why in some circumstances income may not be recognized for income tax purposes in the same period in which it is realized;

4 Identify the four phrases in Sec. 61 of the Internal Revenue Code that affect the tax definition of income; and

5 Identify the more common items of income (broadly conceived) that are excluded from gross income for all taxpayers.

The determination of an *income tax liability* quite obviously must begin with an operative definition of income. Unfortunately, few concepts in the history of economic thought have been more widely debated than the income concept. To make matters even more difficult, as we move from a conceptual plane to the pragmatic and often political world of taxation, no logical explanation of the many distortions to the basic concept can be offered as guidance to either the serious student or the confused taxpayer, who was of special concern to Senator Magnuson, as implied in the headnote to this chapter.

Conceptually, computation of a taxpayer's income tax liability is a simple matter and can be easily reduced to the following formula:

	Income broadly conceived
−	Exclusions
=	Gross income
−	Deductions
=	Taxable income
x	Applicable tax rate
=	Gross tax liability
−	Tax credits and prepayments
=	Net tax payable

The apparent simplicity of this general formula is deceiving because its correct application depends on myriad classifications, definitions, distinctions, and exceptions contained in the Code and the related administrative and judicial interpretations. These authoritative interpretations sometimes give common words a special meaning for tax purposes. Furthermore (and most important), to understand tax provisions, a person often must understand not only the technical definition of the words used in the Code but also the social, economic, and political forces that motivated the enactment of specific provisions, the administrative considerations that attach to a particular interpretation of those provisions, and the personal opinions of the individuals assigned the responsibility of interpreting them. Justice Learned Hand stated this conclusion most explicitly and colorfully:

> as the articulation of a statute increases, the room for interpretation must contract; but the meaning of a sentence may be more than that of the separate words, as a melody is more than the notes, and no degree of particularity can ever obviate recourse to the setting in which all appear and which all collectively create. [1]

Part Two of this text attempts to explain the general income tax formula in broad terms. One major challenge of Part Two is the need to include within it both general concepts and a limited number of specific rules. In studying these five chapters, always keep one fundamental difference in mind. The conceptual portions are analogous to studying geography by looking at a globe of the earth; that is, these discussions give you only the broadest outline of the tax law. The specific rules considered in other portions of these five chapters are more comparable to studying geography by examining a city map; that is, they provide much greater detail for a more limited area. In a few instances, the discussion in Part Two lies somewhere between the analogous globe

---

1 *Helvering v. Gregory*, 69 F.2d 809 (CA-2, 1934).

and the city map; that is, some of the discussion introduces the conceptual idea, illustrates its application with a discussion of one or more specific rules, and then provides a cross-reference to other portions of this text where those some specific rules are considered again in much greater detail. To begin, let us consider the basic income concept.

Goal #1
Understand differences between income concepts in economics, accounting, and income taxation.

_____ INCOME CONCEPTS

There is no single universally accepted definition of the word *income*. Rather there are many definitions, often based on the uses to be made of the income measurement. Each definition depends on concepts and assumptions that may not be totally acceptable for other uses. In this chapter we examine some of the fundamental issues underlying the problem of income definition and measurement. We will begin with major distinctions in the concepts of income found in economics, accounting, and taxation, and we will emphasize the differences between the accounting and tax concepts.

THE INCOME OF ECONOMICS

An ideal concept of income provides a basis for designing a tax system. The definitions of income given by Robert M. Haig and Henry C. Simons some 70 years ago are still used today by tax policy analysts in the U.S. Treasury to assess the merits of proposed tax law changes. Haig's definition of income is simple and straightforward: "Income is the *money value of the net accretion to one's economic power between two points of time*."[2] Simons gave a similar definition: "Personal income may be defined as the algebraic sum of (1) the market value of rights exercised in consumption and (2) the change in the value of the store of property rights between the beginning and end of the period in question."[3]

Professor Harvey Brazer restated the concept held by Simons and Haig in easily understood terms: "Under this concept income is equal to the algebraic sum of consumption plus the change in the individual's net worth during the year or other accounting period. . . . It asks simply, how much could this individual have spent for consumption during the year while remaining as well off in terms of net worth at the end of the year as he was at the beginning of the year."[4] Perhaps the most important aspect of Simons' definition of income, at least from the accountant's viewpoint, is his suggestion that consumption and the net change in the individual's store of claims ideally are "both evaluated at market price, with the latter [increase in store of claims] computed on an accrual rather than on a realization basis."[5]

---

2 Robert M. Haig, "The Concept of Income—Economic and Legal Aspects," *The Federal Income Tax* (New York: Columbia University Press, 1921), p. 7.

3 Henry C. Simons, *Personal Income Taxation* (Chicago: University of Chicago Press, 1921), p. 50.

4 Harvey E. Brazer, "The Economics of Tax Reform," *Proceedings of the Fifty-Sixth Annual Conference* (1963) *of the National Tax Association,* p. 47.

5 Melvin I. White, "Consistent Treatment of Items Excluded and Omitted from the Individual Income Tax Base," *1959 Compendium,* p. 318. (The complete reference is *Tax Revision Compendium: Compendium of Papers on Broadening the Tax Base,* submitted to the Committee on Ways and Means, beginning November 16, 1959. To simplify the footnotes, all subsequent references simply cite the *1959 Compendium.)*

The major difficulty in using this definition for such practical purposes as taxation is in obtaining reliable measures of net worth and consumption. In other words, the big problem is one of valuation. Although the great bulk of income in the economy is rather easily valued (for example, wages, salaries, interest, and dividends), a substantial gray area is the focus of considerable dispute (fixed assets, for example). The worth of assets in the gray zone is a subjective characteristic that depends on someone's estimate of the present value of the satisfaction to be derived from the object in question. [6]

Another practical problem implicit in this economic concept of income is distinguishing between *monetary* income and *real* income. This difference refers to the familiar problem caused by changes in the value of the monetary unit—in accounting, the problem is commonly called the *price-level problem.* A changing price level may not cause a serious problem in measuring consumption, but it may be very important in measuring the change in an accumulation in value during the year if the price level has changed markedly. Most economists stress *real* capital accumulation, measured by the increase in command over scarce resources. Presumably, gains that merely reflect an increase in a price level can be eliminated by deflating the income measure using a price index.

A broad economic definition of income would include *all* receipts from *all* sources, including such gratuitous receipts as gifts, inheritances, and bequests. The underlying rationale is that gratuitous receipts are available for consumption or savings (and thus includable in the Haig-Simons scheme), which fundamentally enhance an individual's "ability-to-pay." In a practical sense, including such items also eliminates the need to differentiate among an individual's receipts according to the intentions of other parties.

An alternative scheme that continues to be actively considered by the U.S. Treasury is based on taxing consumption. Under this concept, generally associated with Professor Irving Fisher, realization is ultimately represented only by *consumption,* because only when an item is consumed is there a logical stopping place among a sequence of economic relations.[7] From this viewpoint, the appropriate tax base is satisfaction derived from consumption and is measured in monetary terms by the amount spent on consumer goods "consumed" during the period. As envisioned by tax policy analysts, a consumption tax could be implemented by modifying the present income tax system to exclude changes in net worth (thus making use of the arithmetical result that a person's after-tax income is either spent on consumption or saved.)[8]

The low national savings rate in the United States virtually ensures consumption taxes, whether through modification of the income tax system or the addition of a national VAT, will continue to be seriously considered. Presently, the U.S. income tax has many features of a consumption tax. Recent proposals such as increasing the capital gains rate differential and increasing IRA deductions would move the system more toward a consumption approach. As Treasury officials have observed, the

---

6 See *Blueprints for Basic Tax Reform,* U.S. Department of Treasury, January 17, 1977, pp. 21–22, for a detailed discussion.

7 See Irving Fisher, *The Nature of Capital and Income* (New York: Macmillan, 1906); "Income in Theory and Income Taxation in Practice," *Econometrica, 5, No. 1 (January 1937), pp. 1–55; and* (with Herbert W. Fisher), *Constructive Income Taxation* (New York: Harper, 1942).

8 See *Analysis of Proposals Relating to Comprehensive Tax Reform,* Joint Committee on Taxation, (U.S. Government Printing Office), September 21, 1948, p. 28.

current tax system is already closer to a consumption tax than to a comprehensive income tax. According to their analysis,

> two important sources of saving for many Americans—home ownership and employer contributions to retirement annuities (or contributions of individuals to Keogh Plans and IRAs)—are treated under the current law almost exactly the same way they would be treated under a consumption tax which allows deduction for savings.[9]

THE INCOME OF ACCOUNTING

The income concepts discussed in the preceding section differ greatly from computation of income following generally accepted accounting principles. The primary difference is the complete absence of any "realization" criterion in the economic definition of income.

Generally accepted accounting principles suggest income should be measured on the basis of *completed transactions*. Note the importance of this distinction: Economists define income in terms of *value*, depending essentially on expectations about the *future*. Accountants define income basically in terms of the *past*, expressed in money measurement. They are concerned with the flow of transactions because completed transactions—presumably at arm's length—provide independent judgments of value on which accountants can rely. Accountants consider the economists' concept too impractical to apply and too lacking in objectivity and accuracy to provide a basis for measuring periodic income. The recognition of unrealized gains and losses (requiring detailed, annual, subjective valuations of all assets and liabilities) is unsatisfactory to most accountants, who are steeped in the virtues of practicality and conservatism and who may share liability for the accuracy of certified financial statements. Thus, accountants have developed a comprehensive and well-defined body of literature that contains concepts and specific rules for measuring income. Almost all of these rules are based on both a realization concept and a matching concept.

The student of accounting may be surprised to discover economists frequently fail to appreciate accountants' reluctance to use subjective valuations to the same extent as economists do. Professor Simons, for example, once charged that accountants prefer to sacrifice relevance for accuracy. On the other hand, he admitted that "outright abandonment of the realization criterion would be utter folly; no workable scheme can require that taxpayers reappraise and report all their assets annually; and while this procedure is implied by the underlying definition of income, it is quite unnecessary to effective application of that definition. . . ."[10]

The Realization Criterion in Accounting

The verb "to realize" has several possible meanings. Perhaps the three most common are (1) to make real; (2) to convert into cash (money); and (3) to understand clearly.[11] Obviously, the second definition is the one pertinent to this discussion. When the realization concept is first introduced into a freshman or sophomore accounting course, the text—and often the instructor—hasten to illustrate the concept with an

---

9 U.S. Department of Treasury, *op.cit.*, pp. 10–11.

10 See Simons, *op. cit.*, pp. 207–208.

11 The *Random House Dictionary of the English Language*, 2nd unabridged ed. (New York: Random House, 1987), p. 1607 lists six different meanings.

example that usually goes something like this: "On August 10, Jones purchased 100 shares of ABC common stock for $600. On December 31, these shares had a fair market value of $700. What is Jones' income for the year from this investment?" The instructor hopes the student will reply that Jones has no income because his $100 gain has not been "realized."

Applying the second definition to the above example, a student would be correct in assuming that until the shares are sold for cash (or money), no income is "realized." An accountant probably would not be as demanding as this definition. He or she likely would be willing to admit that income is realized as soon as the shares are converted into another property that has a high degree of liquidity and measurability. *Kohler's Dictionary for Accountants* defines *realize* as follows:

> To convert into cash or a receivable (through sale) or services (through use): to exchange for property which at the time of its receipt may be classified as, or immediately converted into, a current asset.[12]

The American Institute of Certified Public Accountants' pronouncement on the matter of realization comes reasonably close to the tax position. In its Statement No. 4, the Accounting Principles Board assigned the concept of realization the position of a pervasive measurement principle and then described it as follows:

> Revenue is generally recognized when both of the following conditions are met: (1) the earning process is complete or virtually complete, and (2) an exchange has taken place.[13]

This statement differs from the accountant's definition offered earlier, with less emphasis placed on the liquidity of the asset received and more emphasis on the completion of the earning process.

Although we could write more about the realization concept in accounting, we have covered the most important facts. Accountants generally hold that income (revenue) is not realized until a transaction has been consummated and a measurable, liquid asset received. Usually income is "recognized" (included in the financial statements prepared for the period) in the same period in which it is realized. In limited circumstances, for financial accounting purposes, income may be recognized prior to realization. For example, when a product has an assured market at a fixed price, it might be argued that income should be recognized when the product is completed. Similarly, in some cases, recognition may occur after realization. For example, if there is no reasonable basis for estimating the degree of collectability of a receivable or note, recognition of income might be deferred for accounting purposes until collection actually takes place.

THE INCOME OF TAXATION

We have noted that the income of economics is too subjective to be used by the accountant in measuring income for financial accounting purposes. It is also too subjective to be used generally as a basis for determining taxable income. Nevertheless, the all-inclusive approach to income measurement attributed to Simons and Haig

---

12 *Kohler's Dictionary for Accountants*, 6th ed. (Englewood Cliffs, NJ: Prentice-Hall, 1983), p. 421.

13 *ABP Statement No. 4*, "Basic Concepts and Accounting Principles Underlying Financial Statements of Business Enterprise" (New York: American Institute of Certified Public Accountants, 1970), p. 59.

approaches a method the IRS uses to reconstruct the income of taxpayers who lack adequate accounting records. The **net-worth method** relies heavily on the basic assumption that all inflows of wealth are taxable unless specifically excluded by laws. Essentially this method of measuring income compares the taxpayer's net worth at the beginning and end of a period. The change in net worth is then added to estimated consumption expenditures for the period to get an estimate of total income.

Although the net-worth method of estimating income for tax purposes is subject to criticism on the grounds that the taxpayer has the burden of proving any portion of the computed income was derived from excluded sources, it is sometimes the only realistic alternative available to the IRS. The possibility of its use certainly encourages taxpayers to keep a set of reasonable financial records for tax purposes.

The net-worth method of estimating income for tax purposes yields different results than does the economist's concept of income. This difference occurs largely because of (1) the use of the realization criterion for tax purposes; (2) the exclusion under tax law of certain types of income; and (3) the allowance of certain specified deductions in arriving at taxable income.

Although the measurement of income as computed under generally accepted accounting principles comes much closer to yielding a basis on which income taxes can be computed, there are many differences between income determined under generally accepted accounting principles and income computed for tax purposes. Most of the differences between the realization concept in accounting and realization concept in income taxation are best explained by practical constraints—that is, by the accountant's potential liability for accurate financial statements on the one hand and by the objectives and administrative considerations common to income taxation on the other.

> The **net-worth method** determines a taxpayer's taxable income by adding the change in net worth to consumption for the period.

> **Goal #2**
> Explain the differences between realization for accounting purposes and income tax purposes.

The Realization Criterion in Income Taxation

The realization criterion of income taxation is a blend of statutory, administrative, and judicial law. In Sec. 61, which contains the general definition of gross income, the word "realization" does not appear. The Code provides only that "gross income means all income from whatever source *derived.*"[14] The Treasury Department's interpretation of this statute, however, introduces the realization concept. It follows:

> (2) General definition. Gross income means all income from whatever source derived, unless excluded by law. Gross income includes income *realized* in any form, whether in money, property, or services. Income may be *realized,* therefore, in the form of services, meals, accommodations, stock, or other property as well as in cash.[15]

Observe that this administrative interpretation of the Code suggests that realization requires the receipt of some new service, property, or property right but does not specify anything relative to either the liquidity or the measurability of the item. This broad interpretation of realization is a practical necessity. In its absence, taxpayers would seek out obscure ways of avoiding income taxation by earning their income through barter transactions of infinite variety.

The realization criterion has received judicial support from the beginning. The most celebrated statement is contained in a 1920 U.S. Supreme Court decision:

---

14 Sec. 61(a) (emphasis added).

15 Reg. Sec. 1.61-1(1) (emphasis added).

> Here we have the essential matter; not a gain accruing to capital, not a growth or increment of value in the investment; but a gain, a profit, something of exchangeable value proceeding from the property, severed from the capital however invested or employed, and coming in, being 'derived,' that is, received or drawn by the recipient (the taxpayer) for his separate use, benefit and disposal;—that is income derived from the property. Nothing else answers the description.[16]

These words of the Supreme Court, like those of the regulation quoted earlier, seem to require a transaction or some significant event in addition to appreciation. The important question remains: Exactly what is required before income is realized for tax purposes?

For purposes of income taxation, the singular requirement pertinent to the realization concept is the consummation of an "external transaction." In *United States v. Davis,* the Supreme Court found that a taxpayer who transferred appreciated shares of stock to his former wife "in full settlement and satisfaction of any and all claims and rights against the husband"[17] realized gain equal to the difference between the fair market value of the rights received and the adjusted basis of the property surrendered. Because the "rights received" were unique, and certainly not liquid or easily measured, the Court found that the value of the rights could be presumed equal to the (estimated) value of the property surrendered. Although the specific conclusion of the *Davis* decision has been nullified,[18] it still suggests that, in income taxation, the realization concept does not require the receipt of a measurable, liquid asset.

As illustrated by the *Davis* decision, the word **transaction** must be defined broadly and positively for income tax purposes. A transaction can be defined as any significant change in the form or the substance of any property or property right. An **internal transaction** involves only one taxpayer, an **external transaction,** two or more taxpayers. For income tax purposes, **realization** ordinarily demands an external transaction. To illustrate, the discovery of oil (with a dramatic increase in property values) does give rise to income, using the economist's definition of income. It does not, however, create gross income for tax purposes either (1) because there is no new property or property right or (2) because no second taxpayer is involved. The discovery of buried treasure, on the other hand, does give rise to gross income because there is an increase in value *and* the existence of possible adverse interests in that treasure, by a second taxpayer, is sufficient to find realization.

Another interesting aspect of the realization criterion of income taxation can be observed in the transfer of property between business entities. Business entities recognized for tax purposes are not necessarily the same entities that are recognized for accounting purposes. For example, the transfer of a building from a personal account to a sole proprietorship would most likely give rise to an accounting entry and, possibly, accounting income. It would not, however, give rise to gross income for tax purposes because the sole proprietorship is not viewed as an entity distinct from the individual owner. On the other hand, the transfer of a building from an individual to a corporation could give rise to gross income for tax purposes, as well as to accounting income, because the corporation is deemed to be a separate taxable entity. The word *could* in the preceding statement is important. Realization is ordinarily a necessary but not sufficient condition for recognition of income.

> A **transaction** can be defined as any change in the form or substance of a taxpayer's property or property right.
>
> An **internal transaction** involves only one taxpayer.
>
> An **external transaction** involves two or more taxpayers.
>
> **Realization** usually requires an external transaction.

---

16 *Eisner v. Macomber,* 252 US 189 (1920), p. 207.

17 370 US 65 (1962), p. 67.

18 Sec. 1041 provides that no gain or loss shall be recognized on the transfer of property either between spouses or between former spouses if the transfer is incident to a divorce or separation.

For tax purposes, income generally must be recognized in the accounting period in which it is realized. However, there are numerous exceptions to this general rule. Because sophisticated taxpayers have attempted to use lack of realization as an avenue for avoiding tax, Congress has moved toward taxing some income *before* realization. For example, in 1969, Congress first required periodic inclusion in gross income of the amortization of discount on original issue discount bonds. In 1981, Congress adopted a **mark-to-market system** of taxation for commodity futures contracts, thereby effectively taxing the unrealized (or paper) gains on commodity contracts held at year end. Most recently, in 1984, Congress extended the mark-to-market system of taxation to many options transactions.[19]

For tax purposes, income is more likely to follow, rather than to precede, realization. This significant difference between accounting and taxation can be explained by the tax tenet called **wherewithal to pay.** This tenet suggests that, under many circumstances, the income tax shall impinge at whatever time the taxpayer has funds with which to pay the tax. In numerous situations, wherewithal to pay seems to outrank in importance more sophisticated refinements of income measurement that would cause income to be recognized other than when the funds are readily available.

> In a **mark-to-market system** income is recognized based on changes in market value during a period.
>
> The **wherewithal to pay** concept holds that a taxpayer should be taxed on income when he or she has funds to pay the tax.

EXAMPLE 4-1

In December of this year Frank sold Sharon five acres of land he had acquired years ago for $2,000. The terms of the sale were that Sharon would pay $10,000 down and $40,000 (plus interest) next June. Frank has realized a gain of $48,000. However, tax accounting rules will allow Frank to recognize the $48,000 gain as cash is received (20% this year and 80% next year). This provision is explained in Chapter 7.

> **Goal #3**
> Explain why income may not be recognized for tax purposes when it is realized.

The wherewithal to pay concept merely affects the timing of income recognition. In limited instances, permanent deferrals or **exclusions** are allowed. These exclusions are granted for numerous reasons. A number of exclusions relate to social objectives. Examples include the exclusion of many employee fringe benefits and student scholarships. In some cases, the exclusion is granted to prevent double taxation of the same income. Gifts are excluded for this reason. Other exclusions seem to have arisen because of sympathy for taxpayers in difficult circumstances. Included in this category are the exclusion of life insurance proceeds paid on the death of the insured and of some payments to present and former members of the armed forces. Although controversial, interest on the obligations of state and local governments has been excluded from the federal income tax since 1913. Likewise, Social Security benefits traditionally had been excluded from gross income until a few years ago. As we will learn later in this chapter and in Chapter 9, the scope of many exclusions has been narrowed as Congress, often under pressure to raise revenues, has reexamined the basis for granting the exclusions.

> **Exclusions** grant permanent nonrecognition of income. Excluded income is not part of gross income.

Summary of the Income Concept for Tax Purposes

The preceding discussion of the income concept for federal tax purposes can be summarized as follows. Before any taxpayer must report income for federal income tax purposes, he or she must answer three fundamental questions in the affirmative.

---

19 Joint Committee on Taxation, *op. cit.*, p. 24.

1. Did the taxpayer have any income?

2. Was the income realized?

3. If the income was realized, must it be recognized immediately?

> **Income** can be defined for tax purposes as either (1) an increase in net worth or (2) consumption, during the tax year.
>
> For income tax purposes **realization** can be defined as (1) a change in the form or substance of a taxpayer's property or property right *if* (2) that change involves a second taxpayer.

Perhaps the best possible test for the presence (or absence) of **income** is the one suggested by economists: Did the taxpayer experience *either* an increase in net worth or consumption? If the answer to this question is yes, one should ordinarily presume that income is present. The conclusion that income is present, however, is not sufficient to trigger the income tax. To be taxable, income generally must also be realized.

Realization usually requires both (1) a change in the form or the substance of the taxpayer's property (or property rights) and (2) the involvement of a second party. There are at least three pervasive exceptions to our definition of realization for tax purposes: (1) borrowing, (2) gifts, and (3) death. To illustrate, consider the case of a taxpayer who borrows $10,000 by mortgaging land with a cost basis of $2,000 and a fair market value of $14,000. The $12,000 appreciation in the value of the land, between the time it was purchased and the time the mortgage was placed against it, most certainly represents income, using the economist's definition of income. The courts have held, however, that the act of mortgaging that land does *not* constitute realization for the debtor who mortgages property even though it clearly involves both (1) a change in the owner's property rights and (2) a second taxpayer (the bank or other creditor making the loan).[20] Similarly the courts have held that a taxpayer who makes a gift of an appreciated property does not need to recognize the income associated with the prior appreciation in value even though the donor (the person making the gift) clearly has modified his or her property rights in a transaction involving a second taxpayer.[21] Transfers made at death are likewise deemed to be beyond the realization concept.[22]

Income is most commonly realized when a service has been rendered or a property has been sold, exchanged, or leased, Thus, the receipt of any form of payment—whether cash or noncash property—for a service rendered, is generally sufficient to cause the realization of income, as is the exchange of one property for another. Not every item of realized income is subject to an immediate income tax. To be taxed, realized income must also be recognized for federal income tax purposes.

In general, income must be recognized for tax purposes, at the time that it is realized. There are many exceptions to this general rule. Tax nonrecognition, when it occurs, may be either temporary or permanent. Permanent nonrecognition is typically due to an exclusion provision in the Code. Temporary nonrecognition may be attributed either to (1) specific accounting methods or (2) special provisions that allow income deferral. These provisions usually provide for income taxation at the time the taxpayer has the wherewithal to pay. Details associated with accounting methods are discussed in Chapter 7; details of the most common nonrecognition provisions are explained in Chapter 17. We now turn to our city map view of what does and does not constitute gross income.

---

20 See, for example, *Helvering v. F. & R. Lazarus & Co.,* 308 US 252 (1939) and *Woodsam Associates v. Com'mr.,* 198 F.2d 357 (2nd Cir. 1952).

21 See *Taft v. Bowers,* 278 US 470 (1929) and Rev. Rul. 55-410, 1955-1 CB 297.

22 See O.D. 667, 3 CB 52 (1920); Rev. Rul. 55-117, 1955-1 CB 233. See also Graetz, "Taxation of Unrealized Gains at Death—An Evaluation of Current Proposals," 59 *Virginia Law Review* 830 (1973).

GROSS INCOME FOR TAX PURPOSES— INCLUSIONS AND EXCLUSIONS

INCLUSIONS

The general concept of gross income for tax purposes stems from the Internal Revenue Code, the administrative interpretations of the Code, and the judicial decisions in tax disputes. Although Sec. 61 of the Code purports to define gross income, the definition that it provides—gross income means all income—does not tell us much; it clearly implies that any doubtful items are to be included within the definition. This conclusion is supported by three other phrases in Sec. 61(a), which reads as follows:

(a) GENERAL DEFINITION. Except as otherwise provided in this subtitle, gross income means all income from whatever sources derived, including (but not limited to) the following items:

(1) Compensation for services, including fees, commissions, fringe benefits, and similar items;

(2) Gross income derived from business;

(3) Gains derived from dealings in property;

(4) Interest;

(5) Rents;

(6) Royalties;

(7) Dividends;

(8) Alimony and separate maintenance payments;

(9) Annuities;

(10) Income from life insurance and endowment contracts;

(11) Pensions;

(12) Income from discharge of indebtedness;

(13) Distributive share of partnership gross income;

(14) Income in respect of a decedent; and

(15) Income from an interest in an estate or trust.

> **Goal #4**
> Understand how Sec. 61 defines income.

The four statutory phrases that collectively support an expansive interpretation of "gross income" for tax purposes are

1. *Except* as otherwise provided. . .

2. Gross income means *all* income. . .

3. From *whatever* source derived. . .

4. Including (but *not limited to*). . .

In view of this all-inclusive definition, a taxpayer must look to the phrase "except as otherwise provided" as a basis for omitting an item from gross income. The statutory exceptions are collectively identified as **exclusions.** In other words, *any item of income that is not included in gross income is known as an exclusion.* The words

> For income tax purposes an **exclusion** is any item of income that is *not* included in gross income.

of Sec. 61 clearly suggest that all exclusions must have a statutory base and that these provisions must be found within Subtitle A of the Internal Revenue Code.

A careful examination of a detailed table of contents of the Code might suggest that all of the exclusions are neatly contained within Part III of Subchapter B of Chapter 1. The title for that part of the Code reads Items Specifically Excluded from Gross Income. Part III includes Secs. 101–135 the titles of which read as follows:

Sec. 101.	Certain death benefits.
Sec. 102.	Gifts and inheritances.
Sec. 103.	Interest on state and local bonds.
Sec. 104.	Compensation for injuries or sickness.
Sec. 105.	Amounts received under accident and health plan.
Sec. 106.	Contributions by employer to accident and health plans.
Sec. 107.	Rental value of parsonages.
Sec. 108.	Income from discharge of indebtedness.
Sec. 109.	Improvements by lessee on lessor's property.
Sec. 110.	Income taxes paid by lessee corporation.
Sec. 111.	Recovery of tax benefit items.
Sec. 112.	Certain combat pay of members of the Armed Forces.
Sec. 113.	Mustering-out payments for members of Armed Forces.
Sec. 114.	Sports programs conducted for the American National Red Cross.
Sec. 115.	Income of States, municipalities, etc.
Sec. 117.	Qualified scholarships.
Sec. 118.	Contributions to the capital of a corporation.
Sec. 119.	Meals or lodging furnished for the convenience of the employer.
Sec. 120.	Amounts received under qualified group legal services plans.
Sec. 121.	One-time exclusion of gain from sale of principal residence by individual who has attained age 55.
Sec. 122.	Certain reduced uniformed services retirement pay.
Sec. 123.	Amounts received under insurance contracts for certain living expenses.
Sec. 124.	Qualified transportation provided by employer.
Sec. 125.	Cafeteria plans.
Sec. 126.	Certain cost-sharing payments.
Sec. 127.	Educational assistance programs.
Sec. 128.	Interest on certain savings certificates.
Sec. 129.	Dependent care assistance programs.
Sec. 130.	Cross references to other Acts.
Sec. 130.	Certain personal injury liability assignments.
Sec. 131.	Certain foster care payments.
Sec. 132.	Certain fringe benefits.
Sec. 133.	Interest on certain loans used to acquire employer securities.
Sec. 134.	Certain military benefits.
Sec. 135.	Income from United States Savings bond used to pay higher education tuition and fees.

The seemingly concise list of 15 inclusions provided in Sec. 61(a), coupled with the specific exclusions located in Secs. 101 through 135, may give the student who is unfamiliar with the myriad controversies surrounding the measurement of income a false or unwarranted sense of security. As you will discover throughout the remainder of the text, these few specific items of inclusion and exclusion are merely the tip of a very interesting iceberg. In Part Three of the text we will consider exclusions that apply only to individual taxpayers. In the remainder of this chapter, we will discuss some of the important items that all taxpayers may exclude in determining taxable income.

EXCLUSIONS THAT APPLY TO ALL TAXPAYERS

Before we investigate the details of any exclusion provision, it may be helpful to distinguish between exclusions and returns of capital. An exclusion inevitably involves either (1) an appreciation in net worth or (2) consumption. A **return of capital** involves nothing more than a change in the form of a property or a property right. For example, suppose a taxpayer sells a property with a $5,000 tax basis for $5,000 cash. After making the sale, the taxpayer has more cash. The cash, however, represents a mere return of the capital the taxpayer had previously invested in the property sold. There is no amount of gross income present in this transaction. A sale of that same property for $5,500 cash involves both (1) a $5,000 return of capital and (2) a $500 gain, or income. A sale for $4,000 involves (1) a $4,000 return of capital and (2) a $1,000 loss. The accounting concept of "gross revenues" can easily be confused with the tax concept of "gross income." That would be a mistake. The regulations clearly provide that the cost of goods sold is to be treated as a return of capital and that gross income includes only the profit element (if any) in a transaction.[23]

Sometimes the amount of capital recovery is less obvious than in the previous example.

> A **return of capital** is a recovery of the taxpayer's investment on the sale or exchange of an asset.

> **Goal #5**
> Identify and explain some of the items of income that may be excluded by all taxpayers.

EXAMPLE 4-2

Jane Field worked for a salary and each payday invested a portion of her after-tax pay in a simple annuity. During her working life, she invested a total of $10,000 in the annuity. She has reached age 60 and under the contract, is now to be paid $2,000 per year for eight years. How will the $2,000 payments be taxed? A portion of each payment represents a return of her original investment, and a portion represents income. To determine the part that is a tax-free return of capital, she divides the total investment of $10,000 by the number of years (eight) over which she receives payment and finds, in this way, that each year she may exclude $1,250 as a return of capital. The remaining $750 is taxable income.

In many situations, determination of the taxpayer's investment (or tax basis) is even more difficult. In tax parlance, the term *basis* normally is substituted for investment. Basis is somewhat equivalent to the accountant's book value, but there are important differences which we discuss in Chapter 8.

Contributions to Capital

Section 118 excludes from income any contribution to the capital of a corporation. There is, unfortunately, no simple definition of the term **contribution to capital.** Based on administrative and judicial authorities, the term encompasses transfers of property to corporations. The transferors (persons who transfer the property) may be either stockholders in the corporate transferee or other persons, that is, persons who own no part of the corporation receiving the property. Most transfers of property from shareholders to their own corporations are made nontaxable for the corporation by operation of Sec. 1032, rather than by operation of Sec. 118. Transfers from non-shareholders are typically covered by Sec. 118. For example, a community development group might donate property to a corporation to encourage it to locate a manufacturing plant within the community. From the standpoint of the recipient

> A **contribution to capital** increases a corporation's net worth without increasing its income.

23 Treas. Reg. 1.61-3(a).

corporation, the donation would be a contribution to its capital. A real estate developer's contribution of land to a prospective corporate tenant was also found to be a contribution to the capital of the prospective tenant.[24] Sec. 118(b) goes on, however, to exclude from the meaning of the term any "contribution in aid of construction or any other contribution as a customer or potential customer." Thus the definitional boundary of this exclusion remains uncertain in many circumstances. In those instances found to involve a contribution to capital, Sec. 362(c) provides that the property received will have a zero basis for federal income tax purposes.

Discharge of Indebtedness

Taxpayers who settle debts for less than their book amount have an increase in net worth. However, if the taxpayer is insolvent both before and after the debt forgiveness, the income is excluded from taxation by Sec. 108. The amount of indebtedness eliminated in bankruptcy proceedings is also excluded from income. When creditors reach a compromise agreement, however, the forgiveness of all or part of the taxpayer's debt may result in taxable income, but not in excess of the amount by which the taxpayer is solvent after the compromise.

EXAMPLE 4-3

Westwood Hardware has assets of $100,000 and liabilities of $120,000. As a result of a compromise settlement, Westwood's creditors agree to reduce the debt to $87,000. Westwood must report $13,000 of the forgiveness as taxable income.

Improvements Constructed by Tenant

Section 109 stipulates that a property owner generally has no income either when a tenant constructs improvements on the lessor's property or when the property, including improvement, reverts to the lessor on termination of the lease. If the improvements are constructed *in lieu of rents,* however, the lessor must report as income the fair value of the improvements when they are placed on the property.

Gifts and Inheritances

Section 102 provides that "gross income does not include the value of property acquired by gift, bequest, devise, or inheritance." These exclusions usually are supported by the theory that such transfers of property are a redistribution of a donor's or deceased taxpayer's income rather than the creation of new income, especially in the case of transfers to close relatives. In addition, cumbersome administrative problems would arise if items such as small Christmas and birthday gifts were included in taxable income. On the other hand, the exclusion of gifts creates the administrative problem of separating donative transactions from nondonative ones—in many cases a difficult line to draw. The donee who renders any service to the donor will likely have a difficult time proving that what he or she received was in reality a tax-free gift rather than taxable compensation.

Although gifts seem more likely to arise in a personal rather than a business setting, in certain business situations individuals may receive nontaxable gifts. For example,

---

24 See *Brown Shoe v. Com'mr.,* 339 US 583 (1950) and *May Department Stores Co. v. Com'mr.,* 33 TCM 1128 (1974).

an employer may give each employee a holiday gift such as a turkey or ham.[25] Also, some employers pay death benefits to the survivors of a deceased employee. Provided the payment is not compensation for services the employee performed before death, Sec. 101(b) allows exclusion of up to $5,000 of such payments. Presumably, larger tax-free payments could be made to the survivors provided that donative intent is established.

Some tax scholars favor including all transfers by gift, bequest, or inheritance in gross income. Others do not support taxation of the total value of such transfers but suggest that unrealized gains on property transferred by gift or death should be taxed at the time of the transfer, arguing that current laws act as a deterrent to the transfer of assets because taxpayers are encouraged to retain assets that have increased in value. If these assets are sold, taxable gains would result. On the other hand, if they retain the assets until death, no income tax is paid on the gain. In addition, a degree of inequity is involved because these provisions benefit primarily those who can arrange their affairs in such a way as to avoid realizing the gains prior to death. Transfer taxes on gifts and estates are levied by the federal government and by most states, but these taxes are sometimes less than the income taxes that would result if unrealized gains were taxed at the time of transfer. Furthermore, many feel there should be no direct relationship between income tax issues and other tax issues, whether sales taxes, property taxes, or transfer taxes.

Compensation for Business Injuries

Taxpayers may be compensated for business or personal injuries. The tax treatment of compensation for personal injuries will be discussed in Chapter 9. In general, the tax treatment of payment for business injuries is determined by the nature of the claim that gave rise to the payment.

EXAMPLE 4-4

> Hernandez Construction Company, Inc., received $100,000 from a subcontractor as compensation for income lost when the subcontractor failed to complete its part of a project. The $100,000 is taxable to Hernandez.

EXAMPLE 4-5

> Hernandez Construction Company also received $75,000 reimbursement from its insurance company as compensation for damage caused when an inexperienced operator ran one of the company's construction cranes into a bridge. The $75,000 equals the cost to repair the crane. The $75,000 is not taxable income because the payment merely returns the taxpayer to its former position.

Damages are monetary compensation recovered by a person who has suffered loss or injury. The compensation is sometimes tripled in antitrust cases; these damages are known as treble damages.

In *Commissioner v. Glenshaw Glass*,[26] the Supreme Court held that the punitive two-thirds of treble **damages** must also be included in income. In the words of the Court, "the mere fact that the payments were extracted from the wrongdoers as punishment for unlawful conduct cannot detract from their character as taxable income to the recipient."

---

25 Sec. 274(b)(1) limits the *deduction* for such gifts to $25 per donee per year.

26 348 US 426 (1955).

Exclusions and Intergovernmental Relations

A traditional aspect of the U.S. tax structure has been immunity of governmental units from taxation by other units. As a result of this concept, Sec. 115 specifically excludes the following from the federal income tax:

> (1) income derived from any public utility or the exercise of any essential governmental function and accruing to a State or any political subdivision thereof, or the District of Columbia; or
> (2) income accruing to the government of any possession of the United States, or any political subdivision thereof.

One of the most controversial provisions of the Code is Sec. 103, which provides that interest on "the obligations of a State, a Territory, or a possession of the United States, or any subdivision" is excluded form gross income. This exclusion, a part of our tax laws since 1913, has been supported on a number of bases—most vigorously on the basis of an alleged constitutional relationship between government units.

The constitutional issue was settled by the Supreme Court in *South Carolina v. Baker*.[27] In this case the state of South Carolina contended that a provision of the Tax Equity and Fiscal Responsibility Act of 1982, requiring that tax exempt bonds be issued as registered bonds, was unconstitutional. The Court held there is no constitutional barrier to the imposition of federal income taxes on interest received by holders of state and local securities. As one observer remarked, "the decision says this sacred cow's status has been judged not to be 'holy' or divinely inspired but to flow from eminently adjustable 'custom and law.' "[28]

In effect, the tax-exempt status of state and local bonds is a subsidy by the federal government of the governmental units that issue the bonds. Recall that in Chapter 1 we introduced the notion of implicit taxes. Implicit taxes arise because before-tax rates of return on tax-favored investments decrease relative to before-tax rates of return on less tax-favored investments. This reduced rate of return occurs because investors bid up the price of tax-favored investments. Tax-exempt bonds offer an excellent example of this phenomenon.

Casual observation reveals that the return on tax-exempt municipal bonds is somewhat lower than before-tax return on fully taxable U.S. government bonds of similar risk and maturities. In mid-1991, for example, AA rated tax-exempt bonds maturing in ten years were yielding approximately 6% whereas U.S. Treasury bonds maturing in ten years were yielding approximately 8%. The implicit tax rate on the investment in tax-exempt bonds relative to the taxable bonds (the benchmark bond) is 25%, calculated as follows:

$$\frac{\text{Before-tax return }(B) - \text{Before-tax return }(I)}{\text{Before-tax return }(B)} = \frac{8\% - 6\%}{8\%} = 25\%$$

In another way of expressing this idea, if the rate of tax on the taxable bonds was 25%, the after-tax return would be equal to the 6% return on the tax-exempt

---

27 108 S.Ct. 1355 (1988).

28 Dennis Zimmerman, "Tax-Exempt Bonds: A Sacred Cow That Gave (Some) Milk," *National Tax Journal,* September 1989, p. 283.

bond [8% x (1 – .25) = 6%]. Owners of tax-exempt bonds do not pay an explicit tax to the government, but they do pay an implicit tax by accepting a lower return. The beneficiary of this implicit tax is the state or local government, which is able to borrow money at a lower rate than it could without the tax-exempt status.[29]

Critics complain that the tax-exempt status of state and local bonds is an inefficient subsidy by the federal government. The federal government loses 25–30% more in revenue than the state and local governments gain by way of lower borrowing rates. This loss occurs because the bonds are most attractive to high-income taxpayers, who find the return on tax-exempt securities superior to that on taxable securities. For example, a taxpayer with a combined federal and state marginal income tax rate of 40% would earn only 4.8% after tax on the 8% taxable bond described above but would earn 6% on the tax-exempt bond (provided it was exempt from state tax). On the other hand, a taxpayer with a combined federal and state tax rate of 20% would prefer the taxable bond with its after-tax return of 6.4%.

This phenomenon is called the **clientele effect.** High-bracket taxpayers form the natural clientele for tax-exempt bonds; low-bracket taxpayers form the natural clientele for taxable bonds.[30] In addition to making tax-exempt bonds an inefficient subsidy, the clientele effect leads to vertical inequity because high-bracket taxpayers convert their statutory tax rates into relatively low implicit tax rates.

The loss of revenue caused by tax-exempt bonds vexes federal officials who have had little control over the extent and magnitude of the subsidized state and local projects. State and local tax-exempt bonds were used sparingly by our frugal ancestors, but their popularity soared between 1965 and 1985. During that period volume rose from $11 billion to over $200 billion.[31] Legislation attempting to restrict and control the issuance of municipal bonds has been enacted by Congress seven times in a span of 20 years (in 1968, 1969, 1980, 1982, 1984, 1986, and 1987).

The Tax Reform Act of 1986 seems to have had the most pronounced effect as the volume of municipal bonds dropped in half, from $200 billion in 1985 to $100 billion in 1987. Bond demand and supply forces were affected by the 1986 legislaiton. On the demand side, two features of the Act made municipal bonds less attractive. First, the drastic drop in the top marginal income tax rate from 50% to 28% made their tax-exempt status less of a tax break for high-income investors. Second, private-activity municipal bonds, the largest part of the municipal-bond market, are no longer tax exempt for the alternative minimun tax (AMT) (discussed in Chapter 19). Inclusion of private-activity municipal bond interest in the AMT base substantially reduces the desirability of this type of municipal bond for wealthy taxpayers.

On the supply side, the 1986 Act also contained two important changes. First, an explicit cap of $50 per resident was imposed on the volume of private-activity bonds that a state can issue. Second, by their very nature, private-activity bonds generally finance activities of private investors for some quasi-public purpose (low-income housing, sports stadiums, convention centers, airports, docks, wharves, parking, industrial parks, and so on). Prior to the Tax Reform and Fiscal Responsibility Act of 1982, many investors had been financing the acquisition of capital projects with tax-exempt private-activity bonds and then taking advantage of the accelerated

> The **clientele effect** is the natural affinity of certain types of taxpayers (based on their marginal tax rates) for certain types of investments.

---

29 For a thorough discussion of implicit taxes, see Mryon S. Scholes and Mark A. Wolfson, *Taxes and Business Strategy: A Global Planning Approach* (Englewood Cliffs, NJ: Prentice-Hall, 1991), Ch. 5.

30 For a discussion of the clientele effect, see Scholes and Wolfson, *op. cit.,* Ch. 6.

31 Zimmerman, *op. cit.,* p. 284.

depreciation preferences available for private investment.[32] The 1982 Act required the portion of an asset financed with tax-exempt bonds to be depreciated using a less generous depreciation method (specifically, using the straight-line rather than the declining balance method). The 1986 Act amplified this penalty by requiring tax-exempt assets to use lengthened asset lives.

What does the future hold? No one seems satisfied with the status quo. As one congressional analyst observed, "there appear to be no easy solutions and no early end to ferment in this area."[33] Advocates of using tax-exempt bonds would like to see some of the restrictions of the past 25 years eased to facilitate financing infrastructure projects such as highways and water treatment plants. Others want to move in the opposite direction, taxing all municipal-bond interest for federal purposes and then making direct federal grants to state and local governments for particular types of public capital formation, such as highways.

A final historical note on tax exemption should be of interest. Before 1941, interest on all bonds issued by the United States (federal government) was exempt from federal income taxation as part of the overall philosophy of government tax immunity. Before 1939, even the salaries and wages of state and local government employees were exempt from the federal income tax. The tremendous pressure for tax funds during those years was largely responsible for elimination of these two exclusions. The current pressure for increased tax revenues likewise may spell the end of some remaining exclusions in the near future.

———— KEY POINTS TO REMEMBER

✓ The economist's definition of income is often viewed as the ideal basis for designing an income tax system. Simply put, the economist defines income as the change in net worth between the beginning and end of the period in question plus the value of goods and services consumed during that same period.

✓ The accountant's definition of income includes a realization concept; that is, accountants generally contend that there is no income without a completed transaction and receipt of a measurable, liquid asset. Income generally is recognized by accountants in the same period in which it is earned.

✓ The realization criterion in income taxation is similar to the accounting criterion. However, receipt of a measurable, liquid asset is not required. Any change in any property or property right can trigger the realization of previously unrecognized income for tax purposes. In most cases the involvement of a second taxpayer is also required.

✓ In some situations the recognition of income for income tax purposes does not occur in the same period in which it is realized. The wherewithal to pay concept is often used to justify collection of tax when the taxpayer has the funds to pay the tax.

✓ In a few situations permanent deferral (or exclusion) of income is allowed for tax purposes. A number of exclusions that affect all taxpayers are discussed and explained.

---

32 See Chapter 14 for a discussion of depreciation.

33 Zimmerman, *op.cit.,* p. 290.

———— RECALL PROBLEMS

1. What are the major obstacles to using the economic concept of income as a measure of income for accounting and tax purposes?

2. Briefly describe the consumption expenditures approach to income measurement. Is it suitable as a basis for taxation? Explain.

3. What is meant by the term *recognition* in accounting? In taxation?

4. Rosman does a lot of baby-sitting while attending college. During the current year, Rosman received the following for baby-sitting services rendered:

Cash	$3,000
Clothing	500*
Room	1,200*

*Estimated fair market value

What amount of income has Rosman realized for federal income tax purposes?

5. Tom T. Mouse, a university student 22 years of age, lives with his parents, who provide him a room, food, laundry, etc., free of charge (these items have a fair market value of $6,500) during the year. Tom earned $1,000 in cash from a part-time job. Also, in return for setting up accounting records for a neighbor's business, Tom was given a television with a fair market value of $450. During the year Tom's uncle gave him 100 shares of C corporation stock. On the date of the gift, the stock had a fair market value of $32 per share. Later in the year, the uncle died and Tom inherited additional property worth $64,700.

   a. What is the amount of Tom's economic income?

   b. What is the amount of his income for taxation purposes?

6. Define the word *realization* as it is used in *accounting*. Define the word as it is used in *taxation.*

7. What are some of the major factors that cause differences between accounting income and taxable income?

8. Is *realization* necessary for *recognition* of income for tax purposes?

9. Explain the wherewithal-to-pay concept. How does this concept affect income tax recognition for tax purposes?

10. In general, what income is to be included in gross income for tax purposes?

11. Corporation DEF discovered a large oil deposit worth $20 million on its lands. Does DEF have any income? If so, has the income been realized? (Assume that DEF has not extracted any of this oil.)

12. Taxpayer B borrowed $5,000 cash from City National Bank. What income, if any, has Taxpayer B realized? Explain.

13. Art has been in business for many years. Because of his illness in the current year, Art's corporation suffered severe losses. On September 1, the corporation's assets totaled only $180,000, and its liabilities were $231,000. Because Art has been a valuable customer for many years, and because he had recovered from his illness and the outlook for future profits was good if Art could correct the

immediate insolvency, the creditors agreed to reduce the corporation's debt. How much gross income does the corporation have

  a. if the debts were reduced to $200,000?

  b. if the debts were reduced to $171,000?

`#4` `#5`

14. Salmonson owned a small plot of land in Midcity. In 1960, she leased the land to Acme Company, which built a small building on the property at a cost of $24,000. This amount was also considered to be the building's fair market value. When the lease expired in the current year, the building became Salmonson's property. At that time the building's fair market value was $18,000.

  a. How much income did Salmonson have in 1960 as a result of the building's construction?

  b. How much income did she have in the current year when the lease expired?

`#4` `#5`

15. At the time of his retirement, Jeremy invested $40,000 in an annuity sold by an insurance company. He will receive a monthly payment of $500 for the next ten years. How much of the $6,000 annual annuity will be taxed? Explain

`#4` `#5`

16. Which of the following events would increase a taxpayer's gross income? Explain each answer.

  a. Finding a $100 bill on the sidewalk.

  b. Scalping four 50-yard-line seats at a big football game for $100 each. The tickets cost $6 each. (Scalping tickets is illegal in the state in which they were sold and in which the game was played.)

  c. Having a $100 debt forgiven by a business creditor. (The creditor hoped in this manner to encourage your to do more business with him in the future.)

  d. Embezzling $100 from your employer's check-cashing fund.

  e. Having a $100 debt gratuitously forgiven by your brother.

  f. Selling a fishing boat for $100. (The boat originally cost you $200.)

THOUGHT PROBLEMS

`#1`

1. Imagine that you are a special agent from the IRS investigating the tax affairs of a notorious gambler. You have decided that the net-worth method must be used. Develop a list of the information you would need and suggest some possible sources of such information.

`#2`

2. Which of the following eight events constitute realization of gain for tax purposes by a cash-basis taxpayer? To understand the question better, assume that the property involved is the taxpayer's private residence with a fair market value of $100,000, a tax basis of $60,000, and that it is

  a. sold for $100,000 cash.

  b. sold for $40,000 cash and $60,000 promissory notes.

  c. exchanged for land worth $100,000.

  d. mortgaged for $75,000 cash. The cash was invested in the stock market.

  e. given to a daughter and her husband.

f. left to a church (a charitable organization) by will, at death.

g. converted to rental property.

h. exchanged for corporate stocks valued at $100,000.

3. David Byrd owns and manages a small motel on a lake in Minnesota. The motel has a basis of $70,000 and a fair market value of $200,000. Byrd would like to exchange the motel for similar property in Florida. Assuming he can find such a property and arrange an exchange

   a. from an accounting perspective has he realized a gain? How will he account for the exchange for his accounting records?

   b. from a tax perspective has he realized a gain? If so, do you believe he will be required to recognize it? Explain.

4. It has been suggested that homeowners should be required to include in gross income the rental value of their homes. What practical and theoretical arguments can be given against this proposal?

5. Farmer Brown raises fruits and vegetables. Does Brown realize income for tax purposes when he and his family consume part of the crop? Must he recognize the income (if any)?

6. Ellen has just been notified that she will receive $20,000 as a bequest from her former employer's estate. The will refers to Ellen's "years of faithful service and friendship." Does Ellen have income? Explain.

7. Biondi Construction Company was required to move its equipment to a new site after it learned that the old site was a toxic waste dump. Biondi sued the seller of the property, who did not reveal its former use. The seller agreed to buy the property back from Biondi for $30,000 (the same amount the company had paid for the property) and to pay $10,000 to cover the "cost and inconvenience" of relocating the equipment. Does Biondi have income? Explain.

8. AJ's marginal income tax rate is 28%.

   a. What rate must he earn on a taxable bond to make the after-tax return on the taxable bond equivalent to that on a tax-exempt bond yielding 6.5%?

   b. Regardless of your answer above, assume that AJ can purchase a taxable bond of equivalent risk yielding 8.5%. What is the implicit tax rate on the tax-exempt bond?

   c. Explain the relation between the implicit tax rate and the clientele for tax-exempt bonds.

CLASS PROJECTS

1. Aretha purchased an old trunk in a second hand store for $25. Upon careful inspection, she discovered a letter from Abraham Lincoln under the lining of the trunk lid. The letter has been appraised at a value of $50,000. Further, the trunk itself, which now appears to have belonged to Lincoln's wife, has been appraised at a value of $5,000. Does Aretha have taxable income? If so, how much? Your answer should include references to relevant Code section(s), administrative authority, and judicial authority.

2. Charles, an outstanding high school athlete, was actively courted by a number of colleges. In addition to scholarships, Charles was offered various other inducements to attend these colleges and play football. Most of these offers came from alumni of the schools involved. One individual gave Charles a $9,000 automobile before he made his decision. Charles eventually signed with another college. Does Charles have income equal to the value of the automobile? Your answer should include references to relevant Code section(s), administrative authority, and judicial authority.

The passage of the bill will mark the dawn of a brighter day, with more of sunshine, more of the songs of birds, more of that sweetest music, the laughter of children well fed, well clothed, well housed. Can we doubt that, in the brighter, happier days to come, good, even-headed, wholesome democracy shall be triumphant? God hasten the era of equality in taxation and in opportunity. And God prosper the Wilson bill, the first leaf in the glorious book of reform in taxation, the promise of a brightening future for those whose genius and labor create the wealth of the land, and whose courage and patriotism are the only sure bulwark in the defense of the Republic.

CONGRESSMAN DAVID A. DE ARMOND, CONGRESSIONAL RECORD (1894)

DEDUCTIONS: GENERAL CONCEPTS

CHAPTER OBJECTIVES

In Chapter 5 you are introduced to the income tax treatment of deductions, including the deduction of losses. To the extent possible, emphasis is placed on rules with general rather than specific application. In some instances, discussion of complex details is left to later chapters.

LEARNING GOALS

After studying this chapter, you should be able to

1 Distinguish between an expense for accounting purposes and a deduction for tax purposes;

2 Explain the general provision that authorizes most deductions related to the conduct of a trade or business;

3 Distinguish between a trade or business, an investment, and a hobby and deductions allowed for each;

4 Explain the general provision that allows deductions related to investment motivated transactions;

5 Identify and explain the most common positive and negative criteria that must be satisfied before a deduction can be taken for tax purposes;

6 Recognize some of the specific provisions that supplement or permit exceptions to the general deduction provision;

7 Understand that many deductions apparently allowed by general or specific rules may be disallowed or limited by other provisions;

8 Explain both what is meant by a loss and how the tax treatment of losses relates to deductions;

9 Define what a net operating loss is and explain how it is treated for tax purposes;

10 Explain the origin of the passive activity loss (PAL) limitations and, in general, understand how they operate to limit deductibility of PALs;

11 Explain how losses on the sale or exchange of capital assets are treated for tax purposes; and

12 Explain both how the amount of a casualty or theft loss is determined and how these losses are treated for tax purposes.

_____ DEDUCTIONS

As explained in Chapter 4, the income tax is levied against taxable income, a statutory and legalistic quantity determined by subtracting authorized deductions from gross income. Authorized deductions are spawned by such diverse forces as accounting concepts, common sense, tradition, politics, social justice, and administrative convenience, and they are as complex as the forces that created them. The advocates of new deductions inevitably forecast, as in the headnote to this chapter, the dawn of a new and better world if Congress will but grant their request.

> **Goal #1**
> Distinguish between accounting expenses and tax deductions.

The term *deductions,* as used in federal income taxation, can be defined procedurally as those items that collectively constitute the difference between the quantity called *gross income* and the quantity called *taxable income.* Two considerations implicit in this purely procedural definition are important. First, note that the two quantifications—gross income and taxable income—describe purely statutory concepts; outside the realm of federal income taxation, neither has any meaning. Second, it is a widely accepted notion in federal income taxation that *nothing is deductible unless it is authorized by the Code or the regulations.*

At this point, a well-grounded accounting student is apt to have serious misgivings. Income is a *net* concept, generally conceded to be the difference between properly matched revenues and expenses for a specified time period. Good accounting implies that all properly matched expenses must be deductions for purposes of determining taxable income. Ignoring possible differences in timing—that is, ignoring tax accounting refinements to the matching concept—the accounting student's intuition is only partially correct for matters of federal income taxation. In general, most of the items that fall into the accountant's expense classification are also deductions for tax purposes; however, the Code provides for many other deductions in the calculation of taxable income. The concept of a *deduction* is much broader, more generic and legalistic than the concept of an *expense* in accounting. This conclusion is especially true for the individual taxpayer and also has limited relevance for the corporate taxpayer.

The deductions allowed a corporate taxpayer generally are deemed to be business-related and are roughly comparable to the expenses that appear on the corporation's annual income statement prepared in accordance with generally accepted accounting principles. This generalization also applies to the computation of taxable income earned by a sole proprietorship or partnership. There are, however, numerous and major exceptions to this general rule. Some of these exceptions relate to differences in the timing of deductions; others involve definitional or permanent differences. In this chapter, we will examine some of the more important permanent differences between tax deductions and accounting expenses. In addition, we present an introductory discussion of the deductions granted to individual taxpayers. (See Part III for a detailed consideration of these deductions.) A detailed discussion of timing differences can be found in Chapter 6.

Allowable deductions may be grouped into three broad categories:

1. Deductions applicable to a trade or business, including an employee's business-related expenses;

2. Nonbusiness deductions related to investments and to the production of nonbusiness income; and

3. Purely personal deductions specifically provided for individual taxpayers.

THE BASIC AUTHORIZATION: THE REVENUE CODE

Before a taxpayer can deduct anything, the taxpayer must be able to cite some provision of the Code that authorizes the deduction. It is not necessary that the statute list the specific item by name, but the item to be deducted must clearly fall under one of the statutory provisions. A mere reading of the Code will not reveal whether an item is deductible because Treasury Regulations, revenue rulings, and court decisions constantly interpret the meaning of the statue.

The Code provides for a multitude of deductions for very dissimilar items including expenses, losses, and special items not necessarily involving monetary outlays. The deduction provisions can be usefully divided into two major categories—the general (or universal) provisions and the specific deduction authorizations.

The General Provisions

Two Code sections serve as a common authority for deductions: Sec. 162, Expenses of Carrying on a Trade or Business, and Sec. 212, Expenses for Production of Income. The former section applies equally to sole proprietorships, corporations, partnerships, and all other forms of business organization; the latter section applies only to individual taxpayers. The importance of these two generally applicable sections warrants a closer examination.

> **Goal #2**
> Explain the general provisions that allow trade or business deductions.

EXPENSES OF TRADE OR BUSINESS.   The broadest provision pertaining to deductions—and, incidentally, the provision that comes closest to approximating the expense concept in accounting—is located in Sec. 162(a), which reads in part as follows:

> (a) In General.—There shall be allowed as a deduction all the ordinary and necessary expenses paid or incurred during the taxable year in carrying on any **trade or business** [emphasis added], including—
> (1) a reasonable allowance for salaries or other compensation for personal services actually rendered;
> (2) traveling expenses (including amounts expended for meals and lodging other than amounts which are lavish or extravagant under the circumstances) while away from home in the pursuit of a trade or business; and
> (3) rentals or other payments required to be made as a condition to the continued use or possession, for purposes of the trade or business, of property to which the taxpayer has not taken or is not taking title or in which he has no equity.

> A **trade or business** is an activity involving substantial personal effort by a taxpayer with the intention of making a profit.

Although these apparently straightforward words may suggest that virtually every "business expenses" is deductible, an investigation of the interpretations tax administrators and courts give these words would not support such a simple conclusion. Among the words and phrases that have caused special problems in interpretation are ordinary, necessary, and trade or business.

The definitional boundary of a trade or business—of particular importance to the individual taxpayer since corporations generally are presumed to be engaged in a trade or business—is as elusive as the definitions of ordinary and necessary. The intention to make a profit is necessary; the actuality of a profit is not. Yet the intention to make a profit is not a sufficient condition for a trade or business. Many transactions and most business ventures are profit-oriented, yet they do not constitute a trade or business for tax purposes. A substantial personal effort of an entrepreneurial nature must exist on a continuing basis before an income-producing activity can be said to constitute a

> **Goal #3**
> Distinguish a trade or business from a hobby.

> A **hobby** is an activity conducted by a taxpayer more for personal enjoyment than for profit.

trade or business. A "holding out" of one's self to third parties has also been required in some cases. The distinction between a trade or business and a mere income-producing activity is particularly difficult to draw with respect to relatively passive investments in real estate, stocks, bonds, and other properties.

Another common problem arises in determining whether a particular venture constitutes a trade or business or a **hobby**. Many individual taxpayers, particularly those of financial means, enjoy expensive endeavors such as racing automobiles, breeding racehorses, and feeding beef cattle. Obviously, such endeavors may be either real business ventures or simply hobbies. When a taxpayer consistently reports losses, the tax administrators may suspect that the real motivation is purely personal enjoyment rather than a desire to conduct a profitable business. Whenever the IRS can prove its suspicions, a host of otherwise deductible expenses is lost. Section 183 limits the deductions attributable to hobbies to the amount of gross income from the hobby.

EXAMPLE 5-1

Anna, a school teacher, makes quilts in her spare time. Her quilting frame and other materials and supplies occupy a room in her house. This year, total expenses attributable to the quilt making were $3,000; gross revenues from the sale of quilts was $1,800. If the activity is deemed to be a hobby, Anna can deduct no more than $1,800 of her expenses. Further, Sec. 183 specifies that she must first deduct amounts that would be deductible without regard to the hobby (such as home mortgage interest); second, out-of-pocket expenses (such as materials and supplies); and third, depreciation of fixed assets used in the hobby (such as her quilting frame). As we will learn in Chapter 10, the rules for itemized deductions may further limit amounts deductible with respect to a hobby.

The determination of whether an activity is a trade or a business or a hobby has often been adjudicated. The Regulations[1] list a number of a relevant factors that must be considered, including

1. the manner in which the taxpayer carries on the activity,

2. the taxpayer's expertise,

3. the time and effort expended by the taxpayer in carrying on the activity,

4. the expectation that the assets used in the business may increase in value,

5. the success of the taxpayer in carrying on similar activities,

6. the taxpayer's history of losses with respect to the activity,

7. the amount of occasional profits, if any, that are earned from the activity,

8. the amount of income from other sources, and

9. elements of personal pleasure or recreation from the activity.

All of these facts and circumstances are to be taken into account. If a clear determination cannot be made based on these factors, according to Sec. 183(d), an activity will

---

1 Reg. Sec. 1.183-1(b).

be *presumed* to be engaged in for profit if gross income exceeds related expenses for three or more out of five consecutive years (two out of seven years if the activity is horsebreeding, racing, showing, or training). This presumption is important to the taxpayer because it shifts to the IRS the burden of proving that the activity is not profit motivated if the three-of-five-year test is satisfied. Otherwise, the burden of proof belongs to the taxpayer.

A few **employee business expenses** also are deductible under Sec. 162, because being an employee is considered to be a trade or business. Generally, before deducting expenses for tax purposes, an employee must demonstrate that any expenses deducted are *directly* related to the performance of duties or are required by an employment agreement. Nonreimbursed costs of special clothing not suitable for off-duty wear, union dues, tools of trade, and membership dues in professional organizations are examples of deductible employee business expenses. Travel, transportation, and entertainment also are common employee business expenses.

The difficulty in this area of the law lies in the many arbitrary distinctions between what constitutes a direct cost of earning income and what constitutes a personal expense. It might be argued, for example, that every person employed outside the home incurs extra costs because of his or her job. The cost of commuting to work, the extra expense incurred in eating restaurant meals, the additional costs of wearing appropriate clothing and of personal grooming all result from the taxpayer's employment, but they are all considered to be nondeductible expenses. The distinction between business-related expenses and nondeductible personal expenditures is examined in greater detail in Part Three.

EXPENSES FOR PRODUCTION OF INCOME. As already noted, many business-oriented activities do not qualify as a full-fledged trade or business for tax purposes. Until the Revenue Act of 1942, taxpayers frequently were denied deductions for expenses related to income-producing activities because they did not qualify as a trade or business. In 1941, for example, the Supreme Court found that expenses incurred by a wealthy taxpayer to maintain an office for the purpose of managing his securities and real estate were not those of a trade or business and were, therefore, nondeductible personal expenses.[2] Following this decision, Congress enacted the first two paragraphs of the current Sec. 212. (The third paragraph, relating to deduction of expenses related to taxes, was added by the Revenue Act of 1954.) The section currently reads as follows:

> Sec. 212. Expenses for Production of Income.
> In the case of an individual, there shall be allowed as a deduction all the ordinary and necessary expenses paid or incurred during the taxable year—
> (1) for the production or collection of income;
> (2) for the management, conservation, or maintenance of the property held for the production of income; or
> (3) in connection with the determination, collection, or refund of any tax.

This section makes many income-related expenses deductible for individual taxpayers even though those expenses are not incurred in a trade or business. For example, an expense attributable to a single rental property may not be deductible under Sec. 162 because such limited rental activity may not constitute a trade or business. Nevertheless, Sec. 212(2) authorizes a deduction for the expenses incurred in connection with

Employee business expenses are directly related to an employee's performance of duties or are expenses required by the employment agreement.

Goal #4
Explain the general provisions that allow deductions related to investment transactions.

---

2 *Higgins v. Com'mr.*, 312 US 212 (1941).

that property. The Regulations help delineate what is meant by "production of income."

> The term "income" for the purpose of section 212 includes not merely income of the taxable year but also income which the taxpayer has realized in a prior taxable year or may realize in subsequent taxable years; and is not confined to recurring income but applies as well to gains from the disposition of property. For example, if defaulted bonds, the interest from which if received would be includible in income, are purchased with the expectation of realizing capital gain on their resale, even though no current yield thereon is anticipated, ordinary and necessary expenses thereafter paid or incurred in connection with such bonds are deductible. Similarly, ordinary and necessary expenses paid or incurred in the management, conservation, or maintenance of a building devoted to rental purposes are deductible notwithstanding that there is actually no income therefrom in the taxable year, and regardless of the manner in which or the purpose for which the property in question was acquired. Expenses paid or incurred in managing, conserving, or maintaining property held for investment may be deductible under section 212 even though the property is not currently productive and there is no likelihood that the property will be sold at a profit or will otherwise be productive of income and even though the property is held merely to minimize a loss with respect thereto . . . .[3]

Section 212 is the primary authority for the deduction of such expenses as safety deposit box rental and investment counsel fees that relate to investments in securities. Many other expenses associated with property ownership and with other activities intended to produce income are also deductible under Sec. 212. In determining whether any of these expenses are deductible, the major consideration is whether they relate to an activity entered into with the hope of making profit or merely engaged in for personal reasons.

Goal #5
Identify and explain the positive and negative criteria for deductions.

GENERAL PROVISIONS: POSITIVE CRITERIA. In both Secs. 162 and 212, the terms **ordinary expense** and **necessary expense** are used. In addition, Sec. 162 contains a "reasonableness" test. The meanings of these three terms in income taxation differ somewhat from customary usage. An expense need not recur frequently to be *ordinary*. In fact, an expenditure may be labeled an ordinary expense for tax purposes if no more than, say, one in 100 taxpayers even incurs the expense and if he or she incurs it only once in a lifetime. The essence of the ordinary criterion seems to be that it would be commonplace among other taxpayers who find themselves in comparable circumstances even if the "comparable circumstances" are indeed extraordinary, In *Welch v. Helvering* the Court, struggling with the meaning of the word ordinary, said that the "decisive distinctions are those of degree and not of kind. One struggles in vain for any verbal formula that will supply a ready touchstone. The standard set up by the statute is not a rule of law; it is rather a way of life. Life in all its fullness must supply the answer to the riddle."[4]

An **ordinary expense** is one that would be commonplace for other taxpayers in similar circumstances.

A **necessary expense** is one that is capable of making a contribution to the profitability of a trade or business or income-producing activity.

To be *necessary,* an expense must be capable of making a contribution to a trade or business. Fortunately for the taxpayer, the courts and tax administrators do not insist that necessity be determined on an *ex post* basis; it is sufficient if the expense appeared to be necessary when it was incurred. The courts generally do not second-guess taxpayers on the necessity of making expenditures. As a practical matter this

3 Reg. Sec.1.212-1(b).

4 290 US 111 (1933), pp. 114–15.

positive criterion is probably the least significant of the three considered here. When invoked in the past, it frequently related to illegal activities. For example, fines paid for overweight trucks were found to be unnecessary and to frustrate public policy, and therefore to be nondeductible.[5] In more recent years other Code provisions have been enacted to deal specifically with illegal acts and, therefore, the relative importance of the necessary test has declined.

Even an ordinary and necessary expense incurred in a trade or business or in connection with the production of income must be *reasonable in amount* before it can be deducted for tax purposes. Technically, this requirement is stated in Sec. 162(a)(1) only in relation to compensation, but the courts have found that "the element of reasonableness was inherent in the phrase 'ordinary and necessary.' "[6] The **reasonableness criterion** is most frequently important for related taxpayers. For example, a corporation may attempt to pay its sole stockholder–employee (or his or her children) an unreasonably large salary, interest, or rental payment. If allowed, these expenses could disguise payments that in reality are dividends—a result of particular tax importance since dividends, unlike business expenses, are not deductible to the corporation paying them. Therefore, the IRS constantly screens transactions between related parties to determine their reasonableness.

> Under the **reasonableness criterion**, an expense is reasonable if the same amount would have been paid to an unrelated party.

GENERAL PROVISIONS: NEGATIVE CRITERIA.   In addition to the three positive criteria, four negative criteria must also be satisfied before any unspecified expense may be deductible. Any expense or loss not specifically authorized as a deduction is disallowed if it is *purely personal, a capital expenditure, related to tax-exempt income, or contrary to public policy.* The Code sections pertaining to nondeductible expenses and losses include

Sec. 262. Personal, living, and family expenses.
Sec. 263. Capital expenditures.
Sec. 265. Expenses and interest relating to tax-exempt income.
Sec. 162. Expenses contrary to public policy. (See Sec. 162 (e), (f), and (g).)

Other Code provisions prohibit specific expenses such as selected taxes (Sec. 275) both direct and indirect contributions to political parties (Sec. 276). As explained earlier, our concern at this point in this textbook is limited to the provisions of general application.

Personal, living, and family expenses.   Section 262 states that "except as otherwise expressly provided in this chapter, no deduction shall be allowed for personal, living, or family expenses." All personal expenditures incurred without any intention of profit are thus categorically disallowed unless some section of the law specifically provides for their deduction. In fact, other provisions of the Code specifically allow deduction of a number of purely personal expenses. Some of these deductions can be classified as large, unusual, involuntary personal expenditures. Examples are medical expenses and casualty losses above certain threshold amounts. Others can be classified as subsidies of specific groups. Examples are charitable contributions and home mortgage interest. Still others cannot be easily classified (state income taxes, for example).

---

5 *Hoover Motor Express Co., Inc. v. United States,* 356 US 38 (1958).

6 *Com'mr. v. Lincoln Electric Co.,* 176 F.2d 815 (CA-6, 1949), p. 815.

Itemized deductions are a set of deductions allowed individual taxpayers even though many are personal in nature.

A **standard deduction** amount is allowed individual taxpayers in lieu of "itemizing" deductions.

Individual taxpayers are permitted by specific provisions in the Code to deduct these and many other expenditures as **itemized deductions**. Alternatively, individuals are permitted to deduct a **standard deduction** if the allowed amount is larger than the total of itemized deductions. The amount of the standard deduction depends on the taxpayer's marital status, age, and certain other factors. For example, in 1992, the amounts are $6,000 for a married couple filing jointly and $3,600 for a single person. These amount are adjusted for inflation each year.

EXAMPLE 5-2

Cora, a single person with itemized deductions for taxes, contributions, and interest of only $920 would be able to deduct the larger standard deduction in lieu of itemizing. On the other hand, Ben, a single person with actual itemized deductions of $8,000, could deduct that amount.

In addition, to being allowed to deduct various personal expenditures, individual taxpayers also are allowed to deduct *personal and dependent exemption amounts*. Conceptually, these exemptions permit a basic tax-free living allowance for individual taxpayers. The number of exemptions an individual may claim depends on the taxpayer's family situation and other factors explained in Chapter 10. The amount deductible for each exemption changes as the price level changes. For 1992, the amount is $2,300.

As just illustrated, there are many exceptions to Sec. 262's prohibition on the deduction of "personal, living, and family expenses." The point is the taxpayer must find *specific* statutory authority for the deduction of items that are personal in nature. Frequently, the taxpayer and the IRS disagree as to whether an item is personal or business in nature.

Capital outlays or expenditures create or increase the value of assets. These costs may be deducted later through depreciation or other cost-recovery techniques.

Capital outlays.   **Capital outlays** are defined as those expenditures that must be charged, at least temporarily, to an asset account before they can be deducted. Section 263(a) states that

No deduction shall be allowed for —
(1) any amount paid out for new buildings or for permanent improvements or betterments made to increase the value of any property or estate . . . . [or]
(2) any amount expended in restoring property or in making good the exhaustion thereof for which an allowance is or has been made.

Omitted portions of Sec. 263 recognize that still other Code provisions sometimes specifically authorize the immediate deduction of certain expenditures that ordinarily would be classified as capital expenditures and sometimes require capitalization of specific items. Any student acquainted with financial accounting is aware of the practical difficulties in determining whether an expenditure is a capital expenditure or an expense. In general, the tax solutions to such riddles parallel the accounting solutions; therefore, we present no detailed consideration of them here.

However, the mere fact that a capital outlay is not deductible at the time of the outlay does not prevent its recovery (as a deduction against income) at a later date through depreciation, amortization, depletion, or some other cost-recovery technique. These possibilities are discussed in Part Four.

Expenses related to tax-exempt income. Section 265 disallows a deduction for interest or any other expense that is paid or incurred in order to realize tax-exempt income. This provision closes a loophole that would otherwise exist for persons in high marginal tax brackets. Without this provision a person in a top bracket might, because of income taxation, actually obtain a positive cash flow by borrowing high-interest money and investing it in low-interest state or local obligations.

EXAMPLE 5-3

To illustrate, assume that Zelda, a taxpayer in the 28% marginal tax bracket, borrowed $1 million at 12% and invested the proceeds in a 10% state bond issue. The annual interest expense would amount to $120,000 which, without Sec. 265, might reduce Zelda's tax lability by $33,600 (28% of $120,000). The tax-exempt interest earned on the state bonds would amount to $100,000, producing a net positive cash flow of $13,600 per year (that is, $100,000 + $33,600 – $120,000). As stated above, Sec 265 prevents this kind of tax legerdemain.

Expenses contrary to public policy. Prior to 1969 no statutory authority specifically disallowed such expenses as bribes, kickbacks, and fines. Nevertheless, the courts frequently disallowed such expenses on the grounds that they were not necessary and that allowing their deduction would frustrate public policy. Taxpayers frequently had to litigate to determine whether various items were contrary to public policy. Now, Sec. 162 specifies several types of expenditures that controvert public policy and specifically are disallowed. That list includes

1. Fines or penalties for violation of law. (Sec. 162(f))
2. A portion (usually two thirds) of treble damages paid under antitrust laws in criminal proceedings. (Sec. 162(g))
3. Illegal bribes or kickbacks paid to public officials. (Sec 162(c)(1))
4. Payments such as kickbacks and bribes other than to government officials and employees if such payments are illegal under any generally enforced United States or state law providing for a criminal penalty or loss of license or privilege to engage in trade or business. (Sec. 162(c)(2))
5. Any kickback, rebate, or bribe, under medicare or medicaid. (Sec. 162(c)(3))

Kickbacks, bribes, and similar payments, other than those specified above, may still be deductible if they are commonly paid and there is no general effort to stop them. Payments to foreign government officials are not deductible if such payments violate U.S. laws.

Section 162(e) authorizes a taxpayer to deduct what are generally called lobbying expenses—the costs incurred in connection with appearances before congressional committees or in communicating with individual members of Congress about proposed legislation. That provision does not, however, extend to costs incurred in a political campaign or in attempts to influence the general public on political matters. The latter costs remain nondeductible expenses.

These provisions buried in subsections of Sec. 162 do not solve all the questions involving public policy. The boundaries of the general prohibition are difficult to specify because courts have consistently held that expenses are deductible even if the income the expense produces is illegal. For example, the expenses incurred by a gambler are deductible for tax purposes even if the gambler operates in a state that prohibits gambling. This is equitable because illegal income is fully taxable. On the other hand, the granting of deductions makes the activity more profitable (after taxes) and to that extent serves to controvert laws of the state. However, Congress draws the line with regard to trafficking in illegal drugs. Expenses related to these activities are not deductible.[7]

In summary, an expense is ordinarily deductible in the computation of taxable income if it either is authorized by a specific Code section or satisfies each of eight general criteria. An unspecified expense may be deducted if it is

1. ordinary;

2. necessary;

3. reasonable in amount; and

4. incurred in connection with trade or business or in the production of income

and if it is *not*

5. a capital expenditure;

6. a personal expenditure;

7. related to tax-exempt income; or

8. contrary to public policy.

Goal #6
Recognize some specific provisions that allow deductions.

The Specific Provisions

In addition to the general provisions Sec. 162 and Sec. 212, Part VI of Subchapter B authorizes almost 30 specific deductions in Secs. 163–191. Some of these provisions are of near universal importance; for example,

Sec. 163	Interest.
Sec. 164	Taxes.
Sec. 167	Depreciation.
Sec. 168	Accelerated cost recovery systems.
Sec. 170	Charitable, etc., contributions and gifts.

On the other hand, some sections apply to very few taxpayers; for example,

Sec. 184	Amortization of certain railroad rolling stock.
Sec. 186	Recoveries of damages for antitrust violations, etc.
Sec. 188	Amortization of certain expenditures for child-care facilities.
Sec. 192	Contribution to Black Lung Benefit Trust.

Most deductions are roughly comparable to the expenses appearing on published financial statements. On the surface there is little problem in determining either the nature or the amounts of many items that may be deducted as business expenses. Unfortunately for the student, this general observation is not always true. A detailed examination of each section in Part VI of Subchapter B would yield a lengthy list of exceptions, exceptions to exceptions, limitations, and special definitions. Some of the

---

7 Sec. 280E.

limiting provisions are examined in detail; others are examined in subsequent chapters of this text, and still others are not discussed because of their limited application.

LIMITS ON DEDUCTIONS

Section 162 states that there "shall be allowed as a deduction *all* the ordinary and necessary expenses paid or incurred . . . in carrying on a trade or business." Section 212 provides that *all* ordinary and necessary expenses related to nonbusiness income shall be deductible. One should not be misled by this all-inclusive language. Some expenses, even though they are incurred in trade or business, are disallowed in whole or in part by other provisions. In addition, many special limitations are placed on the deduction of losses. These limitations are discussed later in this chapter.

Goal #7
Recognize some provisions that limit or disallow deductions.

Limitations on Specific Deductions

Both the Code and the Regulations place limits on the amounts that may be deducted for certain items. These limitations in effect specify the maximum amount considered ordinary and reasonable. Four examples follow. Additional details are found in later chapters.

1. Corporate taxpayers may deduct charitable contributions only to the extent of 10% of taxable income determined before the contributions deduction and certain other deductions.

EXAMPLE 5-4

If Z corporation had taxable income of $100,000 before deducting charitable contributions and during the year Z made charitable contributions of $25,000, Z would be allowed a contributions deduction of $10,000 for the year. Z could carry forward the $15,000 excess to the five succeeding years and treat it as contributions made in those years.

2. Deductions by employers for contributions paid to employee pension and profit-sharing plans are generally limited to 15% of salaries and other compensation paid to "covered employees" during the year.

EXAMPLE 5-5

If X corporation paid covered compensation of $1,000,000 during a year and made contributions of $200,000 to a profit-sharing plan, only $150,000 would ordinarily be deductible by X. The remaining $50,000 could be carried over and added to X's contributions made in the succeeding year. There is no limit on the number of years that such excesses can be carried forward.

3. Generally only 80% of business-meal and business-entertainment expenses are deductible. This includes the cost of meals furnished by an employer to employees on the employer's premises as well as costs of meals for employees traveling away from home. The 20% disallowed is never deductible.

4. A limit is placed on the amount of investment interest that can be deducted by a noncorporate taxpayer. For our purpose, **investment interest** can be defined as interest on monies borrowed to fund all income-producing activities of the taxpayer

Investment interest is paid or incurred on loans used to acquire or maintain investment properties.

that (1) are not subject to the passive-activity loss limitation and (2) are not directly related to trade or business activities in which the taxpayer materially participates. The deductible investment interest is limited to the amount of net investment income (income from investments to which the investment interest limitations applies, minus deductible expenses related to that income).

EXAMPLE 5-6

If Ken Mayer paid investment interest of $45,000 and had net investment income (disregarding interest paid or accrued) of $9,000, only $9,000 would be deductible. Ken would be allowed to carry forward the disallowed interest of $36,000 and treat it as investment interest incurred in subsequent years.

Carryover of Disallowed Deductions

Most of the limitations imposed on specific deductions provide that amounts not deductible in one taxable year can be carried forward (or, in a few instances, back) to other years and deducted in those years. Sometimes the disallowed amounts can be carried to an indefinite number of future years. In other cases there is a limit on the number of years to which the item can be carried; if the amount carried over cannot be fully deducted during that limited carryover period, any unused amount simply expires.

For example, in the preceding discussion of limitations and disallowances of deductions we saw that charitable contributions made by corporations in excess of the amount deductible in a tax year may be carried forward for five years; if the carryover cannot be deducted in that time, the unused amount expires. On the other hand, there is no limit on the number of years that disallowed investment interest on excess contributions to a profit-sharing plan may be carried forward.

<table>
<tr><td>

Goal #8
Explain the relation between losses and deductions.

</td></tr>
</table>

_____ LOSSES

Losses may arise because of one of two disparate circumstances. Some losses occur because a business venture fails to yield expected results for reasons largely beyond the taxpayer's control. Other losses occur simply because of a decline in the value of property. The correct tax treatment of the former losses seems to be a logical extension of the ideas introduced earlier in this chapter regarding the treatment of deductions. The correct tax treatment of the latter losses could be viewed conceptually as a logical extension of Chapter 4 (Income: General Concepts) or also of the treatment of deductions. In other words, at least in theory, some losses could be defined either (1) as negative income (translate, a decrease in net worth during period of time) or (2) as a possible deduction.

The tax implications of this fundamental distinction are both subtle and significant. To the extent that losses are simply negative income, they automatically reduce income (the positive element in the tax measurement process) by definition. On the other hand, to the extent that losses are a deduction (the negative element in the tax measurement process), they are a matter of legislative grace and may be narrowly constrained by the law.

To illustrate the significance of the distinction, return for a moment to a basic concept introduced in Chapter 4. There we learned that

1. (Fact 1) A taxpayer pays $10 for a property;

2. (Fact 2) The property increases in value over time from $10 to $14; and

3. (Fact 3) The taxpayer exchanges the first property for either a second property or a service;

4. (Conclusion) For tax purposes, the taxpayer is attributed with a $4 income deemed to be realized and immediately recognized, absent some special Code provision to the contrary.

Now change the scenario in regard to Fact 2 only and allow the property to decline in value from $10 to $6. Under the revised facts, does this taxpayer experience $4 of negative income (that will automatically decrease positive income) or must the taxpayer search the Code to determine whether or not the $4 loss can be deducted in the calculation of taxable income?

The answer to this problem in logic is made clear in the U.S. Internal Revenue Code. All losses are categorized as deductions regardless of how they are derived. Consequently, losses can be defined and interpreted as a special set of the more general deduction rules introduced earlier in this chapter. Over the years, Congress has enacted many provisions for the explicit purpose of minimizing the deduction of losses. Many of these provisions overlap, and the Code frequently gives the taxpayer no advice to determine in what order the loss rules should be applied or how one loss limit might modify another.

The loss provisions have, for all practical purposes shifted the United States from a unitary tax system to a **schedular tax system**. Even though the government claims to tax all income, from whatever source derived, in exactly the same manner as all other income, because of the various loss limitation rules, some income may be treated in a very different manner from other income earned in the same tax year by the same taxpayer.

In this chapter we introduce four of the most significant statutory provisions involving loss deductions. These are Sec. 172, which authorizes a net operating loss (NOL) deduction; Sec. 469, which limits passive activity losses (PALs); Sec. 1211, which restricts the amount of net capital loss that taxpayers may deduct; and Sec. 165, which authorizes the deduction of most business losses, but forbids the deduction of personal losses except for casualties and thefts.

NET OPERATING LOSSES

A progressive tax rate structure, together with annual tax intervals, can sometimes mean that those with steady income streams will pay less taxes overall than those with wildly fluctuating incomes. The ability to pay taxes, in an ideal sense, is best measured over a span of years rather than within the artificial constraint of a yearly time interval. In addition, risk taking may be dampened by a tax system in which the government shares in profitable years but not in lean years. With these considerations in mind, Congress enacted a provision in 1918 allowing net operating losses to be carried back or forward one year and offset against profits in those two years.

The **net operating loss (NOL)** provision has been modified many times since 1918. The most severe modification involved outright repeal of the provision in the 1930s when rampant business losses threatened the flow of tax revenue to the federal government. The **NOL deduction** was reinstated in 1952. Since 1981, a taxpayer has been allowed to spread an NOL deduction over a total of up to 18 other years (3 years back and 15 years forward).

Goal #9
Explain the treatment of net operating losses.

A **schedular tax system** is one in which different types of income are taxed at different rates whereas in a unitary, or global system, all income is subject to the same rate schedule.

A **net operating loss (NOL)** is negative taxable income adjusted to reflect the real economic loss from a trade or business.

An **NOL deduction** is the amount of a net operating loss that a taxpayer is permitted to deduct against income recognized in other years.

The actual NOL deduction eligible to be carried back or forward is restricted in two important ways. First, rather than the negative total at the bottom of the tax return, the deduction is limited to an amount meant to reflect the real economic loss incurred in a genuine trade or business for the year. For individuals, this means the NOL deduction will not be increased by deductions unrelated to the trade or business loss of the taxpayer. Deductions such as capital losses from investments, personal and dependent exemption deductions, and other nonbusiness deductions are disallowed to the extent they exceed nonbusiness income. Other special rules apply to certain taxpayers (for example, regulated transportation corporations, real estate investment trusts, and bank cooperatives) and to certain types of losses (for example, product liability losses and bad debt losses of commercial banks).

A second important restriction involves the continuity of a corporate entity utilizing an NOL deduction. Congress does not like the idea that the most valuable asset a defunct business might have to sell is a whopping NOL carryover. To prevent the purchase and sale of defunct corporate shells for their large NOLs, numerous restrictions have been added over the years. The most important of these restrictions is a limitation on the amount of income that may be offset in any year by an NOL deduction if an ownership change of 50% or more occurred in the prior three years.

Congress has specified an exact sequence for the carryover of an NOL. Unless the taxpayer elects to forgo the carryback, the NOL is carried back and deducted from any taxable income reported in the third prior year, then the second prior year, and then the prior year, in that order. Any remaining NOL is then carried forward up to 15 years. A carryback generally is advantageous because the taxpayer is eligible for an immediate refund of all income tax paid in the three prior years if the NOL deduction is greater than the taxable income reported during those three years.

EXAMPLE 5-7

A 1993 NOL would first be carried back and used as a deduction to offset 1990 taxable income, generating a refund for taxes paid in that year. If the NOL is greater than the taxable income reported in 1990, any excess is carried to 1991, and then, if need be, to 1992. If the NOL still is not exhausted, it is carried forward to 1994, then 1995, and so on, up to 2008.

Goal #10
Explain the origin of the passive activity loss limitations and how they operate.

Multiple NOLs follow the same carryover scheme and use a FIFO (first in, first out) basis for calculating the sequence in which NOLs are offset against taxable income. This scheme is most favorable to the taxpayer because it helps to protect the oldest NOLs from expiring. The computational complexities of the NOL deduction for individual taxpayers are too detailed for discussion here.

PASSIVE ACTIVITIES AND THE PASSIVE LOSS LIMITS

A **tax shelter** is an investment or activity that produces tax losses that can be used to offset other sources of taxable income.

To understand the provisions of Sec. 469, which limit the deductibility of passive activity losses, it is helpful to understand the tax milieu that existed in the United States prior to 1986. At that time, some individuals who earned relatively high incomes managed legally to pay little or no income tax largely because of opportunities to invest in a **tax shelter.** These investments, which were aggressively promoted between approximately 1960 and 1985, were characterized by a combination of four basic ingredients, namely

1. Mismatching of gross income and deductions, with expenses deducted earlier or income recognized later than under generally accepted accounting rules;

2. Use of one or more preferential tax provisions (tax preferences);

3. Use of a business form (partnership, for example) that allowed tax losses to flow through to the owners' personal tax returns; and

4. The opportunity to use leverage, that is, to borrow some part of the amount needed to make the investment.

In most cases the taxpayer had no personal involvement in the activity that produced the tax losses but was instead a passive investor.

A typical tax shelter investment allowed the individual taxpayer to offset operating losses from an investment against income earned from other sources, such as salary or interest. The popularity of tax shelters grew until the **passive activity loss (PAL)** provisions were enacted in 1986. These provision, plus the repeal of many of the tax preferences that made the tax shelters possible, have all but eliminated the tax shelter investment industry in the United States.

The most important factor in the demise of the tax shelter industry was the enactment of Sec. 469. It provides that most non-corporate taxpayers cannot offset passive activity losses (PALs) against income from either active or portfolio sources. Instead, PALs can be offset only against passive activity income. Any disallowed (suspended) PALs can be carried forward indefinitely and offset against passive activity income in future years. A simple example will illustrate the operation of Sec. 469.

> A **passive activity loss (PAL)** is a loss arising from a business activity in which the taxpayer does not materially participate.

EXAMPLE 5-8

Anh Ho has three sources of income:

Activity 1	$250,000	income
Activity 2	50,000	loss
Activity 3	100,000	loss

Depending on the correct classification of the three activities, Anh may have taxable income of

$100,000	($250,000 – $50,000 - $100,000);
$150,000	($250,000 – $100,00);
$200,000	($250,000 – $50,000); or
$250,000	($250,000 – $0).

Obviously, Anh would prefer that neither Activity 2 nor Activity 3 be classified as a PAL unless the income from Activity 1 is also from a passive activity.

As Example 5-8 illustrates, the definition of a passive activity is critical to understanding this provision. Section 469(c)(1) defines a passive activity as

> any activity—(A) which involves the conduct of any trade or business and (B) in which the taxpayer does not materially participate.

Emphasis is on the individual's level of participation in the activity. Thus, a partner who does not materially participate in an active trade or business conducted by a partnership is considered a passive investor. Material participation is in turn defined in Sec. 469(h)(1) as *regular, continuous,* and *substantial* involvement in the activity. Lengthy regulations provided by the Treasury Department attempt to explain just what these terms mean. For example, more than 500 hours of participation in an activity in one year is considered material. On the other hand, limited partners are automatically treated as non-material participants.

Because the rules of Sec. 469 were considered somewhat unfair to individuals who were encouraged by pre-1987 tax law to invest in real estate, Sec. 469(i) allows deduction of up to $25,000 of real estate losses by some individuals who "actively participate" in real estate activity. A more detailed discussion of this and other complexities of Sec. 469 is deferred to Chapter 19.

CAPITAL LOSSES

Goal #11
Explain how capital losses are treated for tax purposes.

Prior to 1987 the United States, for many years, gave very preferential tax treatment to any income that could be reported as net long-term capital gain. Although the statutory provisions that resulted in preferential treatment were repealed in 1986, the old ordinary-versus-capital classification was retained "to facilitate reinstatement of a long-term capital gains rate differential. . . ."[8] A recurring theme of the Bush administration has been reinstatement of preferential tax treatment for long-term capital gains. In 1990 Congress enacted a slight capital gains rate differential for years after 1990. The Act provides a top statutory marginal tax rate on individual taxpayers' **net capital gains** of 28% whereas other income (ordinary income) is subject to a maximum statutory rate of 31%. Corporate capital gains do not receive preferential treatment. However, corporations, like individuals, must separate capital gains and losses from ordinary gains and losses.

Net capital gains are the excess of net long-term capital gains over net short-term capital losses.

A **net capital loss** is an excess of capital losses over capital gains.

An **ordinary loss** is any non-capital loss.

Capital assets are defined in Sec. 1221 as all assets *except* designated assets including inventory, trade receivables, real estate or depreciable property used in a trade or business, and a few other assets.

Aside from the slight preferential treatment afforded net capital gains for individuals, a more important reason for the separate accounting for capital gains and losses is because a **net capital loss** is treated much less favorably than an **ordinary loss.** The most significant difference is that net capital losses generally cannot be offset against ordinary income. Individuals and fiduciaries can deduct net capital losses of up to $3,000 per year against ordinary income. Corporations cannot deduct capital losses against ordinary income at all but carry them back three years and forward five years to offset capital gains in those years.

The reason for limiting the deductibility of capital losses is to avoid what is sometimes called the cherry-picking problem.[9] To illustrate the problem, assume that a taxpayer holds a portfolio of **capital assets,** some of which have increased in value and others that have decreased in value. As explained in Chapter 4, realization must occur in order for the taxpayer to experience any tax consequences from these gains and losses. In such a tax regime, without loss limitation rules, taxpayers could sell depreciated capital assets in order to reduce current taxes while deferring the sale of appreciated capital assets. Current rules encourage the sale of some appreciated capital assets at the same time that depreciated assets are sold since capital losses can be offset in full against capital gains. Unfortunately, the rules provide little relief for taxpayers with large capital losses and no appreciated capital assets.

8 Staff of the Joint Committee on Taxation, *General Explanation of the Tax Reform Act of 1986,* (U.S. Government Printing Office), May 4, 1987, p.179.

9 For a discussion of this topic, see Martin D. Ginsburg, "Income Tax Complexity: Capital Gain and Loss Issues," in *Proceedings of the Invitational Conference on Reduction of Income Tax Complexity* ed. Silvia A. Madeo (AICPA and American Bar Association Section of Taxation, 1990), pp. I-V-4.

EXAMPLE 5-9

> James Campbell has just sold shares of stock in a savings and loan company at a loss of $50,000. Unfortunately, James owns no capital assets that have appreciated in value. He may deduct $3,000 of his loss against other sources of income this year and must carry the remaining $47,000 forward to be offset against income in future years. Had James owned any appreciated capital assets, he could have sold them this year and offset the resulting capital gain against his $50,000 capital loss.

As suggested in the introduction to this section, both passive loss limits and the capital loss limits may apply simultaneously.

EXAMPLE 5-10

> Assume that a single passive activity generates $20,000 of ordinary income and a $25,000 capital loss. Sec. 469 would allow deduction of $20,000 of the capital loss but require suspension of $5,000 because of the passive loss rules. The capital loss limitations, however, allow deduction of only $3,000 of the $25,000 capital loss (assuming no other capital gains and losses). Therefore the taxpayer would report $20,000 of passive income, a $3,000 capital loss, and carry forward $22,000 of the capital loss.

Thus, the passive loss rules may act as an added constraint, and they never mitigate the impact of the capital loss limit.

CASUALTY AND THEFT LOSSES

As explained earlier in this chapter, Sec. 262 denies deduction of purely personal expenses. In general, this prohibition extends to personal losses as well as to expenses. The only type of personal loss that can be deducted is for casualty or theft losses of the taxpayer's property.

In this section, we examine the general provisions controlling casualty and theft loss deductions and explore some common definitional and computational problems. In addition, the tax treatment of personal versus business casualty and theft losses is distinguished.

> **Goal #12**
> Explain how the amount of a casualty or theft loss is determined and how these losses are treated for tax purposes.

General Provisions for Deduction of Casualty and Theft Losses

Section 165(a) permits the deduction of losses sustained during the year to the extent of any amount "not compensated for by insurance or otherwise" if the loss is incurred in a trade or business or in a transaction entered into for profit. In addition, a deduction of losses of property not related to trade or business has been allowed since 1913 if the loss results from fire, storm, or shipwreck. In 1916, this deduction was extended to include losses from "other casualties, or from theft." Today, for individual taxpayers Sec. 165(c)(3) provides for the deduction of unreimbursed losses, as follows:

> (c) Limitation on Losses of Individuals—. In the case of an individual, the deduction under subsection (a) shall be limited to—
>> (1) losses incurred in a trade or business;

(2) losses incurred in any transaction entered into for profit, though not connected with a trade or business; and

(3) except as provided in subsection (h), losses of property not connected with a trade or business, if such losses arise from fire, storm, shipwreck, or other casualty, or from theft.

Subsection 165(h) contains the specific rules relating to personal casualty and theft losses. These rules will be discussed in Chapter 10 along with other personal deductions.

The deductions for losses of personal use property is intended to provide tax relief to taxpayers suffering unusual, involuntary losses large enough "to have a significant effect upon an individual's ability to pay Federal income taxes."[10] Generally, property held by a corporation is deemed to be used either in a trade or business or acquired as the result of a transaction entered into for a profit. Thus, for a corporation, losses on such property come under the general loss recognition rules of Sec. 165(a).

DEFINING CASUALTY *AND* THEFT. Subsection 165(c) specifically includes "fire, storm, or shipwreck" in the definition of casualties, and it provides for the general inclusion of "other casualties." However, "other casualties" are not identified, and it is often difficult to determine if loss of property resulting from a particular event constitutes a casualty for tax purposes. In general, the law requires a sudden, unexpected, or unusual event as well as an external force before a given event can be considered a casualty. Thus, losses caused by vandalism, car and boat accidents, earth slides, hurricanes, and sonic booms are deductible. No deduction is allowed for breakage of china, glassware, furniture, and similar items under normal conditions, apparently because these involve no external force. Tax deductions have also been disallowed for damage due to rust, corrosion, termites (although some courts have allowed deductions for termite damage), insects, disease, and other destructive forces, apparently because they do not involve a sudden event. Because of the imprecision of the general criteria pertinent to the determination of a deductible casualty loss, litigation of specific facts is commonplace.

The definition of a theft loss is somewhat clearer, but whether a theft has occurred is still a matter of factual determination. The term *theft* is deemed to include, but is not limited to, larceny, embezzlement, and robbery. No deduction is allowed for property the taxpayer simply lost or misplaced. The reasons for the stringent rules are apparent if you consider the multiple opportunities for tax evasion that would arise under more lenient rules.

A deduction is allowed for loss to the taxpayer's own property only; no deduction is allowed for damage caused by the taxpayer to the property or body of another. The regulations under Sec. 165 state clearly that a loss to the taxpayer's property may be deductible even through the taxpayer is at fault, but not if the loss is due to the willful act or willful negligence of the taxpayer.

DETERMINING THE BASIC AMOUNT OF LOSS. The amount of loss for physical damage to the taxpayer's property is basically the decrease in value of the property resulting from the casualty (but the deduction cannot be in excess of the "adjusted basis" of the property).

---

10 House Report No. 749, House Ways and Means Committee, 88th Congress, 1st Session, (U.S. Government Printing Office, 1963), p. 52.

EXAMPLE 5-11

If Reed Smith's property had a fair market value of $6,000 just before a casualty and a fair market value of $2,000 just after the casualty, the basic measure of the economic loss sustained would be $4,000. However, if Reed's damaged property had a basis of only $1,000, the tax-deductible loss would be restricted to $1,000.

In some cases, the cost of repairs to the property damaged is acceptable as evidence of the loss of value if (1) the repairs are necessary to restore the property to its condition immediately before the casualty, (2) the amount spent for such repairs is not excessive, (3) the repairs do not improve the property beyond the damage suffered, and (4) the value of the property after the repairs does not exceed the value immediately before the casualty.

No provision is made for deduction of premiums paid for insurance against purely personal casualty losses. Tax scholars often charge that the nondeductibility of casualty insurance premiums paid by individuals discriminates against the insured taxpayer. Any insurance proceeds received as a result of the loss reduce the amount otherwise deductible and actually may result in gain to the extent that the proceeds exceed the adjusted basis of the property.

DETERMINING THE AMOUNT DEDUCTIBLE. The amount of loss deductible from casualty or theft of the taxpayer's property depends on a number of factors: the decrease in value; whether the property is used in a trade or business, for income production, or for purely personal purposes; whether the property is completely destroyed or only partially destroyed; and the amount of insurance or other reimbursement received.

Business property completely destroyed. If property used in a trade or business or held for income production is completely destroyed, the adjusted basis of the property, less any amount of reimbursement, is deductible.

EXAMPLE 5-12

Assume that a property with an adjusted basis of $20,000 and a fair market value of $15,000 is used in Gus Garcia's business and is completely destroyed by fire. Gus collects insurance proceeds of $12,000 for the loss. The amount of Gus's deductible loss is $8,000—the $20,000 adjusted basis less the insurance received.

Business property partially destroyed. When property is only partially destroyed, the amount of loss is the adjusted basis of the property or its decrease in fair market value, whichever is less, reduced by insurance proceeds or other reimbursements.

EXAMPLE 5-13

Assume that a property used in Y Corporation's business is damaged by fire. The property's fair market value before the fire was $8,000; after the fire, it was appraised at $2,500. Insurance proceeds of $3,000 were received, and the adjusted basis of the property was $5,000. The amount deductible by Y Corporation is $2,000 as shown on the following page.

Continued

EXAMPLE 5-13 (Con't.)

Value before fire	$8,000
Value after fire	2,500
Decline in value	$5,500
Basis of property	$5,000
Lesser of basis or value decline	$5,000
Less insurance proceeds	3,000
Deductible loss	$2,000

Nonbusiness property.   For property neither used in a trade or business nor held for income production, the initial measure of the loss is always the smaller of the property's basis or the decline in value resulting from the casualty. This is true whether the property is completely destroyed or only partially destroyed.

EXAMPLE 5-14

Susan Moy's uninsured pleasure boat was completely destroyed in an accident. The basis of the boat was $14,000, but its fair market value just before the accident was only $9,000. The amount of Susan's casualty loss is $9,000.

In Example 5-14, the amount of Susan's casualty loss *deduction* will be less than $9,000 because of special limitations that apply to *personal* casualty and theft losses. These limitations are discussed in Chapter 10.

Casualty gains.   In some circumstances, a casualty or theft may result in a gain. Casualty gain will occur when insurance proceeds or other reimbursement exceeds the basis of the damaged or stolen property. Taxpayers are required to net personal casualty gains and losses together. If gains exceed losses, then all of the transactions are treated as capital gains and losses. If losses exceed gains, then the net amount is treated according to the rules discussed in Chapter 10. Casualty gains and losses from business or investment property also must be netted together. If gains exceed losses, then all the transactions *may* be treated as capital gains according to rules explained in Chapter 16. If losses exceed gains, then all the transactions are treated as ordinary (not capital) gain and losses.

OTHER CONSIDERATIONS

A number of other factors may complicate the proper tax treatment of casualty and theft losses. A few of the more common factors are briefly summarized in the following paragraphs.

In measuring the loss from casualty or theft related to business property, each single identifiable item damaged or destroyed is treated separately in measuring the decrease in value. For example, if a storm damages a building used in a trade or business and also damages or destroys ornamental shrubs on the premises, the decrease in the value of the building is computed separately from the decrease in value of the shrubs. However, for property not used in a trade or business, the real property and any improvements must be considered an integral part of one property. Thus, if a storm damaged the building and shrubs on a personal residence, the decline in value would not be computed for each item, but a single figure for the total decline in overall value of the property would be determined.

A number of complications arise regarding the year in which a casualty or theft loss should be deducted. In general, a loss is allowed as a deduction only for the year in which the loss is sustained. A loss arising from theft, however, is sustained in the year the theft is discovered, rather than in the year the actual theft took place. If a claim for reimbursement exists and there is a reasonable prospect of recovery, no portion of the loss with respect to which reimbursement may be received is deductible until it can be determined with reasonable certainty whether reimbursement will be received. Any portion of the loss not covered by a claim for reimbursement is deductible, however, in the year the casualty occurred or the theft was discovered.

In some cases, if a loss results from a disaster in an area that the president of the United States subsequently declares a "disaster area" warranting federal assistance, the taxpayer may deduct the loss in the year the loss occurs or may deduct the loss on the tax return for the year preceding the one in which the loss actually occurred.

EXAMPLE 5-15

If Brad Flink's home were destroyed by a flood in February 19X2, and the area was declared a "disaster area," then Brad could claim the loss on his 19X1 tax return.

A taxpayer who deducts a loss in one year and in a subsequent tax year receives reimbursement does not recompute the tax for the year in which the deduction was taken. Instead the taxpayer includes the reimbursement income for the year it is received to the extent that the reimbursement represents recovery of an amount that gave rise to a tax benefit when the deduction was taken.

_____ CONCLUSION

The word *deduction*, as it is technically used in the context of federal income taxation, must be carefully distinguished from several other, closely related, yet distinctly different concepts, such as business expenses, monetary expenditures, personal expenses, and losses of many origins. Figure 5-1 illustrates some of the more important differences between these concept. The difficult task for both the student of taxation and the taxpaying public is the ability to relate everyday events into this conceptual framework. In other words, it is often very difficult to determine whether specific expenditures—business expenses or personal expenses—are or are not deductible for tax purposes. The rapidly expanding set of tax rules associated with the deduction of losses is especially difficult.

In terms of settled law, NOLs and casualty losses are at one end of the spectrum and passive losses and capital losses at the other end. The passive activity guidance is extremely complex and taxpayers appear to be taking very aggressive positions on whether they meet the material participation standards and how they define an activity. We can expect the next few years to see a flurry of courtroom activity in this area, rivaling the volume of tax shelter litigation that so burdened the judicial system in the early 1980s. Rather than court action, in view of President Bush's staunch support for a substantial capital gains rate cut, Congressional action is possible on this issue. If this happens, we can expect to see significant taxpayer repositioning as those in business/investment situations argue the investment (hence, capital gains) side rather than the business (hence, ordinary loss) side. In addition, enactment of a more preferential capital gains rate (especially if accompanied by a higher marginal rate on ordinary income) could breathe new life into the semicomatose tax shelter industry and thus intensify taxpayer efforts to avoid the passive loss limits.

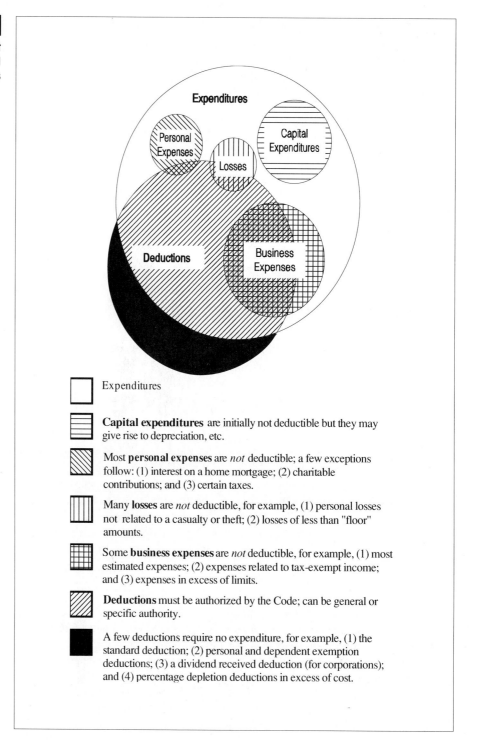

Expenditures

Capital expenditures are initially not deductible but they may give rise to depreciation, etc.

Most **personal expenses** are *not* deductible; a few exceptions follow: (1) interest on a home mortgage; (2) charitable contributions; and (3) certain taxes.

Many **losses** are *not* deductible, for example, (1) personal losses not related to a casualty or theft; (2) losses of less than "floor" amounts.

Some **business expenses** are *not* deductible, for example, (1) most estimated expenses; (2) expenses related to tax-exempt income; and (3) expenses in excess of limits.

Deductions must be authorized by the Code; can be general or specific authority.

A few deductions require no expenditure, for example, (1) the standard deduction; (2) personal and dependent exemption deductions; (3) a dividend received deduction (for corporations); and (4) percentage depletion deductions in excess of cost.

──── KEY POINTS TO REMEMBER

✓ Deductions are a matter of legislative grace. Nothing is deductible unless authorized by the Code or the Regulations.

✓ Two Code sections grant broad authority for deductions. Section 162 allows deduction of ordinary, necessary, and reasonable expenses related to the conduct of a trade or business. Section 212 allows deduction of ordinary and necessary expenses related to an activity that is not a trade or business but is conducted for the production of income.

✓ The distinctions between a trade or business, an investment activity, and a hobby are important because the deductions allowed for each vary significantly.

✓ The Code contains a number of provisions that authorize specific deductions. It also limits some deductions and disallows others.

✓ The rules for losses can be viewed as a special set of the more general rules for deductions. Additional rules modify the tax treatment of net operating losses, passive activity losses, capital losses, and casualty and theft losses.

──── RECALL PROBLEMS

1. Explain how the concept of a tax deduction differs from the concept of an accounting expense.

2. What is meant by the terms *reasonable, ordinary,* and *necessary*?

3. This year Green Grow Chemicals made a $1,000 contribution to the campaign of each candidate for Congress in states in which agriculture is a significant aspect of the economy. Is this an ordinary, necessary expense? Is it deductible? Explain.

4. Xavier is a self-employed manufacturer of electronics equipment. During the year, he had the following expenditures that he thinks may be somewhat questionable when preparing his tax return. Indicate whether each is potentially deductible or is nondeductible.

   a. Trip to Washington, D.C., to testify before congressional committee holding hearings on proposed legislation to restrict foreign imports of electronics equipment. Xavier is very interested in curtailing imports and asked to be heard. Transportation, $280; lodging, $260; meals, $108.

   b. Cost of telephone calls, letters, and telegrams to members of Congress from his state urging them to vote for the import restrictions bill recommended by the congressional committee, $118.

   c. Contribution to electronics manufacturing association to help pay for television campaign to urge public support for anti-import bill.

   d. Gift (a new television set costing $600) to Congressman Doe. Xavier expects Doe to support the anti-import bill.

   e. Cost of television ads purchased for an opponent of Congressman Doe, who after all did not support the anti-import bill.

5. Indicate whether each of the following items is potentially deductible. If only part is deductible, indicate the amount to be deducted.

a. Stinchcomb, an attorney, also operates a farm. During each of the past five years, his expenses on the farm were $9,000, and farm income was only $4,000. During the current year, he has income of $4,800 and expenses of $9,200.

b. Toledo owns 60% of Ace Corporation's outstanding stock. During the current year, Ace Corporation paid Toledo a salary of $82,000. Executives in similar situations earn about $40,000 per year, and that amount is considered reasonable.

c. Black borrowed $50,000 from the First State Bank and used the money to buy City of Blanksville bonds. She paid interest of $4,200 on the borrowed funds. Interest received on the bonds was $3,500.

d. White purchased a piece of land for $45,000 for his new office building. However, he had to tear down an old building on the property, paying $3,200 to a demolition company for clearing the land.

e. Benson is married and has three children. Normal living costs for the home, utilities, food, and clothing total $12,000 for the current year.

 6. a. What tax treatment is given expenses of a hobby?

      b. How do we distinguish between a hobby and a business venture?

 7. Distinguish between a "trade or business expense" and a "nonbusiness expenses related to income production."

 8. Under what conditions could an individual taxpayer deduct the cost of maintaining a safety deposit box?

 9. List and explain the general criteria (positive and negative) that may be applied to determine whether many expenditures are deductible or nondeductible.

 10. Indicate whether each of the following items is potentially deductible. If only part is deductible, indicate the amount to be deducted.

a. Taxpayer operates a truck on a contract basis. While hauling gravel under a contract, he was stopped for speeding. He paid a fine of $25 for speeding and a fine of $30 for carrying an overweight load.

b. Assume the same facts as in part a, except that the taxpayer is an employee instead of an independent contractor. He was not reimbursed by his employer for either fine.

c. Agnew operates a contracting business. During the year, he gave a member of the city council a new watch, which cost $200. Agnew hopes that the council member "throws some city business" his way.

d. A gambler won $45,000 during the year. To earn this income, however, she incurred expenses for travel and other items totaling $10,200.

 11. Explain how the rules for deductibility of losses relate to the rules for deductions.

 12. In calculating an NOL deduction, individuals are not allowed personal or dependent exemption deductions. Explain why.

 13. A taxpayer reports the following:

	Active	Passive	Portfolio	Total
Gross income	$100,000	$50,000	$25,000	$175,000
Deductions	30,000	60,000	5,000	95,000
Net income	$ 70,00	($10,000)	$20,000	$ 80,000

a. Assuming the taxpayer is a single individual and none of the passive income involves rental properties, what amount of taxable income should she report from these activities?

b. Assuming the taxpayer is a C corporation engaged in a mercantile business and none of the passive income involves rental properties, what amount of taxable income should it report?

14. Compare the treatment of passive activity losses with the treatment of capital losses.

15. This year an individual derives $10,000 of ordinary income from passive activity X, no gains from the sale or exchange of capital assets or assets used in a trade or business, $12,000 of capital loss from passive activity Y, and no income, gain, deductions, or losses from any other passive activity.

a. Based on the facts, is any amount suspended because of the passive activity loss rules?

b. What amount can the taxpayer deduct under the capital loss rules?

16. Salad Shooter, Inc., experienced a $50,000 capital loss this year. Taxable income from other sources is $450,000.

a. What is Salad Shooter's income for the year?

b. How much is Salad Shooter's capital loss carryover and when may it be deducted?

17. This year Jack Warren, an individual taxpayer, experienced net short term capital gains of $10,000 and net long term capital losses of $22,000. Jack's taxable income from all other sources is $80,000.

a. What is Jack's taxable income for the year?

b. How much is Jack's capital loss carryover? When may he deduct it?

18. Explain why the loss limitation rules exist for capital losses.

19. What differences, if any, are found in measuring the amount of a casualty loss on property held for personal use and property used in a trade or business?

20. Under what circumstances, if any, may the taxpayer treat the amount of a repair bill as a measure of loss from a casualty.

21. In each of the following cases, indicate the amount of the casualty loss.

a. Berry owned a lake cabin with an adjusted basis of $16,000. On March 18, the cabin had a fair value of $14,000. On the next day a tornado completely demolished the cabin, which was not insured. The cabin was held solely for personal use.

b. Same facts as in part a, except the cabin had a value of $5,000 after the tornado.

c. Greenscape Lawn Care, Inc., owned a garden tractor with a basis of $2,000 and a fair market value of $1,500. Recently, the tractor was destroyed in an accident.

d. Dempsey Corporation's warehouse had an adjusted basis of $150,000 and fair market value of $200,000. On June 15, it was destroyed by fire. Dempsey received $130,000 from its insurance policy.

e. Same facts as in part d, except the proceeds from the insurance policy were $200,000.

_____ THOUGHT PROBLEMS

1. A taxpayer who owns a textile manufacturing plant in New York is visited by an important customer. The taxpayer wines and dines this customer and spouse during their stay in New York. Total cost of this entertainment is $900. Might this be a reasonable, ordinary, and necessary expense? Explain.

2. It is conceivable that the cost of a taxpayer's subscription to the *Wall Street Journal* would be tax deductible, whereas the cost of a subscription to the *New York Times* would be disallowed. Explain the circumstances that would lead to such a situation. Explain other circumstances that might justify the deduction of the cost of a subscription of to the *New York Times.*

3. Which of the following expenditures do you think would be potentially deductible? Explain why or why not.

   a. Current research and development expenses related to a business.

   b. Payment of damages to a client based on failure to meet the terms of a contract.

   c. Cost of investigating the possibility of starting a new business in another city.

4. a. Make an educated guess as to whether each of the following expenditures would be potentially deductible by a corporate taxpayer.

   (1) Cost of prizes given away by a television manufacturer as a part of a sales contest.
   (2) Cost of uniforms and equipment for a company-sponsored baseball team.
   (3) Assessment for benefits paid to union employees during periods of illness.
   (4) Estimated charge for self-insurance program in lieu of commercial insurance coverage.
   (5) Fee paid to a senator from the taxpayer's state to speak on the subject of competitiveness to a gathering of a large corporation's managers.
   (6) During a severe cold wave this last winter, the taxpayer paid $50,000 to officers of a natural gas pipeline company to ensure that gas supplies were not curtailed. Although supplies to competitors were greatly reduced, the taxpayer had no curtailment.

   b. Make an educated guess as to whether or not each of the following expenditures would be potentially deductible by an individual taxpayer.

   (1) Contribution to purchase a fiftieth birthday gift for an employee's supervisor.
   (2) Cost of subscription to *Journal of Accountancy.* (Taxpayer is employed by a local CPA firm.)
   (3) Wages paid caretaker of former residence that is currently listed "for sale or rent."

5. This chapter covers various tests that must be met before an amount is deductible under Sec. 162 or 212. Each independent situation below describes a payment made by a taxpayer. Give the test that is crucial to the decision of deductibility for each item. Do not worry about whether the expense is deductible—only state the most relevant test.

   a. T went to Africa on a legitimate business trip. He took Mrs. T with him. Costs allocated solely to Mrs. T's trip were $4,500.

   b. Mrs. T has a greenhouse in her backyard. She raises flowers and sells some of them to local florists and to neighbors. For the tax year her sales were

$3,000. Expenses of the greenhouse, including depreciation, amounted to $5,500.

c. During the year T paid interest on borrowed money of $10,000. The borrowed money was used for various investments, including the purchase of city of Dallas bonds.

d. T holds a patent on Gismos. National Corporation sold some Gismo look-alikes. T sued National to stop this infringement. He paid a lawyer $10,000 to bring the suit.

e. T owns a nursing home. He paid $5,000 to Dr. Switch during the year as referral fees for elderly patients sent to the home.

f. T breeds racehorses for a living. This year T donated $10,000 to the Texas Horse Racing Association. This money was used to lobby for a horse racing bill in Texas.

g. T runs a mortuary. This year he paid his 16-year-old son $8,000 to help at the business.

6. Sec. 262 specifically disallows the deduction of "personal, living, and family" expenses. Yet many persons may deduct a purely personal contribution to a local charity. Explain the apparent contradiction. `#6`

7. Some of the most significant (in terms of dollars deducted) personal deductions of individual taxpayers are criticized as inequitable subsidies to specific groups. Perhaps the most notorious of these are the deductions for state and local real estate taxes and the deductions for interest paid on home mortgages. What groups are being subsidized by these deductions? Why might each of these deductions be considered inequitable? Why might they be considered desirable? `#6`

8. One of the social costs associated with multiple deductions is the complexity of the tax laws. What social advantages accrue to offset this social cost? `#6` `#7`

9. The amount of interest deductible on money borrowed to purchase investment property is limited to the amount of income earned from investment property. What is the likely reason for this restriction? `#7`

10. Explain why a taxpayer might forgo the opportunity to receive an immediate tax refund by carrying back a net operating loss deduction to the three prior years. `#9`

11. Make an argument for removing restrictions on the sale of NOLs by defunct corporations. `#9`

12. Since 1987, taxpayers have sought to invest in passive income generator (PIGs). Describe the characteristics that a PIG should possess. `#10`

────── CLASS PROJECTS

1. Michael Franklin, CPA, gave bad tax advice to a client. As a result, the client paid $30,000 in penalties and interest to the IRS. Franklin has agreed to reimburse the client rather than file a claim against his malpractice insurance policy. Franklin fears that filing a claim would dramatically increase his annual premium or even result in cancellation of his policy. Will he be allowed to deduct the $30,000 paid to his client? Your answer should cite relevant Code section(s), administrative authority, and judicial authority.

2. Three years ago, Jack and Caroline Wilson purchased a $100,000 home in a new subdivision. Early this year their home was worth approximately $135,000 based on sales of similar homes in the neighborhood. However, heavy rains in March caused extensive flooding in the area. The news media reported that the storm sewer system was inadequate for the rapidly growing area and that it would take years to correct the problem. Most homes in the neighborhood required new carpet and paint. The Wilsons were fortunate to have escaped damage to their home because it is on a slight hill. They have learned, however, that buyers are now less interested in homes in the area. An appraiser has told them they could not sell their home for more than $90,000. Have the Wilsons experienced a casualty loss? If so, what is the amount? Your answer should cite relevant Code section(s), administrative authority, and judicial authority.

In consequence of this perversion of the word Being, philosophers, looking about for something to supply its place, laid their hands upon the word Entity, a piece of barbarous Latin, invented by the schoolmen to be used as an abstract name, in which class its grammatical form would seem to place it; but being seized by logicians in distress to stop a leak in their terminology, it has ever since been used as a concrete name.

JOHN STUART MILL, A SYSTEM OF LOGIC (1843)

TAXABLE ENTITIES, RATES, AND TAX CREDITS

CHAPTER OBJECTIVES

In chapter 6 you will (1) study the provisions which establish the basic taxpaying units, or taxable entities, for federal income tax purposes and (2) learn how the income earned by other entities is or is not taxed under U.S. law. You will next be introduced to the current tax rates paid by each of the taxable entities and then you will discover how the gross tax liability of any entity may be reduced by tax credits and prepayments. The chapter ends with a brief introduction to some tax planning opportunities introduced by this taxable-entity and tax-rate regimen.

LEARNING GOALS

After studying this chapter, you should be able to

1 Determine who must pay the income tax on any item of gross income or on any general business income stream;

2 Distinguish between taxable and nontaxable entities for federal income tax purposes;

3 Explain how any income earned by nontaxable entities may or may not be taxed by the United States;

4 Understand the definitional distinctions between (a) corporations and partnerships and (b) corporations and

trusts, whenever that classification is uncertain for federal income tax purposes;

5 Describe the current tax-rate structure that is generally applied to determine the gross tax liability of each taxable entity each year;

6 Comprehend the major difference between deductions and tax credits; and

7 Begin to appreciate some of the tax planning opportunities implicit in the taxable entity and tax rate paradigms utilized for federal income tax purposes.

This chapter addresses three important questions: Who are the taxpayers? How are they taxed? What is a tax credit? Let us begin with the first question. The income tax can be levied on many different entities. Innumerable legal, economic, natural, and cultural entities exist in our society. A list of some of the more important ones illustrate the diversity:

individuals and family units;

business entities, such as sole proprietorships, partnerships, and corporations;

groups of corporations, and other business ventures with related owners;

trusts and estates; and

other governmental units and social organizations of an infinite variety.

Theoretically any of these entities could serve as a taxable entity and that entity's annual income could be used as the basic unit for calculating an income tax. Practically, however, some of these entities can almost automatically be excluded from consideration. To use cities as a taxable entity, for example, would create major and difficult problems of determining how much income was earned within the city and of reallocating the tax imposed on the city to its residents.

The chapter is divided into three major parts. In the first part the authors distinguish taxable entities from nontaxable ones and explain how the income initially earned by nontaxable entities may still be taxed. This material also contains the definition of several words and phrases that are critical to understanding who pays the income tax. The second part of the chapter is a description of current tax rate structure that is used to determine the amount of income tax that must be paid by the various taxable entities. In the third part of this chapter the authors introduce some of the many tax planning opportunities made possible by the entity and rate regimens described earlier.

> **Goal #1**
> Identify the taxpayers.

> A **fiduciary** is any legal or human person to whom property has been entrusted for the benefit of another.
>
> A **tax-exempt entity** is an entity whose income is, by law, either partially or wholly exempt from U.S. income taxation.
>
> A **tax conduit** is any legal or business entity that is not subject to tax but whose gross income, deductions, and tax credits are immediately attributed to its owners and taxed to them.

_____ WHO ARE THE TAXPAYERS?

From the earliest days of the income tax in the United States, there have been only three taxable entities: individuals, corporations, and certain **fiduciaries** (that is, certain estates and trusts). The taxable income earned by other entities is either partially or wholly excused from U.S. income taxation or immediately taxed on the tax returns filed by those entities' owners. The former set of entities are commonly called **tax-exempt entities;** the latter, **tax-conduit entities.** Observe that in this chapter the sole concern is with who pays the income tax in a mechanistic sense and not with who ultimately bears the tax burden in an economic sense. In other words, this chapter is concerned solely with the correct identification of who writes the income tax checks and ignores the issue of tax incidence, a wholly separate topic introduced briefly in Chapter 1.

THE STATUTORY FOUNDATION

The generally accepted conclusion that there are only three basic taxpaying entities in the U.S. income tax system derives from the words used in Secs. 1 and 11. Section 1 (a) through (d) imposes an income tax on individuals; Sec. 11 on corporations; and Sec.1(e) on certain estates and trusts. Numerous other provisions scattered throughout the Code spin a complex set of exceptions and modifications to the two initial provisions. Let us first examine the general rules and then introduce the most important exceptions to those general rules, defining the more important words and phrases used in the Code.

The Individual Taxpayer

The very first sentence of the Code begins with the following words:

> There is hereby imposed on the taxable income of—
>
> (1) every married individual . . . who makes a single return jointly with his spouse under section 6013, and
>
> (2) every surviving spouse . . . .[1]

Study these precise words carefully. They are important for at least two reasons. First, they impose a tax on **taxable income.** These words, from the first sentence of the Code clearly establish taxable income as a tax base. Second, these words further identify *every* "married individual" (who files one return jointly with his or her spouse) and *every* "surviving spouse" as a possible taxpayer. The income tax is extended to *every* "head of household" in Sec. 1(b); to *every* "individual (other than a surviving spouse . . . or the head of a household . . .) who is not a married individual" in Sec 1(c) and, finally, to *every* "married individual . . . who does not make a single return jointly with his spouse" in Sec. 1(d). Putting these four subsections together, we can safely conclude that every individual—whether married or single, head of household or surviving spouse, filing jointly or filing separately—is a potential taxable entity. In summary, the taxable income of every individual is subject to tax under the authority of Secs. 1(a) through (d).

> **Taxable income** is the arithmetic difference between gross income and deductions for a tax year. It is also the tax base for the federal income tax.

We need many important definitions to make Sec. 1 operative. For example, before we can apply these words to real world events we must know how tax law defines (among other terms) taxable income, married individual, surviving spouse, head of household, and filing jointly. Most of the missing definitions are provided later in this chapter because they merely modify the tax rate to be used in the calculation of an individual's tax liability. The critical point for now is the fact that *every individual* is a potential taxable entity for purposes of the U.S. income tax.

In general, income derived from a service must be taxed to the person who rendered the service, and income from property must be taxed to the person who owns the property. Income earned by one cannot be assigned to another. For instance, if Mary, who is to receive interest income from a note receivable, directs the debtor to pay the interest to Mary's mother, the interest is nevertheless taxable to Mary. In spite of the general rule that income of one taxpayer cannot be assigned to another taxpayer, it is possible for one taxpayer to transfer to another the *property* that generates income, with the income earned thereafter taxed to the transferee. Thus if, in the preceding example, Mary had made a bona fide gift of the entire note to her mother, interest earned after the date of the gift would be taxed to Mary's mother.

The Uniform Gift to Minors Act permits an adult to give a minor child gifts of intangible property such as cash, savings accounts, certificates of deposits, bonds, and stocks. The Act permits the adult to be the custodian of the fund even though the income belongs to, and is ordinarily taxed to, the child.

---

1 Sec.1(a)

Note also that the regulations provide that compensation for the personal services of a child—regardless of the provisions of state law, which sometimes hold that a parent is entitled to the earnings of the child, and whether or not the income is received by the child—deemed to be the gross income of the child and not the gross income of the parent. The income of a minor child is ordinarily not included in the gross income of the parent for income tax purposes.

The Corporate Taxpayer

The first sentence of Sec. 11 is easier to read and understand than the first sentence of Sec. 1. It reads in its entirety as follows:

> A tax is hereby imposed for each taxable year on the taxable income of every corporation. [2]

In spite of its apparent simplicity, you should also read this sentence carefully. Note that it (1) once again imposes a tax on taxable income; (2) identifies a year as the appropriate measurement period, an idea not explicitly stated in Sec.1; and (3) identifies *every* corporation as a potential taxable entity. To make this sentence meaningful we will need a tax definition of taxable income, taxable year, and corporation. Chapters 4 and 5 define taxable income in a general way as the arithmetic difference between gross income and deductions. Chapter 7 defines a tax year in alternative ways. The definition of a corporation appears later in this chapter. For now let us observe only the simple fact that, like every individual, every corporation is potentially a taxable entity.

The separation of corporations from their owners is in accord with financial accounting practice and legal realities. By both custom and law, a corporation is a separate legal person that can own property, contract in its own name, and be sued for nonperformance. It is this separate status that gives corporations the sometimes desirable attributes of limited liability, unlimited life, and readily transferrable shares. Attendant with these financial and legal advantages of incorporation are the formal rules that must be observed in the formation and operation of the entity: for example, obtaining a charter, maintaining stock transfer records, holding necessary meetings of shareholders and directors, and recording the minutes of such meetings, to name only a few.

Approximately three million corporations file federal income-tax returns each year. The vast majority are closely held and relatively small corporations. Fewer than 30,000 corporations hold assets in excess of $25 million. An even smaller number are public corporations, that is, those subject to federal or state security regulations because of public trading. The large number of closely held corporations is due partly to the legal advantages of that form and partly to the several tax advantages that accompanied incorporation before 1987.

Today the most significant reasons for the popularity of corporations derive from *nontax* considerations. Most important, the corporation generally provides limited liability for the owners. That is, business creditors may generally look only to the assets of the corporation in satisfaction of any debts. The shareholder's personal assets, other than those invested to acquire the corporation's stock, remain beyond the reach of the corporation's creditors. Hence, individuals with a substantial amount of

---

2 Sec. 11(a).

personal assets are effectively forced to utilize a corporate entity, particularly when engaging in a trade or business with significant risk.

For small businesses, the limited liability attribute is frequently overstated. The active owner-manager of a small corporation is likely to find that bankers and other lenders, as well as major vendors, are almost certain to require the majority owner(s) to sign a written personal guarantee for the corporation's debts. However, minor suppliers of capital and of merchandise and most suppliers of services may not impose this requirement for credit. As a result, the shareholder of the small corporation is likely to receive at least some benefit from the limited liability attribute in dealing with general creditors. The corporation may or may not offer a shield against debts arising from lawsuits filed for negligence, nonperformance of contract, and so on. In some cases involving a small corporation, the lawsuit is likely to name the owner-manager, the directors, the officers, and even employees as defendants along with the corporation.

Corporations are also popular because they are generally characterized by free transferability of ownership interests, meaning that the shareholders are free to buy and/or sell their interest in a corporation at any given time. Normally, it is far easier to transfer shares of stock than it is to transfer the ownership interest in a partnership. Partnership interests generally can be sold or purchased only with permission of the other partners. Technically, the sale of a partnership interest terminates the old partnership and creates a new one, requiring the new partner to sign the partnership agreement. The sale of corporate shares has no such impact, even though the transfer of shares may carry restrictions requiring the seller to first offer to sell the shares to other existing shareholders or to the corporation itself. One special benefit of this free transferability is that it makes transferability of ownership from the owner to his or her beneficiaries very simple.

Other attributes that make the corporation popular as an entity are the centralization of management and the continuity of life. These characteristics mean that the corporation will continue uninterrupted even though particular shareholders and managers may come and go with some regularity. All of the unique corporate characteristics mentioned previously are especially important in raising large sums of money from diverse sources.

The Fiduciary Taxpayer

In both common parlance and the law generally, a fiduciary is any human or legal person to whom property has been entrusted for the benefit of another. [3] For federal income tax purposes, when the adjective *fiduciary* modifies the noun *taxpayer,* this everyday definition may not suffice. For tax purposes, the term fiduciary includes only certain estates and trusts.

When an individual who owns property dies, an estate is created. Local law and the terms of the decedent's will (if any) determine whether title to the property passes first to the estate and later to the beneficiaries, or directly to the heirs or devisees of the decedent taxpayer. If title passes to the estate and the will directs the administrator of the estate to pay debts of the estate, any income earned on the property during a reasonable period of administration will ordinarily be taxed to the estate and paid from assets of the estate. If a will does not direct the administrator to pay the debts of the estate, and title passes directly to the heirs or devisees, those individuals rather than

---

3 In tax jargon the word *person* is not restricted to humans but includes individuals, trusts, estates, partnerships, corporations, associations, and other entities. See Sec. 7701(a)(1).

the estate will usually pay any federal income tax attributable to whatever income is derived from the property during the period of administration.

The estates of wealthy individuals owning many properties may require several years to settle. In this instance, the estate will typically continue to be recognized as a separate taxpayer until all administrative matters are resolved and all assets distributed.

A few of the terms commonly associated with an estate include the following words and phrases:

> *Decedent:*   the person who died.
>
> *Devisee:*   an individual specifically designated in a will as one to receive some part or all of the property of a decedent.
>
> *Executor (male) or executrix (female):*   the individual legally responsible for the administration of a decedent's estate.
>
> *Heir:*   an individual who may, by operation of local law and/or the terms of a will, receive part or all of a decedent's estate.
>
> *Intestate:*   dying without a will.
>
> *Law of descent and distribution:*   local law that determines, in absence of a will, how the property of a decedent must be distributed.
>
> *Testate:*   dying with a will.

Understanding these terms is often helpful in interpreting tax provisions pertinent to the taxation of estates.

A **trust** is a legal person created by a transfer of property to a trustee who temporarily holds title to the property for the benefit of another. The property put into trust is called the *corpus* (or body) of the trust. The person who puts the property in trust may be referred to as either the **grantor** or **settlor** of the trust. The instructions given by the grantor to the trustee, which generally established both the powers of the trustee and the eventual disposition of any residual property remaining at the termination of the trust, are referred to as the trust *indenture*. Because a trust may exist for many years, it is common to name a corporate person (such as a bank, or a professional legal firm) as trustee simply to ensure the trustee's existence to carry out all of the terms of the trust indenture. Persons designated by the grantor as potential recipients of trust benefits are called beneficiaries. A **life beneficiary** is one who can benefit from a trust only so long as he or she lives; at death, a life beneficiary has no remaining interest in any of the trust assets. The person who will receive whatever property is left at the termination of a trust is called the **remainderman.** The fundamentals of a typical trust are illustrated in Figure 6-1.

The statutory foundation for the income taxation of fiduciary taxpayers is found in Sec. 1(e). It reads in part as follows:

> There is hereby imposed on the taxable income of—
>
> (1) every estate, and
>
> (2) every trust,
>
> taxable under this subsection . . . .[4]

A **trust** is a legal person, created by the transfer of property to a trustee, who holds title to the property for the benefit of another.

The **grantor** (or **settlor**) is the person who puts property in trust for the benefit of another.

A **life beneficiary** is a person who can benefit from a trust for only so long as he or she lives.

A **remainderman** is a person who receives whatever residual property is left at the termination of a trust.

---

4 Sec. 1 (e)

FIGURE 6-1

**Trust
Fundamentals**

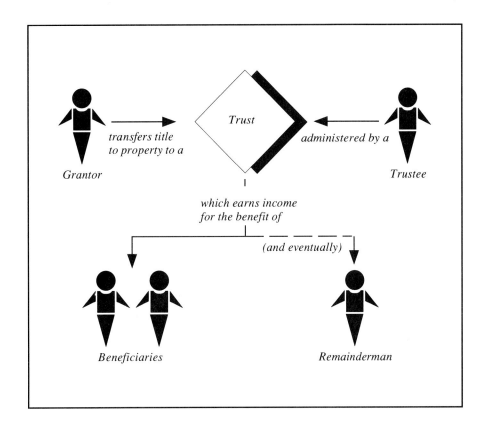

A careful reading of this section is once again wise. Note that Sec. 1(e) both (1) imposes a tax on taxable income and (2) identifies only certain estates and trusts as potential taxpayers. The words *every estate* and *every trust* are subsequently modified by the phrase "taxable under this subsection." That phrase should alert you to the fact that not every estate and trust is a taxable entity. Rather, only those estates and trusts taxable under this subsection are subject to the income tax. Obviously, you must look elsewhere to separate the taxable estates and trusts from the nontaxable ones. In general, the most important of these rules are located in Subchapter J (Secs. 641–692), entitled Estates, Trusts, Beneficiaries and Decedents. For the moment observe only that certain estates and trusts—commonly called fiduciary taxpayers—are made subject to the federal income tax by operation of Sec. 1(e).

In summary, Secs. 1 and 11 of the Code impose only one common tax (the federal income tax) on three distinct taxable entities (individuals, corporations, and certain fiduciaries). We believe that it is important for you to understand this fundamental fact because so many people erroneously conclude that there are two separate and distinct income taxes: (1) the individual income tax and (2) the corporate income tax. Once you understand that there is only one income tax, but that this tax is imposed on three different taxpayers, you will soon appreciate more of the tax opportunities and tax traps that arise whenever one taxable entity engages in a transaction with another taxable entity. Income tax questions related to such issues as dividends, stock redemptions, and corporate reorganizations, for example, are commonly thought of as issues related to corporate taxation. They are far more correctly viewed as straight forward income tax questions involving corporate taxpayers and individual taxpayers, concurrently. This conclusion assumes, of course, that one or more of the corporation's shareholders are individuals. If a parent corporation engages in a transaction with its wholly owned subsidiary, no individual taxpayers are involved. Nevertheless, that transaction involves only one tax (the income tax) but two taxpayers (the parent and the subsidiary corporations).

> **Goal #2**
> Distinguish between taxable and nontaxable entities.

STATUTORY EXCEPTIONS TO THE GENERAL RULE

The need for numerous exceptions to the general rule—that *every* individual, *every* corporation, and certain estates and trusts, must pay the federal income tax—is readily apparent if we focus on the word *every*. How, for example, will the United States manage to tax the income earned by a citizen of China who has no connection with the United States? And how will our federal government impose an income tax on Lincoln, Nebraska, an incorporated city? In addition to these two obvious exceptions, many others exist. We will review the more important exceptions to the conclusion that every individual and every corporation must pay the federal income tax.

S Corporations

> **S corporations** are ordinary corporations that have made a valid election to be taxed as a tax conduit entity for federal income tax purposes.
>
> **C corporations** are all corporations other than S corporations.

Ordinary corporations that satisfy criteria detailed in Subchapter S of the Code may elect to be treated as a tax-conduit entity for federal income tax purposes.[5] These corporations are known as **S corporations** for so long as a valid election is in effect. Corporations that either cannot or do not make the election are known as **C corporations.**[6] All gross income, deductions, and tax credits initially recognized by an S corporation ordinarily pass directly through the corporate entity and are reported on the tax returns filed by the corporation's shareholders.

EXAMPLE 6-1

Bet-Cha Corporation is equally owned by Betty Vick and Charles West. Immediately after receiving its charter, Bet-Cha Corporation, Betty Vick, and Charles West filed the papers necessary to make Bet-Cha Corporation an S corporation for federal income tax purposes. During 19X1 Bet-Cha Corporation recognized gross income of $200,000 and deductions of $160,000, or taxable income of $40,000. Because Bet-Cha is an S corporation, it will not be treated as a taxable entity; however, Betty and Charles must each report an additional $100,000 of gross income and can each claim an additional $80,000 in deductions (giving them each an additional taxable income of $20,000) on their individual income tax returns simply because they each own 50% of Bet-Cha's outstanding stock. Incidentally, Betty and Charles must report this additional taxable income whether or not Bet-Cha Corporation distributes any cash or other assets to them at the end of the year.

The Subchapter S election is available only when the following conditions are met:

1. The corporation must be a domestic corporation with only one class of stock outstanding;

2. All stockholders must be individual citizens or residents, estates, or certain trusts;

---

5 Subchapter S includes Secs. 1361 through 1379.

6 Sec. 1361(a)(2).

3. There must be 35 or fewer stockholders;

4. The corporation cannot own 80% or more of the stock of another corporation; and

5. Every stockholder must consent in writing to the original election.[7]

Once made, the election applies to all subsequent years unless the shareholders agree to revoke the election or it is terminated by operation of law. Once revoked, a new S election cannot generally be made for five years. Revocation of an election requires the positive action of shareholders owning more than one half of the stock. An election automatically is terminated when the corporation ceases to meet any of the conditions listed above.

An S corporation originally was a hybrid entity with some of the characteristics of both C corporations and partnerships. When Subchapter S was added to the statute in 1958, Congress intended to provide taxpayers with a vehicle they could use to obtain the financial benefits of a corporation (primarily limited liability for the shareholders) without the burden of double taxation. Under the rules adopted in 1958, the taxable income of an electing S corporation was taxed directly on the returns of its shareholders. Similarly, an S corporation's net operating losses were deductible by its shareholders, subject to certain limits. Except for the flow-through of taxable income and net operating losses, S corporations were subject to the usual separate-entity rules generally applicable to corporations. The rules adopted in 1958 were complex and often resulted in tax effects that reduced the benefits of the S corporation election.

In 1982, Subchapter S was substantially revised. Congress adopted rules for S corporations identical in many ways to those applicable to partnerships. Each shareholder reports his or her share of the S corporation's taxable items for the S corporation's year that ends during the shareholder's taxable year. Taxable items are allocated pro rata to stock ownership. Recall that S corporations have only one class of stock, a requirement that facilitates this allocation. Taxable items of income, gains, losses, and deductions that are not subject to special tax rules are grouped together as the S corporation's "nonseparately computed" taxable income or loss. All items subject to special rules are separately allocated among the shareholders. S corporation losses reported by shareholders are limited to each shareholder's basis in his or her stock.

Other S corporation rules that parallel partnership rules are that (1) accounting elections are made at the S corporation level, not by each shareholder; (2) the tax character of items is determined at the corporate level; (3) shareholders of an S corporation who own more than 2% of the corporate stock cannot be treated as employees of the corporation for fringe-benefit purposes; and (4) S corporations must generally use the calendar year as their tax year. The usual corporate rules, however, still apply to the formation of S corporations and to some corporate distributions. Other corporate rules sometimes may apply because a corporation may change from C status to S status, or vice versa, during its life.

Affiliated Corporations

The wording of Sec. 11 clearly implies that each and every corporation is to be treated as a separate taxable entity. The initial, separate-entity implication of Sec. 11 is overridden for many corporations by Secs. 1501–1505. These latter sections permit

---

7 See Secs. 1361 and 1362.

An **affiliated group** of corporations includes a common parent corporation and one or more subsidiary corporations, connected to the common parent through specified ownership arrangements, that elect to file a single consolidated income tax return.

An **includible corporation** is any corporation that is eligible to file a consolidated tax return if it is a member of an affiliated group.

certain corporations (1) to ignore their individual legal identities and (2) to elect to file one consolidated tax return for all corporate members of an affiliated group. The definition of an **affiliated group** includes a common parent corporation and at least one subsidiary corporation that is connected to the common parent through specified stock ownership arrangements.[8] Although the details of the definition can be complex, in very general terms an affiliated group consists of a common parent that directly owns (1) 80% or more of the voting power of all classes of stock entitled to vote, and (2) 80% or more of the value of every class of nonvoting stock, of at least one other (includible) corporation. This simple, two-member, corporate chain can be extended to many other corporations so long as at least 80% (by vote and by value) of the stock of other (includible) corporations are owned by either the common parent or by other members of the affiliated group.

Figure 6-2 illustrates just three of an infinite variety of ownership arrangements that could qualify for membership in an affiliated group if all other statutory requirements are also satisfied. Paramount among the other requirements is the requirement that each of the corporations be an **includible corporation.** The following corporations are not includible corporations:

1. S corporations:

2. Exempt corporations;

3. Foreign corporations;

FIGURE 6-2

Three Possible Affiliated Groups of Corporations

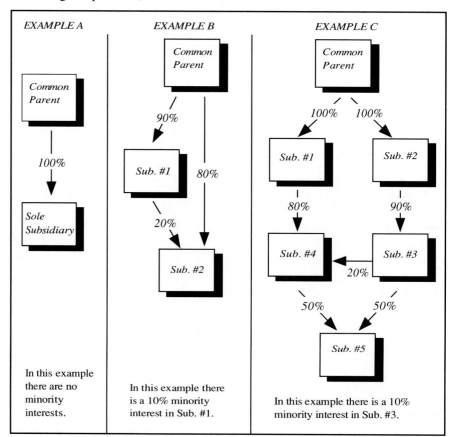

4. Domestic sales corporations (DSCs);

5. Insurance companies;

6. Corporations organized in a U.S. possession if they elect the tax benefits available in Sec. 936; and

7. Regulated investment companies.[9]

The definition of some of the nonincludible corporations—such as exempt corporations and foreign corporations—are included later in this chapter; others must remain outside the confines of this text.

The important conclusion is the fact that corporations that elect to be part of an affiliated group may ignore their separate status and file one consolidated tax return with other members of their affiliated group. The taxable income recognized on the consolidated return is *not* simply the sum of the taxable income of the several members of the group; rather, it is an income measure that more-or-less ignores intercompany transactions and treats the entire group as if it were one separate taxpayer. The very complicated rules that determine the amount of taxable income to be reported by the affiliated group are largely contained in Treasury regulations.[10] If you have studied the preparation of consolidated financial accounting statements you should recognize many parallels between the tax and the accounting rules used in making this income measurement. The two sets of rules are not, however, identical.

Tax-Exempt Entities

Many corporations and many trusts are created for various nonprofit purposes. Most of these are exempt from the federal income tax operation of Sec. 501(a), which reads as follows:

> An organization described in subsection (c) or (d) or section 401(a) shall be exempt from taxation under this subtitle unless such exemption is denied under section 502 or 503.

The list of organizations specifically mentioned in Secs. 501(c) and (d) is very long and includes

civic leagues;

labor and agricultural organizations;

business leagues, chambers of commerce, real-estate boards, and professional football leagues;

recreational clubs and fraternal societies;

cemetery companies;

religious and apostolic organizations;

hospitals;

educational institutions.

Sec. 401(a) describes most pension and profit-sharing trusts. Although many organizations created primarily for religious, charitable, scientific, or educational purposes are generally exempt from federal income taxation, they may still have to pay

---

9 Sec. 1504(b).

10 See Treas. Regs. 1.1502-1 through 1.1502-100.

Unrelated business income (UBI) is that part of an otherwise tax-exempt entity's income that is subject to the federal income tax.

the income tax if and to the extent that they recognize some amount of **unrelated business income** (UBI).[11] The definition of UBI is, obviously, of great interest to those who create and manage otherwise tax-exempt organizations.

In very general terms, tax-exempt organizations can earn passive income—such as interest, dividends, and capital gains—tax-free. If an otherwise exempt organization engages in an active trade or business, however, any income that it earns on those activities will generally be subject to tax *unless* the activity is directly related to the organization's tax-exempt purpose.

EXAMPLE 6-2

Zorba University, a tax-exempt organization, offers a degree program in hotel administration. As part of this program, Zorba University also operates a hotel as a training facility. If this hotel activity earns a profit that is utilized by Zorba in its educational activities, it need not pay any federal income tax on the hotel operation. If Zorba University discontinued its degree program in hotel administration, but continued to operate the hotel on a profitable basis, Zorba would very likely have to pay income tax on the profit from the hotel operation because it then would be unrelated business income.

Prohibited transactions are transactions that may cause a tax-exempt entity to lose its tax-exempt status.

Domestic corporations are corporations created by the authority of a U.S. (federal or state) government.

Foreign corporations are corporations created by the authority of any non–U.S. governmental body.

Tax-exempt organizations can lose their tax exemption by engaging in any of several **prohibited transactions.**[12] Among the forbidden transactions are those between the exempt organization and the individual (or any member of his or her family) who created that entity if the transaction is not made at arm's length. For example, if an exempt organization were to loan any part of its income or corpus to its creator at a less than reasonable rate of interest, or without adequate security, that loan would be a prohibited transaction and the organization would lose its tax-exempt status. For additional details concerning tax-exempt organizations, examine Subchapter F of the Code.[13]

Foreign Corporations

Corporations are legal entities, or legal persons, created by the authority of a government. Corporations created by the authority of either the U.S. (federal) government or any one of our 50 state governments are known as **domestic corporations.** Corporations created under the authority of almost any other (foreign) government are, for purposes of the U.S. income tax, known as **foreign corporations.** As a general rule, a foreign corporation is exempt from U.S. income tax if (1) it has no income from any U.S. source and (2) it is not controlled by U.S. taxpayers. A controlled foreign corporation (CFC) may be subject to an immediate U.S. tax on some portion or all of its income. Any meaningful interpretation of the general rules just stated require a detailed definition of U.S. source rules and control concepts. Unfortunately, the investigation of even these two topics exceeds the scope of this chapter. We must, therefore, be satisfied with a few simplified examples.

---

11 Sec. 501(b).

12 Sec. 503(b).

13 Subchapter F encompasses Secs. 501 through 528.

EXAMPLE 6-3

Brit, Ltd., is a corporation chartered in the United Kingdom. All of Brit's stock is owned by Elizabeth and Charles Laughton, who are British citizens. Brit, Ltd., has no connection with any U.S. trade or business and make no investments in the United States. Brit, Ltd., is exempt from U.S. income taxation.

EXAMPLE 6-4

Maple Leaves, Inc., was chartered by the Canadian Province of Ontario. Maple Leaves, Inc., is wholly owned by Netty and Lee Flowers, who are citizens of Canada. Approximately 40% of Maple Leaves' income is effectively connected with a business that is conducted in the United States. Maple Leaves, Inc., is subject to the U.S. income tax on its U.S. sourced income.

EXAMPLE 6-5

Outbound, Inc., is a wholly owned subsidiary of a U.S. (domestic) corporation. Outbound, Inc., got its charter from the Korean government. Because Outbound, Inc., is a controlled foreign corporation—that is, because it is wholly owned and controlled by the U.S. corporation—it is subject to the U.S. income tax. Incidentally, under most circumstances, neither Outbound, Inc., nor its (U.S.) parent corporation will immediately pay any U.S. income tax on the income Outbound, Inc., earns so long as none of that income is repatriated to the parent corporation. Outbound, Inc., may, however, be required to pay some amount of U.S. income tax currently if it earns any certain Subpart F income.

Examples 6-3, 6-4, and 6-5 illustrate the inordinate complexity of income taxation of income earned across international borders, as well as introducing many new and undefined words and phrases. Although the general topic of international taxation is of growing importance, most of the details must be left for more advanced courses. (See Subchapter N of the code for more details).[14]

Figure 6-3 summarizes the long reach of U.S. income tax over both domestic and foreign corporations. The illustration emphasizes the fact that all domestic corporations—regardless of who owns them or where they earn their income—are subject to the U.S. income tax. Foreign corporations that earn some or all of their income from U.S. sources are also subject to U.S. income tax. And, finally, even foreign corporations with no U.S.-source income may be immediately subject to the U.S. income tax on some part or all of their income if they are a CFC.

Under U.S. tax law, domestic corporations are taxed on their worldwide income. This system of income taxation is known as **global income taxation.** Many other nations tax only the income earned within their boundaries. Those tax systems are know as **territorial income taxes.** Because both the U.S. government and one or more foreign governments may tax the foreign-source income of domestic corporations, that income would be subject to double taxation were it not for a complex system of foreign tax credits. In general, the U.S. government allows domestic corporations

> Governments that impose **global income taxation** ordinarily tax their taxpayers on worldwide income.
>
> Governments that impose **territorial income taxes** ordinarily tax their taxpayers on only that part of their income that is earned from within the taxing government's territory.

---

14 Subchapter N includes Secs. 861 through 999.

FIGURE 6-3

**U.S. Income
Taxation of
Corporations**

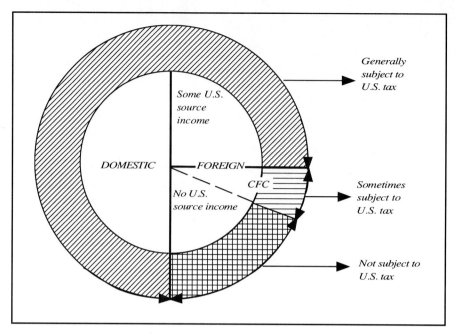

to claim a foreign tax credit for any income taxes paid to foreign governments.[15] This foreign tax credit cannot, however, be greater than the U.S. tax would have been on that same amount of taxable income.[16] In other words, the foreign tax credit cannot exceed the product in the following multiplication:

$$\frac{\text{Foreign-source income}}{\text{Worldwide income}} \times \text{U.S. tax on worldwide income}$$

EXAMPLE 6-6

Bigtime, Inc., a domestic corporation, earns a worldwide income of $20 million this year. Of this $20 million, $5 million is foreign-source income. Bigtime paid foreign income taxes of $2 million; U.S. taxes on Bigtime's worldwide income are $6.8 million before credits. Bigtime's maximum foreign tax credit for this year is $1.7 million.

Any excess foreign tax credit may be carried forward and claimed in subsequent years, but only to the extent that the total credit claimed in any year does not exceed the general limit illustrated above.

Foreign corporations generally pay the U.S. income tax on only their U.S.-source income.[17] If a foreign corporation earns income that is effectively connected with a U.S. trade or business, it will pay tax on that income in a manner similar to any other U.S. business.[18] If a foreign corporation earns only passive income from U.S. sources, the United States insures its taxation of that income by imposing a withholding tax on

15 Sec. 27.

16 Sec. 904.

17 Secs. 881 and 882.

18 Sec. 882.

the income earned by the foreign corporation.[19] If the U.S. person paying the passive income to the foreign corporation fails to withhold the proper amount of tax, then the U.S. person making the payment (rather than the foreign taxpayer) is held responsible for the underpayment of tax actually owed by the foreign corporation.[20]

Perhaps the most important observation to note at this point is the aggressiveness of the U.S. government in taxing worldwide income. The only foreign corporations not subject to the U.S. income tax are those that are not controlled by U.S. taxpayers and those with no U.S.-source income. Only in these relatively extreme circumstances does the United States find it impossible to obtain jurisdiction to tax, either directly or indirectly.

Nonresident Alien Individuals

For U.S. income tax purposes, all individual taxpayers can be classified either as citizens or as aliens. Individuals who are not U.S. citizens are, by definition, aliens. **Alien** taxpayers can be further subclassified either as resident aliens or nonresident aliens. Aliens are deemed to be resident aliens if they meet any one of three tests: (1) if they obtain a green card by lawful admission to the United States; (2) if they have a "substantial presence" in the United States (that is, they are here for at least 31 days during the year or for at least 183 days during a three-year period) or (3) they make a special, first-year election to be treated as a resident.[21]

> For U.S. income tax purposes, an **alien** is any individual who is not a U.S. citizen.

In general, all citizens and resident aliens are fully subject to the U.S. income tax on their worldwide income. Nonresident aliens are subject to tax only if they have some amount of income from U.S. sources.[22] Nonresident aliens engaged in a trade or business in the United States will be taxed like U.S. citizens on that part of their income that is effectively connected with a U.S. trade or business.[23] Nonresident aliens also may be taxed if they receive passive income from U.S. sources.[24] The tax on passive income is assured by requiring the U.S. payor to withhold tax from payments made to nonresident aliens. Failure to withhold may shift the liability for the tax from the nonresident alien to the U.S. person making the payment.

Figure 6-4 illustrates the worldwide taxation of individuals by the U.S. government. A careful comparison of Figures 6-3 and 6-4 will suggest numerous parallels between the U.S. taxation of corporations and individuals who earn income across international boundaries. The only individuals who wholly escape the U.S. income tax are nonresident aliens with no income from U.S. sources.

The foreign-source income of both citizens and resident aliens may be subject to taxation by both the U.S. government and one or more foreign governments. These taxpayers are, therefore, entitled to the foreign tax credit in the same manner as described above for domestic corporations.

Grantor Trusts

> A **grantor trust** is any trust whose taxable income is attributed to, and taxed to, its grantor.

For federal income tax purposes, a **grantor trust** must be distinguished from other trusts because a grantor trust is *not* treated as a taxable entity whereas other trusts (other than tax-exempt trusts) are. To the misfortune of tax students, the definition of

---

19 Secs. 1441 and 1442.

20 Sec. 7501.

21 Sec. 7701(b).

22 Sec. 871.

23 Sec. 871(b).

24 Sec. 871(a).

FIGURE 6-4

U.S. Income
Taxation of
Individuals

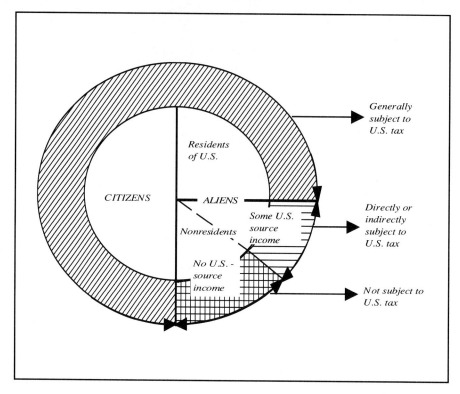

grantor trusts was significantly changed as of March 1, 1986. Trusts in existence on March 1, 1986, are defined under prior law if no additional property is transferred to the trust after that date. All trusts created on or after March 1, 1986, are subject to the current definition. The following two statements summarize the definitional distinctions between taxable trusts and grantor trusts:

1. For trusts created after March 1, 1986 (as well as trusts created before that date *if* any additional property is transferred to the trust after March 1, 1986), the trust will be recognized as a separate taxpayer *only if* the value of any trust property that may revert to the grantor (or the grantor's spouse) is 5% or less of the value of all trust property.

2. For trusts created on or before March 1, 1986 (and to which no additional property has been transferred since that date), the trust will be recognized as a separate taxpayer so long as no trust property *can* revert to the grantor—

   a. In 10 years or less, or

   b. Until the death of a designated life beneficiary.

   These trusts are generally known as Clifford trusts.

EXAMPLE 6-7

On February 1, 1986, Marie Ramirez transferred a $100,000 certificate of deposit, paying 10% interest, into a trust and named her son, Raul, as income beneficiary. At the end of 10 years and one day, the trustee was instructed to return the entire

Continued

EXAMPLE 6-7 (Con't.)

corpus of the trust to Marie, the grantor. Because this trust was created before March 1, 1986, it would not be a grantor trust today unless additional property was added to the trust after March 1, 1986. Had the same trust been created on or after March 1, 1986, or had additional property been added to the prior trust, that trust would be a grantor trust.

The income earned by a grantor trust is taxable to the grantor regardless of who receives the income.[25] The taxable income of a trust that is not a grantor trust (and that is not a tax-exempt trust) will be taxed to the trust if none of that income is distributed to an income beneficiary. Taxable trusts are, however, generally entitled to a deduction for any taxable income distributed to an income beneficiary.[26] Thus, even taxable trusts may escape income taxation if they distribute their entire taxable income to a beneficiary. Under those circumstances the beneficiary becomes the taxpayer on income initially recognized by a trust.

EXAMPLE 6-8

To continue the illustration introduced in Example 6-7, let us assume that for 19X1 the Ramirez Trust earned a taxable income of $10,000 and distributed $8,000 of this $10,000 income to Raul Ramirez. If the Ramirez Trust is properly classified as a grantor trust, the entire $10,000 must be reported as taxable income by Marie Ramirez, as the grantor of the Ramirez Trust. If the Ramirez Trust is not a grantor trust, Raul Ramirez will report $8,000 of taxable income and the ramirez Trust will report the remaining $2,000 of taxable income.

Although a cursory reading of Sec. 1(e) suggests that every trust (other than a grantor trust or a tax-exempt trust) is a taxable entity, the right of a taxable trust to deduct taxable income distributed to a trust beneficiary makes the taxable trust, for all practical purposes, a "half entity" at best. In other words, even taxable trusts must pay the federal income tax only if and to the extent that they do not distribute their taxable income to trust beneficiaries. These general rules, though oversimplified, provide a general introduction to the taxation of income earned by trusts other than foreign trusts.

Foreign Trusts

For federal income tax purposes, a foreign trust is any trust whose foreign-source income is not subject to U.S. tax.[27] The classification of trusts as domestic trusts or foreign trusts is uncertain, at best. This classification turns on factors such as the physical or legal residence of the trustee, the physical location of the trust's assets, the country under whose laws the trust was apparently created, as well as other considerations.[28] Ignoring many details, let us safely conclude that the U.S. income taxation of

25 Sec 671.

26 See Secs. 651 and 661.

27 Sec. 7701(a)(31).

28 For example, see Rev. Rul. 60-181, 1960-1, C.B. 257.

foreign trusts is in many ways similar to the U.S. income taxation of nonresident alien individuals. That is, foreign trusts will wholly escape U.S. income taxation only if they have no income from U.S. sources.

SUMMARY

The entities treated as taxable entities under federal income-tax law can be summarized as follows:

1. *Every* individual other than nonresident aliens who have no income from U.S. sources;

2. *Every* corporation other than

    a. S corporations,

    b. Affiliated corporations,

    c. Exempt corporations, and

    d. Foreign corporations that

       (1) Are not controlled foreign corporations and

       (2) Have no income from U.S. sources; and

3. *Every* estate and trust other than

    a. Exempt trusts,

    b. Grantor trusts, and

    c. Foreign trusts

    but only to the extent that the taxable trust does not distribute its taxable income to a beneficiary. The fact that other entities are not taxable entities does not mean, however, that the income earned by those entities escapes the U.S. income tax.

THE TAXATION OF INCOME EARNED BY OTHER ENTITIES

Goal #3
Understand how the income earned by nontaxable entities is taxed.

Based solely on the information included so far in this chapter, an overly optimistic tax planner might think that the easiest way to avoid the U.S. income tax is to arrange one's affairs so that no income will be recognized by any individual, corporation, estate, or trust. That conclusion is unjustified because any taxable income recognized by most of the other entities must be allocated directly to one or more of the taxable entities. The allocation rules are most readily understood in the context of sole proprietorships and partnerships.

Sole Proprietorships

Financial accounting rules require a separate accounting and reporting for businesses operated as sole proprietorships. Financial statements prepared for a proprietorship do not include the proprietor's nonbusiness income, expenditures, assets, and liabilities, thus providing a clear picture of the business operations.

For tax purposes, a sole proprietorship has no standing as an entity. All items of income, deductions, and tax credits of a proprietorship are reported directly on Schedule C (F for farming) of the proprietor's tax return, that is, on the individual owner's Form 1040. Taxpayers engaged in the operation of more than one trade or business should file more than one Schedule C (or F) and may use different accounting methods for each business. An attorney, for example, may use the cash method of accounting for his or her law practice, even though he or she is required to use the accrual method for the operation of a second business, say an office supply house, where inventory is a material income-producing factor.

Partnerships

A partnership is not a taxpaying entity even though it must report to the IRS all of its gross income, deductions, and tax credits. Although a partnership must file an information return (specifically, Form 1065), the actual tax on the income earned by a partnership must be paid by the *taxable* partners (that is, by the individuals, corporations, estates, or trusts who directly or indirectly own the partnership). Incidentally, tax law says absolutely nothing about the need of a partnership to distribute any part or all of its real economic income. In other words, tax law is solely concerned with the reporting of tax numbers, not with the distribution of real economic income. Consequently, the partners in a financially successful partnership may discover that, because of their mere ownership of a partnership interest, they owe federal income tax on an income that they have not yet received. The decision of the partnership's management group to retain or to distribute its real economic income is a matter of financial management, not an issue of tax law. Figure 6-5 illustrates the essential tax concepts related to partnerships.

The figure assumes that the XYZ Partnership is owned by four equal partners: an individual, I; a corporation, C; a trust, T; and another partnership, the AB Partnership. As 25% partners, each of these entities (I,C,T, and AB) must also report one-fourth of any taxable income reported to the IRS by the XYZ Partnership. However, because

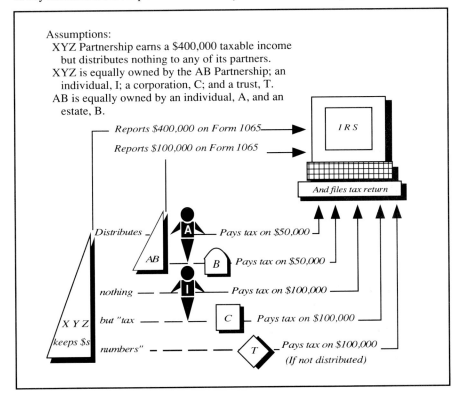

FIGURE 6-5

Partnership Taxation Illustrated

Assumptions:
XYZ Partnership earns a $400,000 taxable income but distributes nothing to any of its partners.
XYZ is equally owned by the AB Partnership; an individual, I; a corporation, C; and a trust, T.
AB is equally owned by an individual, A, and an estate, B.

Reports $400,000 on Form 1065
Reports $100,000 on Form 1065
I R S
And files tax return
Distributes — Pays tax on $50,000
AB — *B* — Pays tax on $50,000
nothing — Pays tax on $100,000
XYZ but "tax — *C* — Pays tax on $100,000
keeps $s numbers" — *T* — Pays tax on $100,000
(If not distributed)

the AB Partnership is itself *not* a taxable entity, any income that AB reports as a partner in the XYZ Partnership will also pass directly through the AB Partnership until it reaches a taxable entity. In Figure 6-5 it is assumed that the AB Partnership is equally owned by individual A and the estate of B. Hence, A and the estate of B indirectly pick up one-eighth of the taxable income originally generated by the XYZ Partnership. Note that the income generated by XYZ results in the filing of seven tax returns—one each by XYZ, AB, A, B, I, C, and T—but only five of these entities (A, B, I, C, and T) actually pay the income tax on the income initially earned by XYZ.

If a partnership reports a loss (because its deductions exceed its gross income) that loss is ordinarily passed through the partnership and claimed as a deduction by the partnership's individual, corporate, and fiduciary partners. The partner's right to deduct a loss generated by a partnership may be restricted by both the PAL rules and certain basis limitations. The PAL rules were explained briefly in Chapter 5; the basis limitation rules are explained in Chapter 8.

Except when policy considerations take precedence, tax rules ignore the existence of the partnership and treat each partner as though the partner owned the underlying assets directly and operated them as a proprietor. As explained in Chapter 7, a partnership generally must use the same tax year that its principal partners use, often a calendar year where the partners are individuals, unless it is willing to pay the special tax associated with the Sec. 444 election. The partnership files a Form 1065 that shows its taxable items of income, gains, losses, deductions, credits, and so on. The return also shows each partner's distributive share of these items. The partners then report their distributive shares on their own tax returns. When the partnership's taxable year is different from that of a partner, the partner reports his or her distributive share for the partnership year that ends within the partner's year.

Distributive shares of taxable items are generally allocated based on each partner's interest in the partnership capital.[29] However, items can be allocated between the partners in any manner that the partners agree on, provided the allocation has "substantial economic effect."[30] This latter term means that the allocations are properly recorded in the capital accounts and that capital accounts are used to determine each partner's share of partnership properties at liquidation.

EXAMPLE 6-9

Assume that partnership CD reports an ordinary loss (excess of ordinary deductions over ordinary income) of $12,000 and a capital gain of $8,000. If C and D are equal partners each reports an ordinary loss of $6,000 and a capital gain of $4,000. If the partners agree, the entire ordinary loss could be allocated to C, for example, provided the loss is properly recorded in C's capital account and provided the capital accounts reflect C's interest for purposes of liquidation. Note that the tax character of an item does not change because of the partnership. The capital gain is still a capital gain to the reporting partner. The tax attributes of all items flow through the partnership to its partners.

The effective administration of the income tax requires that the partnerships be treated as separate entities for some purposes. With only minor exceptions, elections relative to accounting periods and methods must be made at the partnership level. If

29 Sec. 704(a).

30 Sec. 704(b).

a partnership uses the accrual method, then each partner must use that method for reporting partnership items even though a particular partner might otherwise use the cash method. The partnership is a reporting unit for tax purposes, and use of a single method for partnership items is an administrative necessity.

Partnerships are also treated as separate entities for purposes of determining the character of partnership items. If property is held by a partnership as inventory, gain on the disposition is ordinary income, even if the inventory would be a capital asset if held directly by the partners.

Finally, a partnership usually has a continuing existence for tax purposes, even when some event occurs that terminates a partnership under local law. Admission of a new partner, retirement of an old partner, or sale of an existing partnership interest to a new partner (if less than 50% of partnership capital) does not terminate a partnership for tax purposes. The statute provides for continuation of a partnership unless it ceases to do business or unless control of the partnership changes hands by sale within a 12-month period.

CRITICAL DEFINITIONS

To state that a corporation and a trust are taxable entities, whereas a partnership is not, begs three critical definitions. What, exactly, is a corporation, a trust or a partnership, for federal income tax purposes? In the vast majority of all cases the answer is obvious. Entities organized and classified as a corporation under state law will ordinarily also be treated as a corporation for federal income tax purposes; those organized and classified as a partnership will usually be treated as a partnership; and so on. In rare circumstances, however, that general conclusion is not valid.

Furthermore, the definitions provided in the Code are of little practical value in making difficult decisions in questionable cases. The Code purports to define a corporation as follows:

> The term corporation includes associations, joint-stock companies, and insurance companies.[31]

Although this purported definition may put the reader on alert that the definition of a corporation must be broadly construed, it lacks operational utility. In other words, the statutory definition helps very little in trying to decide whether certain business organizations should or should not be considered to be corporations in questionable cases. The definition of a partnership in the statute is equally vague:

> The term partnership includes a syndicate, group, pool, joint venture, or other unincorporated organization through or by means of which any business, financial operation, or venture is carried on, and which is not, within the meaning of this title, a corporation or a trust or estate.[32]

Fortunately, both an early Supreme Court decision and subsequent treasury regulations give substantially more guidance in defining a business entity of uncertain classification.[33] These authorities are especially helpful today in determining how various foreign business entities, with no direct U.S. counterpart, must be classified

---

Goal #4
Distinguish corporations from trusts and partnerships.

---

31 Sec. 7701(a).

32 Sec. 761(a).

33 See *Morrissey et al. v. Comm'r*, 296 US 344 (1935) and Treas. Regs. Sec. 301.7701-2.

for U.S. federal income tax purposes. The general approach of both the judicial and the administrative authorities is to require that uncertain classifications be made on the basis of a careful analysis of all the facts and circumstances, with particular emphasis given to six specific characteristics summarized as follows:

1. What is the primary objective of the entity?

2. Are associates present?

3. Is the entity's life independent of the owners' lives?

4. Are the owners' interests freely transferable?

5. Is the owners' liability limited?

6. Is management of the entity centralized?

Corporation versus Trust

In *Morrissey* the Supreme Court had to decide whether an apparent trust (that is, a legal entity that had many of the trappings of a trust) should be treated for federal income tax purposes as a trust or as a corporation. After analyzing all of the facts and circumstances, the court concluded that both trusts and corporations had lives that were independent of their owners; both had free transferability of ownership interests; both had limited the owners' liability; and both had centralized management. Thus, the two characteristics that distinguish a trust form a corporation were found to be (1) the objective of the entity and (2) the presence or absence of associates. The primary objective of a corporation is to carry on a business, for profit; the primary objective of a trust is to protect assets for beneficiaries. A corporation has associates; a trust does not.

Based on this analysis the court concluded that the entity in *Morrissey* should be treated as a corporation rather than as a trust largely because the primary objective of that entity was to carry on a business for profit rather than to protect assets for beneficiaries. The alleged trust was found to be a "business trust" that should be taxed as a corporation. This decision was of great importance because it demonstrated that a business organization that lacks a corporate charter can still, in unusual circumstances, be treated as a corporation for federal income tax purposes. That basic conclusion of the court is still applicable today.

Corporation versus Partnership

In subsequent cases several courts had to decide whether various business entities should be treated as a partnership or as a corporation for federal income tax purposes.[34] In reaching their decisions the courts reviewed both prior judicial law and several iterations of regulations promulgated after the various judicial decisions were rendered. The judicial decisions noted that corporations and partnerships both share the profit motive and are characterized by the presence of associates. On the other hand, corporations have lives independent of their owners; have free transferability of owners' interests, have limited liability for owners, and have centralized management. Ordinary partnerships have none of these last four characteristics. The courts observed that in the classic partnership the life of the partnership depends on the life of its

34 See, for example, *U.S. v. Kintner*, 216 F.2d 418 (CCA9, 1954); *Zuckman v. U.S.*, 524 F.2d 729 (Ct. Cl., 1975); and *Philip G. Larson*, 66 TC 159 (1975).

owners; a partner's ownership interest is *not* freely transferable; a partner's liability is *not* limited; and the management of a partnership is shared by all partners.

The current regulations provide that an entity that might be classified as either a corporation or a partnership will be treated for tax purposes as a corporation if it has a *majority* of corporate characteristics.[35] For some time there was a question concerning the proper interpretation of majority. Did the term *majority* refer to any four of the six characteristics of a corporation or did it refer to any three of the four *noncommon* characteristics?

The courts eventually accepted the latter position. Today, therefore, an organization is treated for tax purposes as a corporation rather than as a partnership if it is characterized by any three of the following four corporate characteristics: (1) unlimited life, (2) free transferability of ownership interests, (3) limited liability for owners, and (4) centralized management.

In summary, although the Code provides in Secs. 1 and 11 that *every* individual, *every* corporation, and certain estates and trusts are subject to the federal income tax, other authorities significantly modify a literal interpretation of those two sections. Some business ventures organized in corporate form may escape income taxation either by electing to be treated as an S corporation or by virtue of their tax-exempt status; under still other circumstances, an unincorporated association may be taxed as if it were a corporation. Similarly, many individuals—generally nonresident aliens with no income from U.S. sources—also escape the U.S. income tax. Many trusts are taxed as trusts while others may be tax exempt or taxed as a corporation. In short, the literal words of the Code must be interpreted with great care. Disregarding the special cases, let us turn our attention to a determination of the tax rates that are applied to the taxable income recognized by each of the three taxable entities.

AT WHAT TAX RATE ARE TAXPAYERS TAXED?

Sections 1 and 11 provide six different tax-rate tables for the three taxable entities. Four tax-rate tables are applicable to individual taxpayers; one, to corporate taxpayers; and one, to fiduciary taxpayers. Each of the six tax-rate tables are progressive; that is, each tax-rate table provides lower tax rates for lesser amounts of taxable income. In addition, each of the tax-rate tables may be modified by other statutory provisions under special circumstances. In the next few pages of this chapter, we will examine both the ordinary tax-rate tables and the more important modifications to those six tables.

TAX RATES FOR INDIVIDUAL TAXPAYERS

Goal #5
Understand the tax rates.

Subsections 1 (a) through 1 (d) provide four tax-rate tables for individual taxpayers; one each for (1) married persons (including surviving spouses) who file a joint return with their spouse; (2) heads of households; (3) single persons; and (4) married persons who file separate returns. Each of these four tax-rate tables have three steps of progression. Each taxes the initial amounts of taxable income at 15%; an intermediate amount of taxable income, at 28%; and all remaining taxable income, at 31%. The point at which the tax rates increase from 15 to 28% and from 28 to 31% differ for

35 Treas. Regs. Sec. 301-7701-2.

FIGURE 6-6

U.S. Tax Rates
for Individual
Taxpayers

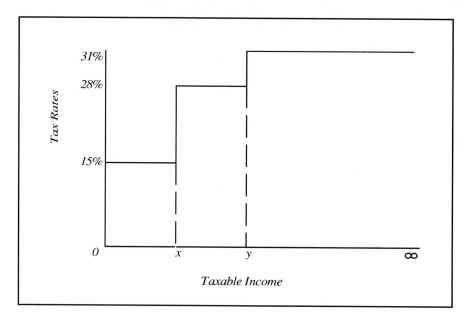

each of the four tax-rate tables. Figure 6-6 illustrates the general structure of the individual tax-rate tables.

To complicate matters still more, the point at which the marginal tax rates increase from 15 to 28% and from 28 to 31% change from year to year to reflect changes in the consumer price index (CPI). Or, in terms of Figure 6-6, points x and y vary from year to year. The exact points for 1991 and 1992 are

Applicable to	Point x for		Point y for	
	1991	1992	1991	1992
Married persons filing separate returns	$17,000	$17,900	$41,075	$43,250
Single persons	20,350	21,450	49,300	51,900
Heads of households	27,300	28,750	70,450	74,150
Married persons filing joint returns	34,000	35,800	82,150	86,500

The technical distinctions that determine which of the four tax-rate tables an individual must use is postponed to Part Three where such critical terms as *dependent* can be defined. For purposes of this chapter the distinction between married persons and single individuals is assumed to be self-evident. Married individuals may file either (1) one tax return as a couple, called a joint return, or (2) two separate tax returns. In addition, a surviving spouse may use the tax-rate table otherwise reserved for married person filing a joint return. For federal income tax purposes the term *surviving spouse* requires more than simply outliving one's wife or husband. In very general terms, it refers to an individual who has been widowed for less than three years and who pays at least 51% of the cost of maintaining a home for self and at least one dependent child who lives with the taxpayer for the entire year.[36] A head of household

---

36 The definition of a dependent can be found in Chapter 9. Note that status as a surviving spouse specifically requires the taxpayer to have a dependent *child*; other dependents do *not* suffice for this purpose.

is ordinarily an individual who pays at least 51% of the cost of maintaining a home for self and one or more dependents who live with the taxpayer for more than half of the year. In most instances a head of household is unmarried; however, married individuals who live apart from their spouse may (under some circumstances) qualify. Additional details and missing definitions are, as noted above, deferred to Part Three.

EXAMPLE 6-10

Amy and Brad Smith were married at 7 P.M. on December 31, 1991. If Amy and Brad are calendar-year taxpayers, they may elect to file either one joint or two separate tax returns for 1991. If they elect to file jointly and their combined taxable income amounted to $30,000, their gross tax liability for 1991 would be $4,500 (that is, 15% of $30,000). If their combined taxable income had amounted to $40,000 (rather than $30,000) and they filed a joint return, their gross tax liability for 1991 would have been $6,780 (that is, 15% of $34,000 plus 28% of $6,000). If Amy and Brad remain married on December 31, 1992, they may elect to file either one joint or two separate returns for 1992. In other words, the marital status of an individual at the end of the year determines their filing status for the entire year. In addition, the election to file joint or separate returns is an annual election that can be changed each year by married persons.

EXAMPLE 6-11

Hoa Thi Lam is a single individual who recognized a taxable income of $30,000 in 1992. Lam's gross tax liability for 1992 will be $5,611.50 (that is, 15% of $21,450 plus 28% of $8,550).

EXAMPLE 6-12

Carlos Lopez was widowed on May 3, 1991. Carlos's mother, Lora Lopez, lived with him throughout 1992 and qualified as his dependent. If Carlos has no other dependents, he will qualify as a head of household (but not as a surviving spouse) for 1992. Thus, if Carlos has a taxable income of $30,000 for $1992, his gross tax liability will be $4,662.50 (or 15% of $28,750 plus 28% of $1,250).

Historical Reasons for Four Different Rates

The reason we have four tax-rate tables for individual taxpayers is most easily understood in historical context. Prior to 1948 there was only one tax-rate schedule for all individual taxpayers, regardless of their marital or family status. Tax rates remained relatively low and the fact that all individuals paid the same tax rate was deemed to be equitable. After tax rates rose dramatically during World War II, a gross inequity between residents of community-property states and common-law states became apparent. Eight states (Arizona, California, Idaho, Louisiana, Nevada, New Mexico, Texas, and Washington) are **community-property states**; their laws affect both the property rights and the income taxation of married persons. The other 42 states are referred to as separate-property or **common-law states.** Those laws also affect the property rights and the income taxation of married persons.

The single most important difference between community-property and common-law states, for income tax purposes, is that federal tax law follows state law in

A **community-property state** is any one of eight states that have special laws governing the property rights of married persons who reside within the state.

A **common-law state** (or separate-property state) is any state other than a community-property state.

determining the person to whom income earned by married persons is taxable. Consequently, in the eight community-property law states, any income earned by either spouse during marriage is deemed to be equally earned by each spouse. In other words, in these eight states, one-half of any wage or salary earned by the wife is taxed to the husband; and one-half of any wage or salary earned by the husband is taxed to the wife. In the 42 common-law states the income earned by any individual is taxed solely to that individual; none of it is attributed to a taxpayer's spouse. The impact of this legal distinction on income taxation 50 years ago was especially significant because, in those days, (1) most families included only one individual who worked outside the home and (2) the income tax rates were highly progressive.

To illustrate the potentially significant impact of community-property laws on income taxation, assume that there is only one tax-rate table for individual taxpayers, and that the tax-rate table is as follows:

Tax on first $20,000 of taxable income, 10%;

Tax on next $30,000 of taxable income, 25%; and

Tax on all remaining taxable income, 50%.

Given this imaginary tax-rate table and assuming a married couple with a taxable income of $100,000, earned solely by either spouse, the gross liability for the couple living in one of the 42 common-law states would be $34,500 (or $20,000 x 10% + $30,000 x 25% + $50,000 x 50%). On the other hand, the gross liability for a couple living in one of the eight community-property law states would be only $19,000 (or 2 x [$20,000 x 10% + $30,000 x 25%]). In other words, in the community-property states the husband and the wife would each report an income of $50,000 and each pay a tax of $9,500 (for a total of $19,000) whereas in the common-law state the husband or the wife would report an income of $100,000 and pay a tax of $34,500. In this example the tax on the couple in the common-law state is 181% of the tax on the same income earned by the couple in the community-property state. The actual tax penalty that existed prior to 1948 depended most importantly on (1) the absolute size of a couple's income; (2) the employment status of the two individuals; and (3) the disparity in the amount of income earned by each of the two individuals if both individuals worked as paid employees. Note that, in the prior illustration, there would be no penalty whatsoever between a couple living in a community-property state and a couple living in a common-law state if both the husband and the wife each earned a taxable income of exactly $50,000. That very special case was not, however, the 1948 norm and pressures grew rapidly for a change in the law.

In order to thwart a rapidly growing movement among the common-law states to adopt community-property laws, in 1948 Congress enacted a second tax-rate table that could be used only by married persons filing a joint return. This second tax-rate table originally had income brackets that were exactly twice the width of the tax brackets applicable to all other (single) individuals. In other words, if the tax rate on the first $20,000 of taxable income earned by a single person was 10%, then the tax rate on the first $40,000 (or exactly 2 x $20,000) of taxable income earned by a married person filing a joint return would also be 10%. The second tax-rate table effectively permitted all married persons to file one joint return and to pay tax as if one-half of their aggregate income had been earned by each spouse, regardless of how their income was actually earned, and regardless of where they lived.

This change solved the community-property dilemma and satisfied taxpayers for a while. It soon became apparent that the death of a spouse in a family with growing children often resulted in drastic tax increases. Furthermore, the increased taxes usually came at a time when the widow or widower was required to incur additional personal expenses (which remained nondeductible) for the care of family members. This draconian result led Congress in 1953 to adopt a third tax-rate table that could be used only by heads of households. The tax brackets in this table were originally arranged so that exactly one-half of the benefit available to married couples filing joint returns was available to heads of households. In other words, if single persons paid 10% tax on their first $20,000 of taxable income and married persons (filing joint returns) paid 10% on their first $40,000 of taxable income, heads of households paid 10% on their first $30,000 of taxable income. Or, in terms of Figure 6-6, if the distance $0x$ were $20,000 for single persons, it would be $30,000 (or 150% x $20,000) for heads of households, and $40,000 (or 200% x $20,000) for married persons filing a joint return. Incidentally, in 1954, the tax-rate table for single taxpayers had 24 tax brackets starting at 20% and rising to 91%! The 91% marginal tax bracket applied to all taxable income in excess of $200,000 for single taxpayers.

Singles were the next group to complain about tax rates. They observed that a growing number of married couples had no family responsibilities, yet they benefited greatly from the tax-rate table available only to married persons filing joint returns. To satisfy this group, in 1971 Congress agreed to reduce the disparity in the income taxation of married couples and single individuals by readjusting the tax brackets in such a manner that single persons would never be required to pay more than 120% of the tax paid by a married couple earning the same amount of income. To accomplish this policy objective without reintroducing the old community-property state bias, Congress had to create a new (fourth) tax-rate table for married persons filing separate returns. The tax brackets in this newest table are exactly one-half the width of the taxable income brackets in the table used by married persons filing a joint return. Note that this most recent change also required that the width of the taxable income brackets for married persons filing jointly be reduced to less than 200% of the width of the brackets for single persons. (Similarly, the width of the brackets for heads of households had to be reduced to less than 150% of the width of the brackets for single taxpayers.)

This last change created a new problem. The present tax-rate tables sometimes impose an extra tax on those individuals who decide to marry. Today, two single persons who each earn an identical amount of income will pay a penalty (in increased income taxes) if they marry. In other words, the tax on a married couple reporting a $100,000 taxable income is now greater than the tax on two single individuals each reporting a taxable income of $50,000. In short, even four different tax-rate tables for individual taxpayers are inadequate to resolve the complex issues of equitable taxation of individual taxpayers with varying personal and family obligations.

Exceptions to the Ordinary Tax Rates for Individuals

In somewhat unusual circumstances, individual taxpayers may be either permitted or required to ignore the normal tax-rate tables and to compute their federal income tax liability using any one (or some combination) of five alternative methods. The five special cases involve (1) a maximum tax on net capital gains; (2) the alternative minimum tax; (3) a "kiddie tax"; (4) lump-sum distributions from qualified pension and profit-sharing plans; and (5) withholding taxes on passive income earned by nonresident aliens. The maximum tax on capital gains is discussed in Chapter 16; the alternative minimum tax, in Chapter 19; the kiddie tax, in Chapter 9; and lump-sum distributions, in Chapter 12.

Persons remitting passive or investment income, derived from U.S. sources, to nonresident alien individuals are generally required to withhold the U.S. federal income tax at a flat rate of 30% of the gross amount remitted.[37] Numerous tax treaties between the United States and foreign governments provide for lower withholding rates. Any nonresident alien eligible for taxation at a lower rate must file Form 1001 with the withholding agent if he or she wants income tax to be withheld at that more favorable rate. In some instances the U.S. tax rate has been reduced to zero. In these cases, obviously, no withholding may be required.

To facilitate the computation of the gross tax liability of individual taxpayers, the IRS has prepared two different sets of tables. The two current tables are reproduced in Appendices A and B at the end of this textbook. The tax-rate schedules that appear as Appendix A can only be used by individuals reporting a taxable income in excess of $50,000. Individuals reporting a taxable income of $50,000 or less must use the tax-rate tables in Appendix B. By removing the need to multiply, the tax tables in Appendix B are supposed to reduce the number of arithmetic errors on tax returns prepared and filed by individuals. Modifications to the basic tax-rate tables required by any of the five special-exception cases are achieved by the use of one or more special IRS forms that must be attached to the basic Form 1040 submitted by the individual taxpayer.

TAX RATES FOR CORPORATE TAXPAYERS

Section 11 provides only one tax-rate table for most corporate taxpayers.[38] That tax-rate table initially appears to have three progressive rates, namely

a 15% rate applicable to the first $50,000 in taxable income;

a 25% rate applicable to the next $25,000 in taxable income; and

a 34% rate applicable to all additional taxable income.

Figure 6-7 illustrates these apparent corporate tax rates.

FIGURE 6-7

Apparent U.S. Tax Rates for Corporate Taxpayers

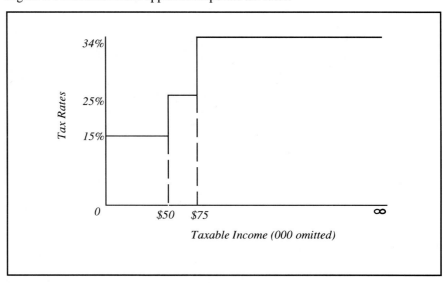

---

37 See Secs. 871, 872, and 1441.

38 Sec. 11(b).

Subsection 11(b)(1) goes on, however, to impose effectively a 5% surtax on any corporate taxable income in excess of $100,000 and less than $335,000. Thus, for corporate taxpayers earning any amount of taxable income between $100,000 and $335,000, there effectively is a fourth marginal tax rate of 39%. Thus the real or effective tax rates for corporate taxpayers are more accurately illustrated in Figure 6-8.

The intent of the additional 5% surtax is to recapture the tax advantage associated with the two lower marginal tax brackets from all corporations earning a taxable income in excess of $335,000 per year. For corporations earning less than $335,000 but more than $100,000, only some fraction of the tax advantage associated with the two lower marginal rate brackets is recaptured. The closer the corporations's taxable income is to $335,000, the greater the portion of the benefit that is recaptured. For all corporate taxpayers earning a taxable income in excess of $335,000, the only real tax rate is one (flat) rate of 34%. This rate is depicted in Figure 6-9.

Figure 6-10 illustrates how the 5% surtax effectively recaptures any potential benefit associated with the two lowest marginal tax rates for corporate taxpayers. In contrast, recall that individual taxpayers generally do not forfeit the benefit of the two lower tax brackets available to them, regardless of how large their income may grow to be. Individuals may, however, lose other tax benefits as their taxable income increases. These possibilities are explained in Part Three.

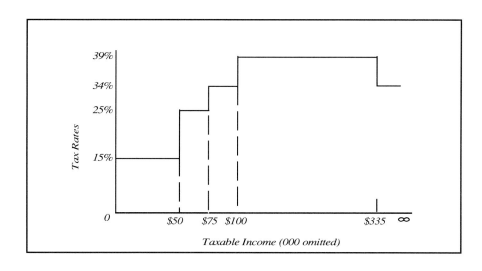

FIGURE 6-8

Real Tax Rates for Corporate Taxpayers with a Taxable Income between $100,000 and $335,000

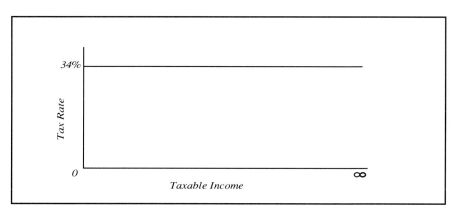

FIGURE 6-9

Effective Tax Rate for Corporations with a Taxable Income in Excess of $335,000

FIGURE 6-10

**Illustration of
How the 5%
Surtax
Recaptures
Potential
Benefit
Associated with
Two Lowest
Marginal Tax
Rates**

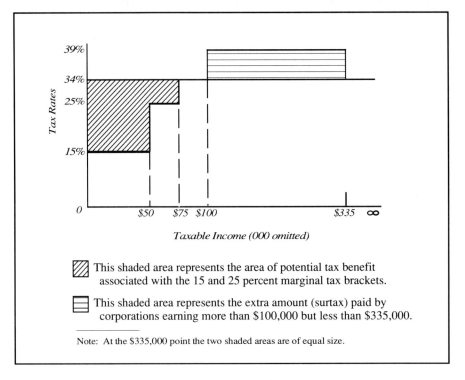

This shaded area represents the area of potential tax benefit associated with the 15 and 25 percent marginal tax brackets.

This shaded area represents the extra amount (surtax) paid by corporations earning more than $100,000 but less than $335,000.

Note: At the $335,000 point the two shaded areas are of equal size.

Exceptions to the Ordinary Tax Rates for Corporations

In somewhat unusual circumstances, corporate taxpayers (like individual taxpayers) are required to ignore the normal tax-rate table and to compute their federal income tax liability in some other manner. The five special corporate cases involve (1) qualified personal service corporations; (2) the alternative minimum tax; (3) corporations that are a member of a controlled group of corporations; (4) foreign corporations (other than CFCs) that earn some amount of passive income, from U.S. sources, that is not effectively connected to a U.S. trade or business; and (5) S corporations in rare circumstances. Four of the five special cases are discussed very briefly, below; the AMT (or alternative minimum tax) is discussed in Chapter 19.

A **personal service corporation** (PSC) is a C corportion (1) engaged in a professional service business if (2) that service is rendered in significant part by shareholders in their capacity as employees.

Personal service corporations. Subsection 11(b)(2) requires qualified **personal service corporations (PSCs)** to pay a flat 34% tax on their entire taxable income. In other words, qualified personal service corporations, regardless of how little they may earn, pay a tax comparable to the tax paid by other C corporations earning more than $335,000 in taxable income. (See Figure 6-9.) A PSC is defined as

any corporation—

(A) substantially all of the activities of which involve the performance of services in the fields of health, law, engineering, architecture, accounting, actuarial science, performing arts, or consulting, and

(B) substantially all of the stock of which (by value) is held directly (or indirectly through one or more partnerships, S corporations, or qualified personal service corporations . . .) by—

(i) employees performing services for such corporations in connection with the activities involving a field referred to in subparagraph (A),

(ii) retired employees who had performed such services for such corporation,

(iii) the estate or any individual described in clause (i) or (ii), or

(iv) any other person who acquired such stock by reason of the death of an individual described in clause (i) or (ii) (but only for the 2-year period beginning on the date of the death of such individual).[39]

This definition includes most professional corporations (or PCs) formed by doctors, dentists, attorneys, accountants, and others. The taxation of professional corporations at the highest applicable corporate rate is a recent phenomenon. Most PCs were formed several years ago when the taxation of income earned by those entities was far more favorable than the taxation of equivalent amounts of income earned by individual taxpayers. In other words, most PCs would never have been formed had today's laws been in effect in those years. In order to escape the high tax rate on PSCs, most PCs today either (1) make the subchapter S election or (2) pay sufficiently large salaries to reduce the PC's taxable income to zero.

Foreign corporations.   The taxation of foreign corporations (other than CFCs) with passive income, from U.S. sources, that is not connected to a U.S. trade or business is highly comparable to the taxation of passive income earned by nonresident alien individuals. That is, these foreign corporations are generally subject to a 30% withholding tax on their gross passive income.[40] The 30% rate may, however, be reduced to some lesser rate by a tax treaty.

S corporations.   Although S corporations ordinarily are not taxed as a separate taxable entity, they may be required to pay a corporate income tax if they either (1) recognize income from a "built in gain" or (2) recognize "excess net passive income." The definition of the two critical terms given in quotation marks must be deferred to more advanced courses in federal income taxation. For now, suffice it to say that whenever S corporations are subject to either of these two conditions, they pay taxes at the highest corporate rate.[41] This means that in those rare instances when S corporations must pay the federal income tax as a separate taxable entity, they pay that tax at a flat 34% rate.

Corporate members of a controlled group.   Although the separate identity of each corporation is ordinarily honored, in the absence of a consolidated return election, corporations that are members of a **controlled group of corporations** must compute their federal income tax liability based on the aggregate taxable income recognized by all of the members of the controlled group, excluding the NOL (net operating loss) of any member.[42]

Unfortunately, the definition of a controlled group is not easily explained. Because of its pervasive influence on small businesses, we have elected to include an explanation of the definition in the next few pages.

A controlled group of corporations can exist in any one of three forms: (1) parent-subsidiary; (2) brother-sister; or (3) combined group.[43] A parent-subsidiary group exists whenever one or more chains of corporations are connected with a common 80% corporate parent. This definition is virtually identical to that suggested earlier for members of an affiliated group. Parent and subsidiary corporations that do

> A **controlled group of corporations** is any two or more legally separate corporations whose gross tax liability must be determined as if their separate taxable income had been earned by a single corporate entity, but only if the ownership of the separate corporations is held in a way uniquely described in Sec. 1563.

39 Sec. 448(d)(2).

40 See Secs. 881, 882, and 1442.

41 Secs. 1374 and 1375.

42 Sec. 1561.

43 Sec. 1563(a)(1), (2) and (3), respectively.

not or cannot elect to file a consolidated return are automatically members of a controlled group. In other words, the three sets of parent-subsidiary corporations illustrated in Figure 6-2 (as well as many others) will be deemed members of an affiliated group if they elect to file one consolidated tax return and members of a controlled group if they do not make that election.

EXAMPLE 6-13

Corporations A, B, C, and D are all members of the same controlled group of corporations. Their separately determined taxable incomes for the year are

Corporation A	$60,000
Corporation B	50,000
Corporation C	40,000
Corporation D	(80,000)(an NOL)

The tax liability for corporations A, B, and C will be calculated for the group as if it had been earned by one corporation with a taxable income of $150,000. The total tax of $41,750 (or 15% x $50,000 + 25% x $25,000 + 34% x $25,000 + 39% x $50,000) must be divided between the three corporations (A, B, and C) in a reasonable manner.[44] Note that the total tax to be allocated among the three corporations is significantly greater than the tax would have been had each corporation been allowed to determine its own tax independently. That total would have been only $23,5000, determined as follows:

Corporation	Taxable Income	Gross Tax
A	$60,000	$10,000
B	50,000	7,500
C	40,000	6,000
Total tax		$23,500

This means, of course, that corporations ordinarily want to avoid being a member of a controlled group.

The brother-sister form of the controlled group of corporations is defined by two tests—an 80% test *plus* a 50% test. The former test requires that five or fewer persons (who are individuals, estates, or trusts) own at least 80% of the stock of the two or more corporations being tested for their inclusion within a controlled group.[45] The 50% test requires that the same five or fewer persons own *more than* 50% of the stock of the two or more corporations being tested "taking into account the stock ownership of each such person only to the extent such stock ownership is identical with respect to each such corporation."[46] The meaning of the 50% requirement is unusually obtuse, even for the Internal Revenue Code. To unravel the statutory syntax, a few examples can be most helpful.

---

44 See Treas. Regs. Sec. 1.1561-3 for details.

45 Sec 1563 (a)(2)(A).

46 Sec. 1563 (a)(2)(B).

EXAMPLE 6-14

Assume that individual I owns 100% of the outstanding stock of Corporations A and B. This ownership arrangement is illustrated in Figure 6-11. In this illustration it is obvious that both the 80% and the 50% tests are satisfied because one person (individual I) owns 100% of both corporations being tested (that is Corporations A and B). Hence, in this example, Corporations A and B are members of a controlled group.

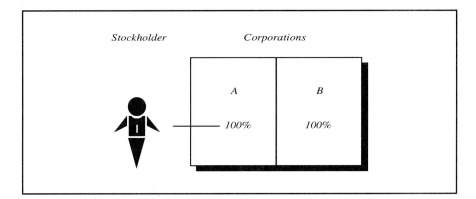

FIGURE 6-11

Simple Example of Two Brother-Sister Corporations

EXAMPLE 6-15

Next, assume that individual I owns 60% of Corporation A and 40% of Corporation B, and that individual J owns 40% of Corporation A and 60% of Corporation B (see Figure 6-12). In this example the 80% test presents no special problem of interpretation because the two individuals (I and J) collectively own 100% of the stock of the two corporations. The meaning of the 50% test is not as apparent because the words used in the Code are themselves unclear. However, Treasury Regulations effectively state that we can apply this test by simply looking across each row in a simple ownership matrix, identifying the *smallest* number that appears there for each shareholder, and then adding together these numbers to determine their identical ownership. [47] Following this administrative guidance, we can conclude that the identical ownership of individual I must be 40% (because I owns only 40% of Corporation B) and that the identical ownership of individual J must also be 40% (because J owns 40% of Corporation A). When we sum (or add together) the two identical ownerships of 40% each, we conclude that the total identical ownership in this example must be 80%. Because 80% is clearly more than 50% we can safety conclude that Corporations A and B in Figure 6-12 are once again members of a controlled group of corporations.

EXAMPLE 6-16

If we were to change slightly the ownership assumed in Figure 6-12 and assume that individual I owned 75% of Corporation A and 25% of Corporation B, and

Continued

---

47 Treas. Regs. Sec. 1.1563-1; give particular attention to the examples included therein.

FIGURE 6-12

Second Example of Two Brother-Sister Corporations

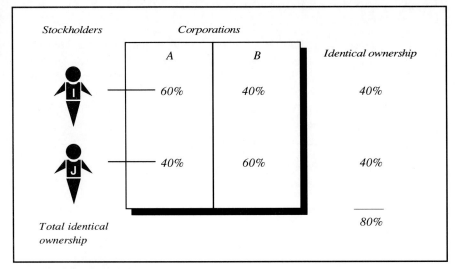

EXAMPLE 6-16 (Con't.)

that individual J owned 25% of A and 75% of B, then Corporations A and B would no longer be members of a controlled group because their identical ownership (combined) is *not more than* 50%. This result is depicted in Figure 6-13.

EXAMPLE 6-17

The ownership arrangement depicted in Figure 6-14 presents a very interesting question in statutory interpretation. In this illustration, individual I owns 100% of Corporation A and 79% of Corporation B. An unrelated individual J owns only 21% of Corporation B. If both I and J can be considered in making the controlled-group tests, Corporations A and B would be members of a controlled group because two individuals clearly own 100% of both corporations and the 50%

Continued

FIGURE 6-13

First Example of a Noncontrolled Group

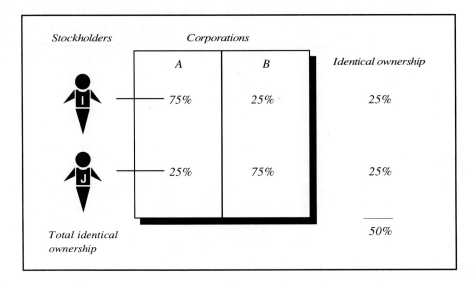

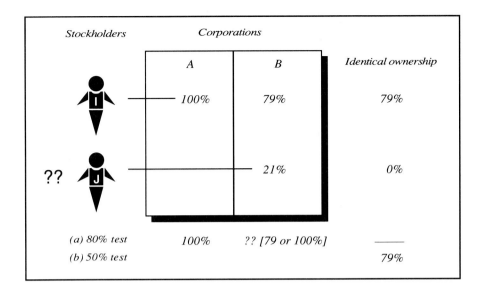

FIGURE 6-14

Second Example of a Noncontrolled Group

EXAMPLE 6-17 (Con't.)

identical-ownership test is satisfied by I's 79% identical interests by itself. The question: Must the stockholders who are included in this procedure own some stock (however little) in both corporations being tested for their inclusion in a controlled group? If individual J cannot be included in making the test, Corporations A and B will not be a controlled group because the 80% test will not be satisfied. Individual I owns only 79% of Corporation B; hence, the inclusion or exclusion of individual J becomes critical. The answer to the question was provided by the Supreme Court in *Vogel Fertilizer*.[48] The Court concluded that an individual who owns no stock in one of two corporations being tested must be excluded from the test. Consequently, Corporations A and B in Figure 6-14 are not members of a controlled group.

As complicated as Examples 6-14 through 6-17 are, they only begin to scratch the surface of complications related to the definition of a controlled group of corporations. The attribution of stock ownership from one stockholder to another is one major source of additional complications.[49] A second major complication involves overlapping groups.[50] In the latter situation one corporation belongs to two or more (different) controlled groups. The question: In which of the overlapping groups should the offending corporation's taxable income be included for purposes of making the income tax calculation? These and other definitional complications must be reserved for further study. To complete our discussion, we will simply note in passing the meaning of a combined group of controlled corporations.

A combined group consists of a combination of a parent-subsidiary group and a brother-sister group. Figure 6-15 illustrates one such possibility. Individual I owns 100% of both A and B Corporations and A Corporation also owns 100% of C

---

48 455 US 16 (1982).

49 See Secs. 1563 (d), (e), and (f).

50 See Treas. Regs. Sec. 1.1563-1(c) and Sec. 1563(b)(4).

FIGURE 6-15

Illustration of a
Combined
Group

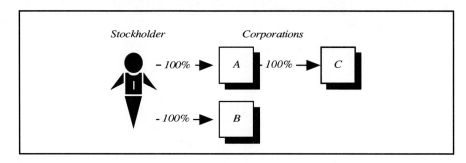

Corporation. Hence, Corporations A and B are brother-sister corporations and Corporations A and C are parent-subsidiary corporations. In this illustration Corporations A, B, and C constitute a combined group of controlled corporations.

The relationship between a *controlled group* of corporations and an *affiliated group* of corporations—discussed earlier in this chapter, as an aberration to the concept that *every* corporation is a separate taxable entity—is very easily confused. Table 6-1 explains the most important differences between these two corporate groups.

Tax Rate for Fiduciary Taxpayers

The tax-rate table applicable to fiduciary taxpayers is highly comparable to the four rate tables applicable to individual taxpayers. The fiduciary table, like the individual tables, has three progressive steps at 15, 28, and 31%.[51] Hence, Figure 6-6 is equally illustrative of fiduciary tax rates. The taxable income represented by distances $0x$ and $0y$ in Figure 6-6 are adjusted annually for changes in the CPI. The exact points for 1991 and 1992 are

Point *x* for		Point *y* for	
1991	1992	1991	1992
$3,450	$3,600	$10,350	$10,900

The benefit of the two lower marginal rates is *not* recovered via a 5% surtax (like it is for corporations) but the brackets are of such narrow width that they have little impact except on very small estates and trusts. Fiduciary taxpayers, like individual taxpayers, are eligible for the 28% maximum tax on net long term capital gains.[52]

Generally, estates and trusts compute their gross income, deductions, and credits using the same rules used by individuals. The many exclusions, deductions, and credits that, by their nature, are intended for individuals only are not available to fiduciaries. On the other hand, the law contains a few special deductions applicable to fiduciaries only. Instead of the individual exemption deduction, estates get an exemption deduction of $600. Simple trusts, defined as those that must distribute all their income to beneficiaries currently, are allowed an exemption deduction of $300. All other trusts get a $100 exemption deduction. Of more importance is the deduction allowed for distributions of income to beneficiaries.

As previously explained, a taxable estate or trust that distributes income to its beneficiaries is not taxed on that income. Instead, the beneficiaries receiving the distributed income declare it on their individual returns. What about the tax charac-

---

51 Sec. 1(e).

52 Sec. 1(h).

	Affiliated Group	Controlled Group
1. Types	1. Parent-subsidiary only	1. Parent-subsidiary* 2. Brother-Sister 3. Combined (a combination of 1 and 2, above)
2. How achieved?	1. By election (if qualified)	1. Automatic (by definition)
3. Important implications	1. File only one consolidated tax return for all of the members of an affiliated group. 2. Eliminate intercompany profits and losses. 3. Can offset any member's NOL against other members' income.	1. Each member files its own corporate tax return. 2. The tax liability is determined for the group based on a taxable income equal to the sum of the taxable incomes earned by members, *excluding* any NOL recognized by member corporations. 3. There is no elimination of profits on intercompany transactions.
4. Is the result desirable?	1. Sometimes, largely because of the right to offset losses and to eliminate intercompany profits. 2. Result is a practical necessity for all large ("Fortune 500") corporate organizations.	1. Never; the result can only "hurt" member corporations by increasing their tax liability (unless the entire group earns $50,000 or less, in which case the result is "neutral").

*Corporate members of a parent-subsidiary group *that elect to file a consolidated return* are *not* subject to the provisions otherwise applicable to controlled groups of corporations. Parent-subsidiary corporations that do *not* elect to file a consolidated return are automatically treated like any other members of a controlled group.

TABLE 6-1

Two Important Corporate Groups Compared

teristics of the distributed income? Consider these facts: A complex trust realizes $3,000 of interest income on corporate bonds, $2,000 of interest on municipal bonds, and $5,000 of gain on capital assets. The trust pays various expenses of $1,000 and distributes the $9,000 remaining current income to its beneficiaries. Does the beneficiary retain the classification for the municipal bond interests and the capital gain? Yes, the character of the income items is not changed but flows through the trust to the beneficiary. Thus, ($2,000/$10,000), or 2/10, of the $9,000 distribution is excluded by the beneficiary, and 5/10 of the distribution is treated as a capital gain.

This completes our introduction to the tax rates paid by the three taxable entities. In the next few pages you will discover how the gross tax liability of any taxable entity may be reduced by tax credits and prepayments.

Goal #6
Distinguish tax credits from tax deductions.

A **tax credit** is a specifically authorized direct (dollar-for-dollar) reduction in a taxpayer's tax liability, other than a tax prepayment.

A **tax prepayment** is any advance payment made by a taxpayer as a partial prepayment of a current tax liability.

WHAT ARE TAX CREDITS AND PREPAYMENTS?

The multiplication of the appropriate tax rates times taxable income yields the gross tax liability for each taxable entity. **Tax credits** are direct (dollar-for-dollar) reductions in a taxpayer's gross tax liability, granted by Congress to taxpayers for some special reasons. **Prepayments,** on the other hand, are advance deposits (usually mandatory) made by taxpayers as a partial payment of their current tax liability. Thus, tax credits and prepayments reduce a taxpayer's gross tax liability to the net tax payable due at the time the tax return is filed. Deductions differ conceptually from prepayments and tax credits. Tax deductions reduce a taxpayer's tax liability but only by some fraction of the deduction, the precise reduction dependent on the taxpayer's marginal tax rate. The economic values of tax credits and prepayments, on the other hand, do not vary with differences in a taxpayer's marginal tax rate.

EXAMPLE 6-18

To illustrate the important distinction between deductions and tax credits, let us consider the example of a taxable C corporation that recognizes a $500,000 taxable income during a year. This corporation would be in a marginal tax bracket of 34% (See Figure 6-9). Suppose that sometime after the corporate officers had computed the corporation's taxable income and gross tax liability, they discovered that a $10,000 payment had been omitted from their computations. Suppose too that they have a legitimate question of whether the payment is considered a deduction or a credit. The two tabulations below demonstrate the significant difference in impact on the corporation's net tax payable resulting from this difference in classification.

	Payment Treated as Deduction	Payment Treated as Credit
Taxable income before considering payment	$500,000	$500,000
Payment treated as deduction	(10,000)	---
Revised taxable income	$490,000	$500,000
Marginal tax rate	x 34%	x 34%
Gross tax liability	$166,600	$170,000
Payment treated as credit	---	(10,000)
Net tax payable	$166,600	$160,000

Observe that if the $10,000 payment is a credit, the entire $10,000 reduces the net tax payable. If the payment is a deduction, the decrease in the net tax payable is only $3,400 (that is $170,000 – $166,600, or 34% x $10,000).

TAX CREDITS

The statutory provisions governing tax credits are generally located in Part IV of Subchapter A. That part includes seven subparts and 27 sections with the following titles:

Subpart A—Nonrefundable Personal Credits

    Sec. 21   Expenses for household and dependent care services necessary for gainful employment.

    Sec. 22   Credit for the elderly and the permanently and totally disabled.

    Sec. 25   Interest on certain home mortgages.

    Sec. 26   Limitation based on tax liability; definition of tax liability.

Subpart B—Foreign Tax Credit, Etc.

    Sec. 27   Taxes of foreign countries and possessions of the United States; possession tax credit.

    Sec. 28   Clinical testing expenses for certain drugs for rare diseases or conditions.

    Sec. 29   Credit for producing fuel from a nonconventional source.

Subpart C—Refundable Credits

    Sec. 31   Tax withheld on wages.

    Sec. 32   Earned income.

    Sec. 33   Tax withheld at source on nonresident aliens and foreign corporations.

    Sec. 34   Certain uses of gasoline and special fuels.

    Sec. 35   Overpayments of tax.

Subpart D—Business Related Credits

    Sec. 38   General business credit.

    Sec. 39   Carryback and carryforward of unused credits.

    Sec. 40   Alcohol used as fuel.

    Sec. 41   Credit for increasing research activities.

    Sec. 42   Low-income housing credit.

    Sec. 43   Enhanced oil recovery credit.

    Sec. 44   Expenditures to provide access to disabled individuals.

Subpart E—Rules for Computing Investment Credit

    Sec. 46   Amount of credit.

    Sec. 47   Rehabilitation credit.

    Sec. 48   Energy credit; reforestation credit.

    Sec. 49   At-risk rules.

    Sec. 50   Other special rules.

Subpart F—Rules for Computing Targeted Jobs for Credit

    Sec. 51   Amount of credit.

    Sec. 52   Special rules.

Subpart G—Credit against Regular Tax for Prior Year Minimum Tax Liability

    Sec. 53   Credit for prior year minimum tax liability.

Even a cursory reading of these subpart and section titles can be instructive. For example, some credits are only available to individual taxpayers (note the title of Subpart A); some credits are refundable—the government will actually *pay the taxpayer* if these credits exceed the taxpayer's gross tax liability (note the title of Subpart C, and contrast it with the wording of Subpart A); and other credits are clearly business related (note the title of Subpart D).

The section titles also give us a hint of the special reasons Congress gives tax credits. Many of those titles reflect issues of great national concern. For example, the credits authorized by Secs. 29, 34, 40, 43, and 48 appear to be associated with concern for greater diversity in domestic energy sources; Secs. 22, 28, 42, and 44 with concern over the economic plight of the underprivileged; Secs. 28 and 41 for the desire to increase research and developmental activities; and Sec. 48 to stem the defoliation of the earth's surface.

To focus on appropriate issues, we defer our discussion of the tax credits that are unique to individual taxpayers to Part Three, and the tax credits that relate primarily to business operations to Part Four. Recall also that the general topic of foreign tax credits has already been introduced in this chapter because it applies equally to all taxpayers with some amount of foreign-source income that is taxed by both the United States and by a foreign government. At this point we simply expect you to understand how both deductions and tax credits can reduce a taxpayer's income tax liability but realizing that they do so in very different ways.

TAX PREPAYMENTS

Although the Code includes prepayments along with tax credits in Secs. 31 and 35, prepayments are not conceptually like tax credits. Credits are usually intended as a special reward for taxpayers who do something the government thinks is particularly important to national interests; prepayments are intended simply to ensure that most taxpayers will pay the tax they owe. If the government waited until the end of each year, and then asked all taxpayers to pay in one lump-sum the amount of their gross tax liability, most taxpayers would be unable to do so simply because they would not have sufficient cash available to make such a large payment. Individual taxpayers who earn most or all of their annual income in the form of wages and salaries achieve their tax prepayments through a payroll withholding system. This system requires every employer to withhold from each employee's wages an amount that will, at the end of the year, closely approximately the employee's gross tax liability. A series of IRS forms and tables are prepared and distributed each year to facilitate the implementation of this withholding system. In general, employers are required to transfer almost immediately to the government any amount withheld from their employees' paychecks as tax prepayments. This requirement reduces any incentive to over-withhold and minimizes the risk of an employer's misappropriation of those funds.

Self-employed individuals, corporations, and fiduciaries achieve their prepayments through a system of quarterly payments. These taxpayers must estimate in advance their gross tax liability for each year and make four advanced deposits throughout the year to reflect their estimates. Because of the interest charges and penalties assessed for any significant underestimation, there is little or no incentive for noncompliance. And, because the government does not pay interest for advanced deposits in excess of the actual tax liability, there is no incentive for overestimation either.

Critics of the income tax frequently argue that the prepayment system is socially undesirable because it tends to mask the real size of a taxpayer's annual gross liability by substituting a series of small payments each payday for one large payment at the end of the year. These critics argue that voters would not be so tolerant of government spending if they were more aware of how much income tax they really pay. Whether or not this conclusion is correct, there is little doubt that the average employee thinks and acts in terms of take-home pay, rather than in terms of gross wages or salaries. Those taxpayers who must make quarterly payments of their estimated tax are generally more aware of their actual tax liability.

Income tax prepayments can also be generated from excess social security tax payments made by the employee. Employees who work for more than one employer during a year, and who earn in total an amount that is in excess of the maximum social security tax base, can claim their excess social security tax payments as an income-tax credit. The excess payments attributable to the *employer's* matching payments are, however, not creditable to either the employee or the employer.

In the remaining pages of this chapter we will introduce (1) some of the tax-planning opportunities that are inherent in our tax-entity and tax-rate regimen, and (2) some of the special provisions put into the Code to reduce or eliminate most of the more obvious opportunities.

_____ USE OF ENTITIES IN TAX PLANNING

The tax environment explained in this chapter is admittedly complicated. From a planning perspective, the large number of alternatives, along with the diversity of the rules, are useful. Except where legal or financial factors dictate otherwise, one usually has a choice of the legal entity used, if any, and the challenge is to select the one that gives the best tax results. Before turning to a summary of the uses that have been made of legal entities, consider the following illustration.

> **Goal #7**
> Introduce some tax
> planning ideas.

COMPREHENSIVE ILLUSTRATION

Assume that Missy and Buz Ness are actively engaged in several business ventures and own a substantial number of corporate stocks. During the current year their activities encompassed five ventures:

1. Buz Cleaners—a chain of drive-in laundry and dry-cleaning establishments organized as a corporation. Mr. Ness receives a $20,000 annual salary from Buz Cleaners. After paying all of its expenses, including the owner-employee's salary, Buz Cleaners, Inc., reports a $22,000 taxable income. The corporation paid $1,200 in dividends to Mr. and Mrs. Ness, the sole owners of Buz Cleaners stock.

2. Goode-Ness Manufacturing Company—a new venture intended to produce commercial washing machines that will reduce waiting time by 50%. Goode-Ness is owned equally by James Goode and Buz Ness, who are not related. During the current year, Goode-Ness reported a taxable loss of $16,000. The firm is organized as a corporation but has elected S corporation treatment for tax purposes. Neither Goode nor Ness receives any salary from the firm, and no other assets were distributed by Goode-Ness during the year.

3. B.R.E.D. Board—a retail pastry shop organized as a partnership. Missy Ness owns a one-fourth interest in the partnership assets and profits. As one of four partners, she draws a $6,000 annual salary. After paying partners' salaries and all other operating expenses, B.R.E.D. Board reports a net income of $8,000, which is reinvested in the business.

4. Loc-Ness Trust Fund—a collection of assets put into trust by Buz Ness's parents prior to their deaths several years ago. The trust agreement provides that the trustee can make distributions of trust income, at his discretion, to Mr. or Mrs. Ness or to any of their children. On the death of the last of Buz Ness's children, the remaining assets are to be distributed to their heirs. During the current year, the trust earned a total income of $60,000. Of this, the trustee distributed $10,000 to each of the four Ness children. He retained $20,000 of the income within the trust fund.

5. Ness Insurance—an insurance agency operated as a sole proprietorship. During this year, the agency earned an income of $30,000. Buz withdrew $1,000 a month from the agency for personal living expenses. The remaining $18,000 was reinvested in a new office building to house the insurance agency.

The Nesses' five business ventures and the related cash flows between these ventures and the individual members of the Ness family are diagrammed in Figure 6-16. In terms of economic and physical realities, this arrangement obviously involves at least five distinct business operations and six people. In terms of taxable entities, however, there is one corporation (Buz Cleaners), one fiduciary (Loc-Ness), and six individuals (Mr. and Mrs. Ness and their four children). Two of the businesses (Goode-Ness and B.R.E.D. Board) must file information tax returns, but they are not liable for any tax as separate entities.

In terms of tax calculations, Mr. and Mrs. Ness probably file one joint tax return on which they report the following items of gross income:

From Buz Cleaners, Inc.:	
As salary	$20,000
As dividend	1,200
From Goode-Ness Manufacturing Co.:	
Half of the net operating loss	(8,000)
From Loc-Ness Trust Fund:	
Nothing	
From B.R.E.D. Board:	
As salary	6,000
As operating income (1/4 interest)	2,000
From Ness Insurance:	
As operating income	30,000
Total from all sources	$51,200

Observe that although the total cash received by Mr. and Mrs. Ness is only $39,200, they must report as gross income a total of $51,200 from their several business interests. Both Ness Insurance and B.R.E.D. Board contributed more to their gross income than to their cash flow; Goode-Ness Manufacturing Company, on the other hand, provided a tax deduction even though it did not require a cash contribution from either Mr. or Mrs. Ness.

On their joint tax return, Mr. and Mrs. Ness probably claim dependent exemption deductions for each of their four children as well as a personal exemption deduction for themselves. Additionally, each of the children must file his or her own tax return.

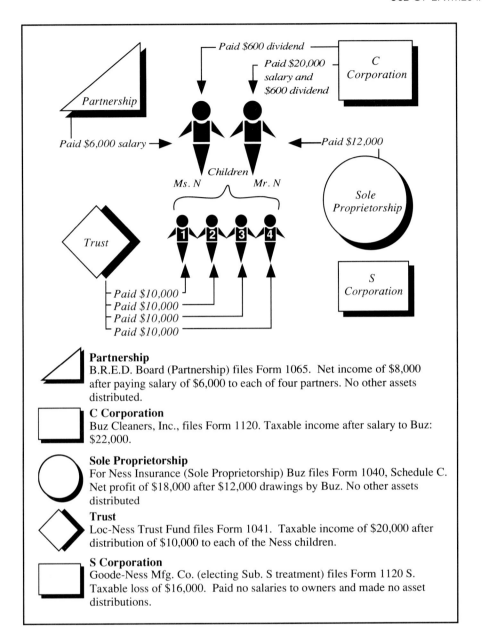

FIGURE 6-16

**Ness Family
Interests and
Cash
Distributions**

Partnership
B.R.E.D. Board (Partnership) files Form 1065. Net income of $8,000 after paying salary of $6,000 to each of four partners. No other assets distributed.

C Corporation
Buz Cleaners, Inc., files Form 1120. Taxable income after salary to Buz: $22,000.

Sole Proprietorship
For Ness Insurance (Sole Proprietorship) Buz files Form 1040, Schedule C. Net profit of $18,000 after $12,000 drawings by Buz. No other assets distributed

Trust
Loc-Ness Trust Fund files Form 1041. Taxable income of $20,000 after distribution of $10,000 to each of the Ness children.

S Corporation
Goode-Ness Mfg. Co. (electing Sub. S treatment) files Form 1120 S. Taxable loss of $16,000. Paid no salaries to owners and made no asset distributions.

Buz Cleaners, Inc., would file a tax return and pay tax on an income of $22,000. Observe that Buz Cleaners gets a tax deduction for the salary it paid to its owner-employee but that it does not get a deduction for the dividend it paid to Mr. and Mrs. Ness. Had Buz elected to do so, he might have been able to increase his salary to reduce or even eliminate any taxable income for Buz Cleaners, Inc. This action would have increased his personal tax and reduced the corporation's tax accordingly.

Unlike Buz Cleaners, Loc-Ness Trust is treated as a separate taxable entity only to the extent that it retains its income. Thus, by paying out $10,000 to each of the four Ness children, Loc-Ness Trust reduces its taxable income from $60,000 to $20,000.

MATCHING ENTITY ATTRIBUTES WITH OBJECTIVES

The important questions left unanswered in the previous illustration follow: Why did the Ness family use the particular entities actually employed? Would other legal arrangements be preferable from a tax standpoint? The selection of the best entity is no easy task. Although we cannot set out a simple set of rules that can be followed to solve the problem, some general statements with examples are helpful, understanding that generalization of a complex subject carries unavoidable risks.

Remember that the business form used may be dictated by legal or economic considerations. A multinational conglomerate with numerous owners and vast re-sources requires the corporate form. Two oil companies that join together to drill a single oil or gas well may want the simplicity of a partnership. And the parent who wants to protect a spendthrift child from his or her own foolishness will use a trust. Here, we are concerned solely with the tax attributes of the entities and with choosing the one with the proper attributes for the circumstance.

The business owner who chooses the corporate form of doing business because of the nontax benefits must be aware of possible disadvantages to such a choice. To begin with, there are possible non-income tax penalties. For example, the cost of state franchise taxes on corporations can be substantial. Social security taxes can also be affected. To illustrate, if the owner hires his or her minor children as employees, the children's earnings are subject to social security taxes if the employer is a corporation. On the other hand, if the owner operates as a sole proprietorship, no social security taxes on wages paid to the owner's minor children are required.

Another disadvantage is that the organizational costs of forming a corporation may be substantially higher than those of forming a partnership. In addition, the records that may be required by state law and various reports that must be filed by corporations can be burdensome and costly.

Perhaps the greatest disadvantage is the risk of double taxation. Corporate income is taxed at the corporate level; and if the corporation's after-tax income is distributed to the shareholders as a *dividend*, the payments are taxed again at the shareholder level. Also, in cases where the taxpayer seeks to allocate income between the shareholder and the corporation in a most beneficial and yet contrived way (through payments for salaries, rents, and so on), the IRS has rather wide power to disallow unreasonable payments to various family members and to tax such payments as disguised dividends to the shareholder, resulting in nondeductible payments at the corporate level.

The C corporation generally requires the active conduct of a trade or business. Furthermore, in the case of relatively small businesses, this form can be used only when the problem of double taxation can be solved. The double tax on C corporations is usually avoided by not paying dividends and by reinvesting the after-tax earnings in the business. Such constant reinvestment of earnings delays any double tax until the corporation is liquidated. If the eventual liquidation, and the resulting double tax, is far enough in the future, the present value (penalty) of a second tax may be insignificant. The reinvestment of C corporation earnings may, however, create other tax problems. The law contains two special penalty taxes that are levied when retained earnings are not reinvested in an active business. The first is the tax on personal holding companies (PHC). Originally added to the law to prohibit the incorporation of investment portfolios, this penalty tax applies when more than 60% of a corporation's income is from passive activities (or, more technically, PHC income, which may include income from personal service contracts). The second possible penalty, the accumulated earnings tax, may apply when a corporation accumulates its earnings and profits beyond the reasonable needs of the business. Further details concerning these two penalty taxes must be deferred to other courses.

To understand how a corporation can still be a useful tax-planning vehicle for a small business venture, you must reflect on at least two basic tax concepts:

1. A corporation is a separate taxable entity, entirely distinct from both owners and employees; and, as a separate taxable entity, it is subject to all of the normal rules concerning gross income, deductions, exclusions, and tax credits for corporate taxpayers.

2. Individuals who incorporate their trades or businesses may cause their own corporations to hire them back as corporate employees; and, as employees, those owner-employees are subject to all of the normal rules concerning gross income, deductions, exclusions, and tax credits for individual taxpayers.

Finally, it is necessary to recall specific Code provisions that can work to the advantage of a particular taxpayer. To illustrate, assume that farmer Brown earns a taxable income of $40,000 each year. As a sole proprietor, Brown cannot deduct many of his personal living expenses—such as the depreciation on his home; the cost of his homeowner's insurance; utilities to heat, cool, and light his home; or the food he eats (Sec. 262).

If farmer Brown were to incorporate his farming business; transfer title to his home to the corporate entity; cause the corporation to employ him to feed cattle, plant crops, and do all of the things that farmers normally do; and then cause the corporation to require that he live in the farmhouse as a condition of his employment for the benefit of the corporation—so that he would be available to attend to emergencies with the livestock as well as provide round-the-clock security—the corporation should be eligible to deduct depreciation on the farmhouse, the insurance on the house, the utilities, food costs, and so on under either a general rule, such as Sec. 162 (for all ordinary and necessary business expenses), or a specific rule, such as Sec. 167 (for depreciation). Farmer Brown, under the proper conditions, might be able to exclude the value of these same items from his own personal gross income under the authority of Sec. 119, which allows an employee to exclude the value of employer-provided meals and lodging in certain circumstances.[53] The net effect of this tax plan, when successful, is the transmutation of what started out as taxable income for farmer Brown into thin air, with the help of a corporate entity.[54]

The illustration just completed is, perhaps, an example of the pinnacle of federal income tax planning because it converted taxable income into nontaxable income without, in any way, reducing the enjoyment of the ultimate consumer (farmer Brown). Because the exclusion provisions of the U.S. federal income tax law are in fact quite limited, there are relatively few opportunities to be this successful in tax planning. There are, however, multiple opportunities to reach somewhat lesser states of tax euphoria. In a much larger number of cases it is possible to lower the effective tax rate or defer the time at which the income tax is payable. One example of lowering the effective tax rate involves **multiple corporations.**

> **Multiple corporations** are corporations with some degree of common ownership that avoid classification as both a controlled group of corporations and as affiliated corporations.

---

53 Sec. 119 is explained in greater detail in Chapter 9.

54 For two real-life examples of this illustration, see *J. Grant Farms Inc., et al.,* paragraph 85, 174 P-H Memo TC and *Denny L. Johnson, et al.,* paragraph 85, 175 P-H Memo TC.

MULTIPLE CORPORATIONS

Prior to 1970, a much used tax-planning strategy was to divide a business or a group of businesses with common ownership into several separate C corporations. For example, in a chain of retail outlets, each outlet would be organized as a separate C corporation. Under this arrangement, each corporation enjoyed the lower rates on the first dollars of taxable income.

There is an obvious advantage to having the income of one corporation spread among two or more corporations, with each taxed on its first dollars of income at the lowest marginal rate, if that is possible. The potential value of splitting a $200,000 income equally between four corporate entities—rather than reporting all of it in one entity—is clearly demonstrated in Figure 6-17. Observe that there is no tax benefit whatsoever in multiple corporations as long as the aggregate amount of taxable income recognized within the corporation(s) does not exceed $50,000. If the recognized income exceeds that amount, however, some tax benefit is inevitable. The larger the corporate taxable income, in general, the greater the number of corporations desired. For example, if the corporate taxable income is $300,000 each year, splitting that taxable income equally among six corporations would yield a tax saving of $55,250, or 55% of the total corporate tax liability!

However, as explained earlier in this chapter, if multiple corporations are members of a *controlled group* of corporations, the taxable income of the several corporations will have to be combined and taxed as if the total were earned by a single taxable entity.

Is it possible for multiple corporations to exist without creating a controlled group? The answer is yes, but only at a price. Today, one possibly beneficial ownership plan involves a distribution like that depicted in Figure 6-18. One individual I owns 79% of the stock of three corporations. Each of three other, unrelated individuals owns 21% of the stock in one corporation. Individual I provides the necessary capital for the three businesses, whereas individuals J, K, and L provide the day-to-day management of the businesses. So long as the four stockholders are not related family members, no

FIGURE 6-17

Tax Advantage of (Four) Multiple Corporations

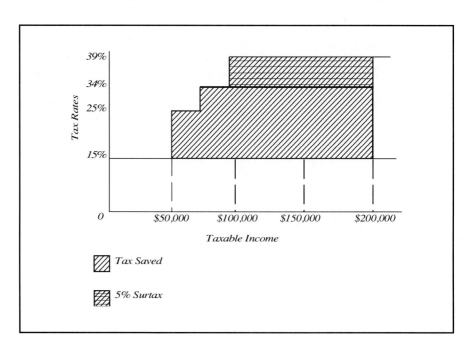

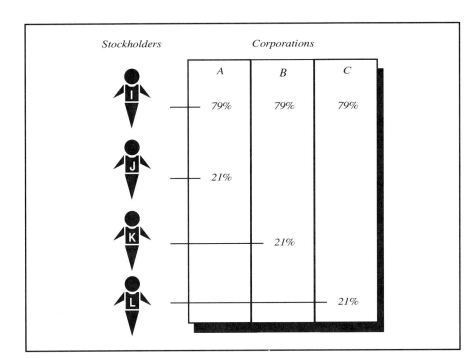

FIGURE 6-18

Example of Nonfamily Ownership Arrangement That Avoids Controlled-Group Status

controlled group exists per *Vogel Fertilizer.*[55] Incidentally, even if J, K, and L are sons- or daughters-in-law of person I, there is no attribution because these relationships do not fall within the purview of family as defined in Sec. 1563(e)(6).

The existence of these rules illustrates an important point about the use of corporations and other artificial entities. Some corporations, indeed, have an existence apart from their owners, though that existence is often threatened by takeover bids and unprofitable operations leading to bankruptcy. Most smaller, closely held C corporations are not really separate entities. Separate treatment of them in our tax law is to some extent unreal, and the fiction creates many problems and a few opportunities.

OTHER ENTITIES

The most common use of partnerships traditionally was for leveraged investments that produced tax losses. Due in large part to tax rules, these investments were often in oil and gas, farming, and real estate. The partnership form permitted deduction of the losses by the partners to the extent of the partner's basis in the partnership interest. Tax rules for partnerships also permitted the special allocation of gains, losses, and so on. In real estate, for example, partner-investors were often allocated all depreciation, which increases their current losses, with the expectation that capital gains would be allocated to them later to recoup these losses.

The passive loss rules diminish the importance of partnerships. Recall from Chapter 5 that rental real estate is by definition passive. Furthermore, a limited partner by definition has a passive role without regard to the partner's actual participation. On the other hand, many practitioners only now are gaining an appreciation of the use of special allocations as well as other partnership attributes beyond our scope here. Because of changes in the tax law, some profitable C corporations were liquidated and transferred their assets to limited partnerships. Because the partnership form permits

---

55 See again discussion on pages 195–200 and footnote 48, *supra.*

a single tax on the income at the partner level. Note also that the limited partnership gives many of the legal advantages of incorporation, especially limited liability, to all but the general partner. Other C corporations resisted these changes to partnership status because it could convert nontaxable dividend income to taxable UBI for their otherwise tax-exempt stockholders.

S corporations are used in various ways. Like partnerships, S corporations may be used to avoid the higher marginal tax rates generally applicable to C corporations. They may also be used to pass losses through to shareholders in some circumstances. S corporations resulting from elections made by prior C corporations may encounter special tax rules enacted to minimize tax avoidance possibilities.

Tax motivations for the use of trusts were reduced substantially by the 1986 act. For trusts, the 15% rate applies only to a very small amount of taxable income. The advantages of the 15% rate might be expanded by creating several trusts for the same beneficiary. Congress, however, has declared war on multiple trusts, and the IRS will not treat multiple trusts separately unless nontax reasons justify their existence. The trust also has only limited usefulness to shelter income of beneficiaries younger than 14 whose unearned income is largely taxed at their parents' marginal rates.

While the role of artificial entities in tax planning is complex, their proper use is a most important subject for the serious tax student. In fact, most of the subject matter in graduate tax programs deals with the use of entities.

KEY POINTS TO REMEMBER

✓ Although *every* individual is a potential taxpayer, for federal income tax purposes, nonresident aliens may escape the U.S. income tax by avoiding any income from U.S. sources.

✓ Although *every* corporation is a potential taxpayer for federal income tax purposes, some corporations escape the U.S. income tax . Among the corporations whose income may be partially or wholly exempt from the U.S. income tax are S corporations, foreign corporations, and tax-exempt corporations.

✓ Although *every* fiduciary is a potential taxpayer, for federal income tax purposes, grantor trusts and foreign trusts may escape the U.S. income tax.

✓ Corporations that are members of an affiliated group of corporations may elect to file one consolidated income tax return for federal purposes.

✓ Although sole proprietorships and partnerships are not taxable entities, any income that they earn will be taxed immediately to the persons who own those entities, even if no assets are distributed by the entities to the owners.

✓ Trusts created solely to make a profit in a trade or business are taxed like corporations.

✓ Business entities that have some of the characteristics of a corporation, and other characteristics of a partnership, will be classified as a corporation only if a *majority* of the four non-common characteristics are corporate characteristics.

✓ The taxable income recognized by individual taxpayers is ordinarily taxed at marginal tax rates of 15, 28, or 31%. The amount of taxable income taxed at each rate varies depending on the year and the classification of the individual.

✓ The taxable income recognized by corporate taxpayers earning less than $335,000 per year is ordinarily taxed at marginal rates of 15, 25, 34, or 39%; corporations earning more than $335,000 pay a flat tax rate of 34%.

✓ The taxable income recognized by fiduciary taxpayers is ordinarily taxed at marginal tax rates of 15, 28, or 31%. The exact amount of taxable income taxed at each of these rates varies slightly because of year-to-year changes in the CPI.

✓ Special tax rates may apply to the net capital gains recognized by both individual and fiduciary taxpayers.

✓ An alternative minimum tax rate of 24% (for individual and fiduciary taxpayers) or 20% (for corporate taxpayers) may apply to taxpayers in special circumstances.

✓ Personal service corporations pay a flat 34% tax on their entire taxable income.

✓ The gross tax liability of any corporation that is a member of a controlled group of corporations is determined in a special manner.

✓ Although S corporations ordinarily pay no federal income tax, they may be required to pay such a tax if they recognize a built-in gain or have excess passive investment income.

✓ Passive income earned by foreign corporations and nonresident aliens may be taxed at a flat rate of 30%, or at some lesser rate if a tax treaty so provides.

RECALL PROBLEMS

1. Chris made a $10,000 loan to his friend, Andy. The loan agreement provided for interest at 12% per year. Chris directed Andy to pay the $1,200 interest for this year directly to his 15-year-old daughter, Ann. Who must pay the income tax due on the interest paid by Andy this year?

2. Periodically, Mrs. Sand makes deposits to a savings account at the Federal Savings and Loan Association. Mrs Sand opened the account in the following name: Mrs. R. T. Sand, Trustee for William Sand. William Sand is her 6-year-old son. The trust was created under the Uniform Gift to Minors Act. Mrs. Sand intends to continue such deposits until William becomes an adult, at which time he will have full control of the account. During the current year, Federal Savings and Loan Association credited the account with $43 interest. To whom is the interest taxed?

3. Amy and Ben, a married couple, own 100% of four different active businesses. Amy, Ben, or both participate in each business in a material, continuous, and substantial manner. Each business is operated in a different legal form. Details of the four businesses for this year can be summarized as follows:

Business	Legal Form	Taxable Income (Loss) before Salary Paid to the Owner(s)	Salary Paid to Owner(s)	Taxable Income (Loss) after Salaries
1	Sole proprietorship	$10,000	$4,000	$ 6,000
2	S corporation	(20,000)	5,000	(25,000)
3	Partnership	30,000	9,000	21,000
4	C corporation	40,000	7,000	33,000

Assume that Amy and Ben had an unrecovered investment (or tax basis) of $50,000 in *each* of these four businesses on January 1. Further, assume that no amounts of cash, other than salaries, were distributed from these businesses to the owners during the year.

a. What amount of gross income must Amy and Ben report on their joint federal income-tax return because of these four businesses?

b. Who must report any gross income, generated by these four businesses, that is not included on Amy and Ben's joint (individual) tax return?

 4. Bill Blestt created the Blestt Trust by transferring $10,000 to City Bank as trustee. The trust indenture provided that (1) the corpus of the trust would be returned to Bill Blestt in 12 years; (2) any income up to $6,000 per year is to be distributed to Bill's daughter, Beverly; (3) any remaining income is to be retained in the trust or distributed to Beverly, at the trustee's discretion. This year the Blestt Trust earned a taxable income of $9,500; the trustee distributed $7,000 of this income to Beverly (age 20) and retained the remaining $2,500.

a. If the Blestt Trust was created on December 24, 1985, what portion (if any) of the $9,500 taxable income will be taxed to Bill Blestt, Beverly Blestt, and the Blestt Trust, respectively?

b. If the Blestt Trust was created on December 24, 1986, what portion (if any) of the $9,500 taxable income will be taxed to Bill Blestt, Beverly Blestt, and the Blestt Trust, respectively?

 5. This year The Book Store earned a taxable income of $330,000. Who must pay the income tax on this $330,000 if The Book Store is

a. A sole proprietorship owned by Li Sung?

b. A partnership equally owned by Roosevelt Brown, a single individual; The Think Tank, a C corporation; and the estate of Karl Book, an individual who died 18 months ago but whose estate has not yet been distributed to the heirs named in his will.

c. A C corporation wholly owned by Lea Horwitz?

d. An S corporation equally owned by Mary and Juan Lopez, a married couple that file separate returns?

 6. Each of the following individuals earned a gross income of $100,000 this year. Which of the six individuals, if any, would not be a taxable entity subject to the U.S. income tax?

Name	Age	Citizenship	Residency	Source of Income
Carlos	30	Italy	U.S.	100% Italy
Mark	2	U.S.	Brazil	100% U.S.
Anita	50	U.S.	Spain	100% Spain
Di	22	U.K.	U.K.	50% U.K.; 50% U.S.
Ian	75	Burma	Burma	100% Australia
Helga	1	Holland	U.S.	80% Holland; 20% U.S.

7. Each of the following legal entities earned a gross income of $500,000 this year. Which of the eight legal entities, if any, would *not* be a taxable entity, subject to the U.S. income tax?

Entity	Legal Form	S Election?	Chartered by	Source of Income
1	Corporation	No	State of Iowa	50% U.S.; 50% Foreign
2	Corporation	Yes	State of Utah	100% Foreign
3	Corporation	No	State of Texas	100% Foreign
4	Partnership	N/A	State of Florida	100% U.S.
5	Trust (tax exempt)	N/A	State of Nevada	100% U.S.; no unrelated business income
6	Corporation (tax exempt)	No	State of Vermont	100% U.S.; 10% unrelated business income
7	Corporation	No	Dutch Government	100% Foreign
8	Corporation	No	French Government	90% Foreign; 10% U.S.

8. Church of the Good Shephard, a local congregation that is part of the Methodist Church, a tax-exempt corporation, earned interest of $32,000 and dividends of $8,000 on its capital investments this year. Who, if anyone, must pay the tax on this $40,000 income?

9. During the current year, State University (a tax-exempt corporation) earned capital gains of $700,000; interest of $200,000; and a profit of $100,000 on a food-service operation. Who, if anyone, must pay the tax on this $1 million income if

   a. The food service operation is an integral part of the university's tax-exempt function?

   b. The food service operation is not related to the tax-exempt purpose of the university?

10. AtoyotA, a Japanese corporation, earned an income of $1 million this year. Of this amount, $900,000 was from Japanese sources; the other $100,000 was from interest income on a loan made to an unrelated U.S. corporation that supplies parts to AtoyotA. What part of AtoyotA's $1 million income, if any, will be subject to U.S. income taxation? (Explain briefly how the United States will tax that income if AtoyotA carries on no trade or business within the United States.)

11. Each of the big six accounting firms in the United States can be characterized as having the following attributes:

   Objective: To carry on a business for profit

   Associates: Yes

   Life independent of owners: Yes

   Free transferability of owners' interests: No

   Owners' liability limited: No

   Management: Centralized

For federal income tax purposes, will these firms be treated as corporations or as partnerships? Explain briefly.

12. South African laws provide for a legal entity called a close corporation. The characteristics of this entity can be characterized as follows:

Objective: To carry on a business for profit

Associates: Yes

Life independent of owners: Yes

Free transferability of owners' interests: No

Owners' liability limited: Yes

Management: Shared by all members

Will a South African close corporation be treated as a corporation or as a partnership for U.S. federal income tax purposes?

13. Calculate the gross tax liability on a taxable income of $350,000 per year if it is recognized by

a. A single individual.

b. A married couple who file a joint return.

c. A C corporation.

d. A trust that distributes no income to any beneficiaries.

14. Assume that four single individuals each earn the following amounts of taxable income during a year:

Person	Taxable Income
Bob	-0-
Ted	$ 50,000
Carol	100,000
Alice	50,000

Calculate the income tax savings or the income tax penalty that would be created by Bob and Carol's marriage and Ted and Alice's marriage. In making these calculations, simply assume that the taxable income of each couple would be the sum of the taxable incomes earned by the two individuals.

15. Calculate the gross tax liability on a taxable income of $60,000 per year if it is recognized by

a. A C corporation.

b. A professional service corporation.

16. C corporations can be subject to as few as one or as many as four different marginal tax rates. Explain briefly.

17. Foreign income taxes paid by U.S. taxpayers can either be deducted under the authority of Sec. 164(a)(3) or claimed as a tax credit under the authority of Sec. 901(a). Sec. 275(a)(4)(A) denies the taxpayer the right to deduct these taxes if the

tax credit has been claimed. The vast majority of all taxpayers who pay foreign income taxes elect to claim the tax credit rather than the deduction. Explain why this is true.

18. The circumstances of two single individuals, relative to the federal income tax, can be summarized as follows:

#6

Individual	Taxable Income	Nonrefundable Tax Credits
Sandra	$20,000	$ 2,900
Betty	60,000	10,000

How would the net tax payable by Sandra and Betty (that is, their gross tax less their tax credits for this year) be affected by

a. An additional deduction of $1,000?

b. An additional nonrefundable tax credit of $1,000?

c. An additional refundable tax credit of $1,000?

19. Tx, a single taxpayer, expects to have *taxable income* of $80,000 this year, of which $60,000 will be net income from the operation of a small retail store. The remaining $20,000 is net interest income. An attorney advised Tx to incorporate his retail store. This attorney further advised Tx to take a salary of $30,000 from the business and would reinvest the remaining after-tax income in the business. Based on the attorney's recommendations, calculate the income taxes saved each year by Tx from incorporation.

#7

20. A U.S. taxpayer who uses a domestic corporation to obtain lower rates for a business cannot afford the distribution of dividends. Why is this true? In your explanation, use current tax rates to demonstrate your conclusion.

#7

21. Three unrelated individuals—Able, Baker, and Cooke—together own 100% of three corporations. Each corporation operates a separate discount store located in three different cities. Each store has an annual income of $80,000.

#7

a. If each shareholder owns 33 ⅓% of each corporation's stock, compute the additional tax liability due for the current year compared with an arrangement in which Able, Baker, and Cooke each owned 100% of one of the three corporations.

b. Devise a scheme of ownership whereby Able, Baker, and Cooke jointly could own the three corporations and still avoid treatment as a controlled group.

c. Discuss why the three individuals might hesitate to adopt the pattern of ownership you devised in part b. For this purpose, assume that each of the stores have been in existence only for a brief period.

22. Herman and Betty Irish have two small children who are dependent on their parents for support. For the current year, the parents expect to receive the following income:

#7

Salaries	$80,000
Dividends from taxable domestic corporations	6,000

The dividends are paid on stock owned jointly by Herman and Betty. They also expect to claim the following deductions:

Itemized deductions	$10,000

A tax consultant has recommended that the stock owned by Herman and Betty be transferred to two trusts, one for each child. The trustees would initially accumulate income and later pay the accumulated income, as needed, for the college education of the children. (This arrangement creates a complex trust entitled to annual exemption of $100 per trust.) The trust corpus, plus any accumulated income, would be paid to each child when he or she reaches the age of 30.

a. Compute Herman and Betty's tax liability for the current year, assuming they do not create the trusts.

b. Compute the combined liabilities of Herman, Betty, and the two trusts, assuming the trusts are established on January of the current year (ignore any federal gift taxes).

c. How much tax is saved by the trust arrangement?

——— THOUGHT PROBLEMS

1. a. As one extreme alternative to our current entity structure, we could exclude corporations from the list of entities recognized for tax purposes on the grounds that all corporate income ultimately belongs to individuals and that, until that income is distributed by the corporation, it ought not to be subject to tax. What practical consequences would follow from this extreme alternative? Explain.

b. As another alternative to our present corporate income tax, we could currently allocate all corporate incomes to the (ultimate) individual stockholders, whether or not the corporation distributed any income. We could then exclude corporations from any income tax. (In other words, we could treat all corporations the way we treat S corporations for tax purposes.) What practical reasons preclude the general acceptance of this alternative?

c. Finally, as another alternative to our current corporate income tax, we could recognize the corporation as a separate entity only to the extent that the corporation retained income. This could be accomplished simply by allowing the corporation a deduction for dividends paid. (In essence, this is the way we treat trusts for tax purposes.) Why do you suppose that Congress has never accepted this alternative?

2. Many foreign countries levy very high taxes on corporate earnings that are not distributed to stockholders as dividends. Compare this option with the U.S. treatment of corporate income and explain the probable effects of both alternatives on the source of corporate funds.

3. Nel owns a 10% interest in a business that pays her an annual salary of $20,000. Except for salaries, this business has never distributed any profits to its owners. The after-salary profits of the business were $100,000 in 19X1 and $200,000 in 19X2. What amount of income must Nel include on her personal tax return in these two years if

a. The business operates as a partnership?

b. The business operates as a C corporation?

c. The business operates as an S corporation?

4. Ted's basis in the TB Partnership is $50,000 as of December 31,19X1. The TB Partnership, which is engaged in an active business, reports a $150,000 net operating loss for 19X1. If Ted owns a 50% interest in the partnership, what maximum amount of the total TB loss may Ted deduct for 19X1? Will this be treated as an active or passive loss on Ted's personal return?

5. Prior to 1987, the top marginal tax rate on corporate taxpayers had always been lower than the top marginal tax rate on individual taxpayers. After that situation was reversed, several commentators suggested that U.S. businesses would *disincorporate*. In other words, after 1986 it made little sense for the owners of U.S. businesses to pay the federal income tax at 34% when it could be reduced to 28% by disincorporating a previously incorporated business. The S election was a solution for businesses with less than 36 individual stockholders; the partnership, for businesses with more owners, or with corporate owners. Some large corporations—the Community Psychiatric Centers in California, for example—actually took initial steps to convert their legal form from a corporation to a limited partnership. When they discovered, however, that about 30% of their stock was held by tax-exempt entities—such as pension funds and universities—they suddenly changed their minds and retained the corporate form. Explain the apparent reason for their change in plans. (Hint: The answer is related to the definition of UBI or unrelated business income.)

6. State whether each of the following statements is true or false. Explain any false statements.

   a. A C corporation can be a partner in a partnership.

   b. An S corporation can be a partner in a partnership.

   c. A C corporation can be a stockholder in an S corporation.

   d. An S corporation can be a stockholder in a C corporation.

   e. A trust can own an active business and still be taxed as a trust.

   f. A trust can own an active business and be taxed as a C corporation.

   g. A partnership engaged in an active trade or business could create portfolio income for one or more of its partners.

   h. An S corporation engaged in an active business could create a passive loss for one of its shareholders.

7. Determine for the current year the maximum amount of taxable income that will be taxed at a marginal rate of 28% for

   a. Married persons who file a joint return.

   b. Heads of households.

   c. Single individuals.

   d. Fiduciary taxpayers.

8. ABC Corporation received the following items of gross income in the current year:

Revenue from merchandise sales	$230,000
Interest from State of New Jersey bonds	50,000

ABC Corporation also incurred the following deductible expenses:

Cost of merchandise sold	$120,000
Other operating expenses	20,000

Given this information, what is ABC corporation's

a. Marginal tax rate?

b. Average tax rate?

c. Real or effective tax rate?

#6   9. Politicians who are more interested in the interests of taxpayers who earn lesser amounts of taxable income than those who earn relatively large amounts of income are apt to prefer tax credits over tax deductions. Briefly explain this preference for tax credits.

#6   10. For many years, the federal income tax law authorized individual taxpayers to claim a deduction for child-care costs if those costs were incurred to permit the parents to be gainfully employed. Today a child-care credit has replaced the former child-care deduction. Why is this switch from a deduction to a credit important to many individuals?

#7   11. Sue, a single taxpayer, wholly owns and personally operates an active business as a C corporation. Sue's business earned a $300,000 taxable income before paying Sue any salary for her efforts during the year. Given only these facts, would Sue prefer to pay herself a salary of $50,000 or $250,000? Explain your answer carefully assuming that Sue has no other significant income sources but that she can live easily on $50,000 per year.

#7   12. If Congress were suddenly to enact a change in our current tax laws that would treat sole proprietorships and partnerships as separate taxable entities, as they are treated in financial accounting, what would you expect to happen if

a. These new taxable entities were subject to the same tax rates as unmarried individual taxpayers?

b. These new taxable entities were subject to the corporate tax rates?

Under either part a or b, would the concept of *controlled corporations* have to be extended to proprietorships and partnerships as well? Explain.

#7   13. A, B, and C are three corporations owned by four individuals. This year A had $80,000 taxable income, B had $70,000, and C had $50,000. How much income tax will A, B, and C save if they are not classified as a controlled group?

#7   14. In each of the following situations state (1) whether a controlled group exists; (2) if so, which corporations are part of the controlled group; (3) and what type of controlled group it is (that is, parent-subsidiary, brother-sister, or a combination). Unless specifically stated, assume that none of the parties are related or own any other stock.

a. Corporation X owns 80% of Corporation Y; Individual I owns the other 20% of Corporation Y. All other stock in X and Y is widely held.

b. Corporation X owns 80% of Corporation Y; Corporation Z owns the other 20% of Corporation Y; Corporation Z does not own any stock in Corporation X. The stock of both X and Z is widely held.

c. Corporation X owns 80% of Corporation Y; Corporation Z owns the other 20% of Corporation Y. Corporation Z owns 85% of Corporation X. Individual I owns 100% of Corporation Z and 20% of Corporation X.

d. Mr. T owns 80% of Corporation A and 80% of Corporation B. Corporation B own 90% of Corporation C.

e. Individual A owns 20% of Corporation X and 80% of Corporation Y. Individual B, unrelated to Individual A, owns 80% of Corporation X and 20% of Corporation Y.

f. Indivudal A owns 20% of Corporation X and 80% of Corporation Y. Individual B, related to Individual A under the provision of Sec. 1563(e)(6), owns 80% of Corporation X and 20% of Corporation Y.

g. Individual A owns 51% in each of three corporations: X, Y, and Z. Individual B owns the other 49% of Corporation X; Individual C owns the other 49% of Corporation Y; Individual D owns the remaining 49% of Corporation Z. None of the individuals are related.

15. Charles Goodnight owns a successful men's clothing store which he operates as a proprietorship. Charles estimates that the net profits of the business will be $110,000. He wonders if he can gain a tax advantage by incorporation. He has no other source of income and would need a salary of $60,000 to live comfortably. Calculate the tax savings from incorporation if Charles is single, under 65 with no dependents, and claims personal deductions that total $10,000 per year. Use current tax rates.

16. Refer to problem 15. Assume that it has been five years since Charles incorporated his clothing store. The business has been very successful and he now owns several branch stores. Corporate earnings are now about $400,000 annually (after payment of a $100,000 salary to Charles—the largest amount considered "reasonable"). Calculate the tax saving (or penalty) attached to having his business incorporated as opposed to a sole proprietorship. Use current year's tax rates. What action would you suggest Charles take?

#7

17. Joan Jacks is the majority shareholder of Jacks, Inc. On Joan's 1990 personal return, her marginal tax rate was 28%. After deducting Joan's salary of $320,000, Jacks, Inc., had taxable income of only $50,000. When examining the 1990 corporate return, the IRS agent proposed to disallow $220,000 of Joan's salary as unreasonably high. Using current rates, calculate the tax cost if the agent disallows the deduction and a court sustains this adjustment.

#7

_____ **CLASS PROJECTS**

1. The introduction of four tax-rate tables did not solve all of the federal income tax problems associated with community-property laws. To illustrate some of the remaining complications, divide the class into three groups of roughly equal size. Assume that each group represents residents of different states, as follows:

   Group A: Individuals assumed to live in common-law states.

   Group B: Individuals assumed to live in Arizona, California, Nevada, New Mexico, and Washington.

Group C: Individuals assumed to live in Idaho, Louisiana, and Texas.

Explain or define the following terminology before any group begins to solve this assignment:

Community property: any property owned by residents of a community-property state to the extent that the property is either (a) acquired from community income after marriage, or (b) is a commingled property. (A commingled property is a property that would have been separate property had it not been converted to community property by placing it in a joint account, such as a joint bank account, or by taking title to the property in the name of both individuals.)

Separate property: any property deemed to be owned solely by one indiviudal.

Finally, ask each group to (1) calculate the federal income tax liability for each of the two individuals described below, and (2) identify some practical problems that would likely be encountered in these circumstances:

Names: Helen and Zack Williams

Date of divorce: September 30

Income earned during the year is $180,000 (detailed as follows):

Source of Income	Amount of Income	Tax Withheld
Helen's salary	$80,000	$18,000
Zack's salary	40,000	9,000
Helen's separate property	10,000	-0-
Zack's separate property	30,000	-0-
Community property/joint property	20,000	-0-
Estimated tax payments made by		
Helen		14,000
Zack		7,000

Total income tax deductions authorized: $20,000. (To simplify an already difficult problem assume that these deductions can be divided equally between Helen and Zack). Ask one individual from each group to summarize the findings for their group. Compare and contrast the difficulties encountered in each group.

2. Based on library research beyond this text identify two reasons why married individuals may elect to file separate returns. Work on this assignment in groups of four. See how many different reasons you can identify.

3. Divide the class into three groups of approximately equal size. Challenge each group to be the first to explain, in language that anyone can understand, why closely held C corporations rarely invest in tax-exempt bonds. To focus attention, suggest that each group consider the following case:

Learning, Inc., a C corporation wholly owned by Mr. and Mrs. Quicksand, recognized a taxable income of $200,000. In addition, Learning, Inc., earned

$50,000 interest on its investment in municipal bonds. Although the $50,000 from gross interest income can be excluded from gross income by Learning, Inc., it increases the current earnings and profits of Learning, Inc. Furthermore, any distribution made by a C corporation to its shareholders will be deemed a dividend to the extent that the corporation has either current or accumulated earnings and profits. How much federal income tax must be paid on this $250,000 income if Learning, Inc., distributes all of its after-tax income to Mr. and Mrs. Quicksand at the end of the year?

Observe due measure, for right timing is in all things the most important factor.

HESIOD, WORKS AND DAYS (C. 700 B.C.)

TAX ACCOUNTING

CHAPTER OBJECTIVES

In Chapter 7, you will gain insight into various aspects of tax accounting and discover how tax accounting differs from financial accounting. You will learn that tax accounting pertains to the *timing* of income recognition and expense deduction and timing depends on the taxpayer's tax year and method of accounting as well as various other doctrines and concepts.

LEARNING GOALS

After studying this chapter, you should be able to

1 Recognize why tax accounting and financial accounting differ;

2 Understand the importance of timing;

3 Appreciate the major implications of adopting and changing an accounting period;

4 Appreciate the major implications of adopting and changing an accounting method;

5 Explain and apply such overall accounting methods as the cash method, the accrual method, and the hybrid method as well as selected special methods; and

6 Define and apply various tax concepts and doctrines, such as the annual accounting concept, the claim of right doctrine, the tax benefit rule, the constructive receipt doctrine, and the treatment of prepayments.

Chapters 4 and 5 addressed the questions (1) *what* is included in and excluded from gross income and (2) *what* is deductible in calculating taxable income? Tax accounting concerns the *timing* of income and deductions. Accordingly, this chapter focuses on the questions (1) *when* is income recognized and (2) *when* are deductions allowed? Timing depends on both the taxpayer's accounting *period* and accounting *method*. In this chapter, we identify the alternative periods a taxpayer may choose for a tax year and the accounting methods most commonly used to determine taxable income in the year chosen.[1] Before proceeding, let us briefly examine the contrast between tax accounting and financial accounting.

TAX ACCOUNTING VERSUS FINANCIAL ACCOUNTING

Goal #1
Recognize differences between tax and financial accounting.

Businesses in general and corporations in particular rarely report the same amount of income in their financial statements as they do in their tax returns. In the next several paragraphs, we explore some reasons for these differences.

REASONS FOR DIFFERENCES

Tax accounting is driven by different goals than financial accounting. Although in some instances tax accounting conforms with generally accepted accounting principles (GAAP), in many cases it differs markedly from GAAP. The Supreme Court in *Thor Power Tool Co. v. Comm.* clearly articulated the reason why tax accounting and financial accounting must necessarily diverge.

> The primary goal of financial accounting is to provide useful information to management, shareholders, creditors, and others properly interested; the major responsibility of the accountant is to protect these parties from being misled. The primary goal of the income tax system, in contrast, is the equitable collection of revenue; the major responsibility of the Internal Revenue Service is to protect the public fisc. Consistently with its goals and responsibilities, financial accounting has as its foundation the principle of conservatism, with its corollary that "possible errors in measurement [should] be in the direction of understatement rather than overstatement of net income and net assets." In view of the Treasury's markedly different goals and responsibilities, understatement of income is not destined to be its guiding light. Given this diversity, even contrariety, of objectives, any presumptive equivalency between tax and financial accounting would be unacceptable.[2]

Several basic tenets and goals of taxation introduced in Chapter 1—such as wherewithal to pay, certainty, administrative convenience, and influencing social and economic behavior—help explain differences between tax and financial accounting. The following examples illustrate this point:

1. *Wherewithal to pay.* On certain installment sales, taxpayers may defer gain recognition primarily because, until they receive the installment payments, taxpayers may not have the wherewithal to pay taxes.

---

1 For a complete treatise on tax accounting, see Stephen F. Gertzman, *Federal Tax Accounting* (Boston: Warren, Gorham & Lamont, 1988).

2 439 US 522 (1979).

2. *Certainty.* Financial accounting prescribes the use of estimates to accomplish the goal of matching, as in the case of warranty and bad debt expenses. Because of the uncertainty they create, tax law rarely permits such estimates and allows expenses to be deducted only when paid or when the liability can be computed with mathematical accuracy and legal certainty (the all-events test).

3. *Administrative convenience.* The certainty criterion and the prohibition against estimates also ease tax administration because the IRS does not have to concern itself with auditing estimated amounts.

4. *Influencing social and economic behavior.* Tax law provides many social and economic incentives in the form of rapid writeoffs. For example, to encourage pollution control, the Code allows the cost of a certified pollution control facility to be amortized over a period (60 months) that is usually shorter than the facility's economic life. Similarly, to stimulate investment, the Code allows taxpayers to use accelerated depreciation methods.

CATEGORIES OF DIFFERENCES

Variations between tax and financial accounting can be categorized as either timing or permanent differences. **Timing differences** can be divided into four subcategories.

> **Timing differences** are variations between tax and financial accounting that occur because income is recognized (or expenses are deducted) in one period for tax purposes and a different period for accounting purposes.

1. *Income is recognized in an earlier period for taxation than for financial reporting.* For example, amounts received in advance for services to be performed in a subsequent period must be recognized for tax purposes in the year received. Financial accounting requires recognition only as the services are rendered.

2. *Income is recognized in a later period for taxation than for financial reporting.* For example, profit on an installment sale is generally recognized at the time of sale for financial reporting. For tax purposes, however, the profit may sometimes be deferred and recognized when cash collections are received on the installment contract.

3. *Expenses and losses are deducted in an earlier period for taxation than for financial reporting.* For example, accelerated cost recovery rules may allow assets to be depreciated over a shorter period and at a more accelerated rate for tax purposes than that permitted by financial accounting principles.

4. *Expenses and losses are deducted in a later period for taxation than for financial reporting.* For example, financial accounting principles require that businesses, under normal circumstances, estimate their uncollectible accounts and expense the estimated amount in the year of sale. Tax rules, however, forbid the allowance or reserve method and permit bad debt deductions only as individual accounts receivable become worthless.

Other variations between taxable income and financial net income represent **permanent differences**. These differences can also be divided into four sub-categories.

> **Permanent differences** are variations between tax and financial accounting that occur largely because of definitional differences in income and expenses for financial purposes as compared to income and deductions for tax purposes.

1. *Income is excluded from taxable gross income but included in financial income,* for example, interest earned on state and local bonds.

2. *Income is included in taxable gross income but excluded from financial income,* for example, imputed interest on intercompany loans.

3. *Certain items are deductible for tax purposes but are not expensed for financial reporting*, for example, the 70% or 80% dividend received deduction allowed to certain corporations.

4. *Expenses and losses are not deductible for tax purposes but are expensed for financial reporting*, for example, interest on amounts borrowed to purchase or carry tax-exempt state and local bonds.

Although permanent differences cause taxable income and financial net income to vary, technically, they are not within the scope of tax accounting because they do not involve timing.

Goal #2
Understand the importance of timing.

Time value of money means that a dollar now is worth more than a dollar in the future.

Tax deferral entails postponing taxes to a future year through the timing of income and deductions.

THE IMPORTANCE OF TIMING

Timing usually has little effect on the total income ultimately reported or the aggregate tax liability ultimately paid by the taxpayer. However, because of the **time value of money,** taxpayers generally prefer to defer their tax liability as long as possible. On a present value basis, **deferred taxes** are less costly than taxes paid currently.

EXAMPLE 7-1

Assume that Mr. Able and Ms. Baker each pay tax at a flat 30% rate. Assume also that the appropriate discount rate is 10%. Each taxpayer has a business that begins in Year 1 and ends in Year 3. Mr. Able's business generates $100,000 of taxable income in each of the three years for a total of $300,000. Ms. Baker's business also earns $300,000 of taxable income, but because of her method of accounting, she reports all $300,000 at the end of Year 3. Their schedule of earnings and taxes follows:

	Year 1	Year 2	Year 3	Total
Mr. Able				
Taxable income	$100,000	$100,000	$100,000	$300,000
Tax at 30%	30,000	30,000	30,000	90,000
PV at 10%	27,273	24,793	22,539	74,605
Ms. Baker				
Taxable income			$300,000	$300,000
Tax at 30%			90,000	90,000
PV at 10%			67,618	67,618

On a present value basis, Ms. Baker pays $6,987 less in taxes ($74,605 – $67,618) than Mr. Able. By deferring her tax liability, Ms. Baker, in effect, receives an interest-free loan from the government, the proceeds of which she can invest at 10%.

Tax authorities have long been aware of the potential for manipulating the timing of income recognition and expense deduction. Normally a taxpayer can defer taxes by either accelerating deductions to early periods or deferring income to late periods. A taxpayer can sometimes reduce taxes by accelerating income and deferring deductions if tax rates increase in future years. Many of the tax laws discussed in this chapter are designed to prevent taxpayers from manipulating tax accounting periods or tax accounting methods to artificially defer or reduce taxes.

Congress's attention to deferral and time-value-of-money issues became particularly acute in 1984 when it enacted the Deficit Reduction Act of 1984. To prevent the premature accrual (acceleration) of deductions, the 1984 Act grafted an economic performance criterion onto the so-called all-events test (defined and discussed later in this chapter). Congress continued its attack on perceived accounting abuses in the Tax Reform Act of 1986. This later act, among other things, restricted use of the cash method of accounting for certain taxpayers; restricted the choice of fiscal years for partnerships, S corporations, and personal service corporations; repealed the reserve method of accounting for bad debts; and repealed the completed contract method.

THE ACCOUNTING PERIOD

To determine when income is included and when deductions are allowed, we must first know the taxpayer's accounting period, typically referred to as the tax year. In the next several pages, we examine the annual accounting concept and survey the rules for adopting and changing the tax year.

THE ANNUAL ACCOUNTING CONCEPT

The tax year approach to measuring taxable income originates in the **annual accounting concept**, which looks to fixed, regular accounting periods rather than to the conclusion of a taxpayer's economic activity. Economic behavior is usually a continuous activity that does not begin and end at convenient intervals. The most accurate measurement of an activity's outcome occurs when the activity is concluded and aggregate net cash flow can be ascertained. However, the concluded economic activity approach is inappropriate for tax reporting because the activity may extend over several years or even the taxpayer's lifetime, thereby delaying the taxpayer's ultimate settlement with the taxing authorities. The annual accounting concept, on the other hand, is analogous to the periodicity assumption in financial accounting: "the economic activities of a firm can be meaningfully related to arbitrary time periods that are shorter than the firm's life."[3]

The annual accounting concept was first articulated by the Supreme Court in *Burnet v. Sanford & Brooks Co.*[4] From 1913 through 1916, the taxpayer (S&B) carried out a dredging contract for the United States. During this period, S&B incurred an aggregate net loss of $176,272 for which S&B obtained no deduction. In 1916, S&B brought a breach of warranty suit against the United States. In 1920, S&B recovered $176,272 plus $16,305 of interest. S&B failed to report any of the recovery as income, and the government assessed a tax deficiency. The Court of Appeals held that only the interest was gross income while the $176,272 was a nontaxable return of losses. The Supreme Court reversed the Court of Appeals and included the entire recovery in S&B's 1920 gross income with no offset against the prior year losses.

The Supreme Court addressed the question of whether income should be determined on the basis of fixed accounting periods or on the basis of concluded activities. It opted for fixed accounting periods, holding that a system of taxation must produce

Goal #3
Appreciate the implications of changing the accounting period.

Goal #6
Define and apply the annual accounting concept.

The **annual accounting concept** requires periodic (annual) reporting of income and payment of taxes.

3 Jan R. Williams, Keith G. Stanga, and William W. Holder, *Intermediate Accounting,* 4th ed. (Fort Worth: Dryden Press, 1992), p.44.

4 282 US 359 (1931).

revenue that is ascertainable and payable to the government at regular intervals. "Only by such a system is it practicable to produce a regular flow of income and apply methods of accounting, assessment, and collection capable of practical operation."[5]

As the taxpayers in *Stanford & Brooks* painfully discovered, the annual accounting concept, if strictly applied, can be quite harsh. To alleviate the type of hardship that occurred in this case, Congress enacted the net operating loss (NOL) provisions. Under current law, NOLs may be carried back three years and carried forward 15 years (see Chapter 5). With NOL rules in place, a taxpayer in circumstances similar to those in *Stanford & Brooks* simply carries over the prior year losses to offset subsequent income.

The annual accounting concept is now codified in Sec. 441(a), which states that "taxable income shall be computed on the basis of the taxpayer's taxable [tax] year." It also pervades the Code in numerous other sections that refer to a taxpayer's taxable (tax) year.

THE TAX YEAR

The Code contains many rules that dictate what tax year a taxpayer may use. The range of choices depends on (1) whether the taxpayer keeps adequate books and records; (2) the type of taxpayer (for example, an individual, corporation, or partnership); and (3) the taxpayer's business purpose for desiring a particular year.

The term **tax year** generally means the taxpayer's annual accounting period if that period is a calendar or fiscal year. The **annual accounting period** is the period used by the taxpayer for keeping books; a **calendar year** is the 12-month period ending on December 31; and a **fiscal year** is usually any 12-month period ending on the last day of any month other than December.[6]

The definition of a fiscal year also includes a so-called **52–53 week year,** which may end on either (1) the same weekday that last occurs in any calendar month (for example, the last Friday in October) or (2) the same weekday occurring nearest the last day of the calendar month (for example, the Friday occurring nearest to October 31 each year).[7] Although a tax year may generally not exceed 12 months, a 52–53 week year occasionally extends to 53 weeks.

Under the general rule, the tax year must conform to that used for bookkeeping purposes if the book year ends on the last day of a month or corresponds to a proper 52–53 week method. A taxpayer who keeps no books or does not have an acceptable annual accounting period is precluded from using a fiscal year and must use a calendar year for tax purposes.[8]

SPECIAL RULES FOR CERTAIN ENTITIES

With no restrictions, partners of a partnership could gain a tax deferral benefit by having the partnership use a fiscal year different than its partners. This benefit could occur because, as discussed in Chapter 6, all partnership income flows through the entity to the partners at the end of the partnership's tax year.

> A **tax year** is the taxpayer's annual accounting period for reporting income and paying taxes.
>
> The **annual accounting period** is the period used for bookkeeping.
>
> A **calendar year** is a tax year ending on December 31.
>
> A **fiscal year** is a tax year ending at the end of any month other than December.
>
> A **52–53 week year** is a tax year ending on a specific weekday each year.

---

5 *Ibid.*

6 Sec. 441(b), (c), (d), and (e).

7 Sec. 441(f).

8 Sec. 441(g).

EXAMPLE 7-2

Assume the partners of AB Partnership have calendar tax years and the partnership has a January 31 fiscal year. Partner A and Partner B share partnership income equally. Partnership income for the year February 1, 19X1, through January 31, 19X2, is $240,000. If the partnership had a calendar year and earned the $240,000 in 19X1, each partner would report $120,000 in his or her 19X1 individual tax return. However, with the assumed fiscal year, the $240,000 ($120,000 each) flows into the partners' 19X2 returns. Consequently, the partners report the income in a year later than 19X1. As shown in the top portion of Figure 7-1, each partner defers taxes on the first 11 months of partnership income.

Shareholders of S corporations could obtain a similar deferral advantage because these special corporations are treated as flow-through entities much like partnerships (see Chapter 6). Tax deferral could also be accomplished with a personal service corporation, which is a corporation whose principal activity is the performance of personal services largely rendered by the individuals who own the corporation's stock. Although a personal service corporation is not a flow-through entity, its owner-employees might obtain a deferral advantage by having the fiscal-year corporation delay paying salaries and bonuses until the end of its fiscal tax year so that the owner-employees receive the cash after the end of their calendar tax year. In the Tax Reform Act of 1986, Congress responded to what it considered improper deferrals by imposing special restrictions on the tax years available to partnerships, S corporations, and personal service corporations.

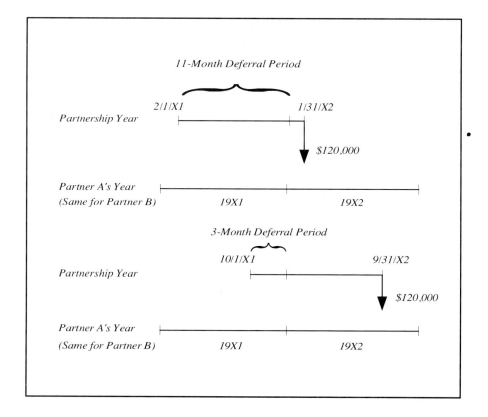

FIGURE 7-1

Deferral of Partnership Income (EXAMPLE 7-2)

The Code now provides a set of hierarchical rules for establishing a partnership tax year in reference to the partners. First, the partnership must use the same tax year as those partners having a majority interest (over 50%) in partnership profits and capital. Second, if the majority partners have different tax years, the partnership must use the same year as all its principal partners (those with at least a 5% interest in the partnership). Third, if the principal partners have different years, the partnership must use a year that results in the least aggregate deferral of income.[9]

A partnership may have a tax year other than one prescribed by this hierarchy if it can establish to the IRS's satisfaction that a business purpose exists for a different tax year. A major factor in determining business purpose is the partnership's annual cycle of business activity, in other words, whether a *natural business year* exists. Deferral of income to partners is not considered a business purpose.[10] Moreover, the IRS has ruled that "the use of a particular year for financial reporting purposes is not sufficient to establish that the business purpose for that year has been met."[11]

Because of 1986 Act changes, an S corporation must now use a calendar year unless, like a partnership, the corporation can establish a business purpose for a different tax year.[12] Similar rules apply to personal service corporations.[13] A tax year imposed on a partnership, S corporation, or personal service corporation, aside from deviations allowed by the business purpose exception, is called a **required tax year.**

> A **required tax year** is any tax year imposed on partnerships, S corporations, and personal service corporations.

The required-tax-year rules enacted in the 1986 Act created a furor in the accounting industry. The American Institute of Certified Public Accountants (AICPA), in an intense lobbying effort, spearheaded a letter-writing campaign to encourage elected officials to support legislation that would allow partnerships, S corporations, and personal service corporations to retain their fiscal years. The AICPA raised the following objections to the 1986 provisions:

1. The 1986 requirements are stringent, unnecessary, and unworkable, thereby imposing hardships on small businesses;

2. The 1986 requirements create hardships on CPA firms during tax season because filing dates occur at the same time rather than being spread throughout the year;

3. The entities affected have important business reasons for using fiscal years; and

4. The compliance costs of the 1986 requirements far exceed any benefits.[14]

The AICPA's political strategy paid off, at least in part, when Congress enacted Sec. 444 as part of the Revenue Act of 1987. Section 444 allows the three designated entities to use a year other than a required tax year if the deferral period does not exceed three months.[15]

---

9 Sec. 706(b)(1)(B); Temp. Reg. Sec. 1.706-1T.

10 See Sec. 706(b)(1)(C); Temp. Reg. Sec. 1.706-1T(b); Reg. Sec. 1.442-1(b); Rev. Proc. 74-33, 1974-2 CB 489; and Rev. Proc. 87-32, 1987-2 CB 396.

11 Rev. Rul. 87-57, 1987-2 CB 117.

12 Sec. 1378.

13 Sec. 441(i); also, trusts other than tax-exempt trusts and wholly charitable trusts must use the calendar year (see Sec. 645).

14 "Washington Update," *Journal of Accountancy,* September 1987, p. 84.

15 Under a special transitional rule, entities having a fiscal year in 1986 could have elected to retain that year even if the deferral period exceeded three months (see Temp. Reg. Sec. 1.444-1T(b)(3)).

EXAMPLE 7-3

> The required year for the AB Partnership in Example 7-2 is a calendar year. However, AB Partnership may elect a fiscal year ending September 30, October 31, or November 30. A September 30 tax year would result in a three-month deferral period as shown in the bottom portion of Figure 7-1.

Despite Sec. 444, partnerships and S corporations gain no real tax advantage because they must pay a deposit, called a *required payment*, that approximates the monetary value of the deferral afforded by the fiscal year.[16]

ADOPTING A TAX YEAR

A taxpayer adopts a tax year by establishing that year on or before the due date (not including extensions) for filing the first tax return. The least controversial way to adopt a tax year is to file the first return by this unextended due date. For example, an individual adopting a calendar year must file his or her *first* return by April 15 of the immediately following year.

EXAMPLE 7-4

> New Corporation begins its legal existence on October 3, 19X1, and wishes to adopt a fiscal year ending on June 30. Thus, its first year runs from October 3, 19X1, through June 30, 19X2, and its first return is due September 15, 19X2.

Although timely filing of the first return ordinarily determines the tax year chosen, the tax year technically depends on the taxpayer's annual accounting period, which in turn depends on the taxpayer's year for maintaining its books. Therefore, the taxpayer must also establish a bookkeeping year by the unextended due date of the initial return. As discussed earlier in this chapter, a taxpayer who maintains no books must adopt a calendar year.

In any case, the taxpayer need not actually file a tax return by the prescribed due date. For example, in Rev. Rul. 68-125,[17] the taxpayer adopted a fiscal accounting period prior to the time its first return was due, and this period was reflected in the taxpayer's books and records. However, the taxpayer failed to file its initial tax return on a timely basis. The IRS held that even though "the taxpayer did not file its initial return within the time prescribed by law . . . such filing does not, of itself, preclude the adoption of a fiscal taxable [tax] year. . . ."[18] The IRS has also ruled that the filing of an extension request for the initial return confirms the adoption of a tax year.[19]

Individuals rarely keep sufficient books to warrant a fiscal year and therefore have little alternative to a calendar tax year. Corporations other than S corporations, on the other hand, have a great deal of latitude in selecting a tax year. These corporations must consider business as well as tax reasons for making their selection.

---

16 Sec. 7519.

17 1968-1 CB 189.

18 *Ibid.*

19 Rev. Rul. 57-589, 1957-2 CB 298 and Rev. Rul. 69-563, 1969-2 CB 104.

EXAMPLE 7-5

Ski Corporation operates a ski lodge in Colorado. The lodge's peak business occurs in December, January, and February. If Ski Corporation adopted a calendar year it would have to close its books in the middle of its busiest season when employees have the least time for performing accounting functions. Moreover, the revenue for a single season would be split between two tax years, and expenses of one season might be mismatched against revenue from another. Thus, income distortions would result. For these reasons, Ski Corporation should consider a fiscal tax year. On the other hand, Ski Corporation might obtain a tax advantage by cutting off its first year early, thereby keeping its taxable income for that year in low tax brackets. The corporation must assess both the tax and nontax factors.

Finally, a corporation needs to determine exactly when its first year begins under state law because a tax year may not exceed 12 months (except in the case of a 52–53 week year). If this beginning point occurs earlier than corporate officials realize, they may inadvertently attempt to adopt an incorrect tax year.

CHANGING THE TAX YEAR

> A **short year** is a tax year having fewer than 12 months.
>
> **Annualization** is a method of computing tax for a short year that eliminates any advantage of low rates on low short-year income.

The tax year initially adopted must be retained for all subsequent years unless the taxpayer obtains prior approval from the IRS to change to a different year.[20] To obtain prior approval, the taxpayer must file Form 1128, Application for Change in Accounting Period, by the 15th day of the second calendar month following the beginning of the **short year** resulting from the change. As part of the application, the taxpayer must establish a substantial business purpose for the change.[21] In addition, the taxpayer must file an income tax return for the short year, and the tax liability must be computed on an annualized basis.[22] **Annualization** is not required for short years resulting from a taxpayer's initial or final year.

The annualization procedure involves the following three steps:

1. Multiply the short-year taxable income by 12, and divide the result by the number of months in the short year;

2. Compute the tax on annualized taxable income from Step 1; and

3. Multiply the tax from Step 2 by the number of months in the short year, and divide the result by 12.

This procedure assumes that income and expenses will occur throughout a 12-month period at the same rate as during the short year and is designed to prevent taxpayers from taking advantage of low-bracket tax rates.

Annualization will overstate the tax if the short year contains an unusually large amount of income compared to a full 12-month period. For example, the taxpayer may have recognized a large, nonrecurring gain during the short year. Section 443 allows the taxpayer to elect an alternative method for computing the short-year tax if the

---

20 Sec. 442.

21 Reg. Sec. 1.442-1(b)(1); Rev. Proc. 87-32, 1987-2 CB 396 provides special guidance for partnerships, S corporations, and personal service corporations desiring to change their tax years.

22 Sec. 443.

alternative method results in a lower tax than does the normal method of annualization. The tax under the alternative method equals the greater of the (1) tax computed on the actual 12-month taxable income times short-year taxable income divided by the actual 12-month taxable income or (2) tax on the short-year taxable income without annualization. The applicable 12-month period begins on the first day of the short year.

EXAMPLE 7-6

Delta Corporation currently uses a calendar year but has a substantial business purpose for changing to a May 30 fiscal year. Delta wants to make the change in 19X1. The change will create a short year from January 1, 19X1, through May 30, 19X1. Delta's taxable income for this period is $50,000. Delta must file Form 1128 by July 15, 19X1, and file a short-year tax return by August 15, 19X1. However, Delta may want to obtain an automatic extension to file the tax return late so that it can first receive the IRS's response to the change application.

If Delta were not required to annualize its short-year income, its tax liability would be only $7,500 (15% x $50,000). With the annualization procedure, however, the short-year tax liability is $12,521 computed as follows:

1. $50,000 x 12/5 = $120,000;

2. Tax on $120,000 is $30,050 [$22,250 + (39% x $20,000)]; and

3. $30,050 x 5/12 = $12,521.

This procedure ensures that Delta's short-year taxable income is taxed at marginal tax rates as high as 39% rather than at one low rate of 15%.

THE CLAIM OF RIGHT DOCTRINE AND THE TAX BENEFIT RULE

Two important concepts, the claim of right doctrine and the tax benefit rule, affect the timing and treatment of income. We define and explain them in the next several pages.

THE CLAIM OF RIGHT DOCTRINE

A taxpayer has a *claim of right* when he or she "acquires earnings, lawfully or unlawfully, without the consensual recognition, expressed or implied, of an obligation to repay and without restriction as to their disposition. . . ."[23] The Supreme Court first enunciated the **claim of right doctrine** in *North American Oil Consolidated v. Burnet* as follows:

> If a taxpayer receives earnings under a claim of right and without restriction as to its disposition, he has received income which he is required to [report], even though it may still be claimed that he is not entitled to retain the money, and even though he may still be adjudged liable to restore its equivalent.[24]

> **Goal #6**
> Define and apply the claim of right doctrine.

> The **claim of right doctrine** holds that income is recognized upon receipt if the taxpayer has an unrestricted claim to the income.

---

23 *James v. U.S.*, 366 US 213 (1961).

24 286 US 417 (1932).

Accordingly, a taxpayer includes amounts in gross income when they are received provided the taxpayer has unrestricted use of the funds. In short, the taxpayer has a claim to the income and a right to use it freely. For example, an attorney must report professional fees received even if those fees must be returned in the event a favorable decision is later appealed and overturned. However, the claim of right doctrine does not apply if, on receiving the item, the taxpayer is obligated to make repayment. For example, a taxpayer does not recognize income upon receipt of a security deposit that must be returned at a future date (if the rental property is returned in good condition or if all rental payments are made during the contract period).

The claim of right doctrine applies to both cash- and accrual-basis taxpayers (defined later in this chapter) and results from strict compliance with the annual accounting concept, which

1. Requires that income be determined at the close of the tax year regardless of *subsequent* events;

2. Precludes reopening the year of receipt if an item is subsequently repaid; and

3. Requires that items be deducted in the year repaid (or, for accrual-basis taxpayers, in the year the liability to repay becomes fixed).

In *United States v. Lewis*,[25] the Supreme Court applied these principles. The taxpayer (Lewis) received and reported as income a $22,000 employee bonus in 1944. Subsequent litigation found that the bonus had been computed improperly, and Lewis had to repay $11,000 to his employer in 1946. Until repayment, Lewis "had at all times claimed and used the full $22,000 unconditionally as his own, in the good faith though 'mistaken' belief that he was entitled to the whole bonus."[26] The court invoked the claim of right doctrine as stated in *North American Oil* and held that the full $22,000 remained taxable in 1944. Although the court did not allow Lewis to reopen his 1944 tax return by recomputing income for that year, it did allow him an $11,000 deduction in 1946.

In one circumstance, the claim of right doctrine may benefit the taxpayer. If upon repayment the taxpayer had to recompute prior-year income, rather than take a current deduction, the benefit of the recomputation would be unavailable if the prior year were closed by the statute of limitations.

With a current deduction on repayment, the only real detriment to a taxpayer occurs when the tax rate in the prior year is higher than in the repayment year. In that event, the taxpayer would have paid a high tax rate on the income but obtains a tax benefit for the deduction at a low rate. Section 1341, enacted after the *Lewis* case, alleviates this hardship if

1. The item was included in gross income in a prior year because the taxpayer apparently had an unrestricted right to the item;

2. The deduction is allowed for the current year because, after the close of the prior year, someone establishes that the taxpayer did not have an unrestricted right to the item; and

3. The amount of the deduction exceeds $3,000 (this precludes the taxpayer from making Sec. 1341 computations for small amounts).

---

25 340 US 590.

26 *Ibid.*

If all three of these conditions hold, the current year tax equals the *lesser* of (1) the current-year tax computed with the deduction or (2) the current-year tax computed without the deduction minus the reduction in tax that would result if the item were excluded from gross income in the prior year.

EXAMPLE 7-7

In 19X1, Ms. Justice agreed to represent a client in a lawsuit. Under the terms of the engagement, her fee was contingent on her successful defense of the suit. In 19X1, the trial court decided in favor of Ms. Justice's client, and the client paid her a $40,000 contingent fee. In 19X3, the appeals court overturned the trial court's decision, and Ms. Justice repaid the $40,000 fee to her client. In 19X1, Ms. Justice had $90,000 of taxable income aside from the fee, and in 19X3 she had $70,000 of taxable income before taking the deduction for repayment of the fee. For simplicity, assume that in both years a taxpayer's first $50,000 of taxable income is taxed at 15%, and any excess over $50,000 is taxed at 30%.

Under the claim of right doctrine, Ms. Justice includes the $40,000 fee in 19X1 income so that total taxable income for that year equals $130,000, and she pays $31,500 in taxes [($50,000 x 15%) + ($80,000 x 30%)]. If she had excluded the $40,000 from 19X1 taxable income her tax liability would have been $19,500 [($50,000 x 15%) + ($40,000 x 30%)], a reduction of $12,000. Her taxable income in 19X3 with the deduction is $30,000 ($70,000 - $40,000), which results in a tax of $4,500 ($30,000 x 15%). Her tax without the deduction would be $13,500 [($50,000 x 15%) + ($20,000 x 30%)]. Under Sec. 1341, her 19X3 tax is the lesser of (1) $4,500 or (2) $13,500 - $12,000 = $1,500. Therefore, her 19X1 tax is $31,500, and her 19X3 tax is $1,500. Had Ms. Justice been in a lower tax bracket in 19X1 than she was in 19X3, her lowest 19X3 tax liability would have resulted from taxable income computed with the deduction. Thus, Sec. 1341 may work to the taxpayer's advantage but never to her detriment.

> **Goal #6**
> Define and apply the tax benefit rule.

THE TAX BENEFIT RULE

In some ways, the **tax benefit rule** is the flip side of the claim of right doctrine. It applies when a deduction is taken in one year and a recovery of the deducted item occurs in a subsequent year. Rather than reopen the prior year, the taxpayer includes the recovery in the gross income of the recovery year. This treatment, which is sometimes referred to as the *inclusionary* component of the tax benefit rule,[27] represents strict compliance with the annual accounting concept. Inclusion in the recovery year, however, generates two potential hardships. First, tax rates in the recovery year may be higher than in the deduction year. No Code section comparable to Sec. 1341 alleviates this inequity. Second, the original deduction may not have given the taxpayer a tax benefit. The *exclusionary* component of the tax benefit rule, codified in Sec. 111, mitigates this second hardship and can be stated as follows: Gross income *excludes* the recovery to the extent the prior deduction did not reduce income taxes. Thus, the complete tax benefit rule ensures that the taxpayer recognizes income only to the extent of a previous tax benefit.

> The **tax benefit rule** holds that the recovery of a previously deducted item is recognized as income to the extent the deduction produced a tax benefit (reduced taxes) in an earlier year.

---

27 See, for example, *Hillsboro National Bank v. Comm.,* 460 US 370 (1983).

> **EXAMPLE 7-8**
>
> Mr. Swanson lives in Wisconsin, which imposes a state income tax. In 19X1, Mr. Swanson paid $2,000 in state income tax through payroll withholding. When Mr. Swanson filed his 19X1 Wisconsin tax return in 19X2, he owed only $1,500 so the state paid him a $500 refund in 19X2. Mr. Swanson itemized deductions on his 19X1 federal income tax return and deducted the entire $2,000, thereby reducing his 19X1 federal taxes. Under the tax benefit rule, Mr. Swanson must include the entire $500 refund in his 19X2 federal gross income. If Mr. Swanson had claimed the standard deduction instead of itemizing in his 19X1 federal tax return, he would not have to include any of the $500 in his 19X2 federal gross income because he would have received no tax benefit for the state income taxes paid in 19X1.

Interestingly, the Supreme Court did not apply the tax benefit rule in the *Sandford & Brooks* case, discussed earlier in this chapter. If the court had, the taxpayer could have excluded the $176,272 recovery because it obtained no tax benefit from the prior years' net losses.

The tax benefit rule does not apply if the taxpayer took an erroneous or improper deduction in the prior year. If the taxpayer ascertains that a previous deduction was improper, he or she should file an amended return, within the period allowed by the statute of limitations, and pay any additional tax due.[28]

> **Goal #4**
> Appreciate the implications of changing methods of accounting.

> A taxpayer's **method of accounting** determines the tax year in which a taxpayer recognizes income and claims deductions.

METHODS OF ACCOUNTING—GENERAL REQUIREMENTS

The taxpayer's **method of accounting** determines in which year income is recognized and deductions are allowed. To provide a framework for a later discussion of specific methods, we first outline the general requirements for all tax accounting methods as follows:[29]

1. The method of accounting must *conform* to that used for book purposes.

2. The method of accounting must *clearly reflect income* (in practice, the IRS makes this judgment for the Secretary of the Treasury).

3. Subject to Requirements 2 and 3, taxpayers may use any of the following methods of accounting:

   a. The cash receipts and disbursements method;

   b. An accrual method;

   c. Any other permitted method (for example, the installment method and the percentage of completion method); or

   d. Any combination of these methods permitted under Regulations (a hybrid method).

4. A taxpayer engaged in more than one trade or business may use a different method of accounting for each trade or business.

28 Reg. Sec. 1.461-1(a)(3)(i).

29 Sec. 446.

5. Unless provided otherwise, taxpayers must obtain the IRS's permission to change their accounting method.

These rules seem to give all taxpayers much leeway in selecting an accounting method. However, as you will see later, the Code denies the cash method to certain business entities.

THE BOOK CONFORMITY REQUIREMENT

The term *method of accounting* pertains to an overall method as well as to the accounting treatment of any particular item. The cash, accrual, and hybrid methods (discussed later in this chapter) are examples of overall methods. Depreciation and LIFO (last-in-first-out) inventory accounting are examples of particular methods.

Section 446 provides that "taxable income shall be computed under the method of accounting on the basis of which the taxpayer regularly computes his income in keeping his books." In addition, taxpayers must maintain sufficient records so that they can file correct tax returns. Accounting records include the books, supporting documentation, and reconciliations of differences between the books and the tax return.[30] Thus, by requiring a taxpayer to maintain records, the **book conformity requirement** enhances the IRS's ability to verify taxable income.

> The **book conformity requirement** requires a taxpayer to determine taxable income in a manner consistent with (or reconcilable to) book income.

The book conformity requirement should not be read too literally, however. Many taxpayers keep their books in strict conformity with generally accepted accounting principles (GAAP). Nevertheless, these taxpayers may not use GAAP numbers for tax reporting purposes. Therefore, we need a broad definition of both *the books* and *conformity* to correctly interpret the book conformity requirement.

A special problem arises when a taxpayer keeps books on the accrual basis and reports taxable income on the cash basis (or vice versa). Regulation Sec. 1.446-1(a)(4) includes reconciliations in its definition of accounting *records* but does not explicitly include these reconciliations in the definition of *the books*. Consequently, the following question arises: Does the definition of the books include reconciling workpapers for purposes of applying the book conformity requirement?

The answer to this question has been clarified for taxpayers who initially adopt the same method for book and tax purposes but subsequently change their book method. In *Patchen v. Comm.*,[31] the taxpayer initially kept its books and filed its tax return on the cash method. Several years later, the taxpayer changed to the accrual method for book purposes. To prepare its tax return, the taxpayer's accountants prepared memorandum journal entries (the entries were not booked) to convert all items of income and expense to the cash method. The accountants kept these entries as part of the permanent records and made them available to the IRS upon audit. Nevertheless, the IRS attempted to change the taxpayer to the accrual method for tax reporting. The Tax Court conceded that both methods clearly reflected income but held that the taxpayer had violated the book conformity requirement. The Appeals Court, which reversed the Tax Court, concluded that the memorandum journal entries were an integral part of the taxpayer's accounting system and that the taxpayer's books and records were entirely adequate even though the taxpayer's accountants possessed the reconciling workpapers.

The IRS subsequently yielded to this view in several Revenue Rulings. These rulings allowed taxpayers to continue their prior tax method after changing their book

---

30 Reg. Sec. 1.446-1(a)(4).

31 258 F.2d 544 (CA-5, 1958).

method. In so ruling, the IRS cautioned that the taxpayer's "permanent books and records must clearly reflect a proper reconciliation between the accrual method used for book purposes and the cash receipts and disbursements method used for filing its Federal income tax returns."[32]

The authorities for *initially adopting* one method for books and another for tax are not as clear as those involving *subsequent changes* in the book method. The legislative history of Sec. 448, which restricts certain entities to the cash method, states that the book conformity requirement is satisfied if the taxpayer maintains sufficient records to allow someone to reconcile the books and tax return.[33] Also, in a recent Technical Advice Memorandum, the IRS ruled that, because a corporation maintained adequate reconciling documentation, the corporation, which used the cash method for tax reporting and the accrual method for bookkeeping, did not violate the book conformity requirement.[34] These authorities seem to allow a taxpayer to *adopt* one method for keeping books and another for tax reporting if the taxpayer maintains adequate supporting records. However, legislative history is not law, and **technical advice** from the IRS applies only to the particular taxpayer under audit, which means that it does not have the same precedential value as a published Revenue Ruling. Thus, the answer is not perfectly clear although, in applying the book conformity requirement, the IRS seems to be moving in the direction of including reconciling workpapers in its broad definition of the books.

> A **technical advice** memorandum is guidance furnished by the IRS National Office on any question that arises during and IRS proceeding (e.g., an audit).

The cases and rulings discussed so far pertain to overall methods of accounting. No controversy exists for particular items, such as depreciation, that are treated differently for tax purposes than for book purposes. The Regulations clearly allow book-tax differences for these items as long as the taxpayer maintains adequate supporting records.[35] In fact, Schedule M-1 of the corporate tax return (Form 1120) specifically requires a reconciliation of book income and taxable income (computed without certain deductions).

We should make two other points. First, the book conformity requirement does not imply financial statement conformity (except for LIFO).[36] For example, a taxpayer could both keep books and file tax returns using the cash method and still prepare accrual method financial statements using unbooked supporting adjustments.[37] Query: Under these circumstances, could the IRS claim that the supporting adjustments are part of the books, thereby producing a book-tax nonconformity? We leave this question for students, attorneys, and the courts to ponder. Second, a taxpayer may use different tax accounting methods for separate and distinct businesses, but each business must keep complete, separate books and records.[38] The separate businesses must also meet the clear reflection of income requirement discussed below.

The *Patchen* case raises another interesting issue. A taxpayer may change its book method at will; a taxpayer may not change its tax method without IRS permission. If the taxpayer changes its book method but chooses not to obtain permission to change its tax method, can the IRS on audit require the taxpayer to change its tax method as part of the book conformity requirement? The Appeals Court in *Patchen* held that the IRS cannot require that change if both methods clearly reflect income. However, if

32 Rev. Rul. 74-383, 1974-2 CB 146, and Rev. Rul. 68-83, 1968-1 CB 190.

33 H. Rep. No. 99-426, 99th Cong., 1st Sess. (1985) and S. Rep. No. 99-313, 99th Cong., 2nd Sess. (1986).

34 TAM 9113003 (1991).

35 Reg. Sec. 1.446-1(a)(1) and (4).

36 Gertzman, p. 2-18.

37 See *Wolfe Bakery & Cafeteria Co.,* 5 TCM 389 (1946).

38 Reg. Sec. 1.446-1(d).

the retained tax method does not clearly reflect income, the IRS can force a change. These matters are examined below.

THE CLEAR REFLECTION OF INCOME REQUIREMENT

The Regulations recognize that no one can prescribe a uniform accounting method that is suitable to all taxpayers. Nevertheless, the Code and Regulations state that no method is acceptable unless that method *clearly reflects income* in the opinion of the Secretary of the Treasury (or his or her agent, the IRS).[39] The **clear reflection of income requirement** seems deceptively simple but is actually difficult to define.

> The **clear reflection of income requirement** holds that a permitted method must be applied consistently, accurately, fairly, and honestly in the IRS's opinion.

The Regulations provide that generally accepted accounting principles will ordinarily be regarded as clearly reflecting income if items of gross income and expense are treated consistently from year to year.[40] This last statement can easily be misinterpreted. It appears to say that GAAP as well as specifically permitted accounting methods (for example, the accrual, cash, and hybrid methods) all clearly reflect income. As we pointed out early in this chapter, however, the Supreme Court in *Thor Power Tool* limited the applicability of GAAP as a tax method. Thus, the statement in the Regulations that GAAP clearly reflects income cannot be read literally.

Citing two well-known cases, the Tax Court attempted to summarize the criteria for clear reflection of income as follows:

> An accounting method clearly reflects income if income is stated with as much accuracy as standard methods of accounting practices permit, . . . and the books are kept fairly and honestly. . . .[41]

But even here we note difficult-to-define terms, such as *accuracy, fairly*, and *honestly*. Thus, the definition of the phrase *clearly reflects income* remains highly subjective.

That subjectivity initially resides with the taxpayer on the adoption of an accounting method. The tax law gives the taxpayer much leeway in selecting a method. Ultimately, however, the IRS exercises subjectivity on audit or when the taxpayer requests a change of accounting method. The Code states that every taxpayer's accounting method must clearly reflect income, *in the opinion of the Secretary* (IRS). The Regulations and courts have interpreted this phrase as giving the IRS broad discretion in determining whether an accounting method clearly reflects income. Citing a long string of cases, the Supreme Court in *Thor Power Tool* stated that the IRS's "interpretation of the [Code's] clear-reflection standard 'should not be interfered with unless clearly unlawful.'"[42]

The IRS's discretion in its interpretation of this critical phrase has limits, however. As we saw in *Patchen*, the IRS was not permitted to require a change in accounting method where the book conformity requirement was satisfied and both the cash and the accrual methods clearly reflected income. The IRS does not have the authority to change a method that clearly reflects income to a method that "more clearly reflects income" simply because the second method increases revenue to the government.[43]

---

39 Sec. 446(b) and Reg. Sec. 1.446-1(a)(2).

40 Reg. Sec. 1.446-1(a)(2).

41 Jerry Fong, 48 TCM 689 (1948), affirmed in an unpublished decision (CA-9, 1987); the Tax Court cites *Caldwell v. Comm.*, 202 F.2d 112 (CA-2, 1950) and *Osterloh v. Lucas*, 37 F.2d 277 (CA-9, 1930).

42 *Thor Power Tool Co. v. Comm.*, 439 US 522 (1979).

43 *Maloney v. Hammond*, 176 F.2d 780 (CA-9, 1949) and *W.P. Garth*, 56 TC 610 (1971).

One criteria paramount in determining whether an accounting method clearly reflects income is consistency. The IRS will consider no method as clearly reflecting income unless the taxpayer treats all items of gross income and deduction consistently from year to year.[44]

The forgoing discussion demonstrates the elusive nature of the phrase *clearly reflects income*. Nevertheless, we attempt to summarize the criteria as follows: (1) the method must be among those permitted by law (cash, accrual, hybrid, and special methods); (2) the method must be applied consistently over time; (3) the method must be applied accurately; (4) the books must be kept fairly and honestly; and (5) the IRS must agree that the method clearly reflects income.

METHODS OF ACCOUNTING— SPECIFIC METHODS

<table><tr><td>

Goal #5
Explain and apply the overall accounting method—the cash method.
</td></tr></table>

As just explained, every accounting method, to be accepted for tax purposes, must satisfy such general criteria as the book conformity and the clear-reflection-of-income requirements. The tax law also imposes other specific requirements on each permissible accounting method.

THE CASH METHOD

<table><tr><td>

A taxpayer using the **cash method** recognizes income when actually or constructively received and deducts expenses when actually paid.

The **constructive receipt doctrine** holds that income is deemed received whenever it is available to the taxpayer without restriction.
</td></tr></table>

Most individual taxpayers and many partnerships use the *cash receipts and disbursements method* of accounting, commonly called the **cash method**. This method is relatively simple, requires less record keeping than other methods, and gives the taxpayer limited control over the timing of income and deductions. Under the cash method, taxpayers generally include all items of income, gain, and profit in gross income when *actually or constructively received* and take allowable deductions in the year paid.[45] Cash receipts include cash equivalents such as marketable property.

The Constructive Receipt Doctrine

The cash method opens the possibility of deferring income recognition by a taxpayer's merely choosing the year in which cash is reduced to physical possession. For example, a taxpayer could wait until January 2, 19X2, to pick up a paycheck that was available to her on December 31, 19X1. To prevent this kind of manipulation, the Regulations impose the **constructive receipt doctrine**:

<table><tr><td>

Goal #6
Define and apply the constructive receipt doctrine.
</td></tr></table>

> Income although not actually reduced to a taxpayer's possession is constructively received by him in the taxable [tax] year during which it is credited to his account, set apart for him, or otherwise made available so that he may draw upon it at any time, or so that he could have drawn upon it during the taxable [tax] year if notice of intention to withdraw had been given. However, income is not constructively received if the taxpayer's control of its receipt is subject to substantial limitations or restrictions.[46]

The constructive receipt doctrine applies only to cash-basis taxpayers and, as set out in the quoted Regulation, has three elements. First, the payee (taxpayer) must be

---

44 Reg. Sec. 1.446-1(c)(2)(ii).

45 Reg. Sec. 1.451-1(a) and Reg. Sec. 1.461-1(a).

46 Reg. Sec. 1.451-2(a).

able to control the income without substantial limitations or restrictions. Second, the payor must credit or set aside the funds for the payee. Third, the funds must be available to the payee on demand, that is, the payor must be able to make payment. The following four examples illustrate the constructive receipt doctrine. Each recipient in these examples uses the cash method.

EXAMPLE 7-9

Mr. Thrifty has a savings account at First National Bank, a solvent bank. On December 30, 19X1, the bank credited $500 of interest to his account, but Mr. Thrifty did not withdraw it until sometime in 19X2. Mr. Thrifty has constructive receipt and must report the interest in 19X1.[47]

EXAMPLE 7-10

On each Friday, employees of Alpha Company can pick up their paychecks for the prior week's work at the secretary's desk. Although paychecks were available on December 30, 19X1, Ms. Defer waited until January 2, 19X2, to pick up her last paycheck. Ms. Defer has constructive receipt and must report those wages in 19X1.

EXAMPLE 7-11

On December 30, 19X1, Dire Straits Company issued a check to Mr. Argyle for accounting services rendered. Because Dire Straits was overdrawn at the bank, the company's manager asked Mr. Argyle not to cash the check until January 5, 19X2. Mr. Argyle agreed and cashed the check in 19X2. Mr. Argyle does *not* have constructive receipt in 19X1 because the payor had insufficient funds.[48] Thus, Mr. Argyle reports this income in 19X2. Moreover, he does not have the option to report the income in 19X1.

EXAMPLE 7-12

On December 10, 19X1, Flush Corporation declared a dividend, payable on December 31, 19X1. The corporation followed its usual practice of mailing these dividend payments so that shareholders did not receive them until 19X2. The shareholders do *not* have constructive receipt in 19X1 and must report the dividend income in 19X2.[49] Moreover, they do not have the option to report the dividends in 19X1.

Time for Deducting Expenses

Under the cash method, a taxpayer generally takes deductions for expenses in the tax year they are paid. Payments by check are deemed paid in the tax year the check is

47 See Reg. Sec. 1.451-2(b).

48 See *L. M. Fischer*, 14 TC 792 (1950) and *A. V. Johnston*, 23 TCM 2003 (1964).

49 See Reg. Sec. 1.451-2(b).

delivered or mailed to the payee, not in the year the payee receives or cashes the check or in the year the check clears at the bank.[50] In addition, a cash-basis taxpayer may sometimes deduct expenses that involve no cash disbursements in the tax year. For example, as explained in Chapters 5 and 14, the cost of a depreciable asset is **capitalized** in the year the asset is placed in service, but the depreciation expense related to that asset is deductible over a given number of years even though the taxpayer makes no additional cash payments for that asset.[51]

Prepaid expenses raise a particularly difficult problem for the cash-basis taxpayer. Must they be capitalized or may they be deducted when paid? For example, may payments of otherwise deductible expenses—payments for rent, interest, and taxes that relate to a period beyond the end of the tax year—be deducted in the year paid or must they be allocated to and deducted in the period to which they relate? The IRS and Tax Court generally maintain that such expenditures create an asset having a useful life that extends substantially beyond the tax year and should be capitalized and allocated accordingly.[52] Other courts, particularly the Ninth Circuit Court of Appeals in *Zaninovich v. Comm.*,[53] have accepted the so called **one-year rule**, which holds that certain prepayments relating to a future period no longer than 12 months may be fully deductible when paid even though the 12-month period straddles two tax years. The court, however, was not clear as to whether the relevant 12-month period refers to the entire prepayment period beginning with the date of prepayment or just the prepayment period remaining at the end of the tax year (see Example 7-14).[54] A subsequent Ninth Circuit case, *Bonaire Development Co. v. Comm.*,[55] added the requirement that the prepayments be mandatory under the terms of the lease or other agreement rather than voluntary. The court held that voluntary prepayments may distort income.

> **Capitalization** means that an expenditure must be treated initially as an asset rather than as an expense.
>
> **Prepaid expenses** invlove current payments for services or goods to be received or used in a later tax year.
>
> The **one-year rule** allows a cash-basis taxpayer to deduct certain prepaid expenses currently if they relate to a future period no longer than 12 months.

Goal #6
Define and apply the concept of prepaid expenses.

EXAMPLE 7-13

Mr. Lessee, a cash-basis taxpayer, decides to rent a building for business purposes. On September 30, 19X1, Mr. Lessee enters into a 12-month lease that runs from October 1, 19X1, through September 30, 19X2. The rent equals $1,000 per month, but the lease requires that Mr. Lessee prepay the entire $12,000 on October 1, 19X1. The IRS would likely hold that Mr. Lessee should deduct $3,000 in 19X1 and $9,000 in 19X2. Certain courts, however, would invoke the one-year rule and allow the entire $12,000 deduction in 19X1. Consequently, Mr. Lessee might have to litigate to obtain the entire deduction in the year paid. If the lease did not require prepayment and Mr. Lessee voluntarily prepaid the entire $12,000, he would *not* likely obtain the benefit of the one-year rule.

---

50 *Modie J. Spiegle Est.,* 12 TC 524 (1949); *Eli B. Witt Est. v. Fahs,* 160 F.Supp 521 (DC Fla., 1956); and Rev. Rul. 73-99, 1973-1 CB 412.

51 Reg. Sec. 1.461-1(a)(1).

52 See, for example, Rev. Rul. 80-70, 1980-1 CB 104, and *Zaninovich v. Comm.,* 69 TC 605 (1978), reversed in 616 F.2d 429 (CA-9, 1980).

53 616 F.2d 429 (CA-9, 1980).

54 *Ibid.,* especially footnote 6 in the court's opinion.

55 679 F.2d 159 (CA-9, 1982).

EXAMPLE 7-14

Ms. Renter, a cash-basis taxpayer, decides to rent a building for business purposes. On September 30, 19X1, Ms. Renter enters into an 18-month lease that runs from October 1, 19X1, through March 31, 19X3. The rent is $1,000 per month, but the lease requires that Ms. Renter prepay the entire $18,000 on September 30, 19X1. The one-year rule does not apply. Therefore, Ms. Renter must deduct $3,000 in 19X1, $12,000 in 19X2, and $3,000 in 19X3.

Suppose instead that the 18-month lease runs from March 1, 19X1, through August 31, 19X2. Although the entire lease period exceeds 12 months, only eight months remain at the end of 19X1. As mentioned earlier, the case law is unclear as to whether the one-year rule applies in this situation. Nevertheless, the IRS (and the Tax Court) would likely hold that Ms. Renter must deduct $10,000 in 19X1 and $8,000 in 19X2, especially if she resides outside the Ninth Circuit.

Although the treatment of prepaid expenses is controversial, we can make this general statement: All prepaid expenses must be allocated over the periods to which they relate if doing otherwise results in a material distortion of income. Despite the general controversy, the treatment of certain prepayments is clear because of mandatory rules in the Code. For example, Sec. 461(g) requires that a cash-basis taxpayer allocate and deduct prepaid interest over the period of the loan. This rule for interest, however, does not apply to **points** paid by the purchaser of a home (principal residence) if (1) the payment of points is an established practice in the area, (2) the payment does not exceed the amount generally charged in the area, and (3) the payment does not pertain to a refinanced mortgage. Accordingly, a cash-basis taxpayer may deduct points in the year paid even though they are a form of interest pertaining to the entire loan period.

> **Points** are payments made at a real estate closing that constitute prepaid interest but which may, in some cases, be deducted in the year of payment.

A cash-basis taxpayer may deduct the entire cost of *incidental supplies* in the year paid even though the supplies are not completely used in that year.[56] However, a taxpayer may not deduct normal inventory costs until the inventory items are sold. We will examine inventory methods later in this chapter. And, as we mentioned earlier, expenditures for long-lived assets, such as equipment and buildings, must always be capitalized and depreciated.

Restrictions on the Use of the Cash Method

With some exceptions, Sec. 448 forbids the following entities from using the cash method: (1) C corporations, (2) partnerships having a C corporation as a partner, and (3) tax shelters. (Remember, a C corporation is a regular corporation that has not elected to be treated as an S corporation.) These entities—defined and discussed in Chapter 6—must use the accrual method of accounting. The Code makes exceptions for (1) certain farming businesses, (2) personal service corporations, and (3) C corporations and partnerships with C corporation partners if they qualify as *small businesses*.[57] Entities meeting these exceptions may use the cash method. Note also that individuals, S corporations, and partnerships without C corporation partners may also use the cash method because they are not among those listed in Sec. 448.

---

56 Reg. Sec. 1.162-3.

57 See Sec. 447 and Sec. 448(b) for further details and definitions pertaining to these exceptions.

The small business exception requires that entities meet a $5 million gross receipts test. Entities meet this test for a given tax year if average gross receipts for the three years preceding the tax year do not exceed $5 million. If a corporation has not been in existence for three years, gross receipts are averaged over the years of existence.

EXAMPLE 7-15

Gamma Corporation, a C corporation, was formed on January 2, 19X1, and had the following gross receipts in years preceding 19X5:

19X1	$4,000,000
19X2	4,900,000
19X3	5,200,000
19X4	5,400,000

Average prior-year gross receipts are as follows:

19X1	$ -0-	
19X2	4,000,000	[($4,000,000)/1]
19X3	4,450,000	[($4,000,000 + $4,900,000)/2]
19X4	4,700,000	[($4,000,000 + $4,900,000 + $5,200,000)/3]
19X5	5,166,667	[($4,900,000 + $5,200,000 + $5,400,000)/3]

Thus, Gamma Corporation may use the cash method in 19X1, 19X2, 19X3, and 19X4 but must use the accrual method in 19X5.

Congress enacted Sec. 448 because it believed that the cash method often fails to reflect accurately a taxpayer's economic performance over a tax year. Congress felt that the cash method mismatches revenue and expenses and thus fails to accord with generally accepted accounting principles. At the same time, Congress recognized the simplicity of the cash method and felt that individuals and small businesses should be allowed to use the cash method. Congress also retained the cash method for personal service corporations and entities, such as S corporations and partnerships without C corporation partners, whose income flows through to individuals. Finally, Congress believed that tax shelters in any form should be precluded from using the cash method because these entities may obtain unwarranted tax benefits from the cash method.[58]

Goal #5
Explain and apply the overall accounting method—the accrual method.

Under the **accrual method,** a taxpayer recognizes income when the right to receive income is fixed (and the amount is determinable with reasonable accuracy) and deducts expenses when the liability is fixed and determinable.

THE ACCRUAL METHOD

Under the **accrual method,** a taxpayer includes an item in gross income when (1) all events have occurred that fix the right to receive the income and (2) the amount of income can be determined with reasonable accuracy. A taxpayer deducts expenses when (1) all events have occurred that establish the fact of the liability and (2) the amount of the liability can be determined with reasonable accuracy.[59]

Time for Reporting Income

According to this *all-events test*, a taxpayer using the accrual method recognizes income before receiving cash. The tax accrual method comes close to the accrual

---

58 Staff of the Joint Committee on Taxation, *General Explanation of the Tax Reform Act of 1986* (U.S. Government Printing Office), May 4, 1987, pp. 474–76.

59 Reg. Sec. 1.446-1(c)(1)(ii), Reg. Sec. 1.451-1(a), and Reg. Sec. 1. 461-1(a)(2).

method required by generally accepted accounting principles, but, as previously discussed, many differences still arise.

Although, prepaid expenses cause special problems for the cash-basis taxpayer, **prepaid income** raises thorny issues for the accrual-basis taxpayer. Should prepaid amounts be recognized in the year received or deferred until actually earned? This problem differs slightly from the claim of right doctrine because amounts subject to that doctrine are already earned when received. The IRS takes the position that all events that fix the right to receive income happen at the earliest of three points: (1) the required performance occurs, (2) payment is due, or (3) payment is received.[60] Also, the Regulations specifically require that a taxpayer include advance rentals in gross income when received regardless of the taxpayer's method of accounting.[61]

Prepaid income means that a taxpayer receives payment before performing services or delivering goods.

EXAMPLE 7-16

Suppose that Ms. Renter in Example 7-14 rents the building from Mr. Lessor, an accrual-basis taxpayer. Based on the facts in that example, Mr. Lessor must include the entire $18,000 in his 19X1 gross income.

Goal #6
Explain and apply the concept of prepaid income.

Figure 7-2 shows four possible combinations that can occur regarding prepayment for cash- and accrual-basis taxpayers. Note that Cells 1 and 4 seem most consistent with the taxpayer's overall method of accounting while Cells 2 and 3 do not. In fact, the combination of Cells 2 and 3 presents the worst of all worlds. An accrual-basis taxpayer must accelerate recognition of prepaid income; a cash-basis taxpayer must defer the deduction of prepaid expenses. Note that the IRS's position deters taxpayers from using prepayments. If the IRS did not adopt this position, accrual-basis taxpayers could defer taxes on prepaid income even though they have enjoyment of the cash, and cash-basis taxpayers could defer taxes by accelerating deductions even though the prepaid expenses relate to future periods.

	Cash-Basis Taxpayer	Accrual-Basis Taxpayer
Prepaid Income	1 Included in gross income in year received. Treatment consistent with overall method.	2 Included in gross income in year received.* Treated as if on cash basis.
Prepaid Expense	3 Allocated over related periods.⁺ Treated as if on accrual basis.	4 Allocated over related periods. Treatment consistent with overall method.

* *Exceptions to this rule exist as discussed in text.*
⁺ *Unless the one-year rule applies.*

FIGURE 7-2

Comparison of Prepayments for Cash- and Accrual-Basis Taxpayers

60 Rev. Rul. 84-31, 1984-1 CB 127.

61 Reg. Sec. 1.61-8(b).

The rule against deferred recognition of prepaid income by accrual-basis taxpayers is not absolute, however. Some courts have allowed taxpayers to prorate income over future years instead of recognizing it in the year received. For example, in *Artnell v. Comm.*,[62] the Seventh Circuit Court of Appeals allowed the owners of the Chicago White Sox to defer recognition on the advance sale of baseball tickets. The games to which the tickets related were played after the end of the accrual-basis taxpayer's fiscal year. In distinguishing *Artnell* from a trilogy of Supreme Court cases,[63] the Seventh Circuit Court asked the following questions:

> Has the Supreme Court left an opening for a decision that under the facts of a particular case, the extent and time of future performance are so certain, and related items properly accounted for with such clarity, that a system of accounting involving deferral of prepaid income is found clearly to reflect income, and the [IRS's] rejection deemed an abuse of discretion? Or has it decided that the [IRS] has complete and unreviewable discretion to reject deferral of prepaid income where Congress has made no provision?[64]

The Court answered the first question in the affirmative and allowed the deferral.

The Code and the IRS also allow specific exceptions to the immediate recognition of prepaid income by certain accrual basis taxpayers. For example, Sec. 455 allows publishers to recognize prepaid subscription income over the period of the subscription, and Sec. 456 allows certain membership organizations a similar deferral for prepaid dues income. Regulation Sec. 1.451-5 contains complex rules that permit a seller of goods to defer recognition of prepaid income until the year in which the payments are properly accrued under the seller's tax accounting method (but never to a year later than the year recognized for financial reporting).

Revenue Proc. 71-21[65] also allows accrual-basis taxpayers to defer recognition of income from services. The deferral under this procedure is optional; the taxpayer may always recognize all prepaid income in the year of receipt. To obtain the deferral, however, the taxpayer must perform the services (pursuant to an agreement with the client or customer) before the end of the year following the year of receipt. If the taxpayer properly defers income but determines in the second year that the services cannot be completed by the end of the year, the taxpayer must recognize all remaining income in the second year regardless of when the services are performed. Furthermore, the taxpayer must recognize the entire amount of prepaid income in the year of receipt if the original agreement specifies that (1) any services be performed after the second year or (2) any services be performed at an unspecified future date that may occur after the second year. Revenue Proc. 71-21 does not apply to prepaid rental income, prepaid interest income, or amounts under guaranty or warranty contracts.

EXAMPLE 7-17

> Mr. Debit, an accrual-basis accountant, agrees to perform accounting services for Client Corporation. Mr. Debit is to perform the services during the period
>
> Continued

---

62 400 F.2d 981 (CA-7, 1968).

63 *Automobile Club of Mich. v. Comm.*, 353 US 180 (1957); *American Automobile Association v. U.S.*, 367 US 687 (1961); and *Schlude v. Comm.*, 372 US 128 (1963).

64 *Artnell v. Comm.*, 400 F.2d 981 (CA-7, 1968).

65 1971-2 CB 549.

EXAMPLE 7-17 (Con't.)

October 1, 19X1, through September 30, 19X2, and Client Corporation prepays $12,000 for the services. Mr. Debit may recognize $3,000 in 19X1 and $9,000 in 19X2. (If he chooses, Mr. Debit may recognize all $12,000 in 19X1.) If in 19X2 Mr. Debit discovers that he cannot complete the services until 19X3, he must recognize the remaining $9,000 in 19X2 even though the services extend beyond the end of 19X2.

EXAMPLE 7-18

Suppose instead that the original agreement specifies that Mr. Debit is to receive $18,000 in 19X1 for services performed during the period October 1, 19X1, through March 31, 19X3. Mr. Debit must recognize the entire $18,000 in 19X1 because the services will not be performed by the end of 19X2 (the second year).

EXAMPLE 7-19

Suppose that Mr. Lessee in Example 7-13 rents the building from Ms. Lessor, an accrual-basis taxpayer. Revenue Proc. 71-21 does not apply to prepaid rental income. Therefore, Ms. Lessor must include the entire $12,000 in her 19X1 gross income even though the rental period does not extend beyond 19X2.

Time for Deducting Expenses

As noted above, under the accrual method a taxpayer deducts an expense when (1) all events have occurred that establish the fact of the liability and (2) the amount of liability (expense) can be determined with reasonable accuracy.[66] According to this *all-events test*, the liability must be *fixed and determinable*. The fixed and determinable criterion is more stringent than criteria used to accrue liabilities and expenses under generally accepted accounting principles. Consequently, it frequently denies taxpayers the right to deduct immediately many estimated expenses mandated by GAAP.

EXAMPLE 7-20

Appliance Corporation, an accrual-basis taxpayer, offers warranties for its products. Based on historical data, the corporation estimates that customers will make $20,000 worth of claims on appliances sold in 19X1. Accordingly, the corporation makes the following journal entry at the end of 19X1:

Warranty expense	$20,000	
Estimated liability for warranties		$20,000

This liability is not fixed and determinable because no customer yet has a legal claim against the corporation. Therefore, the corporation may *not* deduct the $20,000 in 19X1. However, suppose that by the end of 19X2, customers have made actual claims against Appliance Corporation totaling $12,000, but, because of processing delays, the corporation has not yet honored the claims. The corporation may deduct the $12,000 in 19X2.

---

66 Reg. Sec. 1.446-1(c)(1)(ii) and Reg. Sec. 1.461-1(a)(2).

Under the **reserve method** (no longer allowed for tax purposes) the taxpayer estimates expenses and liabilities and establishes allowance accounts.

Under the **direct-writeoff method** the taxpayer deducts bad debts in the year accounts receivable become worthless.

Most businesses similarly estimate uncollectible accounts receivable and record a bad debt expense and an allowance for uncollectible accounts for financial reporting. Before the Tax Reform Act of 1986, these businesses could use a similar **reserve method** for tax purposes. The 1986 Act, however, repealed this provision so that today bad debt accounting for tax purposes is consistent with the treatment of other deductions under the all-events test.[67] Taxpayers (other than financial institutions) must now use the **direct-writeoff method** for tax purposes, deducting bad debts in the year they become worthless. However, the 1986 Act added a provision that allows certain accrual-basis taxpayers to estimate bad debts under the *nonaccrual experience method*. This method applies only to receivables arising from services and allows the taxpayer to exclude from gross income (rather than deduct) amounts they are unlikely to collect.[68]

Thus, aside from limited exceptions such as the nonaccrual experience method, the tax law generally precludes the deduction of estimated amounts. The Supreme Court in *Thor Power Tool* gave the following clear and succinct reason for denying a taxpayer the right to estimate deductions:

> Financial accounting, in short, is hospitable to estimates, probabilities, and reasonable certainties; the tax law, with its mandate to preserve the revenue, can give no quarter to uncertainty. This is as it should be. Reasonable estimates may be useful, even essential, in giving shareholders and creditors an accurate picture of a firm's overall financial health; but the accountant's conservatism cannot bind the [IRS] in [its] efforts to collect taxes.[69]

Under the all-events test, a taxpayer may not deduct an expense related to a *contingent* liability, but a taxpayer may deduct an expense related to a *contested* liability if certain conditions are met.[70] Any recovery on a contested liability is subject to the tax benefit rule.

If a taxpayer computes a deduction with reasonable accuracy and *properly* accrues it under the all-events test but determines in a subsequent year that the exact amount differs from the original determination, the taxpayer recognizes the difference in the later year.[71] However, if the original deduction was improperly claimed, the taxpayer must file an amended return.[72]

In 1984 Congress became concerned that the fixed and determinable criterion was insufficient to prevent premature accruals. Although a fixed and determinable liability may exist at the end of a year, a taxpayer or provider may not yet have performed on the contract. Congress believed that a properly accrued deduction "should take into account the time value of money and the time the deduction is economically incurred."[73] Accordingly, the Deficit Reduction Act of 1984 added an **economic performance** criterion to the all-events test. Section 461(h) sets out this additional criterion and reads as follows:

Economic performance occurs when goods are delivered or services are provided to the taxpayer.

---

67 Staff of the Joint Committee on Taxation, *General Explanation of the Tax Reform Act of 1986* (U.S. Government Printing Office), May 4, 1987, pp. 531–32.

68 Sec. 448(d) and Temp. Reg. Sec. 1.448-2T.

69 *Thor Power Tool Co. v. Comm.,* 439 US 522 (1979).

70 Sec. 461(f).

71 Reg. Sec. 1.461-1(a)(2).

72 Reg. Sec. 1.461-1(a)(3)(i).

73 Staff of the Joint Committee on Taxation, *General Explanation of the Revenue Provisions of the Deficit Reduction Act of 1984* (U.S. Government Printing Office), December 31, 1984, p. 260.

(h) Certain liabilities not incurred before economic performance—

  (1) In general.—For purposes of this title, in determining whether an amount has been incurred with respect to any item during any taxable year, the all events test shall not be treated as met any earlier than when economic performance with respect to such item occurs.

  (2) Time when economic performance occurs.—Except as provided in regulations prescribed by the Secretary, the time when economic performance occurs shall be determined under the following principles:

    (A) Services and property provided to the taxpayer.—If the liability of the taxpayer arises out of—

      (i) the providing of services to the taxpayer by another person, economic performance occurs as such person provides such services.

      (ii) the providing of property to the taxpayer by another person, economic performance occurs as the person provides such property, or

      (iii) the use of property by the taxpayer, economic performance occurs as the taxpayer uses such property.

    (B) Services and property provided by the taxpayer.—If the liability of the taxpayer requires the taxpayer to provide property or services, economic performance occurs as the taxpayer provides such property or services.

Committee reports suggest that Congress also believed that the economic performance criterion may be too harsh on ordinary businesses that typically do not abuse the fixed and determinable criterion. This concern was expressed as follows:

> Congress . . . recognized that in many ordinary business transactions, economic performance may not occur until the year following the year in which the deduction may be taken under the all events test. Therefore, to avoid disrupting normal business and accounting practices and imposing undue burdens on taxpayers, Congress believed that an exception to the economic performance requirement should be provided for certain recurring items.[74]

Accordingly, Sec. 461(h) allows an exception to the economic performance criterion provided that

1. The item meets the fixed and determinable part of the all-events test;

2. Economic performance with respect to the item occurs within a reasonable period (not to exceed 8 ½ months) after the tax year closes;

3. The item is recurring in nature and the taxpayer consistently treats the item as incurred in the tax year in which the fixed and determinable requirement is met; and

4. Either (1) the item is not material or (2) the accrual of the item reflects a more proper matching against income than would deduction in the year of performance.

In determining materiality, the taxpayer (and the IRS) must look to "the size of the item, both in absolute terms and in relation to the taxpayer's income and other

---

74 *Ibid.*, p. 261.

expenses, and the treatment of the item on the taxpayer's financial statements."[75] Treatment in the taxpayer's financial statements must also be considered for the matching requirement.[76]

HYBRID METHODS

A taxpayer may use a combination of the cash and accrual methods along with other special methods discussed later in this chapter. Nevertheless, every **hybrid method** must clearly reflect income and must be consistently applied.[77] If a taxpayer engages in a business in which inventories are a material income-producing factor, the taxpayer must use the accrual method for sales and purchases. However, that same taxpayer may use the cash method for other items, in which case the taxpayer would be applying a hybrid method.[78] A taxpayer may also use the accrual method for all business items and the cash method for nonbusiness items. Finally, as mentioned earlier, a taxpayer may use different methods for separate trades or businesses. However, a taxpayer may not use the cash method for income and the accrual method for expenses. This treatment defers income and accelerates deductions; consequently, it blatantly fails the clear reflection of income requirement.

SPECIAL METHODS

The Code also allows taxpayers to use other special methods. We examine only two of them here: the installment method and the percentage-of-completion method.

The Installment Method

On the sale of property, a taxpayer generally recognizes gain or loss in the year of the sale. However, if the taxpayer sells the property under an installment contract, he or she may not have the wherewithal to pay tax. An **installment sale** is one in which the seller receives at least one payment after the year of sale.[79] Thus, in the year of sale, the taxpayer may not have sufficient cash to pay tax on the entire gain. To alleviate this potential hardship, the Code allows certain taxpayers to use the **installment method**.

Under the installment method, the seller recognizes gain as installment payments are received, based on the following formulas and definitions:

1. Gross profit = sales price − adjusted basis of property sold (adjusted basis is defined in Chapter 8);

2. Contract price = sales price − seller's liabilities assumed by the purchaser;

3. Gross profit ratio = gross profit ÷ contract price; and

4. Gain recognized = installment payment received (excluding interest) x gross profit ratio.

---

75 *Ibid.*, p. 263.

76 *Ibid.*, p. 264 and Sec. 461(h)(3)(B).

77 Reg. Sec. 1.446-1(c)(1)(iv).

78 Reg. Sec. 1.446-1(c)(1)(iv) and 1(c)(2)(i).

79 Sec. 453(b)(1).

EXAMPLE 7-21

Ms. Collector, a cash-basis taxpayer, purchased a painting five years ago for $12,000. She is not an art dealer so she purchased this painting for her own enjoyment and as an investment. On November 1, 19X1, Ms. Collector sold the painting for $20,000 on an installment contract. Mr. Sotheby, the purchaser, agreed to pay her $4,000 on the date of sale and $4,000 on November 1 for each of the next four years. Mr. Sotheby also agree to pay 12% per year interest on the unpaid balance of the installment contract. The painting was not encumbered by any liabilities. Therefore, Mr. Sotheby assumed no liabilities, and the contract price equals the sales price. Relevant computations are as follows:

Gross profit	= $20,000 – $12,000 = $8,000
Contract price	= $20,000
Gross profit ratio	= $8,000 ÷ $20,000 = .4
Gain recognized each year	= $4,000 x .4 = $1,600

In addition, Ms. Collector recognizes interest income each year. The first five columns of Table 7-1 summarize these results. Over the term of the contract, Ms. Collector recognizes $4,800 of interest income and $8,000 of gain, totaling $12,800. However, the installment method rules allow Ms. Collector to recognize the $8,000 gain over five years even though all of it was realized in 19X1. Also, Ms. Collector's cash method allows her to defer recognition of a part of the interest income until the year that she receives it.

TABLE 7-1

Installment
Method
(EXAMPLES 7-21
and 7-22)

1	2	3	4	5	6
	Total			Gain on Sale[+]	Gain on Sale[#]
	Cash	Installment	Interest	(Original	(Revised
Year	Received	Payment	Income*	Contract)	Contract)
19X1	$ 4,000	$ 4,000	$ 0	$1,600	$ 2, 065
19X2	5,920	4,000	1,920	1,600	3,055
19X3	5,440	4,000	1,440	1,600	2,808
19X4	4,960	4,000	960	1,600	2,560
19X5	4,480	4,000	480	1,600	2,312
Total	$24,800	$20,000	$4,800	$8,000	$12,800

*Unpaid Balance x .12.
[+]Amount in Column 3 x .4.
[#]Amount in Column 2 x .51613.

The installment method has several possible advantages over immediate recognition. First, as already mentioned, it defers recognition until the seller receives cash, thereby alleviating the potential cash-flow problems inherent in immediate recognition. Second, total recognition in the year of sale may push the seller into a high marginal tax bracket while spreading the gain over several years may keep the gain in low marginal tax brackets. Third, a carefully written installment contract allows the seller to choose the years in which to recognize gain. Thus, if the seller expects tax rates to be lower in future years than in the current year, the installment method may provide a tax rate reduction as well as a deferral advantage.

The installment method may also have disadvantages. For example, the seller risks loss of remaining installment payments if the purchaser defaults on an installment contract. Also, tax rates may increase rather than decrease in future years, thereby causing an increase in the seller's total tax liability. For these and other reasons, the seller may prefer immediate recognition rather than deferral.

In Example 7-21, notice that the installment sale generates both interest income and a gain on the sale of the asset. As we explain in Chapter 16, certain gains—called net capital gains—are sometimes taxed at lower rates than ordinary income (for example, interest income). Under those circumstances, the seller in an installment contract has an incentive to maximize capital gains and minimize ordinary income.

EXAMPLE 7-22

As shown in Example 7-21 (Table 7-1, Column 2), Ms. Collector received total cash payments (sales price plus interest) of $24,800 over the term of the installment contract. Suppose instead that Ms. Collector and Mr. Sotheby structured the contract so that the entire $24,800 was considered the sales price, to be received in installments as depicted in Table 7-1, Column 2. That is, suppose the contract specified no stated interest. If the tax law imposed no restrictions on this transaction, the relevant computations would be as follows:

Gross profit =	$24,800 – $12,000 = $12,800
Contract price =	$24,800
Gross profit ratio =	$12,800 ÷ $24,800 = .51612
Gain recognized each year =	see Table 7-1, Column 6.

Ms. Collector still recognizes $12,800 over the five-year period, but now the entire amount is capital gain.

Example 7-22 demonstrates how taxpayers might manipulate the sales price and stated interest on installment contracts to convert ordinary income into capital gains. However, the Code prevents this type of abuse by requiring a taxpayer to impute interest if stated interest is insufficient.[80] These rules, in effect, convert part of the selling price back into interest. Although complex, the rules impute interest by comparing the total actual payments (including stated interest, if any) to the total present value of the payments. The present value is determined by discounting at the applicable federal rate, which the IRS publishes monthly. If the stated principal amount of the installment contract does not exceed $2.8 million, the taxpayer discounts at the lesser of the applicable federal rate or 9%.[81]

---

80 Sec. 483 and Sec. 1274.

81 Sec. 1274A; For discounting purposes, the applicable rates are compounded semiannually.

The purchaser's tax situation may present other factors that the parties to a transaction should consider when setting stated interest rates. Example 7-23 illustrates two possibilities.

EXAMPLE 7-23

In Example 7-21, Mr. Sotheby may be able to deduct the interest paid if, for example, he is an art dealer. In Example 7-22, Mr. Sotheby has no interest deduction, but he obtains an increased cost basis in the painting, which reduces gain or increases loss on a subsequent sale. In these circumstances, Mr. Sotheby may not be willing to structure the transaction to Ms. Collector's advantage. On the other hand, if Mr. Sotheby is not an art dealer and is not allowed an interest deduction, he may prefer the increased cost basis in Example 7-22. But again, the imputed interest rules prevent this kind of interest rate manipulation.

The opportunity to defer gain via an installment sale is sometimes reduced or eliminated because of certain depreciation recapture rules, explained in Chapter 16.[82] Moreover, the installment method is *not* available for all transactions. First, it does not apply to *dealer dispositions*, which the Code defines as (1) dispositions of personal property by a person who regularly sells on the installment plan and (2) any disposition of real property ordinarily held for sale in the taxpayer's business. The Code provides exceptions for certain farm property, residential lots, and timeshares sold on installment plans. Thus, taxpayers may use the installment method for sales of these properties. In general, then, the installment method applies only to nondealer sales of real property and personal property that is not inventory. Second, the installment method does not apply to sales of stocks and securities traded on established markets.[83] Third, the installment method also does not apply to losses; it applies only to gains.

An installment sale of any qualifying property is *automatically* to be reported using the installment method unless the taxpayer explicitly elects to have the installment method not apply.[84] The taxpayer may *elect out* of the installment method by reporting the entire gain in the year of sale. Valid elections, once made, may be revoked only with the consent of the IRS.

Under the installment method, a seller always defers the tax liability on the recognized gain. Manifesting its awareness of the time value of money, Congress enacted Sec. 453A, which requires the seller to pay interest on the deferred tax liability if certain conditions prevail. The interest payment requirement applies if (1) the sales price of a property sold exceeds $150,000 *and* (2) the aggregate face value of all such installment obligations outstanding at the end of the year exceeds $5 million. Any item selling for less than $150,000 is not included in the $5 million ceiling. The interest rate used for this computation is the same as the rate used for computing the penalty for tax underpayments. This interest payment requirement does not apply to sales of either *personal-use property* or *farm property*. Personal-use property is any real or personal property that is not used in a business or not held for the production of income. For example, a taxpayer's home or personal automobile is personal-use property. Because of the $150,000 and $5 million ceilings as well as the personal-use exemption,

---

82 Sec. 453(i).

83 Sec. 453(k)(2).

84 Sec. 453(d).

most taxpayers may use the installment method without incurring this additional interest charge.

The Percentage-of-Completion Method

A **long-term contract** involves the manufacture, building, installation, or construction of property started in one tax year but not completed until a subsequent year. Prior to the Tax Reform Act of 1986, contractors could use the **completed contract method** and thereby defer both the recognition of any income and the deduction of all associated costs until the year in which the contract was completed. This method was an obvious exception to the annual accounting concept because the taxpayer reported income and deductions on completion of a contract rather than periodically. Congress concluded that this method permitted an unwarranted deferral of income and repealed it.[85] Consequently, contractors may now use only the **percentage-of-completion method**.

The percentage-of-completion method requires taxpayers to recognize in each year of the construction period a portion of the total gross profit from the contract.[86] The taxpayer first determines the percentage of completion by comparing (1) costs allocated to the contract by year end to (2) estimated total contract costs. The taxpayer applies this percentage to the total gross contract price to determine cumulative gross income. The taxpayer subtracts the gross income recognized in prior years from the cumulative total and includes the remainder in gross income for the current year. The taxpayer then deducts the allocated costs from the included gross income to arrive at the profit from each contract for the year.

> A **long-term contract** involves a contracted activity begun in one year and completed in another.
>
> Under the **completed contract method** (no longer allowed for tax purposes) a contractor recognizes income and deducts expenses in the year a contracted activity is completed.
>
> Under the **percentage-of-completion method** a taxpayer recognizes income and claims deductions related to contracted activity as the project progresses.

EXAMPLE 7-24

Contractor Company entered into a long-term contract to construct a building for a total contract price of $10 million. Construction began in 19X1, and the company incurred $3 million in costs by December 31, 19X1. The company estimates *total* costs to be $8 million. The percentage of completion at the end of 19X1 is 37.5% ($3 million ÷ $8 million), and *cumulative* gross income equals $3.75 million (37.5% x $10 million). Contractor Company includes the entire $3.75 million in 19X1 gross income and deducts $3 million in costs for a profit of $750,000.

In 19X2 the company incurred an additional $4 million in costs and estimates the remaining costs to be $1 million. Cumulative actual costs equal $7 million ($3 million + $4 million), the percentage of completion equals 87.5% ($7 million ÷ $8 million), and *cumulative* gross income equals $8.75 million (87.5% x $10 million). Contractor Company includes $5 million ($8.75 million – $3.75 million) in 19X2 gross income and deducts $4 million in costs for a profit of $1 million.

In 19X3, Contractor Company completes the project, incurring $1 million of actual costs in that year. The company recognizes the remaining $1.25 million gross income ($10 million – $8.75 million) and deducts the $1 million in costs for a profit of $250,000. Thus, Contractor Company recognizes its profit on an annual basis rather than on a contract basis.

85 Staff of the Joint Committee on Taxation, *General Explanation of the Tax Reform Act of 1986* (U.S. Government Printing Office), May 4, 1987, p. 527.

86 Sec. 460.

The Code contains a *look-back* rule to discourage taxpayers from deferring taxes by either overestimating contract costs or underestimating the contract price. On completion of the contract, the taxpayer reallocates gross income and deductions to each year based on the actual contract price and costs. The taxpayer then recomputes the tax liability for each year and compares the recomputed taxes to the reported taxes. Finally, the taxpayer pays interest for any tax underpayments and receives interest for any tax overpayments.[87]

ADOPTING AND CHANGING ACCOUNTING METHODS

> **Goal #3**
> Appreciate the implications of adopting and changing accounting methods.

A taxpayer adopts an accounting method by using the method on the first return filed. If a particular item does not occur in the taxpayer's first year, the taxpayer adopts a method in the first year the item occurs by filing that year's tax return with the adopted method. However, once adopted, the method may not be changed without the IRS's permission.[88] To obtain permission, the taxpayer must file Form 3115, Application for Change in Accounting Method, within the first 180 days of the tax year for which the change is to occur. The taxpayer must even receive permission to change from an incorrect method to a correct one. If the taxpayer uses an incorrect method and does not seek permission to change, the IRS, upon audit, may require the taxpayer to change so that the new method clearly reflects income.

A change in accounting method includes a change in the overall method as well as changes to particular *material* items. An item is material if it involves the proper timing of an inclusion or a deduction. A change in accounting method also includes a change in the taxpayer's overall inventory system or a change in the way the taxpayer treats any material item within that system.

A taxpayer may change from the FIFO to LIFO inventory method without prior permission. A change from LIFO to FIFO or any other inventory change requires permission. A change of accounting does *not* include (1) corrections of computational errors, (2) adjustments to items that do not involve timing, or (3) changes resulting from a change in underlying facts.[89] A taxpayer makes corrections via an amended return filed within the period allowed by the statute of limitations.

The permission requirement gives the IRS a means for monitoring accounting changes so that the IRS can (1) prevent duplication or omission of income or deductions resulting from the change and (2) impose terms and conditions under which the change may be made.[90] In addition, Sec. 481 may require an adjustment in the year of change to prevent amounts from being duplicated or omitted. This requirement leads to so-called **Sec. 481 adjustments**. A Sec. 481 adjustment, if substantial, can itself cause distortion because it does not reflect economic income in the change year. Consequently, Sec. 481 and various Revenue Procedures, including Rev. Proc. 92-20, provide detailed rules and conditions for spreading a Sec. 481 adjustment over several periods, sometimes up to six years.[91] The spread period varies depending on the

> A **Sec. 481 adjustment** is an adjustment in the year of an accounting change to prevent omissions and duplications resulting from the change.

87 Sec. 460(b)(2); the taxpayer uses the overpayment rate, compounded daily, for both overpayments and underpayments.

88 Sec. 446(e) and Reg. Sec. 1.446-1(e)(1) and (2)(i).

89 Reg. Sec. 1.446-1(e)(2)(ii).

90 Rev. Proc. 92-20, I.R.B. 1992-12.

91 *Ibid.* and Sec. 481(b) and (c).

taxpayer's circumstances. For example, the spread period depends on (1) the method being changed, (2) the size of the adjustment, (3) how long the taxpayer has used the old method, (4) how much of the adjustment is attributable to prior years, and (5) whether the change is voluntary (the taxpayer requests change) or involuntary (the IRS requires change).

The IRS sometimes modifies the permission requirement to encourage taxpayers to make changes. For example, Rev. Proc. 85-36 and Rev. Proc. 85-37,[92] which outline procedures for cash-basis taxpayers to change to the accrual method, allow 270 days instead of 180 days to file Form 3115. Also, the Tax Reform Act of 1986 provided special rules for taxpayers required to change accounting method under that act.

EXAMPLE 7-25

Omega Company, a calendar-year taxpayer, has used the cash method for ten years and wishes to change to the accrual method in 19X2. Omega is not a C corporation and is therefore not required to make the change under Sec. 448. At December 31, 19X1, Omega had uncollected accounts receivable of $100,000 and unpaid accounts payable of $40,000. Under the cash method, Omega had not included the uncollected $100,000 in 19X1 income and had not deducted the unpaid $40,000. If Omega changes to the accrual method in 19X2, any collection of the $100,000 accounts receivable would not be included in 19X2 when collected because the receivables pertain to 19X1 and prior years. Similarly, the $40,000 would not be properly deductible in 19X2 when paid. These items represent the type of omissions Sec. 481 was designed to capture, and they create a $60,000 ($100,000 – $40,000) net positive Sec. 481 adjustment. If the entire adjustment is attributable to 19X1, the taxpayer must recognize the entire net adjustment in 19X2. On the other hand, if the adjustment is attributable to a number of prior years, the taxpayer may spread the adjustment over 19X2 and the five subsequent years. If the taxpayer had used the cash method for fewer than six years, the spread period could not exceed the number of years the method was actually used. The rules for determining the exact spread period are complex, and this example does not include sufficient facts to make this determination. In any case, because Rev. Proc. 85-37 applies, the taxpayer has 270 days to file Form 3115. Assuming that 19X2 is not a leap year, the form must be filed by September 27, 19X2.

In summary, we can say that adopting an accounting method is relatively easy. Changing that method can be quite difficult.

_____ INVENTORY METHODS

Goal #5
Explain and apply special
methods—inventory.

The Regulations state that "to reflect taxable income correctly, inventories at the beginning and end of each taxable [tax] year are necessary in every case in which the production, purchase, or sale of merchandise is an income producing factor."[93] Inventory accounting is an accrual method, and, as we pointed out earlier, any taxpayer for whom inventories are a material income-producing factor must use the accrual

---

92 1985-2 CB 434 and 1985-2 CB 438.

93 Reg. Sec. 1.471-1.

method for both sales and purchases. This requirement allows for proper matching of revenue and costs in the familiar formula:

Sales		$XXX
Beginning inventory	$XXX	
Plus purchases or production	XXX	
Less ending inventory	(XXX)	
Cost of goods sold		(XXX)
Gross profit		$XXX

We need to make two observations about this formula. First, as ending inventory increases, cost of goods sold decreases and gross profit increases. Therefore, gross profit (as well as taxable income) moves in the same direction as ending inventory. This relation is important when considering different inventory methods. Second, for manufacturing, merchandising, and mining businesses, gross income means sales minus cost of goods sold.[94] Thus, for tax purposes, gross profit is synonymous with gross income; sales revenue alone does not measure gross income.

Two concepts critical to proper inventory accounting are inventory valuation and inventory flow. Inventory valuation concerns the amounts at which the taxpayer costs inventory, including which direct and indirect costs attach to the inventory. Inventory flow concerns the sequence in which inventory costs flow through the business, for example, FIFO (first-in, first-out) and LIFO (last-in, first-out). Inventory flow assumptions can be considered part of the valuation concept, but, for the sake of exposition, we treat the two concepts separately.

INVENTORY VALUATION

The Regulations allow two basic **inventory valuation** methods: (1) cost and (2) lower of cost or market.[95] For purchased goods, cost means the invoice price minus trade discounts plus charges to acquire possession of the goods (such as transportation costs) plus allocated indirect costs. For manufactured goods, cost means direct production costs plus allocated indirect costs.[96] Cost allocation is dictated by the *uniform capitalization* requirements, which we address later in this section. For purchased goods, market means the current bid price prevailing at the inventory date in quantities usually purchased by the taxpayer. For manufactured goods, market means total reproduction cost at current prices.[97] A taxpayer may value goods below market if they are unsalable at normal prices or unusable in the normal way because of damage, imperfections, changes in style, and so on.[98] A taxpayer may also value goods below market if, in the ordinary course of business, the taxpayer offers the goods for sale at prices lower than the current bid price. If the actual sales price is less than this below-market valuation, the IRS will not accept the below-market valuation.[99]

> **Inventory valuation** refers to the cost method or the lower-of-cost-or-market method.

---

94 Reg. Sec. 1.61-3(a).

95 Reg. Sec. 1.471-2(c).

96 Reg. Sec. 1.471-3.

97 Reg. Sec. 1.471-4.

98 Reg. Sec. 1.471-2(c).

99 Reg. Sec. 1.471-4(b).

Within this framework, the inventory method must meet two tests: (1) it must conform as nearly as possible to the best accounting practice in the taxpayer's particular trade or business and (2) it must clearly reflect income.[100] When applying the first test, the IRS recognizes that inventory rules cannot be uniform for all taxpayers and therefore must conform to industry standards. When applying the second test, the IRS places great weight on consistency from year to year.[101]

Note that tension exists between the two tests. A method that meets industry accounting standards may not clearly reflect income in the IRS's opinion. This tension became apparent in *Thor Power Tool*, a Supreme Court case mentioned frequently in this chapter. The taxpayer (Thor) wrote off some obsolete, defective, and damaged parts. The IRS allowed this writeoff because Thor scrapped the parts soon after removing them from the ending inventory. Thus, these writeoffs were not contested in court. However, Thor also wrote down some spare parts that it retained in inventory for sale at the original prices. Thor wrote down these spare parts because they exceeded any "reasonably foreseeable future demand." The IRS disallowed this writedown because it did not meet the tests for below-market valuation. Thor contested the IRS's position in the Tax Court, which held for the IRS. Thor appealed to the Seventh Circuit Court of Appeals, lost there, and appealed to the Supreme Court. In the Supreme Court's opinion, the term *best accounting practice* is synonymous with generally accepted accounting principles, and the court held that Thor's writedown method met this test. However, the Supreme Court also held that the method did not clearly reflect income (a second test) and upheld the IRS's disallowance of the writedown.

UNIFORM CAPITALIZATION

Prior to 1987, manufacturers were required to use the *full absorption method* to determine inventory costs. This method required the capitalization of direct production costs (direct labor and direct materials) and certain indirect production costs.[102] Capitalized costs are product costs deductible in the year of sale (that is, as part of cost of goods sold) as opposed to period costs, which are deductible in the year paid or incurred (depending on the taxpayer's method of accounting).

Under prior rules, the treatment of indirect costs depended on the category into which they fell. *Category 1* costs had to be capitalized to the extent they were incidental to and necessary in the production process. Examples included indirect labor and materials, repair expenses, maintenance, rent, and utilities. *Category 2* costs did not have to be capitalized; they could be deducted as period costs. Examples included marketing, advertising, and selling expenses; interest; and tax depreciation in excess of financial statement depreciation. *Category 3* costs were capitalized or deducted as period costs depending on how they were treated in the taxpayer's financial statements. Examples included taxes other than income taxes, financial statement depreciation, and officer's salaries.[103]

Congress believed that these pre-1987 rules were deficient for two reasons:

> First, those rules allowed costs that were in reality costs of producing, acquiring, or carrying property to be deducted currently, rather than capitalized into the basis of the property and recovered when the property was sold or as it was used by the

100 Sec. 471(a) and Reg. Sec. 1.471-2(a).
101 Reg. Sec. 1.471-2(b).
102 Reg. Sec. 1.471-11(b).
103 Reg. Sec. 1.471-11(c).

taxpayer. This treatment produced a mismatching of expenses and the related income and an unwarranted deferral of Federal income taxes. Second, different capitalization rules could apply depending on the nature of the property and its intended use. Congress was concerned that these differences could create distortions in the allocation of economic resources and the manner in which certain economic activity was organized.[104]

Accordingly, in the 1986 Act, Congress enacted a set of comprehensive, uniform rules for capitalizing production and acquisitions costs. These **uniform capitalization** (UNICAP) rules are contained in Sec. 263A and associated Regulations. Under these revised rules, many costs that manufacturers could deduct currently under old Categories 2 and 3 must now be capitalized. For example, tax depreciation in excess of financial statement depreciation and taxes other than income taxes must now be allocated to inventory. Some previous period costs remain currently deductible. For example, marketing, advertising, and selling expenses may still be treated as period costs. The UNICAP rules also require taxpayers not engaged in manufacturing to capitalize many indirect costs allocable to property purchased for resale. For example, wholesaler and retailers must now capitalize costs of (1) off-site storage or warehousing; (2) purchasing; (3) handling, processing, assembly, and repackaging; and (4) general and administrative expenses that directly benefit or result from those activities.[105]

> **Uniform capitalization** (UNICAP) is a full costing system under which indirect costs are assigned to inventory rather than deducted as period costs.

Certain taxpayers, property, and expenditures are excluded from the UNICAP rules.[106] The rules do not apply to

1. Personal property acquired for resale if average annual gross receipts of the taxpayer for the immediately preceding three-year period do not exceed $10 million;

2. Property produced by the taxpayer for his or her personal nonbusiness use;

3. Qualified creative expenses of free-lance authors, photographers, and artists;

4. Research and experimental expenditures; and

5. Several other specialized items.

INVENTORY FLOW

The two primary **inventory flow** assumptions allowed for tax purposes are FIFO and LIFO. We avoid detailed explanation of these assumptions because they are adequately covered in most financial accounting texts. Nevertheless, certain aspects of LIFO warrant mention here.

> **Inventory flow** refers to the assumed cost flow as opposed to the actual physical flow of inventory items (e.g., FIFO and LIFO).

LIFO benefits the taxpayer in periods of rising prices because recently incurred high costs flow through cost of goods sold (COGS) while previously incurred low costs remain in inventory. Under LIFO, the flow of costs is the reverse of the actual physical flow of goods. Compared to FIFO, LIFO increases COGS and decreases ending inventory, thereby decreasing gross profit and taxable income. As long as the dollar value of ending inventory does not decrease from year to year (in other words,

---

104 Staff of the Joint Committee on Taxation, *General Explanation of the Tax Reform Act of 1986* (U.S. Government Printing Office), May 4, 1987, p.508.

105 Temp. Reg. Sec. 1.263A-1T(d)(3).

106 Sec. 263A(b)(2)(B), (c), (d), and (h).

as long as LIFO layers are not invaded), LIFO provides cash-flow advantages to the taxpayer.

The adoption of LIFO for tax purposes involves three major requirements. First, a taxpayer must file Form 970, Application to Use LIFO Inventory Method, with the tax return for the adoption year. Although a change from FIFO to LIFO is a change in accounting methods, the change does not require prior IRS approval. Consequently, Form 970 is essentially an information form. Second, a taxpayer using the lower-of-cost-or-market inventory valuation under FIFO must change to the cost-valuation method for LIFO. In the adoption year, the taxpayer values the beginning inventory at cost. The resultant adjustment must be spread ratably over the adoption year and the two succeeding years.[107] Third, the taxpayer must meet the **financial statement conformity requirement**.

Under the financial statement conformity requirement, a taxpayer wishing to use LIFO for tax reporting must also use LIFO for reporting income, profit, or loss (1) to shareholders, partners, or other proprietors; (2) to beneficiaries; or (3) for credit purposes.[108] The Regulations, however, allow the taxpayer to disclose non-LIFO supplemental and explanatory information as long as it does not appear on the face of the income statement. For example, the taxpayer may disclose non-LIFO inventory on the balance sheet, but net worth may not reflect income based on a non-LIFO method. Non-LIFO information may also appear in notes, appendices, and supplements to the financial statements.[109]

Because of the financial statement conformity requirement, many managers refrain from adopting LIFO. These managers fear that reduced earnings per share caused by LIFO will depress their companies' stock prices even though LIFO increases cash flows. To learn whether these fears are justified, accounting researchers have attempted to test whether the stock market reacts positively or negatively to LIFO adoptions. The researchers test two competing hypotheses, the *mechanistic hypothesis* and the *no-effects hypothesis*, by examining abnormal security returns of LIFO adopting firms. An *abnormal return* is the difference between a firm's actual and expected security return. The mechanistic hypothesis suggests that markets will react negatively to a LIFO adoption because accounting earnings will decline. The no-effects hypothesis suggests that markets will not be misled by mere accounting changes. Moreover, because LIFO increases cash flow, the no-effects hypothesis predicts positive abnormal returns, the opposite of the mechanical hypothesis. Although the results of this research are mixed, some researchers have found evidence supporting the mechanistic hypothesis.[110] These results are unsettling because an efficient market should react positively to LIFO changes. Perhaps future research will provide further insights into this issue. Nevertheless, in light of existing evidence, managers seem to be behaving rationally by fearing negative market reactions to LIFO adoptions.

> **The financial statement conformity requirement** provides that taxpayers using LIFO for tax purposes must also use LIFO for financial statement purposes.

_____ KEY POINTS TO REMEMBER

✓ Tax accounting and financial accounting differ because they have different goals. Financial statements provide information to various users and tend to be conserva-

107 Sec. 472(d).

108 Sec. 472(c) and Reg. Sec. 1.472-2(e)(1).

109 Reg. Sec. 1.472-2(e)(3).

110 For a review of these studies see Ross L. Watts and Jerold L. Zimmerman, *Positive Accounting Theory,* (New Jersey: Prentice-Hall, 1986), pp. 99–107.

tive. Taxation generates revenue for the government and must also satisfy various other goals, such as fairness, efficiency, and social policy.

✓ Tax accounting pertains to timing issues: When is income recognized and when are deductions allowed? Timing is important because (1) on a present-value basis, deferred taxes are less costly than taxes paid currently and (2) tax rates may vary from year to year. The timing of income and deductions depends on the taxpayer's annual accounting period (tax year) and accounting method.

✓ The annual accounting concept requires that taxable income be determined periodically on the basis of a tax year. A tax year may be a calendar year, a fiscal year, or a 52–53 week year. The taxpayer's choice of a tax year, however, depends on the existence of books and records, the type of taxpayer, and the taxpayer's business purpose for adopting a particular year. Once a taxpayer adopts a tax year, the taxpayer must obtain the IRS's permission to change that year.

✓ Several important concepts affect the timing and treatment of income. The claim of right doctrine requires that taxpayers include amounts in income when received if the taxpayer claims the receipt as his or her own and has unrestricted use of it. Under the tax benefit rule, a taxpayer includes a recovery of a previously deducted item in income in the year the recovery occurs but only to the extent the original deduction produced a tax benefit (that is, a reduction of taxes). Under the constructive receipt doctrine, which applies to cash-basis taxpayers only, income not actually received is deemed received if the income is available to the taxpayer without restriction.

✓ An accounting method must meet the book conformity requirement and must clearly reflect income. To reflect income clearly, the method must be applied consistently, accurately, fairly, and honestly. Most importantly, the IRS must find the method acceptable; the IRS has broad discretion in making this assessment.

✓ The Code permits the following overall methods of accounting: the cash method, the accrual method, and the hybrid method. Under the cash method, a taxpayer recognizes income when actually or constructively received and deducts expenses when actually paid. Under the accrual method, a taxpayer recognizes income when the right to receive the income is fixed and the amount is determinable with reasonable accuracy and deducts an expense when (1) legal liability is established, (2) the amount is determinable with reasonable accuracy, and (3) economic performance has occurred. A hybrid method is any combination of the cash and accrual methods that does not distort income. For example, a taxpayer for whom inventory is a material income-producing factor must use the accrual method for both sales and purchases even if the taxpayer uses the cash method for all other items of income and deduction.

✓ The Code also allows other special methods for particular transactions, such as the installment method and the percentage-of-completion method. The installment method allows a taxpayer to defer gain recognition on certain sales and exchanges until installment payments are received. The percentage-of-completion method requires a contractor to recognize income on a long-term contract as the project progresses.

✓ Once a taxpayer adopts an accounting method, the taxpayer must obtain the IRS's permission to change that method. The change may create a Sec. 481 adjustment to prevent omissions or duplications.

✓ The Code places severe restrictions on the tax years available to partnerships, S corporations, personal service corporations, and trusts. Also, certain entities may not use the cash method and must use the accrual method. These entities are (1) C corporations, (2) partnerships with a C corporation partner, and (3) tax shelters. The Code provides exceptions from the cash method prohibition for small businesses, personal service corporations, and certain farming business.

✓ Inventory accounting entails two valuation methods: (1) cost or (2) lower of cost or market. It also involves cost flow assumptions, such as FIFO and LIFO.

✓ LIFO provides cash flow advantages in periods of rising prices by matching current costs against current revenue. A taxpayer adopting LIFO must (1) file Form 970 for the adoption year, (2) use the cost valuation method, and (3) meet the financial statement conformity requirement.

✓ The uniform capitalization (UNICAP) rules require many indirect costs to be assigned to inventory rather than deducted as period costs.

———— RECALL PROBLEMS

#1

1. Samantha Wilson, an appliance dealer, included the following expenses in computing her income for financial accounting purposes.

   a. Estimated loss from bad debts, $1,200. This amount was based on assumed losses of one fourth of 1% of net sales.

   b. Estimated expenses arising from guaranties and warranties, $4,000. This amount was based on experience showing that future service costs normally amount to about 2% of the sales price of certain products sold under guaranty and warranty. These sales totaled $200,000.

   c. Estimated repair expense, $800. To prevent large fluctuations in income occurring because major repairs to buildings and equipment tend to occur at irregular intervals, Wilson estimates the average annual repair expense and deducts this estimated amount each year.

   d. Amortization of advertising costs, $3,000. Last year the company spent $15,000 for large magazine advertisements and expected to benefit several years. Wilson decided to defer the cost and charge it off over a five-year period.

   Indicate whether each of the above items could potentially be allowed as a deduction on the tax return. If the item is not deductible for tax purposes, indicate how the amount should be handled on the tax return. (Disregard the question of whether the procedures followed were generally accepted for financial accounting purposes.)

#2

2. If a taxpayer is nearing the end of a year with an unusually large taxable income, to the extent that it is legally possible and administratively convenient, what should the taxpayer try to do about the following:

   a. Additional items of gross income?

   b. Additional deductions?

   Explain briefly.

#3

3. What tax periods are available to the following taxpayers?

   a. An individual

b. A C corporation

c. A partnership

d. An S corporation

4. An individual has used a fiscal year ending October 31 for tax purposes. In June of 19X1, the taxpayer decides to change to a calendar year. Assuming this change, is acceptable, explain how the taxpayer will make the change.

5. What accounting methods are available to the following taxpayers?

a. An individual

b. A C corporation

c. A partnership

d. An S corporation

6. An individual is filing a tax return for the first time. Must the taxpayer obtain permission from the IRS to use the cash basis of accounting?

7. A taxpayer is filing a tax return for the first time. Must the taxpayer obtain permission from the IRS to use the accrual method of accounting?

8. Lambda Company, a calendar-year taxpayer, was formed 20 years ago and has used the cash method since its inception. In 19X1, with the IRS's permission, Lambda changed to the accrual method. During 19X1, Lambda received cash payments of $250,000 and made cash payments of $150,000. Other relevant information follows:

	1/1/X1	12/31/X1
Accounts receivable	$50,000	$60,000
Inventory	40,000	46,000
Accounts payable	22,000	26,000

Assume that cash receipts include collection of beginning accounts receivable and cash payments include purchases of inventory and payment of beginning accounts payable.

a. What amount of net income would Lambda recognize in 19X1 if it remained on the cash method?

b. What amount of net income does Lambda recognize in 19X1 under the accrual method (not counting the net Sec. 481 adjustment)?

c. What is Lambda's net Sec. 481 adjustment? What components of the adjustment prevent omissions? What components prevent duplications?

9. James operates a shoe repair shop. To accommodate his customers, he has a rack on which such items as shoestrings, shoe polish, and shoehorns are displayed for sale. During 19X1, total receipts from shoe repairs were $86,000, and sales of shoestrings and so on were $1,268. May James use the cash basis of accounting? Explain.

10. Wilson, an attorney, uses the cash basis of accounting and a calendar year. In December 19X1, Wilson received $18,000 in cash from clients; billed other clients for $6,000, for which she expects to be paid in 19X2; received from a client

a note receivable with both a principal amount and fair value of $4,000 due in February 19X2; and received a $1,000 City of Chicago bond with a fair market value of $920 in settlement of services of $1,800 billed to the client in July 19X1. How do these items affect Wilson's 19X1 taxable income?

11. Malakoff reports his taxable income using the accrual method of accounting. In 19X1, he had the following items:

Collections on accounts receivable from customers	$290,000
Sales on account to customers	314,000
Cash received on September 1, 19X1, for sublease of part of his office space covering period Sept. 1, 19X1, through Feb. 29, 19X2	6,000
Cash received in February 19X1 representing sublease of part of office space for December 19X0 and January 19X1	2,000

What amount does Malakoff include in 19X1 gross income? What amount would he include in financial accounting revenue?

12. Under what circumstances may a cash-basis taxpayer defer recognition of prepaid income beyond the year of receipt?

13. Under what circumstances may an accrual-basis taxpayer defer recognition of prepaid income beyond the year of receipt?

14. Roscoe opens a cash-and-carry retail grocery store in 19X1. In addition, Roscoe works as an employee for an accounting firm and operates a part-time tax service. Roscoe wishes to use the cash-method of accounting for the retail store because he uses the cash method for his other activities. Will this be possible? Assume, instead, that Roscoe wishes to use the accrual method of accounting for his retail store and continue the cash method for other activities. Will this be possible?

15. Tex Corporation (a C corporation) was formed in 19X1 and properly elected to use the cash basis of accounting. Its gross receipts for the first five years of operations were

19X1	$2,200,000
19X2	3,800,000
19X3	5,900,000
19X4	6,400,000
19X5	8,200,000

In which years is the corporation allowed to use the cash method? Explain your answers.

16. What is meant by the hybrid method of accounting? Give some examples.

17. Terry opened a retail appliance store this year. He recognizes that many of his sales will be on the installment plan. Is he permitted to use the installment method of reporting gross income? Explain.

18. In January of 19X1, Maude Hughes sold 100 acres of unimproved real estate for $1,200 per acre (net of all selling costs). She acquired the property ten years ago for $500 per acre. Three years ago, she mortgaged the property and, at the time

of the sale, the mortgage balance was $30,000. The purchaser agreed to pay $15,000 cash at the closing, assume the mortgage, and pay the remainder in five $15,000 installments (plus interest at 10%) annually on the closing date.

    a. What is Maude's realized gain on this disposition?

    b. How will the gain be recognized?

    c. Does Maude have any alternatives to the treatment in part b?

19. Carl Mays, an employee of Merit Corp., received a salary of $50,000 from Merit in 19X1. In addition, Carl owned a building that he leased to Boss Co. on January 1, 19X1, for a five-year term at $500 per month. As required by the lease, Boss paid Carl $8,000 in 19X1 to cover the following:

Rent for January 19X1 through December 19X1	$6,000
Advance rent for January 19X2	500
Security deposit, to be applied against the final three months' rent in the fifth year of the lease	1,500

How much gross income should Carl report in 19X1?

20. Dr. Wells, a physician, reports on the cash basis. The following items pertain to Dr. Wells's medical practice in 19X1:

Cash received from patients in 19X1	$200,000
Cash received in 19X1 from third-party reimbursers for services provided by Dr. Wells in 19X1	30,000
Salaries paid to employees in 19X1	20,000
Year-end 19X1 bonuses paid to employees in 19X2	1,000
Other expenses paid in 19X1	24,000

What is Dr. Wells's net income in 19X1 from his medical practice?

21. In November 19X1, Yuri received a check from a medical insurance company for $325. The accompanying stub stated: "In payment of your claim No. 123456." Yuri had made no claim, but he nevertheless cashed the check. In June 19X2, Yuri received a letter from the insurance company telling him that the check sent him in the preceding year resulted from a computer error and asking him to repay the $325. Yuri repaid the amount in July 19X2.
    How to these facts affect Yuri's taxable income in 19X1 and 19X2?

22. Surrey owns an apartment building. In addition to the rents applicable to the current year, Surrey receives the following:

    (1) Damage deposits from new tenants. These are refundable when tenants move if no damage is done.

    (2) Payments for the last month's rent on rental contracts. These are prepayments for the final month on each contract.

    a. How do these amounts affect Surrey's income for the year if Surrey uses the cash basis of accounting? If Surrey uses the accrual basis?

    b. How does Surrey treat the damage deposit if, at the end of the contract, he keeps the deposit because of damage done?

#6

23. Jason operates a retail appliance store. He uses the cash basis of accounting except for items related to gross profit from sale of merchandise. Jason offers purchasers of appliances from his store a warranty contract under which Jason agrees to repair free of charge any appliance purchased from him (including parts and labor) for 36 months from date of sale. During 19X1, Jason received $24,000 from the sale of such contracts. An analysis shows that $13,000 relates to work to be performed in 19X2, 19X3, and 19X4.

    a. How much of the $24,000 must Jason include in gross income in 19X1?

    b. Assume the same facts as above, except that Jason uses the accrual method of accounting. How much of the $24,000 must Jason include in gross income in 19X1?

_____ THOUGHT PROBLEMS

#2

1. Why in the 1980s did Congress and the IRS begin taking such a hard look at the time value of money issue?

#2 #5

2. A taxpayer can defer gain recognition on a property sale merely by deferring the sale itself. For example, the seller can simply wait until next year to sell the property. Why would a taxpayer prefer to sell the property in the current year using the installment method rather than selling the property in a subsequent year?

#2 #5

3. Velazquez is a cash-basis, calendar-year individual who is in the 15% tax bracket in 19X1 and expects to be in the 28% tax bracket in 19X2 and subsequent years. Several years ago, he paid $75,000 for some land for investment and now wishes to sell it. The buyer has offered to pay $85,000 in 19X1 or $85,000 plus 12% annual interest in 19X2, with an installment contract signed in 19X1. Assume that Velazquez can invest funds at 12% before taxes.

    a. Should Velazquez accept payment in 19X1 or 19X2? Why?

    b. Suppose the buyer offered to pay the $85,000 plus 12% annual interest ten years after 19X1. Should Velazquez accept payment in 19X1 or ten years later? What factors are important in this decision?

#4

4. Why does the IRS put such great emphasis on consistency in determining whether an accounting method clearly reflects income?

#5

5. The Hard Luck Casino, which is an accrual-basis taxpayer located in Las Vegas, contains several progressive slot machines. A progressive slot machine is one that pays off normally for certain symbol combinations but also pays a large jackpot if a special combination appears. Nevada law forbids casinos from lowering the jackpot. Therefore, it builds up until someone makes the lucky pull. At the end of 19X1, the progressive slot machines had $5 million built up but not yet won. In 19X2, some casino patrons hit the jackpot and won the $5 million. In what year does the Hard Luck Casino deduct the $5 million? What are the important issues in this situation?

#6

6. In many instances, the IRS and the courts require that to reflect income clearly accrual-basis taxpayers must recognize prepaid income when received. Why do these authorities believe that this approach clearly reflects income even though the amounts are not yet earned and are not properly matched against related expenses? Why do the Code, Regulations, and rulings allow exceptions to

immediate recognition for some items (for example, prepaid dues and subscriptions, services, and certain sales of goods) but not for other items (for example, prepaid rent and interest income)?

7. How does the claim of right doctrine differ from the treatment of prepaid income?

8. When do each of the following cash-basis taxpayers recognize income?

   a. Harriet received her paycheck at 5:00 P.M. on December 31, 19X1. Because the banks were closed, she did not cash the check until January 2, 19X2.

   b. On December 31, 19X1, before performing services in 19X2, Jackson entered into an agreement with his employer to defer payment of his 19X2 bonus until 19X3.

   c. On December 31, 19X2, after performing services in 19X2, George entered into an agreement with his employer to defer payment of his 19X2 bonus until 19X3.

   d. On December 31, 19X1, Lena's paycheck was available to be picked up at the reception desk of her employer. However, Lena was home that day so sick that she could not get out of bed. Moreover, she had no one to pick up the check for her. Lena finally picked up the check when she returned to work on January 5, 19X2.

   e. Bob was fired on December 10, 19X1. His employer sent his severance paycheck to him by certified mail. On December 31, 19X1, the postal carrier attempted to deliver the envelope containing the paycheck, but Bob was not home. The postal carrier left a notice of attempt to deliver on Bob's front door, informing Bob that he could pick up the envelope at the post office. By the time Bob returned home, however, the post office was closed. Thus, Bob waited until January 2, 19X2, to pick up the envelope containing his paycheck.

   f. Sasha owned an apartment building, but she retained a real-estate agent to manage the building and collect rents. Following his usual practice, the agent collected the December 19X1 rents and mailed them to Sasha. Sasha did not receive them in the mail until January 3, 19X2.

9. Tom was employed as a salesman for Products Corporation. On December 7, 19X1, the corporation terminated Tom for unsatisfactory performance. On December 14, 19X1, Tom received a $30,000 check. A voucher attached to the check stated: "In full payment of all liabilities of Products Corporation to you for services rendered, a commission check in the amount of $30,000." On receiving the check, Tom computed the amount of commissions due him and found the check was insufficient. He believed that he should have received $40,000. Tom immediately wrote to Products Corporation expressing his concerns and his desire to settle the issue. Tom held onto the check without cashing it. He felt that cashing the check would constitute acceptance of Product's offer of full payment, thereby precluding him from further action against the corporation. In March 19X2, he received another check from Products Corporation in the amount of $10,000, which, in combination with the original check, represented the corporation's new offer of full settlement. Tom then accepted and cashed both checks. What issues and doctrines pertain to this situation? When should Tom recognize the $30,000?

10. Leonardo, a cash-basis, calendar-year taxpayer, operates a sole proprietorship. In December 19X1, he needed to pay $1,000 of business expenses but was short of

cash. Therefore, he borrowed $1,000 from the bank, paid the expenses in 19X1, and repaid the loan in 19X2. When does he deduct the expense? What is your answer if, instead of borrowing the funds from the bank, he charged the expense to a credit card in 19X1 and paid the credit card bill in 19X2?

CLASS PROJECTS

1. Read the following article: Joseph H. Anthony and Steven C. Dilley, "The Tax Basis Financial Reporting Alternative for Nonpublic Firms," *Accounting Horizons*, September 1988, pp. 41–47. When reading the article, be aware that (1) SAS No. 62 has superseded SAS No. 14 and (2) the book-income adjustment does not apply to the alternative minimum tax after 1989. You may also want to read SAS No. 62. After reading the article, prepare a written summary of the authors' main points, including your opinions on the issue.

2. Obtain annual reports for at least three large, publicly held corporations that have adopted LIFO. What LIFO disclosures do they make pursuant to the financial statement conformity requirement? While you have these annual reports, also list some of the major book-tax timing differences reported by these companies.

3. Read the following two articles: (1) James M. Reeve and Keith G. Stanga, "The LIFO Pooling Decision: Some Empirical Results from Accounting Practice," *Accounting Horizons*, June 1987, pp. 25–33 and (2) William R. Cron and Randall B. Hayes, "The Dollar Value LIFO Pooling Decision: The Conventional Wisdom Is Too General," *Accounting Horizons*, December 1989, pp. 57–70. After reading the articles, prepare a written summary of the authors' main points, including your opinions on the issue. When formulating your opinions, consider the following question: How would you advise a company that is considering adopting LIFO to pool its inventories?

In general, the basis of property is the cost thereof. The cost is the amount paid for such property in cash or other property. This general rule is subject to exceptions stated in subchapter O (relating to gain or loss on the disposition of property), subchapter C (relating to corporate distributions and adjustments), subchapter K (relating to partners and partnerships), and subchapter P (relating to capital gains and losses) chapter 1 of the Code.

TREAS. REG. SEC. 1.1012-1(a)

TAX BASIS

CHAPTER OBJECTIVES

By the end of Chapter 8, you should comprehend the often symbiotic relationship between tax basis and the measurement of income derived from property transactions. This chapter provides an important synthesis of those concepts concerning gross income, deductions, entities, and tax accounting periods and methods, each presented as independent notions in the four preceding chapters.

LEARNING GOALS

After studying this chapter, you should be able to

1 Compute the amount of gain or loss realized on the sale, exchange, or other disposition of property;

2 Calculate the adjusted tax basis of property originally acquired by purchase;

3 Calculate the most common basis adjustments made to investments in S corporations and partnerships;

4 Explain how taxpayer's adjusted tax basis may limit a loss deductions from investments in S corporations and partnerships;

5 Determine the tax basis of properties acquired by inheritance; and

6 Determine the tax basis of properties acquired by gift.

Before leaving the general concepts of Part Two and beginning a more detailed discussion of specific statutory provisions in the remainder of this text, we need to examine the basis concept and discover how it relates to the four general concepts—that is, gross income, deductions, taxable and nontaxable entities, and accounting periods and methods—already introduced.

This chapter is divided into four parts. The first part reviews Chapter 4 and expands on the earlier discussion relating to gross income derived from dispositions of property. The second part explains in general how basis is originally acquired in a purchased property and how it may be adjusted over time. The third part discusses how the business entity (or legal form) and the accounting period affect the tax basis of an owner's rights in a business entity. The fourth and final part explains the basis rules for property acquired by inheritance or as a gift.

INCOME FROM PROPERTY DISPOSITIONS

> **Goal #1**
> Compute the amount of gain or loss realized.

We learned in Chapter 4 that the tax concept of gross income includes income derived from property. Although mere appreciation in the value of property constitutes income, appreciation alone will not be taxed until it has been realized in a taxable transaction. In other words, income from appreciation will not be subject to taxation until there has been some change in the form or the substance of the owner's property rights in a transaction that involves a second taxpayer. The moment that a taxpayer disposes of an appreciated property, the general conditions required for income taxation have been satisfied and the taxpayer must determine whether or not one of the nontaxable exchange provisions may apply to the disposition. If not, the taxpayer must then determine the **amount of the gain (or loss) realized.**

> The **amount of gain or loss realized** from the disposition of property equals the amount realized in the disposition *less* the adjusted basis of the property given up.

Section 1001(a) provides that the amount of any gain or loss realized on the disposition of a property is equal to the amount realized less the adjusted basis of the property given up. The two critical phrases in this statutory definition of gain and loss are, obviously, (1) *amount realized* and (2) *adjusted basis*. If the amount realized exceeds the adjusted basis given up, the excess is called a *gain* and becomes part of the taxpayer's gross income. If the amount realized is less that the adjusted basis given up, the difference is called a *loss,* which may or may not be deductible (see Chapter 5).

> The **amount realized** is equal to the sum of (1) any cash received *plus* (2) the fair market value of any noncash property received *plus* (3) any debt relief achieved in a propety disposition.

AMOUNT REALIZED

The **amount realized** is, in common sense terms, a measure of what the taxpayer receives in a transaction. In more technical terms, it is the sum of (1) cash received plus (2) the fair market value of any noncash property received plus (3) any debt relief achieved in a transaction. The first two of these three items are specifically included in the definition of amount realized per Sec. 1001(1); the inclusion of the third item stems from judicial authority—most importantly from *Crane v. Comm'r., 331 U.S.1 (1947).*

The basic notion of the amount realized can be readily illustrated by three examples.

EXAMPLE 8-1

Helen sells her (personal) car for $7,000 cash. Her amount realized is $7,000.

EXAMPLE 8-2

The Li Partnership sells its (business) computer for $10,000 cash plus Trado Corporation common stock that has a fair market value of $8,000. The amount realized by Li Partnership's is $18,000 ($10,000 + $8,000).

EXAMPLE 8-3

Beta, Inc., sells a parcel of land for $100,000 cash and the buyer, Zeldon Industries, assumes Beta's outstanding mortgage on that property in the amount of $300,000. If there are no direct selling expenses, Beta's amount realized is $400,000 ($100,000 + $300,000). Real estate commissions and other *direct* selling expenses are subtracted in the determination of amount realized. Thus, if Beta, Inc., paid a realtor's commission of $20,000 on this sale, Beta's amount realized would be reduced to $380,000.

Note that in each of the three example we determined only the *amount realized* in the sale, *not* the amount of **gain** or **loss realized** in that transaction. To determine the amount of gain or loss realized, it is necessary to subtract from the amount realized the adjusted basis of the property surrendered. Before turning to the meaning of adjusted basis, we should at least note a major practical problem in determining the amount realized in some transactions.

> **Gain realized** is equal to the excess of the amount realized over adjusted tax basis.
>
> **Loss realized** is equal to the excess of the adjusted tax basis over the amount realized.

One of the most difficult administrative problems in income taxation involves the determination of fair market values of noncash properties. Except for properties regularly traded on an organized exchange, there is no easy way to resolve this essentially factual issue in many circumstances. The courts have adequately described the intended value in such terms as an arm's length price involving a willing seller and a willing buyer, acting with full knowledge, and so on. Translating those judicial phrases into operational procedures and, eventually, into a specific number, is no mean task. If a taxpayer and the IRS cannot agree on the fair market value of a property, the dispute may have to be resolved by litigation. Fortunately for students, fair market values are typically given in classroom exercises.

ADJUSTED BASIS

An **adjusted tax basis** in a property is sometimes as difficult to determine as is fair market value. Conceptually adjusted basis is a measure of the taxpayer's potential return of capital; that is, it represents the portion of the amount realized on the disposition of property that is not income by definition. To understand the basis concept, recall that income was defined in Chapter 4 as in increase in net worth plus the value of any items consumed during some time period. If a nonconsuming taxpayer's only asset is a block of common stock purchased for $10,000, that taxpayer will have no income or loss unless and until the stock increases or decreases in value. The $10,000 invested in the stock represents the taxpayer's invested capital and is often called its cost or unadjusted basis. If the value of this stock increases from $10,000 to $13,000 and the taxpayer sells the stock for $13,000 cash, the amount realized is $13,000 but the gain realized is only $3,000 ($13,000 amount realized less $10,000 adjusted basis).

> The **adjusted tax basis** of a property acquired by purchase is a measure of the taxpayer's unrecovered capital investment in that property.

The adjective *adjusted,* when used to modify the noun *basis,* appropriately implies that a taxpayer's original basis in a property may increase or decrease over time. In general, it is a measure of the taxpayer's unrecovered tax cost (or unrecovered capital investment) in a property at any moment in time.

EXAMPLE 8-4

Earl Chapman purchased a building, to be used in his sole proprietorship, for $200,000. Earl paid $20,000 down and assumed a mortgage of $180,000 to acquire this building. He immediately remodeled the building at a cost of $100,000. During the next several years, Earl claimed depreciation deductions for federal income tax purposes totaling $175,000, relative to this building. Given this information, it is reasonable to assume that Earl Chapman's adjusted basis in the building is now $125,000 ($200,000 + $100,000 − $175,000).

The procedure used to calculate adjusted basis is identical to that used by financial accountants in the calculation of book value. The numbers used are, however, tax-generated numbers rather than financial accounting numbers.

A taxpayer's initial or original basis in a property will vary significantly depending on how the taxpayer acquires a property. The notion that adjusted basis represents a measure of the taxpayer's unrecovered (tax) cost in a property is most appropriate in the context of a property that is either purchased in an open market transaction or constructed by the taxpayer. Properties acquired by inheritance or as a gift, as well as properties acquired in a fully or partially nontaxable transaction, do not take a cost basis. The basis of properties acquired in these latter ways is discussed more fully later in this chapter.

> **Goal #2**
> Determine the adjusted basis of purchased property.

COST BASIS IN GENERAL

Section 1012 is statutory authority for the conclusion that the basis of property is generally equal to its cost. It reads in critical part as follows:

> The basis of property shall be the cost of such property, except as otherwise provided in this subchapter and subchapters C (relating to corporate distributions and adjustments), K (relating to partners and partnerships), and P (relating to capital gains and losses).

As implied by the multiple cross references in this one sentence from Sec. 1012, there are many exceptions to the general rule that basis will equal cost, even at the time a property is first acquired. Nevertheless, that is the general rule and you should try to understand the significance of it before worrying too much about the numerous exceptions.

The problems encountered in determining the cost basis of an asset for tax purposes are very similar to those encountered in determining the cost of an asset for financial accounting purposes. Presumably the cost basis of a property includes not only the price initially paid to acquire it but also all of the costs related to getting clear title and making it ready for production. In financial accounting there is an inherent bias to capitalize any questionable expenditures as part of the cost of an asset, because that alternative will tend to improve both the income statement and the balance sheet in the short run. In other words, if a financial accountant charges a questionable expenditure to an asset account rather than an expense account, the immediate consequence is to report a larger income (because of the smaller expense) and to report greater asset values (because of the amount capitalized). In tax accounting the inherent bias runs in precisely the opposite direction. The taxpayer typically wants to reduce taxable income as a means of reducing the income tax and wants to reduce asset values as a means of reducing property taxes. As a consequence, the tax accountant will generally treat a questionable expenditure as a deduction rather than as part of the cost of an asset.

ORIGINAL BASIS

As noted earlier, the original basis of an asset presumably includes the acquisition price, any costs associated with acquiring clear title, and other costs related to getting the asset in place and into production. To illustrate, assume that a taxpayer purchased a large new production machine from a distant vendor and agreed to pay all of the shipping and installation costs. Given this contractual arrangement, the taxpayer's basis in this asset should include all of the costs incurred in getting the new machine from the seller's place of business to the buyer's location as well as the costs incurred in installing the new machine in the taxpayer's factory. If the taxpayer uses its own employees and its own truck to go and get the equipment and to install it in the taxpayer's factory, there is a strong temptation for the taxpayer to charge the various costs incurred to routine expense accounts—and thus to deduct them immediately—at least for income tax purposes.

ALLOCATIONS

A taxpayer often purchases an entire business composed of many assets. Prior to the Tax Reform Act of 1986, the parties to such a transaction had an incentive to whipsaw the government by using inconsistent allocations of the purchase price to the purchased assets. The seller preferred to allocate as much as possible to goodwill and other assets that generated favorable capital gains. The purchaser, on the other hand preferred to allocate as much as possible to inventory and depreciable assets to obtain ordinary deductions. In addition, if the purchaser paid a premium for the business, that is, a price exceeding the total fair market value of identifiable assets, the purchaser might allocate the excess purchase price to the identifiable assets, thereby raising the basis of these assets above their fair market value. To prevent such manipulation, Congress enacted Sec. 1060, which requires *both* sellers and purchasers to use the **residual method** of price allocation.[1] Under the residual method, any price in excess of the total fair market value of identifiable assets must be allocated to goodwill.

> The **residual method** of price allocation requires that any excess of the price paid over the total value of all assets received be allocated to goodwill.

Section 1060 requires that the purchase price be allocated to individual assets so that each asset will have an assigned basis for depreciation, determination of gain or loss, and so on. The purchase price is allocated in hierarchical order: first to Class I assets, then to Class II assets, then to Class III assets, and finally to Class IV assets.[2] Regulations define the four classes as follows:

Class I: Cash, demand deposits, and similar money accounts;

Class II: Certificates of deposit, U.S. Government securities, and other marketable stock and securities;

---

1 Staff of the Joint Committee on Taxation, *General Explanation of the Tax Reform Act of 1986,* (U.S. Government Printing Office), May 7, 1987, pp. 355–60.

2 Sec. 1060 refers to Sec. 338(b) (5), which in turn refers to Regulations. Temp. Reg. Sec. 1.338(b)-2T(b) contains the allocation rules.

Class III: All assets other than those in Classes I, II, and IV; and

Class IV: Goodwill and going concern value.

Within each class, the taxpayer allocates the purchase price in proportion to the fair market value of assets within the class. However, for Classes I, II, and III, the amount allocated to the particular asset may never exceed its fair market value. If the purchase price exceeds the total fair market value of assets, the *residual* is assigned to goodwill (Class IV).

EXAMPLE 8-5

Shark Company purchases all the assets of Target Company except cash. The fair market values (FMV) of the purchased assets are as follows:

Marketable securities	$150,000
Inventories	200,000
Machinery	250,000
Building	350,000
Total	$950,000

Assume three separate cases: in Case 1, Shark pays $950,000; in Case 2, Shark gets a bargain and pays $900,000; in Case 3, Shark pays a premium for a $1,000,000 total. Table 8-1 shows how Shark must allocate the purchase price in each case.

In Case 1, the total purchase exactly equals the total FMV so that each asset's allocated basis equals its FMV. In Case 2, the total purchase price is less than the total FMV. Accordingly, the Class II asset has an allocated basis equal to its FMV, and the balance is allocated to Class III assets in proportion to their relative FMVs. In Case 3, the total purchase price exceeds the total FMV. Accordingly, Class II and III assets are allocated bases equal to their FMVs. The balance (or residual) is allocated to a Class IV asset because the excess purchase price is deemed to be goodwill.

From the seller's perspective, the allocation establishes the selling price of each asset so that the seller can determine gains and losses on the sale. From the purchaser's perspective, the allocation establishes the bases of individual assets purchased.

The Revenue Reconciliation Act of 1990 modified Sec. 1060 to give taxpayers some leeway in allocating a purchase price. The new provision states that if the seller and purchaser agree in writing as to the allocation of the purchase price or to the fair market value of the assets, the written agreement will be binding on both the seller and purchaser unless the IRS determines the allocation or fair market values are inappropriate. This provision recognizes the natural tension between the seller and purchaser concerning the allocation. As mentioned at the beginning of this section, they often prefer different kinds of allocations. Consequently, an agreement reached in an arm's-length transaction should be fair and reasonable. It ordinarily binds both parties, thereby precluding a whipsaw situation in which the two parties use different allocations. Nevertheless, the IRS has the last word on its appropriateness. Also, if

Class	Asset	Case 1	Case 2	Case 3
II	Marketable securities	$150,000	$150,000	$150,000
III	Inventories	200,000	187,500*	200,000
III	Machinery	250,000	234,375*	250,000
III	Building	350,000	328,125*	350,000
IV	Goodwill	0	0	50,000
		$950,000	$900,000	$1,000,000

TABLE 8-1

Allocation of Lump-Sum Purchase Price (EXAMPLE 8-5)

*FMV of Class III assets totals $800,000 ($200,000 + $250,000 + $350,000). Amount allocated among Class III assets equals $750,000 ($900,000 − $150,000). Therefore, the allocation is as follows:

Inventories:	$750,000 x $200,000/$800,000
Machinery:	$750,000 x $250,000/$800,000
Building:	$750,000 x $350,000/$800,000

the parties to the transaction do not reach an appropriate written agreement, the class-by-class allocation scheme discussed above will apply.

SUBSEQUENT ADJUSTMENTS

After a taxpayer has acquired an asset, the tax basis of that asset may increase or decrease because of subsequent events. For example, *capital improvements* made after the acquisition of an asset should be charged to the related asset account and increase the tax basis of that asset, whereas routine *repairs* should be charged to an expense account and deducted for income tax purposes. The Treasury Regulations and numerous judicial authorities have tried for years, with only limited success, to define capital expenditures and to distinguish between routine repairs and capital improvements.[3] However difficult it may be for taxpayers to distinguish between these and other potential adjustments to basis, it is necessary for them to do so because Sec. 1001(a) clearly requires the subtraction of the *adjusted basis* from the amount realized in the measurement of the gain or loss realized.

Tangible Assets

The need to adjust the tax basis of many tangible assets is especially easy to understand. In Example 8-4, for instance, we noted that Earl Chapman had to adjust his original basis in a business building by the amount of depreciation that he claimed on the building during the years that he used it in his sole proprietorship. Similar adjustments must be made to the original basis of many other assets.

EXAMPLE 8-6

The Paddy Wagon, a partnership, acquired a used truck to be used in its delivery business at a cost of $20,000. The partnership immediately had the truck

Continued

---

3 See Treas. Regs. Sec. 1.263(a)-1; Sec. 1.263(a)-2; and Sec. 1.162-4. See also *Wood Preserving Corp. of Baltimore, Inc. v. U.S.*, 233 F. Supp. 600 (D., Md., 1964), aff'd. 347 F.2d 117 (CA-4, 1965).

EXAMPLE 8-6 (Con't.)

overhauled at a cost of $7,000. During the next two years depreciation deductions in the amount of $9,000 (total) were claimed by the partnership relative to this delivery truck. The determination of the adjusted basis of the truck follows common sense: that is, $20,000 original cost *plus* $7,000 capital improvements *less* $9,000 depreciation *equals* $18,000 adjusted basis. Hence the sale of this truck for $21,000 would cause The Paddy Wagon to recognize a gain of $3,000 ($21,000 amount realized *less* $18,000 adjusted basis). On the other hand, the sale of the truck for only $14,000 would cause the partnership to recognize a loss of $4,000 ($14,000 amount realized *less* $18,000 adjusted basis).

The tax basis of some tangible assets, such as land, will only rarely be adjusted after the date of acquisition because these assets are deemed to be nonwasting assets. Although realtors' fees and lawyers' fees must often be added to the purchase price of land—and thus to its basis—at the time it is acquired, very few subsequent events will change the original basis of land. Hence, the adjusted basis of land is usually equal to its original basis or cost.

One cannot assume, however, that no adjustment to the basis of nonwasting, tangible assets is ever appropriate. To illustrate this possibility, consider the following example.

EXAMPLE 8-7

XYZ Corporation purchased a 100–acre plot of land for $1 million with the sole intention of building a research facility on the land. Before beginning construction, however, XYZ discovered that a sizeable mineral deposit existed beneath the surface of this land and decided that it would be more profitable to mine the mineral than to proceed with the original building plans. Given this unexpected turn of events, the XYZ Corporation would likely be required to allocate some portion of its original $1 million purchase price in the land to the newly discovered mineral deposit. Suppose, for example, that XYZ could somehow prove that the minerals located on this building site are worth $3.5 million and that the remaining surface rights are worth only $500,000. Given these values, XYZ should allocate $875,000 of the original basis [or ($3.5 million/$4.0 million) x $1 million] to the mineral rights and leave only $125,000 [or ($500,000/$4 million) x $1 million] of the original basis in the land. In this scenario it would be entirely correct to say that the adjusted basis of XYZ's land is only $125,000.

Intangible Assets

The tax basis of investments in intangible assets—just like investments in tangible properties—may or may not be subject to frequent modification after acquisition. For example, an investment in a copyright or a patent ordinarily will be subject to frequent adjustment because these intangible properties are deemed to be wasting assets, the costs of which may be amortized (and deducted) over their estimated useful life. Goodwill, on the other hand, is generally deemed to be a nonwasting asset and, therefore, an asset whose tax basis only rarely is adjusted prior to disposition of the related business.

The original tax basis in the stock of a C corporation is only rarely changed. The basis will include both the original purchase price and any broker's commission paid to acquire the stock following the cost principles explained earlier. The subsequent payment of an ordinary dividend by the C corporation to its shareholder would not cause the shareholder to adjust the basis of the stock. As explained in Chapter 6, the receipt of the dividend would simply create additional income for the shareholder.

EXAMPLE 8-8

Mr. and Mrs. Garcia purchased 1,000 shares of AT&T common stock for $30,000 and paid a broker's commission of $500 to acquire this stock. If, shortly thereafter, the Garcias received an AT&T dividend check in the amount of $750, their tax basis in the 1,000 shares of stock would remain $30,500. The Garcias would include the $750 dividend as part of their gross income for the year.

Although the tax basis in the stock of a C corporation rarely changes, it can be adjusted in unusual circumstances. One possible explanation for such an adjustment would be the receipt of a *nontaxable stock dividend*. The details of the basis adjustment required on the receipt of a nontaxable stock dividend are explained in Chapter 17. In general, this basis adjustment simply requires the reallocation of the original cost basis over the new and larger number of shares owned.

EXAMPLE 8-9

Mr. and Mrs. Garcia (see Example 8-8) next received a 10% *nontaxable stock dividend* from AT&T. This event increased the number of AT&T shares that the Garcias owned from 1,000 to 1,100. It also adjusts their tax basis down from $30.50 per share ($30,500 cost *divided by* 1,000 shares) to $27.73 per share, ($30,500/1,100).

INVESTMENTS IN TAX CONDUIT ENTITIES

> **Goal #3**
> Calculate the basis adjustments required for investments in S corporations and partnerships.

The tax basis of investments in tax-conduit entities—such as S corporations and partnerships—is substantially more difficult to determine than is the tax basis of investments in C corporations. The increased complexity indirectly attributable to the fact that the owners of conduit entities generally recognize their prorata share of any income or loss, realized by the S corporation or the partnership, whether or not that income is distributed to them. Given this income tax regime, equity demands that the owner's tax basis in an investment in a conduit entity be adjusted frequently to reflect the tax consequences of intervening events. To better understand the complexity of basis associated with investments in conduit entities, let us consider the taxpayer's original basis, subsequent increases in basis, subsequent decreases in basis, and the calculation of gain or loss realized on the disposition of one such investment.

ORIGINAL INVESTMENT

When an individual investor acquires a small fractional interest in a very large business, that interest is ordinarily acquired by purchase. In Example 8-8, for example,

Mr. and Mrs. Garcia purchased their ownership in AT&T through a broker who acquired their 1,000 shares of AT&T stock from an unidentified stockholder who wanted to sell his stock. Acquisition of an interest in smaller businesses may be acquired in any number of ways. The many important details associated with a *non-taxable* acquisition of a business interest are explained very briefly in Chapter 17. Additional details concerning non-taxable acquisitions of business interests are best deferred to more advanced courses in federal income taxation.

To illustrate the points most significant in this conceptual overview of the tax basis concept, we will assume in the following examples that all acquisitions were made in a taxable form. This assumption allows us to concentrate our attention on the most significant differences between a taxpayer's investment in a C corporation and other investments in tax-conduit entities. If a taxpayer acquires an investment in a tax-conduit entity by purchase, his or her *original* investment (and tax basis) will be determined in exactly the same way as would an investment in a C corporation. Investments in tax-conduit entities, however, quickly give rise to numerous adjustments that are not commonly encountered with investments in C corporations.

EXAMPLE 8-10

Assume that on January 1 Mr. and Mrs. Levy purchase 1,000 shares of TA&A stock for $30,500. Assume further that TA&A is a small, closely held, S corporation with only 4,000 shares of outstanding common stock. Given this information the Levys—just like the Garcias in Example 8-8—would take an original tax basis of $30,500 in their 1,000 shares of TA&A stock. The Levy's tax basis in these shares, however, (unlike the Garcias) would almost immediately be subject to adjustment.

SUBSEQUENT INCREASES IN BASIS

Investors in tax-conduit entities must report, as their own taxable income, their proportionate share of any taxable income earned by any tax-conduit entity in which they invest. The owners must report this taxable income whether or not the management of the tax-conduit entity decides to distribute any part (or all) of the income, earned by the entity, to the owners. Because the owners have to report this income on their own income tax returns, the law allows the owners to increase their tax basis in their investment by the same amount that they report as taxable income from the entity on their own returns.

EXAMPLE 8-11

Assume that TA&A recognizes a $20,000 taxable income in the year after the Levys (see Example 8-10) purchased their stock. Even if TA&A distributes nothing to the Levys during the year, they must include an additional $5,000 in taxable income on their own tax return simply because they own 25% of the outstanding TA&A stock. At first glance it may appear grossly unfair to the Levys that they must report $5,000 in taxable income even though they receive nothing in return. To correct this potential tax inequity, the Levys will discover that they may increase their tax basis in their 1,000 shares of TA&A stock from the original $30,500 to $35,500 (in other words, their original $30,500 cost plus the $5,000 taxable income they had to recognize because of this investment.)

Investors in tax-conduit entities can also increase their tax basis in those invest-ments by making additional capital contributions to the entity. If all owners contribute proportionately, each owners' fractional interest will remain constant. If some owners contribute capital and other owners do not, the fractional ownership interests of each owner must be redetermined after a capital contribution.

EXAMPLE 8-12

To illustrate a capital contribution, let us assume that on August 1 of the second year, TA&A requested all of its shareholders to make an additional capital contribution equal to $10 per share. Further assume that the Levys and all other stockholders in TA&A complied with this request. Consequently, the Levys will increase their tax basis by $10,000 (the amount of additional capital that they contributed). After making this capital contribution the Levys' adjusted basis in their TA&A stock would be $45,500 ($30,500 original cost *plus* $5,000 from their share of TA&A's income in year one *plus* $10,000 from the additional capital contribution). Their proportionate interest would still be a 25% interest in TA&A.

SUBSEQUENT DECREASES IN BASIS

Investors in tax-conduit entities must decrease their tax basis in those investments if the entity reports a loss for income tax purposes and the owners deduct their propor-tionate share of that loss on their own tax returns.

EXAMPLE 8-13

Assume that TA&A reports a loss of $36,000 during the second year of the Levys' ownership of 1,000 shares of TA&A's outstanding common stock. As a 25% owner of TA&A, the Levys would be entitled to deduct on their own tax return $9,000 of the $36,000 loss recognized by TA&A (assuming that neither the passive activity loss limitations nor the capital loss limitations applied).[4] Given these facts, the Levys must decrease the adjusted basis in their TA&A stock from $45,500 to $36,500. That is, they must reduce their prior adjusted basis by exactly the same amount that they were permitted to deduct, on their own tax return, because of their ownership of this stock. Note also that this reduction takes place even though the tax-conduit entity (TA&A) still has not distributed anything to its owners.

Investors in tax-conduit entities must similarly decrease their tax basis in those investments whenever the entity makes a property distribution to its owners. Noncash property distributions create special tax problems. In our examples we will, therefore, assume that all distributions made by tax-conduit entities are made in the form of cash. Students interested in the tax consequences associated with noncash distributions must either do additional research beyond this text or enroll in more advanced courses.

---

4 Incidentally this $9,000 reduction in the adjusted basis of TA&A stock is required even if the Levys cannot deduct the $9,000 loss because of a loss limitation rule.

EXAMPLE 8-14

Suppose that on May 1 of their third year of ownership, the Levys finally receive a $12,000 cash distribution from TA&A. Because TA&A is an S corporation, the Levys need not report that $12,000 as dividend income. They must, however, decrease the adjusted tax basis in their 1,000 shares of TA&A stock from $36,500 to $24,500. Note that this result is very different from the result associated with a dividend received from a C corporation. (Compare Example 8-8 to emphasize the distinction.) Note also, however, that this result is entirely consistent with the tax regime explained in Chapter 6 for tax-conduit entities in general.

EFFECT OF DEBT ON INVESTOR'S BASIS

An owner/investor's tax basis in a business entity may or may not be affected by the amount of debt incurred by an entity, depending upon the type of entity involved. Because general partners are liable for all partnership debts, a general partner's basis is increased (or decreased) by his or her pro rata share of any debt incurred (or repaid) by the partnership. The basis of a stockholder's interest in a corporation, however, will not be affected by the debts incurred or repaid by the corporation because a shareholder is not personally responsible for the corporation's debts. The result is equally true for stockholders of C and S corporations.

EXAMPLE 8-15

If, in Example 8-10, we had assumed that TA&A was a partnership, rather than an S corporation, then additional basis adjustments would have been required at the end of each year. In those years in which TA&A's aggregate liabilities increased between the beginning and the end of the year, the Levys could have increased their basis by 25% of the partnership's increased liabilities. And in those years in which TA&A's aggregate liabilities decreased between the beginning and the end of the year, the Levys would have to decrease their basis by 25% of the partnership's decreased liabilities. All other adjustments—described in Examples 8-11 through 8-14—apply equally to investments in partnerships and investments in S corporations.

The different effect of debt on an investor's basis is sometimes a key consideration in the packaging of an investment activity. If it is expected that the venture will incur heavy tax losses—at least in the first few years of operations—it is important for the investors to have as high a basis as possible because losses cannot be deducted to the extent they exceed basis. In general only partnerships have this advantage. Thus, if a joint venture to construct a shopping mall is organized as a partnership (rather than as a C or S corporation), a $10 million bank loan to the partnership will flow through to the investors and increase their basis in proportion to their partnership interest. This will maximize the investors' opportunity to deduct subsequent losses.

DETERMINING GAIN OR LOSS ON SALES DURING THE YEAR

If a taxpayer sells an investment in a tax-conduit entity on any day other than the first day of a new year, that investor will have to make one final adjustment to the tax basis in the investment to bring it "up to date" as of the day of sale.

EXAMPLE 8-16

To illustrate, let us assume that the Levys sell their 1,000 shares of TA&A stock for $50,000 on September 30 of the third year. Their basis in these shares was last adjusted on May 1 of their third year of ownership to reflect their receipt of a $12,000 cash distribution from TA&A. However, as owners of 25% of TA&A's stock for nine months of the year, the Levys must report their prorata share of whatever income or loss TA&A eventually reports for that third year. Because TA&A will ordinarily not measure or report its income for the third year before sometime early in the fourth year, the Levys for several months will be unable to determine the amount of the gain or loss that they realized on September 30 when they sold their 1,000 shares of TA&A stock.

If by February 10 of the fourth year TA&A was able to close its books (as of the prior December 31) and to report that it had earned a $54,000 taxable income during the prior year, the Levys could finally determine that they had realized a $15,375 gain on the sale of the TA&A stock on the prior September 30. They could finally make this determination after February 10 of year four because they would only then know that they will have to include $10,125 in income on their personal tax return because of their ownership of 1,000 shares of TA&A stock from January 1 through September 30 of year three, that is,

$54,000 times 25% times (9 months divided by 12 months) equals $10,125

By reporting this additional amount of income from TA&A for year three, the Levys will also increase their prior adjusted basis in their TA&A stock from $24,500 to $34,625 as of September 30. Hence the gain recognized on the sale of the stock would be $15,375; that is, $50,000 amount realized less $34,625 adjusted basis equals $15,375 gain realized.

To summarize this lengthy illustration, let us review the reasons why the Levys' adjusted basis in their investment in 1,000 shares of TA&A (an S corporation) common stock changed from the day they acquired the stock until the day it was sold and how those basis adjustments eventually came to modify the amount of income reported by the owners in the various years.

If TA&A had been a C corporation rather than an S corporation throughout this same four-year period, the tax results for the Levys would have been very different. The three most important differences can be summarized as follows:

1. The cash distribution received by the Levys on May 1 of year four would have been reported as dividend income rather than as return of capital (assuming that TA&A had sufficient current or accumulated earnings and profits).

2. No amount of income or loss would have been reported by the Levys at the end of each year simply because they owned 25% of the stock in a C corporation. Instead, the corporation itself would have recognized that same income.

3. The gain realized by the Levys on the sale of their stock on September 30 of year four would have been only $9,500 (i.e., $50,000 amount realized *less* $30,500 original basis plus $10,000 increase in basis because of the contribution to capital on August 1, year two).

Date	Event	Adjusted Basis
Jan. 1, Year 1	Purchased stock for $30,500 cash	$30,500
Dec. 31, Year 1	Recognized 25% of TA&A's income for year	5,000
Jan. 1, Year 2	Adjusted basis	$35,500
Aug. 1, Year 2	Made $10,000 additional contribution to capital	10,000
Aug. 1, Year 2	Adjusted basis	$45,500
Dec. 31, Year 2	Recognized 25% of TA&A's loss for year	($9,000)
Jan. 1, Year 3	Adjusted basis	$36,500
May 1, Year 4	Received cash distribution from TA&A	($12,000)
May 1, Year 4	Adjusted basis	$24,500
Sept. 30, Year 4	Sold stock for $50,000 cash	?*
Dec. 31, Year 4	Recognized 25% of TA&A income for three-fourths of the year	10,125
Sept. 30, Year 4	Revised adjusted basis on Sept. 30	$34,625

*Although the stock was sold on September 30, Year 4, the shareholder/investor could not determine the amount of gain or loss realized on this sale until after the end of the year when TA&A's income for the year had been determined.

This lengthy and complex illustration is intended to demonstrate the symbiotic relationship that exists between tax basis and the income recognition rules for taxable and nontaxable business entities. Both taxable and nontaxable entities are allowed limited choice in selecting their own accounting periods and methods. Those choices, along with the selection of a business form, have a dramatic impact on the income taxation of the owners throughout the years of business operation and at the moment any owner disposes of a business investment. Unfortunately for business managers and investors alike, the choice of selecting the most desirable form of business organization is made an extremely difficult task, largely because of the income tax provisions. As complex as this lengthy example has been, it only touches the surface of many alternative possibilities.

LOSS LIMITATION

Goal #4
Explain how loss deductions may be limited by adjusted basis.

Before concluding this introduction to the concept of tax basis, we need to consider briefly how a taxpayer's basis in any investment in a business venture operating in a tax-conduit form may limit the amount of loss that a taxpayer may deduct. The Code generally provides that an investor in a tax-conduit entity cannot claim a tax deduction for his or her prorata share of any loss initially recognized by a nontaxable entity if that loss exceeds the owner's adjusted basis in the investment in the entity.[5]

---

5 See Sec. 704(d) for the limitation applicable to investments in partnerships and Sec. 1366(d) for that applicable to investments in S corporations.

EXAMPLE 8-17

To illustrate, let us assume that Mr. and Mrs. Vun invest $30,500 for a 25% interest in a new business venture, the Nam Restaurant, operating as an S corporation. Further assume that the Nam Restaurant recognizes the following amounts of taxable income or loss during its first four years of operations:

Year	Income or (Loss)
One	($100,000)
Two	(80,000)
Three	20,000
Four	200,000

Given this loss/income pattern for the Nam Restaurant's first four years of operation, Mr. and Mrs. Vun would normally recognize the following amounts of income or loss by virtue of their 25% interest in this S corporation:

Year	Income or (Loss)
One	($25,000)
Two	(20,000)
Three	5,000
Four	50,000

Because of the general basis limitation rule, however, Mr. and Mrs. Vun would *not* recognize loss and gain following the general rules in years two, three, and four. Instead, they would be limited in the amount of loss that they could recognize in year two. The loss recognized in year one would reduce their basis in Nam Restaurant stock from an original basis of $30,500 down to $5,500 ($30,500–$25,000). Then, in year two, the Vuns could recognize only $5,500 of the $20,000 loss that they realized via their ownership of the Nam Restaurant because of the basis limitation rule. The remaining $14,500 would go into suspense pending a subsequent increase in their basis in this stock (or, possibly, be offset against their basis in any loan that they might have made to the Nam Restaurant). The $5,000 income recognized in year three would be entirely offset by the $14,500 put into suspense the year before. It would also reduce the amount of loss remaining in suspense from $14,500 to $9,500. And the $50,000 income recognized via Nam Restaurant in year four would be reduced from $50,000 to $40,500 by virtue of the remaining balance in the suspended loss account. The implication of the loss limitation on the Vuns' taxable income can be summarized as follows:

Year	Income or (Loss) Realized	Income or (Loss) Recognized	Adjusted Basis at Year End	Suspended Loss Carryforward
One	($25,000)	($25,000)	$5,500	-0-
Two	($20,000)	($5,500)	-0-	($14,500)
Three	$5,000	-0-	-0-	($9,500)
Four	$50,000	$40,500	$40,500	-0-

The important consequence of the general basis limitation rule is simply to provide that an investor in a tax-conduit entity cannot deduct losses in excess of the adjusted basis in that particular investment. Disallowed losses can, however, be carried forward and offset against taxable income that would otherwise have been recognized in later years. It might also be noted here that the rule limiting aggregate loss deductions to the partner's adjusted basis in a partnership interest overrides the passive activity loss rules, which simply characterize certain kinds of losses. In other words, if a taxpayer has a total of $50,000 in losses suspended under the passive activity loss rules, but only $30,000 in adjusted basis remaining in a passive activity, that taxpayer cannot deduct more than $30,000 in losses in the year in which the partner disposes of the entire passive activity interest in a taxable transaction.

In each of the prior examples in this chapter it was assumed that the taxpayer's interest in a property was acquired by purchase. Individual taxpayers frequently acquire some property by inheritance or gift. The basis rules for properties acquired in either of these two ways differ significantly from the rules applicable to purchased properties.

PROPERTY ACQUIRED BY INHERITANCE

Goal #5
Determine the tax basis of property acquired by inheritance.

The basis of property received from a decedent is generally the fair market value of the property on the date of the decedent's death. An exception to this general rule applies if the executor or executrix of the estate elects the alternate valuation date for estate tax purposes. In that event, the tax basis is generally the fair market value six months after the decedent's death.

EXAMPLE 8-18

Assume that Tom Tucket purchased stock A for $10,000 on February 5, 19X0, and stock B for $20,000 on September 5, 19X4. Further assume that Tom died on October 16, 19X7, when the fair market value of both stock A and stock B was $15,000. Any beneficiary of Tom's estate who received those shares would take as his or her basis the $15,000 fair market value on Tom's death, assuming that Tom's executor or executrix made no election to value properties on the alternate valuation date. This means that the $5,000 unrealized or paper gain implicit in stock A would forever go unrecognized for income tax purposes, and the $5,000 unrealized or paper loss implicit in stock B would also forever go unrecognized for income tax purposes because death is *not* deemed to constitute a realization event for income tax purposes.

The **alternate valuation** date is the day that is exactly six months after the date of a decedent's death.

If an executor or executrix elects the **alternate valuation** date and also distributes some property prior to that date, then—for the property distributed before the valuation date—the basis is the fair market value of the property on the date it was distributed. For all other property the basis remains the fair market value on the alternate valuation date.

EXAMPLE 8-19

Assume that Len Black died on February 19, 19X8, and that at the time of his death he owned (among other properties) 2,000 shares of V common stock. The

Continued

EXAMPLE 8-19 (Con't.)

value of the V stock was highly volatile. On February 19, 19X8, it sold for $5 per share; on May 1, 19X8, it traded at $9 per share; and on August 19, 19X8, it sold at $4 per share. If the executor of Black's estate elects the alternative valuation date—an election available to the executor only if the aggregate value of all the assets in an estate is greater six months after death than it was on the date of death—and if the executor distributed only the 2,000 shares of V common stock to the sole heir of Black's estate on May 1, 19X8, then the heir's basis in these 2,000 shares would be $18,000 (or $9 per share), even though that same heir's basis in all other assets eventually received from Black's estate would be determined by their fair market value on August 19, 19X8, the alternate valuation date.

In most cases an executor will be reluctant to distribute many assets before an estate is completely settled. Hence this special valuation rule is only rarely encountered in the real world. In the majority of cases the basis of inherited properties is either (1) their value on the date of the decedent's death of (2) their value exactly six months later.

The most difficult practical problem in determining the basis of inherited properties is the problem of the executor in determining the fair market value of many properties that are not routinely traded on an organized exchange. As indicated earlier, that is eventually a factual question and when the IRS and the executor cannot agree, a court may have to settle the issue.

The basis rules for inherited properties are particularly important to good tax planning. In general elderly persons as well as younger persons with a terminal illness are reluctant to sell any highly appreciated properties prior to death because they know that the same properties can be sold by their heirs immediately after death at no income-tax cost. These individuals are often described as locked in to their investments. On the other hand, these same persons are well advised to sell any significantly *depreciated* assets—in other words, assets with a value significantly below their adjusted basis—prior to their own death. Their failure to make such a taxable disposition would mean that an otherwise tax-deductible loss will be lost forever because the heir's basis is, once again, fair market value on the date of the decedent's death.

Goal #6
Determine the tax basis of property acquired by gift.

PROPERTY ACQUIRED BY GIFT

Another common method by which an individual taxpayer acquires property is by gift. January 1, 1921, marked a major change in the rules that determine the basis of property received by gift. A taxpayer's basis for property acquired by gift and disposed of after December 31, 1920, is generally the donor's adjusted basis. A major exception to this general rule applies if the fair market value of the property given is less than the **donor's** basis on the date of the gift. In that event, the **donee's** basis for loss (only) is the fair market value on the date of the gift. This means that a donee may have two different tax bases for properties—one basis for gain and another for loss.

To understand the idea behind the law, observe the possibilities for tax avoidance in the absence of such wording. If the law provided simply that in all cases the donee would take the donor's cost basis (as it did prior to 1921), then a donor in a low marginal tax bracket could give a property with a substantial paper loss to a family member, friend, or acquaintance in a higher marginal tax bracket, and the two individuals combined could achieve a greater tax benefit from the economic or paper loss than the

A **donor** is a person who makes a gift.

A **donee** is a person who receives a gift.

donor alone could have received. On the other hand, if the law provided simply that the donee had to take the lesser of the fair market value of the property on the date of the gift or the donor's cost basis, an unrealistically large gain (in a consolidated sense) would have to be reported if the value of the property were to increase after the date of gift and before the date of sale. Hence the law is written as it is to try concurrently to close a loophole and yet not to create an unduly harsh tax result.

The provisions that relate to gift taxes may further complicate the rules used to determine the cost basis of property acquired by gift. For gifts made after September 2, 1958, and before January 1, 1977, if the donor paid a federal gift tax on the transfer of the property, the donee can increase the donor's basis by the total amount of the gift tax paid so long as the sum of the two (donor's cost and gift tax) does not exceed the fair market value on the date of the gift. If the sum of these two amounts does exceed the fair market value, then the donee's basis is the fair market value on the date of the gift. Note that if the donor's cost alone exceeds the fair market value on the date of the gift, no amount of gift tax can be added to the donee's basis, even if the property is eventually sold for more than the donor's cost. To illustrate the basis rules applicable to gifts made before January 1, 1977, consider the three following examples.

EXAMPLE 8-20

Taxpayer A purchased stock for $15,000. On the date of the gift, June 1, 1976, the stock had a fair market value of $20,000. Gift taxes of $1,000 were paid. In this case, the donee's basis for both gain and loss is $16,000 ($15,000 cost + $1,000 gift taxes).

EXAMPLE 8-21

Taxpayer B purchased stock for $15,000. On the date of the gift, June 1, 1976, the stock had a fair market value of $10,000. Gift taxes of $1,000 were paid. In this case, the donee's basis for gain is $15,000; the donee's basis for loss is $10,000. If the stock is sold by the donee for any amount greater than $10,000 and less than $15,000, the basis is equal to the amount realized on the sale. Under these conditions the taxpayer will recognize neither a gain nor a loss.

EXAMPLE 8-22

Taxpayer C purchased stock for $15,000. On the date of the gift, December 28, 1976, the stock had a fair market value of $15,500. Gift taxes of $1,000 were paid. In this case, the donee's basis for both gain and loss is $15,500 (the sum of the donor's basis plus the gift tax paid, but not in excess of the fair market value of the property on the date of the gift).

The basis rules for property acquired by gift after December 31, 1976, were modified insofar as the step-up in basis for gift taxes is concerned. The law now provides that the amount of gift tax to be added to appreciated property is calculated as follows:

$$\text{Addition to basis} = \text{Gift tax paid} \times \frac{\text{Net appreciation in gift property}}{\text{Total value of gift property}}$$

Net appreciation equals the excess of the fair market value of the gifted property on the date of the gift over the donor's basis at that time. To illustrate the step-up basis for gift taxes paid on gifts made after December 31, 1976, consider the following examples.

EXAMPLE 8-23

Taxpayer X purchased securities at a cost of $20,000 in 1970. This year, he gave the securities to a donee when their fair market value was $50,000. Total gift tax paid on the transfer was $10,000. The donee's basis for gain and loss is $26,000, computed as follows:

Donor's basis	$20,000
Gift tax adjustment:	
$10,000 x $\dfrac{\$50,000 - \$20,000}{\$50,000}$ =	6,000
Total	$\underline{\underline{\$26,000}}$

Under the rules in effect prior to January 1, 1977, the donee's basis would have been $30,000 ($20,000 cost + $10,000 taxes).

EXAMPLE 8-24

Taxpayer Y purchased securities at a cost of $20,000 in 1970. This year, he gave these securities to a donee when their fair market value was $15,000. Total gift tax paid on the transfer was $1,000. No portion of the gift tax can ever be added to the donee's basis because the fair market value on the date of the gift was less than the donor's cost. Thus, the donee's basis for gain is $20,000; the basis for loss is $15,000.

EXAMPLE 8-25

Taxpayer Z purchased securities at a cost of $48,000 in 1970. This year, she gave these securities to a donee when their fair market value was $50,000. Total gift tax paid on the transfer was $10,000. The donee's basis for gain and loss is $48,400, calculated as follows:

Donor's basis	$48,000
Gift tax adjustment:	
$10,000 x $\dfrac{\$50,000 - \$48,000}{\$50,000}$ =	400
Total	$\underline{\underline{\$48,400}}$

For gifts prior to January 1, 1977, the donee's basis for gain and loss would have been $50,000 (the $48,000 cost + $2,000 gift taxes).

What happens if a donor taxpayer dies shortly after giving property to another? Will the recipient determine the basis according to the gift rules or according to the inherited property rules? The answers to these two questions changed several times during the past few years. At the moment, gifts made to a person shortly before the donor's death are generally treated like any other gifts. Inherited property, regardless of how the decedent acquired the property, is generally treated like any other inherited property. One major exception to this rule exists for property given to a decedent within one year of his or her death *if* that same property is subsequently inherited back by the donor or the donor's spouse. In that event, the "heir" must carry over the donor's basis in spite of the fact that he or she technically inherited the property from the deceased donee. This rule eliminates tax benefits previously associated with carefully contrived deathbed giving.

——— CONCLUSION

In summary, the amount of gain or loss realized on the sale or exchange of property is the difference between the amount realized and the adjusted basis of the property on the date it is sold or exchanged. The amount realized is the sum of

1. Money received *plus*

2. Fair market value of other property received *plus*

3. Amount of debt transferred from the seller to the buyer.

The adjusted basis of property acquired by purchase generally is the

1. Cost of the property surrendered *plus*

2. Cost of capital improvements to that property *less*

3. Depreciation or ACRS deductions claimed on the property.

The adjusted basis of property acquired by inheritance or by gift is determined according to special rules explained above. The basis rules for properties acquired in a nontaxable exchange are explained in Chapter 17. Any recognized gains are included as part of gross income; losses recognized are sometimes (but not always) deductible. Because of these rules, any taxpayer engaged in property transactions generally must understand and apply the basis concept both in the determination of income and in the calculation of income taxes. The basis rules are particularly important and difficult to apply as they relate to investments in tax-conduit entities.

——— KEY POINTS TO REMEMBER

✓ The amount of gain or loss realized on the disposition of property is equal to the difference between the amount realized and the adjusted basis of the property given up.

✓ The amount realized is equal to the sum of (1) any cash received; (2) the fair market value of any noncash property received; and (3) the amount of debt relief obtained through the disposition of property.

✓ The adjusted basis of property is generally a measure of the taxpayer's unrecovered tax cost (or unrecovered capital investment) in a property.

✓ The original tax basis of a purchased property is equal to its cost. Cost allocations are required if multiple assets are acquired for one lump-sum purchase price.

✓ The original tax basis of an asset may have to be adjusted upward or downward due to events that transpire after its acquisition. Adjustments to the tax basis of investments in tax-conduit entities are both commonplace and complex.

✓ An investor in a tax-conduit entity generally cannot claim a tax deduction for any part of the loss recognized by the conduit entity to the extent that the loss exceeds the investor's adjusted tax basis in the entity.

✓ The tax basis of property acquired by inheritance or by gift is determined by special rules.

RECALL PROBLEMS

1. On August 10, Linn Berg, an airline pilot, sold 100 shares of Trimotor Aircraft Corporation stock (a C corporation) for $1,000. Determine the gross amount of capital gain or loss that Linn should report if

   a. He purchased the shares on February 15 for $800.

   b. He received the shares as a gift from his Uncle Jim on July 2 when their fair market value was $900. Assume that Jim purchased the shares for $300 in 1962 and that he paid no gift tax on this transfer.

   c. All facts in part b apply, except that Jim purchased the shares for $1,020 rather than for $300.

   d. He inherited the shares from his father, Charles, who died July 8 last year. Charles had purchased the shares for $300 in 1962. The fair market value of the shares on July 8 was $1,200. The executrix of Charles's estate elected to value all estate assets six months after Charles's death. On December 31, the shares had a fair market value of $900. On January 8 (this year), the shares had a fair market value of $880. The shares were distributed by the executrix to Linn on June 21, when they had a fair market value of $1,100.

2. Helen purchased a diamond for $20,000 on February 14. She sold this same diamond for $26,000 on July 4.

   a. What amount of gain did Helen realize on July 4?

   b. Must Helen recognize the gain realized on her income tax return if

     (1) She is a diamond dealer?

     (2) She is an occasional investor in diamonds?

     (3) She bought this diamond as a piece of personal jewelry?

3. On April 2, 19X1, CDE (an S corporation) purchased 1,000 shares of stock in QRS (a C corporation) as a temporary investment of excess cash for $60,000 (including the broker's fee of $600). QRS declared and paid a cash dividend of $2 per share on July 1, 19X1. On January 28, 19X2, QRS reported that it had made a profit of $10 per share during the prior year and declared and paid a cash dividend of $3 per share. On March 3, 19X2, CDE sold its 1,000 shares of QRS stock for $75,000 (after deducting a broker's fee of $750). What amount of gain or loss (if any) did CDE recognize because of its sale of the QRS stock on February 3, 19X3?

#1 #2

4. Several years ago Benita, Inc., acquired a future building site for $30,000 plus a 30-year 10% mortgage note for $220,000. Because of major changes in Benita Inc.'s business needs, management decided this year to give up its building plans and sell the land for $50,000. The buyer assumed the remaining $190,000 mortgage on the property. During the intervening years Benita, Inc., paid $170,000 interest on the mortgage plus $30,000 in property taxes. What amount of gain or loss (if any) must Benita, Inc., report because it sold the land this year?

#2

5. Determine the adjusted basis of a building purchased for $100,000 16 years ago. Taxpayer paid $20,000 down and signed an $80,000 12% note payable. To date, only $35,000 in principal has been paid on this $80,000 note. After acquiring the building, taxpayer incurred $10,000 in repairs (which were expenses) and made $25,000 worth of capital improvements. Taxpayer has claimed depreciation of $50,000 on the building since acquisition.

#3

6. On April 2, 19X1, Song Kim purchased 30% of the outstanding common stock of Freuds, Inc., an S corporation, for $50,000. On April 14, 19X1, Freuds, Inc., distributed $20,000 to its shareholders; Song Kim received $6,000 of the $20,000 distributed. On January 29, 19X2, Freuds, Inc., informed its shareholders that it would report a taxable income of $240,000 for calendar year 19X1. On April 14, 19X2, Freuds, Inc., distributed $80,000 to its shareholders; Song Kim received $24,000 of the $80,000 distributed. On January 31, 19X3, Freuds, Inc., informed its shareholders that it would report a loss of $100,000 for 19X2. On March 14, 19X3, Song Kim sold all of his stock in Freuds, Inc., for $60,000.

What amount of gain or loss, if any, must Song Kim report for 19X3 because he sold the Freuds, Inc., stock if, on January 30, 19X4, Freuds, Inc., reports

   a. A taxable income of $350,000 for 19X3?

   b. A tax loss of $150,000 for 19X3?

#3

7. On January 1, 19X1, Sue Baker purchased for $100,000 cash a 100% interest in an S corporation that reported the following losses and profits during the four (full) years that Sue owned it:

Year	(Loss)/Profit
19X1	($50,000)
19X2	(30,000)
19X3	20,000
19X4	60,000

Given only this information, what will Sue's adjusted tax basis be in this investment on January 1 of each year from 19X1 through 19X5?

8. Assume all facts as stated in problem 7, above, except that Sue paid only $70,000 for her 100% interest in this S corporation. Assuming that Sue works full time for the corporation, and assuming that none of the losses involved capital losses, answer the following questions:

#3

   a. What will Sue's adjusted tax basis be in this investment on January 1 of each year from 19X1 through 19X5?

#4

   b. What maximum amount of loss can Sue deduct (if she has income from other sources) in each of the years from 19X1 through 19X4, because of her ownership of this S corporation?

9. Sandra has owned 40% of the Sweat Shoppe, a partnership, for many years. The partnership's balance sheet at the beginning and the end of this year can be summarized as follows:

	Jan. 1	Dec. 1
Assets	$200,000	$230,000
Liabilities	120,000	160,000
Net worth	80,000	70,000

This partnership reported a loss of $10,000 for the current year. If the partners made no capital contribution during the year, and the partnership distributed no assets to the partners during the year, what amount of partnership loss (if any) may Sandra deduct this year if, at the start of this year, her adjusted basis in the partnership interest was zero *and* Sandra had carried forward (in a suspense account) nondeductible partnership losses from prior years in the amount of $6,000? Ignore any possible PAL and capital loss limitations.

10. Jim inherited four properties from his Aunt Zelda, who died on September 30. The executrix of Zelda's estate valued all properties on the date of death for estate tax purposes. Using the information below, determine Jim's tax basis in each property.

Property	Date Purchased by Zelda	Cost to Zelda	FMV on Sept. 30
Stock A	3/8/62	$10,000	$20,000
Bond B	6/22/68	20,000	10,000
Land	9/1/75	30,000	50,000
Oil painting	11/14/78	2,000	2,500

11. Assume that on February 14 a donee sold, under the alternative conditions detailed below, an investment property she had received as a gift on January 8 (of this year). Assume further that the donor had purchased the property on October 26, 1974. State the amount of capital gain or loss realized.

	Donor's Adjusted Basis	Gift Tax Paid by Donor	Value on Date of Gift	Amount Realized on Sale
a.	$11,000	$ 600	$12,000	$13,000
b.	11,000	1,200	12,000	13,000
c.	11,000	500	10,000	9,000
d.	11,000	500	10,000	12,000
e.	11,000	1,500	10,000	10,500

12. In the six cases that follow, a donee has received property as a gift and subsequently disposed of it through sale. For each case, compute the donee's gain on the subsequent sale if

a. The gifts were made in 1976.

b. The gifts were made today.

Case	Donor's Adjusted Basis	Fair Market Value at Date of Gift	Gift Tax Paid	Amount Realized
1	$10,000	$20,000	$1,000	$21,000
2	10,000	15,000	1,000	15,000
3	10,000	15,000	1,000	9,000
4	10,000	8,000	500	11,000
5	10,000	8,000	500	7,500
6	10,000	8,000	500	9,000

———— THOUGHT PROBLEMS

#1

1. Karen Dougherty purchased a new automobile for $15,000, paying $3,000 down and signing a 12%, 48-month note for the $12,000 balance. During the next several years, Karen's use of this car included 60% business use and 40% personal use. Karen claimed tax depreciation deductions totaling $7,000 for her business use of the car. She sold the car this year for $3,000 cash; the buyer also agreed to assume the $1,000 remaining balance on Karen's original $12,000 note. What amount of gain or loss (if any) should Karen report on her tax return this year because she sold this car? (Hint: The correct solution requires that you treat one car as two separate properties.)

#1

2. Following a recent divorce, Deborah Carr (age 40) began looking for ways to reduced her immediate monthly cash needs and to minimize the time-consuming aspects of home ownership. A realtor friend suggested that Deborah simply exchange the equity in her large home in the suburbs for clear title to a rental duplex (that would provide her with a $1,000 monthly income) and that she move into an $800 per month downtown apartment close to her job to save commuting costs. Because the current owner of the duplex is willing to assume the $120,000 outstanding mortgage on Deborah's home as part of this exchange, the net result should be a major reduction in Deborah's monthly cash requirements. If Deborah's adjusted basis in her home is $140,000 and the duplex has a fair market value of $100,000, how would this exchange affect Deborah's taxable income if no cash changes hands in the deal?

#1

3. Kim purchased a diamond for $20,000 on April 1. She sold this same diamond for $14,000 on November 23 (turkey day).

a. What amount of loss did Kim realize on November 23?

b. May Kim deduct the loss realized on her income tax return if:

(1) She is a diamond dealer?

(2) She is an occasional investor in diamonds?

(3) She bought this diamond as a piece of personal jewelry?

4. This spring Ed Brown purchased 40 acres of land immediately adjacent to the 120 acres that he had farmed for the past 23 years. The 40 acres cost Ed $80,000; the lawyer's fee for the title search added another $1,000. Ed paid the lawyer's bill immediately and also made a $10,000 down payment on the land. The $70,000 balance will be paid in equal monthly installments over the next 20 years with interest at 10%. At the end of the first year Ed had made payments totaling $7,500 on this note; $500 went toward a reduction of debt; the other $7,000 represented interest on the debt.

    During the summer Ed allowed a local builder to remove all of the small rocks lying on the surface of the 40 acres for $200 per truckload. The builder paid Ed $4,000 for the 20 loads that he removed and used in his building business.

    Thereafter Ed put a new fence around the 40 acres at a cost of $12,000. He intends to begin grazing cattle on this land in the near future.

    a. What is Ed's adjusted basis in the land today? Explain briefly any problems that you encountered in answering this question.

    b. Should the cost of the fence be treated as a separate asset (for example, land improvements) or simply be added to the cost of the land? Explain briefly.

    c. Do the monthly mortgage payments affect the adjusted basis of the land?

5. Assuming that money (that is, cash, whether in the form of coin, currency, or demand deposit) is property, why can a taxpayer virtually always acquire a second property for cash without recognizing gain (or loss) for tax purposes whereas making that same acquisition with any other (noncash) property typically triggers both the realization and the recognition of gain (or loss)? To help you understand and analyze this question, study the diagram below, assuming (1) that the fair market values of P_1 and P_2 are always equal and (2) that P_2 is *always* a property other than cash. Your task is to explain why you get a fundamentally different tax result if P_1 is (1) cash or (2) some property other than cash.

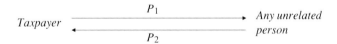

6. Jack and Sue—two single, calendar-year taxpayers—formed a partnership in January 19X1 with each contributing $50,000 cash. They used the cash to make a down payment on a small office building with a cost of $500,000. The balance was financed with a $400,000 mortgage for which Jack and Sue are personally liable. They agreed to share profits, losses, and capital equally. During 19X1 the partnership losses were $15,000. The mortgage balance (the partnership's only liability) at year end was $390,000. Jack and Sue both actively participated in the management of the office building.

    a. What is Jack's basis in the partnership at the end of 19X1? What effect will the partnership investment have on his personal tax return? Assume that Jack's adjusted gross income from all other sources is $90,000.

    b. Explain why this investment probably would not be made through an S corporation.

7. Trevor Farris owns 100% of the Farris Corporation, an S corporation. Trevor's original tax basis in his investment in Farris Corporation has been reduced to zero

by corporate losses recognized in prior years. Trevor expects the Farris Corporation to report another $20,000 this year.

   a. What might Trevor do before the end of the year if he wishes to deduct this year's $20,000 corporate loss on his personal tax return?

   b. Do you recommend that he take that action? Explain briefly.

8. Your grandmother, who is very ill and not expected to live much longer, still owns two investment properties that can be described as follows:

Property	Adjusted Basis	Fair Market Value
A	$ 50,000	$200,000
B	200,000	50,000

Earlier this year your grandmother sold a third investment property (Property C) on which she recognized a $200,000 long-term capital gain. What deathbed tax planning might you recommend to your grandmother under these circumstances? Explain your recommendation briefly.

9. What *new* opportunities for family tax planning would be created if Congress were to amend the extant Code to provide, in the future, that a donee would always take (as his or her adjusted basis) the donor's adjusted basis in any property transferred as a gift?

10. On July 22, 19X3, Aubrey gave 10,000 shares of ABC common stock to his mother, Angela, who was 96 years of age and very ill. Aubrey had purchased this stock in 1963 for $20,000; it had a fair market value of $200,000 on July 22, 19X3. On August 1, 19X3, Angela died. According to the terms of her will, all property was to pass from Angela to her only child, Aubrey. As sole heir, Aubrey received all of his mother's property (including the 10,000 shares of ABC stock) on March 3, 19X4. The fair market value of the ABC shares was $200,500 on August 1, 19X3; $199,000 on February 1, 19X4; and $200,100 on March 3, 19X4. Aubrey, who served as executor of his deceased mother's estate, did *not* elect to value his mother's property, for estate tax purposes, at the alternate valuation date. Given this information, what tax basis do you think Aubrey should have in the 10,000 shares of ABC stock? Explain your answer. (If your instructor specifically asks you to do so, see if you can locate any authoritative answer to this question in your tax library.)

CLASS PROJECTS

1. Divide the class into three groups of approximately equal size, with each group representing one of the groups described below.

   Group 1   Very wealthy individuals who have accumulated large amounts of property over long periods of time. Most of their property has a relatively low adjusted tax basis and a relatively high fair market value. This group has no special needs; hence it has no real reason to sell any of its accumulated property prior to death.

   Group 2   Individuals of *above average* wealth (but *not* "very wealthy" persons) who have accumulated some fair amounts of property over their working lives. Most of this property has a relatively low adjusted tax basis and a relatively high fair market value. This group will consume most of the property it has accumulated during their retirement years; a good part if it will go to pay medical bills and nursing home costs.

Group 3   Ordinary persons who have accumulated little or no property during their lifetime with the possible exception of a home in which they live. The home has appreciated in value but the owners plan to live in the home until their death. If need be, they will sell their home and move to a nursing home during their last few years.

Each group should think of as many reasons as they can to either retain or modify the current tax law relative to the basis of property received through inheritance. Have one spokesperson for each group summarize the ideas generated by their group. After each group has made its presentation, the class should vote on whether or not the present tax law, concerning the adjusted tax basis of inherited property, should be modified.

2. Undertake a field study to determine how much (or how little) taxpayers know about the adjusted tax basis of property they own. Have students interview individual taxpayers; some, employees of small CPA firms that do a lot of tax work for both individual and business taxpayers; and some, large corporations. As part of the interview attempt to review any records that the taxpayers may maintain concerning the adjusted tax basis of the most valuable three or four assets they may own. Based on their findings, students should report on how well (or how poorly) they think the U.S. income tax system works relative to the measurement of income from property transactions.

Part Three

THE INDIVIDUAL TAXPAYER

The mission of Part Three is to explain the tax problems that most frequently confront individual taxpayers. To accomplish this mission we provide four chapters with the following objectives:

CHAPTER 9:
INDIVIDUAL EXCLUSIONS AND ADJUSTED GROSS INCOME—to explain the differences between the tax formula for individual taxpayers and other taxable entities; to identify some of the more common items of income (broadly conceived) that are excluded from gross income by individual taxpayers as well as some of the more common items that are deductible in determining adjusted gross income.

> *"Another example . . . took place within the lifetime of many of us; the revolution of the personal income tax. It has made impossible such displays of ostentatious magnificence as Hearst's Casa Grande in St. Simeon; it has stimulated the creation of foundations and nonprofit institutions; it has reduced the differences between the standards of living of the various socioeconomic classes; it has brought about a clear-cut distinction between wages and take-home pay. And no amount of wishful thinking will ever bring us back to pre-income-tax days."*
>
> J. SAMUEL BOIS, THE ART OF AWARENESS,
> WM. C. BROWN COMPANY, 1966

CHAPTER 10:
DEDUCTIONS FROM AGI—to explain the determination of the standard deduction, itemized deductions, and personal and dependent exemptions.

CHAPTER 11:
CALCULATING THE INDIVIDUAL TAX LIABILITY—to explain calculation of the federal income tax for an individual taxpayer with emphasis on selection of the correct tax rate schedule, determination of marginal tax rates, and calculation of individual tax credits.

CHAPTER 12:
INCENTIVES FOR SAVING—to introduce various tax incentives for saving, particularly for retirement.

The art of taxation consists in so plucking the goose as to obtain the largest amount of feathers with the least amount of hissing.

JEAN BAPTIST COLBERT, FRENCH FINANCIAL MINISTER UNDER KING LOUIS XIV (1638–1715)

INDIVIDUAL EXCLUSIONS AND ADJUSTED GROSS INCOME

CHAPTER OBJECTIVES

In Chapter 9 you will learn to determine gross income and adjusted gross income for individual taxpayers.

LEARNING GOALS

After studying this chapter you should be able to

1 Describe some of the characteristics of typical individual taxpayers;

2 Explain the differences between the tax formula for individuals and other taxable entities;

3 Identify the more common items of income (broadly conceived) that are excluded from gross income by individual taxpayers; and

4 Identify the more common items that are deductible by individuals in determining adjusted gross income.

_____ AN OVERVIEW

In Part Three, we are concerned with the tax problems that most frequently confront individual taxpayers. These problems include the determination of which items of income can be excluded from gross income, which expenditures are deductible and how they are classified, and computation of the tax liability. Part Three concludes with a discussion of tax incentives for individual savings.

From the earliest days of the U.S. income tax, the law has designated individuals, corporations, and fiduciaries (estates and trusts) as taxpayers. The primary purpose of this chapter is to consider in some detail only those provisions that are unique to the determination of gross income and adjusted gross income for *individual* taxpayers. But first, it may be useful to learn more about the statistical profile of a typical individual taxpayer.

Goal #1
Describe some of the characteristics of typical individual taxpayers.

STATISTICAL PROFILE OF THE INDIVIDUAL TAXPAYER

Individuals in their role as taxpayers can be profiled in many different ways. To begin, an examination of income levels might help to define a typical individual taxpayer. Table 9-1 shows percentages of taxpayers who in 1989 had adjusted gross incomes at various levels. While the tax clients of professional accountants and attorneys are mostly drawn from individuals with an AGI of $50,000 or more, this group comprised less than 15% of all taxpayers in 1989. The stakes for these taxpayers are high, however; they paid about 63% of all federal income taxes in that year.

Income sources provide another way of describing taxpayers. Table 9-2 reveals that wages and salaries are by far the most important income source, accounting for 75.4% of AGI in 1989. "All other sources" includes a number of items such as business net income and losses, alimony, partnership gains and losses, rental income and losses, deductions for contributions to retirement plans, and so on. Obviously, the distribution of these sources varies greatly by income level. For example, capital gains are far more significant an income source to high-income than low-income taxpayers. In 1991, 73% of all capital gains were earned by taxpayers with AGIs in excess of $100,000.

A few other descriptive statistics will complete our profile of the typical individual taxpayer. In 1989, only 29% of all taxpayers itemized their deductions, down from 40% in 1986. Approximately 66% of all taxpayers filed Form 1040 (the so-called long form) tax returns; about 18% filed Form 1040-A, and the remainder filed Form

TABLE 9-1

Taxpayers Classified by AGI Level and Percentage of Total Taxes Paid in 1989

AGI	Number of Returns as % of Total	Income Tax Paid as % of Total
< $15,000	42.1%	3.8%
$ 15– 30,000	25.5	12.9
30– 50,000	18.3	20.8
50– 75,000	8.9	18.9
75–100,000	2.6	9.4
100+	2.6	34.2

Source: *Statistics of Income Bulletin,* Summer 1991.

Salaries and wages	75.4%
Interest received	6.7
Dividends in AGI	2.5
Capital gains and losses	4.4
Pensions and annuities	4.5
All other sources and deductions	6.5

Source: *Statistics of Income Bulletin*, Summer 1991.

TABLE 9-2

Income Sources as Percent of AGI—1989

1040-EZ. The last two are both returns that do not permit itemizing. The average age of 1040 filers is estimated at 46.5; of 1040-A filers, 33.4; and 1040-EZ filers, 23.5.[1] Finally, it is estimated that 49% of all taxpayers used paid professional preparers to complete their tax returns in 1990.

Many of the issues discussed in this and the next three chapters are not characteristic of typical taxpayers but are probably more characteristic of taxpayers who hire tax professionals to help with their returns. Nonetheless, the profile provided should help the new student of taxation to put some of the items discussed into perspective.

THE TAX FORMULA REVISED

An expanded version of the formula presented earlier can be used to calculate the tax liability for an individual. Some key terms—such as income, exclusions, deductions, and credits—were discussed at length in earlier chapters, but the definitions of other new terms in this formula are critical to an understanding of the income tax law as it relates to individuals.

With the exception of the multiplication of the tax rates by taxable income to obtain the gross tax, note that every arithmetic operation in this formula is a subtraction. The order of these subtractions is very important. The intermediate remainders—gross income and adjusted gross income—must be correctly calculated before several critical decisions are made about the amount of tax due the government.

Goal #2
Explain the differences between the tax formula for individuals and other taxable entitites.

```
  Income broadly conceived
– Exclusions
= Gross income
– Deductions for adjusted gross income (AGI)
= Adjusted gross income
– Deductions from adjusted gross income
  (the larger of a standard deduction or itemized deductions)
– Personal and dependent exemptions
= Taxable income
x Applicable tax rate(s)
= Gross tax
– Tax credits and prepayments
= Net tax payable
```

1 Bryan Musselman and Paul Grayson, "Individual Income Tax Return, 1983: A Demographic Snapshot." *Statistics of Income Bulletin*, Summer 1986, pp. 57–62.

For the remainder of this chapter we will examine the first two subtractions—exclusions from gross income and deductions for AGI. In particular, we consider exclusions relevant *only* to individual taxpayers. The concept of adjusted gross income applies *only* to individual taxpayers, and therefore deductions for AGI apply *only* to individual taxpayers.

Goal #3
Identify the more common items of income that can be excluded from gross income by individual taxpayers.

EXCLUSIONS FOR INDIVIDUAL TAXPAYERS

Recall that gross income is income broadly conceived after subtracting all allowed exclusions. The correct definition of gross income is important because, among other things, this amount determines which individuals must file income tax returns. The precise amounts of gross income an individual must have before he or she is required to file a return are detailed in Chapter 11. The amount of gross income is also one of the tests used to determine who may be claimed as a dependent, a detail discussed in Chapter 10.

In Chapter 4 we considered exclusions from gross income that can apply to all taxpayers—individuals, corporations, or fiduciaries. These generic exclusions include income from discharge of indebtedness, gifts and inheritances, proceeds of life insurance policies, compensation for business injuries, and tax-exempt interest. In this chapter we will review the more important exclusions that apply only to individual taxpayers.

EXCLUSIONS RELATED TO ILLNESS AND PERSONAL INJURY

Sections 104 (compensation for injuries or sickness), 105 (medical reimbursements), and 106 (health insurance premiums) are important exclusions for individual taxpayers. The complexity of these three provisions demands examination of each with care. To do that, let us proceed in reverse order because (1) the last general rule (that is, Sec. 106) is the simplest, and (2) the other two general rules often involve payments that derive from (and may be influenced by) the plans described in Sec. 106.

Health Insurance Premiums

Section 106 excludes from an employee's gross income the value of any contributions made by the employer to accident or health plans designed to compensate the taxpayer, spouse, or dependents for personal injuries or sickness. Note that Sec. 106 is *not* concerned with the amount *received* by an employee as compensation for injuries or sickness. Rather, it excludes from income either (1) the cost of the premiums paid by the employer to purchase insurance or (2) the employer's contributions to a fund that may later provide for payments to the employee.

EXAMPLE 9-1

James Wilson's employer purchased a health and accident insurance policy that reimburses James and other employees for expenses related to injury or illness. During the tax year, the employer paid a total of $1,200 of premiums on the policy covering James and his family. This $1,200 can be excluded from James's gross income.

Medical Reimbursements

Section 105 excludes some, but not all, amounts received by an employee under an accident and health plan. The following receipts can be excluded:

1. Amounts that "constitute payment for the permanent loss of use of a member or function of the body, or the permanent disfigurement of the taxpayer, his spouse, or a dependent."[2]

2. Amounts that are "computed with reference to the nature of the injury without regard to the period the employee is absent from work."[3]

3. Amounts paid "directly or indirectly to the taxpayer to reimburse the taxpayer for expenses incurred by him for the medical care (as defined in Sec. 213(d)) of the taxpayer, his wife, and dependents."[4]

The last exclusion does *not* apply, however, if the taxpayer receives the medical expense reimbursement in a year following a year in which he or she claimed a medical expense deduction for the item now being reimbursed, to the extent the taxpayer benefited from the earlier deduction.

EXAMPLE 9-2

Maria incurred and paid medical expenses of $10,000 in 19X1. These expenses were reimbursed in 19X1 under an accident and health plan. Maria may exclude the $10,000 reimbursement from gross income. Of course, she cannot claim a medical expense deduction for the amounts reimbursed.

EXAMPLE 9-3

Maria incurred and paid medical expenses of $10,000 in 19X1. She claimed a $6,000 medical expense deduction in 19X1 (4,000 was disallowed by a floor which is explained in Chapter 10). In 19X2 Maria received a $10,000 reimbursement under an accident and health plan for the expenses she incurred in 19X1. She must include $6,000 of the reimbursement in 19X2 gross income; the other $4,000 may be excluded since she received no tax benefit from it in 19X1.

Any amounts received under an accident and health plan, for reasons *other than* the three explicitly stated above, can *not* be excluded from gross income if (1) the premiums on the plan were paid by the employer *and* (2) those premiums were not taxed to the employee (by operation of Sec. 106, discussed above).

EXAMPLE 9-4

Alfred received $9,000 in sick pay under an accident and health plan provided by his employer. Alfred excluded the cost of this insurance plan from his gross income per Sec. 106. The $9,000 payment can *not* be excluded from gross income by Alfred because it is not one of the three items listed above.

---

2 Sec. 105(c)(1).

3 Sec. 106(c)(2).

4 Sec. 105(b).

Compensation for Injuries or Sickness

Section 104 excludes from gross income certain other payments received in compensation for injury or sickness. This list includes

1. Payments "received under workmen's compensation acts as compensation for personal injury or sickness."[5]

2. Payments for "damages received (whether by suit or by agreement and whether as lump sums or as periodic payments) on account of personal injury or sickness."[6]

3. Payments "received through accident or health insurance for personal injuries or sickness" *unless*

   a. paid directly by the employer, or

   b. paid by an insurance company whose premiums were paid by the employer and excluded (under Sec. 106) from the gross income of the employee.[7]

4. Payments received as a pension or other allowance "for personal injuries or sickness resulting from active service in the armed forces" or certain other governmental service.[8]

5. Payments received by government employees for injuries received as a direct result of designated terrorist attacks outside the United States.[9]

Although some overlap exists between item 3 and Sec. 105(b) (described earlier), the former provision can be important to many taxpayers. It allows a taxpayer to exclude from gross income payments received as compensation for injuries or sickness (disability income) under an accident or health insurance plan purchased directly by the taxpayer.

EXAMPLE 9-5

Shao received $15,000 this year as disability income under an insurance plan for which she had paid the premiums. Shao may exclude the $15,000 from gross income. Had her employer paid the premiums under a plan covered by Sec. 106, Shao would be required to include the $15,000 in gross income.

Perhaps the least clear of the exclusions provided by Sec. 104 is item 2, payments for damages received "on account of personal injury or sickness." Traditionally, courts have held that the correct tax treatment of a recovery should be determined by the purpose of the award. That is, an award for lost income should be taxed in the same way as the income replaced, whereas payment for "pain and suffering" would be excluded from gross income as damages received for personal injury. Several recent court cases have addressed the issue of whether recovery for nonphysical personal injuries (libelous statements, for example) may be excluded from gross

---

5 Sec. 104(a)(1).

6 Sec. 104(a)(2).

7 Sec. 104(a)(3).

8 Sec. 104(a)(4).

9 Sec. 104(a)(5).

income as damages for personal injury.[10] In general, the answer has been yes, although some of these cases are complicated by failure of the parties to specify what the payments are for.

EXCLUSIONS RELATED TO DEATH

A number of items of income related to a person's death may be excluded from gross income. As you learned in Chapter 4, proceeds of life-insurance policies generally may be excluded from the gross income of the recipient. In this chapter, we address two additional items that apply only to individual taxpayers.

Employer Paid Premiums on Group-Term Life Insurance

Section 79 provides that premiums paid by an employer for **group-term life insurance**—up to $50,000 face amount of insurance per employee—may be excluded from the employee's income, although premiums paid by the employer on **whole-life insurance** for either an individual or group, as well as premiums paid on individual term policies, are taxable to the employee. If an employee is covered by group-term life insurance with a face value greater than $50,000, the premium applicable to the excess is taxable to the employee.

Death Benefits Paid by Employer

In addition to life-insurance benefits, certain other proceeds paid to beneficiaries because of an employee's death are nontaxable. Section 101(b) provides that beneficiaries of a decedent employee may exclude up to $5,000 of employee death benefits paid by the decedent's employer, or employers, if the payments are made solely on account of death (and not as payment for services performed prior to death). When the decedent has more than one beneficiary who receives payments, the exclusion is prorated among the beneficiaries in proportion to the amount that each receives.

> Term life insurance provides coverage for only a stipulated period of time. Coverage with **group-term life insurance** lasts only as long as the insured is a member of the group.
>
> **Whole-life insurance** provides coverage until the insured dies. Generally, a whole life policy builds cash surrender value.
>
> **Employee death benefits** are amounts paid to a deceased employee's beneficiaries solely on account of the employee's death.

EXAMPLE 9-6

Smith, a long-term employee, dies. Because of his death, the employer makes payments of $8,000 to Smith's widow and $4,000 to each of his two children. The beneficiaries may exclude a total of $5,000, divided among them as follows:

Wife: $\frac{\$8,000}{\$16,000}$ x $5,000 = $2,500

Each child: $\frac{\$4,000}{\$16,000}$ x $5,000 = $1,250

Thus, the widow would include in her taxable income $5,500 of the amount received; each child would include $2,750.

This provision was first enacted in 1951 and was intended to "eliminate the 'hardship' resulting from the fact that the exclusion for death benefits under the then existing law was limited to life insurance."[11] In contrast, the president's 1985 tax

10 See, for example, *Roemer v. Commissioner*, 716 F.2d 693 (CA-9, 1986).

11 Senate Report 781, 82d Congress, 1st Sess.

reform proposal argued that the provision should be repealed because it is an alternative form of employee compensation that is unavailable to many taxpayers such as self-employed individuals. In spite of this recommendation, the provision remains in the law.

EXCLUSIONS RELATED TO AGE—SOCIAL SECURITY BENEFITS

Our tax laws have been freely amended to reflect a growing concern about the social and economic needs of the aged. For example, the taxpayer who is 65 or older is allowed an increased standard deduction. The credit for the elderly, discussed in Chapter 11, permits some taxpayers who are 65 or older to reduce their tax bills. And Sec. 121 allows persons 55 or older to exclude from gross income up to $125,000 of the gain realized on the sale of a personal residence. This provision is examined in detail in Chapter 17.

Prior to 1983, Social Security benefits, which primarily affect older taxpayers, were exempt from taxation as a result of administrative decisions. Today, however, the recipient must include in gross income the lesser of

1. One-half of any Social Security benefits received during the year, or

2. One-half of the amount by which the sum of one-half of Social Security benefits received during the year plus the "modified adjusted gross income" exceeds the "base amount."

Modified adjusted gross income is defined as (1) adjusted gross income before considering Social Security benefits and before the exclusion for U.S. citizens living abroad, plus (2) tax-exempt interest. (*Adjusted gross income* is defined later in this chapter.)

The base amount is $32,000 for a married couple filing jointly; zero for a married person filing a separate return if the married person did not live apart from his or her spouse for the entire year; and $25,000 for a single person or married person filing a single return who lived apart from the spouse for the entire year.

The end result of these complicated rules is that higher income recipients of Social Security benefits may be required to pay tax on as much as one-half of their benefits.

EXAMPLE 9-7

During 19X1 Henry and Susan filed a joint return. During the year they received tax-exempt interest of $4,000 and had adjusted gross income of $26,500 from Susan's salary. Henry was retired and received Social Security benefits of $4,200 during the year. The taxable amount of Social Security benefits is $300.

1.	One-half Social Security benefits	$ 2,100
2.	One-half the sum of one-half of Social Security benefits and modified AGI over the base amount:	
	One-half Social Security benefits	$ 2,100
	AGI from salary	26,500
	Tax-exempt interest	4,000
	Total	$ 32,600
	Less base amount	32,000
	Excess	$ 600
	One-half the excess	$ 300

EXCLUSIONS RELATED TO DOUBLE TAXATION

Several provisions of the law stem from the idea that income should be taxed only once to the person earning it. Prior to 1987, for example, the double taxation of corporate dividends was partially mitigated by a small exclusion allowed individual taxpayers. As discussed in Chapter 4, gifts and inheritances are excluded from the gross income of the recipient by Sec. 102.

Prizes and Awards

Before 1987, certain prizes and awards received for "religious, charitable, scientific, educational, artistic, literary, or civic achievement"[12] were excluded from gross income, provided the recipient was not required to take action in order to receive the award and was not required to perform future services. For years after 1986, this exclusion applies only if the recipient assigns the award to a recognized charity. A taxpayer who receives a Pulitzer Prize, for example, has no gross income if he assigns the award to a charity. Naturally, he gets no charitable deduction—the income is never his (included) to give away. Except for prizes and awards that meet the conditions just mentioned, and certain nominal awards received from employers, all other prizes and awards must be included in gross income at cash or fair market value.

The Tax Reform Act of 1986 created arbitrary, specific rules governing the treatment of employee awards that can be deducted by the employer and excluded from the gross income of the employee. To be excluded (and deducted), an employee achievement award must be based on either the length of service or safety achievements; it must also be part of a meaningful presentation. The dollar limit for an employee achievement award is $400 per year for any employee, unless the award is from a "qualified plan," in which case the limit is increased to $1,600 per year for an employee. A qualified plan is any written plan, that does not discriminate in favor of highly paid employees, if the average award per year per employee does not exceed $400. Awards in excess of these dollar limits are gross income to the recipient and cannot be deducted by the employer. Business gifts costing up to $25 per recipient per year may be deducted by the giver and excluded from gross income by the recipient.[13] Any other "gifts" from an employer to an employee are gross income to the employee.

EXCLUSIONS RELATED TO EDUCATION

Scholarships and Fellowships

One exclusion of special interest to students is that of scholarships and fellowships under Sec. 117. Generally, if a college student who is a candidate for a degree receives an award that does not require him or her to perform duties such as teaching classes or grading papers, the scholarship is not included in the student's gross income to the extent the scholarship is used to pay for tuition and books, fees, supplies, and equipment required by the course of instruction. (Prior to 1987, the exclusion covered the entire scholarship, including amounts for room, board, and other living costs.) Degree candidates can exclude scholarships from gross income even when the scholarship is paid by a corporation or individual not related to the educational institution in which the student is enrolled, provided the payment is not compensation for past or future services. Fellowships received by a taxpayer who is not a candidate for a degree are included in gross income.

---

12 Sec. 74(b).

13 Sec. 274(b)(1).

Educational Assistance Plans

Under Sec. 127, payments made by an employer on behalf of an employee for such costs as tuition and books may be excluded by the employee if made under a nondiscriminatory educational assistance program. Because of budget deficit considerations, this provision recently has been extended (sometimes retroactively) on a year-to-year basis. The current provision will expire on June 30, 1992, if not extended again. The maximum amount that can be excluded is limited to $5,250 per employee per year.

If an employer pays for an employee's educational expenses, and the employer does not have an educational assistance plan, the employee must report the payments as gross income. Individuals may be able to deduct some education expenses as explained in Chapter 10.

EXCLUSIONS RELATED TO EMPLOYMENT

Employer-provided fringe benefits are an important, and tax-free, part of most worker's compensation packages. Fringe benefits generally are excluded from the federal income tax base, the Social Security tax base, and state and local income tax bases—all at an estimated cost to the government in lost revenue of over $100 billion per year.[14] Several important fringe benefits have already been discussed. Here we will consider employer-provided meals and lodging, various other fringe benefits, and income earned abroad.

Employer-Provided Meals and Lodging

Certain forms of compensation are tax-free on the basis that they are "for the convenience of the employer." For example, Sec. 119 excludes the value of meals furnished by an employer to an employee for a "substantial noncompensatory" business reason unless the employee has an option to take cash instead. Under this rule, meals provided to food-service employees generally have been excluded, even though meals are consumed before or after duty hours. Cash allowances in lieu of meals generally are taxable. For example, in a decision involving New Jersey state troopers who were given a mid-shift meal allowance, and were permitted to eat wherever they desired as long as they remained on call in their assigned duty area, the Supreme Court held that the meal allowances were compensation, in part at least, because the meals were not served on the employer's premises.[15] Similarly, the value of lodging provided to an employee is excluded under Sec. 119 only if the employee must accept the lodging on the employer's premises to perform his or her duties properly.

If the exclusion for meals or lodging does not apply, an employee usually must include the fair value of the service received as gross income. The Code contains two exceptions to this general rule. The first exception under Sec. 119(d) provides a special rule for faculty members who are given on-campus lodging as part of their compensation. Although the excess of the fair rental value over the rent paid must be included in gross income, the fair rental value is limited to 5% of the appraised value of the

---

14 Robert Turner, "Fringe Benefits: Should We Milk This Sacred Cow?" *National Tax Journal*, September 1989, pp. 293–300.

15 *Kowalski*, 434 US 77 (1977). The status of "supper money" paid to employees who work overtime is uncertain despite the decision in *Kowalski*.

lodging provided. The second exception provides that employees may exclude from gross income any cost savings gained by eating at food facilities operated by their employer, on or near the employer's premises, so long as the revenues from the activity cover the cost.

Other Fringe Benefits

Section 125 provides for the creation of a *cafeteria plan* under which employees may choose between tax-free and taxable benefits such as cash or property. Expenditures from a cafeteria plan for such benefits as health insurance premiums, premiums on group-term life insurance up to $50,000 in coverage, and group legal services can be excluded from the employee's gross income, as long as the plan does not discriminate in favor of highly compensated employees. Section 125 provides an exception to the constructive receipt rules that normally would apply if an employee could choose between taxable and tax-free benefits. For example, without a nondiscriminatory cafeteria plan if an employe were allowed to select either $600 cash or health insurance coverage costing $600, the $600 value would be taxable under the constructive receipt doctrine even if the employee choose the insurance plan. However, if the same choice were made under a nondiscriminatory cafeteria plan, the employee could exclude the $600 value of the insurance coverage. Of course, the employee would be taxed in either case if $600 cash were selected.

Under Sec. 129 the value of child or dependent care, provided by an employer under a written nondiscriminatory plan, generally is not included in the employee's gross income. For an unmarried taxpayer, the exclusion cannot exceed the amount of the employee's earned income for the year. In the case of married employees, the limitation is based on the earned income of the spouse with the lower earned income. If a spouse is either incapacitated or is a student, earned income is imputed to that spouse at the rate of $200 per month if one qualifying dependent is involved, or $400 per month if more than one qualifying dependent is involved. The maximum amount excluded from gross income for care of dependents is limited to $5,000 per year.

Section 132 provides for exclusion from gross income of no-additional cost fringe benefits (for example, free tickets for airline employees); qualified employee discounts; working condition fringes (items that would be deductible if the employee paid for them, such as uniforms); and *de minimis* fringes (property or service the value of which is "so small as to make the account for it unreasonable or administratively impracticable"). Other excludable fringe benefits specifically mentioned in Sec. 132 are on-premise athletic facilities for employees and their families and free on-premise parking.

Income Earned Abroad

United States citizens are generally taxed on their worldwide income. A foreign government may also levy a tax on a U.S. citizen's income, particularly on income derived from sources within the country of residence. An individual's income may thus be taxed by two governments. The U.S. tax law contains three major provisions aimed at reducing the potential impact of double taxation:

1. Our government has entered into tax treaties with many foreign countries. Various provisions of these treaties are aimed at eliminating or mitigating double taxation.

2. The foreign tax credit, briefly descried in Chapter 11, may be applied against the U.S. tax.

3. As an alternative to the foreign tax credit, a U.S. citizen who is a bona fide resident of a foreign country throughout a taxable year, or who is absent from the United States for a period of 330 days out of 12 consecutive months, may exclude his or her foreign *earned* income up to a maximum of $70,000 per year. An individual who qualifies for the foreign earned income exclusion also may receive tax benefits for excess housing costs incurred while living abroad.

Only income earned from personal services abroad, other than as an employee of the U.S. government or its agencies, qualify for the exclusion. Distribution of corporate earnings do not qualify.

The exclusion of foreign earned income is based partly on the premise that Americans living abroad do not benefit from services and facilities provided by the federal government within the United States; therefore, they should be excused from paying a part of the cost of these services. Other factors that may explain the exclusion are the benefits of international trade and the tendency of Americans working abroad to think and buy American goods.

Payments to Members of Armed Forces and to Veterans

Although regular pay for members of the armed forces is taxable, certain benefits and allowances to service personnel and their dependents may be excluded. For example, the value of living quarters provided to a person in the military service (or the cash payment made to him or her in lieu of quarters) is excluded from gross income. The basic quarters allowance for military dependents can also be excluded. Similarly, the value of any military subsistence allowance (or cash in lieu of subsistence) is not taxable. Uniform and equipment allowances are likewise excluded.

Former military service personnel may also receive certain tax breaks. The mustering-out pay on termination of service is tax exempt. Although pensions paid to military retirees who retire because of length of service are taxable, pensions and other allowances *based on personal injury or sickness resulting from active duty* are exempt. Under Sec. 104, personnel who entered service after September 24, 1975, may exclude these disability pensions only if the benefits are based on a *combat-related injury*. Payments made for education and training (the GI bill) are excluded, as are bonus payments received by veterans from state governments.

To summarize, the first step in the calculation of an individual taxpayer's federal income tax liability is the separation of exclusions from other items of gross income. Once all items of gross income have been identified and quantified, the second step for individual taxpayers is the identification and measurement of all deductions *for* adjusted gross income.

Goal #4
Identify the more common items deductible by individuals in determining AGI.

Adjusted gross income (AGI) is gross income less the deductions specified in Sec. 62.

ADJUSTED GROSS INCOME DEFINED

An important yet troublesome calculation in the tax formula for individuals is that of adjusted gross income (commonly abbreviated AGI). Note from the formula on page 303 that the deductions allowed individuals are divided into two classes—deductions *for* AGI and deductions *from* AGI. The proper classification of deductions is important because, for many taxpayers, the actual amount of the deductions *from* AGI is based in part on the amount of AGI. For example, medical expenses, which are deducted from AGI, can be deducted only to the extent they exceed 7 ½% of AGI.

The term **adjusted gross income** is explicitly defined in Sec. 62, titled Adjusted Gross Income Defined. This section is used for definitional purposes only. Determining whether or not a given expenditure is deductible must be based on the rules and concepts discussed in Chapter 5. Section 62 simply tells the taxpayer whether or not any deductible item can be deducted in the determination of AGI. Thirteen deductions are listed in Sec. 62, which is partially reproduced here:

Sec. 62 Adjusted Gross Income Defined.

For purposes of this subtitle, the term "adjusted gross income" means, in the case of an individual, gross income minus the following deductions:

(1) Trade and business deductions.—The deductions allowed by this chapter (other than by part VII of this subchapter) which are attributable to a trade or business carried on by the taxpayer, if such trade or business does not consist of the performance of services by the taxpayer as an employee.

(2) Certain Trade and Business Deductions of Employees—

    (A) Reimbursed Expenses of Employees.—The deductions allowed by part VI (sec. 161 and following) which consist of expenses paid or incurred by the taxpayer, in connection with the performance by him of services as an employee, under a reimbursement or other expense allowance arrangement with his employer.

    (B) Certain expenses of Performing Artists.—The deductions allowed by section 162 which consist of expenses paid or incurred by a qualified performing artist in connection with the performances by him of services in the performing arts as an employee.

(3) Losses from Sale or Exchange of Property.—The deductions allowed by part VI (sec. 161 and following) as losses from the sale or exchange of property.

(4) Deductions Attributable to Rents and Royalties.—The deductions allowed by part VI (sec. 61 and following), by section 212 (relating to expenses for production of income), and by section 611 (relating to depletion) which are attributable to property held for the production of rents and royalties.

(5) Certain Deductions of Life Tenants and Income Beneficiaries of Property—In the case of a life tenant of property, or an income beneficiary of property held in trust, or an heir, legatee, or devisee of an estate, the deduction for depreciation allowed by section 167 and the deduction allowed by section 611.

(6) Pension, Profit-Sharing and Annuity Plans of Self-Employed Individuals.—In the case of an individual who is an employee within the meaning of section 401(c)(1), the deduction allowed by section 404.

(7) Retirement Savings.—The deduction allowed by section 219 (relating to deduction for certain retirement savings).

(8) Certain Portion of Lump-Sum Distributions from Pension Plans Taxed Under Section 402(e).—The deduction allowed by section 402(e).

(9) Penalties Forfeited Because of Premature Withdrawal of Funds from Time Savings Accounts or Deposits.—. . .

(10) Alimony.—The deduction allowed by section 215.

(11) Reforestation Expenses.—The deduction allowed by section 194.

(12) Certain Required Repayments of Supplemental Unemployment Compensation Benefits.—. . .

(13) Jury Duty Pay Remitted to Employer.—. . .

By omission, Sec. 62 also defines deductions *from* AGI. Any allowable deduction not specifically listed in Sec. 62 is a deduction from AGI. Of the thirteen deductions for AGI identified in Sec. 62, several deserve further attention because of the large number of affected taxpayers.

DEDUCTIONS RELATED TO THE CONDUCT OF A TRADE OR BUSINESS

The tests applied to determine if an activity constitutes a trade or business were discussed in Chapter 5. Recall also that the passive activity loss rules may limit the deductibility of losses from business activities in which the taxpayer does not materially participate. Thus Sec. 62(1), which identifies expenses incurred in a trade or business as deductions for AGI, assumes (1) that the business is an active trade or business, and (2) the passive activity rules permit deduction.

The Tax Reform Act of 1986 added Sec. 162(m), which permits self-employed individuals to deduct 25% of medical insurance premiums paid for the taxpayer and family as deductions for AGI. The amount deducted cannot exceed the taxpayer's earned income from self-employment. Obviously, these amounts cannot also be counted as medical expenses for purposes of determining the taxpayer's deductions from AGI.

Section 164(f), another provision affecting self-employed individuals, allows deduction of one-half of Social Security self-employment taxes. This deduction is designed to put self-employed individuals on a par with employees, for whom one-half the Social Security tax is paid by the employer and not taxed to the employee. The deductible amount is treated as attributable to a trade or business and is therefore a deduction for AGI.

TRADE OR BUSINESS EXPENSES OF EMPLOYEES

As discussed in Chapter 5, certain expenses of employees are allowed as deductions. Only *reimbursed* employee business expenses (unless the employee is a qualified performing artist) are allowed as deduction *for* AGI. All other employee business expenses must be deducted as itemized deductions subject to special limitations discussed in Chapter 10.

EXAMPLE 9-8

> Jan, a CPA who is a sole practitioner, attends a seminar on recent tax developments and incurs the following expenses: registration fee, $105, and transportation, $75. As a sole practitioner, Jan may deduct both of these expenditures *for* AGI because they are trade or business expenses of a self-employed individual.

EXAMPLE 9-9

> Harry, a CPA who is an employee of a large accounting firm, attended the same seminar as Jan and incurred the same expenses. Harry is reimbursed by his employer for the registration fee but not the transportation cost. The registration fee is a deduction *for* AGI whereas the transportation cost is a deduction *from* AGI. The reimbursement is part of Harry's gross income.

LOSSES FROM SALE OR EXCHANGE OF PROPERTY

Section 62(3) refers to the deduction of losses from the *sale or exchange* of property as authorized by Sec. 161 and following. These sections include Sec. 165(c), which limits an individual's losses to (1) those incurred in a trade or business; (2) those from transactions entered into for profit; and (3) purely personal losses arising from theft or casualty.

Since losses of personal-use property arising from a theft or casualty are not the result of a sale or exchange, they generally would not be treated as deductions for AGI under Sec. 62(3). Personal casualty and theft losses, however, may be treated as deductions for AGI (as capital losses) *if* personal casualty gains exceed personal casualty losses. In this situation, all such gains and losses are treated as gains and losses from the sale or exchange of capital assets. *If*, however, personal casualty losses exceed personal casualty gains, then all such losses are treated as deductions *from* AGI, and are subject to the special limits described in the next chapter.

DEDUCTIONS RELATED TO TRANSACTIONS ENTERED INTO FOR PROFIT

A confusing group of deductions are those related to transactions entered into for profit. The deductions authorized by Sec. 212, are those *not* related to a trade or business but which are expenses for the production of income; for the maintenance of income-producing property; and for the determination of a tax liability. The most common transactions in this category involve investments in securities and in unimproved land held for speculation. The distinction between an activity that constitutes a trade or business, as opposed to a transaction entered into for profit, often is a very thin line. This distinction is especially difficult to make for many rental activities. Fortunately, we do not have to reach a decision on the trade or business versus profit-motivated rental activities for purposes of classifying deductions. Section 62(4) provides that all (allowable) deductions related to the production of rents and royalties are deductions for AGI. With this exception, all other deductions authorized by Sec. 212, are deductions from AGI. Examples include the amounts paid for subscriptions to investment services, technical publications, and fees paid to tax consultants.

ALIMONY PAYMENTS

A taxpayer may deduct for AGI amounts paid as alimony. This deduction is supported on two grounds. First, alimony payments may be considered merely a means of dividing income between two taxpayers. Second, they may be considered in the nature of extraordinary, unavoidable expenses that significantly affect the taxpayer's ability to pay income taxes, similar to casualty losses and medical expenses. The major tax controversy surrounding payments between the parties to a divorce is the distinction between payments that represent a sharing of income and those that are property settlements. If a payment is classified as a sharing of income (alimony), it is deductible by the person making the payment and included in the gross income of the recipient. On the other hand, property settlements are neither deductible by the payer nor taxable to the recipient. Likewise, child support payments are neither deductible by the payer nor taxable to the recipient.

Current rules state that, in general, alimony includes only cash payments that the divorce or separation agreement does not specify for something else (such as property settlement or child support). In some cases, the parties may be tempted to disguise property settlements as alimony, especially if the person making the payment is in a higher tax bracket than the recipient. A complex set of recapture rules is designed to prevent so-called front loading of property settlements disguised as alimony during the first three post-separation years. Calculation of recaptured alimony occurs in the third post-separation year. In that third year any amounts determined to have been property settlements as a result of this calculation must be added to the gross income of the person who paid and deducted them in a prior year. They are also treated as deductions for AGI in that same year by the recipient who had previously reported them as income. Any payments that will (per the terms of the divorce or separation agreement) change in amount because of a contingency relating to a child are automatically classified as child support payments. For example, if a divorce decree stipulates that a spouse's payment will decrease by $100 per month when a child reaches age 18, $100 of each monthly payment made prior to that date will not be treated as alimony.

EXAMPLE 9-10

Alma and Charles were divorced this year. They agreed that Charles would pay Alma alimony of $1,000 per month for two years and child support payments of $500 per month until their child reached age 18. These payments began in August and continued through December. In addition, Alma received a property settlement of $30,000. Charles may deduct the $5,000 of alimony payments as a deduction for AGI (and Alma must report $5,000 of income). None of the other payments will result in a deduction to Charles or income to Alma.

Given these general rules, it is easy to understand why the definition of alimony has often been a source of conflict between the IRS and taxpayers and between former spouses.

CONTRIBUTIONS TO RETIREMENT PLANS

Contributions to certain retirement plans, especially Individual Retirement Plans (IRAs) and Keogh plans for self-employed individuals are important deductions *for* AGI. They are discussed in some detail in Chapter 12.

Although Sec. 62 includes several other deductions as deductions for AGI, those deductions are of limited interest to most individuals. Consequently, we will not discuss them here.

——— KEY POINTS TO REMEMBER

✓ Many of the provisions considered in this and the following two chapters apply to a very small percentage of all taxpayers.

✓ A number of exclusions from gross income apply only to individual taxpayers. Gross income is an important concept to individual taxpayers because the amount of gross income determines, in part, who must file an income tax return and who may be claimed as a dependent.

✓ Individuals are permitted to deduct a number of items based on the provisions discussed in Chapter 5. The tax formula for individuals differs from the tax formula for other taxpayers in that deductions are divided into two categories—deductions *for* AGI and deductions *from* AGI.

✓ Section 62 specifies which deductions are classified as deductions *for* AGI.

RECALL PROBLEMS

1. A politician outlines a plan that will give tax relief to the average American taxpayer. Based on Table 9-1, what range of AGI do you think might be included in that category?   #1

2. How does the tax formula used to calculate an individual's tax liability differ from that used to calculate the liability for a corporation or fiduciary?   #2

3. In each of the following independent cases, indicate the amount that the taxpayer would report as gross income for the year: #3

   a. In 19X3, Y's employer paid premiums for a health and accident policy for each employee. During the current year, the employer paid $1,250 on behalf of Y.

   b. Mr. Y has two health and accident policies on which he pays all premiums. During 19X2, when he was hospitalized for hepatitis, his hospital and doctor bills amounted to $500. Y paid these bills and, before the end of 19X2, collected $300 on one policy and $350 on the other policy.

   c. In 19X2 Mr. Y received reimbursement for $3,000 of medical expenses that he had paid in 19X1. Mr. Y claimed a medical expense deduction in 19X1 for the entire $3,000.

   d. Mr Y's employer has a direct health and accident reimbursement plan under which it directly pays medical bills of its employees. The plan is offered on a nondiscriminatory basis to all employees. This year Mr. Y's employer paid $480 of medical bills for him.

4. What is the amount of gross income in each of the cases?   #3

   a. Taxpayer was involved in an accident and as a result received a $5,000 personal damage judgment plus $800 reimbursement for medical costs incurred.

   b. Amos is injured on the job. As a result of his injury, he is paid $400 under workmen's compensation insurance and also receives $800 under health and accident insurance policies to reimburse him for medical costs. Additionally, he receives $500 under a disability income policy that he purchased and paid for himself.

   c. Peter and his wife were injured in an automobile accident during the year. Because of the accident, Peter and his wife were paid $1,300 to reimburse them for medical costs and $8,900 for personal injury and suffering.

   d. Mr. Y's car was struck in the rear by a speeder in September of last year. Mr. Y suffered from whiplash and had severe pains in his neck and upper back. He filed a claim for damages against the speeder and his insurance company. Y went to the doctor with the problem but was never hospitalized because the doctor could not diagnose the ailment. To avoid a costly court fight, the speeder's insurance company settled with Y in February of the current year for $1,000.

e. Z was ill throughout most of the current year. She received $300 per month for nine months from a wage-continuation policy. Z paid all the premiums on the policy.

5. In each of the following independent cases, indicate how much, if any, of the amounts involved must be reported as income by the recipient:

a. Anthony's employer carries a substantial insurance program for his employees. During the current year, the employer paid premiums of $960 on health and hospital insurance policies for Anthony. In addition, the employer pays life insurance premiums of $400 under a group term life insurance program. This life insurance provides for a death benefit of $40,000 payable to Mrs. Anthony in the event of Anthony's death.

b. Taxpayer's employer purchased an ordinary, whole-life insurance policy for every employee. During the current year, the employer paid premiums of $400 on the taxpayer's policy.

6. In each of the following independent cases, indicate the amount that the taxpayer should report as gross income for the year:

a. Mr. Jones, who had been holding two jobs, died during the current year. Because of Mr. Jones's death, the first employer paid Mrs. Jones $8,000, and the second employer paid her $6,000.

b. Mrs. McDonald died during the current year. Her employer paid Mr. McDonald $8,000 and each of her two children $3,500. Payments were made solely on account of her death.

c. Rufus died during the current year. His wife was paid $10,000 under a group term life insurance policy that had been paid for by Rufus's employer. In addition, the employer paid Rufus's wife $4,000 on account of Rufus's death.

7. Herman and Elsie file a joint return. For the year, they had the following items of income:

Dividends on stock in domestic corporations	$14,000
Tax-exempt interest	20,000
Taxable interest	3,000
Social Security benefits	5,000

How much of their Social Security income must be included in their gross income?

8. Friedsam, single, lost his job in August of the current year. He could not secure another job; during August and September, he received unemployment benefits of $380. In October, he qualified for Social Security retirement benefits, and during the remainder of the year he received $980 of Social Security benefits. His only other income was a salary of $19,900 for January through August. What is the amount of Friedsam's gross income this year?

In problems 9-12, give the dollar amount that should be included in the computation of the taxpayer's gross income.

#3

9.   a. Professor Graham was selected by the business students at State University as their outstanding teacher and was given a cash award of $1,000 by the student association.

     b. Sue was chosen Miss City. She won both the bathing suit and the talent contests. Many people speculate that she will ultimately become Miss America. As an award of being chosen Miss City, she was given cash and merchandise totaling $2,000.

     c. Professor Samples was awarded a Pulitzer Prize of $15,000 for writing a book on the history of the Apache Indians.

     d. Professor Goodman was awarded a Nobel Prize in recognition of his contribution to the field of medicine. He assigned the $190,000 award to a charitable organization established to carry on cancer research.

     e. Kamp, a rabid baseball fan, attended every home game of the city team. He was surprised one evening when his ticket stub contained the lucky number and he won an automobile with a fair value of $7,000 in the ticket drawing.

     f. Max received a $300 safety award this year from his employer at the annual recognition banquet. The award was given to all employees who had worked for 10 years without an accident.

10. a. Alice, a university student working on her BBA degree, received a scholarship of $2,000 from the university. Alice's tuition is $2,500. The scholarship was based on grades, and she had no services to render.

#3

     b. Assume the same facts as above in part a, except that the scholarship was awarded by an industrial firm.

     c. Assume the same facts as in part a, except that Alice is working on a PhD.

     d. Assume the same facts as in part a, except that Alice's tuition and course-related supplies amounted to $1,500 during the period covered by the scholarship.

     e. Robert received his PhD in 19X1. Beginning in September 19X1 and continuing to December 19X4 he received a postdoctoral fellowship from a tax-free foundation to continue study and research. The fellowship paid him $500 per month.

     f. Margaret S. is working toward a PhD in chemistry. She receives a $5,000 scholarship from the university. Margaret's tuition is $6,000 per year. To get the scholarship, she must work 10 hours each week in the laboratory. This laboratory work is required of all students working toward the PhD in chemistry at that university. Those students not receiving scholarships are paid $2,000 to do similar work.

     g. Joann, a graduate student at State University, received a $1,000 scholarship grant, $350 for grading accounting papers, and $2,000 from her father. She used the $3,350 to pay tuition ($1,000) and living expenses ($2,350).

     h. Kelly's employer paid $3,000 tuition this year for her to pursue an undergraduate business degree as a part-time student. This plan is available to all employees on a nondiscriminatory basis.

#3

11. a. Taxpayer is a university student. He works in the university cafeteria and receives as payment three meals each day. Total value of the meals consumed during the current year is $1,450.

b. Taxpayer manages an apartment house throughout the year. He is required by his employer to live in one of the apartments, which is given to the taxpayer rent free. Similar apartments are rented to tenants for $3,600 per year. Taxpayer's salary as manager is $12,000 per year.

c. Taxpayer manages an apartment house throughout the year, for which she makes a cash salary of $4,000. In addition, her employer offered to give her another $200 per month in cash or to let her live rent free in an apartment. Choosing the latter, taxpayer received an apartment that has a fair rental value of $4,000 per year.

d. Maude is a waitress at a local cafe. Her income for the year consists of wages of $6,500 and tips of $3,200. In addition, she eats her noon meal while on duty at the cafe, free of charge. She estimates that the value of meals consumed during the year is $650.

e. Guardman lived rent free in a house owned by his employer on the employer's premises during the year. The rental value of the house was $1,800 for the year. Although Guardman lived in the house for the convenience of the employer, he was not required to live there and could have lived somewhere else.

f. Lynn works for an accounting firm. During the busy season she often works until 10:00 P.M. On these occasions, her employer provides a $15 meal allowance. This year, she received $600 as meal allowances. She actually spent $400 for meals on evenings when she worked late.

#3

12. a. Stewart is a flight attendant for Great Fly Airlines. One of his fringe benefits is the right to fly free of charge on the airline, and Stewart takes advantage of this right. He estimates that during 19X1 the flights taken on short vacations would have cost him $1,200 if he had been required to pay for them.

b. Appleton, who is single and earns $38,000 per year, works for a company that provides dependent child care under a nondiscriminatory plan. Preschool-age children of employees are cared for in a day-care facility provided by the employer. The value of the day care provided Appleton's daughter this year was $6,000.

c. Jackson's employer offers a nondiscriminatory cafeteria plan. Jackson can choose from such items as medical insurance, group term life insurance, legal assistance, and disability insurance. In lieu of these items Jackson chose $1,200 extra cash compensation this year.

#3

13. Explain the relationship between cafeteria plans and the constructive receipt doctrine.

#3

14. This year North lived and worked in France as an employee of a U.S. corporation for the entire year. She earned $90,000 salary. North also earned $2,000 interest on a bank account in France and $15,000 dividends and interest on investments in the United States. How much is North's gross income?

#3

15. In the following independent cases, indicate how much, if any, of the amounts involved must be reported as gross income by the recipient.

a. Thompson served in the U.S. Army in Southeast Asia. As a result of combat injury in 1967, Thompson was retired from the military and awarded a pension. During the current year, he received total payments of $8,400 from the pension.

b. On January 1 of the current year, Careerman retired from the U.S. Air Force after 15 years of service. During the current tax year, he received retirement pension payments of $7,600.

16. The correct classification of the various subtractions in the individual tax formula is very important.

a. Why is the accurate calculation of gross income important?

b. Why is the accurate calculation of adjusted gross income important?

17. Explain the difference between the tax treatment of reimbursed and nonreimbursed expenses of taxpayers who are employees.

18. Section 212 authorizes the deduction of expenditures related to transactions entered into for profit. How are these expenditures classified on an individual taxpayer's tax return?

19. Explain why the parties to a divorce are very interested in whether payments are classified as alimony, property settlements, or child support.

20. Indicate how each of the following items will be treated on the individual's tax return (a deduction for AGI, from AGI, or not deductible at all):

a. George Traveler spent $500 for air transportation to a trade show related to his business. George is a self-employed consultant.

b. Same facts as in part a, except that George is employed by a consulting firm. He was reimbursed for the airfare.

c. Same facts as in part b, except that George was not reimbursed by his employer.

d. Mary Smith recently sold 100 shares of GM stock for $700 less than she paid for it two years ago.

e. Al Anderson paid $300 for plumbing repairs to rental property that he owns.

f. Fred Mayer paid $350 this year for a subscription to an investment newsletter related to his stock investment activities.

g. This year Joe Moore paid $5,000 in alimony and $6,000 in child support to his former wife.

h. Alan Spivey, a self-employed statistician, paid $5,000 into his Keogh retirement plan this year.

THOUGHT PROBLEMS

1. Paul, 47 years old, is covered by a nondiscriminatory group-term life insurance policy for which all premiums are paid by his employer. This year Paul's employer paid $1,300 to provide $70,000 coverage (an amount equal to twice his salary). How much, if any, of the $1,300 must Paul include in gross income? (Hint: Consult the regulations associated with Sec. 79.)

2. Lee and Chris were divorced in 1990. As a result of the divorce, Chris paid Lee $20,000 in 1990, $20,000 in 1991, and nothing thereafter. Will Chris and Lee be affected in 1992 by the "excess front-loading of alimony" rules of Sec. 71(f)? Show your calculations and indicate how each will be affected, if at all.

#3

3. Urban University charges its employees $30 per month to park on campus. The money collected is used to pay for road and parking structure maintenance, and safety patrols. The campus parking committee has urged the administration to provide parking as a tax-free fringe benefit to all employees. The administration could do so by transferring money normally available for raises into this parking division. Explain why the employees and the university could be better off with this plan. Consider the specific cases of a single employee earning $15,000 per year and a single employee earning $50,000 per year. Ignore state income taxes in your analysis.

#3

4. H. McGregor Malcolm is president and chairperson of the board of Malcolm Industries. In preparing Malcolm's tax return for the year, you discover the following facts:

    (1) The company provides Malcolm with an automobile for his business and personal use. Each year the automobile is traded in for a new one.

    (2) The company also provides Malcolm's wife, who works on a part-time basis for the company, with an automobile for her exclusive use. Her car is replaced every third year.

    (3) Malcolm Industries has 325 employees. It does not have a general hospitalization insurance plan for employees, but it has secured a medical insurance policy for Malcolm that covers all medical costs for Mr. and Mrs. Malcolm. During this year, premiums on the policy totaled $1,500.

    (4) Malcolm attends many marketing and trade association meetings. His wife always accompanies him because he thinks she is very helpful in making business contacts and in securing sales orders. The corporation pays all expenses for both.

    (5) The company has a dining room for officers, directors, and selected high-level managers. Meals are served at a price that is roughly one half the price charged for similar meals at public restaurants.

    (6) The company frequently receives premiums from suppliers. These premiums are usually resold, but occasionally Malcolm and the other stockholder-employees take premiums for their personal use. During the current year, Malcolm took a color television set, a microwave oven, and a television computer game for his use.

    (7) Malcolm Industries subscribed to many magazines for use in its reception area. Malcolm regularly takes home several of these magazines. After the Malcolms have read them, the magazines are returned to the company's offices.

    (8) During the year, as part of a promotional campaign, one of Malcolm Industries' suppliers offered its customers an all-expense-paid Mediterranean cruise for each $750,000 of merchandise purchased. Malcolm Industries purchased over $1,500,000 during the year and thus was eligible for two free trips, Mr. and Mrs. Malcolm took the cruise.

    a. Comment on the effect of each of the forgoing items on Mr. and Mrs. Malcolm's gross income for the year.

    b. Comment on the effect of each item on the gross income of Malcolm Industries for the year.

——— CLASS PROJECTS

1. Eleanor Dogood, a successful realtor, chaired this year's Charity Ball. Following the event, the local newspaper reported that the Charity Ball had been poorly organized and had raised very little money for charity, primarily because of Dogood's poor management. She brought suit against the newspaper and successfully recovered $100,000 for damage to her "personal and professional reputation." May she exclude any part of the $100,000 from gross income? Your discussion should include relevant administrative and judicial authority.

2. Chuck Hopwood is sole shareholder and manager of Silver Arbor Winery, Inc. Chuck's contract with the winery requires that as manager he live in a house on the premises. The fair rental value of the house is $15,000 per year. May Chuck exclude the value of the house from his gross income? Your discussion should include relevant administrative and judicial authority.

DEDUCTIONS FROM AGI

CHAPTER OBJECTIVES

In Chapter 10 you will learn how to determine the amount of an individual taxpayer's deductions from adjusted gross income.

LEARNING GOALS

After studying this chapter, you should be able to

1 Determine the number of personal and dependent exemptions to which an individual taxpayer is entitled and the amount of the associated deduction from AGI.

2 Calculate the amount of standard deduction to which a taxpayer is entitled.

3 Explain the rules that determine the amount of the itemized deductions most often claimed by individual taxpayers.

4 Determine the amount of an individual taxpayer's total itemized deductions and decide whether the taxpayer should itemize or use the standard deduction.

Itemized deductions are a set of deductions allowed individual taxpayers even though many are personal in nature.

A **standard deduction** amount is allowed individual taxpayers in lieu of itemizing deductions.

A **dependent** is a person for whom a taxpayer may claim a dependent exemption deduction.

Goal #1
Determine number of exemptions and amount of deductions.

After segregating and deducting expenditures allowed *for* AGI, individuals are allowed other deductions for various expenditures. These are deductions *from* AGI, and they are divided into two categories. First, most individual taxpayers are allowed to deduct personal and dependent exemptions. Second, they are allowed to deduct either a standard deduction or alternatively to **itemize deductions**. A taxpayer itemizes deductions when he or she has actual deductions from AGI in excess of the **standard deduction** amounts allowed. The deduction for exemptions is allowed without regard to whether the taxpayer elects to itemize deductions or to claim a standard deduction.

Figure 10-1 should help summarize the discussion to this point. Deductions for AGI were discussed in Chapter 9. In this chapter, we turn our attention to deductions from AGI—personal and **dependent** exemptions and the larger of itemized deductions or the standard deduction.

DEDUCTION FOR PERSONAL AND DEPENDENT EXEMPTIONS

The deduction for personal exemptions is the product of the *number* of exemptions allowed on a return times the exemption *amount*. The amount is an arbitrary figure decided on by Congress. It was $1,000 (adjusted for inflation) for many years prior to 1987. Under the 1986 Act, the exemption amount was increased to $2,000 (inflation adjusted) for 1989 and later years. For 1992, the amount of one exemption deduction is $2,300. Determining the number of exemptions allowed on a return is the complicated part.

EXEMPTIONS FOR TAXPAYERS

One personal exemption is ordinarily allowed for the taxpayer on each return. With one exception, each return has one personal exemption deduction equal to the correct exemption amount for that year. The exception occurs when the taxpayer on a return is also claimed as a dependent on another return. In that case, no personal exemption deduction is allowed on the taxpayer's own tax return. This usually occurs when a child (under 19 or a full-time student under 24) is claimed as a dependent by his or her parents.

As explained later, a married couple usually files a joint return. When a joint return is used, both spouses are taxpayers, and each is entitled to one personal exemption

FIGURE 10-1

Classification of Deductible Expenses for Individual Taxpayers

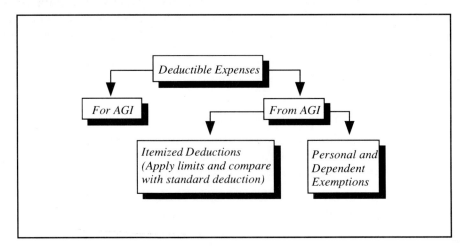

deduction. Thus, there is usually a minimum of two personal exemptions on a joint return. If only one spouse files a return, that spouse may claim an exemption for the other spouse only if the latter has no gross income and is not claimed as a dependent of another taxpayer. Obviously, if spouses file separate returns, neither may take an exemption for the other.

In addition to one personal exemption deduction for each taxpayer, in some cases a taxpayer is entitled to a dependent exemption deduction for each individual who qualifies as the taxpayer's *dependent*.

EXEMPTIONS FOR DEPENDENTS

The rules governing exemption deductions for dependents are much more complex and difficult to interpret and apply than those relating to the personal exemptions for a taxpayer and spouse. As a result, there have been many controversies on this point between taxpayers and the IRS, and numerous court decisions involving dependency exemptions have been reported. Although subject to many exceptions and special interpretations, five basic requirements must be satisfied for the taxpayer to claim an exemption deduction for a dependent:

1. The dependent must *not* be a **nonresident alien.** (An exception exists for dependents who reside in countries contiguous to the United States.)

2. The dependent, if married, must not file a joint return with his or her spouse. (However, if the dependent and spouse are not required to file a return, but do so merely to get a refund of taxes withheld, a joint return is allowed.)

3. A specified relationship must exist between the taxpayers and the dependent.

4. The taxpayer must provide over one half of the dependent's support for the year.

5. The dependent must have gross income of less than the amount of one exemption deduction for the year.

> A **nonresident alien** is a person who is not a U.S. citizen and who does not reside in the United States.

The first two requirements need no interpretation. The last three, however, require further explanation and elaboration.

The Relationship Test

The Internal Revenue Code generally provides that anyone claimed as a dependent must be a *relative* of the taxpayer and delimits the necessary relationship as follows:

(1) A son or daughter of the taxpayer, or a descendant of either,
(2) A stepson or stepdaughter of the taxpayer,
(3) A brother, sister, stepbrother, or stepsister of the taxpayer,
(4) The father or mother of the taxpayer, or an ancestor of either,
(5) A stepfather or stepmother of the taxpayer,
(6) A son or daughter of a brother or sister of the taxpayer,
(7) A brother or sister of the father or mother of the taxpayer,
(8) A son-in-law, daughter-in-law, father-in-law, mother-in-law, brother-in-law, or sister-in-law of the taxpayer.[1]

When a joint return is filed, the relationship test is met if the person claimed as a dependent is a qualified relative of either spouse. Even after termination of a marriage,

---

1 Sec. 152(a)(1–8).

a relationship established by marriage is continued for tax purposes. Finally, an adopted child is treated as a natural child for dependency purposes.

The law also provides for a taxpayer to claim a dependent exemption deduction for an individual who *resides* in the taxpayer's home throughout a tax year, even though the individual is not a relative of the taxpayer, as specified above.

> (9) An individual (other than an individual who at any time during the taxable year was the spouse, determined without regard to section 153, of the taxpayer) who, for the taxable year of the taxpayer, has as his principal place of abode the home of the taxpayer and is a member of the taxpayer's household. . . .[2]

This last provision permits dependency exemptions for persons—such as foster children not legally adopted or foster parents—who do not meet any of the relationship tests in (1) through (8). Foster children and others who pass the residence test are treated in all respects as though they are blood relatives of the taxpayer.

This last provision does *not* apply if the relationship with the taxpayer is contrary to local law. For example, if the state law prohibits common-law marriage, no exemption can be claimed for the taxpayer's consort. Children born into such an arrangement, however, can be dependents.

The Support Test

The taxpayer must provide over one half the dollar value of the dependent's support during the calendar year (or that part of the year that the dependent was alive). Support includes all expenditures for such items as food, clothing, shelter, medical care, education, and child care. A scholarship received by a student *who is the taxpayer's child* is not counted as part of the total support in determining whether the taxpayer provided more than half the student's support. Recall from Chapter 9 that the Code limits the exclusion for scholarships to the amount spent for tuition, books, and incidentals, making scholarships that cover room and board subject to the tax. For purposes of the support test, however, the entire amount of the scholarship grant is excluded from the calculation of support.

The major exception to the support test occurs when two or more persons furnish a dependent's support but no one taxpayer provides over half of the dependent's support. In this event, any one of the taxpayers who (1) provides over 10% of the dependent's support and (2) who satisfies the relationship test may claim the exemption *if* every person who provides more than 10% of the dependent's support during the year, and who also satisfies the relationship test, signs a multiple support statement agreeing *not* to claim an exemption for the dependent. For example, if each of four brothers provides 25% of his father's support, any one of the four may claim the father as a dependent for the year, provided the other three brothers sign a multiple support agreement.

If divorced parents both contribute support for their child or children, the parent who has custody for the major part of the calendar year is generally presumed to have provided more than 50% of the support. These rules may also apply to parents who simply live apart for the last six months of the year. The parent without custody can take the exemption deduction, however, if the custodial parent signs an agreement that she or he will not take the exemption.

---

2 Sec. 152(a)(9).

The Gross Income Test

Section 151(c) provides generally that the dependent's gross income must be less than the amount of one exemption deduction for that year ($2,300 in 1992) if the taxpayer is to claim an exemption deduction for the dependent. This rule does not apply to *a taxpayer's child, or qualified foster child,* who is either under age 19 at year-end or a full-time student under age 24 at year-end. Thus a parent can claim an exemption deduction for a child who is a full-time student through age 23 even if that child's gross income exceeds the exemption amount. Generally, a student is defined as one who during each of any five months of the calendar year was in full-time attendance at an educational institution or took a full-time, on-farm training course during any five months of the year. The taxpayer's child who is either a full-time student or under age 19, and has sufficient gross income, must file his or her own tax return.

This exemption to the gross income test usually means that parents are entitled to a dependency exemption deduction for their child who is a student (under 24) if the parent meets the support test. If the parent claims an exemption for the child, the child is *not* entitled to claim a personal exemption deduction on his or her own tax return.

EXAMPLE 10-1

Gordy, a 20-year-old full-time college student, earned $5,000 this year from a summer job. Gordy's parents provide more than half his support. They are entitled to claim Gordy as a dependent even though his gross income exceeds $2,300. If Gordy were 25 years old, his parents would not be entitled to claim him as a dependent.

The exemption for the taxpayer, plus one for the spouse—where appropriate—plus one for each dependent, *times* the exemption amount equals, the total exemption deduction for the year. This amount, plus the greater of the standard deduction or itemized deductions (discussed below), is deducted from AGI to determine an individual's taxable income.

THE STANDARD DEDUCTION

For 1992, the basic standard deduction amounts generally allowed for taxpayers with good vision, who are less than 65 years of age, are

Single individuals	$3,600
Heads of households	5,250
Married individuals and surviving spouses	6,000
Married individuals filing separately	3,000

> **Goal #2**
> Calculate the amount of a taxpayer's standard deduction.

> A **surviving spouse** is a taxpayer who is entitled to use the married filing jointly rate schedule even though his or her spouse has died.

These basic standard deduction amounts are increased by an additional standard deduction amount equal to $700 if the taxpayer is a married individual (or a **surviving spouse**) who is either 65 or older or blind; or by $900 if the taxpayer is an unmarried individual age 65 or older or blind. Note that one *additional* standard deduction can be claimed for both (1) age and (2) lack of vision, by *each* taxpayer on a tax return. Thus a married individual who is both (1) age 65 or older and (2) blind, can claim a total *additional* standard deduction of $1,400. An unmarried taxpayer who is both (1) age 65 or older and (2) blind would claim an *additional* standard deduction of $1,800.

On the joint return of a couple, both age 65 or older, where one of the two taxpayers is blind, the *additional* standard deduction equals $2,100 (or 3 x $700), and so on. The $700 and $900 amounts are adjusted annually for inflation, with increases rounded *down* to multiples of $50.

EXAMPLE 10-2

Mabel, who is single and age 87, is entitled to a total standard deduction of $4,500 ($3,600 + $900). Mabel's married daughter and son-in-law, ages 65 and 63, are entitled to a total standard deduction of $6,700 ($6,000 + $700).

A taxpayer who can establish actual itemized deductions in excess of the standard amount is entitled to deduct the larger amount. Thus, in 1992, a single individual with good vision and under age 65 who actually incurs $7,200 of itemized deductions is entitled to deduct that amount in lieu of the $3,600 standard deduction. However, a single individual with good vision and under age 65 who incurs only $2,300 of itemized deductions is generally entitled to claim the $3,600 standard deduction for 1992.

In certain situations, the law provides that taxpayers may not be entitled to claim the basic standard deduction. The most common situation in which a taxpayer may not claim the basic standard deduction involves a taxpayer's dependent child who has income and must file a return. In such a case, the child's standard deduction may not exceed the greater of $600 or the amount of his or her earned income (not to exceed the basic standard deduction allowed in more ordinary circumstances).

EXAMPLE 10-3

Jerry, age 15, and Alicia, age 13, are properly claimed as dependents by their parents. Jerry's income this year consisted of $800 interest and $2,100 from an after-school job. Jerry is entitled to a standard deduction of $2,100. Alicia's income consisted of $750 of interest and $450 from babysitting. Alicia is entitled to a standard deduction of $600.

Example 10-3 assumes that the children do not have itemized deductions in excess of their standard deduction, which is usually true of minor children. If a taxpayer, who is claimed as a dependent by another taxpayer, has itemized deductions, the amount of such deductions can be claimed if it exceeds the standard deduction allowed under these circumstances.

An elderly or blind individual, who is claimed as a dependent on another person's tax return, may always claim the *additional* standard deduction of $700 ($1,400 if elderly and blind) if married, or $900 ($1,800 if elderly and blind), if single. This additional standard deduction can be applied against either earned or unearned income.

In addition to the situation just described, if married individuals file separate tax returns, and one spouse itemizes, then the standard deduction for the other spouse is zero. Nonresident aliens, and certain other individuals who have exempt income from U.S. possessions, are also denied a standard deduction.

The proper classification of an individual's deductions between those *for* AGI and those *from* AGI is critical if the maximum deduction *from* AGI is to be obtained. Note first that the standard deduction is not related to the taxpayer's actual expenditures.

Thus, if deductions for AGI are incorrectly classified as from AGI, the taxpayer may elect to take the larger itemized deduction, whereas a correct classification might permit some items to be deducted for AGI and still permit the use of the standard amount.

EXAMPLE 10-4

In 1992, Irving, a bachelor, has gross income of $10,000 and allowable deductions of $4,400, consisting of $1,000 of expenses related to rental income plus $3,400 of charitable contributions. If all of the deductions are classified by Irving as from AGI, he would itemize, giving him total itemized deductions of $4,400. If the $1,000 of rental expenses were correctly classified as a deduction for AGI, Irving's AGI would be $9,000. He would still be entitled to a standard deduction of $3,600. The net effect of making a correct classification is an increase in his total deductions to $4,600 ($1,000 for AGI + $3,600 standard deduction) and a decrease in taxable income of $200.

The correct classification of deductions can also be important for taxpayers whose itemized deductions are clearly greater than the standard amount. As explained in the next section, Sec. 212 deductions (other than those related to rents and royalties) including those related to the production of income and/or the payment of taxes, medical deductions, and personal casualty losses, are all subject to thresholds that are expressed as varying percentages of AGI. Therefore, the correct classification of any deduction that lowers AGI automatically increases the deductible portion of expenditures that must exceed a percentage of AGI in order to be deductible at all.

ITEMIZED DEDUCTIONS

As we have just learned, most individual taxpayers are entitled to a standard deduction in calculating taxable income. However, a taxpayer who can establish that allowable deductions from AGI (not including personal and dependency exemptions) exceed the standard amount can deduct the larger amount.

Table 10-1 lists dollar amounts for the major classes of itemized deductions claimed by taxpayers in 1989 (the most recent year for which data are available) along with the percentage of total itemized deduction represented by each class. Although the Tax Reform Act of 1986 curtailed many of these deductions (and increased standard deduction amounts), many taxpayers continue to find itemizing deductions to be advantageous despite the associated complications. The latest data available (1989) indicate that while only 28% of all taxpayers itemized, more than 85% of taxpayers with AGI of $50,000 or more itemized.

We will discuss itemized deductions in the order of their importance to taxpayers (in other words, in terms of their cost to the government in revenues lost). Interestingly, the three most important deductions—interest, taxes, and charitable contributions—can all be classified as subsidies to some group or groups of taxpayers. Two of the other deductions—medical expenses and casualty losses—are intended to relieve economic hardships. However, these last two deductions are subject to high thresholds and are, therefore, much less important in aggregate than the first three mentioned.

Goal #3
Explain the rules for determining a taxpayer's itemized deductions.

TABLE 10-1

**Itemized
Deductions by
Classes—1989**

Type	Amount (in billions)	Percentage of Total
Interest	$188.4	44.4
Taxes	131.4	30.9
Contributions	55.3	13.0
Medical expenses	20.5	4.8
Others	29.1	6.9

Source: *Statistics of Income Bulletin*, Summer 1991.

INTEREST

Perhaps the most controversial itemized deduction is that for interest,which in 1989 accounted for $188.4 billion, or more than 44% of all itemized deductions. As can be seen in Table 10-2, this deduction grew rapidly (in dollar terms and as a percentage of total itemized deductions) until 1987. Essentially, from the beginning of the modern income tax law in 1913 through 1986, nearly all interest expenses were deductible. Although it is almost unanimously agreed that interest incurred in a trade or business, as well as that incurred in connection with the production of other taxable income, should generally be treated in the same manner as other deductible expenses, there has been less agreement over the propriety of a deduction for interest paid on funds to finance the purchase of personal consumer goods and services. The 1986 Act significantly reduced the amount of such interest that individuals could deduct.

General Rule

The general provision authorizing the deduction of interest is contained in Sec.163, which reads as follows:

(a) General Rule—There shall be allowed as a deduction all interest paid or accrued within the taxable year on indebtedness.

TABLE 10-2

**Deduction for
Interest on
Returns Itemizing
Deductions**

Year	Itemized Interest Deduction (in billions)	As Percentage of Total Itemized Deductions
1970	$ 23.9	27.1
1975	38.9	31.8
1980	91.2	41.8
1985	180.1	44.5
1987	174.4	45.4
1989	188.4	44.4

Source: *Statistics of Income Bulletin*, various dates.

This all-inclusive rule is significantly modified and limited by several other sections disallowing certain types of interest. One of these provisions prohibits the deduction of interest on funds borrowed to earn tax-exempt income and on funds used to purchase single-premium life insurance or endowment policies. Other limiting provisions require that the indebtedness be the taxpayer's if a deduction is to be allowed. Another important restriction, discussed later in some detail, limits the amount of deductible "investment interest." Also, certain "construction period interests" (and taxes) must be capitalized. Finally, the 1986 Act disallowed the deduction for *all* personal interest, except "qualified residence interest," for tax years after 1990. Each of these limitations will be discussed in more detail.

Deductions for Personal Interest

The 1986 Act disallowed the deduction of personal interest, which is defined in Sec. 163(h)(2) as

> any interest allowable as a deduction under this chapter other than—
>
> (A) interest paid or accrued on indebtedness incurred or continued in connection with the conduct of a trade or business (other than the trade or business of performing services as an employee).
>
> (B) any investment interest (within the meaning of subsection (d))
>
> (C) any interest which is taken into account under section 469 in computing income or loss from a passive activity of the taxpayer
>
> (D) any qualified residence interest . . .
>
> (E) any interest payable under section 6601 on any unpaid portion of the tax imposed by section 2001 [the estate tax]. . .

This definition, in effect, provides that any interest that cannot be classified into one of these five categories cannot be deducted. Note that special limitations, discussed below, apply to interest related to investments or passive activities and to qualified residence interest. What is disallowed, of course, is interest in consumer debt, such as personal credit card purchases and automobile loans. Interest on unpaid tax liabilities also is disallowed unless it is interest on estate taxes deferred under Secs. 6163 or 6166.

Qualified Residence Interest

The disallowance of personal interest does *not* include "qualified residence interest" expense. A qualified residence is the taxpayer's principal residence and one second residence, such as a vacation home. A second residence can qualify only if the taxpayer's personal use exceeds the greater of 14 days or 10% of the number of days of rental use. Otherwise, the property probably will be treated under the passive activity rules described later.

Qualified residence interest is fully deductible on up to $1 million of **acquisition debt** (in other words, on debt incurred in acquiring, constructing, or substantially improving the taxpayer's principal or second residence). Additionally, a taxpayer may deduct interest on up to $100,000 of **home equity debt** on either a principal or second residence.

Note that these rules effectively permit taxpayers to circumvent the repeal of the deductibility of personal interest by using home equity loans for purposes such as

Acquisition debt is debt incurred in acquiring, constructing, or substantially improving a taxpayer's principal or second residence.

Home equity debt is debt other than acquisition debt that is secured by the taxpayer's principal or second residence.

purchase of a new automobile. Obviously, not all taxpayers can take advantage of this loophole, either because they are not homeowners or they have insufficient equity in their homes to borrow against the value of the home.

EXAMPLE 10-5

Collins originally acquired her home in 1970 for $100,000. The home now is worth $180,000, and the balance on the original mortgage is $20,000. Collins could deduct interest on up to $120,000 ($20,000 original mortgage plus up to $100,000 of home equity debt) should she choose to borrow against the value of her home.

EXAMPLE 10-6

Patell purchased his $180,000 home this year with a mortgage of $150,000. He may deduct the entire amount of interest on the $150,000 of acquisition debt.

Interest Related to Passive Activities

As described earlier in Chapter 5, the 1986 Act limited the deductibility of losses from such "passive activities" as ownership of rental property, limited partnership interests, and interests in a trade or business in which the taxpayer does not materially participate. Losses from these and other passive activities are allowed only to the extent of gains from similar activities. Disallowed losses can be carried forward to offset income from passive activities in later years. These rules, of course, limit the deductibility of interest associated with passive activities.

Interest Related to Investments

The rules that once permitted deduction of almost all interest expenses permitted taxpayers to incur voluntarily substantial interest expenses on funds borrowed to acquire or carry investment assets. Often these funds were used to purchase securities that had good growth potential, but returned small dividends currently. This investment pattern gave rise to an immediate interest expense deduction and permitted the taxpayer to report gain on sale of the appreciated securities as long-term capital gain. To curtail excessive abuse of this tax break, tax laws limit the amount of interest deductible on funds borrowed by noncorporate taxpayers to purchase investment property. The limit for deductibility of investment interest is the amount of net investment income for the year.

Investment income is defined as the sum of gross income from property held for investment plus any net gain attributable to the disposition of investment property, regardless of the holding period. Investment income does not include income from passive activities. Expenses (other than interest) related to investment properties are deducted from investment income to compute net investment income.

EXAMPLE 10-7

Zalesney paid interest of $45,000 on funds borrowed to purchase investment property. During the year, he received investment income consisting of interest and dividends totaling $5,000 and incurred investment expenses of $2,000. Zalesney may deduct $3,000 of investment interest this year.

Any disallowed investment interest is carried forward by the taxpayer and treated as interest paid or accrued in the succeeding tax year. In effect, an unlimited carryover exists.

Capitalization of Interest (and Taxes) during Construction Period

Prior to 1976, amounts paid or accrued for interest, as well as for property taxes, attributable to the construction of real property were allowed as current deductions unless the taxpayer elected to capitalize those items as carrying costs. Today, the uniform capitalization rules require that all interest costs be capitalized if the debt is paid or incurred to construct, build, install, manufacture, develop, or improve real or tangible personal property that is produced by the taxpayer and that has (1) a long useful life, (2) an estimated production period exceeding two years, or (3) an estimated production period of less than one year and cost exceeding $1,000,000.[3] An asset is deemed to have a long useful life if it is real estate or property with a class life of 20 years or more. These capitalized costs become part of the basis of the asset for purposes of depreciation or determining gain on sale.

Controversies over the Interest Deduction

Presumably, the broad deductibility of interest resulted from the difficulty encountered in trying to distinguish clearly between borrowed funds used for income-producing activities and those used for personal activities. It is extremely difficult to trace the relationship between debts owed by the taxpayer and specific assets or services acquired. In many cases, funds borrowed ostensibly for business purposes are used for personal purchases; alternatively, some funds acquired for consumption purposes may be used in a business venture. In addition, prudent manipulation of the taxpayer's finances could ensure that borrowed funds would be used first in business and that equity capital would be used first for personal expenditures if interest on the former, but not the latter, were deductible.

Proponents of this deduction agree that interest expense represents a reduction of the taxpayer's economic income regardless of why the expense was incurred and, thus, should be deductible in recognition of this difference in wherewithal to pay tax. On the other hand, interest expenses may be considered part of the purchase price of commodities or services acquired—a premium for obtaining the goods and services now rather than waiting until later. This element of price, so the argument goes, should be treated in the same manner as the other portions—that is, interest related to personal expenditures should be nondeductible.

The most difficult aspect of the interest deduction, and the most controversial, has related to interest paid by taxpayers on funds obtained to purchase a home or durable consumer goods. A definite inequity exists between the homeowner and the tenant, which can be seen easily by assuming that one taxpayer makes monthly rental payments of $400 on his residence, whereas a second taxpayer makes mortgage payments of $400 per month, including an average of $300 per month for interest. The former taxpayer can take no deduction on his tax return, but the latter may deduct all of the interest paid; in addition, the homeowner also may deduct property taxes paid. Because the homeowner is not required to include in income the imputed rental value of his owner-occupied home, he or she obviously has a distinct tax advantage over the tenant, even though the two individuals may have essentially the same economic income.

3 Sec. 263(A).

This inequity has been recognized throughout the history of the modern income tax. For example, in the debate over the initial Act in 1913, it was pointed out that

> here is a man . . . who has purchased a home. He has given a mortgage upon it . . . and is paying . . . $1,000 interest. Under this bill that would be deducted from his net income. But if his neighbor has rented a house, and instead of virtually paying what the first-named man does in the form of interest, he pays directly $1,000 rent. He gets no deduction whatever, and yet the situation of the two is to all intents and purposes precisely the same.[4]

Many tax scholars argue that the only real solution to this inequity is to require that the homeowner include in his or her taxable income the imputed rental value of his or her home. Then the interest paid on a home mortgage would be deductible as a cost of earning income. The practical difficulties of this solution are obvious. Additionally, home ownership is highly valued by American taxpayers, many of whom evidently believe that the deductibility of home mortgage interest makes home ownership possible. At any rate, when Congress decided in 1986 to repeal the deductibility of personal interest, there was little serious consideration of also removing the deductibility of home mortgage interest.

TAXES

Taxes have been specifically mentioned as a deduction in every federal income tax law, including the 1861 Act, although the 1865 Act was the first to include specifically taxes not associated with income production. The 1865 law permitted the deduction of all national, state, county, and municipal taxes paid within the year. Similarly, the income tax law of 1913 specifically allowed deductions for all "national, state, county, school, and municipal taxes paid during the year," including the federal income tax itself.

Gradually, however, the number of deductible taxes has been reduced. The deduction for the federal income tax itself was eliminated in 1917; the federal excise tax deduction ended in 1943; the deduction for many state and local taxes (on tobacco, alcoholic beverages, automobile licenses, drivers' licenses, and others) was removed in 1961;[5] and the deduction for state taxes on gasoline was eliminated for taxable years beginning after 1978. The president's 1985 tax reform proposal argued that no deduction should be allowed for state and local taxes unless those taxes related to a trade or business or to the production of income.[6] Arguments were made that the deduction disproportionately benefited high-income taxpayers residing in high-tax states, seriously eroded the tax base, and was an inefficient subsidy to state and local governments. The 1986 Act did not go quite this far, however. Only the deduction for state and local general *sales* taxes was removed from the list of deductible taxes.

---

4 50 *Congressional Record* 3848 (1913), quoted in Samuel H. Hellenbrand, "Itemized Deductions for Personal Expenses and Standard Deductions in the Income Tax Law," 1959 *Compendium*, p. 378.

5 Even though the specific provision authorizing the deduction of automobile licenses was repealed in 1964, the citizens of some states can still claim this as a deduction under Sec. 162(a)(2). If the auto license fee is based on value (an *ad valorem* basis), it can be considered a property tax and, as such, is deductible.

6 *President's Tax Proposals to the Congress for Fairness, Growth, and Simplicity*, May 29, 1985, pp. 62–64.

Although many taxes are no longer deductible, this deduction continues to be significant on returns itemizing deductions. Table 10-1 shows that taxes were the second most important itemized deduction, making up about 31% of all deductions in 1989. As Table 10-3 shows, the amount of taxes deducted grew consistently until 1987 as a result of the rapid growth of state and local property, sales, and income taxes. However, taxes as a percentage of total itemized deductions have been decreasing since 1985.

General Rule

Section 164(a) provides that certain taxes paid to state and local governments not incurred in connection with a trade or business or other income producing activity are still deductible. It reads as follows:

(a) General Rule.—Except as otherwise provided in this section, the following taxes shall be allowed as a deduction for the taxable year within which paid or accrued:

(1) State and local, and foreign, real property taxes.

(2) State and local, personal property taxes.

(3) State and local, and foreign, income, war profits, and excess profits taxes.

(4) The windfall profit tax imposed by section 4986.

(5) The GST [generation skipping transfer] tax imposed on income distributions.

In addition, there shall be allowed as a deduction State and local, and foreign, taxes not described in the preceding sentence which are paid or accrued within the taxable year in carrying on a trade or business or an activity described in section 212 (relating to expenses for production of income). Notwithstanding the previous sentence, any tax (not described in the first sentence of this subsection) which is paid or accrued by the taxpayer in connection with an acquisition or disposition or property shall be treated as part of the cost of the acquired property or, in the case of a disposition, as a reduction in the amount realized on the disposition.

For most taxpayers, these rules mean that they can deduct state and local real and personal property taxes and income taxes.

Year	Amount of Taxes Deducted (in billions)	As Percentage of Total Itemized Deductions
1970	$ 32.0	36.3
1975	44.1	36.1
1980	69.4	31.8
1985	128.1	31.6
1987	118.2	30.8
1989	131.4	30.9

Source: *Statistics of Income Bulletin*, various dates.

TABLE 10-3

Deduction for Taxes on Returns Itemizing Deductions From AGI

EXAMPLE 10-8

Chang, a cash basis taxpayer, paid the following taxes in 1992: Federal income taxes withheld by employer, $9,000; state income tax withheld by employer, $2,000; social security taxes withheld by employer, $3,100; state and local property taxes on home, $1,200; state and local sales tax, $400; 1991 federal income tax paid in April 1992, $300; 1991 state income tax paid in April 1992, $50. On his 1992 federal income tax return Chang may deduct $3,250 ($2,000 state income tax withheld plus $1,200 property taxes on home plus $50 state income tax paid in April 1992).

Rationale for Allowing Deduction of Taxes

Several arguments have been advanced to support the deduction of state and local taxes. Perhaps the most important is that the deduction facilitates the smooth functioning of the federal system, providing a greater flexibility to local governmental units in their own taxing activities. In effect, the deduction represents a federal subsidy to state and local governments because it reduces the net cost of state and local taxes to those taxpayers who itemize deductions on their federal tax returns. Presumably, this permits local governmental units to increase taxes with less opposition from taxpayers. Furthermore, because it tends to reduce intercity and interstate tax differentials, permitting state and local taxes to be deducted reduces the fear, common to many local governmental bodies, that high tax rates will cause business and population to move to areas with lower tax rates.

Before the 1965 reduction of the maximum federal tax rate for individuals to 70% (from a previous high of 91%) it was often suggested that unless some provision were included in the federal tax structure for deduction of taxes paid to state and local governments—especially state and local income taxes—the marginal rate might be more than 100%. Although this extreme is not likely to occur, some degree of coordination between taxing activities of the national and local governmental units is desirable, and the deduction for state and local taxes on the federal tax return gives some relief from multiple taxation and provides limited control of the total tax burden. (Incidentally, state income taxes usually allow a deduction for the federal income tax paid.)

Finally, some persons argue that the taxpayer should not have to pay "a tax on a tax." Essentially, this concept considers taxes in much the same light as medical costs and casualty losses—unavoidable, involuntary payments that reduce the taxpayer's wherewithal to pay the federal income tax.

Arguments against the Deduction for Taxes

Most tax scholars favor the abolition of the deduction for taxes, with the exception, perhaps, of state and local income taxes. They refute most of the arguments supporting the deduction.

First, they point out that taxes paid state and local governments are actually for services such as police protection, schools, streets, and similar services and are very much like payments for services from the private sector of the economy. This argument is sometimes deemed especially pertinent in the case of taxes earmarked for specific direct benefit or services. Most of these taxes (for example, auto licenses and driver's licenses) have been made nondeductible in recent years. The logic may easily be extended to taxes not earmarked for specific purposes.

Most tax experts also point out that making state and local taxes deductible tends to reduce the progressivity that has been deliberately built into the tax structure. This is true because a deduction for state and local taxes generally results in a greater income tax saving for individuals in higher income tax brackets. Moreover, the deduction for state and local property taxes often discriminates between taxpayers with equal incomes and tax-paying ability. For example, it permits the homeowner to deduct taxes but allows no similar deduction to the tenant whose monthly rental surely includes an element for property taxes.

Even the most logical reason for permitting the deduction of state and local taxes—to make it easier for local governmental units to levy taxes—is subject to criticism. Not only is this a helter-skelter and inefficient means of providing a subsidy, but it provides assistance to the wrong communities. Presumably, a greater need for federal aid exists in poor communities, where both income and wealth (property) are relatively low. However, the aid provided by deduction of state and local taxes is of greatest benefit to communities whose taxpayers are in higher income tax brackets and are wealthier.

CHARITABLE CONTRIBUTIONS

Both individual and corporate taxpayers may deduct **charitable contributions** made to qualifying recipients. Most provisions applicable to contributions apply equally to individual and corporate donors. To avoid duplication, the rules of both types of donors are discussed here even though the primary focus of this chapter is itemized deductions for individuals. Rules that are unique to corporations are discussed in Chapter 13. Most questions regarding contribution deductions involve either the determination of the eligibility of a particular gift to qualify for a deduction or the determination of the amount that can be deducted.

> A **charitable contribution** is a gift to or for the use of a qualified donee.

Qualified Donees

Contributions made by individuals or corporations are deductible within limits, if they are made to (or "for the use of") one of the types of organizations listed in Sec. 170(c), which reads as follows:

(1) A State, a possession of the United States, or any political subdivision of any of the foregoing, or the United States or the District of Columbia, but only if the contribution or gift is made for exclusively public purposes.

(2) A corporation, trust, or community chest, fund, or foundation—

   (A) created or organized in the United States or in any possession thereof, or under the law of the United States, any State, the District of Columbia, or any possession of the United States;

   (B) organized and operated exclusively for religious, charitable, scientific, literary, or educational purposes, or to foster national or international amateur sports competition . . . or for the prevention of cruelty to children or animals;

   (C) no part of the net earnings of which inures to the benefit of any private shareholder or individual; and

   (D) which is not disqualified for tax exemption under section 501(c)(3) by reason of attempting to influence legislation, and which does not participate in, or intervene in (including the publishing or distributing of statements), any political campaign on behalf of any candidate for public office.

A contribution or gift by a corporation to a trust, chest, fund, or foundation shall be deductible by reason of this paragraph only if it is to be used within the United States or any of its possessions exclusively for purposes specified in subparagraph (B). . . .

(3)   A post or organization of war veterans, or an auxiliary unit or society of, or trust or foundation for, any such post or organization—

(A)   organized in the United States or any of its possessions, and

(B)   no part of the net earnings of which inures to the benefit of any private shareholder or individual.

(4)   In the case of a contribution or gift by an individual, a domestic fraternal society, order, or association, operating under the lodge system, but only if such contribution or gift is to be used exclusively for religious, charitable, scientific, literary, or educational purposes, or for the prevention of cruelty to children or animals.

(5)   A cemetery company owned and operated exclusively for the benefit of its members, or any corporation chartered solely for burial purposes as a cemetery corporation and not permitted by its charter to engage in any business not necessarily incident to that purpose, if such company or corporation is not operated for profit and no part of the net earnings of such company or corporation inures to the benefit of any private shareholder or individual.

Note that to be deductible, charitable contributions must be made to a qualifying organization that fits into one of the classes listed in Sec. 170(c). Contributions to individuals, no matter how needy, are not tax deductible.

A contribution made to a qualifying organization is just what the words imply—a direct gift to the organization. A contribution made "for the use of" an organization is an indirect gift. For example, an individual might make a gift to a trust and, in turn, direct the trustee to contribute that gift (and, possibly, any income that it produces) to a qualifying charity. Alternatively, an individual might pay a liability originally incurred by a charitable organization. In either of the latter two cases, the gift is "for the use of" the recipient organization and is subject to special rules for tax purposes.

Measuring the Amount Contributed

To be deductible, a charitable contribution must be in money or property; the taxpayer cannot deduct the value of services donated to an organization. Contribution of tangible, personal property must be of "present interest"—that is, a taxpayer cannot get a deduction now for a transfer that takes place at his or her death if the property involved is tangible, personal property. Contributions of "future interest" in real property are, however, possible under certain circumstances.

In some instances, it is difficult to determine if a particular contribution consists of a property or a service; for example, the donation of blood has been held to be a service, not property. Similarly, the law denies a taxpayer the value of "lost rents" as a deduction when the taxpayer permits a charity to occupy rental property free of cost. A taxpayer who uses a personal automobile on behalf of a charitable organization is entitled to deduct only the out-of-pocket costs (gasoline, oil, and so on) or a flat 12 cents per mile. However, the 1986 Act provided that a charitable deduction for travel away from home would not be permitted "unless there is no significant element of personal pleasure, recreation, or vacation in such travel."

When the taxpayer contributes cash, the amount of the contribution cannot be questioned. If the taxpayer contributes other property, the amount deemed to have been contributed depends on both the nature of the property and, in some cases, the nature of the donee organization.

ORDINARY INCOME PROPERTY.   If the sale of contributed property would have resulted in ordinary income (that is, not capital gain), the taxpayer may deduct only the fair market value of the property reduced by the amount of ordinary income that would be recognized if the property were sold. This rule generally results in a deduction equal to the cost or adjusted basis of the property. For example, if an individual who is a sole proprietor contributes routine inventory items that cost $2,000 but had a normal retail sales price of $3,000, the amount of the contribution would be $2,000. This restriction is applied regardless of the nature of the donee organization.

Several other types of property, in addition to inventory, are ordinary income property. For example, the term includes the following:

> **Ordinary income property** is property that would not produce captial gain if sold or exchanged.

1. Capital assets (such as shares of stock and land held for investment) if held for one year or less

2. Art objects, literary works, and so on, produced by the taxpayer

3. Property used in a business or held for investment to the extent that its sale would result in ordinary income (usually through depreciation recapture.) (See Chapter 14.)

4. Inventories of consumable supplies that would be charged to expense when used in the business.

5. Letters and memoranda by or to the taxpayer

Consequently, the donation of any of these properties to a qualifying organization usually creates a deduction that is less than the fair market value of the property.

CAPITAL GAIN PROPERTY.   If the sale of contributed property would have resulted in *long-term* capital gain, the fair market value of the property is deemed to be the amount contributed. Capital gain property is property that would result in long-term capital gain if sold. Examples are shares of stock, land, buildings, and purchased works of art held for more than one year. (See Chapter 16 for a further definition of capital gain property.) There are two exceptions to the rule that donations of capital gain property are equal to the fair market value of the property:

1. Tangible *personalty* (not realty), unrelated to the donee organization's exempt function (for example, an object of art that will be resold by the donee charity).

2. Any capital gain property contributed to a nonoperating *private* foundation that does not meet certain technical requirements (Because this exemption is rarely encountered, we will not discuss it further.)

In the case of property that fits into the two exceptions above, the amount deemed to have been contributed is the property's fair market value reduced by the amount that would have been capital gain had the property been sold.

private foundations, the contributions to public charities must be deducted first. Since the rules are extremely unlikely to affect the "typical individual taxpayer" described at the beginning of Chapter 9, contributions to private foundations will not be considered further.

Time of Deduction

Under most circumstances an individual taxpayer may deduct contributions only in the year in which he or she actually transfers the cash or other property to the qualified recipient. Pledges of contributions are not deductible until paid. This restriction applies equally to accrual-basis taxpayers and to cash-basis taxpayers. Payments by credit card, however, are treated like cash payments in the year the credit slip is signed.

Any contributions to public charities in excess of 50% of the taxpayer's AGI can be carried over to the following year and treated as having been paid in that year. If the sum of the carryover and the actual contributions made to public charities in the second year again exceeds 50% of the taxpayer's AGI, the excess may be carried over to the following year. This procedure can be repeated for up to five years. If because of the percentage limitation a contribution cannot be fully deducted during the five-year carryover period, an unused amount is simply lost as a deduction. In each year, the contributions actually paid during that year must be deducted before any of the contribution carryover is used. If excess contributions are carried over from more than one tax year, the carryovers are used in order of occurrence (a FIFO basis).

Contributions of appreciated capital gains property that exceed the 30% limit may be carried over to future years and added to the capital gain contributions of the future years, subject to a five-year carryover limit. A taxpayer can avoid the 30% limit by electing to reduce the deduction for capital gain property by the amount of the unrealized appreciation.

EXAMPLE 10-12

Arlo gave capital gain property with a fair market value of $10,000 and an adjusted basis of $8,000 at a time when his AGI was only $20,000. If Arlo wishes to deduct the fair market value of the property, he must carry over $4,000 to the succeeding year. On the other hand, he could elect to deduct the adjusted basis ($8,000) all in the current year since this amount is less than 50% of AGI. Of course, there would be no carryover if this election were made.

Importance of the Contributions Deduction by Individuals

Contributions are the third most important group of itemized deductions (following interest and taxes) made by individuals. As shown in Table 10-1 during 1989 deductions for contributions on individual returns totaled $55.3 billion, or about 13% of the total of all itemized deductions on such returns.

It is normally assumed that persons subject to high tax rates are more influenced in their giving by tax considerations than those in lower brackets. Studies by the IRS have shown that contributions are relatively more important in the two highest tax brackets ($500,000 to $1,000,000 and over $1,000,000 AGI) but that a substantial portion of contributions are made by taxpayers with incomes below $10,000. These studies also show a distinct difference in the pattern of giving by large and small contributors. Large contributors give substantial support to educational institutions, hospitals, welfare agencies, and private foundations; low-income taxpayers make most of their contributions to religious groups. For tax years 1982–1986, limited charitable contributions by persons who did not itemize deductions were permitted, but Congress did not renew this provision in the 1986 Act.

Until 1970, wealthy taxpayers were able to use private foundations to achieve some personal financial or other objectives. Today, deductibility of any contributions to private foundations depends on the foundation's compliance with Treasury Department requirements. If a foundation is found to be no longer exempt, a steep penalty tax is imposed unless the foundation's assets are used for charitable purposes. Additionally, excise taxes are levied on certain transactions in which the foundation seeks to achieve such aims as exerting political influence, providing operating capital for donor corporations, and other objectives not compatible with its tax-exempt status.

The Contributions Deduction and Social Welfare

Deductions for contributions to philanthropic organizations were first allowed in 1917 because of the fear that high wartime tax rates would cause a decline in contributions. A deduction allowance for contributions is usually justified as an encouragement to a socially desirable activity. Presumably, contributions provide highly desirable activities with finances that are not adequately provided by other sources and would have to be provided by the state if they were not supplied by voluntary contributions. Many people would describe the charitable deduction as simply a subsidy to charitable causes.

Many tax scholars question the effectiveness of the charitable deduction as an incentive for giving, pointing out that little is known about the actual value of gifts to philanthropies. Professor Harry Kahn has presented evidence to indicate that the relation between contributions and income has been rather stable over the years, regardless of the contribution provisions of the income tax laws in existence.[8] Various studies arrived at conflicting conclusions regarding the impact of deductibility on charitable giving, although there is a general consensus that tax rates and deductibility significantly influence charitable giving.[9]

A possible alternative to the contribution provision might be to eliminate the deduction and, instead, allow the government to match contributions, at a given rate, by refunding the contributor's tax directly to the philanthropy to which the taxpayer made the gift. This would overcome the almost impossible task the IRS now has in auditing contribution deductions, because it would then deal with several thousand philanthropic organizations rather than millions of taxpayers. Also, with this scheme Congress could delineate more clearly the activities it wishes to subsidize.

An important question is whether it is proper for the taxpayer, by making a deductible contribution, to force "the government in effect to make a partial matching grant for a purpose of his own choosing and to an organization whose operations are not subject to government review or control. Sectarian, provincial, eccentric, or frivolous uses of money may be aided along with the most worthy."[10] However, the lack of government control may be a positive advantage because it allows many educational, scientific, and cultural activities to maintain diversity and independence they would not have if Congress scrutinized each deduction. The appropriations process is not well suited to the nourishment of new and unpopular ideas, and the

---

8 C. Harry Kahn, "Personal Deductions in the Individual Income Tax," *1959 Compendium,* pp. 392–95.

9 For a review of these studies, see C. T. Clotfelter, *Federal Tax Policy and Charitable Giving* (The University of Chicago Press, 1985).

10 Richard Goode, *The Individual Income Tax* (Washington, DC: The Brookings Institution, 1964), p. 169.

unusual procedures for handling public funds to finance many activities of philanthropic organizations would be cumbersome and unsatisfactory.

Of course, freedom from control is not completely achieved under the current system of contribution deductions. Professor Melvin White observed this limitation of the current system in the following words:

> The policies and administration of recipient institutions can scarcely be expected to remain independent of the viewpoint of major suppliers of their funds. There are the limitations on the size of deductible contributions, probably rarely reached, and the Government itself sets eligibility requirements for recipient institutions. But . . . the Government's program is biased to expand the influence of the rich as compared to the moderate- and low-income giver.[11]

MEDICAL EXPENSES

The U.S. income tax is filled with special provisions and rules intended to promote the general welfare. The deduction for medical expenses was designed to relieve the economic hardships of individuals whose medical expenses exceed a certain threshold amount.

General Rule

The basic authority for deduction of medical expenses is Sec. 213, which reads in part as follows:

(a) Allowance of deduction—There shall be allowed as a deduction the expenses paid during the taxable year, not compensated for by insurance or otherwise, for medical care of the taxpayer, his spouse, or a dependent (as defined in Section 152), to the extent that such expenses exceed 7 $1/2$% of adjusted gross income.

Medical care is further defined in Sec. 213(d)(1) as follows:

(1) The term "medical care" means amounts paid—

    (A) for the diagnosis, care, mitigation, treatment, or prevention of disease, or for the purpose of affecting any structure or function of the body.

    (B) for transportation primarily for and essential to medical care referred to in subparagraph (A), or

    (C) for insurance . . . covering medical care referred to in subparagraphs (A) and (B).

> **Medical care** is defined in the Code as amounts paid for the diagnosis, care, mitigation, treatment, or prevention of disease, or for the purpose of affecting any structure or function of the body.

Thus, medical costs include unreimbursed amounts paid for medical and dental care, such as physicians' charges, hospital rooms, nursing care, laboratory charges, dentures, optical care, glasses, insulin, prescription drugs and medicines, and premiums on health and hospitalization insurance policies.

Expenses for items such as vitamins and toothpaste—that is, items intended to improve or preserve the general health—are generally not deductible. Vitamins prescribed by a physician, however, are deductible. The cost of birth control pills, as well as the cost of a vasectomy or a legal abortion, is deductible as a medical expense.

---

11 Melvin I. White, "Proper Income Tax Treatment of Deductions for Personal Expense," *1959 Compendium*, p. 371.

Transportation costs "primarily for and essential to" medical care are considered medical costs, as are lodging costs on a trip essential to medical care if the care is provided in a hospital or medical care facility related to a hospital and there is "no significant element of personal pleasure, recreation, or vacation in the travel away from home" [Sec. 213(d)(2)(B)]. In no case can the lodging costs exceed $50 per night for each individual while that individual is an "outpatient." The taxpayer who uses his or her personal automobile for transportation to secure medical care may ether deduct the actual expenses incurred or use the standard allowance of nine cents per mile, plus parking fees and toll charges.

Capital expenditures related specifically to an individual's illness may also be deductible. For example, the cost of a wheelchair would be deductible in the year purchased. However, capital expenditures that increase the value of property are not allowed as a deduction to the extent of the increase in the property's value. For example, the cost of a swimming pool installed in the home of an individual whose doctor recommends daily swimming as therapy is deductible only to the extent that its cost exceeds any increase in the value of the home. Additionally, the Conference Committee Report associated with the Tax Reform Act of 1986 made it clear that specified capital expenditures "incurred to accommodate a personal residence to the needs of a physically handicapped individual, such as construction of entrance ramps or widening of doorways to allow use of wheelchairs, constitute medical expenses . . ." which can be deducted immediately. Evidently Congress believed that these expenditures would not increase the fair market value of a residence and should therefore be fully deductible.

The observant student quickly recognizes the familiar problem of distinguishing between expenses that are purely "personal" and those that are property deductible. The problem has been particularly evident in cases in which pleasure activities are involved in the expenditure. For example, a physician may recommend that the taxpayer leave the cold weather of Michigan and go to the sunshine of Arizona for the winter. Under current rules, only the transportation costs involved would be in question. However, based on the simple facts given before, no hard and fast answer could be given to the question of whether even these costs are deductible. Presumably, if the change in climate is recommended for treatment of a specific or chronic ailment, the costs would be deductible. A change recommended for "general health" reasons would be disallowed.

Note that the medical expense deduction is allowed only for amounts *paid* during the tax year. Thus, if the taxpayer incurs medical expenses in the current year but does not make payment until the next year, no deduction would be allowed until next year. However, if payment is made by credit card, the deduction must be taken in the year charged to the account, regardless of when that account is actually paid. In general no deduction can be taken for prepaid medical expenditures even though insurance premiums are deductible. A possible exception to this rule applies in the case of lump-sum payments to nursing homes and in the case of certain insurance premiums paid by a taxpayer before he or she reaches the age of 65.

Computing the Deduction for Medical Expenses

The taxpayer may take a deduction only for medical expenses paid during the taxable year for himself or herself, a spouse, or dependent[12]—and only to the extent that they

12 Note that for this purpose a person need satisfy only three of the usual five criteria applicable to the determination of dependency status. They are the "support," the "relationship," and the citizen or resident criteria.

are not reimbursed by insurance or otherwise. As previously pointed out, medical expenses are deductible only to the extent they exceed 7 $1/2$% of the taxpayer's adjusted gross income.

EXAMPLE 10-13

Mr. and Mrs. Blue have an AGI of $20,000 and paid the following medical expenses during the tax year for themselves and dependents:

Hospital insurance premium	$1,210
Prescription medicine and drugs	620
Doctor bills	420
Dental care	170
Optical care	150
	$2,570

The Blues are entitled to include $1,070 in itemized deductions:

Medical expenses incurred	$2,570
Less 7 $1/2$% of AGI	1,500
Medical expense deduction	$1,070

REIMBURSEMENT OF MEDICAL EXPENSES SUBSEQUENT TO YEAR OF DEDUCTION. When insurance or other reimbursement for medical expenses is received in a year after that in which the expenses were actually paid, the reimbursement is treated as income only to the extent that it represents repayment of expenditures that resulted in a tax benefit in a prior year.

EXAMPLE 10-14

Last year Fred had AGI of $10,000 and had excess deductions. Fred paid medical costs of $780 and therefore deducted medical expenses of $30 that year. This year he received insurance proceeds of $200 as reimbursement for part of the $780 spent last year. If Fred had received the insurance payment last year, he would have had no medical expense deduction. Thus, of the $200 received, $30 is reported as gross income this year because it represents repayment of an amount deducted last year; the other $170 is not considered gross income because it does not represent a tax benefit in the prior year. Of course, if Fred had not had sufficient itemized deductions to benefit from itemizing in the prior year, no part of the reimbursement received this year would be considered income.

History and Function of the Medical Deduction

Deductions for medical and dental expenses were first permitted in 1942. As stated by the Senate Finance Committee at that time, this provision was recommended "in consideration of the heavy tax burden that must be borne by individuals during the existing emergency and the desirability of maintaining the present high level of public health and morale" [13]

---

13 Senate Report No. 1631, Senate Finance Committee, 77th Congress, 2nd Session (U.S. Government Printing Office, 1942), p.6.

The original legislation relating to medical expenses was proposed by the Treasury and was intended to give more equitable treatment to taxpayers with extraordinary expenses.[14] Much of the public discussion relating to the medical expense deduction has stemmed from its rationale. The basic concept has been that only extraordinary expenses should be deductible, because extraordinary expenses reduce the taxpayer's disposable income and, therefore, his or her ability to pay taxes relative to other taxpayers with the same income. Obviously, however, what is considered ordinary and extraordinary is a matter of personal opinion. Congress apparently believed from 1942–1953 that extraordinary meant something in excess of 5% of AGI. Beginning in 1954, extraordinary meant something in excess of 3% of AGI (or 4%, if we include the 1% exclusion of medicines and drugs). From 1951 to 1966, all medical expenses were extraordinary for the elderly. Today, the tax laws reflect the belief that the taxpayer should be able to bear medical expenses up to $7 \frac{1}{2}$% of his or her AGI without any tax relief.

Many individuals feel that a prime concern of the community should be for the health and physical welfare of the individual and that the community has a responsibility for ensuring that everyone receives adequate medical care. By making all medical costs deductible, the government would be furthering this goal by cutting the cost of medical care and, at the same time, leaving the allocation of funds in the hands of individuals. Following this line of reasoning, it may be argued that the $7 \frac{1}{2}$% floor on medical costs should be abolished.

CASUALTY AND THEFT LOSSES

The deduction for casualty and theft losses of a taxpayer's property like that for medical expenses, is intended to provide tax relief to taxpayers suffering unusual, involuntary losses large enough "to have a significant effect upon an individual's ability to pay Federal income taxes."[15]

Prior to 1964, the full amount of each casualty loss was deductible; since that year, casualty and theft losses on property used in a trade or business have been deductible in full, but the deduction for such losses on nonbusiness property has been limited. In particular, the 10% of AGI floor, introduced in 1983, eliminated almost all deductions for personal casualty losses. In 1987, less than 1% of returns with itemized deduction reported deductible casualty losses.

The general provisions controlling the casualty and theft loss deduction as well as the associated definitional and computational problems were discussed in Chapter 5. Once the *amount* of the casualty loss has been determined, Sec. 165(h) provides the specific rules for determining the deductible portion for an individual taxpayer. Sec. 165(h)(1) and (2) reads:

(h) Treatment of Casualty Gains and Losses—

(1) $100 limitation per casualty.—Any loss of an individual described in subsection c(3) shall be allowed only to the extent that the amount of the loss to such individual arising from each casualty, or from each theft, exceeds $100.

14 Statement of Randolph E. Paul, hearings before House Ways and Means Committee, "Revenue Revision of 1942," 77th Congress, 2nd Sessions. (U.S. Government Printing Office, 1942), pp. 1612–13.

15 House Report No. 749, House Ways and Means Committee, 88th Congress, 1st Session. U.S. Government Printing Office, 1963), p. 52.

(2) Net casualty loss allowed only to the extent it exceeds 10 percent of adjusted gross income—

    (A) In general.—If the personal casualty losses for any taxable year exceed the personal casualty gains for such taxable year, such losses shall be allowed for the taxable year only to the extent of the sum of—

        (i) the amount of the personal casualty gains for the taxable year, plus

        (ii) so much of such excess as exceeds 10 percent of the adjusted gross income of the individual.

    (B) Special rule where personal casualty gains exceed personal casualty losses.—If the personal casualty gains for any taxable year exceed the personal casualty losses for such taxable year—

        (i) all such gains shall be treated as gains from sales or exchanges of capital assets, and

        (ii) all such losses shall be treated as losses from sales or exchanges of capital assets.

EXAMPLE 10-15

A fire in Mr. and Mrs. North's garage destroyed their automobile (value $5,500, basis $11,000); their gardening equipment (value $700, basis $2,000); and the garage itself (value $12,000, basis $5,000). Later in the year a thief snatched Mrs. North's handbag (value of handbag and contents, $500, basis $600). None of these losses was insured, and the North's AGI is $60,000. Following the rules explained in Chapter 5, the loss associated with the fire is $11,200 ($5,500 + $700 + $5,000) and the loss associated with the theft is $500. Each of these losses is first reduced by $100. The resulting total of $11,500 ($11,200 – $100 + $500 – $100) is then reduced by $6,000 (10% of $60,000 AGI). Mr. and Mrs. North can therefore include a $5,500 casualty loss along with their other itemized deductions.

Recall that the deduction for medical expenses includes premiums paid by the taxpayer on health insurance policies. There is no similar provision for deduction of premiums paid for insurance against casualty losses (except, of course, under the general provisions concerning deductions related to trade, business, and income-producing activities). Tax scholars often charge that the nondeductibility of insurance premiums discriminates against the insured taxpayer, especially because any insurance proceeds received as a result of the loss reduce the amount otherwise deductible and actually result in gain to the extent that the proceeds exceed the adjusted basis of the property. Further, individuals who are insured for personal losses must file a timely insurance claim to the extent they are insured with respect to such losses in order to deduct them at all.

Spouses who file a joint return are subject to a single $100 floor for each casualty. Thus, if a single thief stole items belonging to both husband and wife, a single floor of $100 would be imposed if they filed a joint return. However, they each would have a floor of $100 for their personal casualty loss if they filed separate returns.

A number of complications arise regarding the year in which a casualty should be deducted. In general, a loss is allowed as a deduction only for the year in which the loss is sustained. A loss arising from theft, however, is sustained in the year the theft is discovered, rather than in the year the actual theft took place. If a claim for reimbursement exists and there is a reasonable prospect for recovery, no portion of the loss with respect to which reimbursement may be received is deductible until it can be determined with reasonable certainty whether reimbursement will be received. Any portion of the loss not covered by a claim for reimbursement is deductible, however, in the year the casualty occurred or the theft was discovered.

As with medical expenses, if a taxpayer deducts a loss in one year and in a subsequent year receives reimbursement, he or she does not recompute the tax for the taxable year in which the deduction was taken. Instead, the taxpayer includes the reimbursement in income in the year it is received to the extent that the reimbursement represents recovery of an amount that gave rise to a tax benefit when the deduction was taken.

MISCELLANEOUS ITEMIZED DEDUCTIONS

Miscellaneous deductions fall into two categories—those that are subject to the 2% of AGI floor and those that are not. Deductions in the first category include unreimbursed employee business expenses authorized under Sec. 162, some expenses associated with hobbies, and investment expenses authorized under Sec. 212 (other than those associated with rents and royalties, which are fully deductible *for* AGI). Items in the first category are deductible only to the extent that the aggregate amount exceeds 2% of AGI. Items in the second category (miscellaneous deductions not subject to the 2% of AGI floor) include moving expenses, business expenses of handicapped individuals, and gambling losses. We begin by considering those deductions subject to the 2% floor.

Itemized Deductions Subject to the 2% of AGI Floor

The 1986 Act imposed a new 2% of AGI floor on certain itemized deductions. Section 67 states that "miscellaneous itemized deductions for any taxable year shall be allowed only to the extent that the aggregate of such deductions exceeds 2 percent of adjusted gross income." Further, "miscellaneous itemized deductions" are defined negatively as all itemized deductions except the following:

1. The deduction under Sec. 163 for interest

2. The deduction under Sec. 164 for taxes

3. The deduction under Sec. 165(a) for losses from theft and casualties to property held for personal use

4. The deduction under Sec. 170 for charitable contributions

5. The deduction under Sec. 213 for medical expenses

6. The deduction under Sec. 217 for moving expenses

7. Any deduction for impairment-related work expenses

8. The deduction under Sec. 691(c) for estate tax in case of income in respect of the decedent

9. Any deduction allowable in connection with personal property used in a short sale

10. The deduction under Sec. 1341 relating to computation of tax where the taxpayer restores a substantial amount held under claim of right

11. The deduction under Sec. 72(b)(3) relating to deduction where annuity payments cease before the investment is recovered

12. The deduction under Sec. 171 relating to deduction for amortizable bond premium

13. The deduction under Sec. 216 relating to deductions in connection with cooperative housing corporations

Note that only the first six items above are of interest to most taxpayers; the other seven, while important to some taxpayers, occur infrequently. Essentially, any deductible item not on this list and not included in Sec. 62 as a deduction for AGI is subject to the 2% floor. The most common deductions subject to the floor are unreimbursed employee business expenses authorized under Sec. 162 and investment expenses authorized under Sec. 212 (other than those associated with rents and royalties, which are fully deductible *for* AGI per Sec. 62(4). These two categories (and hobby-related expenses) are discussed below.

UNREIMBURSED EMPLOYEE BUSINESS EXPENSES. Section 162 allows the deduction of a number of expenses related to employment. These include travel and transportation, business-related meals, entertainment expenses, education expenses, union dues, uniforms, and various professional expenses such as dues and subscriptions.

The details of what constitutes deductible travel and transportation expenses, business meals, and entertainment expenses will be deferred until Chapter 13. At this point, it is sufficient to note that 20% of business meals and entertainment are disallowed as deductions.

(1) *Education expense.* In recent years, the tax status of education expenses has received much attention because of the substantial increase in educational costs at all levels. Various proposals have been made to grant special tax benefits to taxpayers incurring such costs, especially when related to higher education. These proposals included recommendations that taxpayers with children in college either be permitted to deduct part of the expenses involved or be granted a credit against the tax. It has also been suggested that taxpayers be allowed to capitalize the costs of their college educations and to amortize these costs over their expected productive lives.[16]

At the present time, however, there are stringent limitations on the deduction of education expenses. The basic provisions relating to educational expense deductions are explained in Treas. Reg. Sec. 1.162-5(b). A deduction may be taken for expenditures if the education

(1) Maintains or improves skills required by the individual in his employment or other trade or business, or

(2) Meets the express requirements of the individual's employer, or the requirements of applicable law or regulations, imposed as a condition to the retention by the individual of an established employment relationship, status, or rate of compensation.

---

16 For an interesting discussion of the treatment of education expenses, see Richard Goode, "Educational Expenditures and the Income Tax," in Selma J. Mushken, ed., *Economics of Higher Education*, Bulletin No. 5 (Washington, DC: U.S. Department of Health, Education, and Welfare. Office of Education, 1962), pp. 281–304.

This regulation permits deductions only for education expenses incurred purely for business purposes. This has been interpreted to mean that the costs of acquiring the basic education necessary for the taxpayer's *entrance* into his or her trade, business, or profession are *not* deductible, because they represent personal expenditures. After the taxpayer has attained the minimum educational requirements and is active in a job, however, he or she may deduct expenditures made to maintain or improve job skills. Costs of education undertaken *primarily* to obtain a promotion, an increase in pay, or a new job are nondeductible. It is extremely difficult in many cases to determine why education costs are incurred by the taxpayer. As a result, there have been frequent changes in the regulations and many conflicting court decisions over the deductibility of education costs. Not surprisingly, many tax advisors simply decide that if any doubt exists, they should attempt to take a deduction for educational costs.

One area of controversy between taxpayers and the IRS has been over the deductibility of travel as an education-related expense. Treas. Reg. Sec. 1.162-5(d) states that such expenditures are deductible "only to the extent [they] are attributable to a period of travel that is directly related to the duties of the individual in his employment or other trade or business." The obvious problem with such travel is determining whether it is primarily personal or primarily to obtain education. Code Sec. 274(m)(2), added by the 1986 Act, overrides the regulation cited above and denies any deduction for travel that would be deductible only on the ground that the travel itself constitutes a form of education.

(2) *Other employment-related expenses subject to the 2% floor.*   A number of miscellaneous employment-related deductions are allowed employees. These include union dues, professional fees and dues, work-related uniforms, and, in a few cases, home-office costs. This last deduction is allowed employees only to the extent that a portion of the home is used exclusively and on a regular basis for the convenience of the taxpayer's employer. It is not sufficient that the use of an office at home would be appropriate or helpful. Thus, a school teacher who grades papers at home in the evening would not be permitted a deduction under this provision. For a discussion of the rules applied to calculating home office expenses, see Chapter 13.

EXPENSES RELATED TO A HOBBY.   Recall from Chapter 5 that if an activity is deemed to be a hobby, then deductions attributable to the activity are limited to gross income from the hobby. Further, Sec. 183 specifies that the first amounts deductible are those that would be deductible without regard to the hobby (such as home mortgage interest or property taxes on the home). Other amounts deductible are classified as miscellaneous itemized deductions subject to the 2% floor. Of these expenses, the taxpayer must first deduct out-of-pocket costs and then depreciation of fixed assets used in the hobby.

EXAMPLE 10-16

Anna, a school teacher makes quilts in her spare time. This activity is deemed to be a hobby. Anna's quilting frame and other materials and supplies occupy a room in her house. This year gross revenues from the sale of quilts was $1,800. Expenses were home mortgage interest and taxes attributable to the room used,

Continued

EXAMPLE 10-16 (Con't.)

$1,700; utilities and homeowner's insurance attributable to the room, $500; quilting supplies and materials used, $400; depreciation of quilting frame, $400. The home mortgage interest and taxes are deductible along with other interest and taxes (and would be deductible whether or not Anna engaged in making quilts as a hobby). Only $100 of the out-of-pocket expenses (utilities, insurance, materials and supplies) may be deducted as miscellaneous itemized deductions subject to the 2% floor. None of the depreciation may be deducted. The disallowed expenses may not be carried forward.

INVESTMENT AND TAX PREPARATION EXPENSES ALLOWED UNDER SECTION 212.
A third category of expenses subject to the 2% of AGI floor includes expenses permitted by Sec. 212 for the production or collection of income; the management, conservation, or maintenance of property held for the production of income; or in connection with the determination, collection, or refund of any tax. Typical Sec. 212 expenses relate to portfolio income (interest, dividends, and royalties) as well as to property held for investment that is not a passive activity (for example, vacant land held for speculation). Recall that Sec. 62 permits deductible expenses associated with rents and royalties as deductions for AGI, but other expenses associated with investments are deductions from AGI. Some examples of items included in this category are fees paid for investment counsel, subscriptions to publications such as the *Wall Street Journal*, and the cost of safe-deposit boxes used to hold securities. For tax years after 1986, no deduction is allowed for attending a convention, seminar, or similar meeting if the deduction must be justified under Sec. 212 (that is, related to investments, financial planning, and so on). Thus, a taxpayer who wishes to learn more about investing in the stock market could not deduct the cost of attending a seminar on this subject unless his or her trade or business (as a stockbroker, for example) justifies the deduction. Section 212 also permits the deduction of expenses in connection with the determination, collection, or refund of any tax.

Miscellaneous Deductions Not Subject to 2% Floor

Only a few miscellaneous itemized deduction are not subject to the 2% floor. Those discussed here are moving expenses, business expenses of handicapped individuals, and gambling losses.

MOVING EXPENSES. Section 217 of the Code permits the taxpayer to deduct the expenses of moving either on beginning employment as a new employee or on changing job location in his or her present employment. The moving expense deduction is now available to both employees and self-employed persons. The major requirements of eligibility are as follows:

1. The move must be to a new principal *job site* that is at least 35 miles further from the old residence than was the old *job site*: or at least 35 miles from the taxpayer's former residence if he or she had no former principal place of work.

2. An *employee* must be a full-time employee at the new job location for at least 39 weeks during the 12-month period immediately following arrival at the new job location. A *self-employed* person must perform services on a full-time basis in the new location for at least 78 weeks in the following 24-month period.

Death, involuntary separation, and other job transfers for the convenience of the employer remove the time limitations.

The deductible moving costs fit into two broad groups:

1. Direct costs, deductible without limit. The two main elements of direct costs are (a) transportation of household goods and personal effects and (b) travel costs of the taxpayer and family en route from the former to the new residence. If the taxpayer uses a personal automobile in the move, he or she may deduct the actual out-of-pocket costs incurred (gasoline, oil, and so on) or use an allowance of nine cents per mile.

2. Indirect costs, limited to a total deduction of $3,000. The three main elements of indirect costs are as follows:

   a. Pre-move house-hunting costs at new location after new employment has been obtained;

   b. Temporary living costs for taxpayer and family at new principal job location (up to 30 days);

   c. Costs related to selling old residence, terminating old lease, and obtaining new residence or living quarters.

Meals are subject to the 80% limitation. Furthermore, the amount deductible for house-hunting costs and temporary living quarters [items 2(a) and (b)] is limited to a total of $1,500.

EXAMPLE 10-17

Steve and Patricia French moved from Seattle to Salt Lake City to accept new jobs. They incurred $8,500 of direct moving costs, $1,300 of pre-move house hunting costs, and $6,000 realtor's commission to sell their old house. Their deductible moving expenses are $11,500 ($8,500 direct moving costs plus $1,300 pre-move house-hunting costs plus $1,700 of realtor's commission). The remaining realtor's commission may be deducted in determining the gain on sale of their old house. (See Chapter 17 for a discussion of treatment of gain or loss on sale of a home.)

There are several exceptions to the general rules explained above. Military personnel who must make service-connected moves are not required to meet either the 35-mile test or the 39-week test. If the new place of employment is outside the United States, the period during which temporary living costs may be deducted is 90 days rather than 30 days. Similarly, the overall limit on indirect costs that may be deducted is $6,000 rather than $3,000; the limit on the amount deductible for house-hunting costs and temporary living costs is $4,500 instead of $1,500.

Finally, it should be noted that many employers reimburse all or part of moving expense. Reimbursement of moving expenses does *not* cause these expenses to be classified as deductions for AGI. This classification is available only for expenses paid or incurred by the taxpayer "in connection with the performance by him of services as an employee."[17] Therefore, any reimbursement received by an employee would be

---

17 Sec. 62(a)(2)(A).

treated as part of gross income, and moving expenses would be treated as a deduction from AGI.

BUSINESS EXPENSES OF HANDICAPPED INDIVIDUALS.   Handicapped individuals are allowed to deduct payments for impairment-related work expenses including attendant care services at the individual's place of employment and other expenses necessary for the individual to be able to work.

GAMBLING LOSSES.   Gambling winnings are included in gross income. Losses from gambling are permitted as deductions, but only to the extent of gains from gambling. Therefore, a taxpayer who won $100 in a state lottery could deduct the cost of losing lottery tickets purchased in the same year up to $100. However, gambling losses are deductible only as itemized deductions unless gambling is the taxpayer's trade or business.

Determination of Total Itemized Deductions

Figure 10-2 depicts the determination of deductions from AGI and the comprehensive example illustrates many of the rules discussed in this chapter.

Goal #4
Determine total itemized deductions and compare with the standard deduction.

FIGURE 10-2

Determination of Deductions From AGI

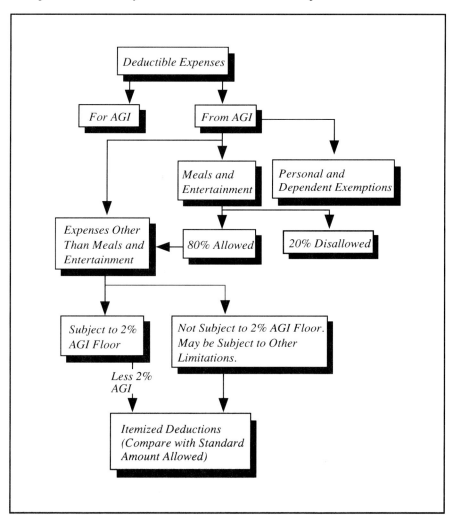

COMPREHENSIVE EXAMPLE.   Ron and Nancy Anderson are both accountants employed by large accounting firms. They have no children, but they do provide 100% of the support for Ron's 25-year-old brother who lives with friends, is not a student, and has no income. The Anderson's adjusted gross income in 1992 was $60,000, including net investment income of $2,000. They incurred the following expenses.

Medical expenses	$1,000
Charitable contributions	3,000
Home mortgage interest (all acquisition debt)	6,000
Interest on auto loan	800
Investment interest	2,500
Casualty loss from auto accident	1,200
Property taxes on home	2,000
General sales tax	600
State income tax	4,000
Unreimbursed professional dues	500
Educational expenses related to Ron's job (all tuition)	1,500
Professional entertainment expense	300
Cost of attending AICPA annual meeting (includes $200 for meals)	1,000
Moving expenses (from St. Louis to Milwaukee), no meals included,	1,400

The Anderson's deductions from AGI consist of personal and dependent exemptions of $6,900 (3 x $2,300) and itemized deductions of $20,400, calculated as follows:

Medical expenses	$1,000		
Less 7 1/2% AGI	(4,500)	$ 0	
Taxes			
State income tax	$4,000		
Property tax on home		2,000	
General sales tax	0	6,000	
Interest			
Home mortgage	$6,000		
Auto loan	0		
Investment interest	2,000	8,000	
Charitable contributions		3,000	
Casualty loss	$1,200		
Less $100 floor	(100)		
	$1,100		
Less 10% AGI	(6,000)	0	
Miscellaneous deductions			
Moving expense	$1,400		
Subject to 2% floor			
Professional dues	$ 500		
Educational expenses	1,500		
Entertainment [80% ($300)]	240		
Annual meeting [$1,000 – 20% ($200)]	960		
	$3,200		
Less 2% AGI	1,200	2,000	3,400
Total itemized deductions			$20,400

Since $20,400 is well in excess of the standard deduction for a married couple filing jointly in 1992 ($6,000), the Andersons obviously will choose to deduct the total itemized deductions of $20,400.

_____ KEY POINTS TO REMEMBER

✓ Deductions from AGI consist of personal and dependent exemptions plus the greater of a standard amount or itemized deductions.

✓ Most individual taxpayers are entitled to a personal exemption deduction. The one exception is a taxpayer who can be claimed as someone else's dependent.

✓ Taxpayers also may claim exemptions for individuals who meet the definition of a dependent.

✓ Most individual taxpayers are entitled to deduct a standard amount from AGI in addition to their deductions for personal and dependent exemptions.

✓ Taxpayers who can establish that allowable deductions from AGI (not including personal and dependent exemptions) exceed the standard amount can deduct the larger amount by itemizing deductions.

✓ By far the most important itemized deductions in aggregate are interest, taxes, and charitable contributions. They account for over 88% of itemized deductions.

_____ RECALL PROBLEMS

1. The correct classification of the various subtractions in the individual tax formula is very important.

   a. Why is the accurate calculation of gross income important?

   b. Why is the accurate calculation of adjusted gross income important?

2. In each of the independent cases below, calculate the number of exemptions for the taxpayer, assuming the current year.

   a. Taxpayer, age 67, and wife, age 63, file a joint return.

   b. Taxpayer, age 68, and wife, age 65, are both blind and file a joint return.

   c. Taxpayer and husband, both 48, spent $3,000 toward living expenses for their son who is 23 and a full-time college student. The son also earned $2,500 during the summer, received a scholarships of $400, and received $450 under the GI Bill. The son used all of these funds for his living costs.

   d. Assume the same facts as in part c, except that the son is 25 years old.

   e. Taxpayer, age 55, provides 100% of the support for her 30-year-old son who is a full-time student.

   f. Taxpayer received her divorce decree on January 8 and has not remarried. The divorce decree requires her ex-husband to pay $3,000 a year for the support of their child, who is 5 years old and lives with the mother. They have not discussed who is to claim an exemption for the child.

   g. Assume the same facts as in part f, except that the divorced couple have agreed in writing that the father is to claim an exemption for the child. The taxpayer is the mother.

   h. Taxpayer is 67 years old. He pays $750 per month to keep his mother, age 88, in a retirement home. The mother also receives Social Security benefits of $300 per month and gross annual rental income of $2,500 (rental expenses consume $1,800 of this amount). She uses all the available funds for living costs.

i. Smith and his wife have great compassion for orphaned children. Currently, they have living in their home and are completely supporting five children, all of whom are in school. The five foster children have been living in Smith's home all year, but none of them have been adopted. None of the children has any income.

j. Williford and his wife have a foster child living in their home for the entire year for whom they provide major support. The foster child, age 15, has gross income of $2,600.

k. An unmarried taxpayer provides over half the support for his 18-year-old sister, who does not live with him. The sister earned $3,000 during the year.

#1

3. For each of the following independent situations, determine the proper number of exemptions to be taken, assuming the current tax year.

a. Taxpayer, age 66, and spouse, age 62, file a joint return. They have one son, age 22, who is a full-time student at State University. The son earned $2,100 in a summer job and received a $1,000 scholarship from State University. During the year, the son's total support cost $5,300, of which $2,200 was paid by his parents.

b. Taxpayer and spouse, both under 65, file a joint return. They provided more than half the support of two unmarried children, both under 19. One child earned $2,400 from a part-time job. Taxpayer also provided most of the support for his blind mother, who is over 65. The mother received $3,500 in Social Security benefits.

c. Taxpayer, unmarried, under 65 and with good vision, provides more than half the support of his brother and sister-in-law, who attend State University. The brother earned $2,800 from a part-time job. The sister-in-law had no income. The brother filed a separate tax return, claiming one exemption.

d. Taxpayer, unmarried, under 65, provides more than half the support for his nephew and the nephew's wife, both of whom attend State University. The nephew earned $2,800 from a part-time job. The nephew filed a separate return in order to receive a refund of taxes paid. He did not claim an exemption.

#1

4. Determine the correct number of exemptions for each situation described below.

a. John Smith, a 66-year-old bachelor, maintains a home in which his deceased friend's 21-year-old son has lived for the past 14 years. The young man is a full-time college student who earned $2,700 during the year. John can prove that he furnishes 65% of the young man's support.

b. Jacques, a widower for four years, age 63, maintains a home that is the principal abode for himself, his married daughter Joan, and his grandchild Zed. Jacque's son-in-law is a wandering bum. Jacques provides more than half the support of all those who live with him. Joan and her husband file a joint return, but they do not claim Zed as their dependent because their joint earnings are only $7,800.

c. Alan Standard contributes more than half the support of his mother and father, who live with him. Alan is 38 and single; his father is 66 and his mother 64. Alan's father earned $2,500 during the year and filed a separate return claiming himself as an exemption.

d. Jack and Jill, who file a joint return, provide more than half the support for their two children. Andrea, who is 5 years old, models clothes for a local department store. Because Andrea earned $3,000 during the year, she filed her own tax return. Their son, Don, who is 2 years old, was born blind. Jack and Jill also have been raising (without adopting) 6-year-old Ted, who was orphaned by an automobile accident. The total expenditures for Ted amounted to $2,500 during the year. Of the $2,500, Jack and Jill paid $1,500 from their personal funds; the remainder was provided by a county welfare program.

5. Discuss two situations in which taxpayers are not entitled to take full advantage of the standard deduction.

#2

6. Which of the following individuals will benefit from itemizing deductions? In each case, indicate the standard deduction to which the individual is entitled.

#2

a. Mary, a single individual, who has actual itemized deductions of $3,500.

b. Mary, a head of household, who has actual itemized deductions of $5,500.

c. Mary, a surviving spouse, who has actual itemized deductions of $5,500.

d. Mary, who is married and files separately from her spouse, who itemizes his deductions. Mary has actual itemized deductions of $900.

e. Mary, a single individual, who is blind and age 72 and has actual itemized deductions of $4,600.

f. Mary and Jack, who are married and file jointly, have actual itemized deductions of $7,300. They have four dependent children.

g. Mary is a 10-year-old dependent child. This year her only income is $700 of interest. She has no actual itemized deductions.

h. Mary is a 10-year-old dependent child. This year her income consists of $700 interest and $400 from babysitting. She has no actual itemized deductions.

i. Same facts as in part h, except that Mary earns $750 from babysitting.

7. In each of the following independent cases, indicate the amount that the taxpayer may deduct as interest on his or her federal income tax return:

a. Alexander paid interest of $2,100 on a loan secured to purchase City of Midville bonds on which he received interest of $2,800.

b. Elmot made the following interest payments during the year: $60 on a loan obtained to buy his wife some jewelry on their 25th wedding anniversary: $670 on his home mortgage (acquisition debt); $45 on a loan obtained at the bank by his dependent 23-year-old son (Elmot also paid the loan principal to protect the family name even though he had no legal liability for the note or interest); $48 to the life insurance company on the loan value of his policy withdrawn to pay for his daughter's high school graduation present; and $92 on amounts owed on gambling debts.

c. Eileen is a majority stockholder in Town Corporation. In 19X1, Town suffered a financial reverse. To protect the corporation's good name, Eileen paid $6,000 of interest owed by the corporation to a local bank.

d. Cox paid $50,000 for his home ten years ago. Today, it is worth $100,000 and the balance due on his original mortgage is only $30,000. Cox recently (1991) borrowed $25,000 on a home equity mortgage, using the proceeds to buy a new car and travel to Europe. This year, interest payments on the original mortgage were $2,400, while interest payments on the home equity mortgage were $2,500.

e. Anderson paid $200,000 for her home 20 years ago. Today it is worth $500,000 and the balance due on her original mortgage is $80,000. Anderson recently borrowed $250,000 against the value of the home. Interest payments on the original mortgage were $4,000 while interest payments on the home equity mortgage were $25,000.

8. In the current year, Lemon and her husband filed a joint return showing adjusted gross income of $80,000. Included in their tax information were the following items:

Interest paid on funds borrowed last year to purchase stock and bonds	$48,000
Investment income	12,000
Investment-related expenses	800
Interest paid on home mortgage (acquisition debt)	6,200
Interest on personal loans	3,500

Compute the Lemons' interest deduction for the year.

9. Which of the following taxes are deductible for federal income tax purposes?

   a. Gift tax

   b. FICA tax on business employees

   c. State gasoline (excise) tax on gasoline used in family auto

   d. Federal gasoline tax on gasoline used in family auto

   e. State income tax

   f. Property tax on family residence

   g. State excise tax on cigarettes for personal consumption

   h. State excise tax on liquor consumed while entertaining business clients

   i. State excise tax on liquor for private consumption

   j. Automobile license (your state) for family auto

   k. State general sales tax on goods purchased for private consumption

10. In each of the following independent cases, indicate the amount that the taxpayer may deduct as taxes on his or her federal income tax return. Indicate whether any amount deductible is *for* AGI or *from* AGI.

   a. In July of this year, Atkins inherited some property from a deceased aunt. He paid a state inheritance tax of $1,200 on the inheritance.

   b. During the year, Bartholomew purchased various bottles of alcoholic beverages for personal use. The amount he paid for these beverages included $118 federal excise taxes, $32 state excise taxes, and $8 state retail sales tax.

   c. During the year, Irma paid the following real estate taxes on her home: state, $69; county, $64; city, $345; school district, $360. In addition, the city made a special assessment for paving the street and installing a curb and gutter in front of her home, $280.

d. Farmer had the following expenditures for taxes during 19X2: payment of 19X1 state income tax, $84; quarterly estimates of his 19X2 federal income tax, $4,600; final payment of net amount due on 19X1 federal income tax return, $310.

e. Goodman purchased real estate on May 1 of this year for $18,000. The estimated taxes for the year were prorated and the cash payment to the seller was reduced by $80, the estimated taxes through April 30. In December, Goodman paid the real estate taxes due for the year, $272.

11. In each of the following independent cases, indicate the amount that may be deducted as charitable contributions:

a. Adamson had AGI of $22,000. During the year, he made the following cash contributions:

Boy Scouts	$3,000
Local church	6,000
Local university	4,200

b. Bartholomew had AGI of $16,500. During the year, he made the following cash contributions:

Boy Scouts	$5,000
Democratic party	2,000
Needy family in neighborhood	400
London School of Economics (England)	800
Local Catholic hospital	1,000

c. Converse owns 1,000 shares of X Corporation stock for which she paid $10,000 in 1962. During the current year, she contributed 600 shares of this stock to the First Church of Centertown. On the date of the contribution, the shares had a market price of $25 per share. Converse's AGI this year was $25,000.

d. Farley operates a retail furniture store as a sole proprietorship. In July of this year, he contributed to the local hospital a number of items of furniture from his merchandise inventory (tables, chairs, and sofas). These items had cost him $3,800 but had a normal retail value of $7,400. Farley's AGI is $40,000.

e. Inglewood is active in the Boy Scouts. During the past year, he served as a scoutmaster. At year-end, he calculated that he had spent $80 for various scout activities such as fund-raising drives. In addition, he had driven his automobile an estimated 300 miles in connection with scout work. He also had lost 38 working hours from his job, with a loss in pay of $190.

f. Robb and three other adults traveled with a youth group from her church for a four-day ski trip in Colorado. Robb spent $150 for airfaire; the church paid for her food and lodging while in Colorado.

12. Burns contributed to the local art museum a painting that she had purchased several years ago for her private collection at a cost of $1,500. At the time of the gift, the painting was appraised at a value of $5,000. She also made cash gifts this year of $6,000 to various charities. Her AGI for the year is $80,000, and she itemizes deductions. Determine her total charitable contributions deduction for the year under the following two assumptions:

a. The museum intends to hang the painting in its permanent collection.

b. The museum intends to sell the painting.

#3

13. This year Abdul gave $50,000 worth of securities that he had owned for five years to State University. Abdul's AGI is $100,000. Assuming no other charitable contributions, what is the amount that he may deduct on this year's tax return?

#3

14. Which of the following items are deductible as medicine or medical costs?

a. Aspirin

b. Cost of dental plate

c. Contact lenses

d. Artificial limb

e. Vitamins prescribed by doctor

f. Transportation to and from doctor's office

g. Health food purchased by vegetarian

h. Bill for having teeth cleaned by dentist

i. Annual trip to Arizona to give the sinuses a rest

j. A legal abortion

k. A wheelchair

l. Repairs to the wheelchair

m. Nonprescription antihistamines taken to combat allergies

#3

15. In 19X1, taxpayer deducted medical expenses of $1,400. In 19X2, she received a $1,200 reimbursement of the expenses incurred in 19X1. If the reimbursement had been received in 19X1, the taxpayer's deduction for medical expenses that year would have been $200. What part of the reimbursement in 19X2, if any, is treated as gross income to the taxpayer?

#3

16. Marcus and Tania reported AGI of $20,000 in a year in which they incurred the following medical expenses:

Dentist's charges	$ 450
Physician's charges	900
Hospital costs	1,800
Prescription drugs	180
Medical insurance premiums	700
Remodeling home to accommodate Tania's wheelchair	5,000

The insurance company reimbursed Marcus and Tania for $1,700 of their hospital bill and $800 of their physician's charges. What is their medical expense deduction for the year?

17. John Beal, age 65, and wife, Miriam, age 39, filed a joint return for the current tax year showing an AGI of $45,000. Mrs. Beal's son by a former marriage is now a full-time university student and is fully dependent on the Beals. The Beals also provide over 50% of the support of Mr. Beal's mother, who is 85 and bedridden. Grandmother Beal receives $2,500 annual interest from a savings

account. Medical expenses in excess of reimbursements were paid by John and Miriam in the amounts stated below:

	John	Miriam	Son	Mother
Hospital insurance premium	$1,240	$ 0	$ 0	$ 0
Prescription drugs	150	350	10	400
Medical expenses	200	300	100	300
Nurse	0	0	0	5,200

Show your computation for the medical expense deduction that can be taken on Mr. and Mrs. Beal's joint tax return.

18. Ted Granger retired from Chicago to Miami, Florida, after 50 years of service with Bidwell Corporation. Each June, Ted flies back to Chicago for an annual physical examination by Dr. Knowbetter, a heart specialist who treated Ted 10 years ago. This annual physical requires approximately one week to complete. Between trips to the physician's office, Ted visits family and friends. The trip costs him $500 for transportation, $300 for a hotel ($50 per day), $140 for food, $200 of medical expenses, and $100 for incidentals. Which of these costs, if any, might Ted deduct? Explain your answer.

19. In each of the following cases, indicate the amount of casualty loss deductible and indicate how the loss would be handled on the income tax return. Assume there are no other casualties or thefts and that the taxpayer's AGI is $14,000 in each case.

   a. Hoover was vacationing in Miami. While Hoover was swimming, a thief stole his wristwatch (cost $220, with a fair market value of $180) and his billfold. The billfold contained $120 cash, which was not recovered. The billfold itself, with a value of $5, cost $10. Hoover was not insured.

   b. Berry owned a lake cabin with an adjusted basis of $16,000. On January 18, the cabin had a fair value of $14,000. On the next day, a tornado completely demolished the cabin, which was not insured. The cabin was held solely for personal use.

   c. Maranto fell asleep at the wheel of her new BMW and drove off the road, causing extensive damage to the car. Repairs cost $5,500. As this was Maranto's third accident in five years, she chose not to make a claim against her insurance policy for fear of cancellation of the policy. Presumably, she could have collected all but the $100 deductible on the policy.

   d. Jackson's home was burglarized. The thief took Mrs. Jackson's jewelry, which had a fair market value of $1,800 and a basis of $1,200. He also took Mr. Jackson's watch, which had a fair value of $150 and a basis of $300. Mr. Jackson and his wife, who filed a joint return, were not insured.

   e. Assume the same facts as in part d, except that the Jacksons filed separate returns. Jackson's AGI was $10,000; his wife's AGI was $4,000.

20. What common justification is given for permitting the deduction of both medical expenses and casualty losses?

#3

21. How does the tax treatment of insurance premiums for health and hospitalization insurance compare with the tax treatment of insurance premiums for fire, theft, and other casualty insurance on non-income-producing assets (for example, a home)? Comment.

#3

22. Elliot, a bank vice president, is not reimbursed for job-related entertainment expenses. This year she incurred $3,000 of entertainment expenses. Elliot is able to itemize deductions.

    a. Assuming Elliot's AGI is $70,000 and she has no other miscellaneous itemized deductions, how much of the $3,000 will she be able to deduct on her tax return?

    b. Assuming that Elliot is in the 31% marginal tax bracket, how much did the entertainment cost her after tax?

#3

23. Peterson, whose hobby is bird watching, paints pictures of birds in his spare time. He uses one room in his house solely for this activity. In recent years he has sold some of his paintings for as much as $400 each, but to date he has never earned a profit from this activity. This year, he earned $2,800 from the sale of his paintings. The costs he incurred were as follows:

Painting supplies	$ 650
Commissions to galleries	600
Trips to galleries	850
Use of room in home	
10% of mortgage interest	1,000
10% of utilities	350
10% of property taxes	200
10% of insurance premium	60

    Which of these costs may Peterson deduct on his tax return this year? In addition to the limits on hobby-related expenses, what other limits will apply?

#3

24. In each of the following independent cases, indicate whether the amount involved is (1) deductible *for AGI*, (2) deductible *from* AGI, or (3) not deductible at all. Put an asterisk next to items in category (2) that are subject to the 2% AGI floor.

    a. Taxpayer paid $8 rent on a bank safety deposit box in which he kept the few shares of stock that he owned.

    b. Taxpayer paid expenses of $1,200 applicable to rental property that he owned.

    c. Taxpayer replaced the roof on rental property that he owned. The new roof cost $1,000.

    d. Taxpayer purchased a vacant lot for investment. During the year, she paid $50 to have it mowed and cleaned.

    e. Taxpayer, a nurse, is employed at a local hospital. She spent $105 for uniforms during the year and was not reimbursed.

    f. Millsaps, a public school teacher, spent $40 for magazine subscriptions and was not reimbursed. The magazines were used in his classroom activities.

    g. Herman, a department store buyer, attended an out-of-town market at which he examined new merchandise. His total costs were $308 (meals $50, lodging $200, transportation $58). He was not reimbursed by his employer.

h. Taxpayer paid $650 real estate taxes on property used in his business.

i. Harry pays $500 per month in alimony and $200 per month in child support to his former wife Victoria.

j. Bill and Jane Rollins were divorced during the current year. The divorce decree provided that Bill should pay Jane a $42,000 lump-sum property settlement, which he paid this year.

25. Indicate how each of the following items will be treated on the individual's tax return. Your answer should include an indication of whether or not the item (or a portion of it) is subject to the 2% AGI floor.

a. Jake spent $1,200 this year on work-related eduction expenses, including $800 for tuition and $400 for transportation. Jake's employer reimbursed the $800 tuition.

b. George spent $800 entertaining prospective customers. George is a self-employed consultant.

c. Same facts as in part b, except that George is an employee of a consulting firm. He was not reimbursed for the entertainment.

d. Tillie is employed by an accounting firm. This year she traveled out of town on several audit engagements. She spent $1,500 on airfare, $600 on hotel costs, and $450 on meals. Tillie was reimbursed for all of these costs.

e. Same facts as in part d, except that Tillie is a self-employed accountant.

f. Taxpayer's employer provides uniforms, but she has to pay to have them dry-cleaned. This year she spent $130 having the uniforms cleaned.

g. Taxpayer is a self-employed special duty nurse. He spent $120 for nursing uniforms.

26. Indicate how much, if any, is deductible as educational expenses in each of the following independent cases. Briefly explain your answer, and indicate in each case whether the amount deductible is *for* AGI or *from* AGI. Ignore the 2% of AGI floor.

a. Haskins is a senior in college majoring in accounting. His college expenses for the current year were:

Tuition	$1,200
Books and supplies	340
Room	540
Meals	1,680

b. Bernard was a practicing certified public accountant in the tax department of a national accounting firm. During July of this year, Bernard decided that he should secure a law degree to further his career, so he resigned from the accounting firm and entered law school. His expenses relating to law school this year were $950.

c. Raymond works for an accounting firm. During this year, he attended several professional development programs sponsored by the American Institute of Certified Public Accountants. These programs were two- or three-day seminars or workshops held in other cities (requiring overnight travel), dealing with areas of accounting in which Raymond is involved. His expenses in attending these programs totaled $800, and they were not reimbursed by his employer.

The costs were as follows: registration fees, $200; transportation, $400; lodging, $110; and meals, $90.

d. Assume the same facts as in part c, except that Raymond is a self-employed accountant with his own public accounting firm.

e. Clifton, unmarried, is employed as a public school teacher. He possesses a BA degree, but the school board has stipulated that each teacher in the school system must return to college for additional course work at least each third summer. During this year, Clifton returned to the state university. His costs were as follows: tuition, $120; meals, $540; lodging, $285; transportation from his home town to the university and return, $23; and books, $40.

f. Dennis, who lives in Milwaukee, is a high school teacher. This January he traveled to Phoenix to attend a seminar entitled "How to Become a Millionaire by Investing in Real Estate." Dennis has not previously invested in real estate, but he is interested in doing so, especially if he can become wealthy. He paid $250 for airfare, $300 for lodging, $200 for food, and a $500 registration fee for the seminar.

g. Elsie, a high school French teacher, spent three weeks in France this summer for the purpose of improving her command of the French language and her understanding of French culture.

#3

27. John Farmer, whose AGI is $35,000, incurred the following expenses this year: unreimbursed employee travel costs, $1,000 (includes $300 for meals); reimbursed employee travel costs, $3,000; unreimbursed business entertainment costs, $400; unreimbursed tuition for job-related course, $300; tax preparation fee, $120; depreciation and other expenses associated with rental property Farmer owns, $2,000. Assuming that Farmer can itemize total deductions in excess of the standard amount, calculate his deductible miscellaneous itemized deductions.

#3

28. In each of the following independent cases, indicate whether the taxpayer is entitled to deduct expenses (depreciation, utilities, insurance, and so on) applicable to an office in the home:

a. Pete is an accounting professor at a state university. One room in his home has been converted into an office used by Pete solely for such tasks as grading papers, preparing exams, and reading journals.

b. Joe is a law professor in a state university. One room in his home has been converted into an office used solely by Joe for grading papers and other class-related activities and also for writing and revising textbooks from which Joe receives substantial royalties.

#3

29. Arno Grey has lived in New Orleans for five years and worked in an electrical manufacturing plant. In August of last year, he moved to St. Louis to take a new job and was still employed there at year-end. A review of Grey's records revealed the following facts related to his move and new job.

In June, Grey decided that he was tired of the hot weather in New Orleans, so he read the classified ads in the local newspaper and found a help-wanted ad by the St. Louis employer. He wrote the St. Louis company and was told that all applicants must appear in person at the company's home office, but that the company could not pay his travel costs for an interview. Grey went to St. Louis in early July for the interview. Cost of the plane ticket was $260, and he paid $20 for limousine service to and from airports. He arrived in St. Louis on Sunday evening, spent the night, and visited the company on Monday morning. He was immediately hired and planned to return to New Orleans on Monday evening. However, the employer suggested that Grey find a place to live. He therefore spent Tuesday and Wednesday looking at apartments and houses, spending $30 for taxi fares and telephone calls. Finding no suitable apartment, he purchased a house for $104,000. Grey's hotel room was $68 per night, and he spent $28 each day for food (Monday, Tuesday, and Wednesday). He returned to New Orleans on Wednesday evening.

   Grey sold his home in New Orleans for $48,000 (it had cost him $19,000) but had to pay a real estate commission of $2,880 on the sale. Other selling costs included an abstract fee of $120 and legal fees of $105.

   Grey shipped most of his furniture by truck, at a cost of $1,820, but he also rented a trailer for $98 and moved some himself. He and his family drove to St. Louis, spending $52 for meals and $64 for one night in a motel. He spent $84 for gasoline and $1.20 for oil on the trip. On arriving in St. Louis, Grey was shocked to find that the former owner of his house had not moved out, so Grey and his family had to live in a hotel for 18 days. Their costs while living there totaled $900 for room and $808 for meals. In addition, Grey paid $96 to have his furniture stored, and another $157 to have it delivered when he got possession of the house. Determine Grey's moving expense deduction.

30. In June of this year Steve Duffy completed his college education at the University of Michigan and accepted a job with a bank in Dallas. After accepting the job, Steve incurred the following expenses related to his move:

#3

   Airfare ($250), lodging ($60), and food ($50) incurred on a trip to find an apartment

   Rental of a van to move his household possessions and tow his automobile from Ann Arbor to Dallas ($1,100)

   Food ($100) and lodging ($80) on trip from Ann Arbor to Dallas

   Temporary living costs during first two weeks in Dallas while Steve waited for the apartment he had rented to be vacated (food, $500; hotel, $800).

   Cost of storing household possessions while waiting for apartment ($100)

   Cost of new lightweight wardrobe for Dallas climate ($1,500)

Steve's new employer reimbursed the costs of renting the van ($1,100) but none of the other costs associated with the move. Compute Steve's moving expense deduction assuming he has sufficient itemized deductions to exceed his allowed standard deduction.

31. This year David and Susan Martin had an adjusted gross income of $50,000. Determine the Martins' itemized deductions using the following list of unreimbursed expenses:

#4

Medical expenses	$ 900	Moving expenses (Houston to Omaha)	$2,000
Interest on home mortgage	7,200		
Interest on auto loan	150	Cost of attending professional meeting (including $100 for meals)	300
Uninsured theft loss from burglary	3,000	Tax return preparation fee	100
Charitable contributions	900	Union dues	150
State sales tax	300	Education costs related to Susan's job (tuition and transportaion)	800
Property tax on home	1,700		

_____ **THOUGHT PROBLEMS**

#3

1. Once a taxpayer has purchased a home, he or she almost always has excess itemized deductions. Explain why this statement generally is accurate.

#3

2. To what extent, if any, does the quality of medical care or its luxuriousness determine the extent to which it is deductible? For example, are different rules applied in determining deductibility of a bed in a hospital ward compared with one in a private room in an exclusive hospital? For contact lenses versus ordinary glasses?

#3

3. Taxpayer provided $600 per month during 19X1 toward the cost of maintaining his mother in the Sunshine Nursing Home. The home was chosen primarily because it had a physician and nurse on duty at all times. Taxpayer's mother had a series of heart attacks in recent years, and although her situation was not critical and she was not confined to her bed, the taxpayer felt it necessary to have immediately available medical care for her. In addition to the $7,200 provided by taxpayer, the mother also received $3,600 from Social Security benefits and $2,000 from a fully taxable pension during 19X1, all of which was used for the mother's living costs. What part, if any, of the $7,200 will the taxpayer be allowed to treat as medical expenses on his 19X1 tax return?

#3

4. Two types of floors for determining the amount of involuntary costs (medical expenses and casualty losses, for example) deemed to be extraordinary or unusual are discussed in this chapter. Compare the two, discussing their relative effects on taxpayers of different income levels.

#3

5. In 19X1, Jones had AGI of $30,000. He made the following contributions during the year:

   (1) Cash of $5,000 to his church.
   (2) Shares of stock that cost him $10,000 in 1960 to Stanford University. Fair market value at date of gift was $12,000.
   (3) A painting that cost him $3,000 in 1950 to a local hospital. Fair value at the date of the gift was $7,000. The hospital immediately sold the painting.

   a. What amount may Jones deduct as a contribution in 19X1?

   b. What amount, if any, does Jones carry forward to 19X2?

#3

6. Billie Sue Barnes, who is employed as a sales representative for a book publisher, receives an annual salary of $75,000. She makes a $2,000 deductible contribution to an IRA account each year. Her other deductions consist of mortgage interest of $6,000 and charitable contributions of $2,000. Billie Sue is reimbursed for her traveling expenses, which amount to about $5,000 per year (including $1,000 for meals). She is single and has no dependents.

   Billie Sue's employer is concerned about the rising costs associated with sales representatives' traveling expenses. In an attempt to control these costs, the company has decided to stop reimbursing these expenses. In lieu of reimbursement, each sales representative will receive a raise and will thereafter be responsible for his or her own traveling expenses. Billie Sue has been told she will receive a $6,000 raise.

   a. Assuming that Billie Sue's deductions and traveling expenses remain the same, by how much is she better or worse off after taxes because of this new plan?

b. What is the smallest pay increase Billie Sue could accept in lieu of reimbursement and be as well off after taxes as she is now?

c. What is the largest pay increase Billie Sue's employer could give her and be as well off as with the current plan? Assume the employer is in the 34% tax bracket.

CLASS PROJECTS

1. If a taxpayer builds an indoor swimming pool at a cost of $194,660 "to prevent paralysis from . . . a spinal injury," what part of that cost do you think that taxpayer might deduct as a medical expense? After you have made a guess, read and prepare a short report on *Ferris v. Commissioner*, 582 F.2d 1112 (CA-7, 1979) *rem'dg* TC Memo 1977–186.

2. When Charlotte's employer moved her to Houston, she purchased her first home for $90,000. Three years later, she was transferred to Chicago. Charlotte tried to sell her house but received no offer in excess of $75,000. Charlotte's employer had agreed to purchase her house for her cost if she was unable to sell it for at least that much. After the house had been on the market for six months, the employer purchased Charlotte's home for $90,000. Does Charlotte have any taxable income as a result of this transaction?

CALCULATING THE INDIVIDUAL TAX LIABILITY

CHAPTER OBJECTIVES

In Chapter 11 you will learn how to calculate the federal income tax for an individual taxpayer.

LEARNING GOALS

After studying this chapter, you should be able to

1 Select the correct tax-rate schedule for an individual taxpayer;

2 Calculate the tax liability for a dependent child;

3 Determine marginal tax rates for individual taxpayers;

4 Calculate the amount of an individual's tax credits;

5 Decide whether or not a taxpayer must file a return; and

6 Determine whether a taxpayer must pay estimated taxes, and, if so, how much.

Chapters 9 and 10 explored tax problems peculiar to individual taxpayers. These problems include determination of exclusions from gross income and of deductions for and from adjusted gross income. The end result of this process is, of course, taxable income. In this chapter, you will learn how an individual taxpayer calculates his or her tax liability given that taxable income has already been determined. Let us begin with selection of the appropriate tax rate schedule.

NOMINAL RATE SCHEDULES FOR INDIVIDUAL TAXPAYERS

Goal #1
Select the correct rate schedule.

INTRODUCTION

As you learned in Chapter 6, four different tax rate schedules are now available to individual taxpayers, whereas prior to 1948 there was only one. The three additional rate schedules were added to the law in an attempt to resolve complex issues of equitable taxation of individual taxpayers with varying personal and family obligations. The correct choice of filing status can be very important to a taxpayer.

EXAMPLE 11-1

Kelly, whose taxable income is $40,000, incorrectly assumes that he must use the single rate schedule. He calculates his tax for 1992 to be $8,411.50. In fact, Kelly is entitled to file as a head of household, and his correct tax is $7,462.50.

FILING STATUS

Joint Returns and Surviving Spouses

As explained in Chapter 6, the joint return originally was designed to give the split income advantage of citizens in community property states to those residing in common law states. As originally conceived, filing a joint return resulted in the same tax as combining the income of a husband and wife, dividing it in half, computing a tax on that half using the basic rate schedule, and then doubling that amount.

As Congress added other rate schedules, this original objective has become less evident, though the taxes obtained from using Schedule Y-Joint are still lower than from using the other schedules (see Appendix A). For 1992, the rate rises from 15% to 28% at $35,800 on joint returns, compared to $21,450 on single returns, and $28,750 for heads of household.

The statute provides criteria that must be met before a taxpayer may use the joint return schedule. Two taxpayers may file a joint return if

1. They are married (not divorced or legally separated on the last day of their taxable year) or they were married at the date of death of one spouse during the taxable year, and

2. Neither spouse is a nonresident alien at any time during the year unless an irrevocable election is made to include the worldwide income of both spouses on the return.

Note that a joint return is permitted for the year within which one spouse dies, provided the survivor does not remarry before year end.

In 1954, Congress recognized that the death of a spouse often causes economic hardship and extended the benefits of income splitting by permitting the surviving spouse to use Schedule Y-Joint in the two years following the tax year in which the spouse dies, provided the surviving spouse has a dependent child or stepchild who lives with the taxpayer in the home. Of course, an exemption for the deceased spouse is not available on the surviving spouse's return during those two years. The special status of surviving spouse automatically terminates after the two-year period, by remarriage during the period, or by the loss of dependency status of the child or stepchild.

EXAMPLE 11-2

In 19X1 Joe's wife died, leaving a 14-year old child who qualifies as Joe's dependent. In 19X1, Joe is entitled to file a joint return and claim three exemptions (one each for Joe, his deceased wife, and dependent child). If the child continues to live in Joe's home and to qualify as a dependent, Joe may use Schedule Y-Joint in 19X2 and 19X3, as well, but he is entitled to only two exemptions (one for himself and one for the dependent child) in those two years.

Heads of Household

Rate Schedule Z, created in 1951, gave qualified taxpayers approximately 50% of the tax saving available from income splitting to married taxpayers filing jointly. The major requirements for using the head-of-household rate schedule are given below.

1. At the end of the tax year, the taxpayer cannot be classified as a married taxpayer or a surviving spouse. (However, as discussed later in this section, certain married persons living apart may use the head-of-household rate schedule. In addition, in certain circumstances, a taxpayer married to a nonresident alien may qualify.)

2. The taxpayer must maintain a home that, for more than one half of the year, is the principal place of abode of a dependent of the taxpayer. If the taxpayer maintains a home for a child or other direct descendant, such person need not be a dependent if the descendant is unmarried. If the descendant is married, he or she must qualify as a dependent. *Child* includes stepchild and adopted child for this purpose (but not foster child). If the taxpayer supports his or her parents and maintains the parents' home, the taxpayer need not live in the same residence.

3. The taxpayer must pay more than 50% of the cost of maintaining the home.

4. The taxpayer must be a U.S. citizen or resident alien.

As mentioned previously, the head-of-household rates may also be used by a married person who meets certain special tests. These requirements are listed here.

1. The taxpayer must file a separate return.

2. The taxpayer must maintain a home that for one half of the taxable year is the principal place of abode of a dependent child or stepchild for whom the taxpayer is entitled to a dependency exemption.

3. The taxpayer must furnish more than half the cost of maintaining the home.

4. The taxpayer's spouse must not live in the household during the last half of the taxable year.

This provision is apparently designed to provide a tax break for abandoned spouses but is brcad enough to include other married persons who simply choose to live apart and for some reason do not wish to file a joint return.

EXAMPLE 11-3

> Returning to the facts of Example 11-2, assume that Joe filed as a surviving spouse for 19X2 and 19X3. In 19X4 and later years, Joe may use the head-of-household rate schedule if the child continues to reside in the household and Joe provides more than half the cost of maintaining the household. Should the child cease to qualify as Joe's dependent but continue to live with him, Joe still may file as head of household unless the child is married.

Single Individuals

Since 1971, single individuals who are not heads of household have used Rate Schedule X, which was created by Congress to recognize that joint returns may have given too great a tax break to some married taxpayers relative to single taxpayers. Taxes obtained from Rate Schedule X are lower than those from Rate Schedule Y-Separate. The rate rises to 28% at $21,450 on Schedule X as compared to $17,900 on Schedule Y-Separate. This slight difference is all that remains of the singles' lobbying efforts for lower taxes.

Because of the differences just noted, however, two single individuals with approximately equal income pay a lower tax than a married couple in comparable circumstances.

EXAMPLE 11-4

> In 1992 M and F, two individuals, each have taxable income of $30,000. Each would pay a tax of
>
> | | |
> |---|---:|
> | On $21,450 at 15% | $3,217.50 |
> | On ($30,000 – 21,450) at 28% | 2,394.00 |
> | | $5,611.50 |
>
> Together, M and F would pay a tax of $11,223 on their combined taxable income of $60,000. If M and F were married and filed a joint return, their tax for 1992 would be (assuming the taxable income on the joint return were $60,000)
>
> | | |
> |---|---:|
> | On $35,800 at 15% | $ 5,370.00 |
> | On ($60,000 – 35,800) at 28% | 6,776.00 |
> | | $12,146.00 |
>
> M and F's taxes would increase by $923 ($12,146 – $11,223) as a result of marriage. This increase occurs because after their marriage $7,100 of their income is taxed at 28% rather than 15%.

Is this marriage penalty enough to discourage marriage? For a few couples, perhaps. The penalty will not apply, and instead, a benefit will result from the use of Schedule Y-Joint if the income belongs primarily to one of the partners.

Married Individuals Filing Separately

The law provides that married individuals may file separate returns. Only under most unusual circumstances do separate returns result in a lower tax, because Congress has taken great pains to close possible loopholes. Note that on separate returns the standard deduction is half the amount for joint returns. In a similar manner, most other possible advantages are eliminated by the statute. For the most part, married individuals filing separate returns do so because of marital or financial disagreements that have not yet reached the point of divorce or legal separation. On a joint return, both spouses are jointly and severally liable for the *combined* tax, a legal obligation that one spouse may be unwilling to assume even if it results in a lower tax on his or her own income.

> **Goal #2**
> Calculate the tax liability for a dependent child.

UNEARNED INCOME OF MINOR CHILDREN

Since 1987, a special rate schedule has existed for children under age 14 who have **net unearned income**. Such income is taxed at the highest marginal rate of the child's parents (of the custodial parent in the case of divorce or separation). Congress adopted this rule to curtail the shifting of income from family members subject to higher marginal tax rates to those subject to lower marginal tax rates. Wealthy parents traditionally have transferred income-producing properties such as stocks, bonds, and savings accounts to children and grandchildren to reduce total family taxes.

> **Net unearned income** is unearned income less $1,200 (in 1992).

To determine how much of a child's income will be taxed at the parents' rate, the first step is to calculate the child's *taxable income*. Recall that a child who is claimed as a dependent of another is not entitled to claim a personal exemption. Further, in 1992 such a child is entitled to a standard deduction that is the greater of $600 or earned income, but no more than the maximum standard deduction allowed ($3,600 for a single individual in 1992).

EXAMPLE 11-5

> Billie, a 12-year-old child, is supported entirely by her parents. Her income this year consists of interest income of $4,000 and earned income from a part-time job of $900. Billie's taxable income is $4,000 ($4,000 + $900 - $900 standard deduction).

Once the child's taxable income is determined, the second step is to calculate the amount of taxable income subject to the parents' marginal rate. This amount is referred to as net unearned income and is the child's gross unearned income (dividends, interest, and so on) less $1,200.[1] The net unearned income cannot, of course, exceed the child's taxable income, and any taxable income that the child has in excess of net unearned income is taxed at the child's rate—15% on taxable income up to $21,450 in 1992.

Computation of the tax is more complicated when more than one child of a parent has unearned income and more than one marginal rate applies to the net unearned income. Since 1989, parents have been able to elect to include the income of a child under 14 on their tax return, thereby avoiding the necessity of filing a separate return for the child. The child must have income between $500 and $5,000, all from interest

---

1 The $1,200 is increased in the unlikely event that the child can itemize deductions in excess of the standard deduction, and the child's itemized deductions directly connected with the production of the *unearned* income exceed $600.

and dividends. The parents simply add the child's gross income over $1,000 to their taxable income and pay an additional tax equal to the lesser of $75 or 15% of the child's income over $1,000.

EXAMPLE 11-6

Returning to the facts in Example 11-5, Billie's net unearned income is

Unearned income	$4,000
Less deduction allowed	1,200
Net unearned income	$2,800

Assuming Billie's parents' marginal tax rate is 28%, Billie's income tax is

$2,800 at 28% (parents' rate)	$ 784
($4,000 – 2,800) at 15% (child's rate)	180
Total tax	$ 964

MARGINAL TAX RATES FOR INDIVIDUAL TAXPAYERS

Goal #3
Determine a taxpayer's marginal tax rate.

Several factors may complicate calculation of a taxpayer's marginal tax rates. Among these factors are a limitation on itemized deductions and the phase out of personal and dependent exemptions for high income taxpayers, both instituted in 1991 after a great public debate over the fairness of a "bubble" in the individual rate schedules. This bubble resulted from a phase out of the benefits of the 15% tax bracket and the personal and dependent exemptions for high income taxpayers. Once those benefits were phased out, the taxpayer's marginal rate dropped, creating a lower marginal tax rate for the highest income individuals than for those taxpayers whose income was in the phase-out range. Congress responded to criticism of the bubble by eliminating the phase out of the 15% bracket and personal and dependency exemptions as part of the nominal rate structure.

As you will see, instead of a bubble in the rate schedules, high income taxpayers now face two adjustments to taxable income. The first is a phase out of personal and dependency exemptions and the second is a reduction in itemized deductions. As a result of these adjustments a bubble in the *effective* rate schedules has replaced a bubble in the *nominal* rate schedules.

THE LIMITATION ON ITEMIZED DEDUCTIONS

The limitation on itemized deductions affects only high-income taxpayers. For 1992, high income is defined as AGI of $105,250 ($52,500 for married filing separately). The same threshold applies to married taxpayers filing jointly, single taxpayers, or heads of household.

For affected taxpayers, itemized deductions (excluding medical expenses, investment interest, casualty losses, and wagering losses) are reduced by 3% of the excess of the taxpayer's AGI over the threshold amount. However, the itemized deductions subject to the threshold cannot be reduced by more than 80%.

A taxpayer subject to the limitation of itemized deductions will find that his or her marginal tax rate is greater than the apparent marginal rate from the nominal rate schedules because the base for the tax will increase by more than the amount of additional income.

EXAMPLE 11-7

Walter and Ruth Ryan have AGI of $220,000. They file a joint return and have two dependents. Their itemized deductions consist of

Mortgage interest	$20,000
Investment interest	4,000
Charitable contributions	12,000
State income tax	8,000
Total	$44,000
Less deductions not subject to limitation	−4,000
	$40,000
	x 80%
Maximum reduction	$32,000

The Ryan's actual reduction in itemized deductions is $3,442.50 [3% x ($220,000 − $105,250)] because this amount is less than $32,000. Their itemized deductions amount to $40,557.50 ($44,000 − $3,442.50).

THE PHASEOUT OF PERSONAL AND DEPENDENT EXEMPTIONS

Personal and dependency exemptions also are phased out for high-income taxpayers, but the definition of high income for this purpose is different than the definition of high income for limiting itemized deductions. For 1992, the threshold for phasing out exemptions occurs when AGI reaches the following amounts:

Married filing jointly and surviving spouse	$157,900
Head of household	131,550
Single individual	105,250
Married filing separately	78,950

These amounts are adjusted each year for inflation.

The deductible amount of a taxpayer's personal and dependency exemptions is reduced by 2% for each $2,500 (or fraction thereof) of AGI above the threshold amounts above. Therefore, a single taxpayer with AGI of $100,001 can deduct only 98% of his or her $2,300 personal exemption.

EXAMPLE 11-8

Walter and Ruth Ryan from Example 11-7 are subject to the phase out of personal exemptions. Their AGI of $220,000 is $62,100 above the threshold of $157,900 for married couples filing jointly. Their $9,200 (4 x $2,300) deduction for personal and dependent exemptions will therefore be reduced by 50% [$62,100/$2,500 = 24.84; 25 x 2 = 50%]. Their 1992 taxable income is $174,842.50 [$220,000 AGI − $40,557.50 itemized deductions − $4,600 exemptions] and their 1992 tax liability is $46,952 [$19,586.00 + .31 ($174,842.50 − $86,500].

In Example 11-8, note that the taxpayers' *apparent* marginal tax rate is 31%. However, any additional income will increase their tax base by more than the amount of income.

EXAMPLE 11-9

Assume that Walter and Ruth Ryan from Example 11-8 won $10,000 from the state lottery on December 31, increasing their AGI to $230,000, their reduction in itemized deductions to $3,742.50 [3% x ($230,000 − 105,250)], and their reduction in exemptions to 58% [$72,100/$2,500 = 28.84; 29 x 2 = 58%]. Their taxable income with the windfall becomes $185,878.50 [$230,000 AGI − $40,257.50 itemized deductions − $3,864 exemptions] and their 1992 income tax liability becomes $50,373. The Ryans' tax liability has increased by $3,421 [$50,373 − $46,952], and their marginal tax rate on the $10,000 of additional income is over 34% [$3,421/$10,000] rather than the apparent 31%. This increase in marginal tax rate results from the fact that while the Ryans' income increased by $10,000, their taxable income increased by $11,036 ($185,878.50 − $174,842.50).

As Example 11-9 shows, there is still a bubble in the tax rate schedules. At some level of income (depending on the number of exemptions and the amount of itemized deductions), a taxpayer loses both the entire benefit of the personal and dependent exemptions, and the maximum 80% of itemized deductions is phased out. At that point, the taxpayer's marginal rate returns to 31%.

OTHER FACTORS THAT CHANGE EFFECTIVE AND MARGINAL TAX RATES

Several other factors can cause a taxpayer to have a different marginal tax rate than is apparent from the rate schedules. For example, as you will learn in Chapter 16, an excess of net long-term capital gains over net short-term capital losses is subject to a maximum tax rate of 28%. However, this amount also increases AGI and therefore may cause the taxpayer to lose some portion of deductions for personal and dependent exemptions and itemized deductions.

A number of other phase-out provisions affect various taxpayers. For example, several of the credits discussed later in this chapter are phased out as income increases. The $25,000 realty rental loss allowance for active owners of a 10% or greater interest is phased out for AGI over $100,000. For older taxpayers with income over certain amounts, Social Security benefits are partly taxed. In each of these cases, the taxpayer's base for the tax increases by more than the increase in income. Several articles have demonstrated that a taxpayer's real marginal rate can be much higher than 31% because of the cumulative effect of various phase out provisions.[2]

---

2 For more detailed discussion of these circumstances and sample calculations see Dennis D. Bensinger, Helen M. Savage, and Raymond J. Shaffer, "Marginal Tax Rates of Self-Employed Taxpayers," *Tax Notes,* August 19, 1991, pp. 957–64 and John R. Gist and J. Mulvey, "Marginal Tax Rates and Older Taxpayers," *Tax Notes,* November 5, 1990, pp. 679–94. The first article demonstrates marginal rates of over 50%; the second article rates of over 60%.

TAX CREDITS FOR INDIVIDUALS

Application of the appropriate rates to taxable income gives the gross tax liability, which is reduced by the allowed tax credits and prepayments to determine the net tax that should be paid when the return is filed. Recall from Chapter 6 that an important distinction exists between a credit and a deduction. Although credits yield a dollar-for-dollar tax reduction, the tax decrease resulting from a $1 deduction depends on the marginal tax rate applied to net taxable income. A given deduction can have widely varying effects on the dollar amount of tax liability of taxpayers at different marginal rate levels. On the other hand, a tax credit has the same dollar effect on the amount of net taxes payable, no matter what the taxpayer's marginal tax rate may be.

At present, only four important credits apply to an individual: the earned income credit, the child-care credit, the foreign tax credit, and the credit for the elderly. These credits are explained in the following sections.

EARNED INCOME CREDIT

Added to the tax law in 1975, the earned income credit contains many characteristics of a **negative income tax**. Congress had several objectives in mind when enacting the credit, and these objectives are reflected in the technical aspects of this provision.[3]

To qualify for the earned income credit, a taxpayer must maintain a household in the United States that is the principal place of abode of the taxpayer and the taxpayer's dependent child, stepchild, foster child, or descendant of the taxpayer's child. The credit is available only to married taxpayers and to taxpayers qualified to file either as a surviving spouse or head of household. The credit is based on earned income, defined as salaries, wages, other employee compensation, and earnings from self-employment. Unlike the other personal credits, the earned income credit is a **refundable credit**. If this credit (plus any prepayments) exceeds the gross tax liability, the taxpayer receives a refund.

> ### EXAMPLE 11-10
> Janet Diggs is entitled to an earned income credit of $950. Janet's tax liability this year is $300, and her employer withheld no income tax from her paychecks. Janet will receive a refund of $650 after she files her tax return.

Goal #4
Calculate the amount of an individual's tax credits.

A **negative income tax** is a welfare program under which individuals who have no income receive a basic grant. The grant is reduced by a fraction of total income so that at some amount of income the grant is reduced to zero and the individual begins to pay tax.

A **refundable credit** is treated as a tax prepayment so that the taxpayer receives the credit even if his or her tax liability is zero.

For 1992, the basic credit equals 16.7% (17.3% for taxpayers with two or more qualifying children) of earned income up to $7,520,[4] giving a maximum credit of $1,256 ($1,301 for taxpayers with two of more qualifying children). The credit is phased out at a rate of 11.93% (12.36% for taxpayers with two or more qualifying children) of AGI above $11,840. Thus a taxpayer with one qualifying child and AGI of $22,368 receives no earned income credit [11.93% × ($22,368 − $11,840) = $1,256].

The earned income credit can be increased by 5 percentage points if the taxpayer has a qualifying child who is less than one year old. The phase-out percentage is increased by 3.57 percentage points.

3 Sec. 32.

4 This amount is adjusted each year according to the change in the Consumer Price Index between August 31 of the preceding year and August 31 of the current year. Additionally, the upper and lower limits of the phase-out range are adjusted each year.

EXAMPLE 11-11

Joe Dixon, a single parent who qualifies as a head of household, has one 3-year-old child. Joe's AGI, all earned income, is $9,500. Joe is entitled to an earned income credit of the maximum amount ($1,256). Had Joe's AGI been $13,000, his earned income credit would have been $1,118 [$1,256 − 11.93% × ($13,000 − $11,840)].

EXAMPLE 11-12

Jean Dixon, a single parent who qualifies as a head of household, has one 3-month old child. Jean's AGI consists of salary income of $12,000 and interest income of $1,000. Her basic credit is $1,632 [$7,520 × (16.7% + 5%). This amount is reduced by 15.5% (11.93% + 3.57%) of the $1,160 excess of Jean's $13,000 AGI over $11,840, giving a credit of $1,452 ($1,632 − $180).

The law also provides for a supplemental health insurance credit calculated in the same way as the earned income credit except the credit percentage is 6% and the phase-out percentage is 4.285%. This credit may be claimed for amounts paid for health insurance coverage that includes at least one qualifying child. Therefore the credit cannot exceed the actual amount paid by the taxpayer for health insurance coverage.

Obviously, the earned income credit is designed to benefit low-income taxpayers. It was passed specifically to offset partially the rapidly growing impact of Social Security taxes. As noted previously, the real significance of this credit is that it provides a form of negative income tax. It differs from a true negative income tax in that the credit increases as the taxpayer's earned income increases, and a taxpayer with no earned income receives no credit. Most proposals for a negative income tax provide a smaller subsidy as income increases. However, one intent of the earned income credit is to encourage individuals to obtain employment. Presumably, Congress felt that the credit would effectively increase the wage rate for low-income taxpayers, thereby providing added incentive to work.

Taxpayers are not required to make the calculations shown above but instead use tables provided by the IRS. Despite this assistance, many eligible taxpayers do not claim the earned income credit. The Revenue Reconciliation Act of 1990 requires the Treasury to establish a taxpayer awareness program to inform the public of the availability of the earned income, dependent care, and health insurance tax credits.

CREDIT FOR CHILD-CARE EXPENSE

A taxpayer who is employed outside the home may incur substantial expenses for the care of children. Such expenses are especially common when young parents both work outside the home. Congress enacted the child-care credit to mitigate this hardship. The credit also works as an incentive to encourage the proper care of children during the working day. Although the credit commonly applies to working parents having children under age 13, the credit also is available for any **qualifying individual** such as a spouse or a dependent who is physically or mentally incapable of self-care, regardless of age.

The credit equals 30% of **qualified expenses** up to $2,400 for one qualifying individual, or $4,800 for two or more qualifying individuals. Thus, the maximum

A **qualifying individual** is a dependent child under age 13 or a spouse or dependent who is incapable of self-care.

Qualified expenses include any expenses for the care of, or housekeeping related to, a qualifying individual in the taxpayer's household.

credit is $720 when there is one qualifying individual or $1,440 when there are two or more qualifying individuals. However, the basic 30% rate decreases by one percentage point for each $2,000 increment (or part thereof) of adjusted gross income in excess of $10,000. The rate is never reduced below 20%.

EXAMPLE 11-13

Taxpayers A, B, and C each pay $3,000 for child care, and each has one qualifying dependent. A's AGI is $9,000; A is therefore entitled to a credit of $720 (30% of $2,400). B's AGI is $17,000; B's credit is $624 (26% of $2,400). C's AGI is $35,000; C's credit is $480 (20% of $2,400).

The base for the credit is the amount of certain employment-related expenses paid during the taxable year to enable the taxpayer to work either full- or part-time as an employee or as a self-employed individual. Qualified expenses on which a credit may be based are those for the care of, or housekeeping related to, a qualifying individual in the taxpayer's household.[5] A qualifying individual may be (1) a dependent under 13 years of age, (2) a person physically or mentally incapable of self-care and for whom the taxpayer is entitled to claim a dependency exemption (or would be entitled to claim an exemption except that the person has gross income in excess of the amount of the deduction allowed for a dependent), or (3) the taxpayer's spouse who is physically or mentally incapable of care.

Qualified expenses can be for care outside the taxpayer's residence if the qualifying dependent is (1) under age 13 or (2) another qualifying individual who regularly spends at least eight hours per day in the taxpayer's household. Payments for food, clothing, and education do not qualify. However, if the care provided includes expenses that cannot be separated, the full amount paid is considered for the qualifying individual's care. Thus, the full amount paid to a nursery school is considered for the care of the child even though the school also provides lunch and some education. Educational expenses for a child in the first or higher grade level are not considered expenses for the child's care.

Generally, qualifying expenses cannot exceed the earned income of the taxpayer. Special rules apply to married individuals. First, married couples must file joint returns. Second, the amount used as the base is the lesser of the husband's or wife's earned income. For purposes of this last test, in cases in which one spouse is a full-time student (five months out of any calendar year) or one spouse is incapable of self-care, some earned income is imputed to that spouse. If one qualifying individual lives in the household, the earned income imputed to the unemployed spouse is $200 monthly (or $2,400 per year). If there are two or more qualifying individuals, the earned income imputed to the unemployed spouse is $400 monthly (or $4,800 per year).

EXAMPLE 11-14

Pat and Chris, a married couple filing jointly, have a 2-year old child named Jan. Chris earns $30,000 per year. Pat is a full-time student. Pat paid a neighbor $2,000
Continued

---

5 Child-care costs qualify even though paid to a relative of the taxpayer (relative being defined in the same manner as for the dependency test) and even though the relative lives in the taxpayer's household, *provided* the relative is not a dependent of the taxpayer or the taxpayer's spouse. An exception to this last prohibition applies if the dependent rendering the child-care service is a child of the taxpayer who is at least 19 years of age at the end of the taxable year.

> **EXAMPLE 11-14 (Con't.)**
>
> to care for Jan while Pat attended school. The amount of earned income imputed to Pat is $2,400, but the base for the earned income credit is $2,000, the amount of actual qualified expenses. Assuming that Pat and Chris have AGI of $30,000, their child-care credit is $400 (20% of $2,000).

Prior to the introduction of the child-care credit in 1976, the law permitted some workers to treat child-care payments as deductions from AGI. The availability of that child-care deduction was severely restricted by its classification as an itemized deduction and by its complexity. The treatment of child-care expenditures as itemized deductions denied any beneficial tax recognition to taxpayers who did not itemize deductions. This denial of benefits was especially typical for low-income taxpayers, who are in greatest need of a tax benefit from such payments. Although changing the deduction provision to a credit may provide greater relief for low-income taxpayers, it can be argued that the law still discriminates in favor of those with higher incomes because those in low-income groups cannot afford such services as child care or household help.

Taxpayers' deductions for child-care expenses have steadily increased. In 1987, the child-care credit was by far the most important credit available to individual taxpayers.[6] The importance of the child-care credit extends beyond the amount involved, however. It established a precedent that unavoidable work-related personal expenditures may be deductible or give rise to a credit. Similar treatment of other personal expenses—such as clothing, transportation to work, and even food consumed during working hours—might just as logically be justified on the basis of necessity, even though the law currently contains no provisions for such deductions.

CREDIT FOR ELDERLY AND DISABLED

The statute provides a limited credit for taxpayers who are 65 years old before the end of the year, or who are retired because of a permanent disability. Because of a restrictive income phase out explained below, the credit offers tax relief only for those with very low incomes.

Although this provision is technically a credit, its practical effect is that of an exclusion. The taxpayer computes gross tax in the usual way but reduces the tax by an amount equal to 15% of the amount subject to the credit. The base for the credit is what the statute calls an "initial amount," which is as follows:

> $5,000 for a single person or for a married couple filing jointly when only one spouse is 65 or older, or

> $7,500 for a married couple filing jointly when both are 65 or older ($3,750 on separate returns)[7]

The initial amount is reduced by the following items to arrive at the base for the credit: (1) Social Security retirement benefits, (2) railroad retirement benefits, and (3) veterans' pensions and certain payments from U.S. government life insurance. In addition, the initial amount is reduced by one half of the AGI on the return in excess

---

6 In 1989, child-care credits of over $2.4 billion were claimed on more than 6 million returns. Total credits claimed by individuals in 1989 amounted to about $6 billion with the second largest credit being the foreign tax credit ($1.2 billion).

7 Sec. 22(c).

TAX CREDITS FOR INDIVIDUALS **383**

of $7,500 for a single individual and $10,000 for married individuals ($5,000 if separate returns are filed).

The initial amounts described above apply to taxpayers 65 or older. For a disabled taxpayer who has not attained age 65, the initial amount is limited to the taxpayer's **disability income**. Special rules apply to the determination of the initial amount for married taxpayers when one is 65 and the other is disabled.

> **Disability income** is income received by an individual on account of a permanent disability.

EXAMPLE 11-15

Reginald, unmarried and age 68, had the following income this year:

Interest	$1,510
Wages	7,800
Social Security benefits	400
Total	$9,710

Because the Social Security benefits may be excluded, Reginald has AGI of $9,310. A retirement income credit of $554.25, computed below, may be subtracted from his tax liability.

Initial amount		$5,000
Less: Social Security benefits	$400	
One-half of AGI in excess of $7,500	905	– 1,305
Balance subject to credit		$3,695
Tentative credit: 15% x $3,695		$ 554.25

Because the credit is nonrefundable, it is limited to the taxpayer's gross tax. Note from Example 11-15 that substantial Social Security benefits will eliminate the credit, as will substantial amounts of any income. Therefore, Social Security benefits are indirectly taxed.

Prior to 1976, this credit existed in the form of a *retirement income credit* and applied only to selected types of retirement income. Originally, the main purpose of the credit was to equalize the tax burden between those who received retirement income from Social Security and railroad retirement plans (both of which were tax free) and those who received retirement income from interest and other taxable income sources. In addition, the system imposed severe limits on the amounts of earned income that could be received without reducing the credit. The 1976 Tax Reform Act increased the coverage by making the credit applicable to gross income from any source and drastically increased the amount of earnings that a retired person could receive without affecting the amount of the credit.

FOREIGN TAX CREDIT

Citizens and residents of the United States generally must pay the U.S. tax on their worldwide income. Exceptions to this rule include the exclusion for foreign-earned income and income excluded from double taxation by treaty. With these exceptions, a citizen or resident often is subject to the U.S. tax and a tax by the host country for foreign-source income. The U.S. law therefore provides a credit against the U.S. tax for income taxes paid to foreign countries.

All foreign taxes, including income taxes, are often deductible by taxpayers as trade or business expenses under Sec. 162 or as taxes under Sec. 164. Taxpayers, therefore, can either elect to take a credit or to deduct foreign income taxes. The credit, with rare exceptions, results in the greatest reduction in the U.S. tax liability.

The foreign tax credit is limited by several provisions beyond the scope of this text. In no event can the credit claimed for foreign taxes exceed the taxes assessed by the United States on the foreign-source income. The general limit is calculated as follows:

$$\text{Limit} = \frac{\text{Foreign-source income}}{\text{Worldwide taxable income}} \times \text{U.S. tax before credits}$$

EXAMPLE 11-16

Jose, a single taxpayer with one exemption, has taxable income of $120,000 for 1992. The U.S. tax on that amount of income would be $32,845.50. Jose derived $50,000 of his income from a foreign country to which he paid an income tax of $12,000. The limit for the foreign tax credit is computed as follows:

$$\frac{\$50,000}{\$120,000} \times \$32,845.50 = \$13,685.63$$

Jose can claim a $12,000 credit, the taxes actually paid, because the foreign taxes did not exceed the limit.

As an alternative to the foreign tax credit, an individual taxpayer may elect to exclude foreign-source *earned* income of up to $70,000 per year. The taxpayer must be a bona fide resident of the foreign country or live in the country at least 330 days out of any 12 consecutive months. An election to exclude foreign-earned income rather than take the credit may be revoked for any taxable year after the year for which the election was made, but the taxpayer may not make another election before the sixth year after the revocation tax year.

THE ORDER FOR SUBTRACTING CREDITS

Nonrefundable personal credits can reduce the tax liability to zero, but cannot create a refund.

The statute specifies an order for the subtraction of credits. First, the **nonrefundable personal credits** (such as the credit for child and dependent care and the credit for the elderly) are deducted from the calculated tax. An excess of these credits over the tax liability will not result in a refund. Further, the excess cannot be carried over to a later year. Next, other nonrefundable credits, such as the foreign tax credit, are deducted. Unused foreign tax credit can be carried back two years and forward five years; thus it is to the taxpayer's advantage that this credit be taken into account after the nonrefundable credits that cannot be carried back or forward. In no case can the tax liability be reduced to less than zero by nonrefundable credits.

The earned income credit *is* refundable and is taken into account only after deduction of the nonrefundable credits and the addition of other taxes (such as Social Security self-employment taxes). Essentially, the earned income credit is treated in the same way as income taxes withheld from wages.

EXAMPLE 11-17

> Dan's tax liability before any credits is $340, none of which has been paid in advance through withholding or estimates. Dan also is entitled to a child-care credit of $400 and an earned income credit of $500. The child-care credit reduces the $340 tax liability to zero, with $60 of the credit unusable. Dan is then entitled to a refund of $500 because of the earned income credit.

SOME MISCELLANEOUS PROCEDURES

The final section of this chapter covers some miscellaneous procedural rules related to individual tax returns. It begins with rules outlining who must file returns and ends with a discussion of the requirements for payment of the tax.

WHO MUST FILE?

As mentioned earlier, an individual whose gross income is below a specified amount is not required to file a tax return. Given the rules for exemptions and the standard deduction amounts, certain taxpayers obviously would not have a gross tax liability for 1992 if their gross incomes were as follows:

Single, under 65 years of age	$ 5,900
Single, 65 years or older	6,800
Surviving spouse under 65	8,300
Surviving spouse over 64	9,200
Married filing jointly, both under 65	10,600
Married filing jointly, one over 64	11,300
Married filing jointly, both over 64	12,000

> **Goal #5**
> Decide whether or not a taxpayer must file a return.

Note that these amounts are the sum of the taxpayer's standard deduction and personal exemptions (but not dependent exemptions). For example, a surviving spouse over age 64 would be entitled to a standard deduction of $6,000 plus a personal exemption of $2,300, for a total of $8,300. This individual would not be required to file a return if his or her gross income were equal to or less than $8,300. As explained earlier, a single individual who is a dependent of another and has unearned income (dividends, interest, and so on) must file a return if 1992 gross income exceeds $600. In addition, a taxpayer who has net income of $400 or more from self-employment must file a return. Individuals whose gross incomes are below these amounts may, of course, file a return to obtain a refund of taxes withheld from wages or to take advantage of the earned income credit.

USE OF TAX TABLES

As indicated in Chapter 6, the IRS provides tax tables to make the tax computation simpler for individuals. In fact, individual taxpayers with taxable incomes of $50,000 or less are required to use the tax tables, which appear in Appendix B.

Payment of the Tax

United States tax law contains a pay-as-you-go system for the payments of federal income taxes. Employers withhold the federal income tax from the salaries and wages of employees. Taxpayers with income not subject to withholding pay estimated quarterly taxes. Finally, the net tax liability due when the return is filed can be reduced by excess Social Security taxes paid and by taxes paid on fuel used off the highways.

Withholding

Every employer must withhold from an employee's wages an amount of income tax based on the employee's marital status, number of exemptions claimed, and earnings and then remit the withholding to a depository of the federal government within specified time periods. Essentially, the withholding provision is designed to put the employee on a pay-as-you-go basis as far as his or her income tax is concerned. Wages include all remuneration for services performed by an employee for an employer, including the fair market value of all remuneration paid in any medium other than cash. Each January the employer must give the employee two copies of Form W-2, showing the total amount of remuneration subject to income tax paid the employee during the year, the amount of income tax withheld, the amount of earnings subject to Social Security taxes, and the amount of Social Security tax withheld. The employee attaches one copy of this form to his or her income tax return sent to the IRS. The amount withheld for income taxes is, of course, a prepayment that is subtracted from the gross tax payable, after tax credits, to arrive at the net tax payable (or refundable).

Estimated Taxes

Goal #6
Determine whether a taxpayer must pay estimated taxes.

Individuals who have income from sources not subject to withholding are required to declare and pay estimated income taxes during the tax year. Payment of estimated tax also is required of individuals whose withholding is insufficient, although such individuals generally request that their employers adjust withholding. The *estimated tax* is the excess of a taxpayer's gross tax over his or her credits and withholdings. A taxpayer must make quarterly payments of his or her estimated tax if such amount exceeds $500.

EXAMPLE 11-18

Della expects her tax liability this year to be $8,000. Her employer will withhold $6,000 of income taxes from her salary. Della may be required to make quarterly estimated tax payments in addition to withholding.

For calendar year taxpayers, quarterly payments of the estimated tax are due April 15, June 15, and September 15 of the taxable year, and January 15 of the following year. To avoid a penalty on underpayment of the estimated quarterly amount, a taxpayer must pay each quarter an amount equal to

1. 22.5% (¼ of 90%) of the actual taxes shown on the return for the year, or

2. 25% of the actual tax liability for the prior year,[8] or

---

8 For 1992–1996, taxpayers whose current year's AGI (with certain modifications) exceeds their prior year's AGI by more than $40,000 cannot avoid penalty by paying 100% of the prior year's tax *if* their current year's AGI exceeds $75,000. These taxpayers must pay 90% of the current year's liability to avoid penalty unless they have neither paid estimated tax nor received a penalty for underpayment of estimated tax in the preceding three years. There are a number of exceptions to these special rules which were enacted in 1991 to help pay for a 20-week extension of unemployment benefits to jobless workers.

3. 22.5% of the tax due for the current year computed on an annualized basis given the actual transactions of the taxpayer for the months of the year preceding the due date of the installment. This provision protects taxpayers whose taxable income unexpectedly increases after the payment of earlier installments.

EXAMPLE 11-19

Clark is retired, and none of his income is subject to withholding. His actual tax liability for 1992 is $16,000. He will not be assessed a penalty for underpayment of estimated taxes if at least $3,600 (22.5% of $16,000) of estimated tax is paid each quarter. If Clark's 1991 tax liability had been $13,000, he would escape penalty in 1992 by paying at least $3,250 (25% of $13,000) each quarter.

The penalty is computed using the federal short-term interest rate (determined on a quarterly basis) plus three percentage points. The penalty applies separately to each quarter's underpayment and is treated as an additional tax, not as deductible interest.

Refund for Nonhighway Use of Fuel

When a consumer purchases gasoline or lubricating oil, the purchase price includes a federal excise tax imposed on users of highways to provide funds for construction and maintenance of roads. When the gasoline or oil is purchased for nonhighway uses, such as farming or operating a motorboat, the taxpayer must pay the tax on purchase but may file a refund claim for the amounts paid. Section 34 allows the taxpayer to take a credit against his or her federal income tax for the amount of excise taxes paid on gasoline and oil bought for nonhighway use, thereby providing a simple refund procedure. In essence, these amounts are treated as prepayments of income taxes.

Excess Social Security Tax

Employees pay a Social Security tax on their wages. In 1992, the tax equals 6.2% of wages up to $55,500 for the Old Age, Survivors and Disability portion plus 1.45% of wages up to $130,200 for the Medicare portion. Employees who work for more than one employer during the year and have combined wages greater than the $55,500 ($130,200) threshold overpay their Social Security tax. Such overpayments are treated as prepayments of the income tax.

────── KEY POINTS TO REMEMBER

✓ Four possible tax rate schedules apply to individual taxpayers depending on their marital status and family responsibilities.

✓ A special rate schedule applies to dependent children under age 14 who have net unearned income. Such income is taxed at the parents' highest marginal tax rate.

✓ Marginal tax rates for individuals may be higher than those apparent from the nominal rate schedules because of several rules phasing out benefits such as personal and dependent exemptions and itemized deductions.

✓ Individuals' gross tax liabilities may be reduced by several tax credits including the earned income credit, the child care credit, the credit for the elderly, and the foreign-earned income credit.

✓ Some taxpayers are not required to file a tax return because their gross income is less than the sum of their standard deduction and personal exemption(s).

✓ Our tax system requires most individuals to pay at least 90% of their tax liability in advance, either through employer withholding or payment of estimated taxes.

——— RECALL PROBLEMS

1. For each of the following independent situations, can John and Marsha file a joint return for 19X1? Explain your answers.

   a. John and Marsha married on December 10, 19X1, after a whirlwind courtship. Following a violent argument on December 28, 19X1, Marsha went home to mother, vowing never to return. No legal action was taken during 19X1.

   b. After years of marriage, John and Marsha were legally separated on December 30, 19X1.

   c. While on temporary assignment in England for a large corporation. John married Marsha, a citizen of Great Britain. They were still in London at the end of 19X1, but they returned to the United States in January 19X2. They made no election for 19X1 to include Marsha's worldwide income on a U.S. return.

   d. John died on January 2, 19X1, after years of happy marriage to Marsha.

2. Indicate in each of the following cases whether taxpayers may file a joint return. If they are not allowed to do so, indicate the reason.

   a. Jones, a widower, and his mother live in the same house. Jones has gross income of $8,000; mother has income of $6,000.

   b. Kuehn, an American citizen, married Greta while he was stationed in Germany. Kuehn and his wife now life in New York. Greta is not yet an American citizen, but at the end of the tax year she was taking steps to become an American citizen.

   c. Smith's wife died in the preceding year, and he has not remarried. Smith's 3-year-old daughter lives with him.

   d. Bellmon's wife died on January 2 of the current year. He has not remarried.

   e. Ratliff and his wife were divorced on December 18 of the current tax year.

   f. Whitlaw and his wife are both U.S. citizens. Whitlaw's wife's parents live in England and are seriously ill. His wife spent the entire tax year in England with her parents.

3. In the following situations, can Mac use Rate Schedule Z (head of household) for the year involved?

   a. Mac, a widower, maintains a home, and his unmarried grandson lives with him. The grandson is 23 years old, has a good job, and therefore does not qualify as Mac's dependent.

   b. Mac maintains a home for his two dependent children. Mac's wife died last year.

   c. Mac's parents live in an apartment at a resort center in Florida. They have no income, so Mac, who is a bachelor and lives and works in New York, supports them.

d. Mac is a widower living in New York. His wife died five years ago. Mac pays all the living costs of his 18-year-old unmarried daughter, who has no income and lives in Miami, Florida.

4. Indicate in each of the following independent cases whether the taxpayer may file a surviving-spouse return.

   a. Taxpayer's husband died in the preceding tax year. Taxpayer maintains a home in which resides her unmarried 20-year-old daughter, a college student, who qualifies as taxpayer's dependent.

   b. Taxpayer's husband died in the preceding tax year. Taxpayer maintains a home in which resides her unmarried 20-year-old sister, a college student, who qualifies as taxpayer's dependent.

   c. Taxpayer's wife died during this tax year. Taxpayer maintains a home in which resides his unmarried 18-year-old daughter, who qualifies as taxpayer's dependent.

   d. Taxpayer's husband died during the preceding year. Taxpayer maintains a home in which reside her married 17-year-old daughter and the daughter's 18-year-old husband. Taxpayer supports both her daughter and son-in-law and properly claims both of them as her dependents.

   e. Taxpayer's wife died four years ago. Taxpayer has not remarried and maintains a home in which reside his two stepchildren, ages 7 and 8. Taxpayer properly claims both stepchildren as dependents.

5. Which rate schedule (X, Y—Joint, Y—Separate, or Z) *should* each of the following taxpayers use?

   a. Sue's husband died last year. She maintains a home in which her married son and his wife live. Both of them qualify as Sue's dependents.

   b. Mary's husband died last year. She maintains a home in which her married son and his wife live. Mary supports both of them, but the son and daughter-in-law file a joint return.

   c. Herman and Victoria were married on December 31 of the current tax year. Herman earned $18,000 during the year, and Victoria earned $7,200. Victoria is a resident alien and has income in several countries.

   d. Wilma's husband died four years ago. Wilma maintains a home in which reside her 6-year-old daughter, her 21-year-old son, and her 20-year-old daughter-in-law. The son and daughter-in-law file a joint return. Wilma provides all the support for everyone in the household.

   e. Jones, whose wife died earlier in the current tax year, has not remarried. He has no children or other dependents.

   f. Joe, a bachelor, maintains a home in which resides his nephew. The nephew is not a dependent.

   g. Thomas was divorced from his wife in November of the current tax year. Thomas's unmarried dependent daughter lives with him.

6. Mary and John are married residents of New York and have two small children. They depend on John's salary of $50,000 per annum for their livelihood. In January 19X2, Mary learned that John was in hock to his bookie to the tune of $200,000 and that the bookie was getting impatient. New York is not a com-

munity-property state. Mary has no current income, but her family is quite wealthy and she expects to inherit substantial amounts in the near future. What would you advise Mary about filing status for 19X1?

#1

7. The Whiten family consists of Herman, Joann, husband and wife, and their 4-year-old son, Junior. Herman earns $35,000 as a warehouse foreman. Joann earned $15,000 as a Tupperware representative. Junior has interest income of $4,500 from money given to him by his grandmother.

   a. How many taxpayers are there in this family?

   b. What minimum number of returns must the family file?

   c. Should Herman and Joann file separate returns?

   Explain all answers.

#1

8. Hank, a lawyer, expects to have gross income of $40,000 for the year. Debbie works for an advertising agency and her gross income will be $30,000. Neither has dependents nor deductions for AGI. After an extended courtship, the two plan to marry before the year-end.

   a. Calculate their combined tax liability if they decide to forgo marriage.

   b. What amount of additional tax results from the marriage?

#2

9. Jason is 13 years old and is a dependent of his parents. This year he earned $2,000 interest income plus $1,500 from an after-school job.

   a. Calculate Jason's taxable income. How much will be taxed at his parent's marginal rate? How much will be taxed at his rate?

   b. Assume that Jason earned $3,000 from his after-school job. Calculate his taxable income. How much of his taxable income will be taxed at his parent's rate and how much at his rate?

#2

10. Hermie is 12 years old and a dependent of his parents. This year he received interest income of $6,000, his only source of income. Hermie's parents file a joint return showing taxable income of $110,000.

    a. What is Hermie's tax liability?

    b. Answer part a assuming that Hermie earns $1,200 during the year on a paper route in addition to the interest income.

#3

11. Jason and Anne Bell, both MDs, have 3 dependent children. Their AGI this year will be $250,000. Their itemized deductions (before the phase out) consist of

Mortgage interest	$25,000
Investment interest	3,000
Charitable contributions	9,000
State income tax	6,000
Property tax on home	5,000

   a. Calculate the Bell's deductible itemized deductions.

   b. Calculate the Bell's personal and dependent exemptions.

   c. Calculate their tax liability for the current year.

   d. How much tax will the Bells pay if they earn an additional $1,000 this year?

e. What is the Bell's effective average tax rate?

f. What is their marginal tax rate?

12. One provision that Congress has often considered is the substitution of a $400 credit instead of a $2,000 exemption deduction.

   a. Would taxpayers with a marginal rate of 15% prefer the credit or the deduction? taxpayers with a 28% marginal rate?

   b. How would adoption of the credit affect the relative tax burdens of low-income taxpayers relative to high-income taxpayers?

13. H and W are married and file a joint return showing adjusted gross income of $35,000. During the year H and W spent $6,000 to care for their two dependent children, ages 4 and 6, in a qualified child-care center. What is the amount of the dependent-care credit if H is employed as an accountant but

   a. W is not gainfully employed during the year?

   b. W has a part-time job and earns $2,000 during the year?

   c. W is a full-time student?

   d. W is physically incapable of self-care, and the $6,000 includes amounts spent for her care?

   e. W earns $10,000 as a model?

14. In each of the following independent cases, compute the earned income credit for the current year.

   a. Taxpayer and spouse file a joint return. They have no dependents. Their income consists of salaries of $6,800 and interest of $600.

   b. Taxpayer and spouse file a joint return. They maintain in the U.S. a household for their dependent 14-year-old child. Their combined adjusted gross income is $7,400, all from wages. Gross tax liability is zero.

   c. Same facts as in part b, except that their total adjusted gross income of $14,400 is made up of $12,800 wages and $1,600 interest. Gross tax liability is $225.

   d. Same facts as in part b, except that their adjusted gross income is $3,600 consisting solely of wages. Gross tax liability is zero.

   e. Same facts as in part b, except that their adjusted gross income is $3,800, consisting solely of taxpayer's net profit from a small motor repair shop. Gross tax liability is zero.

15. In each of the following independent cases, determine the amount, if any, of the taxpayer's credit for child-care expenses. Assume that payment is made to enable taxpayer to be gainfully employed unless otherwise stated.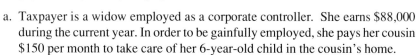

   a. Taxpayer is a widow employed as a corporate controller. She earns $88,000 during the current year. In order to be gainfully employed, she pays her cousin $150 per month to take care of her 6-year-old child in the cousin's home.

   b. Taxpayer is unmarried, earns $17,000 per year, and supports her two younger brothers, ages 8 and 17. During the year she paid a baby-sitter $250 per month to care for the 8-year-old.

   c. Sue is divorced. She earned $8,200 during the current year, but had to pay a housekeeper $200 per month to care for her two children, ages 4 and 5, while she worked. The housekeeper also cleaned the house and prepared all the meals. It is estimated that the housekeeper spends one half of her time caring for the children and the other half doing housework.

d. Margaret is unmarried. She has two dependent children, ages 8 and 14. Both children attend school, but she paid the 14-year-old $480 during the year to take care of the younger child after school until 5:30 P.M. each day. Margaret earned $8,000 during the year.

e. John is a bachelor and supports his aged parents who live with him. John pays a neighbor $300 per month during the year to take care of his parents, both of whom are bedridden, while John works. John's income was $18,000 for the year.

|#4|

16. Matte Harmon, a widow, age 67, had adjusted gross income of $8,000 during the current year. Matte also received $1,800 during the year from Social Security.

    a. What is Matte's credit for the elderly?

    b. What is her credit if her Social Security benefits amount to $5,500?

|#4|

17. Dave, a bachelor, suffered a severe heart attack last year at the age of 60. His employer retired Dave on a disability pension. Dave has no income except for his pension and Social Security payments. He also uses the standard deduction. Calculate the amount of Dave's disability credit for this year if

    a. the disability pension is $4,500 and Dave receives $3,600 from Social Security.

    b. the disability pension is $7,000 and Dave receives $3,600 from Social Security.

    c. the disability pension is $7,000 and Dave receives $6,000 from Social Security.

|#4|

18. In each of the following independent cases, compute the taxpayer's credit for dependent-care expenses. Assume the payments are necessary for gainful employment unless otherwise stated.

    a. Macomb and his wife have five small children, ranging in age from 2 to 9. During the current year Macomb earned $7,400; his wife earned $8,200. They paid a baby-sitter $200 per month to care for the children while they both worked. They filed a joint return.

    b. Assume the same facts as in part a, except that they paid the sitter $410 per month for caring for the children.

    c. Ann, a widow, was employed throughout the year, earning $10,200. She paid a baby-sitter $70 per month throughout the year to care for her two children. The younger is 9, the older became 15 on August 1 of this year.

    d. The taxpayer, a widow, works as an interior decorator and has income of $50,000. During the year she paid $400 per month for maid service including care of her two dependent children, ages 10 and 12. The amount allocated to child care was $1,500.

    e. The taxpayer, a widow with AGI of $12,000, paid her mother $100 per month during the year to care for her 5-year-old dependent child. The mother is not a dependent of the taxpayer.

    f. John and Sue are married and file a joint return. John is a full-time student but earned $1,000 from part-time jobs during 19X1. Sue is employed and earned

$9,400 during the year. In order for Sue to work and John to attend classes, they paid a baby-sitter $900 ($75 per month) to take care of their 2-year-old child.

g. Ray and Ellen are married and file a joint return. Ray is employed and earned $20,000 during 19X1. Ellen is not gainfully employed but paid a college student $600 during the year to take care of her small child while Ellen did her shopping, attended meetings, and so on.

19. T's taxable income for the current year is $80,000, and his gross tax for 1992 as a single individual is $20,454.50 T had dividend income of $5,000 from a Canadian corporation that withheld $750 of the dividend under Canadian income tax law.

#4

a. Should T claim the $750 as a deduction (and reduce his taxable income to $79,250), or should he claim a foreign tax credit?

b. If he claims the credit, what amount is allowed?

20. Rebecca Ellis is a head of household with a 4-year-old dependent child. This year she earned $10,000 from her job and received $3,000 in alimony from her former husband. She paid $1,000 to a neighbor who baby-sat for her son while she worked. Her itemized deductions amount to only $2,300. Her employer withheld $500 in federal income taxes from her wages. Calculate the following:

#4

a. Rebecca's taxable income

b. Her tax liability before credits

c. The amount of refund she can expect to receive

21. Which of the following taxpayers must file a return?

#5

a. Mrs. X, a widow over 65, who has income of $150,000, all interest on tax exempt state bonds.

b. Mrs. Y, a widow over 65, with rental income of $18,000, deductible expenses related to the rental property of $16,500 and Social Security benefits of $5,000.

c. Z, a 15-year-old with taxable interest income of $1,500, who is claimed as a dependent by his parents.

d. Mr. and Mrs. Z, married with 3 dependent children, with gross income of $14,000.

22. Daniel, unmarried, is a retired teacher. This year his pension (all taxable) amounted to $17,000. He also earned $6,000 interest and dividends and received $9,000 in Social Security benefits. Daniel has no dependents, and he does not itemize deductions.

#6

a. What is the amount of Daniel's taxable income? (Refer to Chapter 9 for a discussion of taxability of Social Security benefits.)

b. What is the amount of Daniel's estimated tax?

c. How much estimated tax must Daniel pay in order to avoid penalty for underpayment assuming last year's tax liability was the same as this year's?

d. Answer part c above assuming last year's tax liability was $2,400.

_____ THOUGHT PROBLEMS

#1

1. Which couple described below will experience the largest tax marriage penalty in 1992? Explain. (This problem does not require any calculations but does require inspection of the rate schedules.)

   a. Dave earns $300,000 and Linda earns $300,000.
   b. Nick earns $30,000 and Elsie earns $35,000.
   c. Jim earns $14,000 and Mary earns $14,000.
   d. Joe earns $60,000 and Pat earns $10,000.

#3

2. Refer to Recall Problem 11. Assuming no change in deductions, what amount of income would the Bells have to earn in 1992 in order to have a marginal tax rate of 28%.

#1 #3

3. Karen Hilton, a single taxpayer with no dependents, has AGI of $115,000 after taking into account a $10,000 rental loss from a two-unit apartment that Karen actively manages. She also has $10,000 of itemized deductions (contributions, taxes, and interest).

   a. What is Karen's taxable income and her income tax liability for 1992?
   b. What would be your answer to part a above if Karen earned an additional $10,000 with no change in deductions?
   c. What is Karen's marginal tax rate?

#6

4. Herman's tax liability after credits last year was $8,000, the tax due on Herman's income from the operation (as a sole proprietor) of a pool hall. Because of police harassment, Hermans' business was slow. Based on his business through March annualized for the year, Herman paid a quarterly estimate of $1,000 on April 15. Using the same procedure, he paid $1,000 on June 15. After a new police chief was elected, business began to improve in the summer and continued at unprecedented levels for the remainder of the year, resulting in a tax liability of $15,000. For the last two installments on September 15 and January 15, Herman paid $3,000 per installment.

   a. Calculate Herman's underpayment for each quarter.
   b. Is Herman subject to the underpayment penalty? Explain.

_____ CLASS PROJECT

Amy, age 30, and Bob, age 28, Dink (double income, no kids) earned the following during 1992:

Amy's Salary (123-45-6789)	$55,000
Bob's Salary + Self-employment (987-65-4321)	50,000*
Interest on joint account at ABC Bank	1,500
Interest on State of Arizona Bonds	500
Dividends of XYZ Co.:	
Amy $800; Bob $2,700	3,500
Sale of GHI stock	(15,000)
Sale of KLM stock	5,000
Total Income	$98,550

*See part d for details. GHI stock was purchased jointly on 5/20/92 for $50,000; sold on 10/21/92 for $35,000. KLM stock was purchased jointly on 2/15/90 for $10,000; sold on 9/2/92 for $15,000.

The couple also made the following expenditures:

Medical Expenses:

Prescribed drugs	600	
Medical insurance premiums	2,400	
Other medical expenses	5,000	
Total medical expenses		8,000

Interest Expenses:

Personal Interest	6,100	
Home mortgage interest (original debt)	5,000	
Investment interest	2,300	
Total interest expense		13,400

Taxes:

Real property taxes (on home)	2,100	
State income tax	1,000	
State/local sales tax	900	
Federal income tax (U.S.)	24,000*	
Personal property tax (on boat)	150	
Total Taxes		28,150

*$20,000 via withholding; $4,000 via four estimated quarterly tax paymens of $1,000 each.

Charitable Contributions:

United Fund	800	
Salvation Army	300*	
Local Church	1,100	
Oxford University (England)	1,000	
Total contributions		3,200

*Estimated fair market value of old clothes, TV set, refrigerator, etc., given this year.

Travel Expenses (Amy's business travel away from home):

Airfare	2,200	
Lodging	600	
Entertainment (business)	750	
Food	650	
Total	4,200	
Employer's reimbursement	3,000*	
Remainder		1,200

*Amy's employer would not pay first-class airfare and allowed her only $300 for business entertainment. Hence, the $1,200 remainder represents a $750 difference between coach and first-class airfares plus $450 additional business entertainment expenses. Amy made a complete accounting of all travel expenses to her employer before she was reimbursed. Hence, the $3,000 was *not* included on Amy's Form W-2.

In addition to the above, the following items *may* be pertinent to answering the questions:

a. The Dinks own two cars which were driven a total of 18,000 miles during 1992. Included in that 18,000 mile total are 1,250 miles related to medical care;

1,600 miles related to charity; and 3,000 miles related to business (i.e., 3,000 transportation miles).

b. While the Dinks were away from their home on June 20, 1992, a burgular broke in and took the following items:

	Cost	FMV
TV set	$ 600	$ 300
Guns	500	400
Jewelry	2,000	3,800
Stereo	900	500
Total	$4,000	$5,000

The Dinks' homeowners' policy reimbursed them a total of $2,200 (TV set, $300; guns, $400; jewelry, $1,000—maximum for unlisted jewelry; stereo, $500).

c. Amy Dink paid her ex-husband (S. Nerd, 928-12-6101) alimony of $7,000 and child support of $3,600. Her ex-husband has custody of their child; he also claims the dependent exemption deduction for their child.

d. Bob Dink earned salary of $40,000 plus $10,000 (gross) from CCB, a small computer consulting business he conducts out of his home. Bob uses the kitchen table for his desk. Bob received a total of $10,000 in consulting fees ($7,000 from one client; $3,000 from the other). His 1992 expenses—in addition to the 3,000 miles he put on his car—were

Supplies	750
Dues and Publications	570
Total	1,320

e. The Dinks file a joint return. Assume that if they have overpaid, they desire a refund; if they have underpaid, they will enclose a check for the amount owed. The Dinks reside at 20 Yuppie Drive, Scottsdale, AZ 01010.

REQUIRED

Use Form 1040, Form 2106, and Schedules A, B, C, and D to complete this assignment. Sign your name as the "Paid Preparer" (on bottom, back of Form 1040). Also, put your name in the top right-hand corner of page 1 of the Form 1040.

If you should put even a little on a little and should do this often, soon this too would become big.

HESIOD, WORKS AND DAYS (C. 700 B.C.)

INCENTIVES FOR SAVING: RETIREMENT PLANS AND DEFERRED COMPENSATION ARRANGEMENTS

CHAPTER OBJECTIVES

In Chapter 12 you will gain an insight to various incentives for saving, particularly for retirement. You will learn the basic requirements and tax consequences of life insurance contracts, annuities, qualified retirement plans, and other deferred compensation arrangements.

LEARNING GOALS

After studying this chapter, you should be able to

1 Understand the basic concepts of life insurance;

2 Determine the tax consequences of an annuity contract;

3 Recognize the tax advantages of a qualified retirement plan;

4 Recall the requirements for a qualified retirement plan;

5 Recognize the difference between a defined-contribution plan and a defined-benefit plan;

6 Determine the tax consequences to the various parties to a qualified retirement plan;

7 Determine the tax consequences of an individual retirement account (IRA); and

8 Be familiar with other retirement and deferred compensation arrangements.

A long-term concern of some economists and policy makers has been the effect of the income tax on individual savings. In Keynes's model of how economies work, savings are ultimately translated into new investment, the motor force behind economic growth and overall health. High individual income tax rates, many believe, have decreased the propensity to save, with the possible long-run problem of inadequate growth.

United States tax policy, at least prior to the Tax Reform Act of 1986, has generally dealt with the problem of economic growth by trying to encourage investment in new plant and equipment. For example, prior law allowed accelerated depreciation and an investment tax credit to stimulate new investments. Provisions such as accelerated depreciation may increase the return on investments and thus serve as incentives to acquire assets. The incentive for savings is indirectly increased by these investment incentives because of increased demand for needed funds. Still, the incentives for investment were not concerned with savings except indirectly.

A recurring theme during the Reagan administration was that low tax rates would encourage the savings necessary to ensure a high level of investment. The Economic Recovery Tax Act of 1981 provided a combination of investment incentives and reduced tax rates. Contrary to expectations, personal savings as a percentage of disposable income declined steadily from a rate of 7.5% in 1981 to 3.2% in 1987. Although the 1986 Act further reduced tax rates, it also reversed much of the 1981 Act by eliminating or weakening investment incentives. However, tax rate reductions were nominal or nonexistent for middle income groups, particularly when combined with the Social Security tax; the Reagan administration expected new saving to occur among the wealthy.

Instead, while the U.S. personal savings rate seems to have stabilized, it has shown no appreciable increase. Many worry that low levels of personal savings will result in a future of crisis for individuals as they have inadequate funds to retire and that the United States will experience a period of sustained decline as world position erodes due to declining productivity and growth. The current level of Social Security benefits may be deluding younger workers who project that the same relative levels of benefits will be available upon their retirement. Current benefits are based on a system that has historically experienced high productivity and growth and that now has more than four workers for every retiree. But Social Security benefits are not contractual. They are political, depending on the laws in effect during a worker's retirement years. The political nature of Social Security, the low present savings rate resulting in less future pie to divide, and the demographic projections that 30 years from now there will be fewer than two workers for every retiree, have led congressional budget analysts to speculate that the United States may face intergenerational war over public retirement funding. The issue of adequate private retirement funding is a sleeper in terms of public awareness, especially among younger workers because the most important element of personal savings is retirement savings.

Qualified pension and profit-sharing plans are by far the most important tax provisions that serve directly as incentives for savings, so most of this chapter is devoted to these plans. Pension and profit-sharing plans have enormous clout in society, controlling about 23% of U.S. stocks and 15% of U.S. bonds.[1] However, before discussing these plans, let us consider life insurance and annuity contracts, which control over $1 trillion of assets in the United States. Because many individuals

---

1 James White, "The Decade of Phenomenal Growth for Institutions. . ." *The Wall Street Journal*, December 26, 1989, p. C1.

rely on public retirement plans, especially Social Security, we also give brief attention to these plans. The last part of the chapter describes several other savings incentives, such as nonqualified retirement plans, deferred compensation arrangements, and incentive stock options.

LIFE INSURANCE AND ANNUITY CONTRACTS

Because of their ability to defer taxes, life insurance and annuity contracts can function as savings incentives. The following paragraphs describe these two arrangements.

> **Goal #1**
> Understand basic concepts of life insurance.

LIFE INSURANCE CONTRACTS

An ordinary **whole-life insurance** contract works as follows: The policy owner pays premiums to the insurance company either for a stated period of years or for the life of the insured. The owner and insured are usually the same person. The insurer contracts to pay a fixed sum to the named beneficiary upon death of the insured. In lieu of the death payment, the owner may borrow against the policy, cash it in for its cash surrender value, or elect to draw down the cash value over a period of years as an annuity.

> **Whole-life insurance** has both a life insurance component and an investment component.

Premium payments by the owner are not deductible for tax purposes. If insurance proceeds are paid at the death of the insured, the proceeds are excluded from gross income of the beneficiary, as explained in Chapter 4. If the owner borrows against the policy, the loan principal, as opposed to interest paid on it, has no tax effect because it does not change the borrower's net worth. If the owner takes the cash value as a lump sum or as an annuity, gross income includes the amount received in excess of total premiums paid.

We ignore here the exclusion of the death benefit as a saving incentive although it can be a powerful incentive where the owner is not the insured but is the beneficiary. The tax benefit that accrues to the owner, even though he or she later pays tax on the gain when the policy is cashed in, is the deferral of tax on the income earned over the life of the policy. The policy owner pays premiums, which are invested by the insurance company. Over the years, the policy value increases, but the owner reports no income until the policy is surrendered. Thus, *before-tax* earnings are reinvested. In contrast, if the policy owner buys **term-life insurance** and makes separate investments in stocks and bonds, the interest and dividends on these investments are taxed currently, leaving only the *after-tax* earnings available for reinvestment.

> **Term-life insurance** is pure life insurance with no investment component.

Compared to the typical pre-1986 tax shelter, life insurance did not perform well even where the insurance company guaranteed high returns. In the typical competing shelter, income was deferred to later years and was eventually realized as a capital gain. The life insurance contract also provides deferral but produces ordinary income, a fact of less concern after 1987.

Following the 1986 Act, life insurance companies actively promoted single-premium life insurance policies as tax shelters. These policies take maximum advantage of the tax-free buildup by getting funds into the policy immediately. The 1988 Act discouraged the use of single-premium and other front-loaded policies as tax-sheltered investments by making policy withdrawals and loans against the policies taxable to the extent of accumulated tax-free income inside the policy.[2]

---

2 Secs. 72(e)(10), 72(v), and 7702A.

EXAMPLE 12-1

Assume that a taxpayer purchased a single-premium policy in 1990 for $50,000. Two years later, when the policy had an accumulated value of $59,000, the taxpayer withdrew $10,000 to pay his child's college tuition. Under former rules, the withdrawal would have been a tax-free return of investment. Under the new rules, the $10,000 withdrawal creates taxable income of $9,000 and a $1,000 return of capital. Additionally, unless the taxpayer is at least age 59 1/2 at the time of the withdrawal, he will also be subject to a 10% early withdrawal penalty of $900 (10% of the taxable distribution).

> **Goal #2**
> Determine the tax consequences of an annuity.

ANNUITY CONTRACTS

> An **annuity** is a series of payments made at regular intervals.

An **annuity** is simply a contract calling for a series of monetary payments at stated intervals for either a fixed or a contingent time period.

EXAMPLE 12-2

An individual purchased from an insurance company the right to receive $100 per month for a period of 10 years beginning on January 1, 1992, with the last payment made on December 1, 2001. If the purchaser paid for this contract with a single lump-sum payment on July 1, 1988, the annuity might be diagrammed with a time line as in Figure 12-1.

Types of Annuities

> A **simple** or **term annuity** provides payments for a fixed time period.
>
> A **life annuity** provides payments for as long as the annuitant lives.
>
> A **joint-and-survivor annuity** provides payments for as long as the annuitant and a designated survivor live.

The annuity illustrated in Figure 12-1 is commonly known as a **simple annuity** or a **term annuity**; that is, an annuity that is payable for a fixed time period (ten years in this case). Because most individuals use annuities as a source of retirement income, they are not interested in simple annuities; instead, they typically desire life annuities. A **life annuity** is payable for as long as the annuitant (the person designated to receive the payment) lives. Married individuals usually want retirement income for as long as either spouse lives so they arrange for a **joint-and-survivor annuity.** The amount of the payments may vary depending on whether only one or both spouses are living. For example, a joint-and-survivor annuity might provide $800 a month for as long as both spouses live and a lesser amount (for example, $500) for as long as either spouse survives.

No one knows, of course, exactly how long any individual may live. An insurance company's actuaries, however, know how long an average person will live, and that knowledge is necessary to their writing life annuity contracts with literally thousands of individuals. The fundamental idea behind a life annuity is shared risk—some

FIGURE 12-1

Annuity Time Line (EXAMPLE 12-2)

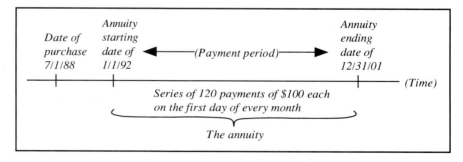

annuitants will die shortly after their payments begin; others will live for many years. Because of the risk of death shortly after the starting date of any annuity, some individuals desire a guarantee that they or their heirs will receive at least a minimum amount in return. For example, if an individual has $75,000 invested in an annuity, he or she might insist on a contract that will return (either to the annuitant or heirs) the $75,000 cost, even if the annuitant dies shortly after the annuity starting date. To satisfy these demands, **refund annuities** have been created.

In Figure 12-1, we assumed that an annuitant purchased an annuity with a single payment. Most individuals, however, do not acquire their retirement annuity in that manner. Instead, nearly all private annuities accumulate from a series of payments made during an individual's working years. In some cases, only the annuitant's employer contributes to the fund that eventually pays the retirement annuity; this annuity agreement is a **noncontributory plan**. If the annuitant makes some or all of the contributions to the fund that eventually pays the annuity, the plan is **contributory**.

Figure 12-2 illustrates a typical contributory annuity plan where both the employer and employee make contributions. Note that the income earned on the contributions is not a set amount (a straight line) because the earnings of the plan vary depending on the success of the plan managers. Alternatively, in the typical commercial annuity, the insurance company guarantees a set rate of return.

Taxation of Annuity Contracts

Although the taxpayer's purchase cost or premiums are not deductible, the income earned on the invested amount *is* sheltered from taxation until withdrawal. Thus, the taxpayer does not report the increase in value as income. With the exception of the employer's contributions to qualified plans, the taxpayer acquires the annuity contract with *after-tax* dollars. In other words, neither premiums paid for a commercial annuity nor employee contributions to an annuity plan are deductible for tax purposes (with several exceptions relevant primarily to employees of tax-exempt organizations). Consequently, the taxpayer recovers the cost basis in the contract as he or she collects the benefits.

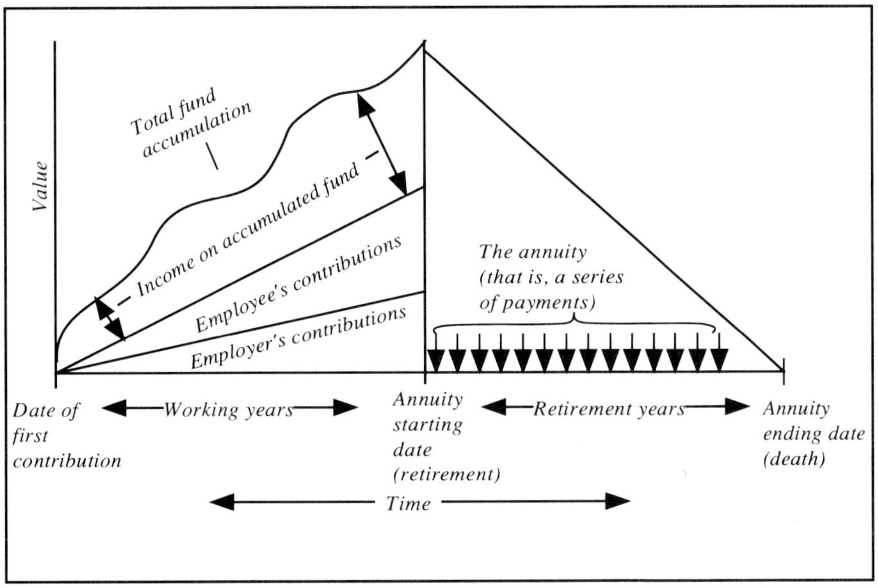

A **refund annuity** provides for the refund of the invested amount if the annuitant dies shortly after entering into the contract.

In a **noncontributory plan,** only the employer makes contributions.

In a **contributory plan,** the employee as well as the employer makes contributions.

FIGURE 12-2

Annuity Contributions and Payments

From the inception of the income tax in 1913 until 1934, taxpayers were allowed to apply the first returns from an annuity to recovery of capital. No income was recognized until the returns exceeded the annuity's total premiums or cost. This treatment of annuities had a major drawback because it often created taxable income for the oldest taxpayers when inflation had already reduced the adequacy of their annuity. In 1934, Congress enacted a 3% rule. Under this procedure, an annuitant included 3% of the annuity's total cost in income each year. The portion of the annual return exceeding 3% of the cost was treated as a return of capital. After total capital was recovered, however, the annuitant treated the entire amount received as income. The rule was unfavorable to taxpayers because 3% actually exceeded the interest paid by insurance companies at that time, and it still taxed the oldest taxpayers at the most inopportune time.

Since 1954, proceeds from an annuity are assumed to consist partly of a return of investment and partly of interest income on the investment. Using the following formula, the taxpayer excludes the portion of the proceeds that represents return of investment:[3]

$$\text{Exclusion ratio} = \frac{\text{Investment in contract}}{\text{Total expected return}}$$

Regulations provide actuarial tables for computing the expected return under annuity contracts involving life expectancies.[4] These tables indicate a multiple to be applied to the annual payments received by taxpayers of various ages at the annuity's starting date. Table 12-1 provides the life multiples for a single-life annuity. Note that Table 12-1, which applies to annuities beginning after July 31, 1986, is a unisex table that does not distinguish between males and females as earlier tables did. Regulations also contain tables for joint-life and joint-survivor annuities. The life multiples from the tables must be adjusted by yet another table when the annuity contains a guaranteed feature.

EXAMPLE 12-3

Assume that an employee of a state government contributed a total of $27,000 to the state retirement program during his working years. Assume further that this program provides for a retirement annuity of $200 per month, or $2,400 per year, beginning at age 65, for as long as the annuitant lives. Table 12-1 shows that, for an annuitant age 65 at the annuity starting date, the appropriate multiple is 20.0. Thus, the total expected return under the contract is $48,000 ($2,400 x 20.0) and the exclusion ratio equals 56.25% computed as follows:

$$\frac{\text{Investment in contract}}{\text{Total expected return}} = \frac{\$27,000}{\$48,000} = 56.25\%$$

Each year the taxpayer *excludes* $1,350 (56.25% x $2,400) and *includes* the remaining $1,050 in gross income.

Prior to 1987, once the exclusion ratio was set, it applied to all amounts received under the contract, whether the taxpayer recovered more or less than the actual

---

3 Sec. 72(b).

4 Reg. Sec. 1.72-9.

Age	Multiple	Age	Multiple	Age	Multiple	Age	Multiple	Age	Multiple	Age	Multiple
5	76.6	24	58.0	43	39.6	62	22.5	81	8.9	100	2.7
6	75.6	25	57.0	44	38.7	63	21.6	82	8.4	101	2.5
7	74.7	26	56.0	45	37.7	64	20.8	83	7.9	102	2.3
8	73.7	27	55.1	46	36.8	65	20.0	84	7.4	103	2.1
9	72.7	28	54.1	47	35.9	66	19.2	85	6.9	104	1.9
10	71.7	29	53.1	48	34.9	67	18.4	86	6.5	105	1.8
11	70.7	30	52.2	49	34.0	68	17.6	87	6.1	106	1.6
12	69.7	31	51.2	50	33.1	69	16.8	88	5.7	107	1.4
13	68.8	32	50.2	51	32.2	70	16.0	89	5.3	108	1.3
14	67.8	33	49.3	52	31.3	71	15.3	90	5.0	109	1.1
15	66.8	34	48.3	53	30.4	72	14.6	91	4.7	110	1.0
16	65.8	35	47.3	54	29.5	73	13.9	92	4.4	111	.9
17	64.8	36	46.4	55	28.6	74	13.2	93	4.1	112	.8
18	63.9	37	45.4	56	27.7	75	12.5	94	3.9	113	.7
19	62.9	38	44.4	57	26.8	76	11.9	95	3.7	114	.6
20	61.9	39	43.5	58	25.9	77	11.2	96	3.4	115	.5
21	60.9	40	42.5	59	25.0	78	10.6	97	3.2		
22	59.9	41	41.5	60	24.2	79	10.0	98	3.0		
23	59.0	42	40.6	61	23.3	80	9.5	99	2.8		

TABLE 12-1

Ordinary Life Annuities One Life—Expected Return Multiples

investment in the contract. These rules still apply to annuities with pre-1987 starting dates. For annuities starting after 1986, however, the exclusion ratio applies only until the entire investment is recovered. Afterward, the annuitant includes the total received in gross income. If the annuitant dies before recovering the investment, the unrecovered amount is deducted on his or her final return.

The rules for annuities, like life insurance, permit the deferral of taxes on earnings over the life of the contract. This advantage applies to both commercial annuity contracts and annuities from retirement plans.

PUBLIC RETIREMENT PROGRAMS

Undoubtedly the most important public pension and retirement plan in the United States today is that provided under the Old Age, Survivors, and Disability Insurance Act (OASDI) of the federal government. OASDI provides for old-age retirement benefits, disability benefits, benefits for survivors of the insured, and hospital insurance benefits. This program, generally referred to as Social Security, increases in social and economic importance each year as a growing portion of the citizenry becomes subject to its provisions, as both the number and percentage of the population actually receiving benefits increase, and as the payroll taxes levied to finance the plan increase. The tremendous growth in the Social Security program through 1988 is reflected in Table 12-2.

Many taxpayers do not think of the Social Security program as a tax-induced saving program because the benefits are not closely tied to total contributions. Social Security

TABLE 12-2

Federal Receipts
and Payments of
Benefits from
Social Security
and Railroad
Retirement Plans
(in millions of
dollars)*

	1940	1950	1960	1970	1980	1988
Benefits paid						
Old-age retirement benefits	$100	$ 838	$ 8,790	$21,883	$ 80,836	$160,889
Disability benefits	31	77	715	3,286	16,001	22,162
Survivorship benefits	7	321	2,517	7,852	28,026	37,427
Total	$138	$1,236	$12,022	$33,021	$124,963	$220,478
Receipts	$725	$2,656	$10,818	$36,170	$120,011	$259,898

Sources: U.S. Bureau of the Census, *Statistical Abstracts of the United States*, various years. (U.S. Government Printing Office), and Joint Economic Committee, *The Federal Tax System: Facts and Problems*, 1964 (U.S. Government Printing Office), p. 293.

*Figures do not include the hospital insurance program nor the supplementary medical program.

is still relatively new, particularly its expensive medical provisions. Most current retirees receive benefits in excess of their contributions, introducing an element of welfare into the program. Nevertheless, for many citizens the Social Security program represents their only significant savings for old age and medical disaster. Refer to Chapter 1 for additional details concerning Social Security.

───── PRIVATE RETIREMENT PLANS

Perhaps no aspect of American economic life has had more far-reaching social implications than the tremendous growth in formal private retirement plans during the past 30 years. This growth is reflected in Table 12-3. The total assets of these plans in 1989 amounted to $1,986 billion, a significant portion of total U.S. wealth invested in securities. Many factors account for the growth of pension plans since 1940. Some of these factors reflect general social and demographic changes in our society; others result directly from tax laws.

First, during and immediately following World War II, wages were subject to direct governmental controls. As a result, workers became increasingly interested in various fringe benefits, including pensions. Employers were eager to hold trained employees and considered pensions and other fringe benefits a relatively cheap method of doing so, especially because such costs were deductible in computing taxable income, which was subject to very high tax rates. In recent years, organized labor groups have also placed great emphasis on fringe benefits, especially pension and profit-sharing arrangements. In addition, business managers have realized that favorable retirement plans may be a powerful incentive to workers, resulting in greater efficiency and a reduction in employee turnover.

Increases in life expectancies, coupled with early retirement ages, have led not only to a large population of retirees but also to a great increase in the average number of years spent in retirement—a time during which some source of income is essential to replace the loss of wages. Growth in general awareness and concern for economic security has been both a result and a cause of the widespread use of formal retirement plans. Another important factor has been the decline in rural populations and the

Year	Coverage[†] End of Year	Employer Contributions	Employee Contributions	Number of Beneficiaries End of Year	Amount of Benefit[†] Payments	Assets End of Year (in billions)
1940	4.1	$ 180	$ 130	0.20	$ 140	$ 2.4
1950	9.8	1,750	330	0.45	370	12.1
1955	14.2	3,280	560	0.98	850	27.5
1960	18.7	4,710	780	1.78	1,720	52.0
1965	21.8	7,370	990	2.75	3,520	86.5
1970	26.3	12,580	1,420	4.74	7,360	137.1
1975	30.3	27,560	2,290	7.05	14,810	212.6
1980	N.A.	N.A.	N.A.	N.A.	N.A.	641.6
1985	N.A.	N.A.	N.A.	N.A.	N.A.	1,248.1
1989	N.A.	N.A.	N.A.	N.A.	N.A.	1,986.3

TABLE 12-3

Private Pension and Deferred Profit-Sharing Plans 1940–1989 (estimated in millions)*

Source: Data for 1940 from Daniel M. Holland, "Some Characteristics of Private Pensions Plans," *1959 Compendium*, p. 1305. Data for 1950 and subsequent years from *Statistical Abstract of the United States*, various years.

*Includes pension funds of corporations, nonprofit organizations, unions, and multi-employer groups. Also includes various other funds.
[†]Excludes annuitants.
[‡]Includes refunds to employees and their survivors and lump sums paid under deferred profit-sharing plans.

concomitant increase in the number of urban dwellers. This demographic shift requires comparatively more complete and complex arrangements for financing retirement living costs.

Unfortunately, many of the private pension and profit-sharing plans developed after World War II existed almost solely on paper. A congressional committee investigation in 1974 disclosed that, frequently, pension plans were not adequately funded, that vesting schedules precluded many participants from ever receiving the full benefits they anticipated, and that requirements of plans made job changes difficult and costly for employees. This investigation resulted in widespread public and congressional demand for reform of the entire private pension system and led to passage of the Employee Retirement Income Security Act of 1974 (ERISA).

ERISA established detailed and complex rules governing such pension plan provisions as the maximum waiting period before an employee is covered, schedules for vesting of benefits from employee and employer contributions, financial reporting and disclosure of pension trust funds, and minimum funding requirements. It also established a program for providing insurance for pension funds and developed many other rules designed to safeguard employee benefits and rights.

QUALIFIED PLANS—GENERAL RULES

One major factor in the growth of retirement plans is the income tax law. A plan that qualifies—that is, meets the tests discussed later—provides the following tax advantages:

Goal #3
Recognize the advantages of qualified retirement plans.

1. The employer claims a current deduction for employer contributions to the plan.

2. The employee excludes or deducts plan contributions from gross income, thereby deferring income taxation on these amounts until withdrawn from the plan.

3. The earnings on plan contributions escape income taxation until withdrawn from the plan. Consequently, earnings accumulate at before-tax rates of returns.

4. The employee may elect various methods of withdrawal. For example, he or she may receive either a lump-sum distribution or an annuity. Moreover, the recipient may roll over a lump-sum distribution into another vehicle, such as an Individual Retirement Account (IRA).

Given these potential benefits, Congress has had a difficult time fashioning rules that give the desired economic and social effects without wholesale abuse. Although ERISA was a comprehensive overhaul, Congress has modified the rules many times since. Recent changes, including the 1986 Act, have generally restricted the benefits for highly paid employees and have provided for wider required participation. Detailed coverage of specific rules is beyond the scope of this text, but generally current rules require that a qualified corporate retirement plan have the following attributes.[5]

> **Goal #4**
> Know the requirements of qualified retirement plans.

> A **nondiscriminatory** plan does not treat highly-paid employees, stockholders, etc., more favorably than rank-and-file employees.
>
> **Coverage** or participation refers to the number of employees eligible to participate in a qualified plan.
>
> **Vesting** occurs when a participant's right to receive benefits becomes nonforfeitable.

1. *Be **Nondiscriminatory**.* The qualified plan generally cannot treat certain corporate officers, stockholders, business owners, and highly paid executives in a way that is preferential to that given the rank-and-file employee. (Note, however, that this does *not* require equal treatment. For example, contributions equal to 6% or 8% of every employee's salary would be *non*discriminatory even though some employees earn much larger salaries than others.)

2. *Satisfy **Coverage** Requirements.* Nearly all full-time employees of any trade or business must be included (participate) in the plan.

3. *Satisfy **Vesting** Requirements.* A participant's right to receive benefits under the qualified plan must become nonforfeitable—even if the participant should change jobs before retirement—within a reasonably short time period. This requirement is satisfied by either of two vesting provisions in the 1986 Act. The first vesting schedule requires that a participant must have a nonforfeitable right to 100% of the participant's accrued benefit derived from the employer's contributions upon completion of five years service. The second acceptable vesting schedule gives participants at least 20% of the accrued benefit each year after three years service so that each participant is 100% vested at the end of seven years service. (Note, however, that vesting does *not* mean that an annuitant is necessarily entitled to withdraw his or her accumulated benefits prior to retirement or death. It simply means that some benefits are guaranteed at the time specified in the plan.)

> **Funding** means that cash or property is actually set aside to cover future retirement obligations.

4. *Provide Immediate **Funding**.* Cash must be put aside currently to cover the payment of promised future benefits; the full-faith-and-credit promise of an employer is not adequate.

5. *Account and Report to Designated Persons.* A qualified plan must keep written records of all details associated with the plan and make periodic reports to both the beneficiaries of that plan and to the government (specifically, the IRS and the Department of Labor).

---

5 Sec. 401(a).

6. *Meet Distribution Requirements.* Distributions from a qualified plan may not begin before the employee reaches age 59½ (with exceptions for death and separation from service), and they must begin no later than April 1 after the year in which the employee attains age 70½. Excise taxes, generally at a 10% rate, apply to improper distributions.

The most important qualified plans are those of corporations, particularly the large corporate units in our economy. Other types of qualified plans include self-employment plans, individual retirement accounts, and simplified employee plans. The rules for qualification of these other types vary somewhat from corporate plans, as explained below.

CORPORATE QUALIFIED PLANS

Although we are primarily concerned with pension plans, other types of corporate plans exist, including profit-sharing and stock-bonus plans. As its name suggests, a **pension plan** provides an income for an individual during his or her retirement years. A **profit-sharing** plan is also just what is name suggests—a plan by which an employer shares profits with its employees. The same ERISA requirements that apply to qualified pension plans also cover qualified profit-sharing plans, except for the funding provisions. Contributions to qualified pension plans are mandatory whether or not the employer makes a profit. Contributions to profit-sharing plans depend on profit and typically vary with the amount of profit earned by the employer. Because no contribution is guaranteed in a profit-sharing plan, it really cannot be considered a true pension plan, but the two are given generally comparable tax treatment.

A **stock-bonus plan** is one in which the employer contributes its own stock rather than cash. In recent years, however, a great deal of publicity has been given to a special form of stock bonus plan called an **employee stock ownership plan (ESOP).** The increased popularity of ESOPs is due in part to their value in defending against a hostile takeover. Under an ESOP, the employer corporation usually contributes its stock to a tax-exempt employees' trust, deducting the value of the stock. Under another form of ESOP, a trust borrows money from a lending institution to purchase stock of the employer corporation. The loan, usually guaranteed by the employer, is repaid by cash contributions made by the employer to the trust. The employer corporation deducts both interest *and* principal payments. Further dividends paid on stock held by an ESOP are also deductible from corporate income. Because the value of an ESOP depends wholly on the value of the employer corporation's stock at the time of an employee's retirement, these plans are not considered to be true retirement plans although they receive generally equivalent tax treatment.

Finally, qualified corporate plans fall into two distinct groups: defined-contribution plans and defined-benefit plans.[6] As its name implies, a **defined-contribution plan** requires specified contributions to the plan during the participant's working years but does not guarantee the amount the participant will receive upon retirement. For example, the contribution may be a fixed dollar amount or a percentage of annual compensation. The amount available upon retirement then depends on earnings those contributions generate. In short, the contributions are fixed (defined), but the retirement benefits may vary depending on fund performance.

On the other hand, a **defined-benefit plan** contractually specifies what the participant will receive upon retirement. The benefit usually depends on the employee's salary and years of service.

> **Goal #5**
> Differentiate defined-contribution versus defined-benefit plans.

> A **pension plan** provides retirement benefits for employees.
>
> A **profit-sharing plan** is a deferred compensation or retirement plan that allows employees to share in the company's profits.
>
> A **stock-bonus plan** is one into which the employer contributes the corporation's stock.
>
> An **employee stock ownership plan (ESOP)** is a typical example of a stock-bonus plan.
>
> A **defined-contribution plan** requires specified contributions to an employee's account with no guarantee of specific retirement benefits.
>
> A **defined-benefit plan** provides for specific retirement benefits with contributions actuarially determined to achieve the targeted benefits.

---

6 Sec. 414(i) and (j).

EXAMPLE 12-4

Roger Retire participates in a qualified defined-benefit plan that allows him to retire at age 65. The plan's benefit formula provides that a retiring employee shall receive an annual benefit equal to 2% times his or her average salary for the last five years of service times his or her years of service. Roger retires in 1992 after 30 years of service, and his average salary for his last five years equals $70,000. Accordingly, Roger's annual retirement benefit (before taxes) equals $42,000 ($70,000 x .02 x 30).

> An **actuary** computes premium rates, risks, etc., based on probabilities and statistical records.

An **actuary** determines how much the employer must contribute currently to deliver the promised future benefits to a large group of individual employees. Thus, depending on such factors as economic conditions, employee turnover, life expectancies, and employee retirements, contributions to a defined-benefit plan may vary significantly from year to year. In short, contributions vary to achieve a targeted (defined) benefit.

A pension plan may be either a defined-contribution or defined-benefit plan. Profit-sharing and stock-bonus plans, however, are always defined-contribution plans.

With this introduction to qualified corporate plans, we now turn to tax rules that apply to the corporate employer, the employee, and the trust. These rules are far too complicated to cover in detail here, so we limit our discussion to generalities and basics.

The Corporate Employer

> **Goal #6**
> Determine the tax consequences of qualified retirement plans.

The employer deducts contributions as they are made to qualified retirement plans. The maximum deduction depends on whether the plan is a pension, profit-sharing, or stock-bonus plan.

The allowable deduction for pension plans is determined by Sec. 404 and is tied to funding standards under Sec. 412. However, the deduction may not exceed the limits on defined-contribution and defined-benefit plans imposed by Sec. 415.[7] Section 415(c) limits annual contributions to defined-contribution plans to the lesser of $30,000 (in 1992) or 25% of the participant's compensation. Section 415(b) limits a participant's annual benefit from a defined-benefit plan to the lesser of $112,221 (in 1992) or 100% of average compensation for his or her highest three years. If the Sec. 415 limits are exceeded, the IRS can disqualify the plans until contributions and benefits no longer exceed the limits. As a practical matter, however, plan disqualification can be avoided by including provisions in the plan instrument that automatically adjust contributions or benefit accruals so that limits are never violated.

Contributions to profit-sharing and stock-bonus plans are limited to 15% of compensation.[8] The limit increases to 25% of compensation if the profit-sharing or stock-bonus plan is combined with a defined-benefit plan.[9] Compensation for purposes of computing the forgoing limits may not exceed $228,860 (in 1992).[10] Most of the numbers in these limits change annually because of inflation adjustments.

Because of funding standards and other factors, the limit on the corporate deduction under Sec. 404 may be less than the maximum amounts imposed by Sec. 415. Consequently, the employer's contributions could exceed the deduction limit without

---

7 Sec. 404(j).

8 Sec. 404(a)(3).

9 Sec. 404(a)(7).

10 Sec. 401(a)(17).

disqualifying the plan. Nevertheless, Sec. 4972 imposes a 10% excise tax on such excess contributions.

The Employee (Participant)

An *employer's* contributions made on behalf of an employee to a qualified retirement plan are excluded from the employee's income when the contribution is made. Income earned by the trust is also excluded from the employee's income. Only when benefits are distributed to the employee does he or she have taxable income. Most *employee* contributions to a plan (if any) are treated as personal expenditures and are not deductible. In other words, the employee contributes after-tax dollars.

If the employee receives retirement benefits from a qualified plan as an annuity, the exclusion ratio applies to each payment received. The employee's investment in the annuity is the amount he or she contributes to the plan. These contributions represent a recoverable investment because they were made from after-tax income. The employer's contributions, on the other hand, were not previously taxed to the employee and, therefore, do not constitute a recoverable investment. If the employee made no after-tax contributions to the plan, he or she includes all benefits in gross income.

EXAMPLE 12-5

Rhonda Gomez worked for the National Company from 1950 through 1992. During this period, National Company contributed $20,000 to a qualified pension fund for Rhonda's benefit. Rhonda also contributed $20,000 to the fund. Because the fund was qualified, the contributions made by National were not taxable to Rhonda when made. But Rhonda's cost, which she is entitled to recover tax free, is the $20,000 that she has contributed. Rhonda began drawing benefits of $333.33 per month ($4,000 per year) in 1992 when she was 65 years old. Table 12-1 shows that the appropriate multiple is 20.0 (essentially meaning that Rhonda's life expectancy is 20 years). Thus, Rhonda *excludes* $1,000 from income each year, computed as follows:

$$\frac{\$20,000 \quad \text{investment}}{\$80,000 \text{ expected return } (\$4,000 \times 20)} \times \$4,000 = \$1,000$$

Rhonda *includes* the remaining $3,000 in gross income. (If Rhonda had made no contributions to the fund, the entire amount received would be taxable to her because she would have no recoverable investment. If Rhonda lives long enough to recover her entire investment (20 years), she must include the entire $4,000 in gross income from that point on.

Section 402(e) provides an exception to annuity treatment. When the employee or beneficiary receives a **lump-sum distribution** of the accumulated benefits under a qualified plan. The taxable portion of a lump-sum distribution in a year beginning on or after January 1, 1974, equals the total amount of the distribution less the amounts contributed to the plan by the employee and less any unrealized appreciation of employer securities. The unrealized appreciation of employer securities is taxed when the employee sells the securities. The cost basis of any employer securities contributed to the plan by the employer and distributed to the employee is included in the taxable portion of the distribution.

> A **lump-sum distribution** is the payment of an employee's retirement benefit within one tax year on account of death, disability, separation from service, or the attainment of age 59 1/2.

For distributions made after 1986, the taxable portion of a lump-sum distribution is generally taxed using a 5-year forward averaging rule. This new 5-year rule, which is illustrated in Example 12-6, replaces a more favorable 10-year averaging rule effective before 1987 and a rule that permitted some part of the distribution to be treated as capital gain. The new 5-year rule can only be used once by a taxpayer during his or her lifetime and only for distribution received after reaching the age of 59 1/2. (A special transition rule applies to taxpayers who were at least 50 years old on January 1, 1988.) Other lump-sum distributions are taxed as ordinary income without 5-year averaging.

The 5-year averaging rule works as follows: First, the taxpayer computes the tax using regular rates on taxable income *excluding* the lump-sum distribution. To this amount is added the tax on the distribution. The taxable distribution is first reduced by the minimum distribution allowance, an arbitrary amount concocted by Congress to reduce the tax on smaller distributions. The minimum distribution allowance is 50% of the first $20,000 of the taxable distribution but is phased out at the rate of 20% as the distribution rises from $20,000 to $70,000. After subtracting the minimum distribution deduction, the remaining distribution is divided by five (5-year averaging), a partial tax is computed on this one fifth using Rate Schedule X—Single, and this tax is multiplied by five to obtain the total tax on the distribution.

EXAMPLE 12-6

In 1992 a married taxpayer with two exemptions and a standard deduction has taxable income of $55,000 before considering a lump-sum distribution of $100,000. This $100,000 is also the taxable distribution because the taxpayer did not contribute to the plan and the plan held no securities of the employer. The tax for 1992 is computed as follows:

Taxable distribution		$100,000
Less: Minimum distribution deduction		
(.5 x $20,000)	$10,000	
Less .20 ($100,000–$20,000)		
(limit $10,000)	10,000	–0–
Net distribution		$100,000
One fifth of above		$ 20,000
Tax on $20,000 (Schedule X—Single)		$ 3,000
Multiply by five		x 5
		$ 15,000
Plus tax on $55,000 (Schedule Y—Joint)		10,746
Total tax on 1992		$ 25,746

Without this special averaging rule, the 1992 tax on $155,000 using Schedule Y—Joint would be $40,801. The savings occurs because the 15% rate applied to most of the lump-sum distribution.

In lieu of electing 5-year averaging under the lump-sum distribution provisions, the recipient may roll over the distribution into an Individual Retirement Account (see below). Such a rollover defers the tax until amounts are withdrawn from the IRA but 5-year averaging may *not* be used for the IRA distribution. Thus, in making this decision, the recipient must compare immediate taxation at low tax rates via 5-year averaging with deferred taxation at possibly higher future tax rates.

The Trust

The trust containing assets of a qualified retirement plan is exempt from taxation. Accordingly, the earnings on those assets compound at *before-tax* rates of return. The following example illustrates the dramatic benefit of the trust's tax-exempt status.

EXAMPLE 12-7

Jack Jacoby worked 30 years for an employer who provided a qualified defined-contribution retirement plan. For each of the 30 years, the employer contributed $2,000 to the plan's trust on Jack's behalf. The trust fund earned a 10% before-tax rate of return for all 30 years. Had the trust been taxable, it would have paid taxes at 40%, thereby generating a 6% after-tax rate of return. Assuming a 10% return in a tax-exempt trust, the $2,000 per year accumulates to approximately $329,000 in 30 years ($2,000 x 164.5 annuity factor). Alternatively, assuming a 6% return in a taxable trust, the same $2,000 per year accumulates to only $158,000 in 30 years ($2,000 x 79 annuity factor). Now suppose that Jack received the accumulation and was subject to a 40% tax rate (assume no 5-year averaging). Because neither the contributions nor the earnings of the tax-exempt trust were ever taxed, the entire $329,000 would be taxable to Jack, leaving an after-tax distribution of $197,400 ($329,000 x .6). Of the $158,000 distribution from the taxable trust, only the $60,000 ($2,000 x 30) portion representing the yet untaxed contributions would be taxable to Jack, leaving an after-tax distribution of $134,000 [$158,000 − (.4 x $60,000)]. In sum, Jack's after-tax distribution from a tax-exempt trust equals $197,400 compared to only $134,000 from a taxable trust.

The benefit of deferring taxes in a tax-exempt trust can be further improved if Jack leaves the accumulation in the trust and receives retirement payments as an annuity over a number of years. He can obtain a similar extended deferral by rolling over the entire accumulation into an IRA.

SELF-EMPLOYMENT RETIREMENT PLANS (KEOGH PLANS)

For many years, critics complained that the tax laws permitting *employees* to benefit from retirement programs were unfair to *self-employed* individuals. In 1962, after much controversy and conflict, Congress passed a law that permits self-employed persons to establish retirement plans for their own benefit and to deduct all or a part of the contributions made to such plans. These plans are popularly known as either **Keogh plans** or **H.R. 10 plans.**

Prior to 1984, Keogh plans were subject to numerous restrictions and limitations that did not apply to qualified corporate plans. The restrictions generally reflected Congress's reluctance to provide qualified plans for self-employed individuals. Under old rules, for example, a self-employed person could only deduct contributions to the plan up to 15% of earned income, limited to $15,000 per year. Changes made by the Tax Equity and Fiscal Responsibility Act of 1982 (TEFRA) provide for general parity between Keogh plans and corporate plans. In particular, Keogh plans are now subject to the same Sec. 415 limitations as corporate plans.[11]

> A **Keogh** or **H.R. 10 plan** is a qualified retirement plan available to self-employed individuals.

---
11 TEFRA repealed old Sec. 404(e).

A **top-heavy plan** is one in which key employees receive a high percentage of benefits compared to other employees.

The 1982 Act also introduced a new safeguard against the abuses of qualified plans that stack the benefits in favor of key employees and owners. This new safeguard, which affects *all* plans, requires **top-heavy plans** to meet many restrictions on vesting and benefits that formerly applied only to Keogh plans.[12]

Funds contributed to Keogh plans may be put in a trust or custodial account (usually administered by a bank or savings and loan association), invested directly in individual annuity contracts issued by an insurance company, or invested in special retirement bonds issued by the federal government. Contributions for a taxable year must be made by the due date for filing the taxpayer's federal tax return for that year, not including extensions.

Generally, distributions to self-employed persons are taxed the same way as distributions from employee trusts. However, payments must not begin before the taxpayer reaches age 59 1/2, unless he or she is permanently disabled. The 5-year averaging rules also apply here, subject to the once-in-a-lifetime rule.

Shareholder-employees of S corporations have traditionally been treated as self-employed individuals for purposes of qualified plans. Before 1984, the restrictions on contributions and deductions for Keogh plans applied also to employees of S corporations who owned more than 5% of the corporate stock. Because of the general parity between corporate plans and Keogh plans after 1983, shareholder-employees are treated like other employees. Plans for small S corporations are subject to the new restrictions on top-heavy plans.

Goal #7
Determine the tax consequences of individual retirement accounts.

INDIVIDUAL RETIREMENT ACCOUNTS (IRAs)

An **individual retirement account (IRA)** is a special retirement vehicle available to individuals who earn income.

Section 408 permits an individual to establish his or her own **individual retirement account (IRA)** and *contribute* up to $2,000 per year to the account ($2,250 for a spousal IRA).[13] Prior to 1982, IRAs were available only to individuals *not* covered by a qualified private or government retirement plan. The Economic Recovery Tax Act of 1981 (ERTA), however, extended coverage to individuals already participating in some other qualified plan. Under post-ERTA IRAs, individuals can also *deduct* up to $2,000 per year.[14] The Tax Reform Act of 1986 continued to allow individuals covered by other plans to establish IRAs, but Sec. 219(g) enacted in the 1986 Act restricts the deductibility of contributions if the AGI of such individuals exceeds certain amounts. Accordingly, contributions to post-1986 IRAs may be fully deductible, partially deductible, or nondeductible.

In general, the annual deduction to an IRA is limited to the lesser of $2,000 or 100% of the individual's compensation (including earned income). This amount is deductible *for* AGI and is therefore beneficial even if the individual does not itemize deductions.

A **spousal IRA** allows an earning spouse to make contributions to an IRA of a nonearning spouse.

Congress also recognized that a spouse who does not earn outside the home nevertheless performs valuable household work and should also have the privilege of a tax-sheltered retirement program. Accordingly, an earning spouse may establish a **spousal IRA** in lieu of a traditional IRA. Contributions to the spousal IRA are deductible only if the couple files a joint tax return.[15] The earning spouse may establish either one IRA in joint names or a separate account for each spouse. In either case, the maximum deduction equals the lesser of $2,250 or the earning spouse's compensation.

---

12 Sec. 416.

13 Sec. 408(a).

14 Sec. 219.

15 Sec. 219(c).

However, if the couple establishes separate accounts, no more than $2,000 may be contributed to either account. Note, however, that if both spouses work outside the home they each may establish their own IRA subject to separate $2,000 limits.

If an individual or an individual's spouse participates in an employer's retirement plan (including a government plan), the dollar limits on deductibility must be reduced (but not below zero).[16] The reduced limit equals the original limit minus the reduction amount, and the reduction amount equals

$$\frac{\text{AGI} - \text{Applicable dollar amount}}{\$10,000} \times \text{Original limit.}[17]$$

AGI for this formula is computed before the IRA deduction. The applicable dollar amounts are (1) $40,000 for married filling jointly, (2) $0 for married filing separately, and (3) $25,000 for other filing statuses. The phase-out rule applies to the $2,250 spousal IRA limit as well as the usual $2,000 dollar limit. In short, once AGI reaches a threshold amount, the IRA deduction phases out over a $10,000 range and reduces to zero when AGI reaches $50,000 for married couples filing jointly, $35,000 for single individuals and heads of households, and $10,000 for married couples filing separately.

EXAMPLE 12-8

A married couple files a joint return and has $46,000 of AGI before claiming an IRA deduction. One spouse participates in an employer pension plan. If each spouse has a separate IRA, the dollar deduction limit for each IRA reduces to $800 (Reduction amount = $2,000 x ($46,000 − $40,000)/$10,000 = $1,200; Limit = $2,000 − $1,200 = $800). If the couple has just one spousal IRA, the dollar deduction limit reduces to $900 (Reduction amount = $2,250 x ($46,000 − $40,000)/$10,000 = $1,350; Limit = $2,250 − $1,350 = $900).

Deductible IRAs offer two benefits: (1) contributions are immediately deductible, thereby deferring taxation until withdrawn and (2) earnings within the IRA also escape taxation until withdrawn. Even though the 1986 Act reduces or eliminates the deductibility of contributions, individuals may nevertheless contribute to such non-deductible IRAs and achieve the second benefit.

IRA funds can be invested in (1) a custodial or trust account with a bank, savings association, or similar institution; (2) an individual annuity contract with an insurance company; or (3) special retirement bonds issued by the federal government. Excess contributions are subject to a 6% excise tax.[18] An excess occurs when contributions exceed the $2,000 limit ($2,250 for spousal IRAs) without regard to the reduction amount described above.

Nondeductible contributions must be kept in separate accounts from deductible contributions to ensure proper treatment upon distribution. Distributions from deductible IRAs are fully taxable as ordinary income when withdrawn. Distributions from nondeductible IRAs receive annuity treatment because nondeductible contributions represent a recoverable investment.

---

16 Sec. 219(g).

17 Also, the reduced limit may not go below $200 unless it zeros out, and a reduction amount that is not a multiple of $10 is rounded to the next lowest $10 (Sec. 219(g)(2)(B) and (C)).

18 Sec. 4973.

Distributions from an IRA made before the taxpayer attains age 59 1/2 are subject to a 10% penalty except in the case of death or disability.[19] The recipient can avoid the 10% penalty as well as income taxation by rolling over the IRA distribution into another IRA within 60 days. On the other hand, no deduction is allowed for contributions made after the individual attains age 70 1/2,[20] and distributions must *begin* by April 1 of the year following the year the individual reaches age 70 1/2. Distributions below this minimum distribution requirement are subject to a 50% penalty.[21] As mentioned earlier, distributions from an IRA may not receive 5-year averaging.

SIMPLIFIED EMPLOYEE PENSIONS (SEPs)

> **Goal #8**
> Recognize other retirement and deferred compensation arrangements.

> A **simplified employee pension (SEP)** allows an employer to make contributions to an employee's IRA.

To simplify some of the rules surrounding qualified retirement plans, the Revenue Act of 1978 greatly liberalized provisions by allowing *employers* to make contributions to an employee's individual retirement account via a **simplified employee pension (SEP).**[22] The employer takes a deduction, which is limited to the lesser of $30,000 or 15% of the participant's compensation.[23] For years after 1986, the *employee* excludes the contribution from gross income and takes no deduction.[24] The employee may also elect a salary reduction arrangement, subject to certain requirements and restrictions.[25] If the *employer* contributes less than the maximum amount permitted as a deduction by the employee under a regular IRA plan (100% of compensation or $2,000, whichever is less), the *employee* may contribute and deduct the difference.

The rules governing SEPs contain strict nondiscrimination provisions. The plan must not discriminate in favor of officers, shareholders, self-employed individuals, or highly compensated individuals. In addition, employer contributions must be based on a written, specific allocation formula and must bear a uniform relationship to the total compensation of each employee maintaining a SEP. Contributions must be made to the plan for each employee who has (1) attained age 21, (2) performed services for the employer in at least three of the preceding five calendar years, and (3) received at least $300 of compensation for the year (adjusted for inflation; $374 in 1992). In addition, withdrawals from the IRA by the employee must not be prohibited, the employee's rights to employer contributions must be 100% vested, and employer contributions must not be conditional on the retention in the IRA of any amount contributed by the employee. If the employer makes contributions on behalf of employees that are discriminatory, the $2,000 limit applies.

401(k) PLANS

> A **401(k) plan** is a special deferred compensation arrangement that qualifies as a retirement plan.

Another particularly popular form of tax deferral is the so-called **401(k) plan,** which is also known as a cash or deferred arrangement (CODA). These plans are established by employers to allow employees to defer taxes on part of their salaries, generally until retirement. The maximum annual amount that can be contributed to a 401(k) plan is $7,000 (adjusted for inflation; $8,728 in 1992). The employee excludes the contribution from gross income usually through a salary reduction arrangement. Further,

---

19 Sec. 72(t).
20 Sec. 219(d)(1).
21 Sec. 4974.
22 Sec. 408(k).
23 Sec. 404(h) and 408(j).
24 Sec. 219(b)(2).
25 Sec. 408 (k)(6).

earnings on the account are not taxed until the money is withdrawn. In many cases, the employer contributes an amount equal to some percentage of the amount contributed by the employee.

As with IRAs, withdrawals from 401(k) accounts can be made without penalty after age 59 1/2; withdrawals must begin by age 70 1/2. Earlier withdrawals are permitted in cases of immediate and heavy financial need for such purposes as medical expenses and tuition for a child. In these cases, the taxpayer must prove that other sources of funds (such as borrowing) are not available. Because all contribution are from before-tax dollars and income to the account is not taxed as it accumulates, amounts withdrawn are fully taxable. A lump sum withdrawal is eligible for 5-year averaging.

NONQUALIFIED CORPORATE PLANS

The tax rules for nonqualified plans are much simpler than those for qualified plans. We briefly consider them for each of the three possible major parties to the nonqualified corporate plan—the corporate employer, the employee, and (possibly) the trust.

The Corporate Employer

Contributions made by the employer to plans that are not qualified may be deducted if the employee's rights in the plan are nonforfeitable. If the employee's rights are not vested when the employer makes the contributions, a deduction can be taken later when the rights become nonforfeitable.

The Employee

For a nonqualified retirement plan, the employee must report as income the employer's contribution when it is made if the employee's rights are vested at that time. If the employee's rights do not vest when the employer's contribution is made, but do vest at a later date, the employee reports such contributions as income at the time of vesting.

If benefits from a nonqualified plan are paid to the employee as an annuity, the employee generally treats the annuity proceeds the same way as annuity proceeds from a qualified plan. If the employee reported the employer's contributions as income when they vested, the employee's investment in the contract increases by the amount of employer's contributions previously included in the employee's income. Alternatively, the excess of a lump-sum distribution from a nonqualified plan over the employee's investment is treated as ordinary income in the year of distribution, and the 5-year averaging rules do not apply.

The Trust

A nonqualified employees' trust must pay tax on its income in the same manner as any other taxable trust (see Chapter 6).

CONTROVERSIES OVER TREATMENT OF QUALIFIED PLANS

The tax rules for qualified plans provide a strong incentive for savings. The employer gets a current deduction, the trust funds escape taxation, and the employee usually pays taxes after retirement, often at favorable rates. These incentives are so powerful that Congress has been forced to pass restrictive rules, particularly to curb abuses for smaller corporate units with owners also functioning as key employees. The rapid growth of these plans raises some intriguing and troublesome social and economic questions, especially the effects on savings and investment and on the mobility of labor and capital.

Effects on Savings

Table 12-3 on page 405 shows that at the end of 1989 the accumulated assets of private retirement funds totaled $1,986 billion. Evidence is inadequate to show clearly how these accumulated reserves have affected the total volume of personal savings, and no accurate way exists to determine whether retirement fund reserves represent, in whole, in part, or not at all, savings that would have been accumulated some other way in the absence of such plans.[26]

To the extent taxpayers have in mind a definite amount of total savings, presumably the retirement fund would be considered merely a means of achieving these savings. On the other hand, if individuals have a given propensity to save a certain portion of their current cash income, the retirement fund probably represents additional savings, at least in part. The degree of consideration individuals give to retirement funds in reaching decisions about the magnitude of their personal savings is a relatively unknown factor. Self-employment retirement funds, as well as deferred compensation contracts negotiated between an individual employee and the employer, may be important in the individual's decision on how much to save, whereas group retirement plans are less important. There seems to be little correlation between the percentage of wages contributed by employers to retirement plans and the relationship between personal savings and personal income. On balance, however, retirement funds seem to add, at least marginally, to the total volume of savings.

Effects on Investment

Proponents of tax laws that encourage retirement funds often base their arguments on the notion that these plans increase the supply of available funds for investment in industry. This theory was the basis of the Reagan administration's 1981 saving incentive programs. Statistical evidence showing an increase in the percentage and amount of retirement funds invested in corporate stock supports this conclusion.

In the 1980s, the enormous assets of overfunded corporate pension funds made them a tempting target for corporate raiders. These excess funds could be used to help finance a takeover. To help discourage this behavior, Congress in 1988 passed a 15% tax on reversions of pension funds.[27] Another concern related to the economic clout of pension funds in society is fear over their potential economic power. Some 276 pension funds hold more than $1 billion each. The California Public Employee Retirement System alone controls $56 billion in assets.[28] Because pension funds account for 30% of stock market trading, politicians have recently begun to scrutinize the impact of pension funds on the volatility of the stock market. Especially suspect are program trading techniques used by fund managers.

Mobility of Labor

Reduction of employee turnover is one major advantage sought by employers in establishing retirement plans. This effect is also one of the chief criticisms levied against such plans—the adverse effects on labor mobility.

Most employee plans provide full vesting of the employee's rights only after several years of participation in the plan. Employees who change jobs after only a few years of coverage may lose all or part of their rights under the plan. Because employees cannot transfer rights from one plan to another, labor mobility may be severely

---

26 Peter T. Scott, "A National Retirement Income Policy," *Tax Notes* (August 21, 1989), pp. 913–26; and Steven F. Venti and David A. Wise, "The Evidence on IRAs," *Tax Notes* (January 25, 1988), pp. 411–16.

27 See "The Power of Pension Funds," *Business Week* (November 6, 1989), pp. 154–58.

28 *Op. cit.*, James White.

restricted. Unfortunately, ERISA (1974) did not solve this problem even though it did require minimum vesting schedules that provide improved vesting of benefits. The 1986 Act requires more rapid vesting than the 1974 Act did, but immediate vesting still is not required. Thus, the existing law does not resolve the conflict between the social goals of providing pension income for retired individuals and freedom of individuals to change jobs. On the other hand, some mobility exists if an employee vests in a retirement plan because he or she, upon termination of service, can roll over a lump-sum distribution into an IRA, thereby continuing deferral of taxes.

Retirement plans may also create a bias against the hiring of older employees. Qualified plans must not discriminate against workers on account of age, but hiring older workers may necessitate increased employer contributions, causing some resistance to their employment.

Even with individually negotiated plans, labor mobility is curtailed. Key employees with deferred compensation contracts may forgo high current salaries to obtain the contract, especially when income tax advantages are significant. The employee may have to give up rights under the deferred payment contract or suffer unfavorable tax consequences upon a change of employment. In addition, the high cost to a new employer of matching the employee's income given up under an old employment contract may be prohibitive.

OTHER SAVINGS INCENTIVES

As we said in the introduction to this chapter, the treatment of retirement plans is the major saving incentive in the tax law. Other incentives for savings not covered above also deserve some mention.

DEFERRED COMPENSATION

One procedure commonly used by executives, athletes, entertainers, and other highly paid employees is a **deferred compensation arrangement**. A typical deferred compensation arrangement works as follows: For a fixed number of years the employer and employee enter into an employment contract that provides for a specified amount of current compensation and an additional amount of nonforfeitable deferred compensation. The deferred compensation is credited to a reserve account on the employer's books and is paid in a specified number of installments after the employee's retirement.

Revenue Ruling 60-31[29] describes in detail various types of arrangements that the IRS considers eligible for tax deferral. In general, the employee may not have the right to receive the compensation immediately, and the plan must be unfunded. As long as these two requirements are met, the employee is not deemed to have constructive receipt, and, therefore, no tax is payable until the money is received. Also, because the deferred compensation arrangement is not a qualified plan, the employer's deduction is also deferred until the compensation is paid.

Deferred compensation usually means deferred consumption. Therefore, the deferred amounts are atypical savings because they are not available for new investment through the usual institutions.

> A **deferred compensation arrangement** can take the form of a nonqualified plan that nevertheless allows the employer to delay payment of an employee's salary.

INCENTIVE STOCK OPTIONS (ISOs)

Many high-ranking executives receive far more compensation from **incentive stock options (ISOs)** than from their annual salary. The 1980s saw generally rising stock

> **Incentive stock options (ISOs)** are compensation arrangements whereby key employees receive options to purchase the employer corporation's stock; qualified ISOs have special tax advantages.

29 1960–1 CB 174.

prices and record-shattering executive compensation packages. The reinstatement of tax-favored status to ISOs in 1981 was a major factor in the rising level of executive compensation.

Pushing equity considerations aside to provide incentives for executives, Congress in 1981 enacted Sec. 422, whereby an employee recognizes no income on exercise of an incentive stock option. Also, the employer corporation must agree to take no deduction for employee compensation in connection with the stock option. The option must be for a stock price greater than or equal to the current market price of the stock on the day the option is granted. If the employee holds the stock for more than one year (and until a date at least two years after the option was granted), any gain qualifies for long-term capital gains treatment (see Chapter 16).

EXAMPLE 12-9

The president of a company is granted an option to purchase shares of the company at $100 per share, which is equal to or more than the market price of the shares on the date the option is granted. Two years after the option is granted the president exercises the option, paying $100 per share when the stock's fair market value is $125. The $25 bargain element is not income. If the president later sells the stock for $150 after holding the stock for more than a year, the gain of $50 per share is recognized as a capital gain. The incentive option thus permits the deferral of income and the conversion of compensation into capital gains.

The 1986 Act made several changes in the rules for incentive stock options; for example, one change clarifies the annual dollar limit on options for each employee. Another makes the bargain element at time of exercise subject to the alternative minimum tax. Elimination of the net capital gain deduction by the 1986 Act also had an important indirect effect on ISOs. With no capital gains preference, the options merely serve to defer income (assuming the stock price rises and the alternative minimum tax is not a problem). Beginning in 1991, some capital gain advantage was restored to the Code. If this advantage increases through future legislation, the conversion element of ISOs will once again become a major benefit.

___ KEY POINTS TO REMEMBER

✓ A whole-life insurance contract has a savings and investment element while a term-life policy does not. Taxation is deferred until the whole-life policy is cashed in, or income taxation is permanently avoided if the beneficiary collects insurance proceeds upon the death of the insured.

✓ A portion of each annuity payment is a nontaxable return of investment determined by the following exclusion ratio: (investment in contract)/(total expected return). The balance of each payment is ordinary income.

✓ A qualified retirement plan (1) allows the employer to deduct contributions currently, (2) allows the employee to exclude or deduct the contributions from gross income, and (3) allows the earnings on contributed amounts to grow at before-tax rates of returns. Hence, taxation on both contributed amounts and earnings is deferred until retirement.

✓ A qualified corporate plan must meet numerous requirements concerning nondiscrimination, coverage, vesting, funding, reporting, and distributions.

✓ A corporate retirement plan can be structured as a pension plan, profit-sharing plan, or stock-bonus plan. Also, a plan may be either a defined-contribution plan or a defined-benefit plan.

✓ Distributions from qualified retirement plans are treated as annuities except that, if the employee has made no investment, the entire retirement payment is ordinary income. Also, under certain circumstances, employees may elect 5-year averaging for lump-sum distributions.

✓ Other retirement vehicles exist for individuals. These options include Keogh plans, individual reitrement accounts (IRAs), simplified employee pensions (SEPs), 401(k) plans, nonqualified corporate plans, and deferred compensation arrangement.

✓ Corporate employees may receive compensation in the form of incentive stock options (ISOs), which allow the employee to defer income recognition and convert income into capital gains.

RECALL PROBLEMS

1. Thirty years ago, Tom began payments to a 30-year endowment policy. This policy provides $50,000 life insurance coverage plus various options for conversion during life. Tom paid total premiums of $19,000. In the current year (after 1986), Tom surrenders the policy and receives its cash value of $36,000. #1

    a. How must he treat the receipt of the $36,000 for tax purposes?

    b. In what way, if any, has this policy sheltered Tom's income from taxation?

    c. Is a shelter such as this more useful now than in earlier years? Explain.

2. Taxpayer purchased a single premium life insurance policy in 1990 for $100,000. Three years later, the value of the policy had grown to $121,000. At that time, Taxpayer borrowed $30,000 against the policy. Assuming Taxpayer is age 50, what are the tax implications of the loan? #1

3. a. A taxpayer contributed $20,000 and his employer contributed $30,000 to a retirement annuity, which pays the taxpayer $5,000 during each of his retirement years. The employer's contributions were *not* treated as taxable income of the employee at the time they were deposited in a tax-free employee trust fund. Assume that 18.4 is the appropriate multiple to be used in computing expected return. How much of his annual $5,000 retirement income must the employee report as taxable income? #2

    b. B. D. Evers retired from employment on December 31, 19X0. Beginning on January 10, 19X1, Evers received monthly payments of $320 from his employer's qualified profit-sharing and pension plan. In recent years, the employer had made all contributions to the fund. Several, years ago, however, the plan provided for optional contributions by the employee, and during that time Evers contributed $8,000 to the plan. At the date of retirement, Evers was 65 years old. Compute the amount Evers will include in income in 19X1.

    c. Roger invested $20,000 in an annuity. Beginning in 19X1 and continuing through 19Y0, a total of 10 years, he is to be paid $3,000 each year. How much, if any, of the $3,000 received in 19X1 must be included in gross income?

4. Refer to part a of problem 3 above:

   a. What happens if the taxpayer lives more than 18 years? Assume he collects $5,000 in the nineteenth year.

   b. What happens if the taxpayer dies in the middle of the sixteenth year?

5. For a qualified plan, explain how the following are treated for tax purposes:

   a. Employer contributions

   b. Trust income

   c. Annuity-type distributions

6. Tom Executive began employment with Grosso Corporation on July 5, 1958, and retired from the company on June 30, 1992. He was covered by his employer's qualified retirement plan. While Tom was employed, he contributed $18,000 to the plan and his employer contributed $62,000. On September 1, 1992, Tom withdrew his cash benefits of $124,000 in a lump-sum distribution and invested the proceeds in a new business venture.

   Tom and his wife file a joint return. During 1992 he has other net taxable income of $60,000. Compute his tax liability for 1992 assuming he elects 5-year averaging on the entire distribution.

7. Elaine's employer sponsors a 401(k) plan. This year Elaine contributed 2% of her salary to the plan and her employer contributed 1% on her behalf (total contribution, $1,500). Explain how the contribution will affect Elaine's taxable income. How will earnings on the account affect her taxable income?

8. In 1992 Harris received a $60,000 lump-sum distribution from a noncontributory plan. Harris is married, and his taxable income, excepting the distribution, is $50,000.

   a. Assume that Harris is 65 years old at the time of the distribution. Compute his tax for the year.

   b. How is Harris taxed on the distribution if he is only 56 years old? What are his alternatives?

9. Determine the maximum deduction in an IRA account for each of the following independent cases:

   a. Howard, a bachelor, has earned income of $30,000 and has an adjusted gross income of $32,000. Howard is not covered by an employer's plan.

   b. Same as in part a except that Howard is covered by an employer's plan.

   c. Same as in part a except that Howard is married, but his wife has no earned income.

   d. Same as in part b except that Howard is married, but his wife has no earned income.

   e. Helen works and earns $44,000. Her husband has no earned income. The AGI on their joint return is $44,000 also. Helen is covered by an employer's plan.

   f. John, bachelor, lives mainly on interest but earned $1,500 during the year. His AGI is $20,000.

10. David retired in the current year; he is 60 years old. He had contributed $21,000 to his IRA account, all deductible. The balance of the IRA account is $38,000.

   a. How is David taxed if he withdraws this balance in a lump sum?

   b. How is he taxed if he withdraws the balance as an annuity of $4,000 a year?

   c. Are your answers to parts a and b the same if David retires at the age of 55?

11. City Manufacturing Company has established a nonqualified pension trust. Contributions are made each year for each employee who has been employed by the company for more than one year. These contributions are forfeitable by the employee if he or she leaves the company at any time before five full years of employment. Howard McVey began work for the company in June 19X0. In 19X1, 19X2, 19X3, and 19X4, the company contributed $200 each year (in December) to the fund on behalf of McVey. On June 12, 19X5, McVey's rights in the plan became nonforfeitable.

   a. How much income, if any, did McVey report in 19X1, 19X2, 19X3, and 19X4?

   b. How much income, if any, did McVey report in 19X5?

12. In January 19X1, Big Dome Corporation issued to its president, H. Bellows, a qualified incentive stock option to purchase 2,000 shares of the corporation's stock at $20 per share. On the date of issue, the stock had a value of $19 per share. Bellows exercised the option on March 15, 19X2, when the stock had a market value of $22 per share. He sold the stock on April 1, 19X3, for $30 per share. How much income and what kind of income does Bellows have in 19X1, 19X2, and 19X3?

THOUGHT PROBLEMS

1. What is an annuity? What income tax problems does a typical employee's retirement annuity present?

2. Many political and economic writers deplore the concentration of economic power in the hands of a relatively few people who manage the assets of huge retirement funds. Explain how the tax laws have contributed to the growth of these funds.

3. Why is the rapid growth in retirement plans receiving so much critical attention from scholars? What are the important tax aspects of retirement plans? What nontax aspects of retirement plans are of major importance?

4. Why are vesting and funding requirements important for retirement plan qualification?

5. In 19X1, Willford Manufacturing Company established a pension program for its employees. Mr. Willford, the president, was especially interested in this program, and the final proposed plan largely reflected his desires. The plan's basic feature was a trust fund to which annual contributions would be made. Each employee with more than five years of service would be eligible to participate. A contribution equal to 5% of the employee's compensation would be made for each employee with earnings in excess of $25,000; contributions of 4% of compensation would be made for each employee with earnings in excess of $15,000 but less than $25,000; and contributions of 3% of compensation would be made for employees with earnings of $15,000 per year or less. Is this likely to be a qualified plan? Explain.

6. Discuss the relative advantages and disadvantages of a defined-contribution plan versus a defined-benefit plan.

7. Consider two possible forms an individual retirement account (IRA) might take. IRA Form 1 allows a deduction for contributions but taxes the entire accumulation (contributions plus earnings) when distributed. IRA Form 2 does not allow a deduction for contributions but allows the entire accumulation (contributions plus earnings) to be distributed without taxation. Show that these two forms are equivalent. Under what conditions would they not be equivalent?

8. Consider a deferred compensation arrangement that is not a qualified retirement plan. Under what conditions would an employee prefer to receive deferred compensation rather than current salary (assuming the employee can afford to defer salary) and vice versa? Under what conditions would an employer prefer to pay deferred compensation rather than current salary and vice versa? Would an employer's and employee's preference ever conflict?

———— CLASS PROJECTS

1. Interview local businesses to determine how their retirement plans have changed over the last ten years. Among other questions you might ask, consider the following:

   a. Have businesses eliminated defined-benefit plans with no replacement of alternative plans? If so, why?

   b. Have businesses replaced defined-benefit plans with defined-contribution plans? If so, why?

   c. Have businesses changed their participation formulas or vesting schedules? If so, how and why?

   d. What changes in reporting requirements would businesses recommend to reduce the compliance burden of qualified retirement plans?

2. Investor earns $60,000 per year, which she receives on the first day of each year. Of this $60,000, she is able to save $2,000 on a before-tax basis. That is, she can save all $2,000 if she invests in a deductible IRA but can save only the after-tax amount if she invests in a nondeductible IRA or saves outside the IRA. Taxes are payable immediately upon receiving her paycheck. Investor's tax rate is 30%. Investor begins saving at the beginning of Year 1. At the beginning of Year 8, when she is 65, she withdraws her savings and retires. She receives no paycheck in Year 8. In parts a and b assume that the tax rate and before-tax rates of return remain constant over the investment horizon.

   a. Prepare a spreadsheet that shows how much Investor would accumulate after taxes by the beginning of Year 8 under the each following three alternatives: (1) she invests in a deductible IRA, (2) she invests in a nondeductible IRA, or (3) she invests in a money market fund. Assume a 7% before-tax rate of return under each alternative. What conclusions can you draw from this analysis?

   b. Assume the same facts as in part a except that Investor has just two alternatives: (1) a nondeductible IRA that yields 6.75% before tax or (2) a money market fund that yields 7% before tax. Again using a spreadsheet, determine how Investor should invest her money each year to maximize her after-tax retirement accumulation. What is the final after-tax accumulation from her investments? What conclusions can you draw from this analysis?

Part Four

THE TAXATION OF BUSINESS INCOME

The mission of Part Four is to expand your comprehension of the income tax provisions that most generally impact business ventures. Part Four provides important details to flesh out some of the more important general rules introduced briefly in Part Two. To accomplish this mission, we provide three chapters with these overriding objectives:

CHAPTER 13:
CHALLENGING TAX ISSUES IN BUSINESS—to illustrate the substantial intellectual challenge associated with the determination of a defensibly correct measure of taxable income for any business venture.

> *"Taxpayers may be forbidden to deduct entertainment expenses because they are suspected of enjoying dinners and theater parties with their business customers, for example, but even the most puritanical definition of business expense is not likely to prevent self-employed taxpayers from deducting the cost of air conditioning their offices, upholstering their swivel chairs, or adding gadgets to their telephones, even if they derive personal pleasure from these amenities."*
>
> *BORIS BITTKER, JOURNAL OF LAW AND ECONOMICS (1973)*

CHAPTER 14:
DEPRECIATION AND COST RECOVERY—to provide a historical and economic basis for depreciation deductions; to explain the depreciation, ACRS, and MACRS provisions; and to introduce the broad outline of the depletion provisions.

CHAPTER 15:
RELATED-PARTY TRANSACTIONS—to demonstrate why the IRS may carefully scrutinize transactions between various related parties and sometimes recast the apparent form of those transactions in a way that may modify the tax liability of the parties to the transaction.

To some extent, of course, every repair or restoration, no matter how minor or how soon after acquisition it is done, will add some value and will prolong the useful life of the thing repaired or restored.

SAM C. EVANS, (CA-5, 1977) 557 F.2d 1095

CHALLENGING TAX ISSUES IN BUSINESS

CHAPTER OBJECTIVES

In Chapter 13 you will be introduced to the intellectual challenges that confront business taxpayers who must determine what the Internal Revenue Code provides relative to their business operations. You will also become more familiar with several statutory provisions that are of particular importance to business ventures.

LEARNING GOALS

After studying this chapter, you should be able to

1 Understand the definitional challenges that face anyone who attempts to interpret the Internal Revenue Code;

2 Explain the definitional difficulties encountered in determining whether an expenditure should be capitalized or expensed for tax purposes;

3 Evaluate the definitional issue of capitalization versus expensing in the specific instances of (a) repairs; (b) professional fees; (c) rental payments; (d) interest expense; (e) feasibility studies; (f) valuation studies; (g) start-up costs; (h) organization costs; (i) environmental cleanup costs; and (j) package design costs;

4 Describe why even a good knowledge of general rules is not sufficient to determine the tax consequences of common business transactions;

5 Explain the burden of proof that rests with taxpayers and the reason that they bear the burden of proof;

6 Describe the kind of detailed records that must be maintained if business ventures are going to meet the burden of proof required to support the tax deductions that they are entitled to claim;

7 Explain generally the rules governing deductions for business travel and entertainment; and

8 Identify the more important tax credits that may be available to business ventures today.

Part Four of this text is limited to the income tax implications of relatively routine business transactions. Because most businesses are free to select any legal form of organization—including C corporations, partnerships, S corporations, or sole proprietorships—Part Four, like Parts One and Two, is entity generic. In other words, the tax provisions discussed in this part of the text have only one factor in common: they all involve business transactions. The primary intellectual challenge of Chapter 13, the first of the three chapters in this part, involves the need for you to apply fundamental tax concepts to everyday business events. Or, in other words, Chapter 13 requires you to think further about some of the tax terminology introduced in Part Two—terms like capital improvement, repair expense, ordinary and necessary, and reasonable in amount—as those terms relate to common business events. The chapter illustrates clearly the significance of definitions to the determination of a defensibly correct income tax liability. This chapter also explains the importance of good records to the determination of the tax liability for any business venture.

> **Goal #1**
> Understand the definitional challenges in interpreting the Internal Revenue Code.

DEFINITIONAL CHALLENGES

All tax law—statutory, administrative, and judicial—is expressed in relatively simple, everyday English words. This veritable library of prose determines the tax consequences of an infinite variety of highly complex economic and social events. Because of the complexity of the events, the specialized meanings often attached to the words used in the law, the syntactical complexity of the Code, and the interactions between the various provisions, the correct tax treatment of certain business transactions may be unclear. The first portion of this chapter is concerned with the definitional challenges faced by those who must interpret tax law.

Taxpayers and their advisers generally prefer to interpret the application of the law to given economic events in a manner that will minimize their own tax liabilities. IRS agents and Justice Department attorneys, on the other hand, generally prefer to interpret the same words in a way that will maximize tax revenues for the government. Hence differences in the interpretation and application of words to specific economic events is inevitable. Conflict and uncertainty forever will be an integral part of the tax process.

> **Goal #2**
> Explain the definitional difficulties in determining whether an expenditure should be capitalized or expensed for tax purposes.

To illustrate just a few of many recurring tax challenges that are common to everyday business events, let us begin by reconsidering the application of a fundamental tax concept introduced in Chapter 5. We learned there that Sec. 263 generally provides that capital expenditures are not deductible. Although that sweeping conclusion is valid as a general rule, any practical application of the general rule is typically fraught with problems when applied to the taxation of income earned in both large and small business ventures.

> The term **capital expenditure** refers to any expenditure which is expected to benefit more than one accounting period.

In both financial accounting and income taxation the term **capital expenditure** refers conceptually to any expenditure which is expected to benefit more than one accounting period. The requirement that those expenditures be capitalized rather than expensed—or, in bookkeeping terms, the requirement that those expenditures be charged to an asset account, rather than to an expense account—is necessitated if one is to avoid an understatement of income in the year the expenditure is incurred, and an overstatement of income in one or more subsequent years, when the remainder of the benefit is realized. Although the fundamental concept is simple, its application to everyday business transactions is sometimes difficult. Much of the difficulty involves the inability to determine whether an expenditure creates or enhances a separate and distinct asset. Sometimes the difficulty involves the distinction between ongoing and entirely new trades or businesses. Sometimes the problem is one of matching income and deductions correctly. The following categories illustrate these definitional problems.

REPAIRS

Amounts expended solely to repair a business property are deductible under Sec. 162. However, differentiating between deductible **repair** expenses and capitalized repair costs can be a difficult task because the fundamental distinction between the two is not always easy to apply. In general, a repair does not either (1) appreciably increase an asset's value or (2) significantly increase its useful life. A repair just keeps an existing asset in its normal operating condition. Repainting a business car or truck damaged in a hailstorm is a good example. Capital expenditures, on the other hand, usually significantly prolong an asset's life, materially increase an asset's value, or make an old asset available for a new or different use in the business. A routine replacement of a part in a machine that produces ceramic tiles would be a repair. The cost of a drastic modification designed to make a machine capable of producing pottery rather than tile would, in contrast, be a capitalized cost. A major overhaul of a machine is often difficult to classify; the cost could be in part an expense and in part a capital expenditure. There is no ready touchstone to provide an easy answer and reasonable persons may disagree as to the correct classification in common business settings.

> The term **repair** means an action that just keeps an existing asset in its normal operating condition.

> **Goal #3**
> Evaluate the definitional issue of capitalization versus expensing in specific instances.

PROFESSIONAL FEES

Professional fees, such as those paid to an accounting firm to audit annual financial statements or to prepare an income tax return, are immediately deductible under Sec. 162. The deductibility reflects the short-term benefits received. However, if a professional fee clearly generates benefits to the business beyond those to the current period, it generally will not be immediately deductible. For example, a payment to an architect for designing an office building must be capitalized as part of the cost of the building. Fees paid to an accounting or a law firm for long-range tax planning are more difficult to categorize correctly. Some portion of those fees may be currently deductible; some portion arguably may be capital in nature; and, at least in the case of individual taxpayers, still other parts could be a nondeductible personal expense. For example, the cost of preparing a will, as part of a tax plan, is a nondeductible personal expense. In these situations a detailed billing for the professional services received may be required to reach the correct tax treatment of a single professional invoice (or bill).

In the business setting, the correct tax treatment of professional fees is sometimes even more complex than is suggested above. Suppose, for example, that as part of its professional engagement, an accounting or law firm provides not only tax planning advice for the business entity, but also tax advice for the most highly compensated members of the business management team and (perhaps) the members of the board of directors who select the accounting or law firm to be engaged by the business. Can this special service—which may be a good marketing tool for the accounting or law firm—properly be considered an expense of the business venture that is paying the professional fee? And how likely is it that the accounting or law firm would prepare an accurate summary (in a detailed professional invoice) for the time that they actually spent on the personal tax matters of their client's management group? The ethical implications of this rhetorical question should be of more than passing interest to all future professionals.

Finally, even if one concludes that a business entity can properly pay the professional fee for services that are primarily of personal benefit to the business owners and/or managers, rather than to the business entity per se, someone must still decide whether or not the value of those professional services should be included as part of the compensation of the individuals who benefited from the service. In other words, should the business entity's accounting department deduct this part of the invoice that it receives for professional services as additional *executive compensation* expense rather than as a *professional service* expense? If the correct tax classification is one of executive compensation, that fact must also be reflected on the W-2 forms that the employer files at the end of the year with the IRS. This means, of course, that the income tax liabilities of the individual officers and directors will increase accordingly. And how likely is it that the CFO (chief financial officer) will make the correct definitional call on this fuzzy of an issue if that call means an increase in the CFO's personal income tax liability as well as the CFO's bosses' personal tax liabilities?

RENTAL PAYMENTS

Rental payments made for property used in a taxpayer's trade or business generally may be deducted by the taxpayer under Sec. 162. For example, amounts paid for the rental of a large computer system will usually be a deductible expenditure. However, when a lease is actually a disguised purchase of a property, a taxpayer who leases property must recast the transaction as a purchase and treat the alleged rental payments as amounts actually paid to purchase the property and payments of interest. The rules which mandate capitalization for accounting purposes are not necessarily the same as those used for federal income tax purposes. The IRS has elected to pursue this issue on a case-by-case basis. Hence the correct classification of a lease versus a purchase depends on all of the facts and circumstances surrounding each alleged lease agreement.

In business transactions that involve the utilization of non-depreciable property, such as land, the lessee has a strong tax incentive to treat any questionable acquisition as a lease rather than as a purchase.

EXAMPLE 13-1

Fun-in-the-Sun Hotels Corporation has recently located a prime ocean-front acreage on the island of Kauai. The asking price for the acreage is $100 million. The construction costs are anticipated to approach $500 million. The corporation has two options for gaining the right of possession of the land.

   a. A 99-year lease at a rate of $10,000,000 per year.

   b. An outright purchase for $100,000,000.
       [The present values of these arrangements are approximately equal at a 10% discount rate, not considering tax consequences.]

If the lease is accepted by the IRS as a true lease, the $10,000,000 in annual lease payments yield a $3,400,000 tax savings to the corporation. In contrast, if Fun-in-the-Sun has purchased the property for $100,000,000, no deductions will be allowable because land is a nondepreciable asset.

Generally speaking, the presence of any one or more of the following factors in a lease agreement suggests that the correct tax classification of an uncertain transaction is really a purchase:

- The lessee has the option to acquire title to the property, at little or no additional economic cost, at the end of the lease term;

- The periodic lease payments (or rents) are substantially larger than the usual rents paid for similar properties in the general locale;

- Some portion of the rent payment is either specifically designated as interest or is readily identifiable as an equivalent of interest; or

- The total of the rents payable plus any optional final payments, under the terms of the lease, are roughly equal to the sum of the purchase price of the leased property plus interest over the term of the lease.

In brief, governmental authorities will not necessarily accept the apparent form of a business lease if it is reasonably obvious that the form of the transaction does not fairly represent the economic substance of the events that have transpired. Hence large corporations and other businesses that frequently engage in lease transactions must pay particular attention to the correct classification of each lease agreement for tax purposes as do the business ventures who lease those same properties.

INTEREST EXPENSE

The UNICAP rules of Sec. 263A, noted earlier in Chapter 7, provide in subsection (f) that the interest expense incurred by a trade or business must be capitalized to the extent that it is paid or incurred during the production period of a fixed asset. The Treasury Department's proposed regulations under this relatively new statutory provision take a rather expansive view of the events that signal the start of the production process. Land developers almost immediately protested the Treasury Department's interpretation which would require the capitalization of interest for an entire project the moment that any work was started on any element of a project involving multiple units or steps. Thus, for example, the cost of clearing a small part of a large land development project could be sufficient to terminate further interest expense deductions. For business ventures short on cash and heavy on interest payments, this one capitalization requirement alone could be sufficient to scuttle the entire project.[1]

FEASIBILITY STUDIES

Successful businesses frequently investigate the commercial feasibility of expanding their product line, moving into a new geographical territory, doing business in a new way, or acquiring another business. Are the costs incurred in making these feasibility studies to be treated as an ordinary and necessary expense of an on-going business or as a capital expenditure of a new and separate trade or business? Once again there is no ready answer to this relatively straight-forward conceptual question for either taxpayers or tax advisers. The only way the question can be properly resolved is

---

1 See "Ten Witnesses to Testify at Nov. 20 Hearing on Interest Capitalization Rules," BNA *Daily Tax Report*, November 11, 1991, pp. G-2, G-3. See also Scott R. Schmedel, "Tax Topics," *The Wall Street Journal*, November 11, 1991, p. A-1.)

through careful research of legal precedents involving other taxpayers in similar circumstances. Even after careful research the correct answer may not be apparent. For example, the Fourth and Fifth Circuit Courts of Appeal currently disagree on the proper tax treatment of costs incurred, by successful banks and savings and loan companies, investigating additional branch banks in new geographical areas. The Fourth Circuit held, in *NCNB Corp. v. U.S.,* that those costs were deductible as an ordinary and necessary expense of an existing trade or business.[2] The Fifth Circuit, in *Central Texas Saving and Loan Association v. U.S.,* held that very similar costs must be capitalized as part of the cost of a new business venture.[3] It is surprising to the authors that this conflict in judicial opinion has not yet reached the Supreme Court.

VALUATION STUDIES

A somewhat analogous definitional question was decided by the Supreme Court in the case of *INDOPCO Inc.* (formerly, *National Starch and Chemical Corp.) v. Comm'r.*[4] The crux of the definitional question was whether an expenditure must be capitalized only if it creates or enhances a "separate and distinct asset." The taxpayer argued for that definition with respect to its expenditure of $2 million in consulting fees paid to determine the fair market value of stock in a friendly takeover.

The Tax Court, Third Court of Appeals, and now the Supreme Court have all disagreed with the taxpayer's position. The Supreme Court opined that because these expenditures were incurred for the purpose of changing corporate ownership and capital structure, significant future benefits would be realized; thus, the expenditures must be capitalized. This case is of significant interest to the many business ventures that have been involved in corporate takeovers during the last decade.[5]

START-UP COSTS

Once it is determined that a given trade or business is best classified as a *new* trade or business, rather than as an extension of an existing trade or business, another set of tax provisions may come into play. **Start-up costs** are defined as the costs incurred in investigating or creating a *new* business. The costs that are subject to a special amortization election under Sec. 195 fall into two general categories:

> **Start-up costs** are the costs incurred in investing or creating a *new* business.

1. Investigatory costs incurred to study or survey potential markets; to determine labor supply or the availability of transportation; to review state and local tax laws; and so on. These costs are normally incurred *before* a decision has been made to acquire or create the new business.

2. Start-up costs incurred *subsequent* to a decision to acquire or establish a particular business, *but prior to* the time the business begins, include advertising; salaries

---

2 684 F.2d 942, 1982.

3 731 F.2d 1181, 1984.

4 U.S. Sup. Ct. No. 90-1278, 60 U.S.L.W. 4173 (U.S. Feb. 26, 1992).

5 See J. Phillip Adams and J. Dean Hinderliter, "INDOPCO, Inc. v. Comm'r.: Impact Beyond Friendly Takeovers," *Tax Notes,* April 16, 1992, pp. 93–103, for an in-depth analysis of the INDOPCO, Inc. case and related issues.

and wages paid to employees who are being trained and to their instructors; travel and other expenses incurred in lining up prospective distributors, suppliers, or customers; and salaries or fees paid or incurred for executives, consultants, and similar professional services.

In brief, start-up costs include many of the costs associated with either the creation of a new business or the acquisition of an existing business. The costs of feasibility studies, found to be associated with the acquisition of a new trade or business rather than an extension of an existing trade or business, are properly included with other start-up costs. The amortization and deduction of these costs cannot begin until the taxpayer actually enters into the active conduct of the trade or business being created or acquired. The exact date on which that event occurs is once again based on all of the facts and circumstances surrounding each specific business venture. As soon as a business has begun, the taxpayer can elect any amortization period of 60 months or more. If the taxpayer fails to make this election by the due date of the first tax return (including possible extensions) for the new trade or business, the opportunity to amortize these costs is lost forever.

A question frequently arises as to the correct tax treatment to be given costs incurred in investigating a business if the investigation is fruitless and no business is created or acquired. If the cost is incurred by a corporation, it generally can be deducted. If the cost is incurred by an individual, the proper treatment is not so clear. If the business being investigated is in the same field as the taxpayer's current business, it usually will be allowed as a business deduction. If the prospective business is in a new field, the individual will apparently be allowed to deduct the accumulated costs as a business loss (under Sec. 165) assuming the expenditures were not a thinly veiled disguise for personal enjoyment activities. Similarly, a taxpayer can ordinarily deduct any accumulated costs that remain unamortized if an active trade or business is terminated before the expiration of the 60-month (or longer) write-off period.

ORGANIZATION COSTS

If a newly created or acquired trade or business involves the creation of a new legal entity, a taxpayer will typically incur some amount of **organization costs.** Organization costs are those costs *directly* related to the creation of a new corporation or a new partnership. These costs create an asset that exists for the remaining life of the entity. Conceptually, the value of this asset expires only at the termination of the entity. To allow current expensing of these costs, Sec. 248 provides that a corporation may amortize costs such as any state fees for obtaining a corporate charter; fees paid to attorneys in connection with drafting bylaws, the charter, and minutes of the organizational meeting; expenses of any temporary directors' meetings; organizers' fees; and similar costs. In contrast, costs incurred in connection with raising capital—such as commissions and fees for selling the corporation's stock and securities and the printing costs related to these stocks and bonds—do not qualify as organization costs. They are treated as a reduction of contributed capital. The amortization period for the qualifying costs is 60 months or more, beginning with the month in which the corporation begins business.

Under Sec. 709, a partnership likewise may elect to deduct its organization costs over a period of not less than 60 months. The costs involved must be incident to the partnership's creation. This election does not apply to syndication fees, commissions on sale of partnership interests, costs of issuing partnership units, or marketing costs, which must be capitalized for the duration of the partnership.

> **Organization costs** are those costs *directly* related to the creation of a new corporation or a new partnership.

EXAMPLE 13-2

Flatirons Corporation was organized on February 1, 1992, and began business on August 1, 1992. The corporation uses a calendar year for accounting and tax purposes. Expenses incurred in the organization were:

Attorney's fees in drafting incorporation documents	$ 1000
Accountant's fees to set up initial bookkeeping system	1200
State fee for corporate charter	200
Underwriter's fee for initial stock offering	10,000

Amortizable organization costs are $2400 ($1000 + $1200 + $200). If the taxpayer elects to amortize these costs over 60 months, $200 can be deducted in 1992.

($2400/60 months x 5 months = $200)

For 1993, 1994, 1995 and 1996, $480 may be deducted each year. The remaining $280 is deductible in 1997.

ENVIRONMENTAL CLEANUP COSTS

The correct tax treatment of many environmental cleanup costs is likely to become an increasingly important topic in the years ahead. These costs commonly include, among others, legal fees, criminal fines, and restitution payments. Generally speaking, restitution payments and legal fees are deductible; criminal penalties are not.[6] The correct tax treatment of monies paid for environmental reasons is likely to depend in significant part on how carefully the taxpayer drafts any settlement agreement. Congressman Guarini (D-NJ), who chairs the House Budget Task Force on Urgent Fiscal Issues, is reported as having said that Exxon Corporation managed to manipulate most of the criminal penalties it incurred in connection with the *Valdez* oil spill as tax deductible expenditures.[7] Exxon's second settlement in that case calls for additional payments of somewhere between $900 million and $1 billion. The corporation claims that it has already paid out some $2.5 billion relative to this one event.[8]

The correct tax treatment of payments made by business ventures in response to EPA (the Environmental Protection Agency) mandated "Superfund Cleanups" are currently unclear. As noted above, amounts clearly designated as fines or penalties are made nondeductible by Sec. 162(f). Taxpayers that still own the property that is being cleaned up may well have to capitalize some part (or all) of many environmental costs as capital costs under Sec. 263(a). Taxpayers who have already disposed of the polluted property, but who incur cleanup costs to avoid further liability, may be in a better position than continuing owners to deduct similar costs currently.[9] It is rumored that the IRS is currently working on two revenue rulings in this area; one involves the cost of asbestos removal; the other, clearing land of toxic waste.

6 See Sec. 162(f).

7 See "Exxon Valdez Fine Largely Tax Deductible, House Budget Task Force Chairman Charges," BNA *Daily Tax Report,* November 1, 1991, pp. G-7, –8.

8 *Ibid.*

9 For further discussion of this interesting issue, see Mark W. March and Julia K. Brazelton, "Superfund Cleanup: The Financial Costs Are High, the Tax Treatment Uncertain," *Taxes,* November 1991, pp. 682–88.

PACKAGE DESIGN COSTS

For many years the IRS appeared to accept most taxpayers' current deduction of package design costs as routine selling expenses under Sec. 162. Three years after the enactment of the UNICAP rules of Sec. 263A, however, the IRS retroactively changed its mind. In Rev. Rul. 89-23 (1989-1 CB 85), the IRS announced its intention to require all taxpayers to capitalize package design costs retroactively. Under this ruling all taxpayers were required to reopen their prior-year tax returns and to capitalize all package design costs that they had incurred and deducted. Furthermore, the IRS said, these costs could not be amortized under Sec. 167 because it would be impossible to estimate the useful life of a package design with any reasonable degree of certainty.

At least in part to minimize future disputes and to quell the strong negative reaction of many taxpayers and tax advisers to Rev. Rul. 89-23, the IRS subsequently modified its initial position. In Rev. Proc. 90-63 (1990-2 CB 664) it announced that taxpayers could, in fact, amortize certain package design costs over a period of either 48 or 60 months (on a pool-of-cost or a design-by-design basis, respectively) if they complied with all of the other requirements of the revenue procedure. Although the authors of your text accept this latest modification as a reasonable interpretation of Sec. 263A, we continue to question whether the small, one-time increase in government revenues is a sufficient justification for the additional administrative complexity and taxpayer compliance cost introduced by the enactment of this new provision.

This completes our discussion of the definitional tax issues implicit in common business transactions. Although the preceding discussion is far from exhaustive, your authors believe that it illustrates how challenging it can be to determine the correct tax treatment of various business transactions. The words of the Code, as well as the fundamental tax concepts implicit within those words, frequently appear to overlap. Thus taxpayers and government personnel frequently disagree as to which section or sections of the Code should control the tax consequences of specific economic events. The significant challenge for every tax expert is to identify, advocate, and sustain the one interpretation that is most beneficial for his or her client, whether that client is a confused taxpayer or a government hungry for additional tax revenues.

STATUTORY CHALLENGES

Even after a tax expert has determined that one Code section, rather than some other section, should govern the tax consequences of a given business transaction, he or she must frequently read and reread the governing Code section(s) with great care to be certain that it does not include a unique rule that modifies the general tax result for this particular transaction. In other words, an unfortunately large number of Code sections include not only a general rule, but also numerous exceptions to the general rule; exceptions to the exceptions (which returns one to the general rule, of course); and even exceptions to the exceptions to the exceptions. Subsections typically provide special rules and definitions for each specific Code section. Furthermore, other sections, which may or may not be adequately cross-referenced, may further modify the Code section being reviewed. The general syntax of the Code is quite possibly more convoluted than any other document written in the English language.

An example of a Code section that requires careful reading is Sec. 162, the statutory provision that generally authorizes the deduction of all ordinary and necessary expenses paid or incurred in a trade or business. This section includes 14 subsections [Sec. 162(a) through Sec. 162(m)]. Subsection (a) provides the general rule; the

> **Goal #4**
> Describe why knowledge of general rules is not sufficient to determine the tax consequences of common business transactions.

remaining subsections provide exceptions modifying the general rule, exceptions modifying other exceptions, and special rules and definitions. It is impossible—and in the authors' view, undesirable—to review in an introductory textbook all of the many Code sections that apply to even routine business transactions. Hence we will demonstrate the types of statutory challenges to be met in working with the Internal Revenue Code in the context of a single example introduced earlier in this chapter: the general rule that prohibits the expensing of capital expenditures.

CAPITAL EXPENDITURES REVISITED

The general rule that capital expenditures are not deductible is a paraphrasing of only the first sentence of Sec. 263(a). The actual statutory provision is considerably more complex than our general rule implies. This complexity is readily apparent in subsection (a), alone, which reads in its entirety as follows:

> Sec. 263(a) GENERAL RULE.—No deduction shall be allowed for—
>
> (1) Any amount paid out for new buildings or for permanent improvements or betterments made to increase the value of any property or estate. This paragraph shall not apply to—
>
> (A) expenditures for the development of mines or deposits deductible under section 616,
> (B) research and experimental expenditures deductible under section 174,
> (C) soil and water conservation expenditures deductible under section 175,
> (D) expenditures by farmers for fertilizer, etc., deductible under section 180,
> (E) expenditures for removal of architectural and transportation barriers to the handicapped and elderly which the taxpayer elects to deduct under section 190,
> (F) expenditures for tertiary injectants with respect to which a deduction is allowed under section 193; or
> (G) expenditures for which a deduction is allowed under section 179.
>
> (2) Any amount expended in restoring property or in making good the exhaustion thereof for which an allowance is or has been made.

The seven exceptions to the general rule of Sec. 263(a) found in subparagraphs (A) through (G) obviously refer to selected cases that have been deemed, for one reason or another, to justify special treatment. The details of the special treatment (usually, the right to claim an immediate deduction for what otherwise would be a nondeductible capital expenditure) are located in another cross-referenced section. For example, Sec. 263(a)(1)(A) refers to Sec. 616 for details concerning the right of a taxpayer to claim an immediate deduction for expenditures incurred in the development of mines or other mineral deposits; Sec. 263 (a)(1)(B) refers to Sec. 174 concerning deductions related to certain research and experimental expenditures; and so on. The one exception to this relative statutory clarity is found in subparagraph (G) which simply refers the reader to Sec. 179 for details regarding an otherwise unexplained deduction. That apparent oversight in English composition is probably attributable to the fact that tax technicians have over the years come to refer to the Sec. 179 deduction as if it were somehow self-explanatory. Obviously, it is not. We will explain the Sec. 179 deduction in the next chapter of this text. The details of the other six exceptions of Sec. 263(a)(1) must largely remain outside the confines of our discussion.

To complicate matters even more, Sec. 263 goes on to provide numerous other details related to the general rule of Sec. 263(a) in subsections (c), (d), (f), (g), (h), and (i). The general content of these six subsections can be implied from simply scanning their titles, which read as follows:

> Sec. 263(c). Intangible Drilling and Development Costs in the Case of Oil and Gas Wells and Geothermal Wells.
> Sec. 263(d). Expenditures in Connection with Certain Railroad Rolling Stock.
> Sec. 263(f). Railroad Ties.
> Sec. 263(g). Certain Interest and Carrying Costs in the Case of Straddles.
> Sec. 263(h). Payments in Lieu of Dividends in Connection with Short Sales.
> Sec. 263(i). Special Rules for Intangible Drilling and Development Costs Incurred Outside the United States.

Subsections (b) and (e) have been repealed; hence they are of no continuing interest. Subsections (c), (d), and (f) effectively authorize the deduction of otherwise capitalizable costs; subsections (g) and (h) require the capitalization of interest in certain financial transactions; and subsection (i) limits certain preferential oil and gas provisions to domestic wells.

The single most important lesson to be learned from this brief discussion of Sec. 263 is not the detail concerning various exceptions to the general rule, but the clear warning that no statutory general rule can be assumed to be free of numerous exceptions. Any taxpayer engaged in business has very little choice in deciding whether or not to engage an income tax professional. The complexity common to many provisions mandates the need for expert tax assistance. Accountants in general practice, as well as audit specialists in larger CPA firms, should understand how limited their own tax knowledge is likely to be. As demonstrated here, the correct income tax treatment of many apparent capital expenditures simply cannot be inferred from either general tax rules or from GAAP.

RECORD-KEEPING CHALLENGES

> **Goal #5**
> Explain the burden of proof that rests with taxpayers and the reason that they bear the burden of proof.

Complex tax laws present a further challenge to every business venture. This challenge involves the need for every business taxpayer to create and maintain records that will support the income tax result that the taxpayer believes is the correct result for the economic events that have transpired. In the absence of adequate records, the conclusion of the IRS will almost always prevail over the conclusion of the taxpayer if a dispute arises and proceeds to litigation. In other words, the taxpayer will be deemed guilty in the absence of adequate records. This general presumption against the taxpayer in contested cases seems to be unduly harsh and patently unfair. Upon further reflection, however, it is easy to understand what has driven the judicial authorities to this apparently extreme position. If the government had to prove in detail exactly what every taxpayer had done, before it could collect any amount of an income tax, very few accounting or legal records would ever be maintained and near economic chaos would prevail simply as a taxpayer's best method of avoiding taxes. Furthermore, because the taxpayer can usually control what happens (the facts), it seems reasonable to require the taxpayer to record and prove what did happen. In short, the taxpayer must generally carry the burden of proof in most tax disputes. Whether fair or not, that is the law; hence every business venture must carefully document all of the economic events which implicitly harbor income tax consequences.

To illustrate just one of the record-keeping challenges faced by most business ventures, we will review here the rules that determine the correct tax treatment of

T & E refers to travel and entertainment expenses.

travel and entertainment expenses. This area of tax law, commonly referred to as **T & E,** is particularly interesting because it requires an uncommon degree of communication and understanding between a business manager and diverse employees. Business managers must explain various requirements of the income tax law in order to get the support and cooperation of the employees who actually incur the travel and entertainment expenses. If the employees fail to document their T & E expenditures in the manner required by law, the business venture stands to pay a much larger income tax liability than would be payable were better records available. When auditing large corporations, IRS agents typically review the T & E records of a headquarters group because their expenditures for these two items are unusually large. Based on the percent of record inadequacies discovered in that audit, the IRS will apply the same percentage disallowance to the total T & E deduction claimed by the entire business venture. This audit procedure can prove to be financially disastrous to any business that fails to understand the important challenge of adequate record-keeping to the income tax determination process.

TRAVEL AND TRANSPORTATION EXPENSES

The basic authority for deducting travel costs rests in Sec. 162(a)(2) of the Code, which reads as follows:

> Sec. 162(a) IN GENERAL.—There shall be allowed as a deduction all the ordinary and necessary expenses paid or incurred during the taxable year in carrying on any trade or business, including—
> (1) . . .;
> (2) traveling expenses (including amounts expended for meals and lodging other than amounts which are lavish or extravagant under the circumstances) while away from home in the pursuit of a trade or business; . . .

Although the controlling statutory provision in this instance appears to be simple enough, the administrative and judicial law that has fleshed out the basic provision over many years is both voluminous and highly detailed. To begin to unravel those complexities, we should note that most business related travel costs can be correctly categorized for tax purposes in one of three ways:

Commuting expenses are the costs incurred in traveling between home and work.

1. **Commuting expenses**: that is, the costs incurred by most individuals in getting from home to work and, sometime later, back home again. In general, these costs are deemed to be nondeductible personal expenses per Sec. 262;

2. Transportation expenses: that is, the cost of moving an individual from one work location to another—as well as the cost of transporting work-related equipment and material, including those costs related to getting *equipment* from an individual's home to a work location, but excluding any meal costs—which are deductible under Treas. Reg. 1.162-1(a); or

The term **away from home** means that the taxpayer is working at a temporary work location.

3. Travel expenses: that is, a multitude of costs—including meals and lodging; taxi fares; air, train, and bus fares; auto expenses; etc.—associated with business trips that require an individual to be **away from home** overnight, all of which can be deducted under Sec. 162(a)(2).

This three-way categorization of travel/transportation costs once again appears to make reasonable common sense. Its application to everyday business events, however, proves to be vastly more challenging than it initially appears.

To begin, any application of these rules requires several new definitions. Where, for example, is an individual's home? For most people, that sounds like a silly question. For a few, it is not. Individuals who maintain two or three residences, itinerant workers and traveling sales persons, military personnel, and persons on temporary but indefinite work assignments frequently discover that the meaning of the word *home* for federal income tax purposes may be quite different from its usual meaning in everyday conversation.

EXAMPLE 13-3

Professor Mariana Lopez, a tenured physics professor at State University, is invited by Premier University to visit PU for the purpose of lecturing and doing research for the 1992-1993 academic year. She accepts, leases her home to a student for $500 a month, and rents an apartment near the campus of Premier University for the academic year.

Is Professor Lopez at home or away from home during this year at Premier University? The question is significant because if she is away from home, her travel expenses (defined to include many ordinary living expenses) are deductible; if she is at home, those expenses are nondeductible personal expenses.

There is no simple answer to the question raised in this example. The test revolves around the taxpayer's intent that the new location will be a temporary one. The actual events that transpire may affect a determination of intent. If Professor Lopez returns to State University, her contention that she always intended to return is likely to be more credible than if she subsequently accepts a permanent position at Premier University. However, if her true intent originally was to return—even if she stays on at PU permanently—she should be entitled to some amount of away from home deductions.

Furthermore, the general tax rules for travel and transportation costs—like all others—contain a number of exceptions. For example, although commuting expenses generally are not deductible, the IRS has created an exception to this general rule for individuals who maintain at least one regular place of business but who are traveling from their home to some other temporary work location. In these circumstances the IRS treats the cost of getting an individual from his or her home to the temporary work location and back home again as a deductible transportation expense.[10]

Although many travel costs are deductible if they are incurred purely in connection with business away from home, a fact question is often raised when the travel is for both business and personal purposes. For example, if an individual, while on a business trip, takes time out for sightseeing or other pleasure activities, the question may arise whether all travel costs should be deductible as business expenses. The reverse situation may also be found: an individual may take a pleasure trip and, while traveling, take time out for certain business activities. The question in this case is whether any part of the travel costs is deductible as a business expense.

The answer to this question depends importantly on where the individual is going. Domestic travel deductions are based on rules that differ significantly from those applicable to foreign travel. For domestic travel, if the trip is primarily for business purposes, incidental sightseeing or other pleasure activities do not change the character of the trip, and, therefore, all expenses incurred—except those directly related to the

---

10 Rev. Rul. 53-190, 1953-2 CB 303.

pleasure activity—are deductible. On the other hand, if the primary purpose of the trip is pleasure, incidental business activities do not change the nature of the trip, and only the expenses directly associated with the business activity are deductible.

In many cases it is difficult, if not impossible, to determine the taxpayer's true intent. A taxpayer may not even know the real purpose of a trip. This is especially true of attendance at meetings or conventions of trade associations and professional organizations. Business conventions often are held in resort areas or other pleasant surroundings to encourage attendance by members. In some cases, the convention may be merely a sham, whereas other business conventions may be invaluable to the participants.

Special rules apply to the individual who travels on business or attends a convention or seminar in a foreign country. If the travel does not exceed one week, or if the portion of the taxpayer's time outside the United States that is not attributable to trade or business activity is less than 25% of the total time of such travel, all of the *transportation costs* may be deductible. If more than one week is spent abroad and 25% or more of the time is spent on nonbusiness activities, the transportation costs must be allocated on the basis of time spent, and the nonbusiness portion is not deductible. Of course, all expenses attributable to nonbusiness activities are nondeductible. Allowable deductions for transportation (including meals and entertainment) by "luxury water transportation" are limited to a daily amount equal to twice the per diem travel allowance for U.S. government executive branch employees away from home but within the United States. Furthermore, if the purpose of foreign travel is to attend a convention or seminar, no deduction whatsoever is allowed unless it is as *reasonable* for that meeting to be held outside the North American area as within it. And, in these cases, air travel costs are restricted to coach fares.

What kind of records must an individual maintain to document (1) the primary purpose of a domestic trip, and (2) just how they spent their time (and money) while on that trip? Unfortunately there are no hard and fast answers. The IRS can (and does) demand some kind of proof in questionable cases. Hence every business person should give serious thought to the need for adequate documentation in any doubtful case.

Many businesses that employ individuals who are required to travel frequently on company business furnish those employees with company-owned or company-leased automobiles. The individuals who drive those automobiles may (with or without company approval) use those same automobiles for purely personal purposes. At a minimum, they often use the company car to commute from home to work and back home again. In these circumstances the employee can be deemed to have received some additional amount of personal compensation for the value of a company car to the extent that it was used for purely personal purposes. Self-employed individuals face essentially the same tax problem when they use their own car(s) for both business and personal use. The costs related to their business use of **mixed-use** cars are generally deductible; those related to personal use are not.

The documentation of business versus personal use of automobiles remains a difficult problem. A few years ago the IRS announced that it would require individuals to maintain a daily odometer log in order to deduct any costs related to the business use of automobiles. Because of a massive negative political response to this IRS announcement, it was subsequently withdrawn. Nevertheless, the IRS continues to require that individuals maintain some reasonable form of documentation for the business use of automobiles.

The maximum amount that can be deducted for transportation costs is, in general, the larger of (1) actual costs or (2) a standard mileage rate. The opportunity to deduct

Goal #6
Describe the kind of detailed records that must be maintained.

Mixed use means there is part business and part personal use of an asset.

actual costs stimulated many taxpayers to purchase and drive very expensive automobiles for business purposes. Congress eventually limited the opportunity of individuals to do this by enacting what we now know as Sec. 280F. This section limits the amount of depreciation that can be deducted on "luxury automobiles" and certain other "listed property." Further details concerning Sec. 280F are included in the next chapter of this textbook.

Many individuals find it more convenient to use the standard mileage allowance than to keep track of the actual cost of using an automobile for business purposes. The danger of not getting (or of losing) gasoline receipts, road and bridge tolls, and repair invoices, in addition to adequate mileage records, is simply too great for many individuals. Hence they opt for the **standard mileage rate**. This rate varies depending upon the purpose for the trip. Table 13-1 gives these rates for 1992. An individual can deduct parking fees and road and bridge tolls in addition to the standard mileage rate.

> The **standard mileage rate** is a per-mile allowance specified by the IRS as an acceptable alternative to calculating actual automobile costs.

MEAL EXPENSES

The cost of eating a meal is ordinarily deemed to be a nondeductible personal expense. However, as noted earlier, the cost of meals eaten by an individual who is away from home overnight on a business trip can be deducted. In general, only 80% of any meal expenses are deductible. Although Sec. 162(a)(2) specifically disallows any deduction for meals (and other travel expenses) that are "lavish or extravagant under the circumstances," the right to deduct expensive business meals taken in high-priced restaurants and luxurious resorts appears to be firmly entrenched in current U.S. business practice. The right to include the cost of wine and alcoholic beverages in the cost of a meal appears to be equally well established.

The meal expense of a spouse or other family member or friend who may accompany a business traveler is ordinarily not deductible. The travel expenses incurred for those individuals can be deducted only if there is a genuine *business* reason for those individuals to be present. Thus it is frequently necessary for business travelers to document clearly and correctly the amounts spent by and for various individuals traveling together.

Because complete and accurate records are often difficult to obtain and preserve, the IRS will allow individuals to base the deductible meal expense on a standard allowance rather than on actual cost. The standard meal allowance is based on the amount paid by the government to federal employees who are on travel status. That amount varies by location and is periodically adjusted. The current standard meal allowance ranges from $34 a day in such high cost cities as New York, Chicago, and Los Angeles, to $26 a day in more rural locations. For business meals eaten outside

	Cents per Mile
Ordinary business use	28
Rural mail carrier	42
Charitable use	12
Medical use and moving	9

Source: Rev. Proc. 91-67.

TABLE 13-1

1992 Mileage Rates

the 48 contiguous states the standard allowance is equal to 40% of the total federal per diem rate; the other 60% is deemed to be lodging. This rate also varies from location to location. Special rules apply to the meal expense of individuals who work in the transportation industry.

ENTERTAINMENT EXPENSES

Few areas of income tax law present more opportunity for controversy than the area of entertainment expense. The authority for the deduction of entertainment costs stems from Sec. 162(a). The problem—as illustrated in Exhibit 13-1—is that it is very difficult to determine in any realistic way what is truly *ordinary* and *necessary* when it comes to business entertainment expenses. The telling line can be found in the next to last paragraph of Exhibit 13-1: ". . .if Washington thinks I didn't have to entertain them that way to get that order. . .they don't know [my customers]." The tax question can then be clearly understood: assuming such entertainment is in fact both ordinary and necessary, is it deductible or not?

EXHIBIT 13–1

Documenting Ordinary and Necessary Entertainment Expense

In the early 1960s, the IRS attempted to improve documentation practices for entertainment expenses. To qualify as a tax deduction, the entertainment expenses had to be necessary and ordinary, and full details were required to support the deduction.

Tax advisers found an unusual way to deal with their frustrations in following the new IRS edicts. They copied, recopied, and circulated what purported to be a first-person account that is part urban legend and part shaggy dog story. In it the narrator complains bitterly about "Mortimer's Instructions." (Mortimer Caplin was the IRS commissioner from 1961 to 1964.) The narrator describes the problem:

"The trouble with you boys in Washington is you've got no idea of all the hell some businessmen have to go through to get business. You can tell that from the example you give of how a businessman ought to report his entertainment. The example you sent out reads this way:

> Lunch with Jones, Green, Brown, and Smith, trustees of P.Q. Real Estate Investment Board. Discussed architectural plans submitted for proposed Claremont Village Apartment Building. No other persons entertained.

"Now that's fine and dandy, if you're entertaining trustees, but if you're entertaining the clowns I have to do business with you've got to go into all the sordid details or you don't get your deduct."

To prove his point, the narrator reads from a carbon copy of the expense report he just turned in. A minor work of folk art, it tells how the business entertainment begins staidly enough at a business dinner between the narrator and his clients. The business purpose of the meal is to discuss retooling costs at the clients' machinery company. After too many drinks, the narrator and his clients lurch to a night club where they become even wilder. One client "figures retooling costs on table cloth. No ink, uses ketchup. Waiter objects. [Client] tells waiter what he can do with tablecloth." The three clients pull two women into their sway, and beat a hasty retreat from the club, followed by the narrator. The clients orchestrate

EXHIBIT 13-1 (Con't.)

an impromptu and unwelcome party in the apartment of one of the women. When that party ends disastrously, the clients start off back to their hotel but instead stumble into an all-night bar. They finally return to the hotel at 4 A.M. Once in the lobby, one client crawls on all fours, baying like a dog, while another blockades the elevator. It takes another half hour for the narrator to get his clients upstairs and into their rooms.

Expenses include meals, drinks, lavish tips to outraged waiters and bartenders, and payments to repay injured parties for the damage and destruction the clients have left in their wake. "And if Washington thinks I didn't have to entertain them that way to get that order," the narrator concludes, "they don't know [my customers]."

· · ·

The 1960s were arguably a more hedonistic decade than the 1990s. How the original document embodies certain attitudes—about alcohol and sexual philandering, for example—could strike today's readers as politically incorrect. Yet the main point of the story is still valid today. Many business people and their accountants are still challenged by the demand of tracking entertainment expenses accurately. In reviewing expenses, the tax professional must make a strong effort to separate the unnecessary and extraordinary from the necessary and ordinary. And whether or not the story is fictional, the implied frustrations of the narrator are not. When the IRS guidelines were issued, many tax advisers wished that they could spout off to the powers that be in Washington, just as the narrator purports to do.

Source: Unknown. Privately circulated document, circa 1962.

Sec. 274 specifically disallows the right of anyone to deduct various specified entertainment expenses and, in subsection (d), it explicitly mandates adequate records and other corroborating evidence for any entertainment deductions claimed. In addition, the IRS frequently publishes a booklet entitled "Travel, Entertainment and Gift Expenses" to help taxpayers understand the law and the documentation requirements. Nevertheless, even with the best explanatory aids, business ventures are continuously faced with a major challenge in getting individuals to understand and comply with these laws.

Entertainment expenses—that is, the cost of food, liquor, theater tickets, sporting events, and similar activities—are often more difficult to relate specifically to business purposes than are travel costs. Eighty percent of business entertainment costs are generally deductible; nonbusiness costs are personal expenditures and are therefore not deductible at all. As a general rule, to be classified as a business-related activity, the entertainment must involve customers or others with whom the taxpayer has, or may be expected to have, a business relationship.

Most of the criticisms of expense account spending as a means of tax avoidance have dealt with entertainment costs. The reasons are obvious, as the following example illustrates. Suppose the taxpayer enjoys the theater (or a nightclub or any other particular form of entertainment). An individual with whom he has some business connection is coming to town, so the taxpayer purchases theater tickets for himself, his wife, and the visiting businessperson. Is this expenditure really for business? Was the attendance of the taxpayer's wife reasonable and necessary? As a result of this entertainment and the goodwill generated, the taxpayer may very well achieve important business objectives even though the two do not directly discuss business during the evening. As noted, the inherent problems are obvious.

The question of whether entertainment costs are ordinary, necessary, and reasonable is largely a subjective one. For this reason, Sec. 274 of the Code contains unusually detailed rules for determining which costs should not be allowed. Portions of this section are quoted below to indicate the nature of its restrictions:

> [Sec. 274(a)] (1) IN GENERAL.—No deduction otherwise allowable under this chapter shall be allowed for any item—
>
> (A) Activity—With respect to an activity which is of a type generally considered to constitute entertainment, amusement, or recreation, unless the taxpayer establishes that the item was directly related to, or, in the case of an item directly preceding or following a substantial and bona fide business discussion (including business meetings at a convention or otherwise), that such item was associated with, the active conduct of the taxpayer's trade or business, or
>
> (B) Facility—With respect to a facility used in connection with an activity referred to in subparagraph (A).
>
> [Sec. 274(a)] (2) Special Rules—For purposes of applying paragraph (1)—
>
> (A) Dues or fees to any social, athletic, or sporting club or organization shall be treated as items with respect to facilities.
>
> (B) An activity described in sec. 212 shall be treated as a trade or business.
>
> (C) In the case of a club, paragraph (1)(B) shall apply unless the taxpayer establishes that the facility was used primarily for the furtherance of the taxpayer's trade or business and that the item was directly related to the active conduct of such trade or business.
>
> [Sec. 274(b)] Gifts.—
>
> (1) Limitation.—No deduction shall be allowed under sec. 162 or sec. 212 for any expense for gifts made directly or indirectly to any individual to the extent that such expense, when added to prior expenses of the taxpayer for gifts made to such individual during the same taxable year, exceeds $25. For purposes of this section, the term "gift" means any item excludable from gross income of the recipient under sec. 102 which is not excludable from his gross income under any other provisions of this chapter. . .
>
> [Sec. 274(d)] Substantiation Required.—No deduction shall be allowed—
>
> (1) under sec. 162 or 212 for any traveling expenses (including meals and lodging while away from home),
>
> (2) for any item with respect to an activity which is of a type generally considered to constitute entertainment, amusement, or recreation, or with respect to a facility used in connection with such an activity, or
>
> (3) for any expense for gifts,
>
> (4) with respect to any listed property (as defined by sec. 280F(d)(4)), unless the taxpayer substantiates by adequate records or by sufficient evidence corroborating his own statement, (A) the amount of such expense or other item, (B) the time and place of the travel, entertainment, amusement, recreation or use of the facility, or the date and description of the gift, (C) the business purpose of the expense or other item, and (D) the business relationship to the taxpayer of persons entertained, using the facility or property, or receiving the gift. . .

Note that, to be deductible, entertainment costs must be either "directly related to" or "associated with" the active conduct of a trade or business. According to the regulations,[11] directly related expenditures must meet the following standards:

---

11 Treas. Reg. 1.274-2(b)(2).

1. The taxpayer must have "more than a general expectation of deriving some income or other specific trade benefit (other than the goodwill of the person or persons entertained)" from the expenditure.

2. During the entertainment, the taxpayer must actively engage in a "business meeting, negotiation, discussion, or other bona fide business transaction other than entertainment."

3. The "principal character or aspect" of the combined business and entertainment must be the active conduct of the taxpayer's business.

4. The costs associated with the expenditure must be allocable to the taxpayer and a person or persons with whom the taxpayer is engaged in the active conduct of a trade or business.

An expenditure that is "associated with" but not "directly related to" the active conduct of a trade or business is deductible only if it was directly preceded or followed by a substantial and bona fide business discussion. This rule applies to entertainment conducted in an atmosphere that is not conducive to business discussion, such as a sporting event.

Special restrictions apply to deductibility of the costs of owning and maintaining entertainment facilities such as yachts and hunting lodges. Section 274 denies deduction of these costs. However, out-of-pocket costs (such as food and beverages) associated with using these facilities for business entertainment can be deducted. Additionally, membership dues and fees paid to social, athletic, or sporting clubs or organizations are not deductible unless the primary use of the facility is for business purposes. Primary use can be established if more than 50% of the total calendar days of actual use are for business purposes. In this case, fees or dues attributable to the days of business use can be deducted.

The committee reports associated with the 1986 Act indicate that Congress intended that deductions for meals should be subject to the same business-connection requirement as other entertainment expenses. Under prior law taxpayers could deduct the cost of entertainment such as a lunch with a potential client even though business was not actually discussed, so long as the atmosphere was considered conducive to business discussion (Reg. Sec. 1.274-2(f)(2)(i)). Under the new rules, such meals are not deductible unless business is discussed during, or directly before or after, the meal. If the taxpayer is traveling away from home, a business discussion is not required unless the taxpayer dines with business associates. For example, it would be permissible for a traveling salesman to deduct the cost of a meal eaten alone or with nonbusiness associates so long as a deduction is claimed only for the taxpayer's meal.

Taxpayers also are subject to special limitations on the deductibility of entertainment tickets and skyboxes at sports arenas. Like other entertainment costs, these expenditures are subject to the 20% reduction rule. Additionally, no more than face value can be deducted for entertainment tickets. Thus, a taxpayer who purchases two football tickets from a scalper at $100 each when the face value is $25 each can deduct only $40 (80% of $50), provided all other requirements for a deduction are met. Since 1988, deductions for skybox seats leased for more than one event have been limited to the face value of nonluxury box seat tickets.

REPORTING AND ACCOUNTING REQUIREMENTS

The regulations associated with travel and entertainment expenses are relatively precise in specifying the reporting and accounting requirements for these deductions.

Because of the great amount of detail and because they are frequently changed, these reporting requirements are not detailed here. Basically, however, the employee who *accounts* to his employer and refunds to the employer any excess advanced funds need not report business expenses or reimbursements on his own return. If the employee is not required to substantiate expenses or to refund excess advanced funds to the employer, then the employer must include all of the reimbursed expenses on the employee's W-2 form. Employees who do not account to their employers must report details of both the expenses and the reimbursements on their returns. In this case, the employee's deductions would be subject to the 2% floor rather than treated as deductions for AGI as explained in Chapters 9 and 10. Additionally, meals and entertainment expenses would be reduced by 20%. If expenses exceed reimbursement and the employee claims a deduction for the excess, some of the details must be reported. An *accounting* includes either (1) a detailed record of expenses or (2) the utilization of a standard per diem allowance and mileage allowance described earlier in this chapter. Figure 13-1 summarizes these reporting requirements for employees. Examples 13-4 and 13-5 demonstrate the application of these requirements.

EXAMPLE 13-4

Johnny Appleseed works for Better Apples, Inc., a company that develops and promotes genetically superior apple seeds. He travels extensively with this job, educating growers and the public about apples. In 1992, his travel costs were as follows:

Continued

FIGURE 13-1

Determination of Deductible Employee Meals and Entertainment Expenses

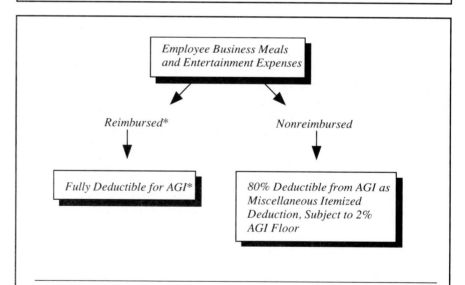

* Note, however, that if the employee adequately accounts to his or her employer, no record of either the reimbursement or the deduction will appear on the employee's personal tax return. Note also that it is the employer, rather than the employee, who loses the right to deduct 20% of meal and entertainment expenses if the employee is reimbursed and an adequate accounting is made to the employer. These same rules apply to independent contractors who are reimbursed for travel costs that they incur.

EXAMPLE 13-4 (Con't.)

Transportation	$18,000
Lodging	10,000
Meals and Entertainment	8,000

Better Apples, Inc., makes travel advances to employees, but requires that they properly account for expenditures and return unused funds to the company. Johnny's tax return will not reflect any of the expenses or reimbursements connected with his travel. The corporation may take a deduction on its tax return of $18,000 for transportation, $10,000 for lodging, and $6,400 ($8,000 x 80%) for meals and entertainment.

EXAMPLE 13-5

Mary Peachseed works for Peachy Future, Inc. She regularly entertains business associates at local restaurants. These occasions always meet the standards for qualifying entertainment costs, but her employer does not reimburse her for the expenditures. Her expenses for such entertainment totalled $2,500. Assuming that she does not claim a standard deduction, she may deduct $2,000 ($2,500 x 80%) as an itemized deduction subject to the 2% floor. If her employer provides her with a $1,500 entertainment allowance each year, that amount will be reported on her W-2 form as income, and she will still deduct the expenses as described above.

This completes our discussion of business travel and entertainment expenses. The ability of taxpayers to deduct these two expenses depends importantly on the existence of good accounting records. All persons interested in business should understand the record-keeping challenges implicit to the correct tax determination of the many dollars spent each year for travel, transportation, meals, and entertainment. The final tax-related challenge to be discussed in this chapter relates to tax credits.

TAX CREDITS RELATED TO BUSINESS

During the past 25 years, the Congress and various presidential administrations have used business credits to stimulate the economy and to encourage investment in specific assets or expenditures for specific activities. These credits are, in essence, subsidies to business. Since December 31, 1985, however, credits have assumed far less importance because of the repeal of the investment tax credit. Their impact may also have been reduced because Congress keeps extending most of these credits on a piecemeal basis, sometimes retroactively. In fact, a number of them are currently scheduled to expire before this book will be published. It is likely, however, that some or all of them will once again be extended. Hence this brief review.

The most important credits available to business have been placed under a general umbrella in Sec. 38(a) of the Code. The general business credit is defined in that section as the sum of the following otherwise separate seven tax credits:

1. The investment tax credit determined under Sec. 46(a);

2. The targeted jobs credit determined under Sec. 51(a);

Goal #8
Identify the more important tax credits that may be available to business ventures today.

3. The alcohol fuels credit determined under Sec. 40(a);

4. The research credit determined under Sec. 41(a);

5. The low-income housing credit under Sec. 42(a);

6. The enhanced oil recovery credit under Sec. 43(a); and

7. In the case of an eligible small business (as defined in Sec. 44(b)), the disabled access credit under Sec. 44(a).

In addition to individual limits on each of the business credits, there is a limit on the overall general business credit. The limit for the overall business credit is equal to 100% of the net regular tax liability up to $25,000 and 25% of the net regular tax liability in excess of $25,000 for the year. (There is also a limit equal to the excess of the taxpayer's net regular tax liability for the taxable year over the tentative minimum tax for the taxable year. In other words, the business credit cannot reduce the regular tax liability below the amount of the alternative minimum tax, discussed in Chapter 19). The general business credit in excess of the limit (the unused credit) is carried back 3 years and then forward 15 years, subject to the overall limitation in each of those years.

THE INVESTMENT TAX CREDIT

The investment tax credit (ITC) was originally initiated in the early 1960s by the Kennedy administration as a means of encouraging businesses to invest in new productive machinery and equipment. The credit was modified in almost every year and was finally repealed by the 1986 Act for property acquired after December 31, 1985. As we write this manuscript (in the spring of 1992), numerous members of Congress and several economists are once again calling for a reinstitution of the ITC to get the U.S. economy out of its most recent recession.

Although the investment tax credit was generally repealed for properties acquired after December 31, 1985, certain properties acquired under binding contracts as of December 31, 1985, were made subject to transition rules. Thus, it is possible that some assets placed in service as late as December 31, 1990, were eligible for the ITC. In addition, any ITC unused as of December 31, 1985, may be allowable (after certain adjustments) for years after that date under the 15-year carryover provision.

CREDIT FOR REHABILITATION OF OLDER STRUCTURES

As a means of arresting urban decay, Congress has provided a tax credit to taxpayers who rehabilitate older structures for business use. The rehabilitation credit is treated in the Code as though it were part of the ITC. This provision, like the basic ITC, has been changed several times since its inception. Currently, the credit to be taken for building rehabilitation expenditures applies to buildings placed into service prior to 1936 and to "certified historical structures." The credit for the former is 10% of rehabilitation costs; the credit for rehabilitation of certified historical structures is 20% of such costs.

To qualify for the credit, the building must have been substantially rehabilitated after being placed in service. Generally, the expenditures for rehabilitation must be greater than the building's adjusted basis. The taxpayer must retain at least 75% of the existing external walls and 75% of the existing internal structure. No credit is allowed for the original cost of acquiring the structure or for the cost of additions or enlargements. Any credit taken reduces the structure's basis for depreciation or cost recovery. (Rehabilitation expenditures are subject to straight-line depreciation over a period of 27.5 or 31.5 years, depending on the use of the structure.)

EXAMPLE 13–6

Assume that in 1991 the taxpayer acquired for $100,000 an old building built in 1929. In 1992, the taxpayer had the building remodeled and rehabilitated at a cost of $250,000. The rehabilitation met all the requirements to qualify for the credit. The taxpayer will be entitled to a credit of $25,000. The basis for depreciation of the rehabilitation expenditures will be $225,000 ($250,000 – $25,000), and this basis can be depreciated by the straight-line method over the appropriate period.

THE TARGETED JOBS CREDIT

The targeted jobs credit gives a credit to employers who employ individuals who were members of groups with high unemployment rates, including such groups as Vietnam veterans, the economically disadvantaged, and ex-convicts. The credit is generally 40% of the first $6,000 of wages paid to qualifying individuals during the first year of employment. At one time in the past, this credit was allowed to expire, only to be retroactively reinstated. During the lapse many taxpayers failed to get and retain the paperwork necessary to claim this credit. Surprisingly, the IRS did not allow taxpayers to retroactively obtain and use the missing records. Hence our best advice is that every business assume that this credit will remain until Congress clearly acts to kill it.

THE ALCOHOL FUELS CREDIT

Section 40 provides a credit to taxpayers who produce, sell, or use alcohol or alcohol-blend fuels for years prior to January 1, 2001. A taxpayer who uses alcohol in the production of a qualified fuel mixture is generally entitled to a credit of 60 cents per gallon for alcohol used in the production. Similarly, the credit for alcohol used as fuel in trade or business is 60 cents per gallon if the alcohol is not blended with petroleum fuels. For lower-proof alcohol the credit is 48 cents per gallon.

THE RESEARCH CREDIT

The "credit for increasing research activities" is another credit that has frequently been scheduled to expire. This credit is currently 20% of the excess of qualified expenditures for the year over a base amount determined with respect to expenditures for the four previous tax years. The amount of R&D expenditures that could otherwise be charged to expense must be reduced by 100% of the R&D credit taken. Expenditures that qualify are those that are technological in nature and whose application is intended to be useful in the development of a new or improved business component of the taxpayer. The Code lists examples of activities that do not qualify. The activities that do not qualify include research after commercial production has started, adaptation of existing business components, duplication of existing business components, marketing and other routine surveys, foreign research, and research in the social sciences.

THE LOW-INCOME HOUSING CREDIT

Section 42 authorizes a tax credit designed to encourage construction of housing for low-income families. It is available for low-income housing that is constructed, rehabilitated, or acquired after 1987 but before 1992. The credit is generally available if at least 20% of the units are rented to persons with income of 50% or less of certain specified amounts, or if at least 40% of the units are rented to persons with incomes 60% or less of the specified amounts. These specified amounts define low-income by location and family size. The rent charged to a tenant in a qualified unit may not exceed 30% of the qualifying income level for the tenant's family size.

To qualify, expenditures on any building in a 24-month period must average at least $2,000 per qualified unit. The credit rate is a percentage computed under a technical formula. The percentage is changed each month, and the rate to be used depends on the announced rate for the month in which the building is placed in service. Like several other credits, the low-income housing credit is currently scheduled to expire in the near future.

THE ENHANCED OIL RECOVERY CREDIT

In order to encourage additional domestic oil production, Congress enacted Sec. 43. It generally provides a tax credit equal to 15% of qualified costs expended on a domestic EOR (Enhanced Oil Recovery) project. To be eligible, there must be a reasonable expectation of more than an insignificant increase in the amount of crude oil to be recovered due to "tertiary recovery methods" (as defined in Sec. 193(b)(3)). These methods involve the injection of liquids, gases, or other matter into extant wells.

THE DISABLED ACCESS CREDIT

In order to encourage small businesses to make themselves more accessible to disabled persons, Congress enacted Sec. 44. This provision generally allows a tax credit equal to 50% of the amount spent for "eligible access expenditures" in excess of $250 but less than $10,250 per year. The amount of any deduction of these expenditures must be reduced by the amount of tax credit claimed. In general this credit is available to businesses with (1) less than $1 million in gross receipts during the prior year or (2) less than 31 full-time employees during the prior year.

It should be clear from the above discussion that business credits have had a checkered life. They are complex, they are instituted and then discontinued, they are often scheduled to expire and then extended at the last moment, and, above all, they are subject to economic fortunes and political whims. What is written today about these credits may not be true tomorrow. Hence part of the tax challenge for any business is determining what tax credits currently exist and making the most of them.

_____ KEY POINTS TO REMEMBER

✓ Differences in the interpretation and application of tax laws to specific economic events are inevitable in any tax system.

✓ Definitional difficulty commonly exists in the distinction between expenditures that must be capitalized and those that may be expensed. The sources of the difficulty lie primarily in two areas: (1) the inability to determine whether certain expenditures create or enhance an asset and (2) problems associated with the proper matching of gross income and deductions.

✓ General rules should not be applied casually and at face value. Tax law embodies many exceptions, special rules and definitions that modify virtually every general rule. Taxpayers and their advisers must proceed with great care to be certain there is no unique rule that would modify a generally applicable tax result for a particular transaction.

✓ Every taxpayer bears the burden of proof in documenting the facts related to tax sensitive transactions.

✓ Record-keeping requirements are especially important in the area of business travel and entertainment expenses. The rules governing these deductions are quite specific.

✓ Tax credits related to business are subsidies that have been used to provide incentives for specific business activities or investments. The most important credits that have recently been available to businesses are (1) the investment tax credit; (2) the targeted jobs credit; (3) the alcohol fuels credit; (4) the research credit; (5) the low-income housing credit; (6) the enhanced oil recovery credit; and (7) the disabled access credit.

———— RECALL PROBLEMS

1. The text states that tax law "is expressed in relatively simple, everyday English words." If that is true, why is there so much concern about the complexity of the tax law? In your response to this question, discuss issues both with respect to the structure of the written language and format of the law and with respect to the incentives presented to the users of the law.

2. Financial accounting and tax accounting rules use the term *capital expenditure* to refer to an expenditure that is fundamentally different from an expense. What are the factors that differentiate a capital expenditure from an expense? Provide specific examples to illuminate your factors.

3. In the context of the categories of expenditures listed below, explain the conditions under which the expenditure should be deducted as a current expense. Include the rationale for these conditions.

   a. Expenditures made for work done on a machine used in manufacturing the principal product of the business.
   b. Expenditures made for work done on a computer used to maintain a business's accounting records, including inventory records.
   c. Fees paid to a lawyer.
   d. Rental payments for the land and building that house a company's administrative offices.
   e. Costs incurred to conduct a feasibility study relative to the acquisition of a new line of business.
   f. Environmental cleanup costs.

4. Andersmith Corporation was organized this year. In connection with its organization and the beginning of its business, Andersmith incurred the following costs in October:

a. A $1,000 attorney's fee for preparing articles of incorporation ($800) and for preparing bylaws ($200).

b. Fee charged by state for corporation's charter, $500.

c. Costs of printing stock certificates, $40.

d. Costs for corporate record books, $100.

e. Fees paid brokers for selling shares of stock to certain investors, $1000.

f. Costs charged for by organizers for time spent on corporation, $4000.

If the corporation is a calendar-year taxpayer and it began business in November, which of these costs can the corporation deduct this year? Next year?

5. Joan Creek owns a cash-basis, calendar-year comedy club. The club operates as a sole proprietorship that incurs the following expenditures this year. Which of these expenditures will be deductible in 1992? For those that will not be deductible, explain generally how the expenditure should be treated.

a. $600 paid to attorneys for drafting contracts between the club and the guests performing at the club.

b. $4500 ($300 per month) paid for rental of the club. The rent covers a 15-month period beginning January 1.

c. $500 paid for repairing some broken club furniture.

d. $1000 paid for a whole-life insurance policy on Joan's life.

e. $2000 paid for advertising the club on a local radio station. It is expected that the advertising will benefit the club for at least two years.

f. $1000 in premiums paid for worker's compensation insurance. The insurance covers club employees.

g. $1000 paid for legal fees connected with the acquisition of land adjoining the club. The land will be paved and used for a parking lot.

h. $2500 in interest paid on money borrowed to purchase the land. Construction of the parking lot will begin in 1993.

6. What is the general rule presented in Sec. 263? Explain why relying on this general rule alone would place a tax adviser in a precarious position.

7. Taxpayers bear the burden of proof in documenting business expenditures. Why does the burden of proof rest with taxpayers?

8. What types of records must taxpayers maintain to substantiate their tax deductions?

9. In the current year, Mr. A. Big Shot, who operates an advertising agency, paid $1600 for membership dues in a hunting lodge in Canada for the purpose of entertaining clients and prospective clients. In November, Shot took three clients to the hunting lodge. He paid their transportation costs, totalling $1200; their meals for the three-day period at the lodge, $460 for the guests and $181 for Shot; their room costs, $900 for the guests and $300 for himself; $220 for a hunting guide; $210 for guns and ammunition; and $120 for miscellaneous items such as phone calls and drinks. What part of the expenditures listed above is deductible by Shot?

10. Indicate how each of the following items will be treated on the individual's tax return. Your answer should include an indication of whether the item (or a portion of it) is subject to the 20% disallowance and/or the 2% AGI floor.

a. Terry, an employee of a major defense contractor in St. Louis, was sent to Memphis to inspect a new plant. Terry had grown up in Memphis, so he took advantage of the trip to visit with several high school friends and out to dinner with them. The cost of Terry's share of the dinners was $45. The second night that Terry was in Memphis he went to dinner with a business associate, a supplier of parts for the Memphis plant. They did not discuss business. Terry paid for both meals at a total cost of $70. Terry was not reimbursed for any of these meals.

b. Nick, an employee, spent $1000 for gasoline, insurance, and repairs during the year. In addition, Nick calculated $500 in depreciation attributable to the business use of his car. Of this amount, 3000 miles were attributable to going from home to work sites and back, while 2000 miles were driven going between work sites during the day. In addition, Nick spent $200 in tolls. There are no toll gates between his work and home. None of these costs was reimbursed. What options does Nick have in calculating his deduction? What documentation is required to substantiate any of Nick's auto deductions?

c. Linda, a self-employed physician, attended two professional conventions on the West Coast connected with her practice. The first convention was held on Monday, Tuesday, and Wednesday in Los Angeles. The second was held on Monday and Tuesday of the following week in San Francisco. Between the two conventions, Linda stayed at Carmel for a short vacation. The costs were air travel from her home to Los Angeles and from San Francisco to her home, $450; hotel for three days in Los Angeles, $500; meals for three days in Los Angeles, $180; auto rental for trip from Los Angeles to Carmel and from Carmel to San Francisco, $180 (Linda estimates that one third of this cost represents the cost of pleasure trips while in Carmel); hotel for two days in San Francisco, $300; meals for two days in San Francisco, $120.

d. Jim paid an accountant $300 to prepare his tax return, including his Schedule C, this year.

11. Explain the purposes behind each of the following tax credits:

#8

a. Investment tax credit.

b. Credit for rehabilitation of older structures.

c. Targeted jobs credit.

d. Alcohol fuels credit.

e. Research credit.

f. Low-income housing credit.

g. Enhanced oil recovery credit.

h. Disabled access credit.

_____ THOUGHT PROBLEMS

#1

1. a. Discuss the definitional challenges implicit in determining the deductibility of travel and entertainment expenses.

    b. Discuss the substantiation challenges implicit in determining the deductibility of travel and entertainment expenses.

    c. Recommend ways in which the travel and entertainment provisions could be made simpler.

#2 #3

2. Three different methods by which we might account for the cost of an asset that benefits more than one accounting period are listed below. Give an example to illustrate each method. If financial and tax accounting treat a particular item differently, explain a possible reason for the different treatments.

    a. Deduct entire cost when incurred.

    b. Deduct nothing until asset is disposed of; the expenditure increases basis, affecting the calculation of gain or loss.

    c. Select an arbitrary method of allocating the costs to multiple periods.

#1 #4

3. Analyze the following dimensions of Sec. 263 in terms of their contribution to the complexity of the tax law.

    a. Understandability of individual words and phrases.

    b. Cross-referencing.

    c. Structure of using exceptions to the general rule.

#2 #3 #7

4. Identify some deductions that are likely targets for modification when Congress goes searching for new sources of revenue. Explain why you think these deductions might be likely targets.

#5

5. Some T & E expenses incured by individuals are deductible on Schedule C, others only on Schedule A. Summarize the conditions under which these expenses are deductible on either schedule. Does it make any difference to the taxpayer where these expenses are deducted? If so, is one schedule always preferred over the other?

#8

6. Some of the credits listed in the text have been enacted with expiration dates that have been extended one or more times. Explain why these credits are enacted with expiration dates and why those extensions tend to occur in short time intervals.

#3

7. Buffalo Corporation entered into a 30-year lease agreement on a small office building. The agreement provides that the lease payments will be $6000 per month for the entire period of the lease. The lease rate for equivalent office space is approximately $5000 per month with CPI index increases every three years, up to ten years (when the lease terms must be renegotiated). When the lease was being negotiated 6 months ago, the lease rate was originally to be $6500 per month. Buffalo negotiated a lower lease rate because it argued that the fall in interest rates should be reflected in lower lease payments. The lease further specifies that Buffalo will have the right to purchase the property for $100,000 at the termination of the lease.

    Assume that you are an IRS agent examining this arrangement. What issues would you raise upon reviewing the arrangement? What tax consequences are dependent upon your conclusions? Without trying to draw a firm conclusion about this arrangement, list the factors that you would consider to be important in analyzing this agreement.

———— CLASS PROJECTS

1. Divide into two groups to study advertising costs and to recommend to Congress the correct income tax treatment of these costs. One group represents the government and is responsible for developing arguments in favor of the capitalization of all advertising expenses. The other group represents the Advertising Council and is responsible for developing arguments in favor of expensing those costs. As background, read any articles you can find on the topic. Discuss the issues in your group and develop a position paper.

2. Big Bad Wolf Corporation (BBW) launches a takeover attempt against Little Red Riding Hood Corporation (LRRH). LRRH incurs $3 million in expenditures in its successful effort to protect itself against BBW. Find authoritative sources that analyze the issue of deductibility of such expenditures. Write a short paper evaluating whether these expenditures will be deductible, referencing and comparing both positive and negative authorities.

Time wastes things away, and all things grow old through time.

ARISTOTLE (384–322 B.C.), PHYSICS

DEPRECIATION AND COST RECOVERY

CHAPTER OBJECTIVES

In Chapter 14, you will acquire both an economic and historical framework for understanding current tax depreciation rules and learn how to determine a taxpayer's deduction for depreciation and depletion.

LEARNING GOALS

After studying this chapter, you should be able to

1 Analyze various depreciation methods using present value techniques;

2 Explain the difference between immediate expensing and economic depreciation, and present the central arguments in the expensing versus economic-depreciation debate;

3 Recognize the role of implicit taxes in depreciation policy;

4 Understand the implications of inflation on depreciation deductions;

5 Appreciate the historical development of depreciation tax law;

6 Compute depreciation deductions under pre-1981 rules;

7 Compute depreciation deductions under the Accelerated Cost Recovery System (ACRS);

8 Compute depreciation deductions under the Modified Accelerated Cost Recovery System (MACRS); and

9 Compute the depletion deduction.

This chapter focuses primarily on depreciation (or cost recovery) and provides a brief overview of amortization and depletion. However, before delving into depreciation rules, we examine some economic aspects of depreciation and then survey the historical development of depreciation rules. We intend the economic and historical discussion to provide a framework for understanding the tax law of depreciation. This framework is important because depreciation policy involves issues other than merely matching costs to revenue. Much depreciation policy focuses on issues such as economic growth and problems caused by inflation.

A capital expenditure may be treated in one of three ways: (1) capitalized when paid or incurred and deducted when the taxpayer disposes of the property, (2) capitalized when paid or incurred and deducted over several periods as depreciation or amortization, or (3) deducted in the year paid or incurred.

Land is an example of the first category. A taxpayer may not deduct or depreciate the cost of land but instead retains a cost basis in the property. When the taxpayer sells the land, he or she subtracts the original cost basis from the amount realized to arrive at gain or loss realized. This subtraction of basis constitutes the taxpayer's cost recovery (or return of capital).

Most capital expenditures fall into the second category and are the topic of this chapter. As we discussed in Chapters 5 and 7, taxpayers generally may not deduct such expenditures in the year paid or incurred but must spread (allocate) cost recovery deductions over a number of periods. Depending on the type of expenditure, this interperiod cost allocation may be based on (1) the income generated by the property, as in the case of percentage **depletion**; (2) the usage of property, such as hours operated or units produced; or (3) a somewhat arbitrary time period, such as the property's estimated useful life or a statutory recovery period. These last two methods are referred to as **depreciation** (or **cost recovery**) for tangible assets and as **amortization** for intangible assets.

The last category, immediate deduction (expensing), is least common for capital expenditures although the Code allows expensing in a few cases. For example, a taxpayer may elect to currently deduct research and experimental expenditures and certain intangible drilling costs.[1] In addition, a taxpayer may elect to expense, within limits, the cost of personal property used in a trade or business (discussed later in this chapter). Some economists and other commentators advocate immediate expensing of all capital expenditures. We discuss the policy issue of immediate expensing in the next section.

> **Depletion** is the removal of natural resources from the earth. It may also be a cost recovery method.
>
> **Depreciation** is the allocation of a tangible asset's cost over time (**cost recovery**). It is also a decline in value (economic depreciation).
>
> **Amoritization** is the allocation of an intangible asset's cost over time.

THE ECONOMICS OF DEPRECIATION

In this section, we examine four economic aspects of depreciation: (1) how depreciation affects returns on capital investments, (2) the issue of immediate expensing versus economic depreciation, (3) the role of implicit taxes in depreciation policy, and (4) the problem of depreciating historical cost in an inflationary environment.

> **Goal #1**
> Analyze various depreciation methods using present value techniques.

HOW DEPRECIATION AFFECTS RETURNS ON CAPITAL INVESTMENTS

Because depreciation affects the timing of deductions, it involves the time value of money. As a general rule, the more accelerated the depreciation deductions, the greater

---

1 Sec. 174 and Sec. 263(c), respectively.

the present value of tax savings created by those deductions. Consequently, depreciation timing impacts the present value of after-tax cash flows from investments.

EXAMPLE 14-1

Mr. Swanson invests $10,000 in a business asset that will generate cash flows at the end of each year for five years. Mr. Swanson has three options for depreciating the cost of the asset: (1) the **straight-line depreciation** method with one-half year's depreciation taken in the first and last years, (2) an **accelerated depreciation** method with one-half year's depreciation taken in the first and last years, and (3) **immediate expensing**. Assume the following: (1) Mr. Swanson pays taxes at a flat 30% rate; (2) if he chooses immediate expensing, he obtains the tax benefit of expensing at the beginning of the first year, but if he chooses depreciation, he obtains the tax benefits of depreciation at the end of each year; and (3) he can offset negative taxable income from the investment against income from other sources, thereby receiving a tax benefit.

    Tables 14-1, 14-2, and 14-3 present the results of the three options. Column 2 of each table lists the expected before-tax cash flows. Column 3 shows the **net present value (NPV)** of these cash flows discounted at the **internal rate of return (IRR).** The IRR is the rate that equates the present value of cash flows with the cost of the investment (in other words, it forces the NPV to zero). Note that the before-tax IRR is 10% in all three cases. Column 4 provides the depreciation schedule for each option, and Column 5 shows the present value of depreciation deductions. Note that the more accelerated the depreciation deductions, the higher the total present value. (Think of expensing as highly accelerated depreciation.) Columns 6, 7, and 8 present taxable income, the tax liability, and after-tax cash flows, respectively. Finally, Column 9 presents the NPV of after-tax cash flows discounted at the after-tax IRR. These IRRs follow:

Straight-line depreciation	6.555%
Accelerated depreciation	7.005
Immediate expensing	10.000

    This example demonstrates that the more accelerated the depreciation deductions, the higher the after-tax IRR. Accelerated depreciation deductions reduce early income streams more than late income streams and thus increase the attractiveness of the investment by deferring taxes. This conclusion assumes that tax rates remain constant. If current tax rates are low and future tax rates are high, the taxpayer may want to defer depreciation deductions.

Straight-line depreciation occurs when the cost of an asset is allocated (depreciated) evenly over time.

Accelerated depreciation occurs when depreciation deductions in early years exceed those in later years.

Immediate expensing occurs when the entire cost of an asset is deducted in the first year.

Net present value (NPV) equals the present value of cash flows minus the cost of investment.

The **internal rate of return (IRR)** is the discount rate that equates the present value of cash flows with the cost of investment.

    Example 14-1 assumes that the taxpayer's choice of depreciation methods does not alter the market price (cost) of the asset. Later in this chapter, we explore the effects of depreciation policy on asset prices along with a discussion of implicit taxes.

TABLE 14-1

Effect of
Straight-Line
Depreciation on
Present Values
and Internal Rates
of Return
(EXAMPLE 14.1)*

1 Year[†]	2 BTCF	3 NPV BTCF (10%)	4 SLD	5 PV SLD (10%)	6 TI[‡]	7 Tax (30%)	8 ATCF[§]	9 NPV ATCF (6.555%)
0	$(10,000)	$(10,000)	$ 0	$ 0	$ 0	$ 0	($10,000)	$(10,000)
1	3,300	3,000	1,000	909	2,300	690	2,610	2,450
2	3,025	2,500	2,000	1,653	1,025	308	2,717	2,393
3	2,660	2,000	2,000	1,503	660	198	2,462	2,035
4	2,200	1,500	2,000	1,366	200	60	2,140	1,660
5	1,610	1,000	2,000	1,242	(390)	(117)	1,727	1,257
6	0	0	1,000	564	(1,000)	(300)	300	205
Total		$ 0	$10,000	$7,237				$ 0

*BTCF = before-tax cash flows; ATCF = after-tax cash flows; PV = present value; NPV = net present value; SLD = straight-line depreciation; TI = taxable income.
[†]Year 0 refers to the beginning of Year 1. Investment occurs at the beginning of Year 1, and cash flows occur at the end of each year.
[‡]Column 2 minus Column 4 for Years 1 through 6. Tax benefit of depreciation occurs at the end of each year.
[§]Column 2 minus Column 7 for Years 0 through 6.

TABLE 14-2

Effect of
Accelerated
Depreciation on
Present Values
and Internal Rates
of Return
(EXAMPLE 14-1)*

1 Year[†]	2 BTCF	3 NPV BTCF (10%)	4 Accel. Depr.	5 PV Depr. (10%)	6 TI[‡]	7 Tax (30%)	8 ATCF[§]	9 NPV ATCF (7.005%)
0	$(10,000)	$(10,000)	$ 0	$ 0	$ 0	$ 0	($10,000)	$(10,000)
1	3,300	3,000	2,000	1,818	1,300	390	2,910	2,719
2	3,025	2,500	3,200	2,645	(175)	(53)	3,078	2,688
3	2,660	2,000	1,920	1,443	740	222	2,438	1,990
4	2,200	1,500	1,152	787	1,048	314	1,886	1,438
5	1,610	1,000	1,152	715	458	137	1,473	1,050
6	0	0	576	325	(576)	(173)	173	115
Total		$ 0	$10,000	$7,733				$ 0

*BTCF = before-tax cash flows; ATCF = after-tax cash flows; PV = present value; NPV = net present value; TI = taxable income.
[†]Year 0 refers to the beginning of Year 1. Investment occurs at the beginning of Year 1, and cash flows occur at the end of each year.
[‡]Column 2 minus Column 4 for Years 1 through 6. Tax benefit of depreciation occurs at the end of each year.
[§]Column 2 minus Column 7 for Years 0 through 6.

1	2	3	4	5	6	7	8	9
Year[†]	BTCF	NPV BTCF (10%)	Expense	PV Expense (10%)	TI[‡]	Tax (30%)	ATCF[§]	NPV ATCF (10%)
0	$(10,000)	$(10,000)	$10,000	$10,000	$(10,000)	$(3,000)	$(7,000)	$(7,000)
1	3,300	3,000	0	0	3,300	990	2,310	2,100
2	3,025	2,500	0	0	3,025	908	2,117	1,750
3	2,660	2,000	0	0	2,660	798	1,862	1,399
4	2,200	1,500	0	0	2,200	660	1,540	1,051
5	1,610	1,000	0	0	1,610	483	1,127	700
6	0	0	0	0	0	0	0	0
Total		$ 0	$10,000	$10,000				$ 0

*BTCF = before-tax cash flows; ATCF = after-tax cash flows; PV = present value; NPV = net present value; TI = taxable income.
[†]Year 0 refers to the beginning of Year 1. Investment occurs at the beginning of Year 1, and cash flows occur at the end of each year.
[‡]Column 2 minus Column 4 for Years 1 through 6. Tax benefit of depreciation occurs at the end of each year.
[§]Column 2 minus Column 7 for Years 0 through 6.

TABLE 14-3

Effect of Immediate Expensing on Present Values and Internal Rates of Return (EXAMPLES 14-1 and 14-3)*

Goal #2
Explain the difference between immediate expensing and economic depreciation.

Economic depreciation measures an asset's decline in economic value.

IMMEDIATE EXPENSING VERSUS ECONOMIC DEPRECIATION

Economists and policymakers have long debated whether the cost of an asset should be expensed immediately or whether the asset should be depreciated according to its decline in economic value. This latter method is referred to as **economic depreciation**, which in a given year can be defined as follows. Economic depreciation equals

1. Present value of remaining before-tax cash flows at the beginning of the year, minus

2. Present value of remaining before-tax cash flows at the end of the year.

Economic depreciation reflects the change in an asset's price or value from one period to the next because the present value of expected future cash flows equals an asset's price or value.

EXAMPLE 14-2

Using the same facts and assumptions as Example 14-1, Table 14-4 presents the investment results using economic depreciation. Column 4 and the associated footnote demonstrate the calculation of economic depreciation. In this example, the cost of the asset ($10,000) equals the present value of expected cash flows at the time of acquisition. Total economic depreciation also equals the cost of the asset because the final value of the asset is zero (that is, no future cash flows are expected). If the investor revises expected cash flows each year because of changing economic conditions, these revised cash flows become the basis for computing economic depreciation in periods following the revision. Neverthe-
Continued

EXAMPLE 14-2 (Con't.)

less, total economic depreciation will still equal the asset's original cost if the asset's value ultimately becomes zero. Thus, economic depreciation allocates an asset's cost over the investment horizon based on the changes in value from year to year. We will make additional observations about Table 14-4 in Example 14-3.

The immediate expensing versus economic depreciation debate centers primarily on the issue of **tax neutrality**. Broadly defined, neutrality means that taxes do not distort investment decisions. That is, if taxes are neutral, investors make the same decisions on an after-tax basis as they would on a before-tax basis. The following two quotations exemplify the polar extremes between immediate expensing and economic depreciation:

> **Tax neutrality** occurs when taxes do not alter or distort a taxpayer's decision.

A tax that permits instantaneous depreciation leaves the internal rate of discount unchanged. It is a perfectly neutral solution, so neutral in fact as to be a zero tax.[2]

If, and only if, true loss of economic value is permitted as a tax-deductible depreciation expense will the present discounted value of a cash-receipt stream be independent of the rate of tax.[3]

TABLE 14-4

Effect of Economic Depreciation on Present Values and Internal Rates of Return (EXAMPLES 14-2 and 14-3)*

1 Year[†]	2 BTCF	3 NPV BTCF (10%)	4 Econ. Depr.[‡]	5 PV Depr. (10%)	6 TI[§]	7 Tax (30%)	8 ATCF[#]	9 NPV ATCF (7%)
0	$(10,000)	$(10,000)	$ 0	$ 0	$ 0	$ 0	$(10,000)	$(10,000)
1	3,300	3,000	2,299	2,090	1,001	300	3,000	2,803
2	3,025	2,500	2,255	1,864	770	231	2,794	2,440
3	2,660	2,000	2,115	1,589	545	163	2,497	2,038
4	2,200	1,500	1,867	1,275	333	100	2,100	1,602
5	1,610	1,000	1,464	909	146	44	1,566	1,117
6	0	0	0	0	0	0	0	0
Total		$ 0	$10,000	$7,727				$ 0

*BTCF = before-tax cash flows; ATCF = after-tax cash flows; PV = present value; NPV = net present value; TI = taxable income.

[†]Year 0 refers to the beginning of Year 1. Investment occurs at the beginning of Year 1, and cash flows occur at the end of each year.

[‡]The numbers in Column 4 are derived by subtracting the PV of cash flows at the end of a year from the PV of cash flows at the beginning of the year. For example, the calculation for Year 1 is $10,000 − ($3,025/1.1 + $2,660/1.1^2 + $2,200/1.1^3 + $1,610/1.1^4 = $10,000 − $7,701 = $2,299; the calculation for Year 2 is $7,701 − ($2,660/1.1 + $2,200/1.1^2 + $1,610/1.1^3 = $7,701 − $5,446 = $2,255; and so on.

[§]Column 2 minus Column 4 for Years 1 through 6. Tax benefit of depreciation occurs at the end of each year.

[#]Column 2 minus Column 7 for Years 0 of through 6.

---

2 Richard A. Musgrave, *The Theory of Public Finance,* (New York: McGraw-Hill, 1959), p. 343.

3 Paul A. Samuelson, "Tax Deductibility of Economic Depreciation to Insure Invariant Valuations," *Journal of Political Economy*, December 1964, p. 604.

Musgrave (the first quotation) advocates *immediate expensing* while Samuelson (the second quotation) espouses *economic depreciation*. But as another economist points out:

> Samuelson neutrality and Musgrave neutrality are two quite different things. Samuelson neutrality comes when the government is truly taxing; Musgrave neutrality comes when the government is in effect a true partner in the enterprise.[4]

This quotation means that, under the Samuelson definition, the difference between the taxpayer's before-tax and after-tax rates of return reflects the taxpayer's statutory tax rate. Stated another way, the taxpayer's **effective tax rate** will equal the taxpayer's **statutory tax rate**. Under the Musgrave definition, the before-tax and after-tax rates of return are the same, making the effective tax rate equal to zero. The effective tax rate (ETR) for a particular investment (I) can be defined as follows:

> The **effective tax rate** is the percentage difference in before-tax and after-tax rates of return using the investment return in the denominator.
>
> **Statutory tax rates** are specified in the Code and are applied to taxable income.

$$\text{Effective tax rate} = \frac{\text{Before-tax return (I)} - \text{After-tax return (I)}}{\text{Before-tax return (I)}}$$

EXAMPLE 14-3

In Table 14-4, the before-tax IRR equals 10% and the after-tax IRR equals 7%. Therefore, the investor's ETR equals .30 or 30% [(10% – 7%)/10%]. The difference between the two IRRs reflects effective taxation at the investor's statutory rate (Samuelson neutrality). In Table 14-3, however, the ETR equals zero [(10% – 10%) / 10%]. Thus, under immediate expensing, the investor is not being effectively taxed (Musgrave neutrality). In Table 14-3, the first row of Column 7 shows that the government actually invests $3,000 ($10,000 x 30%) in the project by giving the investor a $3,000 immediate tax benefit. The taxes in Year 1 through Year 5 represent the government's return on its investment. The first row of Column 8 indicates the investor's net investment of $7,000, and the after-tax cash flows in Year 1 through Year 5 represent his return on investment. Thus, the government and the investor act as 30:70 partners. In the next section, we will show that this analysis is incomplete because it ignores implicit taxes.

Advocates of immediate expensing offer several reasons for their position, some of which economic depreciation advocates can counter.[5] We present these arguments without attempting to resolve the conflict between the two points of view. Regardless of the merits of the arguments, the government, when formulating depreciation policy, accepts economic depreciation as neutral and considers immediate expensing as distortive.

---

4 Arnold C. Harberger, "Tax Neutrality in Investment Incentives," in *The Economics of Taxation*, eds., Henry J. Aaron and Michael J. Boskin, (Washington, DC: The Brookings Institution, 1980), p. 307.

5 For example, see Norman B. Ture, "The Accelerated Cost Recovery System: An Evaluation of the 1981 and 1982 Cost Recovery Provisions," in *New Directions in Federal Tax Policy for the 1980s*, eds. Charles E. Walker and Mark A. Bloomfield (Cambridge: Ballinger, 1983) and Department of the Treasury, *Blueprints for Basic Tax Reform*, (U.S. Government Printing Office, 1977).

Neutrality

Advocates of immediate expensing claim that it is neutral and does not distort the investment decision because the present value of depreciation is independent of the economic life of the asset. The longer the period over which depreciation is spread, the lower the present value of the deductions. Consequently, any depreciation method, including economic depreciation, that extends over time discriminates *against* long-lived assets. Conversely, advocates of economic depreciation might counter that expensing distorts investment decisions *in favor* of long-lived assets because the benefit of expensing is greater for long-lived assets than for short-lived assets. Moreover, economic depreciation does not alter before-tax rates of return (Samuelson neutrality). As we will demonstrate later, expensing may change before-tax rates of return, thereby creating implicit taxes.

Simplicity

Expensing is simple because the taxpayer does not have to keep depreciation records and does not have to determine adjusted basis upon a subsequent disposition. The basis of an expensed asset is always zero. Economic depreciation, on the other hand, is difficult to determine. An asset usually interacts with other assets so that isolating its cash flows becomes problematical.[6] Also, economic depreciation relies on estimates of future cash flows and discount rates, both of which introduce uncertainty. Advocates of economic depreciation claim, however, that adequate means exist for estimating or modeling changes in asset valuation.[7]

Inflation

Inflation is the general rise in price levels.

Expensing is **inflation** proof because the taxpayer deducts the cost of an asset currently. Advocates of economic depreciation counter that their method is also inflation proof because it uses current values instead of historical cost. However, economic depreciation measures the change in a specific asset's value, which may not coincide with the general inflation rate. We will examine the problem of inflation and historical cost later in this chapter.

Matching

We should mention one negative aspect of immediate expensing: it makes no attempt to match an asset's cost against the income generated by that asset. Economic depreciation, if determinable, exactly matches depreciation deductions against related income and therefore conforms to economic and accounting concepts of net income.

DEPRECIATION AND IMPLICIT TAXES

Goal #3
Recognize the role of implicit taxes in depreciation policy.

The analysis of immediate expensing in the last section ignores implicit taxes. As described in Chapters 1 and 4, implicit taxes occur when before-tax rates of return on tax-favored investments decrease compared to those on a benchmark investment as investors bid up the prices of tax-favored investments.[8] The relevant formulas follow:

---

6 For a thorough discussion of the asset interaction problem, see Arthur L. Thomas, *The Allocation Problem in Financial Accounting Theory*, (Sarasota: American Accounting Association, 1969).

7 For example, see Charles R. Hulten and Frank C. Wykoff, "The Measurement of Economic Depreciation" in *Depreciation, Inflation, and the Taxation of Income from Capital,* ed. Charles R. Hulten (Washington, DC: The Urban Institute Press, 1981).

8 For a thorough discussion of implicit taxes, see Myron S. Scholes and Mark A. Wolfson, *Taxes and Business Strategy: A Planning Approach,* (Englewood Cliffs, NJ: Prentice-Hall, 1992) Ch. 5.

Implicit tax rate =

$$\frac{\text{Before-tax return (B)} - \text{Before-tax return (I)}}{\text{Before-tax return (B)}}$$

Explicit tax rate =

$$\frac{\text{Before-tax return (I)} - \text{After-tax return (I)}}{\text{Before-tax return (B)}}$$

Total tax rate = Implicit tax rate + Explicit tax rate =

$$\frac{\text{Before-tax return (B)} - \text{After-tax return (I)}}{\text{Before-tax return (B)}}$$

> The **implicit tax rate** is the percentage decrease in before-tax rates of return arising from tax-favored status of investment.
>
> The **explicit tax rate** is the percentage difference in before-tax and after-tax rates of return using the benchmark investment in the denominator.
>
> The **total tax rate** is the sum of the implicit and explicit tax rates.

The parenthetical expression (B) refers to the benchmark investment, which usually is a relatively riskless fully-taxable bond, and (I) again refers to the particular investment under consideration, whose return is adjusted to the same risk level as the benchmark investment. Note that the *explicit* tax formula differs from the *effective* tax rate formula in that the denominator contains the before-tax rate of return for the benchmark investment rather than for the investment under consideration. The same denominator for the implicit and explicit tax rate fractions allows them to be added to attain the total tax rate. If the implicit tax rate equals zero, the explicit and effective tax rates will be equal. Otherwise, the explicit and effective tax rates will differ.

If one asset must be depreciated over time (for example, economic depreciation) and another asset may be expensed, investors will initially prefer the second asset because it is tax-favored (assuming all other factors being equal). If markets are perfectly competitive, investors will bid up the price of the expensed asset until the after-tax rates of return of the two assets are equal for **marginal investors**.[9] The after-tax rates of return equalize because the increased price of the expensed asset reduces its before-tax rate of return.

> **Marginal investors** are willing to invest only at the rate of return where supply and demand curves intersect. Other investors are willing to accept returns other than the equilibrium rate of return.

EXAMPLE 14-4

Assume that the before-tax rate of return on both a benchmark investment and the asset subject to economic depreciation is 10%. In Example 14-3, the before-tax IRR on the expensed asset remained at 10%, which is unrealistic in a competitive market. Investors should bid up that asset's price so that Mr. Swanson pays $10,725 instead of $10,000. Table 14-5 presents the investment results for this scenario. Note that both the before-tax and after-tax IRRs for the expensed asset are now 7%. The investor's effective and explicit tax rates on this asset are still zero, but his implicit tax rate is 30% [(10% − 7%)/10%]. Therefore, contrary to Musgrave's statement, the investor *is* taxed, but implicitly rather than explicitly. Moreover, an investor in the 30% bracket will be indifferent as to which asset to acquire because both assets yield a 7% after-tax rate of return.

In effect, the increased price of a tax-favored asset is a subsidy paid to the seller. Thus, immediate expensing *creates* an incentive for persons to produce and sell tax-favored assets. (An advocate of expensing would claim that expensing *removes* a disincentive to produce and sell the asset.)

9 *Ibid.*

TABLE 14-5

Effect of Immediate Expensing and Implicit Taxes on Present Values and Internal Rates of Return (EXAMPLE 14-4)*

1 Year[†]	2 BTCF	3 NPV BTCF (7%)	4 Expense	5 PV Expense (7%)	6 TI[‡]	7 Tax (30%)	8 ACTF[§]	9 NPV ATCF (7%)
0	$(10,725)	$(10,725)	$10,725	$10,725	$(10,725)	$(3,218)	$(7,508)	$(7,508)
1	3,300	3,084	0	0	3,300	990	2,310	2,159
2	3,025	2,642	0	0	3,025	908	2,117	1,850
3	2,660	2,172	0	0	2,660	798	1,862	1,520
4	2,200	1,679	0	0	2,200	660	1,540	1,175
5	1,610	1,148	0	0	1,610	483	1,127	804
6	0	0	0	0	0	0	0	0
Total		$ 0	$10,000	$10,000				$ 0

*BTCF = before-tax cash flows; ATCF = after-tax cash flows; PV = present value; NPV = net present value; TI = taxable income.
[†]Year 0 refers to the beginning of Year 1. Investment occurs at the beginning of Year 1, and cash flows occur at the end of each year.
[‡]Column 2 minus Column 4 for Years 1 through 6. Tax benefit of depreciation occurs at the end of each year.
[§]Column 2 minus Column 7 for Years 0 of through 6.

TABLE 14-6

Effect of Economic Depreciation on Present Values and Internal Rates of Return (EXAMPLE 14-5)*

1 Year[†]	2 BTCF	3 NPV BTCF (10%)	4 Econ. Depr.[‡]	5 PV Depr. (10%)	6 TI[§]	7 Tax (40%)	8 ATCF[#]	9 NPV ATCF (6%)
0	$(10,000)	$(10,000)	$ 0	$ 0	$ 0	$ 0	$(10,000)	$(10,000)
1	3,300	3,000	2,299	2,090	1,001	400	2,900	2,736
2	3,025	2,500	2,255	1,864	770	308	2,717	2,418
3	2,660	2,000	2,115	1,589	545	218	2,442	2,050
4	2,200	1,500	1,867	1,275	333	133	2,067	1,637
5	1,610	1,000	1,464	909	146	59	1,551	1,159
6	0	0	0	0	0	0	0	0
Total		$ 0	$10,000	$7,727				$ 0

*BTCF = before-tax cash flows; ATCF = after-tax cash flows; PV = present value; NPV = net present value; TI = taxable income.
[†]Year 0 refers to the beginning of Year 1. Investment occurs at the beginning of Year 1, and cash flows occur at the end of each year.
[‡]See note [‡] in Table 14-4.
[§]Column 2 minus Column 4 for Years 1 through 6. Tax benefit of depreciation occurs at the end of each year.
[#]Column 2 minus Column 7 for Years 0 of through 6.

1	2	3 NPV BTCF (7%)	4 Expense	5 PV Expense (7%)	6 TI[‡]	7 Tax (40%)	8 ATCF[§]	9 NPV ATCF (7%)
Year[†]	BTCF							
0	$(10,725)	$(10,725)	$10,725	$(10,725)	$(10,725)	$(4,290)	$(6,435)	$(6,435)
1	3,300	3,084	0	0	3,300	1,320	1,980	1,851
2	3,025	2,642	0	0	3,025	1,210	1,815	1,585
3	2,660	2,172	0	0	2,660	1,064	1,596	1,303
4	2,200	1,679	0	0	2,200	880	1,320	1,007
5	1,610	1,148	0	0	1,610	644	966	689
6	0	0	0	0	0	0	0	0
Total		$ 0	$10,000	$10,000				$ 0

TABLE 14-7

Effect of Immediate Expensing and Implicit Taxes on Present Values and Internal Rates of Return (EXAMPLE 14-5)*

*BTCF = before-tax cash flows; ATCF = after-tax cash flows; PV = present value; NPV = net present value; TI = taxable income.

[†]Year 0 refers to the beginning of Year 1. Investment occurs at the beginning of Year 1, and cash flows occur at the end of each year.

[‡]Column 2 minus Column 4 for Years 1 through 6. Tax benefit of depreciation occurs at the end of each year.

[§]Column 2 minus Column 7 for Years 0 of through 6.

If asset prices are pegged to 30% taxpayers (in other words, 30% taxpayers are the marginal investors), taxpayers with tax rates other than 30% will not be indifferent as to which asset they prefer.

EXAMPLE 14-5

Suppose, as in Example 14-4, an asset subject to economic depreciation costs $10,000, and an asset subject to expensing costs $10,725. These prices occur because 30% taxpayers are the marginal investors who have bid up the price of the tax-favored asset. Suppose another taxpayer, Ms. Schwartz, pays taxes at 40%. Will she be indifferent as to which asset to acquire? Tables 14-6 and 14-7 present the investment results of the two choices. The after-tax IRR on the asset subject to economic depreciation drops to 6% so that Ms. Schwartz's effective and explicit tax rates equal 40% [(10% – 6%)/10%], the same as her statutory rate. This result is consistent with Samuelson's statement. However, the IRR on the expensed asset remains at 7%. Instead of paying an explicit tax of 40%, Ms. Schwartz incurs an implicit tax of 30%. Therefore, she will prefer the expensed asset over the depreciated one.

As we pointed out in Chapter 4, the phenomenon in Example 14-5 is known as the **clientele effect**.[10] Taxpayers in high tax brackets will prefer tax-favored investments whose prices are determined by marginal taxpayers in low tax brackets. The former are in the tax-favored investment clientele. By investing in tax-favored assets, the taxpayer converts his or her high statutory tax rate into a relatively low implicit tax

The **clientele effect** occurs when taxpayers join groups that prefer investments with particular tax attributes.

10 For a thorough discussion of the clientele effect, see Scholes and Wolfson, *op. cit.*, Ch. 6.

<table>
<tr><td>Goal #4
Understand the implications of inflation on depreciation deductions.</td></tr>
</table>

rate. This conversion is good investment strategy, but from a policy perspective, it violates vertical equity because the taxpayer is not paying the statutory tax rate. Conversely, taxpayers with tax rates below that of the marginal investors will prefer assets that are *not* tax favored. If the low-bracket taxpayer invests in tax-favored assets, he or she converts a low statutory tax rate into a relatively high implicit tax rate—a poor investment strategy.

DEPRECIATION AND INFLATION

The **nominal interest rate** is the stated rate that contains an inflation component.

The **real interest rate** is a deflated rate.

The **inflation rate** is the change in general price level measured with a standard index.

Inflation erodes the present value of depreciation deductions based on historical cost because inflation increases the nominal discount rate. The **nominal interest rate** is a combination of the **real interest rate** and the **inflation rate** and can be computed as follows:

Nominal interest rate =
$$[(1 + \text{inflation rate}) \times (1 + \text{real interest rate})] - 1$$

EXAMPLE 14-6

Consider the straight-line depreciation schedule in Column 4 of Table 14-1. Assume a 10% real interest rate and a 5% inflation rate. The nominal interest rate equals .155 or 15.5% [(1.05 × 1.1) – 1)]. Table 14-8 displays the depreciation deductions discounted at 10% and 15.5%. In this case, inflation erodes the present value of depreciation deductions by $419 ($7,237 – $6,818).

In response to this inflation problem, many policy commentators have recommended indexing either the basis of assets or the depreciation deductions by the inflation rate. Such indexing restores the present value of depreciation deductions to the amount that would occur in a noninflationary environment.

TABLE 14-8

Effect of Inflation on Present Value of Depreciation Deductions with No Indexing (EXAMPLE 14-6)

1 Year	2 Depreciation Deduction	3 Discounted at 10%	4 Discounted at 15.5%
1	$ 1,000	$ 909	$ 866
2	2,000	1,653	1,499
3	2,000	1,503	1,298
4	2,000	1,366	1,124
5	2,000	1,242	973
6	1,000	564	421
Total	$10,000	$7,237	$6,818

EXAMPLE 14-7

Assume that the annual depreciation deductions are indexed for inflation as shown in Column 3 of Table 14-9. The indexed depreciation deductions discounted at the nominal interest rate (Column 4) are now the same as unindexed deductions discounted at the real interest rate with no inflation (Table 14-8, Column 3). Indexing has eliminated the effect of inflation.

Note that an immediate expense requires no indexing because the expense requires no discounting; the expensed amount *is* the present value. As mentioned earlier, immediate expensing is inflation proof.

EVOLUTION OF DEPRECIATION REQUIREMENTS

Tax policymakers and lawmakers have long recognized the importance of depreciation provisions for economic growth and revenue generation. As a result, the tax laws governing depreciation have changed continuously with shifts in economic and social objectives. These changes affect both the timing of depreciation deductions and the detailed requirements for record keeping and tax return preparation. Moreover, depreciation changes are never made retroactively. A taxpayer adopts a required or permitted depreciation method when an asset is placed in service. If the tax law subsequently changes, the taxpayer must continue using the depreciation method originally adopted for existing assets. Consequently, many existing assets are still being depreciated under old methods. In addition, lawmakers usually construct new depreciation rules using underlying principles established under old rules. For these reasons, taxpayers and tax return preparers must have a basic knowledge of prior depreciation concepts and methods. Accordingly, this section highlights the evolution of depreciation requirements from around 1913 to the present.

Goal #5
Appreciate the historical development of depreciation tax law.

EARLY HISTORY: DEVELOPMENT OF THE STRAIGHT-LINE CONCEPT, 1913–1932

Even before the Revenue Act of 1913, accountants recognized the need for systematically spreading or allocating the cost of a wasting asset over the accounting periods

1 Year	2 Depreciation Deduction	3 Indexed at 5%	4 Discounted at 15.5%
1	$ 1,000	$ 1,050	$ 909
2	2,000	2,205	1,653
3	2,000	2,315	1,503
4	2,000	2,431	1,366
5	2,000	2,553	1,242
6	1,000	1,340	564
Total	$10,000	$11,894	$7,237

TABLE 14-9

Effect of Inflation on Present Value of Depreciation Deductions with Indexing (EXAMPLE 14-7)

benefited by the asset. Around the turn of the century, accounting textbooks and manuals usually recommended the following formula for determining the periodic charge against revenue:

$$\text{Depreciation} = \frac{\text{Cost to be allocated}}{\text{Estimated life of asset}}$$

An alternative expression is

$$\text{Depreciation} = \frac{1}{\text{Estimated life of asset}} \times \text{Cost to be allocated}$$

These formulas allow a constant charge for each period during which the taxpayer uses the asset. The fraction in the second formula is the straight-line rate of depreciation. Despite textbook formulas, many businesses, without the influence of tax laws, ignored this systematic approach and deducted varying amounts of depreciation from year to year. For example, in high-income years, businesses might take large depreciation deductions in anticipation of years when income would be insufficient to absorb depreciation charges.[11]

When drafting the Revenue Act of 1913, Congress thought of expenditures as either revenue charges (current expenses) or capital charges (related to acquisition of property). Taxpayers divided capital charges on a common sense basis between property that did not wear out or waste away (nondepreciable) and property that did (depreciable). For depreciable property, the 1913 Act provided "a reasonable allowance for depreciation by use, wear and tear of property, if any." Later acts use substantially identical language but included obsolescence along with use, wear, and tear.[12]

From 1913 to 1933, the Bureau of Internal Revenue (predecessor of the IRS until 1953), directed its efforts toward establishing systematic straight-line depreciation. The Bureau allowed taxpayers maximum freedom in selecting rates of depreciation (or estimated lives of assets). In 1920, the Bureau summarized its view in Bulletin F as follows:

> It is considered impracticable to prescribe fixed, definite rates of depreciation which would be allowable for all property of a given class or character. . . . The taxpayer should in all cases determine as accurately as possible according to his judgment and experience the rate at which his property depreciates.[13]

If taxpayers used a rate systematically, their deductions were allowed unless the Bureau could produce clear and convincing evidence that the deductions were unreasonable. Thus, the burden of proof was on the Bureau. Clear and convincing evidence rarely arose, giving taxpayers much latitude in establishing depreciations rates.

11 Dorothy A. Litherland, "Fixed Asset Replacement a Half Century Ago," *The Accounting Review*, October 1951, p. 475.

12 Eugene L. Grant and Paul. T. Norton, Jr., *Depreciation*, (New York: Ronald Press, 1955), p. 209. This book contains a good discussion of the early history of depreciation.

13 *Ibid.*, p. 216.

THE ERA OF BULLETIN F, 1933–1953

In 1933, the Roosevelt administration sought new sources of revenue to finance its ambitious domestic programs. In partial response, a subcommittee of the House Ways and Means Committee proposed a one-fourth across-the-board reduction in depreciation deductions for three years. However, the Bureau proposed and ultimately adopted a solution more equitable than the House proposal. Specifically, the Bureau increased its control over depreciation deductions by (1) requiring taxpayers to furnish detailed depreciation schedules with their tax returns, (2) shifting to taxpayers the burden of proving the reasonableness of depreciation rates, and (3) issuing a revised Bulletin F that specified reasonable depreciation rates for many assets (the rate equals one divided by the asset life, that is, straight-line depreciation).

After the adoption of these procedures, depreciation deductions became a constant source of controversy between taxpayers and the Bureau. Taxpayers claimed that (1) asset lives dictated by Bulletin F were unrealistically long, (2) long asset lives prevented them from recovering their investments rapidly enough, and (3) long lives inhibited investment in new plant assets. The Bureau, however, remained adamant, claiming that the Bulletin F rates were based on empirical evidence. Moreover, taxpayers could use shorter lives (and faster rates) than specified in Bulletin F if circumstances warranted and if they could sustain the burden of proof.

THE EMERGENCE OF ACCELERATED DEPRECIATION, 1954–1980

The era of accelerated depreciation began with the enactment of the Internal Revenue Code of 1954. For years beginning after 1953, the new Code allowed taxpayers to use the declining-balance method (with rates up to twice the straight-line rate) and the sum-of-the-years-digits method, as well as the straight-line method. In addition, the IRS adopted a policy of not challenging depreciation rates (useful lives) unless "clear and convincing" evidence indicated that the taxpayer's rates were unreasonable.[14]

In 1962, the IRS replaced Bulletin F with *Guidelines for Depreciation*.[15] *Guidelines* grouped assets into fewer than 100 classes instead of using the item-by-item approach employed by Bulletin F. For example, *Guidelines* established a 10-year class for "office furniture, fixtures, machines, and equipment"; an 8-year class for "manufacturing—aerospace industry"; and a 20-year class for "manufacturing—cement manufacture." Thus, the classes represented broad categories of business assets as well as categories for entire industries. In addition, the asset lives in *Guidelines* were "30 to 40 percent shorter than those suggested in Bulletin F and 15 percent shorter than the useful lives actually being used at the time the new procedure was released."[16] Thus, *Guidelines* along with accelerated methods substantially liberalized depreciation deductions for taxpayers.

Continuing the class-life principles begun in *Guidelines*, Congress in 1971 enacted the **Class Life Asset Depreciation Range (CLADR) system**.[17] Like *Guidelines*, the CLADR system provided for a limited number of classes. However, the CLADR system allowed the taxpayer to use any asset life within a specified range. This range varied from 20% below to 20% above the midpoint of the range, with the midpoint

> The **Class Life Asset Depreciation Range (CLADR) system** is a formal system in which the government publishes the time range over which assets may be depreciated.

---

14 Joint Economic Committee, *The Federal Tax System: Fact and Problems*, (U.S. Government Printing Office, 1964).

15 Rev. Proc. 62–21, 1962-2 CB 418.

16 Joint Economic Committee, *op. cit.*, p. 91.

17 Sec. 167(m).

being the asset life specified in *Guidelines*.[18] For example, the class life for office furniture, fixtures, and equipment ranged from 8 years to 12 years, with a 10-year midpoint. The CLADR system was optional for taxpayers and was "designed to minimize disputes between taxpayers and the Internal Revenue Service as to the useful life of property, and as to salvage value, repairs, and other matters."[19] However, because of its elective nature, taxpayers could avoid the CLADR system and base their useful life decisions on facts and circumstances. As a result, disputes between taxpayers and the IRS continued until the advent of the Accelerated Cost Recovery System discussed in the next section. Although the CLADR system applies to assets placed in service before 1981, it remains important after 1980 because cost recovery periods under ACRS depend on midpoint class lives.

Depreciation before 1981 was based on **useful life** concepts, and assets generally could not be depreciated below their estimated **salvage value**. Useful life connotes economic life, and salvage value reflects remaining cash flows. Therefore, pre-1981 depreciation approximated economic depreciation more than it resembled immediate expensing. With the Accelerated Cost Recovery System, the pendulum swung toward expensing.

THE ERA OF ACCELERATED COST RECOVERY, 1981–PRESENT

As part of the Economic Recovery Tax Act of 1981 (ERTA), Congress enacted the **Accelerated Cost Recovery System (ACRS)**, which is still applicable to property placed in service by the taxpayer from 1981 through 1986. Congress modified the system in 1986 for property placed in service after 1986. This latter system is referred to as the **Modified Accelerated Cost Recovery System (MACRS)**.

Congress originally enacted ACRS for several reasons. First, Congress wanted to stimulate capital formation and improve United States competitiveness in international trade. Second, it realized that prior depreciation rules were unnecessarily complicated. Third, it wanted to alleviate the declining value of depreciation deductions caused by inflation.[20]

Original ACRS eliminated the need to determine an asset's useful life (although a taxpayer still needs to know the asset's CLADR class life). **Recovery periods** were set by statute, and were considerably shorter than those previously allowed. Thus, ACRS represented a move toward immediate expensing. In fact, ACRS in conjunction with the now repealed investment tax credit sometimes provided tax benefits as good as or better than expensing. Statutory recovery periods eliminated the controversies between taxpayers and the IRS over useful life determinations. Finally, shortened recovery periods mitigated the effects of inflation.

ACRS classified property into very few categories and specified the depreciation method for each class. The depreciation rates for each class of property appeared in tables, thereby simplifying depreciation calculations. ACRS also eliminated the need for estimated salvage value so that a taxpayer depreciates the entire cost of an asset. In addition, elimination of salvage value ended taxpayer-IRS disputes over this issue, further simplified depreciation calculations, and reflected movement away from economic depreciation.

Useful life is the period over which an asset is expected to be used in a taxpayer's business or in the production of income.

Salvage value is the estimated amount that the taxpayer will realize upon disposal of the asset when it is no longer useful to the taxpayer.

The **Accelerated Cost Recovery System (ACRS)** is a rapid depreciation system that applies to assets placed in service from 1981 through 1986.

The **Modified Accelerated Cost Recovery System (MACRS)** depreciation system is less rapid than ACRS and applies to assets placed in service after 1986.

The **recovery period** is the period over which the taxpayer recovers an asset's cost through depreciation deductions.

---

18 Rev. Proc. 83-35, 1983-1 CB 745, sets forth the class-life ranges under the CLADR system.

19 Reg. Sec. 167(a)-11(a)(1).

20 Staff of the Joint Committee on Taxation, *General Explanation of the Economic Recovery Tax Act of 1981,* (U.S. Government Printing Office, December 29, 1981), p. 75.

Congress introduced MACRS with the Tax Reform Act of 1986. MACRS retained most features of ACRS, but MACRS increased the recovery period for most assets. On the other hand, MACRS increased depreciation rates for personal property by allowing more accelerated methods than did ACRS, but it repealed accelerated methods for real property. MACRS represents a movement back in the direction of economic depreciation. In fact, "Congress believed ACRS could be made more neutral by increasing the recovery period for certain long-lived equipment, and by extending the recovery period of real property."[21] This remark indicates Congress' acceptance of economic depreciation, rather than expensing, as the means to achieve tax neutrality.

Because of the changes outlined in this brief historical survey, many taxpayers must continue to apply three sets of depreciation rules: pre-1981 depreciation, ACRS (1981 through 1986), and MACRS (post-1986). The date any property is placed in service by the taxpayer ordinarily determines which set of rules applies. Acquisition of property from a related taxpayer may require the new owner to continue the use of a depreciation method initiated by a former owner. The next three sections describe the three different sets of rules most frequently encountered today.

Before proceeding, however, we need to emphasize that the first year for depreciating property is the year it is **placed in service**, not necessarily the year the taxpayer acquires it. Property is placed in service "when first placed in a condition of readiness and availability for a specifically assigned function. . . ."[22] Thus, mere acquisition is insufficient to meet the placed-in-service requirement. For example, a taxpayer may acquire machinery at the end of one taxable year but not install it until the next taxable year. The machinery is placed in service in the installation year, not the acquisition year.

> An asset is deemed **placed in service** when it is ready and available for its assigned function.

DEPRECIATION OF PROPERTY PLACED IN SERVICE BEFORE 1981

> **Goal #6**
> Compute depreciation deductions under pre-1981 rules.

Section 167(a) contains the following general rule for depreciation:

> There shall be allowed as a depreciation deduction a reasonable allowance for the exhaustion, wear and tear (including a reasonable allowance for obsolescence)—
>
> (1) of property used in a trade or business, or
>
> (2) of property held for the production of income.

Note that depreciation applies to the same type of activities for which deductions are allowed under Sec. 162 and Sec. 212 (see Chapter 5).

The general rule applies to both personal and real tangible property as well as to intangible property, unless the intangible property does not have definite life. As used in this context, the adjective *personal* means property, other than realty; it does *not* refer to personal use property, such as clothing or a private residence. Depreciation does not apply to goodwill, corporate securities, inventory, or land. Nor does it apply to property held for personal use, such as personal automobiles and residences.

---

21 Staff of the Joint Committee on Taxation, *General Explanation of the Tax Reform Act of 1986*, (U.S. Government Printing Office, May 7, 1987), p. 98.

22 Reg. Sec. 1.167(a)-11(e)(1).

DEPRECIATION METHODS

Section 167(b) prescribes the following permissible depreciation methods:

1. The straight-line method;

2. The declining-balance method, but never to exceed twice the straight-line rate;

3. The sum-of-the-years-digits method; and

4. Any other consistent method that, for the first two-thirds of the asset's useful life, does not result in cumulative depreciation in any year exceeding the depreciation that would have resulted under the fastest permissible declining-balance method.

The availability of methods other than straight line depends on (1) whether the property is personal or real, (2) whether the property is tangible or intangible, (3) whether the property is new or used, (4) whether real property is residential rental property or nonresidential commercial property, and (5) the useful life of the property. Table 14-10 illustrates the permissible methods for various types of property.

Depreciation deductions are limited to cost or other basis. In other words, an asset may not be depreciated below zero. Also, under pre-1981 rules, an asset may not be depreciated below its salvage value. A special rule for salvage value applies to personal property placed in service after October 10, 1962, but before 1981. A taxpayer may reduce salvage by 10% of the property's basis. Thus, if salvage value is equal to or less than 10% of basis, it may be ignored completely. This rule is elective and available only for property having a useful life of at least three years.[23] The rule eliminates disputes between taxpayers and the IRS when salvage value is insignificant relative to cost. Example 14-8 demonstrates this rule.

The depreciation period begins when the asset is placed in service and ends when the asset is disposed of, or retired from service. Therefore, a taxpayer deducts a proportionate part of one year's depreciation in the first and last years.[24] If the taxpayer accounts for property on an item-by-item basis, depreciation is normally computed to the nearest full month. If the taxpayer uses group accounts, an **averaging convention**

> An **averaging convention** is a standardized method of determining the amount of depreciation allowed in the first and last years.

TABLE 14-10

Pre-1981 Depreciation Methods

| Type of Property | Depreciation Method* | |
	New Property	Used Property
Tangible personal property	SL, 200% DB, SYD, Other (units of production)	SL, 150% DB
Real property— residential rental	SL, 200% DB, SYD, Other (units of production)	SL, 125% DB[†]
Real property— nonresidential	SL, 150% DB, Other (units of production)	SL
Intangible property	SL	SL

*SL = straight-line; DB = declining balance; SYD = sum-of-the-years-digits. Useful life must be at least three years for methods other than SL to apply.
†Useful life must be at least 20 years for 125% DB to apply.

---

23 Sec. 167(f).

24 Reg. Sec. 1.167(a)-10(b).

may be used. For example, the taxpayer may take a half-year's depreciation in the first and last years.[25]

Straight-Line Method

Under the straight-line method, the taxpayer reduces an asset's cost (including commissions, fees, and other acquisition costs) by applicable salvage value and allocates equal amounts of the balance over the property's estimated useful life.[26]

EXAMPLE 14-8

On January 2, 1980, Sigma Company places in service a machine costing $20,000. The machine has a five-year estimated useful life and a $1,500 estimated salvage value. Because the estimated salvage value does not exceed $2,000 (10% x $20,000), Sigma elects to ignore it in computing depreciation. The straight-line depreciation rate equals 20% (1 ÷ 5), so Sigma's annual depreciation deduction equals $4,000 (20% x $20,000).

If estimated salvage value is $5,000 instead of $1,500, Sigma may elect to reduce the applicable salvage to $3,000 [$5,000 – (10% x $20,000)]. In this case, Sigma's annual depreciation deduction equals $3,400 [20% x ($20,000 – $3,000)]. Over the five years, Sigma deducts a total of $17,000 ($3,400 x 5), leaving $3,000 of the cost undepreciated because of salvage value.

Declining-Balance Method

Under the **declining-balance method**, the taxpayer applies a constant rate to the property's unrecovered cost.[27] Unrecovered cost equals the cost less accumulated depreciation (adjusted basis). Thus, the taxpayer applies a constant rate to a declining balance. The Code allows a maximum of twice the straight-line rate, referred to as either the 200% declining-balance method or the double declining-balance method. However, in certain cases, the law limits the taxpayer to the 125% or 150% declining-balance method (see Table 14-10).

> The **declining-balance method** is an accelerated depreciation method whereby a constant rate is applied to a declining balance.

EXAMPLE 14-9

Assume the same facts as in the first part of Example 14-8 (Sigma ignores the $1,500 estimate salvage under the 10% rule). Assume also that, instead of the straight-line method, Sigma uses the double declining-method Accordingly, the depreciation rate equals 40%, and Sigma deducts depreciation as follows:

1980	$ 8,000	($20,000 x 40%)
1981	4,800	($12,000 x 40%)
1982	2,880	($ 7,200 x 40%)
1983	2,160	($ 4,320 x 40%)
1984	2,160	($ 4,320 x 40%)
Total	$20,000	

Continued

---

25 *Ibid.*

26 Reg. Sec. 1.167(b)-1.

27 Reg. Sec. 1.167(b)-2.

EXAMPLE 14-9 (Con't.)

Note that Sigma did not use the double-declining method for the last two years. If it had, the deductions would have been $1,728 in Year 4 and $1,037 in Year 5, and Sigma would not have deducted the full $20,000 over the five-year period. To alleviate this problem, the Code allows a taxpayer to switch to the straight-line method without the IRS's prior approval.[28] The taxpayer should make the switch in the first year that straight-line depreciation exceeds declining balance depreciation, or Year 4 (1983) in this example. At the beginning of Year 4 the asset's remaining useful life is two years, so the straight-line rate equals 50% and applies to the unrecovered cost at that time.

If the applicable salvage value had exceeded zero, Sigma would still apply the declining-balance rate to the full cost unreduced by salvage value. Still, Sigma may not depreciate the asset below the applicable salvage value.

If the machine had been used property rather than new, Sigma would have been limited to the 150% declining-balance method. Accordingly, the depreciation rate would have been 30%.

Sum-of-the-Years-Digits Method

> The **sum-of-the-years digits method** is an accelerated depreciation method whereby a declining fraction is applied to a constant balance.

Under the **sum-of-the-years-digits method**, the taxpayer applies a declining rate to the property's cost less applicable salvage value. The declining rate is a fraction whose numerator is the asset's remaining useful life at the beginning of the year and whose denominator is a constant equal to the sum of digits in the asset's useful life.[29] The denominator can be calculated with the following formula: $[UL \times (UL + 1) / 2]$, where UL equals the useful life.

EXAMPLE 14-10

Assume the same facts as in the first part of Examples 14-8 and 14-9 (Sigma ignores the $1,500 estimate salvage under the 10% rule). Assume also that Sigma uses the sum-of-the-years-digits method. The denominator equals 15 [1 + 2 + 3 + 4 + 5; alternatively, 5 × (5 + 1)/2], and Sigma deducts depreciation as follows:

1980	$ 6,667	($20,000 x 5/15)
1981	$ 5,333	($20,000 x 4/15)
1982	$ 4,000	($20,000 x 3/15)
1983	$ 2,667	($20,000 x 2/15)
1984	$ 1,333	($20,000 x 1/15)
Total	$20,000	

Sigma has no reason to switch to the straight-line method because the company recovers the entire depreciable basis over the five-year period. If applicable salvage value exceeded zero, Sigma would apply the fractions to cost less the salvage value.

---

28 Sec. 167(e) and Reg. Sec. 167(e)-1.

29 Reg. Sec. 1.167(b)-3.

Other Depreciation Methods

The most common depreciation method other than those already discussed is the units-of-production (or use) method. Under this method, the taxpayer spreads the depreciable basis (for example, cost) over the estimated units of use or output. For instance, the depreciation rate of equipment might be based on barrels of oil produced, tons of ore mined, or hours of machine time used.

EXAMPLE 14-11

Mining Company placed in service some mining equipment costing $500,000. The company estimates that the mine will produce one million tons of ore. Thus, depreciation equals $.50 per ton produced ($500,000/1,000,000 tons). In Year 1, the company produces 80,000 tons of ore. Therefore, depreciation for Year 1 equals $40,000 (80,000 tons x $.50 per ton).

CHANGES IN DEPRECIATION METHOD AND USEFUL LIVES

As mentioned above, taxpayers using pre-1981 rules may change from a declining-balance method to the straight-line method without the IRS's permission. Taxpayers changing from the sum-of-the-years-digits method to the straight-line method have similar freedom for property subject to depreciation recapture (see Chapter 16).[30] Other changes in method require prior approval as described in Chapter 7.[31]

Also, Regulations allow a taxpayer to subsequently re-estimate the useful life of an asset if the change in the estimated useful life is significant *and* the taxpayer has clear and convincing support for the change.[32] Generally, the taxpayer spreads the unrecovered cost over the remaining useful life as redetermined.

Goal #7
Compute depreciation deductions under ACRS.

ACCELERATED COST RECOVERY SYSTEM FOR PROPERTY PLACED IN SERVICE IN YEARS 1981 THROUGH 1986

Section 168, before modification by the Tax Reform Act of 1986, contains the rules for the Accelerated Cost Recovery System (ACRS). When speaking of ACRS, we refer to Old Sec. 168; when speaking of Modified ACRS (MACRS), we simply refer to Sec. 168.

Under ACRS, a taxpayer determines the depreciation (cost recovery) deduction for any year by applying an **applicable percentage** to the **unadjusted basis of recovery property**.[33] We discuss each of the boldfaced terms in the following paragraphs.

RECOVERY PROPERTY

Recovery property is property that meets the following four tests:[34]

1. It is placed in service after 1980 (and before 1987);

Recovery property is property subject to the Accelerated Cost Recovery System (ACRS).

The **applicable percentage** is applied to the unadjusted basis of recovery property to obtain annual depreciation deductions under ACRS.

The **unadjusted basis of recovery property** is unreduced by depreciation deductions but is reduced by the Sec. 179 expense.

---

30 Sec. 167(e) and Reg. Sec. 167(e)-1.

31 See also Rev. Proc. 74-11, 1974-1 CB 420.

32 Reg. Sec. 1.167(a)-1(b).

33 Old Sec. 168(b).

34 Old Sec. 168(c)(1) and (e).

2. It is tangible property (as opposed to intangible property);

3. It is either (1) used in a trade or business or (2) held for the production of income; and

4. It is of a character normally subject to depreciation.

The last two tests are the same as those under pre-1981 depreciation rules. Thus, recovery property is subject to wear, tear, or obsolescence and does not include inventory or land. In addition, ACRS makes no distinction between new and used property.

The Code also excludes from the definition certain property that might otherwise qualify under ACRS. These exclusions are as follows:[35]

1. Property for which the taxpayer elects to use the units-of-production method or any other method not expressed in terms of years;

2. Property involved in a churning transaction;

3. Property used by public utility unless the utility uses the normalization method of accounting (wherein tax depreciation is consistent with the depreciation expense used for rate-making purposes); and

4. Motion picture films and video tapes.

Point 2 needs additional clarification. Anti-churning rules deter manipulative transactions between entities owned by the same taxpayers or between related taxpayers. Such taxpayers might *churn* property to obtain ACRS benefits for property actually placed in service before 1981.

EXAMPLE 14-12

Mr. Jones owns 100% of Churn Corporation stock. Mr. Jones acquired property in 1980 and, in a nontaxable transaction, transferred the property to his controlled corporation in 1981. The property is not recovery property to the corporation. Therefore, it is not allowed to use ACRS; it must use pre-1981 depreciation.

UNADJUSTED BASIS

The unadjusted basis for ACRS is cost or other basis unreduced by depreciation deductions. Also, salvage value is ignored under ACRS. Therefore, a taxpayer can recover the entire cost through depreciation deductions. However, the unadjusted basis *is* reduced by the amount expensed under Sec. 179 (discussed later in this chapter).[36] In addition, a special basis reduction rule sometimes applied in the years 1983 through 1985. If a taxpayer claimed a full investment tax credit (ITC), the taxpayer had to reduce the unadjusted basis by 50% of the ITC claimed. However, no basis reduction was required if the taxpayer elected to claim a reduced ITC.[37] As we will explain below, the unadjusted basis is a constant amount to which declining or straight-line percentages are applied.

The unadjusted basis of real property is the total cost of the entire property, excluding the cost of the land. Taxpayers may not treat components of a building, such

---

35 Old Sec. 168(e).

36 Old Sec. 168(d)(1).

37 Sec. 48(q).

as central air conditioning and heating units, as separate property to obtain short recovery periods. Accordingly, structural components of a building must be recovered as a whole and treated as constituent parts of the building.[38] However, a substantial improvement made to a building before 1987 is treated as separate property. A substantial improvement is one completed within a 24-month period with the cost equal to or exceeding 25% of the building's adjusted basis.[39]

If a taxpayer converts property from personal use to business or income producing use, the property is deemed placed in service on the date of conversion.[40] The unadjusted basis for ACRS is the lower of the asset's cost or fair market value on the conversion date.

APPLICABLE PERCENTAGE UNDER ACRS

To obtain the annual depreciation deduction, the taxpayer applies the applicable percentage to the unadjusted basis of recovery property. The applicable percentage depends on the class of recovery property and the underlying depreciation method. The percentages appear in published tables constructed with various combinations of accelerated and straight-line methods. Appendix 14A at the end of this chapter reproduces selected ACRS tables. To select the proper table and percentage, the taxpayer needs to know (1) the class of recovery property, (2) the recovery year, and (3) when the property was placed in service.

Classes of Recovery Property

The class of recovery property depends on the type of property and its class life under the previous CLADR system. The following list outlines the eight classes:[41]

1. *3-year property.* Tangible personal property having a CLADR class life of four years or less. Examples include automobiles, light trucks, and property used for research and experimentation.

2. *5-year property.* Tangible personal property that does not fall into any other class. Examples include machinery and equipment, furniture and fixtures, single-purpose agricultural structures, storage facilities (other than buildings) used in petroleum distribution, and public utility property not falling into the 10-year and 15-year classes.

3. *10-year property.* Tangible real property having a CLADR class life of 12.5 years or less, public utility property having a CLADR class life of more than 18 years but less than 25 years, manufactured homes, railroad cars, recreational facilities, theme parks, and other specialized property.

4. *15-year public utility property.* Public utility property with a CLADR class life exceeding 25 years.

5. *15-year property—low-income housing.* Rental real property qualifying as low-income housing placed in service in 1981 through 1986.

---

38 Prop. Reg. 1.168-2(e)(1).

39 Prop. Reg. 1.168-2(e)(4). This rule does not apply to improvements and additions made after 1986 (see Sec. 168(i)(6)).

40 Prop. Reg. 1.168-2(j)(l).

41 Old Sec. 168(c)(2) and Prop. Reg. Sec. 1.168-3(c).

6. *15-year real property.* Depreciable real property having a CLADR class life exceeding 12.5 years (other than low-income housing) placed in service from January 1, 1981 through March 15, 1984.

7. *18-year real property.* Depreciable real property having a CLADR class life exceeding 12.5 years (other than low-income housing) placed in service from March 16, 1984, through May 8, 1985.

8. *19-year real property.* Depreciable real property having a CLADR class life exceeding 12.5 years (other than low-income housing) placed in service from May 9, 1985, through December 31, 1986.

ACRS property used by most taxpayers falls into the 3-year, 5-year, 15-year real, 18-year real, and 19-year real property classes. The other classes contain highly specialized property. After the enactment of ACRS, Congress became concerned that 15 years was too short a recovery period for real property. Congress subsequently extended the recovery period to 18 years and then 19 years, which explains the three classes of real property and applicable dates. As we will show later, Congress further extended the recovery period under Modified ACRS.

Methods and Conventions

Table 14-1A contains the applicable percentages for property in the first four classes. The table percentages reflect the 150% declining-balance method with a switch to straight-line in the optimal year. The taxpayer may take one-half year's depreciation in the first year regardless of when during the year the property is placed in service. This **half-year convention** is built into the tables. The Code allows no depreciation in the year of disposition.[42]

> The **half-year convention** is an averaging convention that considers an asset to have been placed in service and disposed of at the midpoint of the year.

EXAMPLE 14-13

Fabco, Inc., acquired a lathe for its metal fabricating business for $20,000. The company placed the lathe in service on March 3, 1986. The CLADR system assigns a 12-year class life to property in this industry. Therefore, under ACRS, the lathe is 5-year property. Fabco makes no expensing or straight-line elections for this asset (discussed later in this chapter). If Fabco retains the lathe for its entire recovery period, it will deduct depreciation as follows (Table 14-1A):

Year	Amount	Computation
1986	$ 3,000	($20,000 x 15%)
1987	4,400	($20,000 x 22%)
1988	4,200	($20,000 x 21%)
1989	4,200	($20,000 x 21%)
1990	4,200	($20,000 x 21%)
Total	$20,000	

The applicable percentages are applied to a constant unadjusted basis. The declining-balance computations are built into the table percentages. For example, the first year percentage equals 15%, which is 30% for one-half year. The 30% figure equals the 20% straight-line rate times 150%. Note also that, because the

Continued

---

42 Old Sec. 168(d)(2)(B).

EXAMPLE 14-13 (Con't.)

property was placed in service before 1987, Fabco continues to use ACRS even though recovery periods extend into years after 1986.

Suppose that Fabco sells the lathe in 1988 instead of holding it for five years. Fabco deducts no depreciation in 1988, and the adjusted basis of the lathe at the time of sale equals $12,600 [$20,000 – ($3,000 + $4,400)].

Tables 14-2A through 14-5A contain the applicable percentages for 15-year, 18-year, and 19-year real property. All four tables reflect the 175% declining-balance method with a switch to straight-line in the optimal year. Monthly conventions are built into the tables. However, Tables 14-2A and 14-3A assume property is placed in service at the beginning of the month (**full-month convention**) while Tables 14-4A and 14-5A assume property is placed in service in the middle of the month (**mid-month convention**). The change in convention created two subclasses of 18-year real property. If the taxpayer disposes of real property before it is fully depreciated, the taxpayer may take a prorata deduction using a convention consistent with the table.

> The **full-month convention** is an averaging convention that considers an asset to have been placed in service and disposed of at the beginning of the month.
>
> The **mid-month convention** is an averaging convention that considers an asset to have been placed in service and disposed of at the midpoint of the month.

EXAMPLE 14-14

Safe Bank, Inc., acquires a bank building for $500,000 and places it in service on August 3, 1986. Thus, the building is 19-year real property. The bank sells the building on March 25, 1992. The bank makes no straight-line election. The bank's depreciation deductions using Table 14-5A are as follows:

1986	$ 17,500	($500,000 x 3.5%)
1987	44,500	($500,000 x 8.9%)
1988	40,500	($500,000 x 8.1%)
1989	36,500	($500,000 x 7.3%)
1990	33,000	($500,000 x 6.6%)
1991	30,000	($500,000 x 6.0%)
1992	5,729	($500,000 x 5.5% x 2.5/12)
Total	$207,729	

The bank uses the applicable percentages from Column 8 throughout the recovery period because the property was placed in service in August. In the disposition year, the bank uses the percentage from Column 8 (5.5%) to obtain a full year's depreciation but then prorates that amount based on the time in 1992 it held the property. Because of the mid-month convention, the bank is deemed to have sold the building in the middle of March. Therefore, in 1992, the bank is allowed depreciation for two and a half months (2.5/12). The adjusted basis of the building at the time of sale equals $292,271 ($500,000 – $207,729).

By now, businesses holding 3-year and 5-year property will have fully depreciated these assets. However, many business are still depreciating other classes of ACRS recovery property

Elective Straight-Line Rates

In lieu of accelerated cost recovery, taxpayers could elect to take straight-line depreciation over certain optional recovery periods.[43] Table 14-11 lists these optional

---

43 Old Sec. 168(b)(3).

TABLE 14-11

ACRS Optional Straight-Line Recovery Periods (1981–1986)

Property Class	Recovery Periods
3-year property	3, 5, or 12 years
5-year property	5, 12, or 25 years
10-year property	10, 25, or 35 years
15-year public utility property	15, 35, or 45 years
15-year property—low income housing	15, 35, or 45 years
15-year real property	15, 35, or 45 years
18-year real property	18, 35, or 45 years
19-year real property	19, 35, or 45 years

periods. For example, taxpayers owning 5-year property could elect to depreciate that property using the straight-line method over 5, 12, or 25 years. Except for 15-year, 18-year, and 19-year real property (and low-income housing), the election applies to all property in the class placed in service during the year. The election applies on a property-by-property basis for 15-year, 18-year, and 19-year real property (and low-income housing). Once elected, the taxpayer must use the optional method throughout the elected recovery period. The election affects only applicable percentages and recovery periods. Thus, other ACRS rules remain in effect.

SECTION 179 EXPENSE ELECTION

Under ACRS, taxpayers could elect to expense up to $5,000 of a property's cost. The election applied only to personal property used in a trade or business and placed in service in years 1982 through 1986. The taxpayer had to reduce the unadjusted basis of the property for the portion expensed under Sec. 179. Because a similar provision exists under Modified ACRS, we will present an example of expensing when discussing that system.

Goal #8
Compute depreciation deductions under MACRS.

MODIFIED ACCELERATED COST RECOVERY SYSTEM FOR PROPERTY PLACED IN SERVICE AFTER 1986

As mentioned earlier in this chapter, Congress enacted the Modified Accelerated Cost Recovery System (MACRS) as part of the Tax Reform Act of 1986. Under ACRS, 3-year and 5-year recovery periods for most personal property, and a 19-year recovery period for most real property, were quite short compared to historical depreciation rates, particularly in conjunction with the investment tax credit (ITC) for personal property. The 1986 Act repealed the ITC for property placed in service after 1985, and introduced MACRS for property placed in service after 1986. MACRS retains most features of ACRS but lengthens recovery periods, allows the double-declining method for some personal property, allows only straight-line depreciation for real property, increases the Sec. 179 expensing limit to $10,000, and modifies the averaging conventions for personal property.

PROPERTY SUBJECT TO MACRS

Section 168(a) states the following general rule for property placed in service after 1986:

> Except as otherwise provided in this section, the depreciation deduction provided by section 167(a) for any tangible property shall be determined by using—
>
> (1) the applicable depreciation method,
>
> (2) the applicable recovery period, and
>
> (3) the applicable convention.

The reference to Sec. 167(a) means the property must be subject to exhaustion, wear, tear, and obsolescence. The property must also either (1) be used in the taxpayer's trade or business or (2) be held for the production of income. These requirements are consistent with those under pre-1981 rules and ACRS.

The MACRS rules contain a new set of anti-churning rules. Under these rules, property subject to ACRS continues to be subject to ACRS if transferred after 1986 in certain related party and nontaxable transactions.

CLASSES OF MACRS PROPERTY

The applicable depreciation method, recovery period, and convention depend on the class in which MACRS property falls. As with ACRS, the MACRS classes depend on the type of property and its class life under the previous CLADR system. However, the Code specifically assigns some property to classes other than the class conforming to the asset's CLADR life. The Code prescribes the following nine classes of property:[44]

1. *3-year property*. Property having a CLADR class life of four years or less. However, the Code specifically excludes automobiles, light trucks, and property used for research and experimentation from this class. Consequently, this class contains few assets. Examples of properties still remaining in this class include certain race horses, breeding hogs, and over-the-road tractors.

2. *5-year property*. Property having a CLADR class life of more than four years but less than ten years. This class also includes automobiles, light and heavy trucks, personal property used for research and experimentation, semiconductor manufacturing equipment, and qualified technological equipment, and certain other specialized property.

3. *7-year property*. Property having a CLADR class life of ten or more years but less than 16 years. This class also includes *personal* property (1) having no CLADR class life and (2) not classified by the Code into a specific group. Examples of 7-year property include office furniture, fixtures, and equipment; most manufacturing machinery and equipment; and any railroad track.

4. *10-year property*. Property having a CLADR class life of 16 or more years but less than 20 years. This class also includes single-purpose agricultural structures and any tree or vine bearing fruit or nuts.

---

44 Sec. 168(e).

5. *15-year property.* Property having a CLADR class life of 20 or more years but less than 25 years. This class includes municipal wastewater treatment plants and telephone distribution plants.

6. *20-year property.* Property having a CLADR class life of 25 or more years. This class includes municipal sewers. This class does not include real property having a CLADR class life of 27.5 years or more.

7. *Residential rental property.* A building or structure that generates 80% or more of its gross rental income from dwelling units.

8. *Nonresidential real property.* Real property having a CLADR class life of 27.5 years or more, which is not residential rental property. This class also includes *real* property (1) having no CLADR class life and (2) not classified by the Code into a specific group.

9. *Railroad grading or tunnel bores.* The Technical and Miscellaneous Revenue Act of 1988 added this special class.

Table 14-12, taken from Rev. Proc. 87-56,[45] shows a few classes of depreciable assets. A taxpayer needing to classify property must refer to Sec. 168(e), Rev. Proc. 87-56, and any Regulations the Treasury Department might issue. In Table 14-12, the column labeled Class Life refers to CLADR midpoint class lives, the column labeled **General Depreciation System** refers to normal MACRS, and the column labeled **Alternative Depreciation System** refers to an alternative system discussed later in this chapter.

MACRS property used by most taxpayers fall into the 5-year, 7-year, residential rental, and nonresidential real property classes. The other classes contain highly specialized property.

> The **General Depreciation System** is the normal depreciation system under MACRS.
>
> The **Alternative Depreciation System** under MACRS allows slower depreciation deductions than the General Depreciation System.

APPLICABLE METHODS, RECOVERY PERIODS, AND CONVENTIONS

Table 14-13 summarizes the applicable methods, recovery periods, and conventions for the nine classes of property. This table refers only to the MACRS General Depreciation System with no special elections (discussed later in this chapter). Using the applicable methods, recovery periods, and conventions, the IRS published tables in Rev. Proc. 87-57 containing appropriate depreciation percentages.[46] Appendix 14B at the end of this chapter reproduces selected MACRS tables, which are labeled Tables 14-1B through 14-7B. As with ACRS, the taxpayer applies these percentages to the unadjusted basis of MACRS property.

A taxpayer must depreciate an improvement or addition to existing property the same way the underlying property would be depreciated if placed in service at the time the taxpayer makes the improvement or addition.[47] For example, if the taxpayer improves ACRS property after 1986, the improvement is treated as MACRS property.

---

45 1987-2 CB 674.

46 1987-2 CB 687.

47 Sec. 168(i)(6).

TABLE 14-12

Illustrative Class Lives and Modified ACRS Recovery Periods

Asset Class	Description of Assets Included	Class Life (in years)	Recovery Periods (in years) General Depreciation System	Recovery Periods (in years) Alternative Depreciation System
SPECIFIC DEPRECIABLE ASSETS USED IN ALL BUSINESS ACTIVITIES, EXCEPT AS NOTED:				
00.11	Office Furniture, Fixtures, and Equipment: Includes furniture and fixtures that are not a structural component of a building. Includes such assets as desks, files, safes, and communications equipment. Does not include communications equipment that is included in other classes.	10	7	10
00.12	Information Systems: Includes computers and their peripheral equipment used in administering normal business transactions and the maintenance of business records, their retrieval and analysis. Information systems are defined as: 1) Computers: A computer is a programmable electronically activated device capable of accepting information, applying prescribed processes to the information, and supplying the results of these processes with or without human intervention. It usually consists of a central processing unit containing extensive storage, logic, arithmetic, and control capabilities. Excluded from this category are adding machines, electronic desk calculators, etc. and other equipment described in class 00.13. 2) Peripheral equipment consists of the auxiliary machines which are designed to be placed under control of the central processing unit. Nonlimiting examples are: Card readers, card punches, magnetic tape feeds, high speed printers, optical character readers, tape cassettes, mass storage units, paper tape equipment, keypunches, data entry devices, teleprinters, terminals, tape drives, disc drives, disc files, disc packs, visual image projector tubes, card sorters, plotters, and collators. Peripheral equipment may be used on-line or off-line. Does not include equipment that is an integral part of other capital equipment that is included in other classes of economic activity, i.e., computers used primarily for process or production control, switching, channeling, and automating distributive trades and services such as point of sale (POS) computer systems. Also, does not include equipment of a kind used primarily for amusement or entertainment of the user.	6	5*	5*
00.13	Data handling Equipment, except Computers: Includes only typewriters, calculators, adding and accounting machines, copiers, and duplicating equipment.	6	5	6
00.21	Airplanes (airframes and engines), except those used in commercial or contract carrying or passengers or freight, and all helicopters (airframes and engines).	6	5	6
00.22	Automobiles, Taxis.	3	5	5
00.23	Buses.	9	5	9
00.241	Light General-Purpose Trucks: Includes trucks for use over the road (actual unloaded weight less than 13,000 pounds).	4	5	5
00.242	Heavy General-Purpose trucks: Includes heavy general-purpose trucks, concrete ready mix-truckers, and ore trucks, for use over the road (actual unloaded weight 13,000 pounds or more).	6	5	6

*Property described in asset class 00.12 which is qualified technological equipment as defined in section 168(i)(2) is assigned a recovery period of 5 years notwithstanding its class life.

TABLE 14-13

MACRS—General
Depreciation
System

Property Class	Applicable Recovery Period (Years)	Applicable Method*	Applicable Convention[†]
3-year property	3	200% DB w/switch to SL[‡]	HY or MQ
5-year property	5	200% DB w/switch to SL[‡]	HY or MQ
7-year property	7	200% DB w/switch to SL[‡]	HY or MQ
10-year property	10	200% DB w/switch to SL[§]	HY or MQ
15-year property	15	150% DB w/switch to SL	HY or MQ
20-year property	20	150% DB w/switch to SL	HY or MQ
Residential rental property	27.5	SL	MM
Nonresidential real property	31.5	SL	MM
Railway grading and tunnel bores	50	SL	MM

*DB = declining balance; SL = straight-line.
[†]HY = half-year; MQ = mid-quarter; MM = mid-month.
[‡]Limited to 150% DB for any property used in a farming business.
[§]Limited to SL for trees or vines bearing fruit or nuts.

Conventions

The applicable methods and recovery methods in Table 14-13 are self-explanatory. The applicable conventions, however, require further explanation. The Code defines three conventions as follows:[48]

1. *Half-year convention.* Treats property placed in service (or disposed of) during the taxable year as placed in service (or disposed of) at the midpoint of the year.

2. *Mid-month convention.* Treats property placed in service (or disposed of) during any month as placed in service (or disposed of) at the midpoint of that month.

3. *Mid-quarter convention.* Treats property placed in service (or disposed of) during any quarter of the taxable year as placed in service (or disposed of) at the midpoint of that quarter.

The half-year convention applies to all but the last three classes in Table 14-13. The mid-month convention applies to the last three classes and operates the same way as described above for ACRS 19-year real property.

The half-year convention differs slightly from that used under ACRS. Under ACRS, the applicable percentages were adjusted so that all cost recovery occurred by the end of the recovery period. Under MACRS, a half-year's depreciation trails into an extra taxable year. For example, depreciation for MACRS 5-year property extends over six taxable years with a half-year's depreciation in the first and sixth years. Also, ACRS allowed no depreciation in the year the taxpayer disposed of personal property.

48 Sec. 168(d).

Under MACRS, the taxpayer may claim a half-year's depreciation in the disposition year if the asset is not already fully depreciated.

The **mid-quarter convention** applies *in lieu of* the half-year convention if the aggregate bases of property placed in service during the last three months of the taxable year exceed 40% of the aggregate bases of property placed in service during the entire taxable year. With exceptions noted in the next two sentences, the mid-quarter convention, when applicable, applies to all property placed in service during the year, not just property placed in service during the last three months. The mid-quarter convention and the 40% computation do *not* apply to residential rental property, nonresidential real property, railroad grading, and tunnel bores. In addition, the 40% computation does not apply to property placed in service and disposed of during the same taxable year. Congress added the mid-quarter convention to prevent taxpayers from claiming a half-year's depreciation when large amounts of property are placed in service near the end of the year.

> The **mid-quarter convention** is an averaging convention that considers an asset to have been placed in service and disposed of at the midpoint of the quarter.

Examples

The following examples demonstrate the operation of the MACRS rules under the General Depreciation System.

EXAMPLE 14-15

Fabco, Inc., acquired a lathe for its metal fabricating business for $20,000. The company placed the lathe in service on March 3, 1992. Rev. Proc. 87-56 assigns this asset to the 7-year property class. Fabco makes no special elections for this asset and acquires no other property during the year. If Fabco retains the lathe for its entire recovery period, it will deduct depreciation as follows (Table 14-1B):

1992	$ 2,858	($20,000 x 14.29%)
1993	4,898	($20,000 x 24.49%)
1994	3,498	($20,000 x 17.49%)
1995	2,498	($20,000 x 12.49%)
1996	1,786	($20,000 x 8.93%)
1997	1,784	($20,000 x 8.92%)
1998	1,786	($20,000 x 8.93%)
1999	892	($20,000 x 4.46%)
Total	$20,000	

Note that the depreciation deductions are spread over eight taxable years with a half year's depreciation in the first and last years.

As with ACRS, the MACRS percentages are applied to a constant unadjusted basis. The declining-balance computations are built into the table percentages. For example, the double declining rate equals 28.58%, which is the 14.28% straight-line rate ($1/7$) times 200%. The percentages for the first three years are

Year 1(half-year): .5 x 28.58% = 14.29%
Year 2: 28.58% x (100% – accum. depr. of 14.29%) = 24.49%
Year 3: 28.58% x (100% – accum. depr. of 38.78%) = 17.49%

Continued

EXAMPLE 14-15 (Con't.)

Suppose that Fabco sells the lathe in 1994 instead of holding it for eight years. Fabco deducts $1,749 ($3,498 x .5) in 1994, and the adjusted basis of the lathe at the time of sale equals $14,495 [$20,000 – ($2,858 + $4,898 + $1,749)].

Compare these results to those in Example 14-13.

EXAMPLE 14-16

Safe Bank, Inc., acquires a bank building for $500,000 and places it in service on August 3, 1992. The building is nonresidential real property. The bank sells the building on March 25, 1998. The bank's depreciation deductions using Table 14-7B are as follows:

1992	$ 5,950	($500,000 x 1.190%)
1993	15,875	($500,000 x 3.175%)
1994	15,875	($500,000 x 3.175%)
1995	15,875	($500,000 x 3.175%)
1996	15,875	($500,000 x 3.175%)
1997	15,875	($500,000 x 3.175%)
1998	3,307	($500,000 x 3.175% x 2.5/12)
Total	$88,632	

The bank uses the MACRS percentages from Column 8 throughout the recovery period because the property was placed in service in August. The table uses the mid-month convention. For example, the straight-line rate equals 3.1746% (1/31.5), and the first year rate equals 1.19% (3.1746% x 4.5/12). In the disposition year, the bank uses the percentage from Column 8 (3.175%) to obtain a full year's depreciation but then prorates that amount based on the time in 1998 it held the property. Because of the mid-month convention, the bank is deemed to have sold the building in the middle of March. Therefore, in 1998, the bank is allowed depreciation for two and a half months (2.5/12). The adjusted basis of the building at the time of sale equals $411,368 ($500,000 – $88,632).

Compare these results to those in Example 14-14.

EXAMPLE 14-17

In 1992, Aleph Company placed in service the following items of 5-year property:

January 12	$ 30,000
May 6	20,000
September 23	10,000
December 18	60,000
Total	$120,000

Because the company placed more than 40% of the total property in service during the last three months ($60,000/$120,000 = 50%), it must use the mid-

Continued

EXAMPLE 14-17 (Con't.)

quarter convention for all the property. Aleph's depreciation deduction for 1992 is as follows:

Asset 1	$10,500	($30,000 x 35% from Table 14-2B)
Asset 2	5,000	($20,000 x 25 from Table 14-3B)
Asset 3	1,500	($10,000 x 15 from Table 14-4B)
Asset 4	3,000	($60,000 x 5 from Table 14-5B)
Total	$20,000	

If the company could have used the half-year convention, the depreciation deduction would have been $24,000 ($120,000 x 20% from Table 14-1B) rather than $20,000. This reduction is the most common result of the mid-quarter convention; that is, it generally reduces the amount of the MACRS deduction otherwise available. However, the mid-quarter convention can be advantageous to the taxpayer. For example, suppose Aleph placed $70,000 in service in the first quarter and $50,000 in the last quarter. The mid-quarter convention still applies ($50,000/$120,000 = 41.67%), and the depreciation deduction is as follows:

Asset 1	$24,500	($70,000 x 35% from Table 14-1B)
Asset 2	2,500	($50,000 x 5 from Table 14-5B)
Total	$27,000	

The total deduction now exceeds the half-year amount.

Return to the original example and assume the company sells Asset 3 on April 2, 1993. For this asset, the company deducts $1,275 in 1993 ($10,000 x 34% from Table 14-4B x 1.5/4). The company could have used 4.5/12 instead of 1.5/4 in this calculation because the property is deemed sold in the middle of May, the midpoint of the second quarter.

STRAIGHT-LINE ELECTION

A taxpayer may elect to use straight-line depreciation instead of the declining-balance method.[49] The recovery periods and conventions remain the same as under the MACRS General Depreciation System discussed above. Rev. Proc. 87-57 contains applicable tables, which are not reproduced in this text. The taxpayer may make the election for one or more classes of property. Once made, the election is irrevocable and applies to all assets in that class placed in service during the taxable year. Although this election is not widely used, it has been an important option for a few large international corporations characterized by domestic losses and large foreign tax credits.

EXAMPLE 14-18

In 1992, Beth Company places in service several items of 5-year property and 7-year property. The company elects the straight-line method for the 7-year property. The company must continue using the straight-line method over the

Continued

---

49 Sec. 168(b)(5).

EXAMPLE 14-18 (Con't.)

entire recovery period for all 7-year property placed in service in 1992. However, if the company acquires 7-year property in 1993, it uses accelerated MACRS for that property unless the company makes another straight-line election for property placed in service in 1993. Thus, the election must be made on a year-by-year basis for newly acquired property.

ALTERNATIVE DEPRECIATION SYSTEM

Section 168(g) prescribes an Alternative Depreciation System (ADS) that taxpayers must use for the following property:

1. Tangible property used predominantly outside the United States;

2. Property leased to a tax-exempt entity;

3. Property financed with tax-exempt bonds; and

4. Property imported from countries maintaining trade restrictions or engaging in discriminatory acts if covered by an Executive order.

In addition, taxpayers must use the ADS for determining corporate earnings and profits and a modified version of the ADS for calculating the alternative minimum tax (see Chapter 19). Finally, taxpayers may *elect* to use the ADS even if not required.

Taxpayers determine the ADS depreciation deduction by using the straight-line method with the applicable convention over the applicable ADS recovery period. The conventions under the ADS are the same as under the General Depreciation System. If a taxpayer elects the ADS, the taxpayer may also elect to use the 150% declining-balance method instead of straight-line depreciation for property other than residential rental property, nonresidential real property, railroad grading, and tunnel bores.[50]

The recovery period under the ADS is similar to that under the General Depreciation System with notable exceptions. For example, the ADS recovery period for personal property with no class life is 12 years instead of seven, and the ADS recovery period for residential rental property and nonresidential real property is 40 years instead of 27.5 and 31.5 years. Section 168(g)(3) lists a number of other special ADS recovery periods. The ADS column of Rev. Proc. 87-56 reflects these recovery periods, and Rev. Proc. 87-57 contains appropriate percentage tables for taxpayers using the ADS.

For property other than residential rental property and nonresidential real property, a taxpayer makes an ADS election on a class-by-class, year-by-year basis. Thus, the election applies to all property in the elected class placed in service during the taxable year. For residential rental property and nonresidential real property, a taxpayer makes an ADS election on a property-by-property basis. Once made, the ADS election is irrevocable.[51]

Generally, an ADS election is not advantageous to the taxpayer because depreciation deductions are slower than under the General Depreciation System. However, because the Code requires the ADS for the alternative minimum tax (AMT) calculation, taxpayers may consider an ADS election for regular tax purposes to avoid an

---

50 Sec. 168(b)(2)(C), (b)(5), and (c)(2). The 150% declining-balance method also applies to the alternative minimum tax calculation (Sec. 56(a)(1)).

51 Sec. 168(g)(7).

AMT adjustment (see Chapter 19). Also, taxpayers who expect substantial future tax rate increases might benefit by postponing depreciation deductions under the ADS.

OTHER DEPRECIATION METHODS AFTER 1986

Under Sec. 168(f), MACRS does not apply if the taxpayer *elects* to exclude property that is depreciated using the units-of-production method or any other method not expressed in terms of years. MACRS also does not apply to certain public utility property not using the normalization method, films and video tapes, sound recordings, and property to which the anti-churning provisions apply. Accordingly, a taxpayer would apply the pre-1981 rules of Sec. 167(b) to these properties. However, the Revenue Reconciliation Act of 1990 repealed Sec. 167(b) for property placed in service after October 27, 1990. The 1990 Act made an exception for property involved in a churning transaction but makes no reference to other property excluded from MACRS by Sec. 168(f). The 1990 Act, therefore, introduces ambiguity as to how a taxpayer should depreciate property excluded from MACRS.

SECTION 179 EXPENSE ELECTION

The Tax Reform Act of 1986 retained the **Sec. 179 expense** *election* for depreciable personal property used in a trade or business and placed in service after 1986, but the 1986 Act made several changes. Section 179 now allows taxpayers to expense up to $10,000 of the asset's cost in the year the asset is placed in service. However, the $10,000 limitation must be reduced dollar-for-dollar by the amount that total Sec. 179 property placed in service during the year exceeds $200,000. Accordingly, a business that places in service Sec. 179 property costing over $210,000 in a given year obtains no benefit from Sec. 179. The reduction under this rule is lost forever; it may not be carried over. Also, the unadjusted basis for MACRS deductions must be reduced by the amount expensed under Sec. 179.

> The **Sec. 179 expense** is an elective first-year deduction of an asset's cost, limited to $10,000.

The Code imposes several other restrictions on the Sec. 179 election. First, if the potential expense exceeds taxable income from the taxpayer's trade or business (computed without regard to the Sec. 179 expense), the expense deduction is limited to taxable income. If the expense is reduced under this rule, the taxpayer carries the disallowed portion over to the next taxable year, subject to limitations in that year. Second, if the taxpayer converts Sec. 179 property from business to personal use before the recovery period ends, special recapture rules require the taxpayer to recognize the Sec. 179 benefit as income. The benefit equals the excess of the amount expensed over the cumulative depreciation deductions on the expensed portion of the asset's cost that would have been allowed without the Sec. 179 election. Third, the Code treats a married couple as one person for the $10,000 limitation. Therefore, if a couple files separate returns, they must divide the limitation equally unless they elect a different allocation. Finally, special rules apply to flow-through entities and controlled groups of corporations.

The taxpayer may choose which property to expense. However, to be eligible, property must be purchased tangible personal property used in the taxpayer's trade or business. For example, the Sec. 179 election cannot apply to real property or property acquired in nontaxable or partially taxable exchanges. Once made, the taxpayer may not revoke the election without the IRS's consent.

EXAMPLE 14-19

As in Example 14-15, assume that Fabco, Inc., acquired a lathe for its metal fabricating business for $20,000 and placed the lathe in service on March 3, 1992. Assume also that on May 5, 1992, Fabco placed in service another item of 7-year property costing $182,000. Fabco makes a Sec. 179 expense election for the lathe. The total cost of Sec. 179 property is $202,000 ($20,000 + $182,000). Because this total exceeds $200,000 by $2,000, Fabco may only expense a maximum of $8,000 ($10,000 – $2,000). Because it made the election, Fabco applies the Table 14-1B percentages to $12,000 ($20,000 – $8,000). If Fabco retains the lathe for its entire recovery period, it will deduct depreciation on the lathe as follows:

1992 Expense	$ 8,000	
1992	1,715	($12,000 x 14.29%)
1993	2,939	($12,000 x 24.49%)
1994	2,099	($12,000 x 17.49%)
1995	1,499	($12,000 x 12.49%)
1996	1,072	($12,000 x 8.93%)
1997	1,070	($12,000 x 8.92%)
1998	1,071	($12,000 x 8.93%)
1999	535	($12,000 x 4.46%)
Total	$20,000	

Compare this result to that in Example 14-15; the total deduction still equals $20,000, but expensing accelerates depreciation deductions. Fabco also depreciates the $182,000 paid for the other property using Table 14-1B.

SPECIAL LIMITATIONS ON LISTED PROPERTY AND LUXURY AUTOMOBILES

> **Listed property** is specific property subject to the limitations of Sec. 280F.
>
> **Luxury automobiles** are those of sufficiently high cost that the depreciation deduction limitations of Sec. 280F(a) apply.

Section 280F imposes special limitations on **listed property** and **luxury automobiles.**[52] Congress enacted the limitation because it believed that

> accelerated cost recovery should be directed to encourage capital formation, rather than to subsidize the element of personal consumption associated with the use of very expensive automobiles.... Congress was also concerned that many taxpayers claimed...accelerated depreciation with respect to automobiles and other property used primarily for personal or investment use rather than in the conduct of a trade or business.[53]

Listed Property

Listed property includes

1. Any passenger automobile;

---

52 Although Sec. 280F generally applies to property placed in service after June 18, 1984, we are restricting our discussion to that portion of Sec. 280F that applies to property placed in service after 1986.

53 Staff of the Joint Committee on Taxation, *General Explanation of the Revenue Provisions of the Deficit Reduction Act of 1984,* (U.S. Government Printing Office, December 31, 1984), p. 559.

2. Any other property used as a means of transportation;

3. Any property used for entertainment, recreation, or amusement;

4. Any computer or peripheral equipment;

5. Any cellular telephone; and

6. Any other property specified in Regulations.

A passenger automobile means any four-wheeled vehicle manufactured for street and highway use and weighing 6,000 pounds or less. The definition includes a truck or van (unless exempted under Regulations) but does not include ambulances, hearses, and vehicles used in the business of transporting persons or property. Computer and peripheral equipment is not considered listed property if used exclusively at a regular business establishment and is owned or leased by the person operating the business establishment.

 If the taxpayer's *business use* of listed property *exceeds* 50%, the taxpayer may claim the general MACRS deduction for the portion of property used for business and for the production of income. Regulations refer to combined usage as business/investment use.[54] Production-of-income (investment) use, however, does not count toward the 50% business use test. Therefore, listed property whose investment use equals or exceeds 50% can never satisfy the 50% business use test. If business use does not exceed 50%, the taxpayer must use the Alternative Depreciation System (straight-line only) on the business/investment portion. Moreover, the taxpayer may not make the Sec. 179 expense election.

EXAMPLE 14-20

Ms. Garza is a self-employed consultant and also manages her own portfolio of investments. In 1992, she placed in service computer equipment costing $15,000. She uses the equipment 60% for the consulting business, 30% for investment analysis, and 10% for personal use. Because business use (60%) exceeds 50%, she may claim the general MACRS deduction on 90% (60% + 30%) of the cost ($13,500). She may also make the Sec. 179 election with respect to $9,000 of the cost. Section 179 applies only to business use ($15,000 x 60%).[55]

 Suppose instead that Ms. Garza uses the equipment 40% for business, 40% for investment analysis, and 20% for personal use. Business use does not exceed 50%. Therefore, Ms. Garza must use straight-line depreciation under the Alternative Depreciation System for 80% of the cost, and she may not make a Sec. 179 election.

 The Code allows no depreciation for listed property owned and used by an employee unless the property (1) is used for the convenience of the employer *and* (2) is required as a condition of employment. For example, if an individual employed by a CPA firm takes work home and uses his or her personal computer, the CPA may not depreciate any portion of the computer's cost.

---

54 Temp. Reg. Sec. 1.280F-6T(d)(3).

55 Sec. 179(d)(1) and Reg. Sec. 1.179-1(d) and (e).

Luxury Automobiles

Section 280F(a) imposes limitations on the amount of depreciation allowed on passenger automobiles. This Code section does not define luxury automobile. It merely prescribes the limitations, and any automobile subject to the limitations is by implication a luxury automobile. During the MACRS recovery period, the taxpayer deducts the lesser of the Sec. 280F(a) limitation or the MACRS deduction (including the Sec. 179 expense). For years after the normal recovery period, the taxpayer depreciates the automobile at a specified rate until the vehicle is fully depreciated. The Code requires the Sec. 280F(a) limitations to be adjusted for inflation each year. For automobiles placed in service in 1991, the limitations follow:[56]

First year	$2,660
Second year	4,300
Third year	2,550
Each succeeding year	1,575

EXAMPLE 14-21

Rich Company provides its Chief Executive Officer (CEO) with an automobile exclusively for business purposes. Thus, business use is 100%. On June 30, 1991, the company placed in service an automobile (5-year property) costing $20,000. The company makes no Sec. 179 expense election. Table 14-14 schedules the allowable depreciation deductions. The company still recovers the full $20,000, but because of Sec. 280F the depreciation deductions occur much more slowly than under MACRS.

If business use were 80% instead of 100%, Rich Company would deduct 80% of the amounts in Column 5. Column 6 shows the depreciation deductions for 80% business use. In fact, whenever business use is less than 100%, the taxpayer computes the depreciation deductions based on 100% business use and then applies the actual business use percentage to the resulting amounts.

AMORTIZATION OF INTANGIBLE ASSETS

The cost of intangible assets having a definite, limited life may be written off over the life of the asset. This interperiod allocation of intangibles is called amortization rather than depreciation. Intangibles may be amortized on the straight-line basis only; taxpayers may not use accelerated methods, ACRS, or MACRS. The lives of some intangible assets are limited by law (for example, patents—17 years and copyrights—the life of the author plus 50 years), and this legal life is normally the recovery period for amortization. The lives of other intangible assets (such as trademarks, franchises, and covenants not to compete) are sometimes limited by contractual agreement. Finally, the lives of some intangible assets are arguably limited by economic conditions.

The cost of intangible assets having no definite life may not be amortized under current law. For example, goodwill acquired in a business combination may not be amortized for tax purposes even though it is amortized for financial reporting. The government is currently rethinking this policy because of (1) an increasing amount of

56 Rev. Proc. 91-30, 1991–30 IRB 27.

1 Year	2 MACRS*	3 Sec. 280F(a) Limitation	4 Unrecovered Cost†	5 Deduction 100%‡	6 Deduction 80%§
1991	$ 4,000	$2,660	$20,000	$ 2,660	$ 2,128
1992	6,400	4,300	17,340	4,300	3,440
1993	3,840	2,550	13,040	2,550	2,040
1994	2,304	1,575	10,490	1,575	1,260
1995	2,304	1,575	8,915	1,575	1,260
1996	1,152	1,575	7,340	1,575#	1,260
1997		1,575	5,765	1,575	1,260
1998		1,575	4,190	1,575	1,260
1999		1,575	2,615	1,575	1,260
2000		1,575	1,040	1,040	832
Total	$20,000			$20,000	$16,000

*From Table 14-1B.
†Unrecovered cost as of the beginning of the year; reduced each year by the previous year's deduction from Column 5.
‡Years 1991–1995: lesser of Column 2, Column 3, or Column 4.
Years 1996–2000: lesser of Column 3 or Column 4.
§Column 5 times 80%
#The company may deduct $1,575 in 1996 (Year 6) even though it exceeds the MACRS deduction ($1,152). Post-recovery period depreciation is the lesser of the Sec. 280F(a) limitation or the unrecovered cost.

litigation over the amortization of various intangibles and (2) international competition with countries that allow tax deductions for the amortization of goodwill and other intangible assets. Furthermore, the Code already allows the arbitrary amortization of a few costs that might otherwise be unamortizable. For example, a taxpayer may elect to expense research and experimental expenditure or alternatively elect to amortize the expenditures over 60 months or more.[57] As another example, a corporation may elect to amortize certain organizational expenditures over 60 months or more.[58] Hence, more changes in this area of the law seem very likely in the next few years. Revenue considerations are likely to control the speed of change to the present law.

DEPLETION IN THE EXTRACTIVE INDUSTRIES

Goal #9
Compute the depletion deduction.

The removal through production of irreplaceable natural resources, such as metal ores, oil, gas, and other minerals, is referred to as physical *depletion*. As the resources are produced and sold (or used in making products), the owner of the mineral property interest from which the resources are produced is allowed a deduction for depletion. Conceptually, the depletion deduction is a cost-recovery concept similar to depreciation. However, throughout the history of tax law, various political, economic, and

57 Sec. 174.
58 Sec. 248.

national security factors have combined to produce a depletion system very unlike depreciation systems. In most cases, owners of economic interests in natural resources are now allowed a depletion deduction based on amortization of costs or, if larger, a deduction based on income from that property (either gross income from the property involved or net taxable income before depletion). The subject of depletion in the extractive industries is far more complex than suggested in the following discussions, which merely summarizes the basic aspects of the depletion process.

DEPLETION FOR THE PRODUCER

Taxpayers who operate mines or producing oil and gas wells customarily acquire the physical properties by leasing them from the mineral owners, who may or may not be the owners of the land surface. In relatively few instances, the producer may obtain the mineral rights through purchase of both land and mineral rights. The owner of the operating interest is allowed a deduction for depletion as the natural resource is produced and sold. Depletion is computed separately for each individual mineral property. Essentially, each mine is a separate property and each oil and gas lease is a separate property. However, in certain instances mines may be combined or leases may be combined into a single property. Similarly, in narrowly defined instances, a single lease may be divided into more than one mineral property.

Determining the Cost of the Mineral Rights

The basis for computing cost depletion is the capitalized costs of the mineral rights. Determination of the mineral rights cost varies slightly between mining operations and oil and gas producing operations.

Oil and Gas Operations.   The lessee of an oil and gas lease pays the lessor a *bonus* to sign the lease contract. This bonus, along with any related expenditures, such as brokers' fees, legal fees, and recording fees, must be capitalized as mineral rights costs and become part of the basis for *cost depletion*. Normally, the only other capitalized costs of an oil and gas property are *exploration costs*. Exploration costs are costs incurred in finding underground formations on which to drill a test well. They include the costs of geological and geophysical surveys, including such activities as gravimetric surveys, magnetic surveys, soil chemical analysis, seismic activities, and aerial photography. Exploration costs incurred in an area must be capitalized and allocated to any mineral properties (leases) acquired in the area.

Exploratory wells are drilled to see whether oil or gas deposits exist.

Developmental wells are drilled to extract oil and gas deposits.

Intangible drilling costs (IDC) are incurred to prepare a well for production.

The costs of drilling wells, including both **exploratory wells** (drilled to determine whether oil or gas deposits exist) and **development wells** (drilled to produce any oil or gas found) are divided into two classes. The first classification is **intangible drilling costs (IDC).**[59] These costs have no salvage value and are incurred in getting the well drilled and ready to produce. Taxpayers have an option to charge all IDC to expense at the time paid or incurred. Another option is to capitalize all IDC incurred. A final option is to capitalize the IDC of productive wells and to expense the IDC related to dry holes. Rarely will an operating company make any election except to charge all IDC to expense as incurred. If, however, the operator does make the once-in-a-lifetime irrevocable election to capitalize IDC, the capitalized costs become part of the depletable basis of mineral rights.

---

59 Sec. 263(c) and Reg. Sec. 1.612-4.

The law prescribes certain required or elective modifications to the basic IDC elections, but these requirements or elections generally have no effect on depletable cost. For example, an oil or gas producer who has specified levels of (1) refining activity or (2) retail sales of petroleum products, and who has elected to charge all IDC to expense, must presently capitalize 30% of IDC incurred. However, the costs capitalized under this provision are subject to special amortization rules and do not become part of the depletable mineral cost. Similarly, because of the alternative minimum tax (see Chapter 19), taxpayers who have made the irrevocable election to expense all IDC as incurred may nevertheless now make an annual election to capitalize all or any part of the IDC that they would otherwise have expensed under their basic election. Any amounts capitalized under this special election are amortized over a ten-year period and do not affect the depletable basis of the property.

The second classification is *physical assets*. All costs of physical assets, including casing in the well, must be capitalized and are subject to the usual cost recovery or depreciation rules of Sec. 167 or Sec. 168. The labor and other costs incurred to install equipment in the well are part of the IDC subject to the election to expense. However, labor costs to install equipment outside the well are treated as part of the depreciable asset cost.

In summary, the producer's capitalized depletable costs for an oil and gas property will normally be the leasehold bonus costs, miscellaneous costs related to acquiring proper legal title, and exploration costs.

Mining Operations. Mine operators must also capitalize the bonus payment made to acquire the mineral property. Unlike the oil and gas operator, the mine operator may elect to either (1) charge exploration costs to expense at the time paid or incurred or (2) capitalize the costs. If the mine reaches the production stage, however, all exploration expenses related to the mine that have been previously deducted must be recaptured. This may be accomplished either by (1) reporting as gross income the amounts previously deducted as exploration expense or (2) electing to forgo otherwise deductible depletion allowances until the total allowance not taken equals the exploration expenditures that provided a tax benefit.

Mine development costs are those costs incurred in developing a mine after a mineral deposit (other than oil or gas) is found. The costs to acquire tangible property and install it are depreciable costs under Sec. 167 or Sec. 168. Intangible development costs, such as costs of mine operating shafts or clearing the land surface to get access to the minerals, may either be deducted in the year paid or incurred or be deferred and deducted proportionately as the mine's products are produced. A third election, if an initial election was made to deduct the costs at the time paid or incurred, is to capitalize the costs and amortize them over a ten-year period.

Thus, the depletable costs of a mine will customarily be only the costs of acquiring the mineral interest, the bonus paid the mineral-right owner, and the related miscellaneous fees and charges.

Cost Depletion

The depletion allowable on a mineral property for the year is the larger of **cost depletion** or percentage depletion. The producer's cost depletion is determined simply by determining a cost per unit for minerals available to be sold from the property and multiplying this unit cost by the number of units sold during the year. The cost per unit is found by dividing the unrecovered costs at the end of the year (initial basis of the mineral property minus any depletion taken in prior years) by the number of units of reserves at the

Cost depletion is a units-of-production method of charging off the property's cost.

beginning of the year. The beginning reserves are computed by adding together the reserves left at the end of the year and the units sold during the year.

EXAMPLE 14-22

Assume that the unrecovered cost of the mineral property at the end of the year (before the current year's depletion) is $100,000, that the operator's share of current year's production is 25,000 barrels of oil, and that the operator's share of reserves at the end of the year is estimated to be 375,000 barrels. Thus, the cost per unit is $.25 ($100,000/400,000 barrels), and the current year's cost depletion is $6,250 ($.25 per barrel x 25,000 barrels).

Any changes in estimated reserves during the year will be reflected in the beginning reserves. The impact on depletion per unit resulting from the change in estimate will be reflected in the year of the change and in future years.

Percentage Depletion

Percentage depletion is based on a percentage of income from the property.

Percentage depletion on income from a property is determined as the smaller of two amounts:[60]

1. A specified percentage of the taxpayer's gross income from the property for the year (the percentage for each natural resource is specified in the Code and ranges from 5% to 22%); or

2. 50% (100% for oil and gas properties after 1990) of the taxpayer's net income from the property for the year (net income for the year is equal to gross income from the property, less all direct operating expenses of the property, and less an allocated portion of almost all overhead of the company).

Generally, percentage depletion does not apply to large oil and gas wells. However, independent oil and gas producers and royalty owners may use percentage depletion, subject to limitations.[61] For example, oil producers with significant refining or retail operations are not eligible for percentage depletion, and a limit of 1,000 barrels per day of depletable production is imposed on other independent producers.

Illustration of the Depletion Computation

The following extended example illustrates the depletion provisions.

EXAMPLE 14-23

An independent producing company owns the operating interest in an oil lease. Under the standard lease terms, the lessor is entitled to receive payment for one eighth of the gross proceeds from production from the property. This payment is referred to as the *royalty interest*. However, the royalty holder does not pay any portion of the costs to develop or produce the mineral. The producer's capitalized depletable costs of the mineral property are $100,000. During 1992, the first year of production from the property, the operator's share of oil produced and sold is

Continued

---

60 Sec. 613.

61 Sec. 613A.

EXAMPLE 14-23 (Con't.)

25,000 barrels, which sells for a total of $400,000. Note that the royalty owner's share of production is not considered by the operator. The total direct and allocated expenses (other than depletion) applicable to the lease for the year are $423,000, so the operator has a net loss of $23,000 on the property for the year. Assume that the entire production from the property is subject to 15% percentage depletion. At the end of the year, the operator's estimated share of oil in the ground is 375,000 barrels. Cost depletion of $6,250 is computed on the property as follows:

$$\text{Cost depletion} = \$100,000/400,000 \text{ barrels} = \$.25 \text{ per barrel}$$
$$\$.25 \text{ per barrel} \times 25,000 \text{ barrels} = \$6,250$$

Percentage depletion is limited to the smaller of

1. 15% of gross income = 15% x $400,000 = $60,000, or

2. 100% of net income = 100% x ($400,000 – $423,000) = $0.

No percentage depletion is available because the property had a net loss. Therefore, cost depletion of $6,250 is allowed on the property.

In 1993, the operator's share of production is 30,000 barrels, which sells for $15 per barrel so that total gross income is $450,000. Operating expenses are $390,000, and the operator's net income is $60,000 before deducting depletion. Reserve estimates are not changed. At the end of the year, estimated reserves are 345,000 barrels. Depletion for 1993 is $60,000, computed as follows:

$$\text{Cost depletion} = (\$100,000 - \$6,250)/(345,000 \text{ barrels} + 30,000 \text{ barrels})$$
$$= \$.25 \text{ per barrel depletion}$$
$$\$.25 \text{ per barrel} \times 30,000 \text{ barrels} = \$7,500$$

Percentage depletion is the smaller of

1. 15% x $450,000 = $67,500, or

2. 100% x $60,000 = $60,000.

Percentage depletion is limited to $60,000. Depletion allowable is $60,000 because that amount is larger than cost depletion of $7,500.

In 1994 the operator's share of production is 40,000 barrels, it sells for $16 per barrel, and at the end of 1994 the operator's estimated share of reserves is 260,000 barrels. Note that a change in reserve estimate is made so that the new beginning-of-year reserve figure is 300,000 barrels (260,000 barrels plus the 40,000 barrels produced). Expenses applicable to the lease are $100,000, and net income is $540,000.

Depletion for 1994 is $96,000, computed as follows:

$$\text{Cost depletion} = (\$100,000 - \$6,250 - \$60,000)/300,000 \text{ barrels}$$
$$= \$.1125 \text{ per barrel}$$
$$\$.1125 \text{ per barrel} \times 40,000 \text{ barrels} = \$4,500$$

Continued

EXAMPLE 14-23 (Con't.)

Percentage depletion is the smaller of

1. 15% x $640,000 = $96,000, or

2. 100% x $540,000 = $540,000.

Percentage depletion for 1994 is $96,000, and this amount also is the allowable depletion for the year because it exceeds cost depletion.

It may seem strange that the entire $96,000 is allowable in 1994 because the depletion in the first three years of production totals $162,250 while the property had capitalized costs of only $100,000. Recall, however, that percentage depletion is not a cost recovery concept, and it can be continued for as long as the property produces. However, once depletion has been allowed in an amount equal to the capitalized cost, no further *cost depletion* is allowed. In this example, no cost depletion is allowed on this property in 1995 or subsequent years because total depletion exceeds capitalized costs.

DEPLETION FOR THE ROYALTY OWNER

The royalty owner also has a depletable interest in the mineral property and is eligible for either cost depletion or percentage depletion. However, the royalty owner rarely computes cost depletion because of the difficulty in determining the tax basis of the mineral interest. Consequently, almost all royalty owners use percentage depletion. Because the royalty owner bears no production costs, percentage depletion is generally based on gross income.

Oil and gas royalty owners are subject to the same limitations on percentage depletion as operating interest owners. Thus, the royalty owner who has specified amounts of refining activity or of retail sales of petroleum products will be ineligible for percentage depletion.

——— KEY POINTS TO REMEMBER

✓ Capital expenditures for tax purposes may be (1) capitalized and then deducted when the taxpayer disposes of property, (2) capitalized and then depreciated or amortized over time or with production, or (3) deducted currently. The particular treatment depends on the type of expenditure and the applicable tax law.

✓ Depreciation affects the timing of deductions and therefore involves the time value of money. Assuming that tax rates do not increase substantially, the more accelerated the depreciation deductions, the greater the present value of the tax savings and the greater the internal rate of return from the investment.

✓ Immediate expensing and economic depreciation represent two polar extremes in tax policy debates. Under immediate expensing, the taxpayer deducts the entire cost of an asset in the current year. Under economic depreciation, annual depreciation deductions reflect the decline in the asset's economic value.

✓ Advocates of each method claim that their method does not distort investment decisions (the neutrality argument). Advocates of expensing also claim that their method is simple to administer and is inflation proof. Expensing, however, fails to match costs and revenues.

✓ Assets that receive tax-favored treatment are likely to have lower before-tax rates of return (adjusted for risk) than non-tax-favored investments. This reduced before-tax rate of return imposes an implicit tax on the investor. In a competitive market, after-tax rates of return should equalize.

✓ Taxpayers in higher tax brackets than marginal investors can reduce their tax burden by investing in tax-favored investments. They convert their high statutory tax rate into a relatively low implicit tax rate. This phenomenon is the called the clientele effect.

✓ Inflation erodes the present value of depreciation deductions based on historical cost. Indexing of either asset bases or depreciation deductions alleviates this problem.

✓ Before 1953, taxpayers had to use straight-line depreciation. The 1954 Code introduced accelerated depreciation methods; the Economic Tax Recovery Act of 1981 (ERTA) introduced the Accelerated Cost Recovery System (ACRS); and the Tax Reform Act of 1986 modified ACRS.

✓ Pre-1981 depreciation rules allowed various methods: the straight-line method, the declining-balance method, the sum-of-the-years-digits method, and the units-of-production method. The applicable method depended on the type of property being depreciated.

✓ Original ACRS applies to property placed in service from 1981 through 1986. To determine annual depreciation deductions, the taxpayer applies the applicable percentage to the unadjusted basis of recovery property. Recovery property is divided into several classes, each with its own depreciation method and recovery period.

✓ Under original ACRS, taxpayers use the half-year convention for personal property and the full- or mid-month convention for real property. For personal property, the taxpayer is allowed no deduction in the year of disposition. For real property, the taxpayer is allowed a prorata deduction in the year of disposition.

✓ MACRS applies to property placed in service after 1986. Taxpayers determine annual depreciation deductions by using the applicable depreciation method, recovery period, and convention. Table 14-13 summarizes these items. Rev. Proc. 87-56 lists class lives pertaining to MACRS, and Rev. Proc. 87-57 contains tables of applicable depreciation percentages.

✓ Under MACRS, the taxpayer is allowed a prorata depreciation deduction in the year of disposition for both personal and real property.

✓ Under both ACRS and MACRS, the taxpayer ignores salvage value. Thus, the taxpayer depreciates the entire cost of property.

✓ The taxpayer may *elect* to use the straight-line method under the MACRS General Depreciation System. The taxpayer may also *elect* to use the Alternative Depreciation System (ADS). In some cases, and for certain tax purposes, the taxpayer *must* use the ADS.

✓ Under Sec. 179, taxpayers may elect to expense up to $10,000 of personal property used in a trade or business. The $10,000 expense limitation must be reduced dollar-for-dollar by the amount total Sec. 179 property placed in service during the year exceeds $200,000. Other limitations and special rules also apply.

✓ Section 280F places special limitations on depreciation deductions for listed property and luxury automobiles. These limitations restrict the taxpayer to ADS straight-line depreciation if business use of listed property does not exceed 50%. These limitations also provide depreciation deductions for high-priced automobiles that are less than MACRS deductions.

✓ The cost of intangible assets having a definite, limited life must be amortized on a straight-line basis. The cost of intangibles having an indefinite life may not be amortized.

✓ Special depletion rules apply to industries that extract natural resources, such as oil, gas, ores, and other minerals.

——— RECALL PROBLEMS

1. An asset costing $10,000 will generate before-tax cash flows of $4,380 per year for three years. The investment occurs at the beginning of the year, and the cash flows occur at the end of each year. What is the before-tax internal rate of return for this asset?

2. International Machines, Inc., is considering investing $1 million in one of two alternative projects. The cost of Project A can be recovered in five years using double-declining-balance depreciation. The cost of Project B must be amortized over ten years on a straight-line basis. Assume that a full year's depreciation or amortization may be claimed in the first year. Both projects are expected to yield the same amount of net cash flow before depreciation, the present value of which is $1 million using a 12% internal rate of return. Assume that the alternative depreciation or amortization methods do not alter the cost of the projects. The corporation's marginal tax rate is 34%. Compute the amount of the economic advantage arising from the rapid capital recovery of Project A as contrasted with Project B.

3. Under depreciation methods in effect before 1981, estimated useful life was the critical variable in determining the amount of depreciation. How does estimated life come into play under MACRS?

4. What advantages do the ACRS and MACRS rules have over the pre-1981 depreciation rules?

5. Maximum Mining Co. installed certain mining equipment in 1989. The mine was opened and began producing when the equipment was installed. The equipment cost $200,000 and had no salvage value. The recoverable reserves of the mine were one million tons of ore. In 1989 a total of 7,000 tons of ore was produced and processed.

   a. What is the allowable depreciation in 1989 using the units-of-production method?

   b. Assuming that the equipment is still in use in 1992 and that the original estimate of reserves has not changed, what will be the allowable depreciation in 1992 if 100,000 tons of ore are produced?

6. On which of the following properties may a taxpayer claim a depreciation or amortization deduction?

a. Personal residence.

b. A building used in business.

c. The land on which the business building is located.

d. A former residence, which the taxpayer now rents to another individual.

e. A car used 25% of the time for personal reasons and 75% for business purposes.

f. A building leased from another taxpayer and used in the lessee's business.

g. Goodwill acquired in a merger.

7. Marks Company is considering adding a new wing to its manufacturing plant. The old building has been in use since 1965 and has been depreciated under the straight-line method. The building has an adjusted basis of $1 million on January 1, 1992. The new wing will cost $600,000. Assuming the new wing is placed in service in March 1992, how will its cost be recovered?

8. Jones began construction of a new apartment house in 1984. Total cost of the building when it was completed in April 1986 was $2.5 million. Rental of units began on May 15, 1986.

a. What is the maximum ACRS deduction in 1984?

b. What is the maximum ACRS deduction in 1986?

c. Assuming the maximum ACRS deduction has been taken in past years on the building, what is the maximum ACRS deduction in 1992?

9. Limbo Corporation, a soft drink bottler, acquired and placed in service the following assets in 1986:

Description	Estimated Life (years)	Cost
Automobile	3	$ 10,000
Truck (light)	5	40,000
Cement mixer truck	8	16,000
Office copying machine	10	8,000
Bottling machine	15	120,000

The estimated lives are taken from the CLADR System.

a. If Limbo elected to expense the maximum amount of the acquired assets under Sec. 179, how much could be expensed in 1986?

b. If the costs were expensed under the Sec. 179 election, what was the maximum ACRS allowance for 1986, assuming Limbo selected the most beneficial assets to expense? What is Limbo's total deduction for 1986?

c. If no costs were expensed under the Sec. 179 election, what was the maximum ACRS allowance for 1986?

d. If the costs were not expensed under the Sec. 179 election in 1986, what is the ACRS deduction in 1989? 1991?

e. Assume that all of the assets were acquired in the year 1992 rather than in 1986.

(1) What is the maximum amount that could be expensed in 1992 under Sec. 179?

(2) If the maximum cost was expensed under Sec. 179, what is the maximum allowance under MACRS for 1992 assuming that Limbo selected the most beneficial assets to expense?

(3) If no costs were expensed under the Sec. 179 election, what is the maximum MACRS allowance for 1992 and 1993?

10. A taxpayer acquired light-weight trucks in 1986 at a cost of $400,000 with no salvage value. The assets were ACRS 3-year property. Because the taxpayer had huge amounts of operating loss carryovers, she wanted to take the smallest amount of depreciation possible during 1986 and subsequent years. What amount of depreciation should she have deducted in 1986? 1992? What amount would the taxpayer deduct in 1992 and 1993 if the trucks were placed in service in early 1992? Again, assume that she wished to minimize her deduction.

11. In December 1986, Mabel acquired and placed in service 5-year property costing $50,000. She used maximum ACRS recovery in 1986. She sold the assets in November 1990. Mabel made no Sec. 179 election.

a. What is the cost recovery deduction in 1986?

b. What is the cost recovery deduction in 1990?

c. Assume that the assets had been acquired in December 1988 instead of 1986 and were sold in 1992 instead of 1990.

(1) What is the maximum cost recovery deduction in 1988?

(2) What is the maximum cost recovery deduction in 1992?

12. In July 1992, Zeno Corporation purchased and placed into service the following assets:

Description	Cost
5 light trucks	$80,000
10 office desks	4,500
25 chairs	3,750

These were the only assets placed in service in 1992. No election was made under Sec. 179.

a. What is the maximum MACRS allowance for 1992?

b. What is the maximum MACRS allowance in 1993?

c. If Zeno had placed all of the assets in service in December 1992, what would have been the maximum MACRS allowance in 1992?

13. A corporation purchased and placed in service the following assets in 1992:

Month	Property Class	Cost
January	7-year	$100,000
December	7-year	60,000

The corporation made no Sec. 179 election.

a. What is the maximum MACRS allowance for 1992?

b. Assume the same property was placed in service except that the property costing $100,000 was placed in service in December 1992, and the property costing $60,000 was placed in service in January 1992. What is the maximum MACRS for 1992?

c. Assume the same property was placed into service in 1992 except that the property costing $100,000 was placed in service in January and the property costing $60,000 was placed in service in September. What is the maximum MACRS for 1992?

14. Robert acquired and placed in service a new apartment complex in March 1992. The complex cost $3 million. [#8]

a. What is Robert's maximum MACRS allowance for 1992?

b. What is Robert's maximum MACRS allowance for 1993?

c. Assume that Robert sells the complex in July 1995. What, if any, will be the MACRS allowance in 1995? What is the property's adjusted basis at the time of sale?

15. Mega S&L acquired a $40,000 Mercedes automobile for its president in 1991. Mega expects that the president will use the automobile 100% for business. Ignoring the luxury automobile limits and Sec. 179, how much depreciation could Mega deduct in 1991 and 1992? How much will Mega actually be able to deduct? [#8]

16. Derive all the percentages for 5-year property in Tables 14-1B through 14-5B. In Tables 14-6B and 14-7B, derive the percentages for the first year for months 1 through 12. [#8]

17. On February 3, 1992, the taxpayer placed in service 7-year property costing $200,000. On December 30, the taxpayer placed in service nonresidential real property costing $2 million. What convention applies to each property? [#8]

18. On February 28, 1992, a taxpayer purchased a new home and converted her old home into rental property. At the time of conversion, the old home had an adjusted basis of $125,000 and a fair market value of $150,000. [#8]

a. What amount of depreciation may she claim in 1992?

b. What is your answer if on the date of conversion, the old home had a $100,000 fair market value?

19. Mine No. 1 of Big Run Mining Company had an adjusted basis for depletion of $20,000 on January 1, 1992. During 1992, the company's share of production was 40,000 tons, sold at $20 per ton. Direct and indirect expenses applicable to the mine were $760,000 for the year. At the end of the year, the company's share of recoverable product in the mine was 360,000 tons. [#9]

a. Assuming the product is subject to a percentage depletion rate of 10%, what is the deduction for depletion for 1992?

b. Assume the same facts as above except that expenses were $892,000 for the year. What is the company's deduction for depletion for 1992?

c. Assume the same facts as given except that expenses for the year were $240,000. What is the company's deduction for depletion for 1992?

d. Assume that the owner of the royalty interest in the mine received royalty payments of $84,000 during 1992. What is the amount of depletion deductible by the royalty owner?

——— THOUGHT PROBLEMS

#1

1. In May 1992, the taxpayer placed in service one item of 5-year property and one item of 7-year property. Each property cost $50,000. Assume that all tax benefits occur at the end of the year and that tax rates remain constant throughout the recovery period.

   a. Assuming a 10% discount rate, determine the present value of deductions under each alternative.

   b. Which asset should the taxpayer select for the Sec. 179 election?

#1 #8

2. On January 2, 1992, the taxpayer placed in service 7-year property costing $100,000. The taxpayer plans to place in service another item of 7-year property costing $70,000. The taxpayer has the option of placing the second asset in service on September 30, 1992, or October 2, 1992. The taxpayer makes the Sec. 179 election. If the taxpayer wants to maximize her first year deduction what date should she choose, and which asset should she select for the Sec. 179 election?

#1 #8

3. On January 4, 1992, the taxpayer placed in service 5-year property costing $30,000. In 1992, the taxpayer is in the 30% tax bracket. Assume for this problem that Congress has enacted new tax rates for future years. Accordingly, the taxpayer expects to be in the 40% tax bracket in 1993, the 50% tax bracket in 1994, and the 60% tax bracket thereafter. The taxpayer's discount rate is 12%. Under MACRS, the taxpayer has the option of using the *General Depreciation System*, the *Alternative Depreciation System* with 150% declining-balance depreciation, or the *Alternative Depreciation System* (ADS) with straight-line depreciation. Assume that this particular asset also has a 5-year life under the ADS. The applicable percentages for the two ADS alternatives are

Year	150% DB	SL
1	15.00%	10%
2	25.50%	20%
3	17.85%	20%
4	16.66%	20%
5	16.66%	20%
6	8.33%	10%

Provide an analysis showing which depreciation system (method) the taxpayer should elect. Should the taxpayer elect expensing under Sec. 179?

#1 #2 #3

4. Consider two assets, one with a 3-year economic life and another with a 7-year economic life. The 3-year asset yields cash flows of $4,021 per year for three years, and the 7-year asset yields cash flows of $2,054 per year for seven years. Discounted at a 10% before-tax IRR, each of these cash flow streams yield a present value of $10,000. The investor pays taxes at a 30% tax rate. Investment occurs at the beginning of the year, and cash flows occur at the end of each year.

a. Assume that each investment costs $10,000. For each asset, perform an analysis as presented in Tables 14-3 and 14-4 or the text.

b. Determine the price that each asset would have to obtain under immediate expensing to reflect implicit taxes, and then perform an analysis as presented in Table 14-5 of the text.

c. Suppose that *both* assets are subject to economic depreciation. Will the investor prefer one over the other? Why or why not?

d. Suppose that *both* assets are subject to immediate expensing. Will the investor prefer one over the other? Why or why not?

e. What conclusions regarding asset life and neutrality can you draw from your answers in parts c and d?

5. Do you favor immediate expensing, economic depreciation, or some other method? Give the rationale for your answer.

6. In 1984, the Treasury Department released its proposal for tax reform, *Tax Reform for Fairness, Simplicity, and Economic Growth* (commonly called Treasury I). In criticizing ACRS, the proposal presented a table showing that effective tax rates varied considerably depending on the class of property (Table 6-2 in the proposal). The table (in part) provided the following data:

Asset Class (Years)	Effective Tax Rate
3	–90%
5	–51%
10	–5%
15	9%
18	28%

The Treasury table assumed a 46% tax rate and 4% after-tax rate of return on all assets. Assuming that a benchmark investment yields 7.4% before taxes, determine the following:

a. The before-tax rate of return for each asset class.

b. The implicit tax rate for each asset class.

c. The explicit tax rate for each asset class.

d. The total tax rate for each asset class.

e. What conclusions can you draw from this analysis concerning the variability of tax rates across different asset classes?

7. If either asset bases or depreciation deductions are indexed for inflation, should the interest deduction on debt used to finance the property also be indexed? Give the rationale for your answer.

8. Suppose the tax law required taxpayers to use the same depreciation method for tax purposes that they use for financial statement reporting. What conflicts might this requirement cause? Why do depreciation methods differ for tax and financial accounting?

—————— CLASS PROJECTS

1. Locate the latest *Budget of the United States Government* and, within the budget, locate the analysis of tax expenditures.

   a. Define a tax expenditure in general.

   b. How does the tax expenditure analysis in the budget treat accelerated depreciation?

   c. What amounts are the accelerated depreciation tax expenditures for the years disclosed?

2. Choose a major industrialized country other than the United States and research how that country's tax laws treat expenditures for equipment and structures.

3. Read the following article: Martin Feldstein, "Adjusting Depreciation in an Inflationary Economy: Indexing Versus Acceleration," *National Tax Journal*, March 1981, pp. 29–43. Prepare a written summary of the author's main points (ignore ITC). What does the author conclude about accelerated depreciation as a means to correct for inflation? How does immediate expensing fit into his conclusions?

4. Locate Rev. Proc. 89-15, 1989-1 CB 816, and use the information in the procedure to answer the following two problems:

   a. Able Corporation began business on January 2, 1992. It elected a fiscal year ending September 30, so its first taxable year was a short period running from Janaury 2, 1992, through September 30, 1992. On Janaury 4, 1992, the company placed in service 7-year property costing $100,000. The company makes no Sec. 179 expense election, and the company retains the property for its entire recovery period. Compute the depreciation deduction for each year in the recovery period.

   b. Baker Corporation began business on March 1, 1992. It elected a fiscal year ending June 30, so its first taxable year was a short period running from March 1, 1992, through June 30, 1992. On March 3, 1992, the company placed in service 5-year property costing $100,000, and on May 20, 1992, the company placed in service another item of 5-year property costing $200,000. The company makes no Sec. 179 expense election (it would not receive a benefit even if it did make the election), and the company retains both assets for their entire recovery period. Compute the depreciation deduction for each year in the recovery period.

APPENDIX 14A: SELECTED ACRS TABLES (1981–1986)

Recovery Year	Property Class			
	3-Year	5-Year	10-Year	15-Year Public Utility
1	25	15	8	5
2	38	22	14	10
3	37	21	12	9
4		21	10	8
5		21	10	7
6			10	7
7			9	6
8			9	6
9			9	6
10			9	6
11				6
12				6
13				6
14				6
15				6

TABLE 14-1A

ACRS Basic Recovery Percentages for 1981–1986

Recovery Year	Month Placed in Service											
	1	2	3	4	5	6	7	8	9	10	11	12
1	12	11	10	9	8	7	6	5	4	3	2	1
2	10	10	11	11	11	11	11	11	11	11	11	12
3	9	9	9	9	10	10	10	10	10	10	10	10
4	8	8	8	8	8	8	9	9	9	9	9	9
5	7	7	7	7	7	7	8	8	8	8	8	8
6	6	6	6	6	7	7	7	7	7	7	7	7
7	6	6	6	6	6	6	6	6	6	6	6	6
8	6	6	6	6	6	6	5	6	6	6	6	6
9	6	6	6	6	5	6	5	5	5	6	6	6
10	5	6	5	6	5	5	5	5	5	5	6	5
11	5	5	5	5	5	5	5	5	5	5	5	5
12	5	5	5	5	5	5	5	5	5	5	5	5
13	5	5	5	5	5	5	5	5	5	5	5	5
14	5	5	5	5	5	5	5	5	5	5	5	5
15	5	5	5	5	5	5	5	5	5	5	5	5
16	-	-	1	1	2	2	3	3	4	4	4	5

Note: Placed in service after December 31, 1980, and before March 16, 1984.

TABLE 14-2A

ACRS Recovery Percentages for 15-Year Real Property (other than low-income housing)

TABLE 14-3A

ACRS Recovery Percentages for 18-Year Real Property

Recovery Year	Month Placed in Service												
	1	2	3	4	5	6	7	8	9	10	11	12
1	10	9	8	7	6	6	5	4	3	2	2	1
2	9	9	9	9	9	9	9	9	9	10	10	10
3	8	8	8	8	8	8	8	8	9	9	9	9
4	7	7	7	7	7	7	8	8	8	8	8	8
5	6	7	7	7	7	7	7	7	7	7	7	7
6	6	6	6	6	6	6	6	6	6	6	6	6
7	5	5	5	5	6	6	6	6	6	6	6	6
8	5	5	5	5	5	5	5	5	5	5	5	5
9	5	5	5	5	5	5	5	5	5	5	5	5
10	5	5	5	5	5	5	5	5	5	5	5	5
11	5	5	5	5	5	5	5	5	5	5	5	5
12	5	5	5	5	5	5	5	5	5	5	5	5
13	4	4	4	5	5	4	4	5	4	4	4	4
14	4	4	4	4	4	4	4	4	4	4	4	4
15	4	4	4	4	4	4	4	4	4	4	4	4
16	4	4	4	4	4	4	4	4	4	4	4	4
17	4	4	4	4	4	4	4	4	4	4	4	4
18	4	4	4	4	4	4	4	4	4	4	4	4
19	-	-	1	1	1	2	2	2	3	3	3	4

Note: Placed in service after March 15, 1984, and before June 23, 1984.

TABLE 14-4A

ACRS Recovery Percentages for 18-Year Real Property

Recovery Year	Month Placed in Service												
	1	2	3	4	5	6	7	8	9	10	11	12
1	9	9	8	7	6	5	4	4	3	2	1	0.4
2	9	9	9	9	9	9	9	9	9	10	10	10
3	8	8	8	8	8	8	8	8	9	9	9	9
4	7	7	7	7	7	8	8	8	8	8	8	8
5	7	7	7	7	7	7	7	7	7	7	7	7
6	6	6	6	6	6	6	6	6	6	6	6	6
7	5	5	5	5	6	6	6	6	6	6	6	6
8	5	5	5	5	5	5	5	5	5	5	5	5
9	5	5	5	5	5	5	5	5	5	5	5	5
10	5	5	5	5	5	5	5	5	5	5	5	5
11	5	5	5	5	5	5	5	5	5	5	5	5
12	5	5	5	5	5	5	5	5	5	5	5	5
13	4	4	4	5	4	4	5	4	4	4	5	5
14	4	4	4	4	4	4	4	4	4	4	4	4
15	4	4	4	4	4	4	4	4	4	4	4	4
16	4	4	4	4	4	4	4	4	4	4	4	4
17	4	4	4	4	4	4	4	4	4	4	4	4
18	4	3	4	4	4	4	4	4	4	4	4	4
19	-	1	1	1	2	2	2	3	3	3	3	3.6

Note: Placed in service after June 22, 1984, and before May 9, 1985.

TABLE 14-5A

(1) ACRS Recovery Percentages for 19-Year Real Property

Recovery Year	1	2	3	4	5	6	7	8	9	10	11	12
1	8.8	8.1	7.3	6.5	5.8	5.0	4.2	3.5	2.7	1.9	1.1	.4
2	8.4	8.5	8.5	8.6	8.7	8.8	8.8	8.9	9.0	9.0	9.1	9.2
3	7.6	7.7	7.7	7.8	7.9	7.9	8.0	8.1	8.1	8.2	8.3	8.3
4	6.9	7.0	7.0	7.1	7.1	7.2	7.3	7.3	7.4	7.4	7.5	7.6
5	6.3	6.3	6.4	6.4	6.5	6.5	6.6	6.6	6.7	6.8	6.8	6.9
6	5.7	5.7	5.8	5.9	5.9	5.9	6.0	6.0	6.1	6.1	6.2	6.2
7	5.2	5.2	5.3	5.3	5.3	5.4	5.4	5.5	5.5	5.6	5.6	5.6
8	4.7	4.7	4.8	4.8	4.8	4.9	4.9	5.0	5.0	5.1	5.1	5.1
9	4.2	4.3	4.3	4.4	4.4	4.5	4.5	4.5	4.5	4.6	4.6	4.7
10	4.2	4.2	4.2	4.2	4.2	4.2	4.2	4.2	4.2	4.2	4.2	4.2
11	4.2	4.2	4.2	4.2	4.2	4.2	4.2	4.2	4.2	4.2	4.2	4.2
12	4.2	4.2	4.2	4.2	4.2	4.2	4.2	4.2	4.2	4.2	4.2	4.2
13	4.2	4.2	4.2	4.2	4.2	4.2	4.2	4.2	4.2	4.2	4.2	4.2
14	4.2	4.2	4.2	4.2	4.2	4.2	4.2	4.2	4.2	4.2	4.2	4.2
15	4.2	4.2	4.2	4.2	4.2	4.2	4.2	4.2	4.2	4.2	4.2	4.2
16	4.2	4.2	4.2	4.2	4.2	4.2	4.2	4.2	4.2	4.2	4.2	4.2
17	4.2	4.2	4.2	4.2	4.2	4.2	4.2	4.2	4.2	4.2	4.2	4.2
18	4.2	4.2	4.2	4.2	4.2	4.2	4.2	4.2	4.2	4.2	4.2	4.2
19	4.2	4.2	4.2	4.2	4.2	4.2	4.2	4.2	4.2	4.2	4.2	4.2
20	0.2	0.5	0.9	1.2	1.6	1.9	2.3	2.6	3.0	3.3	3.7	4.0

Note: Placed in service after May 8, 1985, and before January 1, 1987.

(2) Straight-Line ACRS Method over a 19-Year Period

Recovery Year	1	2	3	4	5	6	7	8	9	10	11	12
1	5.0	4.6	4.2	3.7	3.3	2.9	2.4	2.0	1.5	1.1	0.7	0.2
2–13	5.3	5.3	5.3	5.3	5.3	5.3	5.3	5.3	5.3	5.3	5.3	5.3
14–19	5.2	5.2	5.2	5.2	5.2	5.2	5.2	5.2	5.2	5.2	5.2	5.2
20	0.2	0.6	1.0	1.5	1.9	2.3	2.8	3.2	3.7	4.1	4.5	5.0

APPENDIX 14B: SELECTED MACRS TABLES (1987 AND AFTER)

TABLE 14-1B

MACRS Recovery Percentages Half-Year Convention

Recovery Year	Property Class					
	3-Year	5-Year	7-Year	10-Year	15-Year	20-Year
1	33.33	20.00	14.29	10.00	5.00	3.750
2	44.45	32.00	24.49	18.00	9.50	7.219
3	14.81	19.20	17.49	14.40	8.55	6.677
4	7.41	11.52	12.49	11.52	7.70	6.177
5		11.52	8.93	9.22	6.93	5.713
6		5.76	8.92	7.37	6.23	5.285
7			8.93	6.55	5.90	4.888
8			4.46	6.55	5.90	4.522
9				6.56	5.91	4.462
10				6.55	5.90	4.461
11				3.28	5.91	4.462
12					5.90	4.461
13					5.91	4.462
14					5.90	4.461
15					5.91	4.462
16					2.95	4.461
17						4.462
18						4.461
19						4.462
20						4.461
21						2.231

TABLE 14-2B

MACRS Recovery Percentages Mid-Quarter Convention (First Quarter)

Recovery Year	Property Class					
	3-Year	5-Year	7-Year	10-Year	15-Year	20-Year
1	58.33	35.00	25.00	17.50	8.75	6.563
2	27.78	26.00	21.43	16.50	9.13	7.000
3	12.35	15.60	15.31	13.20	8.21	6.482
4	1.54	11.01	10.93	10.56	7.39	5.996
5		11.01	8.75	8.45	6.65	5.546
6		1.38	8.74	6.76	5.99	5.130
7			8.75	6.55	5.90	4.746
8			1.09	6.55	5.91	4.459
9				6.56	5.90	4.459
10				6.55	5.91	4.459
11				0.82	5.90	4.459
12					5.91	4.460
13					5.90	4.459
14					5.91	4.460
15					5.90	4.459
16					0.74	4.460
17						4.459
18						4.460
19						4.459
20						4.460
21						0.557

Note: Property placed in service during *First* quarter.

Recovery Year	Property Class					
	3-Year	5-Year	7-Year	10-Year	15-Year	20-Year
1	41.67	25.00	17.85	12.50	6.25	4.688
2	38.89	30.00	23.47	17.50	9.38	7.148
3	14.14	18.00	16.76	14.00	8.44	6.612
4	5.30	11.37	11.97	11.20	7.59	6.116
5		11.37	8.87	8.96	6.83	5.658
6		4.26	8.87	7.17	6.15	5.233
7			8.87	6.55	5.91	4.841
8			3.33	6.55	5.90	4.478
9				6.56	5.91	4.463
10				6.55	5.90	4.463
11				2.46	5.91	4.463
12					5.90	4.463
13					5.91	4.463
14					5.90	4.463
15					5.91	4.462
16					2.21	4.463
17						4.462
18						4.463
19						4.462
20						4.463
21						1.673

Note: Property placed in service during *Second* quarter.

TABLE 14-3B

MACRS Recovery Percentages Mid-Quarter Convention (Second Quarter)

Recovery Year	Property Class					
	3-Year	5-Year	7-Year	10-Year	15-Year	20-Year
1	25.00	15.00	10.71	7.50	3.75	2.813
2	50.00	34.00	25.51	18.50	9.63	7.289
3	16.67	20.40	18.22	14.80	8.66	6.742
4	8.33	12.24	13.02	11.84	7.80	6.237
5		11.30	9.30	9.47	7.02	5.769
6		7.06	8.85	7.58	6.31	5.336
7			8.86	6.55	5.90	4.936
8			5.53	6.55	5.90	4.566
9				6.56	5.91	4.460
10				6.55	5.90	4.460
11				4.10	5.91	4.460
12					5.90	4.460
13					5.91	4.461
14					5.90	4.460
15					5.91	4.461
16					3.69	4.460
17						4.461
18						4.460
19						4.461
20						4.460
21						2.788

Note: Property placed in service during *Third* quarter.

TABLE 14-4B

MACRS Recovery Percentages Mid-Quarter Convention (Third Quarter)

TABLE 14-5B

MACRS Recovery Percentages Mid-Quarter Convention (Fourth Quarter)

Recovery Year	3-Year	5-Year	7-Year	10-Year	15-Year	20-Year
			Property Class			
1	8.33	5.00	3.57	2.50	1.25	0.938
2	61.11	38.00	27.55	19.50	9.88	7.430
3	20.37	22.80	19.68	15.60	8.89	6.872
4	10.19	13.68	14.06	12.48	8.00	6.357
5		10.94	10.04	9.98	7.20	5.880
6		9.58	8.73	7.99	6.48	5.439
7			8.73	6.55	5.90	5.031
8			7.64	6.55	5.90	4.654
9				6.56	5.90	4.458
10				6.55	5.91	4.458
11				5.74	5.90	4.458
12					5.91	4.458
13					5.90	4.458
14					5.91	4.458
15					5.90	4.458
16					5.17	4.458
17						4.458
18						4.459
19						4.458
20						4.459
21						3.901

Note: Property placed in service during *Fourth* quarter

TABLE 14-6B

MACRS Recovery Percentages: Residential Rental Property (27.5 years)

Recovery Year	Month Placed in Service											
	1	2	3	4	5	6	7	8	9	10	11	12
1	3.485	3.182	2.879	2.576	2.273	1.970	1.667	1.364	1.061	0.758	0.455	0.152
2	3.636	3.636	3.636	3.636	3.636	3.636	3.636	3.636	3.636	3.636	3.636	3.636
3	3.636	3.636	3.636	3.636	3.636	3.636	3.636	3.636	3.636	3.636	3.636	3.636
4	3.636	3.636	3.636	3.636	3.636	3.636	3.636	3.636	3.636	3.636	3.636	3.636
5	3.636	3.636	3.636	3.636	3.636	3.636	3.636	3.636	3.636	3.636	3.636	3.636
6	3.636	3.636	3.636	3.636	3.636	3.636	3.636	3.636	3.636	3.636	3.636	3.636
7	3.636	3.636	3.636	3.636	3.636	3.636	3.636	3.636	3.636	3.636	3.636	3.636
8	3.636	3.636	3.636	3.636	3.636	3.636	3.636	3.636	3.636	3.636	3.636	3.636
9	3.636	3.636	3.636	3.636	3.636	3.636	3.636	3.636	3.636	3.636	3.636	3.636
10	3.637	3.637	3.637	3.637	3.637	3.637	3.636	3.636	3.636	3.636	3.636	3.636
11	3.636	3.636	3.636	3.636	3.636	3.636	3.637	3.637	3.637	3.637	3.637	3.637
12	3.637	3.637	3.637	3.637	3.637	3.637	3.636	3.636	3.636	3.636	3.636	3.636
13	3.636	3.636	3.636	3.636	3.636	3.636	3.637	3.637	3.637	3.637	3.637	3.637
14	3.637	3.637	3.637	3.637	3.637	3.637	3.636	3.636	3.636	3.636	3.636	3.636
15	3.636	3.636	3.636	3.636	3.636	3.636	3.637	3.637	3.637	3.637	3.637	3.637
16	3.637	3.637	3.637	3.637	3.637	3.637	3.636	3.636	3.636	3.636	3.636	3.636
17	3.636	3.636	3.636	3.636	3.636	3.636	3.637	3.637	3.637	3.637	3.637	3.637
18	3.637	3.637	3.637	3.637	3.637	3.637	3.636	3.636	3.636	3.636	3.636	3.636
19	3.636	3.636	3.636	3.636	3.636	3.636	3.637	3.637	3.637	3.637	3.637	3.637
20	3.637	3.637	3.637	3.637	3.637	3.637	3.636	3.636	3.636	3.636	3.636	3.636
21	3.636	3.636	3.636	3.636	3.636	3.636	3.637	3.637	3.637	3.637	3.637	3.637
22	3.637	3.637	3.637	3.637	3.637	3.637	3.636	3.636	3.636	3.636	3.636	3.636
23	3.636	3.636	3.636	3.636	3.636	3.636	3.637	3.637	3.637	3.637	3.637	3.637
24	3.637	3.637	3.637	3.637	3.637	3.637	3.636	3.636	3.636	3.636	3.636	3.636
25	3.636	3.636	3.636	3.636	3.636	3.636	3.637	3.637	3.637	3.637	3.637	3.637
26	3.637	3.637	3.637	3.637	3.637	3.637	3.636	3.637	3.636	3.636	3.636	3.636
27	3.636	3.636	3.636	3.636	3.636	3.636	3.637	3.637	3.637	3.637	3.637	3.637
28	1.970	2.273	2.576	2.879	3.182	3.485	3.636	3.636	3.636	3.636	3.636	3.636
29	0.000	0.000	0.000	0.000	0.000	0.000	0.152	0.455	0.758	1.061	1.364	1.667

TABLE 14-7B

MACRS Recovery Percentages: Nonresidential Real Property (31.5 years)

Recovery Year	| Month Placed in Service											
	1	2	3	4	5	6	7	8	9	10	11	12
1	3.042	2.778	2.513	2.249	1.984	1.720	1.455	1.190	0.926	0.661	0.397	0.132
2	3.175	3.175	3.175	3.175	3.175	3.175	3.175	3.175	3.175	3.175	3.175	3.175
3	3.175	3.175	3.175	3.175	3.175	3.175	3.175	3.175	3.175	3.175	3.175	3.175
4	3.175	3.175	3.175	3.175	3.175	3.175	3.175	3.175	3.175	3.175	3.175	3.175
5	3.175	3.175	3.175	3.175	3.175	3.175	3.175	3.175	3.175	3.175	3.175	3.175
6	3.175	3.175	3.175	3.175	3.175	3.175	3.175	3.175	3.175	3.175	3.175	3.175
7	3.175	3.175	3.175	3.175	3.175	3.175	3.175	3.175	3.175	3.175	3.175	3.175
8	3.175	3.174	3.175	3.174	3.175	3.174	3.175	3.175	3.175	3.175	3.175	3.175
9	3.174	3.175	3.174	3.175	3.174	3.175	3.174	3.175	3.174	3.175	3.174	3.175
10	3.175	3.174	3.175	3.174	3.175	3.174	3.175	3.174	3.175	3.174	3.175	3.174
11	3.174	3.175	3.174	3.175	3.174	3.175	3.174	3.175	3.174	3.175	3.174	3.175
12	3.175	3.174	3.175	3.174	3.175	3.174	3.175	3.174	3.175	3.174	3.175	3.174
13	3.174	3.175	3.174	3.175	3.174	3.175	3.174	3.175	3.174	3.175	3.174	3.175
14	3.175	3.174	3.175	3.174	3.175	3.174	3.175	3.174	3.175	3.174	3.175	3.174
15	3.174	3.175	3.174	3.175	3.174	3.175	3.174	3.175	3.174	3.175	3.174	3.175
16	3.175	3.174	3.175	3.174	3.175	3.174	3.175	3.174	3.175	3.174	3.175	3.174
17	3.174	3.175	3.174	3.175	3.174	3.175	3.174	3.175	3.174	3.175	3.174	3.175
18	3.175	3.174	3.175	3.174	3.175	3.174	3.175	3.174	3.175	3.174	3.175	3.174
19	3.174	3.175	3.174	3.175	3.174	3.175	3.174	3.175	3.174	3.175	3.174	3.175
20	3.175	3.174	3.175	3.174	3.175	3.174	3.175	3.174	3.175	3.174	3.175	3.174
21	3.174	3.175	3.174	3.175	3.174	3.175	3.174	3.175	3.174	3.175	3.174	3.175
22	3.175	3.174	3.175	3.174	3.175	3.174	3.175	3.174	3.175	3.174	3.175	3.174
23	3.174	3.175	3.174	3.175	3.174	3.175	3.174	3.175	3.174	3.175	3.174	3.175
24	3.175	3.174	3.175	3.174	3.175	3.174	3.175	3.174	3.175	3.174	3.175	3.174
25	3.174	3.175	3.174	3.175	3.174	3.175	3.174	3.175	3.174	3.175	3.174	3.175
26	3.175	3.174	3.175	3.174	3.175	3.174	3.175	3.174	3.175	3.174	3.175	3.174
27	3.174	3.175	3.174	3.175	3.174	3.175	3.174	3.175	3.174	3.175	3.174	3.175
28	3.175	3.174	3.175	3.174	3.175	3.174	3.175	3.174	3.175	3.174	3.175	3.174
29	3.174	3.175	3.174	3.175	3.174	3.175	3.174	3.175	3.174	3.175	3.174	3.175
30	3.175	3.174	3.175	3.174	3.175	3.174	3.175	3.174	3.175	3.174	3.175	3.174
31	3.174	3.175	3.174	3.175	3.174	3.175	3.174	3.175	3.174	3.175	3.174	3.175
32	1.720	1.984	2.249	2.513	2.778	3.042	3.175	3.174	3.175	3.174	3.175	3.174
33	0.000	0.000	0.000	0.000	0.000	0.000	0.132	0.397	0.661	0.926	1.190	1.455

RELATED-PARTY TRANSACTIONS

CHAPTER OBJECTIVES

In Chapter 15 you will discover why the IRS may carefully scrutinize even relatively routine business transactions between related parties and sometimes recast the apparent form of those transactions in a way that will modify income tax consequences. The details of the specific transactions and the statutory provisions explained in this chapter are not as significant as the general concept that they illustrate.

LEARNING GOALS

After studying this chapter, you should be able to

1 Understand why related-party transactions are subject to special scrutiny by the IRS;

2 Define the term *related-party transaction* as we use it in this chapter;

3 Identify the two statutory provisions that are explained in this chapter as possible authority for an IRS challenge to a related-party transaction, and describe in general how these two provisions operate;

4 Explain what judicial authority means and identify the tax principles supported by the three benchmark cases discussed in this chapter;

5 Explain why transactions between a legal entity and its owners present so many difficult tax issues.

Describe some of the more common ways in which these transactions provide tax avoidance opportunities as well as the ways in which the IRS can address them;

6 Analyze the fundamental tax issue involved in stock-redemption transactions and describe the basic approach of the two statutory provisions designed to address the fundamental issue;

7 Describe some of the common tax avoidance possibilities endemic to family partnerships; and

8 Explain the ways in which multiple corporations or those engaged in foreign operations provide opportunities for tax avoidance.

<table>
<tr><td>

Goal #1
Understand why related party transactions are subject to special scrutiny by the IRS.

</td></tr>
</table>

The vast majority of all business transactions that occur daily involve unrelated parties dealing with one another at arm's length. Under these conditions it is generally safe to conclude that the form of the transaction clearly represents the economic event that occurred because no one has reason to act in anything other than his or her own self-interest. On the other hand, any time that the parties to a transaction are closely related, there is good reason to question whether the apparent form in which the transaction was cast truly reflects the economic event that occurred. Recognizing that there are golden opportunities for tax avoidance in many transactions between related parties, the IRS may carefully scrutinize these transactions. If the IRS concludes that a related-party transaction does not properly reflect economic reality, it will not hesitate to recast the transaction in a manner that more correctly represents what, in the opinion of the IRS, actually transpired. And if a taxpayer refuses to accept the IRS' recharacterization as an accurate representation of what really happened, the resolution of that conflict may ultimately have to be decided by a court of law.

Goal #2
Define the *related party transaction* as used in this chapter.

_____ WHO IS RELATED TO WHOM?

A **related-party transaction** is one that fails to represent economic reality because tax consequences have *unduly influenced* the form of the transaction.

Bona fide means in (or with) good faith.

Statutory law refers to the body of law created by acts of a legislature.

Common law refers to legal *rules* derived from judicial decisions.

Judicial precedents are fundamental principles established in previous cases.

Landmark decisions are judicial decisions that significantly extend or change existing law.

The biggest problem in trying to police how well or how poorly accounting and legal records document economic reality lies in our inability to define, with an adequate degree of precision, the set of suspect relationships. Transactions that have tax consequences, by definition, involve at least two persons.[1] The fact that two persons are engaged in the same transaction automatically creates some kind of relationship between the two parties. For example, the two parties to a simple sale transaction automatically create a buyer-seller relationship; writing a paycheck automatically involves an employer-employee relationship; and a rental agreement automatically involves a lessor-lessee relationship. Hence, in one sense, every transaction involves related parties. The challenge of this chapter—and one challenge of tax law more generally—is to define related party transactions more narrowly. For purposes of taxation, a **related-party transaction** is any transaction that fails to represent economic reality because tax consequences have *unduly influenced* the precise form in which the transaction was arranged and recorded. A major problem is that the IRS and legal authorities will sometimes accept a transaction that was very carefully orchestrated to achieve specific tax results as a fair representation of economic events. At other times, and in other circumstances, those same authorities will reject the details of a very similar transaction as inappropriate and proceed to adjust the tax consequences according to the rules applicable to the restructured transaction.

The legal authorities cited by the IRS in challenging the ***bona fide*** quality of any transaction may be anything from a very narrowly prescribed rule of **statutory law** to a very widely applicable rule of **common law**. The term common law refers to general rules derived from **judicial precedents**. Over relatively long periods of time, a few judicial decisions become known to legal scholars as **landmark decisions** or *benchmark decisions* because subsequent courts so frequently cite them as authority to justify the judge's decision in the subsequent case. These landmark cases establish principles broader than the specific facts of the case considered. Thus landmark cases may be cited as controlling, even if the facts of the subsequent case are really quite different from the facts in the landmark decision.

---

1 Remember that the word *persons* includes not only individuals but also various legal entities, at least for federal income tax purposes.

A skilled tax adviser eventually develops a sixth sense (or smell test) that alerts her or him to the existence of a transaction that is likely to be challenged by the IRS. Once a transaction with a risky tax result has been identified, a tax adviser can then evaluate the applicability of both statutory and common law to the transaction under consideration. The primary purpose of this chapter is to alert you to the broad issues of related-party transactions and to introduce to you a few of the statutory provisions that are of general interest in this context. This introduction is intended to help you develop that same sixth sense, or the ability to employ a **smell test**, so that you can engage the skilled tax adviser for timely professional advice whenever you or your client is involved in a transaction that the IRS is likely to challenge.

Practitioners employ a **smell test** when they use their intuition to test whether the stated tax result of a transaction is likely to be upheld by tax authorities.

───── LEGAL AUTHORITIES

As noted earlier, the IRS has ample legal authority to challenge any related party transaction. In the following discussion we will examine very briefly some of the statutory and judicial authority that is most likely to substantiate the IRS' recasting of a related party transaction so that it will have different income tax consequences from those preferred by the taxpayer. We will begin our discussion with a look at statutory authority.

STATUTORY AUTHORITIES

The statutory authority that can be cited by the IRS, whenever it challenges a related party transaction, may involve either (1) a Code provision of very general application or (2) a narrow provision of very limited application. This diverse pattern of statutory authority should be familiar to you because it replicates what you learned in Chapters 5 and 13 relative to the statutory provisions which authorize deductions. In that regard, the Code ranges from provisions like Sec. 162, which are widely applicable to many business ventures, to Sec. 263(i), which is solely applicable to domestic oil and gas producers. Relative to related party transactions, Sec. 482 is almost certainly the provision of most general interest.

Goal #3
Identify the two statutory provisions that are explained in this chapter as potential authority for an IRS challenge, and describe in general how they operate.

Section 482

A careful reading of Sec. 482, which has only two sentences, will reveal why it may apply to such a diverse set of business ventures. The provision reads in its entirety as follows:

> Sec. 482. Allocation of Income and Deductions among Taxpayers.
>
> In any case of two or more organizations, trades, or businesses (whether or not incorporated, whether or not organized in the United States, and whether or not affiliated) owned or controlled directly or indirectly by the same interest, the Secretary may distribute, apportion, or allocate gross income, deductions, credits, or allowances between or among such organizations, trades, or businesses, if he determines that such distribution, apportionment, or allocation is necessary in order to prevent evasion of taxes or clearly to reflect the income of any of such organizations, trades, or businesses. In the case of any transfer (or license) of intangible property (within the meaning of section 936(h)(3)(B)), the income with respect to such transfer or license shall be commensurate with the income attributable to the intangible.

Note that Sec. 482 can be applied to virtually any transaction between any two persons that are directly *or indirectly* owned *or controlled* "by the same interests." (Emphasis added.) Sec. 482 gives "the Secretary"—that is, the Secretary of the Treasury and, through the Secretary, to the Commissioner of the IRS—the authority to "distribute, apportion, or allocate" literally any component of the set of numbers (or measurements) that determine a taxpayer's federal income tax liability. The Code simply requires that the Secretary determine that some modification of the facts as reported is necessary "to prevent evasion of taxes or to clearly reflect income" of the parties to any transaction. Once the Secretary has made that determination, he has the statutory authority to recast any transaction in the way deemed necessary to prevent the alleged wrong; that is, either the evasion of taxes or a clear reflection of income.

The concept implicit in Sec. 482 is very similar to that embodied in sec. 446(b). As we learned in Chapter 7, page 238, the latter section gives the Secretary authority to prescribe a general method of accounting if, in his opinion, the taxpayer's method does not "clearly reflect income." Sec. 482 clearly goes a step further by giving the Secretary the authority to reallocate or reapportion *any component of income* even if the accounting method does (more generally) provide a good income measurement. The components specified in Sec. 482 include any item of gross income, deduction, credit, or "allowance." Although the intended meaning of the word *allowance* is unclear to the authors of your text, the breadth of the three other components is sufficient to cover every imaginable related-party transaction.

Section 267

Section 267 differs significantly from Sec. 482. Section 267 applies only to transactions that involve (1) losses, (2) expenses, or (3) interest, between parties that are specifically related in the manner defined in subsection (b). Thus Sec. 267 is a good example of a provision of limited application whereas Sec. 482 is a provision of very general application. Perhaps because of its limited application, Sec. 267 is significantly longer and more complex than Sec. 482. In fact, Sec. 267 is so long and detailed that we will not even reprint here. Neither will we describe, in any detail, many interesting facets of its application to specific business ventures. The general thrust of Sec. 267, however, is of widespread interest to everyday business.

Section 267 has seven subsections that can be explained as follows:

- Sec. 267(a)(1) disallows any deduction for a loss if the sale or exchange of property that creates the loss, involves parties that are related in a manner detailed in subsection (b). See Example 15-1 for an illustration of how this rule works.

- Sec. 267(a)(2) provides that both parties to any transaction involving either an expense or interest, must recognize the tax impact of the transaction in the same accounting period if the parties are related in a manner detailed in subsection (b). See Example 15-3 for an illustration of this provision.

- Sec. 267(b) defines the set of related parties that may be subject to (1) having a loss disallowed or (2) having any expense or interest item recognized in an accounting period other than the period that it would ordinarily be recognized, were it not for this special rule. Examples 15-1 through 15-4 illustrate just a few of the relationships specified in Sec. 267(b).

- Sec. 267(c) provides a set of attribution rules that extend the related-party concept, introduced in Sec. 267(b), as that concept applies to corporate stockholders. The

attribution rules effectively make certain shareholders the indirect owners of shares directly owned by certain other persons. In still other words, in determining whether any stockholder owns a statutorily set percentage of a corporation, every shareholder must include shares that are deemed to be constructively owned as well as shares directly owned by the stockholder under investigation. The two terms— *attribution rules* and *constructive-ownership rules*—are used interchangably. See Example 15-4 for an illustration of Sec. 267(c).

> **Attribution** (or constructive ownership) **rules** describe the circumstances that will cause one stockholder's ownership interest to be attributed to another party.

• Sec. 267(d) provides that a loss deduction that was disallowed by operation of Sec. 267(a)(1) may, under some circumstances, be used to offset a gain subsequently recognized by the related person who initially acquired a property in a transaction that involved a disallowed loss. See Example 15-2 for an illustration of how Sec. 267(d) relates to Sec. 267(a).

• Sec. 267(e) provides a host of special rules, to modify the general rules of Sec. 267(a), for transactions involving pass-thru entities (partnerships and S corporations).

• Sec. 267(f) provides a host of special rules, to modify the general rules of Sec. 267(a), for transactions involving a controlled group of corporations. The provisions of Sec. 267(f) modify very slightly the controlled group definition introduced in Chapter 6, page 195.

• Sec. 267(g) provides a special rule, to modify the general rule of Sec. 267(a), for transactions between spouses involving transfers of property that are incident to a divorce.

Even this relatively lengthy description of the seven subsections of Sec. 267 does not begin to capture the intrigue of the actual Code provision. Omitted details provide (among others) very special rules for certain foreign currency losses; transfers to a DISC, or Domestic International Sales Corporation; transactions involving low-income housing; and partners who own less than a "qualified 5-percent interest." Although we cannot investigate any of the more exotic special rules, the following examples will illustrate just how important Sec. 267 can be to relatively routine business transactions between certain related parties.

EXAMPLE 15-1

Big Brother owns a van used 100% of the time in his computer consulting business. The van's adjusted basis is $15,000 and its fair market value is $10,000. He sells the van to Little Sister in 19X2 for $9,000. Although Brother and Sister are not related for all tax purposes, they are considered related for purposes of Sec. 267. Thus, because there has been a sale between related persons, none of the $6,000 loss realized by Big Brother may be recognized on his return for tax purposes.

EXAMPLE 15-2

Little Sister tired of the van in 19X3, and decided that she wanted a sports car. She sold the van to an unrelated third-party for $7,500. Her $1,500 loss ($9,000 basis – $7,500 selling price) is deductible if she used the van solely for business purposes.

Continued

EXAMPLE 15-2 (Con't.)

Had Little Sister sold the van for $11,000, the special provision in Sec. 267(d) would allow her to use the loss previously disallowed on the initial sale from Brother to Sister to offset her gain. Thus, in this example, her realized gain would be calculated as $2,000 ($11,000 selling price – $9,000 basis). Her taxable gain is $0 because she can offset the $2,000 gain by $2,000 of the $6,000 loss disallowed to Big Brother in Example 15-1. The remainder of the loss disallowed in Example 15-1 is, however, lost forever.

EXAMPLE 15-3

Ace Cargyle is a 75% shareholder in Runners, Inc. The accrual basis corporation has a March 31 year end. On December 31, 19X2, the corporation accrues an $8,000 monthly salary which is paid to Ace on January 1, 19X3. Under the rules defining related parties for purposes of Sec. 267, an individual who owns more than 50% of a corporation is considered related to that corporation. Section 267(a)(2) requires that any transaction between two related parties that generates an expense deduction for one and income for the other must be given special accounting treatment if the accounting methods of the two parties would allow a deduction in a year earlier than the year in which the income reported would. Sec. 267(a) provides that the deduction is not allowable until such time as the income is includable in the payee's taxable income. Therefore, since Ace owns more than 50% of Runners, Runners may not deduct the $8,000 accrual until Ace takes it into income in 19X3.

If Runners had a March 31 year end, made the accrual March 30, 19X3, and paid the amount on April 30, 19X3, the $8,000 would not be deductible by Runners, Inc., until the year ended March 31, 19X4.

EXAMPLE 15-4

John Adams sells a plot of land to Quincy Corporation for $50,000. John's tax basis in this land is $60,000. Although John does not personally own any stock in Quincy Corporation, his wife (Abigail) owns 60% of Quincy Corporation's outstanding stock. The other 40% of Quincy is owned by JA, Inc. John Adams owns 100% of the outstanding stock of JA, Inc. Given these facts, John Adams cannot recognize any part of the $10,000 loss that he realized on the sale of land to Quincy Corporation. By application of the constructive ownership rules of Secs. 267(c)(2) and (c)(4) John is deemed to indirectly own the 60% of Quincy Corporation that is directly owned by his wife, Abigail. And by application of Sec. 267(c)(1) John is also deemed to indirectly own the 40% of Quincy Corporation that is directly owned by his corporation, JA, Inc. Thus, even though John does not *directly* own any part of Quincy Corporation, he is deemed to own 100% of Quincy indirectly. This means of course, that John cannot recognize the $10,000 loss realized on this sale to Quincy Corporation by operation of Sec. 267(a)(1), as explained in Example 15-1.

In addition to various statutory provisions, like Secs. 267 and 482, the IRS may also rely on any of several rules of common law whenever they deem it necessary to recast a transaction between related parties to better reflect economic reality (at least in the perception of that amorphous government bureaucracy). Common-law rules, by their very nature, can be applied to almost any form of relationship between any two persons relative to almost any transaction. In short, like Sec. 482, common-law rules can be very generally applied.

JUDICIAL AUTHORITIES

There is no single generally accepted set of benchmark cases relative to federal income tax law. Most tax authorities would, however, include no less than 20 cases in any reasonably comprehensive list. Because our intent is simply to illustrate how any of these cases might be applied to related-party transactions, we will examine only three rules of common law in a very cursory manner.

> **Goal #4**
> Explain what judicial authority means and identify the tax principles supported by the three benchmark cases discussed in this chapter.

Lucas v. Earl

The case of *Lucas v. Earl* has come to stand for the general proposition that income must be recognized by the taxpayer who earns it, regardless of who actually receives it.[2] In very general terms, income derived from rendering a service must be recognized by the person rendering the service; income from property, by the person who owns the property. If applied literally, this apparently straightforward rule would mean that an individual taxpayer could not, acting alone, create a wholly-owned, personal-service corporation and have any part of the income derived from his or her services be recognized by (and taxed to) the corporation. We know from the material introduced in Chapter 6, however, that this conclusion is *not* correct. In other words, personal service corporations have been recognized as separate taxpayers for many years, even when they are wholly owned and operated by one individual. The potential for tax problems created under these circumstances is clearly reflected in the headnote to this chapter. As usual, therefore, the real difficulty is that of identifying correctly the circumstances under which the IRS is likely to challenge, and a court to sustain, the contention that there has been an improper assignment of income and that either the statutory rule of Sec. 482 or the judicial rule of *Lucas v. Earl* should be used to reallocate that income from one apparent taxpayer to another.

EXAMPLE 15-5

Larry and Silvia Marathon are successful CPAs who have organized their tax practice as a partnership (they each own 50%). Larry and Silvia have a son, Sylvester, who is in his third year of a five-year accounting program at State University. Sylvester has decided to take the Spring semester off from school to work in his parents' practice during tax season. He made this decision because he is having some trouble choosing an area of accounting specialization.

At the beginning of 19X3, Larry and Silvia gave Sylvester a ⅓ interest in the partnership. In addition, for 19X3 Larry and Silvia were each paid $50,000 (even though they were each paid $90,000 in the prior year), and Sylvester was also paid $10,000 for 19X3.

Continued

---

2 281 US 111 (1930).

EXAMPLE 15-5 (Con't.)

An IRS agent assessing this situation is likely to raise the issue of assignment of income. Recall that net income of a partnership in excess of payments to partners for services is allocated to partners in accordance with their profit-sharing ratios. By making Sylvester a partner under circumstances in which he is not yet qualified to be a partner and by underpaying themselves for their services to the partnership, the Marathons make it appear as if they are attempting to shift the taxability of a portion of partnership income from themselves to their son.

The IRS is likely to make an adjustment based on an argument that the partnership is underpaying Larry and Silvia for their services. The probable result will be an allocation of more of the income to Larry and Silvia as payments for services.

The chart below shows in the left column the results the Marathons hope to achieve. In the right column, the chart shows how the IRS might restructure the allocation of income.

	With Sylvester as Partner	Without Sylvester as Partner
Partnership Income (before payments to Larry, Silvia and Sylvester for services)	$260,000	$260,000
Payments for services	110,000	110,000
Net Income to be allocated according to profit-sharing ratios	$150,000	$150,000
Share of income allocated to		
Larry	$ 50,000	$ 75,000
Silvia	$ 50,000	$ 75,000
Sylvester	$ 50,000	$ -0-

Gregory v. Helvering

The case of *Gregory v. Helvering* has come to stand for the general proposition that a transaction must have a valid business purpose, above and beyond a reduction in taxes, if it is to be recognized for federal income tax purposes. [3] **Judge Learned Hand** summarized the intent of *Gregory v. Helvering* simply in the following words:

> The doctrine . . . means that in construing words of a tax statute which describe commercial or industrial transactions we are to understand them to refer to transactions entered upon for commercial or industrial purposes and not to include transactions entered upon for no other motive but to escape taxation. [4]

U.S. v. Phellis

The case of *U.S. v. Phellis* has come to stand for the general notion that the real substance of a transaction should control over its apparent form when tax results are

---

3 293 US 465 (1935).

4 *Comm'r. v. Tansport Trading & Terminal Corp.*, 176 F.2d 570, 572 (CA-2, 1979).

in question.[5] Once again, however, this general rule should not be interpreted too literally or, more precisely, it cannot be applied to each and every tax-motivated transaction. In a large number of transactions, the courts will give the full tax effect to the form in which it has been so carefully cast. In these instances, therefore, it may appear that form controls over substance in tax matters. Under other and sometimes similar circumstances, however, the IRS and the courts may rearrange the tax consequences of a transaction and justify the modification in part or in total on the judicial rule of substance-over-form. The difficult part is predicting correctly the circumstances under which the IRS is likely to raise this issue.

Rules of common law frequently overlap. Any of several different judicial rules might apply to a single transaction. In addition, statutory rules can overlap with judicial rules. As a student just beginning to study the fascinating subject of taxation, therefore, you should not worry too much about the need to identify precisely which rule of law is most likely to apply to any specific transaction. It is far more important for you to understand why the tax consequences of business transactions between related parties may or may not be subject to challenge by the IRS.

EXAMPLE 15-6

To examine the problem of determining which doctrine applies, consider the case of Manuel Gonzalez, a 100% shareholder in Computer Link, Inc. Computer Link was formed ten years ago to provide computer repair and maintenance services. The corporation has grown substantially and Manuel now has 30 employees. The corporation has for several years been paying Manuel a $100,000 salary per year and has accumulated $700,000 in earnings. The balance sheet shows that the company has about $500,000 in excess cash and marketable securities. Manuel wants to take that $500,000 out of the corporation to buy his dream house; so, for one year, he increases his salary to $500,000.

What happens if you smell this transaction? You probably get a whiff of something strange. Why? Upon closer examination, we are hard pressed to discover any possible benefit to be gained by the corporation if it pays such a large salary to Manuel for just one year. Therefore, Computer Link, Inc., is likely to run into trouble justifying a deduction for a $500,000 payment that appears to have no *business purpose,* despite the fact that the literal requirements for paying salaries and withholding income and employment taxes are met. Furthermore, we know that certain distributions from corporations to their shareholders are dividends. If we can identify no business purpose for this payment, we probably should conclude that although the *form* of the transaction is that of a salary payment, the *substance* of the transaction is a dividend to the extent that the salary is excessive. In addition to these two judicial principles, we can find extensive administrative authority that attempts to flesh out the concepts of business purpose and substance-versus-form in the specific case of "unreasonable compensation" to shareholders.

In the rest of this chapter we will investigate the tax consequences of a few transactions that are typical of a much larger set of problematic business events. To provide some degree of organization to this discussion, we will consider a few of the more common species of the genus that we categorize as the related-party transaction.

---

5 257 US 156 (1921).

OWNER-ENTITY TRANSACTIONS

Subchapter C is the part of the Internal Revenue Code concerned with transactions between a corporation and its shareholders in their role as shareholders.

Subchapter K is the part of the Internal Revenue Code concerned with transactions between a partnership and its partners in their role as partners.

Goal #5

Explain why transactions between a legal entity and its owners present so many difficult tax issues.

Transactions between a legal entity and its owners, *in their role as owners*, present many difficult tax issues. These tax issues are, in fact, so complex that entire subchapters of the Code have been reserved for them. The two subchapters of most general interest to business are Subchapters C and K. **Subchapter C**, which includes all of the sections numbered in the 300 series (all sections from Sec. 301 to Sec. 399), generally governs the tax consequences of transactions between a corporation and its shareholders in their role as shareholders. **Subchapter K**, which includes all of the sections numbered in the 700 series (all sections from Sec. 701 through 799), generally governs the tax consequences of transactions between a partnership and its partners in their role as partners.

Two aspects of this statutory classification scheme must be emphasized. First, the clause—"in their role as shareholders" (or as partners)—is very important. Transactions between corporations and their shareholders in other roles are *not* governed by the provisions located in Subchapter C. To illustrate, if a corporation compensates an individual, who is concurrently both a shareholder and an employee of the corporation, for services rendered by the individual in his or her role as an employee, that transaction will *not* be governed by any section in the 300 series so long as the compensation is reasonable in amount. Instead, that transaction will be governed by Secs. 1, 61, and 162, the same sections that govern all other compensation-for-services transactions. The fact that an employee just happens also to be a shareholder is of no tax significance because the transaction does *not* involve a shareholder *in his or her role as a shareholder.*

Second, Subchapter C is *not* the locus for all corporate tax rules, and Subchapter K is *not* the locus for all partnership tax rules. This common misconception is due to the fact that so many academic courses, concerned with the transactions governed by the rules located in Subchapters C and K, are referred to as courses in Corporate Taxation and Partnership Taxation, respectively. The common misconception is more than unfortunate for at least two reasons: (1) it sometimes causes newcomers to tax work to search futilely for statutory authority in the wrong portions of the Code, and (2) it often causes those same people to overlook the fact that many of the provisions in Subchapters C and K apply equally to individuals, estates, and trusts, as well as to corporations, partnerships, and other legal persons. This conclusion is true because corporate shareholders and partners are found in widely verigated forms. In still other words, the tax consequence of a transaction between an individual and a corporation, in that individual's role as a shareholder, is most correctly classified as an issue of individual taxation (not as an issue of corporate taxation) even though the governing statutory provision is located in Subchapter C. Similarly, a transaction between a partnership and a C corporation, in the partnership's role as a stockholder, is an issue of partnership taxation, not corporate taxation, even though the statutory authority governing the transaction is found in Subchapter C, rather than in Subchapter K, of the Code.

SYMBOLS

The study of owner-entity transactions can be facilitated by the use of a few simple symbols. To begin, let us represent an individual with a stickfigure; a corporation, with a rectangle; a partnership, with a triangle; and a fiduciary, with a diamond. Further refinement of these four basic symbols may also be useful. For example, the area of a rectangle or a triangle can be used to represent the net assets of a corporation or partnership, respectively. The capital letter C inside a rectangle can designate a C corporation; the letter S, a corporation that has elected to be taxed under the rules of Subchapter S. An E inside a diamond would signify an estate; a T, a trust. These symbols are summarized in Figure 15-1.

Arrows between entities can represent either (1) critical relationships or (2) the item(s) being exchanged in a specific transaction. The words used, and the context of the symbol, will suggest which use of the arrow is intended. For example, in Figure 15-2 arrows are used to represent the ownership of an imaginary C corporation. There, individual I owns 30% of Corporation C's outstanding stock; trust T, 20%; and partnership P, the other 50%. In Figure 15-3, on the other hand, arrows are used to identify the items being exchanged in a transaction. There, an individual (I) is selling a property to a C corporation for $10 cash. As noted in Figure 15-3, the individual (I) has a $3 tax basis in the property being sold.

If the individual designated by the capital letter I in both Figures 15-2 and 15-3 is one and the same person, then the transaction in Figure 15-3 is a transaction between

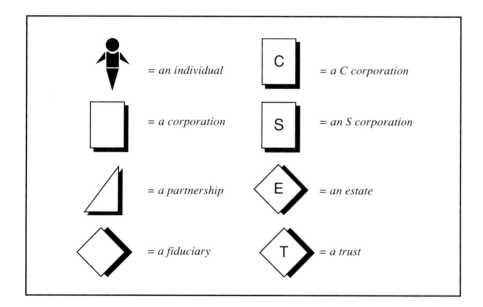

FIGURE 15-1

Common Symbols

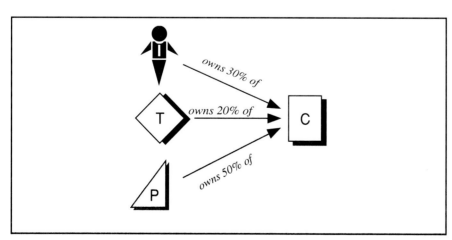

FIGURE 15-2

An Example of Ownership Details

FIGURE 15-3

A Sales
Transaction?

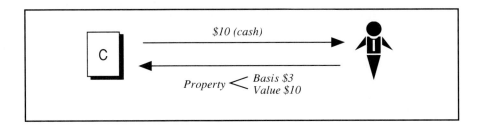

a C corporation and one of its own shareholders. As explained earlier, however, that fact alone will not automatically bring the transaction of Figure 15-3 within the jurisdiction of Subchapter C, even though it might raise some general skepticism about whether the transaction is *bona fide*. Before we can conclude that the rules of Subchapter C will govern the tax consequences of the transaction illustrated in Figure 15-3, we must determine whether or not individual I is acting in his or her role as a shareholder of Corporation C. Sometimes, of course, the true facts will not be readily discovered.

SALE TRANSACTIONS

To make the issue of related-party transactions both more interesting and more realistic, let us assume that the $10 (cash) in Figure 15-3 represents not just $10, but $10 million. Let us further assume that individual I owns 100% of Corporation C, not just 30% as depicted earlier in Figure 15-2. As revised, the real question implicit in the apparent sale transaction (diagrammed in Figure 15-3) becomes much clearer. That is, if the property that I is selling to C is actually worth $10 million, then the transaction in Figure 15-3 can properly be described as a sale, and the tax provisions that generally govern sales transactions ought to apply. On the other hand, if the property that I is transferring to C is really worth something more or less than $10 million, it would be incorrect to describe the transaction as a simple sale. A correct description of the transaction under those circumstances would depend on a careful analysis of all the facts surrounding the transaction.

Because the tax provisions pertinent to property transactions have not yet been discussed in our text—those discussions are located in Part Five—you are not yet prepared to understand the potentially significant impact of alternative interpretations of the facts surrounding Figure 15-3 if C actually gives I $10 million cash for a property worth only (say) $5 million. Several aspects of that analysis will be clearer to you after you have had an opportunity to study the next chapter (Chapter 16) and you learn more about the income tax treatment of capital gains and losses. For now, therefore, we will suggest only that the IRS might interpret C's transfer of $10 million to I, for a property worth only $5 million, as more realistically being described as

1. (Part A) A sale of property for $5 million; plus

2. (Part B) A $5 million dividend.

Under these circumstances, the IRS might argue that Figure 15-4 is a more realistic diagram of the true economic facts than is Figure 15-3. If the IRS did recast the transaction as depicted in Figure 15-4, the tax consequences to both C and I would differ significantly from the tax consequences that would flow from a simple $10 million sale. The major differences can be summarized as follows:

Tax Consequences	If a $10M Sale	If a $5M Sale Plus a $5M Dividend
For C	Basis in property is $10 million	Basis in property is $5 million
For I	A $7 million gain (possibly a capital gain)	A $2 million gain (possibly a capital gain) plus a $5 million dividend

Having just finished your study of the depreciation provisions, you should understand clearly why Corporation C would prefer to have a $10 million basis (rather than only a $5 million basis) in the property that it acquired from I. After you study the next chapter, and possibly Chapter 19 (where the passive activity loss (or PAL) rules are further explained), you will also understand why I might prefer a $7 million capital gain to a $2 million capital gain plus a $5 million dividend.

The IRS could challenge the treatment of a transaction structured as a simple $10 million sale of property under either (or both) Sec. 482 and/or the judicial rule of substance-over- form. If the dispute proceeded to trial, the court's conclusion would rest on its holding as to the true fair market value of the property transferred from I to C. As we noted in Chapter 13, the taxpayer generally carries the burden of proof in tax cases. Hence, I should be prepared to prove the real value of the property sold. Incidentally, a court might hold that the true value was some amount between $5 and $10 million. If so, the tax results would be adjusted accordingly.

Before leaving this discussion of an apparent sale, from an owner to an entity owned by the seller, we should recall briefly the facts that would most likely raise suspicions within the IRS. In our original diagram (Figure 15-2), we started with a corporation that was 30% owned by I; 20%, by T; and 50%, by P. Thereafter, we modified our assumed facts to give I a 100% ownership of Corporation C. This modification of the assumed facts should have triggered your sixth sense (or the smell test), suggesting the presence of a questionable related party transaction. In other words, as originally diagrammed in Figure 15-2, if trust T and partnership P are truly independent of individual I, they (as 70% owners of C) would not allow Corporation C to pay $10 million for a property worth only $5 million. On the other hand, if I owns 100% of C, or if I is the sole beneficiary of T and a 90% partner in P, their presence might be

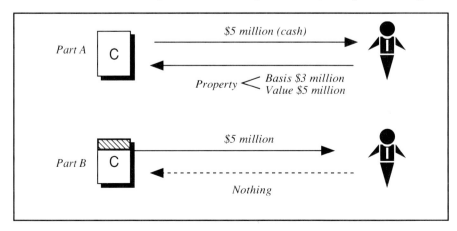

FIGURE 15-4

An Alternative Interpretation of Figure 15-3

ignored as insignificant. This last possibility illustrates clearly why attribution rules (or constructive ownership rules) are needed in the Code.

COMPENSATION TRANSACTIONS

As a second example of a suspect related-party transaction, let us consider the economic reality of a typical payroll transaction between a corporation and its employee-president, who is also the corporation's sole shareholder. This example will illustrate, via diagrams, the concept introduced earlier in Example 15-6. If we were to draw a simple employer-employee compensation transaction between two imaginary taxpayers, it might be depicted as in Figure 15-5. That illustration would at first glance suggest that this is a routine transaction governed by the normal Code rules located somewhere outside of Subchapter C. That is, the corporation would appear to be entitled to a $250,000 salary expense deduction, by way of Sec. 162, and the individual would recognize salary income of that same amount via Secs. 1 and 61.

On the other hand, the IRS just might believe that a more accurate presentation of the true facts is the presentation implied by Figure 15-6. In that figure, individual I is being paid a salary of $50,000 (in Part A) and a dividend of $200,000 (in Part B). Obviously the second transaction would be a transaction governed by the rules of Subchapter C because dividends are only paid to shareholders in their role as shareholders.

For those of you who understood the message implicit in the tax planning portion of Chapter 6, the reasons that a taxpayer like individual I in Figures 15-5 and 15-6 would have for preferring the former interpretation of the facts over the latter interpretation are obvious. For the benefit of those not blessed with such intuition, let us add a few more details. Suppose that we were to discover, for example, that Corporation C in Figure 15-5 had earned a taxable income of approximately $325,000 *before giving any consideration to compensating individual I.* Hence, if the facts are

FIGURE 15-5

A Compensation Transaction?

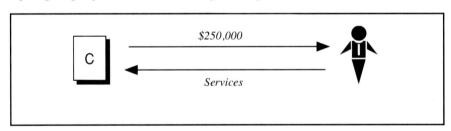

FIGURE 15-6

An Alternative (IRS) Interpretation of Figure 15-5

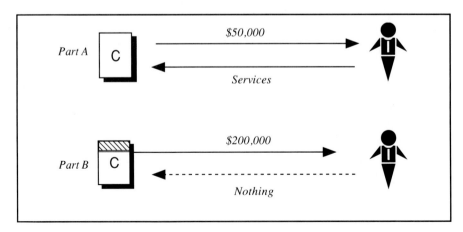

really as depicted in Figure 15-5, Corporation C will owe an income tax liability of only $13,750 ($50,000 x 15% plus $25,000 x 25%). On the other hand, if the facts of Figure 15-6 are correct, C will owe a tax of $90,500 ($50,000 x 15% plus $25,000 x 25% plus $25,000 x 34% plus $175,000 x 39%). Individual I will owe the same amount of income tax either way because his or her gross income will be $250,000 total in both cases—either $250,000 in salary plus no dividends or $50,000 in salary plus $200,000 in dividends. The potential double tax implicit in Figure 15-6 will, however, effectively cost Corporation C an extra $76,750 in taxes for the year ($90,500 – $13,750). Similar opportunities for tax avoidance are commonplace in many owner-entity transactions.

Based on the two preceding examples you may be inclined to believe that every transaction between an entity and a *sole* shareholder is automatically a suspect transaction. Unfortunately the conundrum of related-party transactions is not solved that easily. At least a few transactions between a corporation and its sole shareholder can be accepted at face value because they hold little or no opportunity for tax avoidance. Others are automatically suspect because tax avoidance opportunities are innate to the transaction. The ability to distinguish the one from the other requires a reasonably sophisticated understanding of our federal income tax laws. The dividend transaction is a good example of this ambiguity.

DIVIDEND TRANSACTIONS

The word *dividend* is commonly used to describe any distribution of a corporation's assets to its shareholders, in their role as shareholders, so long as the corporation making the distribution receives nothing in return. At least in its conversational usage, the term dividend is often applied to distributions by S corporations as well as by C corporations. The opportunity for tax avoidance in these two very similar transactions is quite different.

Dividends Paid by C Corporations

If a C corporation has either (a) **current** or (b) **accumulated earnings and profits** (or **E&P**), any distribution of its assets to its shareholders, in their role as shareholders, is ordinarily deemed to be a dividend to the extent of the E&P.[6] Although the term **earnings and profits** is not specifically defined in the Code, it is a tax law *approximation* of the same concept that financial accountants describe as retained earnings. If the shareholder of a C corporation, with adequate E&P, were to cause the corporation to distribute a $200,000 cash dividend, that transaction would ordinarily have no tax avoidance potential. The essence of this dividend transaction can be diagrammed simply, as in Figure 15-7.

> **Current E&P** refers to E&P earned in the immediate tax year.
>
> **Accumulated E&P** refers to E&P earned and accumulated in previous tax years.
>
> **E&P (earnings and profits)** is a tax law *approximation* of the concept financial accountants describe.

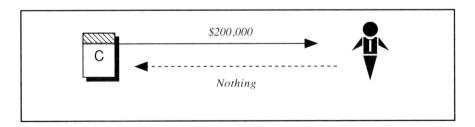

$200,000

Nothing

FIGURE 15-7

An *Innocuous* Dividend Transaction

---

6 See Secs. 301 and 316.

FIGURE 15-8

A *Loaded*
Dividend
Transaction

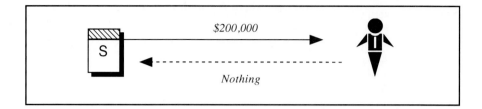

Observe that in Figure 15-7 the net assets of Corporation C are being reduced by $200,000; hence, the size of the rectangle representing C is also being reduced (by the size of the cross-hatched rectangular area in the diagram). The tax consequences, assuming that C has either current or accumulated E&P of at least $200,000, are to require I to recognize $200,000 in the form of dividend income but to give C no deduction because the Code does not authorize most C corporations to deduct any part or all of the dividends that they pay. (An exception may apply to dividends paid by utility companies.) An almost identical transaction between an S corporation and its shareholders, or between a family partnership and its family-member partners, yields dramatically different tax consequences.

Dividends Paid by S Corporations

If an S corporation distributes some of its assets to its shareholders, in their roles as shareholders, the distribution is ordinarily treated as a return of capital.[7] This tax result is consistent with the pass-thru or conduit status given to both S corporations and partnerships, as described in Chapter 6. That is, the entity's taxable income is taxed to the owners when earned, not when distributed. Therefore, there is no double tax potential (assuming that the S corporation never operated as a C corporation) and no tax reason to avoid distribution of accumulated S corporation earnings. In fact, as you will see below, a $200,00 cash dividend distribution to the sole shareholder of an S corporation can hold surprising and significant tax avoidance potential. This result occurs even though, as illustrated in Figures 15-7 and 15-8, a diagram of the two transactions appear to be virtually identical.

Because of the potential of a double tax on dividends paid by C corporations—that is, having an income stream first made subject to the federal income tax at the corporate level, and then subjecting that same income stream to a second federal income tax on the dividend at the shareholder level—small, closely held C corporations very rarely (if ever) pay any dividends. Because an S corporation's dividends ordinarily are not subject to the potential of a double tax, the owners of S corporations have a strong incentive to distribute as little as possible of the corporations's earnings as salary, and as much as possible as a dividend, because this transformation can sometimes minimize the owner's liability for his or her self employment (or FICA) taxes. In other words, if in Figure 15-8, individual I owns 100% of the S corporation, the IRS might have good reason to step in and recast this same transaction as diagrammed in Figure 15-9. Although the *income tax* consequences of Figures 15-8 and 15-9 would *not* change, the FICA tax consequences certainly would.

If you recall from Chapter 1 that the self-employment tax can currently exceed $10,000 per year for each self-employed individual, you will understand why a dividend paid by an S corporation holds far more tax avoidance potential than does a doubly-taxed dividend paid by a C corporation.

---

7 See Sec. 1378.

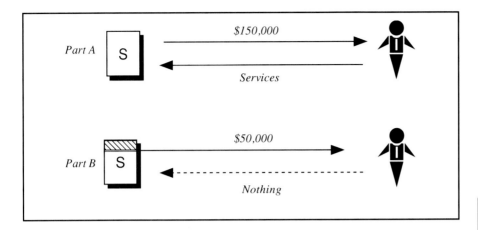

FIGURE 15-9

An Alternative (IRS) Interpretation of Figure 15-8

Once again, based on the prior examples, you might conclude that transactions between an owner and an entity are suspect only if the owner is a sole owner. As stated earlier, however, the presence of more than one owner of a legal entity does not *automatically* make a related-party transaction less suspect, from a tax point of view, even if the multiple owners are *not* otherwise related to one another. This conclusion can be illustrated through the careful analysis of a stock redemption transaction.

> **Goal #6**
> Analyze the fundamental tax issue involved in stock-redemption transactions and the two statutory provisions designed to address the issues.

STOCK-REDEMPTION TRANSACTIONS

Any transaction in which a C corporation purchases shares of its own outstanding stock can be described as a **stock redemption**. The term *stock redemption* is ambivalent, however, relative to the income tax consequences of the transaction so far as the shareholder (whose stock is being acquired) is concerned. From the standpoint of the selling stockholder, a stock redemption can be treated for income tax purposes as either (1) a dividend or (2) a capital gain or loss. Although we cannot investigate all of the tax nuances innate in stock redemptions, we can look briefly at the statutory provisions that generally determine the income tax consequences of this interesting transaction. To understand the primary tax issue, study Figure 15-10 carefully.

> A **stock redemption** is a purchase by a corporation of its own outstanding stock from its shareholders.

The most important tax question implicit in the transaction diagrammed in Figure 15-10 can be stated as follows: For federal income tax purposes, should I treat the stock redemption as a sale of stock or as a dividend? If the correct answer is "as a sale of stock," I will report a $20,000 capital gain. On the other hand, if the correct answer is "as a dividend," I must report a $100,000 dividend! The reasonableness of this second alternative is most easily demonstrated in the context of a wholly-owned corporation. In that extreme case, the fact that a sole stockholder gave up some of his or her stock in the corporation is a totally meaningless gesture; hence the result has to be a dividend if the acquiring corporation has the requisite E&P. If unrelated owners are present, the conclusion as to the correct treatment of the transaction is much less obvious. In this latter instance, however, statutory rules are provided to resolve any doubt concerning the correct tax treatment of the redemption transaction.

Section 302

The correct tax treatment for any shareholder involved in a routine stock redemption is usually found in Sec. 302. Although this provision is far more complex than the oversimplified discussion below implies, Sec. 302 would generally provide that an individual (in a situation comparable to that depicted for I in Figure 15-10) treat the

FIGURE 15-10

Dissecting a
Stock Redemption

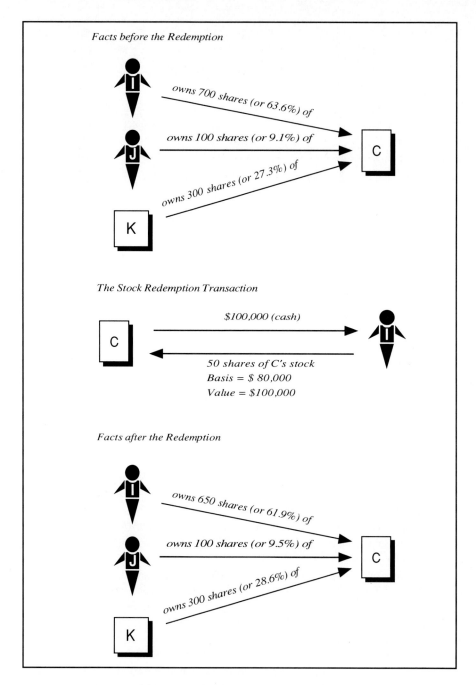

apparent sale of his or her stock as a corporate distribution, rather than as a sale, and I must, therefore, recognize the $100,000 dividend. The rationale for this general conclusion is that I's interest in C has not changed *significantly* even though his or her share of ownership in C has declined from 63.6% before the stock redemption to 61.9% after the redemption. The mere presence of two unrelated parties (represented by individual J and corporation K in Figure 15-10) as unrelated minority stockholders would usually not be sufficient to modify the tax result if, as in this example, the shareholder whose stock is redeemed continues to own more than 50% of the outstanding stock of the corporation after the stock redemption.

In determining whether a shareholder owns 50% or more of the stock in a corporation that is party to a stock redemption, a tax adviser typically must apply a set of constructive ownership rules with great care. In our example (Figure 15-10) we simply assumed that the three shareholders (I, J, and K) were wholly unrelated to one another. In real-world stock redemption transactions, you cannot make that assumption. Instead, you must thoroughly investigate a veritable network of possible relationships (similar to those that we explored earlier in this chapter relative to Sec. 267) between each and every shareholder of the corporation making the stock redemption. As interesting as that exercise is, we cannot undertake it as part of this course simply because it requires too much time and because it would add little or nothing to our conceptual understanding of related-party transactions. At the same time, however, a few words of caution are in order.

Section 318

Unfortunately the Code includes not just one but several different sets of attribution rules. Earlier in this chapter we noted the attribution rules found in Sec. 267(b). As explained there, those rules are solely applicable to transactions involving losses, expenses, or interest. Hence the rules of Sec. 267(b) would *not* apply to a stock-redemption transaction. The attribution rules found in Sec. 318 might apply, however. To determine whether Sec. 318 applies to a stock-redemption transaction is a difficult task in statutory interpretation.

The key to the solution of this syntactical riddle must begin with a careful reading of the first sentence of Sec. 318(a). It reads as follows:

> Sec. 318. Constructive Ownership of Stock.
>
> (a) GENERAL RULE—For purposes of those provisions of this subchapter to which the rules contained in this section are expressly made applicable—
>
> (1) MEMBERS OF FAMILY—
>
> (A) IN GENERAL—An individual shall be considered as owning the stock owned, directly or indirectly, by or for—
>
> (i) his spouse (other than a spouse who is legally separated from the individual under a decree of divorce or separate maintenance), and
>
> (ii) his children, grandchildren, and parents.

Note that this sentence says that the constructive ownership rules of Sec. 318 will apply (1) only to the "provisions of this subchapter" and (2) only if they are "expressly made applicable." Paraphrased, this sentence says that (1) Sec. 318 will apply only to transactions governed by Subchapter C—that is, since Sec. 318 is part of the 300 series, the reference to "this subchapter" must mean Subchapter C—and (2) it will apply only if another section specifically says that it does apply.

A careful examination of Sec. 302(c) would uncover the following sentence: "Except as provided in paragraph (2) of this subsection, section 318(a) shall apply in determining the ownership of stock for purposes of this section." In other words, because it is expressly provided in Sec. 302, the attribution rules of Sec. 318 must be applied to stock-redemption transactions, but with some modification (as detailed in Sec. 302(c)(2)).

The significance of this discussion of Sec. 318 attribution rules is once again not the statutory detail that governs the tax treatment of stock redemptions, but rather the convoluted concept of related-party transactions. In other words, before you begin to investigate any transaction between a business entity and one or more of its owners, you will very likely have to investigate every possible relationship that might exist among or between any or all of the owners of that entity. Never assume that the mere presence of *apparently* unrelated owners is sufficient to make an owner-entity transaction an innocuous transaction from an income tax point of view. And never assume that one set of attribution rules is exactly like another set. They differ significantly. For example, in some attribution rules brothers and sisters are deemed to be related persons; in others, they are not.

Section 303

One final word of caution relative to stock-redemption transactions is necessary. In Chapter 13 we learned that (1) more than one Code section may sometimes apply to the same business transaction, and (2) the several applicable sections may not be adequately cross-referenced. These same two problems are equally applicable to related-party transactions. It is entirely possible that a stock redemption, like that diagrammed in Figure 15-10, could be governed by Sec. 303 rather than Sec. 302. In that event, the correct tax treatment for I is the sale treatment, with a $20,000 capital gain, not the $100,000 dividend. Section 303, which may override the general rules of Sec. 302, only governs stock redemptions made to pay death taxes. The details of that very special case must once again be deferred to more advanced tax courses.

As a final example of owner-entity transactions that are likely to be challenged by the IRS, let us examine the opportunities for tax avoidance in a family partnership. As the following example will illustrate, the IRS sometimes has good reason to recast the real economic results of a family partnership business in a way that is very different than the way in which it was initially reported on the partnership tax return.

FAMILY PARTNERSHIPS

Goal #7
Describe some of the common tax avoidance possibilities endemic to family partnerships.

The partners of a family partnership frequently include parents, children, grandparents, and grandchildren. These family partnerships can be capital intensive, labor intensive, or involve a combination of both capital and labor as material income producing factors. They can engage in almost any kind of business and they commonly include such diverse ventures as family farms and professional medical service organizations. The partner's individual participation in the partnership's business can vary from no participation whatsoever to total involvement. The partnership agreement can be anything from a carefully drafted legal document to an oral promise or a handshake. A partner's interest may have been acquired by purchase, as a gift, through personal effort, or in any of several other ways. Given this wide diversity among family partnerships, the IRS has good reason to suspect that at least some family partnerships are created largely as an income-splitting device to achieve inappropriate tax advantages.

To illustrate, let us expand on the idea introduced earlier in Example 15-5 and consider a labor-intensive family partnership that is equally owned by five individuals: a middle-aged couple, an older parent, a college-age child, and a younger child. Assume that this partnership earns approximately $150,000 per year, before allocating any amount of income to any of the partners. The partnership tax return might initially allocate the $150,000 as follows:

Partner	Salary	Remainder	Total
The couple	$75,000	$20,000	$95,000
Older parent	10,000	10,000	20,000
Child in college	12,000	10,000	22,000
Younger child	3,000	10,000	13,000

This reported allocation of taxable income earned by the partnership could be a wholly legitimate reflection of economic reality if all five of the family members actually work in the business. For example, the partnership might be engaged in a restaurant and bar business, and the relative value of services contributed by each of the five family members may be correctly reflected in the salary schedule identified above.

On the other hand, the partnership's business might alternatively involve a highly skilled professional service where only one of the two parents (that is, the couple) is legally authorized to practice that profession. The spouse of the professional might perform some less valuable office assistance function while none of the other partners ever make an appearance on the partnership's premise. The elder parent could reside in a nursing home; the college age child might live a thousand miles from home for 12 months each year; and the younger child might be a carefree participant in high school extracurricular activities. In the latter event, the reported salary structure certainly does not reflect the economic value of the services contributed by each family member. Given the facts assumed in the second scenario, the conclusion of the IRS would almost certainly be sustained in court. Given those facts, it would be virtually impossible for the family to prove that their initial representation correctly reflected economic reality. In fact, with such an extreme distortion of economic reality, the partner responsible for the tax aspects of the partnership's tax return would likely be charged with fraud and risk the possibility of a jail term. Each of the other family members would likely be subject to penalties and interest for underpayment of the income tax.

This completes our discussion of owner-entity transactions. Although transactions between a business entity and one or more of its owners do represent a significant portion of all related-party tax problems, the IRS will sometimes challenge the tax consequences of transactions between persons who are less directly related.

OTHER RELATED-PARTY TRANSACTIONS

To round out our discussion of related-party transactions, let us consider two examples that do not directly involve transactions between an entity and its owners. The first example concerns multiple corporations; the second, foreign operations. Historically, the IRS has found it appropriate to monitor everyday business transactions between multiple entities and foreign operations because they present unusually large opportunities for tax avoidance.

Goal #8
Explain the ways in which multiple corporations or those engaged in foreign operations provide opportunities for tax avoidance.

MULTIPLE CORPORATIONS

Figure 15-11 illustrates a set of three (multiple) corporations that are *not* members of a controlled group. In this figure, the ownership of each of four, unrelated, individual stockholders (identified as I, J, K, and L) was very carefully controlled. The goal of such a contrived ownership distribution is usually to achieve tax savings comparable

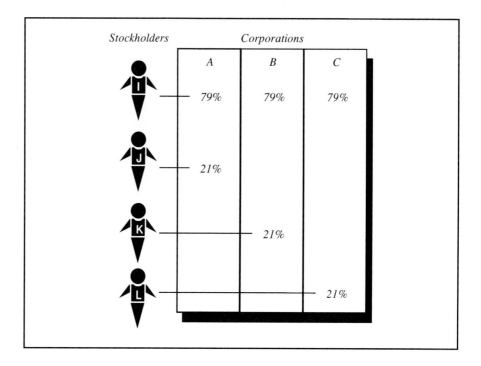

FIGURE 15-11

Example of Nonfamily Ownership Arrangement That Avoids Controlled Group Status

to those illustrated in Figure 15-12. This tax saving idea will work, however, only if the taxable income of each corporation is also carefully controlled or monitored.

To illustrate the importance of the intra-corporate distribution of taxable income between three corporations, consider the two alternatives outlined below:

| | Taxable Income or (Loss) | |
Corporation	Alternative A	Alternative B
X	$200,000	$ 50,000
Y	(50,000)	50,000
Z	-0-	50,000
Total Taxable Income	$150,000	$150,000
Total Tax Liability	$ 61,250*	$ 22,500

*Ignores any possible tax value of Y's NOL.

Suppose that one individual (for example, individual I in Figure 15-11) owned 79% of Corporations X, Y, and Z. Under these circumstances, individual I in the situation detailed as *Alternative A*, would have a very strong tax motivation to cause X Corporation to enter into various dubious transactions with corporations Y and Z. The objective of these dubious transactions would be to move taxable income out of X Corporation and into Y and Z Corporations until the optimal result (identified as *Alternative B*) had been achieved. The specific transactions utilized to achieve this optimal result could take any of several forms. For example, Corporation X could do the following:

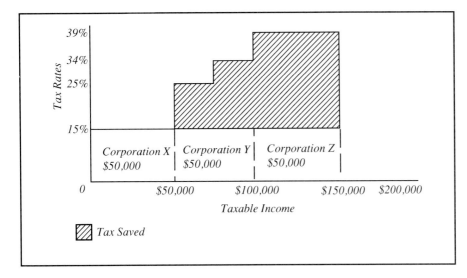

FIGURE 15-12

**Tax Advantage of
Three Multiple
Corporations**

- Sell property to corporations Y and Z at below-market prices and allow them to resell those same properties to unrelated parties at their true fair market values.

- Provide critical management services to corporations Y and Z at little or no cost.

- Make interest-free loans to corporations Y and Z.

- Rent equipment or buildings to corporations Y and Z at below market prices.

None of these (or any of several other possible) transactions would *directly* involve a transaction between an entity and an owner of that entity. Nevertheless, each of these transactions would fail to reflect economic reality, and each would have been unduly influenced by tax avoidance objectives.

Although the presence of an unrelated, minority stockholder—identified as individual J in Figure 15-11—adds some degree of internal reliability to any transaction negotiated by X Corporation, the dominant position of individual I (who owns 79% of X) makes those same transactions potentially suspect. In other words, individual I may indirectly stand to gain more from the potential tax savings to X, Y, and Z combined, than individual J would lose via his or her 21% ownership in X. Furthermore, I might indirectly compensate J for any loss in the value of his or her stock in X that is attributable to the dubious transactions.

If the IRS can prove that any of the transactions between X and either Y or Z do not reflect economic reality, both Sec. 482 and/or the judicial doctrine of business purpose provide sufficient authority for the IRS to reallocate income and deductions in a way that more clearly reflects the true economic incomes of each of the three corporations.

Foreign Operations

Large corporations increasingly engage in multinational operations. In the prototype case, goods are manufactured in a country with low labor costs and/or abundant raw materials. The manufactured goods are shipped to, and sold in, other countries. Because the tax laws of various countries differ widely, the multinational parent corporation may have good tax reasons for dictating inter-company pricing policies in a way that will minimize its overall tax costs rather than in a way that reflects economic reality.

To illustrate this possibility (see Figure 15-13), consider the tax opportunity of Corporation P to dictate the intercompany prices between Subsidiary MFG (the manufacturing operation) located in country A; Subsidiary HVN, a paper or shell corporation located in country B, a country with very low income tax rates, often called a tax-haven country; and Subsidiary SAL (the final sales operation) located in country C. Assume, as illustrated in Figure 15-13, that Corporation P, which owns 100% of the stock of each subsidiary corporation (MFG, HVN, and SAL), is a (U.S.) domestic corporation.

FIGURE 15-13

An Example of Foreign Operations

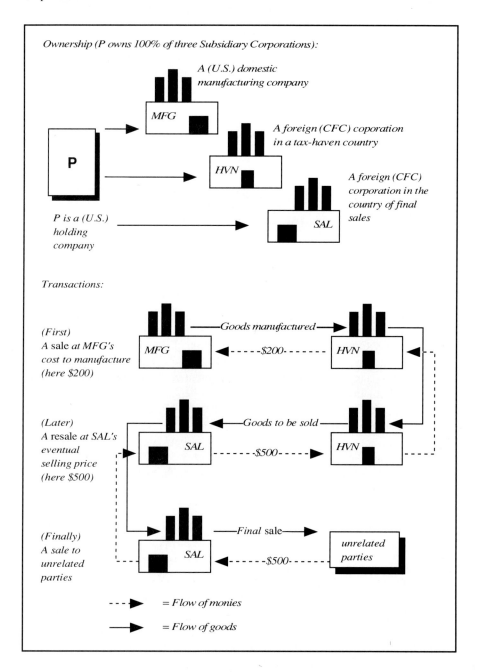

If there were no Sec. 482 and no CFC (Controlled Foreign Corporation) rules, P might dictate that MFG first sell its product to HVN at a price equal to MFG's cost to manufacture the product. P might further dictate that HVN resell that same product to SAL at a price equal to the eventual sales price that SAL will charge its customers. Given this series of purchase and sale transactions, P would attempt to move all of the taxable income associated with the manufacture and eventual sale of its product to tax-haven country B. Note that none of these transactions were made *directly* between an entity and an owner of that entity. Nevertheless, the apparent bookkeeping (or accounting) results do not reflect economic reality. To prevent exactly this sort of tax legerdemain, Sec. 482 gives the IRS the authority to reallocate all income and deduction items between the various subsidiaries using **arm's-length prices.** Because an arm's length price may be a difficult number for anyone to establish, the Code also includes special provisions that will penalize any CFC that operates in the manner described for Subsidiary HVN in this example. The penalty extracted by the **subpart F** rules, which are solely applicable to CFCs, would be to make 100% of HVN's taxable income immediately taxable to the parent corporation (P) even if HVN distributed nothing to P during the year in question.

No multinational management team would be so foolish, as in our highly contrived example, to try and trap 100% of its profits in one tax-haven country. There is reason to suspect, however, that carefully monitored pricing policies have caused a less extreme shifting of taxable income among the nations of the world for many years. When the top U.S. marginal corporate tax rates were higher than those in many other countries, the issue of intercompany pricing primarily affected outbound transactions. For the past few years—specifically, after the major reduction in the top U.S. marginal tax rates in 1986—the transfer-pricing problem has been increasingly associated with inbound transactions. Much of the current debate on intercompany pricing involves foreign manufacturers with growing U.S. sales. Some commentators suggest that these multinational corporations are not paying their fair share of the U.S. income tax; others disagree.[8]

As noted earlier, the primary objective of this chapter is simply to acquaint you with some of the routine business transactions that may be subject to careful scrutiny by the IRS. In general, these are transactions between closely related parties. Although transactions between a business entity and one or more of its owners are almost automatically subject to special IRS scrutiny, those transactions are not the only ones subject to this dubious honor. We hope the examples that we have provided in this chapter will give you a good feel for the tax issues involved. The better that you become at spotting those related-party transactions that are most likely to be challenged, the more likely you are to understand tax planning opportunities in general.

> **Arm's-length prices** are prices that would be charged between taxpayers who are not related parties or who do not otherwise have incentives to either understate or overstate prices.
>
> **SubpartF** of the Internal Revenue Code establishes special tax rules applicable to CFC's.

_____ KEY POINTS TO REMEMBER

✓ Related-party transactions are subject to special IRS scrutiny because these transactions present many opportunities for tax avoidance.

---

8 For example, see Gregory J. Millman, "The Trauma of Transfer Pricing," *CFO*, November 1991, pp. 30–34; Lauren Chambliss, "Holier Than Thou," *Financial World*, May 29, 1990, pp. 20-21; Larry Martz with Rick Thomas, "The Corporate Shell Game," *Newsweek*, April 15, 1991, pp.48–49; and Howard Gleckman with Ted Holden, "Can Uncle Sam Mend this Hole in His Pocket?" *Business Week,* September 10, 1990, pp. 48–49.

✓ As we use it, the term *related-party transaction* means a transaction that fails to represent economic reality because tax consequences have *unduly influenced* the precise form in which the transaction was arranged and recorded.

✓ Section 482 gives the IRS the power to reallocate any item(s) affecting net taxable income among organizations, trades, or businesses that are directly or indirectly owned or controlled. A Sec. 482 reallocation is allowable if it prevents the evasion of taxes or more clearly reflects the income of each organization, trade, or business.

✓ Section 267 alters the tax results in transactions, between related parties, that involve losses, expenses, or interest.

✓ Three important judicial authorities provide broad powers for the IRS to restructure transactions. The first, *Lucas v. Earl*, holds that income must be taxed to the taxpayer who earned it. The second, *Gregory v. Helvering*, holds that transactions will be given tax effect only if there is a valid business purpose in addition to tax avoidance. The third, *U.S. v. Phellis*, holds that for tax purposes the substance of a transaction should control over its form.

✓ Transactions between a legal entity and its owners, *in their role as owners*, present difficult tax issues because both sides of the transaction may be under the control of owners who may structure the transaction in ways that do not reflect economic reality. Three common examples have to do with the sale, compensation, and dividend transactions.

✓ A stock redemption is a purchase by a corporation of its own outstanding stock from its shareholder. The tax effects of stock redemptions are governed by statutory provisions that determine whether the transaction will be treated as a sale of stock or as a dividend. These provisions were generally designed to provide a test of whether a taxpayer has given up enough control through the redemption to justify non-dividend treatment.

✓ Attribution (or constructive ownership) rules indirectly assign (and sometimes reassign) direct ownership among certain related parties for purposes of determining the assumed effective ownership of every possible related-party owner.

✓ Family partnerships are sometimes used by taxpayers to split income among family members. The IRS often investigates various aspects of family partnerships to test whether they reflect economic reality.

✓ Corporations and other entities with foreign operations provide many opportunities to alter the calculation of taxable income in ways that do not reflect economic reality.

───── RECALL PROBLEMS

1. Define the term *related-party transaction*. Explain why related-party transactions are viewed with skepticism by the IRS.

2. Assume that individual I owns 100% of the outstanding stock of a C corporation. If I also owns real estate which she leases to C at an arm's-length

    a. Will C corporation be allowed to deduct the monthly rent payments made to I?

    b. Will the tax rules that govern this transaction be found in Subchapter C of the Code? Explain briefly.

c. If C earns a taxable income in excess of $75,000 each year, why would I be tempted to raise the rent on this property to something greater than an arm's-length price?

d. What is meant by the phrase arm's-length price?

3. In outline form, identify some of the circumstances under which the IRS might invoke Sec. 482. If Sec. 482 is invoked, what can the IRS do?

4. In 19X1, Ted purchased 100 shares of General Food's 7 million shares of outstanding common stock for $7,000. In 19X7, Ted sold these 100 shares in General Foods to Wink, Inc., for $5,000. Assume that Ted owns 75% of Wink's outstanding stock. In 19X8, Wink, Inc., resold the same 100 shares of General Foods to Tom Foolery, an unrelated individual.

a. What amount of gain or loss, if any, should Ted report in 19X7?

b. What amount of gain or loss, if any, should Wink, Inc., report in 19X8 if it sold the share to Tom for $6,500?

c. What amount of gain or loss, if any, should Wink, Inc., report in 19X8 if it sold the shares to Tom for $7,500?

5. Antoinette and Phillipe (a married couple) are 50/50 shareholders in Albertville Corporation, a June 30 year end, accrual basis corporation. When they formed the corporation, they capitalized it with $50,000 identified as a capital contribution and $100,000 identified as a loan. On June 30, 19X2, Albertville accrued $12,000 in interest payable on the note to Antoinette and Phillipe (cash basis taxpayers). Describe the tax consequences of this transaction. Explain the rationale for these consequences.

6. Name the benchmark case that is most closely associated with each of the following propositions. Describe how these three propositions might overlap.

a. The substance of a transaction should control over its form.

b. For the tax outcome of a transaction to be respected, there must be a legitimate reason for the transaction other than tax avoidance.

c. Income must be taxed to the taxpayer who earns it.

7. Joseph works for a small retail shop. After his daughter (Josephine) started college, Joseph arranged to have his employer pay half of his earnings directly to Josephine. Withholdings for income tax and social security tax were correctly made from the payments made to both Joseph and Josephine and the income was properly reported to each on W-2 forms at the end of the year.

a. Does this salary arrangement meet your smell test? Explain why or why not.

b. What statutory or judicial authority might be applicable in determining the appropriate tax outcome for this arrangement?

8. Consider the following transactions and describe your reaction to each transaction assuming that you are a skeptical IRS agent. Explain the tax avoidance opportunities (if any) present in these transactions.

a. Shareholder A owns 2% of the stock in XYZ Corporation (a C corporation). A's salary is $350,000. This is a far greater amount than any survey data would predict A's salary should be given his job description.

b. Shareholder B owns 80% of the stock in PQR Corporation (an S corporation). B's responsibilities include acting as general manager and director of sales. B supervises a staff of 35 employees. B's salary is $3,000. Net income of PQR Corporation is $250,000; $150,000 of this is distributed as a dividend to PQR's shareholders on the last day of the year.

c. Partner C owns 35% of LMN Partnership. In lieu of receiving a salary payment (or guaranteed payment) of $20,000 for the services that C rendered to the partnership, C arranges to sell a piece of depreciable property to the partnership for $70,000. This property was recently appraised at $50,000. C's basis in the property is $70,000.

d. Shareholder D owns 100% of ABC Corporation (a C corporation). D sells property to ABC Corporation for $1 million. His basis in the property is $250,000; its fair market value is $600,000.

e. Shareholder E owns 90% of DEF Corporation. E's salary has been set at $40,000 per year, plus a bonus equal to DEF Corporation's *pre-bonus* taxable income in excess of $50,000.

9. Determine who is related to whom for purposes of Sec. 318(a) in the following examples:

   a. Mother and daughter.

   b. Husband and wife.

   c. Wife and mother-in-law.

   d. Brother and sister (child 1 and child 2).

   e. Husband's father and child 1.

10. AT is a 75% shareholder in PC Corporation. On January 1 of 19X3, AT sold one-third of his stock to PC Corporation for $100,000. AT's basis in the PC stock that he sold is $60,000. What are the tax effects of this apparent sale under the scenarios described below?

    a. None of the other PC shareholders are related in any way to AT.

    b. All of the other shareholders are AT's children.

    c. The other 25% shareholder (before the transaction) is a longtime friend but is otherwise unrelated to AT.

    d. Same as part c, above, except that the other (25%) shareholder is AT's grandfather.

11. Closely held businesses that operate in partnership form often include relatively young children among the partners.

    a. What tax reasons might help to explain this phenomenon?

    b. Would children under 14 or children over 13 be most effective in achieving any tax objectives in this plan? Explain briefly.

    c. In auditing family partnerships, the IRS often gives careful attention to the salaries paid to the family members who do most of the work in the business. Are they usually looking for unreasonably large or unreasonably small salaries in this situation? Explain briefly.

12. Corporation A is a dealer in hospital supplies. Corporation B is a dealer in laboratory supplies. Corporation C manufactures certain hospital and laboratory products. Chin Chee owns 75% of each corporation. May Lee owns 25% of A; Kim Lin owns 25% of B; and Chee Chow owns 25% of C. Corporation C manufactures several products that are also manufactured by many other companies. However, three of its products are manufactured only by Corporation C. These three products are expected to be extremely profitable to Corporation C in the future, but the corporation is generating large losses currently. The other two corporations are profitable, but Corporation A is less profitable than B because its market is much more competitive. Estimates of the current and next year's income for each corporation are:

    Corporation A: $100,000

    Corporation B: $400,000

    Corporation C: ($200,000)

  a. Calculate the aggregate tax liability for the three corporations.

  b. What distribution of income would produce an optimal tax liability for this group of corporations?

  c. What aspects of the net income calculation would you investigate in planning to minimize the aggregate tax liability of the group? Explain the tax planning possible in such an arrangement.

  d. What limits are there on your tax planning suggestions in part c, above?

———— THOUGHT PROBLEMS

1. Design and describe three related party transactions (other than those presented in this chapter) that should trigger a smell test by an IRS agent. Explain the basis upon which the IRS might challenge these three transactions.

2. Mommy Corporation is the 100% (U.S.) domestic, parent corporation of Daughter Corporation. Daughter is incorporated in a Caribbean country with low income tax rates. Clothing manufacture is done in Daughter because of low labor costs. Daughter Corporation sells all of the clothing that it manufactures to Mommy Corporation through wholesalers in the United States. Assume that Daughter Corporation's average cost for this clothing is from $25 to $35 per unit, and that the selling price in the United States is $100 per unit. Mommy Corporation has asked your advice on intercompany prices for the transactions between it and Daughter.

  a. If there were no constraints on setting prices, what might you recommend to Mommy Corporation?

  b. What constraints exist?

  c. What approach should you take in giving advice to Mommy Corporation?

  d. What position would you expect an IRS agent to take if he or she challenges the prices that you recommend.

3. Stonewall and Michael Jackson are brothers. Michael owns some farm land that he thought would become targeted for residential development because the city was growing in that direction. However, with the economic downturn, new

residential development virtually stopped and Michael's land lost 50% of its value (from a $200,000 purchase price to an appraised $100,000 by an MAI appraiser). Michael needs money to fund a nationwide tour. Stonewall wants Michael's land to raise a few hogs and cattle. What are the tax consequences of a sale from Michael to Stonewall? Can you think of another way to structure this transaction to achieve a better tax outcome?

4. Both Secs. 482 and 267 provide statutory authority governing related-party transactions. Would the IRS be able to challenge the related-party transactions described in those provisions without such statutory authority? Explain.

5. Review Example 15-5. The problem presented in that example is discussed in the context of the assignment of income. Could the IRS alternatively have questioned that transaction on its business purpose? Taking this approach, the IRS might argue that the gift was not a valid transfer of an interest because the transfer satisfied only a tax avoidance purpose; that is, it lacks a valid business purpose. The taxpayer's counter-argument in that event might be that there is a business purpose that is not apparent to the IRS; that is, that the parents are interested in seeing that Sylvester maintains his interest in an accounting career and they hope that, by transferring an ownership interest to him, he will be more likely to become a full-time participant after graduation in the firm's activities. How do you think Judge Learned Hand would have responded to these arguments? What variation on these facts might strengthen or weaken the taxpayer's position?

6. Omega Corporation is being organized by Alpha and Beta. Together, Alpha and Beta have $100,000 to invest. In the process of organizing the corporation, they discover that making long-term loans to the corporation can be more beneficial (from a tax standpoint) than making equity investments. Upon further investigation, they discover that the state of incorporation requires a minimum of $5,000 in equity capital. Therefore, when they incorporate their business, they issue $5,000 in stock and $95,000 in loans to the corporation.

a. What is the apparent form of this transaction?

b. Does the real substance correspond to the apparent form? Why or why not? Explain both current and subsequent events that might bear on this conclusion.

7. Bev owns 100% of the outstanding stock of PAR Corporation; PAR, in turn, owns 100% of SUB Corporation. In 19X6 Bev sold 500 of her 1,000 share of PAR stock to SUB for $200,000. Bev's basis in these 500 shares of PAR stock was $50,000. Assuming that both PAR and SUB have operated a very successful business for several years before this sale, how do you think Bev should report her sale of stock in 19X6? Explain briefly.

8. Lucille Lee operates an apron manufacturing business as a sole proprietorship. She started this business in 1970, when her children were small. Her eldest child, Ron, has just graduated from college with a marketing degree. Ron plans to join Lucille in another three years, after working in the marketing department of a medium-sized corporation that sells specialty products to restaurants. Her younger child (April) has just begun college. April has been actively involved in various aspects of the business (manufacture, delivery, accounting, etc.) since she was 12. April will continue to work for the business during summer vacations and will make sales calls at restaurants in the town where she attends college.

Lucille's apron business has been so successful that she has invested $1 million in machinery and equipment to improve the efficiency of the operation. Her other assets include the land and building for the manufacturing operation and an office building.

Lucille has decided to organize her business as the Ap-Ron-Lee partnership by transferring a one-third interest in the business to each of her children, despite the fact that they will provide only nominal services for the business during the next several years.

Describe any problems that you see with this arrangement. Analyze those problems and explain the conditions under which this arrangement might be respected for tax purposes.

CLASS PROJECTS

1. a. Divide the class into several Supreme Courts (of 9 or fewer members each) and ask each "court" to evaluate the two cases presented below. Each court must decide (1) who should report the income and (2) reasons for their conclusions.

   Case A: Shayne is a lawyer. She enters into an agreement with her husband, Monty (currently a student in medical school), which provides that any future income of either party will be treated as belonging equally to each. In fact, half of Shayne's earnings were turned over to Monty in 19X2 and 19X3 when he had no income.

   Case B: Calvin is Jerry's father. Calvin is an eccentric inventor whose creations are not always highly valued by the marketplace. However, Calvin did stumble onto a clever invention: a robotic system that removes and stacks dishes from a dishwasher into their appropriate places. After many expensive trials, he was able to patent this system. Calvin believes it has tremendous potential, but he does not know how to market his invention. Therefore, Calvin transfers his patent to Jerry. Jerry collects the royalties on this patent.

   b. After a preliminary evaluation of these cases allow each "court" to read *Lucas v. Earl* 281 US 111 (1930), *Helvering v. Eubank* 311 US 122 (1940), and *Heim v. Fitzpatrick* 262 F. 2d 887 (2d Cir. 1959). Compare the real Court's decisions to theirs.

   c. Tell each court to be prepared to discuss the critical issues and to defend their decisions.

2. The issue of unreasonable compensation frequently arises in situations in which a sole shareholder of a C corporation attempts to avoid the double taxation on dividend income by paying himself or herself a large salary. Locate court cases and articles in tax journals that deal with this issue. Discuss the issues in small groups. Have each group collectively prepare a two-page paper that (1) identifies the primary factors that raise the issue with the IRS upon examination of a tax return and (2) summarizes the planning opportunities that can be used to sustain a taxpayer position. Award the group that writes the best paper in an appropriate manner.

Part Five

PROPERTY TRANSACTIONS

> "*That which flows from capital, like interest, rent and other items of income, is separate and distinct from the capital which produces it as gathered fruit is separate from the tree that bore it. While income may be transformed by accumulation into capital, like fruit, the seed of which produces another tree, the growth itself of neither capital nor the tree is income.*"
>
> *GODFREY N. NELSON, "THE QUESTION OF TAXING CAPTIAL GAINS" (1940)*

The mission of Part Five is to explain the tax consequences of taxable and nontaxable dispositions of property with emphasis on the underlying rationale. To accomplish this mission, we provide two chapters with the following objectives:

CHAPTER 16:
CAPITAL GAINS AND LOSSES—To present a conceptual framework for understanding and applying capital gain and loss rules in the pure case and with modifications to the pure case.

CHAPTER 17:
NONTAXABLE EXCHANGES—To provide insight into the basic principles of nontaxable exchanges and to present the general rules for five common transactions.

The root of the problem is that the capital gains concept itself is clear and consistent neither in practice nor in principle.

PETER MILLER, "CAPITAL GAINS ON PERSONAL EFFORTS" (1954)

CAPITAL GAINS AND LOSSES

CHAPTER OBJECTIVES

In Chapter 16, you will acquire a conceptual framework for understanding current rules for taxing capital gains and losses and will learn how to apply the capital gain and loss rules in the pure case and with modifications to the pure case.

LEARNING GOALS

After studying this chapter, you should be able to

1 Recognize some of the different capital gain concepts;

2 Present the central arguments for and against the preferential treatment of capital gains;

3 Define a capital asset for federal income tax purposes;

4 Apply the netting rules to capital gains and losses realized by individual and corporate taxpayers;

5 Determine the tax liability of individual and corporate taxpayers who recognize capital gains and losses;

6 Understand the important planning implications of capital gains and losses;

7 Apply Sec. 1231 in conjunction with Secs. 1245, 1250, and 291;

8 Determine the proper tax consequences when a taxpayer incurs personal casualty (and theft) gains and losses;

9 Determine the tax consequences of worthless securities; and

10 Apply Sec. 1244 rules to losses realized on the disposition of small business stock.

> **Capital gains and losses** arise under tax law when a taxpayer sells or exchanges a capital asset.

This chapter focuses on the taxation of **capital gains and losses**. We first examine the capital gain concept from the perspective of the law, economics, and accounting. We then outline the arguments for and against preferential treatment of capital gains. This conceptual framework leads to an examination of the pure case of capital gains and losses, including current definitions and rules for taxing capital gains and losses. After considering the pure case, we examine some common modifications to the pure case, especially rules concerning the disposition of depreciable property. We also describe the tax consequences of realizing both business and personal casualty gains and losses. Finally, we briefly discuss several other topics related to capital gain and loss taxation, including the treatment of losses realized on the disposition of small business stock.

Tax experts and legislators have long debated the correct or preferred tax treatment of gains and losses realized on the sale or exchange of property other than inventory. The debate raises two threshold questions:

1. Should gains and losses from property transactions be included within the definition of income?

2. If so, should they receive special treatment for income tax purposes?

If the answers to both of these questions are yes, the following two additional questions arise:

3. Precisely which property transactions should be eligible for special tax treatment?

4. Exactly what special tax treatment should be extended to these gains and losses?

In the United States, these four questions make up the core of what can best be described as the capital gain controversy. Over the last century and a half, the United States has moved from one extreme to another. During the years of the Civil War income tax, the United States wholly excluded certain property gains from income taxation. From 1913 through 1921, capital gains were taxed as ordinary income. From 1922 through 1987, capital gains were either taxed partially or taxed at preferential rates. From 1988 through 1990, capital gains were again taxed as ordinary income. Beginning in 1991, certain capital gains of noncorporate taxpayers once again receive **preferential treatment** although the current preference is very modest compared to the treatment prior to 1988. During the years of capital gains taxation, capital losses have always received unfavorable treatment by being subject to stringent limitations. These limitations were noted in Chapter 5 and are again discussed later in this chapter.

> **Preferential treatment** means a tax advantage in the form of an exclusion, a deduction, a credit, or a tax rate lower than ordinary rates.

THE CAPITAL GAIN CONCEPT

> **Goal #1**
> Recognize capital gain concepts.

The American concepts of ordinary income and capital gain evolved primarily from the essential features of the economies prominent in the temperate zones of Europe during the eighteenth and nineteenth centuries.[1] In these agricultural economies, income was the value of an annual harvest, and capital was the land, which was almost never sold. Under these conditions, income and capital could be specifically identified, at least conceptually, as separate physical phenomena.

---

1 For an interesting development of this theme, see Lawrence H. Seltzer, *The Nature and Tax Treatment of Capital Gains and Losses* (New York: National Bureau of Economic Research, 1951).

Although the English concept of capital gain laid the foundation for the American concept, the American economy developed quite differently from the English economy. In America, the population was both growing and mobile. These conditions contributed to a rapid increase in the market value of business enterprises and real estate, and entrepreneurs often realized substantial gains by selling their basic assets and reinvesting the proceeds in other ventures and in other locations. This frequent turnover of the capital base blurred the distinction between income and capital.

JUDICIAL CONCEPT OF A CAPITAL GAIN

Despite the diversity between the early European and American economies, the first American courts to struggle with problems of income taxation applied English common law and concluded that any gain realized on the sale of a capital investment was not income. In fact, little or no attention was given to the pecuniary measurement of capital investments. This English legal concept prevailed in *Gray v. Darlington* (1872) in which Justice Field said,

> the mere fact that property has advanced in value between the date of its acquisition and sale does not authorize the imposition of the tax on the amount of the advance. Mere advance in value in no sense constitutes the gains, profits, or income specified by the statute. It constitutes and can be treated merely as increase in capital.[2]

By 1918, however, the U.S. Supreme Court modified its earlier position and held that under the Revenue Act of 1913 the sale of an investment or capital asset resulted in a taxable gain or loss equal to the difference between the sale proceeds and the asset's cost (or adjusted basis). The most widely quoted judicial statement of this revised position is found in *Eisner v. Macomber*. There the Court, adopting a definition used in two earlier cases, said,

> "Income may be defined as the gain derived from capital and from labor, or from both combined," provided it be understood to include profit gained through a sale or conversion of capital assets.[3]

As a consequence, between 1913 and 1922 any gain or loss realized on the sale or exchange of a capital asset was subject to income taxation in precisely the same manner as ordinary forms of income. The Revenue Act of 1921, which became effective on January 1, 1922, provided the first special treatment for capital gain. Some distinction between the income tax treatment of ordinary income and capital gain was retained from 1922 through 1987 and from 1991 to the present.

One commentator summarized the essential judicial concept of a capital gain as follows:

> In both law and common speech, capital gains are generally regarded as the profits realized from increases in the market value of any assets that are not part of the

---

2 15 Wall. 63 (1872).

3 252 US 189 (1920). Quoted in the decision are words used earlier in Stratton's *Independence v. Howbert,* 231 US 399 (1913) and *Doyle v. Mitchell Bros. Co.,* 247 US 179, 185 (1918).

owner's stock in trade or that he does not regularly offer for sale, and capital losses as the losses realized from declines in the market value of such assets.[4]

This definition of a capital gain emphasizes the nature of the asset owner's trade or business or, more basically, the owner's intended use or disposition of specific property. If the owner intends to hold a particular asset only until it can be resold at a price that returns a satisfactory profit, then, according to the legal concept, any gain realized on sale or other disposition constitutes ordinary income, Alternatively, if the owner holds the asset either for the production of recurring income or as a long-range investment, with little or no intention of offering the basic asset for resale in the short run (even if the asset were to increase in value), the asset would constitute a capital asset, and the gain realized on its sale would constitute a capital gain.

ECONOMIC CONCEPT OF A CAPITAL GAIN

In the classical economists' model of free enterprise, capital gains and losses do not exist. In this model, assumed conditions—such as perfect competition, perfect knowledge, conditions of certainty, and freedom of entry—ensure the rapid and perfect adjustment of costs and prices throughout the market to eliminate pure economic profit. In the real world, however, the assumed conditions do not occur. Economists concerned with divergences of the real world from the model sometimes define, often indirectly, the capital gain (or loss) as the gain attributable to one or more imperfect conditions. One important imperfection is inflation, which we discuss later in this chapter.

ACCOUNTING CONCEPT OF A CAPITAL GAIN

To the accountant, capital gains and losses are best described as those gains and losses that occur only at irregular intervals and are attributable to imperfect knowledge and imperfect income measurement. Thus, the accounting concept of capital gain is comparable to the economic concept in that it denies the theoretical existence of a distinct thing called a capital gain. Like the economist, the accountant observes certain phenomena that do not fit into an ideal model. The accountant recognizes the imperfections of the real world and defines capital gains and losses loosely as those items that are attributable to real-world imperfections.

Accountants are concerned with presenting financial information fairly to third parties. Although accountants must distinguish between routine income items and other material amounts of nonrecurring gains and losses, they may characterize such gains and losses as capital only if this terminology has meaning to financial statement readers. In presenting financial data, accountants accept the notion that recurrence is a necessary condition of operating income and that nonrecurrence is a necessary condition of capital gain.

TAX CONCEPT OF CAPITAL GAIN

Unfortunately, the most desirable tax treatment of a capital gain is not determined any more easily than is the concept of a capital gain. Once we accept the notion that a given transaction warrants special tax treatment, we must define the transaction so

---

4 Lawrence H. Seltzer, *The Nature and Tax Treatment of Capital Gains and Losses* (New York: National Bureau of Economic Research, 1951), p. 3.

that it may be recognized among the many transactions subject to the income tax. Ideally, this definition would be subject to objective tests, render equitable results, and contribute to administrative simplicity. These objectives conflict, however desirable they might be individually.

The frequency and severity of change in the capital gain and loss tax provisions and the lack of a sound theoretical framework for these changes, implies that, at least for tax purposes, it is best to accept the notion that capital gains and losses are what the Code says they are—and nothing more or less. Concepts of capital gain differ in other disciplines, and the greatest danger in comparing these concepts lies in failing to realize that what constitutes a sound concept for one purpose may be wholly inadequate for another purpose.

ARGUMENTS FOR PREFERENTIAL TREATMENT OF CAPITAL GAINS WITH COUNTERARGUMENTS

Goal #2
Present arguments for preferential treatment.

As mentioned earlier in this chapter, policy options for capital gains treatment range from complete exclusion of capital gains to full taxation as ordinary income. Historically, the preferential taxation of capital gains has ranged from partial inclusion at regular rates to full inclusion at reduced rates. For example, prior to the 1986 Act the Code allowed individual taxpayers to deduct 60% of net long-term capital gains from gross income, thereby explicitly taxing only 40% of that gain. Alternatively, preferential treatment sometimes has been accomplished by taxing capital gains at tax rates lower than those applying to ordinary income. For example, prior to the 1986 Act net long-term capital gains of corporations were subject to a maximum 28% rate while other corporate income was taxed at rates as high as 46%. Similarly, in the 1920s the maximum tax rate on an individual's capital gains was much lower than the top rate on ordinary income. This section briefly outlines the arguments *for* subjecting capital gains to some form of special treatment. Each argument is accompanied by at least one counterargument because the issue of preferential treatment is often hotly debated with no clear answer emerging.[5]

THE LOCK-IN EFFECT

Argument

High capital gains rates deter investors from selling capital assets, thereby locking investors into existing investments. The higher the capital gains tax rate, the higher the rate of return necessary on alternative investments to induce investors to sell existing capital assets currently instead of later. The high required alternative rates of return induce the **lock-in effect**, which ties up funds that could be invested in new ventures.

The **lock-in effect** occurs when taxation of capital gains induces investors to hold capital assets rather than sell them.

The lock-in effect is exacerbated by the basis rules for inherited property. As discussed in Chapter 8, the basis of inherited property is usually its fair market value at the decedent's death. Consequently, a taxpayer has an incentive to hold capital gains

5 Although many books and articles have been written on this subject, we recommend the following two references: (1) Joint Committee Print: Staff of the Joint Committee on Taxation, *Proposals and Issues Relating to Taxation of Capital Gains and Losses,* (U.S. Government Printing Office, 1990), pp. 21–26 and (2) Walter J. Blum, "A Handy Summary of the Capital Gains Arguments," *TAXES—The Tax Magazine,* April 1957, pp. 247–266.

property to achieve a stepped-up basis at death, thereby escaping tax on any capital gains accruing during the taxpayer's lifetime.

Counterarguments

First, little empirical evidence yet exists to strongly support the lock-in effect argument. Second, the real culprit is not high capital gains tax rates but is instead the realization principle. If taxpayers were required to recognize capital gains as they accrue rather than when they are realized, any tax bias that favors retaining capital assets would disappear, including the incentive to hold assets until death. Of course, a *mark-to-market* system that taxed unrealized capital gains at the end of each year or at the time of a taxpayer's death would introduce valuation and cash-flow problems.

INCENTIVES

Argument

Preferential treatment of capital gains provides investors an incentive to channel funds into equity investments such as corporate stock. Incentives are particularly needed to attract venture capital to new businesses. The resultant incentive effect contributes to economic growth and thereby provides a social benefit.

Counterarguments

First, a broad capital gains preference is too general to target specific types of equity investments. Second, a question arises as to whether equity investments should be automatically classified as capital assets. For some investors, equities are more like inventory (or property held for resale) than capital investments. Third, many investors are tax-exempt entities (for example, pension funds) for which a tax preference has no incentive effect. Fourth, incentives to acquire capital assets distort investment decisions toward assets that appreciate in value and away from those that generate current interest and dividend income. Fifth, preferential treatment encourages taxpayers to convert ordinary income into capital gains. As a result, many resources are expended planning and engaging in transactions that might not otherwise occur. Taxpayers may also tend to misclassify their income to take advantage of the capital gains preference.

When evaluating the incentive argument, you must remember the role of implicit taxes. If capital gains receive preferential treatment, the investment's before-tax rate of return should decrease so that the investment yields an after-tax rate of return equal to that of the benchmark investment (see Chapters 1, 4, and 14). In this event, the venture capitalist incurs an implicit tax and is not as well off as suggested by the incentive argument. However, a high-tax-bracket venture capitalist may nevertheless receive a benefit via the clientele effect (see Chapters 4 and 14).

COMPETITIVENESS

Argument

Preferential treatment is necessary for U.S. firms to compete for capital in the international arena, especially when some countries tax capital gains at relatively low rates. Investors in tax-favored ventures require a lower before-tax rate of return from the firm than investors in nonfavored ventures. Therefore, a firm that directly obtains tax-favored invested funds receives an implicit tax subsidy, which reduces its cost of capital and improves its competitiveness.

Counterargument

The cost of capital entails more than just capital gain taxation. Other factors associated with a nation's overall tax system—such as taxes on dividends, interest, net wealth, and corporate income—also affect the cost of capital and, hence, the U.S.'s competitiveness in international capital markets.

BUNCHING

Argument

Bunching occurs because, under U.S. tax law, capital gains are not taxed until realized. Consequently, a taxpayer may realize in a single year a large gain that has accrued over many years. If a large realized gain pushes the taxpayer into a high tax bracket, the taxpayer's tax burden may be larger than it would have been had the gain been taxed as it accrued.

> **Bunching** occurs when a large capital gain is recognized at the time an asset is sold or exchanged rather than gradually as the gain accrues.

Counterargument

The bunching effect has been mitigated in recent years because tax rates since 1986 have been much less graduated than they were in earlier years. Even in years of steeply graduated rates, the bunching effect can be alleviated to some extent by income averaging. Income averaging reduces marginal tax rates by spreading high income over a number of tax years. It can take the form of statutory income averaging, which existed before the 1986 Act, or a taxpayer can self average by spreading gain realizations over several years.

INFLATION

Argument

Proponents claim that preferential treatment is necessary to compensate taxpayers because all or part of a realized capital gain may be due to inflation rather than a real increase in value or income.

EXAMPLE 16-1

Assume that a taxpayer purchased an asset 20 years ago for $10,000 and sold it this year for $15,000. If during the 20-year interval the general price level increased by 50%, then in terms of that taxpayer's command over goods and services, the $5,000 gain realized on the sale is illusory. Today, it would cost the full $15,000 to repurchase goods or services equivalent to those that could have been purchased 20 years ago for $10,000. If a tax is imposed on the illusory gain, the taxpayer will be worse off after the sale because the after-tax proceeds are insufficient to repurchase goods or services equivalent in value to those sold. Any tax would constitute a tax on capital rather than a tax on income.

Counterarguments

First, preferential capital gains tax rates usually either over-compensate or under-compensate for inflation. The effects of inflation can better be alleviated by adjusting the basis of the underlying capital asset with an index tied to the inflation rate although indexing would further complicate the tax law.

Second, inflation affects many transactions other than capital gains (for example, inventories, plant and equipment, and wages). Specifically, an unindexed system taxes nominal rather than real profit and wages. Moreover, inflation also affects debtors and creditors. A debtor who is allowed an interest deduction may, under current tax law, deduct both the real and the inflationary components of the interest expense. Conversely, the creditor must include both components in gross income. A taxpayer who is allowed a capital gains tax preference (including indexing) to compensate for inflation, but whose interest deductions are not indexed, obtains a double benefit. The taxpayer pays tax on only the real component of the gain but deducts both the real and inflationary components of the interest. Therefore, preferential treatment for only capital gains may be an incomplete and unfair solution to the inflation problem. On the other hand, a completely indexed tax system may be costly in terms of revenue and will certainly be complex.

REVENUE

Argument

Unlocking capital gains would increase gain realizations, the tax base, and tax revenues.

Counterargument

Empirical evidence for this supply-side effect is inconclusive.

ARGUMENTS AGAINST PREFERENTIAL TREATMENT OF CAPITAL GAINS WITH COUNTERARGUMENTS

Goal #2
Present arguments against preferential treatment.

This section briefly outlines the arguments *against* subjecting capital gains to some form of special treatment. As before, each argument is accompanied by at least one counterargument.

DEFERRAL OF GAIN

Argument

Any special treatment of capital gains, such as a reduced tax rate, is unnecessary because, under the realization principle, capital gains already enjoy the benefit of deferred taxation.

Counterargument

The deferral benefit may be insufficient to offset disadvantages such as bunching and inflation.

SIMPLICITY

Argument

Much complexity in the tax law stems from defining and treating capital asset transactions differently than other transactions. The tax law would be much simpler if capital gains and losses were treated the same as other income and losses.

Counterargument

Even in years in which capital gains were taxed as ordinary income, the tax law continued to limit the deductibility of capital losses. Thus, the capital gains distinction remains in the Code, thereby keeping the tax law complex. Because of the cherry-picking problem described in Chapter 5, Congress is not likely to remove restrictions on the deductibility of capital losses. Therefore, the Code will retain a certain degree of complexity regardless of how capital *gains* are treated.

EQUITY

Argument

Preferential treatment fosters inequity. Horizontal inequity may occur because capital gains are taxed more favorably than other income, and the clientele effect may produce vertical inequity because high-bracket taxpayers prefer tax-favored investments. Moreover, introducing preferential treatment of capital gains may provide *current* holders of appreciated capital assets with an unexpected and undeserved benefit. This windfall benefit occurs because introduction of the preference induces investors to bid up the capital asset's price. The increased price reduces the before-tax rate of return earned by *new* purchasers, thereby creating an implicit tax. But at the same time, the increased price enhances the wealth of current holders of capital assets and allows them to realize an additional windfall gain upon the sale of the assets.

Counterargument

The vertical equity and windfall benefit arguments are valid. The horizontal equity argument, however, ignores implicit taxes. Although the *explicit* tax on capital gains may be less than the *explicit* tax on other income, capital assets that are taxed favorably may bear an *implicit* tax in the form of reduced before-tax rates of return. Consequently, the *total* tax on the two forms of income may be equal or nearly equal.

CURRENT PROVISIONS: THE PURE CASE

The statutory provisions governing the tax consequences of gains or losses realized on sales or exchanges of capital assets can be divided into two general categories: (1) a pure case and (2) modifications to the pure case. This somewhat unusual categorization is suggested by the way Subchapter P—the portion of the Code that deals with capital gains and losses—is organized. Parts I, II, and III of Subchapter P (Secs. 1201–1223) provide some reasonably straightforward rules for the pure case. Thereafter, Parts IV, V, and VI (Secs. 1231–1297) provide a lengthy series of often complex exceptions to (and extensions of) the basic concept. Many Code sections outside of Subchapter P also modify the pure concept of capital gains and losses. In the next few pages of this chapter, we summarize and illustrate the general rules found in Parts I through III of Subchapter P. Thereafter, we will examine a few common modifications to the pure case.

Goal #3
Define a capital asset.

CAPITAL GAIN AND LOSS DEFINED

The Code does not define capital gains and losses per se; instead, it defines a capital asset and then states that a capital gain or loss is simply the gain or loss realized on the sale or exchange of a capital asset. Moreover, the Code defines a capital asset negatively—that is, it states that all properties except those specifically exempted by the Code are capital assets. The complete statutory definition of a **capital asset** is contained in Sec. 1221 and reads as follows:

> For purposes of this subtitle, the term "capital asset" means property held by the taxpayer (whether or not connected with his trade or business), but does not include—
>
> (1) stock in trade of the taxpayer or other property of a kind which would properly be included in the inventory of the taxpayer if on hand at the close of the taxable year, or property held by the taxpayer primarily for sale to customers in the ordinary course of his trade or business;
>
> (2) property, used in his trade or business, of a character which is subject to the allowance for depreciation provided in section 167, or real property used in his trade or business;
>
> (3) a copyright, a literary, musical, or artistic composition, a letter or memorandum, or similar property, held by—
>
> (A) a taxpayer whose personal efforts created such property,
>
> (B) in the case of a letter, memorandum, or similar property, a taxpayer for whom such property was prepared or produced, or
>
> (C) a taxpayer in whose hands the basis of such property is determined, for the purpose of determining gain from a sale or exchange, in whole or in part by reference to the basis of such property in the hands of a taxpayer described in subparagraph (A) or (B);
>
> (4) accounts or notes receivable acquired in the ordinary course of trade or business for services rendered or from the sale of property described in paragraph (1);
>
> (5) a publication of the United States Government (including the Congressional Record) which is received from the United States Government or any agency thereof, other than by purchase at the price at which it is offered for sale to the public, and which is held by—
>
> (A) a taxpayer who so received such publication, or
>
> (B) a taxpayer in whose hands the basis of such publication is determined, for purposes of determining gain from a sale or exchange, in whole or in part by reference to the basis of such publication in the hands of a taxpayer described in subparagraph (A).

> A **capital asset** is any property held by the taxpayer *other than* inventory, real and depreciable property used in a trade or business, artistic property created by the taxpayer, trade receivables, and certain U.S. publications.

This definition raises numerous vexing questions. Phrases such as "stock in trade," "primarily for sale," and "trade or business" contain enough ambiguities to guarantee ample controversy between taxpayers and the government. For instance, suppose a taxpayer inherited some jewelry that he or she had no intention of keeping and, in fact, promptly disposed of through another party. Would those jewels be "property held by the taxpayer primarily for sale to customers"? If so, the gain on their sale would be ordinary income; if not, the gain would be capital gain.[6]

An interesting corollary issue is the definition of a taxpayer's trade or business. Many challenging tax problems arise because of this phrase. For instance, can a

6 For a decision of the First Circuit Court of Appeals on this issue, see *R. Foster Reynolds v. Comm.*, 155 F.2d 620 (1946).

taxpayer have more than one trade or business concurrently?[7] Specifically, suppose that a salaried employee also owns and rents a single dwelling unit to another individual. Does this rental activity constitute a second and separate trade or business for the taxpayer? If it does, the dwelling is depreciable property used in the trade or business and not a capital asset. If the rental activity is not a trade or business, the property is a capital asset.[8]

Perhaps the most illogical aspect of the capital asset definition is the Sec. 1221(2) exclusion of depreciable and real property used in a trade or business. If asked to give an example of a capital asset, most business-oriented persons uninitiated in federal taxation would quickly respond with such examples as plant, equipment, and business real property, or the things financial accountants often describe as fixed assets. Yet these items are clearly eliminated from the statutory definition. We will explain the reason for excluding depreciable assets from the definition of capital assets later in the chapter when we discuss the historical background of Secs. 1231, 1245, and 1250.

The Sec. 1221(3) exclusion is an interesting example of a conceptual problem inherent in capital gain taxation. The only way that most individuals can earn a living is by selling a service that involves a physical or mental process or both. For example, a person might dig a ditch, diagnose an illness and prescribe a medication, or repair an automobile. Some individuals, however, create property that, when sold, provides an income. For example, artists create art objects, authors and composers create copyrighted works, and inventors create patentable ideas. If all property were capital assets, individuals whose efforts resulted in property would reap the benefits of the capital gains tax, whereas all other taxpayers would be subject to the less favorable ordinary tax rates (assuming the tax law contains a preferential treatment for capital gains). To preclude this result, Congress inserted Sec. 1221(3) into the Code. Observe that the current statute does *not* exclude patents and that the exclusion extends only to individuals whose efforts created the property and to those who assume the creator's tax basis. For example, if a private art collector (not a dealer) *purchases* a painting from an artist, the artist would have ordinary income, but the collector would possess a capital asset. On the other hand, if the artist *gifts* the painting to a friend, the painting remains an ordinary asset to the friend because the friend takes the artist's basis.

Congress enacted the Sec. 1221(3)(B) exclusion to end the large tax deductions previously available to former presidents of the United States. Under prior law, whenever an ex-president contributed his papers and other memorabilia to a specially created library named in his honor, a major charitable deduction was created. After lengthy debate, Congress decided that Lyndon Johnson was to be the last president to be so privileged. Because ordinary income property creates a charitable deduction equal only to the taxpayer's basis in the property and because a president's basis in his papers is generally zero, Sec. 1221(3)(B) ensures that presidents no longer receive major personal tax benefits from their public service. Richard Nixon's attempt to claim a charitable contribution deduction for the alleged donation of his vice presidential

---

7 Apparently so. See John H. Saunders, *Trade of Business—Its Meaning Under the Internal Revenue Code*, 12th Annual Institute on Federal Taxes, University of Southern California, 1960, p. 693.

8 Initially, the Tax Court maintained that the mere ownership of improved rental property constituted a trade or business. See, for example, *Hazard*, 7 TC 372 (1946). However, other courts required continuous, systematic, and substantial taxpayer activity with the property—in addition to mere ownership—before there could be a trade or business. See, for example, *Union National Bank of Troy, Exec.* 195 F. Supp. 382 (DC NY, 1961). In a later decision, the Tax Court modified its original position in *Hazard*. See *Edwin R. Curphey*, 73 TC 424 (1979). Today, the mere leasing of real estate will often not qualify as an active trade or business.

papers before the effective date of this change in the tax law was widely reported in the daily press.

One final observation relative to the definition of capital assets demonstrates that care must be exercised in dealing with this portion of the Code. Suppose a local accountant sells his entire practice to another accountant for a fixed sum, payable immediately. Is all or any part of the sale proceeds to be allocated to the sale of a capital asset? More specifically, if the proceeds exceed the fair market value of the tangible assets and uncollected receivables, does the excess represent the sale of goodwill, and, if so, is this intangible asset a capital asset? As a general rule it is; however, a slight difference in facts may modify this conclusion. If, for example, the sale agreement includes a covenant not to compete, all or a part of the excess may be ordinary income. Careful tax planning by an expert is absolutely essential to guarantee the tax rights of both the purchaser and seller in these and other similar arrangements.

For tax purposes, the most numerically important group of capital assets is stocks and bonds. Except when held for resale by securities dealers, these assets generally are capital assets, and the gain or loss on their sale or exchange is a capital gain or loss. Personal use assets such as residences, family automobiles, and pleasure boats are also common forms of capital assets. Observe that a single asset may be both capital and noncapital—for example, a car that is used 75% of the time in a trade or business and 25% of the time for family driving is treated for tax purposes as two separate assets: one capital (the personal use portion), the other ordinary.

TAX TREATMENT OF CAPITAL GAINS AND LOSSES

Goal #4
Apply the netting rules to capital gains and losses.

Prior to 1987, the distinction between long-term and short-term capital gains and losses was extremely important because the excess of net long-term capital gains over net short-term capital losses (called a net capital gain) received highly preferential treatment. As mentioned earlier, individual taxpayers,[9] by taking a 60% deduction, paid taxes on only 40% of net capital gains.[10] Corporations, whose ordinary income was subject to a 46% top rate, paid a maximum of 28% on net capital gains. The Tax Reform Act of 1986 repealed preferential treatment for both individuals and corporations so that all capital gains were taxed as ordinary income, albeit at lower ordinary tax rates than existed before the 1986 Act. For years beginning after 1990, however, the Revenue Reconciliation Act of 1990 raised the top individual tax rate to 31% and retained a 28% maximum tax rate for net capital gains. Corporations still pay ordinary tax rates on their capital gains. Consequently, for individual taxpayers, the long-term versus short-term distinction becomes at least marginally important because of this small difference in tax rates. If Congress further raises individual tax rates or reduces the capital gains rate, the distinction becomes increasingly important. Accordingly, in this section we examine the rules for proper treatment of capital gains and losses.

Definitions and the Netting Process

Section 1222 provides the following definitions:

1. *Short-term capital gain (STCG).* Gain from the sale or exchange of a capital asset held one year or less.

---

9 Rules similar to those for individuals also apply to estates and trusts.

10 In 1987, a transitional year, an individual's net capital gains were subject to a 28% maximum tax rate.

2. *Short-term capital loss (STCL)*. Loss from the sale or exchange of a capital asset held one year or less.

3. *Long-term capital gain (LTCG)*. Gain from the sale or exchange of a capital asset held *more than* one year.

4. *Long-term capital loss (LTCL)*. Loss from the sale or exchange of a capital asset held *more than* one year.

5. *Net short-term capital gain (NSTCG)*. Excess of STCG over STCL.

6. *Net short-term capital loss (NSTCL)*. Excess of STCL over STCG.

7. *Net long-term capital gain (NLTCG)*. Excess of LTCG over LTCL.

8. *Net long-term capital loss (NLTCL)*. Excess of LTCL over LTCG.

9. *Capital gain net income*. Excess of capital gains over capital losses.

10. *Net capital loss*. Excess of capital losses over the amount of capital losses allowed as a deduction.

11. *Net capital gain (NCG)*. Excess of NLTCG over NSTCL.

> A **net capital gain (NCG)** is the excess of a net long-term capital gain over a net short-term capital loss; an NCG receives modest preferential treatment under current law.

The phrase **net capital gain** is a confusing choice of words because the phrase conjures the same image as the phrase capital gain net income. Nevertheless, a net capital gain occurs only when net *long-term* capital gains exceed net *short-term* capital losses in the process described below. The net capital gain definition is important because only this amount receives modest preferential treatment after 1990.

Both short-term and long-term capital gains and losses are netted initially. If one set of transactions results in a net gain and the other a net loss, the two net amounts are netted against each other. Alternatively, if the two net amounts are either both positive or both negative, they are *not* netted again. Figures 16-1 and 16-2 depict this netting process as a mixing apparatus that clears out at the end of each tax year. Long-term gains and losses enter the left receptacle and exit that receptacle as either a long-term capital gain or a net long-term capital loss. Similarly, short-term gains and losses enter the right receptacle and exit that receptacle as either a net short-term capital gain or a net short-term capital loss. The output of these two receptacles then combine and enter one of six mutually exclusive channels in Figure 16-1 or one of two channels in Figure 16-2.

Capital Gains

For individual taxpayers, if the netting process results in capital gains exceeding capital losses (Channels 1 through 3 in Figure 16-1), any short-term component of the excess receives ordinary income treatment, and any long-term element (net capital gain) becomes subject to the 28% maximum tax rate (see Figure 16-3, which appears on page 565).[11] We make the following observations about Figure 16-3:

> **Goal #5**
> Determine tax liability when capital gains and losses are present.

1. In Graph 1, no special computation is necessary because taxable income does not exceed the top of the 28% bracket.

2. In Graphs 2 and 3, taxable income is split into two components: ordinary income (OI) and net capital gain (NCG). The OI component is taxed at ordinary rates,

---

11 Sec. 1(h).

and the NCG component is taxed at 28%. The two amounts are added to attain the total tax.

3. In Graph 4, the OI component does not exceed the top of the 15% bracket. Splitting taxable income between OI and NCG would subject the shaded portion of NCG to a 28% rather than a 15% tax rate. To prevent this result, taxable income must be split at the top of the 15% bracket.

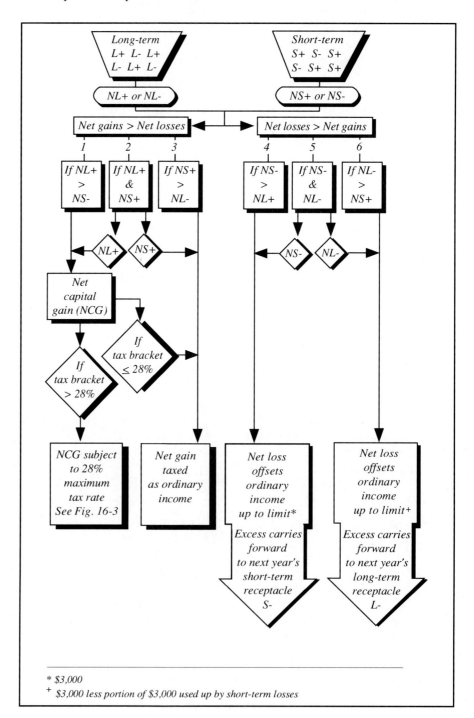

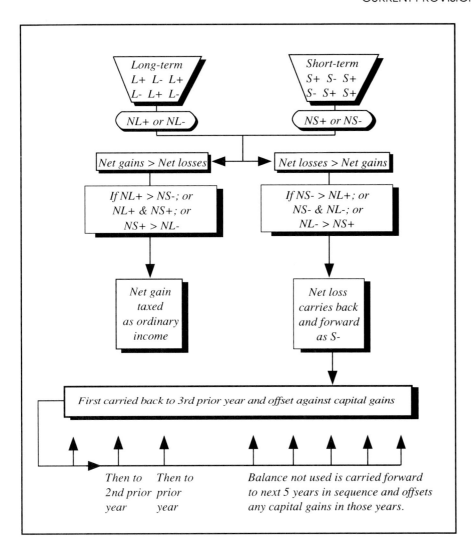

FIGURE 16-2

Consequences of Corporations' Capital Gains and Losses

For corporate taxpayers, all excess gains are taxed as ordinary income regardless of their long-term or short-term character. The following examples demonstrate these principles.

EXAMPLE 16-2

For 1992, Mr. and Mrs. Gainer have a combined salary of $115,500 and total itemized deductions and exemptions of $28,000 (after required phaseouts). They file a joint tax return. In addition, they sold the following stocks during 1992:

Stock	Acquired	Sold	Cost	Selling Price
A Corp.	2/11/92	7/14/92	$ 40,000	$100,000
B Corp.	10/12/91	1/31/92	250,000	160,000
X Corp.	5/12/84	7/20/92	150,000	200,000

Continued

EXAMPLE 16-2 (Con't.)

Stock	Acquired	Sold	Cost	Selling Price
Y Corp.	7/8/88	8/14/92	250,000	225,000
Z Corp.	3/10/91	12/28/92	75,000	140,000

These sales result in the following capital gains and losses (Channel 1 in Figure 16-1):

A Corp.	STCG	$ 60,000	
B Corp.	STCL	(90,000)	
	NSTCL		$(30,000)
X Corp.	LTCG	$ 50,000	
Y Corp.	LTCL	(25,000)	
Z Corp.	LTCG	65,000	
	NLTCG		90,000
	NCG		$ 60,000

The Gainers' taxable income is $147,500 computed as follows:

Salary	$115,500
NCG	60,000
AGI	175,500
Itemized deductions and exemptions	(28,000)
Taxable income	$147,500

With no special NCG provision, the Gainers' 1992 tax liability would be $38,476 {$19,566 + [31% x ($147,500 – $86,500)]}. However, because they have a net capital gain and are in the 31% tax bracket, they compute their tax as follows (see Figure 16-3, Graph 2):

Tax on $87,500 ordinary income	
{$19,566 + [31% x ($87,500 – $86,500)]}	$19,876
Tax on $60,000 NCG (28% x $60,000)	16,800
Total tax	$36,676

Thus, the Gainers' tax liability is $36,676 rather than the $38,476 it would have been without the 28% limit on net capital gains. Figure 16-4 shows the Gainers' tax calculation graphically with the shaded area representing the $1,800 tax savings ($38,476 – $36,676)

If the taxpayer had been a corporation, the entire $60,000 net capital gain would have been taxed as ordinary income (see Figure 16-2). Corporations do not currently enjoy preferential treatment for their capital gains.

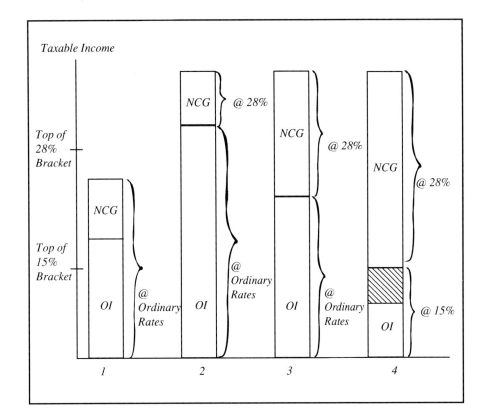

FIGURE 16-3

Applicable Tax Rates for an Individual's Net Capital Gain

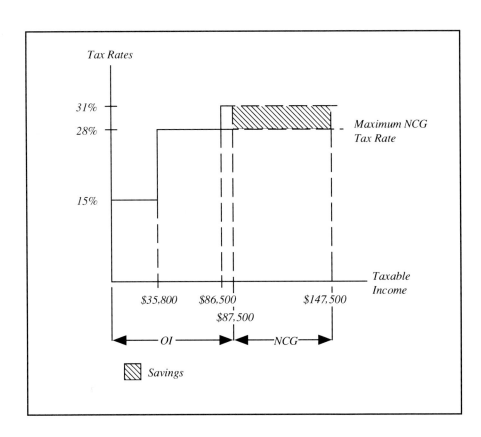

FIGURE 16-4

Computation of Tax for an Individual's Net Capital Gain— (EXAMPLE 16-2)

EXAMPLE 16-3

Assume the same facts as in Example 16-2 except that (1) the A Corp. stock sold for $155,000 instead of $100,000 and (2) the Z Corp. stock sold for $85,000 instead of $140,000. The sales now result in the following capital gains and losses (Channel 2 in Figure 16-1):

A Corp.	STCG	$115,000	
B Corp.	STCL	(90,000)	
	NSTCG		$25,000
X Corp.	LTCG	$ 50,000	
Y Corp.	LTCL	(25,000)	
Z Corp.	LTCG	10,000	
	NLTCG (and NCG)		$35,000

The Gainers' taxable income is $147,500 computed as follows:

Salary	$115,500
NSTCG	25,000
NCG	35,000
AGI	175,500
Itemized deductions and exemptions	(28,000)
Taxable income	$147,500

The Gainers compute their tax as follows (See Figure 16-3):

Tax on $112,500 ordinary income	
{$19,566 + [31% x ($112,500 − $86,500)]}	$27,626
Tax on $35,000 NCG (28% x $35,000)	9,800
Total tax	$37,426

Note that only the $35,000 net capital gain is taxed at the preferential 28% tax rate. The $25,000 net short-term capital gain is taxed as ordinary income. Therefore, ordinary income equals $112,500 ($147,500 − $35,000).

Although a net capital gain is taxed at 28%, the marginal tax rate on the net capital gain may actually exceed this percentage. Recall from Chapter 11 that exemptions and itemized deductions must be phased out once AGI reaches certain threshold levels. Thus, a net capital gain, which increases AGI, may result in reduced exemptions and itemized deductions. The tax calculation demonstrated in Examples 16-2 and 16-3 separated the net capital gain from the ordinary component of taxable income, but the tax on ordinary income was computed without altering the original phaseout calculations. Consequently, the total marginal tax rate on a net capital gain will equal 28% plus the marginal tax rate attributable to the reduction in exemptions and itemized deductions.

Capital Losses

To prevent the cherry-picking problem described in Chapter 5, the Code limits the deductibility of capital losses (see Channels 4 through 6 in Figure 16-1). Individual taxpayers may deduct capital losses to the extent of gains (via the netting process). If capital losses exceed capital gains, individuals may offset up to $3,000 ($1,500 if married filing separately) of the excess against ordinary income with the offset occurring in a particular order.[12] Specifically, excess net short-term capital losses offset ordinary income before excess net long-term capital losses do. Capital losses that exceed these limitations carry forward to succeeding years and retain their net short-term or net long-term character in the carryforward year.[13] The carryforward period for individuals is indefinite; the losses never expire.

Corporations treat capital losses differently than do individuals. They deduct capital losses only to the extent of gains and may not offset excess capital losses against ordinary income.[14] A corporation carries an excess capital loss back three years and forward five years (see Figure 16-2). Accordingly, a corporation is not allowed an indefinite carryforward, as are individuals. If the corporation does not use the carrybacks and carryforwards to offset capital gains within the prescribed period, the unused capital losses expire permanently. The capital losses carry back and forward as short-term capital losses regardless of their character in the loss year. The following examples demonstrate the operation of the capital loss rules for individuals and corporations.

EXAMPLE 16-4

For 1992, Mr. and Mrs. Loser have a combined salary of $100,000 and file a joint tax return. After netting their capital gains and losses, they realize a $15,000 net short-term capital loss and a $10,000 net long-term capital gain. These amounts further net to a $5,000 excess loss (Channel 4 in Figure 16-1). The Losers offset $3,000 of the $5,000 excess capital loss against their salary so their 1992 AGI is $97,000. The remaining $2,000 excess capital loss carries forward to 1993 as a short-term capital loss and enters the short-term receptacle for that year. If the Losers have no capital gains in 1993, they may offset the $2,000 carryforward against their 1993 ordinary income. If the taxpayer were a corporation, the corporation would carry back the entire $5,000 excess loss to 1989 as a short-term capital loss (see Figure 16-2).

EXAMPLE 16-5

Assume the same facts as Example 16-4 except that the Losers realize a $2,000 net short-term capital loss and a $7,000 net long-term capital loss (Channel 5 in Figure 16-1). Again, the Losers offset $3,000 of the $9,000 excess capital loss against their salary so their 1992 AGI is $97,000. The $3,000 ordinary income offset first uses up the entire $2,000 net short-term capital loss and then absorbs $1,000 of the net long-term capital loss. Therefore, the Losers carry forward a $6,000 long-term capital loss to 1993. If the taxpayer were a corporation, the corporation would carry back the $9,000 excess loss to 1989 as a short-term capital loss.

---

12 Sec. 1211(b).

13 Sec. 1212(b)(1).

14 Sec. 1211(a).

The netting rules discussed so far assume that capital losses are deductible in the first place. However, taxpayers may realize losses that are not deductible at all. These losses may not offset capital gains or any portion of ordinary income. For example, if an individual sells a personal automobile or residence at a *gain,* he or she realizes a taxable capital gain because these properties are capital assets. On the other hand, if the individual sells these personal use assets at a *loss,* the losses are nondeductible and may not offset capital gains from other transactions. This asymmetrical treatment occurs because of limitations imposed on personal losses by Secs. 165(c) and 262 (see Chapter 5).

PLANNING IMPLICATIONS

<table>
<tr><td>

Goal #6
Understand planning implications of capital gains and losses.

</td></tr>
</table>

Planning around the capital gain and loss rules involves both characterization and timing. Generally, capital gains are preferable to ordinary income because net capital gains are taxed at a top rate of 28% rather than 31%. If Congress raises the top ordinary tax rate or reduces the net capital gains rate, the differential will increase, making net capital gains increasingly attractive. Also, except for the $3,000 ordinary income offset, the taxpayer must realize capital gains to offset capital losses. Therefore, taxpayers with realized capital losses may want to structure their financial affairs to generate capital gains rather than ordinary income. Conversely, deductible ordinary losses are better than capital losses because they are not limited. Therefore, taxpayers with no realized capital gains may want to structure their financial affairs to generate ordinary losses rather than capital losses.

Timing affects planning in two ways. First, a taxpayer must hold capital assets for more than one year to achieve long-term capital gains. Second, the taxpayer needs to decide in which year to realize capital gains and losses.

EXAMPLE 16-6

Ms. Planner realized a $50,000 long-term capital gain early in 1992. She holds another stock that stands to generate a $45,000 long-term capital loss if sold. She owns no other capital assets. If she sells the second stock in 1992 she may offset it against the $50,000 gain. However, if she waits until 1993, she may offset only $3,000 against ordinary income in 1993 and the subsequent 14 years (assuming no other capital gains in the future). Remember, individual taxpayers may not carry back capital losses. Good planning dictates that Ms. Planner realize the capital loss in 1992 rather than 1993.

EXAMPLE 16-7

Smart Corporation has a $20,000 capital loss carryforward that arose from a transaction in 1987. Thus, the carryforward expires after 1992. If possible, Smart Corporation should realize a capital gain in 1992 to use the carryforward before it expires.

These examples are just two of many possible situations involving the timing of capital gains and losses. Such year-end tax planning is an important part of a tax practitioner's responsibilities. In addition, the planner must remain aware of nontax considerations. For example, delaying a stock sale increases the risk of unfavorable changes in the stock market. Also, a transaction that appears wise from a tax perspective may fit poorly into the taxpayer's overall investment goals.

CURRENT PROVISIONS: MODIFICATIONS TO THE PURE CASE

The preceding section of this chapter introduced the general rules that determine the tax consequences of realizing capital gains and losses. The Code contains many other provisions that modify the pure case. Sometimes a modifying provision, such as Sec. 1244, excludes a definitionally pure capital asset from capital loss treatment. Other modifying exceptions, such as Sec. 1231, provide capital gain treatment for assets that do not satisfy the statutory definition of a capital asset. The number of such modifying Code sections ranges in the dozens. This portion of Chapter 16 examines the most important modifications to the pure case of capital gain and loss taxation. Sections 1231, 1245, 1250, and 291 receive major attention because they deal with a broad set of assets, namely, depreciable and real property used in a trade or business. We then briefly examine five other Code sections: Sec. 165(h), personal casualty gains and losses; Sec. 1272, original issue discount; Sec. 165(g), worthless securities; and Sec. 1244, losses on small business stock.

A HISTORICAL AND CONCEPTUAL OVERVIEW OF SECTION 1231 AND THE DEPRECIATION RECAPTURE PROVISIONS

Section 1231 and the depreciation recapture rules, which pertain to the sale of depreciable assets, can best be understood in a historical context. Congress enacted the provisions at different times for different reasons with the end result, seemingly, a disparate patchwork of complex definitions and concepts. First we will explain the basic concepts as they developed chronologically. Later, we will add some of the detail that exists in the law today.

> **Goal #7**
> Apply Sec. 1231 in conjunction with Secs. 1245, 1250, and 291.

Exclusion from Capital Asset Definition

As mentioned earlier in this chapter, Sec. 1221(2) excludes depreciable and real property from the definition of a capital asset. This exclusion was motivated by the specific economic realities that existed in the late 1930s. Up to that time, depreciable assets were defined as capital assets and consequently were subject to the limitation on capital losses. During the depression years, Congress decided that the capital loss limitation unduly restricted the sale of plant and equipment purchased during the 1920s. To remove this impediment, Congress enacted the definitional exclusion and thereby transformed losses on the sale of such assets into ordinary losses, which were deductible without limitation. But the definitional exclusion also transformed gains into ordinary income, which was taxed less advantageously than capital gains.

Section 1231 before Advent of Depreciation Recapture

By the early 1940s, taxpayers viewed ordinary income treatment of gains as an increasingly important problem because, as the nation emerged from the depression, the gains and concomitant tax liabilities were becoming sizable. Pressure for change built until Congress again modified the Code by adding what is now Sec. 1231. This provision gave taxpayers the best of both worlds. Net losses on the sale of depreciable and real property still resulted in ordinary deductions, but net gains were afforded capital gain treatment even though the assets were technically not capital assets.

EXAMPLE 16-8

Recap Corporation sold a machine that it purchased several years earlier for $10,000. At the time of sale, accumulated depreciation was $6,000 and the adjusted basis was $4,000 ($10,000 - $6,000). Assume two *separate* cases in which the sales price is either (1) $9,000 or (2) $3,000. The gain or loss under each case is as follows:

	Case 1	Case 2
Sales price	$9,000	$ 3,000
Adjusted basis	4,000	4,000
Gain (loss)	$5,000	$(1,000)

Under Sec. 1231 as originally enacted, Recap would recognize a $5,000 long-term *capital* gain in Case 1 and a $1,000 *ordinary* loss in Case 2.

EXAMPLE 16-9

Suppose Recap Corporation sold two depreciable assets during the year. Under Sec. 1231 as originally enacted, if one asset generated a $10,000 gain and the second asset generated a $3,000 loss, the $7,000 net gain would receive long-term capital gain treatment. Alternatively, if the first asset generated a $9,000 loss and the second a $4,000 gain, the $5,000 net loss would be ordinary.

Advent of Section 1245

The asymmetrical treatment of Sec. 1231 seemed to work fine for a while, but in 1954 Congress enacted the first accelerated depreciation provisions. Accelerated depreciation produces ordinary deductions and, at the same time, quickly reduces the adjusted basis of the assets. The combination of accelerated depreciation and Sec. 1231 produced a great tax-savings device for taxpayers. They could deduct the depreciation expense from ordinary income, producing tax benefits at high tax rates, and then sell the low-basis assets with the gains taxed at favorable capital gains rates under Sec. 1231. To prevent this conversion of ordinary deductions into capital gains, Congress enacted Sec. 1245 in 1962. At the time, Sec. 1245 applied to depreciable personal property.

Section 1245 produces the following symmetrical result: Gain recognized on the disposition of depreciable personal property is treated as ordinary income to the extent of depreciation claimed. In effect, Sec. 1245 overrides Sec. 1231 and reconverts a portion of the gain to ordinary income, a process called **depreciation recapture**. However, recapture may not exceed the gain realized.[15] Thus, **potential Sec. 1245 recapture** equals total accumulated depreciation, and **actual Sec. 1245 recapture** equals the lesser of (1) potential Sec. 1245 recapture or (2) the gain realized.[16] With

> **Depreciation recapture** means that gain on the disposition of depreciable property is ordinary income to the extent of a defined amount of depreciation previously claimed.
>
> **Potential Sec. 1245 recapture** equals the total accumulated depreciation claimed on Sec. 1245 property.
>
> **Actual Sec. 1245 recapture** equals the lesser of potential Sec. 1245 recapture or the gain realized.

---

15 Sec. 1245(a)(1).

16 The Sec. 1245 rules discussed in this chapter apply only to Sec. 1245 property placed in service after 1961. Special rules apply to such property placed in service before 1962.

Sec. 1245 in place, only gains in excess of depreciation recapture become subject to Sec. 1231. Section 1245, however, does not apply to losses. Therefore, any losses remain within the scope of Sec. 1231.

Figures 16-5 and 16-6 graphically illustrate the combined rules of Secs. 1231 and 1245. In each graph the distance *OC* represents the cost of Sec. 1245 property purchased at the date t_0, and the curve represents the adjusted basis of this asset between t_0 and t_1, the date that asset was sold or exchanged. Figure 16-5 represents the Sec. 1231 and 1245 rules for any depreciable personal property that was depreciated on a straight-line basis. The linear function in Figure 16-5 implies that this property is depreciated on a straight-line basis. If this asset were sold on date t_1 for any amount less than that represented by distance *OB* (the adjusted basis of the property on the date of sale), the resulting loss would be a **Sec. 1231 loss.** If that same asset were sold on t_1 for any amount greater than that represented by distance *OC* the portion of the gain equal to distance *BC* would be recaptured as ordinary income by operation of Sec. 1245, and the remainder of the gain (that is, gain in excess of *OC*) would be **Sec. 1231 gain.** Figure 16-6 is similar to Figure 16-5. In Figure 16-6, however, the property is depreciated using an accelerated method, as suggested by the nonlinear function.

> A **Sec. 1231 loss** is a recognized loss on the dispostion of Sec. 1231 property.
>
> A **Sec. 1231 gain** is a recognized gain on the disposition of Sec. 1231 property in excess of depreciation recapture.

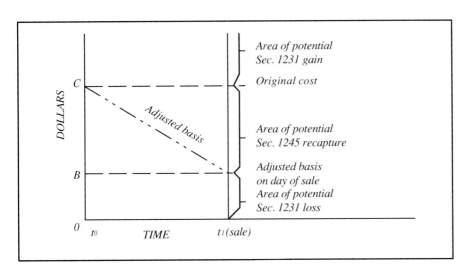

FIGURE 16-5

Sections 1231 and 1245: Combined Rules If Straight-Line Depreciation Was Used

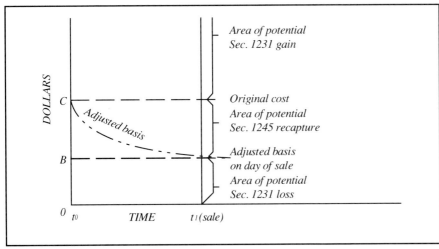

FIGURE 16-6

Sections 1231 and 1245: Combined Rules If Accelerated Depreciation Was Used

EXAMPLE 16-10

Assume the same facts as Example 16-8. The potential Sec. 1245 recapture is $6,000. If Recap sells the machine for less than the $4,000 adjusted basis, it recognizes a Sec. 1231 loss, which is ordinary. If the sales price ranges between $4,000 and $10,000 (original cost), all gain is ordinary because of Sec. 1245. If the sales price exceeds $10,000, $6,000 of the gain is ordinary income (Sec. 1245 recapture) with the balance being a Sec. 1231 gain. Specifically, assume three *separate* cases in which the sales price is either (1) $9,000, (2) $3,000, or (3) $12,000. The gain or loss under each case is as follows:

	Case 1	Case 2	Case 3
Sales price	$9,000	$ 3,000	$12,000
Adjusted basis	4,000	4,000	4,000
Gain (loss)	$5,000	$(1,000)	$ 8,000
Depreciation recapture— ordinary income	$5,000	$ 0	$6,000
Sec. 1231 gain (loss)	$ 0	$(1,000)	$2,000

Economic Rationale for Sections 1231 and 1245

Although Sec. 1231 and 1245 arose in different times in response to different problems, the end result seems theoretically correct. Depreciable assets are wasting assets because they are consumed over time in a taxpayer's business, which is why depreciation deductions offset ordinary income. In Cases 1 and 2 of Example 16-10, the gain or loss actually reflects the difference between tax depreciation and economic depreciation. In Case 1, tax depreciation ($6,000) exceeds the economic decline in value ($1,000) by $5,000. Conversely, in Case 2, tax depreciation ($6,000) lags the economic decline in value ($7,000) by $1,000. Thus, the gain or loss merely adjusts for the difference between tax and economic depreciation and, therefore, should be treated as ordinary. In Case 3, on the other hand, the asset *increased* in value. Consequently, the $6,000 gain attributable to tax depreciation should be ordinary because the asset experienced no economic decline. The remaining $2,000 is treated as capital gain because it represents a real economic increase in value (ignoring inflation).

Advent of Section 1250

In 1964, Congress added Sec. 1250 to the crazy quilt of gain and loss rules. Section 1250 introduced the recapture rules for depreciable real property. Historically, Congress has treated real property more favorably than personal property because the real estate industry has always wielded strong political power. Consistent with this bias, Sec. 1250 was not as harsh (and perhaps not as theoretically correct) as Sec. 1245.

Additional or **excess depreciation** is the excess of actual depreciation over straight-line depreciation; this amount is potential depreciation under Sec. 1250.

As a general rule under Sec. 1250, *potential* depreciation recapture is limited to the excess of actual depreciation over what depreciation would have been had the taxpayer used the straight-line depreciation method. The Code refers to this excess as **additional depreciation**, but we prefer to use the phrase **excess depreciation** because it is more descriptive than the Code's choice of words.

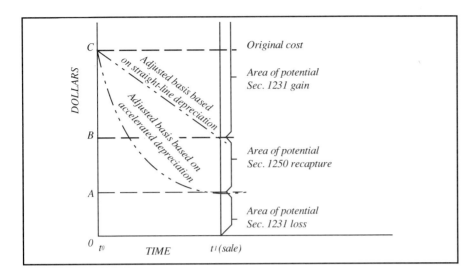

FIGURE 16-7

Sections 1231 and 1250: Combined Rules for Certain Sec. 1250 Property Described in This Chapter

Figure 16-7 graphically illustrates the combined rules of Secs. 1231 and 1250. Distance *OC* represents the initial cost of depreciable real property. The straight-line represents the adjusted basis of the Sec. 1250 property based on straight-line depreciation. The curve represents the actual adjusted basis of the property based on the accelerated depreciation method. The vertical difference between the line and the curve at any time represents the excess depreciation claimed. Thus, at t_1, the date of sale, the excess depreciation is represented by the distance *AB*. If the property were sold at t_1 for more than that represented by the distance *OA* but for less than that represented by the distance *OB*, the entire gain would be ordinary income by operation of Sec. 1250. If the property were sold at t_1 for something more than that represented by the distance *OB*, part of the gain—that represented by the distance *AB*—would be ordinary income via Sec. 1250, and the remainder would be Sec. 1231 gain.

Section 1250 is more favorable than Sec. 1245 because it subjects only excess depreciation to potential recapture rather than all depreciation. Under Sec. 1245, the portion of the gain represented by the distance *AC* in Figure 16-7 would be potential recapture, but under Sec. 1250 only the gain represented by the distance *AB* is potential recapture. Furthermore, if the taxpayer holds the property for a long period of time, the distance *AB* decreases so that potential Sec. 1250 recapture diminishes over time. Also, if the taxpayer uses the straight-line method, the curve coincides with the straight line, and no potential recapture exists.

EXAMPLE 16-11

Ivan Investor sold an apartment building that he purchased several years earlier for $100,000. At the time of sale, accumulated depreciation was $40,000 and the adjusted basis was $60,000 ($100,000 – $40,000). He used an accelerated depreciation method. Had he used the straight-line method, however, accumulated depreciation would have been $25,000. Thus, *potential* Sec. 1250 recapture is $15,000 ($40,000 – $25,000). If the sales price is less than the $60,000 adjusted basis, Ivan recognizes a Sec. 1231 loss, which is ordinary. If the sales price ranges between $60,000 and $75,000 (adjusted basis if straight-line depreciation had been used), all gain is ordinary because of Sec. 1250. If the sales price exceeds $75,000, $15,000 of the gain is ordinary income (Sec. 1250 recapture) with the balance being a Sec. 1231 gain.

SECTION 1231: SOME ADDITIONAL DETAILS IN CURRENT LAW

Recall from the overview that Sec. 1231 contains the following two general rules:

1. If Sec. 1231 gains exceed Sec. 1231 losses, the gains are treated as long-term capital gains, and the losses are treated as long-term capital losses;[17] and

2. If Sec. 1231 losses exceed Sec. 1231 gains, the gains are treated as ordinary income, and the losses are treated as ordinary losses.[18]

But several factors further complicate the application of Sec. 1231. First, a number of seemingly diverse transactions fall within the scope of this Code section. Second, the outcome of applying Sec. 1231 cannot be determined until the end of the tax year, at which time the relevant transactions are subject to a multi-tiered netting process. Third, as already mentioned, depreciation recapture rules must be applied before Sec. 1231 gains can be determined. Fourth, previously deducted Sec. 1231 losses may have to be recaptured.

Section 1231 originally applied to depreciable and real property. However, because it gave taxpayers the dual advantage of capital gains and ordinary losses, many special interests naturally sought Sec. 1231 treatment for their transactions. Also, the government wanted to provide some relief to taxpayers experiencing casualties, thefts, and other involuntary conversions. As a result, Sec. 1231 expanded over the years to cover an increasingly diverse set of property and transactions. Thus, as we define **Sec. 1231 property** below, notice that the definition embraces an array of seemingly unrelated types of property.

Section 1231 encompasses three classes of transactions:[19]

> **Section 1231 property** is real property or depreciable property used in a trade or business that is held for more than one year; the definition also includes other specialized property.

1. *Sales and exchanges.* Recognized gains (in excess of depreciation recapture) and recognized losses from the sales or exchange of property used in a trade or business. We define trade or business property below.

2. *Casualties and thefts.* Recognized gains (in excess of depreciation recapture) and recognized losses from casualties or thefts of (1) property used in a trade or business and (2) capital assets held for more than one year. These transactions are included in Sec. 1231 only if casualty and theft gains exceed casualty and theft losses. Also, the capital assets must be held in connection with a trade or business or in connection with a transaction entered into for profit. Casualties and thefts are defined and discussed in Chapter 5.

3. *Other involuntary conversions.* Recognized gains (in excess of depreciation recapture) and recognized losses from involuntary conversions other than casualties or thefts of (1) property used in a trade or business and (2) capital assets held for more than one year. Involuntary conversions in this category include seizures and condemnations. These transactions are included in Sec. 1231 even if they generate a net loss. Again, the capital assets must be held in connection with a trade or business or in connection with a transaction entered into for profit.

Property used in a trade or business includes various kinds of property held for various lengths of time. Specifically, this definition includes the following items:[20]

---

17 Sec. 1231(a)(1).

18 Sec. 1231(a)(2).

19 Sec. 1231(a)(3).

20 Sec. 1231(b).

1. Real property (whether or not depreciable) and depreciable personal property used in a trade or business if held for more than one year;

2. Timber, coal, and domestic iron ore to which Sec. 631 applies;

3. Cattle and horses held for draft, breeding, dairy, or sporting purposes if held for more than 24 months;

4. Livestock other than cattle, horses, and poultry held for draft, breeding, dairy, or sporting purposes if held for more than 12 months; and

5. Unharvested crop on land used in a trade or business and held for more than one year if the crop and land are sold, exchanged, or involuntarily converted at the same time and to the same person.

Figure 16-8 presents another mixing apparatus to represent the Sec. 1231 netting process. Several observations are in order before proceeding to an example.

First, casualty (and theft) gains and losses on long-term business property never get to the Sec. 1231 netting process unless they net to a gain. Otherwise, they exit the Sec. 1231 apparatus as ordinary gains and losses.

Second, *gains* from involuntary conversions (casualties, thefts, condemnations, and seizures) occur if the taxpayer receives compensation in excess of the property's adjusted basis. For example, an insurance company may remit insurance proceeds to the taxpayer for the fair market value of property destroyed in a casualty. Similarly, a governmental unit may reimburse the taxpayer for condemned property. The *gain* is always measured in relation to the adjusted basis of the property. If the taxpayer receives insufficient compensation, the *loss* is measured in relation to (1) the adjusted basis if the business property is *totally* destroyed or (2) the lesser of the adjusted basis or decrease in fair market value if the business property is *partially* destroyed (see Chapter 5).

Third, short-term transactions never enter the Sec. 1231 apparatus at all. They generally receive ordinary income and loss treatment unless they involve capital assets, in which case they generate short-term capital gains and losses. Personal casualty gains and losses also never enter the Sec. 1231 apparatus. Chapter 5 describes the treatment of personal casualty losses, and, later, this chapter explains the treatment of personal casualty gains.

Fourth, even after obtaining a **net Sec. 1231 gain**, the taxpayer may not receive long-term capital gain treatment because of another set of recapture rules. Prior to 1985, taxpayers could take advantage of Sec. 1231 by selling loss assets in one year and selling gain assets in the next year. By using this *straddle* technique, taxpayers could obtain ordinary deductions on the loss assets and long-term capital gain treatment on the gain assets. In the Deficit Reduction Act of 1984, Congress attempted to eliminate this strategy by enacting Sec. 1231 loss recapture rules.[21] Under these rules, a net Sec. 1231 gain is treated as ordinary income to the extent the net Sec. 1231 gain fails to exceed **nonrecaptured net Sec. 1231 losses**. Nonrecaptured net Sec. 1231 losses equal the excess of aggregate **net Sec. 1231 losses** for the five tax years immediately preceding the current year over the portion of those losses recaptured under this provision. Note that the recapture rule operates in only one direction. Taxpayers can still work the straddle by selling gain assets first and then selling loss

> A **net Sec. 1231 gain** is the excess of Sec. 1231 gains over Sec. 1231 losses.
>
> **Nonrecaptured net Sec. 1231 losses** equal the excess of aggregate net Sec. 1231 losses for the past five years over the portion of such loss already recaptured.
>
> A **net Sec. 1231 loss** is the excess of Sec. 1231 losses over Sec. 1231 gains.

---

21 Sec. 1231(c).

FIGURE 16-8

Section 1231 and Business Casualty Gains and Losses

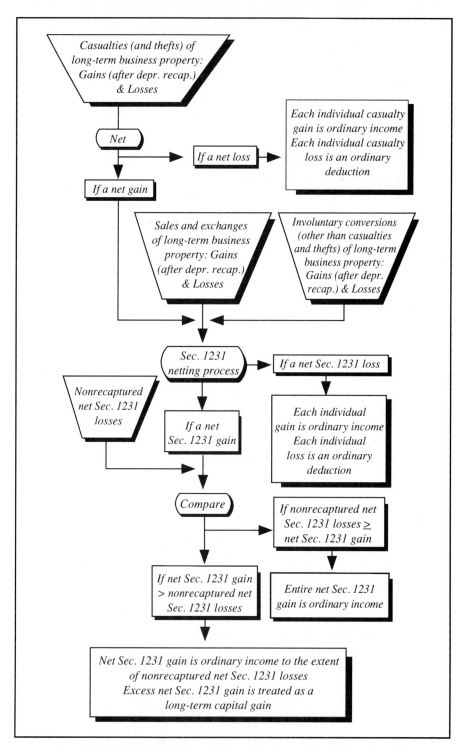

assets in the subsequent year. Taxpayers do not have to carry back net Sec. 1231 losses to prior years. The following example demonstrates the operation of Sec. 1231.[22]

---

22 This example is adapted from Kenneth E. Anderson, "Sec. 1231 and Involuntary Conversions after the DRA," *The Tax Adviser,* June 1985, pp. 326–331.

EXAMPLE 16-12

Hardluck Company, which is not a corporation, incurred the following transactions in 1992. All properties were held for more than one year. No depreciation recapture occurs on the factory building because it was depreciated using a straight-line method.

1. Business automobile partially wrecked:

Insurance recovery	$ 10,000
Lesser of adjusted basis or decrease in FMV	15,000
Casualty loss	$ (5,000)

2. Factory building completely destroyed by fire:

Insurance recovery	$ 90,000
Adjusted basis	78,000
Casualty gain	$ 12,000

3. Sale of factory machine (total accumulated tax depreciation is $20,000):

Selling price	$ 55,000
Adjusted basis	25,000
Gain	$ 30,000
Sec. 1245 recapture	$ 20,000
Sec. 1231 gain	$ 10,000

4. Sale of computer equipment (total accumulated tax depreciation is $15,000):

Selling price	$ 60,000
Adjusted basis	72,000
Sec. 1231 loss	$(12,000)

5. Land condemned by the city:

Condemnation proceeds	$ 74,000
Adjusted basis	65,000
Condemnation gain	$ 9,000

In addition, Hardluck Company had the following Sec. 1231 gains and losses from the immediately preceding five tax years:

1987	$10,000
1988	(6,000)
1989	(8,000)
1990	11,000
1991	(5,000)

Continued

EXAMPLE 16-12 (Con't.)

Because nonrecaptured net Sec. 1231 losses do not carry back, Hardluck's nonrecaptured net Sec. 1231 losses from prior years equal $8,000 (net of 1988 through 1991 gains and losses). Application of Figure 16-8 yields the following results:

Casualty loss on automobile	$ (5,000)
Casualty gain on factory building	12,000
Net casualty gain	$ 7,000
Net casualty gain (from above)	$ 7,000
Sec. 1231 gain on sale of machine	10,000
Sec. 1231 loss on sale of computers	(12,000)
Sec. 1231 gain on condemnation of land	9,000
Net Sec. 1231 gain	14,000
Recaptured net Sec. 1231 losses	(8,000)
Excess net Sec. 1231 gain	$ 6,000

Thus, Hardluck Company's 1992 gains and losses are characterized as follows:

Ordinary income:	
Sec. 1245 recapture on machine	$20,000
Recapture of net Sec. 1231 losses	8,000
Net LTCG treatment:	
Excess net Sec. 1231 gain	6,000

Because Hardluck recaptured the entire $8,000 of nonrecaptured net Sec. 1231 losses, no such losses carry forward to 1993.

Section 1245 property is depreciable personal property and certain depreciable real property (referred to as Sec. 1245 recovery property).

Section 1245 recovery property is real property that meets three conditions: (1) it is ACRS recovery property, (2) it is depreciated using ACRS accelerated tables, and (3) it is nonresidential real property.

DEPRECIATION RECAPTURE: SOME ADDITIONAL DETAILS IN CURRENT LAW

Section 1245

As explained in the overview, Sec. 1245 requires that, despite Sec. 1231, gain recognized on the disposition of **Sec. 1245 property** be treated as ordinary income to the extent of depreciation claimed. The Sec. 179 expense (see Chapter 14) is treated as depreciation for purposes of the Sec. 1245 recapture rules.[23]

Prior to 1981, Sec. 1245 applied to depreciable *personal* property, as opposed to *real* property, such as buildings and building components,[24] and Sec. 1250 applied to depreciable *real* property. However, certain ACRS real property placed in service from 1981 through 1986 may be subject to Sec. 1245 recapture instead of Sec. 1250 recapture. This special category of property is called **Sec. 1245 recovery property**.

---

23 Sec. 1245(a)(2)(C).

24 Section 1245 also applies to other specialized properties that may not be personal property but which also are not buildings or building components.

Real property is classified as Sec. 1245 recovery property if it meets *all three* of the following conditions:[25]

1. It is ACRS recovery property, that is, 15-year, 18-year, or 19-year real property placed in service between January 1, 1981, and December 31, 1986;

2. The taxpayer used ACRS accelerated tables rather than a straight-line option; and

3. The property is nonresidential real property.

If any one of these conditions is *not* met, the real property is Sec. 1250 property.

EXAMPLE 16-13

In 1986, Taxpayer A placed in service an office building and depreciated it using an ACRS accelerated table. The office building is Sec. 1245 recovery property. In 1986, Taxpayer B placed in service a warehouse and elected to depreciate it under a straight-line option. The warehouse is Sec. 1250 property. In 1986, Taxpayer C placed in service an apartment building and depreciated it using an ACRS accelerated table. The apartment building is Sec. 1250 property. In 1987, Taxpayer D placed in service an office building and depreciated it under MACRS. The office building is Sec. 1250 property.

The effect of having ACRS real property classified as Sec. 1245 recovery property can be dramatic. If the property is Sec. 1245 recovery property, *all* depreciation (cost recovery) is potential Sec. 1245 recapture. If, on the other hand, the property is Sec. 1250 property, only the depreciation in excess of straight-line depreciation is potential Sec. 1250 recapture. If the property is Sec. 1250 property because the taxpayer elected a straight-line option, *none* of the depreciation is potential recapture.

Section 1250

Section 1250 property refers to any depreciable *real* property that is not Sec. 1245 property. When originally enacted in 1964, Sec. 1250 applied to virtually all real property. Congress modified the Sec. 1250 rules in 1969, 1976, 1981, 1982, and 1986, with the changes *not* being retroactive. Consequently, a given item of real property may be subject to any one of six different sets of rules depending on when it was placed in service and when it was sold. To simplify matters, we have discussed in this chapter only Sec. 1250 rules applicable to the following two cases of major importance today:[26]

> **Section 1250 property** is any depreciable real property that is not Sec. 1245 property.

1. Depreciable nonresidential real property placed in service after December 31, 1969, unless the property is Sec. 1245 recovery property; and

2. Depreciable residential rental property placed in service after December 31, 1975.

Sec. 1250 applies only to the gain attributable to depreciable property, such as buildings. Gain attributable to the sale of land used in a trade or business is always a Sec. 1231 gain. Therefore, the allocation of the sales price between the land and the building can be important.

---

25 Sec. 1245(a)(5) before repeal by the Tax Reform Act of 1986.

26 Anyone interested in other possibilities may want to refer to the instructions for Form 4797.

As explained in the overview, only excess depreciation is subject to Sec. 1250 recapture. Therefore, real property depreciated under the straight-line depreciation method is never subject to either Sec. 1245 or Sec. 1250 recapture (although Sec. 291 may apply). The usual Sec. 1250 rule, however, applies only to property held for more than one year.[27] The potential recapture for Sec. 1250 property held for one year or less equals the *total* depreciation claimed.

Section 291

The Tax Equity and Fiscal Responsibility Act of 1982 (TEFRA) added complexity and additional recapture for *corporate* taxpayers that sell Sec. 1250 property after 1982. Section 291, added by TEFRA, requires additional recapture equal to

20% x (actual recapture as if the property were Sec. 1245 property – actual Sec. 1250 recapture).

EXAMPLE 16-14

In 1986, Chi Corporation acquired an apartment building for $500,000 (we ignore the land in this example). The building, which is ACRS 19-year property was placed in service on September 4, 1986. The corporation used the accelerated ACRS tables to depreciate the building and claimed total depreciation of $205,700. On March 4, 1992, Chi Corporation sold the building for $400,000, at which time the adjusted basis equaled $294,300 ($500,000 – $205,700). Thus, the corporation recognizes a $105,700 gain ($400,000 – $294,300). If the corporation had used straight-line depreciation, the total accumulation depreciation at the time of sale would have been $145,500 instead of $205,700. Therefore, excess depreciation (and potential Sec. 1250 recapture) is $60,200 ($205,700 – $145,500). Because this amount does not exceed the gain recognized, it also represents the actual Sec. 1250 recapture before application of Sec. 291. In addition, recapture under Sec. 291 equals $9,100. This amount is determined as follows: (1) actual recapture if the property were Sec. 1245 property would equal $105,700; (2) actual Sec. 1250 recapture equals $60,200; and (3) 20% x ($105,700 – $60,200) = $9,100. Consequently, $69,300 ($60,200 + $9,100) of the $105,700 gain is ordinary income while the remaining $36,400 is a Sec. 1231 gain. Had the taxpayer *not* been a corporation, the total recapture would have been only $60,200. Also, had the property been nonresidential real property rather than residential rental property, it would have been Sec. 1245 recovery property instead of Sec. 1250 property, in which case the entire $105,700 gain would have been ordinary income.

Installment Sales

As explained in Chapter 7, a taxpayer may defer gain recognition by electing the installment method. According to this method, the taxpayer recognizes a portion of each installment payment when it is received. The recognized portion is the ratio of total gain to the contract price (that is, the gross profit ratio). Section 453(i) modifies this treatment if the property sold is subject to depreciation recapture. Under Sec. 453(i), any gain treated as ordinary income because of Sec. 1245 or 1250 recapture

---

27 Sec. 1250(b)(1).

(including Sec. 291) must be recognized in the year of sale. Only the remaining gain may be deferred under the installment method. Thus, for installment sales, depreciation recapture not only creates ordinary income, it also accelerates gain recognition.

Summary

Section 1221 excludes real and depreciable property used in a trade or business from the definition of a capital asset. Nevertheless, part or all of the gain from the sale or exchange of these properties could receive long-term capital gain treatment under Sec. 1231. However, the depreciation recapture rules of Secs. 1245, 1250, and 291 override Sec. 1231, reconverting some or all of the gain on depreciable property to ordinary income. To determine the characterization of gains and losses from the sale of depreciable assets, one must understand the interrelationship of these provisions.

In addition to the Sec. 1231 and depreciation recapture rules, the Code contains other provisions that modify the pure case of capital gains and losses. We discuss several of these variations in the following paragraphs.

SECTION 165(h): PERSONAL CASUALTY (AND THEFT) GAINS AND LOSSES

Chapter 5 described the tax treatment of *personal* casualty (and theft) losses, and the present chapter has explained how *business* casualty gains and losses fit into the Sec. 1231 netting process. If a taxpayer incurs both gains and losses from property held for personal use, the gains and losses must be netted to determine the proper tax treatment. This netting, however, is done separately from the netting of business casualty gains and losses under Sec. 1231.

Goal #8
Determine the tax consequences of personal casualty gains and losses.

Recall from Chapter 5 that the amount of a personal casualty loss equals the lesser of (1) the decrease in fair market value of the property resulting from the casualty or (2) the adjusted basis of the property. This amount is further reduced by insurance proceeds and $100 per casualty. On the other hand, a taxpayer will realize a casualty (or theft) *gain* to the extent the insurance proceeds exceed the adjusted basis of the property. Should the taxpayer incur both casualty gains and losses, the following netting rules apply:

1. If the losses (after applying the $100 floor to each separate casualty) exceed the gains, the net loss is a deduction *from* AGI (in other words, an itemized deduction) to the extent the net loss exceeds 10% of AGI.

2. If the gains exceed the losses (after applying the $100 floor to the losses), individual gains and losses are treated as capital gains and losses. The capital gains will be long-term or short-term depending on the holding period of the property and will be netted with other capital gains and losses recognized by the taxpayer.

EXAMPLE 16-15

Ms. Fortune owned a valuable painting that was damaged by vandals on February 3, 1992. She paid $30,000 for the painting on November 29, 1980. An appraisal indicated the painting had a $90,000 fair market value (FMV) before the casualty and a $42,000 FMV after the casualty. She received $45,000 from the insurance company. Because this amount exceeds the adjusted basis of the painting, she realizes a $15,000 casualty gain ($45,000 – $30,000).

Continued

EXAMPLE 16-15 (Con't.)

On March 2, 1992, Ms. Fortune purchased an automobile for $22,000 to be used entirely for personal enjoyment. On September 24, 1992, the automobile was totaled in an accident in which Ms. Fortune was not injured. The automobile was worth $20,000 before the accident and nothing after the accident. Her loss before insurance is $20,000, which is the lesser of (1) the decrease in FMV ($20,000 – $0) or (2) the adjusted basis of the automobile ($22,000). She received $10,000 from the insurance company. Thus, she has a $9,900 loss after insurance and the $100 floor ($20,000 – $10,000 – $100).

Her $15,000 casualty gain and $9,900 casualty loss produce a net casualty *gain* of $5,100. Therefore, she recognizes a $15,000 long-term capital gain and a $9,900 short-term capital loss. These amounts are netted with other capital gains and losses recognized by Ms. Fortune in 1992 (see Figure 16-1).

EXAMPLE 16-16

Assume the same facts as in Example 16-15 except that Ms. Fortune receives only $32,000 from the insurance company for the damaged painting. In this case, she realizes a $2,000 casualty gain ($32,000 – $30,000). Her $2,000 casualty gain and $9,900 casualty loss produce a net casualty *loss* of $7,900. If her 1992 AGI equals $50,000, she may claim a $2,900 casualty loss itemized deduction [$7,900 – (10% x $50,000)].

SECTION 1272: ORIGINAL ISSUE DISCOUNT

> **Original issue discount** on a debt instrument equals the excess of the stated redemption price at maturity over the issue price.
>
> **Market discount** on a debt instrument equals the excess of the stated redemption price at maturity over the basis of the instrument immediately after an acquisition other than original issue.

Investments in corporate stocks and bonds are normally treated as capital assets. Furthermore, the amount received by a creditor on the retirement of any bond (or other evidence of indebtedness) is usually considered as the amount received in exchange for the bond. Given only the two facts just stated, a taxpayer might assume that any discount feature of a corporate bond (or other evidence of indebtedness) would give rise to a capital gain when the bond is sold, exchanged, or retired. In other words, the amount realized (usually equal to the face value of the bond at maturity) would be greater than the taxpayer's cost basis in the bond by the amount of any discount existing when the bond was acquired. Section 1272, however, generally requires a creditor (bondholder) to amortize any **original issue discount** (OID) and to recognize part of any OID as ordinary (interest) income each year from the date of acquisition to the date of retirement (or other disposition). The amortization of OID must be done using a constant interest method, rather than a straight-line method, to avoid the possibility of deducting inappropriately large amounts of interest expense during the early years of the debt. The same idea is extended in Sec. 1276 to **market discount** that occurs when a bond is resold by the original owner.

Because the creditor (bondholder) must report the amortized discount as ordinary income each year, the creditor also receives an equivalent increase in the basis of the bond. If the bond is held to maturity, the adjusted basis of the bond will equal the face of the debt, and no amount of capital gain remains to be recognized.

SECTION 165(g): WORTHLESS SECURITIES

An entirely different kind of problem was resolved by Sec. 165(g). A meticulous study of Sec. 1222 would reveal the critical importance of a few words contained there. Capital gain (or loss) is defined as the gain (or loss) from the *sale or exchange* of a capital asset. Given this choice of words, what happens when a taxpayer experiences a loss because a **security** has become totally worthless? If the security is truly worth nothing, the taxpayer can neither sell it nor exchange it for anything else of value. Does this fact deny the taxpayer the right to deduct any loss? Much to their surprise, taxpayers once found this to be the conclusion of the IRS and the courts.

To correct this obvious misinterpretation of the law, Congress passed the predecessor of Sec. 165(g) to create an artificial sale or exchange in the event of worthlessness. Section 165(g)(1) now reads as follows:

> If any security which is a capital asset becomes worthless during the taxable year, the loss resulting therefrom shall, for purposes of this subtitle, be treated as the loss from the sale or exchange, on the last day of the taxable year, of a capital asset.

Observe that this Code section does more than create the artificial sale or exchange. It also determines the end of the holding period by deeming the security sold on the last day of the year regardless of when during the year it becomes worthless. Unfortunately it cannot, and does not, solve the problem of determining when a security finally becomes worthless. Therefore, taxpayers and IRS agents continue to disagree frequently over the exact year in which a taxpayer should claim a loss deduction on worthless securities.

> A **security** is either (1) a share of corporate stock; (2) a right to receive stock; or (3) a corporate or government bond, debenture, note, etc., issued with coupon interest or in registered form.

> **Goal #9**
> Determine the tax consequences of worthless securities.

SECTION 1244: LOSSES ON SMALL BUSINESS STOCK

Section 1244 removes, to a certain extent, a disincentive to form small corporations by allowing holders of **Sec. 1244 stock** an ordinary loss deduction instead of a capital loss on the sale, exchange, or worthlessness of the stock. Ordinary loss treatment is limited, however, to $50,000 per year ($100,000 for married taxpayers filing a joint return). Nevertheless, this $50,000 (or $100,000) limitation is much more favorable than the $3,000 per year limitation on capital losses.

For stock (either common or preferred) to qualify as Sec. 1244 stock, three conditions must be met:[28]

1. At the time the stock is issued, the corporation must be a small business corporation (defined below);
2. The stock must be issued for money or other property (except stock or securities); and
3. During the five taxable years immediately preceding the loss year, the corporation must derive more than 50% of its total gross receipts (not gross income) from sources other than royalties, rents, dividends, interest, annuities, and sales or exchanges of stocks or securities (in other words, the corporation must be predominantly an operating rather than an investment entity).

> **Section 1244 stock** is common or preferred stock issued for money or other property by an active (based on a 50% gross receipts test) small business corporation.

> **Goal #10**
> Apply Sec. 1244 to dispositions of small business

---

28 Sec. 1244(c).

> A **small business corporation** is one whose total paid-in capital does not exceed $1 million.

The five-year requirement is reduced if the corporation is not in existence five years before the loss.[29] A corporation is a **small business corporation** if the total amount of money or other property received by the corporation (1) for the stock, (2) as a contribution to capital, and (3) as paid-in surplus does not exceed $1 million.[30] If the total capital and paid-in surplus exceeds $1 million, the stock attributable to the first $1 million still qualifies as Sec. 1244 stock.[31] Section 1244 operates automatically if the stock meets the requirements; the shareholders do not have to make an election.

Ordinary loss treatment under Sec. 1244 applies to two categories of taxpayers:[32]

1. Individuals to whom the small business corporation stock was issued; and

2. Individual partners who were partners when their partnership acquired the issued small business corporation stock.

Corporate, trust, or estate shareholders are not entitled to Sec. 1244 treatment, nor are individuals who acquire their stock by purchase, gift, or means other than original issue. In short, the individual or partnership must have acquired the stock from the small business corporation and must hold it continuously from the date of issuance.[33]

EXAMPLE 16-17

Mr. Solo has $75,000 he wishes to invest in a business. Suppose he operated as a sole proprietorship and used the invested funds for business expenses. His investment would be deductible as an ordinary business expense under Sec. 162. Suppose instead that he decided to operate the business as a corporation. He contributes the $75,000 to the newly formed corporation in exchange for the corporate stock. After the exchange, the stock has a $75,000 basis (see Chapter 17). If the corporation incurs losses, Mr. Solo cannot deduct them (assuming the corporation did not elect S corporation status). Now suppose the corporation becomes worthless so that Mr. Solo holds stock having a zero fair market value but a $75,000 basis. If Sec. 1244 did not exist, Mr. Solo would have a $75,000 capital loss in the year of worthlessness, deductible at $3,000 per year for the current year and the next 24 years (assuming Mr. Solo has no capital gains). The possibility of such an outcome would deter many taxpayers from incorporating their businesses. With Sec. 1244, however, Mr. Solo could claim an ordinary deduction (*for* AGI) of $50,000 in the year of worthlessness as well as $3,000 of the remaining $25,000 capital loss. If Mr. Solo filed a joint return, he could deduct the entire $75,000 in the year of worthlessness. Thus, Sec. 1244 partially removes the impediment to operating in corporate form.

If an S corporation owns small business corporation stock, its shareholders are not entitled to Sec. 1244 treatment unlike partners in a partnership that acquires Sec. 1244 stock.[34] However, shareholders of an S corporation that is itself a small business corporation may obtain Sec. 1244 treatment for the S corporation stock. Combining

---

29 Sec. 1244(c)(2).

30 Sec. 1244(c)(3).

31 Reg. Sec. 1.1244(c)–2(b).

32 Reg. Sec. 1.1244(a)–1(b).

33 *Ibid.*

34 TAM 9120003.

Sec. 1244 with an S corporation election increases the benefits of incorporation. If the S corporation incurs losses, they flow through to the shareholders as ordinary deductions and reduce the basis of the shareholders' stock (see Chapter 8). If the corporation becomes financially successful and the market value of the stock increases, the shareholder can sell the stock at a gain, thereby converting ordinary loss deductions (via early-year S corporation losses) into long-term capital gains. Meanwhile, the shareholders are partially protected against further downside market risk by Sec. 1244. Consequently, these two provisions working together enhance the ability of small corporations to raise venture capital.

—— KEY POINTS TO REMEMBER

✓ Proponents argue that preferential treatment of capital gains (1) reduces the lock-in effect, (2) creates incentives for investment, (3) increases U.S. competitiveness in international markets, (4) alleviates the bunching effect, (5) mitigates the effects of inflation, and (6) increases tax revenues. Opponents discount these arguments and further argue that (1) capital gains already enjoy a deferral advantage, (2) capital gains provisions add complexity to the tax laws, and (3) preferential treatment reduces equity in the tax system.

✓ Under the tax law, capital gains and losses arise from the sale or exchange of capital assets, where a capital asset is defined as any property held by the taxpayer other than inventory, real property and depreciable property used in a trade or business, artistic property created by the taxpayer, trade receivables, and certain U.S. publications.

✓ Proper taxation of capital gains and losses requires a netting process as depicted in Figures 16-1 and 16-2.

✓ For individual taxpayers, a net capital gain is taxed at a 28% maximum tax rate as shown in Figures 16-3 and 16-4. Capital losses are deductible to the extent of capital gains plus up to $3,000 of ordinary income. Excess capital losses carry forward indefinitely and retain their short-term or long-term character.

✓ For corporate taxpayers, net capital gains are taxed the same as ordinary income. Capital losses are deductible to the extent of capital gains with no offset against ordinary income. Excess capital losses carry back three years and forward five years as short-term capital losses.

✓ Under Sec. 1231, part or all of the gain from the disposition of real and depreciable business property may receive long-term capital gain treatment even though this property does not meet the definition of a capital asset. Nevertheless, the depreciation recapture rules of Secs. 1245, 1250, and 291 override Sec. 1231 and reconvert some or all of the gain to ordinary income. Proper treatment under Sec. 1231 requires a complex netting process as depicted in Figure 16-8.

✓ Personal casualty gains and losses must be netted. If a net gain results, the individual gains and losses are treated as capital gains and losses. If a net loss occurs, the loss is an itemized deduction to the extent that it exceeds 10% of AGI.

✓ Section 1244 allows ordinary loss treatment on small business corporation stock. The ordinary loss is limited to $50,000 ($100,000 on a joint return).

RECALL PROBLEMS

Note: If no year is stated, assume the transaction occurred in the current year.

#3

1. Harry Fox operates a retail hardware store and owns the property listed below. Indicate whether each property is, for federal tax purposes, a capital asset or a noncapital asset in Fox's hands.

   a. A sailboat used solely for pleasure.

   b. The building that houses his retail store.

   c. A warehouse in which he stores his hardware.

   d. The hardware items in the store.

   e. The hardware items in the warehouse.

   f. His personal residence.

   g. His automobile used 25% of the time for business, 75% for pleasure.

   h. One hundred shares of Alpha Corporation stock.

   i. A valuable painting inherited from a favorite aunt.

   j. Land on which the warehouse is located.

   k. Goodwill purchased by Fox when he acquired the business form its previous owner.

#3

2. The *Washington Dispatch*, a Delaware corporation, sold the following assets during the current year. Which of the sales by the *Washington Dispatch* corporation involved capital assets?

   a. A letter it received a year earlier from a well-known politician.

   b. A letter from a former U.S. president to a New York attorney, which the *Washington Dispatch* purchased (from the attorney) in conjunction with a story it published this year.

   c. A set of 25 photographs taken by a staff photographer, which graphically depict the terror associated with a recent skyjacking,

   d. Above normal sales (say, 100,000 extra copies) of a special edition of the *Dispatch*.

   e. A set of classified government documents given to the *Dispatch* by an anonymous person.

   f. All the common stock of a subsidiary corporation that publishes another newspaper in another city.

   g. A three-year-old printing press deemed obsolete.

   h. Illinois State bonds, which the *Dispatch* treasurer purchased as a temporary investment for excess corporate cash.

#3

3. Helen and Maria, two University of Hartford students, have almost covered the walls of their apartment with oil paintings. Helen's favorite painting is not a capital asset; Maria's favorite is a capital asset. Explain how this could be true.

#3

4. Taxpayer, an individual, realized the following gains and losses during the current year:

   (1) Personal car sold at a $1,600 loss.

(2) Business car sold at a $200 gain.

(3) Personal home sold at a $2,000 loss.

(4) Rental property sold at a $3,000 gain.

(5) Purchased oil painting from personal art collection sold at a $100 gain.

(6) Bronze statue, cast by taxpayer in spare-time hobby, sold at a $20 loss.

a Which of the above gains and losses can be classified as capital gains and losses? Explain any troublesome classifications.

b. Which of the above gains and losses would not be recognized for tax purposes?

5. For tax purposes, does it make any difference to the selling taxpayer whether part of the sales price involved in the sale of a business is allocated to a covenant not to compete rather than to goodwill? Explain.

6. For tax purposes, does it make any difference to the purchasing taxpayer whether part of the purchase price involved in the purchase of a business is allocated to a covenant not to compete rather than to a goodwill? Explain.

7. Listed below are various assets and their uses. In each case, indicate whether the asset is Sec. 1245 property, Sec. 1250 property, or neither.

a. Family automobile.

b. Machine used in a trade or business.

c. Family home.

d. Warehouse of a manufacturing company placed in service in 1978 and depreciated using the 150% declining-balance method.

e. Electric transmission lines of a utility.

f. Apartment house placed in service in 1986 and depreciated using ACRS tables.

g. Warehouse of a manufacturing company placed in service in 1986 and depreciated using ACRS tables.

h. Warehouse of a manufacturing company placed in service in 1986 and depreciated using the straight-line option under ACRS.

i. Apartment house placed in service in 1988.

j. Warehouse of a manufacturing company placed in service in 1988.

8. The tax treatment of property transactions depends on their proper classification in one of the following five categories:

A—Ordinary gain or loss

B—Sec. 1231 gain or loss

C—Casualty gain or loss

D—Long-term capital gain or loss

E—Short-term capital gain or loss

By using the identifying letter indicated above, classify each of the following independent transactions in the way it should be treated initially.

a. Gain from sale of raised livestock held 3 years for breeding purposes.

b. Fire loss on inventory held 4 months.

c. Gain from sale of antique auto held 10 months by classic car dealer.

d. Gain on sale of pleasure boat owned for 14 months.

e. Loss on sale of customers' receivables held 14 months. (Assume an accrual-basis taxpayer.)

f. Loss on condemnation of taxpayer's business parking lot.

g. Gain on sale of depreciable real property used in a business and held 10 months.

h. Gain on the sale of land used in a business and held 10 months.

9. Bud Kister, a cash-basis taxpayer who uses a calendar year, sold the following securities during the current year:

Security	Date Acquired	Purchase Price	Date Sold	Selling Price
Burns Co.	1/7 this year	$10,000	12/18	$7,300
Witten Co.	12/21 last year	2,500	6/4	5,000
Berner Co.	7/2 last year	4,200	9/7	2,100
Christy Co.	6/3 two years ago	16,000	1/5	9,500

In addition, Bud earned income of $54,000 in the year of the sale of the stock. In the following year, Bud had capital gains from the sale of stock amounting to $2,000. He again earned a salary of $54,000. What tax impact will the losses have on Bud's taxable income in the current year and next year?

10. Ralph and Norma, who file a joint tax return, earned a combined salary of $200,000 in 1992. Before phaseouts, they have itemized deductions of $30,000 and exemptions of $11,500. In addition, they realized capital gains and losses in 1992. For each of the following six *separate* cases, compute Ralph and Norma's AGI, taxable income, and tax liability.

	Case 1	Case 2	Case 3	Case 4	Case 5	Case 6
LTCG	$20,000	$20,000	$10,000	$10,000	$10,000	$10,000
LTCL	(6,000)	(6,000)	(16,000)	(6,000)	(16,000)	(26,000)
STCG	8,000	8,000	20,000	8,000	8,000	8,000
STCL	(12,000)	(3,000)	(3,000)	(20,000)	(20,000)	(3,000)

11. The JKL Corporation recognized the following amounts of income, gain, and loss in years 19X1 through 19X5:

	19X1	19X2	19X3	19X4	19X5
Ordinary income	$200,000	$400,000	$800,000	$1,600,000	$3,200,000
Long-term capital gain(loss)	50,000	100,000	200,000	(400,000)	100,000

a. Calculate JKL's tax liability for 19X1 through 19X3 as computed on its original tax return.

b. Calculate JKL's tax liability for 19X4 and 19X5, and determine the impact of the 19X4 capital loss on years 19X1 through 19X5.

12. Baldwell, a calendar-year taxpayer, operates a small manufacturing plant as a sole proprietor. He files a joint return with his wife; both are under 65 and have good vision. They have no itemized deductions and no dependents. During 1992, Baldwell sold the following property (assume no Sec. 179 election):

a. January 23—The family automobile for $7,000; purchased two years ago for $12,000.

b. January 28—A machine for $4,500; purchased in 1986 for $12,000. The machine was 5-year ACRS property.

c. April 3—One hundred shares of ABC, Inc., for $4,000; purchased 16 months ago for $3,400.

d. July 16—A truck for $2,500; purchased in April 1990 for $10,000. The truck was 5-year MACRS property.

All property sold was used in Baldwell's business except for the automobile and the ABC shares. In addition, Baldwell had business income of $52,000 and business deductions (including depreciation) of $12,000. These amounts do not include gains and losses for the above sales. Compute Baldwell's tax liability for 1992.

13. Assuming an individual taxpayer, determine taxable income in each of the following cases. Show details as to character of income, gains, and losses. Also determine the amount and character of any capital loss carryforwards. Assume no non recaptured net Sec. 1231 losses from prior years.

	Case 1	Case 2	Case 3	Case 4
Taxable income excluding all transactions below	$30,000	$40,000	$50,000	$60,000
Property transactions:				
Net LT capital gain (loss)	10,000	(5,000)	(14,000)	(2,000)
Net ST capital gain (loss)	(2,000)	1,000	1,000	(2,000)
Net Sec. 1231 gain (loss)	(3,000)	3,000	13,000	(2,000)
Net casualty gain (loss)—business	1,000	(4,000)	3,000	(2,000)
Taxable income	$	$	$	$

14. In 19X1 through 19X3, a taxpayer incurred the gains and losses shown below:

Item of Income or Loss	19X1	19X2	19X3
Taxable income excluding all transactions below	$30,200	$33,200	$37,200
Property transactions:			
Net short-term capital gain (or loss)*	800	200	1,000

Item of Income or Loss (Con't.)	19X1	19X2	19X3
Net long-term capital gain (or loss)*	(5,000)	4,600	(13,000)
Depreciation recapture under Sec. 1245	1,000	1,100	2,000
Net Sec. 1231 gain (or loss)	(2,000)	3,000	7,000

*Excluding capital loss carrybacks and carryforwards and excluding Sec. 1231 transactions.

a. Assume that the taxpayer is an individual. Compute taxable income for 19X1 through 19X3. Show details as to the character of income, gains, and losses. Determine the amount and character of any carryforward to 19X4.

b. Assume that the taxpayer is a corporation. Compute taxable income for 19X1 through 19X3 *after* capital loss carrybacks and carryforwards. Show details as to the character of income, gains, and losses. Determine the amount and character of any carryforward to 19X4.

15. Assume the following facts for 1992:

	Taxpayers		
	A	B	C
AGI excluding all transactions below	$43,000	$43,000	$43,000
Short-term capital gains	3,000	4,000	12,000
Short-term capital losses	(7,000)		
Long-term capital gains	30,000	13,000	
Long-term capital losses	(19,000)		(29,000)
Sec. 1245 recapture	5,000		10,000
Sec. 1231 gains	2,000		3,000
Sec. 1231 losses	(12,000)	(5,000)	(5,000)
Casualty gains			14,000
Casualty losses (after insurance recovery)		(1,000)	(4,000)

a. Assume that Taxpayers A, B, and C are each married individuals filing a joint return. They have no itemized deductions and no dependents. The casualty gains and losses are from property used for personal purposes. For each set of taxpayers, determine:

(1) AGI.

(2) Taxable income.

(3) The character of income, gains, and losses.

(4) The amount and character of capital loss carryforward, if any.

b. Assume that Taxpayers A, B, and C are each corporations and that income on the first line is taxable income excluding the transactions below instead of AGI. Also assume that casualty gains and losses are business related. For each taxpayer, determine:

(1) Taxable income

(2) The character of income, gains, and losses.

(3) The amount and character of capital loss carryback, if any.

16. On January 10, Ed Burns sold some of his business equipment, which he had purchased for $4,000 several years ago and on which he had properly claimed $3,600 of depreciation since acquisition. The tax consequences of this sale depend on the selling price of the equipment. Indicate, for each of the selling prices listed below, whether the result would be taxable as ordinary income under Sec. 1245 or a Sec. 1231 gain or loss:

    a. $2,500 b. $5,000 c. $100

17. On January 8, Tom Lock sold a small warehouse that he had used in his sole proprietorship. Tom built the warehouse in 1980 for $100,000. Tom claimed $65,000 of actual depreciation since building the warehouse. Straight-line depreciation would have been $60,000.

    a. If Tom sold the warehouse for $50,000, what amount of his gain is ordinary income (Sec. 1250 recapture), and what amount is a Sec. 1231 gain?

    b. If Tom had claimed straight-line depreciation on this warehouse, what amount of his gain would have been ordinary income?

18. Joe Schwartz purchased a small apartment house as an investment on January 1, 1986. Joe paid $50,000 for the land and $200,000 for the apartment house. If Joe were to sell this property on January 1, 1992, the tax consequences of the sale would depend to a great extent on both the selling price and the allocation of that price between the land and building.

    a. Indicate the amount that must be treated as ordinary income (as depreciation recapture) and the amount that must be treated as Sec. 1231 gain or loss if the total sales price were $240,000, of which $60,000 is allocated to the land and $180,000 to the apartment house. (Assume that total ACRS depreciation over the holding period is $87,800 and that straight-line depreciation would have totaled $63,400.)

    b. Assume Joe received $160,000 in the sale, of which $60,000 was allocated to the land and $100,000 to the building. How does your answer differ?

    c. Redo part a assuming Joe sold a warehouse instead of an apartment house.

    d. Redo part a assuming the taxpayer is a corporation instead of an individual (again assume the sale of an apartment building).

19. Redo Example 16-12 assuming the selling price of the computer equipment was $35,000 instead of $60,000, thereby generating a $37,000 loss.

20. Redo Example 16-12 assuming the insurance recovery on the factory building was $80,000 instead of $90,000, thereby generating a $2,000 casualty gain.

21. Recap Company acquired a machine for its business for $100,000. The company placed the machine in service on May 23, 1990. The machine is MACRS 7-year property, and Recap made the Sec. 179 expense election in 1990. Recap Company plans to sell the machine in 1992. Determine the adjusted basis of the machine at the time of sale. What is the amount and character of gain or loss if Recap sells the machine for:

a. $ 40,000

b. $ 80,000

c. $120,000

#7

22. In 1987, Rho Corporation acquired land and a factory building for $900,000, with $200,000 of the purchase price allocated to the land and $700,000 allocated to the building. The building, which is nonresidential real property, was placed in service on February 3, 1987. On May 17, 1994, Rho Corporation sold the land and building for $950,000, with $300,000 of the sales price allocated to the land and $650,000 allocated to the building. Determine the amount and character of gain or loss on the sale.

#8

23. On March 1, 1992, burglars broke into Ms. Diamond's home and stole her jewelry. She discovered the theft after returning home from the opera and immediately reported it to the police. The stolen jewelry had cost Ms. Diamond $100,000, and a recent appraisal indicated the jewelry was worth $90,000. If Ms. Diamond's 1992 AGI is $150,000, indicate the tax consequences in each of the following cases. If the insurance recovery exceeds the jewelry's fair market value, assume that Ms. Diamond had special theft insurance policy that guaranteed the stated recovery regardless of the actual value of the jewelry.

a. Insurance recovery is $80,000.

b. Insurance recovery is $105,000.

c. Insurance recovery is $95,000.

#9 #10

24. On November 15, 1991, Harry Hardluck purchased the stock of Risky Corporation for $20,000. In 1992 Risky Corporation failed, and the stock became worthless on June 15, 1992.

a. What is the amount and character of Harry's loss? How much, if any, of the loss may he deduct in 1992 assuming no other capital transactions?

b. Would the results be any different if Harry had acquired the stock as part of the original issuance of the corporation? Explain.

───── THOUGHT PROBLEMS

#1

1. Courts and tax commentators for years have compared capital to a tree and income to the fruit of that tree; that is, income is viewed as something that can be separated from capital, leaving the productive base unscathed. Discuss the possible weaknesses of this metaphor.

#1

2. On November 14 of the current year the authorities suspended all trading in Equity Funny Corporation stocks. Radcliff had purchased 1,000 shares of Equity Funny on February 13 last year for $32,500. The closing quotation for these shares on November 13 this year was $5 per share. The trading suspension was still in effect on December 13, so Radcliff could not sell his 1,000 shares although he desperately wanted to do so. What amount of capital loss can Radcliff deduct in the current year as far as his Equity Funny stock is concerned? Explain briefly.

#1 #2

3. Twenty years ago, Betty paid $20,000 for Property A, and Bob earned $20,000 for his services. Today, Betty sold Property A for $40,000, and Bob was paid

$40,000 for his services. If the consumer price index (CPI) increased from 100 to 200 in 20 years

a. How much real income has Betty realized on Property A?

b. How much of an increase in real wages has Bob realized after 20 years' work?

c. Do you believe that Betty should pay an income tax on the sale of the property? Explain briefly. (Note: This question asks for personal opinion, not the answer per the Code.)

d. On what amount of income do you believe Bob should pay an income tax? Explain briefly. (Note: State your personal opinion.)

e. Based on our current tax law, will either Betty or Bob automatically get a tax break? If so, which one?

4. Based on your own intuition, how would you define a capital gain? (In responding to this question, ignore this textbook and base your answer on any general notions you might have gathered from your other studies thus far in college.) Why do basic differences in concepts exist?

5. Suppose the tax law taxed ordinary income at 30%, capital gains at 15%, and municipal bond interest at 0%. Consider three taxpayers, A, B, and C. In the current year, A receives $10,000 interest income on a fully-taxable corporate bond, B realizes a $10,000 capital gain, and C receives $10,000 interest on a tax-exempt municipal bond. Accordingly, on their tax returns, A pays $3,000 tax, B pays $1,500 tax, and C pays no tax. Are these taxpayers being treated inequitably? Explain.

6. On March 3 of this year, Walter Caringounce, a real estate dealer, sold a 12-acre tract of land for $120,000. Although Walter had purchased the property for $40,000 as an investment six years ago, he made minor improvements to the land during the past 18 months, and he actively advertised the property for sale for a year before closing the deal this year. How should Walter report his $80,000 gain this year?

7. According to Sec. 1212(b)(2), a technically correct description of the capital loss carryforward rule for individuals is as follows: For determining the carryforward, the lesser of the following two amounts is treated as a net short-term capital gain: (1) excess capital losses allowed to offset ordinary income or (2) adjusted taxable income. Adjusted taxable income equals taxable income plus the amount of capital loss allowed to offset ordinary income plus personal and dependency exemptions. This rule means that excess net short-term capital losses offset ordinary income before excess net long-term capital losses do. It also means that, if the offset against ordinary income exceeds adjusted taxable income, the difference is preserved as a capital loss carryforward. Apply this rule to the following problem:

Mr. and Mrs. Cole are married and file a joint tax return. Mr. Cole runs a business that experienced a net loss in 1992, and Mrs. Cole is a salaried employee. They realized a $7,000 net long-term capital loss during the year. Their 1992 taxable income is as follows:

Salary	$ 50,000
Net business loss	(38,000)
Capital loss deduction (limited to $3,000)	(3,000)

AGI	9,000
Itemized deductions	(10,000)
Personal exemptions	(4,600)
Taxable income	$ (5,600)

Determine the Coles' capital loss carryover to 1993.

#4 #6 #7

8. Cary Clever owns three assets that if sold will generate the following gains and losses:

   Asset #1   Sec. 1231 gain, $50,000

   Asset #2   Sec. 1231 loss, $(50,000)

   Asset #3   Long-term capital loss, $(50,000)

   The first two assets are Sec. 1231 property, and the third asset is a capital asset. Cary can sell some or all the assets in December 1992 or January 1993, but in any case, he will sell all the assets. Describe each possible strategy available to Cary, determine the tax consequences of each strategy, and decide which strategy Cary should adopt. Assume that Cary is in the same tax bracket for both years.

#5

9. Mr. and Mrs. Margin are married, file a joint return, and have two dependent children. Their combined salary for 1992 is $160,000. In 1992, they also recognized a $40,000 long-term capital gain, which is a net capital gain because they recognized no capital losses. The margins incurred $30,000 of itemized deductions (before reduction under phaseout rules). What is their marginal tax rate on the $40,000 net capital gain?

#6

10. On Monday, October 19 of this year, Sigmund Yuppie had one of the worst days of his life. Short on cash, Sigmund decided to sell a large portion of his stock holdings. Unfortunately, on that day the price of stocks fell drastically and, while Sigmund got the cash he needed, he realized capital losses of $31,000 in the process. Always an optimist, Sigmund wants to make the most of the situation. What tax planning opportunities could you suggest to Sigmund to minimize the effect of his losses?

#7

11. "The probability of a taxpayer's being able to recognize a capital gain on the sale of depreciable personal property used in a trade or business has diminished to the point where, today, it is practically zero." True or false? Explain.

#9

12. What problems do you think a taxpayer faces in determining if and when a security becomes worthless? What events might indicate worthless?

#10

13. Do you think Sec. 1244 adequately removes impediments to incorporating a business? If so, explain why. If not, explain why not and recommend changes you would make to Sec. 1244.

——— CLASS PROJECTS

1. Research paper: Write a position paper on how capital gains or losses should be treated under U.S. tax law. Choose what you think is the proper treatment and defend that view in the paper. For supporting authority, use sources other than your own opinion and this textbook.

2. Tax return: For Mr. Dreary Dropout, December 1, 1991, was the worst of times, or so it seemed. Dreary was a CPA who operated his own practice in Minneapolis, Minnesota. He had worked all night on an urgent tax problem for one client and faced an unpleasant lunch with another client. The second client was unhappy about the amount of the latest bill for Dreary's services. Moreover, 14 inches of snow had fallen overnight, making the streets treacherous. However, by 10:00 A.M., snowplows had cleared most streets, so Dreary began his drive to the client's office. Preoccupied with tiredness and the upcoming confrontation, Dreary failed to notice an icy patch on the road. He lost control of his car, slid across the two opposite lanes, and slammed into a light pole. Fortunately, no one was injured, but Dreary's car was totaled. Dreary lived nearby, so he decided to walk home after giving his report to the police and having his mangled car towed away. When he arrived home, he found his house burned to the ground. Heavy ice had broken several electical wires, causing them to fall on his house, igniting the blaze. While sitting on a snowbank across from the charred remains of his home, Dreary's life seemed as bleak as the winter sky of the northern Midwest—until he thought of Ms. Upwardly Mobile.

In the 1980s, Upwardly Mobile was the star of her college. She graduated first in her class in undergraduate and post-graduate studies. She received top offers from every CPA firm with which she interviewed. Within five years of working for one of the top firms, she was promoted to manager—she was on the fast track. By 1991, however, mergers, the economic recession, and increased competition had taken their toll on the accounting firms, and promotions to partner were taking longer than suitable to our heroine—after all, she was Upwardly Mobile. Early in 1991, Upwardly approached Dreary about buying his accounting practice. She believed that, with her superior intelligence, knowledge, motivation, and savoir faire, she could triple the size of Dreary's business. Moreover, the rewards of her efforts would be hers rather than the partners of her current firm. At that time, however, Dreary was not interested.

Sitting on the snowbank with new snow falling around him, Dreary thought about his burned home, his wrecked car, his long work days, his demanding clients, the brutal Midwest winters, and Upwardly Mobile. He decided to sell his practice. Moreover, he decided to sell his entire stock portfolio, use the proceeds from the practice and stock sales to purchase government bonds, and move to Southern California. There, he would realize his lifelong fantasy of bumming around on warm, sunny beaches. With renewed energy, Dreary jumped up and walked to his office, which was three blocks from what used to be his home. His practice was housed in a restored Victorian house that he purchased in June 1986. Dreary hated hermetically sealed office buildings. Arriving at the office, he immediately called Upwardly. They agreed to meet the next day, and on December 17, 1991, they consummated the deal. Dreary collected proceeds from the insurance company on December 18, sold all his stocks on December 19, and moved to Malibu, California, on December 20. Dreary was no longer dreary.

On arriving in California, Dreary swore never to prepare another tax return, so early in 1992 he calls you to prepare his 1991 return and provides you with the following facts pertinent to that year.

a. Dreary's social security number is 123-45-6789. He is single, 45 years old, has no dependents, and his vision has never been better. His home address in Minneapolis was 333 Kafka Lane, Minneapolis, MN 55455. His address in California is 711 Bliss Road, Malibu, CA 90111.

b. The following information is relevant to Dreary's stock portfolio (all common stock):

Company	ABC Corp.	DEF, Inc.	GHI Co.
Shares	1,200	2,000	3,000
Date purchased	11/21/80	2/3/91	12/15/75
Cost per share	$20	$50	$10
Date sold	12/19/91	12/19/91	12/19/91
Selling price per share	$100	$40	$200
Total dividends received in 1991	$5,000	$4,000	$20,000

In addition, Dreary had a $15,000 long-term capital loss carryforward from 1990.

c. Dreary also received interest income of $20,000 from Minneapolis National Bank; $30,000 of income from Dreyfus Liquid Assets; $55,000 of interest income from Fidelity Municipal Bond Fund; and a $1,000 state income tax refund for which he had received a full tax benefit as a deduction in 1990.

d. Dreary incurred the following expenses in 1991, *not* related to the accounting practice:

State income taxes paid	$25,000
Real estate taxed on home	2,000
Interest on home mortgage* (from Form 1098)	15,000
Interest on credit cards	300
Cash contributed to charities[†]	4,900
Safe deposit box for stock certificates	100

---

*His $150,000 mortgage loan was taken out five years ago with a financial institution. He took out no second mortgage or home equity loans.
[†]No more than $3,000 to any one charitable organization.

e. Dreary's 1990 tax liability was $165,000, and he paid $200,000 in 1991 estimated taxes ($50,000 on each of the following dates: 4/15/91, 6/14/91, 9/13/91, and 1/15/92).

f. He made a $25,000 deductible contribution to a Keogh retirement plan.

g. While operating his accounting practice, Dreary was a self-employed individual with his office building located at 1120 Compliance Street, Minneapolis, MN 55455. He practiced under the name Dreary Dropout, CPA. His employee ID number was 36-7654321 and business code was 7858. The business filed Form 941 in 1991. During 1991, his cash-basis practice incurred the following items of revenue and expense:

Fee revenue	$1,000,000
Professional salaries	300,000
Secretarial salaries (no jobs credit)	50,000
Payroll taxes (FICA, FUTA, etc.)	20,000

Premiums for employee medical insurance	3,000
Insurance expense	15,000
Interest on building mortgage (paid to a bank)	40,000
Property taxes	6,000
Building maintenance and repairs	2,500
Office expenses	10,200
Utilities and telephone	12,600
Office supplies	5,000
Business meals	6,500
Travel expenses	7,500
Automobile expenses (excluding depreciation)	1,800
Professional dues	1,100
Depreciation	(*)

*Dreary owned the following depreciable business property:

	Date Placed in Service	Cost
Building*	6/3/86	$600,000
Office equipment*	5/6/89	150,000
Furniture*	12/16/88	100,000
Automobile[†]	10/17/89	20,000

*Dreary used the most accelerated depreciation allowable for each asset. In addition, he made the Sec. 179 expense election for the furniture in 1988 and the office equipment in 1989.
[†]Dreary used this automobile exclusively for business purposes; he owned another car for personal use and commuting. In addition, he had written policy that no employee could use the business vehicle. In 1991, Dreary put 15,000 business miles on the car before wrecking it on December 1, 1991.

h. On December 18, 1991, Dreary received insurance recoveries for the car, the home, and the home's contents. The following information pertains to the casualties:

Item	Automobile	Home	Contents
Date acquired	10/17/89	1985	1985
Cost	$20,000	$200,000	$75,000
FMV immediately before casualty	$ 9,000	$300,000	$60,000
Insurance recovery	$ 8,000	$300,000	$40,000

i. Dreary and Upwardly agreed on a $3,000,000 price for the accounting practice. She paid $600,000 with cash she had inherited from her great grandmother, she assumed the $400,000 mortgage on the building, and she borrowed the remaining $2,000,000 from the bank. The practice consisted of the following explicitly identified assets:

	Tax Basis	FMV and Agreed upon Allocation of Purchase Price
Accounts receivable	$ 0	$ 100,000
Land	250,000	400,000
Building:		
Cost	600,000	750,000
Accum. depr.	(?)	
Office equipment:		
Cost	150,000	60,000
Accum. depr.	(?)	
Furniture:		
Cost	100,000	50,000
Accum. depr.	(?)	
Supplies	0	2,000
Client list	0	1,250,000
Covenant not to compete	0	250,000
Goodwill	0	138,000
Total		$3,000,000

The practice had no nonrecaptured net Sec. 1231 losses from prior years.

j. Tax forms required:

Form 1040

Schedules A&B

Schedule C

Schedule D

Schedule SE

Form 2210

Form 4562

Form 4684

Form 4797

*By just exchange one for the
other given...
There never was a better bargain
driven.*

SIR PHILIP SIDNEY, SONNET (1580)

NONTAXABLE
EXCHANGES

CHAPTER OBJECTIVES

In Chapter 17, you will acquire a general understanding of nontaxable exchanges and will learn how to apply the rules for nontaxable exchanges to various common transactions.

LEARNING GOALS

After studying this chapter, you should be able to

1 Understand the underlying rationale for nontaxable exchanges;

2 Recognize the difference between a taxable and non-taxable exchange;

3 Understand the requirements and determine the tax consequences of a like-kind exchange;

4 Understand the requirements and determine the tax consequences of an involuntary conversion;

5 Understand the requirements and determine the tax consequences of selling a principal residence;

6 Understand the requirements and determine the tax consequences of forming a corporation; and

7 Understand the essential characteristics and tax consequences of corporate reorganizations.

Goal #1
Understand the rationale
for nontaxable exchanges.

A **nontaxable exchange** is
one in which a realized
gain or loss is not
recognized at the time of
the exchange; the gain is
usually deferred until
some future event.

In a **direct exchange,** the
taxpayer receives
comparable property in
exchange for the property
transferred.

In an **indirect exchange,**
the taxpayer disposes of
property, receives cash
payment for the property,
and subsequently reinvests
the cash in comparable
property.

Continuity of interest
means a continuing
investment in property
comparable to that
exchanged.

The title of this chapter, Nontaxable Exchanges, is something of a misnomer. Most of the transactions discussed involve *deferral* of gain or loss recognition rather than *permanent* nonrecognition. As explained in detail later, the deferred gain or loss is reflected in the tax basis of exchanged property. Nevertheless, to conform to common usage, we will use the expression **nontaxable exchange** to designate transactions in which a realized gain or loss is not recognized at the time of exchange.

Nontaxable exchanges can take one of two basic forms: a direct exchange or an indirect exchange. In a **direct exchange**, the taxpayer transfers property and receives comparable or similar property in exchange (although, in certain corporate transactions, a taxpayer may receive stock rather than other property). In an **indirect exchange**, the taxpayer (1) disposes of or loses property; (2) receives cash compensation for the property; and (3) within prescribed time limits, reinvests the cash proceeds in comparable or similar property.

Two doctrines provide the underlying rationale for nontaxable exchanges: the wherewithal-to-pay concept (defined earlier in this text) and continuity of interest. The wherewithal-to-pay concept is important because, in most nontaxable exchanges, the taxpayer either receives property comparable to that exchanged or receives money that is reinvested in comparable property. In either case, the taxpayer does not have money to pay taxes. Imposing taxation at this stage would subject the taxpayer to unnecessary hardship because the taxpayer would have to obtain money to pay taxes from other sources. On the other hand, a taxpayer who receives money (called boot) in an otherwise nontaxable exchange or retains money in a transaction requiring reinvestment should recognize some amount of gain because he or she has at least the partial wherewithal to pay taxes.

Continuity of interest plays a role in nontaxable exchanges because the taxpayer maintains an investment or interest in property similar to that exchanged. In other words, the taxpayer's investment or interest continues, albeit in modified form. This concept allows deferral of gain or loss recognition until continuity of interest is broken. Again, a taxpayer who receives money in an otherwise nontaxable exchange or retains money in a transaction requiring reinvestment must recognize some amount of any gain realized because continuity of interest is at least partially severed.

Both concepts also apply in situations where a taxpayer sells property outright for cash. In such circumstances, the taxpayer fully recognizes gain or loss because he or she has no continuity of interest and has the wherewithal to pay taxes.

This chapter describes five important types of nontaxable exchanges, which share a common characteristic: deferral of gain (and sometimes loss) with the deferral reflected in the basis of property received. These five transactions are

1. Like-kind exchanges (direct);

2. Involuntary conversions (usually indirect; sometimes direct);

3. Sale and replacement of a principal residence (indirect);

4. Formation of a corporation (direct); and

5. Corporate reorganizations (direct).

A **like-kind exchange** is a
direct exchange of
property for other property
of a like-kind where each
property must be held for
productive use in a trade
or business or for
investment.

SECTION 1031: LIKE-KIND EXCHANGES

The **like-kind exchange** is a prototypical transaction that contains all the basic elements of a nontaxable exchange. Therefore, you should thoroughly understand like-kind exchanges before studying other transactions so that these other transactions will be seen as mere variations on the basic model. The essential characteristics of a *simple* like-kind exchange follow:

1. The taxpayer recognizes no gain or loss on the exchange;

2. The basis of like-kind property received equals the basis of like-kind property transferred; and

3. The holding period (HP) of like-kind property received includes the holding period of like-kind property transferred.

The following example illustrates these basic concepts. Although both taxpayers in this and subsequent examples qualify for like-kind exchange treatment, in some transactions only one party may qualify. For example, a dealer in property would *not* qualify.

EXAMPLE 17-1

Xavier owns Machine A, which has a $1,000 fair market value (FMV) and a $600 adjusted basis. He purchased the machine on January 2, 1990. Yolanda owns Machine B, which also has a $1,000 FMV but has a $450 adjusted basis. She purchased the machine on February 9, 1989. For business reasons, they decide to trade machines in a transaction that qualifies as a like-kind exchange. See Figure 17-1 for a diagram of the exchange. Xavier and Yolanda incur the following tax consequences:

	Xavier	Yolanda
Amount realized (FMV of machine received)	$1,000	$1,000
Less: Adjusted basis of machine transferred	600	450
Gain realized	$ 400	$ 550
Gain recognized	$ 0	$ 0
Basis of machine received	$ 600	$ 450

Also, Xavier is deemed to have owned Machine B since January 2, 1990, because the holding period of Machine B includes the holding period of Machine A. Similarly, Yolanda is deemed to have owned Machine A since February 9, 1989.

Although each taxpayer in Example 17-1 *realizes* a gain, neither taxpayer *recognizes* a gain because each lacks the wherewithal to pay and each maintains a continuity of interest in like-kind property. But note a key point: Each taxpayer's basis in the machine received is the same as the basis in the machine given up. Consequently, if Xavier sells Machine B for $1,000 after receiving it in the exchange, he recognizes a $400 gain. Therefore, the gain not recognized on the like-kind exchange is merely *deferred* until the taxpayer sells the new property in a taxable transaction. Alternatively, if Xavier retains Machine B and depreciates it, he recognizes the deferred gain over the recovery period because depreciation based on $400 offsets less income than depreciation based on $1,000. In a similar way, Yolanda has a $550 deferred gain because Machine A, which she received in the exchange, takes

FIGURE 17-1

Like-Kind
Exchange—
EXAMPLE 17-1

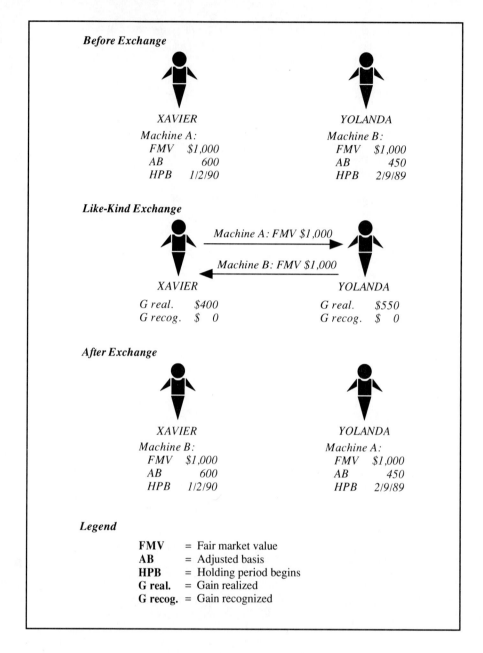

Before Exchange

XAVIER

Machine A:
FMV $1,000
AB   600
HPB   1/2/90

YOLANDA

Machine B:
FMV $1,000
AB   450
HPB   2/9/89

Like-Kind Exchange

Machine A: FMV $1,000 →

← Machine B: FMV $1,000

XAVIER

G real. $400
G recog. $ 0

YOLANDA

G real. $550
G recog. $ 0

After Exchange

XAVIER

Machine B:
FMV $1,000
AB   600
HPB   1/2/90

YOLANDA

Machine A:
FMV $1,000
AB   450
HPB   2/9/89

Legend

FMV   = Fair market value
AB   = Adjusted basis
HPB   = Holding period begins
G real.   = Gain realized
G recog. = Gain recognized

a $450 basis. Essentially, then, the property received in the like-kind exchange retains all the tax characteristics of the property transferred (see Figure 17-1). The taxpayers simply continue their investments in different but comparable property. (We will further describe the basis and holding period rules later in this chapter.)

On the other hand, full gain recognition on an exchange is reflected in basis equal to fair market value and in a new holding period. For example, if the transaction in Example 17-1 had not qualified as a like-kind exchange, Xavier would have recognized the $400 gain immediately. Moreover, he would have a $1,000 basis in Machine B with the holding period beginning on the date of the exchange. Similarly, Yolanda would have recognized the $550 gain immediately and would have a $1,000 basis in Machine A, with the holding period again beginning on the date of the exchange.

Goal #2
Recognize taxable versus
nontaxable exchange.

REQUIREMENTS FOR LIKE-KIND EXCHANGES

Section 1031 governs like-kind exchanges and reads, in part, as follows:

(a) Nonrecognition of Gain or Loss from Exchanges Solely in Kind—

    (1) In General—No gain or loss shall be recognized on the exchange of property held for productive use in a trade or business or for investment if such property is exchanged solely for property of like kind which is to be held either for productive use in a trade or business or for investment.

    (2) Exception—This subsection shall not apply to any exchange of—

        (A) stock in trade or other property held primarily for sale,

        (B) stocks, bonds, or notes,

        (C) other securities or evidences of indebtedness or interest,

        (D) interests in a partnership,

        (E) certificates of trust or beneficial interests, or

        (F) choses in action.

> **Goal #3**
> Understand the requirements for like-kind exchanges.

Several aspects of Sec. 1031(a) must be emphasized. First, nonrecognition applies only to exchanges of like-kind property, defined in the next several paragraphs. Second, the like-kind property must be held either for investment or for productive use in a trade or business. Personal use property does not qualify. Third, nonrecognition treatment is *mandatory* if the exchange satisfies the requirements of Sec. 1031. A taxpayer engaging in a transaction that meets the like-kind exchange requirements may not elect to recognize gain or loss. Fourth, the provisions apply to *direct* exchanges. The taxpayer is denied nonrecognition treatment if he or she sells property and uses the proceeds to acquire like-kind property.[1] Finally, Sec. 1031(a)(2) specifically excludes certain property from the scope of Sec. 1031.[2]

Regulations contain the following general definition of **like-kind property**:

> As used in section 1031(a), the words "like kind" have reference to the nature or character of the property and not to its grade or quality. One kind or class of property may not, under that section, be exchanged for property of a different kind or class. The fact that any real estate involved is improved or unimproved is not material, for that fact relates only to the grade or quality of the property and not to its kind or class. Unproductive real estate held by one other than a dealer for future use or future realization of the increment in value is held for investment and not primarily for sale.[3]

> Whether property is **like-kind property** generally depends on the facts and circumstances; however, Regulations provide automatic like-kind treatment for certain asset classes.

Examples of like-kind exchanges include

1. Real property held for investment exchanged for real property used in a trade or business if the taxpayer is not a dealer in real property;

2. Unimproved real property (for example, land) exchanged for improved real property (for example, land and building) if the taxpayer is not a dealer in real property; and

---

1 Also, see Reg. Sec. 1.1031(k)-1(a).

2 Also, Sec. 1031(f) imposes special rules on like-kind exchanges between related parties. Generally, property acquired from a related party must be held for at least two years after the exchange for nonrecognition treatment to apply.

3 Reg. Sec. 1.1031(a)-1(b).

3. A used truck (plus cash) exchanged (traded in) for a new truck as long as the old and new trucks are business property of a like kind (however, like-kind treatment would not apply to the truck dealer).

Examples of transactions *not* qualifying as like-kind exchanges include

1. Real property used in a trade or business exchanged for personal property used in a trade or business;

2. Inventory exchanged for personal property used in a trade or business;

3. Real property used in a trade or business exchanged for stock; and

4. Livestock of one sex exchanged for livestock of a different sex.[4]

Recently issued Regulations provide additional rules for exchanges of *personal* property (as opposed to real property).[5] The Regulations distinguish two broad categories of personal property: (1) depreciable tangible personal property[6] and (2) intangible personal property and nondepreciable personal property.[7] Depreciable tangible personal property qualifies under Sec. 1031 if it is exchanged for property of a like kind or like class. Properties are of a like *class* if they are classified in either the same General Asset Class or the same Product Class. The Regulations list 13 General Asset Classes derived from Rev. Proc. 87-56 (see Chapter 14). The 13 classes follow (numbers in parentheses refer to asset classes in Rev. Proc. 87-56):[8]

1. Office furniture, fixtures, and equipment (00.11);

2. Information systems, including computers and peripheral equipment (00.12);

3. Data handling equipment, except computers (00.13);

4. Airplanes, except those used in commercial or contract carrying of passengers or freight, and all helicopters (00.21);

5. Automobiles and taxis (00.22);

6. Buses (00.23);

7. Light general-purpose trucks (00.241);

8. Heavy general-purpose trucks (00.242);

9. Railroad cars and locomotives, except those owned by railroad transportation companies (00.25);

10. Tractor units for use over the road (00.26);

11. Trailers and trailer-mounted containers (00.27);

12. Vessels, barges, tugs, and similar water transportation equipment, except those used in marine construction (00.28); and

13. Industrial steam and electrical generation and/or distribution systems (00.4).

4 Sec. 1031(e).
5 Reg. Sec. 1.1031(a)-2.
6 Reg. Sec. 1.1031(a)-2(b).
7 Reg. Sec. 1.1031(a)-2(c).
8 Reg. Sec. 1.1031(a)-2(b)(2).

Product Classes are listed in the *Standard Industrial Classification Manual* (the SIC Manual) published by the Executive Office of the President, Office of Management and Budget. Depreciable tangible personal properties classified within a given four-digit SIC code are in the same Product Class.[9]

Exchanged depreciable tangible personal property falling within a General Asset Class or a Product Class automatically qualifies as like kind. On the other hand, property that does *not* fall within one of these classes or property that falls within different classes nevertheless may qualify as like kind if the facts and circumstances warrant.[10] When relying on facts and circumstances, a taxpayer must look to IRS rulings and court cases to obtain guidance.

No like classes exist for intangible personal property or nondepreciable personal property.[11] Therefore, to qualify as like kind, these properties must also pass muster under the facts and circumstances test. Goodwill and going concern value, however, are never considered like kind.[12] Consequently, if two taxpayers exchange entire businesses, the part of the transaction representing an exchange of goodwill is taxable.

THE ROLE OF BOOT IN LIKE-KIND EXCHANGES

Two taxpayers engaging in a like-kind exchange rarely have property that is exactly equal in value. To equalize the exchange, the taxpayer with the lower-valued property must pay **boot**, which means additional cash or other nonlike-kind property. The taxpayer receiving the boot must recognize gain to the extent of cash and the fair market value of nonlike-kind property.[13] Recognition occurs because the boot recipient has the wherewithal to pay some tax and does not have complete continuity of interest. The gain recognized, however, never exceeds the gain realized. Also, if the boot recipient realizes a loss, he or she recognizes no gain or loss.[14]

> **Boot** is property given or received in an exchange in addition to the property qualifying for nontaxable treatment; it is a *side* payment to equalize the value of the exchange.

EXAMPLE 17-2

Mr. Swapper owns a parcel of land, which he holds for investment. The land cost $300 in 1985 and is now worth $700. Ms. Trader owns another parcel of land, which she also holds for investment. Her land cost $800 in 1990 but is now worth only $600. Neither taxpayer is a dealer in real property. They agree to exchange their parcels of land, which qualify as like-kind property. Because of the difference in fair market values, Ms. Trader also gives Mr. Swapper $100 cash. Their gains and losses follow:

	Swapper	Trader
FMV of land received	$ 600	$ 700
Cash received	100	0

Continued

---

9 However, any four-digit SIC code ending in a "9" (a miscellaneous category) will not be considered a Product Class (Reg. Sec. 1.1031(a)-2(b)(3)).

10 Reg. Sec. 1.1031(a)-2(a). Specifically, the Regulations state that, "in determining whether exchanged properties are of a like kind, no inference is to be drawn from the fact that the properties are not of a like class."

11 Reg. Sec. 1.1031(a)-2(c)(1).

12 Reg. Sec. 1.1031(a)-2(c)(2).

13 Sec. 1031(b) and Reg. Sec. 1.1031(b)-1(a).

14 Sec. 1031(c), Reg. Sec. 1.1031(b)-1(a), and Reg. Sec. 1.1031(c)-1.

EXAMPLE 17-2 (Con't.)

Amount realized	700	700
Less:		
Adjusted basis of land transferred	300	800
Cash paid	0	100
Total given up	300	900
Gain (loss) realized	$ 400	$(200)
Gain (loss) recognized	$ 100	$ 0

Mr. Swapper recognizes a $100 gain because he received $100 of boot and because the amount of boot did not exceed the gain realized. Moreover, Mr. Swapper has the wherewithal to pay taxes on the $100 gain recognized and, to the extent of cash received, does not have a continuity of interest in his land investment.

If Mr. Swapper had paid $850 instead of $300 for his original parcel of land, he would realize a $150 loss but would recognize no gain or loss even though he received boot.

At this point, we should point out that like-kind exchange treatment under tax law differs somewhat from similar-asset exchange treatment under generally accepted accounting principles (GAAP). First, under GAAP a realized loss on the exchange of similar assets is also recognized. Conservatism dictates this reasoning. Second, under GAAP the recipient of boot does not recognize the full amount of gain attributable to the boot. Instead, the gain recognized is computed as follows: gain recognized = gain realized x (boot received ÷ total fair market value received). In effect, GAAP divides the transaction into an exchange portion and a sale portion.

EXAMPLE 17-3

In Example 17-2, Mr. Swapper would recognize a $57.14 gain under GAAP, computed as follows:

$$\$400 \times (\$100 \div \$700) = \$57.14.$$

Under tax law, the *payment* of *cash* boot triggers no gain recognition. However, a person who gives *non*like-kind property as boot instead of cash recognizes gain or loss *as if* he or she sold the nonlike-kind property for fair market value.

EXAMPLE 17-4

Assume the same facts as in Example 17-2 except that, instead of cash, Ms. Trader gives Mr. Swapper stock worth $100. If her adjusted basis in the stock is $80, she recognizes a $20 gain. Alternatively, if her adjusted basis in the stock is $120, she recognizes a $20 loss. In either case, Mr. Swapper is treated as having received $100 boot, the fair market value of the stock. Therefore, he recognizes a $100 gain as in Example 17-2.

EXCHANGES OF PROPERTY SUBJECT TO LIABILITIES

If in a like-kind exchange a taxpayer transfers property subject to a liability, the transferring taxpayer is deemed to have *received* boot equal to the amount of the liability.[15] The taxpayer being relieved of the liability is treated as though he or she received cash and then used the cash to pay off the liability. Conversely, the taxpayer assuming the liability is deemed to have *paid* boot equal to the amount of the liability.

EXAMPLE 17-5

Ms. Alsop owns a parcel of land (Land A), which she holds for investment. The land cost $400 in 1980 and is now worth $1,000. Mr. Brizio owns another parcel of land (Land B), which he also holds for investment. His land cost $1,100 in 1988 and is now worth $1,350. Mr. Brizio's parcel is subject to a $350 mortgage. They agree to exchange their parcels of land, which qualify as like-kind property. In addition to receiving Mr. Brizio's parcel of land, Ms. Alsop assumes the $350 mortgage. The exchange is an equal one because Ms. Alsop gives up land worth $1,000 and receives land having a *net* value of $1,000 ($1,350 – $350). Figure 17-2 depicts the property exchange and the flow of benefits associated with the exchange. Ms. Alsop's and Mr. Brizio's gains follow:

	Alsop	Brizio
FMV of land received	$1,350	$1,000
Mortgage assumed by Ms. Alsop treated as cash received by Mr. Brizio	0	350
Amount realized	1,350	1,350
Less:		
Adjusted basis of land transferred	400	1,100
Mortgage assumed by Ms. Alsop treated as cash paid by Ms. Alsop	350	0
Total given up	750	1,100
Gain (loss) realized	$ 600	$ 250
Gain (loss) recognized	$ 0	$ 250

Mr. Brizio treats the $350 mortgage assumed by Ms. Alsop as boot received because he is relieved of a liability, which is a benefit to him. Conversely, Ms. Alsop treats the assumption as boot paid because she must eventually pay off the liability. Note also that Mr. Brizio recognizes only $250 even though he receives $350 of boot. Gain recognized may not exceed gain realized.

Boot treatment of liabilities may seem harsh because the person assuming the liability does not receive actual cash and therefore may not have the wherewithal to pay taxes on the gain recognized. Nevertheless, the rule exists to prevent taxpayers from abusing the nonrecognition provisions of Sec. 1031. If liabilities were not treated as boot, a taxpayer could borrow money using the property as collateral and then transfer the property in a nontaxable like-kind exchange. By doing so, the taxpayer

---

15 Reg. Sec. 1.1031(b)-1(c).

FIGURE 17-2

Like-Kind
Exchange with
Liability
Assumed—
(EXAMPLE 17-5)

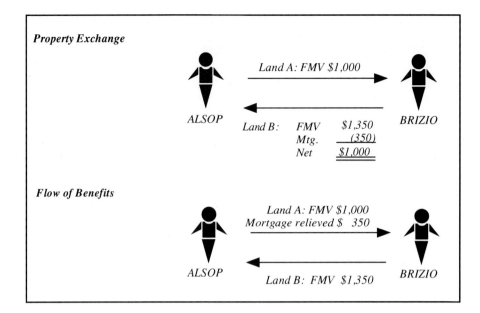

would end up having new like-kind property *and* cash without invoking the boot recognition rule. The rule treating liabilities as boot nullifies this type of manipulation.

The complexity of the exchange increases if both properties are subject to liabilities and/or if some cash is also paid. The following guidelines summarize the rules for determining gain recognition when liabilities are present (including the single liability situation already described).[16]

1. If one party to the like-kind exchange assumes a liability of the other party (or takes property subject to a liability), the party relieved of the liability is considered to have received money (boot), and the party assuming the liability is considered to have paid boot.

2. If each party to the like-kind exchange assumes a liability of the other party (or takes property subject to a liability), the party relieved of the largest liability is considered to have received money (boot) equal to the difference between the two liabilities.

3. For determining the amount of boot received, actual cash (or other nonlike-kind property) *given* reduces consideration *received* in the form of liabilities assumed by the other party.

4. For determining the amount of boot received, actual cash (or other nonlike-kind property) *received* is *not* reduced by consideration *given* in the form of liabilities assumed.

BASIS AND HOLDING PERIOD OF PROPERTY RECEIVED IN LIKE-KIND EXCHANGES

The basis of property received in a like-kind exchange is important because it must reflect the gain or loss deferred on the exchange. Example 17-1 indicated that the basis of like-kind property received equals the basis of like-kind property transferred. In tax

---

16 Reg. Sec. 1.031(b)-1(c) and Reg. Sec. 1.1031(d)-2.

terminology, the like-kind property received takes an **exchanged basis**.[17] The existence of boot and liabilities, however, complicates the basis computation.[18] Accordingly, the basis of like-kind property received may be calculated in either of the two following ways:

Method I[19]

	Adjusted basis of like-kind property transferred
+	Cash paid (including liabilities assumed) and FMV of other boot given
+	Gain recognized on the exchange because of boot received
–	Cash received (including liabilities relieved) and FMV of other boot received
=	Basis of like-kind property received

Method II

	FMV of like-kind property received
–	Gain *not* recognized on the exchange
+	Loss *not* recognized on the exchange
=	Basis of like-kind property received

> Property received in a nontaxable exchange has an **exchanged basis** if it takes the basis of property transferred, with some modifications.

The basis of *non*like-kind property received always equals its fair market value.

To make sense of Method I, you should understand that the sum of the first three items reflects the total basis available to the recipient taxpayer. This total basis must then be allocated to like-kind property received, cash received, and other boot received. The amount subtracted for cash and other boot received is allocated to these assets leaving the remainder to be allocated to like-kind property. Method II, which approaches basis from a different perspective, highlights the deferral aspect of a like-kind exchange. In a fully taxable exchange, the basis of property received equals its fair market value. Method II, however, reduces the fair market value of like-kind property by the gain *not* recognized so that the nonrecognized gain is merely deferred. Similarly, Method II increases the fair market value so that any nonrecognized loss is also deferred. Although Methods I and II are alternative ways to arrive at the same result, you should apply *both* methods as a cross-check on your computations.

Property that acquires an exchanged basis, as in like-kind exchanges, is typically considered to be an extension of the original property for purposes of determining its holding period. Accordingly, the holding period of like-kind property received includes the holding period of like-kind property transferred.[20] This **tack-on holding period** rule applies if the like-kind property transferred is either a capital asset or Sec.

> A **tack-on holding period** means that the holding period of propety received includes the holding period of property transferred (could be called an exchanged holding period to go along with an exchanged basis).

---

17 Practitioners have traditionally called this type of basis a substituted basis. Under Sec. 7701(a)(44), however, the proper terminology is exchanged basis.

18 Sec. 1031(d) and Reg. Sec. 1.1031(d)-1.

19 This calculation simplifies the method used in Reg. Sec. 1.1031(d)-1. An equivalent variation of Method I as described in the Regulations follows:

	Adjusted basis of like-kind property transferred
+	Cash and *adjusted basis* of other boot given
+	Gain recognized on the exchange because of boot received *and* boot given
–	Loss recognized on boot given
–	Cash and FMV of other boot received
=	Basis of like-kind property received

20 Sec. 1223(1).

> A **new holding period** begins on the date of an exchange.

1231 property. Otherwise, the holding period for the property received begins on the date of the exchange (a **new holding period**). Moreover, if the taxpayer recognizes *all* the realized gain because of boot received, the like-kind property received takes a new rather than a tack-on holding period regardless of the type of property transferred. This result occurs because the basis of the like-kind property received equals its fair market value.[21] The holding period of nonlike-kind property received always begins on the date of the exchange regardless of its type. The holding period rule is important for determining the type of gain or loss if the taxpayer subsequently sells the new like-kind property.

   The following three examples demonstrate the basis and holding period concepts. They are based on facts given in previous examples and, therefore, complete Examples 17-2, 17-4, and 17-5.

EXAMPLE 17-6

The basis and holding period results in Example 17-2 follow:

Method I	Swapper	Trader
Adjusted basis of like-kind property transferred	$ 300	$ 800
Cash paid	0	100
Gain recognized	100	0
Cash received	(100)	0
Basis of like-kind property received	$ 300	$ 900

Method II	Swapper	Trader
FMV of like-kind property received	$ 600	$ 700
Gain not recognized on the exchange	(300)	0
Loss not recognized on the exchange	0	200
Basis of like-kind property received	$ 300	$ 900
Holding period (HP)	Tack-on	Tack-on
HP begins in	1985	1990

   Again, note the deferral aspect of the exchange. Assume that after the exchange Mr. Swapper sells Land B for $600 (its FMV). He recognizes a $300 gain ($600 – $300), which equals the gain not recognized on the like-kind exchange. Similarly, assume that after the exchange Ms. Trader sells Land A for $700 (its FMV). She recognizes a $200 loss ($700 – $900), which equals the loss not recognized on the like-kind exchange.

EXAMPLE 17-7

The basis and holding period results in Example 17-4 are the same as in Example 17-6 except that the $100 *fair market value* of the stock is substituted for the cash in the basis calculation. In addition, the basis of the stock to Mr. Swapper is $100,

Continued

---

21 Sec. 1223(1) allows the tack-on holding period if the property received has the same basis *in whole or in part* as the property transferred. Property ending up with a basis equal to its fair market value does not seem to satisfy the *in whole or in part* criterion of this provision.

EXAMPLE 17-7 (Con't.)

its fair market value, because the stock is nonlike-kind property. As an exercise, the student should apply the Method I variation given in footnote 19 (p. 609) to solve this problem (see Thought Problem 4 on p. 637).

EXAMPLE 17-8

The basis and holding period results in Example 17-5 follow:

Method I	Alsop	Brizio
Adjusted basis of like-kind property transferred	$ 400	$1,100
Mortgage assumed by Ms. Alsop treated as cash paid by Ms. Alsop	350	0
Gain recognized	0	250
Mortgage assumed by Ms. Alsop treated as cash received by Mr. Brizio	0	(350)
Basis of like-kind property received	$ 750	$1,000

Method II		
FMV of like-kind property received	$1,350	$1,000
Gain not recognized on the exchange	(600)	0
Loss not recognized on the exchange	0	0
Basis of like-kind property received	$ 750	$1,000
Holding period (HP)	Tack on	New
HP begins	In 1980	On exchange date

Note that Mr. Brizio takes a new rather than a tack-on holding period because the basis of the like-kind property received equals its fair market value.

EXCHANGES OF MULTIPLE PROPERTIES

Up to this point, we have discussed exchanges involving one like-kind property for each taxpayer, along with some boot. The complexity of rules for gain recognition and basis determination increases considerably if either taxpayer exchanges more than one item of like-kind property. A **multiple property exchange** can occur, for example, when two business owners decide to swap their entire businesses or when two real estate owners decide to exchange buildings that also contain personal property such as furniture. Although the details of multiple property exchanges are beyond the scope of this chapter, the appendix to this chapter provides a brief outline of the steps described in the Regulations. Essentially, the taxpayer assigns property to exchange groups and a residual group. Each exchange group contains property of a like kind or like class, and the residual group contains boot-type property. Then, the rules of Sec. 1031 apply separately to each exchange group for determining gain recognized and basis of assets.[22] Although we did not cast them as such, each of the examples

> A **multiple property exchange** occurs when either party exchanges more than one item of like-kind property.

22 Reg. Sec. 1.1031(j)-1(a)(2)(i).

FIGURE 17-3

**Three-Party
Exchange**

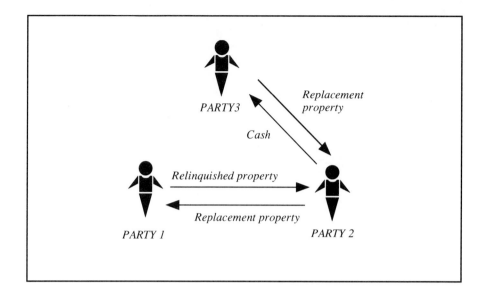

presented earlier in this chapter could be viewed as a transaction involving one exchange group and a residual group. But characterization as a multiple property exchange is unnecessary unless the taxpayer transfers or receives more than one like-kind asset.

THREE-PARTY EXCHANGES AND DEFERRED EXCHANGES

Two-party like-kind exchanges as just described may be difficult to accomplish because the person desiring an exchange (Party 1) must find another party (Party 3) who has suitable replacement property and who also wants Party 1's property. Commonly, Party 3 owns property desired by Party 1, but Party 3 does not want Party 1's property. Still another party (Party 2) wants Party 1's property but does not have property desired by Party 1. In this case, the parties can enter into a **three-party exchange** as depicted in Figure 17-3. Party 3 sells property to Party 2 in a taxable transaction, and then Party 1 and Party 2 enter into a nontaxable like-kind exchange.

A variation on the transaction entails the transfer of Party 1's property (the relinquished property) to Party 2 with Party 2 *subsequently* acquiring Party 3's property (the replacement property) and transferring it to Party 1. This variation introduces a **deferred exchange** between Party 1 and Party 2, and Sec. 1031(a)(3) and associated Regulations place restrictions on the timing of the transaction.[23] To be considered like-kind property, the replacement property must be identified before the end of the identification period and received before the end of the exchange period. The identification period ends 45 days after Party 1 transfers the relinquished property. The exchange period ends on the earlier of (1) 180 days after Party 1 transfers relinquished property or (2) the due date (including extensions) of Party 1's tax return for the year in which the transfer occurs. Regulations provide detailed requirements for identifying replacement property and for other aspects of deferred exchanges. Therefore, anyone engaging in such an exchange must consult these Regulations before proceeding.

A **three-party exchange** occurs when one party purchases property from a second party and then enters into a like-kind exchange with a third party.

A **deferred exchange** occurs when one party receives replacement property sometime after transferring the relinquished property; strict timing requirements must be met for a deferred exchange to qualify as a like-kind exchange.

---

23 Reg. Sec. 1.1031(k).

SECTION 1033: INVOLUNTARY CONVERSIONS

Taxpayers engaging in like-kind exchanges do so voluntarily even though nonrecognition treatment is mandatory if the transaction meets the conditions of Sec. 1031. Section 1033, on the other hand, "applies in cases where property is compulsorily or involuntarily converted."[24] An **involuntary conversion** of property entails one of the following events:[25]

1. Total or partial destruction;
2. Theft;
3. **Seizure**;
4. **Condemnation**;[26] or
5. Sale under threat or imminence of condemnation.

NONRECOGNITION REQUIREMENTS AND BASIS OF REPLACEMENT PROPERTY

The tax consequences of an involuntary conversion depend on whether the property is (1) converted into property similar or related in use (a direct exchange) or (2) converted into money or property not similar or related in use (potentially an indirect exchange).

If property is converted into similar property, the taxpayer recognizes no gain on the conversion, and such nonrecognition is *mandatory*.[27] Conversion into similar property could occur, for example, if a governmental unit condemns a taxpayer's property and replaces it with similar property of equal value. The basis of the replacement property equals the basis of the converted property, that is, an exchanged basis. Thus, conversion into similar property produces tax results similar to those for a like-kind exchange, with one important difference—Sec. 1033 applies only to gains. If the taxpayer realizes a loss on the involuntary conversion, he or she recognizes the loss if such recognition is allowed by other Code sections (for example, a capital loss).

Conversion into similar property is not the typical case, however. Usually, the taxpayer receives money compensation for the involuntary conversion. For example, the condemning governmental unit may pay the taxpayer for the condemned property or an insurance company will reimburse the taxpayer for property destroyed by a casualty or lost by theft. In this case, nonrecognition of gain is completely at the discretion of the taxpayer and depends on two things: (1) whether the taxpayer *reinvests* the proceeds in similar property and (2) whether the taxpayer *elects* to have the nonrecognition provisions of Sec. 1033 to apply. Again, Sec. 1033 applies only to gains.

If the taxpayer replaces the converted property with eligible property within a specified period of time *and* makes the Sec. 1033 election, the taxpayer recognizes gain only to the extent the amount realized on the conversion exceeds the cost of

Goal #4
Understand involuntary conversions.

An **involuntary conversion** is a disposition of property forced on the taxpayer by destruction, theft, seizure, condemnation, or threat of condemnation.

A **seizure** is an uncompensated confiscation of property by a governmental unit.

A **condemnation** is a compensated acquisition of property by a governmental unit.

---

24 Reg. Sec. 1.1033(a)-1(a).

25 *Ibid.*

26 The Code also uses the terms requisition *and* condemnation, but for simplicity we will use just the term condemnation.

27 Reg. Sec. 1.1033(a)-2(b).

replacement property.[28] However, the gain recognized never exceeds the gain realized, which means that the gain recognized is the lesser of (1) the gain realized or (2) the amount *not* reinvested. The basis of the replacement property is computed as follows:[29]

$$
\begin{array}{l}
\text{Cost of replacement property} \\
-\ \text{Gain } not \text{ recognized on the involuntary conversion} \\
\hline
=\ \text{Basis of replacement property}
\end{array}
$$

This formula is equivalent to the Method II approach given earlier except that it excludes nonrecognized losses (because Sec. 1033 does not apply to losses). Accordingly, Sec. 1033 allows the taxpayer merely to *defer* gain recognition, not achieve permanent nonrecognition. Once again, the wherewithal-to-pay and continuity-of-interest concepts provide the underlying rationale for this treatment.

If the taxpayer defers any gain under Sec. 1033, the holding period of the replacement property includes the holding period of the converted property. Specifically, the holding period tacks on if the converted property is either a capital asset or Sec. 1231 property.[30]

EXAMPLE 17-9

On August 3, 1988, Involco Corporation purchased a corporate jet plane to be used exclusively in the corporation's business. On March 15, 1992, the pilot, who was alone in the plane, flew to a neighboring city to pick up some corporate customers. En route, the plane developed engine trouble, and the pilot attempted to land in an open field. In the attempt, the pilot escaped with minor injuries, but the plane was totally destroyed. On May 29, 1992, the corporation received $5 million from the insurance company and purchased a new jet plane on June 3, 1992. The old plane had a $1 million adjusted basis, and the new plane cost $6 million. The corporation made the Sec. 1033 election.

Involco *realizes* a $4 million gain on the involuntary conversion, which equals the insurance proceeds ($5 million) minus the old plane's adjusted basis ($1 million), but the corporation *recognizes* no gain because the amount realized on the conversion ($5 million) did not exceed the cost of the new plane ($6 million). In other words, Involco reinvested the entire amount of insurance proceeds (plus an additional $1 million) in eligible replacement property. Consequently, Involco does not have the wherewithal to pay taxes on the gain, and it has complete continuity of interest in the new plane.

The basis of the new plane is $2 million: its cost ($6 million) minus gain *not* recognized on the involuntary conversion ($4 million). The new plane takes a tack-on holding period and is therefore considered owned since August 3, 1988.

If Involco chose not to make the Sec. 1033 election, the corporation would recognize the entire $4 million gain. The basis of the new plane would be $6 million (its cost), and the new plane would take a new holding period beginning on the purchase date.

---

28 Sec. 1033(a)(2)(A) and Reg. Sec. 1.1033(a)-2(c).

29 Sec. 1033(b).

30 Sec. 1223(1).

EXAMPLE 17-10

Assume the same facts as in Example 17-9 except that the new place cost $3.5 million instead of $6 million. If Involco makes the Sec. 1033 election, it recognizes a $1.5 million gain computed as follows:

Amount realized on conversion	$5.0 million
Cost of new plane	3.5 million
Excess amount not reinvested	$1.5 million

Accordingly, the corporation defers only $2.5 million of the $4 million gain. The basis of the new plane is $1 million ($3.5 million – $2.5 million), and the plane takes a tack-on holding period.

EXAMPLE 17-11

Assume the same facts as in Example 17-9 except that Involco recovers only $600,000 from the insurance company. In this case, the corporation realizes a $400,000 loss. (Remember that, for totally destroyed business property, the amount of loss equals the adjusted basis reduced by insurance proceeds.) Section 1033 does not apply to losses, so the corporation also recognizes a $400,000 casualty loss. The basis of the new plane is $6 million (its cost), and the new plane takes a new holding period beginning on the date it was purchased.

A taxpayer who recognizes a gain or loss on an involuntary conversion must also determine the character of the gain or loss. Depending on the factual circumstances, this determination is made using rules for capital losses, personal casualty and theft losses, business casualty and theft losses, and Sec. 1231 gains and losses.

ELIGIBLE REPLACEMENT PROPERTY

Eligible **replacement property** must be similar or related in service or use to the property involuntarily converted. To determine whether replacement property meets the statutory requirements, the IRS applies one of two tests depending on whether the taxpayer is an owner-user or an owner-investor.[31] An **owner-user** must satisfy the **functional-use test**, which "means that the property acquired must have a close 'functional' similarity to the property converted."[32] Under the functional-use test, the IRS will not consider property as similar or related in service or use "unless the physical characteristics and end uses of the converted and replacement properties [are] closely similar."[33] This test is more restrictive than the like-kind property rules of Sec. 1031.

An **owner-investor** must satisfy a **taxpayer-use-or-services test** under which the IRS examines the following three factors: (1) whether the converted and replacement properties provide a similar service to the taxpayer (such as property held for investment and leased to another party), (2) whether the properties involve similar

> **Replacement property** in an involuntary conversion must be similar or related in service or use.
>
> An **owner-user** uses property directly in his or her business.
>
> The **functional-use test** applies to an owner-user and requires that replacement property have a close functional similarity to the property converted.
>
> An **owner-investor** leases or rents property out to other parties.
>
> The **taxpayer-use-or-services test** applies to an owner-investor and requires that replacement property have the same investment characteristics as the converted property.

---

31 Rev. Rul. 64-237, 1964-2 CB 319.

32 *Ibid.*

33 *Ibid.*

business risks, and (3) whether the taxpayer engages in similar management activities and provides similar services to the lessee.[34]

EXAMPLE 17-12

Mr. Lessor owns a light manufacturing plant, which he *rents* to Ms. Lessee. The plant is destroyed by fire, and Mr. Lessor replaces it with a wholesale grocery warehouse, which he *rents* to Mr. Produce under similar arrangements that he had with Ms. Lessee. The warehouse is eligible replacement property because Mr. Lessor is an owner-investor and each lease arrangement has similar investment attributes. On the other hand, assume that Mr. Lessor *uses* the plant in his own business and replaces it with the warehouse, which he also *uses* in his own business. In this situation, Mr. Lessor is an owner-user, and the warehouse fails the functional-use test.[35]

A taxpayer also can satisfy the eligible replacement property requirements if he or she purchases a controlling interest in a corporation owning property that is similar or related in service or use.[36] Control means the ownership of stock possessing at least 80% of total voting power *and* ownership of 80% of all other classes of stock.[37]

Section 1033(g) provides a special exception to the above replacement property requirements for *real* property used in a trade or business or held for investment. If the involuntarily conversion results from condemnation or seizure (or threat or imminence thereof), the taxpayer applies the like-kind property standard instead of the similar-or-related-in-use-and-service test.[38] Congress enacted this provision when the government was acquiring land on which to construct the interstate highway system. The exception reduced disputes over the qualifications of replacement property acquired by taxpayers whose property was condemned.

TIME REQUIREMENTS

To obtain the nonrecognition benefits of Sec. 1033, a taxpayer must acquire eligible replacement property within a prescribed time period. The replacement period *begins* on the earlier of (1) the disposition date of the converted property or (2) the date when the threat or imminence of condemnation begins.[39] Property or stock purchased *before* the disposition date may be considered eligible replacement property if the property has a cost basis and is held by the taxpayer on that date.[40] The date of threat or imminence poses a practical problem because a taxpayer may have difficulty establishing exactly what event constitutes a threat or imminence of condemnation. For example, rumors may precede a government's actual condemnation action by several years.

The replacement period *ends* two years after the close of the first tax year in which the taxpayer realizes any part of the conversion gain.[41] A taxpayer, however, may

---

34 *Ibid.*

35 *Ibid.*

36 Sec. 1033(a)(2)(A).

37 Sec. 1033(a)(2)(E)(i).

38 The exception does not apply, however, to the purchase of a controlling interest in a corporation owning such real property (Sec. 1033(g)(2)).

39 Sec. 1033(a)(2)(B).

40 Sec. 1033(a)(2)(A).

41 Sec. 1033(a)(2)(B)(i).

apply for and obtain an extension of the replacement period if the taxpayer can show reasonable cause for not being able to replace the converted property within the prescribed time period.[42] Moreover, real property that qualifies for the like-kind exception for eligible replacement property must be replaced within a three-year rather than a two-year period.[43]

EXAMPLE 17-13

In Example 17-9, Involco replaced the plane on June 3, 1992. However, the corporation had until December 31, 1994, to make the replacement assuming that Involco was a calendar-year taxpayer.

A taxpayer elects nonrecognition under Sec. 1033 by filing a tax return that excludes the deferred portion of any gain realized. If the taxpayer fails to acquire eligible replacement property within the prescribed replacement period, the taxpayer must file an amended return that recomputes the tax liability for the year the gain was realized.[44]

SECTION 1034: ROLLOVER OF GAIN ON THE SALE OF A PRINCIPAL RESIDENCE

> **Goal #5**
> Understand the requirements and determine the tax consequences of selling a principal residence.

Section 1034 provides a *mandatory* special rule that defers the recognition of gain on the sale or exchange of a taxpayer's principal residence. As usual, the transaction must satisfy certain conditions for nonrecognition to occur. Notice that the mechanics of Sec. 1034 are similar to those of Sec. 1033.

STATUTORY REQUIREMENTS

A taxpayer who sells his or her principal residence at a gain and purchases a new principal residence within a prescribed time period recognizes gain only to the extent that the adjusted sales price of the old residence exceeds the cost of the new residence. The prescribed time period begins two years before and ends two years after the sale of the old residence.[45] As with the replacement of involuntarily converted property, the taxpayer recognizes no gain if the proceeds from the old residence are entirely reinvested in a new residence. Again, given total reinvestment, the taxpayer does not have the wherewithal to pay taxes and has a continuity of interest in a principal residence. Section 1034 applies only to gains. Any loss on the sale of a principal is disallowed because the residence is personal use property.

Whether property is used by the taxpayer as a **principal residence** depends on the facts and circumstances of the taxpayer's situation. A principal residence may include a houseboat, house trailer, condominium, or cooperative apartment.[46] If a taxpayer's home is used partially as a residence and partially for other purposes (for example, a home office), Sec. 1034 applies only to the residential portion.[47]

> A **principal residence** is one physically occupied by the taxpayer as his or her primary living quarters.

---

42 Sec. 1033(a)(2)(B)(ii) and Reg. Sec. 1.1033(a)-2(c)(3)

43 Sec. 1033(g)(4).

44 Reg. Sec. 1.1033(a)-2(c)(2).

45 Sec. 1034(a).

46 Reg. Sec. 1.1034-1(c)(3)(i).

47 Reg. Sec. 1.1034-1(c)(3)(ii).

FIGURE 17-4

Diagram of
Section 1034

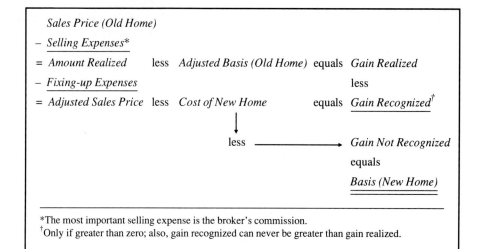

*The most important selling expense is the broker's commission.
†Only if greater than zero; also, gain recognized can never be greater than gain realized.

The **adjusted sales price** equals the amount realized minus fixing-up expenses and represents the amount the seller of a principal residence has available for reinvestment in a new residence.

Fixing-up expenses are expenditures incurred within a specified time period to enhance the salability of the old residence.

Figure 17-4 diagrams the computations dictated by Sec. 1034. The **adjusted sales price** equals the amount realized on the sale minus **fixing-up expenses**,[48] whereas the amount realized equals the sales price reduced by selling expenses.[49] Fixing-up expenses are total expenditures for work performed on the old residence to enhance its salability. Examples include painting and repair expenses. To qualify for this reduction, fixing-up expenses must meet the following conditions:[50]

1. The work must be performed during the 90-day period ending on the day the taxpayer enters into a contract to sell the old residence;

2. The expenses must be paid on or before the 30th day after the taxpayer actually sells the old residence;

3. The expenses may not be of a type normally deductible in computing taxable income;

4. The expenses may not be of a type deductible in computing the amount realized on the sale; and

5. The expenses may not include capital expenditures that constitute adjustments the basis of the old residence.

Note in Figure 17-4 that fixing-up expenses have nothing to do with determining the gain *realized* on the sale of the old residence. These expenses are deducted only to compute the adjusted sales price, an amount that indicates how much the taxpayer has available to reinvest in a new residence. If the taxpayer does not reinvest the entire adjusted sales price in a new residence, he or she faces gain recognition.

The basis of the new residence equals its cost minus the gain deferred on the sale.[51] This formula is exactly like the basis formula for replacement property under Sec. 1033 and serves the same purpose. The deferred gain from the sale of the old residence is *rolled over* into the new residence via the reduced basis. In addition, if the taxpayer defers any gain, the holding period of the new residence includes the holding period

---

48 Sec. 1034(b)(1).

49 Reg. Sec. 1.1034-1(b)(4).

50 Sec. 1034(b)(2) and Reg. Sec. 1.1034-1(b)(6).

51 Sec. 1034(e).

of the old residence (known as a tack-on holding period).[52] A taxpayer who sells the old residence at a *loss* may not recognize the loss because the home is a personal use asset. Nevertheless, the basis of the new residence (if one is purchased) is still its cost. The loss does not increase basis of the new residence because the nonrecognition is *permanent* rather than deferred.

EXAMPLE 17-14

Ten years ago Harry Homeowner purchased a home for $40,000 and has used it as his principal residence ever since. Two years after purchasing it, he added a new room for $8,000 so that his adjusted basis in the home is $48,000. In the current year he sold the home for $64,500, paid a $3,000 sales commission, and incurred $1,500 of fixing-up expenses. As shown in Figure 17-5, Harry's amount realized is $61,500, and he realizes a $13,500 gain. If Harry moves into an apartment rather than purchase a new residence, he would also recognize the $13,500 gain in the current year. In this case, the fixing-up expenses have no impact on the computation. Suppose instead that Harry pays $70,000 for a new residence shortly after selling the old one. Now, the adjusted sales price is $60,000. If he wishes to defer the entire $13,500 gain, the new residence must cost at least $60,000, which it does. Therefore, Harry recognizes no gain in the current year. The basis of the new residence, however, is reduced to $56,500. In addition, the new residence has a tack-on holding period.

Suppose Harry (age 45) sells the *new* residence several years later for $75,000, incurs no selling expenses, and does not purchase another home. He realizes and recognizes a $18,500 gain ($75,000 selling price minus $56,500 adjusted basis). This gain consists of two components, the $13,500 gain deferred on the sale of the first home and the $5,000 appreciation in value of the new home ($75,000 sales price minus $70,000 cost). Because Harry does not purchase yet another residence, he has the wherewithal to pay taxes on the gain, and he no longer has a continuity of interest in a principal residence.

The discussion pertaining to the sale of a principal residence focuses on the basic rules. Section 1034 and associated Regulations provide numerous other special rules and distinctions beyond the scope of this text. These rules pertain to matters such as constructed property, multiple purchases within the replacement period, members of armed forces, taxpayers residing outside the United States, a special election for spouses, and filing procedures if the taxpayer fails to purchase a new residence within the prescribed time period.

SPECIAL EXCLUSION FOR TAXPAYERS AGE 55 OR OLDER

Under Sec. 121, a taxpayer may *exclude* gain from the sale or exchange of a principal residence if all three of the following conditions are met:

1. The taxpayer has attained age 55 before the date of the sale or exchange;

2. The taxpayer has used the property as a principal residence for at least three of the five years immediately preceding the sale or exchange; and

3. The taxpayer *elects* to have this provision apply.

---

52 Sec. 1223(7).

FIGURE 17-5

**Application of
Section 1034—
EXAMPLE 17-14**

$64,500 Sales Price (Old Home)
− 3,000 Selling Expenses
= $61,500 Amount Realized   − $48,000 Adjusted
                               Basis (Old Home) = $13,500 Gain Realized

− 1,500 Fixing-up Expenses   less

= $60,000 Adjusted Sales Price − $70,000 Cost of
                                 New Home   =   0 Gain Recognized

                               less $13,500 Gain
                                                       Not Recognized
                                                  equals
                                                  $56,500 Basis (New Home)

The exclusion, however, may not exceed $125,000. Also, the taxpayer may make only *one* such election in his or her lifetime.

The exclusion is particularly beneficial to taxpayers who have rolled over gains during their younger years. Taxpayers with growing families and wealth tend to purchase increasingly expensive homes allowing for gain deferral under Sec. 1034. When children are grown and leave the home, a couple may decide to sell their large home, thereby triggering a large gain because prior gain deferrals reduced the basis of each successive home. If the taxpayers purchase a small, less expensive home or rent an apartment, they may forfeit some or all the benefits of Sec. 1034. Section 121 alleviates this problem by allowing qualified taxpayers to exclude *permanently* up to $125,000 of their gain. Thus, the benefit is not a mere deferral. Moreover, the excluded amount reduces the adjusted sales price of the old home,[53] which may allow some deferral under Sec. 1034 even if the taxpayers purchase a relatively inexpensive new home.

EXAMPLE 17-15

Mr. and Mrs. Emptynester sell their home, which has a $70,000 adjusted basis, for $260,000. They pay $17,000 in commissions and closing costs but incur no fixing-up expenses. They have owned and used the home as a principal residence for 15 years. Also, Mr. Emptynester is age 62 so they qualify for the Sec. 121 exclusion.[54] Shortly after selling the old residence, they purchase a new one for $108,000. In addition, they make the one-time election under Sec. 121. The tax consequences follow:

Continued

---

53 Sec. 121(d)(7). The exclusion also reduces the amount realized for purposes of Sec. 1033, thereby reducing the required reinvestment.

54 Under certain conditions, if one spouse meets the age, holding, and use requirements, both spouses are deemed to meet the requirements (Sec. 121(d)(1)).

EXAMPLE 17-15 (Con't.)

Sales price of old home		$260,000
Less selling expenses		17,000
Amount realized		243,000
Less adjusted basis of old home		70,000
Gain realized		173,000
Less exclusion under Sec. 121		125,000
Potential gain to be recognized		48,000
Actual gain recognized:		
Amount realized	$243,000	
Less gain excluded under Sec. 121	125,000	
Adjusted sales price	118,000	
Less cost of new home	108,000	
Gain recognized		10,000
Gain deferred under Sec. 1034		$ 38,000
Cost of new home		$108,000
Less gain deferred under Sec. 1034		38,000
Basis of new home (with tack-on holding period)		$ 70,000

In summary, the gain realized consists of the following three components:

Gain excluded under Sec. 121	$125,000
Gain deferred under Sec. 1034	38,000
Gain recognized	10,000
Total gain realized	$173,000

Had the Emptynesters not purchased a new residence, they would have recognized $48,000 of gain.

COMPARISON OF SECTIONS 1031, 1033, AND 1034

Sections 1031, 1033, and 1034 are similar in that each allows for deferral of gain with the deferral reflected in the basis of replacement property. However, these Code sections also differ in important ways. Table 17-1 summarizes the major similarities and differences. In addition, Sec. 1033 and 1034 may overlap if a taxpayer's principal residence is involuntarily converted. If the conversion occurs because of a casualty, Sec. 1033 rather than Sec. 1034 applies. On the other hand, if the conversion occurs because of condemnation or seizure (or sale under threat or imminence thereof), the taxpayer may elect to have Sec. 1034 rather than Sec. 1033 apply.[55] Section 1034 may be more advantageous than Sec. 1033 if, for example, the taxpayer incurred fixing-up

---

55 Sec. 1034(i).

TABLE 17-1

Comparison of Sections 1031, 1033, and 1034

Comparison	Sec. 1031: Like-kind Exchanges	Sec. 1033: Involuntary Conversions	Sec. 1034: Sale of a Principal Residence
1. Gain recognized, if any, is the lesser of the gain realized or…	Boot received	Amount realized *not* reinvested in similar property	Amount realized (net of fixing up expenses) *not* reinvested in another residence
2. Indirect as well as direct conversion permitted?	No	Yes	Yes
3. Time allowed for replacement?	Short delay is allowed	Generally two years after end of year gain was first realized	Generally two years before or after sale of residence
4. Is provision mandatory or elective?	Mandatory	Elective (unless a direct replacement)	Mandatory
5. Is loss recognized if realized?	No; but deferred loss reflected in basis	Yes, if otherwise allowed	Never; home is a personal use asset

expenses before the conversion. Alternatively, Sec. 1033 may be more advantageous than Sec. 1034 because the replacement period under Sec. 1033 can be longer than two years. Also, Sec. 1034 *requires* nonrecognition while Sec. 1033 makes nonrecognition elective. A taxpayer who wants to recognize a gain (for example, to offset a capital loss) would prefer to avoid Sec. 1034.

FORMATION OF A CORPORATION

Goal #6
Understand the requirements and determine the tax consequences of forming a corporation.

Incorporation of a business can take may forms. For example, a taxpayer or group of taxpayers may contribute cash to a corporation in exchange for the corporation's stock. The corporation can then use the cash to acquire business assets. Alternatively, a taxpayer operating a sole proprietorship may wish to incorporate his or her business by transferring the business assets to the corporation in exchange for stock. Similarly, several proprietors may wish to join forces and form a corporation, or an existing partnership may wish to incorporate. Finally, an existing corporation may want to form a subsidiary by transferring assets in exchange for the newly formed subsidiary's stock. In any case, the taxpayers transfer property of some sort to the corporation in exchange for stock (see Figure 17-6). Taxpayers who transfer property other than cash face potential gains or losses if the property's fair market value differs from its adjusted basis. In fact, if no special provisions applied, taxpayers who incorporate a business could incur tax liabilities as the result of the exchange. This possibility would discourage taxpayers from incorporating their businesses. To remove this deterrent and to facilitate incorporations, Congress enacted Sec. 351. As with other nontaxable

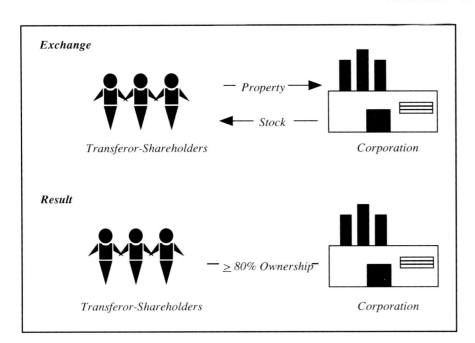

FIGURE 17-6

Formation of a
Corporation

exchanges, the wherewithal-to-pay and continuity-of-interest concepts provide the theoretical underpinnings of Sec. 351. The following statement by the First Circuit Court of Appeals reflects these concepts:

> It is the purpose of [Sec. 351] to save the taxpayer from an immediate recognition of gain, or to intermit the claim of a loss, in certain transactions where the gain or loss may have accrued in a constitutional sense, but where in a popular and economic sense there has been a mere change in the form of ownership and the taxpayer has not really "cashed in" on the theoretical gain, or closed out a losing venture.[56]

STATUTORY REQUIREMENTS

Section 351(a) holds that a transferor-shareholder recognizes no gain or loss if the following three conditions are met:

1. One or more *persons* transfer *property* to a corporation;

2. The transfer is solely in exchange for *stock* of the corporation; and

3. The transferors are in *control* of the corporation immediately after the exchange.

A **person** can be an individual, trust, estate, partnership, association, company, or corporation.[57] **Property** includes money but does not include services provided to the corporation in exchange for stock.[58] **Stock** can be either voting or nonvoting, but the term does not include stock rights or warrants.[59] Shareholders have **control** if they (1) own stock possessing at least 80% of total voting power and (2) own at least 80% of

A **person** is an individual, trust, estate, partnership, association, company, or corporation.

Property in a Sec. 351 transaction includes money but not services.

Stock used in a Sec. 351 transaction may be voting or nonvoting.

Control means aggregate ownership of at least 80% of a corporation's stock.

---

56 *Portland Oil Co. v. Comm.*, 109 F.2d 479 (CA-1, 1940).

57 Sec. 7701(a)(1).

58 Rev. Rul. 69-357, 1969-1 CB 101 and Sec. 351(d)(1).

59 Reg. Sec. 1.351-1(a)(1).

all other classes of stock.[60] In short, the aggregate group of property transferors must own at least 80% of the corporation after the exchange.

Because services are not property, a taxpayer providing only services to the corporation is not included in the transferor group for determining whether control exists. Moreover, the service provider always recognizes compensation income equal to the fair market value of the stock received for services. If the service provider also contributes property having substantial value, that person's entire stock ownership counts toward the control test even though he or she still recognizes compensation income on the portion of stock received for services.[61]

The nonrecognition provisions of Sec. 351 are mandatory, not elective. If the exchange meets the requirements of Sec. 351, the Code section applies automatically. Moreover, a Sec. 351 transaction bears many other similarities to a like-kind exchange.

Although Sec. 351(a) specifies a solely-for-stock requirement, a transferor nevertheless may receive property other than stock from the corporation. For example, the corporation might issue money, notes, or securities along with the stock. In this case, the transferor will have received boot in the exchange. Accordingly, Sec. 351(b) provides that the boot recipient in a transaction that otherwise qualifies under Sec. 351(a) must recognize gain (if any) to the extent of the money or fair market value of other property received. However, the gain recognized may not exceed the gain realized, and losses are not recognized regardless of the amount of boot.

The corporation also engages in an exchange because it issues stock for property. Therefore, some protection against gain or loss recognition is required for the corporation as well as the transferor-shareholder. Section 1032(a) provides that protection. It states that a corporation recognizes no gain or loss on the receipt of money or other property in exchange for its own stock (including treasury stock).

TRANSFERS OF PROPERTY SUBJECT TO LIABILITIES

Property transferred to a corporation is commonly subject to liabilities. Under the like-kind exchange rules, the liabilities were treated as boot that triggered gain recognition. A similar rule in Sec. 351 transactions would again inhibit the incorporation of businesses. Section 357 comes to the rescue with a liability rule that is more lenient than Sec. 1031. As a general rule, Section 357 provides that the corporation's assumption of the transferor's liability (or the corporation's receipt of property subject to a liability) will not be treated as boot received by the transferor. This exception applies only in determining the transferor's gain *recognized*. Liabilities assumed by the corporation are nevertheless taken into account for computing gain or loss *realized* by the transferor and are treated as money received for determining the transferor's basis of stock received.[62]

Section 357 contains two exceptions to the liability nonrecognition rule. First, if the assumption of the liability has a federal tax avoidance purpose or does not have a bona fide business purpose, the total assumed liability will be treated as boot for determining gain recognized.[63] Second, if the sum of liabilities exceeds the total basis of property transferred (including cash), the shareholder recognizes the excess liability as gain.[64]

---

60 Sec. 368(c).

61 IRS guidelines (Rev. Proc. 77-37, 1977-2 CB 568) consider property having a fair market value of 10% or more of the total stock received as having sufficiently substantial value.

62 Sec. 358(d).

63 Sec. 357(b).

64 Sec. Sec. 357(c).

BASIS OF STOCK AND PROPERTY

The basis rules in a Sec. 351 exchange are similar to those for like-kind exchanges. Pursuant to Sec. 358(a)(1), the transferor-shareholder takes an exchanged basis in the stock received, computed as follows:

Method I

Adjusted basis of property (including cash)
    transferred to controlled corporation
+ Gain recognized on the exchange
− Cash received from the corporation (including liabilities
    assumed by the corporation)
− FMV of other property received from the corporation
= Basis of stock received

The shareholder can also use the following second method for determining stock basis, which reflects the deferral aspect of the exchange:

Method II

FMV of stock received
− Gain *not* recognized on the exchange
+ Loss *not* recognized on the exchange
= Basis of stock received

The basis of other property received by the shareholder equals its fair market value.[65]
    The corporation's basis in property transferred to it is called a **transferred basis** and is computed as follows:[66]

Adjusted basis of property in the hands of the
    transferor-shareholder before the exchange
+ Gain recognized by the transferor-shareholder
= Basis of property to corporation

> Property has a **transferred basis** if it retains the same basis as the transferor had immediately before the exchange, with some modifications.

EXAMPLE 17-16

Carmen decides to form a corporation called Newco. She transfers real property to the corporation in exchange for stock worth $40,000. The real property has a $100,000 fair market value, a $75,000 adjusted basis, and is subject to a $60,000 mortgage. Newco assumes the mortgage, which is why Carmen receives only $40,000 worth of stock. After the exchange, Carmen owns 100% of Newco's stock and therefore meets the control test. Accordingly, the tax consequences follow:

Continued

---

65 Sec. 358(a)(2).

66 Sec. 7701(a)(43) and Sec. 362(a).

EXAMPLE 17-16 (Con't.)

Fair market value of stock received	$ 40,000
Liability assumed by Newco	60,000
Amount realized	100,000
Less adjusted basis of real property transferred	75,000
Gain realized	$ 25,000
Gain recognized	$ 0

Basis of Stock—Method I:

Adjusted basis of real property transferred	$ 75,000
Liability assumed by Newco treated as cash received by Carmen	(60,000)
Basis of stock	$ 15,000

Basis of Stock—Method II:

FMV of stock received	$ 40,000
Gain not recognized on the exchange	(25,000)
Basis of stock	$ 15,000

Note that the liability assumed by the Newco is treated as money received by Carmen in the computation of gain realized and stock basis but not in the determination of gain recognized. Moreover, the stock basis reflects the $25,000 gain deferred.

Newco recognizes no gain or loss upon the issuance of its stock and takes a $75,000 transferred basis in the real property. The corporation also assumes the $60,000 mortgage, which does not reduce the real property's basis.

Goal #7

Understand the characteristics and tax consequences of corporate reorganizations.

Example 17-16 also highlights the double-taxation aspect of corporate formations. The corporation receives property with a transferred basis, and the shareholder receives stock with an exchanged basis. Although neither taxpayer recognizes gain on the exchange, they *both* face deferred recognition—the corporation when it sells or depreciates the low-basis property and the shareholder when she sells the stock.

CORPORATE REORGANIZATIONS

A **reorganization** is one of seven specific nontaxable corporate restructurings defined in Sec. 368.

A corporate **reorganization** is one of seven types of readjustments to the structure of one or more corporations. Section 368(a)(1) defines the seven types of reorganizations, which can be described as follows:

1. Type A—A statutory merger or consolidation;

2. Type B—A stock-for-stock acquisition;

3. Type C—A stock-for-asset acquisition;

4. Type D—A divisive reorganization (as well as certain types of nonacquisitive and nondivisive reorganizations);

5. Type E—A recapitalization;

6. Type F—A mere change in identity, form, or place of organization; and

7. Type G—A bankruptcy reorganization.

The first three types (A, B, and C) are acquisitive reorganizations because they entail the acquisition of one corporation by another. The divisive Type D reorganization involves the division of one corporation into two or more corporations. Types E, F, and G usually affect a change in capital structure of only one corporation. A complete discussion of corporate reorganizations is inappropriate here so we focus only on the essential characteristics of acquisitive reorganizations to give you the flavor of this type of nontaxable exchange.

In an acquisitive reorganization, the acquiring corporation acquires either assets (Types A and C) or stock (Type B) of the acquired corporation. In either case, the acquiring corporation uses its own stock to make the acquisition so that the shareholders of the acquired corporation ultimately receive stock instead of cash and therefore retain a continuity of interest in the acquired corporation via ownership in the acquiring corporation. Moreover, a continuity of business enterprise exists because the acquiring corporation either obtains the business assets of the acquired corporation (Types A and C) or the acquired corporation retains its identity (Type B). As with other nontaxable exchanges discussed in this chapter, the lack of wherewithal to pay and the existence of continuity of interest play key roles in the nontaxable status of corporate reorganizations. In fact, Regulations under Sec. 368 explicitly address these points:

> Under the general rule [of taxation], upon the exchange of property, gain or loss must be accounted for if the new property differs in a material particular, either in kind or extent, from the old property. The purpose of the reorganization provisions of the Code is to except from the general rule certain specifically described exchanges incident to such readjustments of corporate structures made in one of the particular ways specified in the Code, as are required by business exigencies and which effect only a readjustment of continuing interest in property under modified corporate forms. Requisite to a reorganization under the Code are a continuity of the business enterprise under modified corporate form, and…a continuity of interest therein on the part of the persons who…were the owners of the enterprise prior to the reorganization.[67]

Section 368 is a purely *definitional* Code section. If a transaction meets the definition of a reorganization, certain *operational* Code sections protect against gain or loss recognition and adjust the basis of stock and assets to reflect the deferral aspects of the transaction. If a transaction fails to satisfy the definition of a reorganization under Sec. 368, the exchanges become taxable.

Figure 17-7 diagrams a **Type A reorganization**, which is one form of asset acquisition. The Type A reorganization is called a statutory merger because it must conform to corporation laws of the United States, a state, a territory, or the District of Columbia.[68] Notice that the merger entails two exchanges: (1) A Corp. (the acquiring corporation) exchanges its stock for the assets and liabilities of T Corp. (the acquired or target corporation) and (2) T Corp. shareholders exchange their stock for A Corp.

> In a **Type A reorganization,** the acquired corporation merges into the acquiring corporation.

---

67 Reg. Sec. 1.368-1(b).

68 Reg. Sec. 1.368-2(b)(1).

FIGURE 17-7

Type A
Reorganization
(Statutory Merger)

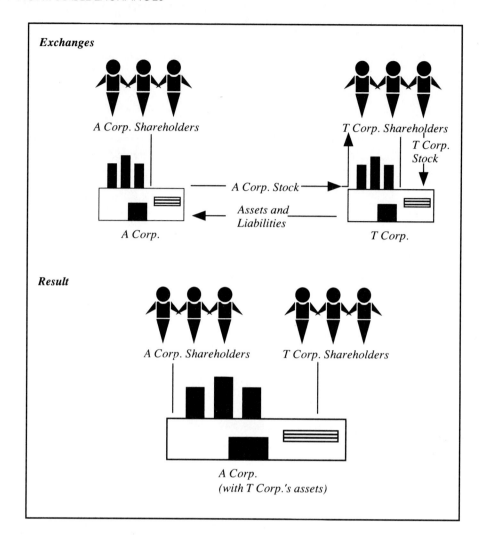

FIGURE 17-7

Type A Reorganization (Statutory Merger)

stock. A Corp. may use voting or nonvoting stock. As a result of the exchanges, T Corp. is absorbed by A Corp. and disappears. The T Corp. shareholders retain a continuity of interest because they now own stock of A Corp., which contains the assets of the old T Corp. The primary tax consequences of the merger follow:

1. Under Sec. 1032, A Corp. recognizes no gain or loss on the issuance of its stock in exchange for T Corp.'s assets (this result holds even if the transaction fails the definition of a reorganization);

2. Under Sec. 361, T Corp. recognizes no gain or loss on the exchange of its assets for A Corp. stock;

3. Under Sec. 357, A Corp.'s assumption of T Corp.'s liabilities triggers no gain recognition to T Corp;

4. Under Sec. 354, T Corp. shareholders recognize no gain or loss on the exchange of their T Corp. stock for A Corp. stock;

5. Under Sec. 362, A Corp.'s basis in the assets is the same as T Corp.'s basis immediately before the exchange (transferred basis); and

6. Under Sec. 358, T Corp.'s old shareholders' basis in the A Corp. stock is the same as their basis in the T Corp. stock surrendered (exchanged basis).

If A Corp. transfers cash in addition to stock, the T Corp. shareholders, under Sec. 356, will have some gain recognition on the receipt of boot. However, if A Corp. pays too much cash, the T Corp. shareholders will lose so much continuity of interest that the acquisition will fail to qualify as a reorganization, in which case the transaction becomes fully taxable. The amount of boot allowed in reorganization depends on its type. Under IRS guidelines, the acquiring corporation can use up to 50% boot in Type A reorganizations.[69]

Figure 17-8 diagrams a **Type B reorganization** (stock-for-stock acquisition). In this transaction, the acquiring corporation issues its *voting* stock in exchange for a controlling interest in the acquired corporation. Control for this purpose has the same meaning as for Sec. 351 transactions described earlier. In this type of acquisition, only one exchange occurs, and T Corp. retains its existence and identity as a subsidiary of A Corp. Unlike the statutory merger, the Code allows no boot in Type B reorganizations except minor amounts in particular circumstances. The primary tax consequences of the Type B reorganization follow:

> In a **Type B reorganization,** the acquiring corporation issues voting stock in exchange for a controlling interest in the acquired corporation.

1. Under Sec. 1032, A Corp. recognizes no gain or loss on the issuance of its stock in exchange for T Corp.'s stock (this result holds even if the transaction fails the definition of a reorganization);

2. Under Sec. 354, T Corp. shareholders recognize no gain or loss on the exchange of their T Corp. stock for A Corp. stock;

3. Under Sec. 362, A Corp.'s basis in the T Corp. stock is the same as that of the T Corp. shareholders immediately before the exchange (transferred basis); and

4. Under Sec. 358, T Corp.'s old shareholders' basis in the A Corp. stock is the same as their basis in the T Corp. stock surrendered (exchanged basis).

A **Type C reorganization** looks similar to a Type A merger except that the acquiring corporation must use *voting* stock to acquire substantially all the assets of the acquired corporation. Also, the Code allows no more than 20% boot and places other specific requirements and restrictions on the reorganization.

> In a **Type C reorganization**, the acquiring corporation issues voting stock in exchange for substantially all the assets of the acquired corporation.

Acquisitive nontaxable reorganizations are among several options available to the acquiring and acquired corporations. The acquiring corporation may also use exclusively cash to purchase the assets or stock of the acquired corporation. However, such a fully taxable transaction triggers gain and loss recognition to the parties selling the assets or stock. Sometimes, the acquiring corporation has no choice but to offer cash as, for example, in a tender offer to acquire the stock of a public corporation. In any case, however, the parties to a corporate acquisition must address three fundamental questions:

1. Should the transaction be structured as a taxable purchase or a nontaxable reorganization?

---

69 Rev. Proc. 77-37, 1977-2 CB 568. The courts have been more lenient than the IRS on how much boot is allowed.

**Type B
Reorganization
(Stock-for-Stock
Acquisition)**

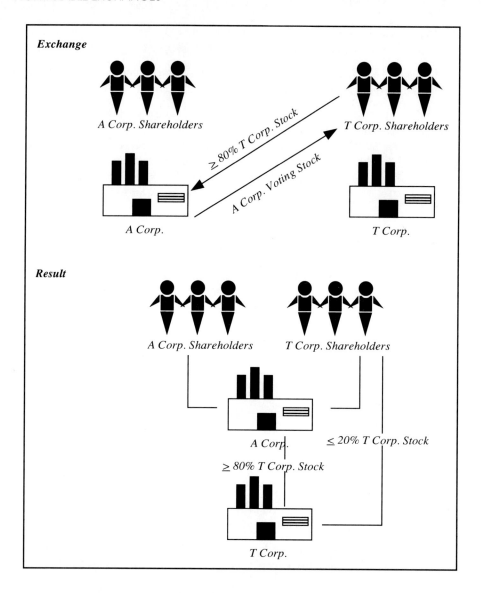

2. Should the acquiring corporation acquire stock or assets?

3. Should the acquired corporation be operated as subsidiary or a division of the acquired corporation?

The tax planner must analyze the tax consequences of each alternative and must also address nontax issues when advising on a corporate acquisition.

_____ KEY POINTS TO REMEMBER

✓ Nontaxable exchanges usually fall into one of two categories: a direct exchange or an indirect exchange. In either case, the exchange is characterized by a deferred gain (and sometimes a deferred loss) with the deferral reflected in the basis of property received.

✓ The underlying principles of the nontaxable exchange are the wherewithal-to-pay and continuity-of-interest concepts.

✓ The like-kind exchange is a prototypical transaction in which the taxpayer transfers property in direct exchange for like-kind property. If no boot is present, the taxpayer recognizes no gain or loss. The property received takes an exchanged basis and a tack-on holding period.

✓ If the taxpayer receives boot in a like-exchange, he or she recognizes gain equal to the lesser of the gain realized or the boot received. The basis of the property received equals its fair market value less gain deferred plus loss deferred.

✓ A taxpayer assuming a liability is deemed to have paid boot, and a taxpayer being relieved of a liability is deem to have received boot.

✓ To defer gain (not loss) in an involuntary conversion, the taxpayer must replace the converted property within a specified time period and make an election under Sec. 1033. Gain recognized on an involuntary conversion equals the lesser of the gain realized or the amount not reinvested. The basis of the replacement property equals its cost less gain deferred.

✓ A taxpayer can defer gain on the sale of a principal residence by purchasing a new residence within a time period beginning two years before and ending two years after the sale of the old residence. Gain recognized equals the lesser of the gain realized or the amount of adjusted sales price not reinvested in a new residence. The basis of the new residence equals its cost less gain deferred.

✓ Taxpayers age 55 or older can permanently exclude up to $125,000 of gain on the sale of their principal residence. The taxpayers must meet certain requirements and make a one-time election under Sec. 121.

✓ Section 351 allows for the nontaxable formation of a corporation if the shareholders transfer property in exchange for stock and the transferor-shareholders control the corporation after the exchange.

✓ Section 368 defines seven nontaxable corporate reorganizations. Types A, B, and C are acquisitive reorganizations; Type D is usually a divisive reorganization; and Types E, F, and G usually involve the restructuring of a single corporation.

APPENDIX 17A: MULTIPLE PROPERTY EXCHANGES

1. *Separate the properties transferred and received into exchange groups.* An exchange group contains all properties of a like kind or like class. Each exchange group must contain at least one asset transferred and one asset received.[70]

2. *Place remaining properties in the residual group.* A residual group occurs if the aggregate fair market value of properties transferred in all exchange groups differs from the aggregate fair market value of properties received. This group contains property that is not of a like kind or a like class, in other words, property normally

---

70 Reg. Sec. 1.1031(j)-1(a)(2) and (b)(2)(i).

categorized as boot. Properties in the residual group are categorized into Class I, II, III, or IV assets as described in Chapter 8.[71]

3. *Offset liabilities assumed against liabilities relieved.* If liabilities assumed exceed liabilities relieved, the excess is allocated among the exchange groups in proportion to the aggregate fair market value of assets in the exchange groups. If liabilities relieved exceed liabilities assumed, the excess is allocated to the residual group as a Class I asset (that is, cash).[72]

4. *Determine the exchange group surplus or deficiency for each exchange group.* The surplus or deficiency for *each* exchange group is computed as follows:

> Aggregate FMV of properties received
> – Excess liabilities assumed allocated to the exchange group in step 2
> – Aggregate FMV of properties transferred
> _____
> = Exchange group surplus (deficiency, if negative)[73]

5. *Compute gains and losses realized and recognized.* Gain or loss realized for each exchange group and for the residual group equals the difference between the aggregate fair market value of properties transferred over their aggregate adjusted basis. The *gain recognized* (if any) for each exchange group equals the lesser of the gain realized or the exchange group deficiency (if any). The total gain recognized equals the sum of gains recognized for each exchange group. No losses are recognized with respect to the exchange groups. A realized gain and loss in the residual group is also recognized.[74]

6. *Compute the basis of properties received.* In the residual group, basis equals the fair market value of the property. The aggregate basis for properties in *each* exchange group is determined as follows:

> Aggregate adjusted basis of properties transferred
> + Gain recognized in the exchange group
> + Excess liabilities assumed allocated to the exchange group
> + Exchange group surplus
> – Exchange group deficiency
> _____
> = Aggregate basis of properties received

This aggregate basis is then allocated to each individual asset within the exchange group in proportion to the fair market value of the assets.[75]

_____ RECALL PROBLEMS

Note: If no year is stated, assume the transaction occurred in the current year.

1. a. On July 8 of this year, Jason Corp. sold a transport truck for $6,000. At that time the truck had an adjusted basis of $9,000. On July 10 of same year, the company purchased a new replacement transport truck for $20,000.

---

71 Reg. Sec. 1.1031(j)-1(b)(2)(iii). Also, a third category of assets could exist if the property does not fit into an exchange group or the residual group. See Reg. Sec. 1.1031(j)-1(b)(3)(ii) and (d) Examples 3 and 5.

72 Reg. Sec. 1.1031(j)-1(a)(2) and (b)(2)(ii).

73 Reg. Sec. 1.1031(j)-1(b)(2)(iv).

74 Reg. Sec. 1.1031(j)-1(b)(3).

75 Reg. Sec. 1.1031(j)-1(c).

    (1) What amount of gain or loss, if any, will Jason Corp. recognize on the sale?

    (2) What will Jason's basis be in the new truck?

  b. Assume the same facts as in part a above except that the old truck had an adjusted basis of $4,200.

    (1) What amount, if any, of gain or loss will Jason Corp. recognize on the sale?

    (2) What will Jason's basis be in the new truck?

  c. What is the answer to part a if Jason instead acquires the new truck with $14,000 and a direct trade in of the old truck?

  d. What is the answer to part b if Jason instead acquires the new truck with $14,000 and a direct trade in of the old truck?

2. What is the holding period of like-kind property received in a nontaxable exchange? What is the holding period of boot property received in a nontaxable exchange?   `#3`

3. Dusty Rhodes, a road contractor, owned a light airplane used in his business. This plane had an adjusted basis of $24,000 when he exchanged it for a smaller plane with a fair market value of $30,000. Dusty received $9,000 cash when he made this trade. Straight-line depreciation claimed on the old plane since acquisition totaled $20,000.   `#3`

  a. How much gain was realized on this exchange?

  b. What minimum gain must be recognized on this exchange?

  c. Is the recognized gain a capital gain, ordinary income, or part of Sec. 1231? Explain.

  d. What is Dusty's tax basis in the new plane?

4. Assume the following facts apply to a like-kind exchange of productive use or investment property and complete the schedule: `#3`

Adjusted Basis of Property Surrendered	Cash Given (or Received)	FMV of Property Received	Recognized Gain (or Loss)	Basis of New Property
a. $19,000	$5,000	$30,000	$ _____	$ _____
b. 8,000	(4,000)	20,000	_____	_____
c. 17,000	0	25,000	_____	_____
d. 17,000	0	15,000	_____	_____
e. 17,000	(5,000)	10,000	_____	_____

5. Tora Corporation owned a machine, used in its business, that had cost $6,000 and on which depreciation of $2,200 had been taken up to January 2 this year. On that date, Tora exchanged the old machine for a new one to serve the same purpose. Using these facts, in each of the following cases compute (1) the recognized gain or loss on the exchange and (2) the tax basis of the new machine: `#3`

a. Value of new asset, $4,000; no boot given or received.

b. Value of new asset, $3,000; boot received, $400.

c. Value of new asset, $3,000; boot given, $300.

d. Value of new asset, $4,000; boot received, $300.

e. Value of new asset, $4,000; boot given, $300.

f. Value of new asset, $3,700; boot received, $300.

#3

6. For each of the independent situations below, determine (1) the amount of gain or loss realized; (2) the amount of gain or loss recognized; and (3) the tax basis of the new land. Assume that during the current year the taxpayer exchanged one parcel of farmland for another; further assume that the taxpayer had held the original land for six years and that it had an adjusted basis of $50,000 at the time of the exchange.

a. Taxpayer received only the new land, which had a fair market value of $60,000.

b. Taxpayer received the new land, with a fair market value of $60,000, and $15,000 cash.

c. Taxpayer gave the other party to the exchange $5,000 cash in addition to the land and received in return land worth $45,000.

d. Taxpayer received only the new land, which had a fair market value of $60,000, and the other party to the exchange assumed taxpayer's $20,000 mortgage on the old land.

e. Taxpayer took the new land and assumed a $10,000 mortgage against that land. The other party to the exchange also assumed taxpayer's $6,000 mortgage on the old land. The new land has an estimated value of $60,000.

f. Taxpayer took the new land and assumed a $6,000 mortgage against that land. The other party to the exchange also assumed taxpayer's $10,000 mortgage on the old land. The new land has an estimated value of $60,000.

#3

7. a. Kleno held for investment a track of land with a basis of $20,000 and a fair market value of $40,000. She exchanged the land for a tract with a fair market value of $50,000. To balance the transaction, Kleno gave the other party as boot 100 shares of Americo Co. stock, which had a fair market value of $10,000 and a basis of $6,200.

(1) What amount, if any, of gain or loss will be recognized by Kleno?

(2) What will be Kleno's basis in the new land?

b. Assume the same facts as in part a, except that the stock's basis to Kleno was $13,000.

(1) What amount, if any, of gain or loss will be recognized by Kleno on the transaction?

(2) What will be Kleno's basis in the new land?

#4

8. What are the beginning date and ending date of the period during which condemned real estate held for investment must be replaced in order for the gain on conversion to qualify as nontaxable?

9. Assume the following facts apply to an involuntary conversion of business property and complete the schedule:

	Adjusted Basis of Property Destroyed	Insurance Proceeds	Amount Expended for Immediate Replacement of Property	Recognized Gain (or Loss)	Basis of New Property
a.	$26,000	$16,000	$24,000	$	$
b.	17,000	21,000	20,000	$	$
c.	20,000	25,000	27,000	$	$

10. On April 18, Tom's Cleaners, Inc., lost one of its delivery vans in an auto accident. The van had an adjusted basis of $3,200 at the time of the accident. Straight-line depreciation of $4,000 had been claimed on the van before the accident. Insurance proceeds of $5,000 were received on May 1. On April 20, Tom's Cleaners, Inc., purchased a new delivery van for $8,000.

   a. What amount of gain did Tom's Cleaners, Inc., realize because of the accident?

   b. What minimum amount of gain must Tom's Cleaners, Inc., recognize because of the accident?

   c. If Tom's Cleaners, Inc., recognizes only the minimum amount of gain, what is the tax basis in the van purchased on April 20?

   d. What maximum amount of gain may Tom's Cleaners, Inc., recognize because of the accident? What kind of gain is this?

   e. If Tom's Cleaners, Inc., recognizes the amount of gain, what is its tax basis in the van purchased on April 20?

11. Investo Corporation purchased several acres of land in 1936 for $400. This year, the state government took the land for highway right-of-way, and the taxpayer was awarded $21,000 for the land. Investo first received notification of the prospective conversion on January 4 and received full payment for the land on November 30. In each of the following cases, compute (1) the recognized gain or loss on the conversion under Sec. 1033 and (2) the tax basis of the replacement property in those cases in which the property was replaced:

   a. The land was not replaced.

   b. New land was purchased on June 1 for $16,000.

   c. New land was purchased on December 1 for $22,000.

   d. New land was purchased on December 1 for $10,200.

   e. New land was purchased on December 1 of the following year for $24,000.

   f. New land was purchased on June 10 of the third following year for $30,000.

12. In 1975, Tom Fahr purchased an $18,000 frame house for his family. Eventually this house was too small for Tom's growing family, so in April of this year, he sold the frame house for $62,000. The broker's fee on the sale was $3,700. Tom

incurred $600 in fixing-up expenses prior to completing the sale. On June 1, the Fahr family moved into their new brick house. What gain must the Fahrs report this year because of the sale of their frame house if

a. the new residence cost them $80,000?

b. the new residence cost them $50,000?

What is the tax basis for the Fahr's brick house in each of the above situations?

13. A taxpayer purchased a mobile home as a residence in 1970 for $10,000. This year he sold the home for $21,000. He incurred and paid fixing up expenses of $300 in the month before sale. He also paid a real estate agent a commission of $1,260. Seven months after the sale of the old residence, the taxpayer purchased a new mobile home for $26,000. (It is a primary residence.)

a. What amount of gain is recognized by the taxpayer under Sec. 1034?

b. What would be the tax basis of the new home under Sec. 1034?

14. Assume the same facts as in problem 13, except that the new mobile home cost $15,400.

a. Under Sec. 1034, what would be the recognized gain on the sale?

b. What would be the tax basis of the new mobile home?

15. This year Mr. Elder (age 64) sold his residence for $140,000. He and Mrs. Elder had lived in this home since 1940. They originally paid $18,000 for the home, but they immediately remodeled it at a cost of $3,000. Since then only routine upkeep was required. The Elders paid a realtor $8,400 commission for selling the house; they also incurred fixing-up expenses of $500 one month prior to the sale. One month after selling their home, the Elders purchased a small cottage on a nearby lake for $48,000. They intend to make this lake cottage their home whenever they are not traveling.

a. What minimum amount of gain must the Elders include on their tax return this year because of the sale of their old home?

b. Would this be a capital gain or ordinary income?

c. If Mr. Elder had been 54, rather than 64, when he sold this home, what minimum amount of gain would he have been required to report as taxable income?

16. Taxpayer, age 57, sold her former home for $162,500. Broker's commission on this sale was $8,000. Taxpayer's basis in her old home was $24,000. What is the minimum amount taxpayer must reinvest in a new home if she is to avoid any recognition of taxable gain this year (assuming that she qualifies for and makes the election to exclude as much of her gain as possible)?

17. In 1987, Sue Near purchased a home for $100,000. In the current year, Sue sold the home for $98,000. In so doing, she incurred a $5,500 sale's commission and $500 of fixing-up expenses. One week after selling the old home, she purchased a new residence for $92,000. What gain or loss does Sue realize and recognize on the sale of the old residence? What is her basis in the new home?

18. James Madison and Henry Clay formed a corporation on July 1 of this year. Madison transferred to the corporation the assets of his existing hardware busi-

ness, which had a basis of $8,000, and Clay transferred assets that had a basis of $18,000. Each individual received 200 shares of stock in the new corporation; each share had a fair market value of $80. In addition, Madison's wife was issued one share of stock on the investment of $80 cash. Discuss the tax consequences of this transaction, including the basis of shares received and the basis of the corporation in the property.

THOUGHT PROBLEMS

1. Although Chapter 17 did not address the formation of a partnership, you should be able to apply your understanding of nontaxable exchanges to a novel situation. Two individuals decide to form a *partnership*. Della transfers real property in exchange for a 50% interest in the partnership. The real property has a $50,000 fair market value, has a $40,000 adjusted basis, and is not subject to a mortgage. Ephraim transfers personal property in exchange for a 50% interest in the partnership. The personal property has a $50,000 fair market value, a $55,000 adjusted basis, and is not subject to a liability. For Della and Ephraim, determine gain or loss realized, gain or loss recognized (if any), and basis of the partnership interest received. For the partnership, determine the gain or loss recognized (if any) and the basis of each property received in the exchange. Explain the underlying rationale for your answer.

2. Explain why Method I for determining basis in a like-kind exchange is equivalent to the variation in Footnote 19. Apply the variation to Example 17-7 in the text and then recast your answer into a journal entry format. Do this problem for both Mr. Swapper and Ms. Trader, and do the problem for each assumed basis for the stock boot ($80 and $120).

3. Sly Avoider decides to incorporate his real estate holdings. He owns real property having a $100,000 fair market value and a $40,000 adjusted basis. Two days before the incorporation, he borrows $20,000 from the bank using the real property as collateral; thus, the real property becomes subject to a mortgage. He transfers the property to the corporation in exchange for stock worth $80,000, and the corporation assumes the $20,000 mortgage. What is Sly's gain realized and gain recognized (if any)? What is his basis in the corporate stock? Explain the rationale for your answer and compare your result with the liability rules for like-kind exchanges.

4. On October 10, 1946, Rancher Alpha purchased 500 acres of land on the Colorado River for $40,000. He used this land to graze cattle until November 1, this year, when he traded the ranch for a small complex of land and buildings that had just been completed in Nearby City. This complex was intended to constitute a neighborhood shopping center. At the time of the trade, the estimated fair market value of the ranch was $250,000; that of the shopping center, $300,000. To equate the exchange, Rancher Alpha gave the builder 1,000 shares of Tractor stock, which had cost him $20,000 in 1965. The shares were worth $50,000 at the time of the exchange.

   Builder Beta, the contractor who constructed the shopping center complex, works independently with a small group of people. She makes her living by building homes and office buildings and selling them to interested parties. Her construction cost in this particular complex was $270,000; she started construction on February 4, last year.

    a. Relative to Rancher Alpha:

       (1) What amount of gain (or loss) did he realize on the exchange of the ranch and Tractor shares for the shopping center?

       (2) What amount of gain (or loss) must be recognize on this same exchange?

       (3) What is the tax basis in the shopping center after the exchange has been completed?

       (4) What is his holding period in the shopping center?

       (5) Is the shopping center a capital asset in Rancher Alpha's hands after the exchange? Explain.

       (6) Can you see any reason why Rancher Alpha may prefer to make this a taxable (rather than a nontaxable) event? Explain.

    b. Relative to Builder Beta:

       (1) What amount of gain (or loss) did she realize on the exchange of the shopping center for the ranch and Tractor stock?

       (2) What amount of gain (or loss) must she recognize on the exchange?

       (3) What is her tax basis in the ranch after the exchange has been completed?

       (4) What is her tax basis in the Tractor shares after exchange?

       (5) What is her holding period in the ranch and the shares?

       (6) Is the ranch a capital asset to Beta? Explain.

       (7) Are the Tractor shares a capital asset to Beta? Explain.

#2 #3

5. Bracket Corporation's board of directors voted to close Plant 12 (acquired in 1975) located in a congested area of New Jersey and to open the same operation in a semirural setting somewhere in the southwestern region of the United States. After making this decision, Bracket sent its secretary and treasurer on a search for the new plant site. The two corporate officers eventually selected an ideal 80-acre tract that was for sale for $75,000. Instead of arranging an outright purchase of the new site, the officers contracted with a New York broker, who agreed to acquire the 80 acres and to exchange it plus $5,000 cash for Bracket's old Plant 12. The parties agreed that the approximate fair market value of Plant 12 was $85,000. Bracket's adjusted basis in old Plant 12 was $54,000 ($100,000 − $46,000; straight-depreciation would have been $60,000). The broker acquired the new 80-acre tract for $72,000.

    a. What amount of taxable gain must Bracket Corporation report in the year it completed this exchange?

    b. What kind of gain—ordinary income, capital gain, or Sec. 1231 gain—does Bracket Corporation report because of this transaction?

    c. What is Bracket's tax basis in the (new) 80-acre tract?

    d. What amount of taxable income must the New York broker report because of his role in this exchange?

    e. Would the broker's income be ordinary income or capital gain? Why?

6. Shark Corporation wishes to acquire Target Corporation in a Type A reorganization (a statutory merger). Target owns property having a fair market value of $50,000 and an adjusted basis of $30,000. Target is wholly owned by Bob. Bob's stock in Target is worth $50,000 and has a $10,000 adjusted basis. Determine the tax consequences to Shark, Target, and Bob in each of the following independent situations:

   a. Shark acquires Target's assets with Shark stock worth $50,000. The stock is transferred to Bob in exchange for Bob's Target stock in liquidation of Target.

   b. Shark acquires Target's assets with Shark stock worth $45,000 plus $5,000 cash. The stock and cash are transferred to Bob in exchange for Bob's Target stock in liquidation of Target. Continuity of interest is maintained in the transaction.

   c. Shark acquires Target's assets with Shark stock worth $12,000 plus $38,000 cash. The stock and cash are transferred to Bob in exchange for Bob's Target stock in liquidation of Target. Because of the large amount of cash, continuity of interest is broken.

7. Shark Corporation wishes to acquire Target Corporation in a Type B reorganization (stock-for-stock acquisition). Target owns property having a fair market value of $50,000 and an adjusted basis of $30,000. Target is wholly owned by Bob. Bob's stock in Target is worth $50,000 and has a $10,000 adjusted basis. Determine the tax consequences to Shark, Target, and Bob in each of the following independent situations:

   a. Shark acquires Bob's Target stock with Shark voting stock worth $50,000.

   b. Shark acquires Bob's Target stock with Shark voting stock worth $45,000 plus $5,000 cash.

8. Items a–j are ten suggested property exchanges. Which of the ten would not qualify as a (nontaxable) like-kind exchange? Explain any of the exchanges that would partially qualify. Assume that none of the property is an inventory item.

   a. Gold jewelry for Dodge van. (Both for personal use.)

   b. Ranch land for fully equipped restaurant (land, building, and equipment).

   c. Stallion for a gelding. (Both used in business.)

   d. Sailboat for a racehorse. (Both held as investment properties.)

   e. Corporate stock for corporate bond.

   f. Personal residence for a rental property.

   g. Silver bullion for gold bullion. (Both held for investment.)

   h. Apartment house for bulldozer. (Apartment is investment; bulldozer is productive-use property.)

   i. Airplane for a heavy general-purpose truck.

   j. Heavy general-purpose truck for a light general-purpose truck.

9. UAS Corporation exchanged land it owned near Tempe, Arizona, for other land near Provo, Utah. UAS's basis in the Arizona land was $800,000; it had a $750,000 mortgage outstanding against this property. The other party to the exchange, YUB Corporation, assumed the $750,000 mortgage. To complete the

exchange, UAS Corporation paid YUB Corporation $300,000 cash (boot). The Utah land was valued at $850,000, had a $250,000 adjusted basis, and was clear of debt; the Arizona land was valued at $1,300,000. Assuming the exchange qualifies as a like-kind exchange, determine gain or loss realized, gain or loss recognized (if any), and basis of land received for both UAS Corporation and YUB Corporation.

#3

10. Samantha Jones has operated a dairy farm on the outskirts of a large city for a number of years. She owns 200 acres of land for which she originally paid $150 per acre. The land is adjacent to a railway track, and a freeway through the area (but not on Samantha's place) was recently completed. Boyce Corporation has approached Samantha about buying her place to use as the site for a large manufacturing plant. They offered Samantha $1,000 per acre. Samantha intends to continue in the dairy business but does not want to sell her land because she will get less than its value after paying the tax. Devise a plan that allows Boyce to obtain Samantha's land and leaves Samantha without diminution of the value of her investment in land.

#3

11. Mr. Smith owns a parcel of land, which he holds for investment. The land cost $70,000 in 1975, is now worth $150,000, and is subject to a $50,000 mortgage. Mr. Jones owns another parcel of land, which he also holds for investment. His land cost $60,000 in 1981, is now worth $135,000, and is subject to a $30,000 mortgage. They agree to exchange their parcels of land, both of which qualify as like-kind property. In addition, they assume each other's mortgage, and Mr. Smith pays Mr. Jones $5,000 cash. For each party, determine the gain or loss realized, gain or loss recognized, and basis of property received.

#3 #4

12. State whether each of the following statements is true or false. If false, explain why.

a. The like-kind requirement of Sec. 1031 is generally interpreted more narrowly than the similar-or-related-in-service-or-use requirement of Sec. 1033.

b. Any item of inventory must be considered as boot in an exchange that otherwise qualifies under Sec. 1031.

c. An exchange of real property for personal property may sometimes qualify as a like-kind exchange under Sec. 1031.

d. Loss may not be recognized following an involuntary conversion if the taxpayer reinvests all proceeds in similar property within the time period specified in Sec. 1033.

e. Giving boot in a like-kind exchange does not necessitate the recognition of gain by the taxpayer giving the boot.

#3 #4

13. Categorize each of the following as (1) a like-kind exchange, (2) a replacement of similar property, or (3) neither:

a. Inventory of a trade or business is exchanged for an automobile to be used in a trade or business.

b. Land and a building used in a trade or business are exchanged for unimproved land that will be held for investment.

c. Common stock held by an individual is traded for land that will be held as an investment.

d. Manufacturing machinery that produces metal tanks is destroyed by fire; proceeds are used to acquire machines that produce combat boots.

e. An office building held as rental property is condemned by the city for a new park. Proceeds are used to acquire farmland, which is rented immediately following acquisition.

f. A dump truck used by a dirt contractor is exchanged for a family car.

g. Machinery that produces farm equipment is exchanged for office furniture that will be placed in rental property.

h. Unimproved land is exchanged for machinery to be used in a trade or business.

i. Four bulls are exchanged for 12 heifers by a rancher.

14. On March 19, 1956, Red inherited a home from his mother. His mother's basis in this home was $40,000; it was valued at $50,000 for estate tax purposes. Red immediately occupied the home as his own primary residence.

   On May 15, 1964, Red sold this home for $60,000. Broker's commission on the sale was $3,600. Two weeks prior to making this sale, Red purchased a new primary residence for $55,000.

   On July 24, 1971, Red's residence was condemned by the State Highway Commission. Red received a condemnation award of $60,000. On November 22, 1971, Red purchased his next primary residence for $56,000 and elected to pay the minimum possible tax for 1971.

   On February 14, 1975, Red gave his primary residence to his daughter as a wedding gift. On the day of the gift, the home was valued at $60,000. Red paid a gift tax of $1,500 before leaving for a round-the-world cruise.

   On December 15 of this year, Red's daughter sold the home, which she had occupied as her primary residence since February 15, 1975, for $65,000. Because she sold the home herself, there was no commission on this sale. She moved into a rented apartment and has no intention of returning to home ownership in the near future. What gain or loss must Red's daughter recognize on the sale she made this year?

15. Kyle, Dan, and Bob decided to pool some assets in a new corporate business to be known as KDB Company. Kyle contributed $4,000 cash plus equipment with a fair market value of $26,000 and a tax basis of $15,000. Dan contributed land with a fair market value of $30,000 and a tax basis of $40,000. Bob contributed $20,000 cash and a good deal of work, which all parties agreed was worth $10,000. In exchange, each transferor received 1,000 shares of KDB stock.

a. If all the contributions are made under a single plan so that the transaction qualifies under Sec. 351(a):

   (1) How much gain or loss does each transferor recognize in the year KDB is incorporated?

   (2) What is the tax basis of the 1,000 shares of KDB each transferor received?

   (3) What is the tax basis of the equipment and land received by KDB Company?

   (4) Why might Dan prefer to arrange the incorporating transaction in a way that would not qualify under Sec. 351(a)?

   (5) Why might Kyle prefer to keep the transaction as it is currently arranged?

b. If the incorporation plans were revised so that initially Dan contributed $30,000 cash and subsequently, in a wholly separate transaction, KDB Company purchased the land from Dan for $30,000, why might both Kyle and Dan be satisfied?

c. Under either plan (a or b, above), each shareholder has contributed $30,000 in cash, equivalent property, and/or services to KDB Company in exchange for 1,000 shares of stock. Nevertheless, in one important sense Kyle has not contributed his fair share. Explain.

16. Three individuals decide to form a corporation called Newco. Alphonso transfers $10,000 cash and real property to the corporation in exchange for stock worth $40,000. The real property has a $90,000 fair market value, has a $45,000 adjusted basis, and is subject to a $60,000 mortgage. Newco assumes the mortgage. Buford transfers inventory in exchange for stock worth $30,000 and a $10,000 two-year note (Buford elects *out* of the installment method). The inventory has a $40,000 fair market value and a $28,000 adjusted basis. Caroline transfers equipment in exchange for stock worth $40,000. The equipment has a $40,000 fair market value and a $55,000 adjusted basis. After the exchange, the three shareholders together own 100% of Newco's stock. For Alphonso, Buford, and Caroline, determine gain or loss realized, gain or loss recognized (if any), and basis of stock received. For Newco, determine the gain or loss recognized (if any) and the basis of each property received in the exchange.

———— CLASS PROJECTS

1. Refer to following material concerning multiple property exchanges: (1) Reg. Sec. 1.1031(j); (2) Larry Witner, "Multiple Asset Exchanges: An Endangered Species?" *The Tax Adviser*, October 1991, pp. 636–45; and (3) any other useful references that address this topic. Prepare an example (different from that in the reference material) that demonstrates the essential characteristics of this type of transaction. Be sure that the example contains at least the following aspects: (1) the transaction should be an exchange of one business for another; (2) property exchanged should include cash, goodwill, and like-kind property subject to a liability as well as other items of like-kind property; and (3) one General Asset Class should contain only one property (either transferred or received but not both) so that an exchange group cannot be formed for that class.

2. Sally Seller sold her home to Barry Buyer on May 1, 1992 (the settlement date). Barry had not owned a home before purchasing this one. Determine the tax treatment of each item on the accompanying settlement statement (Figure 17–9). In particular, determine (a) Sally's amount realized on the sale, (b) Barry's basis in the home, (c) amounts allowed as itemized deductions in 1992, and (d) items that are neither deductible nor additions to basis. Assume that city and county property taxes are paid on January 2 for the upcoming year. For example, Sally paid property taxes for the entire 1992 property tax year on January 2, 1992. Specifically, she paid $540 ($45 per month) in city taxes and $480 ($40 per month) in county taxes. Barry's mortgage payments begin on June 1, 1992. We recommend the following publication to assist you in understanding the settlement statement: U.S. Department of Housing and Urban Development, *Settlement Costs: A HUD Guide*.

FIGURE 17-9

Settlement Statement

		(Exp. 12-31-86) OMB No. 2502-0265
A. U.S. DEPARTMENT OF HOUSING AND URBAN DEVELOPMENT	**B. TYPE OF LOAN:**	
	1. ☐ FHA 2. ☐ FMHA 3. ☒ CONV. UNINS. 4. ☐ VA 5. ☐ CONV. INS.	
	6. FILE NUMBER CP-2	7. LOAN NUMBER 123456
SETTLEMENT STATEMENT	8. MORTG. INS. CASE NO.	

C. NOTE: This form is furnished to give you a statement of actual settlement costs. Amounts paid to and by the settlement agent are shown. Items marked "(p.o.c.)" were paid outside the closing; they are shown here for informational purposes and are not included in the totals.

D. NAME AND ADDRESS OF BORROWER	E. NAME AND ADDRESS OF SELLER	F. NAME AND ADDRESS OF LENDER
Barry Buyer	Sally Seller	First Mortgage Company

G. PROPERTY LOCATION	H. SETTLEMENT AGENT	I. SETTLEMENT DATE:
Somewhere, U.S.A.	Eastside Title Insurance Company PLACE OF SETTLEMENT Somewhere, U.S.A.	5/1/92

J. SUMMARY OF BORROWER'S TRANSACTION		**K. SUMMARY OF SELLER'S TRANSACTION**	
100 GROSS AMOUNT DUE FROM BORROWER:		**400 GROSS AMOUNT DUE TO SELLER:**	
101 Contract sales price	90,000	401 Contract sales price	90,000
102 Personal property		402 Personal property	
103 Settlement charges to borrow (line 1400)	4,900	403	
104		404	
105		405	
Adjustments for items paid by seller in advance:		Adjustments for items paid by seller in advance:	
106 City/town taxes 5/1/92 12/31/92	360	406 City/town taxes to	360
107 County taxes 5/1/92 12/31/92	320	407 County taxes to	320
108 Assessments to		408 Assessments to	
109		409	
110		410	
111		411	
112		412	
120 GROSS AMOUNT DUE FROM BORROWER:	95,580	**420 GROSS AMOUNT DUE TO SELLER:**	90,680
200 AMOUNTS PAID BY OR IN BEHALF OF BORROWER:		**500 REDUCTIONS IN AMOUNT DUE TO SELLER:**	
201 Deposit or earnest money	1,000	501 Excess deposit (see instructions)	
202 Principal amount of new loan(s)	70,000	502 Settlement charges to seller (line 1400)	5,600
203 Existing loan(s) taken subject to		503 Existing loan(s) taken subject to	
204		504 Payoff of first mortgage loan	42,000
205		505 Payoff of second mortgage loan	
206		506	
207		507	
208		508	
209		509	
Adjustments for items unpaid by seller:		Adjustments for items unpaid by seller:	
210 City/town taxes to		510 City/town taxes to	
211 County taxes to		511 County taxes to	
212 Assessments to		512 Assessments to	
213		513	
214		514	
215		515	
216		516	
217		517	
218		518	
219		519	
220 TOTAL PAID BY/FOR BORROWER:	71,000	**520 TOTAL REDUCTION AMOUNT DUE SELLER:**	47,600
300 CASH AT SETTLMENT FROM/TO BORROWER:		**600 CASH AT SETTLEMENT TO/FROM SELLER:**	
301 Gross amount due from borrower (line 120)	95,580	601 Gross amount due to seller (line 420)	90,680
302 Less amounts paid by/for borrower (line 220)	71,000	602 Less total reductions in amount due seller (line 520)	47,600
303 CASH (☐ FROM) (☐ TO) BORROWER:	24,580	603 CASH (☐ TO) (☐ FROM) SELLER:	43,080

HUD—1 (Rev 3-86)
RESPA, HB 4305.2

Continued

FIGURE 17-9 (Con't.)

Settlement Statement

PAGE 2 OF
OMB No. 2502-0265

L. SETTLEMENT CHARGES	PAID FROM BORROWER'S FUNDS AT SETTLEMENT	PAID FROM SELLER'S FUNDS AT SETTLEMENT
700 TOTAL SALES/BROKER'S COMMISSION Based on price $ 90,000 @ 6 %= 5,400		
Division of commission (line 700) as follows		
701 $ 5,400 to Friendly Realty Company		
702 $ to		
703 Commission paid at settlement		5,400
704		
800 ITEMS PAYABLE IN CONNECTION WITH LOAN.		
801 Loan Origination fee 1 %	700	
802 Loan Discount 2 %	1,400	
803 Appraisal Fee to First Mortgage Company	150	
804 Credit Report to First Mortgage Company	30	
805 Lender's inspection fee		
806 Mortgage Insurance application fee to		
807 Assumption Fee		
808		
809		
810		
811		
900 ITEMS REQUIRED BY LENDER TO BE PAID IN ADVANCE.		
901 Interest from 5/1/92 to 6/1/92 @$ 17.90 /day	555	
902 Mortgage insurance premium for mo. to		
903 Hazard insurance premium for 1 yrs. to Home Insurance Company	420	
904 yrs. to		
905		
1000 RESERVES DEPOSITED WITH LENDER		
1001 Hazard insurance 1 mo. @$ 35 per mo.	35	
1002 Mortgage insurance mo. @$ per mo.		
1003 City property taxes 5 mo. @$ 45 per mo.	225	
1004 County property taxes 5 mo. @$ 40 per mo.	200	
1005 Annual assessments (Maint.) mo. @$ per mo.		
1006 mo. @$ per mo.		
1007 mo. @$ per mo.		
1008 mo. @$ per mo.		
1100 TITLE CHARGES:		
1101 Settlement or closing fee to Eastside Title Insurance Company	100	100
1102 Abstract or title search to		
1103 Title examination to		
1104 Title insurance binder to		
1105 Document preparation to Eastside Title Insurance Company		60
1106 Notary fees to		
1107 Attorney's fees to		
(includes above items No.		
1108 Title insurance to Eastside Title Insurance Company	500	
(includes above items No.		
1109 Lender's coverage $ 70,000		
1110 Owner's coverage $		
1111		
1112		
1113		
1200 GOVERNMENT RECORDING AND TRANSFER CHARGES		
1201 Recording fees: Deed $ 10 ; Mortgage $ 20 ; Releases $	30	
1202 City/county tax/stamps: Deed $; Mortgage $		
1203 State tax/stamps: Deed $ 300 ; Mortgage $ 80	380	
1204		
1205		
1300 ADDITIONAL SETTLEMENT CHARGES		
1301 Survey to Land Surveys, Inc.	175	
1302 Pest inspection to Termite Terminator, Inc.		40
1303		
1304		
1305		
1400 TOTAL SETTLEMENT CHARGES (entered on lines 103, Section J and 502, Section K)	4,900	5,600

CERTIFICATION

I have carefully reviewed the HUD 1 Settlement Statement and to the best of my knowledge and belief, it is a true and accurate statement of all receipts and disbursements made on my account or by me in this transaction. I further certify that I have received a copy of the HUD-1 Settlement Statement.

Borrowers | Sellers

The HUD 1 Settlement Statement which I have prepared is a true and accurate account of this transaction. I have caused the funds to be disbursed in accordance with this statement.

Settlement Agent | Date

WARNING: It is a crime to knowingly make false statements to the United States on this or any other similar form. Penalties upon conviction can include a fine and imprisonment. For details see: Title 18 U.S. Code Section 1001 and Section 1010.

Part Six

PERSPECTIVE

> "The phenomenal proliferation of law, loophole litigation, and judicial exegesis has spawned a huge tax industry. It gathers its capital from legal conundrums."
>
> PETER MEYER, HARPERS (1977)

The mission of Part Six is to add perspective to the many, detailed tax provisions already introduced in Parts Two through Five by reviewing the human *process* of taxation. To accomplish this mission, we provide two chapters with these overriding objectives:

CHAPTER 18:
TAX PLANNING, PRACTICES, AND EDUCATION—to explain the economic role and educational background of tax advisers in the United States.

CHAPTER 19:
LEGISLATIVE BACKSTOPS—to explore typical government reactions to the more aggressive tax plans implemented by taxpayers.

Close the loopholes and you will not get a bunch of contented taxpayers; you will get a lot of dropouts from the rat race, and the whole economy will go to hell from sheer despair.

LARRY MARTZ, NEW YORK (1969)

TAX PRACTICE, PLANNING, AND EDUCATION

CHAPTER OBJECTIVES

In Chapter 18 you will become familiar with common career opportunities available in taxation and learn about the educational preparation common to those careers. You will also learn how tax advisers frequently help taxpayers control their tax costs while achieving their personal and business objectives.

LEARNING GOALS

After studying this chapter, you should be able to

1 Identify the more common career paths for individuals interested in tax-related employment;

2 Define tax planning;

3 Understand how most successful tax planning is achieved;

4 Describe the educational preparation common to professional tax advisers; and

5 Explain why many CPAs and attorneys really are not prepared to offer high quality tax services.

This chapter offers a brief perspective of what might lie ahead for those students who go on to make a living from a tax-related endeavour as well as for those who might someday engage an individual for professional assistance. While reading this chapter recall from Part One that the process of taxation redirects nearly 30% of the gross national product from the private to the public sector each year in the United States. An undertaking of such magnitude obviously involves many individuals in many different capacities. The breadth of opportunities available to those who find taxes interesting is truly exceptional. We hope that at least a few of the students who study this textbook will elect to pursue the next step toward a challenging tax career.

The chapter is divided into three major parts. The first part briefly explains the career options available to individuals who are interested in working in the tax field. The second part discusses in greater detail the work done by some of the most technically sophisticated tax advisers in the area of tax planning. The third part examines the educational alternatives available to and generally pursued by those who devote their lives to tax concerns in one way or another.

> **Goal #1**
> Identify career paths in tax-related employment.

TAX PRACTICE

> **Tax practice** is a term frequently used to describe the professional services rendered by accountants, lawyers, and others who devote a significant part of their lives to making our tax system work.

Tax Practice can be defined broadly to include all of the work done by those individuals who devote a significant part of their lives to making our tax system work. Such a broad definition would include people who might otherwise describe themselves as accountants, bureaucrats, computer programmers, employees, judges, lawyers, politicians, and researchers, among other occupations. To make our task more manageable, we will confine most of our remarks in this chapter to the accountants and lawyers who specialize in tax issues while working in public practice, for private industry, or with the government.

PUBLIC PRACTICE

> **Tax compliance work** is the work done by paid tax-return preparers to help others satisfy their legal tax obligaitons.

Approximately 350,000 people sign their names each year as paid preparers of tax returns filed by other taxpayers. This aspect of tax practice is generally described as **tax compliance work**; that is, work done by paid preparers to help other taxpayers satisfy their legal obligation in a self-assessment tax system. The fact that more than 50% of all taxpayers deem it either necessary or desirable to pay someone else to help them comply with the income tax laws is vivid testimony to the complexity most people encounter in preparing and filing a complete and correct income tax return.

Businesses offering tax compliance services vary from self-employed individuals, to nationally franchised operations, to international accounting and law firms. The smallest of these businesses typically offer no services beyond the preparation and filing of returns. The larger firms offer additional assistance in the resolution of administrative disputes between taxpayers and the IRS and in tax planning. In the largest firms most of the tax-related revenues derive from tax planning work, a topic described in greater detail later in this chapter and illustrated in the next chapter.

In the six largest U.S. accounting firms tax endeavors typically generate from 20% to 25% of total revenues. In small CPA firms tax engagements frequently account for 50% or more of the firm's aggregate revenues. We are unaware of comparable figures for law firms. In general, however, we suspect that the national averages would be lower in law than in accounting firms because most law firms tend to do relatively less tax compliance work than do accounting firms.

The degree of specialization in both accounting and law firms tends to increase significantly with the size of the firm. In the smaller firms most tax advisers can be aptly described as general practitioners; that is, they give advice on the widest possible spectrum of tax matters. In the largest firms, on the other hand, most individuals tend to specialize in one or two limited areas of practice. Specialties in **Subchapter C** (corporation–shareholder transactions), **Subchapter K** (partnership–partner transactions), estate and gift taxes, ERISA (pension and profit-sharing plans, etc.), **Subchapter N** (multi-national issues), special industries (such as oil and gas, banking, insurance), and multistate taxation, among others, are commonplace.

The fees charged by tax advisers vary from approximately $30 to $300 or more per hour. The fees charged by specialists tend to exceed those of generalists. Annual earnings of a tax practitioner engaged in public practice vary from as little as $20,000 per year for a new recruit to as much as $500,000 per year for senior partners in the largest law and accounting firms. Litigation specialists, working on a commission basis, sometimes earn even larger incomes through favorable settlements in large-dollar cases.

PRIVATE INDUSTRY

Virtually all the Fortune 500 corporations plus many smaller businesses employ their own (in-house) tax advisers. These businesses also engage additional external tax advisers for assistance on special problems from time to time. The in-house employees may work in a separate tax department or be part of the legal or the controller's staff. The tax department of a smaller business may involve only two or three people; in large corporations it may involve 100 or more tax professionals plus many clerical personnel. In most instances private industry hires tax personnel that have prior practical experience in either public practice or government. Salaries generally range from $30,000 to $300,000 per year.

Persons engaged in tax practice for large corporations frequently develop industry specializations. They also spend a good deal of time complying with property, sales and use, ad valorem, and other state and local taxes, as well as complying with the federal payroll and excise taxes—compliance areas that receive relatively less attention in public practice. The surreal complexity of a large corporation's compliance problems is difficult for most people to imagine. To illustrate, it has been reported that one single income tax calculation required 16 *hours* of computer time for Dow Chemical to resolve. Eventually that one computation became part of a corporate tax return that filled nearly 7,000 pages.[1]

THE GOVERNMENT

The largest single employer of tax professionals is the federal government, specifically the Treasury Department. The IRS alone, which is part of Treasury, employs some 15,000 to 20,000 accountants and lawyers. Many others are employed in such diverse agencies as the Tax Court, the Justice Department, the Office of Tax Policy (in Treasury), various congressional committees, the Commerce Department, and the Office of Management and Budget, to name but a few. In the more policy-oriented government agencies a larger number of tax professionals will have a strong academic background in economics rather than (or in addition to) accounting or law.

> **Subchapter C** is that portion of the Code that stipulates the tax consequences of transactions between a corporation and its own shareholders in their role as shareholders.
>
> **Subchapter K** is that portion of the Code that stipulates the tax consequences of transactions between a partnership and its own partners in their role as partners.
>
> **Subchapter N** is that portion of the Code that stipulates the tax consequences of earning income in more than one country.

---

1 See Robert Norton, "The Corporate Tax Mess," *U.S. News and World Report*, September 26, 1988, pp. 44–45.

The average salaries of employees in the government sector are significantly less than those earned by individuals in public practice and private industry. The range is from about $20,000 to $80,000 per year. In part because of lower salaries, employee turnover tends to be high. The senior policy positions, which are often held by political appointees, are typically vacated every two to five years.

State and local governments also employ a number of tax professionals in various compliance roles. In many instances the salaries paid for these positions are even less than those paid by the federal government for comparable work. Many college professors in both business and law schools are also state employees. For those who teach the income tax courses there are ample opportunities to do consulting and writing, which can substantially supplement base salaries generally in the $30,000 to $100,000 range.

In summary, there are many opportunities for accountants and lawyers to specialize in tax work in both the private and public sectors. Much of this work can be described as compliance oriented. The most challenging assignments in the private sector, however, usually involve tax planning.

———— TAX PLANNING

Goal #2
Define tax planning.

Tax planning is the term used to describe the efforts made to investigate, before taking action, the tax cost associated with various alternatives and the selection and implementation of those alternatives which can achieve the taxpayer's objectives at the minimal cost.

Goal #3
Understand how tax planning is done.

Taxes are but one of many economic costs incurred by living in general and carrying on a business in particular. The intelligent individual as well as the prudent business manager will soon learn to contain tax costs in a manner that is consistent with the achievement of personal and business objectives. The objective of containing tax costs involves more than mere tax minimization. Both suicide and the termination of a viable business venture will unquestionably minimize future tax costs. Those two actions, however, are totally inconsistent with the enjoyment of life and the maximization of profits. This self-evident observation simply emphasizes the fact that efforts made to control tax costs cannot be made independent of other considerations.

Tax planning is the term used to describe the intellectual efforts made to investigate, *before taking action*, the tax cost associated with each of several alternative methods of achieving various personal and business objectives, and the selection and implementation of those alternatives that achieve the desired objectives at minimal tax cost. Tax planning typically requires the involvement and cooperation of both the taxpayer and the tax adviser. The taxpayer best understands the personal and business objectives to be achieved. The tax adviser best understands the tax consequences associated with the different ways of achieving stated objectives.

A final tax liability is a function of three variables—the law, the facts, and an administrative (and sometimes judicial) process. Most of this textbook is an explication of the law; a few pages describe the administrative and judicial processes that operationalize the written rules or law. Except for a few problem assignments, we have given scant attention to the critical role of facts. In this part of Chapter 18, we demonstrate how important the facts are to the determination of any tax liability. In the next chapter we will see how overly zealous and massively successful tax planning may sometimes leads to increased complexity in the law.

Observe that facts are the one variable that almost everyone can do something about. If you are not satisfied with either the law or the administrative and judicial processes, there is relatively little that you can do (unless, of course, you are a veritable mogul in American society).[2] The facts, however, can generally be modified by

---

2 In other words, only very few people have enough money and clout to get a tax law changed by Congress in such a way that it will benefit only themselves. The administrative and judicial processes are similarly

anyone. If you are wise enough to understand when and how to modify them, you may very well reduce your tax liability significantly. The most highly qualified professional tax experts earn most of their lucrative fees by giving advice on alternative ways of arranging facts! In other words, most professional tax planning is little more than the prearrangement of facts in the most tax-favored way.

AVOIDANCE VERSUS EVASION

Successful tax planning, or **tax avoidance**, must be clearly distinguished from **tax evasion.** In tax jargon, the latter term refers to the *illegal* reduction of a tax liability, whereas the former terms encompasses only *legal* means of achieving that same objective. For example, assume a taxpayer claims that he has ten dependent children when filing his federal income tax return even though he actually has only two such dependents. That misrepresentation of fact would constitute a simple form of tax evasion, and the guilty taxpayer would be subject to both criminal and monetary penalties. Backdating an important tax document would constitute an equally obvious form of tax evasion. Deceit, concealment, and misrepresentation are common elements in most illegal tax plans.

On the other hand, the careful investigation of alternatives and full disclosure are common elements in tax avoidance. For example, if a taxpayer can significantly reduce income tax liability by operating a business as a corporation rather than as a partnership or a sole proprietorship, there is, obviously, nothing illegal about making such a change in the facts. Perhaps the most celebrated statement made in defense of tax planning came from the pen of Judge Learned Hand in the following dissenting opinion from *Commissioner* v. *Newman*:

> Over and over again courts have said that there is nothing sinister in so arranging one's affairs as to keep taxes as low as possible. Everybody does so, rich or poor, and all do right, for nobody owes any public duty to pay more than the law demands: taxes are enforced exactions, not voluntary contributions. To demand more in the name of morals is mere cant.[3]

Although this quotation is from a dissenting opinion and, therefore, of no value as legal precedent, it is widely quoted in support of tax planning. Other judges have said essentially the same thing in majority opinions, but their choice of words is less striking.

Unfortunately, the line between avoidance and evasion is not always as clear as the earlier example suggests. Some tax plans so distort the apparent truth that they approach the level of evasion. In this chapter, we are not primarily concerned with making fine-line distinctions. Nevertheless, we encourage students to develop a natural suspicion of anything that sounds too good to be true in tax planning.

THE CRITICAL VARIABLES

There are several ways to approach tax planning systematically. One possibility is to reexamine the general formula used to determine the income tax liability of any taxable entity:

Tax avoidance is the term used to describe wholly legal means of controlling tax costs.

Tax evasion is the term used to describe illegal means of reducing taxes.

(continued from page 650) resistant to personal intervention. Nevertheless, some few people do get the law changed for their personal benefit. In the 1986 Act these unusual provisions benefitted some 650 taxpayers to the tune of $10 billion. For further details, see a series of articles by Donald L. Bartlett and James B. Steele that appeared in *The Philadelphia Inquirer* from April 10 to April 16, 1988.

3 159 F.2d 848 (CCA-2, 1947).

Line Number		Item
1		Income broadly conceived
2	–	Exclusions
3	=	Gross income
4	–	Deductions
5	=	Taxable income
6	x	Applicable tax rate(s)
7	=	Gross tax payable
8	–	Tax credits (and prepayments)
9	=	Net tax payable

Because the ultimate objective of business tax planning is the minimization of the net tax payable, consistent with the achievement of other more general objectives, the rules of simple arithmetic suggest that tax planning must necessarily involve the maximization of tax credits, the minimization of the applicable tax rate(s), and the maximization of deductions and exclusions. In other words, the items on all even-numbered lines in the above formula constitute the critical variables in tax planning. In the next few pages, we consider some fundamental tax-planning ideas implicit in the provisions already introduced in earlier chapters. In some instances, we also consider provisions that have been enacted to preclude the apparent tax plan from being successful. More complex plans—as well as more complex legislative prohibitions—are considered in Chapter 19.

Maximizing Exclusions

Simple illustrations of maximizing exclusions can be readily constructed.

EXAMPLE 18-1

Assume that taxpayer Lucky is a head of household who reports a $200,000 taxable income including $100,000 from interest on bank deposits. If Lucky were to switch his bank deposits to state government bonds the interest could be excluded from taxable income and Lucky's net tax payable would decrease from about $56,038 per year to about $25,038 (that is, to the tax for a head of household reporting $100,000 taxable income). This plan would save Lucky about $31,000 per year in explicit taxes. That fact alone does not, however, support a conclusion that switching investments from bank deposits to state government bonds is necessarily wise.

To determine the wisdom of proposing such a tax plan for Lucky, we must examine the after-tax rate of return on the investment. Let us keep the arithmetic as simple as possible by assuming that Lucky is earning an 8% rate of return on his original investment in bank deposits. To receive a $100,000 annual interest income, Lucky must have $1,250,000 invested ($100,000 ÷ .08 = $1,250,000). If the interest rate on state government bonds is only 6%, Lucky's annual, interest income would drop from $100,000 per year to $75,000 per year, other things being equal. However, the sum of the $31,000 tax savings plus the $75,000 annual interest exceeds the original return by $6,000 per year. Thus, with the assumed interest rates of 8% and 6%, and with Lucky's marginal tax bracket, this tax plan is a favorable plan, assuming no change in the risk of the two investments. Further study of this example explains why tax-exempt securities are especially favorable investments to taxpayers in the highest marginal tax brackets, whereas the same securities are of little or no interest to taxpayers in the low marginal tax brackets. The after-tax rate of return on tax-exempt securities depends directly on the taxpayer's marginal tax bracket.

A more generalized tax plan might be based on exclusions that can be thought of as wage and salary supplements. To illustrate these opportunities briefly, let us consider the case of taxpayer Black, who has operated a small-town mortuary out of his home as a sole proprietorship for many years. Black has always purchased life, health, and accident insurance from his own after-tax funds; he has always provided his own meals and lodging from the same source; and he has never had any death benefits. What would keep Black from forming a corporation (in which he and his family own the entire equity interest) and transferring all (or most) of his assets to the new corporation, which would then hire Black as its principal employee? Couldn't the new corporation provide its employees (including Black) with certain supplemental benefits and get a tax deduction for the cost of the (group-term) life insurance premiums, the health and accident insurance premiums, the casualty insurance, utilities, and upkeep on the home? If Black can exclude the receipt of those benefits from his own gross income (under the conditions stipulated in the statutory authorities noted in Part Three), and if Black's corporation can deduct the cost of those benefits in the calculation of its own taxable income, won't Black have implemented a successful tax plan that involves both the maximization of exclusions (for himself) and the maximization of deductions (via his new corporate entity)?

Under the proper circumstances, the IRS would have a difficult, if not impossible, task in challenging such a tax plan. Although many aspects of this proposal could be subject to attack, if the taxpayer were sufficiently careful in attention to detail—that is, if Black's tax advisor carefully planned, executed, and documented each step in this proposal—there is no fundamental reason why the plan could not succeed. The fringe benefits for highly paid employees must pass muster as nondiscriminatory. Otherwise, the rules explained in Chapter 9 will cause them to be income to the employee. Details of how such a plan might work are beyond our scope here.

Maximizing Deductions

To illustrate how tax planning can be achieved through the maximization of deductions, consider another simplified example.

EXAMPLE 18-2

Suppose that Ionna Stoor is a very successful single businesswoman with an annual taxable income of $200,000. In addition, Stoor is the sole stockholder of the Stoor Corporation, which operates a small brewery. If Stoor were suddenly to inherit a large block of stock in other corporations, which paid her $100,000 in dividends per year, she would discover that Uncle Sam took 31% of her additional income by way of income taxes. Her annual taxable income would have increased from $200,000 to $300,000, and her annual tax liability would have increased from $57,654.50 to $88,654.50. In other words, after paying income taxes, Stoor would have only $69,000 of her $100,000 annual dividend income to reinvest in other property.

Continued

EXAMPLE 18-2 (Con't.)

With a little tax planning, Stoor could transfer her newly inherited stocks to her wholly owned corporation, the Stoor Corporation. As a corporation, the latter taxpayer would be entitled to a 70% dividends-received deduction (or 80% if Stoor owns more than 20% of the corporation). Thus, if the Stoor Corporation were to receive an additional $100,000 in dividends each year, it could deduct $70,000 of that amount and increase its taxable income by only $30,000. The corporation's federal income tax on $30,000 would amount to $10,200 (assuming a 34% marginal corporate tax rate). Thus, by giving the title to the stocks to a corporate entity, and thereby maximizing deductions, Stoor would have reduced the income tax on the $100,000 in annual dividends from $31,000 to $10,200; at the same time, she would have increased her reinvestment potential from $69,000 to $89,800 per year!

The preceding example is a dramatic illustration of how taxes can be saved by maximizing deductions. It is also a dramatic example of how immediate tax savings may be only a part of the critical story. That is, Stoor's stocks are now tied up in a corporate entity and she may encounter major tax costs if she ever tries to get them out of that corporation. Furthermore the Stoor Corporation might also now become subject to the personal holding company tax, a penalty tax not explained in this introductory text.

Many other, sometimes equally convoluted, tax-saving possibilities exist based on the same basic principle. In the discussion of maximizing exclusions, we briefly considered how an imaginary taxpayer, Black (the operator of a small-town mortuary), could decrease his tax liability through the use of such corporate fringe benefits as life, health, and accident insurance; meals and lodging; and certain death benefits. We pointed out that Black benefited from the exclusion provision of the Code because he did not have to report as gross income the value he received in the form of group-term life, health, and accident insurance; meals and lodging; and certain death benefits. Note, however, that the real tax benefits implicit in those examples depend not only on the fact that they can be excluded from the calculation of Black's personal taxable income, but also on the fact that the cost of those same benefits can be deducted as ordinary and necessary business expenses by Black's wholly owned corporation, which pays the bills. In summary, therefore, the tax savings implicit in those examples really stem from the maximization of both exclusions and deductions. Through the use of a corporate entity, Black may be able to convert what would otherwise largely have been nondeductible personal expenditures into tax-deductible expenses without creating any taxable income for himself (because of the statutory exclusion provisions).

Minimizing the Tax Rate

A third critical variable in tax planning is the applicable tax rate. As noted early in the text, the marginal tax rate is to business affairs what the law of gravity is to physics. Just as water seeks its lowest level (due to the laws of gravity), so also taxable income seeks its lowest marginal tax rate (due to tax planning). The tax-planning objective is achieved, of course, when the marginal tax rate is minimized. This principle can once again be readily illustrated through a simple example.

EXAMPLE 18-3

Suppose that Mr. and Mrs. Isadore Safe, a highly successful locksmith and his wife, report an annual taxable income of $200,000. If Mrs. Safe suddenly inherited $100,000 cash from her recently deceased uncle, Willis More, she might be tempted to deposit the inheritance in a bank savings account and to use the interest to finance the education of her two children. If Mrs. Safe received 7.5% interest on her savings account, she would discover that the additional $7,500 in interest each year increased the annual income tax liability payable by her and Mr. Safe by $2,325. In other words, only $5,175 would be left after taxes to apply toward the children's education. With a little planning, Mrs. Safe might give the $100,000 that she inherited equally to her two children. Each of the Safe children would now receive $3,750 per year in interest. If we assume that the children received no other income and that they were each 14 years of age or older, they would each pay an income tax of $472.50. In this way, the aggregate tax liability on the $7,500 of interest each year would have been reduced from $2,325 to $945, and the amount left toward the children's education would have increased from $5,175 to $6,555 per year.

The tax savings implicit in this simple example is attributable to the combined effect of minimizing the tax rate and maximizing deductions. Mr. and Mrs. Isadore Safe were in a 31% marginal tax bracket; their children were in a 15% marginal tax bracket. Transferring the $7,500 annual interest income from their higher marginal tax bracket to the children's lower marginal tax bracket created a tax savings. The aggregate tax savings was further increased because the children could claim an additional $600 standard deduction on their own tax returns. (As discussed in earlier chapters, the Code largely eliminates these tax savings if the child is under 14 years old.)

Taxpayers such as the Safes can also use trusts effectively to lower rates on unearned income. As explained in Chapter 7, the marginal rate for trusts is 15% on the first $5,000 of taxable income. Trusts may be especially useful where the beneficiary is under 14, in which case the child's net unearned income would otherwise be subject to the parents' highest marginal rates. Note that, in this case, to retain the benefit of the 15% marginal rate, the trust cannot distribute very much income to a beneficiary under age 14.

A corporate entity that does not recognize too much taxable income and that pays no dividends may also be a useful vehicle in minimizing tax rates so long as the corporate marginal rate is lower than that of the shareholder. If one individual owns the entire equity interest in a corporation, that corporation is, obviously, a mere alter ego of the sole stockholder. Nevertheless, the IRS and the courts recognize the existence of a separate (corporate) taxpayer as long as it has a legitimate business purpose.

Maximizing Credits

Relative to the three other variables already discussed, the opportunity to save taxes through the maximization of credits is more limited for the average taxpayer. Nevertheless, a taxpayer can help maximize the value of available credits. For example, a taxpayer weighing alternative investment opportunities must consider tax credits carefully before making final decisions. An investment in the rehabilitation of a certified historic structure can give rise to a tax credit of as much as 20% of the amount expended in the rehabilitation, whereas the construction of a new building ordinarily provides no investment credit. Similarly, the purchase of a robot or other piece of industrial equipment generally does not give rise to any credit, but the employment of individuals who meet specified criteria may yield a credit. Whether or not (1) a remodeled old building is a good substitute for a new one, or (2) an employee can replace an industrial robot are difficult and separate questions. Nevertheless, neither decision can be made without giving adequate attention to tax credits.

THE TIMING OF INCOME AND DEDUCTIONS

Observe that our income tax rates start over with each new tax year. Because very few taxpayers have a constant level of taxable income in each year, taxpayers tend to have high-tax years and low-tax years. As explained earlier, the tax value of a deduction is directly dependent on the marginal tax bracket of the party reporting it. Obviously, taxpayers tend to recognize losses and other deductions in high-tax years and tend to defer the recognition of taxable income to low-tax years.

Taxpayers entitled to use the cash method of accounting have the greatest opportunity for shifting income and deductions between years. For example, an attorney faced with a higher marginal rate this year might neglect to send out bills for work done late in the year. In addition, this attorney can pay all deductible expenses late in December. Note that this deferral of income will work only if the rules for constructive receipts are observed. Note also that the taxpayer must consider the time value of money. The financial cost of deferral may be greater than the tax benefits. Under the relatively flat rate schedules in effect now, the benefits of shifting taxable income between years are definitely reduced from years before 1987.

The use of proper tax accounting methods (other than basic cash or accrual methods) can sometimes defer income and accelerate deductions. On the income side, use of the installment method defers recognition of income until cash is collected. During a period of inflation, use of LIFO (last-in, first-out) inventory costing, which is permitted for tax purposes if used for book purposes, can result in a substantial deferral of income. Tax-free exchanges of property can give the same result.

To illustrate the advantages gained from astute timing of income and deductions, consider the case of the wage earner whose itemized deductions nearly always equal the standard deduction. That taxpayer would likely conclude that no tax planning can help. Actually, such a taxpayer does have one albeit minor chance at playing the tax game. Because he or she can itemize deductions in any year and can report taxable income on a cash basis of accounting, he or she can benefit by carefully itemizing deductible expenditures and keeping good records. The basic idea involves itemizing deductions every other year. In years when deductions do not exceed the standard deduction, the taxpayer should defer all tax-deductions to the maximum extent possible. For example, in those years, the taxpayer should

1. Make minimal charitable contributions

2. Defer tax deductible interest payments

3. Defer paying doctor and dentist bills

4. Avoid making property tax payments

In years when deductions exceed the standard deduction, the taxpayer should do just the opposite. This tax plan can be illustrated easily, as in the following diagram. In this way, the taxpayer's aggregate deductions may be greater and tax liability smaller, over several years.

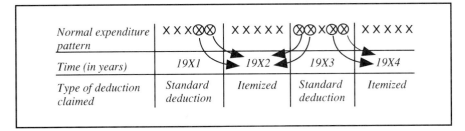

The above illustrations are relatively simple examples of the kinds of changes a tax adviser in public practice might recommend to a client interested in minimizing the tax liability associated with the circumstances depicted in each example. Every tax plan is situation specific. In other words, every tax plan begins with a unique set of facts for a specific taxpayer. The tax adviser's challenge starts with a discovery of facts. This means that successful tax planning cannot occur unless and until the tax adviser knows essentially everything that can be known about a taxpayer's unique circumstances. After the adviser has discovered and assimilated the taxpayer's unique circumstances, he or she must then identify possible alternatives that can achieve the taxpayer's ultimate objectives. After identifying alternatives, the adviser determines the tax costs associated with each viable option. Finally, the adviser recommends to the client a tax-preferred way of achieving a desired economic or personal objective. The taxpayer may accept or reject the recommended alternative, considering both personal and business constraints. In summary, a tax adviser only recommends; the taxpayer decides.

The greatest challenge of the tax adviser is, probably, the creative genius associated with the identification of alternative ways of achieving a client's business and personal objectives. The next greatest challenge may well be the ability to explain each tax alternative in layman's language. This ability to explain complex tax laws in nontechnical terms is no trivial assignment for even the most accomplished adviser. Successful tax planning clearly requires both creative and explanatory skills. How is a beginner expected to acquire those two diverse skills? Education plays an important role.

TAX EDUCATION

Prior to 1960 virtually all tax advisers acquired whatever technical skills they possessed from practical experience. This was because no U.S. institution of higher learning offered any academic degree specifically intended to develop or improve the knowledge and skills required of a successful tax adviser. Because tax acumen was developed on the job, most early tax advisers had graduated from either a law school or an accounting program in a business school, not because of the academic program but because professional lawyers and accountants were frequently called on by taxpayers to help them resolve their complex tax questions.

In the late 1950s, New York University broke new academic ground by offering the first master of law (LL.M.) degree with a concentration in taxation. Their advanced program of specialized tax studies was soon replicated in several other law schools

> **Goal #4**
> Describe educational preparation for tax professionals.

and, eventually, in a rapidly expanding number of graduate business schools with concentrations in accounting.[4]

Today, therefore, a growing number of tax professionals complete at least one advanced degree that offers a concentration in taxation before they undertake their first professional tax assignment. This national trend notwithstanding, many individuals continue to acquire their tax education through on-the-job training largely because the demand for tax advisers continues to far exceed the supply of graduates from tax-specialized academic programs.

The fact that both lawyers and CPAs are more or less automatically authorized to practice before the IRS in tax matters only serves to confuse the public on the issue of professional tax qualifications. In other words, even though virtually all attorneys and CPAs holding a permit to practice their respective professions are technically or legally able to represent taxpayers in disputes with the IRS, a majority of these individuals are *not* real tax experts in any meaningful sense of the term. That distinction should be reserved for the 15% to 20% of all lawyers and accountants who, by education and experience, have acquired a genuine mastery of the special skills required of a capable tax adviser.

To restate the education issue, qualified tax advisers can still acquire their technical tax education in either of two basic ways. One might be described as exclusively experienced-based; the other, as partially education-based. The former option includes at least the three education/career paths depicted in Figure 18-1. The figure suggests that it is still possible for individuals to become tax experts largely by experience. That experience could come through sufficient and appropriate work with a CPA firm, a law firm, or the IRS.

Alternatively, a growing number of relatively younger tax professionals now acquire at least some of their special tax expertise in one of two education paths depicted in Figure 18-2. This figure emphasizes the fact that a growing number of law

Goal #5
Understand expert qualifications.

FIGURE 18-1
Education by Experience

	Track I	Track II	Track III
Undergraduate major	Accounting	Any	Accounting
Graduate/professional degree	None	Law	None
Tax (work) experience	CPA firm	Law firm	IRS

FIGURE 18-2
Tax Education by Degree

	Track IV	Track V
Undergraduate degree	Any	Accounting
Professional degree	Law	None
Graduate degree	LL.M./Tax	MBA/Tax*

*The specific graduate tax degrees offered in business schools vary greatly among institutions.

4 The *1991 Ernst & Young Guide to Graduate Tax Education*, compiled by Professors Barry C. Broden and Myron S. Lubell, identifies 108 such programs in the United States.

schools and graduate schools of business now offer specialized or graduate masters degrees that permit students to concentrate their studies in the area of taxation. Although graduates of those programs still have a lot to learn through experience, their formal education has taken them well beyond the level of tax specialization held by most lawyers and accountants engaged in general practice.

Although the formal educational opportunities for future tax professionals has improved substantially during the past 20 to 30 years, there is room for additional improvement. Tax practice is an interesting blend of at least four traditionally distinct and unrelated academic disciplines: law, accounting, economics, and government. The significant overlap can be portrayed in a Venn diagram like that of Figure 18-3. That figure emphasizes the fact that a person educated to understand the totality of many tax issues needs to know some part (but not all) of four traditionally separate academic disciplines. A brief explanation of Figure 18-3 follows:

1. Taxes are ultimately based on statutory laws, modified by administrative and judicial interpretations, following traditional legal conventions. Ergo, law.

2. Taxes, especially income taxes, rely heavily on traditional accounting measures, records, and conventions for implementations. Ergo, accounting.

3. Taxes have both macro and micro economic consequences that magnify their significance far beyond the raising of government revenues. Ergo, economics.

4. Taxes are conceived and born in a political milieu that for the uninitiated often confuses more than it clarifies. Ergo, government.

Because of these fundamental facts, no one can truly appreciate any tax issue in its totality without a reasonable comprehension of each of the four apparently separate academic dimensions of the tax problem.

The authors of this text have tried to introduce these four separate dimensions of the income tax. For those who continue their formal study of taxes beyond the confines of this text, a more thorough introduction to legal research methods is essential. This introduction can be obtained in either a law school or a graduate tax program in a business school. Although further investigation of both the economic and political

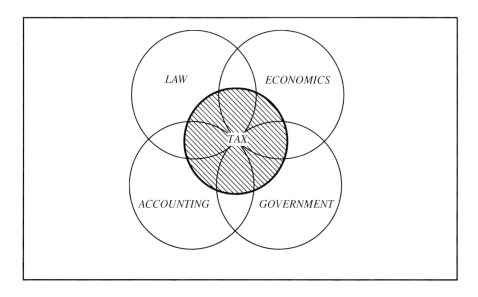

FIGURE 18-3

Tax in the Traditional Academic Disciplines of Law, Economics, Accounting, and Government

aspects of tax issues is highly recommended, those concerns are *not* generally required by the masters degree programs with tax specializations currently offered by schools of businesses or law. In short, at least in the immediate future, would-be tax advisers cannot rely on academic degree requirements to provide an ideal course of study for a lifetime tax pursuit. With self-discipline, however, such a program of study can be designed by the ingenious student attracted to this labor of golden opportunity.

———— KEY POINTS TO REMEMBER

✓ There are numerous, exciting careers available to individuals interested in the process of taxation.

✓ Tax planning should be done *before* a taxpayer begins to implement a business decision or a business plan.

✓ Most successful tax plans involve little more than a rearrangement of the method by which personal and business objectives are to be achieved.

✓ Avoiding taxes is entirely legal; evading them is illegal.

✓ Paying the lowest possible tax bill is, by itself, not good tax planning.

✓ Successful tax planning involves a high degree of cooperation between the taxpayer and the tax adviser.

✓ Special education in taxation typically involves either a masters degree in business, accounting, or law.

✓ A thorough understanding of taxation involves some in-depth study in accounting, law, economics, and government (or politics).

✓ Not every CPA and every attorney is a fully qualified tax adviser even though they may automatically be permitted to practice before the IRS.

———— RECALL PROBLEMS

#1 1. Approximately what percent of gross revenues is derived from tax-related services in

    a. The typical Big-Six accounting firm?

    b. The typical small CPA firm?

#1 2. Approximately what percent of the roughly 110 million federal income tax returns filed by individual taxpayers in 1991 will be prepared by someone other than the taxpayer? What term is commonly used to describe this work done by paid tax-return preparers?

#2 3. Define tax planning and distinguish tax planning work from tax compliance work.

#2 4. Identify the three basic variables that determine any taxpayer's federal income tax liability for a year and specify the one variable that is most commonly involved in successful tax planning.

#2 5. Explain why the minimization of taxes, by itself, is not the ultimate goal of tax planning.

6. Who is primarily responsible for tax planning: the tax adviser or the taxpayer? Explain briefly.

7. Mr. I. M. Rich earned the following income during 19X1:

Operating income from sole proprietorship (Drag Cleaners)	$56,000
Dividends from various domestic corporate stocks (jointly owned by Mr. and Mrs. Rich)	20,200
Interest on state bonds (tax exempt)	10,000
Total income for 19X1	$86,200

Assuming that Mr. Rich is married, has one dependent child, is 45 and of good vision, does not itemize deductions, and files a joint return with his wife (who is 43 and also of good vision), determine Rich's

a. Taxable income.

b. Gross tax liability for 19X1. (Use current rates.)

c. Amount available for reinvestment in Drag Cleaners if the Riches spent $50,000 for personal consumption in 19X1.

Could the Riches reduce their income tax to provide themselves with additional capital for reinvestment in the Drag Cleaners chain? Specifically, could they gain any tax advantages by incorporating the business? Answer the above questions by answering the questions below:

d. If the Riches incorporate the business venture, should they transfer the state bonds to the new corporation? Explain.

e. If they incorporate, should they transfer the dividend-producing investments to the corporation?

Regardless of how you answered any of the questions above, *assume* that the Riches form a corporation and transfer all of their operating assets (those that comprise the chain of cleaners) and most of the corporate investments to this new corporation. The income result (assuming the same operating results as were reported in 19X1) would look something like this:

Corporation		Personal	
Operating income	$56,000	Operating income (all corporation)	$ 0
Less: Salary paid to Mr. Rich	46,000	Salary from corporation	46,000
Operating income after salary	$10,000	Tax-exempt interest on state government bonds	10,000
Dividends received	20,000	Total income	$56,000
Total income	$30,000		

(Note: The combined income, before income taxes, is exactly the same now as it was prior to incorporation in 19X1.) Assuming the above distribution of income and assets, determine the following:

    f. Corporation's taxable income.

    g. Corporation's tax liability.

    h. Personal taxable income. (Assume all facts as before in re dependents, joint return, and so on.)

    i. Personal tax liability.

    j. Total taxes paid (combined personal and corporate).

    k. Amount available for reinvestment in Drag Cleaners. (Assume again that the Riches spent $50,000 for personal consumption items.)

`#4`

8. Baker, Diane, and Jorge are just completing an undergraduate accounting degree program that included one three-semester-hour course in taxation. Because these three students found their tax course to be especially interesting, each is seriously considering a tax career. Personal constraints, however, may well determine their next step in achieving that goal. Baker is not willing to spend any more time or money on education. Diane is willing to spend no more than one or two additional years in school. Jorge is willing to remain on campus as long as it takes to get a really challenging tax job as quickly as possible.

    a. Given the personal constraints outlined above, describe the career path options available to each student.

    b. Which of these three students is most likely to spend

        (1) a longer period doing compliance-oriented work?

        (2) the least time doing compliance-oriented work?

    Explain your answers.

`#4`

9. Why is the formal education of tax advisers under 30 years of age likely to differ significantly from that of tax advisers over 50 years of age?

`#5`

10. The general public often assumes that any lawyer who has passed a state bar exam and is allowed to practice before certain courts, and any accountant who has passed the CPA exam and holds a permit to practice public accountancy in one or more states, is a well-qualified tax adviser.

    a. What fact accounts for this public perception?

    b. Is the public perception really accurate?

——— THOUGHT PROBLEMS

`#1`

1. Why do tax advisers in large public accounting firms tend to specialize more than those in smaller firms?

`#2`

2. Many specific business transactions, as well as business operations in general, are modified significantly by our federal income tax provisions. Demonstrate your understanding of this statement by answering the following questions:

    a. Detail three specific business transactions that would be susceptible to modification for tax reasons and explain how you think the tax provision would affect the transaction.

    b. Cite two recent, major changes in the U.S. tax laws, and explain how these changes modify (or will modify) American business behavior.

3. For years, the Italians did not impose a real property tax on buildings under construction. Discuss the effects of this rule. [#2]

4. For years, the French had a tax based on the number of windows a building had. Discuss the effects of using this tax base. Identify at least two major definitional problems that would likely arise were this tax to be imposed today. [#2]

5. Jesus Urias earns a taxable income of $500,000 each year. That income includes $100,000 from long-term bonds issued by the Ford Motor Company that pay 8% interest. Jesus is thinking seriously about selling the Ford bonds and reinvesting the proceeds in State of California bonds paying interest at 6.5%. Do you recommend that Jesus proceed with these plans? Explain your answer briefly. [#3]

6. The highest marginal tax rate paid by corporations prior to 1981 was 46% while the top marginal rate paid by individual taxpayers was 70%. Today the top, marginal, corporate rate is 34% (sometimes 39% because of the surcharge) whereas the top, marginal, (apparent) individual rate is 31%. Based solely on these rate changes would you anticipate that the number of C corporations, as opposed to S corporations, increased or decreased between 1981 and 1991? Explain briefly. [#3]

7. Wilhamena Delcar, a head of household, typically reports a taxable income of about $35,000 per year. This year, because of the $65,000 that she won on "Wheel of Fortune," Wilhamena will report a taxable income of nearly $100,000. Wilhamena is thinking seriously of making a charitable contribution of $10,000 to her church. If she makes this contribution, do you recommend that Wilhamena make the contribution this year or next year? Explain briefly assuming that Wilhamena itemizes deductions in most years because her home mortgage interest and property taxes typically exceed the standard deduction. [#3]

8. Chow Down, Inc., is a C corporation owned entirely by Lin Chow. *Before paying any salary to Lin*, Chow Down, Inc., earned a taxable income of $300,000 this year. Given this information would Lin be more inclined to set her own salary at $50,000 or at $200,000 for the year? Explain briefly and note a major problem that Lin might encounter if this involves increasing her salary from $100,000 last year to $200,000 this year and this change was made later in this year. [#3]

9. Assume that as part of your decision concerning the wisdom of attending graduate school, to further study taxation before getting your first tax job, you made a thorough study of the educational background of all tax partners in Big Six CPA firms in your city. This study proved that less than 10% of those partners hold an advanced degree with a concentration in tax subjects. Based on these findings can you safely conclude that going on to school makes little economic sense if your long-range goal is to become a tax partner in an international CPA firm? Explain briefly. [#4]

10. Assume that immediately after graduating from college you started a small, entrepreneurial business and engaged Joe Blow, a local CPA, to complete your annual income tax return. During each of these five years your return has never been audited and the IRS has never sent you a notice of deficiency. Your annual encounter with Joe Blow has always been a pleasant one and Joe's fees are very reasonable. Assuming that your business has grown significantly during the past five years, is it reasonable to conclude that you have been getting good tax service from Joe based on these facts? Explain your answer briefly. [#5]

CLASS PROJECTS

1. Identify the three, graduate, tax programs in accounting that are located nearest to you. In what major ways are these three programs alike or different? (Note: This assignment will be much easier if you read footnote 4 on page 657 before you undertake a solution.)

2. Investigate the organization chart of any three Fortune 500 corporations and determine where in each organization the tax department is located.

3. Make a brief investigation into the details of the personal holding company tax and explain how that tax might negate the tax plan suggested for Ioona Stoor and the Stoor Corporation in Example 18-2, page 653. (Note: Any of several sources available in your tax library are likely to include a brief description of this tax.)

4. Undertake a field study to determine the number of advanced degrees in taxation held by the tax practitioners in your locale. Stratify your results by age groups, as follows: (1) under 30; (2) 30–40; (3) 40–50; (4) over 50.

5. Determine from the *SOI* (Statistics of Income) *Bulletin* prepared by the IRS/Department of Treasury—a document that will likely be found in the government documents section of your college library. How many S corporations filed Form 1120-S in 1985 and in 1989, respectively? Suggest a likely explanation for the big difference in these two numbers.

Trying to control tax shelters is like stepping on Jello. It just squeezes out between your toes, and the mess is worse than when you began.[1]

UNIDENTIFIED CONGRESSIONAL AIDE (1983)

LEGISLATIVE BACKSTOPS

CHAPTER OBJECTIVES

In Chapter 19, you will learn about two provisions introduced to provide a backstop against excessive or abusive use of tax incentive provisions. These provisions are the alternative minimum tax and the passive activity loss rules.

LEARNING GOALS

After studying this chapter, you should be able to

1 Explain the circumstances leading up to enactment of minimum taxes;

2 Define tax preferences and describe examples of major alternative minimum tax preferences and adjustments;

3 Describe the concept of an alternative minimum tax;

4 Explain the process of calculating the alternative minimum tax;

5 Describe the reasons Congress enacted the passive activity loss limitations;

6 Explain the taxpayers and types of activities subject to the passive activity loss limitations; and

7 Explain the process by which the passive activity loss limitations are calculated.

---

1 Quoted in Edsall, "Efforts Fail to Control Tax Shelters," *Washington Post*, November 6, 1983, as cited by Michael Graetz in *Federal Income Taxation*, 2nd ed. (Westbury, NY: Foundation Press, 1988), pp. 986–87.

THE NECESSITY FOR BACKSTOP PROVISIONS

The Internal Revenue Code has been shaped by many forces, which we have discussed in earlier chapters. Initially, the law imposed a relatively straightforward tax on income measured by ability to pay. Over time it has been embellished by various provisions intended to affect economic decision making to accomplish social or economic goals. By imposing taxes on certain types of transactions, Congress introduces a disincentive to engage in those transactions. On the other hand, by exempting certain transactions from taxation or by imposing differential rates of tax, it encourages other activities. As you revisit many of the provisions presented in this book, you can often identify an economic or social rationale for the provision. As examples, the earned income credit addresses the social goal of distributing the tax burden according to ability to pay by offsetting the regressive burden of employment taxes; deductions for home mortgage interest and property taxes encourage the purchase of personal residences by reducing the cost of home ownership.

> **Backstop provisions** are enacted to prevent taxpayers from obtaining excessive reduction in tax liability through overuse or abuse of certain tax provisions.
>
> The **fisc** is the treasury of a country, kingdom, or state.

The purpose of this chapter is to explore a final significant category of provisions in the Internal Revenue Code: **backstop provisions** introduced to protect the **fisc** from excessive or abusive use of some tax incentive provisions. One textbook dubs these backstops examples of "Congressional finger crossing" because what Congress gives with one hand, it may take away with the other.[2] Backstops reflect congressional retaliation in the longstanding skirmish between the government on one side and taxpayers and their advisers on the other.

The government's objectives are straightforward. Congress attempts to craft tax law that optimizes the various objectives discussed earlier while adequately funding the budget. The IRS attempts to raise the most amount of money for the least cost while carrying out the intentions of Congress and ensuring the integrity of the tax system. On the other side of the skirmish, taxpayers have clear incentives to maximize their economic welfare by minimizing their tax liabilities. Tax advisers likewise have clear incentives to design tax minimization plans that accomplish a client's economic and personal objectives at the lowest possible legitimate tax cost because that enhances their reputations and increases their income.

> **Goal #1**
> Explain the circumstances leading up to enactment of minimum taxes.

A major goal of tax planning is to position a client's transactions and investment portfolio in such a way that maximizes tax benefits provided by Congress. However, a problem is presented for Congress when taxpayers utilize too many incentive provisions. Aggressive use of beneficial tax provisions can yield a taxable income that is much lower than economic income. This transformation from economic to taxable income occurs in various ways, as you have discovered in this textbook. For example, some income is not taxed at all (such as municipal bond interest), some income is tax-deferred (installment sales), and other income is taxed at preferential rates (capital gains). Furthermore, some deductions are allowed when there is no economic detriment or associated cash flow (depreciation in some cases), and deductions for favored activities (research and development) are allowed over a shorter time frame than that allowed for nonfavored ones. Although members of Congress intended for taxpayers to use these provisions, they have been disturbed and embarrassed by evidence that the distributional design of the tax system has been gutted by excessive use of beneficial tax provisions.

---

2 James J. Freeland, Stephen A. Lind, and Richard B. Stephens, *Fundamentals of Federal Income Taxation: Cases and Materials*, 7th ed., (Westbury, NY: Foundation Press, 1991), p. 488.

Congress has attempted to find ways of addressing this problem since the mid 1960s. The government launched its first backstop weapon, the minimum tax, in 1969. While this initial foray made some inroads in addressing the problem, taxpayers and their advisers proved nimble and dogged in their search for tax reduction ploys. For some, tax avoidance was transformed from the game prize to the game itself. Investment readily flowed into different activities, prompting amendments to the minimum tax provisions. In addition, by 1976, the game of reducing taxable income through investments that created artificial losses became so active, it provided the final impetus for a different type of backstop. The **at-risk rules** were enacted to eliminate tax benefits from losses for which taxpayers bore no real economic burden. Significant changes in both sets of rules (minimum taxes and at-risk rules) continued to be made every few years to counter taxpayer agility in shifting economic activities and to address abuses of the intent of the law. These changes were only fleetingly successful.

> The **at-risk rules** require that an investor can deduct losses from an investment only if there is a true economic burden or risk of loss.

The following statement made by Internal Revenue Commissioner Roscoe Egger in 1981 was specifically targeted at **tax shelters** but was equally applicable to the general problem of trying to stay one step ahead of the taxpayer. Egger analogized the tax shelter problems to Mickey Mouse's problems with mops in *The Sorcerer's Apprentice*. Mickey, in trying his wings as a sorcerer, created a mop to help him with his job of transferring water from a well to a large receptacle. The mop was an extremely effective tool in accomplishing the task; Mickey basked in his success. However, once the receptacle was filled, Mickey was unable to stop the mop. When Mickey tried to use force rather than sorcery to stop the mops, they merely multiplied, out of control.[3] Egger's analogy presents a graphic picture of the frustrations he felt in attempting to find solutions to perceived overuse and abuse of tax favored transactions and investments. In 1986, both the alternative minimum tax and the limitations on loss rules were radically changed as Congress threw up its hands in frustration and launched the tax equivalent of an atomic bomb in its battle to deal with overuse and abuse of tax-favored provisions. The rest of this chapter examines in more detail the current versions of the two broadest backstop provisions in the Code: the alternative minimum tax and the passive loss rules.

> **Tax shelters** are investments that generate deductions that are used to offset other sources of income to reduce current tax liability.

> **Goal #2**
> Define tax preferences and describe examples of major alternative minimum tax preferences and adjustments.

THE ALTERNATIVE MINIMUM TAX

What would your reaction be if you learned that 155 taxpayers with more than $600,000 in adjusted gross income paid no income tax for the previous year? After price-level adjustment to 1992 dollars, that is the announcement President Nixon's Secretary of the Treasury Joseph Barr made in 1969. As you might imagine, there was an overwhelming cry of outrage by the American public.

Congress is generally reluctant to repeal major provisions in the law that favor certain segments of our society. Noting this tendency, the tax specialists in the Treasury and on the staff of the Joint Committee on Taxation decided that a tactic other than direct repeal was needed to increase the tax burden of taxpayers who had managed to significantly reduce their tax liabilities by the perfectly legal approach of taking advantage of favorable provisions in the law. The tactic adopted was a new concept—a tax on **tax preferences**. Tax preferences are provisions in the law that treat certain transactions or investments preferentially. The initial concept of a minimum tax as a backstop to overuse of tax preferences was formally introduced in

> **Tax preferences** are provisions in the law that treat certain transactions or investments preferentially.

---

3 Address by Commissioner Egger, New Directions in Tax Shelters, *Daily Tax Report* BNA No. 210 at J-4 (Oct. 30, 1981), as cited by Michael Graetz in *Federal Income Taxation*, 2nd ed., (Westbury, NY: Foundation Press, 1988), p. 986.

1968 in the Johnson Administration's *Tax Reform Studies.* Public sentiment and bipartisan support lead to the first minimum tax in 1969. The objective of the minimum tax is that no taxpayer may reduce a substantial economic income to little or no taxable income by claiming normal exclusions, deductions, and credits without running afoul of the minimum tax provisions.

The form in which this objective has been accomplished has varied substantially since initial enactment. The first minimum tax applied both to individuals and corporations and was designed as an add-on tax. An **add-on minimum tax** imposes a levy in addition to the regular tax on the excess of certain tax preferences over an exemption amount. For example, the first minimum tax was a 10% tax on tax preferences over the sum of $30,000. *This tax was added on to the regular tax paid.*

This version remained in effect with little change until 1976. At that time an alternative minimum tax was considered as a replacement for the add-on tax. An **alternative minimum tax** is a tax calculation on a tax base that is different from, and an alternative to, the regular tax base. The larger of the two calculations is the amount of tax due. Ultimately, although heavily discussed as a reform measure, the alternative minimum tax was not initiated in 1976. The listing below highlights changes in the form and scope of the minimum tax from 1976 to 1982. In each of these years, the effect of the changes was to subject a larger number of taxpayers to the minimum tax.

> An **add-on minimum tax** imposes a levy in addition to the regular tax on the excess of specified tax preferences over an exemption amount.
>
> An **alternative minimum tax** is a tax calculation on a different tax base as an alternative to the regular tax base.

1976   List of tax preferences extended. The most significant addition to the list of tax preferences was certain itemized deductions.

Increased the tax rate for the add-on tax.

1978   The alternative minimum tax was initiated in addition to the add-on minimum tax.

Preferences for capital gains and itemized deductions were removed from the add-on tax calculation and subjected to the alternative minimum tax.

1982   Add-on tax eliminated for individuals.

Alternative minimum tax base expanded to include tax preferences previously subject to the add-on tax.

Corporations remained subject to an add-on minimum tax.

As momentum for further tax reform increased in the mid 1980s, attention was focused on corporations. The many discrepancies between income measurements as reported for financial accounting purposes and those reported for federal income tax purposes eventually created an interesting policy problem for Congress and the Administration. Various tax lobby groups, such as the Citizens for Tax Justice, attracted a great deal of media attention by pointing out on or about April 15 each year that numerous large corporations paid little or no federal income tax to the IRS even though they reported earning a substantial amount of income to the Securities and Exchange Commission (SEC) and to their shareholders for those same years. These lobby groups, with the aid of the mass media, soon convinced the general public of two so-called facts: (1) that large corporations often paid less federal income tax than did elderly widows, and (2) that the reason for this deplorable state of affairs was attributable to a tax Code riddled with deliberate loopholes for large business interests. To some degree, of course, there was an element of truth in both conclusions. The real facts, however, are vastly more complex and less clear than the simple conclusions seized on by the voting masses and the media. Unfortunately the true story is far too lengthy to investigate here. Suffice it to note that public unrest became a major factor in the design of the Tax Act passed in 1986. Among the specific provisions primarily concerned with this disparity-in-income phenomenon are Sections 55 through 59, the portion of the Code that now imposes an alternative minimum tax (AMT) on certain taxpayers who otherwise would pay little or no regular income tax for one reason or another. It is appropriate to note at least two important conclusions at this early juncture. First, the AMT effectively imposes a second and wholly separate set of accounting records on all but the smallest business taxpayers. Second, the rules for 1987–89 effectively lead, for the first time in U.S. history, to a federal income tax liability based in part on income as measured by generally accepted accounting principles (GAAP) as determined by the SEC and the Financial Accounting Standards Boards (FASB). After 1989, the comparison is no longer between taxable income and financial accounting income. A new measure of income, labeled **adjusted current earnings (ACE)** was devised by Congress as the appropriate measure of a corporation's economic income.

Adjusted current earnings (ACE) is a measure of income used for the calculation of corporate alternative minimum tax.

OVERVIEW OF THE AMT

The alternative minimum tax is exactly what the words suggest; that is, (1) it is an *alternative* to the federal income tax computed in the regular or normal way *and* (2) it is the *minimum* federal income tax that any taxpayer can pay for a year. Hence, if the AMT is larger than the regular tax, the AMT is the amount that must be paid; but if the regular tax is larger than the AMT, the AMT is ignored. The computations that every taxpayer must make in order to determine the AMT payable require, for all practical purposes, a set of accounting records separate and distinct from both the records that must be maintained for regular federal income tax purposes and those required for financial reporting purposes. The added cost of this complexity is substantial. However, the AMT was the technique selected by Congress to put an end to frequent news reports that some of the largest corporations and some of the wealthiest citizens in America had legally paid less in U.S. federal income taxes than did the legendary widow in Dubuque.

Goal #3
Describe the concept of an alternative minimum tax.

The rejuvenated AMT also is viewed as an important element in tax-revenue generation. Under prior law, relatively little tax revenue was generated by the minimum-tax provisions; in the years between 1987 and 1991, the AMT provided the federal treasury with over $30 billion.

BASIC COMPUTATION

Much to our chagrin, there are many terms of art in the statute relating to minimum taxes. We have been unable to find an effective way of avoiding these terms in discussing the calculation, so try to grasp the broad concepts in this discussion without getting too bogged down in the terminology. Section 55 uses the term "alternative minimum taxable income" (AMTI) to refer to the tax base for the AMT calculation. The starting point for the calculation is regular taxable income (TI) as defined in all the other chapters in this text. The basic computation of AMTI is summarized in Figure 19–1. As you can see in that figure, there are two categories of modifications of TI before reaching AMTI. The first modification is for adjustments and the second is for preferences. In addition to these modifications, certain losses are disallowed for AMT

Goal #4
Explain the process of calculating the alternative minimum tax.

FIGURE 19-1

Computation of
the AMT

Taxable income (TI)	\$XXXXX
Plus and/or minus net adjustments	XXXX*
Plus tax preferences	XXXX
Equals AMTI	\$XXXXX
Less exemption (if any)	(XXX)
Equals net AMTI	\$XXXXX
Times tax rate	x XX%[†]
Equals tentative minimum tax (TMT) before foreign tax credits	\$XXXXX
Less AMT credit for foreign taxes	(XXX)
Equals TMT	\$ XXXX
Less regular tax	(XXXX)
Equals AMT (if positive)[‡]	\$ XXXX

*Note that this net amount can be either positive or negative.

[†]The tax rate is 20% for corporations and 24% for other taxpayers.

[‡]Note that an AMT is payable only if TMT exceeds the regular tax. If the regular tax exceeds TMT, only the regular tax is payable. Note also that an AMT credit (discussed under credits) may be available in the latter case.

purposes. Many of the modifications in the minimum tax calculations are too technical for discussion here. However, some of the common and straightforward calculations are included in the next section as examples to help you understand the process.

After determining AMTI, there are a few more steps in the calculation. In recognition that the tax law was designed with the purpose of encouraging taxpayers to take actions that would allow the use of tax preferences and other beneficial provisions, an exemption (subject to a phase-out) eliminates a portion of AMTI from the tax calculation. After the allowable exemption is deducted to find net AMTI, this tax base is multiplied by the appropriate tax rate (lower than the maximum regular tax rate) to find the AMT before allowable credits. The foreign tax credits allowable for AMT are subtracted to find tentative minimum tax.

We are almost at the end of the calculation of the AMT. Let's pause a moment and take this opportunity to reflect on the purpose of the AMT. Recall that we described the AMTI as a tax base that serves as an *alternative* to the regular tax base. Further recall that the AMT is designed to be imposed only when the regular tax base has been seriously eroded by special incentive tax provisions. These factors make the next step you see in the calculation (the subtraction of the regular tax liability) logical. In other words, the final subtraction results in a minimum tax liability for the taxpayer *only* if the tax calculated on the AMT tax base exceeds the tax calculated on the regular tax base. As long as the regular tax base does not vary substantially from a measure of economic income (as measured by the AMT tax base), the taxpayer is deemed to have paid a reasonable amount of tax on his or her net income.

The next sections of this chapter explain the different factors in the calculation of AMT more fully.

ADJUSTMENTS AND PREFERENCES

The first step in the calculation of AMT is to modify TI by adjustments and preferences. As noted, many of these modifications are extremely technical. Further difficulty in mastering these provisions comes in remembering that different taxpayers are affected by various AMT provisions. Table 19-1 provides a list of most adjustments and preferences found in Secs. 56–58 and indicates the taxpayers to whom they apply. The following discussion covers only a sampling of these provisions to help you gain a basic understanding of the way the AMT seeks to redress abuses of tax benefits.

Required adjustments are found in Secs. 56 and 58. Adjustments for the AMT calculation include amounts that must be determined by alternative calculations or alternative accounting methods for AMT purposes. Perhaps the most common AMT adjustment under current law is depreciation (for property placed in service after December 31, 1986). The methods and lives allowable for AMT and regular tax purposes serve different purposes. For regular tax purposes, cost recovery on depreciable assets is accelerated to stimulate investment in capital assets. The AMT allowable depreciation is calculated based on longer lives and the straight-line method, in a rough attempt to remove the incentive component of the depreciation deduction. The procedure followed in making the adjustment for depreciation is to add regular depreciation back to TI and to substitute in its place AMT depreciation. Because differences in the amounts of depreciation taken are merely timing differences, you can see that it is possible for there to be both positive and negative adjustments to TI in the calculation of AMTI.

An extremely important and politically sensitive adjustment for corporate taxpayers, the ACE (or Adjusted Current Earnings) adjustment, was introduced in the 1986 Act. The details of this adjustment have varied since its enactment, but the concept has been constant. The ACE adjustment was Congress's solution to the problem described in the following example.

EXAMPLE 19-1

Dynamic Duo Corporation (DDC) is in an industry in which the possible accounting methods for regular tax purposes allow vastly different patterns of income recognition than those reported for financial accounting purposes. In addition, DDC has large amounts of tax-exempt interest income. For the four years leading up to 1986, DDC reported the following amounts of net income to the IRS for tax purposes and to its shareholders for financial accounting purposes.

	Tax	Financial
	(in millions)	
1982	$(25)	$100
1983	$(50)	$150
1984	$0	$ 75
1985	$10	$ 50

No AMT was due despite these wide discrepancies, because they were created by items not captured in the AMTI calculations.

TABLE 19-1

AMT Adjustments And Preferences

Brief General Description	Applicable to Individuals	Applicable to Corporations	Code Reference
Adjustments for All Taxpayers			
Depreciation of tangible property placed in service after 12/31/86 (requires a longer life and sometimes a less rapid method)	Yes	Yes	Sec. 56(a)(1)
Mining exploration and development costs other than oil and gas properties (requires capitalization with 10-year amortization)	Yes	Yes	Sec. 56(a)(2)
Long-term contracts entered into on or after 31/1/86 (requires use of percentage-of-completion method of accounting)	Yes	Yes	Sec. 56(a)(3)
Net operating loss deduction (limited to 90% of AMTI)	Yes	Yes	Secs. 56(a)(4) and 56(d)
Amortization of pollution-control facilities placed in service after 12/31/86 (requires a longer amortization period)	Yes	Yes	Sec. 56(a)(5)
Disallowance of deferral of gain on certain installment sales after 3/1/86	Yes	Yes	Sec. 56(a)(6)
Gain or loss on sale of certain properties (redetermine basis and, therefore, amount of gain or loss, using AMT depreciation rules)	Yes	Yes	Sec. 56(a)(7)
Adjustments for Noncorporate Taxpayers			
Limitations on certain deductions *from* AGI (some deductions—such as miscellaneous itemized deductions and the standard deduction—disallowed; others, modified—such as medical expenses and interest)	Yes	No	Sec. 56(b)(1)
Circulation and research and experimental expenditures incurred after 12/31/86 (requires capitalization and amortization over 3 and 10 years, respectively)	Yes	No	Sec. 56(b)(2)
Exercise of an incentive stock option (excess of fair market value over option price is included in AMTI)	Yes	No	Sec. 56(b)(3)
Adjustments for Corporate Taxpayers			
Three-fourths of the excess of adjusted current earnings over AMTI before this adjustment	No	Yes	Sec. 56(c)(i) and (g)
Preferences for All Taxpayers			
Percentage depletion in excess of adjusted basis (disallowed)	Yes	Yes	Sec. 57(a)(1)
Intangible drilling costs on oil and gas properties (may be limited to a smaller deduction)	Yes	Yes	Secs. 57(a)(2) and 57(b)
Tax-exempt interest from specified private-activity bonds (included in AMTI)	Yes	Yes	Sec. 57(a)(5)
Charitable contribution of appreciated property (unrealized gain is included in AMTI)	Yes	Yes	Sec. 57(a)(6)
Excess of rapid depreciation over straight-line depreciation on property placed in service before 1/1/87 (mainly Sec. 1250 property)	Yes	Yes	Sec. 57(a)(7)
Denial of Losses			
Deduction of losses from certain tax shelter farm activities (denied for AMT purposes)	Yes	No (unless personal service corporation)	Sec. 58(a)

Disclosure of this type of discrepancy in reported income caused concerns of fairness. Although Congress made some changes in 1986 that directly addressed identified accounting method problems in the measurement of economic income (for example, long-term contract accounting methods), the Senate was not satisfied that the direct, targeted approach would solve the more general problem. The Senate Finance Committee explained in its report the addition of the comprehensive ACE adjustment as follows:

> The minimum tax cannot successfully address concerns of both real and apparent fairness unless there is certainty that whenever a company publicly reports substantial earnings (either pursuant to public reporting requirements, or through voluntary disclosure for substantial non-tax reasons), that company will pay some tax (unless it has sufficient net operating losses to offset its income for the year).
>
> Thus, the committee believes that it is important to provide that the alternative minimum taxable income of a corporation will be increased when book income for the year exceeds alternative minimum taxable income. Such a provision will increase both the real and the perceived fairness of the tax system, eliminate the highly publicized instances in which corporations with substantial book income have paid no tax, and further broaden the minimum tax base to approach economic income more closely.[4]

The committee report referred to book income, and the first version of this adjustment was made with reference to book income. The current version, the ACE adjustment, is calculated with respect to the difference between regular taxable income and a newly defined term, adjusted current earnings.

ACE is similar to the E&P calculation in many respects, but it is not identical. A major difference is that the ACE calculation does not provide for a deduction for federal income taxes. Other differences exist in accounting and depreciation methods allowed. Therefore, corporations must calculate this number in addition to calculating financial income, regular taxable income, and earnings and profits. The procedure for calculating the ACE adjustment is as follows:

Step 1: Start with regular taxable income.

Step 2: Add and/or subtract adjustments and preferences as in Table 19–1 and find the subtotal AMTI before the ACE adjustment.

Step 3: Calculate ACE according to Sec. 56.

Step 4: Calculate the ACE adjustment by multiplying the difference between the ACE calculated in Step 3 and AMTI before the ACE adjustment in Step 3 by 75%: [75% (ACE – AMTI before the ACE adjustment).]

Step 5: Add or subtract the ACE adjustment to find AMTI and continue with the calculation of the AMT as shown in Figure 19–1.

EXAMPLE 19-2

Forbes Corporation has $500,000 in taxable income. The regular tax liability is $170,000 (34% of $500,000). Forbes calculated ACE depreciation to be $75,000; regular depreciation was $50,000. In addition, the corporation earned $700,000

Continued

4 Senate Finance Comm. Rep. No. 313, 99th Cong., 2d Sess. 520 (1986).

EXAMPLE 19-2 (Con't.)

in tax-exempt interest, $125,000 of which was earned on private-activity bonds. ACE is $1,000,000. The calculation of the ACE adjustment is

Step 1: Regular taxable income	$500,000
Step 2: Adjustments: Net ACE depreciation over regular depreciation	–25,000
Preferences: Tax-exempt interest on private activity bonds	+125,000
AMTI before the ACE adjustment	$600,000
Step 3: ACE = $1,000,000 (given)	
Step 4: ACE adjustment: 75% ($1,000,000 – $600,000)	300,000
Step 5: Sum equals AMTI	$900,000

Tax preferences are detailed in Sec. 57. In contrast to adjustments, preferences are always added back to TI in the calculation of AMTI. Tax-exempt interest from certain private-activity bonds is an example of a tax preference. This interest is not included in regular taxable income because it (along with all other sources of tax-exempt interest) is specifically excludable for regular tax purposes. Congress judged that only the portion of tax-exempt interest relating to private-activity bonds is a tax advantage under the law that should enter the minimum tax calculation as a tax preference under Sec. 57. Therefore, this interest is not reflected in TI, but is included in AMTI as a tax preference addition to TI.

An important practical problem is presented by the method of requiring calculation of many items in more than one way. Many of these adjustments and preferences effectively require a separate set of tax accounting records. For example, the accelerated cost recovery methods allowable for regular income tax purposes are not acceptable for AMT purposes. In general, longer lives and straight-line depreciation methods must be used in the calculation of AMT depreciation. These differences lead, of course, to differences in the depreciation deduction, but they also lead to different bases in the assets. Therefore, until the assets are fully depreciated, there will be differences in gains and losses of assets sold or exchanged.

The requirement that a separate set of records be maintained for AMT purposes means that many business taxpayers must now keep four (for corporations) or three (for noncorporate business taxpayers) different sets of accounting records for the following organizations and purposes:

1. The SEC and/or other users who wish to see records reflecting financial accounting conventions:

2. The IRS for regular income tax calculations;

3. The IRS (and, perhaps, the general public) for AMT purposes, including a calculation of Adjusted Current Earnings (ACE) for regular corporations.

4. The IRS for determining the earnings and profits (E&P) of ordinary corporations.

Predicting the impact of the AMT on taxpayers is difficult because of the great diversity in the adjustments and preferences in Table 19–1. Corporate taxpayers engaged in businesses that are capital intensive are the most affected by depreciation adjustments. Many corporations face problems in dealing with the ACE adjustment. Businesses involved in the extraction of oil, gas, and other minerals lose the benefits of several favorable tax provisions targeted specifically at that industry.

For individuals who derive their income from personal services, the disallowance or limitation for the AMTI calculation of many of the deductions that an individual taxpayer can claim in the computation of taxable income (item 8) and the inclusion in AMTI of unrealized gain on charitable contributions (item 15) will have the greatest impact. The adjustments for personal deductions such as the standard deduction, personal exemptions, and itemized deductions are so restrictive that individuals can only claim the following deductions for AMTI purposes:

1. Home mortgage interest, but with modifications;

2. Charitable contributions;

3. Gambling losses;

4. Medical expenses and casualty losses (in relatively rare situations).

Commonly utilized deductions that are notably missing from this set of allowed deductions are income and property taxes, the standard deduction, and personal exemptions.

We continue by considering the next aspect of the AMT calculation, the AMT exemption.

THE AMT EXEMPTION

To exempt literally millions of average taxpayers from the need to make the complex AMT calculations, Congress provided a relatively generous exemption. The amount of the initial (or tentative) exemption varies from one taxpayer to another, based on both entity and filing-status differences. The initial exemptions are phased out (at the rate of 25 cents on the dollar) for taxpayers with a sufficiently large AMTI. The exemption levels and phase-out ranges are summarized as follows:

Entity	Filing Status	Initial Exemption	Phaseout Begins at AMTI of	No Exemption If AMTI Exceeds
Corporation	N.A.	$40,000	$150,000	$310,000
Fiduciary	N.A.	20,000	75,000	155,000
Individual	Single persons and heads of households	30,000	112,500	232,500
Individual	Married persons filing jointly and surviving spouses	40,000	150,000	310,000
Individual	Married persons filing separate returns	20,000	75,000	155,000

As a practical matter, these numbers mean that even though the average individual taxpayer may still be able to ignore totally the AMT provisions with little risk, individuals in the upper-middle income group, as well as many corporations, will have to give them a considerable amount of time and attention. For most of these taxpayers, a competent tax adviser is no longer a luxury; one is now a virtual necessity.

AMT CREDITS

In general the only tax credit that can be used by all taxpayers to reduce the tentative AMT is the foreign tax credit. In addition, an AMT credit may be used to reduce a taxpayer's *regular* income tax in future years. These two credits are explained below.

Foreign Tax Credit

The United States allows citizens, resident aliens, and domestic corporations the right to claim a foreign tax credit on income earned abroad to avoid the double taxation of a single earnings stream. This provision generally applies equally to the regular tax liability and the AMT liability. However, when the foreign tax credit is used to reduce a taxpayer's AMT, a special maximum is imposed by Sec. 59(a). The limit is equal to 90% of a tentative AMT. This 90% limit was specifically designed to keep a U.S. taxpayer, earning a substantial amount of foreign-source income, from using the foreign tax credit to totally avoid any U.S. federal income tax liability.

The AMT Credit against the Regular Tax

In many instances, a taxpayer will be required to pay the AMT solely because of timing differences. In other words, many of the AMT adjustments and some preferences will balance themselves out over enough years. In general, the AMT provisions require a taxpayer (1) to accelerate the recognition of gross income and (2) to defer the recognition of deductions, as compared to the regular income tax provisions. If, because of these provisions, a taxpayer must pay the AMT (because it is larger than the regular tax), that taxpayer might eventually be subject to a second tax on the same item when the situation is reversed and the regular tax exceeds the AMT. This unfortunate consequence can be illustrated easily by reference to depreciation rules.

EXAMPLE 19-3

A taxpayer who acquired ACRS property last year is entitled this year to an ACRS allowance that is generally greater than the depreciation that is allowed for the AMT. As a result, a positive adjustment must be made to taxable income to arrive at AMTI. Assume that this adjustment results in an AMT greater than the regular tax, which the taxpayer is required to pay. In a later year, ACRS depreciation for that same property will be less than the AMT depreciation, and the regular tax would be greater than the AMT. With no AMT credit, the taxpayer would pay a higher AMT in the early years of the property's life and the regular tax later when the ACRS deduction is lower.

To eliminate (or minimize) this result, Sec. 53 was added to the Code. It creates an AMT credit that can be used in subsequent years to reduce *only* the regular tax liability; that is, it cannot be used to reduce the AMT payable in subsequent years. Although this credit cannot be carried back, it can be carried forward indefinitely. The problem described in the example illustrates a timing difference that caused Congress to enact the AMT credit, but the credit is now allowable in any succeeding year in which the regular tax exceeds the AMT, whether for timing or for other reasons.

THE AMT AND TAX PLANNING

The very existence of the AMT is a tribute to the success of tax planning in years past. Because of this successful planning, Congress decided to (1) eliminate many of the advantageous provisions that had been part of the Code for years and (2) tighten up the provisions of the AMT. The overall impact of the changes is clearly to make tax planning more difficult; it will not, however, put an end to those activities. Although the general objective may still be the maximization of wealth via, other things being equal, the minimization of taxes, today's tax planner understands that the price of too large a reduction in the regular income tax may well be an increase in the AMT. Therefore, successful tax planning requires a careful consideration of both the ordinary and the AMT rules, as well as of economic consequences more generally.

One planning strategy for taxpayers who expect to be subject to the AMT is exactly the opposite of the usual strategy for regular tax. Generally, taxpayers try to accelerate deductions and defer income. Because the tax rate for AMT is lower than that for the regular tax, a taxpayer may prefer to defer deductions to a non-AMT year and accelerate income to an AMT year.

EXAMPLE 19-4

Michael is a tax consultant who has been working on several projects that are currently incomplete. By arrangement with his clients he may bill work-in-progress as frequently as monthly. In November, he evaluates his tax situation and determines that he will be subject to the alternative minimum tax in the current year. He estimates that he could bill $50,000 and receive approximately $30,000 by December 31. He decides to do so because his tax rate will be 24% under the alternative minimum tax this year and 31% under the regular tax if the income is attributable to the next year.

Because of the complexities of the AMT, especially the effects of the AMT credits, the basic planning strategies beyond that presented in Example 19-4 are often unclear. Such basic questions as whether a taxpayer should forgo the use of favorable tax accounting methods for the regular tax to avoid the AMT cannot be answered in a general way. For example, should a taxpayer use the alternate method of depreciation in order to avoid the AMT? General answers to such questions are not possible. For now, the only reliable planning technique is use of long-term projections that show the effects of alternative courses of action on the regular tax and the AMT.

PASSIVE ACTIVITIES AND THE PASSIVE ACTIVITY LOSS LIMITS

> **Goal #5**
> Describe the reasons Congress enacted the passive activity loss limitations.

Motivations for enacting the other backstop provision discussed in this chapter, the limits on deductibility of losses from passive activities, have some similarity to those that led to the minimum tax provisions. Specifically, reports that many taxpayers were substantially reducing their tax liabilities through tax shelters created perceptions of inequity in those taxpayers who could not make such investments. However, there was also a more troubling element: a significant group of tax shelters emerged that were abusive. These tax shelters were ones whose promoters represented to investors tax consequences that were unlikely to be sanctioned by the IRS or upheld by a court. In addition, another subset of shelters was not clearly abusive, but investors in these shelters were clearly taking extremely aggressive positions where there was ambiguity in the law. Enormous numbers of taxpayers were involved in all types of tax shelters, making identification of problem shelters and other tasks of administration a nightmare.

The numbers of taxpayers and dollars involved were staggering. Between 1982 and 1984, investments in publicly registered shelters more than doubled from about $5 billion to about $11 billion. Private offerings were estimated to involve an additional 25%. IRS resources were so consumed by tax shelter examinations that regular audits dwindled to almost nothing in some regions of the country.

Trying to find solutions to this problem required a great deal of effort by Congress and the IRS. The earliest efforts at disallowing losses involved hobby-loss rules and limits on investment interest. These rules were partial and therefore inadequate solutions, particularly as tax shelter activities saw such startling growth. The free-flowing capital that flooded in from investors eager to get a piece of the action attracted unethical syndicators who often sold otherwise poor economic investments solely on the basis of their purported tax benefits.

In 1976, after rejecting proposals to place "limitations on artificial losses" (proposals conceptually similar to the passive activity loss rules that this section is about) because it believed such an approach would unfairly penalize legitimate investments, Congress enacted at-risk rules to deny deductions for which the taxpayer bore no risk of true economic loss. Congress tinkered with these provisions over the next 10 years in an attempt to tighten them up and close loopholes. All the while tax shelter investments ballooned.

> **PALs** are **passive activity losses;** *passive activity* will be defined shortly.

The final solution is Sec. 469, a highly effective weapon that operates through severe limits on **passive activity losses (PALS).** As you will see, the new rules go far beyond the control of tax shelters and profoundly affect the investment patterns of many citizens. These new rules have virtually eliminated the promotion of abusive shelters. But that victory was won at the cost of penalizing the many legitimate investments Congress strove to protect in previous legislation.

WHAT IS A TAX SHELTER?

You probably heard the term *tax shelter* before you ever enrolled in this tax course. (You probably even hoped that if you got nothing else out of the course, at least you would be able to improve your own financial future through the use of tax shelters.) But what is a tax shelter? The words mean different things to different people. They can mean anything from a routine investment in municipal bonds that generate tax-exempt income or a purchase of a personal residence to more exotic investments in cattle-feeding operations, Hollywood movies, or foreign currencies.

Generically, a tax shelter is any investment governed by tax rules that protect or shelter economic benefits from immediate taxation. This generic definition is much too simplistic to suggest the nature of the tax shelter abuses that evolved, as you will discover. Perhaps the definition captures the simple purpose Congress had as it enacted various provisions as investment incentives for taxpayers. Congress probably expected that small groups of taxpayers would band together to pool capital for such investments; it could hardly have anticipated what would be created by those who had enormous economic incentives to put these various parts of tax law together in a way that attracted large investment pools.

In the following discussion, prior law must be discussed because some aspects of it were important ingredients in the chemistry of tax shelters. Without viewing important historical structural characteristics of prior law, you cannot begin to understand the power of the mighty engines that drove the tax-shelter mania of the 1970s and early 1980s.

Congress was not concerned with the generic form of a tax shelter when it created the at-risk and PAL rules. Rather, Congress was concerned with a special breed of tax shelter created to generate losses to uninvolved or passive investors in one activity that they could use to offset profits in their other endeavors. The concern was particularly great in cases where the losses were paper losses generated only by nonrecourse debt (debt for which no one had any personal liability). The use of the term tax shelter evolved to describe more specifically investments that created paper or artificial losses used to shelter a taxpayer's profitable enterprises or activities from taxation. Example 19-5 provides an example of this evolved definition of tax shelter.

EXAMPLE 19-5

Tory is a medical doctor. He had $300,000 of earned income from his practice. Distressed over the level of taxes that he was paying, he followed the advice of his investment adviser and purchased for $100,000 a 10% interest in a real estate tax shelter partnership that bought and managed apartment complexes. The partnership purchased an apartment building from the previous owner:

Cash investment	$ 1,000,000
Nonrecourse note	15,000,000
Purchase price	$16,000,000
Allocated to Land	$ 1,000,000
Allocated to Building	$15,000,000

The note carried an interest rate of 10% and no principal payments were required for the first five years. The project produced sufficient cash flow to cover operating expenses and debt service for the first five years. Therefore, net losses represented the depreciation (15-year, straight-line) on the building:

Cost of building	$15,000,000
Cost recovery period	15
Partnership's annual depreciation	$ 1,000,000
Tory's share of annual depreciation	$ 100,000

Tory's tax losses were $100,000 per year (10% of the total of $1,000,000 per year) for the first five years. Thus, at a probable tax rate at that time of 50%, Tory saved $50,000 in taxes each year by using the losses from the partnership to offset a portion of his $300,000 earned income.

Dissection of the arrangement presented in Example 19-5 will help you understand the economics of tax shelters. Tax shelters have three main components: leverage, deferral, and conversion. Each of these components is discussed below.

1. **Leverage.** Leverage through high proportions of debt is a good investment tool as long as appreciation in the asset leveraged is greater than the carrying costs of the debt. Most tax shelters were highly leveraged; that aspect of tax shelters was attractive

Leverage is the use of debt to finance part of an investment.

to investors who were unable to make such arrangements individually. In addition to the straight investment benefits of leverage, debt is part of the basis calculation, thus generating deductions for the investor in excess of cash invested. In Tory's case, you can see that he recovered his $100,000 cash outlay through tax savings associated with those deductions in the first two years of the project. (If the opportunity cost on the $100,000 is incorporated, the calculation will show that Tory would not have recovered his investment plus forgone income until the third year.)

> **Deferral** means the postponement of tax to a later period.

2. **Deferral.** In a sound economic investment, at the point of sale the equity owner will be able to repay creditors and receive in return more than was invested. The investor will have a taxable gain at the point that the investment is sold. In other words, an investor hopes that deductions today will be recovered by gains in the future. By choosing to invest in a tax shelter, Tory was attempting to trade a dollar of taxes payable today (by offsetting medical practice earned income with real estate net loss net deductions) for a dollar of taxes payable in the future. In other words, Tory was hoping to achieve a deferral of his tax liability.

EXAMPLE 19-6

When the note from Example 19-5 came due, the partnership sold the building for $24,000,000. The calculation of the gain is

Selling Price		$24,000,000
Cost	$16,000,000	
Acc. Depr.	(5,000,000)	
Adjusted basis		11,000,000
Gain		$13,000,000
Tory's share of gain (10%)		$ 1,300,000
Components of gain:		
Recovery of reductions in basis through depreciation deductions		$ 500,000
"Real" gain through increases in value over purchase price		$ 800,000

Deferral in the tax shelter sense occurs with respect to the $500,000 portion of the gain. That is, Tory was able to offset his other earned income by $500,000 partnership losses over the five-year period of the investment, saving $250,000 in taxes in the short-run. Assuming Tory faces the same 50% tax bracket in the year of sale, he must pay back the $250,000 of taxes he saved. The benefits of deferral come into play in that he (rather than the government) has the use of the money over the investment period.

> **Conversion** means that when a deferred gain is ultimately recognized, the tax character of the gain is more favorable than that of the income originally sheltered.

3. **Conversion.** You can see through the particular examples of Tory's investments that leverage and deferral can create enormous economic gains to taxpayers. There was still more to come in certain tax shelters investments: the ability to *convert* the character of the deferred income into a more tax-favored form when recognized than that of the income originally sheltered. To understand how this is accomplished, review the deferral case. Deferral generates benefits through the time value of money. What if the gain attributable to previous depreciation were to be taxed not at ordinary

income rates, but at then favorable capital gains rates? That is, instead of paying taxes on $500,000 of gain attributable to recovery of depreciation reductions in basis, Tory's taxable income were to be increased by only 40% (the capital gains inclusion percentage) of the $500,000, or $200,000. This was possible and even probable with certain types of investments in which the deductions were taken against ordinary income, but the gain attributable to recovery of those deductions was characterized as Sec. 1231 (which may have been taxed as capital gain) rather than as Sec. 1245 or 1250 recapture (taxed as ordinary income). If Tory's investment qualified for this treatment, he could *convert* a $250,000 tax savings through ordinary income deductions into a $100,000 tax bill if the Sec. 1231 gain was taxed as capital gain.

So, through leverage, deferral, and conversion, taxpayers like Tory were able to reap large benefits through tax shelters. If Congress enacted all those provisions, why should they be concerned that they were being used by taxpayers? Many of the details are much too complex to explore here, but some of the most important issues can be discussed conceptually.

First, Congress did not anticipate the magnitude of the investment that would flow into tax shelters or the size of the syndicates that would be formed. Administration of the tax law as it related to tax shelters was extremely cumbersome and ineffective. The earliest attempt to stem tax shelters was a legal argument that the syndicated tax shelters were associations taxable as corporations. Had the government won this argument, losses could not have flowed through to owners, dramatically (perhaps fatally) decreasing the attractiveness of the investment. However, the IRS argument failed in court.

Second, anticipating the possible failure of the argument concerning the tax treatment of the tax shelter entity and its owners, IRS focused on the problem of leverage and appealed to Congress to address this problem by statute. The aggressive use of leverage had led to arrangements with nonrecourse debt that had no economic reality. Because debt is included in a taxpayer's basis, debt that does not reflect an arm's-length transaction can generate deductions the taxpayer is not entitled to. As briefly mentioned in the introduction to this section, Congress saw this as the greatest specific problem with tax shelters and sought to cure the most egregious tax shelter problems by introducing at-risk rules. The intent of these rules was to limit deductions to the amounts a taxpayer had personal liability for, that is, to amounts for which the taxpayer was at-risk. While the idea sounds good in theory, taxpayers devised a myriad of ways of circumventing the intent of the statute. Congress regularly tried to patch the rules, but the pressure on the at-risk dike was too great for these patches to hold.

Finally, these failures caused tax shelters to gain more momentum. The tax shelter attracted greater and greater numbers of less than ethical syndicators who understood the administrative hurdles the IRS faced in auditing tax shelter partnerships and their partners. They sold these investments (many times, ones with no chance of being economically sound on their merits) by stating tax benefits that they knew, or should have known, would not be sustained upon audit. Taxpayers who had never invested in tax shelters joined the investment pools as they were made available to individuals with smaller amounts of money than ever before. Many of these investments were made with very little or no professional investment advice because taxpayers were so eager to join those who were reaping large tax benefits (legitimate as well as not legitimate) from these widely hailed investment opportunities. The government lost tax dollars because taxpayers filed returns based on fraudulent representations; the investors lost their investment dollars; and the syndicators were often the only ones who came out ahead.

CONGRESSIONAL RESPONSE—THE PAL SLEDGEHAMMER

Congress took several steps in the 1986 Act in addition to the PAL rules that reduce the attractiveness of tax shelters. Think about how each of these steps would influence Tory's investment decision in Example 19-5. First, the tax rate structure was flattened and the top rate was significantly reduced. Second, tax incentives in various areas were reduced. The prime example for purposes of this discussion is methods of depreciation on real property. Finally, the preferential rate for capital gains was essentially eliminated. All of these changes mean that the attractiveness of the economic benefits of a tax shelter investment must rely much less heavily on tax consequences.

Unconvinced that these measures were enough to stall tax shelter mania, Congress erected the backstop of passive activity loss limitation in Sec. 469. The enactment of these rules institutes a policy of isolating different types of financial activities engaged in by taxpayers and restricting the possibilities for blending the financial results of these different activities in the calculation of taxable income. As an example, these rules disallow the offset of real estate losses generated by a syndicated partnership against earned income of a taxpayer. Thus, these rules address the concern of Congress demonstrated in the discussion above.

The means of accomplishing this objective are extremely restrictive. The severity of the limitations eliminates the use of even most modest, legitimate tax shelters—thus, the reference to the PAL sledgehammer. The provisions are also extremely technical and fraught with terms whose definitions are difficult to decipher. Congress delegated authority to the Treasury to flesh out the details of the Sec. 469 rules in regulations. Those regulations are extensive and quite detailed. They reflect a period in regulation writing in which the philosophy was that the best way to provide guidance to taxpayers is to spell out every possible detail and address every possible anticipated problem so that there is little room for interpretation or argument. The mood shifted somewhat when Internal Revenue Commissioner Fred Goldberg took office and declared a policy of "rough justice" in which guidance from the IRS should take broader positions so that taxpayers and advisers do not have to master such a plethora of detail. New Internal Revenue Commissioner Shirley Petersen is reputed to adhere to the former policy.

At any rate, the regulations under Sec. 469 are clearly very specific and intended to be all-encompassing. The following sections take you through some of this detail in the explanation of the regulations' definitions and operating rules for several key terms, in particular: passive activity, material participation, activity, and undertaking. Before that, we examine the taxpayers who are subject to the limits.

TAXPAYERS SUBJECT TO THE LIMITS

All noncorporate taxpayers are subject to the limits on passive losses, including individuals, estates, and trusts. As discussed in Chapter 7, because the limits are imposed at the taxpayer level, partnerships and S corporations that pass their tax items through to owners are not affected directly by the rules—these entities do not *deduct* losses.

The law divides C corporations into three groups for purposes of applying the passive loss limits. First, publicly held C corporations are not affected but closely held C corporations generally are. However, a closely held C corporation (that is not a personal-service corporation) is permitted to offset passive losses against income from the active conduct of a business, but such losses cannot be used to offset portfolio income. For this purpose, a closely held corporation is one where 50% or more in value of its stock is owned by 5 or fewer individuals at any time during the last half of the tax year. Uses of this exception for planning purposes are illustrated later.

C corporations that are personal-service corporations are subject to the limits, even if they are not closely held. A personal-service corporation is a corporation (1) where the principal activity is the performance of personal services; (2) where those services are substantially performed by employee owners; and (3) where more than 10% of the corporate stock is owned by all employee-owners combined. While there exist many uncertainties about the definition just given, the term personal-service corporation clearly covers all professional corporations employed by doctors, lawyers, accountants, architects, and others. Without a rule that subjects personal-service corporations to the passive loss limits, an individual who earned income by performing services could incorporate, include the passive activity in the corporation, and thus avoid the limits.

To summarize, individuals, estates, trusts, and personal-service C corporations are subject to the new rules. Publicly held C corporations are exempt. Closely held C corporations are partly covered, but with the important exception that permits passive losses to be offset by active income.

> **Goal #6**
> Explain the types of activities subject to the passive activity loss limitations.

PASSIVE ACTIVITIES DEFINED

The statute defines a **passive activity** as one that involves the conduct of any trade or business in which the taxpayer does not materially participate. To understand this new concept we must first recognize that income is first classified into **baskets** containing either **portfolio income** or **activity income**. The latter category is then classified as active or passive (giving us, courtesy of a confused legislature, the nonsense term *active activity*).

Portfolio income consists of interest, dividends, and royalty income provided the asset that produces the income is held as an investment. Portfolio income also includes gains from the disposition of property that produces portfolio income. Note that interest income is not automatically portfolio income. Interest earned on notes arising from the active conduct of a business is active income. Similarly, royalty income and dividends are portfolio only if the asset is held for investment and not used in a business.

Once portfolio income is distinguished from activity income, the active-passive classification generally depends on material participation.

> A **passive activity** is one in which the taxpayer's participation in the activity's operations does not rise to the required level of material participation.
>
> **Baskets** are tax categories for various income and loss items.
>
> **Portfolio income** is income from an investment asset such as stocks or bonds.
>
> **Activity income** is income from trade or business activities.

Material Participation

Material participation is a critical term in determining the active/passive status of most activities. The following items are exceptions established by Congress:

- Rental activities are passive. A rental activity is one where payment is for the use of tangible property as opposed to payment for services. For this purpose, hotels and car rentals are active businesses because significant services are performed.

- Working interests in oil and gas deposits are always active. A working interest is that held by an operator of a property, as opposed to holding a nonactive royalty interest.

- A limited partnership interest is usually passive. The degree of participation by the partner or the type of activity does not affect this passive classification. Thus, a limited partner in a partnership that holds only a working interest in oil and gas has passive income or loss.

- Certain low-income housing projects are temporarily classified as active businesses to deter owners from abandoning these projects.

All activities other than those just listed are active or passive with respect to a taxpayer depending on whether that taxpayer meets the test of **material participation**. A taxpayer meets that test only if he or she is involved in the activity's operations on a *regular, continuous,* and *substantial* basis. Reflecting the general approach adopted for the PAL regulations (writing extensive, detailed regulations) the test of material participation became a test of meeting one of seven largely mechanical, hours-based tests. Those tests are reproduced here to satisfy your curiosity, but note that the first test (the 500-hour test) is the one most frequently used to demonstrate material participation. Under the regulations, an individual materially participates in a trade or business activity in any taxable year if *any* one of the following seven tests are met.

> **Material participation** means that the taxpayer is involved in the activity's operations on a regular, continuous, and substantial basis.

1. The individual participates in the activity for more than 500 hours during the taxable year.

2. The individual's participation in the activity for the taxable year constitutes substantially all the participation in such activity of all individuals (including nonowners) for such year.

3. The individual participates in the activity for more than 100 hours during the taxable year and such individual's participation is not less than the participation in the activity of any other individual—including nonowners.

4. The activity is a significant participation activity and the individual's aggregate participation in all significant participation activities during the year exceeds 500 hours.

5. The individual materially participates in the activity for any 5 taxable years during the 10 preceding taxable years.

6. The activity is a personal service activity and the individual materially participated in the activity for any 3 taxable years (whether or not consecutive) preceding the taxable year.

7. Based on all the facts and circumstances, the individual participates in the activity on a regular, continuous, and substantial basis during such year. However, for this test, an individual's services performed in the management of an activity shall not be taken into account in determining whether such individual is treated as materially participating unless the two following conditions are satisfied:

   a. No other person receives compensation by performing such services; and

   b. No individual performs services in connection with the management of the activity that exceed (by hours) the amount of such services by such individual.

In view of the statutory language requiring regular, continuous and substantial participation, the 500-hour requirement is surprisingly liberal. It is particularly liberal when the activities of a spouse are counted toward the material participation of the individual owning the interest in the activity.

EXAMPLE 19-7

The 500-hour requirement in combination with the spouse rule means that an individual could own a farm and meet the material participation requirement by

Continued

EXAMPLE 19-7 (Con't.)

> working on the farm for five hours each Saturday and Sunday during the year. Or, if the individual has a spouse, if both work for five hours each Saturday, the taxpayer will meet the 500-hour requirement for the year.

The forgoing discussion assumes that the taxpayer is an individual, capable of material participation. The law contains rules for application of the test with the artificial entities. For partnerships and S corporations, the partner or shareholder reporting the taxable items must meet the test. For trusts, the trustee must participate, and for estates, the executor must meet the test. For C corporations that are also personal-service corporations, the material participation test is met only if stockholders owning more than 50% in value of the corporate stock meet the test. For closely held corporations that are not personal-service corporations, an alternate test of material participation requires that at least one employee of such corporation devotes full time to the management of the activity, that at least three nonowner employees of the corporation devote full time to the activity, and that the activity has Section 162 deductions that exceed 15% of the activity's gross income. For practical purposes, these rules mean that the owner-employees must perform the requisite services for personal-service corporations. Other closely held corporations (that are not personal-service corporations) meet the test if the requisite services are performed by employees.

Separation of Activities

The new limits on passive losses can be applied properly only if *each* **activity** of a taxpayer is accounted for as a separate entity. The identification and separation is necessary because the rules listed below apply on an activity-by-activity basis.

> An **activity** is an integrated and interrelated economic unit.

1. The active-passive determination based on material participation is made *each* year for *each* activity. An activity that was classified as passive last year may be active this year, for example.

2. Disallowed (suspended) passive losses from an activity are fully deductible when an activity is entirely disposed of in a taxable transaction.

3. The rental of real estate by an individual, while passive, enjoys a special relief provision, as explained below.

Congress intends that this separation of activities be made in a realistic economic sense. In making the decision of what constitutes a separate activity, "the question to be answered is what undertakings consist of an integrated and interrelated economic unit, conducted in coordination with or reliance upon each other, and constituting an appropriate unit for the measurement of gain or loss."[5] Treasury issued almost 200 pages of Regulations under Sec. 469 attempting to define the term activity. The Regulations adopt a building-block approach. The smallest unit that can constitute an activity is an undertaking. The next step aggregates undertakings into an activity. Although the aggregation rules vary depending on the nature of the undertaking (trade or business, rental real estate, professional service, or oil and gas operations), the identification of an activity is critically dependent on three factors: (1) location, (2) ownership, and (3) income production.

---

5 Senate Finance Committee Report (accompanying H.R. 3838), TRA 1986, p. 739.

Of the three factors, overriding importance is attached to the location factor. Business operations carried out at different locations are considered to be separate activities, regardless of common ownership, if the operations represent a separate source of income. Thus, two grocery stores owned by the same person but located one mile apart would be considered separate activities.

The Treasury Regulations on passive activities clearly lean toward a broad definition of activity. Forcing a taxpayer to aggregate different income-producing operations at the same location actually makes it easier for the taxpayer to meet the material participation test (which causes the activity to be classified as active rather than passive). However, greater aggregation defers the timing of most dispositions—to the taxpayer's detriment if there are suspended losses. But, if a timely election is filed, it is possible for the taxpayer to disaggregate undertakings in order to free suspended losses upon disposition of an operation.

We hope this peek at the difficulty of definition in this setting gives you an inkling of the complexity of the activity rules and the importance that a taxpayer be well advised.

> **Goal #7**
> Explain the process by which the passive activity loss limitations are calculated.

APPLYING THE LIMITS ON PASSIVE LOSSES

Once a taxpayer's activities are divided into separate activities using the above rules and it is determined that some of these activities are passive, then the combination/limitation process begins. Net losses from passive activities may only be used to offset net income from passive activities. Disallowed net losses from a passive activity are deferred to later years to offset passive income, and any unused losses are fully deductible when the activity is completely disposed of.

Accounting for Disallowed Losses

Passive losses in excess of passive income must be accounted for on an activity-by-activity basis for two purposes: (1) to determine when a deferred loss is fully deductible because the activity is disposed of or (2) to account for losses when an activity becomes active. The deferred loss from a given year is allocated pro rata to the loss activities for that year based on the amounts of their losses.

EXAMPLE 19-8

Assume that a taxpayer has four passive activities that produce the results below in 1991:

Activity	Gross Income	Deductions	Net	Carryover
1	$1,000	$1,800	$(800)	$(214)
2	1,800	900	900	–
3	1,300	2,000	(700)	(186)
4	200	–	200	–
	$4,300	$4,700	$(400)	$(400)

The net losses from activities 1 and 3 are deductible to the extent of $1,100 (the net income from activities 2 and 4), but the net passive loss of $400 is deferred to later years. What if activity 1 is disposed of early in 1992? How much of the $400 disallowed is attributable to activity 1? A pro rata allocation is necessary: for activity 1, $800/$1,500 x $400 = $214; for activity 3, $700/$1,500 x $400 = $186.

The separate accounting for each activity is also important if a particular activity is later reclassified because the owner materially participates.

EXAMPLE 19-9

Assume that activity 1 in Example 19-8 becomes an active activity in 1992 and that all four activities produce the same gains and losses as above. Now the passive loss of $700 from activity 3 is fully deductible against the income from activities 2 and 4. The $800 loss from activity 1 in 1992 can be deducted against any income, either active or portfolio. While the suspended 1991 loss of $214 from activity 1 cannot be deducted against active and portfolio income in 1992, this passive loss can be deducted against the net passive income in 1992:

Activity 2—1992	$ 900
Activity 3—1992	200
Passive income	$1,100
Less: 1992 passive loss, activity 3	(700)
Suspended loss, activity 1	(214)
Net passive income	$ 186

Alternatively, the suspended loss for activity 1 could be deducted against active income derived from that same activity in a later year.

Special Limits for Rental of Real Estate

Because of the many individuals with investments in rental real estate, Congress provided a limited relief provision available to most individual taxpayers. Individuals who actively participate in the management of rental real estate may deduct net passive losses attributable to such activities, subject to several qualifications.

This provision does not create a deduction but instead excepts net passive loss on real estate rentals up to $25,000 per year from the overall limit of passive income. This $25,000 limit is reduced by 50% of the amount by which the taxpayer's AGI (with certain adjustments) exceeds $100,000. The benefit is totally phased out when AGI reaches $150,000.

This special rule applies only to individuals (and certain estates) who own at least 10% of the property. Furthermore, the individual must actively participate in the management of the property. **Active participation** is a much less stringent test than material participation. The operation of rental real estate involves only limited management decisions and the taxpayer need only participate in this way. Actual work on the property can be relegated to the taxpayer's agents. On the other hand, if the taxpayer furnishes substantial services, for example, the operation of a motel, the activity may be something more than real estate rental and ineligible for the rental activity exception. In this instance, note that the entire activity may be active, not passive, depending on the material participation test.

Active participation is the level of participation required for the limited real estate exception to the passive loss rules. The test for active participation is less stringent than the test for material participation.

EXAMPLE 19-10

Assume that an individual with AGI (as adjusted) of $90,000 owns 100% of an apartment house that the individual actively manages, his only passive activity.

Continued

EXAMPLE 19-10 (Con't.)

If the taxpayer's current loss from this activity is $20,000, the entire loss is allowed; if the loss if $30,000, $25,000 is allowed currently and the remaining $5,000 is postponed. If the taxpayer's AGI is $120,000, the limit of this special provision is $15,000 [$25,000 − .5($120,000 − $100,000)], and only that amount is deductible currently. A taxpayer who engages in several passive activities must first net passive losses against passive income before applying this special limit for rental real estate.

RECOUPMENT OF LOSSES AT DISPOSITION

The rules for passive losses do not permanently disallow losses but instead defer or suspend them indefinitely until one of two events occurs. First, passive income in later years will trigger the use of suspended losses. Second, suspended losses become fully deductible when the taxpayer disposes of the passive activity that generated the suspended losses. A disposition triggers the deduction of suspended losses only if such disposition is complete, fully taxable, and not made to a related party.

To be *complete*, the taxpayer must dispose of his or her entire interest in the passive activity. If the passive activity is owned through a partnership interest, the sale of the partnership interest would be a complete disposition. On the other hand, take the case of a taxpayer engaged in several activities, one of which is passive, as a proprietor. In this case, a complete disposition presumably requires the sale of all assets used in the passive activity.

Only fully taxable dispositions cause the deduction of suspended losses. Transfers of passive activities, or assets used in such activities, to a partnership or a corporation in a nontaxable exchange or in a like-kind exchange only result in association of the suspended losses with the new property received in the nontaxable exchange. Similarly, a gift of assets used in a passive activity is not a taxable disposition. For gifts, suspended losses are allocated to and increase the basis of the property in the donee's hands, giving recognition of the deferred passive losses when the donee eventually sells the property. Transfers at death, however, though nontaxable, are effective dispositions for this purpose and the decedent's executor can deduct suspended losses on the final return. Such losses must be reduced by the amount by which the basis of the property used in the passive activity is increased by the fair-market-value rule that applies to property passed at death.

EXAMPLE 19-11

If a taxpayer dies leaving to his heirs a farm classified as passive, the farm having a fair market value of $5,000,000, a basis of $4,000,000, and suspended loss of $2,500,000, only $1,500,000 passive loss is deductible on the final return, with the remaining $1,000,000 being absorbed by the increase in basis from $4,000,000 to $5,000,000.

Finally, dispositions to related parties do not trigger the deduction of suspended losses. This rule is consistent with the general rule for related parties that disallows losses on sales to family members, controlled corporations, and other related entities. The technical definition of relatedness, found in Section 267(b) was discussed in Chapter 15.

For bookkeeping purposes, the losses suspended because of the limits on passive activities effectively become a new basis account that contains losses attributable to disallowed current expenses as well as depreciation and amortization of property used in the activity. When a property is sold or otherwise disposed of, the amount realized on the disposition is offset by any remaining basis for the properties used in the activity plus the suspended losses.

IS THE TAX SHELTER EXTINCT?

Having ground your way through the framework of Sec. 469, do you think tax shelters can possibly exist in the current climate? Although the form is quite different and the possibilities for huge gains more limited, consider the possibility of a personal residence as a tax shelter. Recall the factors involved in tax shelters: leverage, deferral, and conversion.

Leverage exists in home ownership when the purchaser takes out a mortgage to finance the purchase. He or she reaps benefits if the gains eventually realized exceed the interest paid over the life of the loan.

Deferral exists in a somewhat different way than discussed before. Here, the interest payments and property taxes are out-of-pocket costs that no one else will absorb, in contrast to the example of the apartment building which produced enough cash flow from tenants to cover out-of-pocket expenses. The house cannot be depreciated because we are assuming it is all used for personal use. Nevertheless, the interest and taxes are deductible (although subject to some potential disallowance). Therefore, even if the appreciation on the house only equals exactly the amount of interest and taxes paid, those amounts were deductible in each year when paid and the increments to value in each year are not taxable until realized in a taxable sale. Thus, the deferral aspect with a personal residence relates to the nontaxability of unrealized gains.

Finally, the factor of conversion is perhaps the best part about this tax shelter. That is, the carrying costs are immediately deductible, but the gain may escape tax altogether. There are three escape routes from paying taxes on the gain: (a) death, because gains are not realized upon the event of death and the basis in the asset is stepped-up to fair market value (a great tax plan but one that is not particularly attractive from a non-tax standpoint); (b) qualifying reinvestment of proceeds defers recognition of realized gain; (c) the over-55 exemption can be used to shelter all or part of the gain realized.

The continuing allowance of the tax shelter benefits of home ownership continue to come under fire in Congress as the pressure to find new sources of revenue causes them to look at big ticket tax expenditure items. Reducing benefits of home ownership is politically unpalatable. In fact, early in 1992, credits for new home owners were proposed as a means of aiding the economy and promoting family values. However, for high income individuals, the benefits of the last great tax shelter in America continue to be eroded.

PIGs AND PTPs

As draconian as the PAL rules were, taxpayers did not take them sitting down. The Code established a presumption that limited partners were passive investors, paving the way for the master limited partnership to rise from its death as a loss generator to a new life as a **passive income generator (PIG)**. Congress quickly responded with new legislation in 1987 that provides that **publicly traded partnerships (PTPs)**

PIGs is the acronym for **passive income generators.** PIGs were formed to generate passive income sought by investors with passive losses.

PTPs are **publicly traded partnerships,** defined as a partnership traded on an established securities market or readily tradable on a secondary market.

formed after December 17, 1987, will be taxed as corporations. There is an exception if 90% of the gross income is portfolio income. Section 7704(b) defines a PTP as a partnership which is traded on an established securities market or is readily tradable on a secondary market. PTPs in existence on December 17, 1987, will continue to be treated as a partnership for tax purposes until 1998. These partnerships are subject to separate rules under Sec. 469(k). These rules, as explained in the Senate Report, mean that each PTP effectively has its own basket; net income from PTPs is treated as portfolio income.

CONCLUSION

Congress enacts some provisions to affect economic decisions by taxpayers. Taxpayers respond by taking advantage of tax favored investments to maximize their investment returns. In some cases, taxpayer utilization of these provisions is viewed as excessive because taxable income becomes so much lower than economic income. In other cases, taxpayers have abused tax advantages. This chapter examined the alternative minimum tax which was enacted to serve as a backstop against excessive use of beneficial tax provisions. It also examined the passive activity loss rules which were motivated by perceptions that too many taxpayers were getting too great a tax advantage from tax shelters, both in legitimate and abusive uses of shelters. These provisions appear to be relatively effective in accomplishing their goals, but add a great deal of complexity to the system. In the case of passive activity loss rules, there has also been a negative effect on legitimate activities that were not primary targets of the legislation.

Other backstop provisions exist in the Code as well (such as, Sec. 382 dealing with corporate acquisitions of loss subsidiaries) but the details of most of these provisions are beyond the scope of this textbook. You may expect to see other similar legislative movements in areas where there is perceived abuse (for example, intercompany allocations). The issue of ensuring that taxpayers pay a reasonable amount of tax on their annual economic increments to wealth will probably continue to be played out through the existing alternative minimum tax system, if not through the regular tax system. Responding to calls for a level-playing field, in the 1986 Act, Congress made significant changes in moving to the measurement of income for regular tax purposes to a more economic basis. Perhaps that direct approach will persist. However, in the heat of the 1992 presidential campaign, candidates will be pressured to increase tax incentives to jump-start the economy. Movement toward more incentives will again widen the gap between taxable and economic income.

KEY POINTS TO REMEMBER

✓ The tax incentive provisions that are enacted to affect economic decision making can lead to situations in which a taxpayer's taxable income is substantially lower than economic income.

✓ The alternative minimum tax (AMT) requires a tax calculation in addition to the regular tax calculation. The alternative calculation adds specified tax preferences and makes certain adjustments to the tax base of regular taxable income to generate a tax base that is a truer measure of economic income. The higher of the two tax calculations is the tax liability.

✓ Congress enacted passive activity rules as a last resort in its attempts to put a stop to abusive tax shelters. The rules have proven to be effective for that purpose, but have also captured legitimate transactions in the web.

✓ The passive activity loss rules require that taxpayers categorize income and deductions in separate baskets. These baskets contain portfolio income, passive and active income and loss. Passive losses can only be used to offset passive income. At disposition of the activity, any unused losses may be utilized.

——— RECALL PROBLEMS

1. What is a backstop provision and why are backstops necessary?

2. What problem was the minimum tax specifically designed to address?

3. What is the difference between an add-on minimum tax and an alternative minimum tax?

4. Describe briefly the transitional stages leading up to our current version of the minimum tax.

5. The 1986 Act made a significant change in the minimum tax calculation for corporations by creating a new tax preference item for 75% of the difference between ACE and AMTI before the ACE adjustment. What prompted Congress to add this tax preference item?

6. For the following items, identify whether each involves an adjustment, a preference, or neither. Explain why each item is or is not an adjustment or preference in calculating the alternative minimum tax base.

   a. Tax-exempt interest from private activity bonds.

   b. Net operating loss deduction.

   c. Personal exemption deductions.

   d. Percentage depletion in excess of cost.

   e. Tax-exempt interest from public activity bonds.

   f. Depreciation on assets acquired before 1/1/87 (generally applies to excess depreciation).

   g. Depreciation on assets acquired after 12/31/86.

   h. Charitable contribution deduction.

7. Antoine Corporation has provided you with the following financial information for preparation of the 1992 tax return. Determine the amount of the AMT, if any.

Taxable Income	$ 500,000
Tax Preference Items	100,000
Tax Adjustment Items (+)	200,000
Adjusted Current Earnings	1,000,000

8. Compute the tentative minimum tax (gross AMT) for

   a. A corporation with gross AMTI of $100,000.

   b. A corporation with gross AMTI of $200,000.

    c. A corporation with gross AMTI of $400,000.

    d. A married couple with gross AMTI of $150,000.

    e. A single individual with gross AMTI of $150,000.

    f. A fiduciary with gross AMTI of $30,000.

9. In 1992, Jorge Valasquez had a regular tax liability of $42,000 and a gross AMT of $35,000. Jorge's minimum tax credit from 1991 is $10,000.

    a. What is Jorge's 1992 tax liability?

    b. How much minimum tax credit will be available to Jorge in 1993?

10. What circumstances motivated the enactment of the PAL rules?

11. Homer and Amy Wagner operate a sporting goods store and engage in various other economic activities listed below. Income (losses) for the current year appear at the right.

Net profit—sporting goods store	$50,000
Dividends on stock held as investment	3,100
Loss on rental house managed by Homer	(1,500)
Limited partnership interest in an apartment house	(4,500)
General partnership interest in a cattle operation—managed by agent	3,000
Working interest in oil well	(3,500)
Amy's loss on Tupperware sales	(1,000)

    a. Calculate the Wagners' AGI.

    b. What is the AGI if Homer materially participates in the cattle operation?

12. John Witte engaged in the following passive activities during the *current* year (no rental real estate):

Activity	Gross Income	Deductions	Net
1	$ 8,000	$11,000	$(3,000)
2	15,000	10,000	5,000
3	16,000	20,000	(4,000)
	$39,000	$41,000	$(2,000)

    a. How much may Witte deduct against active income this year?

    b. If Witte disposes of his interest in activity 3 on the first day of next year, how much of the suspended loss is deductible?

13. Currently, Norma Lisa has a basis in an interest in a limited partnership of $40,000. Accumulated suspended losses relative to this interest amount now to $30,000. What are the tax consequences if Norma

    a. Sells the interest for $25,000 to an unrelated party?

    b. Dies, leaving the interest to her friend, Tammy, when the interest has a FMV of $45,000?

c. Contributes the interest to a general partnership in a transaction where no gain or loss is recognized?

14. Tx, a dentist, invested $20,000 for a partnership interest in an apartment house. Tx's interest represents 10% of the capital and profits. In 1991 Tx's share of the loss was $16,000, and in 1992 his share of the loss was $15,000. Under what conditions can Tx deduct these losses currently?

15. Listed below are various taxpayers along with their operations and investments. Which ones are subject to the limits on passive losses? Explain any special provisions that may apply.

a. An individual owns and operates a rental business where personal property (TVs, dishes, tractors, etc.) is leased to the public.

b. A C corporation engages in retail sales but also owns and rents several shopping centers. One individual owns 30% of the stock, but the remainder is spread among numerous shareholders with a top percentage of 2% owned.

c. Three CPAs operate as a professional corporation. The corporation owns a partnership interest in a cattle ranch. The ranch is operated by one partner, and the CPAs visit it rarely to help with management decisions.

d. A C corporation is owned entirely by two brothers engaged in electrical contracting. The corporation owns and operates an office building.

16. Lyndon, an individual, owns two partnership interests. Both were purchased in 1985. Activity 1 is an apartment house, and Lyndon actively participates in its management. Activity 2 is a group of thoroughbred race horses (no participation). In 1992, his share of the loss from activity 1 was $45,000; his share of the profit from activity 2 was $10,000.

a. How do these activities affect Lyndon's 1992 return if AGI before considering these investments is $90,000?

b. Assume the same situation as (a) except that his AGI is $120,000. How is his return affected?

17. Which of the following individuals would be treated as materially participating? If they are deemed to materially participate, which of the seven tests is relevant?

a. F, an individual, owns an interest in a partnership that feeds and sells cattle. The general partner of the partnership periodically mails F a letter setting forth certain proposed actions and decisions with respect to the cattle-feeding operation. Such actions and decisions include, for example, what kind of feed to purchase, how much to purchase, when to purchase it, how often to feed cattle, and when to sell cattle. The letters explain the proposed actions and decisions, emphasize that taking or not taking a particular action or decision is solely within the discretion of F and the other partners, and ask F to indicate a decision with respect to each proposed action by answering certain questions. The general partner receives a fee for managing the cattle-feeding operation. Will F be treated as materially participating?

b. In 1990, D, an individual, acquired stock in an S corporation engaged in a business activity. For every taxable year from 1990 through 1994, D is treated as materially participating in the activity. At the beginning of 1995, D retires and is no longer involved with the business. Will D be treated as materially participating in 1995?

c. B, an individual, is employed full-time as a carpenter. B also owns an interest in a partnership engaged in a van conversion activity, which is a business activity. B and C, the other partner, are the only participants in the activity for the taxable year. The activity is conducted entirely on Saturdays. Each Saturday throughout the taxable year, B and C work for eight hours in the activity. Will B be treated as materially participating?

d. A, a calendar-year individual, owns an interest in a restaurant. During the taxable year, A works for an average of 30 hours per week in connection with the restaurant activity. Will A be treated as materially participating?

e. C, an individual, is employed full-time as an accountant. C also owns interests in a restaurant and a shoe store. The restaurant and shoe store are located across town from each other and constitute separate activities under the regulations. Each activity has several full-time employees. During the taxable year, C works in the restaurant activity for 400 hours and the shoe store activity for 150 hours. Will C be treated as materially participating in the restaurant activity? Will C be treated as materially participating in the shoe store activity?

———— THOUGHT PROBLEMS

1. Consider alternatives to using a minimum tax approach to overcome problems of overuse of beneficial tax provisions. Write a brief essay presenting other possible solutions and supporting your position as to the best approach.

2. Review the list of tax preferences and adjustments. Consider planning problems the alternative minimum tax system presents for individual taxpayers and for corporate taxpayers. Prepare brief statements explaining several planning problems for each type of taxpayer. Discuss how planning under the AMT differs from planning under the regular tax structure.

3. Explain why you think Congress adopted the approach of using ACE as the appropriate measure of corporate economic income rather than relying on income as reported for financial accounting purposes.

4. Explain why you think Congress used the concept of ACE as an additional AMT adjustment item for corporations rather than identifying specific tax preference items that cause a corporation's economic income to differ from taxable income and including those items as tax preferences or adjustments to the AMTI calculation.

5. Consider alternatives to PALs for dealing with the problems of abusive tax shelters and excessive utilization of provisions that generate losses that are not accompanied by economic detriment. Write a brief essay presenting alternative solutions to the problem Congress faced. Support your position as to the best approach.

6. The Treasury has issued almost 200 pages of Regulations in an attempt to define the term *activity*. Why does the definition of an activity play such a crucial role in the administration of the PAL rules?

7. While the new limits on passive losses make many past tax shelters ineffective under some circumstances, sheltering income from the tax is still good planning sometimes. Explain how the following investments can be effective shelters for individuals under current tax law.

    a. Investment in a general partnership that explores for oil and gas.

    b. Purchase of a rental house.

    c. Investment in a general partnership that engages in farming and ranching.

    d. Purchase of a personal residence.

    e. Purchase of a second home.

8. Considering the restrictions on deducting passive losses, what general planning ideas would you suggest to a potential client who

    a. Wishes to invest in a limited partnership (not a PTP) that will generate $30,000 in losses for at least 5 years.

    b. Wishes to invest in a rental property because he believes such properties are undervalued at the present time, and he thinks rental properties will show a much larger economic return than CDs or mutual funds. The required investment is $150,000. He can borrow up to 80% of that amount at 10% or pay for the property in cash. Cash flow before interest is expected to be $15,000. His AGI is $150,000 and is comprised largely of active income. Would your recommendation change if his AGI is $50,000?

    c. Wishes to invest in a partnership activity that he could either materially participate in, or not. The activity is expected to generate $20,000 in income to him each year.

    First, evaluate each of these items independently. Then, evaluate them together, under the assumption that AGI will be $50,000 before consideration of the returns on these investments.

CLASS PROJECTS

1. Locate hearings, committee reports, and articles published defending or protesting the institution of the initial minimum tax in 1969. Find the same types of materials for the 1986 Act. Summarize the statistics presented and arguments raised. Compare, contrast, and evaluate the credibility of the arguments made in the two different time periods in a short essay.

2. Locate articles written since the passage of the 1986 Act assessing the impact of the PAL rules on the economy and the financial well-being of individual investors. Summarize your conclusions about the wisdom of enacting the PAL statutes based on your reading. Prepare a brief presentation of your conclusions, highlighting the evidence you found most convincing.

Appendixes

APPENDIX A: 1992 Tax Rate Schedules

APPENDIX B: 1991 Tax Tables (Caution: These tables cannot be used to determine
              1992 tax liabilities. They are included here only to indicate format
              and for use with 1991 tax forms that might be utilized during summer
              or fall 1991 terms.)

APPENDIX C: 1991 Earned Income Credit (Caution: The actual credit should be
              computed from a table that is not yet available. This information will
              however, permit the student to determine the amount of the credit.)

APPENDIX D: Gift and Estate Tax Rates

Appendix A

1992 Tax Rate Schedules

Schedule X—Use if your filing status is Single

If the amount on Form 1040, line 37, is: *Over—*	*But not over—*	Enter on Form 1040, line 38	*of the amount over—*
$0	$21,450	. . . 15%	$ 0
21,450	51,900	$ 3,217.50 + 28%	21,450
51,900	. . .	11,743.50 + 31%	51,900

Schedule Y-1—Use if your filing status is Married filing jointly or Qualifying widow(er)

If the amount on Form 1040, line 37, is: *Over—*	*But not over—*	Enter on Form 1040, line 38	*of the amount over—*
$0	$35,800	. . . 15%	$0
35,800	86,500	$ 5,370.00 + 28%	35,800
86,500	. . .	19,566.00 + 31%	86,500

Schedule Y-2—Use if your filing status is Married filing separately

If the amount on Form 1040, line 37, is: *Over—*	*But not over—*	Enter on Form 1040, line 38	*of the amount over—*
$0	$17,900	. . . 15%	$0
17,900	43,250	$2,685.00 + 28%	17,900
43,250	. . .	9,783.00 + 31%	43,250

Schedule Z—Use if your filing status is Head of household

If the amount on Form 1040, line 37, is: *Over—*	*But not over—*	Enter on Form 1040, line 38	*of the amount over—*
$0	$28,750	. . . 15%	$0
28,750	74,150	$ 4,312.50 + 28%	28,750
74,150	. . .	17,024.50 + 31%	74,150

1992 Exemption, Standard Deduction, and Phaseout Amounts

Exemption Deduction	$ 2,300
Standard Deduction:	
Basic Amounts:	
Single	$ 3,600
Married Filing Jointly	6,000
Married Filing Separately	3,000
Head of Household	5,250
Minimum Standard Deduction	$ 600
Additional Standard Deduction for Persons	
Age 65 or Older or Legally Blind:	
Single or Head of Household	$ 900
Married	700
Phaseout of Personal Exemption Deduction	
Begins at adjusted gross income of:	
Single	$105,250
Married Filing Jointly	157,900
Married Filing Separately	78,950
Head of Household	131,550
Phaseout of Itemized Deductions Begins at adjusted gross income of:	
Married Filing Separately	$ 52,625
All Other Returns	105,250

Appendix B
1991 Tax Tables
Section 7.

1991
Tax Table

Use if your taxable income is less than $50,000.
If $50,000 or more, use the Tax Rate Schedules.

Example: *Mr. and Mrs. Brown are filing a joint return. Their taxable income on line 37 of Form 1040 is $25,300. First, they find the $25,300–25,350 income line. Next, they find the column for married filing jointly and read down the column. The amount shown where the income line and filing status column meet is $3,799. This is the tax amount they must write on line 38 of their return.*

Sample Table

At least	But less than	Single	Married filing jointly *	Married filing separately	Head of a household
			Your tax is—		
25,200	25,250	4,418	3,784	4,853	3,784
25,250	25,300	4,432	3,791	4,867	3,791
25,300	25,350	4,446	(3,799)	4,881	3,799
25,350	25,400	4,460	3,806	4,895	3,806

If line 37 (taxable income) is—		And you are—				If line 37 (taxable income) is—		And you are—				If line 37 (taxable income) is—		And you are—			
At least	But less than	Single	Married filing jointly *	Married filing separately	Head of a household	At least	But less than	Single	Married filing jointly *	Married filing separately	Head of a household	At least	But less than	Single	Married filing jointly *	Married filing separately	Head of a household
			Your tax is—						Your tax is—						Your tax is—		
$0	$5	$0	$0	$0	$0	1,300	1,325	197	197	197	197	2,700	2,725	407	407	407	407
5	15	2	2	2	2	1,325	1,350	201	201	201	201	2,725	2,750	411	411	411	411
						1,350	1,375	204	204	204	204	2,750	2,775	414	414	414	414
15	25	3	3	3	3	1,375	1,400	208	208	208	208	2,775	2,800	418	418	418	418
25	50	6	6	6	6	1,400	1,425	212	212	212	212	2,800	2,825	422	422	422	422
50	75	9	9	9	9	1,425	1,450	216	216	216	216	2,825	2,850	426	426	426	426
75	100	13	13	13	13	1,450	1,475	219	219	219	219	2,850	2,875	429	429	429	429
100	125	17	17	17	17	1,475	1,500	223	223	223	223	2,875	2,900	433	433	433	433
125	150	21	21	21	21	1,500	1,525	227	227	227	227	2,900	2,925	437	437	437	437
150	175	24	24	24	24	1,525	1,550	231	231	231	231	2,925	2,950	441	441	441	441
175	200	28	28	28	28	1,550	1,575	234	234	234	234	2,950	2,975	444	444	444	444
200	225	32	32	32	32	1,575	1,600	238	238	238	238	2,975	3,000	448	448	448	448
225	250	36	36	36	36	1,600	1,625	242	242	242	242						
250	275	39	39	39	39	1,625	1,650	246	246	246	246	**3,000**					
275	300	43	43	43	43	1,650	1,675	249	249	249	249	3,000	3,050	454	454	454	454
300	325	47	47	47	47	1,675	1,700	253	253	253	253	3,050	3,100	461	461	461	461
325	350	51	51	51	51	1,700	1,725	257	257	257	257	3,100	3,150	469	469	469	469
350	375	54	54	54	54	1,725	1,750	261	261	261	261	3,150	3,200	476	476	476	476
375	400	58	58	58	58	1,750	1,775	264	264	264	264	3,200	3,250	484	484	484	484
400	425	62	62	62	62	1,775	1,800	268	268	268	268	3,250	3,300	491	491	491	491
425	450	66	66	66	66	1,800	1,825	272	272	272	272	3,300	3,350	499	499	499	499
450	475	69	69	69	69	1,825	1,850	276	276	276	276	3,350	3,400	506	506	506	506
475	500	73	73	73	73	1,850	1,875	279	279	279	279	3,400	3,450	514	514	514	514
500	525	77	77	77	77	1,875	1,900	283	283	283	283	3,450	3,500	521	521	521	521
525	550	81	81	81	81	1,900	1,925	287	287	287	287	3,500	3,550	529	529	529	529
550	575	84	84	84	84	1,925	1,950	291	291	291	291	3,550	3,600	536	536	536	536
575	600	88	88	88	88	1,950	1,975	294	294	294	294	3,600	3,650	544	544	544	544
600	625	92	92	92	92	1,975	2,000	298	298	298	298	3,650	3,700	551	551	551	551
625	650	96	96	96	96							3,700	3,750	559	559	559	559
650	675	99	99	99	99	**2,000**						3,750	3,800	566	566	566	566
675	700	103	103	103	103	2,000	2,025	302	302	302	302	3,800	3,850	574	574	574	574
700	725	107	107	107	107	2,025	2,050	306	306	306	306	3,850	3,900	581	581	581	581
725	750	111	111	111	111	2,050	2,075	309	309	309	309	3,900	3,950	589	589	589	589
750	775	114	114	114	114	2,075	2,100	313	313	313	313	3,950	4,000	596	596	596	596
775	800	118	118	118	118	2,100	2,125	317	317	317	317						
800	825	122	122	122	122	2,125	2,150	321	321	321	321	**4,000**					
825	850	126	126	126	126	2,150	2,175	324	324	324	324	4,000	4,050	604	604	604	604
850	875	129	129	129	129	2,175	2,200	328	328	328	328	4,050	4,100	611	611	611	611
875	900	133	133	133	133	2,200	2,225	332	332	332	332	4,100	4,150	619	619	619	619
900	925	137	137	137	137	2,225	2,250	336	336	336	336	4,150	4,200	626	626	626	626
925	950	141	141	141	141	2,250	2,275	339	339	339	339	4,200	4,250	634	634	634	634
950	975	144	144	144	144	2,275	2,300	343	343	343	343	4,250	4,300	641	641	641	641
975	1,000	148	148	148	148	2,300	2,325	347	347	347	347	4,300	4,350	649	649	649	649
						2,325	2,350	351	351	351	351	4,350	4,400	656	656	656	656
1,000						2,350	2,375	354	354	354	354	4,400	4,450	664	664	664	664
						2,375	2,400	358	358	358	358	4,450	4,500	671	671	671	671
1,000	1,025	152	152	152	152	2,400	2,425	362	362	362	362	4,500	4,550	679	679	679	679
1,025	1,050	156	156	156	156	2,425	2,450	366	366	366	366	4,550	4,600	686	686	686	686
1,050	1,075	159	159	159	159	2,450	2,475	369	369	369	369	4,600	4,650	694	694	694	694
1,075	1,100	163	163	163	163	2,475	2,500	373	373	373	373	4,650	4,700	701	701	701	701
1,100	1,125	167	167	167	167	2,500	2,525	377	377	377	377	4,700	4,750	709	709	709	709
1,125	1,150	171	171	171	171	2,525	2,550	381	381	381	381	4,750	4,800	716	716	716	716
1,150	1,175	174	174	174	174	2,550	2,575	384	384	384	384	4,800	4,850	724	724	724	724
1,175	1,200	178	178	178	178	2,575	2,600	388	388	388	388	4,850	4,900	731	731	731	731
1,200	1,225	182	182	182	182	2,600	2,625	392	392	392	392	4,900	4,950	739	739	739	739
1,225	1,250	186	186	186	186	2,625	2,650	396	396	396	396	4,950	5,000	746	746	746	746
1,250	1,275	189	189	189	189	2,650	2,675	399	399	399	399						
1,275	1,300	193	193	193	193	2,675	2,700	403	403	403	403			Continued on next page			

* This column must also be used by a qualifying widow(er).

(Caution: These tables cannot be used to determine 1992 tax liabilities. They are included here only to indicate format and for use with 1991 tax forms that might be utilized during summer or fall 1991 terms.)

1991 Tax Table—*Continued*

If line 37 (taxable income) is—		And you are—				If line 37 (taxable income) is—		And you are—				If line 37 (taxable income) is—		And you are—			
At least	But less than	Single	Married filing jointly *	Married filing separately	Head of a household	At least	But less than	Single	Married filing jointly *	Married filing separately	Head of a household	At least	But less than	Single	Married filing jointly *	Married filing separately	Head of a household
5,000						**8,000**						**11,000**					
5,000	5,050	754	754	754	754	8,000	8,050	1,204	1,204	1,204	1,204	11,000	11,050	1,654	1,654	1,654	1,654
5,050	5,100	761	761	761	761	8,050	8,100	1,211	1,211	1,211	1,211	11,050	11,100	1,661	1,661	1,661	1,661
5,100	5,150	769	769	769	769	8,100	8,150	1,219	1,219	1,219	1,219	11,100	11,150	1,669	1,669	1,669	1,669
5,150	5,200	776	776	776	776	8,150	8,200	1,226	1,226	1,226	1,226	11,150	11,200	1,676	1,676	1,676	1,676
5,200	5,250	784	784	784	784	8,200	8,250	1,234	1,234	1,234	1,234	11,200	11,250	1,684	1,684	1,684	1,684
5,250	5,300	791	791	791	791	8,250	8,300	1,241	1,241	1,241	1,241	11,250	11,300	1,691	1,691	1,691	1,691
5,300	5,350	799	799	799	799	8,300	8,350	1,249	1,249	1,249	1,249	11,300	11,350	1,699	1,699	1,699	1,699
5,350	5,400	806	806	806	806	8,350	8,400	1,256	1,256	1,256	1,256	11,350	11,400	1,706	1,706	1,706	1,706
5,400	5,450	814	814	814	814	8,400	8,450	1,264	1,264	1,264	1,264	11,400	11,450	1,714	1,714	1,714	1,714
5,450	5,500	821	821	821	821	8,450	8,500	1,271	1,271	1,271	1,271	11,450	11,500	1,721	1,721	1,721	1,721
5,500	5,550	829	829	829	829	8,500	8,550	1,279	1,279	1,279	1,279	11,500	11,550	1,729	1,729	1,729	1,729
5,550	5,600	836	836	836	836	8,550	8,600	1,286	1,286	1,286	1,286	11,550	11,600	1,736	1,736	1,736	1,736
5,600	5,650	844	844	844	844	8,600	8,650	1,294	1,294	1,294	1,294	11,600	11,650	1,744	1,744	1,744	1,744
5,650	5,700	851	851	851	851	8,650	8,700	1,301	1,301	1,301	1,301	11,650	11,700	1,751	1,751	1,751	1,751
5,700	5,750	859	859	859	859	8,700	8,750	1,309	1,309	1,309	1,309	11,700	11,750	1,759	1,759	1,759	1,759
5,750	5,800	866	866	866	866	8,750	8,800	1,316	1,316	1,316	1,316	11,750	11,800	1,766	1,766	1,766	1,766
5,800	5,850	874	874	874	874	8,800	8,850	1,324	1,324	1,324	1,324	11,800	11,850	1,774	1,774	1,774	1,774
5,850	5,900	881	881	881	881	8,850	8,900	1,331	1,331	1,331	1,331	11,850	11,900	1,781	1,781	1,781	1,781
5,900	5,950	889	889	889	889	8,900	8,950	1,339	1,339	1,339	1,339	11,900	11,950	1,789	1,789	1,789	1,789
5,950	6,000	896	896	896	896	8,950	9,000	1,346	1,346	1,346	1,346	11,950	12,000	1,796	1,796	1,796	1,796
6,000						**9,000**						**12,000**					
6,000	6,050	904	904	904	904	9,000	9,050	1,354	1,354	1,354	1,354	12,000	12,050	1,804	1,804	1,804	1,804
6,050	6,100	911	911	911	911	9,050	9,100	1,361	1,361	1,361	1,361	12,050	12,100	1,811	1,811	1,811	1,811
6,100	6,150	919	919	919	919	9,100	9,150	1,369	1,369	1,369	1,369	12,100	12,150	1,819	1,819	1,819	1,819
6,150	6,200	926	926	926	926	9,150	9,200	1,376	1,376	1,376	1,376	12,150	12,200	1,826	1,826	1,826	1,826
6,200	6,250	934	934	934	934	9,200	9,250	1,384	1,384	1,384	1,384	12,200	12,250	1,834	1,834	1,834	1,834
6,250	6,300	941	941	941	941	9,250	9,300	1,391	1,391	1,391	1,391	12,250	12,300	1,841	1,841	1,841	1,841
6,300	6,350	949	949	949	949	9,300	9,350	1,399	1,399	1,399	1,399	12,300	12,350	1,849	1,849	1,849	1,849
6,350	6,400	956	956	956	956	9,350	9,400	1,406	1,406	1,406	1,406	12,350	12,400	1,856	1,856	1,856	1,856
6,400	6,450	964	964	964	964	9,400	9,450	1,414	1,414	1,414	1,414	12,400	12,450	1,864	1,864	1,864	1,864
6,450	6,500	971	971	971	971	9,450	9,500	1,421	1,421	1,421	1,421	12,450	12,500	1,871	1,871	1,871	1,871
6,500	6,550	979	979	979	979	9,500	9,550	1,429	1,429	1,429	1,429	12,500	12,550	1,879	1,879	1,879	1,879
6,550	6,600	986	986	986	986	9,550	9,600	1,436	1,436	1,436	1,436	12,550	12,600	1,886	1,886	1,886	1,886
6,600	6,650	994	994	994	994	9,600	9,650	1,444	1,444	1,444	1,444	12,600	12,650	1,894	1,894	1,894	1,894
6,650	6,700	1,001	1,001	1,001	1,001	9,650	9,700	1,451	1,451	1,451	1,451	12,650	12,700	1,901	1,901	1,901	1,901
6,700	6,750	1,009	1,009	1,009	1,009	9,700	9,750	1,459	1,459	1,459	1,459	12,700	12,750	1,909	1,909	1,909	1,909
6,750	6,800	1,016	1,016	1,016	1,016	9,750	9,800	1,466	1,466	1,466	1,466	12,750	12,800	1,916	1,916	1,916	1,916
6,800	6,850	1,024	1,024	1,024	1,024	9,800	9,850	1,474	1,474	1,474	1,474	12,800	12,850	1,924	1,924	1,924	1,924
6,850	6,900	1,031	1,031	1,031	1,031	9,850	9,900	1,481	1,481	1,481	1,481	12,850	12,900	1,931	1,931	1,931	1,931
6,900	6,950	1,039	1,039	1,039	1,039	9,900	9,950	1,489	1,489	1,489	1,489	12,900	12,950	1,939	1,939	1,939	1,939
6,950	7,000	1,046	1,046	1,046	1,046	9,950	10,000	1,496	1,496	1,496	1,496	12,950	13,000	1,946	1,946	1,946	1,946
7,000						**10,000**						**13,000**					
7,000	7,050	1,054	1,054	1,054	1,054	10,000	10,050	1,504	1,504	1,504	1,504	13,000	13,050	1,954	1,954	1,954	1,954
7,050	7,100	1,061	1,061	1,061	1,061	10,050	10,100	1,511	1,511	1,511	1,511	13,050	13,100	1,961	1,961	1,961	1,961
7,100	7,150	1,069	1,069	1,069	1,069	10,100	10,150	1,519	1,519	1,519	1,519	13,100	13,150	1,969	1,969	1,969	1,969
7,150	7,200	1,076	1,076	1,076	1,076	10,150	10,200	1,526	1,526	1,526	1,526	13,150	13,200	1,976	1,976	1,976	1,976
7,200	7,250	1,084	1,084	1,084	1,084	10,200	10,250	1,534	1,534	1,534	1,534	13,200	13,250	1,984	1,984	1,984	1,984
7,250	7,300	1,091	1,091	1,091	1,091	10,250	10,300	1,541	1,541	1,541	1,541	13,250	13,300	1,991	1,991	1,991	1,991
7,300	7,350	1,099	1,099	1,099	1,099	10,300	10,350	1,549	1,549	1,549	1,549	13,300	13,350	1,999	1,999	1,999	1,999
7,350	7,400	1,106	1,106	1,106	1,106	10,350	10,400	1,556	1,556	1,556	1,556	13,350	13,400	2,006	2,006	2,006	2,006
7,400	7,450	1,114	1,114	1,114	1,114	10,400	10,450	1,564	1,564	1,564	1,564	13,400	13,450	2,014	2,014	2,014	2,014
7,450	7,500	1,121	1,121	1,121	1,121	10,450	10,500	1,571	1,571	1,571	1,571	13,450	13,500	2,021	2,021	2,021	2,021
7,500	7,550	1,129	1,129	1,129	1,129	10,500	10,550	1,579	1,579	1,579	1,579	13,500	13,550	2,029	2,029	2,029	2,029
7,550	7,600	1,136	1,136	1,136	1,136	10,550	10,600	1,586	1,586	1,586	1,586	13,550	13,600	2,036	2,036	2,036	2,036
7,600	7,650	1,144	1,144	1,144	1,144	10,600	10,650	1,594	1,594	1,594	1,594	13,600	13,650	2,044	2,044	2,044	2,044
7,650	7,700	1,151	1,151	1,151	1,151	10,650	10,700	1,601	1,601	1,601	1,601	13,650	13,700	2,051	2,051	2,051	2,051
7,700	7,750	1,159	1,159	1,159	1,159	10,700	10,750	1,609	1,609	1,609	1,609	13,700	13,750	2,059	2,059	2,059	2,059
7,750	7,800	1,166	1,166	1,166	1,166	10,750	10,800	1,616	1,616	1,616	1,616	13,750	13,800	2,066	2,066	2,066	2,066
7,800	7,850	1,174	1,174	1,174	1,174	10,800	10,850	1,624	1,624	1,624	1,624	13,800	13,850	2,074	2,074	2,074	2,074
7,850	7,900	1,181	1,181	1,181	1,181	10,850	10,900	1,631	1,631	1,631	1,631	13,850	13,900	2,081	2,081	2,081	2,081
7,900	7,950	1,189	1,189	1,189	1,189	10,900	10,950	1,639	1,639	1,639	1,639	13,900	13,950	2,089	2,089	2,089	2,089
7,950	8,000	1,196	1,196	1,196	1,196	10,950	11,000	1,646	1,646	1,646	1,646	13,950	14,000	2,096	2,096	2,096	2,096

* This column must also be used by a qualifying widow(er).

Continued on next page

1991 Tax Table—Continued

14,000

At least	But less than	Single	Married filing jointly*	Married filing separately	Head of a household
14,000	14,050	2,104	2,104	2,104	2,104
14,050	14,100	2,111	2,111	2,111	2,111
14,100	14,150	2,119	2,119	2,119	2,119
14,150	14,200	2,126	2,126	2,126	2,126
14,200	14,250	2,134	2,134	2,134	2,134
14,250	14,300	2,141	2,141	2,141	2,141
14,300	14,350	2,149	2,149	2,149	2,149
14,350	14,400	2,156	2,156	2,156	2,156
14,400	14,450	2,164	2,164	2,164	2,164
14,450	14,500	2,171	2,171	2,171	2,171
14,500	14,550	2,179	2,179	2,179	2,179
14,550	14,600	2,186	2,186	2,186	2,186
14,600	14,650	2,194	2,194	2,194	2,194
14,650	14,700	2,201	2,201	2,201	2,201
14,700	14,750	2,209	2,209	2,209	2,209
14,750	14,800	2,216	2,216	2,216	2,216
14,800	14,850	2,224	2,224	2,224	2,224
14,850	14,900	2,231	2,231	2,231	2,231
14,900	14,950	2,239	2,239	2,239	2,239
14,950	15,000	2,246	2,246	2,246	2,246

15,000

At least	But less than	Single	Married filing jointly*	Married filing separately	Head of a household
15,000	15,050	2,254	2,254	2,254	2,254
15,050	15,100	2,261	2,261	2,261	2,261
15,100	15,150	2,269	2,269	2,269	2,269
15,150	15,200	2,276	2,276	2,276	2,276
15,200	15,250	2,284	2,284	2,284	2,284
15,250	15,300	2,291	2,291	2,291	2,291
15,300	15,350	2,299	2,299	2,299	2,299
15,350	15,400	2,306	2,306	2,306	2,306
15,400	15,450	2,314	2,314	2,314	2,314
15,450	15,500	2,321	2,321	2,321	2,321
15,500	15,550	2,329	2,329	2,329	2,329
15,550	15,600	2,336	2,336	2,336	2,336
15,600	15,650	2,344	2,344	2,344	2,344
15,650	15,700	2,351	2,351	2,351	2,351
15,700	15,750	2,359	2,359	2,359	2,359
15,750	15,800	2,366	2,366	2,366	2,366
15,800	15,850	2,374	2,374	2,374	2,374
15,850	15,900	2,381	2,381	2,381	2,381
15,900	15,950	2,389	2,389	2,389	2,389
15,950	16,000	2,396	2,396	2,396	2,396

16,000

At least	But less than	Single	Married filing jointly*	Married filing separately	Head of a household
16,000	16,050	2,404	2,404	2,404	2,404
16,050	16,100	2,411	2,411	2,411	2,411
16,100	16,150	2,419	2,419	2,419	2,419
16,150	16,200	2,426	2,426	2,426	2,426
16,200	16,250	2,434	2,434	2,434	2,434
16,250	16,300	2,441	2,441	2,441	2,441
16,300	16,350	2,449	2,449	2,449	2,449
16,350	16,400	2,456	2,456	2,456	2,456
16,400	16,450	2,464	2,464	2,464	2,464
16,450	16,500	2,471	2,471	2,471	2,471
16,500	16,550	2,479	2,479	2,479	2,479
16,550	16,600	2,486	2,486	2,486	2,486
16,600	16,650	2,494	2,494	2,494	2,494
16,650	16,700	2,501	2,501	2,501	2,501
16,700	16,750	2,509	2,509	2,509	2,509
16,750	16,800	2,516	2,516	2,516	2,516
16,800	16,850	2,524	2,524	2,524	2,524
16,850	16,900	2,531	2,531	2,531	2,531
16,900	16,950	2,539	2,539	2,539	2,539
16,950	17,000	2,546	2,546	2,546	2,546

17,000

At least	But less than	Single	Married filing jointly*	Married filing separately	Head of a household
17,000	17,050	2,554	2,554	2,557	2,554
17,050	17,100	2,561	2,561	2,571	2,561
17,100	17,150	2,569	2,569	2,585	2,569
17,150	17,200	2,576	2,576	2,599	2,576
17,200	17,250	2,584	2,584	2,613	2,584
17,250	17,300	2,591	2,591	2,627	2,591
17,300	17,350	2,599	2,599	2,641	2,599
17,350	17,400	2,606	2,606	2,655	2,606
17,400	17,450	2,614	2,614	2,669	2,614
17,450	17,500	2,621	2,621	2,683	2,621
17,500	17,550	2,629	2,629	2,697	2,629
17,550	17,600	2,636	2,636	2,711	2,636
17,600	17,650	2,644	2,644	2,725	2,644
17,650	17,700	2,651	2,651	2,739	2,651
17,700	17,750	2,659	2,659	2,753	2,659
17,750	17,800	2,666	2,666	2,767	2,666
17,800	17,850	2,674	2,674	2,781	2,674
17,850	17,900	2,681	2,681	2,795	2,681
17,900	17,950	2,689	2,689	2,809	2,689
17,950	18,000	2,696	2,696	2,823	2,696

18,000

At least	But less than	Single	Married filing jointly*	Married filing separately	Head of a household
18,000	18,050	2,704	2,704	2,837	2,704
18,050	18,100	2,711	2,711	2,851	2,711
18,100	18,150	2,719	2,719	2,865	2,719
18,150	18,200	2,726	2,726	2,879	2,726
18,200	18,250	2,734	2,734	2,893	2,734
18,250	18,300	2,741	2,741	2,907	2,741
18,300	18,350	2,749	2,749	2,921	2,749
18,350	18,400	2,756	2,756	2,935	2,756
18,400	18,450	2,764	2,764	2,949	2,764
18,450	18,500	2,771	2,771	2,963	2,771
18,500	18,550	2,779	2,779	2,977	2,779
18,550	18,600	2,786	2,786	2,991	2,786
18,600	18,650	2,794	2,794	3,005	2,794
18,650	18,700	2,801	2,801	3,019	2,801
18,700	18,750	2,809	2,809	3,033	2,809
18,750	18,800	2,816	2,816	3,047	2,816
18,800	18,850	2,824	2,824	3,061	2,824
18,850	18,900	2,831	2,831	3,075	2,831
18,900	18,950	2,839	2,839	3,089	2,839
18,950	19,000	2,846	2,846	3,103	2,846

19,000

At least	But less than	Single	Married filing jointly*	Married filing separately	Head of a household
19,000	19,050	2,854	2,854	3,117	2,854
19,050	19,100	2,861	2,861	3,131	2,861
19,100	19,150	2,869	2,869	3,145	2,869
19,150	19,200	2,876	2,876	3,159	2,876
19,200	19,250	2,884	2,884	3,173	2,884
19,250	19,300	2,891	2,891	3,187	2,891
19,300	19,350	2,899	2,899	3,201	2,899
19,350	19,400	2,906	2,906	3,215	2,906
19,400	19,450	2,914	2,914	3,229	2,914
19,450	19,500	2,921	2,921	3,243	2,921
19,500	19,550	2,929	2,929	3,257	2,929
19,550	19,600	2,936	2,936	3,271	2,936
19,600	19,650	2,944	2,944	3,285	2,944
19,650	19,700	2,951	2,951	3,299	2,951
19,700	19,750	2,959	2,959	3,313	2,959
19,750	19,800	2,966	2,966	3,327	2,966
19,800	19,850	2,974	2,974	3,341	2,974
19,850	19,900	2,981	2,981	3,355	2,981
19,900	19,950	2,989	2,989	3,369	2,989
19,950	20,000	2,996	2,996	3,383	2,996

20,000

At least	But less than	Single	Married filing jointly*	Married filing separately	Head of a household
20,000	20,050	3,004	3,004	3,397	3,004
20,050	20,100	3,011	3,011	3,411	3,011
20,100	20,150	3,019	3,019	3,425	3,019
20,150	20,200	3,026	3,026	3,439	3,026
20,200	20,250	3,034	3,034	3,453	3,034
20,250	20,300	3,041	3,041	3,467	3,041
20,300	20,350	3,049	3,049	3,481	3,049
20,350	20,400	3,060	3,056	3,495	3,056
20,400	20,450	3,074	3,064	3,509	3,064
20,450	20,500	3,088	3,071	3,523	3,071
20,500	20,550	3,102	3,079	3,537	3,079
20,550	20,600	3,116	3,086	3,551	3,086
20,600	20,650	3,130	3,094	3,565	3,094
20,650	20,700	3,144	3,101	3,579	3,101
20,700	20,750	3,158	3,109	3,593	3,109
20,750	20,800	3,172	3,116	3,607	3,116
20,800	20,850	3,186	3,124	3,621	3,124
20,850	20,900	3,200	3,131	3,635	3,131
20,900	20,950	3,214	3,139	3,649	3,139
20,950	21,000	3,228	3,146	3,663	3,146

21,000

At least	But less than	Single	Married filing jointly*	Married filing separately	Head of a household
21,000	21,050	3,242	3,154	3,677	3,154
21,050	21,100	3,256	3,161	3,691	3,161
21,100	21,150	3,270	3,169	3,705	3,169
21,150	21,200	3,284	3,176	3,719	3,176
21,200	21,250	3,298	3,184	3,733	3,184
21,250	21,300	3,312	3,191	3,747	3,191
21,300	21,350	3,326	3,199	3,761	3,199
21,350	21,400	3,340	3,206	3,775	3,206
21,400	21,450	3,354	3,214	3,789	3,214
21,450	21,500	3,368	3,221	3,803	3,221
21,500	21,550	3,382	3,229	3,817	3,229
21,550	21,600	3,396	3,236	3,831	3,236
21,600	21,650	3,410	3,244	3,845	3,244
21,650	21,700	3,424	3,251	3,859	3,251
21,700	21,750	3,438	3,259	3,873	3,259
21,750	21,800	3,452	3,266	3,887	3,266
21,800	21,850	3,466	3,274	3,901	3,274
21,850	21,900	3,480	3,281	3,915	3,281
21,900	21,950	3,494	3,289	3,929	3,289
21,950	22,000	3,508	3,296	3,943	3,296

22,000

At least	But less than	Single	Married filing jointly*	Married filing separately	Head of a household
22,000	22,050	3,522	3,304	3,957	3,304
22,050	22,100	3,536	3,311	3,971	3,311
22,100	22,150	3,550	3,319	3,985	3,319
22,150	22,200	3,564	3,326	3,999	3,326
22,200	22,250	3,578	3,334	4,013	3,334
22,250	22,300	3,592	3,341	4,027	3,341
22,300	22,350	3,606	3,349	4,041	3,349
22,350	22,400	3,620	3,356	4,055	3,356
22,400	22,450	3,634	3,364	4,069	3,364
22,450	22,500	3,648	3,371	4,083	3,371
22,500	22,550	3,662	3,379	4,097	3,379
22,550	22,600	3,676	3,386	4,111	3,386
22,600	22,650	3,690	3,394	4,125	3,394
22,650	22,700	3,704	3,401	4,139	3,401
22,700	22,750	3,718	3,409	4,153	3,409
22,750	22,800	3,732	3,416	4,167	3,416
22,800	22,850	3,746	3,424	4,181	3,424
22,850	22,900	3,760	3,431	4,195	3,431
22,900	22,950	3,774	3,439	4,209	3,439
22,950	23,000	3,788	3,446	4,223	3,446

* This column must also be used by a qualifying widow(er).

Continued on next page

1991 Tax Table—*Continued*

If line 37 (taxable income) is— At least	But less than	Single	Married filing jointly*	Married filing separately	Head of a household
23,000					
23,000	23,050	3,802	3,454	4,237	3,454
23,050	23,100	3,816	3,461	4,251	3,461
23,100	23,150	3,830	3,469	4,265	3,469
23,150	23,200	3,844	3,476	4,279	3,476
23,200	23,250	3,858	3,484	4,293	3,484
23,250	23,300	3,872	3,491	4,307	3,491
23,300	23,350	3,886	3,499	4,321	3,499
23,350	23,400	3,900	3,506	4,335	3,506
23,400	23,450	3,914	3,514	4,349	3,514
23,450	23,500	3,928	3,521	4,363	3,521
23,500	23,550	3,942	3,529	4,377	3,529
23,550	23,600	3,956	3,536	4,391	3,536
23,600	23,650	3,970	3,544	4,405	3,544
23,650	23,700	3,984	3,551	4,419	3,551
23,700	23,750	3,998	3,559	4,433	3,559
23,750	23,800	4,012	3,566	4,447	3,566
23,800	23,850	4,026	3,574	4,461	3,574
23,850	23,900	4,040	3,581	4,475	3,581
23,900	23,950	4,054	3,589	4,489	3,589
23,950	24,000	4,068	3,596	4,503	3,596
24,000					
24,000	24,050	4,082	3,604	4,517	3,604
24,050	24,100	4,096	3,611	4,531	3,611
24,100	24,150	4,110	3,619	4,545	3,619
24,150	24,200	4,124	3,626	4,559	3,626
24,200	24,250	4,138	3,634	4,573	3,634
24,250	24,300	4,152	3,641	4,587	3,641
24,300	24,350	4,166	3,649	4,601	3,649
24,350	24,400	4,180	3,656	4,615	3,656
24,400	24,450	4,194	3,664	4,629	3,664
24,450	24,500	4,208	3,671	4,643	3,671
24,500	24,550	4,222	3,679	4,657	3,679
24,550	24,600	4,236	3,686	4,671	3,686
24,600	24,650	4,250	3,694	4,685	3,694
24,650	24,700	4,264	3,701	4,699	3,701
24,700	24,750	4,278	3,709	4,713	3,709
24,750	24,800	4,292	3,716	4,727	3,716
24,800	24,850	4,306	3,724	4,741	3,724
24,850	24,900	4,320	3,731	4,755	3,731
24,900	24,950	4,334	3,739	4,769	3,739
24,950	25,000	4,348	3,746	4,783	3,746
25,000					
25,000	25,050	4,362	3,754	4,797	3,754
25,050	25,100	4,376	3,761	4,811	3,761
25,100	25,150	4,390	3,769	4,825	3,769
25,150	25,200	4,404	3,776	4,839	3,776
25,200	25,250	4,418	3,784	4,853	3,784
25,250	25,300	4,432	3,791	4,867	3,791
25,300	25,350	4,446	3,799	4,881	3,799
25,350	25,400	4,460	3,806	4,895	3,806
25,400	25,450	4,474	3,814	4,909	3,814
25,450	25,500	4,488	3,821	4,923	3,821
25,500	25,550	4,502	3,829	4,937	3,829
25,550	25,600	4,516	3,836	4,951	3,836
25,600	25,650	4,530	3,844	4,965	3,844
25,650	25,700	4,544	3,851	4,979	3,851
25,700	25,750	4,558	3,859	4,993	3,859
25,750	25,800	4,572	3,866	5,007	3,866
25,800	25,850	4,586	3,874	5,021	3,874
25,850	25,900	4,600	3,881	5,035	3,881
25,900	25,950	4,614	3,889	5,049	3,889
25,950	26,000	4,628	3,896	5,063	3,896

If line 37 (taxable income) is— At least	But less than	Single	Married filing jointly*	Married filing separately	Head of a household
26,000					
26,000	26,050	4,642	3,904	5,077	3,904
26,050	26,100	4,656	3,911	5,091	3,911
26,100	26,150	4,670	3,919	5,105	3,919
26,150	26,200	4,684	3,926	5,119	3,926
26,200	26,250	4,698	3,934	5,133	3,934
26,250	26,300	4,712	3,941	5,147	3,941
26,300	26,350	4,726	3,949	5,161	3,949
26,350	26,400	4,740	3,956	5,175	3,956
26,400	26,450	4,754	3,964	5,189	3,964
26,450	26,500	4,768	3,971	5,203	3,971
26,500	26,550	4,782	3,979	5,217	3,979
26,550	26,600	4,796	3,986	5,231	3,986
26,600	26,650	4,810	3,994	5,245	3,994
26,650	26,700	4,824	4,001	5,259	4,001
26,700	26,750	4,838	4,009	5,273	4,009
26,750	26,800	4,852	4,016	5,287	4,016
26,800	26,850	4,866	4,024	5,301	4,024
26,850	26,900	4,880	4,031	5,315	4,031
26,900	26,950	4,894	4,039	5,329	4,039
26,950	27,000	4,908	4,046	5,343	4,046
27,000					
27,000	27,050	4,922	4,054	5,357	4,054
27,050	27,100	4,936	4,061	5,371	4,061
27,100	27,150	4,950	4,069	5,385	4,069
27,150	27,200	4,964	4,076	5,399	4,076
27,200	27,250	4,978	4,084	5,413	4,084
27,250	27,300	4,992	4,091	5,427	4,091
27,300	27,350	5,006	4,099	5,441	4,102
27,350	27,400	5,020	4,106	5,455	4,116
27,400	27,450	5,034	4,114	5,469	4,130
27,450	27,500	5,048	4,121	5,483	4,144
27,500	27,550	5,062	4,129	5,497	4,158
27,550	27,600	5,076	4,136	5,511	4,172
27,600	27,650	5,090	4,144	5,525	4,186
27,650	27,700	5,104	4,151	5,539	4,200
27,700	27,750	5,118	4,159	5,553	4,214
27,750	27,800	5,132	4,166	5,567	4,228
27,800	27,850	5,146	4,174	5,581	4,242
27,850	27,900	5,160	4,181	5,595	4,256
27,900	27,950	5,174	4,189	5,609	4,270
27,950	28,000	5,188	4,196	5,623	4,284
28,000					
28,000	28,050	5,202	4,204	5,637	4,298
28,050	28,100	5,216	4,211	5,651	4,312
28,100	28,150	5,230	4,219	5,665	4,326
28,150	28,200	5,244	4,226	5,679	4,340
28,200	28,250	5,258	4,234	5,693	4,354
28,250	28,300	5,272	4,241	5,707	4,368
28,300	28,350	5,286	4,249	5,721	4,382
28,350	28,400	5,300	4,256	5,735	4,396
28,400	28,450	5,314	4,264	5,749	4,410
28,450	28,500	5,328	4,271	5,763	4,424
28,500	28,550	5,342	4,279	5,777	4,438
28,550	28,600	5,356	4,286	5,791	4,452
28,600	28,650	5,370	4,294	5,805	4,466
28,650	28,700	5,384	4,301	5,819	4,480
28,700	28,750	5,398	4,309	5,833	4,494
28,750	28,800	5,412	4,316	5,847	4,508
28,800	28,850	5,426	4,324	5,861	4,522
28,850	28,900	5,440	4,331	5,875	4,536
28,900	28,950	5,454	4,339	5,889	4,550
28,950	29,000	5,468	4,346	5,903	4,564

If line 37 (taxable income) is— At least	But less than	Single	Married filing jointly*	Married filing separately	Head of a household
29,000					
29,000	29,050	5,482	4,354	5,917	4,578
29,050	29,100	5,496	4,361	5,931	4,592
29,100	29,150	5,510	4,369	5,945	4,606
29,150	29,200	5,524	4,376	5,959	4,620
29,200	29,250	5,538	4,384	5,973	4,634
29,250	29,300	5,552	4,391	5,987	4,648
29,300	29,350	5,566	4,399	6,001	4,662
29,350	29,400	5,580	4,406	6,015	4,676
29,400	29,450	5,594	4,414	6,029	4,690
29,450	29,500	5,608	4,421	6,043	4,704
29,500	29,550	5,622	4,429	6,057	4,718
29,550	29,600	5,636	4,436	6,071	4,732
29,600	29,650	5,650	4,444	6,085	4,746
29,650	29,700	5,664	4,451	6,099	4,760
29,700	29,750	5,678	4,459	6,113	4,774
29,750	29,800	5,692	4,466	6,127	4,788
29,800	29,850	5,706	4,474	6,141	4,802
29,850	29,900	5,720	4,481	6,155	4,816
29,900	29,950	5,734	4,489	6,169	4,830
29,950	30,000	5,748	4,496	6,183	4,844
30,000					
30,000	30,050	5,762	4,504	6,197	4,858
30,050	30,100	5,776	4,511	6,211	4,872
30,100	30,150	5,790	4,519	6,225	4,886
30,150	30,200	5,804	4,526	6,239	4,900
30,200	30,250	5,818	4,534	6,253	4,914
30,250	30,300	5,832	4,541	6,267	4,928
30,300	30,350	5,846	4,549	6,281	4,942
30,350	30,400	5,860	4,556	6,295	4,956
30,400	30,450	5,874	4,564	6,309	4,970
30,450	30,500	5,888	4,571	6,323	4,984
30,500	30,550	5,902	4,579	6,337	4,998
30,550	30,600	5,916	4,586	6,351	5,012
30,600	30,650	5,930	4,594	6,365	5,026
30,650	30,700	5,944	4,601	6,379	5,040
30,700	30,750	5,958	4,609	6,393	5,054
30,750	30,800	5,972	4,616	6,407	5,068
30,800	30,850	5,986	4,624	6,421	5,082
30,850	30,900	6,000	4,631	6,435	5,096
30,900	30,950	6,014	4,639	6,449	5,110
30,950	31,000	6,028	4,646	6,463	5,124
31,000					
31,000	31,050	6,042	4,654	6,477	5,138
31,050	31,100	6,056	4,661	6,491	5,152
31,100	31,150	6,070	4,669	6,505	5,166
31,150	31,200	6,084	4,676	6,519	5,180
31,200	31,250	6,098	4,684	6,533	5,194
31,250	31,300	6,112	4,691	6,547	5,208
31,300	31,350	6,126	4,699	6,561	5,222
31,350	31,400	6,140	4,706	6,575	5,236
31,400	31,450	6,154	4,714	6,589	5,250
31,450	31,500	6,168	4,721	6,603	5,264
31,500	31,550	6,182	4,729	6,617	5,278
31,550	31,600	6,196	4,736	6,631	5,292
31,600	31,650	6,210	4,744	6,645	5,306
31,650	31,700	6,224	4,751	6,659	5,320
31,700	31,750	6,238	4,759	6,673	5,334
31,750	31,800	6,252	4,766	6,687	5,348
31,800	31,850	6,266	4,774	6,701	5,362
31,850	31,900	6,280	4,781	6,715	5,376
31,900	31,950	6,294	4,789	6,729	5,390
31,950	32,000	6,308	4,796	6,743	5,404

* This column must also be used by a qualifying widow(er).

Continued on next page

1991 Tax Table—Continued

Column headings (apply to all sections below):

If line 37 (taxable income) is—		And you are—			
At least	But less than	Single	Married filing jointly *	Married filing separately	Head of a household
				Your tax is—	

32,000

At least	But less than	Single	Married filing jointly	Married filing separately	Head of a household
32,000	32,050	6,322	4,804	6,757	5,418
32,050	32,100	6,336	4,811	6,771	5,432
32,100	32,150	6,350	4,819	6,785	5,446
32,150	32,200	6,364	4,826	6,799	5,460
32,200	32,250	6,378	4,834	6,813	5,474
32,250	32,300	6,392	4,841	6,827	5,488
32,300	32,350	6,406	4,849	6,841	5,502
32,350	32,400	6,420	4,856	6,855	5,516
32,400	32,450	6,434	4,864	6,869	5,530
32,450	32,500	6,448	4,871	6,883	5,544
32,500	32,550	6,462	4,879	6,897	5,558
32,550	32,600	6,476	4,886	6,911	5,572
32,600	32,650	6,490	4,894	6,925	5,586
32,650	32,700	6,504	4,901	6,939	5,600
32,700	32,750	6,518	4,909	6,953	5,614
32,750	32,800	6,532	4,916	6,967	5,628
32,800	32,850	6,546	4,924	6,981	5,642
32,850	32,900	6,560	4,931	6,995	5,656
32,900	32,950	6,574	4,939	7,009	5,670
32,950	33,000	6,588	4,946	7,023	5,684

33,000

At least	But less than	Single	Married filing jointly	Married filing separately	Head of a household
33,000	33,050	6,602	4,954	7,037	5,698
33,050	33,100	6,616	4,961	7,051	5,712
33,100	33,150	6,630	4,969	7,065	5,726
33,150	33,200	6,644	4,976	7,079	5,740
33,200	33,250	6,658	4,984	7,093	5,754
33,250	33,300	6,672	4,991	7,107	5,768
33,300	33,350	6,686	4,999	7,121	5,782
33,350	33,400	6,700	5,006	7,135	5,796
33,400	33,450	6,714	5,014	7,149	5,810
33,450	33,500	6,728	5,021	7,163	5,824
33,500	33,550	6,742	5,029	7,177	5,838
33,550	33,600	6,756	5,036	7,191	5,852
33,600	33,650	6,770	5,044	7,205	5,866
33,650	33,700	6,784	5,051	7,219	5,880
33,700	33,750	6,798	5,059	7,233	5,894
33,750	33,800	6,812	5,066	7,247	5,908
33,800	33,850	6,826	5,074	7,261	5,922
33,850	33,900	6,840	5,081	7,275	5,936
33,900	33,950	6,854	5,089	7,289	5,950
33,950	34,000	6,868	5,096	7,303	5,964

34,000

At least	But less than	Single	Married filing jointly	Married filing separately	Head of a household
34,000	34,050	6,882	5,107	7,317	5,978
34,050	34,100	6,896	5,121	7,331	5,992
34,100	34,150	6,910	5,135	7,345	6,006
34,150	34,200	6,924	5,149	7,359	6,020
34,200	34,250	6,938	5,163	7,373	6,034
34,250	34,300	6,952	5,177	7,387	6,048
34,300	34,350	6,966	5,191	7,401	6,062
34,350	34,400	6,980	5,205	7,415	6,076
34,400	34,450	6,994	5,219	7,429	6,090
34,450	34,500	7,008	5,233	7,443	6,104
34,500	34,550	7,022	5,247	7,457	6,118
34,550	34,600	7,036	5,261	7,471	6,132
34,600	34,650	7,050	5,275	7,485	6,146
34,650	34,700	7,064	5,289	7,499	6,160
34,700	34,750	7,078	5,303	7,513	6,174
34,750	34,800	7,092	5,317	7,527	6,188
34,800	34,850	7,106	5,331	7,541	6,202
34,850	34,900	7,120	5,345	7,555	6,216
34,900	34,950	7,134	5,359	7,569	6,230
34,950	35,000	7,148	5,373	7,583	6,244

35,000

At least	But less than	Single	Married filing jointly	Married filing separately	Head of a household
35,000	35,050	7,162	5,387	7,597	6,258
35,050	35,100	7,176	5,401	7,611	6,272
35,100	35,150	7,190	5,415	7,625	6,286
35,150	35,200	7,204	5,429	7,639	6,300
35,200	35,250	7,218	5,443	7,653	6,314
35,250	35,300	7,232	5,457	7,667	6,328
35,300	35,350	7,246	5,471	7,681	6,342
35,350	35,400	7,260	5,485	7,695	6,356
35,400	35,450	7,274	5,499	7,709	6,370
35,450	35,500	7,288	5,513	7,723	6,384
35,500	35,550	7,302	5,527	7,737	6,398
35,550	35,600	7,316	5,541	7,751	6,412
35,600	35,650	7,330	5,555	7,765	6,426
35,650	35,700	7,344	5,569	7,779	6,440
35,700	35,750	7,358	5,583	7,793	6,454
35,750	35,800	7,372	5,597	7,807	6,468
35,800	35,850	7,386	5,611	7,821	6,482
35,850	35,900	7,400	5,625	7,835	6,496
35,900	35,950	7,414	5,639	7,849	6,510
35,950	36,000	7,428	5,653	7,863	6,524

36,000

At least	But less than	Single	Married filing jointly	Married filing separately	Head of a household
36,000	36,050	7,442	5,667	7,877	6,538
36,050	36,100	7,456	5,681	7,891	6,552
36,100	36,150	7,470	5,695	7,905	6,566
36,150	36,200	7,484	5,709	7,919	6,580
36,200	36,250	7,498	5,723	7,933	6,594
36,250	36,300	7,512	5,737	7,947	6,608
36,300	36,350	7,526	5,751	7,961	6,622
36,350	36,400	7,540	5,765	7,975	6,636
36,400	36,450	7,554	5,779	7,989	6,650
36,450	36,500	7,568	5,793	8,003	6,664
36,500	36,550	7,582	5,807	8,017	6,678
36,550	36,600	7,596	5,821	8,031	6,692
36,600	36,650	7,610	5,835	8,045	6,706
36,650	36,700	7,624	5,849	8,059	6,720
36,700	36,750	7,638	5,863	8,073	6,734
36,750	36,800	7,652	5,877	8,087	6,748
36,800	36,850	7,666	5,891	8,101	6,762
36,850	36,900	7,680	5,905	8,115	6,776
36,900	36,950	7,694	5,919	8,129	6,790
36,950	37,000	7,708	5,933	8,143	6,804

37,000

At least	But less than	Single	Married filing jointly	Married filing separately	Head of a household
37,000	37,050	7,722	5,947	8,157	6,818
37,050	37,100	7,736	5,961	8,171	6,832
37,100	37,150	7,750	5,975	8,185	6,846
37,150	37,200	7,764	5,989	8,199	6,860
37,200	37,250	7,778	6,003	8,213	6,874
37,250	37,300	7,792	6,017	8,227	6,888
37,300	37,350	7,806	6,031	8,241	6,902
37,350	37,400	7,820	6,045	8,255	6,916
37,400	37,450	7,834	6,059	8,269	6,930
37,450	37,500	7,848	6,073	8,283	6,944
37,500	37,550	7,862	6,087	8,297	6,958
37,550	37,600	7,876	6,101	8,311	6,972
37,600	37,650	7,890	6,115	8,325	6,986
37,650	37,700	7,904	6,129	8,339	7,000
37,700	37,750	7,918	6,143	8,353	7,014
37,750	37,800	7,932	6,157	8,367	7,028
37,800	37,850	7,946	6,171	8,381	7,042
37,850	37,900	7,960	6,185	8,395	7,056
37,900	37,950	7,974	6,199	8,409	7,070
37,950	38,000	7,988	6,213	8,423	7,084

38,000

At least	But less than	Single	Married filing jointly	Married filing separately	Head of a household
38,000	38,050	8,002	6,227	8,437	7,098
38,050	38,100	8,016	6,241	8,451	7,112
38,100	38,150	8,030	6,255	8,465	7,126
38,150	38,200	8,044	6,269	8,479	7,140
38,200	38,250	8,058	6,283	8,493	7,154
38,250	38,300	8,072	6,297	8,507	7,168
38,300	38,350	8,086	6,311	8,521	7,182
38,350	38,400	8,100	6,325	8,535	7,196
38,400	38,450	8,114	6,339	8,549	7,210
38,450	38,500	8,128	6,353	8,563	7,224
38,500	38,550	8,142	6,367	8,577	7,238
38,550	38,600	8,156	6,381	8,591	7,252
38,600	38,650	8,170	6,395	8,605	7,266
38,650	38,700	8,184	6,409	8,619	7,280
38,700	38,750	8,198	6,423	8,633	7,294
38,750	38,800	8,212	6,437	8,647	7,308
38,800	38,850	8,226	6,451	8,661	7,322
38,850	38,900	8,240	6,465	8,675	7,336
38,900	38,950	8,254	6,479	8,689	7,350
38,950	39,000	8,268	6,493	8,703	7,364

39,000

At least	But less than	Single	Married filing jointly	Married filing separately	Head of a household
39,000	39,050	8,282	6,507	8,717	7,378
39,050	39,100	8,296	6,521	8,731	7,392
39,100	39,150	8,310	6,535	8,745	7,406
39,150	39,200	8,324	6,549	8,759	7,420
39,200	39,250	8,338	6,563	8,773	7,434
39,250	39,300	8,352	6,577	8,787	7,448
39,300	39,350	8,366	6,591	8,801	7,462
39,350	39,400	8,380	6,605	8,815	7,476
39,400	39,450	8,394	6,619	8,829	7,490
39,450	39,500	8,408	6,633	8,843	7,504
39,500	39,550	8,422	6,647	8,857	7,518
39,550	39,600	8,436	6,661	8,871	7,532
39,600	39,650	8,450	6,675	8,885	7,546
39,650	39,700	8,464	6,689	8,899	7,560
39,700	39,750	8,478	6,703	8,913	7,574
39,750	39,800	8,492	6,717	8,927	7,588
39,800	39,850	8,506	6,731	8,941	7,602
39,850	39,900	8,520	6,745	8,955	7,616
39,900	39,950	8,534	6,759	8,969	7,630
39,950	40,000	8,548	6,773	8,983	7,644

40,000

At least	But less than	Single	Married filing jointly	Married filing separately	Head of a household
40,000	40,050	8,562	6,787	8,997	7,658
40,050	40,100	8,576	6,801	9,011	7,672
40,100	40,150	8,590	6,815	9,025	7,686
40,150	40,200	8,604	6,829	9,039	7,700
40,200	40,250	8,618	6,843	9,053	7,714
40,250	40,300	8,632	6,857	9,067	7,728
40,300	40,350	8,646	6,871	9,081	7,742
40,350	40,400	8,660	6,885	9,095	7,756
40,400	40,450	8,674	6,899	9,109	7,770
40,450	40,500	8,688	6,913	9,123	7,784
40,500	40,550	8,702	6,927	9,137	7,798
40,550	40,600	8,716	6,941	9,151	7,812
40,600	40,650	8,730	6,955	9,165	7,826
40,650	40,700	8,744	6,969	9,179	7,840
40,700	40,750	8,758	6,983	9,193	7,854
40,750	40,800	8,772	6,997	9,207	7,868
40,800	40,850	8,786	7,011	9,221	7,882
40,850	40,900	8,800	7,025	9,235	7,896
40,900	40,950	8,814	7,039	9,249	7,910
40,950	41,000	8,828	7,053	9,263	7,924

* This column must also be used by a qualifying widow(er).

Continued on next page

1991 Tax Table—*Continued*

41,000

At least	But less than	Single	Married filing jointly*	Married filing separately	Head of a household
41,000	41,050	8,842	7,067	9,277	7,938
41,050	41,100	8,856	7,081	9,291	7,952
41,100	41,150	8,870	7,095	9,307	7,966
41,150	41,200	8,884	7,109	9,322	7,980
41,200	41,250	8,898	7,123	9,338	7,994
41,250	41,300	8,912	7,137	9,353	8,008
41,300	41,350	8,926	7,151	9,369	8,022
41,350	41,400	8,940	7,165	9,384	8,036
41,400	41,450	8,954	7,179	9,400	8,050
41,450	41,500	8,968	7,193	9,415	8,064
41,500	41,550	8,982	7,207	9,431	8,078
41,550	41,600	8,996	7,221	9,446	8,092
41,600	41,650	9,010	7,235	9,462	8,106
41,650	41,700	9,024	7,249	9,477	8,120
41,700	41,750	9,038	7,263	9,493	8,134
41,750	41,800	9,052	7,277	9,508	8,148
41,800	41,850	9,066	7,291	9,524	8,162
41,850	41,900	9,080	7,305	9,539	8,176
41,900	41,950	9,094	7,319	9,555	8,190
41,950	42,000	9,108	7,333	9,570	8,204

42,000

At least	But less than	Single	Married filing jointly*	Married filing separately	Head of a household
42,000	42,050	9,122	7,347	9,586	8,218
42,050	42,100	9,136	7,361	9,601	8,232
42,100	42,150	9,150	7,375	9,617	8,246
42,150	42,200	9,164	7,389	9,632	8,260
42,200	42,250	9,178	7,403	9,648	8,274
42,250	42,300	9,192	7,417	9,663	8,288
42,300	42,350	9,206	7,431	9,679	8,302
42,350	42,400	9,220	7,445	9,694	8,316
42,400	42,450	9,234	7,459	9,710	8,330
42,450	42,500	9,248	7,473	9,725	8,344
42,500	42,550	9,262	7,487	9,741	8,358
42,550	42,600	9,276	7,501	9,756	8,372
42,600	42,650	9,290	7,515	9,772	8,386
42,650	42,700	9,304	7,529	9,787	8,400
42,700	42,750	9,318	7,543	9,803	8,414
42,750	42,800	9,332	7,557	9,818	8,428
42,800	42,850	9,346	7,571	9,834	8,442
42,850	42,900	9,360	7,585	9,849	8,456
42,900	42,950	9,374	7,599	9,865	8,470
42,950	43,000	9,388	7,613	9,880	8,484

43,000

At least	But less than	Single	Married filing jointly*	Married filing separately	Head of a household
43,000	43,050	9,402	7,627	9,896	8,498
43,050	43,100	9,416	7,641	9,911	8,512
43,100	43,150	9,430	7,655	9,927	8,526
43,150	43,200	9,444	7,669	9,942	8,540
43,200	43,250	9,458	7,683	9,958	8,554
43,250	43,300	9,472	7,697	9,973	8,568
43,300	43,350	9,486	7,711	9,989	8,582
43,350	43,400	9,500	7,725	10,004	8,596
43,400	43,450	9,514	7,739	10,020	8,610
43,450	43,500	9,528	7,753	10,035	8,624
43,500	43,550	9,542	7,767	10,051	8,638
43,550	43,600	9,556	7,781	10,066	8,652
43,600	43,650	9,570	7,795	10,082	8,666
43,650	43,700	9,584	7,809	10,097	8,680
43,700	43,750	9,598	7,823	10,113	8,694
43,750	43,800	9,612	7,837	10,128	8,708
43,800	43,850	9,626	7,851	10,144	8,722
43,850	43,900	9,640	7,865	10,159	8,736
43,900	43,950	9,654	7,879	10,175	8,750
43,950	44,000	9,668	7,893	10,190	8,764

44,000

At least	But less than	Single	Married filing jointly*	Married filing separately	Head of a household
44,000	44,050	9,682	7,907	10,206	8,778
44,050	44,100	9,696	7,921	10,221	8,792
44,100	44,150	9,710	7,935	10,237	8,806
44,150	44,200	9,724	7,949	10,252	8,820
44,200	44,250	9,738	7,963	10,268	8,834
44,250	44,300	9,752	7,977	10,283	8,848
44,300	44,350	9,766	7,991	10,299	8,862
44,350	44,400	9,780	8,005	10,314	8,876
44,400	44,450	9,794	8,019	10,330	8,890
44,450	44,500	9,808	8,033	10,345	8,904
44,500	44,550	9,822	8,047	10,361	8,918
44,550	44,600	9,836	8,061	10,376	8,932
44,600	44,650	9,850	8,075	10,392	8,946
44,650	44,700	9,864	8,089	10,407	8,960
44,700	44,750	9,878	8,103	10,423	8,974
44,750	44,800	9,892	8,117	10,438	8,988
44,800	44,850	9,906	8,131	10,454	9,002
44,850	44,900	9,920	8,145	10,469	9,016
44,900	44,950	9,934	8,159	10,485	9,030
44,950	45,000	9,948	8,173	10,500	9,044

45,000

At least	But less than	Single	Married filing jointly*	Married filing separately	Head of a household
45,000	45,050	9,962	8,187	10,516	9,058
45,050	45,100	9,976	8,201	10,531	9,072
45,100	45,150	9,990	8,215	10,547	9,086
45,150	45,200	10,004	8,229	10,562	9,100
45,200	45,250	10,018	8,243	10,578	9,114
45,250	45,300	10,032	8,257	10,593	9,128
45,300	45,350	10,046	8,271	10,609	9,142
45,350	45,400	10,060	8,285	10,624	9,156
45,400	45,450	10,074	8,299	10,640	9,170
45,450	45,500	10,088	8,313	10,655	9,184
45,500	45,550	10,102	8,327	10,671	9,198
45,550	45,600	10,116	8,341	10,686	9,212
45,600	45,650	10,130	8,355	10,702	9,226
45,650	45,700	10,144	8,369	10,717	9,240
45,700	45,750	10,158	8,383	10,733	9,254
45,750	45,800	10,172	8,397	10,748	9,268
45,800	45,850	10,186	8,411	10,764	9,282
45,850	45,900	10,200	8,425	10,779	9,296
45,900	45,950	10,214	8,439	10,795	9,310
45,950	46,000	10,228	8,453	10,810	9,324

46,000

At least	But less than	Single	Married filing jointly*	Married filing separately	Head of a household
46,000	46,050	10,242	8,467	10,826	9,338
46,050	46,100	10,256	8,481	10,841	9,352
46,100	46,150	10,270	8,495	10,857	9,366
46,150	46,200	10,284	8,509	10,872	9,380
46,200	46,250	10,298	8,523	10,888	9,394
46,250	46,300	10,312	8,537	10,903	9,408
46,300	46,350	10,326	8,551	10,919	9,422
46,350	46,400	10,340	8,565	10,934	9,436
46,400	46,450	10,354	8,579	10,950	9,450
46,450	46,500	10,368	8,593	10,965	9,464
46,500	46,550	10,382	8,607	10,981	9,478
46,550	46,600	10,396	8,621	10,996	9,492
46,600	46,650	10,410	8,635	11,012	9,506
46,650	46,700	10,424	8,649	11,027	9,520
46,700	46,750	10,438	8,663	11,043	9,534
46,750	46,800	10,452	8,677	11,058	9,548
46,800	46,850	10,466	8,691	11,074	9,562
46,850	46,900	10,480	8,705	11,089	9,576
46,900	46,950	10,494	8,719	11,105	9,590
46,950	47,000	10,508	8,733	11,120	9,604

47,000

At least	But less than	Single	Married filing jointly*	Married filing separately	Head of a household
47,000	47,050	10,522	8,747	11,136	9,618
47,050	47,100	10,536	8,761	11,151	9,632
47,100	47,150	10,550	8,775	11,167	9,646
47,150	47,200	10,564	8,789	11,182	9,660
47,200	47,250	10,578	8,803	11,198	9,674
47,250	47,300	10,592	8,817	11,213	9,688
47,300	47,350	10,606	8,831	11,229	9,702
47,350	47,400	10,620	8,845	11,244	9,716
47,400	47,450	10,634	8,859	11,260	9,730
47,450	47,500	10,648	8,873	11,275	9,744
47,500	47,550	10,662	8,887	11,291	9,758
47,550	47,600	10,676	8,901	11,306	9,772
47,600	47,650	10,690	8,915	11,322	9,786
47,650	47,700	10,704	8,929	11,337	9,800
47,700	47,750	10,718	8,943	11,353	9,814
47,750	47,800	10,732	8,957	11,368	9,828
47,800	47,850	10,746	8,971	11,384	9,842
47,850	47,900	10,760	8,985	11,399	9,856
47,900	47,950	10,774	8,999	11,415	9,870
47,950	48,000	10,788	9,013	11,430	9,884

48,000

At least	But less than	Single	Married filing jointly*	Married filing separately	Head of a household
48,000	48,050	10,802	9,027	11,446	9,898
48,050	48,100	10,816	9,041	11,461	9,912
48,100	48,150	10,830	9,055	11,477	9,926
48,150	48,200	10,844	9,069	11,492	9,940
48,200	48,250	10,858	9,083	11,508	9,954
48,250	48,300	10,872	9,097	11,523	9,968
48,300	48,350	10,886	9,111	11,539	9,982
48,350	48,400	10,900	9,125	11,554	9,996
48,400	48,450	10,914	9,139	11,570	10,010
48,450	48,500	10,928	9,153	11,585	10,024
48,500	48,550	10,942	9,167	11,601	10,038
48,550	48,600	10,956	9,181	11,616	10,052
48,600	48,650	10,970	9,195	11,632	10,066
48,650	48,700	10,984	9,209	11,647	10,080
48,700	48,750	10,998	9,223	11,663	10,094
48,750	48,800	11,012	9,237	11,678	10,108
48,800	48,850	11,026	9,251	11,694	10,122
48,850	48,900	11,040	9,265	11,709	10,136
48,900	48,950	11,054	9,279	11,725	10,150
48,950	49,000	11,068	9,293	11,740	10,164

49,000

At least	But less than	Single	Married filing jointly*	Married filing separately	Head of a household
49,000	49,050	11,082	9,307	11,756	10,178
49,050	49,100	11,096	9,321	11,771	10,192
49,100	49,150	11,110	9,335	11,787	10,206
49,150	49,200	11,124	9,349	11,802	10,220
49,200	49,250	11,138	9,363	11,818	10,234
49,250	49,300	11,152	9,377	11,833	10,248
49,300	49,350	11,166	9,391	11,849	10,262
49,350	49,400	11,182	9,405	11,864	10,276
49,400	49,450	11,197	9,419	11,880	10,290
49,450	49,500	11,213	9,433	11,895	10,304
49,500	49,550	11,228	9,447	11,911	10,318
49,550	49,600	11,244	9,461	11,926	10,332
49,600	49,650	11,259	9,475	11,942	10,346
49,650	49,700	11,275	9,489	11,957	10,360
49,700	49,750	11,290	9,503	11,973	10,374
49,750	49,800	11,306	9,517	11,988	10,388
49,800	49,850	11,321	9,531	12,004	10,402
49,850	49,900	11,337	9,545	12,019	10,416
49,900	49,950	11,352	9,559	12,035	10,430
49,950	50,000	11,368	9,573	12,050	10,444

* This column must also be used by a qualifying widow(er).

50,000 or over — use tax rate schedules

Appendix C

TABLE A—Basic Credit

1991 Earned Income Credit

This is **not** a tax table.

To find your basic credit: First, read down the "At least — But less than" columns and find the line that includes the amount you entered on line 7 or line 9 of Schedule EIC. Next, read across to the column that includes the number of qualifying children you listed on Schedule EIC. Then, enter the credit from that column on Schedule EIC, line 8 or line 10, whichever applies.

If the amount on Schedule EIC, line 7 or line 9, is—		And you listed—	
At least	But less than	One child	Two children
		Your basic credit is—	
$1	$50	$4	$4
50	100	13	13
100	150	21	22
150	200	29	30
200	250	38	39
250	300	46	48
300	350	54	56
350	400	63	65
400	450	71	74
450	500	79	82
500	550	88	91
550	600	96	99
600	650	104	108
650	700	113	117
700	750	121	125
750	800	129	134
800	850	138	143
850	900	146	151
900	950	154	160
950	1,000	163	169
1,000	1,050	171	177
1,050	1,100	180	186
1,100	1,150	188	195
1,150	1,200	196	203
1,200	1,250	205	212
1,250	1,300	213	221
1,300	1,350	221	229
1,350	1,400	230	238
1,400	1,450	238	247
1,450	1,500	246	255
1,500	1,550	255	264
1,550	1,600	263	272
1,600	1,650	271	281
1,650	1,700	280	290
1,700	1,750	288	298
1,750	1,800	296	307
1,800	1,850	305	316
1,850	1,900	313	324
1,900	1,950	321	333
1,950	2,000	330	342
2,000	2,050	338	350
2,050	2,100	347	359
2,100	2,150	355	368
2,150	2,200	363	376
2,200	2,250	372	385
2,250	2,300	380	394
2,300	2,350	388	402
2,350	2,400	397	411
2,400	2,450	405	420
2,450	2,500	413	428
2,500	2,550	422	437
2,550	2,600	430	445
2,600	2,650	438	454
2,650	2,700	447	463
2,700	2,750	455	471
2,750	2,800	463	480

If the amount on Schedule EIC, line 7 or line 9, is—		And you listed—	
At least	But less than	One child	Two children
		Your basic credit is—	
$2,800	$2,850	$472	$489
2,850	2,900	480	497
2,900	2,950	488	506
2,950	3,000	497	515
3,000	3,050	505	523
3,050	3,100	514	532
3,100	3,150	522	541
3,150	3,200	530	549
3,200	3,250	539	558
3,250	3,300	547	567
3,300	3,350	555	575
3,350	3,400	564	584
3,400	3,450	572	593
3,450	3,500	580	601
3,500	3,550	589	610
3,550	3,600	597	618
3,600	3,650	605	627
3,650	3,700	614	636
3,700	3,750	622	644
3,750	3,800	630	653
3,800	3,850	639	662
3,850	3,900	647	670
3,900	3,950	655	679
3,950	4,000	664	688
4,000	4,050	672	696
4,050	4,100	681	705
4,100	4,150	689	714
4,150	4,200	697	722
4,200	4,250	706	731
4,250	4,300	714	740
4,300	4,350	722	748
4,350	4,400	731	757
4,400	4,450	739	766
4,450	4,500	747	774
4,500	4,550	756	783
4,550	4,600	764	791
4,600	4,650	772	800
4,650	4,700	781	809
4,700	4,750	789	817
4,750	4,800	797	826
4,800	4,850	806	835
4,850	4,900	814	843
4,900	4,950	822	852
4,950	5,000	831	861
5,000	5,050	839	869
5,050	5,100	848	878
5,100	5,150	856	887
5,150	5,200	864	895
5,200	5,250	873	904
5,250	5,300	881	913
5,300	5,350	889	921
5,350	5,400	898	930
5,400	5,450	906	939
5,450	5,500	914	947
5,500	5,550	923	956
5,550	5,600	931	964

If the amount on Schedule EIC, line 7 or line 9, is—		And you listed—	
At least	But less than	One child	Two children
		Your basic credit is—	
$5,600	$5,650	$939	$973
5,650	5,700	948	982
5,700	5,750	956	990
5,750	5,800	964	999
5,800	5,850	973	1,008
5,850	5,900	981	1,016
5,900	5,950	989	1,025
5,950	6,000	998	1,034
6,000	6,050	1,006	1,042
6,050	6,100	1,015	1,051
6,100	6,150	1,023	1,060
6,150	6,200	1,031	1,068
6,200	6,250	1,040	1,077
6,250	6,300	1,048	1,086
6,300	6,350	1,056	1,094
6,350	6,400	1,065	1,103
6,400	6,450	1,073	1,112
6,450	6,500	1,081	1,120
6,500	6,550	1,090	1,129
6,550	6,600	1,098	1,137
6,600	6,650	1,106	1,146
6,650	6,700	1,115	1,155
6,700	6,750	1,123	1,163
6,750	6,800	1,131	1,172
6,800	6,850	1,140	1,181
6,850	6,900	1,148	1,189
6,900	6,950	1,156	1,198
6,950	7,000	1,165	1,207
7,000	7,050	1,173	1,215
7,050	7,100	1,182	1,224
7,100	11,250	1,192	1,235
11,250	11,300	1,189	1,232
11,300	11,350	1,183	1,226
11,350	11,400	1,177	1,220
11,400	11,450	1,172	1,214
11,450	11,500	1,166	1,207
11,500	11,550	1,160	1,201
11,550	11,600	1,154	1,195
11,600	11,650	1,148	1,189
11,650	11,700	1,142	1,183
11,700	11,750	1,136	1,177
11,750	11,800	1,130	1,170
11,800	11,850	1,124	1,164
11,850	11,900	1,118	1,158
11,900	11,950	1,112	1,152
11,950	12,000	1,106	1,146
12,000	12,050	1,100	1,139
12,050	12,100	1,094	1,133
12,100	12,150	1,088	1,127
12,150	12,200	1,082	1,121
12,200	12,250	1,076	1,115
12,250	12,300	1,070	1,109
12,300	12,350	1,064	1,102
12,350	12,400	1,058	1,096
12,400	12,450	1,052	1,090
12,450	12,500	1,046	1,084

If the amount on Schedule EIC, line 7 or line 9, is—		And you listed—	
At least	But less than	One child	Two children
		Your basic credit is—	
$12,500	$12,550	$1,040	$1,078
12,550	12,600	1,034	1,071
12,600	12,650	1,028	1,065
12,650	12,700	1,022	1,059
12,700	12,750	1,016	1,053
12,750	12,800	1,010	1,047
12,800	12,850	1,004	1,041
12,850	12,900	999	1,034
12,900	12,950	993	1,028
12,950	13,000	987	1,022
13,000	13,050	981	1,016
13,050	13,100	975	1,010
13,100	13,150	969	1,003
13,150	13,200	963	997
13,200	13,250	957	991
13,250	13,300	951	985
13,300	13,350	945	979
13,350	13,400	939	973
13,400	13,450	933	966
13,450	13,500	927	960
13,500	13,550	921	954
13,550	13,600	915	948
13,600	13,650	909	942
13,650	13,700	903	935
13,700	13,750	897	929
13,750	13,800	891	923
13,800	13,850	885	917
13,850	13,900	879	911
13,900	13,950	873	905
13,950	14,000	867	898
14,000	14,050	861	892
14,050	14,100	855	886
14,100	14,150	849	880
14,150	14,200	843	874
14,200	14,250	837	868
14,250	14,300	831	861
14,300	14,350	826	855
14,350	14,400	820	849
14,400	14,450	814	843
14,450	14,500	808	837
14,500	14,550	802	830
14,550	14,600	796	824
14,600	14,650	790	818
14,650	14,700	784	812
14,700	14,750	778	806
14,750	14,800	772	800
14,800	14,850	766	793
14,850	14,900	760	787
14,900	14,950	754	781
14,950	15,000	748	775
15,000	15,050	742	769
15,050	15,100	736	762
15,100	15,150	730	756
15,150	15,200	724	750
15,200	15,250	718	744
15,250	15,300	712	738

(Caution: The actual credit should be computed from a table that is not yet available. This information will however, permit the student to determine the amount of the credit.)

1991 Earned Income Credit TABLE A—Basic Credit *Continued*

If the amount on Schedule EIC, line 7 or line 9, is—		And you listed—		If the amount on Schedule EIC, line 7 or line 9, is—		And you listed—	
		One child	Two children			One child	Two children
At least	But less than	Your basic credit is—		At least	But less than	Your basic credit is—	
$15,300	$15,350	$706	$732	$18,500	$18,550	$324	$336
15,350	15,400	700	725	18,550	18,600	319	330
15,400	15,450	694	719	18,600	18,650	313	324
15,450	15,500	688	713	18,650	18,700	307	317
15,500	15,550	682	707	18,700	18,750	301	311
15,550	15,600	676	701	18,750	18,800	295	305
15,600	15,650	670	694	18,800	18,850	289	299
15,650	15,700	664	688	18,850	18,900	283	293
15,700	15,750	659	682	18,900	18,950	277	287
15,750	15,800	653	676	18,950	19,000	271	280
15,800	15,850	647	670	19,000	19,050	265	274
15,850	15,900	641	664	19,050	19,100	259	268
15,900	15,950	635	657	19,100	19,150	253	262
15,950	16,000	629	651	19,150	19,200	247	256
16,000	16,050	623	645	19,200	19,250	241	250
16,050	16,100	617	639	19,250	19,300	235	243
16,100	16,150	611	633	19,300	19,350	229	237
16,150	16,200	605	626	19,350	19,400	223	231
16,200	16,250	599	620	19,400	19,450	217	225
16,250	16,300	593	614	19,450	19,500	211	219
16,300	16,350	587	608	19,500	19,550	205	212
16,350	16,400	581	602	19,550	19,600	199	206
16,400	16,450	575	596	19,600	19,650	193	200
16,450	16,500	569	589	19,650	19,700	187	194
16,500	16,550	563	583	19,700	19,750	181	188
16,550	16,600	557	577	19,750	19,800	175	182
16,600	16,650	551	571	19,800	19,850	169	175
16,650	16,700	545	565	19,850	19,900	163	169
16,700	16,750	539	559	19,900	19,950	157	163
16,750	16,800	533	552	19,950	20,000	151	157
16,800	16,850	527	546	20,000	20,050	146	151
16,850	16,900	521	540	20,050	20,100	140	144
16,900	16,950	515	534	20,100	20,150	134	138
16,950	17,000	509	528	20,150	20,200	128	132
17,000	17,050	503	521	20,200	20,250	122	126
17,050	17,100	497	515	20,250	20,300	116	120
17,100	17,150	491	509	20,300	20,350	110	114
17,150	17,200	486	503	20,350	20,400	104	107
17,200	17,250	480	497	20,400	20,450	98	101
17,250	17,300	474	491	20,450	20,500	92	95
17,300	17,350	468	484	20,500	20,550	86	89
17,350	17,400	462	478	20,550	20,600	80	83
17,400	17,450	456	472	20,600	20,650	74	76
17,450	17,500	450	466	20,650	20,700	68	70
17,500	17,550	444	460	20,700	20,750	62	64
17,550	17,600	438	453	20,750	20,800	56	58
17,600	17,650	432	447	20,800	20,850	50	52
17,650	17,700	426	441	20,850	20,900	44	46
17,700	17,750	420	435	20,900	20,950	38	39
17,750	17,800	414	429	20,950	21,000	32	33
17,800	17,850	408	423	21,000	21,050	26	27
17,850	17,900	402	416	21,050	21,100	20	21
17,900	17,950	396	410	21,100	21,150	14	15
17,950	18,000	390	404	21,150	21,200	8	8
18,000	18,050	384	398	21,200	21,250	2	2
18,050	18,100	378	392				
18,100	18,150	372	385	**$21,250 or more**—you may not take the credit			
18,150	18,200	366	379				
18,200	18,250	360	373				
18,250	18,300	354	367				
18,300	18,350	348	361				
18,350	18,400	342	355				
18,400	18,450	336	348				
18,450	18,500	330	342				

TABLE B—Health Insurance Credit

1991 Earned Income Credit

This is **not** a tax table.

To find your health insurance credit: First, read down the "At least—But less than" columns and find the line that includes the amount you entered on line 7 or line 9 of Schedule EIC. Next, read across and find the credit. Then, enter the credit on Schedule EIC, line 13 or line 15, whichever applies.

If the amount on Schedule EIC, line 7 or line 9, is—		Your health insurance credit is—	If the amount on Schedule EIC, line 7 or line 9, is—		Your health insurance credit is—	If the amount on Schedule EIC, line 7 or line 9, is—		Your health insurance credit is—	If the amount on Schedule EIC, line 7 or line 9, is—		Your health insurance credit is—	If the amount on Schedule EIC, line 7 or line 9, is—		Your health insurance credit is—
At least	But less than		At least	But less than		At least	But less than		At least	But less than		At least	But less than	
$1	$50	$2	$3,600	$3,650	$218	$11,300	$11,350	$425	$14,900	$14,950	$271	$18,500	$18,550	$117
50	100	5	3,650	3,700	221	11,350	11,400	423	14,950	15,000	269	18,550	18,600	115
100	150	8	3,700	3,750	224	11,400	11,450	421	15,000	15,050	267	18,600	18,650	112
150	200	11	3,750	3,800	227	11,450	11,500	419	15,050	15,100	264	18,650	18,700	110
200	250	14	3,800	3,850	230	11,500	11,550	417	15,100	15,150	262	18,700	18,750	108
250	300	17	3,850	3,900	233	11,550	11,600	414	15,150	15,200	260	18,750	18,800	106
300	350	20	3,900	3,950	236	11,600	11,650	412	15,200	15,250	258	18,800	18,850	104
350	400	23	3,950	4,000	239	11,650	11,700	410	15,250	15,300	256	18,850	18,900	102
400	450	26	4,000	4,050	242	11,700	11,750	408	15,300	15,350	254	18,900	18,950	100
450	500	29	4,050	4,100	245	11,750	11,800	406	15,350	15,400	252	18,950	19,000	97
500	550	32	4,100	4,150	248	11,800	11,850	404	15,400	15,450	250	19,000	19,050	95
550	600	35	4,150	4,200	251	11,850	11,900	402	15,450	15,500	247	19,050	19,100	93
600	650	38	4,200	4,250	254	11,900	11,950	399	15,500	15,550	245	19,100	19,150	91
650	700	41	4,250	4,300	257	11,950	12,000	397	15,550	15,600	243	19,150	19,200	89
700	750	44	4,300	4,350	260	12,000	12,050	395	15,600	15,650	241	19,200	19,250	87
750	800	47	4,350	4,400	263	12,050	12,100	393	15,650	15,700	239	19,250	19,300	85
800	850	50	4,400	4,450	266	12,100	12,150	391	15,700	15,750	237	19,300	19,350	82
850	900	53	4,450	4,500	269	12,150	12,200	389	15,750	15,800	235	19,350	19,400	80
900	950	56	4,500	4,550	272	12,200	12,250	387	15,800	15,850	232	19,400	19,450	78
950	1,000	59	4,550	4,600	275	12,250	12,300	384	15,850	15,900	230	19,450	19,500	76
1,000	1,050	62	4,600	4,650	278	12,300	12,350	382	15,900	15,950	228	19,500	19,550	74
1,050	1,100	65	4,650	4,700	281	12,350	12,400	380	15,950	16,000	226	19,550	19,600	72
1,100	1,150	68	4,700	4,750	284	12,400	12,450	378	16,000	16,050	224	19,600	19,650	70
1,150	1,200	71	4,750	4,800	287	12,450	12,500	376	16,050	16,100	222	19,650	19,700	67
1,200	1,250	74	4,800	4,850	290	12,500	12,550	374	16,100	16,150	220	19,700	19,750	65
1,250	1,300	77	4,850	4,900	293	12,550	12,600	372	16,150	16,200	217	19,750	19,800	63
1,300	1,350	80	4,900	4,950	296	12,600	12,650	369	16,200	16,250	215	19,800	19,850	61
1,350	1,400	83	4,950	5,000	299	12,650	12,700	367	16,250	16,300	213	19,850	19,900	59
1,400	1,450	86	5,000	5,050	302	12,700	12,750	365	16,300	16,350	211	19,900	19,950	57
1,450	1,500	89	5,050	5,100	305	12,750	12,800	363	16,350	16,400	209	19,950	20,000	55
1,500	1,550	92	5,100	5,150	308	12,800	12,850	361	16,400	16,450	207	20,000	20,050	52
1,550	1,600	95	5,150	5,200	311	12,850	12,900	359	16,450	16,500	205	20,050	20,100	50
1,600	1,650	98	5,200	5,250	314	12,900	12,950	357	16,500	16,550	202	20,100	20,150	48
1,650	1,700	101	5,250	5,300	317	12,950	13,000	354	16,550	16,600	200	20,150	20,200	46
1,700	1,750	104	5,300	5,350	320	13,000	13,050	352	16,600	16,650	198	20,200	20,250	44
1,750	1,800	107	5,350	5,400	323	13,050	13,100	350	16,650	16,700	196	20,250	20,300	42
1,800	1,850	110	5,400	5,450	326	13,100	13,150	348	16,700	16,750	194	20,300	20,350	40
1,850	1,900	113	5,450	5,500	329	13,150	13,200	346	16,750	16,800	192	20,350	20,400	37
1,900	1,950	116	5,500	5,550	332	13,200	13,250	344	16,800	16,850	190	20,400	20,450	35
1,950	2,000	119	5,550	5,600	335	13,250	13,300	342	16,850	16,900	187	20,450	20,500	33
2,000	2,050	122	5,600	5,650	338	13,300	13,350	339	16,900	16,950	185	20,500	20,550	31
2,050	2,100	125	5,650	5,700	341	13,350	13,400	337	16,950	17,000	183	20,550	20,600	29
2,100	2,150	128	5,700	5,750	344	13,400	13,450	335	17,000	17,050	181	20,600	20,650	27
2,150	2,200	131	5,750	5,800	347	13,450	13,500	333	17,050	17,100	179	20,650	20,700	25
2,200	2,250	134	5,800	5,850	350	13,500	13,550	331	17,100	17,150	177	20,700	20,750	22
2,250	2,300	137	5,850	5,900	353	13,550	13,600	329	17,150	17,200	175	20,750	20,800	20
2,300	2,350	140	5,900	5,950	356	13,600	13,650	327	17,200	17,250	172	20,800	20,850	18
2,350	2,400	143	5,950	6,000	359	13,650	13,700	324	17,250	17,300	170	20,850	20,900	16
2,400	2,450	146	6,000	6,050	362	13,700	13,750	322	17,300	17,350	168	20,900	20,950	14
2,450	2,500	149	6,050	6,100	365	13,750	13,800	320	17,350	17,400	166	20,950	21,000	12
2,500	2,550	152	6,100	6,150	368	13,800	13,850	318	17,400	17,450	164	21,000	21,050	10
2,550	2,600	155	6,150	6,200	371	13,850	13,900	316	17,450	17,500	162	21,050	21,100	7
2,600	2,650	158	6,200	6,250	374	13,900	13,950	314	17,500	17,550	160	21,100	21,150	5
2,650	2,700	161	6,250	6,300	377	13,950	14,000	312	17,550	17,600	157	21,150	21,200	3
2,700	2,750	164	6,300	6,350	380	14,000	14,050	309	17,600	17,650	155	21,200	21,250	1
2,750	2,800	167	6,350	6,400	383	14,050	14,100	307	17,650	17,700	153			
2,800	2,850	170	6,400	6,450	386	14,100	14,150	305	17,700	17,750	151			
2,850	2,900	173	6,450	6,500	389	14,150	14,200	303	17,750	17,800	149	$21,250 or more—you may not take the credit		
2,900	2,950	176	6,500	6,550	392	14,200	14,250	301	17,800	17,850	147			
2,950	3,000	179	6,550	6,600	395	14,250	14,300	299	17,850	17,900	145			
3,000	3,050	182	6,600	6,650	398	14,300	14,350	297	17,900	17,950	142			
3,050	3,100	185	6,650	6,700	401	14,350	14,400	294	17,950	18,000	140			
3,100	3,150	188	6,700	6,750	404	14,400	14,450	292	18,000	18,050	138			
3,150	3,200	191	6,750	6,800	407	14,450	14,500	290	18,050	18,100	136			
3,200	3,250	194	6,800	6,850	410	14,500	14,550	288	18,100	18,150	134			
3,250	3,300	197	6,850	6,900	413	14,550	14,600	286	18,150	18,200	132			
3,300	3,350	200	6,900	6,950	416	14,600	14,650	284	18,200	18,250	130			
3,350	3,400	203	6,950	7,000	419	14,650	14,700	282	18,250	18,300	127			
3,400	3,450	206	7,000	7,050	422	14,700	14,750	279	18,300	18,350	125			
3,450	3,500	209	7,050	7,100	425	14,750	14,800	277	18,350	18,400	123			
3,500	3,550	212	7,100	11,250	428	14,800	14,850	275	18,400	18,450	121			
3,550	3,600	215	11,250	11,300	427	14,850	14,900	273	18,450	18,500	119			

TABLE C—Extra Credit for Child Born in 1991

1991 Earned Income Credit
This is **not** a tax table.

To find your extra credit for a child born in 1991: First, read down the "At least—But less than" columns and find the line that includes the amount you entered on line 7 or line 9 of Schedule EIC. Next, read across and find the credit. Then, enter the credit on Schedule EIC, line 17 or line 18, whichever applies.

At least	But less than	Credit	At least	But less than	Credit	At least	But less than	Credit	At least	But less than	Credit	At least	But less than	Credit
$1	$50	$1	$3,600	$3,650	$181	$11,300	$11,350	$354	$14,900	$14,950	$226	$18,500	$18,550	$97
50	100	4	3,650	3,700	184	11,350	11,400	353	14,950	15,000	224	18,550	18,600	95
100	150	6	3,700	3,750	186	11,400	11,450	351	15,000	15,050	222	18,600	18,650	94
150	200	9	3,750	3,800	189	11,450	11,500	349	15,050	15,100	220	18,650	18,700	92
200	250	11	3,800	3,850	191	11,500	11,550	347	15,100	15,150	219	18,700	18,750	90
250	300	14	3,850	3,900	194	11,550	11,600	345	15,150	15,200	217	18,750	18,800	88
300	350	16	3,900	3,950	196	11,600	11,650	344	15,200	15,250	215	18,800	18,850	87
350	400	19	3,950	4,000	199	11,650	11,700	342	15,250	15,300	213	18,850	18,900	85
400	450	21	4,000	4,050	201	11,700	11,750	340	15,300	15,350	212	18,900	18,950	83
450	500	24	4,050	4,100	204	11,750	11,800	338	15,350	15,400	210	18,950	19,000	81
500	550	26	4,100	4,150	206	11,800	11,850	336	15,400	15,450	208	19,000	19,050	79
550	600	29	4,150	4,200	209	11,850	11,900	335	15,450	15,500	206	19,050	19,100	78
600	650	31	4,200	4,250	211	11,900	11,950	333	15,500	15,550	204	19,100	19,150	76
650	700	34	4,250	4,300	214	11,950	12,000	331	15,550	15,600	203	19,150	19,200	74
700	750	36	4,300	4,350	216	12,000	12,050	329	15,600	15,650	201	19,200	19,250	72
750	800	39	4,350	4,400	219	12,050	12,100	328	15,650	15,700	199	19,250	19,300	71
800	850	41	4,400	4,450	221	12,100	12,150	326	15,700	15,750	197	19,300	19,350	69
850	900	44	4,450	4,500	224	12,150	12,200	324	15,750	15,800	195	19,350	19,400	67
900	950	46	4,500	4,550	226	12,200	12,250	322	15,800	15,850	194	19,400	19,450	65
950	1,000	49	4,550	4,600	229	12,250	12,300	320	15,850	15,900	192	19,450	19,500	63
1,000	1,050	51	4,600	4,650	231	12,300	12,350	319	15,900	15,950	190	19,500	19,550	62
1,050	1,100	54	4,650	4,700	234	12,350	12,400	317	15,950	16,000	188	19,550	19,600	60
1,100	1,150	56	4,700	4,750	236	12,400	12,450	315	16,000	16,050	187	19,600	19,650	58
1,150	1,200	59	4,750	4,800	239	12,450	12,500	313	16,050	16,100	185	19,650	19,700	56
1,200	1,250	61	4,800	4,850	241	12,500	12,550	311	16,100	16,150	183	19,700	19,750	54
1,250	1,300	64	4,850	4,900	244	12,550	12,600	310	16,150	16,200	181	19,750	19,800	53
1,300	1,350	66	4,900	4,950	246	12,600	12,650	308	16,200	16,250	179	19,800	19,850	51
1,350	1,400	69	4,950	5,000	249	12,650	12,700	306	16,250	16,300	178	19,850	19,900	49
1,400	1,450	71	5,000	5,050	251	12,700	12,750	304	16,300	16,350	176	19,900	19,950	47
1,450	1,500	74	5,050	5,100	254	12,750	12,800	303	16,350	16,400	174	19,950	20,000	46
1,500	1,550	76	5,100	5,150	256	12,800	12,850	301	16,400	16,450	172	20,000	20,050	44
1,550	1,600	79	5,150	5,200	259	12,850	12,900	299	16,450	16,500	170	20,050	20,100	42
1,600	1,650	81	5,200	5,250	261	12,900	12,950	297	16,500	16,550	169	20,100	20,150	40
1,650	1,700	84	5,250	5,300	264	12,950	13,000	295	16,550	16,600	167	20,150	20,200	38
1,700	1,750	86	5,300	5,350	266	13,000	13,050	294	16,600	16,650	165	20,200	20,250	37
1,750	1,800	89	5,350	5,400	269	13,050	13,100	292	16,650	16,700	163	20,250	20,300	35
1,800	1,850	91	5,400	5,450	271	13,100	13,150	290	16,700	16,750	162	20,300	20,350	33
1,850	1,900	94	5,450	5,500	274	13,150	13,200	288	16,750	16,800	160	20,350	20,400	31
1,900	1,950	96	5,500	5,550	276	13,200	13,250	286	16,800	16,850	158	20,400	20,450	29
1,950	2,000	99	5,550	5,600	279	13,250	13,300	285	16,850	16,900	156	20,450	20,500	28
2,000	2,050	101	5,600	5,650	281	13,300	13,350	283	16,900	16,950	154	20,500	20,550	26
2,050	2,100	104	5,650	5,700	284	13,350	13,400	281	16,950	17,000	153	20,550	20,600	24
2,100	2,150	106	5,700	5,750	286	13,400	13,450	279	17,000	17,050	151	20,600	20,650	22
2,150	2,200	109	5,750	5,800	289	13,450	13,500	278	17,050	17,100	149	20,650	20,700	21
2,200	2,250	111	5,800	5,850	291	13,500	13,550	276	17,100	17,150	147	20,700	20,750	19
2,250	2,300	114	5,850	5,900	294	13,550	13,600	274	17,150	17,200	145	20,750	20,800	17
2,300	2,350	116	5,900	5,950	296	13,600	13,650	272	17,200	17,250	144	20,800	20,850	15
2,350	2,400	119	5,950	6,000	299	13,650	13,700	270	17,250	17,300	142	20,850	20,900	13
2,400	2,450	121	6,000	6,050	301	13,700	13,750	269	17,300	17,350	140	20,900	20,950	12
2,450	2,500	124	6,050	6,100	304	13,750	13,800	267	17,350	17,400	138	20,950	21,000	10
2,500	2,550	126	6,100	6,150	306	13,800	13,850	265	17,400	17,450	137	21,000	21,050	8
2,550	2,600	129	6,150	6,200	309	13,850	13,900	263	17,450	17,500	135	21,050	21,100	6
2,600	2,650	131	6,200	6,250	311	13,900	13,950	262	17,500	17,550	133	21,100	21,150	4
2,650	2,700	134	6,250	6,300	314	13,950	14,000	260	17,550	17,600	131	21,150	21,200	3
2,700	2,750	136	6,300	6,350	316	14,000	14,050	258	17,600	17,650	129	21,200	21,250	1
2,750	2,800	139	6,350	6,400	319	14,050	14,100	256	17,650	17,700	128			
2,800	2,850	141	6,400	6,450	321	14,100	14,150	254	17,700	17,750	126	$21,250 or more—you may not take the credit		
2,850	2,900	144	6,450	6,500	324	14,150	14,200	253	17,750	17,800	124			
2,900	2,950	146	6,500	6,550	326	14,200	14,250	251	17,800	17,850	122			
2,950	3,000	149	6,550	6,600	329	14,250	14,300	249	17,850	17,900	120			
3,000	3,050	151	6,600	6,650	331	14,300	14,350	247	17,900	17,950	119			
3,050	3,100	154	6,650	6,700	334	14,350	14,400	245	17,950	18,000	117			
3,100	3,150	156	6,700	6,750	336	14,400	14,450	244	18,000	18,050	115			
3,150	3,200	159	6,750	6,800	339	14,450	14,500	242	18,050	18,100	113			
3,200	3,250	161	6,800	6,850	341	14,500	14,550	240	18,100	18,150	112			
3,250	3,300	164	6,850	6,900	344	14,550	14,600	238	18,150	18,200	110			
3,300	3,350	166	6,900	6,950	346	14,600	14,650	237	18,200	18,250	108			
3,350	3,400	169	6,950	7,000	349	14,650	14,700	235	18,250	18,300	106			
3,400	3,450	171	7,000	7,050	351	14,700	14,750	233	18,300	18,350	104			
3,450	3,500	174	7,050	7,100	354	14,750	14,800	231	18,350	18,400	103			
3,500	3,550	176	7,100	11,250	357	14,800	14,850	229	18,400	18,450	101			
3,550	3,600	179	11,250	11,300	356	14,850	14,900	228	18,450	18,500	99			

Appendix D

GIFT AND ESTATE TAX RATES

If the "taxable transfer" is valued:		Then the "gross tax payable" is:		
Over	But not over	Amount	Plus percent	Of the amount over
$ -0-	$ 10,000	$ -0-	18%	$ -0-
10,000	20,000	1,800	20	10,000
20,000	40,000	3,800	22	20,000
40,000	60,000	8,200	24	40,000
60,000	80,000	13,000	26	60,000
80,000	100,000	18,200	28	80,000
100,000	150,000	23,800	30	100,000
150,000	250,000	38,800	32	150,000
250,000	500,000	70,800	34	250,000
500,000	750,000	155,800	37	500,000
750,000	1,000,000	248,300	39	750,000
1,000,000	1,250,000	345,800	41	1,000,000
1,250,000	1,500,000	448,300	43	1,250,000
1,500,000	2,000,000	555,800	45	1,500,000
2,000,000	2,500,000	780,800	49	2,000,000
2,500,000	3,000,000*	1,025,800*	53*	2,500,000*
3,000,000	—	1,298,000*	55*	3,000,000*

* After 1992, any taxable transfer in excess of $2,500,000 will be taxed at a marginal rate of 50%.

For taxable transfers in excess of $10,000,000 but less than $21,040,000 there is an additional surtax of 5%. This means that all taxable estates valued in excess of $21,040,000 are taxed at a flat rate of 55%.

ABA.*See* American Bar Association
Ability to pay. *See* wherewithal to pay
Accelerated Cost Recovery System. *See* ACRS depreciation
Accountants. *See* Professional tax practitioner
Accounting concepts. *See also* Tax concepts
  annual accounting concept, 229–30
  capital gain, 552
  claim of right doctrine, 235–37
  expenses, 138
  generally accepted accounting principles (GAAP), 226, 239, 241, 605
  income, 119–20
  realization criterion, 119–20
Accounting methods
  accrual method, 246–52
  cash method, 242–45
    restrictions on, 245–46
  changing, 239–40, 257–58
  completed contract method, 256
  for disallowed passive activity losses, 686–87
  general requirements, 238–39
    book conformity, 239–41
    clear reflection of income, 241–42
  hybrid methods, 252
  installment method, 252–56
  inventory tracking, 258–59
    FIFO, 261–62
    inventory valuation, 259–60
    LIFO, 261–62
    uniform capitalization, 260–61
  percentage-of-completion method, 256–57
  timing of income and deductions, 228–29
ACE. *See* Adjusted current earnings
ACRS depreciation, 470–71. *See also* Depreciation
  applicable percentage, 477–80
    conventions for, 478–79
    elective straight-line rates, 479–80
    methods of, 478–79
  and CLADR system, 477–80
  expense election, 480
  property excluded from, 476
  recovery property, 475–76
    classes of, 477–80
  unadjusted basis for, 476–77
Add-on minimum tax, 668
Adjusted basis. *See* Tax basis
Adjusted current earnings, 671–73
Adjusted gross income (AGI), modified, 308
  deductions for, 24, 412
    alimony, 315–16

deductions from, 24, 381
  casualty and theft loss, 348–50
  charitable contributions, 339–45
  dependent exemption, 327–29
  individual standard deduction, 329–31
  interest, 332–36
  medical expenses, 345–48
  miscellaneous, 350–56
  personal exemption, 326–27
  taxes, 336–39
  defined, 312–14
  and earned income credit, 379–80
  of individual taxpayers, 302
  and IRAs, 412–13
  and marginal tax rates, 376–78
Adjusted tax basis. *See* Tax basis
Age
  average, of individual taxpayers, 302
  deduction for, 329
  exclusions
    sale of principal residence, 619–20
    Social Security benefits, 308
  tax credit for, 382–83
AGI. *See* Adjusted gross income
AICPA. *See* American Institute of Certified Public Accountants
Alimony. *See* Adjusted gross income; Deductions
Alternative minimum tax (AMT), 22–23
  adjustments to, 671–73
  AMT credit against regular tax, 676
  calculation for, 669–70
  exemptions, 675–76
  foreign tax credit, 676
  history of, 668–69
  overview of, 669
  preferences, 672, 674–75
  reasons for, 667–69
  records maintained for, 674–75
  tax base for, 670
Alternative minimum taxable income (AMTI)
  calculation for, 669–70
  deductions, 675
American Bar Association (ABA), and tax practitioner guidelines, 85
American Institute of Certified Public Accountants (AICPA), 232
  and tax practitioner guidelines, 85
Amortization
  of corporate stocks and bonds, 582
  of intangible assets, 278, 492–93

of new business start-up costs, 431
of organization costs, 431
AMT. *See* Alternative minimum tax
AMTI. *See* Alternative minimum taxable income
Annuities
  defined, 400
  taxation of, 401–403
  types of, 400–401
Assets. *See also* Capital assets
  cost basis of, 274–79
    for intangible assets, 278–79
    for tangible assets, 277–78
  depreciation deductions for, 472
  depreciation period for, 472–73
  immediate expensing of versus economic depreciation,
    459–62
  intangible, amortization of, 492–93
  rate of return on, 463
  reovery periods for, 470
  salvage value of, 470
    special rule for, 472
  straight-line depreciation of, 467–68
  tax-favored, 463–66
  useful life of, 470
Audit
  appeal of, 88–90
  dispute of results, 89–92
  penalties, 80–82
  probability of, by IRS, 86
  process of, by IRS, 87–88
  rates of, 86
  reviewed by Claims Court, 90–91
  reviewed by Court of Appeals for the Federal Circuit, 91
  reviewed by Tax Court, 90
  reviewed by U.S. District Court, 90–91
  reviewed by U.S. Supreme Court, 91
  Taxpayer Compliance Measurement Program (TCMP),
    86–87

Bad debts. *See* Deductions
Base. *See also* Tax base
  for child care credit, 381
  for elderly and disabled credit, 382–83
Basis. *See* Tax basis
Benefits. *See* Business/trade; Deductions; Employees
Bonds
  capital gain/loss on, 582
  worthless, 583
Boot, in like-kind exchanges, 605–606
Brushhaber v. Union Pacific Railroad Co., 51
Bureau of Internal Revenue, 468. *See also* Internal Revenue
  Service
Burnet v. Sanford & Broods Co., 229
Business/trade

AMT, required records for, 674–75
  documentation requirements, 443–45
  documentation responsibilities, 435–45
  employees, gifts to, 309
  entertainment expense deductions, 440–43
  environmental cleanup cost deductions, 432
  expenses
    employee, 314, 351
    of handicapped individuals, 355
  feasibility studies deductions, 429–30
  fringe benefits, 310–11
  interest expense deduction, 429
  meal expense deductions, 439
    documentation of, 439–40
  organization cost deductions, 431
  package design cost deductions, 433
  passive activity, material participation, 685
  professional fee deductions, 427–28
  property, capital gain/loss with, 574–76
  related-party transactions
    compensation transactions, 528–29
    dividend transactions, 529–31
    family partnerships, 534–35
    foreign operations, 537–39
    multiple corporations, 535–36
    owner-entity, 524
    sale transactions, 525–28
    stock-redemption transactions, 531–34
  rental payment deductions, 428–29
  repair cost deductions, 427
  retirement plans, 407–411
  start-up cost deductions, 430–31
  stock, losses on, 583–85
  tax credits, 445–48
  transportation/travel expense deductions, 436–39
    documentation of, 438–39
  valuation studies deductions, 430
  versus hobby, 140

Capital assets. *See also* Assets
  corporate stocks/bonds, 582
  defined, 558–60
  exclusions from, 569
Capital expenditures
  Code regulations for, 434–35
  defined, 426
  tax treatment of, 456
Capital gain/loss. *See also* Deductions; Gain; Loss
  accelerated depreciation provisions, 570
  accounting concept of, 552
  business/trade property, 574–76
  casualty and theft
    business, 574, 576
    personal, 581

controversy over
   bunching, 555
   competitiveness, 554–55
   deferral of gain, 556
   equity, 557
   incentives, 554
   inflation, 555–56
   lock-in effect, 553–54
   revenue, 556
   simplicity, 557
corporate, 152
corporate stocks/bonds, 582
deferred recognition, 580–81
defined, 558–60
depreciation recapture, 570–73, 578–81
   before, 569–70
   installment sales, 580–81
economic concept of, 552
excess depreciation, 572–73
and installment accounting method, 253
involuntary conversions, 574, 576
judicial concept of, 551–52
long-term, 561
loss as deduction, 152–53
net versus ordinary loss, 152
planning for, 568–69
property, as charitable contribution, 341
sale/exchange of property, 574
short-term, 560–61
small business stock, 583–85
tax concept of, 552–53
tax treatment of, 560–68
   capital gain, 561–66
   capital losses, 566–68
   netting process, 560–61
worthless securities, 583
C corporations. *See also* Corporations; S corporations
   double taxation of, 208
   as multiple corporations, 210–11
   passive activity
      loss limits for, 682–83
      material participation, 685
   penalty taxes of, 08–209
   related-party transactions
      dividends, 529–30
      stock redemption transactions, 531–34
Central Texas Saving and Loan Association v. U.S., 430
Charitable contributions. *See also* Deductions
   amount deductible, 342–43
   capital gain property as, 341
   corporate, 147
   as deductions, 339–45
   income property as, 341
   qualified recipients, 339–40

and social welfare, 344–45
Child care
   excluded from gross income, 311
   tax credit for, 380–82
Children. *See* Dependents; Minor children
CLADR system. *See* Class Life Asset Depreciation Range
      system
Class Life Asset Depreciation Range system, 469–70. *See also*
      Depreciation, ACRS depreciation; MACRS
      depreciation
   and ACRS, 477–80
   and MACRS, 481–82
Commissioner v. Glenshaw Glass, 129
Compliance, taxpayer
   noncompliance, 79–80
      penalties for, 80–82
   responsibilities of professional tax practitioners, 82–85
   responsibilities of taxpayers, 77–80
   Taxpayer Compliance Measurement Program (TCMP),
      86–87
   voluntary compliance level (VCL), 79–80
Congress
   Committee on Ways and Means, 72, 74–75
   passive activity loss limits, 682
   as source of tax law, 72
Corporations. *See also* C corporations; S corporations
   affected by AMT, 674–75
   affiliated, taxation of, 173–74
   AMT, required records for, 674–75
   AMT adjustments, Adjusted Current Earnings (ACE)
      statement, 671–73
   capital gains, 153
      tax treatment of, 563
   capital gains and losses, 563
   charitable contributions of, 147
   contributions to capital of, 127–28
   controlled group of, 210–11
      taxation of, 195–200
   deductions, for employee retirement plans, 408
   defined by Code, 185
   disadvantages of, 208
   double taxation of, 208
   foreign
      defined, 176
      subject to U.S. income tax, 176–79
      taxation of, 195
   foreign operations, and related-party transactions, 537–39
   formation of, 622–23
      basis of property, 625–26
      statutory requirements for, 623–24
      transfer of property subject to liabilities, 624
   multiple, and related-party transactions, 535–37
   pay-as-you-go system of taxation, 78
   personal service corporations, taxation of, 194–95

qualified retirement plans of, 407–411
reorganization of, 626–630
securities, capital gain/loss on, 583
statutory provisions applied to, 168–69
Subchapter S criteria, 172–73
tax-exempt, 174–76
tax loopholes for, 668–69
tax rates for, 192–93
    exceptions to, 192–93
tax year for, 231
versus partnerships, 186–87
versus trusts, 186
CPAs. *See* Professional tax practitioner
Crane v. Commr., 331 U.S.1, 272
Credits
AMT credit against regular tax, 676
business, 445–46
    alcohol fuels credit, 447
    credit for structure rehabilitation, 446–47
    disabled access credit, 448
    enhanced oil recovery credit, 448
    investment tax credit, 446
    low-income housing credit, 448
    research credit, 447
    targeted jobs credit, 447
child-care credit, 380–382
defined, 202
earned income credit, 379–80
    supplemental health insurance credit, 380
elderly and disabled credit, 382–83
foreign, 311–12
foreign tax credit, 383–84
    and AMT, 676
investment tax credit, 480
maximizing, 655–56
statutory provisions for, 203–204
subtraction of, for filing, 384–85
versus deductions, 202
versus prepayments, 202
Criminal fraud. *See* Compliance, taxpayer
Criminal penalties. *See* Penalties

Death, exclusions related to, 307–308
Deductions. *See also* Adjusted gross income; Exclusions;
        Exemptions; Income;   individual deductions
ACRS, basis for, 476–77
for AGI, 24, 314, 315, 330–31, 412
from AGI, 24, 312, 330–31, 381
alimony, 315–16
and AMTI, 675
business
    bad debts, 250
    capital expenditures, 434–35
    casualty and theft losses, 155, 156–157

charitable contributions, 147, 339–45
employee expenses, 141
employee retirement plans, 408–409
entertainment expenses, 440 43
environmental cleanup costs, 432
expenses, 139–41
feasibility studies, 429–30
gifts, 309
interest expense, 429
meal expenses, 439–40
meals, 147
net operating loss, 149–50
organization costs, 431
package design costs, 433
pension/profit-sharing plans, 147
personal interest, 333
professional fees, 427–28
rental payments, 428–29
start-up costs, 430–31
transportation/travel, 436–39
valuation studies, 430
versus hobby, 140
capital losses, 152–53
capital outlays, 144
defined, 138
defined by Internal Revenue Code, 138–47
depreciation, 472
disallowed, 148
individual, 143–44
    capitalized interest, 335
    casualty and theft losses, 153–56, 348–50
    dependent exemption, 327–29, 377–78
    investment interest, 147–48, 334–35
    itemized deduction, 144
    medical expenses, 345–48
    passive activities interest, 334
    personal exemption, 326–27, 377–78
    personal interest, 333
    qualified residence interest, 333–34
    standard deduction, 144, 329–34
    taxes, 336–39
interest, 332–33
    controversy over, 335
IRA contributions, 412–14
limits on, 147–48
losses, 148–49
    from passive activity, 150–52
loss limitations for, 284–86
maximizing, 653–54
medical expenses, 305
negative criteria for, 143
nondeductible expenses, 145–46
positive criteria for, 142–43
property losses, 315

state and local taxes, 7
timing of, 656–57
trade or business, 314
transactions for profit, 315
using accrual accounting method, 249–52
using cash accounting method, 243–45
versus credits, 202
Deficit spending, 13
Dependents. *See also* Minor Children
and earned income credit, 379–80
eligibility tests for
gross income test, 329
relationship test, 327–28
support test, 328
and head of household, 373
Depletion, 493–94
computation of, 496–98
cost, 495–96
percentage, 496
for producer, 494–98
for royalty owner, 498
Depreciation. *See also* ACRS depreciation; MACRS
depreciation
accelerated, 469–70
provisions for, 570
accelerated cost recovery, 470–71
and adjusted tax basis, 275, 277
assets, period for, 472–73
Bulletin F, 469
deductions, 472
economic
defined, 459
versus immediate expensing, 459–62
excess, 572–73
expense election, 489
general rule for, 471
Guidelines for Depreciation, 469
and inflation, 466–67, 470
listed property, 490–91
luxury automobiles, 490, 492
methods, 472–73
declining-balance, 469, 473
other, 475, 489
straight-line, 469, 472, 473, 479–80
sum-of-the-years-digits, 469, 473–74
of property, with AMT, 671
recapture, 570–73, 578–81
requirements, evolution of, 467–71
returns on investment affected by, 456–58
straight-line concept, 467–68
and taxes, implicit, 462–66
Discretionary spending, 58
Documentation. *See also* Tax returns; Business/trade;
Tax/taxes

business
entertainment expenses, 440–43
meal expenses, 439–40
transportation/travel, 436–39
deductions, reporting and accounting requirements, 443–45
Double taxation
of C corporations, 208
exclusions for, 309

Education
employee expense, 351–52
exclusions for, 309–310
tax skills, 657–60
Eisner v. Macomber, 551
Employees
benefits, as exclusions, 310–11
business expenses, 351
documentation of business expenses, 444
education expense, 351–52
handicapped, expenses, 355
military, 312
retirement plan income, 409–411
veterans, 312
Employee stock ownership plan (ESOP), 407
Employment Retirement Income Security Act of 1974
(ERISA), 405, 407, 649
Environmental Protections Agency (EPA), 432
EPA. *See* Environmental Protection Agency
ERISA. *See* Employment Retirement Income Security Act of
1974
ESOP. *See* Employee stock ownership plan
Estates, 169–71. *See also* Fiduciaries; Trusts
passive activity, loss limits for, 683
statutory provisions applied to, 169–70
Excise tax
as consumption tax, 30
and 1990 Tax Act, 29
tax base for, 29–30
Exclusions. *See also* Deductions; Adjusted gross income;
Gross income; *specific exclusions*
annuities returns, 402
business
fringe benefits, 310–11
gifts, 309
death benefits, 307–308
educational assistance plans, 310
foreign income, 311–12
health insurance premiums, 304
individual, on sale of principal residence, 619–20
life insurance premiums, 307
maximizing, 652–53
medical compensation, 306–307
medical reimbursements, 305

for military personnel, 312
prizes and awards, 309
scholarships and fellowships, 309–310
Social Security benefits, 308
Exemptions
for AMT, 675–76
dependent, 326–27, 377–78
personal, 326–27, 377–78

Federal government. *See* Congress; Internal Revenue Code;
    Internal Revenue Service; Judicial System; Treasury
    Department; Treasury Regulations
Fiduciaries. *See also* Estates; Trusts
    statutory provisions applied to, 169–72
    tax rates for, 200–201
    tax return requirements, 77–78
FIFO (First-in, last-out), 261–62
Financial accounting
    book value versus adjusted tax basis, 274
    versus tax accounting, 226–28, 426
        permanent differences, 227–28
        timing differences, 227
Flint v. Stone Tracy Co., 50

Gain
    deferral of, 621
    from property dispositions, 272, 273
    on investments, 280–81
    on investment sale, 282–83
    recognition of, 613–14
Generally accepted accounting principles (GAAP). *See*
    Accounting concepts
Gramm-Rudman Act of 1985, 8–9
Gray v. Darlington, 551
Gregory v. Helvering, 522
Gross income. *See also* Adjusted gross income; Income
    child care, excluded from, 311
    defined, 125–26, 127–29
    exclusions from, 125–27, 130–32, 304–312

Head of household, 188, 373–74
Hobby
    expenses as deduction, 352
    versus business, 140

Income. *See also* Adjusted gross income; Gross income
    accounting definition, 119–20
    accounting realization criterion of, 119–20
    disability, as exclusion, 306
    foreign, 311–12
    generally defined, 117–18
    interest, from annuities, 402
    investment, 280
        of nonresident aliens, 192

monetary versus real, 118
negative, 379
passive
    of nonresident aliens, 192
    from tax-exempt organizations, 176
passive income generator (PIG), 689
property, as charitable contribution, 341
from property dispositions, 272–79
reporting
    using accrual accounting method, 246–48
    using cash accounting method, 242–43
from retirement plans, 409–411
sources, of individual taxpayers, 302
taxation definition, 120–24
taxation realization criterion, 121–23
taxation realization of, 124
timing of, 656–57
Income tax, 22–23
    changes in since 1913, 51–62
    during Civil War, 46–47
    corporate, 27–28
        of 1909, 50–51
        tax base for, 28
    enforcement of, 5–6
    evolution of, 45–51
    future of, 62–66
    horizontal equity of, 10
    individual, tax base for, 23–25
    liability formula, 116
    as single entity, 171–72
    vertical equity of, 10–11
Individual Retirement Account. *See* IRA
Individual taxpayers. *See also individually listed taxpayers*
    adjusted gross income of, 302
    capital gains/losses, 562
        computation of, 565
        tax rates for, 565
    dependent exemption for, 377–78
    filing status for, 372–75
    high-income
        itemized deductions limitations for, 376–77
        and personal/dependent exemptions, 377–78
    income sources of, 302
    low-income, and earned income credit, 380
    marginal tax rates for, 376–78
    nonresident alien, 179
    partnerships as, 183–85
    passive activities, material participation, 683–85
    passive activity, loss limits for, 683
    pay-as-you-go system for, 77, 385–86
        estimated ta payments, 77
        withholding, 77
    personal exemption for, 326–27, 377–78
    profile of, 302

rate schedules for, 372–76
resident alien, 179
standard deduction for, 329–34
statutory provisions, applied to, 167–68
tax credits for, 379–84
tax liability formula, 302
tax rates for, 187–89
    exceptions to, 191–92
    history of, 189–91
INDOPCO Inc. (formerly, National Starch and Chemical Corp.) v. Comr., 430
Inflation
    and capital gain, 555–56
    and depreciation, 462, 466–67, 470
    rate of, 466
Insurance
    health, as exclusion, 304
    life
        term, 399
        whole, 399
    supplemental health insurance credit, 380
Interest
    capitalization of, 335
    deduction, controversy over, 335
    as deduction from AGI, 332–33
    on deferred tax liability, 255
    income, from annuities, 402
    investment, 334–35
    from passive activities, 334
    personal, 333
    qualified residence, 333
Interest rates
    nominal, 466
    real, 466
Internal Revenue Code
    backstop provisions, 666–67
    capital expenditures, regulations for, 434–35
    and deductions, 139–47
    dependent defined by, 327–28
    MACRS conventions defined, 484
    organization of, 96–98
    Sec. 1(a), 167
    Sec. 1(e), 170
    Sec. 11(a), 168
    Sec. 62, 313, 353
    Sec. 62(3), 315
    Sec. 62(4), 315
    Sec. 79, 307
    Sec. 104, 306–307
    Sec. 119, 310
    Sec. 125, 311
    Sec. 127, 309
    Sec. 129, 311
    Sec. 132, 311

Sec. 152(a), 327–28
Sec. 161, 315
Sec. 162, 145, 351, 427–28, 433
Sec. 162(a), 139, 436, 440
Sec. 162(a)(2), 439
Sec. 162(f), 432
Sec. 163(a), 332
Sec. 164(a), 337
Sec. 165(c), 153–54, 315
Sec. 165(g), 583
Sec. 165(h)(1-2), 348–49
Sec. 167(a), 471
Sec. 168, 475
Sec. 168(g), 488
Sec. 170(c), 339–40
Sec. 179, 480, 489
Sec. 195, 430–31
Sec. 212, 141, 315, 353
Sec. 213(a), 345
Sec. 213(d)(1), 345
Sec. 213(d)(2)(B), 346
Sec. 248, 431
Sec. 263, 434–35
Sec. 263(a), 144, 432
Sec. 263A, 429, 432
Sec. 267, 518–21
Sec. 274, 441–42
Sec. 302, 531–33
Sec. 303, 534
Sec. 318, 533–34
Sec. 351(a), 623–24
Sec. 357, 624
Sec. 368, 627
Sec. 404, 408
Sec. 412, 408
Sec. 415, 408
Sec. 448(d)(2), 194–95
Sec. 461(h), 251
Sec. 482, 517–18
Sec. 501(a), 175
Sec. 709, 431
Sec. 1031, 603–605, 621–22
Sec. 1033, 621–22
Sec. 1034, 617–19, 621–22
Sec. 1060, 275–76
Sec. 1221, 558–59
Sec. 1231, 569–72, 574–76
Sec. 1244, 583–85
Sec. 1245, 570–73 , 578–79
Sec. 1250, 572–73 , 579–80
Sec. 1272, 582
Subchapter C, 649
Subchapter K, 649
Subchapter N, 649

tax year defined
    for partnerships, 232
    for S corporations, 232
Internal Revenue Code of 1939, 52, 74
Internal Revenue Code of 1954, 52–53, 74
    and depreciation, 469
Internal Revenue Code of 1986, 74
Internal Revenue Service. *See also* Audit; Compliance,
        taxpayer
    ability to verify taxable income, 239–41
    as statutory authority, 517
    audits by, 86–88
    and changes in accounting methods, 257–58
    Guidelines for Depreciation, 469
    and revenue rulings, 76
Inventory
    methods of accounting, 258–59
        FIFO, 261–62
        inventory flow, 261–62
        inventory valuation, 259–60
        LIFO, 261–62
        uniform capitalization, 260–61
Investments
    adjusted tax basis of, 279–84
    capital, 456–58
    expenses, 353
    gain on, 280–81, 282–83
    loss on, 281, 282–83
    rate of return on
        after-tax, 461
        before-tax, 461
    return on, affected by depreciation, 456–58
    taxable income from, 280
IRA (Individual Retirement Account), 412–14
    deduction for, 316
    distribution rollovers to, 410–11
IRS. *See* Internal Revenue Service
Itemized deductions. *See also* Deductions
    capitalized interest, 335
    casualty and theft loss, 348–50
    charitable contributions, 339
    interest, 332–33
    investment interest, 334–35
    limitation on, 376–77
    medical expenses, 345–47
    miscellaneous, 350–56
    passive activities interest, 334
    personal interest, 333
    qualified residence interest, 333–34
    taxes, 336–39

Judicial authorities, 521–23
Judicial system
    and audit appeals process, 89–93

capital gain concept, 551–52
and claim of right doctrine, 235–37
Claims Court, 100
District Court, 100
interpretation of tax law, 430
Tax Court, 99–100

Keogh plan, 411–12
    deduction for, 316
Keynes's economic model, 398

Lawyers. *See* Professional tax practitioner
LIFO (Last-in, first-out)
    accounting methods for, 261–62
    and financial statement conformity, 240
Like-kind exchanges. *See* Nontaxable exchanges
Local taxes. *See* State and local taxes
Loss. *See also* Net operating loss; Capital gain/loss;
        Deductions; Passive activities
    casualty and theft, 153–56, 315
    deduction limits on tax basis, 284–86
    defined, 148–49
    from gambling, 355
    on investments, 281
    on investment sale, 282–83
    from passive activity, 150–52
    property
        deduction on, 315
        from disposition of, 272, 273
    recognition of, 613–14
Lucas v. Earl, 521
Luxury tax, and 1990 Tax Act, 12

MACRS depreciation, 470–71
    alternative depreciation system, 488–89
    and CLADR system, 481–82
    conventions, 484–87
    property
        classes of, 481–82
        subject to, 481
    straight-line election, 487
Marginal tax rates. *See* Rates/rate schedules
Married taxpayers
    filing jointly, 188, 372–73
    filing separately, 188, 375
    surviving spouse, 188, 372–73
Medical
    compensation, 306–307
    expenses
        capital expenditures, 346
        as deduction, 345–48
        deduction for, 305
    health insurance, 304
    reimbursements, 304

Mineral operations
    cost of mineral rights, 494–95
    depletion in, 493–94
Minor children. *See also* Dependents
    rate schedule for, 375–76
    standard deduction for, 330
    support payments for, 315–16
    Uniform Gift to Minors Act, 167
Modified Accelerated Cost Recovery System. *See* MACRS
        depreciation
Multiple corporations. *See* C corporations

NCNB Corp. v. U.S., 430
Net operating loss (NOL), 149–50
Nontaxable exchanges
    corporate reorganizations, 626–30
    direct, 600
    formation of corporations, 622–23
        basis of property, 625–26
        basis of stock, 625–26
        transfer of property subject to liabilities, 624
    indirect, 600
    involuntary conversions
        basis of replacement property, 613–15
        defined, 613
        eligible replacement property, 615–16
        nonrecognition requirements, 613–15
        replacement period, 616–17
    like-kind, 600–602
        basis of property, 608–610
        deferred, 612
        holding period of property, 608–610
        multiple properties, 611–12
        of property subject to liabilities, 607–608
        requirements for, 603–605
        role of boot in, 605–606
        three-party, 612
        versus similar asset exchange, 605
    sale of principal residence, age exclusion, 619–20
    wherewithal-to-pay, 600
North American Oil Consolidated v. Bernet, 235

Oil/gas operations
    depletion in, 494–95
    exploration costs, 494
    intangible drilling costs (IDCs), 494–95
Old Age, Survivors, and Disability Insurance (OASI) Act, 403.
        See also Social Security

PACs. *See* Political action committees
Partnerships
    defined by code, 185
    family, related-party transactions, 534–35
    passive activity, material participation, 685

passive loss from, 211–12
    publicly traded (PTPs), 689–90
    taxation status of, 183–85
    tax year for, 230–31
    versus corporations, 186–87
Passive activities, 150–52. *See also* Tax shelters
    defined, 683
    disallowed losses, accounting for, 686–87
    losses, recoupment of, at disposition, 688–89
    loss limits
        for real estate rental, 687
        for C corporations, 682–83
        for estates, 683
        for individual taxpayers, 683
    material participation, 683–85
    partnerships, 211–12
    passive activity loss (PAL) provisions, 151
        limit on, 678
    passive income generator (PIG), 689–90
    publicly traded partnerships (PTPs), 689–90
    separation of activities for, 685–86
    tax shelters, 689
        defined, 678–79
Patchen v. Comm., 239
Penalties
    criminal, 81–82
    defined, 4–5
    for taxpayer noncompliance, 80–82
Pension plans
    deduction for, 408
    defined, 407
    history of, 404–405
Political action committees (PACs), 14
Pollock v. Farmers Loan and Trust Co., 49
Professional tax practitioner
    and preparation of returns, 93–95
    and audit disputes, 648
    education of, 657–60
    in federal government, 649–50
    filing returns, 82–83
    guidelines for
        by ABA, 85
        by AICPA, 85
    in private industry, 649
    regulation of, 83–85
    salaries of, 649–50
    and tax compliance, 648
    and taxpayer compliance, 82–83
    use of, 83
Profit-sharing plans
    deduction for, 408
    defined, 407
    history of, 404–405
Progressive tax rate, 16

Property
    ACRS, excluded from, 476
    ACRS classified, 470
    adjusted tax basis of, 273–74
    alternative depreciation system, 488–89
    basis of, 625–26
    business/trade, capital gain/loss from, 574–76
    capital gain, as charitable contribution, 341
    community, 189–91
    deduction on loss from, 315
    depreciable, and Revenue Act of 1913, 468
    depreciation of, with AMT, 671
    disposition of, and capital gain/loss, 570
    dispositions
        amount realized from, 272–73
        gain or loss from, 272, 273
    gift, tax basis of, 287–90
    income, as charitable contribution, 341
    inherited, tax basis of, 286–87
    like-kind, 603–605
    like-kind exchange, basis of, 608–610
    listed, 490–91
    MACRS, classes of, 481–82
    principal residence, sale of, 617–22
    real
        recapture rules for, 572–73
        unadjusted basis of, 476–77
    recovery, 578–79
        for ACRS, 475–76
    replacement
        basis of, 613–15
        in involuntary conversion, 615–16
    replacement period, in involuntary conversion, 616–17
    sale/exchange of, capital gain/loss from, 574
    subject to liabilities
        like-kind exchange of, 607–608
        transfer of, 624
Proportional tax rate, 16
Publications
    Congressional, 75
    Federal Income Taxation of Corporations and Shareholders, 103
    Federal Reporter, 100
    Federal Supplement, 100
    Internal Revenue Bulletin, 99
    Tax Court Reports, 100
    U.S. Claims Court Reports, 100
Public versus private goods, 6–7

Rates/rate schedules
    average versus marginal, 17–18
    for corporations, 192–93
        exceptions to, 194–200
    effective tax rate, 461
    explicit tax rate, 463
    for fiduciaries, 200–201
    for head of household, 373–74
    implicit tax rate, 463
    for individual taxpayers, 187–89
        exceptions for, 191–92
        history of, 189–91
    for joint returns, 372
    marginal, affected by Social Security taxes, 26
    marginal, for individual taxpayers, 376–78
    married filing separately, 375
    minimizing tax rates, 654–55
    for minor children, 375–76
    nominal versus effective, 18
    and savings, 398
    Schedule X, 374
    Schedule Y-Joint, 372–73
    Schedule Z, 373
    for single individuals, 374
    statutory tax rate, 461
    for surviving spouses, 373
    total tax rate, 463
Realization criterion. *See* Income
Regressive tax rate, 17
Research and development. *See* Credits
Retirement plans. *See also* Insurance, life; Annuities; Social Security; *individually listed plans*
    corporate, qualified plans, 407–411
    effect on savings of, 416
    effects on investment of, 416
    401(k) plans, 414–15
    income from, taxation of, 409–411
    mobility of labor, 416–17
    nonqualified corporate plans, 415
    private, 404–405
        qualification requirements, 405–407
    simplified employee pensions (SEPs), 414
Retirements plans, public, 403–404
Revenue procedures, 76
Revenue rulings. *See also* Internal Revenue Service
    organization of, 99

Sales tax. *See* State and local taxes
Savings, 398. *See also* Retirement plans
S corporations
    defined, 172
    passive activity, maerial participation, 685
    related-party transactions, dividends, 530–31
    small business stock, capital gain/loss on, 584–85
    taxation of, 195, 212
    tax year for, 232
    versus C corporations, 172–73
Self-employed individuals
    estimated taxes for, 386–87

prepayment of taxes, 204–205
retirement plans for, 316, 411–12
Senate
Committee on Finance, 72–73
and tax law, 72–73
Single taxpayers, 188, 374
Social Security
as public retirement plan, 403–404
benefits as exclusions, 308
retirement benefits, 398–99
Social Security tax
excess, 387
implications for marginal tax rates, 26
tax base for, 25–27
Sole proprietorship, taxation status of, 182–83
Springer v. United States, 47
State and local taxes
deductibility of, 7
sales tax, 30
Statutory regulations. *See* Treasury Regulations, interpretive
versus legislative
Stock
basis of, in formation of corporations, 625–26
capital gain/loss on, 582
exchange
corporate reorganization, 627–30
formation of corporations, 622–23
worthless, 583

Tax/taxes
accounting versus financial accounting, 226–28, 426
permanent differences, 227–28
timing differences, 227
business, documentation responsibilities for, 435–45
capital gain/loss, 560–68
colonial faculties taxes, 46
criteria for, 7–8, 10–14
deduction of, 336–39
defined, 4
disputes over, 648
double taxation, 208
earmarking of, 7
implicit, and depreciation, 462–66
implicit versus explicit, 19–20
interest on unpaid, 81
payment of, 385–86
preparation expenses, 353
prepayments of, 202
estimated, 204–205, 386–87
payroll withholding, 204, 386
refund for nonhighway use of fuel, 387
revenue losses, 78–80
services to aid preparation of, 102–104
transactions, 29

versus penalties, 4–5
versus service fees, 7
Taxable entities, 182. *See also individually listed taxpayers*
corporations, 168–69
fiduciaries, 169–72
individual taxpayers, 167–68
partnerships, 183–85
sole proprietorships, 182–83
tax conduit, 166, 279–84
loss deductions of, 284–86
tax-exempt, 166
Tax base, 15–16, 21–23. *See also individually listed tax bases*
for AMT, 670
benefits excluded from, 310–11
by levels of government, 42–45
formulas for, 23–24, 25–26, 28, 302–304
for retail sales tax, 15–16
Tax basis, 127
adjusted, of property 273–74
adjustments to
for investments, 279–84
of intangible assets, 278–79
of tangible assets, 277–78
cost basis of asset, 274–79
effect of debt on, 282
of gift property, 287–90
of inherited property, 286–87
of like-kind exchange property, 608–610
loss limitations for, 284–86
of property, in formation of corporations, 625–26
of replacement property, 613–15
at sale of asset, 282–84
of stock, in formation of corporations, 625–26
of tax conduit entities, 279–84
unadjusted, for ACRS, 476–77
Tax burden, 19, 20–21
Tax concepts
administrative convenience, 227
avoidance, 651
capital gain, 551–52
certainty, 22
claim of right doctrine, 235–37
deductions, 138
evasion, 651
fixed accounting periods, 229–30
influencing social/economic behavior, 227
realization criterion, 121–23, 124
tax benefit rule, 237–38
tax neutrality, 9, 460
tax preferences, 667–68
wherewithal to pay, 123, 226–27
Tax credits. *See* Credits
Tax Equity and Fiscal Responsibility Act of 1982 (TEFRA), 411

Tax forms
  970, 262
  1040, 77, 78, 302
  1040A, 77, 78, 302
  1040EZ, 77, 78, 302
  1041, 78
  1120, 78
  1128, 234
  3115, 257
Tax gap. *See* Tax/taxes, revenue losses
Tax law. *See also* Internal Revenue Code; Internal Revenue
      Service; Judicial system; Tax legislation
  and accounting method, 241–42
  business
    environmental cleanup costs, 432
    feasibility studies, 429–30
    interest expense, 429
    organization costs, 431
    package design costs, 433
    professional fees, 427–28
    rental payments versus hidden purchase, 428–29
    repair expenses versus capital repair costs, 427
    start-up costs, 430–31
    valuation studies, 430
  capital gain/loss, 574–76
  changes in, 8–9
  committee reports as information source of, 74–75
  common law property, 189–91
  community property, 189–91
  Congress as source of, 72
  formed by Conference Committee, 73
  interpreted by Treasury Department, 75
  judicial authorities, 521–23
  judicial interpretation of, 77
  miscellaneous savings incentives, 417–18
  related-party transactions, 516–17
    compensation transactions, 528–29
    dividend transactions, 529–31
    family partnerships, 534–35
    foreign operations, 537–39
    multiple corporations, 535–36
    owner-entity, 524
    sale transactions, 525–28
    stock redemption transactions, 531–34
  Secretary of the Treasury, role of in, 72
  and Senate, 72–73
  statutory authorities, 517–21
  structure of, 74–75
  and transition rules, 74
Tax legislation
  Current Tax Payment Act of 1943, 52
  Deficit Reduction Act of 1984, 229, 250
  Economic Recovery Tax Act of 1981 (ERTA), 54, 398, 412, 470

  Omnibus Budget Reconciliation Act (OBRA), 57–58
    problems not addressed by, 59–62
  Revenue Act of 1864, 46
  Revenue Act of 1913, 468, 551
  Revenue Act of 1918, 51–52
  Revenue Act of 1921, 551
  Revenue Act of 1942, 141
  Revenue Act of 1978, 53, 54
  Revenue Act of 1987, 232
  Revenue Reconciliation Act of 1990, 276
  Tax Act of 1990, 12
  Tax Reform Act of 1969, 53, 56
  Tax Reform Act of 1976, 32
  Tax Reform Act of 1986
    and ACRS, 475
    and alternative minimum tax, 669
    and business purchase allocations, 275
    and capital gains, 553
    and charitable contributions, 341
    and completed contract accounting method, 256
    and corporate tax base, 28
    creation of Internal Revenue Code of 1986, 74
    and deduction of bad debts, 250
    and depreciation expense election, 489
    and double taxation, 309
    and economic growth, 398
    effects of, 58–59
    effects on Congress, 73
    enactment of, 55–56
    and interest deductions, 332
    and IRAs, 412
    and itemized deductions, 331, 350
    and life insurance, 399
    and MACRS, 471
    and medical capital expenditures, 346
    and private retirement plans, 406
    savings incentives, 418
    and tax shelters, 86
    and tax year restrictions, 231–32
    and timing of income abuses, 229
  Uniform Gift to Minors Act, 167
  Windfall Profits Tax Bill of 1979, 54
Taxpayer Compliance Measurement Program (TCMP), 86–87
Tax planning, 650–51
  under accrual accounting method, 247–52
  avoidance versus evasion, 651
  capital gain/loss, 568–69
  under cash accounting method, 242–45
  deductions
    timing of, 250–52, 656–57
  income, timing of, 656–57
  income tax liability, 651–52
  maximizing credits, 655–56
  maximizing deductions, 653–54

maximizing exclusions, 652–53
  minimizing tax rates, 654–55
  timing of income and deductions, 228–29
Tax policy, objectives of, 8–9
Tax practitioner. *See* Professional tax practitioner
Tax rates. *See* Rates/rate schedules
Tax rate structures. *See* Proportional tax rate; Progressive tax
    rate; Regressive tax rate
Tax returns
  filing status, for individual taxpayers, 372–75
  filing requirements, 385
  prepared by professional tax practitioners, 648
  responsibility to file, 77–80
  statute of limitations on filed returns, 82
Tax shelters, 689. *See also* Passive activities
  components of
    conversion, 680–81
    deferral, 680
    leverage, 679–80
  defined, 678–79
Tax year, 229
  based on annual accounting concept, 229–30
  calendar versus fiscal year, 230
  changing accounting periods, 234–35
  for corporations, 231
  defined, 230
  individual taxpayers, options, 233–34
  for partnerships, 230–31
  S corporations, options, 233–34
Treasury Department, interpretation of tax law, 75–76
Treasury Regulations
  challenged by taxpayers, 75
  interpretive versus legislative, 75–76
  organization of, 99
  on passive activities, 686
  Sec. 1.62-5(b), 351–52
Trusts. *See also* Fiduciaries; Estates
  as retirement plans, 411
  defined, 170
  foreign, 181–82
  grantor
    defined, 179
    taxation of, 179–81
  passive activity, loss limits for, 683
  taxation of, 170–71, 212
  tax-exempt, 174–76
  versus corporations, 186

U.S. Circuit Court of Appeals. *See* Judicial System
U.S. Claims Court. *See* Judicial system
U.S. Congress. *See* Congress
U.S. District Courts. *See* Judicial system
U.S. Senate. *See* Senate
U.S. Supreme Court. *See* Judicial system

U.S. Treasury Department. *See* Treasury Department
U.S. v. Phellis, 522–23
Uniform Gift to Minors Act, 167
United States v. Davis, 122
United States v. Lewis, 236

Value-added tax (VAT), 30–31

Wealth tax, tax base for, 31–32
Wealth-transfer tax, 32–33
  and Tax Reform Act of 1976, 32
Welch v. Helvering, 142
Wherewithal to pay, 123, 226–27
  with nontaxable exchanges, 600
Withholding
  individual taxpayers, 77
  from payroll, 204, 386